League Express

LEAGUE
Publications Ltd

RUGBY LEAGUE 2015-2016

Every minute mattered

League Publications Ltd

First published in Great Britain in 2015 by
League Publications Ltd
Wellington House
Briggate
Brighouse
West Yorkshire HD6 1DN

A CIP catalogue record for this book is available from the British Library
ISBN 978-1-901347-32-6

Designed and Typeset by League Publications Limited
Printed by H Charlesworth & Co Ltd, Wakefield

Contributing Editor
Tim Butcher

Statistics, production and design
Daniel Spencer

Contributors
Thomas Alderson
Malcolm Andrews
Jack Asbury
Patrick Baines
Andrew Belt
Aaron Bower
Martin Butcher
Michael Butcher
Phil Caplan
Joshua Chapman
George Clarke
John Cox
John Davidson
Richard de la Riviere
Andy Donnelly
Paul English
Steve Fox
Ian Golden
Sian Golden
Ryan Gould
Sean Hayes
Phil Hodgson
Andrew Jackson
Chris Jackson
Gareth Jones
Steve Kilmartin
David Kuzio
John Lawless
Lorraine Marsden
Tommy Marsden
Paddy McAteer
Keith McGhie
Grace Mellor
Joe Mills
James Oddy
Dave Parkinson
Arindam Rej
Huw Richards
Ian Rigg
Mike Rylance
Martyn Sadler
David Saffer
Steve Slater
Alex Spindler
Pete Stephenson
James Stott
Gareth Walker
John Walsh
Jordan Weir
James Whaling
Joe Whitley
Ricky Wilby
Gavin Wilson
Ian Wilson
Peter Wilson

Pictures
Rugby League Photos
Action Photographics *(Australia)*
Paul Clayton
Paul English
Steve Gaunt
Magi Haroun
Steve Jones
Paul McCarthy
Peter Morley
David Murgatroyd
Bill Watkinson
Simon Wilkinson

Main cover picture
Steve Gaunt

CONTENTS

ACKNOWLEDGEMENTS

Rugby League 2015-2016 is the 20th of League Publications Ltd's annual series of Rugby League Yearbooks.

In compiling this historical record of the Rugby League year, we rely on the hard work and dedication of all the contributors to *Rugby Leaguer & Rugby League Express* and *Rugby League World* magazine. Without their efforts this yearbook would not be possible.

We are able to include some wonderful action photography provided by, in particular RLphotos.com, Action Photographics in Sydney, Magi Haroun, Steve Gaunt and Peter Morley.

Thanks also to the Rugby Football League for their help during the year, and to the historians and statisticians at clubs who help to keep us on our toes.

Acknowledgement also to the Rothmans Yearbook 1999, compiled by Ray Fletcher, the British Rugby Records Book from London Publications, and to the club officials, and some supporters, who helped us verify records.

The comprehensive statistical review was put together meticulously, as always, by Daniel Spencer, who also designed the book.

Invaluable contributions once again from Gareth Walker and Malcolm Andrews, who wrote the Championship and NRL/State of Origin sections. Thanks also to Opta Sports, who compiled the Opta Index Analysis in our thought-provoking statistical section.

TIM BUTCHER
Contributing Editor

INTRODUCTION

The year 2015 marked a leap into the unknown for Rugby League.

Since the formation of the Northern Union in 1895, with the 120th anniversary of that event marked at Wembley this year, there have been numerous changes to the structure of the leagues and none more radical than the one made for 2015.

The top two divisions of the Rugby Football League both had 12 instead of 14 teams in 2015 and after 23 rounds were split into three divisions of eight, each playing seven league fixtures and each with their own points and play-off systems. To a lot of people it seemed confusing.

The administrators promised the new system would bring in an era of excitement and an end to end-of-season, as well as early season, matches with little or nothing at stake, as well as providing a route for clubs to be promoted into Super League.

The slogan that the marketers came up with was 'Every Minute Matters' and from that point of view the 'two into three' structure appeared to work.

There were near the end of the season plenty of dead rubbers with several teams having little to play for after 23 of the 30 rounds. But there were some thrilling climaxes to several matches. The Super League season began with a rousing draw between Widnes Vikings and Wigan Warriors and ended with a two-point Grand Final between Wigan and Leeds that could have gone either way. And there was a rise in attendances of almost nine per cent, so that has to be regarded as a success. And there was a sell-out crowd on hand to witness what was possibly the best Grand Final to date.

The Kingstone Press Championship experienced a much higher percentage rise in crowds, although much of this could be put down to the Bulls effect, Bradford being one of the teams relegated to accommodate the new system at the end of 2014.

Bradford had the most dramatic and heart-breaking finish to the season when they lost what was billed as 'The Million Pound Game' - a play-off between fourth and fifth placed teams in the Middle Eight, known as 'The Qualifiers' - at Wakefield by the narrowest of margins. It was an exciting way to decide the fourth team that would be in Super League in 2016, but for the fans, players and staff of both clubs it was a painfully anxious experience.

The Middle Eight provided much of the excitement in the last seven rounds of the year although they ended with the four teams - Widnes, Hull KR, Salford and Wakefield - who had finished in positions nine to 12 - retaining their places in Super League in 2016, probably not what the game's bosses would have ideally liked.

Whereas that outcome could be viewed as predictable, there was plenty of unpredictability and out-and-out excitement about 2015.

The season ended with an absorbing Test series between England and New Zealand that concluded with an England win confirmed with a decider in front of a sold-out crowd at Wigan. The second game of the series was played at the Olympic Stadium in London, attracting an attendance of 44,393, second only to the World Cup semi-final crowd of 2013 - also staged in London - in the history of contests between the two nations since 1908.

By the time they came to England, the Kiwis were ranked number-one in the world

England rounded off the 2015 season in style, with a Test Series win against New Zealand

by the Rugby League International Federation and England, under coach Steve McNamara, confirmed they were currently able to now consistently compete with the top League nations.

Domestically, with only four play-off places to compete for, no team could afford to drop league points at any stage of the season. One of Super League's big-hitters, Warrington Wolves, couldn't find any consistency and even though they beat eventual champions Leeds twice and runners up Wigan, they finished sixth and out of contention well before the end of the campaign.

The Rhinos dominated 2015, ending with the treble of Challenge Cup, League Leaders Trophy and Super League Championship, the first time that had been achieved since St Helens did it in 2006. It was a fairytale story with the triumvirate of Kevin Sinfield, Jamie Peacock and Kylie Leuluai all ending their playing careers in fairytale fashion. Another part of their story was the record Challenge Cup Final win at Wembley, where they beat Hull KR 50-0, winger Tom Briscoe finishing with a record five tries and being awarded the Lance Todd Trophy.

Introduction

The Rhinos became the arch exponents of the late finish, closely followed by St Helens. But the way Leeds secured the League Leaders Trophy on a September night in Huddersfield was the stuff of legend.

With the Rhinos trailing the Giants - who themselves went into the game, alongside Wigan, with a chance of finishing top - 16-8 with seven minutes to go, the helicopter with Super League general manager Blake Solly and the Shield on board headed for Wigan, where the Warriors were running away with their game with the Tigers.

Incredibly, the Rhinos snatched the game on the very last play of the game from deep in their own half when Ryan Hall raced onto Danny McGuire's kick down the left wing, necessitating an aerial U-turn and a lengthy wait before the Rhinos players could be awarded the trophy on the pitch. That was one of many amazing nights for Leeds fans.

The Warriors snapped at Leeds' heels all season and could have snatched the Super League trophy but for the Rhinos' incredible resolve. And St Helens suffered the same fate at Headingley in the semi-final, seeing a game they had in their pocket slip away in the last eleven minutes.

The Giants were excellent for long periods of the season but they weren't their best in a heavy semi-final defeat at Wigan. They had the Super League's top try-scorer in Jermaine McGillvary, who deservedly won a first England cap at the end of the year.

Of the four teams outside the top-four, only Castleford Tigers threatened the play-offs in the Super 8s - while also providing some exciting finishes of their own; while Widnes, Salford and Hull KR were never seriously threatened in the The Qualifiers. Wakefield only won three regular-season Super League games, but brought in new coach Brian Smith in mid-season and that was enough to see them retain the status they have clung on to for 17 years.

In the Championship, Leigh Centurions were all-conquering and beat both Salford and Wakefield on a wonderful Cup run that ended in noble defeat at Warrington, but they couldn't beat Super League sides in the Qualifiers and didn't get a sniff of the promotion for which they had been tipped.

Amongst it all there was drama both on and off the field, spectacular tries and limitless excitement. We hope you enjoy reliving it all in this book.

The League Express Yearbook contains the full story of the domestic year, the Australian NRL season and match facts for all Super League, Challenge Cup games involving professional teams, Championship and League 1 games. Every player who has played Super League is also listed along with those players to have made their debuts this year. We have also selected five individuals - though this year it is seven - who we judge to have made the biggest impact on Rugby League in 2015. There are scoring and attendance records for every club. League Publications publishes the weekly newspaper Rugby Leaguer & Rugby League Express, as well as the monthly glossy magazine Rugby League World and the UK's most popular League website 'totalrl.com'.

TIM BUTCHER
Contributing Editor

1
THE 2015 SEASON

DECEMBER 2014
An exciting place

On the back of a re-invigorated England performance in the Four Nations, Rugby Football League chairman Brian Barwick promised that the 2015 season would be the best in living memory. 'I do think we are in an exciting place,' Barwick told Rugby League Express.

'We have some exciting new elements next year, which is bookended by the new three-match World Club Series at the start of the season and a three-match Test series against New Zealand at the end of it. We will have international Rugby League for both club and country and both will take the game forward.

'Every game was a belter in the Four Nations. That is a really positive element and, of course, the new structure of the league in 2015 seems to be gradually winning favour. We are very optimistic about it and the RFL officials have worked very hard to explain it.

'There is a sense of ambition and excitement about the new season, and I'm not just banging the gong for the sake of it. I genuinely believe that we have something very exciting to look forward to.'

The game was on the up if the TV figures were anything to go by. Super League raised its TV audience by more than five per cent in 2014, bucking the trend of many other sports with major TV contracts and the viewing audience for the Grand Final between St Helens and Wigan was 33 per cent up on the previous year.

On the international front, RFL chief executive Nigel Wood announced it would be 'nonsensical' for England to take a leaf out of Australia's book by taking a year off. Demands from Australian players to take a break had spelled the end of a planned Great Britain tour of Australia in 2015. Instead the three-Test series with New Zealand had been arranged.

Wood, however, who was also the Chairman of the Rugby League International Federation (RLIF), was far more definitive on England's attitude towards the international game as he tried to get a calendar sorted for the next 15 years. He said: 'England want to play international Rugby League every year. We think it's nonsensical for the national side to disappear from public view for 24 months. That's not the way to build a sport in our view, and the Kiwis have a similar view.

'Players don't want to be playing in front of 15,000 or 20,000 people. They want to be playing in front of 50,000 or 60,000 people. That's what the international game needs to achieve.

'Australia would prefer to have one year off in every cycle, and that's up to them, but the international calendar can't be built around one country.'

The RLIF, which was handed a £3.5 million profit from the 2013 World Cup, had just suffered a blow when the former chief executive of the International Rugby (union) Board, Mike Miller, rejected the offer of the chief executive's role.

Wigan winger Joe Burgess was awarded the 2014 Albert Goldthorpe Rookie of the Year Medal. Having previously played only two Super League games, Burgess enjoyed a meteoric rise to prominence in 2014, scoring 25 tries in 27 games in all competitions.

Teammate Ben Flower backed the Wigan club's decision to dock him 50 per cent of his wages for three months, following his attack on St Helens' Lance Hohaia in the second minute of the 2014 Super League Grand Final. Flower - who was found guilty of gross misconduct - could have been sacked, but would instead face a rehabilitation programme involving service with young people in the community while he completed his six-month RFL ban.

Huddersfield Giants' impact prop Larne Patrick crossed the Pennines to join Wigan on a season-long loan, in a deal which saw Jack Hughes heading to Huddersfield in the opposite direction. The Warriors released forward Eddy Pettybourne from the last year of his contract so he could return home to care for his ill father. Pettybourne was halfway through his two-year deal, after joining Wigan from Wests Tigers at the start of the 2014 season. Wigan had their pre-season training camp in early December in Florida.

Salford Red Devils announced they would stage a pre-season game against neighbours Swinton Lions in honour of Alan Henning, the Salford taxi driver who was tragically murdered by fanatics in early October after being kidnapped the previous December while delivering aid to Syria.

The Red Devils were already back in training and headed to an Army camp in the second week in December - a contrast from the warm weather training in South Africa before the 2014 season. New signing Cory Paterson said he had his hunger back for Rugby League after a brief stint in professional boxing. Paterson, who spent the 2013 season with Hull KR, had retired abruptly three months before and became a heavyweight boxer after finishing the 2014 NRL campaign with West Tigers. The 27-year old won his second professional bout on November 12th, in the first round against Michael Lua Tama, but decided to hang up the gloves and return to Super League.

But Salford were resigned to losing their assistant coach Sean Long to St Helens. Red Devils owner Marwan Koukash revealed the news on Twitter, tweeting: 'The club has reluctantly agreed to Sean Long's request to leave the club with immediate effect. I personally feel very disappointed. He knows why he is leaving and I wish him all the best. We won't take him back again.'

New Hull KR signing Ryan Bailey said the responsibility that came with the surprise move from Leeds Rhinos would ultimately make him a better player. Within a week of Rovers announcing the departures of forwards Justin Poore and Neville Costigan they had snapped up the former England international, who had been a one-club player since making his Rhinos debut in 2002.

Widnes Vikings coach Denis Betts confirmed that Kevin Brown would captain the club in 2015 after the retirement of 2014 leader Jon Clarke.

The Vikings had accepted the decision of an independent tribunal to fine the club £20,000 for serious breaches of the sport's Operational Rules at the end of the Challenge Cup semi-final with Castleford Tigers at Leigh Sports Village in August. The club and the RFL were continuing work to bring to account the individuals responsible for the violent scenes that followed the conclusion of the match.

At the end of November Leeds captain Kevin Sinfield collected his MBE from the Duke of Cambridge in a ceremony at Buckingham Palace. Sinfield was targeting a playing return in Jamie Peacock's testimonial match early in the new year after post-season knee surgery.

England Academy star Ashton Golding agreed a new four-year deal with Leeds after the 18-year-old was named man of the match against the Australian Schoolboys in England's second Test win at Leigh.

Both England Academy coach Richard Marshall and his Australian counterpart Brian Battese forecast a bright future for the former Stanningley junior, who made his Super League debut in 2014 at London and was named the club's under-19s player of the season in that year.

The Aussie Schoolboys had won the first Test, also at Leigh, 22-18, with Golding the star for England along with Hull pair Jordan Abdull and Jansin Turgut and Wigan centre Oliver Gildart. A week later England got their revenge with a 28-14 victory.

December 2014

Catalans Dragons star halfback Scott Dureau said he was ready to put a difficult two-year spell on the sidelines behind him in 2015. Dureau returned to the Dragons after a mid-season loan stint with the Sydney Roosters. The Australian managed just one Super League appearance in 2014 after rupturing a biceps and spent most of the 2013 season out after having an operation to remove a non-malignant brain tumour.

Keighley Cougars' attempt to overturn their relegation from the Championship at the end of the 2014 season ended after the RFL AGM in December.

The RFL committed itself to reviewing its disciplinary process with a view to incorporating some form of external arbitration. But the Cougars did not have their Championship status restored nor would they receive compensation, despite being relegated after both Batley and Doncaster fielded ineligible dual-registration players. Keighley had been furious at an appeals panel overturning an initial decision to dock both clubs three points.

Wakefield Trinity Wildcats completed the signing of Hull FC halfback Jacob Miller, with the Australian signing a one-year deal. Miller, who joined the Black and Whites in 2013, failed to hold down a place under Lee Radford in 2014, spending time out on dual-registration at Championship club Doncaster. The Wildcats also signed Leeds Rhinos prop forward Ian Kirke.

Wildcats coach James Webster admitted that whilst his pride was hurt following the 50-28 Boxing Day defeat to Leeds, with 18-year-old winger Ash Handley scoring five tries, there was still plenty of time to improve.

In other festive friendlies, Castleford beat Featherstone at home 18-0, while Batley Bulldogs won the Heavy Woollen derby with Dewsbury Rams 18-16. The Warrington-Widnes game was frozen off.

England hooker Daryl Clark won the League Express readers' player-of-the-year award and, unsurprisingly, polled the most votes in the young players category too.

New Wolves signing Clark enjoyed a dream 2014, standing out in a Castleford team that defied most expectations in both league and cup before going on to win England selection and scoring with his first touch against Samoa in the Four Nations.

He became the first winner of the Man of Steel award since it was named after the late Steve Prescott and he also won the Super League Young Player of the Year award.

ACADEMY INTERNATIONAL SERIES

Saturday 6th December 2014

ENGLAND ACADEMY 18 AUSTRALIAN SCHOOLBOYS 22

ENGLAND ACADEMY: 1 Ashton Golding (Leeds Rhinos); 2 Callum Lancaster (Hull FC); 3 Oliver Gildart (Wigan Warriors); 4 Toby King (Warrington Wolves); 5 Ash Handley (Leeds Rhinos); 6 Jordan Abdull (Hull FC); 7 Joe Keyes (London Broncos); 8 Will Maher (Castleford Tigers); 9 Robbie Ward (Leeds Rhinos); 10 Tyler Dickinson (Huddersfield Giants); 11 Olly Davies (St Helens); 12 Nick Gregson (Wigan Warriors); 13 Jansin Turgut (Hull FC). Subs (all used): 14 Luke Waterworth (Wigan Warriors); 15 Ted Chapelhow (Widnes Vikings); 16 Mikey Wood (Huddersfield Giants); 17 Elliot Minchella (Leeds Rhinos).
Tries: Davies (30), Gildart (47, 79), Abdull (70);
Goals: Abdull 1/2, Keyes 0/2.
AUSTRALIAN SCHOOLBOYS: 5 Latrell Mitchell (Sydney Roosters); 2 Connor Cox (Morayfield State High School); 3 Tyrell Fuiaomano (Parramatta Eels); 4 Tevita Cottrell (South Sydney Rabbitohs); 1 Gideon Gela (North Queensland Cowboys); 6 Brock Lamb (Newcastle Knights); 7 Jack Cogger (Newcastle Knights); 8 Hame Sele (St George Illawarra Dragons); 9 Jayden Brailey (Cronulla Sharks); 10 Tom Amone (Parramatta Eels); 11 Ray Stone (Wests Tigers); 12 Ash Nisbet (Cronulla Sharks); 13 Nat Butcher (South Sydney Rabbitohs). Subs (all used): 14 Jacob Liddle (Wests Tigers); 18 Luicano Leilua (St George Illawarra Dragons); 16 Keegan Hipgrave (Brisbane Broncos); 17 Jacob Host (St George Illawarra Dragons).
Tries: Cottrell (9), Mitchell (23, 37), Fuiaomano (59); **Goals:** Lamb 3/4.
Rugby Leaguer & League Express Men of the Match:
England: Jordan Abdull; *Australia:* Brock Lamb.
Penalty count: 9-6; **Half-time:** 4-16; **Referee:** Sam Ansell (England);
Attendance: 1,583 *(at Leigh Sports Village).*

Friday 12th December 2014

ENGLAND ACADEMY 28 AUSTRALIAN SCHOOLBOYS 14

ENGLAND ACADEMY: 1 Ashton Golding (Leeds Rhinos); 2 Jack Johnson (Warrington Wolves); 3 Ash Handley (Leeds Rhinos); 4 Toby King (Warrington Wolves); 5 Jack Logan (Hull FC); 6 Jordan Abdull (Hull FC); 7 Joe Keyes (London Broncos); 8 Ted Chapelhow (Widnes Vikings); 9 Robbie Ward (Leeds Rhinos); 10 Tyler Dickinson (Huddersfield Giants); 11 Olly Davies (St Helens); 12 Jansin Turgut (Hull FC); 13 Sam Wilde (Warrington Wolves). Subs (all used): 14 Luke Waterworth (Wigan Warriors); 15 Will Maher (Castleford Tigers); 16 Mikey Wood (Huddersfield Giants); 17 Elliot Minchella (Leeds Rhinos).
Tries: Handley (2), Logan (27), Turgut (50), Ward (62), Johnson (72);
Goals: Abdull 4/5.
Sin bin: Ward (72) - fighting.
AUSTRALIAN SCHOOLBOYS: 5 Latrell Mitchell (Sydney Roosters); 2 Connor Cox (Morayfield State High School); 3 Braden Robson (Newcastle Knights); 4 Keenan Yorston (Cronulla Sharks); 1 Gideon Gela (North Queensland Cowboys); 6 Brock Lamb (Newcastle Knights); 7 Jack Cogger (Newcastle Knights); 8 Hame Sele (St George Illawarra Dragons); 9 Jayden Brailey (Cronulla Sharks); 10 Tom Amone (Parramatta Eels); 11 Tyrell Fuiaomano (Parramatta Eels); 12 Ash Nisbet (Cronulla Sharks); 13 Ray Stone (Wests Tigers). Subs (all used): 14 Jacob Liddle (Wests Tigers); 16 Keegan Hipgrave (Brisbane Broncos); 17 Jacob Host (St George Illawarra Dragons); 18 Oliver Clark (Penrith Panthers).
Tries: Mitchell (20), Nisbet (32), Liddle (55); **Goals:** Lamb 1/3.
Sin bin: Amone (72) - fighting.
Rugby Leaguer & League Express Men of the Match:
England: Sam Wilde; *Australia:* Brock Lamb.
Penalty count: 7-10; **Half-time:** 10-8; **Referee:** Tom Grant (England);
Attendance: 1,197 *(at Leigh Sports Village).*

JANUARY
Magic Johnson gets Boot

New Zealand halfback Shaun Johnson was the recipient of the 2014 Golden Boot, the prestigious award for the best player of the year selected by Rugby League World magazine. Johnson became only the fourth Kiwi to win the award, following in the footsteps of Hugh McGahan (1987), Stacey Jones (2002) and Benji Marshall (2010).

The big news in the first month of 2015 was that Wigan's 20-year-old winger Joe Burgess, a non-playing member of the England Four Nations squad, would be moving to the NRL to join Sydney Roosters at the end of the season.

Wigan were the 11/4 favourites to be crowned Super League Champions in 2015 according to bookmakers and new Challenge Cup sponsors Ladbrokes. The Warriors were to open Super League XX with a trip to Widnes Vikings, who were priced at 100-1 to win the title.

Champions St Helens, who defeated their arch-rivals in a memorable Grand Final the previous October, were second favourites at 7/2 to stage a successful defence and lift the trophy for a record seventh time, whilst six-time winners Leeds Rhinos were 9/2. Warrington Wolves were third favourites at 4/1.

Other teams that were tipped to make the Grand Final were Catalans Dragons at 11/2, Huddersfield Giants at 11/2 and Salford Red Devils at 10/1.

Wigan winger Josh Charnley was 4/1 favourite to top the try-scoring charts in 2015, closely followed by the Catalans' French fullback Morgan Escaré and last year's top try-scorer, Warrington Wolves newly-appointed captain Joel Monaghan, who were both priced at 6/1.

England and Wigan scrum-half Matty Smith was placed at 6/1 to be crowned Man of Steel, with Catalans Dragons' new recruit Todd Carney quoted at 7/1 along with St Helens playmaker Luke Walsh.

At 16/1 Wigan Warriors were also firm favourites to lift the Super League trophy and the Ladbrokes Challenge Cup in the same year. They were closely followed by St Helens at 20/1, Warrington Wolves at 25/1 and Leeds Rhinos at 28/1.

There were four rule changes, devised by the RFL Rules Committee, concerning the interpretation of the obstruction rule, the interchange in relation to players suffering concussion, changes in the application of the sin bin and new ways in which video referees would make their decisions.

The interpretation of the obstruction rule in particular had caused confusion among spectators in the 2014 season, with several examples of tries being disallowed in situations which defenders could not have prevented. In 2015 the question would be whether the defending team was materially disadvantaged. And if a player who was carrying the ball was tackled or succumbed to the tackle, then there would be no penalty, even if the lead runner appeared to run in front of him.

In 2015 each televised game would incorporate two video referees, while, before they made a decision, the main referee would indicate whether, in his opinion, a try had been scored or not. The video referees would then determine whether there was sufficient evidence to overturn his decision.

The new season would see referees able to sin bin players for foul play that was not deemed serious enough to merit a full red card, but where the offending player deserved to be punished by having some time off the field.

Teams would be allowed an extra 'free' interchange in the event of a player suffering an injury that required a pitchside concussion assessment. The change was designed to safeguard players against the unseen dangers of concussion by removing any subconscious pressure on medical staff to not be over-cautious in removing a player from the field for an assessment.

Leeds Academy star Ash Golding joined the 24 Rhinos players who had been given squad numbers at a warm-weather training camp in Florida.

Castleford Tigers winger Kirk Dixon's retirement was announced at the club's shirt presentation event. The 30-year-old had a disk removed from his neck and an artificial one put in its place after suffering from problems in his hand and arm due to a trapped nerve.

Among a raft of pre-season friendlies, veteran prop Andy Lynch was man of the match in his own testimonial game, in which the Tigers beat his former club Bradford Bulls 22-14. Wigan lost 18-14 Leigh Centurions who, with the Bulls, were expected to mount a serious challenge to be in Super League in 2016 under the new league structure.

Two late tries from Widnes youngster Declan Hulme saw the Vikings come from behind to lift the Karalius Cup against St Helens with a 20-16 win at Langtree Park.

And almost ten thousand fans watched the Hull derby at KC Stadium as new-look Hull KR laid out their intentions for the new Super League season with an impressive second-half display to gain a 28-22 victory to win the annual Clive Sullivan Trophy. A subsequent 40-nil defeat at Warrington burst the Robins' bubble.

Wakefield Trinity Wildcats also showed much promise in a 46-10 home win over Hull FC in a testimonial match for Gareth Ellis. Leeds Rhinos beat Bradford 34-14 in Jamie Peacock's Testimonial match. And St Helens got the better of arch-rivals Wigan in a 28-12 home win.

Local communities came together at Salford's AJ Bell Stadium to celebrate the life of murdered aid worker Alan Henning. For the record the Red Devils beat Swinton Lions 66-4. Before the game there was ninety seconds applause from the fans and players alike and Alan Henning's family were on the pitch to take gifts from both team captains.

LADBROKES CHALLENGE CUP - ROUND 1

Saturday 31st January 2015
British Army 8 Wath Brow Hornets 20
Castleford Lock Lane 64 Sharlston Rovers 0
East Leeds 12 Kells 20
Egremont Rangers 28 Wigan St Judes 0
Elland 26 Leeds Beckett University 0
Hull Dockers 10 Leigh Miners Rangers 6
Loughborough University 16 Hunslet Warriors 42
Normanton Knights 34 Myton Warriors 16
Oulton Raiders 60 Scarborough Pirates 6
Royal Air Force 0 Siddal 48
Royal Navy 32 Saddleworth Rangers 14
Skirlaugh Bulls 27 Aberdeen Warriors 20
Walney Central 28 Hunslet Parkside 8
West Bank Bears 14 South West London Chargers 10
West Hull 14 Thatto Heath Crusaders 12

Sunday 1st February 2015
Great Britain Police 0 Rochdale Mayfield 38
Valley Cougars 27 Leicester Storm 22

Saturday 7th February 2015
Featherstone Lions 46 Queens 10
Nottingham Outlaws 4 Blackbrook 50
Shaw Cross Sharks 18 York Acorn 16

LADBROKES CHALLENGE CUP - ROUND 2

Saturday 14th February 2015
Elland 16 Egremont Rangers 4
Hunslet Warriors 8 West Hull 24
Kells 52 Blackbrook 6
Leigh Miners Rangers 26 Walney Central 18
Normanton Knights 12 Shaw Cross Sharks 4
Oulton Raiders 48 Valley Cougars 0
Siddal 12 Featherstone Lions 31
Skirlaugh Bulls 30 Royal Navy 16
Wath Brow Hornets 27 Castleford Lock Lane 12
West Bank Bears 38 Great Britain Police 16

FEBRUARY
Every minute matters

Round 1

Favourites Wigan opened their campaign on the first Thursday night of the season at Widnes, who were priced at 100-1 to win Super League. Shaun Wane's side looked to be sailing to a first win when they led 16-0 after 35 minutes, with the Vikings down to 12 men after the 23rd minute dismissal of Patrick Ah Van for a high tackle on Josh Charnley and Kevin Brown sidelined with concussion after a thunderous hit from teenage Wigan prop Ryan Sutton.

Many thought the red card from James Child was an over-reaction as Ah Van caught his opposite from behind stopping his surge for the line, though Widnes coach Denis Betts wasn't among them.

On 35 minutes Joe Mellor scooped up a spilled ball on to race away for a try that Danny Tickle converted. From that point Widnes wouldn't be denied, Chris Dean crashing over for a converted try three minutes from time to produce the 22-22 final scoreline.

With former Bradford back-rower John Bateman outstanding, Joel Tomkins, playing at left centre, scored the first try of the season when he brushed off Stefan Marsh on eight minutes and Anthony Gelling helped himself to two tries. Even without Michael McIlorum, not playing because of a hand injury, Wigan looked in fine form.

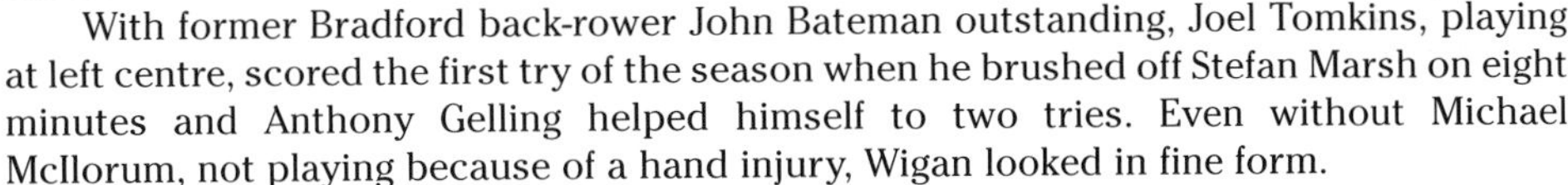

But Mellor's try was a key moment and six minutes into the second half Rhys Hanbury latched onto Mellor's grubber which evaded Matt Bowen to plant the ball behind the uprights, with Tickle's goal reducing the deficit to four points.

Wigan exploited their numerical advantage as Joe Burgess crossed wide on the left. Matty Smith banged over a towering conversion and Wigan looked back in charge at 22-12.

On 65 minutes Declan Hulme was stopped short and bundled into touch at the right corner and the referee ruled that he had been pushed out of play after having already been held. From the ensuing penalty Cameron Phelps crossed for a try on the left flank from a great pass by Hanbury, but Marsh, deputising for the substituted Tickle, was unable to add the difficult conversion.

But there was now a real belief amongst the majority of the 9,286 spectators – Widnes's biggest gate in over ten years – that their team could complete an improbable comeback. And with the Vikings laying siege to the Wigan line, Dean took a short ball from impressive debutant, former Hull halfback Aaron Heremaia, to crash over at the posts, leaving Marsh with a straightforward conversion to level the scores.

Ah Van was suspended for one match and Matty Smith took a one-game early guilty plea after being sin-binned for aiming a kick at Hanbury as he celebrated Dean's winning try under the posts.

Supporters appeared to give a massive thumbs up to the new 12-team structure of Super League, with several clubs posting significant crowd increases as the curtain came up on the 2015 season. The average attendance for the six matches was 10,497, which represented an increase of almost 2,000 per game on the same games the previous season, when the average figure was 8,573.

The biggest crowd of the weekend was at Langtree Park on the Friday night, when 12,008 spectators turned out to see the Champions, St Helens, begin the defence of their trophy, as second favourites, with an 18-7 victory over the Catalans Dragons.

Backrower Atelea Vea, signed from relegated London Broncos, had a debut to remember, opening the scoring in the eighth minute as he crashed onto his fellow debutant Travis Burns' pass to give Saints the lead.

Catalans welcomed back Remi Casty, named co-captain with Greg Mounis, after his year with Sydney Roosters but new signing Todd Carney was left out of the Dragons' matchday 17 because of a calf strain and, with Scott Dureau absent and Luke Walsh still missing for Saints, the game lacked creativity.

The Dragons' other big signing, former Australia centre Willie Tonga, lasted 12 seconds as he was stretchered from the field with concussion after making the first tackle of the game on Saints prop Alex Walmsley. Minutes later Thomas Bosc was hit by Joe Greenwood in a tackle that left the French halfback prone on the floor as the Catalans attacked the Saints' try line. A further five-minute stoppage saw Bosc ordered from the field under the new concussion criteria - leaving the Dragons playing with Ian Henderson and Mounis as makeshift halfbacks, although Bosc did return later.

Catalans had a Zeb Taia try denied by the video referee for an illegal challenge in the air, which puzzled most observers, before Burns' pass sent in Vea to open the scoring. Adam Swift had a try denied by the video ref for a foot in touch and Mark Percival looked a certain scorer but for a superb tackle from Bosc.

That seemed to swing the momentum of the game, as Catalans were then awarded a staggering eight penalties in a row inside the final minutes of the half. Three goal-line drop-outs increased the pressure and, as the penalties kept coming, Greg Richards was shown a yellow card by referee Phil Bentham seconds after the home side had been placed on a team warning.

And from the resulting penalty, Catalans struck as hooker Eloi Pelissier dived over to score just left of the posts, with Bosc nailing the goal to make it 6-6. Just before the break Bosc hit a field goal to make it 7-6.

Immediately after the resumption Saints were awarded two penalties and with the field position they attacked and shifted the ball from left to right to Tommy Makinson, who dived for the corner, only to be forced into touch by Taia and Morgan Escaré. However, the latter was penalised for using a shoulder charge on the St Helens winger.

From that penalty, James Roby, who made 65 tackles in the game, Jon Wilkin and Burns combined to feed Jonny Lomax, who joined into the line before sending Jordan Turner over to score down the left.

St Helens finished the stronger with sub Andre Savelio powering his way over two Dragons defenders to score. And five minutes from the end Makinson touched down in the corner to seal the win.

On the Saturday afternoon, Warrington beat Salford 22-8 in a brutal first-up match. The two teams tore into each other throughout the first quarter, with new Wolves signing Ashton Sims, Gareth Hock and Cory Paterson immersed in a ding-dong battle.

But after the Red Devils missed two clear-cut chances - both down to the defence of the excellent Stefan Ratchford - the Wolves pulled clear of their opponents with a lesson in clinical finishing, which demonstrated their title credentials for 2015.

Red Devils coach Iestyn Harris handed debuts to five new players, including

Paterson and halfback Michael Dobson, back from the Newcastle Knights for a fourth Super League club and starting on the bench, though fullback Kevin Locke missed out with a groin complaint.

Warrington also had three new signings on display in Sims, Daryl Clark and substitute Gary Wheeler.

The Wolves led 12-0 after half an hour before Reds prop Adam Walne was sin-binned for persistent interference. But perversely the Wolves sealed the result when they were a man down after Ben Westwood was sin-binned for a high tackle on Walne on 50 minutes, Ryan Atkins' try and Ratchford's conversion making it 18-0.

Former Leeds winger Ben Jones-Bishop grabbed himself a try double on his Salford debut but Rhys Evans' four-pointer in between was enough for Warrington.

On the Sunday Hull Kingston Rovers attracted a record attendance at the KC Lightstream Stadium for their clash against Leeds, although the Robins went down 30-40 to a late Rhinos' charge.

The Rhinos, with prop Adam Cuthbertson their only debutant, twice fought back from 14-point deficits to eventually win, to claim the best opening-day record in Super League, having lost only two of 20 fixtures.

Rovers suffered a huge blow beforehand with the loss of enforcers Mick Weyman and Ryan Bailey - who it had been hoped would debut against his old club - but they still turned out 11 debutants. Stand-off Terry Campese in particular left a great impression on debut with Albert Kelly a thrilling sidekick.

On the same afternoon, Marc Sneyd produced a man-of-the-match performance in Hull FC's 19-0 win at Huddersfield Giants. Huddersfield could not get out of first gear after a scrappy first half, as the visitors took a meagre 6-0 lead into the interval. In the second period the Airlie Birds took control, with a double to fullback Jamie Shaul putting the match out of reach as the Giants' frustration grew. Shaul's second try on 57 minutes was a lovely dancing effort, which effectively sunk the Giants. Sneyd's 63rd-minute field goal were the concluding points.

Castleford attracted 10,728 fans for their local derby against Wakefield Trinity Wildcats, with the kick-off being delayed by ten minutes to accommodate the crowds.

The Wildcats were just about every pundits tip for the wooden spoon and after 68 minutes, with the Tigers, orchestrated by new halfback Luke Gale, in total control and 22-6 up, the assessment looked sound.

But Pita Godinet's try on 69 minutes, as he raced onto Tim Smith's smart kick to the posts, turned the tide. Six minutes later Ali Lauitiiti was over after a Craig Hall half-break and offload and it was a nightmare for the Wheldon Road faithful as Smith's short pass had the Cas defence in knots and Danny Washbrook tore under the posts at the Wheldon Road end for Hall to convert for a 24-22 victory that saw the Wildcats win the Adam Watene Trophy.

Denny Solomona, signed from London, scored two fine tries on the right wing for the Tigers and there was another impressive debut from back-rower Junior Moors. Ben Roberts was left out of the starting 17. But Hall, Wakefield's signing from Hull KR was the pick of the debutants.

** Former Warrington winger Matt King scored the decisive try in golden-point extra time to secure an 18-14 victory for South Sydney Rabbitohs over Cronulla Sharks in the final of the NRL's Auckland Nines tournament.*

Round 2

Salford Red Devils chairman Marwan Koukash tweeted: 'I have had enough' shortly after the final hooter of his side's highly anticipated Thursday night home clash against St Helens, which ended in a 52-6 thumping. A week later Koukash said he was not walking away and was bringing in Australia coach Tim Sheens to advise the club. Head coach Iestyn Harris's position was not under threat.

Salford were missing Weller Hauraki, suspended for a match for dangerous contact in the round-one defeat at Warrington. But a polished St Helens display in which second-rower Joe Greenwood and centre Mark Percival both stood out, left Salford looking like a rabble by full-time.

Winger Ben Jones-Bishop scored after a brilliant individual effort in the first half as a Saints' attack broke down and he remained Salford's only try scorer after two games. Harris's woes were compounded by key players Michael Dobson (shoulder), Cory Paterson (shoulder), Kevin Locke (groin) and Jones-Bishop (knee) picking up injuries during the course of a night to forget for the Red Devils.

The writing was on the wall with the ease that Percival shrugged off Mason Caton-Brown for the game's opening try after 11 minutes. Luke Thompson's try just before half-time quickly repelled Jones-Bishop's brief response for the home side.

The game turned out the Gareth Hock's last appearance in a Salford shirt. He was sin-binned just after the hour mark for use of the knees in a tackle, having minutes earlier being penalised for the same offence. He was banned for three matches for each offence, meaning a six-week lay-off. Dr Koukash said he thought the former England forward's future might lay outside Rugby League, releasing him a week later. He signed for Championship side Leigh Centurions.

In the Friday-night TV game, Wigan, without the suspended Matty Smith, rallied in the second half to beat the Giants at home, two tries to Joel Tomkins and one each for Ryan Sutton and Michael McIlorum securing a 24-16 victory. It was a tough and niggly affair, with Sam Powell yellow-carded for a chicken-wing tackle and Sutton sin-binned for fighting with Craig Huby. Powell took a one-match early guilty plea. Eorl Crabtree avoided suspension after an early guilty plea for dangerous contact.

John Bateman stood out for the second week running for the Warriors, who drafted Ryan Hampshire into the side after George Williams was injured in the warm-up. The Giants led 16-10 at half-time, having scored three tries to Wigan's two, with the first coming in the seventh minute, with prop Anthony Mullally crashing over from Shaun Lunt's dummy-half feed.

Wigan regained their composure and eventually took the lead thanks to tries from Tomkins and Bateman, after Jamie Ellis had put the Giants in front, before Aaron Murphy pounced on a Jake Connor grubber to extend their advantage.

Wigan struck the crucial blow on 68 minutes when Bateman demonstrated a lethal combination of pace and footwork to break clear on halfway and hooker McIlorum was in support to finish off. Sutton then made sure of the points when he crashed over near the posts, just moments after emerging from the sin bin, and Hampshire rounded off the scoring with the conversion.

On the same night at the KC Stadium, the Wolves continued their perfect start to the season with a tough 7-6 victory over Hull FC. Gareth O'Brien's field goal on the stroke of half-time was all that separated the two best defensive sides in the opening two rounds.

2014 Man of Steel Daryl Clark showed a touch of class to elude the FC defence up the middle to score a trademark try, his first for his new side, on his 100th career appearance. Tom Lineham's 64th minute try, superbly converted by Marc Sneyd led to a tense last quarter of an hour as the Wolves hung on to their one-point lead.

In the third Friday night game, at Headingley, another close contest looked on the cards as the Rhinos and the Vikings finished the first half at 6-all. But in persistent rain, Leeds cut loose with four great touchdowns in a blistering nine-minute spell to overwhelm the gallant but contained Vikings - missing captain Kevin Brown, out with concussion - by 38-6. Adam Cuthbertson's all-round effort – including 45 tackles and telling offloads - sapped the Vikings' resolve. Prop Andy Yates, signed from Hunslet a year earlier but sidelined for 2014 with Achilles and then a biceps injury, made his debut off the bench.

On the Saturday afternoon, Scott Dureau, who last played for the Catalans in the second game of the 2014 season at Castleford, kicked a field goal to seal a 13-12 win over the Tigers in Perpignan. The 2012 Albert Goldthorpe Medal winner earned his first three points of the season with a performance of old.

It was another feisty affair, with Jake Webster avoiding suspension with an early guilty plea and Oliver Elima getting one match after a 35th-minute fight, sparked by a shoulder charge on Cas prop Scott Wheeldon by Eloi Pelissier. Pelissier pleaded guilty and got two matches.

The Tigers had taken a 6-0 lead thanks to Justin Carney's converted try and should have gone further ahead when right winger Denny Solomona was denied a try for offside.

The adoption in 2015 of the Australian system of the referee awarding try or no try, with the onus on the video referees to have conclusive proof to change the decision, proved Castleford's downfall.

The TV cameras could not provide a shot with Solomona in frame at the moment Luke Gale launched a perfect kick to the right corner. It was obvious Solomona was onside and he took the ball over his shoulder on the run for a superb score, but under the letter of the law the referee's decision could not be overturned.

Second-half tries from Morgan Escaré and Elliott Whitehead and a Dureau penalty gave the Dragons a 12-6 lead but a magnificent try from in-form Jordan Tansey after a Carney break from Liam Finn's drop-off and Gale's second conversion levelled with six minutes to go. Dureau settled it with his field goal that skimmed the inside of the post.

Which left only one Sunday game, in which Wakefield made it two from two, winger Chris Riley and halfback Jacob Miller netting a hat-trick of tries each in the Wildcats' 44-24 home victory over Hull KR.

The Wildcats were dominant in their 20-point victory, scoring eight tries, with five coming in the second half. Matty Ashurst crossed for Wakefield's first on his debut after the Robins started the match in a blaze, with Albert Kelly breaking away early on after intercepting Paul McShane's pass. Keal Carlile was then held up in Wakefield's in-goal area as Hull KR were camped on their line, but the home team managed to hold them out and thwart several Terry Campese bombs.

Hull KR broke the deadlock eight minutes in as Kelly hoisted a downtown that was left to bounce by the Wildcats' defence and he raced through to regather and score. After Ashurst's try, Tyrone McCarthy, back from a season in the Queensland Cup, restored Hull KR's six-point lead, but a Miller double just before the break gave Wakefield a 16-12 half-time lead.

It was still nip and tuck as Danny Kirmond - off a short pass from Tim Smith - and strong winger Ken Sio swapped tries, but Riley's genuine hat-trick took the Wildcats clear as the re-built Rovers spilled possession at frequent intervals.

** Leigh won a controversial and thrilling Championship opener 36-24 against Bradford on the Sunday. Six yellow cards were brandished and 26 penalties awarded in front of a bumper 7,449 crowd. Four players were suspended after a first-half brawl.*

World Club Series

A total of 51,902 people attended the three World Club Series games, including a capacity crowd of 17,980 at Langtree Park for the World Club Challenge between St Helens and South Sydney Rabbitohs on the Sunday night. Saints' 39-0 defeat was the biggest in the competition's history, eclipsing Saints' 38-0 defeat to Sydney Roosters in 2003.

The other two World Club Series games had seen St George Illawarra and Brisbane Broncos secure narrow victories, by six points and two points respectively, against Warrington and Wigan.

February

The presence of South Sydney co-owner Russell Crowe as a guest at Langtree Park on the Sunday night gave the game wider exposure. Crowe had made a point of being in St Helens rather than in Los Angeles for the Oscars ceremony the same night. He was happy with his team's performance but critical of the watered down format of the Series, referencing an idea he had put forward in the past to have an eight-team World Club Series with the final potentially being played in Las Vegas.

Brisbane coach Wayne Bennett admitted he was bemused when their World Club Series clash with Wigan Warriors went into golden point extra-time on the Saturday night. The Broncos eventually claimed a 14-12 victory in the second game to give Australia a series win, but the Broncos coach was left a little confused.

Bennett said he was not aware the game was going into extra-time and didn't actually see the point of doing so. But his team still got home after a controversial penalty in the 89th minute that Brisbane goal-kicker Corey Parker slotted home to seal the victory. He also admitted he didn't even realise Brisbane had won the series for the NRL with their win. 'I didn't know it was a series until you just told me,' Bennett said.

The expanded World Club Series was again scheduled to take place in the UK in 2016 and its long-term future was to be determined following a 2015 tournament review.

St Helens head coach Keiron Cunningham was unable to hide his disappointment after the Super League Champions were thumped 39-0 in the World Club Challenge, the third game of the series, on the Sunday night.

The Rabbitohs, with halfback Adam Reynolds in brilliant form, led 24-0 at half-time. New signing from Manly, Glenn Stewart, opened his account for Souths within two minutes of the game kicking off. With fullback Jonny Lomax in no man's land during Souths' first attacking set, a clever kick from Reynolds saw Stewart touch down, with Reynolds' goal making it 6-0. After Greg Inglis superbly prevented Adam Swift from touching down in the corner, Reynolds slotted a penalty goal to make it 8-0.

WORLD CLUB CHALLENGE

Sunday 22nd February 2015

ST HELENS 0 SOUTH SYDNEY RABBITOHS 39

SAINTS: 1 Jonny Lomax; 2 Tom Makinson; 17 Mark Percival; 3 Jordan Turner; 5 Adam Swift; 6 Travis Burns; 12 Jon Wilkin (C); 10 Kyle Amor; 9 James Roby; 8 Mose Masoe; 21 Joe Greenwood; 11 Atelea Vea; 15 Mark Flanagan. Subs (all used): 13 Louie McCarthy-Scarsbrook; 14 Alex Walmsley; 18 Luke Thompson; 25 Andre Savelio.
RABBITOHS: 1 Greg Inglis (C); 2 Alex Johnston; 3 Dylan Walker; 4 Bryson Goodwin; 5 Joel Reddy; 6 Luke Keary; 7 Adam Reynolds; 8 George Burgess; 9 Issac Luke; 10 David Tyrrell; 11 Glenn Stewart (D); 12 John Sutton; 15 Ben Lowe. Subs (all used): 13 Jason Clark; 16 Chris McQueen; 17 Tom Burgess; 20 Chris Grevsmuhl.
Tries: Stewart (2), Walker (20), Inglis (24), Reddy (31, 67), Keary (47), McQueen (59); **Goals:** Reynolds 5/7, Luke 0/1; **Field goal:** Reynolds (78).
Rugby Leaguer & League Express Men of the Match: *Saints:* Atelea Vea; *Rabbitohs:* Adam Reynolds.
Penalty count: 5-6; **Half-time:** 0-24;
Referee: Richard Silverwood; **Attendance:** 17,980 *(at Langtree Park).*

Saints looked to have got back in the game when Mark Percival crossed in the right corner. The video referee was called and it was clear that Issac Luke had not only got his arm under the ball but also slid Percival into touch. In a flash Souths were in again. The NRL champions were cutting Saints open at will and this time a scintillating break from the superb Reynolds carved the home side up in the right centre, with Dylan Walker in support to race home.

Four minutes later, the mercurial Reynolds provided a platform for Inglis to dance his way over. Reynolds' goal took the lead out to 18-0. The Bunnies' fourth try put the result beyond doubt. John Sutton's infield kick bounced and curled in front of the posts, with new winger Joel Reddy the recipient to touch down under the posts.

St Helens' Kyle Amor outnumbered by the Souths defence

Just before half-time Percival again thought he had crossed - and so too did referee Silverwood, who sent the call upstairs with the feeling he had grounded. However, the video referee disagreed, adjudging Percival to have knocked on in the act of scoring.

There was no relaxation from the Rabbitohs after the break. Seven minutes in, Souths crossed again. Reynolds' kicking game had torn the Saints to shreds and, after his deft chip was palmed back by a Souths attacker, halfback partner Luke Keary touched down - the third Souths score from a kick.

Chris McQueen crossed just prior to the hour mark and the Rabbitohs levelled up the 38-point record margin eight minutes later, when a simple finish from Reddy gave him his second try, before Reynolds slotted a field goal to make it 39-0 and send the Rabbitohs into the World Club Challenge record books.

St George Illawarra won a see-sawing 18-12 victory against Warrington Wolves in the opening match of the World Club Series at the Halliwell Jones Stadium on the Friday night.

Only seven penalties were dished out in the entire match, with just one to the NRL side, as several high tackles went unpunished by referee Ben Thaler. St George Illawarra winger Eto Nabuli was lucky not to have been shown a card of any description for a high shot on Warrington counterpart Kevin Penny in the first half, whilst Jason Nightingale escaped sanction for a grab of Rhys Evans off the ball. In the second half, Thaler also failed to show a card to Benji Marshall for a high tackle on Gareth O'Brien.

In the end, halfback Marshall's astute kicking game proved the difference between the two teams in a match that was not short of controversy or talking points.

Warrington, who suffered a blow before kick-off with loss of fullback Stefan Ratchford to injury, with Gary Wheeler taking his place, started poorly, Ashton Sims knocking the ball on just 16 seconds in. A short ball from Marshall put rampaging Welsh international Tyson Frizell over for the first try.

O'Brien pegged the Wolves level 11 minutes later. The halfback threw a great dummy to break through the line and then dummied again to beat Josh Dugan for an impressive solo try. O'Brien then converted to tie the scores up at 6-6.

But Richie Myler's knock on from a play-the-ball on his own 30-metre line helped put St George in again. Gareth Widdop put in a short grubber and Joel Thompson was first to the ball just ahead of Joel Monaghan to put the Dragons back in front.

After Nabuli's reckless challenge on Penny, Warrington tied the scores up again through Ryan Atkins, the former England international busting through a handful of tackles, though O'Brien couldn't convert from the sideline, so the Dragons maintained a two-point lead.

In the second half the aggressive defence and frenetic pace continued. A penalty on 58 minutes after Marshall caught O'Brien once again tied the match up via the boot of the Warrington halfback.

Tempers were flaring before Dugan's try off a cheeky Marshall kick proved to be the winning score. Marshall's banana kick was spilled by Warrington hooker Daryl Clark and Dugan was there to pounce.

Warrington rallied in the final 15 minutes, but the Dragons' defence held firm.

WORLD CLUB SERIES

Friday 20th February 2015

WARRINGTON WOLVES 12
ST GEORGE ILLAWARRA DRAGONS 18

WOLVES: 23 Gary Wheeler; 2 Rhys Evans; 5 Joel Monaghan (C); 4 Ryan Atkins; 24 Kenny Penny; 20 Gareth O'Brien; 7 Richard Myler; 8 Chris Hill; 9 Daryl Clark; 10 Ashton Sims; 17 Ben Currie; 18 James Laithwaite; 12 Ben Westwood. Subs (all used): 3 Chris Bridge; 13 Ben Harrison; 14 Mick Higham; 19 Anthony England.
Tries: O'Brien (12), Atkins (29); **Goals:** O'Brien 2/3.
DRAGONS: 1 Josh Dugan; 2 Eto Nabuli; 3 Dane Nielsen; 4 Dylan Farrell; 5 Jason Nightingale; 6 Gareth Widdop; 7 Benji Marshall; 8 Rory O'Brien; 9 Mitch Rein; 10 Leeson Ah Mau; 11 Tyson Frizell; 12 Joel Thompson; 13 Ben Creagh (C). Subs (all used): 14 Trent Merrin; 15 Jack de Belin; 16 Jake Marketo; 17 George Rose.
Tries: Frizell (1), Thompson (18), Dugan (62);
Goals: Widdop 3/3.
Rugby Leaguer & League Express Men of the Match:
Wolves: Ben Westwood; *Dragons:* Josh Dugan.
Penalty count: 6-1; **Half-time:** 12-10; **Referee:** Ben Thaler;
Attendance: 13,080 *(at Halliwell Jones Stadium).*

Saturday 21st February 2015

WIGAN WARRIORS 12 BRISBANE BRONCOS 14
(after golden point extra-time)

WARRIORS: 1 Matt Bowen; 2 Josh Charnley; 3 Anthony Gelling; 4 Dan Sarginson; 5 Joe Burgess; 6 George Williams; 7 Matty Smith; 8 Dominic Crosby; 9 Michael McIlorum; 28 Ryan Sutton; 11 Joel Tomkins (C); 12 Liam Farrell; 14 John Bateman. Subs (all used): 17 Tony Clubb; 24 Taulima Tautai; 25 Larne Patrick; 26 Logan Tomkins.
Tries: L Farrell (25), Burgess (79); **Goals:** Smith 2/2.
Sin bin: Gelling (90) - charging down penalty attempt.
BRONCOS: 1 Jordan Kahu; 2 Daniel Vidot; 3 Aaron Whitchurch; 4 Justin Hodges; 5 Lachlan Maranta; 6 Anthony Milford; 7 Ben Hunt; 8 Josh McGuire; 9 Andrew McCullough (C); 10 Adam Blair; 11 Alex Glenn; 12 Sam Thaiday; 13 Corey Parker. Subs (all used): 14 Mitchell Dodds; 15 James Gavet; 16 Joe Ofahengaue; 17 Kodi Nikorima.
Tries: McCullough (8), Maranta (57); **Goals:** Parker 3/4.
Rugby Leaguer & League Express Men of the Match:
Warriors: John Bateman; *Broncos:* Corey Parker.
Penalty count: 5-8; **Half-time:** 6-6; **Referee:** Phil Bentham;
Attendance: 20,842 *(at DW Stadium).*

Game two of the new series on the Saturday night at DW Stadium was again played at breakneck speed and had intensity throughout.

There were big hits aplenty in a first half where Andrew McCullough and Liam Farrell traded converted tries, McCullough picking up and grounding under the posts after Joe Burgess lost the ball two metres from his line on a kick-return after only eight minutes. But on 25 minutes, Farrell was quick to react and he collected George Williams' clever kick to touch down to the left of the posts.

Brisbane went back in front in the second half through winger Lachlan Maranta and that looked like sealing the win until Burgess popped up in the dying seconds to send the game into golden point extra time in front of over 20,000 fans.

Both teams had failed field-goal attempts before referee Phil Bentham penalised Joel Tomkins for a high tackle on Corey Parker just seconds before the first period ended and, after Anthony Gelling was sin-binned for trying to charge down the kick, Parker ignored the boos to clinch the win.

Wigan were without captain Sean O'Loughlin and Sam Powell, with the former out for six weeks with a knee problem and the young halfback suspended for a chicken wing tackle in the win over Huddersfield. Dan Sarginson was back in at centre.

The Broncos got a lucky call for an offside just before the hour mark and made that fresh set pay as they spread the ball wide and Maranta was able to collect Justin Hodges' cut-out ball. Parker missed the conversion, but Brisbane led 10-6.

An off-the-ball block from John Bateman then gifted the Broncos a penalty and Parker opted to take the two and extend their lead to 12-6 with 12 minutes remaining. Brisbane were finding holes everywhere now with Anthony Milford being put through a massive gap by Adam Blair - but they could not put the game to bed.

And just as it looked like time was going to beat Wigan, they produced a try out of absolutely nothing. The ball was spread to the left and Burgess, who hadn't had the best of games, broke clear before exchanging passes with Williams to touch down. Crucially, Matty Smith converted to send the game into extra-time.

After forcing a goal-line drop-out, the Broncos won the position to win the game. Referee Phil Bentham penalised Tomkins under the Wigan posts for his innocuous challenge on Parker and the game reached an anti-climactic conclusion.

Round 3

St Helens responded to their 39-0 World Club Challenge humiliation when they bounced back on a five-day turnaround to beat Castleford Tigers 21-14 at Langtree Park on the last Friday night of February.

A spilt bomb by Jordan Tansey and an offside penalty against Luke Gale gifted Saints a first real sniff at the tryline on nine minutes. Atelea Vea, Kyle Amor and Alex Walmsley softened up the Tigers' defence before they shuttled the ball from left to right with some slick handling from Travis Burns and Jonny Lomax, which saw Adam Swift stroll over in the corner and Mark Percival add the goal.

The Tigers had two tries ruled out, the second on 32 minutes when a glorious dummy from Liam Finn opened up Saints in front of their own posts. As the halfback hit the ground he delivered an excellent offload to Ryan Boyle, who touched down, only for the referee to deem it a forward pass, although the replay on the big screen showed otherwise.

Against the run of play Saints had the final word on the stroke of half-time when a Burns bomb was spilled by Michael Channing, resulting in a goal-line drop-out. After Walmsley bulldozed his way downfield, Burns got a lovely short ball out to Lomax, who ghosted through the Tigers' fringe defence before looping a beautiful pass for Tommy Makinson to cruise in at the corner to make it 10-0.

Salford's Adam Walne in the thick of the action against Hull FC

Castleford got off to the worst possible start in the second half when Justin Carney's crazy long pass inside his own ten-metre zone failed to find any of his teammates, leaving Josh Jones to pick up and wrestle his way over to score the simplest of tries on 42 minutes. Percival missed the difficult kick, but at 14-0 the Tigers were up against it.

But Carney went from zero to hero with two tries in three minutes to stun the Langtree Park crowd. The first came on 48 minutes when, after a great burst from Oliver Holmes, Shenton's great offload down the short side at the ruck saw the winger ground the ball in the corner.

Three minutes later an amazing line break and stunning offload from Junior Moors allowed Luke Gale to float a kick over the Saints defensive line, which Carney pouched with ease to touch down. Gale missed both attempted conversions, but at 14-8 the champions were looking over their shoulder.

But after Grant Millington knocked on inside his own '10', Saints capitalised from the scrum as they shifted the ball left on the first play and Percival squeezed in at the corner after a brilliant offload from Jones. At 20-8, the starch was taken out of the Tigers.

Saints then saw the game out with great professionalism and a field goal from Jon Wilkin on 73 minutes was the final nail in the coffin, despite a late try from Tansey, who collected a kick from Gale to touch down under the posts.

Castleford remained point-less but off the field there was good news. Chief executive Steve Gill told League Express that the Tigers were planning to be in a new ground for the 2017 season, after planning permission was approved for the Five Towns Park project.

Leeds Rhinos were the only other team with a perfect start to Super League XX as a Thursday night 28-24 home win against Huddersfield made it three wins from three.

Up until the 63rd minute and a Kyle Wood try, which cemented a near-sensational comeback from initially 18-0 and then ten points down, the Giants had not scored in the second half of a Super League game this season.

Soon afterwards Brett Ferres, who had a discordant night, rumbled over and Danny Brough gave the visitors a lead with his fourth goal, which took him to 3,000 career points.

The score stood at 24-22 to the visitors, as it had finished in the corresponding fixture the previous season. But Paul Aiton, who was busy throughout, chose the perfect time to post his first-ever points in blue and amber, sniping over from dummy-half with six minutes remaining, on his back and just retaining possession of the ball.

Warrington lost their winning record on the Saturday afternoon with a 38-18 defeat at Catalans. Todd Carney made his Dragons debut but it was the other Australian halfback, Scott Dureau, who stole the show.

With both sides lacking several key figures through injury and suspension, the encounter was far from fluent. The Wolves, without Stefan Ratchford, Richie Myler, Rhys Evans and Simon Grix, were forced to think on their feet and gave Gareth O'Brien and Gary Wheeler their first start together in the halves.

The Dragons were also far from full strength, with Olivier Elima, Thomas Bosc, Eloi Pelissier and Rémi Casty unavailable.

Zeb Taia's brace of tries in the space of three minutes on the hour mark gave the Catalans an unassailable 30-12 lead after they had led 18-0 at the break, with the Wolves unable to retain possession.

Wakefield also dropped their first points of the season, in a 58-16 rout at Widnes on the Sunday. It was a St David's Day to remember for Cardiff-born Lloyd White, as the Welshman helped himself to a personal haul of 24 points on his first appearance of the year, including four tries, as the Vikings powered to their first win of the campaign in impressive style, running in ten tries against the shell-shocked Wildcats.

Salford got off the mark in a nip and tuck 32-28 home win over Hull FC. The Red Devils' win was down largely to the brilliant Rangi Chase. Switched to fullback after two injuries in the backline, he created all three of his side's second-half tries plus one in the first, producing the kind of virtuoso performance that won him the Man of Steel in 2011 when at Castleford.

His stunning second-half assist for Josh Griffin's second try was a piece of ball-handling magic, first dummying a drop-off with the ball leaving his hands and somehow returning to them, and then when tackled looping a five-metre pass around his back to Griffin.

Hull centre or second rower Steve Michaels wasn't selected after police in Queensland linked him to a drugs investigation that centred on his former club Gold Coast Titans.

Meanwhile Red Devils fullback Kevin Locke continued to be courted by the Scottish Rugby Union in anticipation of a move to the 15-man code.

Hull KR coach Chris Chester admitted he was a happy man after his side claimed its first win of Super League XX, but he said it was no less than they deserved.

FIRST UTILITY SUPER LEAGUE TABLE
Sunday 1st March

	P	W	D	L	F	A	D	PTS
St Helens	3	3	0	0	91	27	64	6
Leeds Rhinos	3	3	0	0	106	60	46	6
Catalans Dragons	3	2	0	1	58	48	10	4
Warrington Wolves	3	2	0	1	47	52	-5	4
Wakefield T Wildcats	3	2	0	1	84	104	-20	4
Widnes Vikings	3	1	1	1	86	76	10	3
Wigan Warriors	3	1	1	1	66	60	6	3
Hull FC	3	1	0	2	53	39	14	2
Hull Kingston Rovers	3	1	0	2	76	104	-28	2
Salford Red Devils	3	1	0	2	46	102	-56	2
Castleford Tigers	3	0	0	3	48	58	-10	0
Huddersfield Giants	3	0	0	3	40	71	-31	0

The Robins rallied from 20-6 down to snatch a dramatic 22-20 home win against Wigan, thanks to Kieran Dixon's late try and a cool conversion from Italian international winger Josh Mantellato. It was a first victory over Wigan in 15 attempts.

Terry Campese's perfect kicking game was the difference as the Warriors were forced to defend set after set on their line and his three point-show took him the top of the Albert Goldthorpe Medal standings.

MARCH
Moving up

Round 4

Kevin Sinfield moved up into the top-four points scorers in Rugby League history in Leeds' astonishing win at Hull FC in the first Thursday night TV game of March.

Sinfield's personal tally of 15 points from the 43-12 win was enough to take him past John Woods on the all-time scorers list, with just three men now above him on the 120-year-old list. Sinfield was unlikely to catch Neil Fox and Jim Sullivan, the top two, but Gus Risman was likely have his tally of 4,050 points passed by Sinfield, with the Rhinos captain now sat on 3,995.

Leeds produced a stunning second-half display to maintain their perfect start to Super League XX with four wins from four.

Trailing 12-0 at half-time with Hull in seeming command after two tries from Leon Pryce, seven unanswered second-half tries, all converted by Sinfield, condemned Hull to their third straight defeat in front of a frustrated home crowd at the KC Stadium.

Young prop Brad Singleton turned the game on its head in the first four minutes of the second half. With many spectators still returning to their seats from the interval, Danny McGuire was the beneficiary of Singleton's 40-metre break from behind the ruck. On the next attack Singleton took a cut-out pass from Sinfield to score. Sinfield reached his milestone shortly afterwards as he continued to convert an avalanche of Leeds tries.

Rob Burrow completed a double two minutes from time with his 150th Super League try, with a Sinfield field goal sandwiched in between to cap off a remarkable second-half performance that saw Hull concede 43 unanswered points.

St Helens had to show some grit to maintain their perfect start to the domestic season with a 20-16 win in a televised Friday night game at Wakefield.

Saints, already without Travis Burns and Kyle Amor through suspension and Luke Walsh with injury, lost Jonny Lomax and Mark Percival through leg injuries and Luke Thompson, with concussion after a head clash with teammate Mose Masoe, during the game. And the depleted Saints repelled a late Wildcats' comeback to hold on for the win.

Saints won the game up the middle, with Alex Walmsley, Masoe and Atelea Vea outstanding as Paul Wellens played his first game since the 2014 Grand Final in the unfamiliar position of scrum-half.

Wakefield went into the break 12-6 up and should have gone further in front early in the second half when a long pass found Reece Lyne and he strolled in. But the video referee saw an obstruction by Ali Lauitiiti in the lead up and it was no try.

The Wildcats had no luck again a few minutes later when Craig Hall put Riley over in the left corner from a long, flat pass, but it was harshly ruled forward.

Saints made the most of their good fortune when Louie McCarthy-Scarsbrook picked up a loose pass and made 70 metres downfield. On the next tackle, with Wakefield's defence in disarray, Joe Greenwood dived in and the visitors were level.

At the 50-minute mark a Tommy Makinson penalty put St Helens ahead by two points and that became eights points just four minutes later, after Jordan Turner was first to a Jon Wilkin bomb that was allowed to bounce. Video replays suggested Turner was in front of the kicker but the video ref gave the try the green light.

The lead was cut to four points with eleven minutes left, Dean Collis chipping for Richard Owen to score on the right wing.

It was thrilling finish. With the last play of the game Lauitiiti tried to force his way over, taking five St Helens defenders with him, but he was unable to ground as the full-time siren sounded.

Castleford Tigers got off the mark at the fourth attempt, and in some style, with a stunning 42-14 Friday night win over Wigan at the Mend-a-Hose Jungle.

Luke Gale was the star of the show on a night that Wigan coach Shaun Wane described as 'the worst day of my coaching career by far'. Fullback Luke Dorn, in his first match of the season after recovering from injury, added scintillating pace from the rear and had a hand in several of his side's tries in addition to snaring a score of his own.

Winger Justin Carney, who had copped some criticism during the week for a couple of careless errors in the previous outing at St Helens, laid the bogey to rest with two trademark barnstorming tries in the first 13 minutes as the Tigers made the most of an early 4-0 penalty count in their favour.

The Giants got their first win of Super League XX, Danny Brough starring in a 24-12 home verdict over Widnes Vikings.

The Vikings, hugely encouraged by two great home displays against Wigan and Wakefield, but still trying to open their account away from home, took an early lead through Joe Mellor and were still in the game when a converted Manase Manuokafoa try brought it back to 14-12 with 16 minutes remaining. Not until Eorl Crabtree's try with seven minutes left did the Giants look assured of victory.

The Wolves made it three wins from four after edging a home thriller with Hull KR 32-24, Matthew Russell continuing his impressive form on the wing with two tries to his name and Kevin Penny producing a top performance. Stefan Ratchford returned at fullback, to offset the loss of Ryan Atkins early on the Sunday morning due to illness, and he was the game's top performer.

A superb offload from Robins captain Terry Campese - who was excellent again - put Graeme Horne over to reduce the gap to just two points as a thrilling contest entered the final ten minutes. But, with just six minutes left on the clock, the Wolves secured the result. A magnificent ball from the exceptional Ratchford freed Ben Currie, who showed great pace to out-run Ken Sio and touch down.

Todd Carney suffered a broken rib during the 40-40 draw against Salford Red Devils at the Stade Gilbert Brutus, after a late tackle by Salford prop Lama Tasi. Dragons coach Laurent Frayssinous was incensed after the game, but the RFL Match Review Panel found no case to answer.

The highest ever score for a Super League draw ended in even more controversial circumstances. With two minutes to go and under his own posts, Morgan Escaré was penalised for getting up and playing on despite being tackled. The current interpretation was to make the player go back and play the ball, but referee Phil Bentham penalised him for not playing the ball and Josh Griffin added the simple penalty to level the scores.

Frayssinous's incredulity was echoed by many fans, but it didn't stop the RFL fining him £500.

Round 5

Warrington ended Leeds' winning start at four games with an 18-6 home win on the Friday night.

Zak Hardaker was absent, left out of the Leeds squad after it was confirmed police were to interview both him and Leeds teammate Elliot Minchella over an alleged assault in Leeds that had taken place before the start of the season. Hardaker's absence meant a first start and second appearance for Ashton Golding, the top performer when England Academy beat the Australian Schoolboys the previous December.

March

Warrington captain Joel Monaghan was missing from the Wolves squad with a hamstring strain, so Chris Hill took over the role, and Gary Wheeler was left out of the 17-man squad after he suffered a calf injury in training, with Chris Bridge and Ryan Atkins both returning to the side.

Kevin Penny opened the scoring when he threaded across field from the right wing and then accelerated into the clear for a terrific try. Penny was then called upon at the other end, combining with Stefan Ratchford to deny Ryan Hall. The England winger then uncharacteristically bombed another chance after Carl Ablett who, after Joel Moon's departure with a head injury, had moved to centre, had set him up, only for Hall to knock on with the line at his mercy.

Warrington's march became steadily more inexorable, led by the inexhaustible Ben Westwood forcing another drop-out and, when Gareth O'Brien teased a kick to the posts, Ratchford raced through and was awarded the touchdown after a considerable degree of analysis by the video referee.

Warrington's defensive fortitude won them another score in the 56th minute as Kevin Sinfield was hurried into a misplaced pass and O'Brien gathered the ball on the free play to send Atkins over by the posts, with Ratchford goaling.

Sinfield's re-start didn't travel ten metres but Leeds were back in the game soon after with a magnificent try. Sinfield's pass found Hall, who offloaded to Kallum Watkins and Tom Briscoe finished impressively to cap a 60-metre move that Sinfield was able to convert. But it was a fifth consecutive regular-season defeat at the Halliwell Jones for Leeds, who lost winger Briscoe with a long-term shoulder injury.

St Helens sat on top of the Super League table with ten points from five wins, after they came back from a 14-6 half-time deficit at Widnes on the Friday night to score four tries and triumph 30-20, despite having several key players, including James Roby, absent with injury.

Widnes were also without the injured Kevin Brown, Lloyd White, Hep Cahill, Cameron Phelps, Willie Isa and Manase Manuokafoa, with pivots Grant Gore and Danny Craven called up to the 17-man squad along with the returning Alex Gerrard.

Lance Hohaia deputised for Roby and scored two tries in a man-of-the-match performance.

The Red Devils, with Rangi Chase the star, stretched their unbeaten run to three games following Tim Sheens' arrival at the club, with their 24-18 home win on the Sunday against Wakefield moving them up to sixth in the table, Adrian Morley making his 300th Super League appearance. Chase, Greg Johnson, Weller Hauraki and Junior Sa'u all crossed for the home side.

The Wildcats, who scored tries through Jacob Miller, Paul McShane and Craig Hall, picked up yet more injuries. Matty Ashurst was already ruled out for three months following an injury suffered against St Helens. Scott Anderson suffered a medial ligament injury at Widnes the week before and was also a long-term absentee. Lopini Paea was injured in the run-up to the Salford match which saw hooker Pita Godinet withdraw midway through the defeat with a neck injury.

Daryl Powell was left 'speechless' after the Tigers' 22-0 defeat to Huddersfield on the Thursday night in a dour game at the John Smith's Stadium.

Luke Robinson returned after missing Huddersfield's last two games with a back injury to fill the void left by Shaun Lunt, who had surprisingly departed for Hull Kingston Rovers earlier in the week on a season-long loan deal.

Jermaine McGillvary was the gamestar and kept opposing number Justin Carney quiet all game as Aaron Murphy's try as the game entered the final quarter confirmed that Castleford - with captain Michael Shenton out with a shoulder problem - were down and out.

Lunt made a two-try debut for Hull KR at home to Catalans Dragons as despite trailing 20-4 until the 38th minute, the Albert Kelly-inspired Robins emerged 50-20 victors.

Three Rovers tries in five minutes around the hour mark took the score from 22-20 to 38-20, which proved an unassailable lead for the home side. Winger Ken Sio ended with a hat-trick of tries. Mitch Allgood was banned for two games after being sin-binned in the 23rd minute for punching Scott Dureau. Ben Pomeroy also got a one-match ban for running in and punching.

Hull KR had been hit with the news that prop Michael Weyman had been forced into retirement because of an ongoing knee injury

Wigan needed to dig deep to end their run of consecutive Super League defeats with a scratchy 13-12 home victory over Hull FC.

First-half tries from Joel Tomkins and Dan Sarginson put Wigan 12-0 up. Tries from Fetuli Talanoa and Callum Lancaster sandwiched a Matty Smith 66th minute field goal which settled the match in the Warriors' favour.

Hull almost snatched it late on as they piled the pressure on, but Danny Houghton switched the ball to the blind side instead of closer to the posts to secure a draw and Liam Watts' pass to Talanoa was high and into touch as Wigan survived.

** David Collier, the former chief executive of the England and Wales Cricket Board, was appointed first chief executive of the Rugby League International Federation.*

Round 6

St Helens maintained their hundred per cent record when they beat Warrington Wolves 32-24 at Langtree Park in the Thursday-night TV game.

It was at times a thrilling contest and, with both sides showing a willingness to attack from any area of the field, there was a wealth of long-range breaks, desperate cover tackles and terrific tries.

Both coaches acknowledged after the game that St Helens dominated long periods of the match. But trailing by 30-12 with little over ten minutes remaining, the Wolves mounted an unlikely surge that could still have yielded a draw.

With Luke Walsh yet to make his 2015 bow, Jon Wilkin, particularly in the first half, thrived in his makeshift position of scrum-half, creating two tries and scoring another. Prop Alex Walmsley and back-rowers Atelea Vea and Joe Greenwood were again outstanding. Walmsley's explosive start to the season saw him at the top of the Albert Goldthorpe Medal standings.

Saints led 18-6 at the break, with Warrington twice making long-range breaks that produced no tries, Travis Burns lucky not to be sin-binned for a professional foul after Ryan Atkins tore away from deep in only the second minute. Tries from Greenwood, Wilkin and Adam Swift gave St Helens the advantage against Daryl Clark's dummy-half effort for the Wolves.

Burns missed an early second-half penalty attempt before Warrington responded. Again it was a try from dummy-half, with this time Mickey Higham the scorer.

Saints restored their two-score lead through Louie McCarthy-Scarsbrook's barge-over effort and, after Kevin Penny had a spectacular effort correctly disallowed, the home side looked to have sealed matters.

When Vea swooped on a Westwood mistake and charged up field, he swatted off a host of visiting defenders, creating the position for James Roby to send Tommy Makinson over on the next tackle.

But still the Wolves would not surrender. Penny got the try his efforts deserved when he supported Chris Bridge after a charge-down of Wilkin's kick, juggling the ball before racing away from Burns. And when Chris Hill threw a huge dummy to score a third Warrington dummy-half try, the Wolves were suddenly within six points with three minutes still to play.

But their hopes ended when Bridge produced an ill-advised pass in the next set of six and Saints eventually sealed the two points when Burns slotted a last-minute penalty goal.

Leeds bounced back with a 26-14 home victory over Wigan in front of a bumper crowd on the Friday night. Zak Hardaker returned to the Leeds side, playing a key role. The Rhinos had announced that week they were considering action against Hardaker and teammate Elliot Minchella after the police decided not to prosecute them for an incident that took place in a Leeds student hall of residence prior to the start of the season.

After the duo were released by police it emerged they had admitted to an assault charge and had both paid £200 in compensation to their victim, a 22-year-old student, as well as writing a letter of apology. It had been the Rhinos who reported Hardaker and Minchella to the police when images of the incident came to light.

On the Friday, Leeds had teenage winger Ash Handley on home debut in place of Tom Briscoe, whose shoulder injury suffered at Warrington required surgery. Logan Tomkins and Connor Farrell appeared in Wigan's 17 in place of Sam Powell (calf) and Ryan Sutton (concussion).

Prop Adam Cuthbertson's seven offloads, which was half as many as the entire Wigan haul, caused havoc and played a part in three of the Rhinos' touchdowns. He was assisted by the tireless Stevie Ward and hard-working skipper Danny McGuire, who was standing in for hamstring victim Kevin Sinfield.

Narrowly ahead at the break, despite being more dominant than the 16-14 scoreline suggested, Leeds kept the Warriors scoreless in the second half. The first try of the second half, by Liam Sutcliffe on the hour to make it 20-14, on the back of a 5-0 penalty count, sapped Wigan's remaining energy and resolve.

Castleford responded to their previous week's horror show at Huddersfield with a 30-16 home win over Salford. The Tigers were given a boost by the return, much earlier than expected, of captain and centre Michael Shenton, who had suffered a dislocated shoulder in the Wigan match and who had not been named in the 19-man squad. Shenton celebrated his comeback with a try, while stand-off Liam Finn turned on a master-show, with a hand or a foot in all six of his side's touchdowns, two of them going to winger Justin Carney. Carney and former Tigers hero Rangi Chase were both sin-binned after a spat on the half hour.

Catalans suffered a host of injury problems to their outside backs during their 33-22 defeat at Hull FC, again on the Friday night. Todd Carney, making a shock return from broken ribs, suffered a tear to his quadriceps, while Michael Oldfield was taken from the field with a knee injury.

After having won only one from their first five matches, Hull FC put on their best display of the year. Jordan Rankin scored a brilliant solo try to give his side the lead and was heavily involved in his side's following four tries.

Hull scored three tries in ten minutes - through Rankin, Steve Michaels and Fetuli Talanoa - to end the first half and, although Thomas Bosc pegged one back on the stroke of half-time, the 22-10 lead gave them the confidence to go on with the job, a double from Tom Lineham confirming their second-half dominance.

Huddersfield fullback Scott Grix grabbed the plaudits with the fastest hat-trick to start a Super League match, as the Giants recorded a third straight win to see off Wakefield by 44-14 at Belle Vue on the Sunday.

Grix's trio of scores in the first nine minutes put Huddersfield into a lead they would never lose throughout the match, in a game which saw 30 of Huddersfield's 44 points scored by ex-Wakefield players, with Danny Brough grabbing a personal haul of 16 points.

Tries from Dean Collis and Danny Kirmond made it 18-8 at half-time and Jordan Crowther's score narrowed the gap but Giants produced four unanswered tries through Brett Ferres, Danny Brough, Leroy Cudjoe and Ukuma Ta'ai.

Widnes Vikings moved off the bottom of the table with a tense home 20-16 win over Hull Kingston Rovers. Paddy Flynn and Danny Galea scored tries either side of Ben

Cockayne's effort for Rovers to help the hosts take a 14-4 lead at the break. After the turnaround, the Vikings twice went close before Flynn grabbed his second try.

But Rovers fought back through Liam Salter and Kris Welham tries and Albert Kelly looked as if he had grabbed the points to level the match, but play was brought back by referee Matthew Thomason for a shoulder charge in the build-up.

** Amateurs Leigh Miners Rangers beat Kingstone Press League 1 side Oxford 32-6 in the main shock of the fourth round of the Ladbrokes Challenge Cup.*

Round 7

Hull KR head coach Chris Chester hailed his players after they broke St Helens' undefeated record in the Friday TV game at KC Lightstream Stadium to win 24-22. Albert Kelly crossed twice in six minutes in the first half, running 90 metres for both audacious interception tries to help set up a memorable win that the Robins thoroughly deserved. Hemel product Kieran Dixon, playing at fullback, scored a crucial try in the 64th minute.

Saints rallied late in the second half and cut the deficit to just two points on the siren. But former Robin Travis Burns, who was smashed in a shoulder charge by James Green early and was jeered throughout the match, couldn't clinch the draw by potting the conversion from wide out.

Hull KR went into the sheds at half-time with a crucial four-point lead. In the second half the Robins continued their strong defensive display and their intent to shift the ball across the field. Josh Mantellato got the ball down in the 43rd minute but his foot was in touch and the video ruled out the try but the winger nailed a penalty after that for a ball steal to extend Hull KR's cushion.

St Helens' discipline was letting them down and Mantellato slotted another penalty soon afterwards to put the home team 20-12 in front. That came after Greg Richards had clattered Campese after he kicked the ball and the Saints forward was lucky not to go to the sin bin for his clumsy challenge.

With 16 minutes left Dixon shot over, beating two defenders, to score the match-winning fourth try for the Robins and Hull KR seemed to have the game all sewn up, even with Mantellato missing the conversion.

Saints pushed forward in a late charge, but Louie McCarthy-Scarsbrook's try, off a Burns offload, should never have been given as the final pass was a couple of metres forward, before Jordan Turner's score a few minutes later.

For Saints it was an expensive night with James Roby forced off in the 34th minute with a head knock and forward Atelea Vea picking up a shoulder injury in the final minutes which ruled him out for four months.

Huddersfield Giants moved up to third on the ladder after a 29-10 win at Warrington, a result which saw them leapfrog their opponents on the table. It was the first time in twelve attempts that the Giants had beaten Warrington and their fourth SLXX win in a row. Danny Brough twice provided inch-perfect, innovative kicks for impressive winger Aaron Murphy to score.

Paul Anderson's side also defended brilliantly for most of the game, not least during a first half in which the home team had more pressure and position, but turned around 0-7 down. Murphy's second try on 67 minutes put an end to the Wolves comeback and restored a two-score Giants lead. Jermaine McGillvary and Eorl Crabtree tries in the last five minutes finished it off.

Wigan got back to winning ways with a 52-10 home hammering of Wakefield. The Wildcats were down to their last 18 fit players after Jacob Miller pulled out in the build-up to the game with injury, with Jarrod Sammut - on loan at London - and Craig Hall forming the halfback pairing.

Richard Owen moved to fullback with Tom Johnstone starting on the wing for his debut. In the pack, Daniel Smith was promoted from the bench in place of injured skipper Danny Kirmond, while on-loan from St Helens Jordan Hand started from the bench. Wigan named the same 19-man squad ahead of the game that they took to Leeds but on the day Matty Bowen dropped out and Ryan Hampshire took over at fullback.

The game was truly out of Wakefield's reach when Anthony Gelling crossed for Wigan's fourth try just before half-time.

Veteran prop Andy Lynch made his 450th career appearance in the Tigers' 20-14 home win against Hull FC. And there was a match-winning contribution of two tries and two goals by scrum-half Luke Gale, which secured a third win in the last four games for Castleford, as well as shooting him to the top of the Albert Goldthorpe Medal standings.

The Tigers, who lacked forwards Nathan Massey and Matt Cook – both suspended for a game after the previous week's victory over Salford Red Devils – and injured fullback Luke Dorn, were only behind for a four-minute spell around the hour mark.

But they were forced to withstand tremendous pressure in the second half as Hull, with hooker Danny Houghton, scrum-half Marc Sneyd and stand-off Leon Pryce influential, increasingly dominated.

Castleford, who had the better of the penalty count in the opening quarter, subsequently conceded five goal-line drop-outs, forcing none themselves, as former Tiger Sneyd in particular adopted a telling kicking game, forcing a couple of scrums close to the Tigers' line. Visiting winger Tom Lineham benefited from the pressure with a hat-trick but Castleford somehow held out

Sneyd limped off towards the end of the defeat to add to Hull's problems, with captain Gareth Ellis missing with a rib injury and Kirk Yeaman pulling out before kick-off with a groin strain.

Salford were a position above the Tigers in sixth after a one-sided Thursday night game with depleted Widnes ended in a 36-8 home win.

The hosts took the lead inside the first few minutes when Ben Jones-Bishop touched down Rangi Chase's well-weighted kick - his fifth try in five games. Weller Hauraki gathered Michael Dobson's grubber and, after Stefan Marsh was sent to the sin bin after chasing down a long-range Liam Hood break, the Red Devils scored a third out wide as Greg Johnson went over.

Despite the man disadvantage, the Vikings responded as winger Paddy Flynn finished well and then Jack Owens added a penalty before the interval.

After the break, Lama Tasi took a good line from Chase's inside ball to score his first try of the season, before Josh Griffin crashed over from short range. Another Dobson kick was caught and put down by Cory Paterson and then Scott Taylor bulldozed over.

Catalans-Leeds completed the round on the Saturday in Perpignan and the Rhinos took their chance to go top of the table on points difference from St Helens with a 38-22 win, after being 22-10 down 15 minutes into the second half.

The Rhinos were still without their injured skipper Kevin Sinfield, as Liam Sutcliffe continued in the stand-off role, while Ash Handley kept the right-wing spot, with Tom Briscoe out injured.

The Catalans' injury list mounted, with Todd Carney, Michael Oldfield, Greg Mounis and Vincent Duport all out after picking up injuries in the away games against the Hull clubs.

Rob Burrow came off the bench to inspire the Rhinos to a remarkable comeback win, having a hand in three of the Rhinos' five second-half tries. Kallum Watkins' try four minutes from the end sealed the win for Leeds.

FIRST UTILITY SUPER LEAGUE TABLE
Sunday 29th March

	P	W	D	L	F	A	D	PTS
Leeds Rhinos	7	6	0	1	219	126	93	12
St Helens	7	6	0	1	195	111	84	12
Huddersfield Giants	7	4	0	3	159	107	52	8
Warrington Wolves	7	4	0	3	131	143	-12	8
Wigan Warriors	7	3	1	3	159	150	9	7
Salford Red Devils	7	3	1	3	162	198	-36	7
Castleford Tigers	7	3	0	4	140	124	16	6
Hull Kingston Rovers	7	3	0	4	190	198	-8	6
Widnes Vikings	7	2	1	4	146	182	-36	5
Catalans Dragons	7	2	1	4	162	209	-47	5
Hull FC	7	2	0	5	124	137	-13	4
Wakefield T Wildcats	7	2	0	5	142	244	-102	4

APRIL
Wildcats on the slide

Round 8

Two capacity crowds on Good Friday, at Castleford and Wigan, combined with a crowd of over 20,000 at the Hull derby on the Thursday, contributed to a total of 72,670 spectators flocking through the turnstiles for round eight of Super League XX. Despite there being one game fewer than the previous season's Good Friday schedule owing to the reduction of teams in Super League from 14 to 12, the attendance figures represented a significant upturn - in 2014, 59,994 fans attended matches over the first part of the Easter period.

In the Thursday-night TV game, Terry Campese showcased all the attributes of a natural leader behind a brilliant team performance to see Hull KR run out convincing 20-6 winners at the KC Stadium. The Robins' skipper got the opening points in the fourth minute. After supplying a nice pass for Kieran Dixon to scythe through, Campese was on hand on the following play to take Shaun Lunt's pass and plunge over next to the posts.

Hull FC gave as good as they got without the ball as both sides belted each other and had the better of the field position on the back of a strong forward performance, but without the injured Marc Sneyd they were struggling to click in attack. Instead Rovers showed their finesse with the ball again with a well-taken try. After being heavily involved in his side's opening score, the lightning-quick Dixon got on the scoresheet himself after great work by Maurice Blair and Campese, as he beat Jamie Shaul with pace and extended the Robins' lead after a rare foray into Hull's half.

The former London Bronco went from hero to villain shortly afterwards though, as his fumble on his own goal line, whilst under pressure from Shaul to get back into the field of play, allowed Leon Pryce to pounce for the simplest of scores that was awarded by referee Richard Silverwood and confirmed by the video referee. There was an element of controversy about the try, however, with some contending that Dixon had grounded the ball and the tackle was complete.

But Rovers registered the next score. Lunt, playing in his first Hull derby, was the beneficiary as the ball bounced perfectly for him following a knock-on from Fetuli Talanoa, who dropped an Albert Kelly bomb.

A Josh Mantellato penalty was the only score of the second half and despite the best efforts of Pryce and Mark Minichiello, Hull never really looked like breaking through a strong Robins defence.

On the same night Widnes secured a surprisingly one-sided 30-10 home victory against an out-of-sorts Warrington, who were suffering a third consecutive defeat. It was a solid return to form for the Vikings after their reverse at Salford, inspired by a great performance from Kevin Brown after a three-week absence.

Ben Westwood's try put the Wolves ahead before a smoke bomb on the field caused a delay in play as both teams were taken off by the referee. When play re-started, a try from Cameron Phelps and two from Stefan Marsh made it 14-6 at the break.

Lloyd White, Brown and Jack Owens then also crossed after half-time to complete a dominant Widnes display, with teenage back-rower Matt Whitley making a fine debut.

In the other fixture on the Thursday, Wakefield lost their sixth consecutive game in spectacular fashion with Scott Dureau-inspired Catalans Dragons running out 40-4 winners at Belle Vue as winger Damien Cardace scored a hat-trick of tries. Elliott Whitehead's try two minutes before the break gave the Catalans a 26-point lead at half-time and the Wildcats were never in the game in the second half.

Wakefield head coach James Webster was left clutching for players after the game. His injury list that already included Lopini Paea, Reece Lyne, Scott Anderson, Ian Kirke and Matty Ashurst was further extended when former Dragon Mickael Simon was withdrawn on the quarter-hour mark.

The following day, Leeds Rhinos moved two points clear at the top of the table with a 26-12 win at Castleford while St Helens lost 12-4 at Wigan.

All the focus at the Rhinos in the build-up had been the announced departures of first Jamie Peacock, who was to take up the post of football manager at Hull KR at the end of the season, and Kevin Sinfield, who was to switch to Headingley-based Yorkshire Carnegie rugby union club.

Sinfield was still missing with a hamstring injury as 20-year-old Liam Sutcliffe, touted as the heir apparent, was superb in the win. He had a try ruled out for losing the ball as he weaved over, produced a thunderous tackle to barrel Michael Shenton into touch and slipped a grubber over for Stevie Ward's try just before the break to edge his side ten points clear.

Stand-in captain Danny McGuire was again masterful, providing quality passes for two of the Rhinos' five tries. Ryan Hall's second try in the 63rd minute, fashioned by a superb McGuire pass 15 minutes from time, gave Leeds breathing space.

It was blood and thunder at the DW Stadium. The first half was certainly not for the faint-hearted, as Wigan led 6-4 at half-time, with Dom Manfredi going over before Louie McCarthy-Scarsbrook got Saints on the board.

That was the end of the scoring in the first half, but not the action, as both sets of forwards knocked seven bells out of each other in a half that was a throwback to the eighties, with big hits aplenty on a heavy, muddy pitch.

The intensity continued in the second half but more injuries for St Helens, in-form Joe Greenwood breaking a leg and Paul Wellens aggravating a hip injury in the 15th minute, saw them play the last 38 minutes with only two substitutes.

It took until the 71st minute to break the deadlock. Joe Burgess scored the match winner as the Warriors made it six Good Friday victories in succession and moved up to third place on the Super League ladder.

Josh Griffin scored a try and kicked three goals as Salford kept their heads to earn a first away win of the season, an 18-12 success at Huddersfield which lifted them above the Giants into fourth spot. Ben Jones-Bishop scored a try and created another after moving from the wing to fullback following the 14th minute withdrawal of the concussed Kevin Locke.

Jones-Bishop's try on 31 minutes, scored when Rangi Chase kicked direct from a scrum earned through Junior Sa'u having tackled Huddersfield fullback Scott Grix into touch, gave Salford a 10-point lead which the hapless Giants were incapable of overhauling.

Griffin had set his side on course to win midway through the first half, improving his own try before converting Jones-Bishop's four-pointer. For the Giants, Jack Hughes responded before the break, Danny Brough adding the extras. Carl Forster scored on 55 minutes to restore the Red Devils' 10-point lead, then Aaron Murphy replied before a Griffin penalty sealed it.

The big talking point of the game was the injury to Brett Ferres in the 15th minute after a third man 'cannonball' tackle by Chase. The following week, Chase contested the charge of making a grade E dangerous throw but he was found guilty by the panel and banned for seven matches. Ferres was expected to be out for three months with ankle ligament damage.

* *New club Coventry Bears kicked off their League 1 campaign with a 32-10 Good Friday success over Oxford in front of 721 supporters.*

Round 9

Salford Red Devils' 24-18 Easter Monday home victory ended the club's run of 17 successive defeats to Wigan.

Despite Wigan taking the lead with an early Larne Patrick try, Salford's heads never dropped and they hit back before the break through tries from Niall Evalds and Michael Dobson. Then, with the game an hour old, a great solo try from Ben Jones-Bishop, who showed tremendous pace to evade the Wigan defence, just about sealed it for the Red Devils.

But it was not plain sailing for Salford in the final 20 minutes as Ryan Hampshire converted his own try to leave home fans nervous. Evalds' second try of the afternoon eased those nerves and, with Josh Griffin continuing his 100 per cent record with the boot, it meant Joe Burgess's try in the final minute was a consolation for Wigan.

Salford's Weller Hauraki and John Bateman of Wigan had a running battle throughout the game and were sin-binned mid-way through the second half for fighting. Within minutes of returning to the pitch they were both shown red cards for the same offence. Hauraki got a two-match ban plus another two matches for reckless striking in the Good Friday win at Huddersfield. Bateman took a one-match early guilty plea.

Leeds captain Kevin Sinfield became only the fourth player to surpass 4,000 career points with his second goal of the afternoon in a 48-22 home win over Wakefield Trinity Wildcats as the Rhinos took a four-point lead at the top of the table, after Sinfield converted all eight of his side's tries.

Wakefield stayed in contention until the half-hour mark, scoring three tries through Tim Smith, Craig Hall and Jarrod Sammut. But they were no match for the pace of the home backs, for whom Kallum Watkins was again a standout.

First-half scores from Ryan Hall, Zak Hardaker and Rob Burrow's brace - which saw him pass 1,000 career points - as well as further tries after the break from Watkins (two), Ash Handley and Andy Yates saw Leeds ease to victory. Daniel Smith's try six minutes from time reduced the deficit for Wakefield.

Hull KR finished an Easter to remember with a 20-16 home win over Huddersfield Giants - the first time the Robins had taken maximum points over Easter since they were promoted to Super League in 2007.

Darrell Goulding got them off the mark early when he took a superb pass from Albert Kelly to cross. Then the Robins were put under great pressure by the Giants, who could not find a way to score until the half-hour when Joe Wardle found a huge gap and touched down near the posts, making the conversion easy for Danny Brough. However it was Rovers that took a lead into the break after Graeme Horne went over following a bomb by Terry Campese.

Ukuma Ta'ai and Kelly traded tries early in the second half, before Josh Mantellato touched down to extend the home lead. A penalty kick by Mantellato with a minute left on the clock sealed it for Hull KR, before an unconverted consolation try from Aaron Murphy cut the deficit.

Jamie Shaul was a hero for Hull FC as they bounced back from their derby defeat with a 28-20 win over St Helens, who gave debuts to Ricky Bailey and Jack Ashworth at Langtree Park.

With the score tied at 20-20 after 75 minutes, it was a moment of brilliance from Shaul that started the Airlie Birds' celebrations. The fullback broke from deep in his own half and beat his St Helens opposite number Tommy Makinson to touch down under the posts. Jordan Rankin added the goal and then kicked a last-minute penalty to seal a momentous win.

Shaul had also opened the scoring on four minutes, before Makinson and Louie McCarthy-Scarsbrook hit back for Saints. Curtis Naughton, making his Hull debut, reduced the arrears before the break.

In a nip-and-tuck game the lead continued to change hands as Leon Pryce and Jordan Turner traded tries, before Fetuli Talanoa edged Hull in front. A Makinson penalty then levelled the scores before Shaul's match winner.

Castleford bounced back from their Good Friday defeat to Leeds Rhinos with a 22-14 victory at the Halliwell Jones Stadium, which saw Warrington drop out of the top eight.

Luke Gale was again the catalyst for the Tigers and it was his pass that led to Jordan Tansey's opening try, although he could not add the goal. The Wolves thought they had hit back soon afterwards when Joel Monaghan crossed, but Chris Bridge's pass was adjudged forward. However there was nothing wrong when Stefan Ratchford touched down five minutes later and Gareth O'Brien's goal gave the hosts the lead. They soon extended it when Ryan Atkins added to the tally, but a try from Luke Dorn and Gale's conversion made it all-square at the break.

After a tight third quarter, two tries in three minutes from Adam Milner and Ben Roberts, both converted by Gale, gave the Tigers the edge. Kevin Penny then had a try awarded by the video referee, but a missed goal by O'Brien and a further Penny attempt ruled out by the video official saw the Tigers take the points.

Four tries in the opening 20 minutes proved too much of a hurdle for a weakened Widnes Vikings to overcome as the Catalans Dragons made it two wins from two over Easter with a 32-16 home victory.

Willie Tonga opened the scoring and then grabbed a second following Eloi Pelissier's touchdown and by the time Mathias Pala added a fourth try things looked bleak for the Vikings.

But even though they had been reduced to twelve men after Matt Whitley was sent to the bin for a high shot on Scott Dureau, Widnes started to claw their way back into the game with Jack Owens touching down in the corner from a fine Tom Gilmore pass.

That try seemed to give the Vikings a boost and a comeback looked possible when Stefan Marsh scored eight minutes after the restart and Owens added the conversion. However, a second try for Pelissier, goaled by Dureau after Thomas Bosc had landed three earlier conversions, and a touchdown from Damien Cardace put the Dragons back in control. Although Alex Gerrard scored a late consolation try for Widnes, goaled by Owens, the Vikings were never able to overcome their slow start.

Round 10

After four straight losses, Warrington finally got back on the horse with a fourteen-try, 80-0 demolition of a woeful Wakefield side that already looked destined for a long relegation battle.

The scoreline meant the Wolves had equalled the joint record winning margin in Super League, pulling level with the 80-point margin in Bradford Bulls' 96-16 victory over Salford City Reds (as they then were) in 2000 and Leeds Rhinos' 86-6 victory over Huddersfield Giants in 1999.

Nineteen year-old stand-off Declan Patton had a sparkling debut, playing a notable role in several of the Wolves' fourteen tries, and Richie Myler ended with a hat-trick of tries.

Wakefield's eighth straight loss on the back of a run of injuries and Super League's lowest playing budget was already showing a flaw in the new league structure. Their coach James Webster said: 'I hate looking for excuses, but over the last month I think we have spent around two hours as a team training together, for the simple reason I don't have enough people to fulfil training. There are no ifs and buts about that - I just don't have enough players. Maybe we make a decision now to be the first team to get rid of the motto 'every minute matters' and wait until round 24 and try and get our team nice and fit to make a crack at those last seven games - as we will most likely be in the lower one.'

Leeds stayed four points ahead of the pack as Zak Hardaker inspired the Rhinos to a 28-18 victory at Salford Red Devils. Hardaker had been fined a month's wages that week and ordered to undertake voluntary work with the club after his pre-season misdemeanours.

Hardaker started the game in the centres, but reverted to his usual role of fullback magnificently as the game wore on, snuffing out everything Salford threw at him in driving rain and howling winds at the AJ Bell Stadium.

Leeds held a four-point advantage at the break after two converted tries from Jamie Peacock and one for Ash Handley, with Lama Tasi and Niall Evalds replying for Salford.

Rob Burrow then scored Leeds' fourth try, but Evalds reduced the deficit with his second score. Hardaker's converted try as the game entered the final quarter secured a precious two points for the Rhinos.

St Helens had double cause for celebration, as a number of star players returned to their ranks for the Sunday game at Huddersfield, which they won 11-8 to snap their three-game losing streak and maintain second spot in Super League.

The reigning Super League champions saw pivot Travis Burns and captain Jon Wilkin return from injury lay-offs but, most notably, the game marked the first appearance of the season for Australian scrum-half Luke Walsh, who came off the bench in the second half.

Walsh hadn't played since a serious leg injury suffered the previous year against Widnes, but the 25 minutes he spent on the field saw him make a crucial and telling contribution, as one of his few touches produced the long-range field goal that edged St Helens into a lead they would never lose.

Wind and rain also caused havoc at the DW Stadium, but it was the Warriors who handled the elements best in a 34-0 win over Catalans Dragons, winger Dom Manfredi finishing with a hat-trick and fullback Ryan Hampshire excelling, although he could convert only one of his eight conversion attempts.

Tom Lineham scored a spectacular hat-trick as Hull FC continued their derby-day redemption with a second consecutive win, a 22-8 home victory over Widnes. It was a far from emphatic display, with two length-of-the-field interception tries from Lineham crucial to their win but nevertheless it kept the Airlie Birds in touch with the top eight.

It was tough on Widnes, who had been forced into the unnecessary situation of travelling to Catalans on Easter Monday before playing away again just four days later. The home side sealed matters when Jamie Shaul reacted the quickest to Jordan Rankin's kick striking the post, ensuring that Ah Van's spectacular late finish couldn't affect the result.

Luke Gale starred during Castleford Tigers' 25-4 home win against Hull KR on the Saturday. Hull KR, after having gone ahead in the third minute through a Ken Sio try, were second best thereafter as the Tigers pack increasingly dominated. Gale's field goal midway through the second period stretched the home lead to 15 points and clearly put the game beyond struggling Rovers.

The only real negative for Castleford was an injury to rampaging winger Justin Carney who, in landing awkwardly in attempting to score, sustained a dislocated elbow.

Round 11

With the Challenge Cup, sponsored in 2015 by bookmakers Ladbrokes, played on a seeded basis, the Super League clubs that finished the previous season in positions nine to 12 in the table entered the competition at the fifth-round stage, where they joined 12 lower league clubs who had progressed through the earlier rounds. Which meant a truncated round of Super League.

Leeds Rhinos went a whopping six points clear at the top of the table with a convincing 41-16 win at second-placed St Helens, young winger Ash Handley, getting an extended first-team run because of the long-term shoulder injury to Tom Briscoe, scoring a first-half hat-trick in the Friday night TV game.

Coming in to the game with only one defeat all season, suffered at Warrington, Paul Aiton's industrious and skilful performance around the play-the-ball and Liam Sutcliffe, at stand-off ahead of Kevin Sinfield, who started as a substitute for the first time since July 2003, contributed much to a devastating opening Rhinos salvo that put them 24 points ahead before the half-hour mark. Saints pulled to within two converted tries with 19 minutes remaining after half-time substitute Luke Walsh inspired a brief revival, but Sutcliffe stepped through their tiring defence for the decisive try on 67 minutes. Sinfield then slotted a close-range field goal, before Joel Moon, who was another notable Leeds performer, completed the scoring in the final minute.

There had been a party atmosphere at the DW Stadium on the Thursday with the return of Ben Flower after his six-month ban from the previous year's Grand Final and the announcement of the re-signing of Sam Tomkins from New Zealand Warriors, as Wigan celebrated with a 30-20 win over Warrington.

At half-time Wigan Chairman Ian Lenagan announced to the 14,175 crowd that Tomkins would be returning at the start of next season on a four-year deal, with the club paying a transfer fee in excess of £200,000.

Before that there had been 40 minutes of thrilling action, with Tony Smith keeping faith in youngsters Toby King and stand-off Declan Patton. Patton looked a fine young prospect with the ball, but Joel Tomkins targeted him all night and he ended up missing nine tackles in total.

Warrington raced into a 10-0 lead inside the opening eleven minutes thanks to tries from Joel Monaghan and Chris Bridge. But the Warriors recorded back-to-back scores themselves through Liam Farrell and Ryan Hampshire, both made by Joe Burgess, to take a 12-10 lead.

Flower's introduction on 23 minutes had the Wigan fans on their feet, but seconds later they were back in their seats as Bridge went over again. But it was the Warriors who went into the break in front thanks to a try from Dom Manfredi.

Warrington again struck first in the second half, with Ben Currie crossing, but Anthony Gelling went over and Manfredi scored twice to complete his hat-trick, extending Wigan's unbeaten home run in 2015 to six matches.

The Vikings were far too good for Castleford, emerging 46-16 winners at the Select Security Stadium. Widnes had lost all but one of their last ten encounters with the Tigers, but a sparkling eight-try performance ensured their dismal run rarely looked like being extended. With Kevin Brown pulling the strings, Rhys Hanbury was a constant threat from the back and Jack Owens fired over conversions from all angles in windy conditions

Huddersfield climbed into the top five with a convincing 38-14 win at home to the Catalans Dragons on the Sunday. The Giants won the game in the three minutes before half-time, scoring two tries and running out to a convincing 22-8 lead at the break, with Ukuma Ta'ai leading a dominant pack performance

Challenge Cup Round 5

Leigh Centurions, leaders of the Kingstone Press Championship, sent Salford Red Devils, fourth in the Super League table, tumbling out of the Challenge Cup in front of the Saturday-afternoon Sky Sports cameras at Leigh Sports Village. The build-up had been dominated by a wrangle between the Red Devils and Leigh over whether Gareth Hock should be allowed to play against the club that had released him weeks earlier. Hock played off the bench.

The Red Devils, missing the suspended Rangi Chase, ran out of troops as Michael Dobson left the field inside the opening quarter of the 22-18 loss with a knee injury, before

Junior Sa'u followed soon afterwards with a wrist injury. They still led by six points with 15 minutes to go thanks in the main to the efforts of Theo Fages and Niall Evalds.

But then, Ben Jones-Bishop, in his own '20', collected a loose offload from Harrison Hansen and threw a low pass across the face of his attackers. Ryan Brierley snapped the ball up and raced over from 25 metres to crown his 100th Leigh appearance. Martyn Ridyard nudged over the goal and the game was finely poised at 18-all. But the momentum thereafter was with the Centurions and they scored back-to-back tries. Quickly seizing the opportunity, play came down the right from Brierley for Gregg McNally to drift between two defenders and hand on for winger Jonny Pownall to control the low pass and sweep over.

It was the Centurions' 21st successive win in all competitions.

Hull KR went into the hat after fighting back to beat Bradford Bulls 50-30 at Odsal on the Sunday. Josh Mantellato was the star for the Robins, with four tries and a personal points tally of 30, which included some superb goal kicking.

Hull FC also went through, Liam Watts and Kirk Yeaman returning in a hard 34-12 win over third-placed Championship side Sheffield at Bramall Lane. Utility Jordan Thompson once again stood out for the Black and Whites.

Super League basement club Wakefield gained some respite from their survival worries by seeing off Championship promotion hopefuls Halifax 44-16 at Belle Vue on the Friday night, in a dress rehearsal for the late summer 'middle eight' that would determine which clubs played in Super League in 2016.

Four tries in the last 17 minutes, including two from Ian Kirke on his injury-delayed Trinity debut, left the Wildcats with a slightly flattering scoreline from a game that could have gone either way for an hour.

Just 22-16 down at that stage, another try from Fax could have prompted a different outcome. But James Webster's side, which had conceded 264 points in their previous five matches and gone eight without a win, ultimately pulled through with their late flurry.

In the all-Championship game on the Sunday, Dewsbury Rams won a thriller at Hunslet 31-16; while Featherstone won at League 1 North Wales Crusaders 38-12 and Batley had a home 46-16 success over Swinton.

Round 12

Warrington upset the odds to complete a league double over Leeds at Headingley on the Friday night with a dominant 29-10 victory. It was the Rhinos' second defeat of the season, both by Warrington.

Kevin Sinfield's hopes of victory on his 500th appearance for Leeds were scuppered. Although the Wolves dominated most of the opening quarter, racing into a 14-point lead, the stage was set for the Leeds skipper to play his customary hero's role after his men had clawed their way back into the contest just before the break.

But, by the time the Leeds skipper had removed his tracksuit to enter the fray in the 45th minute, the task had become almost insurmountable, thanks to another bench-man, Daryl Clark, with his bursts up the middle which set up a sensational try for Ben Currie straight after the break. From then on the visitors had the points in the bag and a double over the league leaders. Roy Asotasi's 50th-minute converted try made it 28-4 at one stage and Declan Patton's field goal five minutes from time sealed it.

After the game Wolves coach Tony Smith tipped Currie as a future captain of the club.

St Helens narrowed the gap at the top to four points after winning a thrilling tussle with Widnes at home by 34-16. Only Tommy Makinson's 73rd-minute, full-length score after he collected a kick from Joe Mellor finally broke the Vikings resolve after young threequarter Matty Fleming, who had made his debut in the defeat by Leeds, had scored his first try for Saints eight minutes earlier.

April

A rout was expected in the Thursday-night TV game as down-at-heel Wakefield, on the back of their 80-0 hammering at Warrington, entertained Wigan, who had beaten the Wolves in their last match. But Wakefield took a 6-0 lead in the first minute with a long-range try finished off by Craig Hall and the Warriors led only 24-18 at half-time before Joe Burgess scored two tries to complete a hat-trick, as the Warriors shook off their travel sickness to record a first away victory, by 40-22, since July 2014.

The down side for Wigan was a hamstring injury suffered by in-form Anthony Gelling. Wakefield also lost Ian Kirke, who suffered a broken thumb in only his second game for the Wildcats, who had taken Ben Kavanagh on loan from Widnes, and he impressed.

At the KC Stadium on the Friday night, the Giants scored five tries after defending their line impressively for long periods to emerge 24-4 winners over Hull FC. Jermaine McGillvary was outstanding, getting his side on the front foot from early in the set and he was a handful on the flank all night, finishing with a well-deserved try in the final play of the game.

But it was all over well before then, tries to Danny Brough, Ukuma Ta'ai and Jamie Ellis, with two Brough conversions, giving the Giants a 16-0 lead at half-time, Michael Lawrence extending the lead just before the hour mark before Steve Michaels got Hull's only points of the night.

Todd Carney returned to action in Perpignan on the Saturday night after missing six games with a quadriceps injury suffered in the loss to Hull FC in March and, after trailing 12-6 to Hull KR after half an hour, the Dragons won 32-24. Elliott Whitehead's try eleven minutes from the end gave the Catalans a three-score lead and gave them a big enough cushion to secure the win.

Dane Tilse made his debut for the Robins, a week after playing his 201st game for Canberra, despite having not yet visited Hull. The rangy prop had flown into Manchester on the Tuesday afternoon, had two nights there before a night in Barcelona and got into Perpignan on the Friday night.

Twelve of the Catalans' seventeen players were French, including debutant Fouad Yaha, who became, at 18, the youngest Frenchman to play in Super League, taking over from Salford's Theo Fages by two months.

On the Sunday at AJ Bell Stadium, Castleford survived an almighty scare from injury-hit Salford to pick up their sixth win of the season and further cement their position inside Super League's top eight.

The Red Devils were in the midst of a huge barren run with injuries but even without such star power in Rangi Chase, Michael Dobson and Junior Sa'u, a patched-up side gave Castleford more than a few scares before going down 22-20.

Theo Fages and Niall Evalds again showed up well, whilst young England Academy centre Oliver Gildart, who had signed a new four-year deal with Wigan at the start of the year, was Salford's best after signing on loan earlier in the week. Another Wigan loanee, James Greenwood also debuted.

Tigers winger Ash Robson's try on debut, which made it 22-10 with 15 minutes to go, proved to be the score that was the difference between the two sides as Kevin Locke scored for the Red Devils, though crucially he could not convert and Scott Taylor's four-pointer made it a nervous closing minute for the Tigers.

FIRST UTILITY SUPER LEAGUE TABLE
Sunday 26th April

	P	W	D	L	F	A	D	PTS
Leeds Rhinos	12	10	0	2	372	223	149	20
St Helens	12	8	0	4	280	216	64	16
Wigan Warriors	12	7	1	4	293	220	73	15
Huddersfield Giants	12	6	0	6	257	174	83	12
Warrington Wolves	12	6	0	6	284	235	49	12
Castleford Tigers	12	6	0	6	237	234	3	12
Salford Red Devils	11	5	1	5	242	278	-36	11
Catalans Dragons	12	5	1	6	280	325	-45	11
Hull Kingston Rovers	11	5	0	6	258	277	-19	10
Widnes Vikings	12	4	1	7	262	296	-34	9
Hull FC	11	4	0	7	184	209	-25	8
Wakefield T Wildcats	11	2	0	9	190	452	-262	4

MAY
On the Toon

Round 13

Huddersfield overcame a 22-6 deficit to grab a 24-all draw with league leaders Leeds in a pulsating game at the John Smith's Stadium that, both before, during and afterwards, was still in danger of being overshadowed by the sensational omission from the team of the Rhinos' record-breaking captain Kevin Sinfield.

A week earlier Sinfield made his 500th appearance for the Rhinos but on the following Thursday night he was left out of the 17-man squad for the first time in 15 years.

A blistering first half saw the Rhinos lead 22-6 at one point, through tries to Brett Delaney, Carl Ablett, Joel Moon and Kallum Watkins, before the Giants rallied to go 24-22 up as Danny Brough steered the Giants to a wonderful comeback. Tries to Michael Lawrence, Jermaine McGillvary and a second to Joe Wardle, two of them converted by Brough had the Giants two in front.

But a late, controversial Liam Sutcliffe penalty eventually earned Leeds a share of the spoils. And the Leeds fans were left pondering whether Sinfield might have landed a decisive field goal, which Sutcliffe, again impressive in most other aspects, pushed agonisingly wide with two minutes to play.

Leeds could still have pinched it as the ball bounced around like a pin-ball in a frenetic final ten seconds. But Rob Burrow slipped and lost his footing ten metres out, with the line at his mercy.

The draw meant St Helens were able to move within three points of Leeds with their Luke Walsh-inspired 44-4 home win over Wakefield the following evening. Only the erratic goal-kicking of Travis Burns prevented Keiron Cunningham's men hitting a half century against a Wildcats outfit that was always game, but massively outgunned.

Saints had lost Lance Hohaia who had announced his retirement in the week because of 'recurrent post-match concussion-type symptoms'. Cunningham reserved special praise for two-try hooker Lewis 'Duggie' Charnock, who deputised for James Roby in the absence of Hohaia.

Saints also brought in Shannon McDonnell at fullback fresh off the plane from Australia after his re-signing.

On the same night, Hull KR were on the end of a 60-nil TV-thrashing at Wigan. It could have been much worse for the Robins as the Warriors led 34-nil after only 21 minutes. Joe Burgess finished with a hat-trick, though the star of the show was stand-off George Williams.

Rovers coach Chris Chester fielded a depleted squad, with Terry Campese, Dane Tilse and Shaun Lunt all ruled out prior to the match with hamstring, rib and back injuries respectively, while Kevin Larroyer was injured in the warm-up. Josh Mantellato had flown back to Australia to attend his brother's wedding. Which meant that youngsters Connor Robinson and Josh Guzdek were drafted in from the 19-man squad, with Robinson making his debut on the bench.

Off the field, Shaun Wane joined the clamour for the return of a reserve-grade competition for Super League clubs. Another in favour was Warrington coach Tony Smith, whose side moved into the top four on the Sunday, but only just as a last-second try from captain Joel Monaghan earned the Wolves a 22-20 home win over neighbours Widnes.

Kevin Brown became more influential as the game wore on, with the scores locked at 14-all and after the Wolves almost re-took the lead themselves, he produced a moment of magic to nudge Widnes in front. Wolves forward Ben Harrison had the ball pinched out of his pocket by the talismanic Widnes captain and he raced home from 60 metres to put the visitors six points to the good.

But Warrington struck back themselves soon after. After Gene Ormsby went close on the left, Ben Westwood charged his way over the line on the next tackle to reduce the gap to just two, with Declan Patton slicing the conversion attempt to leave it at 20-18.

With the game on a knife edge, Widnes thought they'd extended their lead further when a bullet pass from Brown found its way to Owens, but referee Ben Thaler chalked off the score for an obstruction in the build-up.

Warrington bombarded the Widnes line repeatedly in a bid to grab a game-winning score. They managed to force a drop-out with just 44 seconds left on the clock and, with the last play of the game, they managed to pull off the impossible and seal the most dramatic derby victory.

After sweeping the ball wide, Stefan Ratchford's pass to Joel Monaghan was just about good enough for the Wolves captain to claim off his toes and, when he did assume control of the ball, he barged his way over in the corner to secure two competition points. The kick was missed by Patton - but it was irrelevant.

On the Friday it took 72 minutes for Hull FC to land the telling and crucial blow, as a late Setaimata Sa try gave the Black and Whites the lead for the first time in the game and their fourth win in five matches, by 24-20 against a patched up and committed Salford Red Devils side at the KC Stadium.

Oliver Gildart's try on 58 minutes and Theo Fages' conversion put Salford 20-12 up but Mark Minichiello, Hull's most consistent player in 2015, scored an impressive solo effort to again get Hull within two points and give them all the momentum.

Catalans dropped out of the top eight as they yet again struggled on a visit to England, going down 36-28 on the Sunday at Castleford, despite a hat-trick from Benjamin Garcia. The Tigers made the Dragons pay for a host of penalties mid-way through the first half, running in 20 points in ten minutes to give them a convincing lead at the break that the Dragons couldn't claw back.

Luke Gale produced a top performance for Castleford, while Ryan Bailey made his debut for the Tigers after being released by Hull KR after making only one appearance.

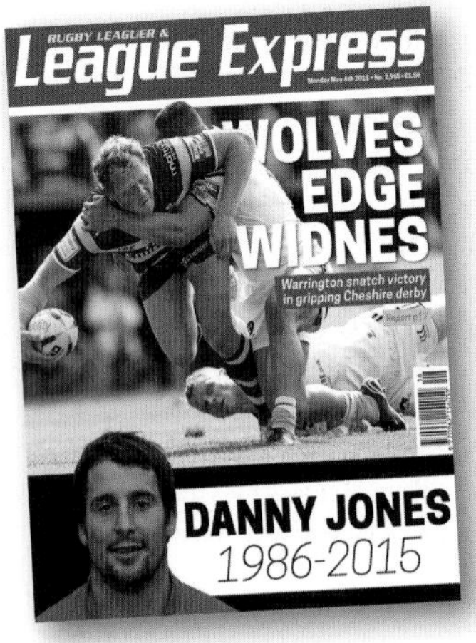

** The world of Rugby League was shocked by the news of the death of Wales and Keighley Cougars player Danny Jones. The 29-year-old suffered a cardiac arrest on the first Sunday of May, shortly after leaving the pitch at the New River Stadium, as the Cougars played League 1 rivals London Skolars.*

Round 14

Leeds were slowly being drawn back to the pack after a shock 38-24, Sunday afternoon defeat at Widnes, as the Vikings stunned the league leaders with a determined and disciplined performance to claim their first victory over the Rhinos in almost twelve years.

The Vikings began the game like the proverbial house on fire. A line-break by Lloyd White in the opening seconds put his team on the attack and for the next four minutes they pounded the Leeds line, aided by a couple of penalties – including Joel Moon being put on report for a tackle on Alex Gerrard - and two repeat sets as desperate defenders knocked down passes.

Eventually the pressure told as loanee Chris Clarkson - playing against his parent club - crashed over from close range from a flat Kevin Brown pass.

It was the sixth minute before the Rhinos got their hands on the ball but they were soon making good use of their possession. A powerful set of six ended with a towering Danny McGuire bomb that Rhys Hanbury mishandled in the swirling wind and moments later Stevie Ward was reaching over to score.

It was a nip and tuck first half that Widnes edged 16-14, but Danny Galea and Manase Manuokafoa tries took the Vikings to a 28-14 lead before Kallum Watkins and Jimmy Keinhorst replies made it 28-24.

Even facing a four-point deficit, the Rhinos looked the likely winners as the game entered the final ten minutes. They were edging field position and stretching the Vikings' defence on nearly every play. But as Watkins juggled a pass in the Leeds defensive third of the field he was hit with a juggernaut tackle by Patrick Ah Van that forced a knock-on. From that play came the opportunity for Chris Dean's match-clinching score.

At 34-24 the game was now as good as over and Aaron Heremaia's bizarre try - he looped behind a knot of several players from either side who were at each others throats and ambled in for a score – was a footnote.

St Helens missed their chance to move within a point of Leeds after a 33-26 defeat in the south of France. The defending champions found themselves 12-4 down inside the opening quarter in Perpignan, but four tries from winger Adam Swift helped them recover and level up at 26-26 as the game entered the final ten minutes.

However, a superb solo score from Zeb Taia and a field goal from Scott Dureau right on the hooter sealed it.

Instead it was Wigan who closed the gap on the Rhinos to two points with a 28-0 home win against Castleford on the Friday. The Warriors were not at their fluent best because of the heavy rain that poured down. But they were patient and backed up their 60-0 win over Hull KR with another complete defensive performance.

An error-strewn first 40 minutes saw Wigan lead 12-0. The game improved slightly after the break, but Castleford struggled to create many clear try-scoring opportunities and the Warriors were able to pick them off and cruise home in the end.

Second-half scores from Michael McIlorum, Dan Sarginson and Dom Manfredi saw Wigan avenge their 42-14 defeat at the Mend-a-Hose Jungle in March.

The Warriors' 17 contained 12 products of their own youth system, with Taulima Tautai the only player from overseas.

In the Thursday TV game, Hull KR bounced back efficiently and professionally from the previous week's 60-0 hammering at Wigan with a much-needed 54-6 home win over Wakefield.

The Robins were led magnificently once again by captain Terry Campese and there was a 22-point haul for winger Josh Mantellato. Graeme Horne's try seven minutes after the break secured a comfortable win early on for Rovers.

It was a straight eleventh league defeat for Wakefield and in the last eight the Wildcats had shipped 40 points or more.

The following night's TV game saw Danny Brough guide his side to a 19-0 victory at Salford with the perfect wet-weather game plan in pouring rain.

All Huddersfield's tries came from kicks by Brough, with his opposite number Theo Fages unable to have the same effect for the Red Devils, in the absence of suspended Rangi Chase and injured Michael Dobson. Brough's 55th-minute field goal put his side three scores ahead and that was always likely to be too much for the Red Devils.

Since beating Wigan on Easter Monday - a victory that took them into the top four - the Red Devils had lost four successive matches, including a Challenge Cup defeat to Leigh, and they dropped into the bottom four.

The Salford club insisted they would hand out life bans to any supporters who were found to be involved in trouble during the game, when spectators appeared to become involved in a fracas that involved both sets of players behind the posts. The incident took place midway through the first half and resulted in the sin-binning of Huddersfield fullback Scott Grix and Salford second-rower Weller Hauraki.

The 1,972 crowd was the lowest Super League gate of the season, with over a third of the club's season ticket holders not attending the match which had been moved from the Sunday afternoon for the TV cameras.

On the Sunday afternoon, Hull FC, boosted by the return of talismanic skipper Gareth Ellis after seven weeks out with a rib cartilage injury, overtook Hull KR back into the top-eight with a stunning 27-26 win at Warrington. The Wolves frittered away a 10-point advantage to succumb to a Marc Sneyd field goal in the final second of the match in a mesmerising ten-try slugfest which capped Hull's best performance of the year to date.

When Ryan Atkins sent Gene Ormsby in at the corner for his brace to make it 26-16 on 62 minutes, the game looked to be going Warrington's way. But Hull refused to go away, and on 69 minutes a glorious offload from Liam Watts saw Setaimata Sa scorch 60 metres downfield, before Mark Minichiello took advantage of some disorganised ruck defending to breeze over from 10 metres out to make it 26-22.

On 75 minutes a set Hull play out to the right from deep inside their own half saw the outstanding Sneyd break the line before racing downfield and coolly slipping the ball to Tom Lineham, who finished off the try of the day to level the scores at 26-26.

Sneyd couldn't convert and, with the clock ticking down, Hull were searching for a crucial one-pointer. With three seconds left, Sneyd looked set to pull the trigger when referee Silverwood halted play due to a Chris Bridge head injury.

Amazingly, from the re-start, Houghton bulleted the pass to Sneyd who thundered over the field goal as the hooter sounded to round off a truly pulsating 80 minutes.

Over 4,000 people crammed into Cougar Park to support Danny Jones's family and pay tribute to the former Welsh international on the Sunday. £10,491 was raised via bucket collections alone at the game against Coventry Bears, while Widnes's clash against Leeds raised in excess of £5,000. Over 100,000 pounds had already been raised via social media fundraising.

** The 2017 Rugby League World Cup qualifying process got underway when Spain beat Latvia 32-12 in a European Championship C qualifying tie at the Upesciema Stadions, just outside the Latvian capital Riga. Spain would join Malta and Greece in the next phase.*

Challenge Cup Round 6

Runaway Kingstone Championship leaders Leigh marched into the quarter-finals of the Ladbrokes Challenge Cup in astounding fashion with a 36-30 win at Super League strugglers Wakefield in the Sunday BBC TV game.

The Centurions were 22-0 down midway through the first half as two tries from Joe Arundel and one each from Chris Riley and Nick Scruton had them seemingly well beaten.

But, inspired by Ryan Brierley, Martyn Ridyard and Bob Beswick, the Centurions got a try back before the break and posted 30 points in the second half to blitz Wakefield.

A Craig Hall penalty made it 24-6 at half-time and just after Wakefield captain Danny Kirmond and former Wildcat Liam Kay were sin-binned for a squabble, winger Jonny Pownall's try started the comeback in earnest.

Hope turned into genuine belief soon afterwards, when Beswick crashed over from close range to make it 24-18. All the momentum was now with Leigh, even with the game restored to full parity at 13 each, and a moment of magic from the mercurial Brierley then completed a quite incredible comeback.

Brierley, seemingly on instinct, chipped over the top and collected with ease, before firing a remarkable pass left to Tom Armstrong, who dived over in the corner to leave Ridyard with a testing conversion to square it up. He didn't fail and at 24-24, Leigh looked unstoppable.

Ridyard sailed a penalty attempt wide soon after, before, against the run of play, Wakefield struck back. Forward Jon Molloy barged over from close range to make it 28-24 and, with Hall's goal, the Wildcats led by six again. Leigh weren't done though, despite that setback, and when Sam Hopkins crashed over, it was 30-30.

From there it only looked like one team would win. And so it proved when former Wakefield man Oliver Wilkes scored after Kay had looped a pass inside to Beswick inches from the left touchline.

After dumping out London, Salford and Wakefield in previous rounds, Paul Rowley's all-conquering Centurions were drawn to play 2012 winners Warrington Wolves at the Halliwell Jones Stadium.

Wakefield coach James Webster cut a desolate figure following the match - he wished the assembled journalists 'the best of luck' following his media call. It was no big surprise when he left the club the following Tuesday.

In the Saturday TV game Leeds dealt efficiently with the Giants by 48-16 at Headingley. It was a first win from four, while ending Huddersfield's run of four games unbeaten and shredded the Giants' record of having the best defence in Super League as Leeds posted eight tries.

The up-tempo victory coincided with the return of Rhinos' skipper Kevin Sinfield, the scorer of eight goals who produced a peach of a pass for Kallum Watkins' second score within the opening 13 minutes. It was Sinfield's first start for four matches, as he replaced the young pretender Liam Sutcliffe.

Bearing in mind Huddersfield's second-half comebacks from similar deficits in both league games between the sides, the first try after the break was crucial and went to Danny McGuire to make the score 28-4.

Wigan's home game with Hull KR the night before had to be moved to Leigh Sports Village because of pitch maintenance work at the DW Stadium. And just two weeks after beating Hull KR 60-0 in Super League, the Warriors slumped to a 16-12 reverse to exit the competition at the first hurdle.

A spirited first-half performance from Hull KR saw them go in level at the break. A well-worked try from Maurice Blair cancelled out a Matty Smith penalty before Joel Tomkins got the Warriors back in the game with a late try as they went into the interval all-square at six apiece.

Hull KR then led 10-8 going into the final quarter and, despite falling behind, they refused to drop their heads and pulled off a great victory late on. Joe Burgess' try in the

64th minute looked to have won it for the Warriors, but a spilled ball five metres from his own line from Dan Sarginson gifted a try to Ken Sio to send Rovers through to the quarter-finals.

On the same night, Warrington comfortably booked their place in the next round with a 52-10 win at Dewsbury. Five first-half tries built up a commanding half-time lead, before the Wolves added another five tries in the second half with a brace apiece for Kevin Penny and Ben Currie.

St Helens progressed comfortably after a 46-6 home win over League 1 York City Knights, with wingers Tommy Makinson and Adam Swift bagging seven tries between them. Underdogs York City Knights, from the third tier, produced a wholehearted effort. James Ford's team never stopped trying to take the game to Saints and winger Tyler Craig's late consolation try brought the night's biggest cheer.

Youngster Curtis Naughton starred with a hat-trick as Hull FC moved into the last eight with a 40-14 Saturday home win against the previous year's runners-up Castleford Tigers.

Widnes coach Denis Betts paid tribute to beaten opponents Batley Bulldogs after a pulsating Challenge Cup affair on the Sunday afternoon. The Vikings booked their spot in a second consecutive quarter-final following a nerve-jangling 26-22 home win. They initially led 26-6 and looked comfortably en route to the last eight, before John Kear's men set up a grandstand finish with a late rally.

It was even closer in Perpignan as Thomas Bosc was the Catalans' saviour as they came from behind to win a titanic tussle with Featherstone Rovers 37-34. Former Dragon Remy Marginet came back to haunt his old side as Featherstone pushed the Dragons all the way. Rovers led 30-24 until Morgan Escaré's 72nd minute try levelled. Then Bosc raced over under the posts to give the Catalans the lead. Bosc's sixth goal took the score to 36-30.

With three minutes remaining Stan Robin dropped a goal to give the Dragons breathing space before Australian prop Ryan Verlinden scored a Rovers consolation.

** In Leeds a court verdict ruled former Bulls coach Francis Cummins was wrongfully dismissed by the club. The 38-year-old was in charge of the club from September 2012 to June 2014, when he was sacked by the current administration with 18 months left on his three-year contract.*

Round 15

Kevin Sinfield became the third highest points' scorer in the sport's history, overtaking the 4,050 scored by Gus Risman, with his third goal in the 20th minute of the Rhinos 36-16 home win over Hull KR.

That touchline conversion gave Leeds a ten-point lead and its worth was emphasised at the break. By the interval, plucky Rovers – who brought in James Greenwood on loan from Wigan and gave a debut to Stephen Holker – had cut the deficit to two points, but they should have been ahead.

Seemingly able to engineer an overlap on either wing, thanks to some effortless distribution - long or short - from Terry Campese and decisive linking from fullback Ben Cockayne, the Robins scored four tries to three in the opening forty minutes but trailed, with Josh Mantellato having missed three shots at goal and Kieran Dixon the other.

In the second half they didn't get a chance to redress their kicking deficit as the Rhinos, with deeper resource on their bench, ran in a further 18 unanswered points. Ryan Hall's second try, just before the hour, and accompanying touchline goal from Sinfield established a decisive 12-point margin.

The Rhinos had finally ended speculation that week about Rob Burrow following Kevin Sinfield and Jamie Peacock out of Headingley when they agreed a new two-year contract with their 32-year-old halfback. They also signed Huddersfield Giants prop forward Anthony Mullally for the 2016 season on a three-year contract.

Ben Currie was a standout in Warrington's 34-18 win at Salford in the Friday night TV game. It was a sixth consecutive defeat for the Red Devils but they played their part in a thoroughly absorbing nine-try contest.

Warrington had paid compensation to bring hooker Brad Dwyer back from a season-long loan at London after Mick Higham joined hometown club Leigh Centurions for £50,000, and he scored the gamebreaking try in the 66th minute. The Wolves had also signed Kurt Gidley from Newcastle Knights for 2016.

There was a hat-trick of tries for left winger Gene Ormsby, his last one of the most spectacular seen for many a year as he leapt high to plant the ball and somehow managed to ground in the corner as he was tackled into touch by Greg Johnson in a vertical position.

Castleford Tigers coach Daryl Powell hit out at the video refereeing system following their home defeat to Huddersfield in the Thursday TV game. Two controversial tries from Craig Huby and Eorl Crabtree were both awarded by the video referee, which proved to be telling as the Tigers slipped to a 24-16 defeat to the Giants.

Referee Richard Silverwood sent both decisions recommending tries and video referee Ben Thaler was unable to find evidence to overturn those decisions.

'There are too many calls being made by people who are guessing - there's just too much guesswork going on,' said Powell.

The most controversial of the visitors' tries was the last, by Crabtree six minutes from time. The veteran prop charged to the line and appeared to have been held just short. Silverwood, however, signalled that in his view the touchdown was probably valid. His colleagues concurred and Danny Brough's fourth conversion from as many attempts secured an eight-point cushion for Huddersfield, which an injury-hit and disjointed Castleford outfit were unable to claw back.

The Tigers lost Frankie Mariano for the season to a serious knee injury as the Giants, who had announced the signing of Kiwi international prop Sam Rapira for 2016, held onto fourth spot.

St Helens coach Keiron Cunningham was effusive in his praise for his relatively inexperienced team after Saints' 17-10 win at Hull FC on the Friday night, with special praise reserved for Lewis Charnock, who was standing in for the injured Luke Walsh at halfback, although the non-stop James Roby was the standout.

A last-minute field goal from former Hull player Jordan Turner finally put St Helens beyond reach after a real arm-wrestle ensued from kick-off. The likes of Liam Watts and Mickey Paea, arguably the form props in Super League at this stage, were matched blow for blow by Alex Walmsley and Kyle Amor, as both sets of players tore into each other in a physical affair.

Hull that week announced they had signed Hull-born prop forward Scott Taylor from Wigan for the 2016 season on a four-year contract.

Catalans made it three wins in a row with a 58-16 demolition of Wigan Warriors in Perpignan on the Saturday. Todd Carney was in magnificent form and he created a host of Dragons tries as the Catalans ran rampant. They scored three tries in the seven minutes leading up to half-time, taking the score from 16-10 to 34-10 and giving Wigan little hope of mounting a comeback.

Zeb Taia and Tony Gigot, re-signed until the end of the season, four years after he left the Dragons, scored hat-tricks, while Scott Dureau kicked nine goals from ten conversion attempts.

Assistant coach Stuart Dickens took the Wildcats' reins after the departure of James Webster but there was little improvement at Belle Vue on the Sunday as Widnes won 30-18 - the Vikings' first away win of the season.

Wakefield's task wasn't made any easier by yet another injury early on. A thunderous tackle left Wildcats captain Danny Kirmond in a heap on the floor and after going off he failed his concussion assessment, meaning Wakefield had to play virtually the entire game without their captain. And just three minutes later, the Vikings broke the deadlock when a sweeping move eventually saw the ball find its way to Rhys Hanbury, the fullback gliding over to make it 4-0.

Three more tries, two to Stefan Marsh and one to Jack Owens, plus a conversion from Lloyd White made it 18-0 after 25 minutes. A try to promising teenage winger Tom Johnstone on the stroke of half-time provided some hope for Wakefield but White scored a try and Marsh completed his hat-trick before Matt Ryan and Dean Collis scored consolations.

** North Wales Crusaders proved to be the Cup Kings of League 1 on the Saturday when a 14-8 success over Swinton Lions at Bloomfield Road saw them lift the iPro Sport Cup. The game was a curtain raiser to the 'Big Bash Weekend' at Bloomfield Road, Blackpool, a magic weekend style event for Championship clubs.*

Round 16 - Magic Weekend

A total of 67,788 fans packed into St James' Park for the two-day sporting spectacular that saw a full round of First Utility Super League fixtures played at the home of Newcastle United on the last Saturday and Sunday of May. The Etihad Stadium in Manchester, which had hosted the previous three Magic Weekends, was unavailable due to work on the stadium.

The figure included a record 40,871 on the Saturday and on the Sunday 26,917 fans were in the stadium for the second day of competition.

The total weekend attendance was also an all-time Magic Weekend record, surpassing the previous best of 64,552 set at the Etihad Stadium in 2014.

The last game of the weekend was the derby game between Castleford and Wakefield, which proved to be predictably one-sided, the Tigers winning 56-16. Four tries for Denny Solomona was the headline story, with the former Melbourne and London winger outdoing Kevin Brown and Fetuli Talanoa's hat-tricks as top try scorer of Magic Weekend 2015.

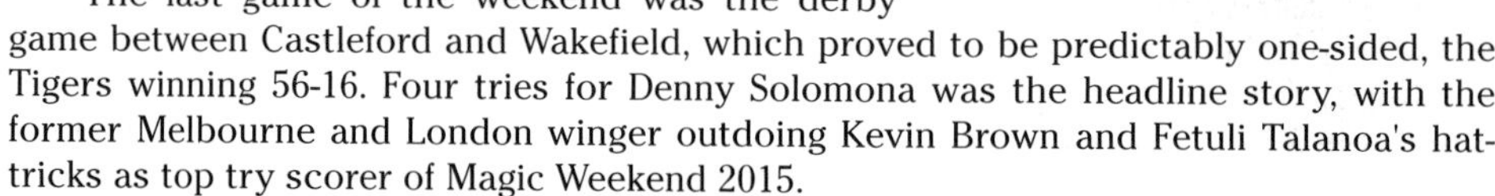

But the build up to the game provided the most dramatic news of the weekend, with Wildcats chairman Michael Carter revealing live on Sky Sports that legendary Australian coach Brian Smith was to take over with immediate effect as head coach, replacing the departed James Webster.

Catalans and Huddersfield opened the Sunday programme, in wet conditions compared to the Saturday and it was a scrappy game that turned into the most exciting of finishes.

In a dour first half, Huddersfield ground out a ten-point advantage and had two tries chalked off in a half that was dominated by Danny Brough's kicking game.

The Giants led 16-0 within four minutes of the second half with Jodie Broughton's try before the Dragons ran in 22-unanswered points to lead with just seconds remaining. Todd Carney led the comeback and scored two tries himself, the second giving the Dragons a 22-16 lead on 72 minutes, before sustaining a pectoral injury three minutes from time.

However, Jermaine McGillvary's last-gasp try gave Brough the opportunity to convert from the touchline and grab a point for the Giants - and he nailed it.

Widnes' Rhys Hanbury weaves through the Salford defence at the Magic Weekend

In the second game, St Helens coach Keiron Cunningham was delighted with the way his side came back from an 8-16 deficit at half-time to beat Warrington Wolves 20-16.

Cunningham praised his side's defensive work that kept Warrington scoreless in the second half after the Wolves had scored three tries to take what looked like a convincing lead at the break. Stefan Ratchford, Ben Harrison and Ryan Atkins scored the tries and Chris Bridge kicked two goals as the Wolves dominated.

St Helens scored first nine minutes into the second half and finally took the lead following with a 58th-minute try from captain Jon Wilkin, before Tommy Makinson added a late penalty to complete the scoring.

There was a knife-edge moment late on. On 72 minutes, with the Wolves trailing 18-16, Gene Ormsby finished off a spectacular score but video replays showed that Ben Harrison had passed off the ground earlier in the move.

Wakefield's defeat to Castleford was their 13th in a row. As well as Solomona's scoring feat (he had one disallowed too), Ashley Gibson scored a hat-trick, with Jake Webster causing much of the damage in the right centre. Teenage winger Tom Johnstone's try-brace was the Wildcats' only highlight as the Tigers moved into the top-eight at the expense of Catalans.

Salford coach Iestyn Harris admitted that the week leading up to their 38-16 loss to Widnes in the first game of the weekend was difficult for his squad, following the death the previous Tuesday of the Griffin brothers' father Martin at the age of 58 to a heart attack.

Any other time there would surely have been cause for celebration within the Salford camp as the return, after six weeks out with a foot injury, of centre Josh Griffin made it the first time that three siblings, Darrell and George also starting, had appeared for the same side in Super League.

Before the game a minute's silence was observed in remembrance and it proved too much for eldest brother Darrell who was shown a red card for a high tackle on Matt Whitley just before half-time. Josh was sin-binned after a punch-up with Cameron Phelps three minutes from full time.

Widnes were always in control of the game, despite Cory Paterson's opening try, as Kevin Brown, who missed the success at Wakefield through illness, made a spectacular return with an inspiring display rewarded by a fine hat-trick. The Vikings had also won local favour by wearing the black and white stripes of Newcastle United, with profits from shirt sales supporting the Bobby Robson Foundation.

Next up, Hull FC triumphed in the derby with a comprehensive 46-20 win thanks to a Fetuli Talanoa hat-trick and a brace from centre Kirk Yeaman. The Black and Whites ran in eight tries to four in front of a vocal St James' Park crowd, blitzing their neighbours with an impressive second-half attacking display.

The match was evenly poised at half-time, after Hull FC had edged in front 22-12. But the Airlie Birds crossed for two tries in the first five minutes of the second half to effectively put the contest to bed. The Robins rallied, cutting Hull's lead back to 14 points, until additional four-pointers to Talanoa and Yeaman finally ended their resistance.

Former St Helens and Salford Tony Puletua prop was solid on debut for the Robins but without Albert Kelly, Shaun Lunt and Dane Tilse they were well beaten and sat in tenth spot on the Super League ladder.

The final, showcase match on the Saturday night was a good one as Wigan went from conceding almost 60 points seven days earlier in Perpignan to producing a masterclass in shutting down the Rhinos' options to emerge 27-12 winners

FIRST UTILITY SUPER LEAGUE TABLE
Sunday 31st May

	P	W	D	L	F	A	D	PTS
Leeds Rhinos	16	11	1	4	468	328	140	23
St Helens	16	11	0	5	387	279	108	22
Wigan Warriors	16	10	1	5	424	290	134	21
Huddersfield Giants	16	8	2	6	346	236	110	18
Warrington Wolves	16	8	0	8	382	320	62	16
Castleford Tigers	16	8	0	8	345	330	15	16
Catalans Dragons	16	7	2	7	421	425	-4	16
Widnes Vikings	16	7	1	8	388	376	12	15
Hull FC	15	7	0	8	291	292	-1	14
Hull Kingston Rovers	15	6	0	9	348	425	-77	12
Salford Red Devils	15	5	1	9	296	393	-97	11
Wakefield T Wildcats	15	2	0	13	234	636	-402	4

Early on, as the Rhinos looked to promote the ball at seemingly every opportunity and built a 12-4 lead that looked the most likely route to Leeds' success. But Wigan forced them back into midfield, not conceding a point after the 18th minute - and counter-attacked with deadly precision.

Dan Sarginson opened the scoring for Wigan before Leeds responded with tries from Adam Cuthbertson and Joel Moon. But George Williams broke through in midfield to race away and go over in the corner before Joe Burgess side-stepped his way to the try line.

Matty Bowen ran 80 metres to touch down for Wigan and added another second-half try, capped by Matty Smith's late field goal. There was a sensational battle between fullbacks Bowen and Zak Hardaker, both making over 200 metres and producing glorious touches.

JUNE
Beware the Tigers

Round 17

At the fourth attempt, by a majority of eight to four, the Super League clubs decided to introduce marquee players into the competition from 2016 onwards. Huddersfield, Castleford, Wakefield and Hull FC all voted against the proposal.

Under the terms of the salary cap rule amendment, clubs would be entitled to sign one marquee player who would have a notional value on their salary cap register of either £100,000 if club trained or £175,000 if non-club trained. Castleford explained their objection to the new rule in a press release, claiming it would further skew the competition in favour of the richer clubs.

The Tigers were starting to find their form in Super League XX after a patchy start and they followed up their big Magic Weekend win over Wakefield with a 30-22 victory at Hull KR on the first Friday night of June.

A close-range try six minutes from time by stand-off Liam Finn, with scrum-half Luke Gale adding his fifth goal from six attempts, put paid to a rousing rally by Rovers, from 24-6 down midway through the first half, leaving them firmly ensconced in the bottom four and the Tigers in the frame for a play-off place.

Castleford were 18 points to the good by the fourteenth minute as their pack, props Nathan Massey, Andy Lynch and Grant Millington making regular inroads, dominated territorially. Ben Roberts, showing fine form at fullback, forced his way over from 15 metres out and Denny Solomona took Gale's high kick to the corner to touch down. Then Roberts broke from his own half to work his way past three defenders before feeding supporting second-rower Oliver Holmes, who powered over in the corner from ten metres, Gale again adding the conversion.

The Tigers' fourth try came after Albert Kelly had opened Hull KR's tally, Solomona's break from deep was supported by Michael Shenton, who sent in Gale for another converted try and a seemingly unassailable 24-6 lead.

Hull KR didn't see it that way. Terry Campese's towering kick to the corner led to a well-taken try by Kieran Dixon on the half-hour, although Dixon's conversion attempt bounced off the top of a post-protector. Rovers, just four minutes later, were firmly back in the game. Impressive winger Ken Sio, turning inside, was well-tackled by Andy Lynch, but Kelly scythed over from 15 metres from the play-the-ball, Dixon this time improving.

The hooter sounded after a Gale penalty attempt from 30 metres bounced out off an upright, leaving the Tigers 24-16 ahead at the break.

The second half was not as free scoring but there was plenty of excitement. On 54 minutes, Rovers found themselves only two points adrift when, after Kelly's last-tackle kick had gone loose, Kris Welham's smart grubber confounded Castleford's defence. Rovers substitute hooker Aaron Ollett pounced and Dixon added the goal from wide out.

Rovers, however, were unable to register the score that could have swung the issue. A Campese break came to nothing when his pass to non-existent support went into touch, and Finn's try duly settled the issue.

That week, Hull KR centre Darrell Goulding announced his retirement at the age of 27. The former England international joined the Robins from hometown club Wigan Warriors for 2015 but hung up his boots on medical advice after suffering a series of concussion injuries. He made eight appearances for the Robins, scoring one try, with his final match against Castleford Tigers in April remembered for his terrific flick pass that sent winger Sio over for a try in the corner.

2013 Albert Goldthorpe Rookie of the Year Tom Lineham was almost dropped by coach Lee Radford for the Thursday night TV game at Widnes, but he scored a thrilling hat-trick of tries to help Hull FC to a crucial 25-12 win, after the Vikings had raced into a 12-0 lead after ten minutes. Lineham produced an off-colour performance - one he described as the worst of his career - during the Magic Weekend win against Hull KR. However, a late injury to Fetuli Talanoa meant Lineham retained his place.

Marc Sneyd and Lineham deservedly earned the spotlight in the backs, but it was the Hull forwards who set the platform and Gareth Ellis and Mark Minichiello were at the heart of it.

In the following night's TV game, Warrington had to dig in to register a 26-18 home win over the Catalans. Ben Currie and Ryan Atkins tries saw the Wolves lead 12-6 at half-time after Tony Gigot had opened the scoring. But Eloi Pelissier sparked an early second-half spell that saw the Dragons lead 18-12 after he and Elliott Whitehead scored tries converted by Scott Dureau. That should have been more when Morgan Escaré broke clear soon after, only to see the supporting Stanislas Robin change direction at the crucial moment and his pass go to ground.

Warrington wrestled control back and three tries in the space of 11 minutes sealed their win. Richie Myler and Gareth O'Brien combined to allow Stefan Ratchford to send Atkins over for his second and close the gap to two points. The home side were then in front when Chris Hill brushed off Ian Henderson - who had just conceded the penalty that put Warrington in position - and charged under the posts.

Victory was effectively secured with the best try of the match. Gene Ormsby launched Ratchford from deep following a kick downfield, and he handed on to Currie, who showed a fine turn of foot to beat Dureau in a 60-metre footrace to the line.

St Helens won a hard-earned 32-12 home victory over a tenacious Salford side. Seeking their first away win against St Helens for over 35 years, Salford threw everything but the kitchen sink at Saints for long periods of the game, with Rangi Chase back after his seven-match ban and on song, but still went in at half-time 24-0 down.

Tommy Makinson once again emphasised his class with a 20-point haul, including two outstanding first-half tries, before suffering a broken fibia late on.

Salford began the second half as brightly as they started the first, only this time they were rewarded for their efforts, with dummy-half Logan Tomkins, back on loan from Wigan for the rest of the season, creating more time and space for his halves Chase and Theo Fages.

Two tries came in five minutes, through Niall Evalds and Chase and suddenly it was all Salford. Another score for the visitors could have changed the complexion of the game completely.

Saints were rattled. In the first 15 minutes of the half they had barely touched the ball, but Harrison Hansen, who was inspirational throughout, turned villain when he flattened Travis Burns late, allowing Makinson to put over a pressure-relieving penalty to put Saints three scores ahead. Finally, Andre Savelio put Shannon McDonnell in on 64 minutes for the final try of the game.

In the week, Salford had been rocked with the news that halfback Fages had handed in a formal transfer request.

Huddersfield coach Paul Anderson defended his skipper Danny Brough after his side's 32-18 home loss to Wigan on the Sunday. The Giants were on the wrong side of a 10-6 penalty count, which went 5-0 to the Warriors in the second half and Brough was caught up in a running battle with referee James Child throughout.

At a sun-drenched John Smith's Stadium in perfect conditions the first 40 minutes was a grinding affair - the score locked at 12-12 at half-time - with few clear attacking opportunities.

But the Warriors put their foot on the accelerator in the second half, Josh Charnley bagging a double and Liam Farrell getting his second try of the afternoon. The Giants, whose fullback Jared Simpson had scored a try on debut after only four minutes - only managed one more try, a 95-metre interception from Brough.

Brian Smith arrived in England in time to watch the Wildcats' 58-26 home defeat to Leeds, who maintained their one-point lead at the top of the table thanks to a rush of seven tries in 20 second-half minutes.

The Rhinos became the first team to pass 500 points in 2015 with some style, the feature a hat-trick from Liam Sutcliffe at fullback, on a day when Danny McGuire reached 250 tries for the club and Kevin Sinfield became the outright top appearance maker in Super League history, moving ahead of Paul Wellens with 440 games.

Round 18

Leeds Rhinos lost their place at the top of the Super League table after their 31-24 home defeat to Castleford Tigers on the Thursday, coupled with St Helens' victory over Wigan the following night at Langtree Park.

Saints were worthy winners over Wigan by 30-14, dominating the battle up front, where their bigger, more enthusiastic forwards impressed again. The Warriors opened strongly but faded under pressure. In the closing 15 minutes individual errors hurt them badly, with mistakes from Matty Bowen and Dan Sarginson leading directly to crucial St Helens tries.

Joe Burgess enjoyed an eventful opening few minutes as he made the game's first break in the Warriors' opening set, before being led to the sidelines for a concussion test after he was caught accidentally by Matt Dawson's boot.

And Burgess would have opened the scoring had he still been on, as Sarginson touched down after having switched to his left wing slot and taking George Williams' cut-out pass. Almost half-an-hour elapsed before Saints did respond, but it sparked a spell of dominance by them. An error at the play-the-ball by Joel Tomkins gifted them field position and, after four defenders had been sucked into a Mose Masoe drive, Saints quickly went left, where Jordan Turner put Adam Swift over out wide. In the next set of six Travis Burns booted a superb 40/20 that allowed a similar attacking platform and this time Turner touched down from Shannon McDonnell's pass.

Saints were attacking again when Wigan hit back against the run of play to lead at the break. Burns' pass wide was flicked on by McDonnell, but only into the arms of Burgess, who sprinted 80 metres up field to make it 8-10 at half-time. Burgess celebrated by throwing the ball into the home supporters, only to see it hit him on the back of the head when it was returned.

St Helens would score three times in the second half and each one came from a Wigan mistake. Bowen made failed to deal with Jon Wilkin's grubber to the in-goal and Burns pounced to score. Tomkins did respond for Wigan soon after, taking a smart pass from Bowen to finish in the right-hand corner. But, after Mark Percival's penalty had edged the home side ahead again, errors continued to haunt the Warriors.

They were denied a try of their own by a remarkable piece of covering from St Helens substitute Masoe, who covered virtually the full length of the pitch in tracking a Sarginson break and being first to his chip over. Bowen then dropped Wilkin's spiralling kick cold in front of his own posts, and McDonnell pounced to score.

Three minutes later, Sarginson's wayward pass - again on the Wigan line - was swooped on by the by-this-time bloodied Wilkin (after taking a cut from a knock from

Michael McIlorum) who celebrated passionately, embracing some of the St Helens supporters at the front of the stand.

Percival added both conversions and a late penalty to send Saints marching to the top of the league with five regular-season matches remaining.

The Rhinos finally succumbed to a late try by Castleford winger Denny Solomona, who was able to capitalise when Leeds winger Ash Handley dropped a Luke Gale bomb near his own line.

The Tigers had started the game like a whirlwind. By the time Leeds got into the Castleford half with ball in hand in the 17th minute, they were 18-0 down. Liam Sutcliffe, again at fullback, knocked on in his own '10'; Michael Shenton stripped the ball from Handley in a similar position and Paul Aiton was pulled up for a forward pass.

The mounting pressure told when Nathan Massey, who bossed the middle, slipped a great short ball to Grant Millington and he stepped clear to the posts. Luke Gale, whose kicking was superb, added the goal and a 40/20 in the next set. Scott Moore's pass to Liam Finn was not crisp, but the halfback readjusted and fooled the defence to dab the ball down from close in. Then Shenton stole the ball from Carl Ablett coming out of dummy half to gather and go over from 30 metres for his 500th point for Castleford in his 300th career appearance.

But Leeds had it back to 18-16 at the break through tries to Carl Ablett, Ryan Hall and Adam Cuthbertson and looked odds-on to go on and win the game. But, from their first penalty, three minutes in to the second half, Castleford scored on a power play last tackle as Finn, Gale and Shenton combined to send Solomona in at the corner, and Gale added a tremendous conversion.

Sub Kevin Sinfield entered the fray at hooker and he, Cuthbertson and McGuire, who held up the ball perfectly, sent Jimmy Keinhorst over, with Sinfield adding the goal. Then Sinfield and Cuthbertson exchanged passes and Ablett was impeded on the last tackle for Sinfield to draw the sides level with twelve minutes to play.

From the restart, Cuthbertson knocked on in his own '30' and, after Junior Moors and Andy Lynch had gone close, Finn dropped a goal to ease the Tigers decisively in front. Then Moors made more good ground and Gale's spiralling kick eluded Handley for Solomona to pounce, allowing Gale to add his fifth conversion.

On the Saturday, Catalans returned to winning ways with a hard-fought 20-14 home win over top-eight rivals Hull FC. With both sides heading into the game level on 16 points and separated on the league table by Hull's positive points difference, it was always going to be a close affair.

Hull went ahead when a sparkling up-the-middle break and offload by Joe Westerman put Jordan Rankin in for the opening score. Fine footwork from Remi Casty and a smart pass to the supporting Thomas Bosc had Catalans level and, after Marc Sneyd kicked a penalty goal to push Hull ahead, Tony Gigot swooped with an intercept try. Greg Mounis punished a ball strip on Elliott Whitehead to cross from Louis Anderson's pass and give Catalans a 18-8 half-time lead.

The Dragons were struggling to make possession and field position count and were punished when the outstanding Mark Minichiello notched the first points of the second half with a powerful drive. But Fetuli Talanoa had a try chalked off for obstruction in the build-up with 10 minutes to play and Dureau's penalty goal was enough to see out the home side's success.

Paul Anderson paid tribute to three-time Albert Goldthorpe Medal winner Danny Brough, who made his 400th career appearance in the Giants' 30-19 home win over Warrington on the Sunday.

It was a spiteful encounter filled with drama. Four players were sin-binned in a frenetic second half that erupted several times as the Giants staged a late comeback. Brough and Anthony England were given yellow cards just after the break and then Jake Connor and Daryl Clark joined them two minutes before full-time as tempers continued to flare.

Castleford's Denny Solomona stretches for the line under pressure from Leeds' Kallum Watkins

Clark crossed from short range to give Warrington the lead, before Connor levelled the scores. Gareth O'Brien's try and field goal made it 13-6 at half-time but Jodie Broughton's score reduced the deficit. Ben Harrison restored Wolves' seven-point lead, but two Jermaine McGillvary tries, one for Jared Simpson and two Jamie Ellis field goals gave Huddersfield the win.

The following Tuesday England was banned for four games for spitting at Brough. That week Warrington had announced the signing of Hull winger Tom Lineham for 2016.

Hull Kingston Rovers snapped a three-game losing streak in emphatic style with a 38-16 home success over Widnes Vikings, despite the injury absence of Terry Campese, who had suffered ACL damage in the Castleford defeat. It turned out to be season-ending.

Rovers went into the game four points behind the top eight after winning just one of their last seven in Super League, but a Ken Sio hat-trick helped them keep alive their Super-Eight hopes. Tries from Kris Welham, Maurice Blair, Josh Mantellato, Albert Kelly and Sio gave Rovers a 26-10 half-time lead. The Robins lost Mantellato to injury after the restart, but Sio led their charge as he went over twice more. Despite Stefan Marsh, Kevin Brown and Chris Dean going over for tries, Widnes were second best for most of the game.

Wakefield, who had seen the departures of star players Lopini Paea and Dean Collis, went down 24-16 to Salford at Belle Vue in an improved display in Brian Smith's first game in charge of the Wildcats.

Early on it looked as though little had changed. The Red Devils were 12-0 up after 15 minutes, Theo Fages over after a Wildcats attack broke down at the other end and Scott Taylor forcing his way over under the sticks. Even after Daniel Smith replied, Wakefield bumbled as Harrison Hansen charged down Tim Smith's clearing kick, collected the ball and raced over.

But within two minutes of the restart, Wakefield did manage to cut the gap. It came when the impressive Pita Godinet, the spark for Wakefield on a low-quality afternoon, provided a great pass for forward Ian Kirke to crash over on just his second league appearance for the club.

Then came the game's pivotal minute. Wakefield, with stacks of pressure and momentum, thought they were in again when Chris Riley looked to have touched down in the corner. But referee Robert Hicks and his officials deemed there was a knock-on whilst Riley grounded the ball.

Still reeling from that call, Wakefield conceded a quick penalty to give Salford field position and when Hansen crashed over after a great ball from Rangi Chase the Wildcats had it all do. Wakefield refused to give in though and they continued to scrap and fight for everything - a huge sign that their performance was markedly better than in recent weeks. And they set up a tense finish as the game entered the final quarter, when captain Danny Kirmond crashed over after another great ball from Godinet.

Round 19

Leeds and St Helens swapped places again the following week, with the rejuvenated Castleford Tigers again the major factor.

A week after toppling Leeds at Headingley, the Tigers hosted Saints in the Thursday night TV game and won the clash 25-24 after the most exciting finish of the season so far.

Castleford's Ben Roberts, the match-winner with a field goal in the last second, had been pivotal in much of a thrilling contest that went into the closing stages with the sides on level terms. Roberts had been involved in a couple of the Tigers' touchdowns and had been partly culpable for at least one of St Helens' tries.

The Australian was under little pressure when collecting a failed field-goal attempt by Saints scrum-half Luke Walsh with only a couple of minutes remaining. But he spilled possession in driving the ball out, giving the table-toppers, who had lost centre Mark Percival to the sin bin with eight minutes remaining, the chance to extend their winning run against Castleford to 16 games. Unaccountably, however, the usually impeccable St Helens hooker James Roby emulated Roberts' role as villain, knocking on at the base of the scrum to give the Tigers, who had braced themselves for a likely field-goal attempt by Walsh, an unexpected lifeline.

Castleford made the most of the escape as prop Andy Lynch spearheaded a drive downfield where, with less than five seconds left on the clock, the ball was spun across field and Roberts assumed a heroic mantle by landing the field goal from 15 metres out to cap a recovery from 18-10 down at the break.

Defeat was tough on several of the visiting side, notably second rower Jon Wilkin and, on their returns after periods on the sidelines through injury, scrum-half Luke Walsh and substitute forward Joe Greenwood. A number of Tigers players too made big impressions on returning to the fold, with Justin Carney and bench forward Matt Cook joining Walsh and Greenwood in making try-scoring come-backs.

The Rhinos made the most of it on the Sunday with a 32-20 home win over Hull FC.

The hosts led at the break thanks to tries from Danny McGuire, Joel Moon and Jimmy Keinhorst, playing in the second row, with Jordan Thompson crashing over for the visitors. Curtis Naughton touched down to give Hull FC hope before Moon ran in again. Danny Houghton and Fetuli Talanoa reduced the arrears but two Kevin Sinfield penalties and Carl Ablett's try on the final hooter gave Leeds the win.

Hull halfback Marc Sneyd and McGuire were sin-binned. Sneyd hauled down McGuire whilst chasing back in the 71st minute and appeared to twist McGuire's leg. He got a two-match ban for dangerous contact the following Tuesday.

Wigan remained third as they came from behind to stun a Salford Red Devils side that deserved more than a 19-12 defeat at the DW Stadium on the Friday.

Cory Paterson's try after nine minutes was the only score of the first half as Wigan were caught in possession on the fifth and made countless handling errors throughout the first half, while finding it hard to contain Rangi Chase. George Griffin scored a try at the start of the second half to put the Red Devils 12-0 in front, but they eventually tired, with Joe Burgess, Liam Farrell and Dan Sarginson all scoring in the second half. Sarginson's try was the main talking point as referee Joe Cobb pointed to the spot after a long consultation with his touch-judges, despite the in-goal judge awarding a drop-out, with Theo Fages claiming to have grounded the ball first from Michael McIlorum's kick, before the referee decided to give the try. The Salford fans behind the posts were adamant it was no try and made their voices known, as did coach Iestyn Harris. Matty Smith's 75th-minute field goal sealed it.

Despite having a numerical advantage for much of the game, Widnes were beaten 30-22 at home by a spirited Giants side in a bad tempered affair, which left the Vikings' top-eight hopes hanging by a thread.

Patrick Ah Van had made it 4-0 before Brett Ferres was shown a red card for punching Rhys Hanbury after just 12 minutes. Ferres, returning to the side after a three-week absence because of a knee injury, aimed a blow at Hanbury after the referee had already blown for a knock on after Aaron Heremaia's break from deep.

The visitors fought back through Ukuma Ta'ai before Jack Owens converted his own try to make it 10-6 at the break. The Giants took the lead for the second time in the match through Craig Kopzcak's four-pointer shortly after the restart only for Kevin Brown to almost immediately reply for the hosts.

However, the Giants would not be denied and scores from Jack Hughes, Luke Robinson and Jodie Broughton, who ran the length of the field after a poor pass by Joe Mellor, proved to be enough to render Brown's second try against his former side purely academic.

Warrington were just two points above the bottom four after a 36-10 defeat at Hull Kingston Rovers on the Friday night. With three of the top five still to play before the split, the Wolves were dangling perilously above danger. With pivotal stand-off and captain Terry Campese out for the season, Albert Kelly and Maurice Blair proved they could steer the Robins into the Super Eights.

The Wolves, in a closely-contested opening, took the lead on nine minutes when, after hooker Daryl Clark charged down a last-tackle kick by Kelly, Ashton Sims sent fellow prop Chris Hill over from 15 metres. Scrum-half Declan Patton added the goal and there was no further score until five minutes before the break, when Rovers scored a try out of nothing.

Warrington didn't appear to be in any danger when the Robins moved the ball wide, but Kelly's long pass to Liam Salter gave the centre the chance to send Ken Sio away down the flank. It was a chance the winger took in style, outflanking the cover from the half-way mark and outfoxing visiting fullback Stefan Ratchford to dive over in the corner. Josh Mantellato's conversion attempt just failed to carry, but Hull KR went in at the break 10-6 ahead, thanks to a bizarre second touchdown.

Warrington winger Joel Monaghan took Kelly's towering bomb coolly enough in the shadow of his own posts, only to lose possession under Rovers centre Kris Welham's strong challenge, the players' heads clashing in the collision. Both were able to continue, with the pair reflecting on a resulting try for Mantellato, who crossed after being fed by the alert Blair, duly converting his own score.

It was pretty much one-way traffic in the second half as Rovers increasingly dominated and the Wolves fell away alarmingly. Kieran Dixon, who was starting to hit form, got the ball rolling after only six minutes, darting onto Blair's telling pass from 15 metres out to round Ratchford, with Mantellato's goal stretching the lead to ten points. Salter's try minutes later helped Hull KR establish a 16-point lead, which was beyond lacklustre Warrington.

In baking Perpignan on the Saturday, the Dragons ran in three late tries to secure a 32-12 win over Wakefield. The Dragons led 12-0 after eight minutes through tries to Ben Pomeroy and debutant Krisnan Inu, the former Kiwi international signed until the end of the season after a spell in French rugby union, and it looked like a humiliation for the Wildcats.

Astoundingly, Wakefield hung on to keep the Catalans scoreless until half-time and by the 55th minute had levelled through Chris Riley and Pita Godinet tries, both converted by Jacob Miller. And they had another try claim by Richard Owen over-ruled by the video referee five minutes later.

Scott Dureau's third goal, a 65th minute penalty, gave the home side some relief before tries in the last seven minutes to Eloi Pelissier, Morgan Escaré and Louis Anderson gave the final score a one-sided look.

The defeat confirmed mathematically that Wakefield would by competing in the Middle Eight at the end of the season.

FIRST UTILITY SUPER LEAGUE TABLE
Sunday 21st June

	P	W	D	L	F	A	D	PTS
Leeds Rhinos	19	13	1	5	582	405	177	27
St Helens	19	13	0	6	473	330	143	26
Wigan Warriors	19	12	1	6	489	350	139	25
Huddersfield Giants	19	10	2	7	424	309	115	22
Castleford Tigers	19	11	0	8	431	400	31	22
Catalans Dragons	19	9	2	8	491	477	14	20
Warrington Wolves	19	9	0	10	437	404	33	18
Hull FC	18	8	0	10	350	356	-6	16
Hull Kingston Rovers	18	8	0	10	444	481	-37	16
Widnes Vikings	19	7	1	11	438	469	-31	15
Salford Red Devils	18	6	1	11	344	460	-116	13
Wakefield T Wildcats	18	2	0	16	288	750	-462	4

Challenge Cup Quarter Finals

Leigh's magical Challenge Cup run finally came to an end on the last Saturday of June when they fell to a 34-24 defeat at Warrington.

It was a superb game for the BBC TV audience that could have gone either way given a handful of crucial turning points. The biggest one was at the start of the second half when the Wolves - trailing 12-14 and in danger of being put under even more scrutiny than of late - came out and stepped up a gear, Kevin Penny scoring twice in the space of four minutes to take the momentum away from the Centurions.

Penny's second was one of the tries of the season as he somehow got the ball down whilst his entire body was in mid-air and suspended outside the touchline.

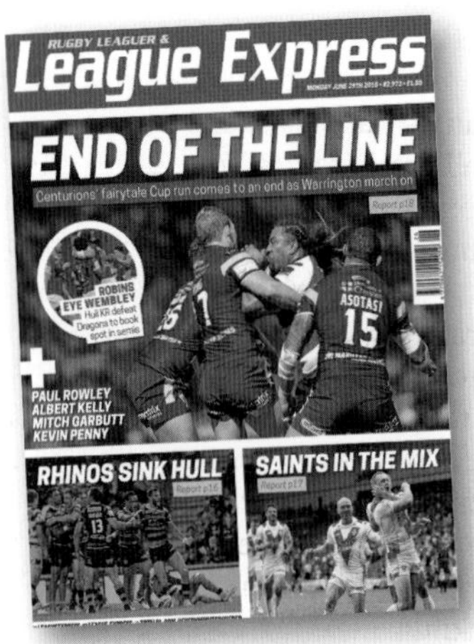

There were other crucial plays later in the game, not least Greg Worthington being ruled to have knocked on at the play-the-ball at 28-20 with 11 minutes to play. In the ensuing set of six, the excellent Ben Currie effectively sealed matters with his second try. Leigh still rallied again in the closing stages, Tom Armstrong getting the last score of the game. But any hopes of their outstanding Challenge Cup run finding a new peak ended when Worthington's delayed pass inside to Liam Kay - after another long range break - drifted forward.

Leigh's halfback Ryan Brierley enhanced his reputation with two tries - the first when he showed blistering pace to round Stefan Ratchford. And Gregg McNally's try at the end of the first half epitomised everything that was good about the Centurions, as they chanced their arm on the last tackle to produce a stunning team try.

On the Thursday night, Hull KR marched into the semi-finals for the first time since 2006 with a 32-26 home win over Catalans Dragons.

The Robins' blistering first-half performance saw them race into a 24-0 lead inside the opening half-hour, a lead from which the Dragons could not recover, although they were angered by a string of refereeing decisions against them.

While the Catalans lost their tempers, the red and whites kept their cool, with Albert Kelly in particular calmly pulling the strings. Tries to Ken Sio, Kieran Dixon, Kelly and Graeme Horne were all converted by Josh Mantellato, who added a last-second penalty goal after Krisnan Inu had opened the Catalans' account.

After half-time the Dragons fought back hard, but Sio's try in the 65th minute gave the hosts enough of a lead to see off the Catalans heading into the closing moments of the game. When Elliott Whitehead's converted try brought the gap back to six points there was too little time left for the Dragons to level.

The night after, in a rain-affected game, Kevin Sinfield's leadership qualities came to the fore in a 24-6 win at Hull FC. Joel Moon made it three tries in two weeks against the Black and Whites as he stole his own bomb off Jordan Rankin to slide over in the wet after only six minutes. Sinfield converted and kicked two penalty goals to make it 10-0 at half-time.

Three minutes after the turnaround, Sinfield turned Kallum Watkins back on the inside for him to cross for a converted try and give the home side an almost impossible task. Leeds added eight more points in the final ten minutes to see them cruise into the semi-finals. Zak Hardaker ghosted over for Leeds' third try of the night before Sinfield was handy with the boot again with another long-range penalty.

Young Hull halfback Jordan Abdull, deputising for the suspended Marc Sneyd, dummied his way over in the final minutes to see Hull escape being kept to zero.

Paul Wellens was given a guard of honour at Langtree Park on the Sunday by the St Helens and Widnes teams, after he had announced he would be quitting the game with immediate effect because of a hip injury that had plagued him for the past twelve months.

Saints' fullback problem was solved temporarily by Mark Percival, who excelled with two tries and six goals in the 36-20 home win, despite having to leave the field in the second half for a concussion check.

For the best part of 65 minutes Widnes were as good as the Saints and led 20-18 after tries to Patrick Ah Van and Chris Dean. But a couple of key moments going against Denis Betts' men and a killer touch from St Helens late on proved to be the telling difference.

With fifteen minutes left on the clock, Jordan Turner appeared to have dropped the ball as Saints launched another attack, but referee Roberts Hicks adjudged there was a ball steal from a Widnes man to give the hosts a huge opportunity. And they duly struck from the following set; James Roby's lightning burst out of dummy-half saw him feed Kyle Amor, with the forward barging his way over to restore St Helens' lead.

Whilst there was an element of controversy surrounding that score, there was less drama concerning Turner's next notable involvement. Following a Widnes error inside their own half, the Saints again shifted wide with pace and Turner was too quick and too strong for Danny Craven, going over for the game-clinching try.

Widnes almost set up a grandstand finish when Ah Van was freed down the left, but Rhys Hanbury couldn't finish off courtesy of some great scrambling defence from the Saints - and when a failed drop-out attempt didn't go the required distance, Percival opted to eat up more time and slot a penalty to add further gloss on the result, before adding a try of his own on the hooter.

JULY
Doing the splits

Round 11

Wakefield Trinity Wildcats ended their losing league run at 16 games in the midweek catch-up game which accommodated the previous year's teams outside the top-eight in the newly formatted Challenge Cup.

The Wildcats beat Hull FC at Belle Vue on a Wednesday night, the first day of July, by 26-16, despite trailing 16-0 following a lacklustre opening quarter. Wakefield, without Tim Smith who was injured in the warm-up, somehow fought back with the kind of performance that had seemed to be on its way during Brian Smith's opening few weeks in charge.

Out-of-favour Salford fullback Kevin Locke had joined Wakefield on a deal until the end of the season and there was also a debut for Jordan Tansey, signed from Castleford Tigers and Samoan hooker Michael Sio. Locke was impressive, though clearly not match fit, and he had great support in the forwards from Mickael Simon and the equally impressive Nick Scruton, Chris Annakin and Danny Washbrook.

It took 90 seconds for Hull to break the deadlock as Jordan Abdull's pass sent Kirk Yeaman through a gaping hole in the Wakefield defence, with Jordan Rankin converting to make it 6-0.

Rankin would again convert four minutes later as Liam Watts got Hull their second try of the evening. It was all too familiar a pattern for Wakefield; penalties handed Hull the field position and they struck again when Rankin ghosted through a tired-looking Wakefield defence.

Wakefield stemmed the Hull FC charge. They then hauled themselves back into it on 33 minutes when former Airlie Bird Jacob Miller produced a brilliant individual effort to dive over under the posts.

Locke's first telling contribution of the evening was to fire a bullet pass out wide for Richard Owen on 45 minutes to make it 16-12, before he picked off a Curtis Naughton pass nine minutes later to help lay the platform for another Trinity try.

Locke was brought down following his break, but Wakefield kept their composure and, three tackles later, another ex-Hull man in Joe Arundel charged his way over. Although Miller missed the conversion, the game was level at 16-16.

After Mickey Paea was placed on report for a dangerous tackle on Washbrook that forced him from the field - Paea was later suspended for two games - another penalty 30 seconds later enabled Miller to take two points from in front of the posts and give Wakefield the lead for the first time on the night.

With ten minutes left the Wildcats finally found some fluidity in attack again and killed the game off. Pita Godinet's pass out wide was good enough to find Matt Ryan in space and he dived over to spark wild scenes amongst the home fans, who knew that they were home and dry.

Off the field, the Wildcats issued the Bank of Ireland, the owner of Belle Vue, with a notice saying they would leave their famous ground on December 24th, with the club now having six months to find an alternative venue to play in 2016.

The defeat left Hull FC, without the direction of Marc Sneyd and Leon Pryce, two points behind Hull KR and Warrington heading into Round 20.

The Robins had gone clear the night before with a 34-28 home win over Salford. Despite trailing 8-10 at the break, Rovers were able to score three tries in seven minutes to launch themselves into a 26-10 lead before the hour mark.

Salford responded to level the game with six minutes remaining with a converted try to Ben Jones-Bishop, before a mix-up from the re-start allowed Albert Kelly the opportunity to race onto the bouncing ball and snatch the win for Rovers and secure the vital two points.

Salford coach Iestyn Harris said he was 'devastated' after the game and before the weekend had begun a period away from the club with illness.

Round 20

Leeds Rhinos went three points clear at the top after a convincing 46-18 home win over St Helens in the Friday night TV game.

Saints had a disastrous opening half as the Rhinos led 22-0 at the break, with Kallum Watkins in sensational form throughout.

Leeds' win was exemplified in a spell just after Rhinos' fullback Zak Hardaker, with the ink still drying on his new four-year deal, had been temporarily red-carded although actually sin-binned for a lifting tackle on Travis Burns in the 50th minute.

A man down, but with their old hands firmly on deck, Jamie Peacock produced another trademark, Herculean charge. Danny McGuire, back from injury, put in a grubber to the in-goal, the bounce troubling Matty Dawson who conceded a drop-out. From it, Watkins fed Carl Ablett, who brilliantly exploited the blindside all game, and he showed great step, balance, power and twist to shrug off Luke Walsh, Adam Swift and Mark Percival to post a remarkable solo try.

From the re-start, Peacock, Brett Delaney and Kylie Leuluai drove in relentlessly. Watkins then shot diagonally and around Jordan Turner and into the clear. McGuire, inevitably, linked and drew in three defenders, with his slipped inside pass sending Ash Handley in for his second try to cap a magnificent 70-metre move. Handley's brilliant solo effort for his hat-trick try in the 69th minute allowed Leeds to breathe easily after Jordan Turner and Kyle Amor tries got Saints back to 32-18.

Wigan stayed a point behind second-placed St Helens as they had fallen 17-6 at the Halliwell Jones Stadium the night before. Richie Myler's moment of genuine magic illuminated a vital win for Warrington's top-eight hopes.

The Wolves had come into the game as significant underdogs, having lost three of their last four Super League matches and with the absence of several key players. But, as they had done in the second half against Leigh just five days earlier, Tony Smith's side showed genuine resilience when it really mattered. Led from the front by the non-stop Ben Westwood and Chris Hill and, with Brad Dwyer again providing spark from the bench, Warrington made fewer mistakes than error-prone Wigan.

Wigan trailed from the 12th minute, when Myler produced his outstanding try. The scrum-half grubbered for himself on the last tackle, then flicked the ball over Matty Bowen soccer-style and regathered it to score.

Warrington broke Wigan again when Joe Philbin went through, only to see his pass to Ryan Atkins go to ground, while at the other end Lee Mossop was held up over the line and Joe Burgess was prevented from scoring by a Kevin Penny cover-tackle - he grounded the ball initially on the Wolves winger's foot.

It stayed at 6-0 until three minutes before the break. First, stand-off Gareth O'Brien kicked an impromptu field goal under the posts, before Dwyer earned a penalty in the next set and then produced a smart pass to put Atkins over and make it 13-0 at half-time.

Dwyer almost scored himself early in the second half, only for Matt Bowen to stop him short, before O'Brien did extend the lead further. After a mistake from Taulima Tautai - one of a number from the Wigan forward after he returned from a mandatory head test following a big collision with George King in the first half - Myler's pass allowed O'Brien the space to dummy his way over.

The stand-off missed the conversion to his own try, but 17-0 looked a long way back for an under-par Wigan side. They hinted at mounting a comeback when Matty Smith's excellent kick behind the defence put Dominic Manfredi over and the Warriors scrum-half booted a 40/20 not long after to give them another attacking platform.

But time after time they put the ball down under little pressure, with Larne Patrick's mistake in a Dwyer and Westwood tackle, after the visitors had forced a drop-out, typifying a frustrating night for the Warriors.

Danny Brough claimed his 100th career try whilst expertly guiding fourth-placed Huddersfield to a 32-14 Sunday afternoon home win over Hull KR. Jermaine McGillvary's try on the hour from Brough's superb kick, in a wet and windy second half, killed off any real hope Rovers had of recovering.

The defeat dropped Hull KR back into the bottom four after three games in eleven days and five in barely three weeks, as back in Hull, FC took revenge for their midweek defeat at Wakefield with a 31-24 victory.

Gareth Ellis was immense for the home side after initially being ruled out for up to six weeks from the previous Wednesday's game and Marc Sneyd's late field goal finally killed off the battling Wildcats, who were in with a shout right until the final minutes.

Castleford's fifth successive victory - by 34-20 over Widnes at home - mathematically confirmed their spot inside the Super Eights. Denny Solomona's hat-trick laid the platform for Castleford, who always had Widnes - missing Kevin Brown with an ankle injury - at arm's length. Justin Carney's try just after the restart left Widnes with too much to do to mount a realistic challenge.

Ian Watson took the reins for the Sunday clash against Catalans Dragons, with an 18-14 victory giving Salford a faint hope that they could scrape into the top eight with three rounds remaining.

Salford owner Marwan Koukash opened the gates to the Salford public and they repaid him with over 5,000 supporters heading through the turnstiles to see the Red Devils snatch a thrilling win with a spectacular late try, even though a sunny summer's day turned cold and wet as the game kicked off.

Rangi Chase was ruled out with a back injury, whilst Olsi Krasniqi made his Salford debut from the bench but by the time he came on Catalans led 12-0 through Remi Casty and Louis Anderson tries. But by half-time Salford only trailed 14-12 after a wonderful try from Niall Evalds try off a Michael Dobson inside pass and one from Dobson, as stand-in fullback Tony Gigot spilled his kick as he hit the ground. Scott Dureau's 37th-minute penalty edged the Dragons back in front.

And that's how it stayed until the 74th minute when Evalds sent Mason Caton-Brown clear down the left wing and Dobson was in support on the inside to the delight of the enthusiastic crowd.

There was much speculation about the future of absent head coach Iestyn Harris, with newly appointed Director of Rugby Tim Sheens to arrive at the club that week.

** Hull FC and Hull Kingston Rovers announced the merger of their Academies, with new players joining the system to become part of an NFL-style draft system.*

Round 21

The live TV fixtures at the start of round 21 saw the top four sides in action. And Leeds were drawn back to the pack after a 26-24 defeat at Wigan on the Friday as St Helens edged fourth-placed Huddersfield 35-34 at Langtree Park.

Wigan had started to look vulnerable in their recent fixtures against St Helens and Warrington but they kept up their unbeaten home record for the season with an edgy win at the end of an exciting game.

The Warriors led 18-12 at half-time despite going behind early on as Paul Aiton opened the scoring. But tries from Liam Farrell, Sean O'Loughlin and Matty Bowen eventually saw them go in ahead at the interval.

Wigan extended their lead with Josh Charnley going over, but Leeds hit back through Ash Handley and Rob Burrow to level matters at 24-24. No one would have complained if that had been the final outcome.

But with seconds to go referee Richard Silverwood opted to hand a controversial penalty to Wigan for obstruction, with Aiton the guilty party. Matty Smith kept his cool to slot over the winning penalty.

Smith produced his performance of the season, providing two assists and kicking five goals. Zak Hardaker was missing from the Leeds side after being suspended for one match for a dangerous throw in the Rhinos' last match against St Helens.

In the 31st minute the Rhinos were denied what would have been possibly the finest try ever scored in Super League, 'scored' by Danny McGuire after a series of mesmerising offloads. Silverwood recommended to the video referees that no try be awarded because of a possible obstruction by Kallum Watkins on Joel Tomkins and the video-referees concurred, much to the consternation of most observers, who believed that Tomkins had made the wrong call defensively.

The following night it was nip and tuck again as second played fourth and new Australian fullback Adam Quinlan's debut hat-trick and Luke Walsh's late field goal helped St Helens keep up the pressure on Leeds at the top with a 35-34 home win against wasteful Huddersfield.

Errors or penalties led directly to almost each of the twelve tries that were scored in a tit-for-tat encounter.

The Giants had easily enough chances to secure a win that would have seen them leap-frog Saints into third, but they failed to take them, most notably in the first half. They also had two late opportunities to win an entertaining contest, with Jamie Ellis recording his only missed conversion to Aaron Murphy's equalising try on 72 minutes - Danny Brough carrying a slight injury into the game - and Brough then pulling a penalty from halfway wide soon after.

When Luke Robinson was adjudged to have knocked on in Joe Greenwood's tackle in the dying stages, Saints took their chance through Walsh.

On the Sunday, Castleford missed the chance to go into fourth spot, with Hull FC doing their Super Eights qualification chances a power of good after a 21-18 home win over the Tigers.

Lee Radford's men looked to be staring down the barrel of another crucial defeat at half-time, trailing 14-10, but three tries in the second half, two from Ton Lineham and one from Jordan Abdull, put them in control and they were just able to hold on. Marc Sneyd's late field goal put Hull out to a seven-point lead late in the game and Ben Roberts late try wasn't enough.

Hull KR were now two points adrift and with a significantly worse points difference after being stunned by a second-half comeback from hosts Salford. Salford assistant coach Ian Watson was again in charge of the team in a 31-18 win, with the future of head coach Iestyn Harris still uncertain.

The Robins were seemingly in charge, 18-4 up at the break. But after Josh Griffin cruised around Ben Cockayne on 51 minutes for a fine try it was one-way traffic, with Liam Hood providing the spark out of dummy half. Theo Fages' 76th minute try gave Salford the lead for the first time and Michael Dobson potted a field goal before Niall Evalds finished it off in the last minute, Dobson's conversion making it 31-18.

Widnes Vikings could still technically make the top eight and ended an unwanted record on the same Sunday afternoon, earning their first ever victory against the Catalans Dragons with a 29-22 home victory, helped by two tries each to wingers Paddy Flynn and Patrick Ah Van.

The Vikings had lost six and drawn two of their previous games against the Dragons since their elevation to Super League in 2012.

Leading 18-12 at half-time, after having gone 0-12 down early in the game, the Vikings held on valiantly in the second half, despite injuries to Stefan Marsh and Chris Dean that reduced the size of their bench.

Warrington indicated they were starting to hit their straps and were only two points behind the top four after a 40-20 win at Wakefield, as the two Smith brothers Brian and Tony coached against each other for the first time in their careers.

Stefan Ratchford and Joe Philbin tries had the Wolves 12-0 up in 13 minutes but it wasn't until back-to-back tries from Daryl Clark and Richie Myler, with the score at 22-14 towards the end of the third quarter, that the Wolves were home and hosed.

Without Tim Smith and Pita Godinet, the Wildcats' creative influence was largely reliant on Jacob Miller, who couldn't be faulted for effort and scored four tries in defeat.

Meanwhile the Wolves were being strongly linked with Parramatta's mercurial scrum-half Chris Sandow, with Richie Myler having agreed to join Catalans for 2016 and Chris Bridge heading for Widnes Vikings.

Round 22

The composition of the inaugural Super Eights was effectively decided when Hull KR were defeated 22-12 by Hull FC in a brutal encounter at the KC Lightstream Stadium in the Friday night TV game.

Hull FC lost both Leon Pryce (shoulder) and Gareth Ellis (achilles tendon) to injury during the first half of the derby, but managed to stay composed and record a vital ten-point victory that secured their place in the top eight. Hull KR could still mathematically retain their place in the Super League if they could win at St Helens on the following Friday and make up a 65-point shortfall on the Catalans Dragons, who had to play their final game against Leeds at Headingley on the Sunday.

Rovers' talismanic scrum-half Albert Kelly, who had been under an injury cloud all week with a medial ligament strain, did his utmost as the home team, playing in a Papua New Guinea-styled kit to support the Stanley Gene Foundation, led 12-4 up to the half-hour mark through tries to Shaun Lunt and Josh Mantellato, the Italy winger picking up Kris Welham's smart flick outside after collecting Kelly's high kick, against one from Steve Michaels, a beauty as the Australian collected Marc Sneyd's overhit kick to the corner with one hand and managed to touch down at speed.

But two tries to Tom Lineham, the first off Jordan Rankin's flat pass, the second when he collected a bouncing pass behind him and powered past Welham, had Hull 16-12 to the good at half-time.

There was only one score in the second half, 14 minutes in when Michaels forced an error from opposite number Ken Sio. Michaels pounced on the ball and touched it down. His try was confirmed by the video referee, who deemed him not to have stripped the ball one-on-one in the build-up.

St Helens, despite losing skipper Jon Wilkin with a broken thumb in the seventh minute, once again broke Warrington's hearts by 20-14 in a five-try rollercoaster derby at Halliwell Jones Stadium on the Thursday night.

It was a tight affair that could have gone either way. The Wolves conceded several penalties as they tried to slow down St Helens' roll early on, resulting in an 8-nil Saints lead on the quarter hour after a short-range converted James Roby try and a Luke Walsh penalty goal.

Saints were also penalised around the ruck - there were 16 in total in the first half -

but it wasn't until the 37th minute that the Wolves capitalised, as Ben Currie hit a good angle to take Gareth O'Brien's pass to crash over.

On 50 minutes, Walsh's improvised last-play cut-out pass down the left flank was intercepted by Kevin Penny who streaked over from 20 metres out to give Wire the lead for the first time at 12-8. But five minutes later a double drive from the wrecking ball Mose Masoe ended with him touching down under the posts - and when Walsh added from the tee the Saints were back in front at 14-12.

Coming into the final ten minutes the game was on a knife-edge. Then, after a spell of frantic play from both sides, Warrington went close when O'Brien's bomb was gathered by Ryan Atkins, who tried to wrestle his way over the line only to be held up by some desperate Saints defence. The upshot of the lengthy video analysis was that Warrington were given a penalty for a ball steal and O'Brien slotted over the penalty to level the scores at 14-14 on 75 minutes.

But then, a line-break from Travis Burns and superb back-up play from fullback Adam Quinlan on 78 minutes scattered the Wire defence. Mark Percival kept the ball alive as he was tackled and as the champions shifted the ball left they took advantage of a massive overlap for Jordan Turner to glide in at the corner.

Huddersfield Giants maintained their fourth position as they joined Leeds as the only two teams to win in Perpignan this season - edging a scrappy encounter 14-12.

The sides were level at 6-6 at the break after a first half of dropped balls and an early ten-minute break as Dragons' Elliott Whitehead was knocked out and stretchered off.

After 31 minutes of deadlock, the Giants moved the ball right where Leroy Cudjoe took play to the line and dropped a one-handed pass to Jermaine McGillvary, who finished in the corner, with Jamie Ellis kicking the touchline conversion. Danny Brough was sin-binned after lashing out when he was knocked over launching a high kick and the Catalans soon equalised as Morgan Escaré slipped a kick into the right corner for Krisnan Inu to race onto and Scott Dureau's touchline kick levelled.

Escaré opened up a six-point home lead when Inu swooped on a loose ball on his own line and sent the fullback racing under the posts. But McGillvary got his second from a long forward-looking Scott Grix pass, Ellis converted again and then kicked a 54th-minute penalty, which provided the winning margin, as not long after Dureau missed a kickable penalty.

The Giants gave a debut to Daniel Smith, 22, who had joined the club from Wakefield on a four-and-a-half-year contract. Giants forward Anthony Mullally had moved to the Wildcats until the end of the season, before he joined Leeds in 2016.

After the game, Dragons Chairman Bernard Guasch hit out at the standard of refereeing in Super League. 'Enough is enough! We have had another two points taken away from us today because of the scandalous and dishonest decisions of the referees,' said Guasch.

Guasch was fined £1,000 by the Rugby Football League for public criticism of a match referee.

Another outspoken club chairman, Salford's Marwan Koukash was also at the centre of post-match talk after league-leaders Leeds Rhinos' 70-6 humbling of the Red Devils at Headingley on the Friday night, as Rhinos coach Brian McDermott aimed a surprise broadside at Koukash. He said: 'Because of the way he has conducted himself, it embarrasses me to be involved in Rugby League when there's an owner of a club conducting himself like he is, saying what he wants, when he wants, how he wants.'

Koukash was not at the game and available for immediate comment, but he did respond on Twitter: 'I sincerely apologise to our fans. Well done to @leedsrhinos but McDermott should keep his mouth shut.'

Defeat ended Salford's hopes of a top-eight finish as Zak Hardaker returned from suspension with a 26-point haul from two touchdowns and nine goals.

Widnes's chance of the Super Eights also ended on the same night at Wigan, where the Warriors won a close game 20-10.

Josh Charnley had given Wigan an early lead in the second minute after Ryan Hampshire collected Charnley's kick through - he was a metre or so offside - raced away and, when tackled short, managed to get the pass back to his winger.

That was cancelled out by Widnes tries from Tom Gilmore - a nice try up the middle after a smart interchange between Aaron Heremaia and Rhys Hanbury - and Chris Dean. Just before the half-time hooter, Joe Burgess raced around the posts after stabbing through and taking Anthony Gelling's subsequent kick through.

The scores were locked at 10-10 for much of the second half and with 12 minutes left Matty Smith missed with a field-goal attempt. But three minutes later Burgess broke down the left and sent in Hampshire. And in the last minute Gelling confirmed the Wigan win.

Winger Justin Carney scored four second-half tries to help Castleford to a comfortable 58-20 derby victory at bottom club Wakefield.

The Tigers were level at 12-12 until they found their groove to run in five tries in a decisive 12-minute spell either side of half-time to clinch the points that took them level with fourth-placed Huddersfield, although with a vastly inferior points difference going into the final round of fixtures.

The Wildcats were expecting star recruit Kevin Locke to be out for the rest of the season after he picked up a serious injury. Locke was replaced after 13 minutes clutching his arm and shoulder after trying to stop Grant Millington from scoring. Tom Johnstone did score twice for the outclassed Wildcats.

Round 23

Leeds Rhinos secured top spot ahead of the Super 8s after beating Catalans 36-22 at Headingley on the last Sunday of July, a result which moved them back ahead of St Helens, who had hammered Hull KR 52-12 the previous Friday.

Leeds' win meant the gap between first and eighth-placed Catalans going into the big split was 13 league-points, after the Rhinos won a 10-try, rain-affected encounter.

Tom Briscoe grabbed a hat-trick after returning from a dislocated shoulder suffered in March but it was Kallum Watkins who scored the game-turning wonder try around the hour mark, an 80-metre charge through centrefield that signalled two more, from Brett Delaney and Briscoe, in six minutes. Aussie prop Mitch Garbutt also got his first try for the club just before half-time.

Luke Walsh and Travis Burns pulled the right strings at Langtree Park as St Helens eased past a tired-looking Hull KR as both sides prepared for Challenge Cup semi-finals the following weekend.

With a host of willing workers in the pack - headed by youngsters Luke Thompson and Joe Greenwood, plus the returning Atelea Vea - Saints had far too much for the Robins, running in nine tries in total.

Both sides rested key men ahead of those semi-finals in James Roby and Albert Kelly, while Rovers handed a debut to newly signed Aussie Dane Chisholm, a French international, at halfback. But the Robins were 24-0 down before they had mounted a serious attack, as Saints completely dominated the opening half-hour.

The win took St Helens above Wigan who had beaten Hull FC 48-12 the night before at the KC Stadium. Coming off the back of the highs of a massive derby win, the Black and Whites were looking for their fourth straight victory to close the gap on fourth place in the last game before the split. But after being out-classed they ended the regular season six points adrift of the top four.

Eight tries, including a double for fullback Matty Bowen on his return to the side, ensured the points for Wigan.

Huddersfield Giants secured fourth place on the Sunday with a 34-24 home victory over bottom side Wakefield Trinity Wildcats.

The hosts led 28-12 at the break thanks to tries from Luke Robinson, Jodie Broughton, Michael Lawrence, Daniel Smith and Leroy Cudjoe's 100th career try. Two tries in four minutes early in the second half - from Matty Ashurst and Lee Smith - put Wakefield back in contention at 28-20. But Danny Brough added a fine solo score to his five goals to settle it before Reece Lyne scored a consolation.

Wakefield boss Brian Smith gave three debuts to recent signings Scott Moore, in a swap deal with Castleford for Paul McShane, Bill Tupou from the Canberra Raiders and the returning Lee Smith, in the light of injuries to Kevin Locke, Tim Smith and Ali Lauitiiti.

Castleford went into their Sunday game at home to Warrington with a slim chance of catching the Giants on points difference, but that went badly wrong as they crashed to a 44-6 defeat.

The Tigers lost Luke Gale on 17 minutes, the in-form scrum-half, who led the Albert Goldthorpe Medal standings, having sustained a heavy knock from Ben Westwood. Westwood was banned for two games the following Tuesday for a reckless high tackle.

The Wolves, with halfbacks Richie Myler and Gareth O'Brien on song, established a lead they were destined not to lose on seven minutes when winger Joel Monaghan, back in action after having recovered from a calf injury, pounced on Myler's kick to the corner. When teenage second-rower Sam Wilde got his first try for the Wolves on 66 minutes it was 40-0, a Junior Moors try eight minutes from the end avoiding the whitewash.

Warrington had been boosted by the news that Chris Sandow had been released by Parramatta Eels to join the Wolves, who registered him before the previous Friday's signing deadline. Injured Simon Grix went to Wakefield on loan to make space on the salary cap. He never played for the Wildcats.

On the same afternoon, Widnes claimed a thrilling 21-20 home victory over Salford to win the battle for ninth place and earn themselves four home games in the Qualifiers. Niall Evalds and Cory Paterson crossed either side of Chris Clarkson's try to put Salford 12-6 in front at the break. Paddy Flynn and Scott Taylor exchanged tries to leave the visitors 10 ahead.

But Stefan Marsh and Aaron Heremaia touched down before Danny Craven's last-minute field goal won it for Widnes, who were to be boosted by the imminent arrival of St George Illawarra centre Charly Runciman, who had signed for the 2016 season.

FIRST UTILITY SUPER LEAGUE TABLE
Sunday 26th July

	P	W	D	L	F	A	D	PTS
Leeds Rhinos	23	16	1	6	758	477	281	33
St Helens	23	16	0	7	598	436	162	32
Wigan Warriors	23	15	1	7	589	413	176	31
Huddersfield Giants	23	13	2	8	538	394	144	28
Castleford Tigers	23	13	0	10	547	505	42	26
Warrington Wolves	23	12	0	11	552	456	96	24
Hull FC	23	11	0	12	452	484	-32	22
Catalans Dragons	23	9	2	12	561	574	-13	20
Widnes Vikings	23	9	1	13	518	565	-47	19
Hull Kingston Rovers	23	9	0	14	534	646	-112	18
Salford Red Devils	23	8	1	14	447	617	-170	17
Wakefield T Wildcats	23	3	0	20	402	929	-527	6

KINGSTONE PRESS CHAMPIONSHIP TABLE
Sunday 26th July

	P	W	D	L	F	A	D	PTS
Leigh Centurions	23	21	1	1	972	343	629	43
Bradford Bulls	23	18	1	4	828	387	441	37
Sheffield Eagles	23	17	0	6	586	451	135	34
Halifax	23	16	0	7	646	377	269	32
Featherstone Rovers	23	13	0	10	633	565	68	26
Dewsbury Rams	23	12	1	10	490	461	29	25
London Broncos	23	12	0	11	538	510	28	24
Workington Town	23	7	1	15	379	631	-252	15
Batley Bulldogs	23	7	0	16	421	539	-118	14
Whitehaven	23	7	0	16	418	671	-253	14
Hunslet Hawks	23	5	0	18	362	769	-407	10
Doncaster	23	1	0	22	282	851	-569	2

The Red Devils had also strengthened their squad ahead of the Qualifiers by landing two deadline day signings. Former Australia international Reni Maitua joined on a deal for the rest of the season from Featherstone Rovers, whilst centre Iain Thornley signed from Wigan, similarly on a deal for the remainder of 2015. But they lost halfback Theo Fages, who resigned from the club in late July.

St Helens' Andre Savelio can't stop Leeds' Jamie Peacock from scoring a memorable semi-final try

** Leigh Centurions were awarded the Kingstone Press Championship League Leaders' Shield after beating Doncaster 66-10 on the Sunday at Leigh Sports Village. Leigh lost only one league game all season, finishing with 44 points from their 23 matches, six points ahead of second-placed Bradford Bulls.*

Challenge Cup Semi-finals

Leeds Rhinos were the first to go through to the Wembley final with a 24-14 win over St Helens in a superb game at the Halliwell Jones Stadium broadcast on BBC2 on the last Friday night of July.

According to Leeds coach Brian McDermott, the opening 20 minutes were the best his side had played all season; their ball movement at pace was at times mesmerising. But Saints not only held on under the almost submerging pressure, they found their way back into the game. Two scores in three minutes saw them just a try away from a remarkable turnaround, only for the Rhinos to find another gear again and return to Wembley to defend their Challenge Cup crown.

Kevin Sinfield led the Rhinos superbly, as usual, but the star of the show was Zak Hardaker, who was making his 150th career appearance. Hardaker made a remarkable 230 metres from 26 carries and made two clean breaks. He scored the opening try in the third minute when he stepped superbly inside Luke Walsh and it was his tackle on Adam Quinlan in the 66th minute that secured a goal-line drop-out and led to Leeds scoring their final try by Kallum Watkins to win the game.

Hardaker's try and Joel Moon's 24th minute effort put Leeds 12-0 ahead although Mark Percival pulled back an unconverted try two minutes before half-time.

An amazingside-stepping effort by Rhinos veteran Jamie Peacock made it 18-4, but another try by Percival kept Saints in touch. However, a 66th minute last-tackle power-play saw Rob Burrow and Danny McGuire combine and Sinfield sent in Watkins on an unstoppable angle, then added the conversion.

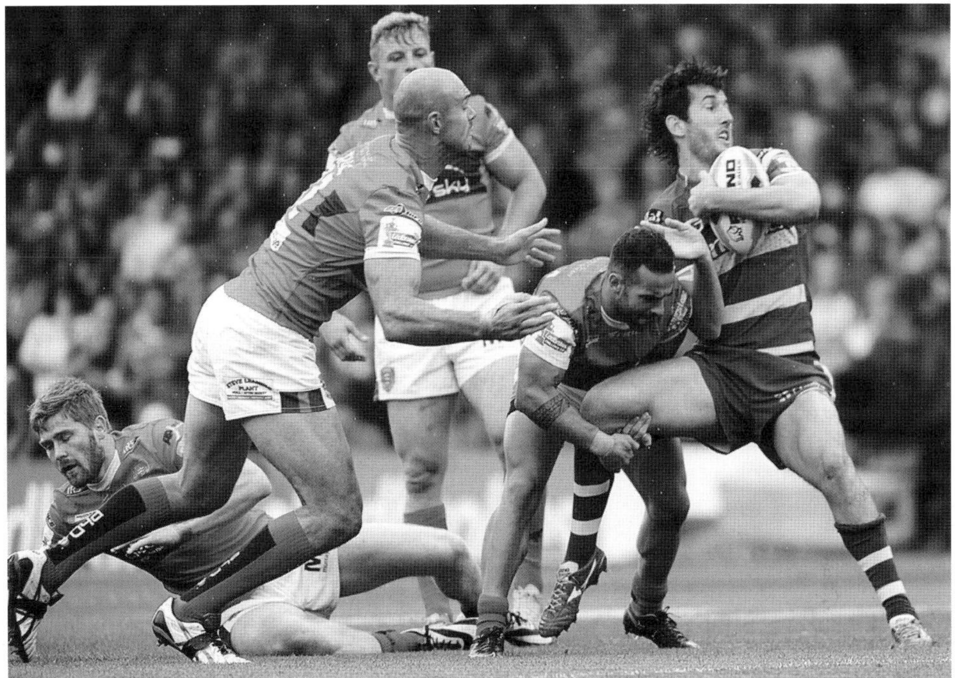

Warrington's Stefan Ratchford halted by Hull KR's John Boudebza as Dane Tilse moves in

The downside for Leeds was a serious knee injury to Jamie Jones-Buchanan in the later stages.

In a major shock, Hull KR, who hadn't qualified for the Super 8s, went through to the Challenge Cup Final for the first time since 1986 by defeating Warrington Wolves 26-18 at Headingley on the Saturday.

The Wolves got off to the perfect start after Gareth O'Brien's kick-off went dead. They took full advantage of their early field position when a sweeping move left enabled Ryan Atkins to force his way over and break the deadlock for O'Brien to convert.

Without captain Terry Campese, Albert Kelly and Josh Mantellato proved to be the key men for Hull KR, as they slowly started to wrestle control of the contest in testing conditions. Teeming rain before the game had left plenty of surface water on the pitch and, when the rain re-started during the match, it made things even more difficult.

The Robins struck when a slick move to the left and a great final pass from Kieran Dixon found Mantellato and, although he couldn't convert from the touchline, it was game on. Two minutes later they were in again when a sublime kick from Kelly was matched with an incredible on-the-run take from winger Ken Sio, who plucked the ball from the murky air and raced home, with Mantellato's goal making it 10-6. And rather than opting to run it when receiving their sixth penalty four minutes from half-time, the Robins left it to the reliable Mantellato to knock over a penalty for 12-6 at the interval.

Seven minutes after the break, Kevin Larroyer somehow managed to get the ball down for a try, despite the efforts of four Wolves defenders to prevent him. Mantellato converted that and then knocked over another penalty heading into the final 25 minutes and, with a 14-point deficit to claw back, the game looked up for Warrington.

But they set up a tense finish with two quick tries. First Richie Myler darted over after Brad Dwyer was held up short of the line, before a neat pass from Myler put Ben Currie over and, with O'Brien converting both, Rovers were now facing a stern test of their resolve at 20-18. But they dug deep, as Shaun Lunt sealed the win with a trademark hooker's try.

AUGUST
Eights a knockout

The Super 8s that began after 23 rounds of Super League and the Kingstone Press Championship comprised three leagues of eight teams, with one fixture against each of the seven other teams and home and away for each club determined by their finishing position in the league table.

The top four clubs in Super League - Leeds, St Helens, Wigan and Huddersfield - each had four home matches, while the teams finishing fifth to eighth had three home matches. Each team's points accrued carried on into the Super 8s.

In the Qualifiers, Widnes and Hull KR had four home fixtures, while fellow Super League clubs Salford and Wakefield had three each.

Leigh and Bradford were rewarded for finishing first and second in the Championship with four home games, while third placed Sheffield and fourth placed Halifax each had three home games. All eight teams started off on zero points, with the top three finishers automatically promoted back to Super League and the fourth and fifth teams playing off for the fourth 'promotion' place.

The bottom eight teams in the Championship – Featherstone, Dewsbury, London, Batley, Whitehaven, Workington, Hunslet and Doncaster - competed for the Championship Shield, with the bottom two teams to be relegated into League 1 for 2016.

Super League General Manager Blake Solly accepted that August and September would be the acid test of the new competition structure introduced by the RFL.

Solly claimed the Championship attendance record had been broken twice and the overall increase in crowds was 70 per cent over 23 rounds, with a 10 per cent increase in Super League crowds.

Super League Super 8s - Round 1

The prospects of a top-four play-off not involving 2012 and 2013 Grand Finalists Warrington Wolves became more likely after a heavy 49-10, Friday night defeat at Leeds in the opening round of the Super 8s.

Only Warrington had done the double over the Rhinos in the regular rounds but going into the Super 8s Leeds did not appear to have a weak link. Fullback Zak Hardaker was at the top of his game, running 256 metres, including four line breaks and two glorious tries; Kallum Watkins was majestic and the guile of Danny McGuire was at its peak. Adam Cuthbertson was so often the catalyst with another six offloads, which was double the Wolves total.

The only downside was the loss of hooker Paul Aiton. Aiton suffered a broken arm, which almost certainly meant he had played his last game for the Rhinos, having signed for Catalans, despite the club having wanted to keep him.

Chris Sandow made his Wolves debut as Kevin Penny's second try six minutes into the second half got Warrington back to 24-10. But the Rhinos' defensive resolve on their own line after that created the platform for Hardaker's wonder, breakout, second try. And Leeds were unstoppable after that. The Wolves also lost Anthony England for the rest of the season with an elbow injury.

The night before, Wigan move into second with a hard-fought 30-22 home win over Huddersfield. It was a thriller at the DW Stadium, with the result in doubt until the final few minutes.

The Giants raced into a 10-0 lead after just twelve minutes, targeting Wigan's left side, and winger Jermaine McGillvary was the happy recipient as he bagged an early double.

A breakaway try from Liam Farrell put the Warriors back in it at 6-10 and they could have gone in at half-time leading as John Bateman was held up inches short twice.

Two tries in the space of two second-half minutes saw Wigan take an 18-10 lead as Dom Manfredi and George Williams went over to put the home side in control. Jack Hughes and Larne Patrick then traded scores as Wigan led 24-16.

Eorl Crabtree then epitomised Huddersfield's fighting spirit by crashing over near the posts to again reduce the gap to two points, but Wigan were not going to be denied, as Dom Crosby barged over from close range in the 78th minute to seal the win.

St Helens slipped into third on the Saturday after a 26-16 defeat in Perpignan, which ended the Dragons' four-match losing run and kept faint hopes of a top-four spot alive for the French side.

Scott Dureau - heading home to Australia at the end of the season - gave the French fans a glimpse of what they would be missing with a superb performance as the Dragons successfully overcame Ben Pomeroy's 43rd-minute red card for a shoulder charge on Josh Jones. He was later suspended for one game.

Saints were chasing the game after Tony Gigot's 12th minute try and could have set up a thrilling finish had Greg Richards' try claim in the 70th minute not have been controversially ruled out for obstruction.

After their loss at Wigan, Huddersfield were in a tight battle for fourth spot, sitting on 28 points, the same as fifth-placed Castleford, who beat Hull FC 36-30 at the Mend-A-Hose Jungle on the Friday night.

Tigers captain Michael Shenton scored four tries and had another touchdown disallowed as Castleford edged a rollercoaster of a match between two sides that could barely contemplate defeat in the battle for a semi-final spot. Shenton could easily have finished on the losing side in a game that Hull led 12-0 after only five minutes. But the Tigers - with prop Andy Lynch setting a huge platform - blasted back to go four points ahead as the interval beckoned.

The home side, however, found themselves 18-16 adrift at the interval when the visitors claimed a controversial try in which former Castleford halfback Marc Sneyd appeared to pass the ball forward in the build-up.

Hull went on to establish a 24-16 lead within three minutes of the restart, but the Tigers roared back to lead 36-24, Ashley Gibson's try four minutes from time giving the Tigers a 12-point cushion, which was needed as Hull rallied immediately through a Jack Logan try. After the game, Hull coach Lee Radford admitted that top-four hopes were almost up this season for the Black and Whites.

Super 8s, The Qualifiers - Round 1

There were no shocks in the first round of the Middle Eight, with two Super League teams winning their clashes with Championship sides.

Leigh Centurions were favourites from the Championship clubs to win promotion and at half-time of their televised Saturday game at the Leigh Sports Village that favouritism looked well placed as they led Hull KR, missing Albert Kelly, who suffered a lateral knee ligament injury in the latter stages of Rovers' win against Warrington in the semi-finals of the Cup, by 24-6 at half-time.

Ryan Brierley, Gregg McNally, Andrew Dixon and Tom Armstrong all scored tries, all converted by Martyn Ridyard, on the back of some open football for which the

Centurions had become renowned.

But all that Leigh could manage in the second half was a Ridyard penalty in the 53rd minute as they hung on for dear life, the Robins emerging 36-26 winners. The final half-hour belonged to Maurice Blair, who stepped up to the plate with his halfback partner Dane Chisholm to ensure Leigh couldn't escape from their own half.

Halifax, still a part-time club, gave Widnes Vikings a bit of a scare at the Shay on the Sunday. The Vikings won 14-0, after the teams were scoreless at half-time, and they were grateful to Australian signing Charly Runciman, who scored two tries on his debut.

The other two Super League clubs, Salford and Wakefield, met at the AJ Bell Stadium and it was the Red Devils who won a crucial victory, by 34-26.

It could easily have gone Wakefield's way. The Red Devils led 16-6 at the break through Josh Griffin's two scores and another from brother George.

Wakefield's Jacob Miller twice touched down before Danny Washbrook gave them the lead, with all three tries set up by former Salford scrum-half Tim Smith. A Lee Smith penalty had the Wildcats in the lead by four.

But after Wakefield had somehow fluffed an opportunity to win the game - Bill Tupou's half-break should have seen him pass to Richard Owen - Rangi Chase stepped, jinked and twisted his way out of two Wakefield defenders' arms, before sprinting the length of the field and sealing a win for the Red Devils. Cory Paterson's second try at the death sealed it.

Bradford Bulls went to the top of the table on points difference after a 42-10 home win over Sheffield Eagles. The returning Lee Gaskell blew off the cobwebs with an eye catching, three-try display.

Super League Super 8s - Round 2

Leeds went four points clear at the top of the table with a 25-18 grinding, home win in wet conditions over second-placed Wigan.

There were some controversial moments in the Friday night TV game. Danny McGuire was awarded his first try by the video-referee after Richard Silverwood had indicated he would have disallowed it on the advice of his touch judge as McGuire appeared to brush the touchline as he went over.

Wigan then struck back with a try by Liam Farrell, and the video-referee awarded it again, despite Dom Manfredi appearing to push Tom Briscoe when the Leeds winger was trying to get back to rescue the situation.

The most controversial try was scored by Ryan Hall just before the interval, when he touched down Kevin Sinfield's kick to the corner, after Sinfield, operating at dummy half with Paul Aiton injured, had dropped the ball and regathered it. Sinfield looked to have knocked the ball on, but the video-referee ruled it had gone backwards.

It was all over by the 65th minute when, following a McGuire break, a brilliant switch of play by Zak Hardaker, in at acting halfback, to send Kallum Watkins scything over put Leeds 24-8 up with 15 minutes to go and out of reach despite John Bateman and Matty Bowen scoring in the later stages.

Michael McIlorum left the field in the 52nd minute when he was accidentally poked in the eye by teammate George Williams.

Champions St Helens blew an 18-6 half-time lead at Langtree Park to lose 32-22 to Hull FC, missing the chance to go into second spot.

Two of Hull's five second-half tries came from 20-year-old winger Curtis Naughton to complete a hat-trick on the night. He was just one of numerous heroes for the Airlie Birds, none more so than Australian back-rower Mark Minichiello.

The result meant St Helens were in third place in Super League, just two points ahead of Huddersfield Giants and Castleford Tigers, with the Giants due to visit Langtree Park the following Thursday.

'We have some people earning big money who just don't want to do it,' said an angry Saints coach Keiron Cunningham.

Castleford edged Warrington at home 17-16 on the Thursday night on the back of an impressive defensive display and a late Liam Finn field goal.

Two tries to Justin Carney helped the Tigers to a 16-6 lead in the second half, as the home team looked to have the two points all sewn up. But an error from Finn, when he kicked the ball straight to Richie Myler, who ran 90 metres to score, helped the Wolves, against the run of play, back into the game.

A late Kevin Penny try then tied the match up and Warrington looked set to steal a draw. However, Finn made amends with a perfectly executed left-footed field goal two minutes from full-time to leave the Castleford faithful crowing.

Jermaine McGillvary struck to score his fifth and sixth tries of the season against the Catalans to seal a 24-12 home win and effectively end the Dragons' hopes of being in the end-of-season semi-finals.

Willie Tonga's decision not to knock a ball dead in his in-goal area was pivotal. The ball stayed in the in-goal area for a chasing McGillvary to touch down with five seconds remaining of the first half and Danny Brough's conversion made it 16-6. The Dragons never recovered after the break. And McGillvary's second with nine minutes to go was a beauty - a 70 metre weave through the Catalans defence.

Super 8s, The Qualifiers - Round 2

Bradford Bulls coach James Lowes insisted he would not give up on his squad despite a dismal performance at Wakefield on the Saturday.

Bradford, who lost Lee Gaskell to a back injury, were blitzed 48-18 by the Wildcats and were 30-0 down after the opening half hour. Lowes insisted the squad could bounce back.

The Wildcats had shown regular signs of improvement since the mid-season arrival of coach Brian Smith and they put all of that together in an accomplished opening half hour. Up front, Nick Scruton and Mickael Simon tore into the Bulls defence in the early stages, while Anthony Mullally would later make an impact from the bench.

Tim Smith thrived in the space they provided, as did halfback partner Jacob Miller and livewire hooker Michael Sio. The only negative for Smith and the Wildcats was a second-half double leg fracture to unlucky winger Richard Owen, the second time in his career he had suffered the injury.

Leigh Centurions were also finding it tough and crashed 46-18 at Salford on the Sunday, with two-try Rangi Chase in magical form. Chase cut down a Leigh revival in the second half to steer Salford to a second straight win in the Super 8s.

Sixteen-nil down at half-time, Leigh had their tails up at 22-12 midway through the second half, but Chase would turn the game on its head with multiple breaks in just three minutes - two of which ultimately ended in Salford tries.

Also on the Sunday, Josh Mantellato collected a hat-trick of tries in a 34-12 home win but Hull Kingston Rovers' clinical touch deserted them for much of the game against a hard-working Halifax side.

Halifax created some discomfort for Rovers by battling back to 10-6 midway through the first half and then gave themselves hope at 22-12 until the closing stages before the fitter home players added gloss to the scoreline. Ken Sio's 76th-minute try finished off a spirited effort from Halifax.

Widnes Vikings condemned Sheffield Eagles to successive heavy defeats in their Super 8s campaign with a 10-try, 48-12 demolition job at the Select Security Stadium, to go top of the Qualifiers.

The game was overshadowed by serious injuries to Widnes loose forward MacGraff Leuluai and Sheffield prop Steve Thorpe, with coaches Denis Betts and Mark Aston confirming after the match that their players had both suffered broken legs.

Five tries in a devastating, 15-minute spell in the first half killed the game off. Kevin Brown controlled proceedings from start to finish, giving Eagles boss Aston food for thought as his club planned an assault on promotion to the top-flight next season with a full-time squad.

Super League Super 8s - Round 3

Huddersfield gave their hopes of a Grand Final debut added credibility with a gritty 28-22 win at St Helens, who fell to their third straight defeat in the Super 8s and whose top-four place was now under real threat. The Thursday night victory lifted them above Saints into third spot on points difference.

At times the Saints attack again lacked direction. Their halfbacks, Travis Burns and Luke Walsh, were outplayed by the visiting pair of Danny Brough and former Saints junior Jamie Ellis.

Ellis scored one superbly taken try and made a crucial effort for Jermaine McGillvary, who displayed excellent finishing skills to go alongside his powerful carries.

St Helens prop Kyle Amor powered over for the first of his side's four tries, but Ellis sidestepped his way through and Ukuma Ta'ai collected Danny Brough's pass to put Huddersfield 12-6 ahead. Brough's penalty stretched their lead, but they could not withstand sustained Saints pressure before half-time.

Having conceded six penalties in quick succession and also having lost Michael Lawrence to the sin bin, their defence was broken by James Roby.

Joe Wardle put the Giants, still playing with 12 men, eight points clear again after half-time, but Saints scored twice in four minutes to level.

Tommy Makinson marked his return from a two-month injury absence with a try in the corner following Mark Percival's break, before Percival's superb offload created a try for Burns. A Luke Walsh penalty goal gave Saints a two-point lead.

But they could not hold on, as McGillvary touched down for his 10th try in seven matches and then Aaron Murphy strolled over from Wardle's pass. Alex Walmsley's late knock-on, confirmed by the video referee as Saints claimed a try, ended the home side's hopes of a share of the spoils.

Leeds looked uncatchable, still four points clear at the top after a 36-22 win at Hull FC on the Friday night. With the Wembley Cup Final to come eight days later there was no Danny McGuire, Kallum Watkins, Adam Cuthbertson, Joel Moon or Brett Delaney. But after Steve Michaels' 47th-minute try gave Hull FC the lead, Jamie Peacock's drive, Kevin Sinfield's guile out of dummy-half combined with flawless goalkicking, as well as Rob Burrow's sniping support play, which brought up his 200th career try, took Leeds home.

On the same night, second-placed Wigan handed Warrington their fourth loss in a row with a record-breaking 28-0 defeat of the Wolves at the Halliwell Jones Stadium.

Warrington failed to score a single point on their home turf for the first time since they moved from Wilderspool in 2004. It was also an unhappy home debut for Chris Sandow, but an impressive display from the Warriors, who were physical, defensively strong and clinical in wet conditions. Matty Bowen was in brilliant form all night and John Bateman ended with two tries to his name.

Wigan coach Shaun Wane claimed that a provocative promotional pie-smashing video released during the week by Warrington, to mark Sandow's inaugural game at the Halliwell Jones, helped motivate his team.

Castleford Tigers' play-off hopes suffered a setback with a 44-26 defeat in Perpignan.

A horror 23rd minute tackle from Ben Pomeroy, returning from a one-game ban, on Ashley Gibson stole the headlines. Pomeroy flipped Gibson on his neck and later received a six-game suspension after pleading guilty to a Grade E dangerous throw.

By that stage the Dragons were already 20-0 up and the Tigers had injury problems -

as well as losing Gibson, Ben Roberts suffered concussion and Michael Shenton sustained a shoulder injury.

Todd Carney showed the Catalans fans what they had been missing in a injury-hit 2015, producing a superb assist for Tony Gigot's second try and getting on the score sheet himself. Gigot's hat-trick try just after the hour effectively sealed the win for the home side, as he intercepted Justin Carney's intended pass to race over and give the hosts a 22-point lead heading into the final quarter of the game.

Super 8s, The Qualifiers - Round 3

A Championship side finally managed to beat a Super League team in the Qualifiers as Bradford Bulls bounced back from the hammering at Wakefield the week before with an astounding 41-10 home win over Salford Red Devils.

Inspired by ex-Salford man Jake Mullaney and Danny Addy the Bulls had too many attacking plays for a Salford side - missing Reni Maitua who had been banned for one game for a dangerous throw in the win against Leigh - who, according to acting head coach Ian Watson, just weren't good enough.

Wakefield Trinity Wildcats shrugged off the sin-binning of Michael Sio at Leigh Sports Village to just hold off Championship Leigh Centurions 17-16 and claim their second win of the competition.

Lee Smith kept a cool head for the visitors, scoring a try and booting the all-important field goal on 69 minutes that led to a tense closing ten minutes. Smith had given the Wildcats the perfect start with an early try.

But Championship winners Leigh, who had beaten Wakefield in the Challenge Cup in May, hit back with tries from Fuifui Moimoi, Jonny Pownall and Liam Kay. Jacob Miller scored either side of half-time to level the scores before Smith won it with the boot.

In the following Monday's League Express, Wildcats Chairman Michael Carter hit back at claims the club had held back money on its salary cap for the Super 8s.

The Wildcats lost 20 of their 23 regular season games to finish bottom of Super League ahead of the split and new coach Brian Smith had brought in ten players since his arrival at the club. But Carter told League Express that the club was spending as much money as during the regular season and pointed out the Wildcats had lost a lot of players, including stars Lopini Paea and Dean Collis.

A textbook display of wet-weather football earned Wembley-bound Hull KR a third win from three in the Qualifiers - by 12-8 - at the expense of Widnes at a rain-soaked Select Security Stadium.

The Robins made wholesale changes, with a raft of starters not risked ahead of the following Saturday's showpiece. Graeme Horne, Kevin Larroyer, Shaun Lunt, Tyrone McCarthy, Tony Puletua, Adam Walker and Ken Sio all sat out as 19-year-old debutant George Lawler scored the 52nd minute try that sealed the win.

There was also a shock in the all-Championship game as Sheffield Eagles beat Halifax 28-24 at their home for 2015, the Keepmoat Stadium in Doncaster. Former Fax winger Rob Worrincy's 76th minute hat-trick try got the Eagles Super 8s campaign up and running.

FIRST UTILITY SUPER LEAGUE - SUPER 8s
Sunday 23rd August

	P	W	D	L	F	A	D	PTS
Leeds Rhinos	26	19	1	6	868	527	341	39
Wigan Warriors	26	17	1	8	665	460	205	35
Huddersfield Giants	26	15	2	9	612	458	154	32
St Helens	26	16	0	10	658	522	136	32
Castleford Tigers	26	15	0	11	626	595	31	30
Warrington Wolves	26	12	0	14	578	550	28	24
Catalans Dragons	26	11	2	13	643	640	3	24
Hull FC	26	12	0	14	536	578	-42	24

SUPER 8s - THE QUALIFIERS
Sunday 23rd August

	P	W	D	L	F	A	D	PTS
Hull Kingston Rovers	3	3	0	0	82	46	36	6
Widnes Vikings	3	2	0	1	70	24	46	4
Bradford Bulls	3	2	0	1	101	68	33	4
Wakefield T Wildcats	3	2	0	1	91	68	23	4
Salford Red Devils	3	2	0	1	90	85	5	4
Sheffield Eagles	3	1	0	2	50	114	-64	2
Leigh Centurions	3	0	0	3	60	99	-39	0
Halifax	3	0	0	3	36	76	-40	0

Challenge Cup Final

Tom Briscoe made history as the first man to score five tries in a Challenge Cup Final as Leeds demolished Hull Kingston Rovers 50-0, a record margin, at Wembley.

Briscoe credited centre Kallum Watkins and his Rhinos teammates for his record-breaking haul that led to him winning the Lance Todd Trophy as the player of the match. He later said he had never scored five tries in a match before, either as a junior or as a professional.

Briscoe's second in the 47th minute, the standout moment of the game, was the highlight. With Leeds leading 16-0 after a complete and professional first half, Hull KR were applying a rare bit of pressure. Much like 12 months before when the Rhinos had a similar lead, an early try for their opponents would have at least tested Leeds' ability to hold on and shut the game out.

But Briscoe leaped highest to snuff out an Albert Kelly kick, racing the length of the field, despite an admirable chase by Ken Sio, to make it 20-0 and hammer a telling nail in the Robins' coffin.

Hull KR froze in the Wembley spotlight. Halfback Kelly, whose participation was in doubt because of a knee injury suffered in the semi-final win over Warrington, was their best player on a fruitless day.

Early in the game Kelly was harshly penalised by referee Ben Thaler for stealing the ball from Ryan Hall. The Rhinos were then able to create the position for their first try, when a nice offload from Adam Cuthbertson found Jamie Peacock, who looked as though he was going to score under the posts until he had the ball stripped by Kevin Larroyer.

Brett Delaney was on the spot to pick the ball up and touch it down for a try that demonstrated that luck was probably going to go Leeds' way. A few minutes later, when the Robins were trying to fight back, their captain Tyrone McCarthy dropped a relatively simple pass from Shaun Lunt.

From that moment the Rhinos swept downfield and scored two tries from Danny McGuire and Briscoe. First a clever short-side move caught the Robins off-guard and allowed Joel Moon, who had looped to the right from his left centre position, to put McGuire over, before, straight from the kick-off, Ryan Hall surged downfield and freed Carl Ablett. The forward was hauled down close to the line, but Leeds showed all their smartness to switch the ball right and put Briscoe in for the first of five.

Hull KR couldn't fight back and fell apart in the second half. Fullback Kieran Dixon, the former London flier, enjoyed a miserable spell. He spilled the ball twice in the opening seven minutes after the break, before allowing Briscoe to pluck the ball out of the air unchallenged and race home for his second. Dixon was powerless to stop Brad Singleton from claiming try number five eleven minutes later. And Rovers just had no answer to a

LADBROKES CHALLENGE CUP FINAL

Saturday 29th August 2015

HULL KINGSTON ROVERS 0 LEEDS RHINOS 50

ROVERS: 1 Kieran Dixon; 4 Josh Mantellato; 19 Kris Welham; 18 Liam Salter; 5 Ken Sio; 6 Maurice Blair; 7 Albert Kelly; 8 Adam Walker; 31 Shaun Lunt; 34 Tony Puletua; 11 Kevin Larroyer; 12 Graeme Horne; 13 Tyrone McCarthy (C). Subs (all used): 24 John Boudebza; 15 James Donaldson; 32 Dane Tilse; 14 Mitchell Allgood.
RHINOS: 1 Zak Hardaker; 2 Tom Briscoe; 3 Kallum Watkins; 4 Joel Moon; 5 Ryan Hall; 13 Kevin Sinfield (C); 6 Danny McGuire; 30 Mitch Garbutt; 17 Adam Cuthbertson; 10 Jamie Peacock; 14 Stevie Ward; 12 Carl Ablett; 15 Brett Delaney. Subs (all used): 7 Rob Burrow; 8 Kylie Leuluai; 16 Mitch Achurch; 19 Brad Singleton.
Tries: Delaney (7), McGuire (17),
T Briscoe (20, 47, 66, 75, 79), Singleton (58), Burrow (73);
Goals: Sinfield 7/9.
Rugby Leaguer & League Express Men of the Match:
Rovers: Albert Kelly; *Rhinos:* Tom Briscoe.
Penalty count: 2-3; **Half-time:** 0-16; **Referee:** Ben Thaler;
Attendance: 80,140 *(at Wembley Stadium).*

Leeds Rhinos get their Challenge Cup party underway in the Wembley dressing room

Leeds defence that was dealing with everything they threw at them.

The Rhinos skipper Kevin Sinfield, along with Peacock playing his last Wembley final, was absolutely superb at dummy-half, directing play brilliantly, often on the short side, especially to the left side of the Robins' defence.

After Briscoe completed his hat-trick following a slick move to the right and an impressive finish, Leeds finished with a flourish. Another electrifying break from the Rhinos was this time finished by Rob Burrow, before Briscoe bagged two more impressive tries in the last five minutes to cement his place in the Wembley record books.

Before the Wembley final a statue immortalising the exploits of five Challenge Cup legends was unveiled at the stadium - on the day that Rugby League celebrated its 120th birthday. Sports Minister Tracey Crouch MP conducted the unveiling ceremony.

The statue, which was commissioned in association with the charity Rugby League Cares, features five of the game's immortals - Eric Ashton MBE, Martin Offiah MBE, Alex Murphy OBE, Gus Risman and Billy Boston MBE and stood on the Wembley Stadium concourse within sight of the statue of England football hero Bobby Moore.

The most moving part of the day was the singing of Abide With Me by Lizzie Jones. The widow of Danny Jones, the Keighley and Wales halfback Danny who had died from a congenital heart condition during a match at London Skolars in May, was afforded a standing ovation midway through the hymn.

SEPTEMBER
Shield of dreams

Super League Super 8s - Round 4

Wigan Chairman Ian Lenagan hailed the club's decision to play a Super 8s game in London on the first Saturday in September. A crowd of 8,101 was at The Den, Millwall to see Wigan secure a 42-16 victory over the Catalans Dragons. It was the biggest attendance for a Super League game in London for nine years.

With the Catalans' poor away record, they elected to leave the private jet at home and travelled to the Den on a Ryanair flight on the morning of the game. It was a move that looked to have paid dividends on the hour mark, as they trailed by only eight points.

The travel then appeared to catch up with them and the Warriors let loose to score 18 points in the final quarter. Matty Bowen was the main man, with a personal haul of 22 points through two tries and seven goals from seven attempts from all over the field.

The win moved Wigan to within two points of leaders Leeds, who had fallen to a 32-18 defeat to St Helens at Headingley the night before. Captain Jon Wilkin's return was instrumental in Saints' victory. His leadership qualities were immediately evident, as he topped his side's tackle count and his presence as an extra halfback freed up Luke Walsh, who had his greatest influence for a while. The scrum-half's kicking game, often early in the tackle count, was a key factor and he kicked six from six goals, as well as scoring a crucial try just after half-time.

Adam Quinlan's superbly crafted try just before the hour to make it 26-12 gave Saints the cushion to complete a determined win that got their title retention bid back on track.

Warrington claimed their first win in the Super 8s in emphatic style as they swept aside a flat and lacklustre Hull FC side by 46-16 in a dead rubber.

With the game locked at 6-all early on, Warrington, with Stefan Ratchford outstanding, scored three back-to-back tries - through Kevin Penny, the first of a hat-trick, Gary Wheeler and Ben Currie - in a blistering six-minute spell to take the game away from Hull, allowing them to cut loose in the second half. Nineteen-year-old Jack Johnson made an impressive debut for the Wolves at fullback.

Huddersfield Giants took another major step towards confirming their semi-final place and put a significant dent in Castleford's hopes, to compound a difficult week for the Tigers.

Winger Justin Carney, who had scored 72 tries in 67 appearances with the Tigers, was missing from the 40-26 Thursday-night defeat, suspended after a breach of club discipline.

Winger Jermaine McGillvary's two terrific tries were the highlight of a ten-minute spell that turned the game decisively in the Giants' favour. They trailed a gutsy Castleford side 10-0 after the opening stages thanks to Luke Gale and Ashley Gibson tries, but then scored 20 unanswered points without the visitors touching the ball while Mike McMeeken was in the sin bin for tripping Joe Wardle.

To their credit, Daryl Powell's side battled back to trail by just four points going into the final quarter after great tries from Luke Dorn and Ben Roberts, only for another flurry of Huddersfield tries to seal matters in the closing stages.

Castleford had the final say with one of the most spectacular tries of the season when Dorn released Denny Solomona on his own line and the winger, showing blistering pace, sprinted 90 metres down the left touchline.

Super 8s, The Qualifiers - Round 4

Kieran Dixon produced an impressive response to his difficult week in the wake of a disappointing display in the Challenge Cup final to score twice and help Hull Kingston Rovers fight back to secure a nervy 20-18 home win against Wakefield Trinity Wildcats.

Dixon's contribution ensured that Rovers kept up their perfect winning record in The Qualifiers. For Wakefield, in contrast, it was a frustrating missed opportunity to strengthen their own survival chances as they allowed Rovers to recover from a 12-0 deficit to score 20 unanswered points, leaving the visiting team with too much to do in the tense closing stages.

The sides finished with four tries apiece - but Wakefield failed to add the extras to any of their opening three tries as Lee Smith and Jordan Tansey missed excellent goal chances - then Josh Mantellato later nailed his testing, late goal attempt at a crucial stage of the contest to establish a 20-12 lead. Lee Smith's second try in the 78th minute and his touchline conversion came too late for Wakefield.

Widnes won a significant 56-12 victory at Bradford Bulls, after leading by only 14-12 at half-time.

The Vikings were just too quick, too fast and too clinical in the second 40 minutes. By the time gamestar Joe Mellor completed his hat-trick on 50 minutes, Bradford looked done. They were. Patrick Ah Van also finished with a hat-trick.

Salford Red Devils officially confirmed the departure of head coach Iestyn Harris, by mutual agreement, over two months after his last game in charge of the club, the 34-28 defeat at Hull KR. The former Wales international had been in charge since succeeding Brian Noble in April 2014, but had been on long-term 'sick leave' with assistant Ian Watson taking charge.

Rangi Chase's future at the club was also clouded. Chase was absent from Salford's 50-26 TV win at Halifax on the Saturday after being suspended by the club pending an internal investigation, with the club coy on the details.

Halifax more than troubled Salford and even looked capable of dumping further misery on the Red Devils after another turbulent week for the club. But they had too much quality in key areas when it really mattered. Niall Evalds, Greg Johnson and Ben Jones-Bishop all stepped up to the plate, each grabbing hat-tricks as Salford made it three wins from four.

Leigh Centurions finally got their Qualifiers campaign going with a comfortable nine-try 52-16 win at home to Sheffield Eagles to keep their hopes of reaching Super League alive. Ryan Brierley's hat-trick was the highlight.

Super League Super 8s - Round 5

The four teams who would compete in the Super League XX play-offs were decided when Castleford's top-four hopes went up in smoke with a 42-38 home defeat to St Helens on the Thursday night.

Fourth-placed Saints quelled a number of fightbacks from Castleford after leading 18-0 after 20 minutes through converted tries, two to Adam Swift, his second created by a beautiful back flick in the build-up from Jon Wilkin, and one to Mark Percival. But two stunning tries from Luke Dorn and another solo effort from Ben Roberts, all converted by Luke Gale, made it 18-18 at half-time.

Just after the break, the Tigers looked to be on their way to keeping their play-off hopes alive when Mike McMeeken caught Travis Burns' kick to the in-goal and tore downfield. He was closed down 40 metres out by four Saints defenders, but managed an audacious backflick to Roberts, who raced home.

It was nip and tuck from then on, Percival crashing through for his second, Gale making it 26-24 with a penalty, Adam Quinlan going through a gap created by a blatant obstruction that was ignored by the video ref, Tommy Makinson's converted try creating a ten-point gap before Denny Solomona and Swift traded converted tries. Cas weren't finished but Junior Moors' try came too late.

Fourteen goals were kicked on the night, not one missed by either kicker, Luke Walsh and Luke Gale.

Gale got two Albert Goldthorpe Medal points and, with two rounds of Super League remaining, was in an unassailable position with 36 points, eight points ahead of second placed Huddersfield Giants captain Danny Brough.

Despite their stated intention not to repeat the post-Wembley wobble of the previous year, Leeds Rhinos lost a second game in a row, this time in Perpignan, where the Catalans put on a power show, with Todd Carney again a stand-out, to win 46-16.

Thomas Bosc, Krisnan Inu and Carney tries put the Dragons 18-0 up at half-time. Bosc and Inu crossed for further tries and Jordan Sigismeau, born on the Indian Ocean island of Le Réunion, went over for a 34-0 lead before Ryan Hall responded. Jeff Lima and Elliott Whitehead then traded tries with Leeds' Danny McGuire and Joel Moon.

The Rhinos' defeat meant that Wigan were level on league points, though with a 60-point inferior points difference, after their 30-24 Friday night home win over Hull FC.

Pre-match, a 50-point mauling had been forecast, as Hull had 12 first-teamers on the sidelines. Academy prop Masi Matongo was handed his debut from the bench, while fellow youngsters Jordan Abdull, Jack Logan, Jack Downs, Brad Fash and Jansin Turgut all featured.

The Warriors led 18-0 at one stage thanks to tries from Oliver Gildart, Josh Charnley and John Bateman and it looked like Wigan were going to put a cricket score past an inexperienced Hull side.

But a long-range try from Jamie Shaul and a neat step and go from centre Logan saw Lee Radford's men trail by just six at the break.

Hull looked dead and buried at 26-12 after a Ben Flower try and two Ryan Hampshire goals but, as in the first half, Wigan took their foot off the gas and tries from Jordan Rankin and Logan put the visitors in with a real shout as they played the final six minutes with a man advantage after Taulima Tautai was sin-binned for a spear tackle on Mickey Paea.

The result was in doubt right until the final whistle, but Wigan sealed victory in the dying seconds as the impressive Bateman, playing in the centre, launched an attack down the left, with George Williams offloading for Joe Burgess to go over in the corner.

The following Tuesday, Tautai pleaded guilty to a Grade D dangerous throw and was suspended for three games.

Jermaine McGillvary scored four tries to take a clear lead in the Super League scoring charts as the Giants hammered the Wolves 48-10 at the John Smith's Stadium on the Sunday. Opposite winger Aaron Murphy also claimed a hat-trick.

McGillvary scored twice before the break, adding to an earlier effort from Murphy, to help the hosts to an 18-0 lead at the interval. McGillvary twice more, Joe Wardle, Murphy with a pair that completed his treble and Jamie Ellis chipped in with further scores after the restart to secure a comfortable win, despite the loss of Jake Connor for ten minutes in the sin bin.

Warrington, who lost their entire right edge after 13 minutes through injuries to skipper Joel Monaghan and Gary Wheeler, replied through Ben Westwood and Roy Asotasi.

Super 8s, The Qualifiers - Round 5

Hull KR made sure they would be back in Super League in 2016 with a 48-4 hammering of Bradford Bulls in the Saturday TV game, Kieran Dixon's four tries the highlight at the KC Lightstream Stadium.

The Bulls' discipline let them down, two yellow cards handicapping their cause, winger Danny Williams slowing down a 20-metre restart in the seventh minute and Epalahame Lauaki sin-binned a minute before half-time for a needless hand in Dixon's face after he'd tackled him.

Two Josh Mantellato tries and one from Dixon gave the Robins a 12-4 half-time lead, despite James Mendeika's try for Bulls. Dixon and Dane Chisholm scored tries while the Bulls were still a man down after the break. Ken Sio, Kris Welham and Graham Horne also got on the scoresheet for Rovers, before Dixon crossed twice more late on.

Adrian Morley confirmed his retirement at the end of 2015, the defeat at Bradford having helped in his decision, although he was to stay with the Red Devils in a new role as a club ambassador from 2016.

On the Sunday, Morley came off the bench in a 53-34 home win over Sheffield Eagles, who had taken a sensational 18-6 lead midway through the first half with tries to Cory Aston, Quentin Laulu-Togagae, Menzie Yere and Rob Worrincy. But Salford led 34-24 at half-time thanks to Josh Griffin's brace and tries from Weller Hauraki, Lama Tasi, Harrison Hansen and Liam Hood.

Duane Straughier and Scott Turner went over for Sheffield with a try in between from Niall Evalds, and Michael Dobson felt it necessary to kick a 74th minute field goal for a 41-34 lead before tries to Iain Thornley and George Griffin in the dying minutes sealed it for the relieved Red Devils who stayed four points clear of Wakefield in third spot.

The Wildcats' chances of avoiding the fourth v fifth play-off 'Million Pound' game were in tatters after an abject 46-4 Saturday night home defeat to Widnes. Rhys Hanbury inspired Widnes who were all but mathematically certain of maintaining their Super League status with a fourth win in five matches.

Halifax provided a major upset the following afternoon when they beat Leigh 34-12 at the Shay for their first two points of the Qualifiers.

Halifax led 20-0 at the break through tries from Dane Manning, Ross Divorty and James Saltonstall and four Steve Tyrer goals. Leigh threatened a fightback as Adam Higson and Fuifui Moimoi replied. But Scott Murrell went over before the outstanding Tyrer crossed to add to three more goals, making it seven from seven attempts.

Super League Super 8s - Round 6

Albert Goldthorpe Medal winner Luke Gale pressed his claim for an England call-up with a wonderful performance against the club which had released him as a junior, to guide Castleford Tigers to a 29-22 win at Leeds.

At the start of each half the Tigers established quickfire 12-point leads. The consecutive touchdowns in the second half will live long in the memory, coming on the back of Kevin Sinfield being forced off with a deadleg.

Matt Cook, back from suspension, was the Tigers' only change and he created the first with a magnificent 60-metre run, swatting off Ryan Hall and taking on Zak Hardaker. Cook found Gale in close support and he swallow-dived in for his second try, which was part of an 18-point haul.

Gale then created an equally breathtaking second. Leeds were again bust up the middle, this time thanks to Ben Roberts' twinkling feet. Gale provided the link and, with an exquisite reverse pass, sent Roberts over to further emphasise the Tigers' attacking class.

The Tigers got home thanks to their outstanding goal-line defence, three times holding the Rhinos up over the line and Luke Dorn producing an outstanding cover tackle in the corner to deny Carl Ablett in the 66th minute.

Roberts' 73rd minute field goal edged the confident Tigers two scores clear and into a fifth-place finish for 2015.

That defeat for the Rhinos meant Wigan had the opportunity to overtake them at the top of the table the following night. But they lost 18-14 at St Helens in the most sensational manner.

Wigan were two points in front with three minutes remaining, having led the vast majority of the game. And the Warriors would have won to move to the top of the table had St Helens winger Tommy Makinson not pulled off a magnificent try-saving tackle on Oliver Gildart just prior to that.

Shortly afterwards Saints marched downfield on the back of their only penalty of the second half and Jon Wilkin produced a towering kick. While Matty Bowen stayed grounded, Josh Jones took to the air to take the ball on the full and score the winning try, sending three sides of Langtree Park into raptures.

Saints' win moved them within a point of both Leeds and Wigan going into the last round before the four team play-off and Huddersfield stayed above the champions on points difference after a 34-20 win at Hull FC on the same night, meaning the League Leaders Shield was still winnable by four teams.

Hull, who had the game's outstanding figure in two-try fullback Jordan Rankin, were only a couple of points adrift with a couple of minutes remaining, only for the Giants to register two late tries, to Jermaine McGillvary and Jamie Ellis, both of which Danny Brough improved in a five-goal contribution. It was the Giants' fourth successive win, which set up a massive home game with current leaders Leeds Rhinos the following Thursday evening.

Warrington Wolves gave their departing players a great send-off in their final home game of the season with a crushing 48-6 defeat of the Catalans Dragons, which ensured a sixth-placed finish.

The departing Joel Monaghan, Richie Myler and Roy Asotasi all made it onto the score sheet and Asotasi's conversion eight minutes from the end created the biggest cheer of the afternoon. Monaghan stole the show with his hat-trick of tries on his final home appearance in a Warrington shirt.

As soon as the Catalans lost Todd Carney to a hamstring injury in the warm-up before the game, the Dragons' heads visibly dropped

Super 8s, The Qualifiers - Round 6

A rugged performance from Salford Red Devils, both in attack and defence, earned them an impressive 24-10 win at Widnes Vikings and secured their Super League status for 2016.

Patrick Ah Van got the hosts back in it after Josh Griffin had put Salford in front in the second minute, but further scores from Scott Taylor and Cory Paterson put the Red Devils 18-4 in front at half-time. Junior Sa'u's powerhouse try early in the second half stretched his side's lead to 24-4 and effectively put the game beyond the reach of the home side. Josh Griffin and Brown were both red-carded after trading punches.

Wakefield came through a week of adversity to secure a place in the Million Pound Game with a 30-12 home victory over Halifax.

Key players Kevin Locke, Tim Smith and Reece Lyne all missed out due to an ongoing internal investigation at the club, after Humberside Police confirmed Smith had been charged with driving without due care and attention and failing to provide a specimen for analysis.

Wildcats coach Brian Smith was quick to praise his team, particularly the young quartet of Tom Johnstone, Max Jowitt, Andy Yates and Anthony Walker. Jacob Miller was a constant thorn in Halifax's side, after having that week signed a two-year contract extension.

A Michael Sio brace and a Mickael Simon effort put Wakefield 18-6 ahead at the break, with Jake Eccleston responding to Sio's opening effort. Wakefield wrapped up the match in the 68th minute. A superb run from Anthony Mullally saw him bust the line from close range to score, with Joe Arundel's conversion opening up a 20-point advantage.

Whilst Halifax did manage to score through crafty halfback Scott Murrell after good work from Ben Johnston, it was Wakefield who had the last word as Jowitt raced away from long distance to end a troubled week for Wakefield in style.

Bradford Bulls would be Wakefield's opponents in the play-off game, although which club would have home advantage was still to be decided, after they won at Leigh Centurions 32-16 in the Saturday TV game.

There were two tries each from Danny Williams and Matty Blythe as Adrian Purtell dominated from stand-off in the absence of Lee Gaskell. Jake Mullaney crossed to put the Bulls ahead, while Williams extended the lead to 10 points with his first try. But Adam Higson and Gregg McNally levelled the scores at half-time. Williams and Blythe touched down to restore the Bulls' lead before Bob Beswick's try put Leigh, missing the injured Martyn Ridyard, back in contention, before Blythe scored again to seal the two points for Bradford.

Sheffield Eagles' chances of playing top-flight rugby in 2016 ended with a 38-28 defeat at Bramall Lane on the Friday night to Hull KR. Ken Sio's second try of a hat-trick just before the half-time hooter gave Hull KR a 16-6 interval lead they never looked like relinquishing, despite a brave Sheffield effort.

* *Oldham won the Kingstone Press League 1 Promotion Final to earn their place in the Championship for 2016 following a 31-20 victory over Keighley Cougars in front of a record 1,405 crowd at their current home Whitebank Stadium.*

Super League Super 8s - Round 7

The League Leaders Shield was decided on the last Friday night of September in the most dramatic way possible.

The Shield, which meant automatic qualification for the World Club Series and could have been won by either of the top four teams, was won by Leeds Rhinos with a last-second 20-16 win at Huddersfield Giants.

With the Rhinos trailing 16-8 with seven minutes to go, the helicopter with Super League general manager Blake Solly and the Shield on board, headed for Wigan, where the Warriors were running away with their game with the Tigers.

Incredibly, the Rhinos snatched the game, necessitating an aerial U-turn and a lengthy wait before the Rhinos players could be awarded the trophy on the pitch. Not many Leeds fans went home and there were scenes of real jubilation.

After three defeats in a row, Leeds weren't pre-match favourites and a win for the in-form Giants coupled with a loss for Wigan would have seen them top the table, with St Helens having lost their chance by losing to Warrington the night before.

The Rhinos went ahead through Stevie Ward's converted try off a Kevin Sinfield flat

Leeds' Ryan Hall races away from Huddersfield's Jermaine McGillvary on the way to a sensational last-gasp score

ball before Jermaine McGillvary was over after a combination between Jack Hughes and Leroy Cudjoe. Danny Brough converted from the touchline. The only other scores until those final monumental minutes, were a penalty from Sinfield just before half-time and one from Brough just after the break.

The Giants went clear on 65 minutes when a Brough kick was allowed to bounce and Hughes and Cudjoe combined again to send Jamie Ellis tearing in for the try. Brough converted that and a penalty goal three minutes later.

It looked up for the Rhinos until the 74th minute when Zak Hardaker's overhead pass allowed Kallum Watkins' brilliant backflick to send Tom Briscoe into the right corner. Sinfield's towering touchline conversion heightened the sense that a comeback was on. Four penalties against the Giants in the last ten minutes didn't help their cause and from one of them, for a shoulder charge by Craig Kopczak, Sinfield levelled with a goal.

There was less than a minute remaining as the Giants kicked off deep. The last play the ball of the game was just in front of the Leeds 30-metre line as Rob Burrow fed Danny McGuire and McGuire launched a speculative chip kick down the left touchline. Amazingly the ball skipped past Scott Grix and was collected by Ryan Hall, who raced into the left corner for his 200th try for the Rhinos.

It was the most amazing finish to a regular season in the Super League's 20-year history.

The drama was disappointing for Wigan fans but at least they secured a home semi-final tie - against the Giants as it turned out - Dom Manfredi finishing with four tries in a 47-12 win over Castleford.

The Tigers led 12-10 at half-time but were unable to stem the flow as Wigan ran in seven tries after the break. The Warriors made a big start, crossing early on through Manfredi and Matty Bowen to lead 10-0. The visitors fought back with Luke Dorn and Junior Moors scores. But Manfredi raced in a further three times and after Matty Smith's field goal, scores from George Williams, Oliver Gildart, Joe Burgess and Larne Patrick sealed the win.

Saints - missing prop Alex Walmsley and stand-off Travis Burns - finished fourth after a 32-16 home defeat to Warrington on the Thursday night. They led after Joe Greenwood's early try, but the Wolves were on form and scored six tries, and had five more disallowed - four of them for winger Kevin Penny. Joel Monaghan and Roy Asotasi both scored on their last Warrington appearance. Jack Johnson, Chris Hill, Ryan Atkins and winger Penny, who eventually got a legitimate try in the final minute, were the Wolves' other try scorers. Chris Sandow added three conversions, while Monaghan added the extras to Penny's try with the game's final act.

In the remaining game, Catalans Dragons earned a 28-24 victory, only their second away win of the season, at Hull FC, despite four tries from Airlie Birds winger Tom Lineham.

Super 8s, The Qualifiers - Round 7

The final round of the Qualifiers was an anti-climax, with the only uncertainty whether Bradford or Wakefield would have home advantage in the 4th v 5th play-off game.

That was decided on the Saturday when Halifax beat Bradford at Odsal by a runaway 52-18, after being 18-16 down at half-time.

Steve Tyrer scored a hat-trick and kicked six goals, Tommy Saxton and Ben Johnston scored two tries apiece, while Dane Manning, Adam Tangata and Ben Heaton also crossed. Ryan Shaw's brace and Matt Ryan's try were in vain for the Bulls, who made nine changes from the week before and saw Lee Gaskell return from injury off the bench.

Wakefield also lost the day after at Bramall Lane, by 24-10 to the Sheffield Eagles. Quentin Laulu-Togagae was a bag of tricks and scored the decisive try on 72 minutes.

Hull KR scored 36 unanswered second-half points to beat Salford Red Devils 46-22 at home and finish top of The Qualifiers with seven wins from seven games. Josh Mantellato scored a try and kicked six goals for Rovers, for whom Kris Welham and Tyrone McCarthy scored tries in their final outings for the club.

Harrison Hansen and Lama Tasi both scored first-half tries in their farewell appearances for the Red Devils, who had needed to win by 16 points to finish top of the table. Greg Johnson and Ryan Lannon also crossed for the visitors, while George Lawler, Ken Sio, Dane Chisholm, Ben Cockayne and Maurice Blair were Hull KR's other try scorers.

Widnes Vikings thrashed undisciplined Leigh Centurions 50-6, who finished bottom of the table, to secure their place in Super League for 2016.

The Centurions led after five minutes through a Ben Reynolds' try. But Widnes hit back to lead 20-6 at the break through Patrick Ah Van, Kevin Brown, Charly Runciman and Paddy Flynn. Alex Gerrard, Rhys Hanbury, Joe Mellor and Jack Owens all crossed after the break, while Ah Van grabbed his second. In the following days Leigh announced the signings of Rangi Chase, Harrison Hansen, Cory Paterson and Reni Maitua from Salford, although it transpired that the announcement on Chase was premature, even though he was released by the Red Devils.

FIRST UTILITY SUPER LEAGUE - SUPER 8s
Final table - Sunday 27th September

	P	W	D	L	F	A	D	PTS
Leeds Rhinos	30	20	1	9	944	650	294	41
Wigan Warriors	30	20	1	9	798	530	268	41
Huddersfield Giants	30	18	2	10	750	534	216	38
St Helens	30	19	0	11	766	624	142	38
Castleford Tigers	30	16	0	14	731	746	-15	32
Warrington Wolves	30	15	0	15	714	636	78	30
Catalans Dragons	30	13	2	15	739	770	-31	28
Hull FC	30	12	0	18	620	716	-96	24

SUPER 8s - THE QUALIFIERS
Final table - Sunday 27th September

	P	W	D	L	F	A	D	PTS
Hull Kingston Rovers	7	7	0	0	234	118	116	14
Widnes Vikings	7	5	0	2	232	70	162	10
Salford Red Devils	7	5	0	2	239	203	36	10
Wakefield T Wildcats	7	3	0	4	153	170	-17	6
Bradford Bulls	7	3	0	4	167	240	-73	6
Halifax	7	2	0	5	162	186	-24	4
Sheffield Eagles	7	2	0	5	152	267	-115	4
Leigh Centurions	7	1	0	6	146	231	-85	2

OCTOBER
Seven up for Rhinos

Super League Semi-finals

WIGAN WARRIORS 32 HUDDERSFIELD GIANTS 8

On the first Thursday of October the challenge of Huddersfield Giants fell away once again at the play-off stage as they failed to trouble in-form Wigan at the DW Stadium.

The Warriors led 12-2 at the break thanks to tries from Ben Flower and John Bateman, with Huddersfield's only reply a Danny Brough penalty on the half-time hooter.

Dom Manfredi extended Wigan's lead after the turnaround and then a controversial decision from video-referees James Child and Phil Bentham to award a penalty try put the game out of Huddersfield's reach and the Warriors were back at Old Trafford.

Flower had announced he would atone for his second-minute red card in the 2014 Grand Final and the way he charged onto Matty Smith's inside ball 25 metres out to burst clear for the posts after only six minutes indicated he was deadly serious. Matt Bowen converted and added a penalty goal after George Williams was held down in a tackle.

With five minutes to the break, Manfredi out-jumped Aaron Murphy to Sam Powell's kick to the corner before somehow getting the ball out for Bateman to use all his strength to score.

The Giants opted to close the gap by two just before the break as Brough slotted over a penalty just seconds after Jermaine McGillvary went close as he collected a Jamie Ellis kick and brushed past Joe Burgess before being brought down.

The next score after the interval was going to be crucial and the Giants went close on two separate occasions as Brett Ferres was held up over the line by Liam Farrell before Oliver Gildart and Burgess pulled off a try saver to stop McGillvary.

Those missed chances came back to haunt the Giants as Manfredi used all his strength to get over the top of Murphy and Jake Connor. Bowen converted and the Warriors led 18-2 after 50 minutes.

Jack Hughes looked as though he was about to get the Giants back into the game but he knocked on close to the line and the Warriors took full advantage. Burgess was sent clear by Bowen and was brought down just over halfway by Michael Lawrence. Moments later controversy reigned as Ben Thaler went upstairs to judge whether Bateman had grounded Matty Smith's kick-through. After a lengthy delay a penalty try was awarded, ruled that Scott Grix had prevented Bateman from grounding the ball cleanly. The decision incensed both fans and players from Huddersfield, as Bowen converted from under the sticks to put Wigan 24-2 in front.

Ferres barged over from close range as he took a short ball from Brough and crashed off the uprights before touching down. Brough converted to make it 26-8, but it was too little too late. The Giants started to throw the ball around with the game gone, but it was the Warriors who had the final say as Tony Clubb took a short ball off Michael McIlorum to wrap the game up.

LEEDS RHINOS 20 ST HELENS 13

On the Friday night the Rhinos left it late to edge the reigning champions at Headingley, Ryan Hall's try eleven minutes from the end putting Leeds in front for the first time in the match after St Helens had looked well capable of going back to Old Trafford, leading 13-8 and seemingly in control.

The Rhinos were looking increasingly ragged trying to get out of their own territory as Saints defended in the style of champions when Kevin Sinfield turned the game with a majestic 40/20, on the back of a magnificent tackle by Jamie Peacock - one of 50 he made - to hold out James Roby on a power play.

Roby had already shown with his extraordinary try in the fifth minute, when he took on and beat a host of would-be defenders with an astonishing twisting surge and step, his threat out of dummy half. Luke Walsh converted and kicked a penalty for offside ten minutes after.

Leeds had levelled by the 26th minute, Kallum Watkins on the loop sending Zak Hardaker sliding in, with Sinfield goaling. Soon afterwards Sinfield tied the scores, taking the two points on offer after Peacock had cleared all-comers and Roby held on to Watkins for too long. But Walsh edged Saints a point ahead with a field goal in the last play of the first half.

A fabulous first half was followed by an even better second. There was no further score until just before the hour. Hall again looked to clear his lines with a strong run, but Joe Greenwood ripped the ball free and, quickly sizing up the free-play option, Jon Wilkin sprinted right, sent Jordan Turner into space and he positioned Mark Percival to the corner.

Peacock's tackle and Sinfield's 40/20 changed the game with barely 13 minutes to play.

From the scrum, a penalty was awarded and, following another superb tackle by Adam Quinlan to deny Watkins, Sinfield built a bridge and Jimmy Keinhorst, who was in for injured Stevie Ward, found McGuire. His low pass was breathtakingly taken by Joel Moon, whose reverse ball sent Hall skittling defenders on his way through to a fingertip touchdown confirmed by video. From near touch Sinfield, with inevitable precision, added the conversion to give his side the lead for the first time.

In their last throw, a Saints power play involving Turner, Walsh, Wilkin, Greenwood and Josh Jones was ended by the final pass from Wilkin being forward.

Burrow found touch on the Saints '10' and, as the defending champions tried to desperately create from deep, Mose Masoe, in his final performance in the Red Vee, offloaded. Walsh palmed the ball back and Watkins swooped to secure the win. Fittingly, Sinfield had the final act, landing the conversion.

Million Pound Game

WAKEFIELD TRINITY WILDCATS 24 BRADFORD BULLS 16

The first Saturday afternoon of October provided the tensest occasion of the season at an unseasonably warm Belle Vue, as the Wildcats eventually joined the other three Super League clubs in the top flight in 2016.

Championship side Bradford had the opportunity to level a gripping game with little under three minutes remaining and send it into golden point extra time. But Danny Addy pushed his difficult penalty attempt wide, leaving the Wildcats ahead by two points.

Moments later, home hooker Scott Moore broke a tired defensive line on the last tackle and somehow made it to the line, sending the Wakefield support into raptures and leaving Bulls players slumped on the floor in despair.

After the game, Bulls coach James Lowes launched a scathing attack on the sport's new structure on live TV, as well as criticising the match officials for missing a ball-steal as his team launched a desperate late attack. He later apologised for the outburst.

It couldn't detract from a gutsy effort from the Wildcats, who had a traumatic build-up with the sacking of their two key players Tim Smith and Kevin Locke for off-field indiscipline. As well as preserving their 17-year Super League stint, victory also completed the short-term assignment set for veteran coach Brian Smith when he arrived at the club in early June.

Wakefield looked the have the game in their pocket five minutes after half-time having soaked up plenty of Bulls pressure - Bradford had two tries, correctly ruled out by the video referee. A terrific cover tackle from Tom Johnstone prevented Matty Blythe from touching down in the right corner before, two minutes later, Danny Kirmond took Pita Godinet's pass to stride over from close range.

Joe Arundel added the conversion and minutes later had a try chalked off after Johnstone, just turned 20, leapt for a Jacob Miller bomb, took it cleanly and looped a pass for Arundel to score. Referee Richard Silverwood was right in line and called a forward pass. Then Arundel missed a 33rd minute penalty and Miller a field-goal attempt just before the hooter.

In between, Addy had a try ruled out for a knock-on - a pass hit his shoulder and rocketed forward - while the first half finished with the Bulls on the attack.

Bradford fell further behind in the 44th minute. Again it was straightforward stuff from the Wildcats, Moore's delayed pass allowing Leeds-bound Anthony Mullally to stroll over with barely a hand being laid on him.

That stirred the Bulls into their first response as the excellent Adrian Purtell produced a wonderful round-his-back offload for Williams to score.

Moments later they were over again. The impressive Jake Mullaney set the position with a midfield break from Lee Gaskell's smart pass and Jay Pitts' pass hit a Wakefield defender and found its way to Blythe, who finished in the corner.

Addy missed the touchline conversion after having kicked the first one via a post and the crossbar, and Bradford now trailed 12-10.

The gap became two scores again when Miller's pass put Danny Washbrook over in his last game for the Wildcats, but Bradford quickly responded, Purtell taking the line on and forcing his way over.

Moore also got over the line - in the excitement the video referee missing that Adam O'Brien had raced back from an offside position to smother his dart from dummy half - but was held up following a Chris Annakin charge. Then the Wildcats were penalised for Reece Lyne not being square at marker, the decision given by the video referee, such was the tension, giving Addy the chance to level matters.

The position of the kick was moved infield after Addy had originally set up for the kick, but the tough angle still proved too much for him, leaving his side trailing 18-16 with a matter of minutes remaining.

Wakefield then regained possession via what Lowes felt was an illegal Godinet ball-steal and within seconds Moore was breaking clear on the last tackle to break Bradford hearts.

Super League Grand Final

Leeds Rhinos completed the treble for the first time since St Helens in 2006, and the club's first ever league and cup double, with a comeback 22-20 win over Wigan Warriors at a sold-out Old Trafford.

A historic seventh Grand Final win was a perfect way for Rhinos legends Kevin Sinfield, Jamie Peacock and Kylie Leuluai to bring a close to their playing careers.

Leeds halfback Danny McGuire won the Harry Sunderland Trophy. Having scored a try in a first half which the Rhinos dominated, he was the architect of the winning try, after Matty Bowen had scored a brilliant solo under the posts and Wigan re-taken the lead at 18-16, a lead then extended by a Bowen penalty goal. McGuire's high kick to the left corner was measured to perfection for Ryan Hall to mount an aerial challenge to Dom Manfredi. Hall won the challenge and managed to tip the ball back to Joel Moon who immediately fed Jimmy Keinhorst and he stepped right to feed Josh Walters for the score. Sinfield kicked the conversion from ten metres to the left of the sticks to edge the Rhinos two points back in front.

Rhinos coach Brian McDermott had gone with Walters on the bench in preference to a second hooker in young Jordan Lilley or Mitch Achurch. Peacock started after being brought off the bench after only seven minutes in the semi-final win over Saints, with Brad Singleton taking up the third prop starting position and Adam Cuthbertson a substitute. Shaun Wane made no changes to the team that beat the Giants so handsomely in the semi-final, which meant starts in the centre for a second-rower in John Bateman and Academy starlet Oliver Gildart. Anthony Gelling and Taulima Tautai were left out of the 19-man squad.

From the off there was evidence it wasn't going to be a conservative affair. On the third tackle, Tom Briscoe drove to the middle of the 30-metre line and got the offload out of a three-man tackle to Zak Hardaker, who was off up the middle of the field before Joel Tomkins stopped his progress. The first set ended with Joe Burgess leaping magnificently to take Sinfield's bomb to the right corner.

In Leeds' next set Singleton got an offload out to Joel Moon, who threatened to break the Wigan line and the attack was snuffed out when Burrow's grubber from a darting run ricocheted all over the shop and somehow ended up in the arms of Liam Farrell.

It seemed inevitable that the Rhinos would soon be over the line.

Instead the Warriors chanced their arm on their own '40' as the Rhinos' defensive line got their numbering horribly wrong. When Sean O'Loughlin and Matty Smith combined to get the ball left, Leeds looked two men short as Smith's smart pass selection saw Farrell sail through a gap as wide as the Manchester Ship Canal and race away. Farrell timed his pass to the supporting Burgess on his outside to perfection and the Roosters-bound flyer

FIRST UTILITY SUPER LEAGUE GRAND FINAL

Saturday 10th October 2015

LEEDS RHINOS 22 WIGAN WARRIORS 20

RHINOS: 1 Zak Hardaker; 2 Tom Briscoe; 3 Kallum Watkins; 4 Joel Moon; 5 Ryan Hall; 13 Kevin Sinfield (C); 6 Danny McGuire; 30 Mitch Garbutt; 7 Rob Burrow; 10 Jamie Peacock; 12 Carl Ablett; 15 Brett Delaney; 19 Brad Singleton. Subs (all used): 8 Kylie Leuluai; 17 Adam Cuthbertson; 20 Jimmy Keinhorst; 21 Josh Walters.
Tries: McGuire (7, 35), Moon (27), Walters (64);
Goals: Sinfield 3/4.
WARRIORS: 1 Matt Bowen; 22 Dominic Manfredi; 14 John Bateman; 34 Oliver Gildart; 5 Joe Burgess; 6 George Williams; 7 Matty Smith; 8 Dominic Crosby; 9 Michael McIlorum; 10 Ben Flower; 11 Joel Tomkins; 12 Liam Farrell; 13 Sean O'Loughlin (C). Subs (all used): 16 Sam Powell; 17 Tony Clubb; 23 Lee Mossop; 25 Larne Patrick.
Tries: Burgess (4), Manfredi (46), Bowen (49);
Goals: Bowen 4/4.
Rugby Leaguer & League Express Men of the Match: *Rhinos:* Danny McGuire; *Warriors:* Matt Bowen.
Penalty count: 5-4; **Half-time:** 16-6; **Referee:** Ben Thaler;
Attendance: 73,512 *(at Old Trafford, Manchester).*

slipped out of Kallum Watkins' despairing tackle to score the first try in the Grand Final for the second year running.

Bowen kicked a fine conversion to cap off a stunning start.

Wigan's balloon was quickly burst. Hardaker's restart kick spun away from Smith at the last moment and Leeds made hay from the scrum. Hall went close but was stopped by a Manfredi tackle; but on the last Sinfield produced a short grubber of real precision for McGuire on his inside to race onto at speed, collect and dive over just to the right of the uprights. Referee Ben Thaler wanted to check the offside but McGuire's run was timed to utter perfection, there was no doubting the try's validity. Sinfield kicked the goal and after only seven minutes it was 6-all.

It wasn't mistake-free football. Wigan knocked on in their own '40' and Cuthbertson dropped the ball cold from the scrum with his first touch after coming off the bench. Smith's pass to Sean O'Loughlin went to ground as Wigan charged for the posts as Sinfield and Cuthbertson cut each other's heads open trying to prevent the pass. Briscoe took a Smith bomb and Leeds won their first penalty to relieve a siege when Hardaker was held down.

Peacock came back on after a small breather and within minutes the Rhinos were in the lead after a frantic passage of play.

George Williams gave Leeds another set of six when he went on too long with the goal-line tackle on Hardaker after held was called.

The ball was zipped from left to right, desperately kept alive - a dive by Watkins to scoop the ball back from the right touchline a highlight. Eventually Leeds came right again and McGuire looked to have knocked on in a tackle by Williams. If the ref had blown for the scrum not many people would have questioned it. But play was allowed to go on. Hardaker half got around Bowen on the right touchline and on his inside was Moon who went over for the score. Thaler thought it was a try and the video referees, after much scrutiny, agreed with him, to the disgust of the Wigan support.

Sinfield edged the conversion just to the right of the posts and Leeds led 10-6.

Wigan threw plenty more at the Rhinos line after McGuire knocked on Cuthbertson's offload on his own '40'.

Gildart was stopped just short and when the ball moved right Hall knocked on Joel Tomkins' grubber. Bowen went close, before Williams' grubber took a bad bounce into dead.

Hall was tackled in-goal off a Smith bomb, but the goal-line drop-out was overruled by the video ref and Leeds got their third penalty for a tackle in the air by Manfredi.

It was a crucial call as, with five minutes to go to half-time, the Rhinos scored a peach of a try.

McGuire looked at his options and found Briscoe on halfway with a long ball. Watkins looped around to the outside and was away down the right and, when he was just caught by Gildart, fed McGuire on his inside with the try-making pass.

This time Sinfield nailed the wide-out conversion for a 16-6 lead as Burgess almost got Gildart away down the left wing but half-time came without any further score.

The third quarter belonged to Wigan. Farrell had already knocked on when Peacock tried an offload on his own '40' that McGuire couldn't pick up cleanly.

Then Leuluai gave away a penalty for a high tackle and, after Farrell was stopped six inches short, Williams' grubber to the posts was slapped dead by Hardaker for Wigan's second GLDO.

Gildart went close again and O'Loughlin this time put up a measured bomb to the right. Hall looked to have taken it but, as he came down, his challenger, Manfredi, pulled the ball away and ran the couple of metres to score.

The Warriors were energised. Two minutes later Gildart's pass to Burgess was knocked down by Briscoe on the Leeds '40'. Within seconds, Bowen was shooting under the sticks off Smith's inside ball, brushing off the tackles of Walters and Peacock and

Wigan's Michael McIlorum burrows towards the Leeds line during the Super League Grand Final

stepping around Hardaker like a spring chicken. He kicked the easy goal and, 18-16 down, Leeds were in a hole.

Bowen, retiring at the end of the game, was looking imperious, threatening every time he had the ball, taking bombs with ease, stopping Hardaker's break up the middle and scooping up low kicks for fun.

Michael McIlorum played a blinder at dummy half, passing into the prone Watkins behind the play the ball to win the penalty and Bowen obliged with the goal from 35 metres straight in front of the posts.

After Walters' try had given Leeds the lead, Wigan didn't panic, but the Rhinos' almost innate ability to close out games took them home.

With four minutes left Tony Clubb's offload on half way went forward in Brett Delaney's tackle and the game was going away from Wigan. Wigan's last possession ended when the ball came to Clubb and his midfield bomb went backwards.

SUPER LEAGUE XX AWARDS

STEVE PRESCOTT MAN OF STEEL
Zak Hardaker
(Leeds Rhinos)

YOUNG PLAYER OF THE YEAR
Joe Burgess (Wigan Warriors)

COACH OF THE YEAR
Brian McDermott (Leeds Rhinos)

CLUB OF THE YEAR
Leeds Rhinos

TOP TRY SCORER
Jermaine McGillvary (Huddersfield Giants) (27)

TOP METRE MAKER
Alex Walmsley (St Helens) (4092)

TOP TACKLER
Danny Houghton (Hull FC) (1359)

(totals include regular season & Super 8s only)

SUPER LEAGUE DREAM TEAM
(previous appearances in italics)
1 Zak Hardaker (Leeds Rhinos) *2014*
2 Jermaine McGillvary (Huddersfield Giants) *Debut*
3 Kallum Watkins (Leeds Rhinos) *2014*
4 Michael Shenton (Castleford Tigers) *2014*
5 Joe Burgess (Wigan Warriors) *Debut*
6 Danny Brough (Huddersfield Giants) *2013*
7 Luke Gale (Castleford Tigers) *Debut*
8 Alex Walmsley (St Helens) *Debut*
9 James Roby (St Helens) *2007, 2010, 2011, 2012*
10 Jamie Peacock (Leeds Rhinos) *2000, 2001, 2002, 2003, 2005, 2007, 2008, 2009, 2013, 2014*
11 Zeb Taia (Catalans Dragons) *Debut*
12 Liam Farrell (Wigan Warriors) *Debut*
13 Adam Cuthbertson (Leeds Rhinos) *Debut*

ALBERT GOLDTHORPE MEDAL
Luke Gale (Castleford Tigers)

ALBERT GOLDTHORPE ROOKIE OF THE YEAR
Andre Savelio (St Helens)

2
CHAMPIONSHIP & LEAGUE 1 2015

CHAMPIONSHIP SEASON
Faltering Centurions

LEIGH CENTURIONS dominated the Kingstone Press Championship for a second consecutive year, again losing just one game - this year at London Broncos - en route to finishing top.

But that didn't tell the full story of their season, as Paul Rowley's side - widely tipped to be the team most likely to earn promotion via the new structure - then fell some way short in the Qualifiers, winning only once to finish bottom.

Those promotion predictions looked well placed when the Centurions led Challenge Cup finalists Hull KR 24-6 at half-time in their opening Qualifiers game, a scoreline that could easily have been wider.

But perhaps an element of naivety at crucial stages cost them a valuable opening win and it was a similar story when they slipped to a one-point loss at home to Wakefield.

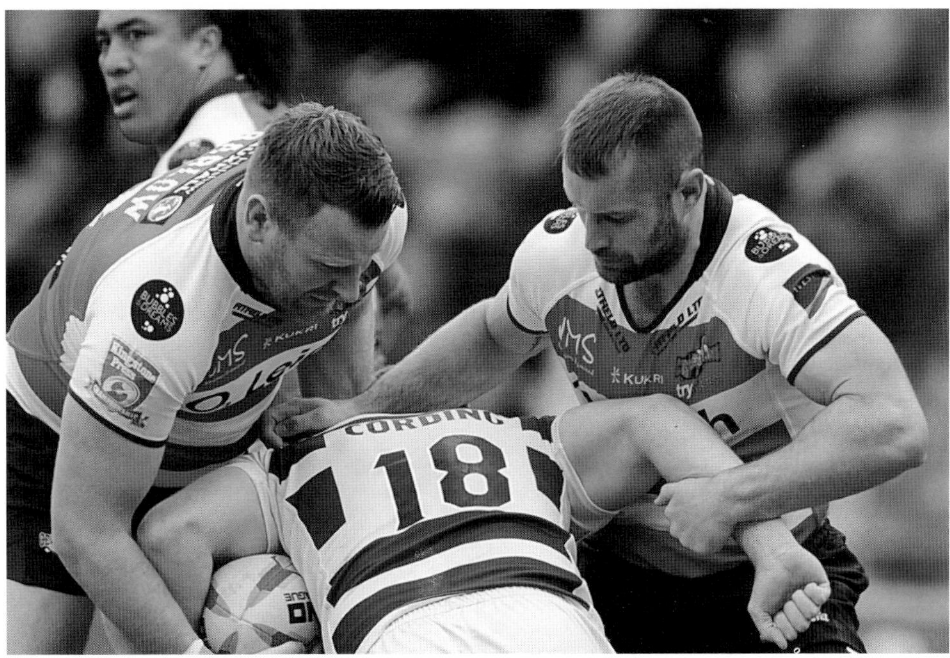

Sam Barlow and Bob Beswick halt Featherstone's Jamie Cording during the Championship Summer Bash

For the second season running, Ryan Brierley was the leading tryscorer in all competitions

Just one win from seven matches was undoubtedly a disappointing return - but it shouldn't completely cloud another season of achievement overall, which included a stunning Challenge Cup run.

RUGBY LEAGUER &

League Express

LEIGH MARCH ON

Moimoi stars as Centurions extend unbeaten run with comfortable win over rivals Featherstone

PLUS
Hardaker latest
Powell lays into Cas
Lunt joins Hull KR
Koukash on Sheens
Weyman retires
& MORE

SAINTS TAKE TOP SPOT

Leigh beat both Salford and Wakefield before running Warrington close in a thrilling quarter-final at the Halliwell Jones, where their expansive approach earned widespread acclaim via terrestrial television.

Fullback Gregg McNally was arguably their best player, though the likes of forward Jake Emmitt and winger Liam Kay ran him close and Ryan Brierley continued to rack up the tries with 37 in all competitions.

CHAMPIONSHIP AWARDS

PLAYER OF THE YEAR
Lee Gaskell
(Bradford Bulls)

YOUNG PLAYER OF THE YEAR
Jordan Baldwinson
(Featherstone Rovers)

COACH OF THE YEAR
Richard Marshall
(Halifax)

CLUB OF THE YEAR
Dewsbury Rams

Jordan Baldwinson

Lee Gaskell was named Championship Player of the Year for 2015

BRADFORD BULLS' ultimate goal of promotion fell agonisingly short in the Million Pound Game, the play-off between fourth and fifth in the Qualifiers.

Had Danny Addy's difficult late penalty attempt drifted just inside the posts instead of wide, a different story could have unfolded, but the Bulls will start 2016 back in the Championship.

James Lowes' side had finished second behind Leigh in the regular season after what became an inconsistent campaign in the second half of the year - they won just one of their final five league matches.

The Bulls were then wildly up and down in the Qualifiers, where they won matches against the Centurions, Sheffield and most impressively Salford, but were also soundly beaten by Widnes, Hull KR, Wakefield and Halifax.

Still, they were within minutes of a return to Super League only for the closing stages of the winner-takes-all shoot-out with the Wildcats to go against them.

One of their problems appeared to be an imbalanced squad in which a number of signings, such as Aussie Karl Davies and Dave Petersen, didn't feature at all and others only minimally.

The Bulls did have the Championship Player of the Year in their ranks in stand-off Lee Gaskell, who terrorised defences throughout the year before hitting injury problems late on.

Hooker Adam O'Brien, utility back Adrian Purtell, loose forward Addy and fullback Jake Mullaney were among their best elsewhere and the club were aiming to go one better next time around.

Cory Aston continued his progress in 2015

SHEFFIELD EAGLES continued their steady progress by making the coveted top four and chalking up two wins in the Super Eights.

Mark Aston's squad would become full-time in 2016 as they looked to continue their long-term aim of earning a place back into the top flight.

News of that transition probably affected the start of their Qualifiers campaign, when they were well beaten by Bradford and Widnes. But they finished the season on a significant high by defeating Wakefield at Bramall Lane.

There were some disappointments within a generally consistent campaign, primarily heavy defeats away at each of their top four rivals and an out-of-character thrashing on the big stage when London beat them 46-6 at the Summer Bash in Blackpool.

Of the class of 2015, Australian prop Steve Thorpe landed the major awards at the club's presentation night after an impressive first year in this country.

Eagles favourite Menzie Yere had another big season in the centres, just edging out Quentin Laulu-Togagae in the top try scorer stakes.

Back-rowers Duane Straugheir, Michael Knowles and Pat Walker all finished the season strongly and there was a cluster of promising young players that continued their progress during the season, not least Aston's talented son Cory.

Dane Manning had an impressive season for Halifax

HALIFAX ended the season on a major high, thrashing local rivals Bradford on their own ground to secure a major windfall of £780,000 next year by finishing sixth in the Qualifiers.

It capped a hugely impressive campaign under the Championship Coach of the Year Richard Marshall in his first term in charge at the Shay. Marshall effectively inherited Karl Harrison's entire squad at the club, making only minimal additions through the course of the season.

But they gradually moulded together as an impressive team and Fax exceeded most people's expectations by making the top four, virtue primarily of a superb nine-match winning run, which included another memorable win over the Bulls at the Shay.

And had it not been for a late defeat to Sheffield in the Qualifiers, they could even have made the Million Pound Game and a shot at Super League.

That might well come next season, although the club has taken the credible stance to remain part-time and build its infrastructure, which is expected to include a reserve team.

In 2015, play-making skipper Scott Murrell led his side throughout, earning a deserved nomination for the Championship Player of the Year.

Overseas props Mitch Cahalane and Adam Tangata were also terrific along with hard-working back-rower Dane Manning, while top try-scorer Steve Tyrer had an outstanding campaign at centre.

Will Sharp was named Featherstone's Player of the Year

FEATHERSTONE ROVERS were strongly tipped to make the Qualifiers given their big central funding and experienced recruitment - but they fell short before regrouping to win the Championship Shield, the end-of-season competition for the third eight.

Inconsistency and some shocking home form hit their league campaign hard. They lost seven from 11 home matches in the regular season, against Bradford, Leigh, London, Halifax, Sheffield, Dewsbury and Whitehaven - a number of them by convincing margins.

Yet the same Rovers team won away at Fax and the Broncos, pushed Catalans all the way in the Challenge Cup with a young side in Perpignan and then won comprehensively away at Bradford.

That win came just days before the mid-season exit of coach Any Hay, following the home Dewsbury defeat, and led to the appointment of Jon Sharp. He oversaw a successful Shield campaign that culminated in a play-off final victory over London at Widnes, and with a significant overhaul of their squad now underway it will be a different-looking Featherstone in 2016.

Jordan Baldwinson and Thomas Minns both earned Young Player of the Year nominations with Baldwinson winning, while Will Sharp took the club Players' award - but all three were to move on as part of that shake-up.

The future lay more in the hands of the likes of youngsters Sam Day, Jack Coventry and Kyran Johnson, who were all given extended opportunities in the Shield under Sharp.

DEWSBURY RAMS briefly threatened their own top-four push before settling in sixth ahead of the mid-season split, and then missing out on the Championship Shield final.

Still, there was much for coach Glenn Morrison to be positive about, not least the introduction of a new reserve side that won its competition against the odds and also provided a host of future first-team players.

Operating on a much lower budget than many of their rivals, the Rams punched above their weight for most of the year, beating full-time London three times, winning at Featherstone and pushing both Leigh and Bradford to within four points.

When they lost 22-18 at the Bulls in June they were in fourth place in the Championship table, but were eventually overhauled by Halifax and Featherstone.

While scrum-half Anthony Thackeray and centre Shane Grady earned most of the public plaudits for their performances, the Rams also had a raft of unsung heroes in their ranks, with the likes of Dale Morton, Scott Hale and Rob Spicer providing terrific levels of consistency.

Top try-scorer was Welsh international winger Dalton Grant in his first season at the club, closely followed by Morton and Thackeray, while loose forward Joel Farrell earned a Young Player of the Year nomination.

Shane Grady

LONDON BRONCOS were also expected to make the top four after dropping down from Super League and enjoying the increased central distribution funding that involved.

But their season suffered from disruption almost from day one, with key signings hit by injury and coach Joey Grima heading back to Australia. He was replaced by a Championship stalwart in Andrew Henderson, assisted by Brian Noble in an advisory roll.

And the pair inspired a definite upturn in fortunes midway through the season, when their Summer Bash thrashing of Sheffield sparked a run of five wins in six, including ending Leigh Centurions' undefeated start to the year.

Andrew Henderson

That also coincided with hooker Henderson coming out of retirement, such were the limited options available to him.

But any hopes of squeezing into the Qualifiers were ended by losing four of their last five, though they did regroup to make the Championship Shield final, ending a run of three straight defeats to Dewsbury by winning there in the semis.

Henderson began the process of making significant changes to his ranks for next season, when the Broncos would remain full-time but start life at yet another new home in West Ealing.

Threequarters Ben Hellewell and Rhys Williams led the try-scoring stakes, while Jamie Thackray and Rhys Lovegrove were impressive up front before injuries hit both.

Brett Phillips was a consistent performer for Workington

WORKINGTON TOWN recovered from a worrying start, with just two wins in 12 hinting at a lengthy relegation scrap.

But their crucial May win at Doncaster began an upturn in fortunes and four wins over local rivals Whitehaven during the course of the campaign kept most of their supporters satisfied.

Two of those were by thumping margins and one a memorable comeback triumph at the Summer Bash, hinting at the potential within Phil Veivers' small squad if he can add a few more numbers next year.

But by the end of the 2015 season they had run out of numbers, with a threadbare side well beaten at Featherstone in the Championship Shield semi-finals.

They were certainly boosted by the late-season arrival of experienced halfback Jarrod Sammut, who produced a number of match-winning performances, scoring nine tries in just eight Shield matches and 11 overall.

That left him just one short of top try-scorer Elliott Miller, while Brett Carter and Jarrad Stack also made double figures in all competitions.

There was good progress made by several local products as well, most notably Steve Scholey and Sam Forrester, who should remain stalwarts of the side for several years.

Elsewhere, back-rowers Brett Phillips and Stack, plus fullback Jack Murphy were among their most consistent performers.

BATLEY BULLDOGS' season was undoubtedly a case of what might have been.

The Bulldogs lost 13 matches by a margin of 12 points or less - which might not have been so bad had the bonus point system not been ditched for 2015.

Those defeats also included a nail-biting 26-22 loss at Widnes Vikings, which almost provided John Kear with another remarkable Challenge Cup upset to add to his collection.

The narrow league losses meant that a genuine top-four push was never on the cards and the Bulldogs' hopes of making the Championship Shield play-offs effectively ended with opening losses to Workington and Dewsbury.

Still, there were plenty of positives as well, though most of them centred around gutsy performances in defeat, such as at home to Bradford early in the campaign.

A run of seven straight league losses in May and June had briefly hinted at a relegation scrap, but the Bulldogs recovered well to end that campaign with three wins from four.

Two serious injuries to Johnny Campbell robbed Kear of one of the best attacking players in the competition, while Wayne Reittie and Shaun Squires had good years in the threequarters and Joe Chandler was a stand-out before his own season-ending injury.

But Batley's best players could be found in the front row, where Alex Rowe, Keegan Hirst and James Brown all had big campaigns up front.

WHITEHAVEN could reflect on a season of hurdles that ended with plenty of positives - apart from their clashes with local rivals Workington.

The main obstacle they had to overcome was the sudden departure of newly-appointed coach Steve Deakin at the beginning of the campaign, meaning that his assistant James Coyle stepped up to his first senior role.

He acquitted himself well enough to earn a Coach of the Year nomination from his peers and guide Haven to their main objective - avoiding relegation.

They finished the league season on a significant high with a hugely creditable 29-0 win away at Featherstone.

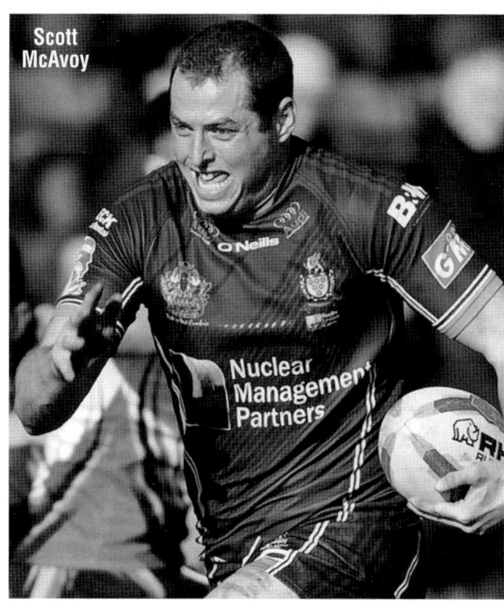

The only major negative for supporters was no less than four defeats to Town - including 40-0 and 60-20 losses.

Even in defeat, Papua New Guinean Dion Aiye was a shining light, scoring a hat-trick in the last of those Workington setbacks and exciting supporters throughout the season with his damaging runs.

Coyle's captures of front rowers Richie Beaumont and Sam Brooks also made a notable difference, helping them to turn their season around after they won just one of their first seven games.

Club stalwarts Craig Calvert and Scott McAvoy both reached double figures for tries, but another potential local hero of the future, John-Paul Brocklebank, missed most of the campaign through injury after a promising start.

Jimmy Watson

HUNSLET HAWKS were always expected to be up against it in terms of avoiding relegation, with fewer financial resources than any of their Championship rivals.

But four wins from their opening 10 matches - including a head-turning result against Dewsbury - suggested they could upset the odds, before injuries set in mid-season, making the Hawks' mountain all the more steeper.

Key losses included centre Luke Briscoe, who had been among the competition's form threequarters, and major signing Andy Kain at halfback.

James Duckworth also missed 12 matches following a string of good performances - and that trio of absences undoubtedly hit coach Barry Eaton's squad hard.

Throughout the whole season fullback Jimmy Watson was coach Eaton's most consistent player and he was among a host of players retained by the club as they looked to bounce straight back into the Championship at the first attempt.

Hooker Jack Lee finished as the top try scorer and the only Hawk to make double figures, in a squad in which Eaton used almost 40 players in total, including six from their partnership with Leeds Rhinos, which has remained solid while others have crumbled.

Hunslet will again be one of the favourites for promotion in 2016; bridging the gap with the Championship remains a long-term goal for a club that does plenty of admirable things on and off the field.

Liam Welham

After a 2014 to remember, **DONCASTER** had a 2015 to forget, never getting going and finishing well adrift at the bottom of the Championship.

Paul Cooke had guided the club into the top four last season, meaning that they actually had greater central funding than Halifax.

But by the time he parted company with the club in May their relegation had all but been confirmed, without a victory to their name.

Not until mid-July, under the newly-appointed Gary Thornton, did the Dons register a win, when they beat fellow strugglers Hunslet 34-26 at home.

Their only other triumph in a long season was a late Championship Shield win at home to Dewsbury in which Peter Fox scored a hat-trick of tries, helping him to finish as their top try scorer despite not arriving until after the start of the season.

Thornton's task immediately looked more of a rebuilding one than a relegation rescue, and the club made good progress in assembling a squad for next year.

In what was undoubtedly a tough season, centre Liam Welham was regularly among the Dons' best, along with hooker Kyle Kesik and overseas forwards Mitch Clark and Matt Groat.

Youngsters Jack Walton, Brad Foster and Sam Doherty all had their moments at different stages as well and promised to play a key role for Thornton's squad in League 1 next year.

LEAGUE 1 SEASON
Roughyeds rejoice

OLDHAM put almost a decade of heartache behind them when they finally clinched promotion to the Championship.

Having lost six out of the previous eight finals at this level - plus the 2001 NFP Grand Final when elevation to Super League was at stake - the Roughyeds supporters and chairman Chris Hamilton had endured more than their fair share of heartache.

But led by deserving League 1 Coach of the Year Scott Naylor, the club finally made the step up back to the second tier by beating Keighley Cougars in the promotion play-off after a hugely impressive campaign.

A Whitebank record crowd of 1,405 was present to see the Roughyeds win 31-20 with a team performance that typified their season as a whole.

Naylor didn't have the established names of some of his rivals, but maintained a strong element of continuity and stuck to his mantra of giving young players a chance.

He also adopted innovative tactics not used elsewhere, including the regular use of three different hookers during a match.

Super-consistent back-row pairing Danny Langtree and Josh Crowley were yet again bedrocks of the team, along with League 1 Player of the Year Lewis Palfrey.

All three and the majority of the rest of the squad would be back next season along with a sprinkling of new additions, meaning there was much to be positive about for the Roughyeds again.

SWINTON LIONS joined their local rivals in achieving promotion after a thrilling play-off final, also against Keighley.

John Duffy's side showed a tremendous amount of defensive steel and resolve in the closing stages of a 29-28 win that saw the Cougars laying siege to their line.

It completed a year of significant progress for the Lions after they decided to move away from their dual-registration partnership with Warrington and go their own way under Duffy and chairman John Roddy.

They were rewarded for that leap of faith by exceeding most people's expectations in finishing third and then completed two thrilling one-point wins in the play-offs.

The first saw them edge out York City Knights, with Chris Atkin kicking the golden-point winning field goal in extra time.

In the final, second-rower Rhodri Lloyd - on loan from Wigan - had an outstanding game in a similarly tight win over the Cougars, which sent the retiring Tommy Gallagher out on a major high.

A memorable season all round also saw the Lions make the final of the iPro Cup earlier in the year at the Summer Bash in Blackpool, where they narrowly lost out to North Wales Crusaders.

Veteran centre Stuart Littler rolled back the clock with some vintage displays, Ben White thrived at halfback and Andy Ackers was a constant handful at hooker as the Lions finally roared again.

League 1 Season

KEIGHLEY COUGARS set out as many people's favourites to earn an immediate return to the Championship, but had more to deal with than any other club.

The devastating death of Danny Jones at the game at London Skolars in early May shook the club to its core and, although in many ways it brought the Cougars closer together, it was a huge amount for Paul March and his squad to contend with.

The club rallied in the following months and honoured Jones' memory in several ways, before ultimately falling just short of earning the promotion they craved with their one-point defeat to Swinton in the play-off final.

The retirement of March and his brother David will mean a further reshaping of the Keighley squad next year, and they have made some eye-catching 2016 recruits.

Prolific winger Paul White was among their best in 2015, finishing with a haul of 30 tries in 25 appearances.

Next in line was Andy Gabriel - one of a host of talented youngsters to emerge - with 21, while Paul Handforth produced some influential performances during the course of the year.

Josh Lynam, Brendan Rawlins and Scott Law were constants in a solid Cougars pack, and they should again be among the front runners for promotion next time around.

YORK CITY KNIGHTS had different kinds of issues to contend with, centring around their lack of a home ground and training facilities during the early part of the campaign.

Jack Aldous

James Ford's introduction to professional first-team coaching involved playing matches on the road and scratching around for training venues before a resolution with the council was reached.

The wrangling between club and local authority dominated the entire first half of the year, with uncertainty surrounding both where the Knights could train and play at the time, and in the future, ahead of the proposed new community stadium in the city.

It made for a tough start for Coach of the Year nominee Ford and his young squad and it was to their great credit that despite that back-drop he steered an inexperienced side to fourth place in League 1.

Now, with stadium issues resolved, the future is looking much rosier for the Knights.

It could have been even better in 2015 but for a heart-wrenching golden point defeat at Swinton in the play-offs, where they were ahead in normal time with 12 seconds remaining.

But the likes of Jonny Presley, Jack Aldous, Mark Applegarth, Ed Smith and Josh Tonks can hold their heads high and a cluster of youngsters should help them kick on next year.

Of those promising players, Greg Minikin, signed by Super League side Castleford for 2016, Kris Brining, Harry Carter and Tyler Craig all deserve credit for their campaigns.

NORTH WALES CRUSADERS were forced to field only 16 players on a number of occasions in the closing stages of the season due to a crippling injury list, but still made the play-offs in Anthony Murray's first full season in charge.

There, they were well beaten by Keighley at Cougar Park despite being level at 6-6 at the break, with the second half seemingly 40 minutes too far for their stretched squad.

The season highlight undoubtedly came with winning the iPro Cup at the Summer Bash weekend in May, with Jamie Dallimore's late try clinching a thrilling 14-8 win over Swinton.

The Crusaders hoped to kick on from that and secure a notable double with promotion, but those injuries hit them hard.

The club had a dual registration partnership with Warrington, but it appeared to be used mainly to give fringe Wolves players the occasional run out - the likes of Gareth O'Brien, Gary Wheeler, Rhys Evans and Gene Ormsby making fleeting appearances.

Welsh international winger Rob Massam topped the Crusaders' try-coring chart, followed by back-rower Jono Smith, who at the end of the season joined rivals Rochdale.

French youngster Benjamin Jullien impressed at centre, Tommy Johnson was a near constant at fullback and Dallimore again the fulcrum of the team for much of the season from scrum-half.

ROCHDALE HORNETS set out with high hopes of a second promotion campaign in three years and highlighted increased investment in their playing squad.

But their target never materialised, with Ian Talbot's side falling just one point short of the top five.

In the final shake-up, a last-minute home defeat to Newcastle in April proved costly, along with key forward Tony Suffolk's 10-match mid-season suspension for a controversial 'crocodile roll' against North Wales.

But they were still in contention to make the play-offs right until the closing stages of the campaign when another narrow home loss, this time to Keighley, was also decisive.

Back-rower Danny Bridge and ever present prop Warren Thompson were among those that ensured Hornets were dangerous opposition for any side, with both players recognised at the club's end-of-season awards night.

Hornets favourites Paul Crook, Wayne English and returning threequarters Lee Paterson and Dale Bloomfield were also influential figures.

Coach Talbot - who had steered Rochdale to promotion two years earlier - parted company with the club at the end of the campaign to be replace by Alan Kilshaw, who has worked both in Warrington's junior system and in Australia and will hope to go at least one better in 2016.

BARROW RAIDERS made a renewed move towards local players under returning coach Paul Crarey, along with a cluster of signings from Leigh.

But like Rochdale they also fell a point short of the play-offs, with a one-point defeat at Keighley in mid-August crucial.

They also lost by two points at home to the Cougars in June - two narrow setbacks that would ultimately prove decisive, and somewhat frustrating given that the Raiders dumped the same side comprehensively out of the Challenge Cup.

Of their arrivals from the Centurions, halfback Josh Ward topped the points-scoring chart and crossed for 10 tries, Joe Bullock, Anthony Bate and Craig Briscoe were big presences in the pack and threequarters Chris Hankinson and Cameron Phelps collected 18 tries in total out wide.

But there was also a large contingent of local products in Crarey's ranks, with experienced duo Liam Campbell and top try scorer Nathan Mossop helping to guide them from the middle of the field.

Others to impress at different stages included Andy Litherland, Liam Harrison and emerging youngster Kyle Doran.

Crarey will use a similar formula in 2016, although the arrival of established Championship pair Oliver Wilkes and Ryan Fieldhouse will significantly bolster their experience.

NEWCASTLE THUNDER started the year with much promise, with a host of talented overseas signings joining coach Stanley Gene at the renamed club.

By mid-June Thunder were flying high in League 1 and threatening a genuine promotion push.

But their season gradually unravelled from that point, with just three wins from their final 11 games seeing them eventually end up in eighth place, a definite disappointment given their excellent start.

By the end of the year Gene had left his post and has been replaced by little-known - in this country at least - Australian coach Michael Matelli, who has worked on Canberra Raiders' backroom staff.

But there was still much to be positive about in 2015, not least an average home attendance of 944 at their new Kingston Park home, up by over 200 per cent on their 2014 figure.

On the field, halfback Matty Beharrell flourished under Gene and was named the League 1 Young Player of the Year, while Dayne Craig and PNG import Jason Tali both finished with a club-high 16 tries.

The mid-season return of Kiwi fullback Jordan Meads down under was a definite blow, but there are enough promising signs in the north east to suggest Thunder's eye-catching start to 2015 was not a false dawn in the longer term.

GLOUCESTERSHIRE ALL GOLDS enjoyed a season of definite progress under new coach Lee Greenwood and finished top of the recently introduced expansion clubs, and of all those in the south.

They also became the first southern team to beat a northern League 1 opponent for over a year when they toppled Newcastle 26-10 in August and the signs are that they could continue that improvement next season.

That was one of three wins in their final five matches, ending a generally encouraging year on a definite high.

Skipper Steve Parry scored two tries in that Newcastle win and was a key figure for Greenwood's side throughout the campaign, topping their try-scoring chart with 14.

He was closely followed by experienced threequarter Lee Mapals and Irish international Callum Mulkeen, who were both important members of the team, along with Phil Cowburn, Oliver Purslow and Aussie Ryan Pywell.

The All Golds also took the admirable stance of standing alone rather than looking at a dual-registration partnership, something they will continue in 2016 with the help of a handful of new recruits, some from overseas.

The challenge for Greenwood and his All Golds squad will be making results like the Newcastle one more frequent.

OXFORD were another club with a new coach in Tim Rumford and their season was characterised by wildly different highs and lows.

Rumford's side were on the end of some of the biggest hammerings in the competition - conceding 96 and 84 points against Swinton and 76 at Rochdale.

But they also recorded a creditable seven wins and were within 10 points of winning at York.

Of those victories, their June triumph over South Wales was a third in five matches, but they were unable to replicate that in the second half of the season.

Some of their best performances coincided with the arrival of Bradford dual-registration players Matty Blythe, Dave Petersen and Vila Halifihi, who brought valuable know-how.

But like most of the other expansion clubs, they struggled with consistency of selection - using a total of 53 players in all competitions.

One of the few constants in the side was halfback Danny Thomas, who provided an experienced head in the middle of the field.

Andrew Hoggins top scored with 10 tries, closely following by Nathan Kitson, while Marcus Brooker, Andrew Jones-Bishop, Andy Matthews and Adam Withington were other regular members of Rumford's side that played important roles in their campaign.

LONDON SKOLARS parted company with their coach Joe Mbu in the wake of an 86-4 home defeat to Swinton in the Challenge Cup in March, having conceded 78 points against York the previous week.

He was replaced by Skolars old boy Jermaine Coleman, who - aided by his own presence on the field - oversaw a steady upturn in fortunes that the club hopes will continue in 2016.

Highlights included three wins in five during the course of July and August and another credible showing in the annual Friday Night Lights game, this year against promotion-chasing North Wales Crusaders in front of over 1,000 fans.

Another Skolars old boy back in the fold was utility back James Anthony, who topped their try-scoring charts with more than double his nearest rival, including a hat-trick in a narrow final-day defeat at Rochdale.

Lamont Bryan, Mike Bishay and Aaron Small were also back in north London along with popular front-rower Dave Williams.

Coleman will be hoping for more stability in 2016 - using almost 50 players is rarely conducive to winning matches regularly - but the signs are promising that Skolars can re-establish themselves as a genuine threat to the established northern clubs at this level.

COVENTRY BEARS can be proud of their efforts in their debut season, not least a flying start that saw them win two of their opening three games.

Comprehensive victories over Oxford and Hemel suggested the Bears could leapfrog several of their fellow expansion clubs in their first year, but they would win just three times more.

They were hardly helped by key Hull KR dual-registration signings Matty Marsh and Josh Guzdek moving onto rival League 1 clubs after playing integral roles in those early wins, while another, Connor Robinson, ended up at Halifax.

Had they all stayed, who knows where Tom Tsang's side would have ended up, but there was still much to be positive about in their opening campaign.

Jamahl Hunte finished as clear top try scorer with 13 from 19 games in all competitions, while other stalwarts of the side included Matt Cooper, James Geurtjens, Dan Parker and Liam Thompson.

But arguably their most notable achievement came off the field at the Championship awards night, when the Bears were handed the League 1 Project of the Year.

That illustrated - as some impressive crowds did - the work that goes on off the pitch from club founder Alan Robinson and his team.

Their average attendance of 458 compared very favourably with much more established clubs, and they will look to continue their early progression in 2016.

Finishing second bottom of League 1 was a definite slide for **HEMEL STAGS**, who had been the highest placed expansion club 12 months earlier.

The highlight of the Stags season' was probably a comprehensive opening day win at London Skolars, though it could have looked a lot different for Troy Perkins' side had they not suffered two high scoring four-point defeats to the All Golds.

Perkins revealed the difficulties southern-based clubs deal with in a revealing interview with League Express midway through the season, but he and the club have come a long way in previous years and shouldn't be written off despite their slide down the table.

Using almost 50 players certainly didn't help the Hemel coach, and there were regular comings and goings throughout the course of the year, several of them from partner club Hunslet Hawks.

Among the few constants were the prolific Alex Anthony, and the hard-working Derrell Olpherts and Eddie Mbaraga and halfback Jy-mel Coleman, whose brother Jermaine's appointment at London Skolars also had an impact.

Perkins has brought in some new faces for 2016 including experienced Australian halfback Chad Isles, and will be hoping that helps him avoid the scramble for southern-based players he says is damaging clubs in the area.

SOUTH WALES SCORPIONS endured another tough season on the field, winning just once, against London Skolars, for the second year running. But that tells little of the story at the outpost club, with coach Mike Grady again working miracles to get a near fully local team on the pitch every weekend.

Grady parted company with the Scorpions late in the year with his head held high and reputation intact, signalling significant changes in the Valleys.

The club is now under different ownership and has a new coach in returning old-boy Phil Carleton, as they look to build on the solid foundations left by Grady and others.

Their admirable stance in relying heavily on inexperienced local talent made chalking up wins difficult, however, with players as young as 17 stepping up to the mark during the course of the campaign.

Assistant coach and halfback Paul Emanuelli was a huge influence on the field alongside hooker Connor Farrer, who again ended the year in the senior Welsh squad for the European Cup.

Farrer, Ian Newbury and Yannic Parker were joint top try scorers with eight each, while Curtis and Connor Davies, Dafydd Hellard, Kyle Scrivens, Jordan Sheridan and northerners Jonny Leather and Ryan Millington were other mainstays of a side that deserves more credit than bottom spot usually brings.

LEAGUE 1 AWARDS

PLAYER OF THE YEAR
Lewis Palfrey
(Oldham)

YOUNG PLAYER OF THE YEAR
Matty Beharrell
(Newcastle Thunder)

COACH OF THE YEAR
Scott Naylor
(Oldham)

CLUB OF THE YEAR
Keighley Cougars

Lewis Palfrey

iPRO SPORT CUP FINAL
Victorious Crusade

North Wales Crusaders lifted the inaugural iPRO Sport Cup with a gritty 14-8 win over Swinton Lions at Bloomfield Road.

The newly-introduced competition took the form of a knock-out cup for League 1 clubs and two amateur sides, with the final being held at the new Summer Bash in Blackpool.

Crusaders saw off West Hull and Rochdale before edging past Oldham 18-16 in a thrilling semi-final.

And it was a similar story in the decider against the Lions, with Jamie Dallimore's 65th-minute try proving crucial.

Anthony Murray's side had trailed 6-8 at the break, with Shaun Robinson opening the scoring for the Lions in the 10th minute before Scott Turner responded for the Welsh.

But Swinton would not trouble the scoreboard again in the second half as the Crusaders' rearguard stood firm after Dallimore's try, despite plenty of pressure.

Coach Murray said: "We set a goal at the beginning of the year to get here and then to win it, so it's really nice when you can set goals and achieve them.

"And that's what we've done, so I'm really pleased.

"Swinton, to be fair to them, threw everything but the kitchen sink at us, and we defended it.

"At half-time, the message was that they've had their best at you and they've only crossed your line once. Complete our sets, finish in good areas of the field and see how much pressure we can put on their line.

"Once we started doing that, I knew we'd get back in the game."

iPRO SPORT CUP FINAL

Saturday 23rd May 2015

NORTH WALES CRUSADERS 14 SWINTON LIONS 8

CRUSADERS: 1 Tommy Johnson; 2 Scott Turner; 4 Matt Reid; 22 Alex Thompson; 5 Rob Massam; 14 Karl Ashall; 7 Jamie Dallimore; 16 Joe Burke; 9 Callum Wright; 8 Jonny Walker; 11 Jono Smith; 12 Stephen Wild; 13 Gary Middlehurst. Subs (all used): 15 Lee Hudson; 23 Mark Hobson; 10 Ryan Duffy; 20 Elliott Davies.
Tries: Turner (30), Dallimore (65); **Goals:** Johnson 3/5.
LIONS: 7 Chris Atkin; 2 Shaun Robinson; 3 Stuart Littler; 22 Chris Rothwell; 1 Ritchie Hawkyard; 6 Ben White; 18 Aaron Lloyd; 24 Jordan James; 9 Andy Ackers; 10 Ben Austin; 30 Josh Barlow; 23 Connor Dwyer; 31 Rob Lever. Subs (all used): 8 Mike Morrison; 12 Darren Hawkyard; 17 Matt Gardner; 29 Mick Govin.
Try: Robinson (10); **Goals:** Atkin 2/2.
Rugby Leaguer & League Express Men of the Match:
Crusaders: Jamie Dallimore; *Lions:* Chris Atkin.
Penalty count: 12-5; **Half-time:** 6-8;
Referee: Michael Woodhead; **Attendance:** 1,200
(at Bloomfield Road, Blackpool).

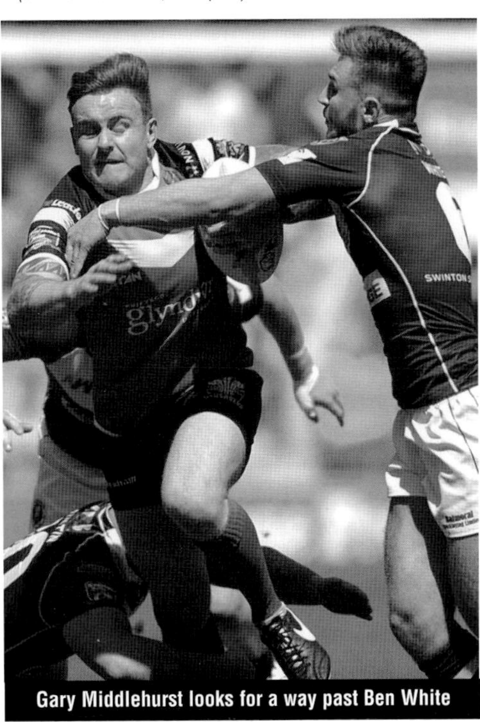

Gary Middlehurst looks for a way past Ben White

LEAGUE 1 PLAY-OFFS
Oldham end heartache

A Whitebank record crowd saw Oldham finally realise their long-held dream by winning the Promotion Final in the sport's new structure.

Rather than have to negotiate another final on neutral ground after six near misses in the previous eight years, the Roughyeds earned the right to host Keighley after topping the League 1 table.

And they took full advantage in front of 1,405 largely success-starved supporters to make the step back up to the Championship.

Scott Naylor's side were ahead from the 12th minute when prolific centre Jon Ford crossed, and led 18-6 at the break after further tries to Adam Neal and Danny Langtree negated Matthew Bailey's 25th minute response.

The Cougars dragged themselves back into the contest when top try scorer Paul White crossed just before the hour mark and were well in the game going into the closing stages when Paul Handforth touched down.

But Oldham kept their noses sufficiently far in front and could begin their promotion party when winger Adam Clay touched down two minutes from the end.

Paul March's Keighley still had a second chance to follow them however, and the following week booked their place in the play-off final with an eventually comprehensive 32-6 win over North Wales Crusaders.

KINGSTONE PRESS LEAGUE 1 PROMOTION FINAL

Sunday 20th September 2015

OLDHAM 31 KEIGHLEY COUGARS 20

OLDHAM: 21 Richard Lepori; 2 Adam Clay; 17 George Tyson; 3 Jonathan Ford; 4 Jack Holmes; 6 Lewis Palfrey; 7 Steve Roper; 10 Adam Neal; 15 Gareth Owen; 8 Phil Joy; 12 Danny Langtree; 11 Josh Crowley; 26 Will Hope. Subs (all used): 13 Liam Thompson; 19 Michael Ward; 14 Adam Files; 16 Kenny Hughes.
Tries: Ford (12), Neal (32), Langtree (38), Tyson (66), Clay (78); **Goals:** Palfrey 5/6; **Field goal:** Palfrey (71).
COUGARS: 36 Josh Guzdek; 25 Andy Gabriel; 4 Danny Lawton; 30 Rikki Sheriffe; 5 Paul White; - Adam Mitchell; 7 Paul Handforth; 8 Scott Law; 13 David March; 35 Tyler Dickinson; 17 Oliver Pursglove; 12 Brendan Rawlins; 11 Ashley Lindsay. Subs (all used): 26 Paul March; 19 Matthew Bailey; 28 Josh Lynam; 34 Samir Tahraoui.
Tries: Bailey (25), White (59), Handforth (69), Gabriel (80); **Goals:** Lawton 2/4.
Rugby Leaguer & League Express Men of the Match: *Oldham:* Steve Roper; *Cougars:* Paul Handforth.
Penalty count: 6-4; **Half-time:** 18-6;
Referee: Michael Woodhead; **Attendance:** 1,405.

Adam Neal beats David March to score

The sides were locked together at 6-6 at the break at Cougar Park after Alex Thompson's try had cancelled out an early White effort.

But the Cougars winger would go on to complete a hat-trick after the restart and, with Bailey, Paul March and winger Andy Gabriel also touching down, Keighley moved smoothly through.

Elsewhere that afternoon it was much, much tighter at Park Lane, as Swinton needed golden-point extra time to edge out York.

The City Knights had looked set to progress when they led 17-16 with just 12 seconds remaining, courtesy of Jordan Howden's 74th minute field goal.

But Ben White responded in kind with the clock ticking down and Chris Atkin then broke York hearts three minutes after the restart, despite the fact that the visitors outscored their hosts four tries to three.

Swinton Lions' experience of late drama in their semi-final against York served them well in the decider a week later, as they clung on to a one-point lead to beat Keighley 29-28 and secure the second promotion spot.

John Duffy's side had led for much of an entertaining game, including 26-16 at the break.

But Keighley roared back in the closing stages and by the end the Lions were hanging on with Cougars laying siege to their line.

Duffy said: "I called the early drop goal from the side line as I knew it was going to get really tight in the end.

"The last five minutes I could barely watch. It's massive for the club – we are trying to change the club and make it more professional and there are a lot of people behind the scenes who do a lot for free, so this is for them.

"It's also for the chairman and a good board that he's got around him who have gone out of their way to make things happen this year."

In a see-saw first half, Chris Atkin, Mike Butt, Ben White, Shaun Robinson and man of the match Rhodri Lloyd all touched down for the Lions, with Scott Law (2) and Josh Lynam responding for Keighley.

The Cougars' defence would not be breached again and they scored further tries through Oliver Pursglove and coach Paul March, but an Atkin penalty and 63rd minute field goal would prove decisive despite a late Keighley onslaught.

March said: "We gave ourselves too much to do in the game.

"All credit to the boys for fighting back because we could have snatched it at the end.

"But I don't think we were smart enough in certain areas and the best side won."

KINGSTONE PRESS LEAGUE 1 PLAY-OFF FINAL

Sunday 4th October 2015

KEIGHLEY COUGARS 28 SWINTON LIONS 29

COUGARS: 36 Josh Guzdek; 25 Andy Gabriel; 4 Danny Lawton; 30 Rikki Sheriffe; 5 Paul White; 26 Paul March; 7 Paul Handforth; 8 Scott Law; 13 David March; 12 Brendan Rawlins; 28 Josh Lynam; 17 Oliver Pursglove; 11 Ashley Lindsay. Subs (all used): 9 James Feather; 19 Matthew Bailey; 15 Neil Cherryholme; 34 Samir Tahraoui.
Tries: Law (12, 15), Lynam (28), Pursglove (50), P March (70); **Goals:** Lawton 4/5.
LIONS: 1 Ritchie Hawkyard; 2 Shaun Robinson; 3 Stuart Littler; 22 Chris Rothwell; 28 Mike Butt; 6 Ben White; 7 Chris Atkin; 24 Jordan James; 9 Andy Ackers; 10 Ben Austin; 17 Andy Thornley; 29 Rhodri Lloyd; 31 Rob Lever. Subs (all used): 13 Tommy Gallagher; 30 Josh Barlow; 23 Connor Dwyer; 18 Aaron Lloyd.
Tries: Atkin (7), Butt (20), White (22), R Lloyd (36), Robinson (40); **Goals:** Atkin 4/6; **Field goal:** Atkin (63).
Rugby Leaguer & League Express Men of the Match:
Cougars: Paul Handforth; *Lions:* Rhodri Lloyd.
Penalty count: 8-4; **Half-time:** 16-26; **Referee:** Chris Kendall.
(at Select Security Stadium, Widnes).

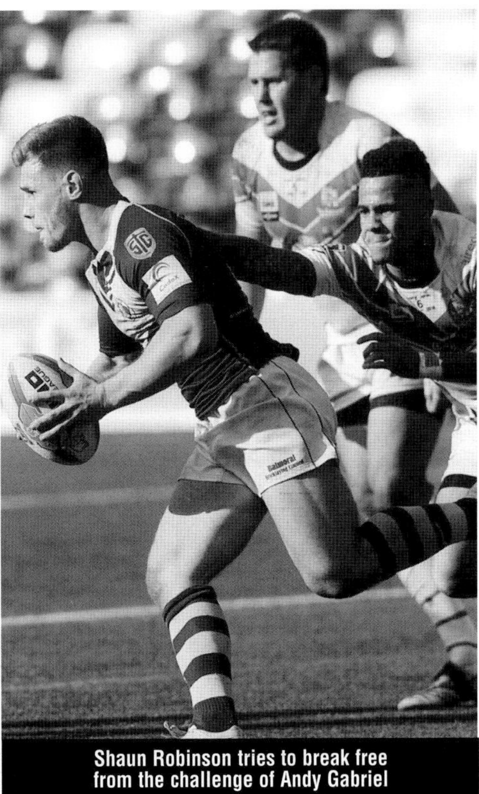

Shaun Robinson tries to break free from the challenge of Andy Gabriel

3
INTERNATIONAL YEAR

TEST SERIES
The future's white

There were seven uncapped players selected in England coach Steve McNamara's England squad for the autumn Test matches against France and New Zealand.

The seven were Castleford halfback and 2015 Albert Goldthorpe Medal winner Luke Gale, Warrington's Ben Currie, Wigan's John Bateman, George Williams and Joe Burgess, St George Illawarra's Mike Cooper and Huddersfield's Jermaine McGillvary. Of the seven, Gale and Currie didn't feature in any of the four Tests.

The England squad was captained by Wigan's Sean O'Loughlin, who after England's 2-1 win was named Man of the Series - and awarded the George Smith Medal.

TEST SERIES SQUADS

ENGLAND: John Bateman (Wigan Warriors); Joe Burgess (Wigan Warriors); Tom Burgess (South Sydney Rabbitohs); Mike Cooper (St George Illawarra Dragons); Leroy Cudjoe (Huddersfield Giants); Ben Currie (Warrington Wolves); Liam Farrell (Wigan Warriors); Brett Ferres (Huddersfield Giants); Luke Gale (Castleford Tigers); James Graham (Canterbury Bulldogs); Ryan Hall (Leeds Rhinos); Zak Hardaker (Leeds Rhinos); Chris Hill (Warrington Wolves); Josh Hodgson (Canberra Raiders); Jermaine McGillvary (Huddersfield Giants); Sean O'Loughlin (Wigan Warriors) (C); James Roby (St Helens); Matty Smith (Wigan Warriors); Sam Tomkins (New Zealand Warriors); Kallum Watkins (Leeds Rhinos); Ben Westwood (Warrington Wolves); Elliott Whitehead (Catalans Dragons); Gareth Widdop (St George Illawarra Dragons); George Williams (Wigan Warriors).

NEW ZEALAND: Gerard Beale (Cronulla Sharks); Adam Blair (Brisbane Broncos) (C); Jesse Bromwich (Melbourne Storm); Lewis Brown (Penrith Panthers); Manaia Cherrington (Wests Tigers); Alex Glenn (Brisbane Broncos); Tohu Harris (Melbourne Storm); Peta Hiku (Manly Sea Eagles); Jordan Kahu (Brisbane Broncos); Shaun Kenny-Dowall (Sydney Roosters); Tuimoala Lolohea (New Zealand Warriors); Isaac Liu (Sydney Roosters); Issac Luke (South Sydney Rabbitohs) (C); Ben Matulino (New Zealand Warriors); Sam Moa (Sydney Roosters); Jason Nightingale (St George Illawarra Dragons); Kodi Nikorima (Brisbane Broncos); Kevin Proctor (Melbourne Storm); Curtis Rona (Canterbury Bulldogs); Sio Siua Taukeiaho (Sydney Roosters); Martin Taupau (Wests Tigers); Roger Tuivasa-Sheck (Sydney Roosters); Dean Whare (Penrith Panthers).

St Helens hooker James Roby, Huddersfield centre Leroy Cudjoe and Warrington's Ben Westwood all returned after missing selection twelve months before through injury, though Cudjoe and Westwood were not selected for the Tests.

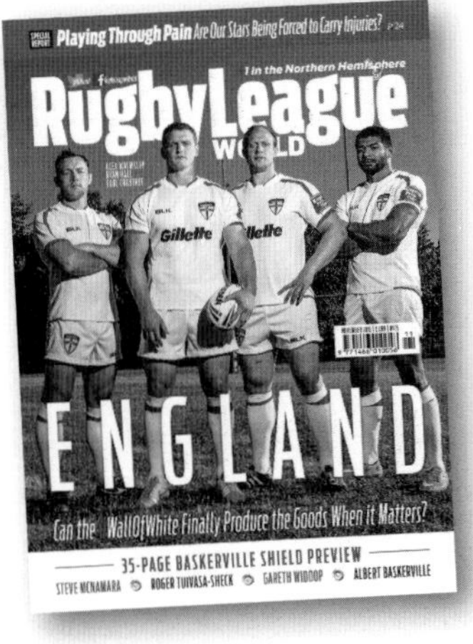

South Sydney's George Burgess, St Helens' Alex Walmsley, Leeds' Stevie Ward, Brisbane Broncos' Jack Reed, Warrington's Stefan Ratchford and Wigan's Joel Tomkins were not considered because of upcoming surgery during the close season. Sam Tomkins was selected but ruled out of the series with a knee injury.

England were based throughout the tournament at the Football Association's St George's Park training facility in Burton-upon-Trent.

New Zealand travelled to England in the autumn as, officially, the best team in international Rugby League, having wrestled top spot away from Australia for the first time since the world rankings began following their 26-12 triumph in the Anzac Test in Brisbane.

Coach Stephen Kearney named Adam Blair and Issac Luke as co-captains, in the absence of Simon Mannering, who pulled out of the tour in an attempt to recover from a gastric illness that had affected him for much of the season.

Kieran Foran (elbow), 2014 Golden Boot winner Shaun Johnson (ankle), Thomas Leuluai (knee) and Jason Taumalolo (knee) also missed the tour through injury.

Benji Marshall, the former New Zealand captain who had played 27 Tests for his country, sustained an ankle injury during St George Illawarra Dragons' NRL elimination semi-final defeat by Canterbury Bulldogs. But coach Kearney made clear that he would not have been selected anyway.

The Kiwis' 23-man squad included seven uncapped players - utility backs Jordan Kahu and Tuimoala Lolohea, wing Curtis Rona, hooker or halfback Kodi Nikorima, hooker Manaia Cherrington and forwards Isaac Liu and Sio Siua Taukeiaho. Rona and Cherrington didn't play in any of the three Tests.

All three games were screened live by the BBC.

England went one up on a murky, misty Sunday night at the KC Stadium, Hull, with an assured 26-12 win.

Steve McNamara's side recovered from a lacklustre opening to peg back a New Zealand team that looked more than capable of steam-rolling the home side with a fast and powerful offload game. But after clawing back to parity by half-time, they scored 14 points after the turnaround, keeping the black and white juggernaut pointless.

A 5-nil penalty count in the second half in their favour helped, but that was more a symptom of England's domination in the second 40 minutes. The Kiwis were a tired bunch by the time that Sean O'Loughlin bumped off Adam Blair's attempted big hit three minutes from time to race over for the final points of the Test.

Gareth Widdop was the guiding force on the back of a mighty effort up front, Tom Burgess immense and Brett Ferres looking international class, finishing with two tries to his name.

McNamara named an unchanged side from the 84-4 win against France the previous Saturday.

Despite the optimistic prognoses up to the previous week, Sam Tomkins was out for the series after aggravating a knee injury he sustained playing for the New Zealand Warriors in August.

With his first-choice halfbacks unavailable through injury, Stephen Kearney turned to Peta Hiku, the Manly centre or winger, who played at fullback when England lost 16-14 to New Zealand in Dunedin in the 2014 Four Nations, and 20-year-old Tuimoala Lolohea, coincidentally making a good fist of playing fullback at the Warriors in 2015 during Sam Tomkins' punctuated campaign.

Lolohea was earning his first Kiwi cap, as were Jordan Kahu, Brisbane dummy-half Kodi Nikorima and Roosters forward Sio Siua Taukeiaho.

FIRST TEST

Sunday 1st November 2015

ENGLAND 26 NEW ZEALAND 12

ENGLAND: 1 Zak Hardaker (Leeds Rhinos); 2 Joe Burgess (Wigan Warriors); 4 Kallum Watkins (Leeds Rhinos); 3 John Bateman (Wigan Warriors); 5 Ryan Hall (Leeds Rhinos); 6 Gareth Widdop (St George Illawarra Dragons); 7 George Williams (Wigan Warriors); 8 James Graham (Canterbury Bulldogs); 9 Josh Hodgson (Canberra Raiders); 10 Chris Hill (Warrington Wolves); 11 Elliott Whitehead (Catalans Dragons); 12 Liam Farrell (Wigan Warriors); 13 Sean O'Loughlin (Wigan Warriors) (C). Subs (all used): 14 James Roby (St Helens); 15 Tom Burgess (South Sydney Rabbitohs); 16 Mike Cooper (St George Illawarra Dragons); 17 Brett Ferres (Huddersfield Giants).
Tries: Hodgson (20), Ferres (35, 60), O'Loughlin (77);
Goals: Widdop 5/5.
NEW ZEALAND: 1 Roger Tuivasa-Sheck (Sydney Roosters); 5 Shaun Kenny-Dowall (Sydney Roosters); 4 Dean Whare (Penrith Panthers); 3 Jordan Kahu (Brisbane Broncos); 2 Jason Nightingale (St George Illawarra Dragons); 6 Peta Hiku (Manly Sea Eagles); 7 Tuimoala Lolohea (New Zealand Warriors); 8 Jesse Bromwich (Melbourne Storm); 9 Issac Luke (South Sydney Rabbitohs) (C); 10 Sam Moa (Sydney Roosters); 11 Kevin Proctor (Melbourne Storm); 12 Tohu Harris (Melbourne Storm); 13 Adam Blair (Brisbane Broncos) (C). Subs (all used): 14 Kodi Nikorima (Brisbane Broncos); 15 Martin Taupau (Wests Tigers); 16 Ben Matulino (New Zealand Warriors); 17 Sio Siua Taukeiaho (Sydney Roosters).
Tries: Harris (6), Moa (16); **Goals:** Luke 2/3.
On report: Moa (59) - alleged shoulder charge on Roby.
Rugby Leaguer & League Express Men of the Match:
England: Gareth Widdop; *New Zealand:* Jesse Bromwich.
Penalty count: 7-2; **Half-time:** 12-12;
Referee: Ben Thaler (England); **Attendance:** 23,526
(at KC Stadium, Hull).

Test Series

Adam Blair, co-captain with Issac Luke, was passed fit to play after shrugging off a calf injury he picked up in the previous Friday's 34-16 warm-up win over Leeds at Headingley. Brisbane club-mate Kahu also recovered from a hamstring injury in the same game.

History was on England's side, with New Zealand never having won at the KC Stadium. England's last win over New Zealand - by 28-6, which remained McNamara's only previous win in nines games against the top-two nations - had come in the 2011 Four Nations at the same venue. Before that, in the 2004 Tri Nations, Brian Noble's Great Britain had edged the Kiwis 26-24, and Tony Smith's Lions had sewn up the 2007 series there with a whopping 44-0 win.

The first half didn't look promising for England, but they somehow found themselves level at half-time at 12-all.

The Kiwis had dominated the first quarter despite England starting strongly, with Widdop's high kick on the first set trapping Jason Nightingale a metre from the New Zealand line.

But early offloads from Jesse Bromwich had first Tuivasa-Sheck causing chaos and then Tohu Harris tearing away in centrefield. It was an uncontainable black and white tide.

Harris opened the scoring in the sixth minute when Blair and Hiku moved the ball left for the big second-rower to bundle over through Hardaker's tackle.

Issac Luke missed the conversion but, ten minutes later, a charge-down of Hiku's kick by the impressive Chris Hill bounced kindly to Dean Whare who sent Hiku away. Jason Nightingale almost got in and, from the play the ball, the ball was moved right for Sam Moa to crash through Hardaker and Liam Farrell's tackle by the post protector.

Luke converted, but minutes later some big drives from Hall and Kallum Watkins had England back upfield and a brilliant inside ball from George Williams put Elliott Whitehead through a hole and charging for the line. The Catalans second-rower desperately offloaded inside to Zak Hardaker, who couldn't take the ball. The referee ruled no try, but the video referees ruled it came off his knee and bounced back off Hiku. As the Kiwis paused, Josh Hodgson was the recipient and over he went.

Luke kicked an easy penalty on 25 minutes when O'Loughlin was pinged for hands in as Martin Taupau, just on the field, tried to play the ball on the England line. It was a relief. If the Kiwis had run the ball it would have been their second repeat set.

England were still in the game but not looking too likely at this stage.

On 34 minutes, sub James Roby was tackled in goal, trapped by Luke's grubber. From the drop-out the Kiwis moved the ball left and Roger Tuivasa-Sheck shot through to put Kahu over.

It looked a telling blow but the video referees ruled that George Williams had been impeded by Harris's decoy run. It proved a lucky break for England as they worked down the other end from the penalty and, when the ball was moved right, Ferres hit a short pass from Williams on a straight run and stepped Tuivasa-Sheck on his way to the posts.

Straight after the turnaround Williams was almost over after two magnificent charges from Tom Burgess. And then Watkins forced Luke to drop the ball in the tackle. And when Luke was penalised shortly after for going on too long with the tackle on Mike Cooper, Widdop gave England the lead for the first time at 14-12.

In the 59th minute Roby was laid out by a tackle from Moa and had to leave the field for a head check. The incident was put on report and it wasn't long before Ferres charged under the posts and rolled out of Taukeiaho's tackle to get the ball down. Widdop's goal made it 20-12 and it could soon have been more after Tuivasa-Sheck was trapped in-goal, but Whitehead couldn't hang onto Hodgson's crash ball on the Kiwis line.

Minutes after, Whitehead shot for the line again but Roger Tuivasa-Sheck and Issac Luke somehow stopped him scoring.

That gave New Zealand some energy, the energy they had sapped out of them in the previous 30 minutes. They got three repeat sets with ten minutes to go, the last from a scrum, but Tuivasa-Sheck couldn't catch Blair's long pass and England were let off again.

A mighty James Graham charge helped take England downfield and it wasn't long before captain O'Loughlin was making the game safe with his converted try.

Eighty minutes of punishing defence from two well-organised lines that were only breached once was the story of the second Test played at the Olympic Park on a dreary day in east London, as New Zealand levelled the series with a 9-2 win.

Conditions played a huge part in a first half that ground to a 2-2 stalemate at half-time. And the game's only try came just over two minutes after the turnaround, with Shaun Kenny-Dowall the scorer. It took something special to create the chance, Tohu Harris collecting Kodi Nikorima's desperate offload out of the tackle off his bootlaces and then feeding Kenny-Dowall, who also took the pass on the half-volley, to squeeze into the right corner.

There could have been plenty more tries but for desperate commitment in defence, New Zealand having two potential scores ruled out by the video referee, and England one. And there were spells where, particularly England, couldn't be rightfully expected to hold out against waves of goal-line attacks.

SECOND TEST

Saturday 7th November 2015

ENGLAND 2 NEW ZEALAND 9

ENGLAND: 1 Zak Hardaker (Leeds Rhinos); 2 Joe Burgess (Wigan Warriors); 3 Kallum Watkins (Leeds Rhinos); 4 John Bateman (Wigan Warriors); 5 Ryan Hall (Leeds Rhinos); 6 Gareth Widdop (St George Illawarra Dragons); 7 George Williams (Wigan Warriors); 8 James Graham (Canterbury Bulldogs); 9 Josh Hodgson (Canberra Raiders); 10 Chris Hill (Warrington Wolves); 11 Elliott Whitehead (Catalans Dragons); 12 Liam Farrell (Wigan Warriors); 13 Sean O'Loughlin (Wigan Warriors) (C). Subs (all used): 14 James Roby (St Helens); 15 Tom Burgess (South Sydney Rabbitohs); 16 Mike Cooper (St George Illawarra Dragons); 17 Brett Ferres (Huddersfield Giants).
Goals: Widdop 1/1.
NEW ZEALAND: 1 Roger Tuivasa-Sheck (Sydney Roosters); 5 Shaun Kenny-Dowall (Sydney Roosters); 4 Dean Whare (Penrith Panthers); 3 Jordan Kahu (Brisbane Broncos); 2 Jason Nightingale (St George Illawarra Dragons); 6 Peta Hiku (Manly Sea Eagles); 19 Kodi Nikorima (Brisbane Broncos); 8 Jesse Bromwich (Melbourne Storm); 9 Issac Luke (South Sydney Rabbitohs) (C); 10 Sam Moa (Sydney Roosters); 11 Kevin Proctor (Melbourne Storm); 12 Tohu Harris (Melbourne Storm); 13 Adam Blair (Brisbane Broncos) (C). Subs (all used): 14 Lewis Brown (Penrith Panthers); 15 Martin Taupau (Wests Tigers); 16 Ben Matulino (New Zealand Warriors); 17 Alex Glenn (Brisbane Broncos).
Try: Kenny-Dowall (43); **Goals:** Luke 1/2, Kahu 1/1;
Field goal: Kahu (77).
Rugby Leaguer & League Express Men of the Match:
England: Chris Hill; *New Zealand:* Tohu Harris.
Penalty count: 6-7; **Half-time:** 2-2;
Referee: Gerard Sutton (Australia); **Attendance:** 44,393
(at Queen Elizabeth Olympic Park, London).

Kiwi coach Stephen Kearney summed it up nicely when he said: 'It wasn't the prettiest game but it was a good old Test match.'

Kearney had surprised everybody, apart from those in the Kiwi camp, by picking Brisbane's Nikorima at scrum-half after announcing in midweek that he wouldn't even be in the 17-man squad, opting instead for the more experienced Lewis Brown as the bench hooker option. He went ahead with that plan and also the one to have Brisbane utility forward Alex Glenn on the bench in place of Sio Siua Taukeiaho.

But when the team was announced on the Saturday, Nikorima was in, with Tuimoala Lolohea dropping out.

As well as resulting in not a single New Zealand Warriors player from 2015 being in the starting 13, it provided a bit of a surprise for the England side. And the 21-year-old, whilst used to playing the last 20 minutes off the bench as a dummy-half for the Broncos, looked more of a natural halfback than the supremely talented Lolohea.

There were some outstanding efforts, none more so than from co-captains Adam Blair and Issac Luke, while the coach wanted to give a post-match mention to back-rower Tohu Harris.

Brisbane prop Blair played first receiver with aplomb, committing the England line every time he took the ball up before releasing. His virtuoso performance included a through-the-legs offload in the first half. And in the second half he produced a no-look one-handed dropped pass in front of the England posts, never before seen, certainly not in a Test match.

Luke was good in the first half and, in the second he came back on the field for the last half-hour to torment England with his kicks to the corner. His only blot was missing a very kickable penalty on 70 minutes that would have given the Kiwis a two-score advantage.

For England, it was a massive disappointment. They weathered a dominant Kiwi side better than the previous week at Hull when they trailed 10-0 at the 20-minute mark. But this week they couldn't get on top, although they tried their damnedest, with Tom Burgess and Mike Cooper again adding impetus off the bench and James Graham and Chris Hill in particular upping the ante in the last quarter.

But in the main New Zealand had the England halves taped, with 21-year-old George Williams not having a happy time and the outside backs given little to go at. Wigan's John Bateman's creative limitations as a centre became more and more apparent as the game wore on after he had starred in the first half with some rock-solid defence and a couple of stirring half-breaks.

The rain had stopped by kick-off and England took a tentative lead in the eighth minute. Blair's interference on Sean O'Loughlin on halfway gave England their first penalty, followed almost instantly by Sam Moa holding down Chris Hill on the second tackle. From 20 metres out, Widdop kicked the goal for 2-0.

But England couldn't find much field position after that, with some poor kicks under pressure. They had to find some special defence to keep the Kiwis out.

A Blair offload allowed Jordan Kahu to find Jason Nightingale - another standout - ten metres out and only a knock down by Joe Burgess saved the try. The pressure did tell with Luke's equalising penalty when, after Blair audacious through-the-legs pass, Graham held down Peta Hiku under the sticks.

New Zealand had another kickable penalty five minutes later for Josh Hodgson's interference on Blair, but they chose to run it and it looked like a smart move as Kahu slid for the line, but he was stopped by Zak Hardaker. After a repeat set the ball was moved left where Harris's inside ball on the line was spilled by Hiku, who would have been a certain scorer. A massive cheer went up from the 44,393 people in the stands.

It was deadlock but the portents for England weren't great at the start of the second half. On the end of the first set a mix-up on halfway saw Roby pass forward from dummy-half to Tom Burgess. It proved to be England's downfall.

New Zealand worked to the right and Nikorima had a tilt at the line. He looked to be held by Widdop and Bateman but managed to drop a pass backwards for Harris to show brilliant handling skills and send Kenny-Dowall in. The video referee confirmed there was no knock-on and Kahu - with Luke off the field having a rest - put the goal over from the touchline.

There was going to be no black and white fade-out this week, even though Tuivasa-Sheck dropped the restart. The Kiwis forced three GLDOs in four minutes after Nikorima dropped Blair's pass as a try beckoned and Joe Burgess had taken Hiku's bomb superbly.

England's defence had to fold and when Hiku brushed off Williams in the left channel it looked game, set and match. But somehow Brett Ferres stopped Hiku grounding the ball one-handed, as proven by the video.

Williams' pass on his own '30' to Ryan Hall's ankles that was knocked on looked like curtains again but Luke put an easy penalty-goal attempt wide after Elliott Whitehead's interference on Hiku.

England could still save it and after Ben Matulino knocked on just inside the England half everybody thought they had. After a great Hill charge, dummy-half Hodgson slid a deft kick under the posts and Graham was first there to drop on the ball.

Referee Gerard Sutton - who had got in the way as Graham went for the ball - gave the try but asked for video confirmation, which, after much scrutiny and to the displeasure of the crowd, showed Graham had overshot the ball and grounded it with the top of his legs.

A minute later at the other end a ricocheted kick down the left ended with Kahu and Nightingale combining at speed to send Nikorima in, but video was again needed to prove Whitehead's amazing tackle from behind had stopped the halfback short of the line and he had then lost the ball.

There was still hope but, after Bateman dropped the ball on contact on halfway, it was all over when Kahu coolly slotted a field goal from 20 metres out. With four minutes to go, that was that.

England wrapped up their first series win since 2007 with a 20-14 victory at Wigan on another rainy and cold Saturday thanks to another mighty defensive effort which kept New Zealand out when they threatened so often.

After the attacking drought of the previous week's game in London, coach Steve McNamara - in the last game of his contract - made two changes. As expected he started the two players he had brought into the squad in midweek with Huddersfield's Jermaine McGillvary replacing Joe Burgess on the right wing and Matty Smith coming in for clubmate George Williams at scrum-half.

McGillvary certainly showed his worth right from the off when his super strong kick return won the game's first penalty. The Kiwis had probably heard he was a strong man but it was obvious they were shocked by how strong, as on several occasions he managed to stay on his feet in four-man tackles. And his majestic defusing of a Peta Hiku bomb into the in-goal under pressure from Jason Nightingale on the hour mark proved crucial, as two minutes later Elliott Whitehead was in for his second try and the Albert Baskerville Shield was on its way back to Red Hall.

Smith provided a great anchor and put in several kicks that turned Kiwi fullback Roger Tuivasa-Sheck around on his own line, as well as providing the pass that gave Whitehead an inch of space for that vital try.

This was another bash-athon that New Zealand would have won but for a mighty effort from England. The Kiwis broke the England line several times in the first half, only for some breathless cover to deny them. And in the third quarter, when they attacked almost incessantly, the England scramble harassed them into mistakes.

New Zealand looked the most threatening with the ball in the first half, even though England led them 8-6 at the break.

Three times they had looked certain scorers down the left wing before Jason Nightingale finally got the ball down in the corner in the 36th minute.

The try was one of the most spectacular in Test history as the Kiwis feigned to kick

THIRD TEST

Saturday 14th November 2015

ENGLAND 20 NEW ZEALAND 14

ENGLAND: 1 Zak Hardaker (Leeds Rhinos); 2 Jermaine McGillvary (Huddersfield Giants); 3 Kallum Watkins (Leeds Rhinos); 4 John Bateman (Wigan Warriors); 5 Ryan Hall (Leeds Rhinos); 6 Gareth Widdop (St George Illawarra Dragons); 7 Matty Smith (Wigan Warriors); 8 James Graham (Canterbury Bulldogs); 9 Josh Hodgson (Canberra Raiders); 10 Chris Hill (Warrington Wolves); 11 Elliott Whitehead (Catalans Dragons); 12 Liam Farrell (Wigan Warriors); 13 Sean O'Loughlin (Wigan Warriors) (C). Subs (all used): 14 James Roby (St Helens); 15 Tom Burgess (South Sydney Rabbitohs); 16 Mike Cooper (St George Illawarra Dragons); 17 Brett Ferres (Huddersfield Giants).
Tries: Whitehead (27, 63), O'Loughlin (72); **Goals:** Widdop 4/4.
NEW ZEALAND: 1 Roger Tuivasa-Sheck (Sydney Roosters); 5 Shaun Kenny-Dowall (Sydney Roosters); 4 Dean Whare (Penrith Panthers); 3 Jordan Kahu (Brisbane Broncos); 2 Jason Nightingale (St George Illawarra Dragons); 6 Peta Hiku (Manly Sea Eagles); 7 Kodi Nikorima (Brisbane Broncos); 8 Jesse Bromwich (Melbourne Storm); 9 Issac Luke (South Sydney Rabbitohs) (C); 10 Sam Moa (Sydney Roosters); 11 Kevin Proctor (Melbourne Storm); 12 Tohu Harris (Melbourne Storm); 13 Adam Blair (Brisbane Broncos) (C). Subs (all used): 14 Lewis Brown (Penrith Panthers); 15 Martin Taupau (Wests Tigers); 16 Ben Matulino (New Zealand Warriors); 17 Alex Glenn (Brisbane Broncos).
Tries: Nightingale (36), Tuivasa-Sheck (75), Kahu (78);
Goals: Luke 1/3.
Rugby Leaguer & League Express Men of the Match:
England: Mike Cooper; *New Zealand:* Jason Nightingale.
Penalty count: 9-6; **Half-time:** 8-6;
Referee: Ben Thaler (England); **Attendance:** 24,741
(at DW Stadium, Wigan).

on the last but instead spread the ball left. Jordan Kahu made the initial half break and fed Kodi Nikorima on the inside and his pass back outside gave Nightingale just enough space this time to beat Zak Hardaker to the line. It was a trademark 21st Century winger's finish as Nightingale leapt to evade Hardaker's challenge and plant the ball down while his body was high in the air.

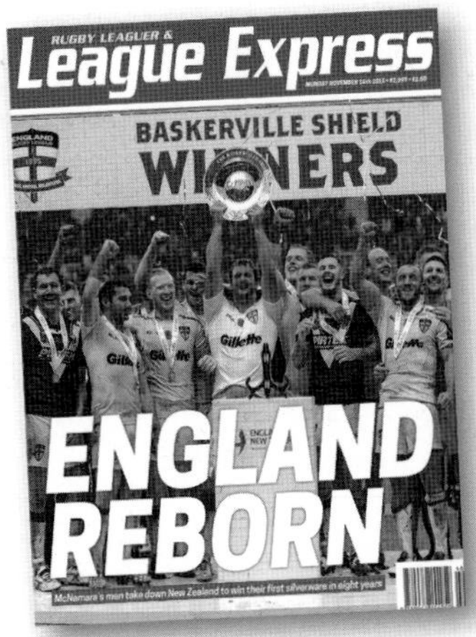

Before that, Hardaker had been one of the heroes of a committed cover defence. Five minutes before the try, Hardaker had tackled Nightingale into touch as he sped for the corner and, as early as the ninth minute, McGillvary and Kallum Watkins had combined to deny the winger after Issac Luke had gone through the England defence like a knife through butter. On their next attack the Kiwis took the same route but Nightingale was again forced into touch.

By that stage England led 2-0 thanks to an easy Gareth Widdop penalty goal as New Zealand struggled to contain the hosts.

Hardaker's kick-off had trapped Tuivasa-Sheck after a daring pass from Shaun Kenny-Dowall to his fullback in his in-goal had kept the ball in play. Widdop's kick on the end of the next set didn't look too promising but when the Kiwis kicked to McGillvary his ferocious return tempted Nightingale to illegally slow down his play-the-ball. In the next set Adam Blair held down Chris Hill under the New Zealand sticks and the two points were impossible to resist.

After Smith was clattered putting up his clearing kick the Kiwis went left again and Nightingale touched down in the left corner but the video referees saw instantly that Kahu's pass inside had been knocked forward by Hiku.

When Hill inexplicably tried to offload on the exit set it seemed certain the Kiwis would claim the game's first try but Whitehead's tackle on Hiku as he tore for the line managed to force a knock on and a rousing break by John Bateman got England on the front foot. Moa held down Hill and then a penalty for a high tackle by Ben Matulino on James Roby would have provided another relatively easy shot at goal, but the ball was worked right from the tap where Watkins beat Kahu, but his inside pass to a static Hardaker fell short of its target.

But when Luke illegally held down McGillvary, England made the breakthrough, Smith's grubber to the line was deflected by Luke's boot to sit up perfectly for Whitehead to collect and dive over. Widdop kicked the goal from ten metres to the right of the posts.

The 8-nil lead lasted seven minutes and it was 8-6 after Luke converted Nightingale's try from the touchline.

As the teams came back after half-time the rain became heavier and a good Smith kick was matched by Peta Hiku as New Zealand turned the screw. England's only ray of light came when Ryan Hall had the chance to collect Bateman's grubber, but he couldn't hold the ball and would probably have been penalised for pushing Tuivasa-Sheck in the back.

Most of the action was at the other end. Widdop had to race back to bring down Tuivasa-Sheck as he broke through the ruck, Hardaker had to put Whare's grubber dead, Hall made a half break from deep but his inside pass went to ground and Watkins knocked on playing the ball just inside the England half.

But in between, Smith's kicking kept New Zealand temporarily in their own half and when they were at the other end they couldn't make the ball stick. Sub Alex Glenn spilled a pass under pressure from Whitehead. And Tuivasa-Sheck lost possession from

Zak Hardaker shows his delight as Elliott Whitehead dives over to score his first try of the Third Test

Nikorima's inside ball thanks to another Widdop tackle.

Hiku tried another strategy on the hour mark with his kick to the corner for Nightingale but McGillvary leapt high with his hands outstretched to catch the ball. A high tackle, the penalty looked harsh, by Hiku on Whitehead took England to the Kiwi '20' and after Blair had scragged a charging Bateman to the ground, James Graham and Smith moved the ball right for Whitehead to get round the on-rushing Kahu and hand off Tohu Harris for a fine try. Widdop's goal made it a two-score advantage.

There was no Kiwi collapse and only a rush-tackle by McGillvary prevented Tuivasa-Sheck creating an overlap. But when Kahu's interference on Whitehead relieved the siege, a superb charge to the posts by Mike Cooper, who had been a standout all series, set up camp for Sean O'Loughlin to charge through a gap at the ruck and score the decisive try by the right upright, the video referee agreeing with Ben Thaler that he had grounded the ball in Tuivasa-Sheck's tackle.

Graham dropped the kick-off, O'Loughlin gave away a penalty and Nightingale's wonder reverse pass as he headed for touch found Tuivasa-Sheck, who video ruled had got the ball down.

Luke couldn't kick the rushed goal attempt. Ten points in it and when another frantic attack by Tuivasa-Sheck down the right ended with Nikorima's kick to open space on the left, it was six points as Kahu collected and slid over. Luke's conversion was this time much more kickable but the ball hit the right upright and bounced out.

It was a relief for England as the Kiwis could now only draw, with 70 seconds of the game left when Hardaker lofted the restart. The hooter had sounded when Tuivasa-Sheck had a tilt down the left. But his pass went to ground and Whitehead hoofed the ball into touch.

There were two games as preparation for the series, played on the weekend before the first Test at Hull.

England hammered France, in a game which had full Test status, 84-4 at Leigh Sports Village.

France coach Richard Agar was denied the services of up to a dozen top stars and the inexperienced line-up was not in the same league as England, who fielded four debutants including Wigan's back-rower John Bateman, who was man of the match playing in the centre. The game was over by the time Bateman scored England's third try after just eight minutes of the match.

There were 15 tries in total, including a hat-trick for Huddersfield back-rower Brett Ferres.

The evening before at Headingley, the Kiwis underwent more of a test against a far from full-strength Leeds side - which included returning guest players in Adrian Morley and Ali Lauitiiti - in front of a near-capacity crowd of over 20,000.

New Zealand won a superb match 34-16.

Fullback Ashton Golding, in a magnificent duel with Roger Tuivasa-Sheck, excelled, vying for home man-of-the-match with fellow 19-year-old halfback Jordan Lilley.

Youth was also the centrepiece for the Kiwis, specifically in the key halfback roles, where unfamiliar pairing Peta Hiku and debutant Tuimoala Lolohea looked to cement their combination ahead of the Test series.

Like their side, they grew into the game, with three tries in five minutes just after the hour turning the outcome the tourists' way, although it was at hooker that they posed the most danger. Co-skipper Issac Luke was magnificent running out of dummy-half and positioning the big men up front into space. Youngster Kodi Nikorima then took over with his explosive speed and tricky footwork to capitalise on the tiring Rhinos.

TEST SERIES WARM-UP MATCH

Friday 23rd October 2015

LEEDS RHINOS 16 NEW ZEALAND 34

RHINOS: 1 Ashton Golding; 2 Tom Briscoe; 3 Jimmy Keinhorst; 4 Joel Moon; 5 Ash Handley; 6 Danny McGuire (C); 7 Jordan Lilley; 8 Kylie Leuluai; 9 Robbie Ward; 11 Adrian Morley (Guest); 14 Ali Lauitiiti (Guest); 12 Josh Walters; 13 Adam Cuthbertson. Subs (all used): 10 Mitch Garbutt; 19 Brad Singleton; 16 Mitch Achurch; 15 Anthony Mullally; 17 Jordan Baldwinson; 18 Rob Mulhern.
Tries: Moon (26, 53), T Briscoe (69); **Goals:** Lilley 2/3.
NEW ZEALAND: 1 Roger Tuivasa-Sheck (Sydney Roosters); 2 Jason Nightingale (St George Illawarra Dragons); 3 Jordan Kahu (Brisbane Broncos); 4 Dean Whare (Penrith Panthers); 5 Shaun Kenny-Dowall (Sydney Roosters); 6 Peta Hiku (Manly Sea Eagles); 7 Tuimoala Lolohea (New Zealand Warriors); 8 Jesse Bromwich (Melbourne Storm); 9 Issac Luke (South Sydney Rabbitohs) (C); 10 Ben Matulino (New Zealand Warriors); 11 Kevin Proctor (Melbourne Storm); 12 Tohu Harris (Melbourne Storm); 13 Martin Taupau (Wests Tigers). Subs (all used): 16 Sam Moa (Sydney Roosters); 15 Adam Blair (Brisbane Broncos) (C); 17 Sio Siua Taukeiaho (Sydney Roosters); 18 Alex Glenn (Brisbane Broncos); 20 Lewis Brown (Penrith Panthers); 14 Kodi Nikorima (Brisbane Broncos).
Tries: Nightingale (33), Kahu (38), Bromwich (61), Whare (63), Tuivasa-Sheck (66, 78), Nikorima (74); **Goals:** Luke 1/2, Lolohea 2/5.
Rugby Leaguer & League Express Men of the Match:
Rhinos: Ashton Golding; *New Zealand:* Issac Luke.
Penalty count: 5-8; **Half-time:** 6-10; **Referee:** Richard Silverwood; **Attendance:** 20,158.

TEST MATCH

Saturday 24th October 2015

ENGLAND 84 FRANCE 4

ENGLAND: 1 Zak Hardaker (Leeds Rhinos); 2 Joe Burgess (Wigan Warriors); 3 Kallum Watkins (Leeds Rhinos); 4 John Bateman (Wigan Warriors); 5 Ryan Hall (Leeds Rhinos); 6 Gareth Widdop (St George Illawarra Dragons); 7 George Williams (Wigan Warriors); 8 James Graham (Canterbury Bulldogs); 9 Josh Hodgson (Canberra Raiders); 10 Chris Hill (Warrington Wolves); 11 Elliott Whitehead (Catalans Dragons); 12 Liam Farrell (Wigan Warriors); 13 Sean O'Loughlin (Wigan Warriors) (C). Subs (all used): 14 James Roby (St Helens); 15 Tom Burgess (South Sydney Rabbitohs); 16 Mike Cooper (St George Illawarra Dragons); 17 Brett Ferres (Huddersfield Giants).
Tries: Watkins (2), Hodgson (6), Bateman (8, 40), Farrell (14), Hall (36, 61), T Burgess (42), Ferres (44, 54, 78), Roby (46, 51), Williams (48), J Burgess (65); **Goals:** Widdop 12/15.
FRANCE: 1 Morgan Escare (Catalans Dragons); 2 Jordan Sigismeau (Catalans Dragons); 3 Jean-Philippe Baile (Bradford Bulls); 4 Benjamin Jullien (North Wales Crusaders); 5 Olivier Arnaud (Avignon); 6 Stanislas Robin (Catalans Dragons); 7 Remy Marginet (Featherstone Rovers); 8 Julian Bousquet (Catalans Dragons); 9 John Boudebza (Hull Kingston Rovers); 10 Antoni Maria (Catalans Dragons); 11 Kevin Larroyer (Hull Kingston Rovers); 12 Ugo Perez (Catalans Dragons); 13 Mickael Simon (Wakefield Trinity Wildcats) (C). Subs (all used): 14 Mourad Kriouache (Toulouse Olympique); 15 Gadwin Springer (Castleford Tigers); 16 Clement Boyer (Halifax); 17 Mickail Gourmand (Avignon).
Try: Arnaud (12); **Goals:** Marginet 0/1.
Rugby Leaguer & League Express Men of the Match:
England: John Bateman; *France:* John Boudebza.
Penalty count: 3-2; **Half-time:** 32-4; **Referee:** James Child (England); **Attendance:** 8,380 *(at Leigh Sports Village).*

OTHER INTERNATIONALS
Wales revived

European Championship

EUROPEAN CHAMPIONSHIP - FINAL STANDINGS	P	W	D	L	F	A	D	Pts
Wales	3	3	0	0	62	22	40	6
France	3	2	0	1	73	46	27	4
Ireland	3	1	0	2	42	83	-41	2
Scotland	3	0	0	3	52	78	-26	0

Wales completed a reversal in fortunes by winning the 2015 80th anniversary European Championship, a year after finishing with the wooden spoon and two years after losing every game in a disappointing World Cup campaign in 2013.

But John Kear's side beat Ireland 30-4 in Bray, just south of Dublin, on the last weekend of the tournament to secure the European crown at the expense of second-placed France.

France temporarily moved top of the group on the same day, eventually finishing second after consigning winless Scotland to the wooden spoon with their 32-18 victory in Avignon. For that game Scotland were without captain Danny Brough, who injured his hand in a 22-24 defeat to Ireland at Galashiels - Scott Grix's sensational try on 72 minutes deciding the outcome.

And by the time they travelled to France, holders Scotland were already out of title contention, having lost to Wales in Wrexham in the first game of the Championship by 18-12.

Two weeks later, Wales stunned France - who were on the back of the friendly mauling by England - at Cardiff Arms Park, Gloucestershire All Golds halfback Courtney Davies' try in the 49th minute proving decisive in a 14-6 win.

France had already got a win under their belt by beating a tenacious Ireland in Albi on the first weekend by 31-14. A John Boudebza field goal seven minutes from time was pivotal and late tries to Theo Fages and Kevin Larroyer gave the score a one-sided look.

In the win over Scotland, Tony Gigot produced a top performance, scoring two tries down the right. France needed Wales to lose by 14 or more points to take the title later that day.

But needing only a draw, Wales sealed the game with two tries just before half-time from Steve Parry and Rhodri Lloyd. When man of the match Elliot Kear went over for a try just before the hour mark it was 30-nil and the destiny of the Championship was in no doubt.

** Keighley and Wales met in a game at Cougar Park on Sunday 25th October 2015 to raise funds for Danny Jones' wife Lizzie and young twins Bobby and Phoebe. The game ended in a 36-20 win for Wales.*

Other Internationals

EUROPEAN CHAMPIONSHIP

Friday 16th October 2015

WALES 18 SCOTLAND 12

WALES: 1 Elliot Kear (London Broncos); 2 Rhys Williams (London Broncos); 3 Michael Channing (Castleford Tigers); 4 Christiaan Roets (North Wales Crusaders); 5 Dalton Grant (Dewsbury Rams); 7 Ollie Olds (Souths Logan Magpies); 24 Courtney Davies (Gloucestershire All Golds); 17 Anthony Walker (Wakefield Trinity Wildcats); 18 Steve Parry (Gloucestershire All Golds); 10 Craig Kopczak (Huddersfield Giants) (C); 11 Rhodri Lloyd (Swinton Lions); 14 Lewis Reece (Gloucestershire All Golds); 13 Phil Joseph (Widnes Vikings). Subs: 12 Morgan Knowles (St Helens); 20 Joe Burke (North Wales Crusaders); 21 Matt Barron (Newcastle Thunder); 25 Jamie Murphy (Gloucestershire All Golds) (not used).
Tries: Parry (9), Grant (37), Walker (64); **Goals:** Davies 3/5.
SCOTLAND: 1 Oscar Thomas (London Broncos); 2 Dave Scott (Doncaster); 3 Ben Hellewell (London Broncos); 4 Harvey Burnett (unattached); 5 Alex Walker (London Broncos); 6 Danny Brough (Huddersfield Giants) (C); 7 Danny Addy (Bradford Bulls); 8 Adam Walker (Hull Kingston Rovers); 9 Liam Hood (Salford Red Devils); 10 Jonathan Walker (London Broncos); 11 Sonny Esslemont (Hull Kingston Rovers); 12 Dale Ferguson (Bradford Bulls); 13 Ben Kavanagh (Widnes Vikings). Subs (all used): 14 Joe McClean (Gloucestershire All Golds); 15 Corbyn Kilday (Central Queensland Capras); 16 Richard Harris (Warrington Wolves); 17 Scott Plumridge (Edinburgh Eagles).
Tries: Ferguson (27), Thomas (78); **Goals:** Brough 2/2.
Rugby Leaguer & League Express Men of the Match:
Wales: Steve Parry; *Scotland:* Liam Hood.
Penalty count: 9-9; **Half-time:** 12-6; **Referee:** Joe Cobb (England);
Attendance: 1,253 *(at Glyndwr University Racecourse Stadium, Wrexham).*

Saturday 17th October 2015

FRANCE 31 IRELAND 14

FRANCE: 1 Morgan Escare (Catalans Dragons); 2 Jordan Sigismeau (Catalans Dragons); 3 Tony Gigot (Catalans Dragons); 4 Benjamin Jullien (North Wales Crusaders); 14 Stanislas Robin (Catalans Dragons); 6 Theo Fages (unattached); 7 Remy Marginet (Featherstone Rovers); 8 Julian Bousquet (Catalans Dragons); 9 John Boudebza (Hull Kingston Rovers); 10 Mickael Simon (Wakefield Trinity Wildcats) (C); 11 Kevin Larroyer (Hull Kingston Rovers); 12 Ugo Perez (Catalans Dragons); 13 Gadwin Springer (Castleford Tigers). Subs (all used): 19 William Barthau (London Broncos); 15 Jean-Philippe Baile (Bradford Bulls); 16 Clement Boyer (Halifax); 17 Antoni Maria (Catalans Dragons).
Tries: Robin (24), Sigismeau (29), Gigot (44, 74), Fages (49), Larroyer (77);
Goals: Marginet 2/4, Barthau 1/2; **Field goal:** Boudebza (73).
IRELAND: 1 Scott Grix (Huddersfield Giants); 2 Bradley Hargreaves (Rochdale Hornets); 3 James Mendeika (Bradford Bulls); 4 Elliott Cosgrove (Batley Bulldogs); 5 Casey Dunne (Athboy Longhorns); 6 Ben Johnston (Halifax); 7 Liam Finn (Castleford Tigers) (C); 8 Danny Bridge (Rochdale Hornets); 9 Bob Beswick (Leigh Centurions); 10 Luke Ambler (Halifax); 11 Haydn Peacock (Carcassonne); 12 Will Hope (Oldham); 13 Oliver Roberts (Huddersfield Giants). Subs (all used): 14 Joe Keyes (London Broncos); 15 Graham O'Keeffe (Gloucestershire All Golds); 16 Callum Mulkeen (Gloucestershire All Golds); 17 Matty Hadden (Rochdale Hornets).
Tries: Dunne (19), Hargreaves (53); **Goals:** Finn 3/3.
Rugby Leaguer & League Express Men of the Match:
France: Tony Gigot; *Ireland:* Liam Finn.
Penalty count: 6-4; **Half-time:** 8-8; **Referee:** Phil Bentham (England);
Attendance: 4,681 *(at Stadium Municipal, Albi).*

Friday 23rd October 2015

SCOTLAND 22 IRELAND 24

SCOTLAND: 1 Dave Scott (Doncaster); 2 Shane Toal (Barrow Raiders); 4 Richard Harris (Warrington Wolves); 3 Ben Hellewell (London Broncos); 5 Alex Walker (London Broncos); 6 Danny Brough (Huddersfield Giants) (C); 7 Oscar Thomas (London Broncos); 8 Ben Kavanagh (Widnes Vikings); 9 Liam Hood (Salford Red Devils); 10 Jonathan Walker (London Broncos); 11 Sonny Esslemont (Hull Kingston Rovers); 12 Dale Ferguson (Bradford Bulls); 13 Danny Addy (Bradford Bulls). Subs (all used): 14 Joe McClean (Gloucestershire All Golds); 15 Corbyn Kilday (Central Queensland Capras); 16 Lewis Clarke (Edinburgh Eagles); 17 Harvey Burnett (unattached).
Tries: Addy (16, 43), Toal (46), Ferguson (59); **Goals:** Brough 3/4.
IRELAND: 1 Scott Grix (Huddersfield Giants); 2 Bradley Hargreaves (Rochdale Hornets); 3 James Mendeika (Bradford Bulls); 4 Elliott Cosgrove (Batley Bulldogs); 5 Casey Dunne (Athboy Longhorns); 6 Ben Johnston (Halifax); 7 Liam Finn (Castleford Tigers) (C); 8 Matty Hadden (Rochdale Hornets); 9 Bob Beswick (Leigh Centurions); 10 Luke Ambler (Halifax); 11 Danny Bridge (Rochdale Hornets); 12 Will Hope (Oldham); 13 Oliver Roberts (Huddersfield Giants). Subs (all used): 14 Callum Mulkeen (Gloucestershire All Golds); 15 Graham O'Keeffe (Gloucestershire All Golds); 16 Joe Keyes (London Broncos); 17 Sean Hesketh (Batley Bulldogs).
Tries: Ambler (8, 33), Hargreaves (13), Grix (72); **Goals:** Finn 4/5.
Rugby Leaguer & League Express Men of the Match:
Scotland: Shane Toal; *Ireland:* Will Hope.
Penalty count: 5-5; **Half-time:** 4-18; **Referee:** Chris Kendall (England);
Attendance: 1,197 *(at Netherdale Stadium, Galashiels).*

Friday 30th October 2015

WALES 14 FRANCE 6

WALES: 1 Elliot Kear (London Broncos); 2 Rhys Williams (London Broncos); 3 Michael Channing (Castleford Tigers); 4 Christiaan Roets (North Wales Crusaders); 5 Dalton Grant (Dewsbury Rams); 7 Ollie Olds (Souths Logan Magpies); 24 Courtney Davies (Gloucestershire All Golds); 17 Anthony Walker (Wakefield Trinity Wildcats); 18 Steve Parry (Gloucestershire All Golds); 10 Craig Kopczak (Huddersfield Giants) (C); 11 Rhodri Lloyd (Swinton Lions); 14 Lewis Reece (Gloucestershire All Golds); 13 Phil Joseph (Widnes Vikings). Subs (all used): 8 Morgan Evans (Coventry Bears); 19 Connor Farrer (South Wales Scorpions); 20 Joe Burke (North Wales Crusaders); 22 Regan Grace (St Helens).
Tries: Grant (23), Burke (45), Davies (48); **Goals:** Davies 1/3.
FRANCE: 1 Morgan Escare (Catalans Dragons); 2 Jordan Sigismeau (Catalans Dragons); 3 Tony Gigot (Catalans Dragons); 4 Jean-Philippe Baile (Bradford Bulls); 5 Olivier Arnaud (Avignon); 6 Theo Fages (unattached); 7 William Barthau (London Broncos); 8 Julian Bousquet (Catalans Dragons); 9 John Boudebza (Hull Kingston Rovers); 10 Mickael Simon (Wakefield Trinity Wildcats) (C); 11 Kevin Larroyer (Hull Kingston Rovers); 12 Ugo Perez (Catalans Dragons); 13 Jason Baitieri (Catalans Dragons). Subs (all used): 14 Stanislas Robin (Catalans Dragons); 15 Antoni Maria (Catalans Dragons); 16 Gadwin Springer (Castleford Tigers); 17 Benjamin Jullien (North Wales Crusaders).
Try: Simon (71); **Goals:** Barthau 1/1.
Rugby Leaguer & League Express Men of the Match:
Wales: Courtney Davies; *France:* Tony Gigot.
Penalty count: 8-13; **Half-time:** 4-0; **Referee:** Robert Hicks (England);
Attendance: 1,028 *(at Cardiff Arms Park).*

Saturday 7th November 2015

FRANCE 32 SCOTLAND 18

FRANCE: 1 Morgan Escare (Catalans Dragons); 2 Jordan Sigismeau (Catalans Dragons); 3 Tony Gigot (Catalans Dragons); 4 Benjamin Jullien (North Wales Crusaders); 5 Olivier Arnaud (Avignon); 6 Stanislas Robin (Catalans Dragons); 7 Remy Marginet (Featherstone Rovers); 8 Julian Bousquet (Catalans Dragons); 9 John Boudebza (Hull Kingston Rovers); 10 Mickael Simon (Wakefield Trinity Wildcats) (C); 11 Kevin Larroyer (Hull Kingston Rovers); 12 Ugo Perez (Catalans Dragons); 13 Jason Baitieri (Catalans Dragons). Subs (all used): 14 William Barthau (London Broncos); 15 Jean-Philippe Baile (Bradford Bulls); 16 Gadwin Springer (Castleford Tigers); 17 Florent Rouanet (Carcassonne).
Tries: Arnaud (3), Gigot (15, 38), Larroyer (22), Escare (26), Robin (30), Perez (60); **Goals:** Marginet 2/7.
SCOTLAND: 1 Dave Scott (Doncaster); 2 Shane Toal (Barrow Raiders); 3 Harvey Burnett (unattached); 4 Richard Harris (Warrington Wolves); 5 Alex Walker (London Broncos); 6 Danny Addy (Bradford Bulls); 7 Oscar Thomas (London Broncos); 8 Joe McClean (Gloucestershire All Golds); 9 Liam Hood (Salford Red Devils); 10 Ben Kavanagh (Widnes Vikings); 11 Sonny Esslemont (Hull Kingston Rovers); 12 Dale Ferguson (Bradford Bulls) (C); 13 Sam Brooks (Whitehaven). Subs (all used): 14 Scott Plumridge (Edinburgh Eagles); 15 Gavin Grant (Coventry Bears); 16 Lewis Clarke (Edinburgh Eagles); 17 Finlay Hutchinson (Edinburgh Eagles).
Tries: Toal (9), Scott (66), Hood (70); **Goals:** Thomas 3/3.
Rugby Leaguer & League Express Men of the Match:
France: Tony Gigot; *Scotland:* Oscar Thomas.
Penalty count: 3-3; **Half-time:** 28-6; **Referee:** Gareth Hewer (England);
Attendance: 5,737 *(at Parc des Sports, Avignon).*

IRELAND 4 WALES 30

IRELAND: 1 Scott Grix (Huddersfield Giants); 2 Bradley Hargreaves (Rochdale Hornets); 3 Callum Mulkeen (Gloucestershire All Golds); 4 Elliott Cosgrove (Batley Bulldogs); 5 Casey Dunne (Athboy Longhorns); 6 Ben Johnston (Halifax); 7 Liam Finn (Castleford Tigers) (C); 8 Matty Hadden (Rochdale Hornets); 9 Bob Beswick (Leigh Centurions); 10 Luke Ambler (Halifax); 11 Danny Bridge (Rochdale Hornets); 12 Will Hope (Oldham); 13 Oliver Roberts (Huddersfield Giants). Subs (all used): 14 Joe Keyes (London Broncos); 15 Rob Mulhern (Leeds Rhinos); 16 Haydn Peacock (Carcassonne); 17 Gareth Gill (Ballynahinch Rabbitohs).
Try: Mulkeen (72); **Goals:** Finn 0/1.
WALES: 1 Elliot Kear (London Broncos); 2 Rhys Williams (London Broncos); 3 Michael Channing (Castleford Tigers); 4 Christiaan Roets (North Wales Crusaders); 5 Dalton Grant (Dewsbury Rams); 7 Ollie Olds (Souths Logan Magpies); 24 Courtney Davies (Gloucestershire All Golds); 17 Anthony Walker (Wakefield Trinity Wildcats); 18 Steve Parry (Gloucestershire All Golds); 10 Craig Kopczak (Huddersfield Giants) (C); 11 Rhodri Lloyd (Swinton Lions); 14 Lewis Reece (Gloucestershire All Golds); 13 Phil Joseph (Widnes Vikings). Subs (all used): 8 Morgan Evans (Coventry Bears); 19 Connor Farrer (South Wales Scorpions); 20 Joe Burke (North Wales Crusaders); 22 Regan Grace (St Helens).
Tries: Grant (7), Reece (20), Parry (33), Lloyd (38), Kear (57);
Goals: Davies 5/6.
Rugby Leaguer & League Express Men of the Match:
Ireland: Will Hope; *Wales:* Elliot Kear.
Penalty count: 8-9; **Half-time:** 0-22; **Referee:** Ben Thaler (England);
Attendance: 1,405 *(at Carlisle Grounds, Bray).*

Anzac Test

The 2015 Anzac Test kicked off 44 hours after it had been originally scheduled, flooding in Brisbane forcing the game to be called off on the Friday night. The postponement didn't bother New Zealand who completely outclassed Australia in a 26-12 triumph at Suncorp Stadium.

It was the Kiwis' first mid-season Test win over the Kangaroos in 17 years, and – following on from their two Four Nations victories at the end of 2014 – their first run of three successive wins over Australia since 1952-53.

Australia coach Tim Sheens took plenty of criticism for fielding an ageing side as the Kangaroos were blown off the park by the Kiwis' attacking brilliance in the second quarter. By half-time they were trailing 26-6. After the break, the Aussies enjoyed 59 per cent possession overall and a wealth of opportunities in the Kiwis' 20-metre zone but, against the committed New Zealand defence, looked totally bereft of ideas.

Australia had no answer to explosive Wests Tigers forward Martin Taupau and wingers Manu Vatuvei and Jason Nightingale. Roger Tuivasa-Sheck was brilliant in his first Test appearance at fullback and Jesse Bromwich was magnificent up front. 2014 Golden Boot winner Shaun Johnson put in another virtuoso Test performance as New Zealand became the highest-ranked nation in Rugby League.

ANZAC TEST

Sunday 3rd May 2015

AUSTRALIA 12 NEW ZEALAND 26

AUSTRALIA: 1 Greg Inglis (South Sydney Rabbitohs); 2 Alex Johnston (South Sydney Rabbitohs); 3 Michael Jennings (Sydney Roosters); 4 Will Chambers (Melbourne Storm); 5 Josh Dugan (St George Illawarra Dragons); 6 Johnathan Thurston (North Queensland Cowboys); 7 Cooper Cronk (Melbourne Storm); 8 Matt Scott (North Queensland Cowboys); 9 Cameron Smith (Melbourne Storm) (C); 10 Aaron Woods (Wests Tigers); 11 Greg Bird (Gold Coast Titans); 12 Sam Thaiday (Brisbane Broncos); 13 Corey Parker (Brisbane Broncos). Subs (all used): 14 Luke Lewis (Cronulla Sharks); 15 Trent Merrin (St George Illawarra Dragons); 16 Nate Myles (Gold Coast Titans); 17 James Tamou (North Queensland Cowboys).
Tries: Thaiday (12), Chambers (58); **Goals:** Thurston 2/2.
NEW ZEALAND: 1 Roger Tuivasa-Sheck (Sydney Roosters); 2 Jason Nightingale (St George Illawarra Dragons); 3 Shaun Kenny-Dowall (Sydney Roosters); 4 Peta Hiku (Manly Sea Eagles); 5 Manu Vatuvei (New Zealand Warriors); 6 Kieran Foran (Manly Sea Eagles); 7 Shaun Johnson (New Zealand Warriors); 8 Jesse Bromwich (Melbourne Storm); 9 Issac Luke (South Sydney Rabbitohs); 10 Ben Matulino (New Zealand Warriors); 11 Tohu Harris (Melbourne Storm); 12 Kevin Proctor (Melbourne Storm); 13 Simon Mannering (New Zealand Warriors) (C). Subs (all used): 14 Thomas Leuluai (New Zealand Warriors); 15 Martin Taupau (Wests Tigers); 16 Sam Moa (Sydney Roosters); 17 Greg Eastwood (Canterbury Bulldogs).
Tries: Vatuvei (20, 28), Johnson (31), Kenny-Dowall (40);
Goals: Johnson 5/6.
Rugby Leaguer & League Express Men of the Match:
Australia: Corey Parker; *New Zealand:* Shaun Johnson.
Penalty count: 7-7; **Half-time:** 6-26; **Referee:** Gerard Sutton (Australia); **Attendance:** 32,681 *(at Suncorp Stadium, Brisbane).*

2017 World Cup Qualifiers

Fourteen teams will contest the 15th Rugby League World Cup to be staged in Australia, New Zealand and Papua New Guinea in 2017, with the qualification process begun in 2015.

Seven of the eight quarter-finalists from the 2013 World Cup qualified automatically; hosts Australia and New Zealand, England, Fiji, France, Samoa and Scotland. The USA, who were also quarter-finalists, were denied automatic qualification after a long-running internal governance dispute saw their RLIF membership temporarily suspended in 2014; they were later accepted to take part in the qualification process once the matter was resolved. Papua New Guinea were to be involved in the qualifying competition but due to becoming co-hosts of the tournament they also automatically qualified. The remaining six spots will come from four different qualification zones; three from Europe, one from Asia/Pacific, one from the Americas and one from Middle East/Africa.

Tonga were the first team to qualify from the qualification stage after winning the Asia-Pacific play-off against Cook Islands in Sydney in October 2015. Lebanon joined them, winning the two-leg Middle East/Africa play-off with South Africa.

USA, Canada and Jamaica were to contest the Americas play-off at the end of 2015, while Wales, Ireland, Russia, Italy, Serbia and Spain will play for the three Euro places at the end of the 2016 season.

2017 WORLD CUP QUALIFIERS

ASIA/PACIFIC
Saturday 17th October 2015
Tonga 28 Cook Islands 8 *(at Campbelltown Stadium, Sydney)*

MIDDLE EAST/AFRICA
Sunday 25th October 2015
South Africa 12 Lebanon 40
Saturday 31st October 2015
South Africa 16 Lebanon 50
(two legs, both at Brakpan, near Pretoria)

European Championship B

Serbia won the 2014-15 European Championship B, which also involved defending champions Russia, Euro B 2012-13 runner-up Italy and Ukraine, who were promoted after winning the 2013 European Bowl. Preparations for the tournament came in the midst of the political crisis involving Russia and Ukraine.

EUROPEAN CHAMPIONSHIP B

Saturday 16th May 2015
Serbia 20 Russia 15
(at Makis Stadium, Belgrade)

Saturday 20th June 2015
Italy 14 Serbia 21
(at Gemona)

Saturday 4th July 2015
Ukraine 20 Russia 34
(at Makis Stadium, Belgrade)

Saturday 18th July 2015
Ukraine 12 Italy 40
(at National University of State Taxation Service of Ukraine)

Saturday 12th September 2015
Russia 26 Italy 6
(at Fily Stadium, Moscow)
Ukraine 4 Serbia 64
(at FC Locomotive Stadium, Chop)

FINAL STANDINGS

	P	W	D	L	F	A	D	Pts
Serbia	6	5	0	1	196	73	123	10
Russia	6	4	0	2	137	92	45	8
Italy	6	3	0	3	142	134	8	6
Ukraine	6	0	0	6	80	256	-176	0

European Championship C

Spain won the European Championship C, which in 2015 formed the opening stages of European Qualification for the 2017 World Cup.

As winner, Spain will join the top three European Championship B nations and 2013 World Cup teams Ireland and Wales in a two-group round robin competition. Spain will also be promoted to European Championship B in 2016, taking the place of Ukraine.

With their country in the midst of a grave economic crisis, 2014 Euro C winners Greece finished last in this year's competition, unable to travel to fulfil their fixture in Malta.

EUROPEAN CHAMPIONSHIP C

Saturday 9th May 2015
Latvia 12 Spain 32
(at Upezhtsiems Stadium, Riga)

Saturday 26th September 2015
Spain 40 Malta 30
(at Polideportivo Cuatre Carreres Stadium, Valencia)

Saturday 10th October 2015
Malta 30 Greece 0
(Greece unable to travel due to national economic crisis)

Saturday 17th October 2015
Greece 4 Spain 76
(at Nikaia Municipality Stadium, Athens)

FINAL STANDINGS

	P	W	D	L	F	A	D	Pts
Spain	2	2	0	0	116	34	82	4
Malta	2	1	0	1	60	40	20	2
Greece	2	0	0	2	4	106	-102	0

MAGELLAN TROPHY

Monday 19th January 2015
Philippines 80 Latin Heat 4
(at Bishop Park, Brisbane)

COLONIAL CUP

Saturday 19th September 2015
Canada 36 USA 28

Saturday 17th October 2015
USA 28 Canada 34

(both at AA Garthwaite Stadium, Conshohocken, Pennsylvania)

PACIFIC TESTS

Saturday 2nd May 2015
Samoa 18 Tonga 16
Papua New Guinea 10 Fiji 22

(both at Cbus Super Stadium, Gold Coast)

NORDIC CUP

Sunday 24th May 2015
Sweden 16 Denmark 30 *(Lund)*

Saturday 13th June 2015
Denmark 24 Norway 12 *(Roskilde)*

Saturday 17th October 2015
Norway 30 Sweden 20 *(Oslo)*

ASIAN CUP

Thursday 15th October 2015
Thailand 30 Japan 6 *(Bangkok)*

OTHER INTERNATIONALS

Saturday 18th April 2015
Belgium 52 Czech Republic 12 *(Brussels)*

Sunday 26th April 2015
South Africa 32 Philippines 28 *(Moorebank)*

Wednesday 29th April 2015
Japan 52 Thailand Stars 16 *(Tokyo)*

Saturday 2nd May 2015
Belgium 60 Netherlands 12 *(Duivensteyn)*

Saturday 2nd May 2015
South Africa 4 Niue 48 *(Campbelltown)*

Sunday 3rd May 2015
Lebanon 34 Malta 16 *(St Mary's, Sydney)*

Friday 22nd May 2015
France A 68 Serbia 8 *(St Esteve)*

Saturday 6th June 2015
Spain 16 Germany 32 *(Valencia)*

Saturday 20th June 2015
Germany 46 Netherlands 12 *(Gnarrenburg)*

Sunday 21st June 2015
Belgium 34 Malta 35 *(Headingley)*

Sunday 12th July 2015
Ireland 34 Belgium 0 *(Bray)*

Saturday 18th July 2015
Samoa Residents 20 Tonga Residents 4 *(Honolulu)*

Saturday 25th July 2015
Czech Republic 12 Sweden 40 *(Brod)*

Saturday 29th August 2015
Serbia 16 Ireland 24 *(Belgrade)*

Saturday 5th September 2015
Malta 22 Ireland 34 *(Pembroke)*

Saturday 26th September 2015
Papua New Guinea PM XIII 12 Australia PM XIII 40 *(Port Moresby)*

Saturday 3rd October 2015
Czech Republic 14 Belgium 4 *(Tiss)*

Saturday 3rd October 2015
Niue 44 Cook Islands 22 *(Wentworthville, Sydney)*

SEASON DOWN UNDER
Simply the best

Queenslander, Queenslander! It was the catch-cry invoked by Australian Test backrower Billy Moore before the State of Origin series in 1995 that inspired the Maroons to a shock victory.

It was also the scream that reverberated around the Olympic stadium at Homebush before, through and after the 2015 Grand Final.

And with good reason. The season's decider created history when, for the first time, two Queensland clubs fought for the ultimate NRL prize. Brisbane Broncos versus North Queensland Cowboys. It stuck in the craw of NSW fans who had watched the Cowboys knock out Cronulla Sharks before Brisbane disposed of the Minor Premiers Sydney Roosters.

It was a packed house, with every available flight from the Sunshine State sold out as fans from north of the border struggled to make it to the season finale and buy tickets from disappointed New South Welshmen. Indeed, xenophobic Queensland fans went to extraordinary lengths to be at Homebush. Many paid massive airfares to fly overseas to Bali in Indonesia or Auckland in New Zealand and back in order to be there. They could have flown to Britain and return for less. Others took advantage of charter flights on aircraft especially flown in from Asia.

They were richly rewarded as they witnessed what many keen judges suggested was the finest Grand Final in history.

The North Queensland Cowboys, inspired by one of the legends of the game, Johnathan Thurston, created a fairytale finish. In decades to come those among the 82,758 in the stands will relate their experiences to their grandchildren. They will explain how they treasured the moment when Thurston inspired a late rally to set up an amazing finish.

The Cowboys were trailing by four points when JT danced away from potential defenders, this way and that, before his halfback partner-in-crime Michael Morgan made an amazing flick pass to right winger Kyle Feldt, who touched down as the final siren was sounding. Thurston then lined up a conversion attempt from near the right sideline which could possibly win the game. The ball bounced off the right upright, sending the game into 'golden-point' extra time. It mattered not. From the kick-off for an extra 10 minutes each way, Broncos half Ben Hunt fumbled. And within a few moments Thurston had snapped the winning field goal to ensure North Queensland Cowboys snared the first Premiership success in their two-decade history.

JT was shaking when interviewed after the success: 'This is unbelievable what we have just done. They (the Cowboys) working so hard every day during the season. I love the club.'

It was a spine-tingling match from the kick-off. The Broncos were obviously expecting a close game when they opted for a Corey Parker penalty goal after five minutes. One wondered why, especially when there was an explosive run from the restart. Big Adam Blair started a move 10 metres from the Brisbane line with a wonderful offload. The ball passed through the hands of Anthony Milford and England Test man Jack Reed before

Corey Oates sped 70 metres down the left flank to score.

It took only a couple of minutes for the Cowboys to hit back. Hooker Jake Granville found a gap in the defence and gave centre Justin O'Neill the advantage to touch down for the try that lifted the North Queensland players. It was razzle-dazzle, something no one had expected after Grand Finals in recent years. Milford and Reed were involved in another exciting run. Backwards and forwards the ball went at lightning speed. Wonderful!

Midway through the half the Cowboys finally edged ahead when Granville, one of the real finds of the season, found a gap for Test prop James Tamou to surge over the tryline. It was a rare mistake by Thurston that gave the Broncos the opportunity to get back in the lead when he lost the ball in a crunching tackle. Young international Matt Gillett snapped up the loose ball and Reed was on hand to score. A video replay ruled against a possible strip.

The Broncos' lead of 14-12 at 'oranges' made sure the result remained in the balance – especially with the exhaustion that was already showing in the faces of those involved in such a stirring season decider.

Brisbane started the second half virtually the same way as they started the first, with winger Jordan Kahu accepting a penalty goal after the Cowboys infringed in a tackle on Reed.

The Cowboys rose when Thurston found a new lease of life midway through the second half. And there was hope for the North Queensland fans when Lachlan Coote swivelled and slammed the ball down behind the tryline.

But it was obviously a double movement. No try ... penalty!

It set up the exciting finish

Here's how the clubs fared during the season.

NORTH QUEENSLAND COWBOYS (Premiers)

Fairytales can come true! It may have been two decades in the making – but the wait was well worth it for the Rugby League enthusiasts in the Queensland tropics, some of whom travel more than 1000 kilometres (625 miles) to watch their beloved Cowboys' home games in Townsville. How sweet was their victory. Those three wooden spoons and a couple more near misses in the first six seasons in the big league are now little more than a faint, distant memory.

The Paul Green-coached Cowboys lost their first three outings in 2015 before stringing together a club record 11 straight victories to show they meant business. They had two big wins in their first two appearances in the finals before the dramatic last-second effort to pull the Grand Final out of the fire. With 17 members of the Grand Final squad still with the club, North Queensland will be hard to beat in 2016.

Co-captains Johnathan Thurston and Matt Scott and New Zealand-born, Aussie Test prop James Tamou were in Australia's line-up for the Anzac Test, while fullback Tautau Moga played for Toa Samoa in the 18-16 Test victory over traditional Pacific rivals Mate Ma'a Tonga. Jason Taumalolo was Dally M Lock (Loose Forward) of the Year, but injury kept him out of the Kiwis squad for the England tour. Of course, Thurston won almost every award possible, including a record fourth Dally M Medal, his first Clive Churchill Medal, and the Cowboys Player of the Year gong. He and Scott shared the Dally M Captain of the Year award.

Michael Morgan was a revelation after switching to stand-off (and made the Queensland State of Origin squad). Fullback Lachlan Coote was in outstanding form after a year on the sideline, making an average of 140 metres in runs each game and an incredible 80 tackle-breaks. Hooker Jake Granville, previously unable to establish himself at the Broncos, had the critics raving with his runs from dummy half.

Brisbane's Darius Boyd can only watch as Kyle Feldt scores North Queensland's last-gasp NRL Grand Final try

BRISBANE BRONCOS (2nd)

The prodigal son returned to Brisbane. And what a difference Wayne Bennett made. After the Broncos scraped into the play-offs in 2014 on points-difference, the inaugural coach returned and helped steer them into second spot on the NRL ladder. Once in the play-offs they hammered Minor Premiers Sydney Roosters 31-12 before the heartbreaking loss to the other Queensland heavyweights, the Cowboys, during 'golden point' extra time in the Grand Final.

Bennett put it all in perspective: 'The bottom line is that the Grand Final was an absolutely outstanding game of football. Someone had to lose. Do we feel beaten? No, we don't. Do we feel disappointed? Yes, we do. But it's not about winning and losing all the time.'

Sadly, the defeat meant Justin Hodges missed out on a Premiership in the final game of his career – but he still had a stellar season as Brisbane's inspirational captain. The Broncos benefited from the return from Newcastle with Bennett of fullback Darius Boyd and the arrival from Canberra of Anthony Milford. Bennett switched him from fullback to stand-off where he established a superb partnership with scrum-half Ben Hunt. Not only did Milford score 13 tries himself he set up another 14 – second only to Hunt's 16.

Loose forward Corey Parker might have been in the twilight of his career, but he was a logical choice as Broncos Player of the Year. He also won the Wally Lewis Medal as Player of the State of Origin Series and was named Dally M Representative Player of the Year. Parker and second-rower Sam Thaiday were in Australia's side beaten in the Anzac Test by the Kiwis. Adam Blair found a new lease of life after a disappointing spell with

Wests Tigers and was chosen as a co-captain of the Kiwis side for the series against England. Also in the New Zealand squad were utility stars Jordan Kahu and Alex Glenn and halfback Kodi Nikorima. Centre Jack Reed would have most certainly played for England but for being forced into reconstruction surgery after injuring his right shoulder in the Grand Final. Josh McGuire turned out for Samoa in May while Joe Ofahengaue made his international debut for Tonga in the World Cup qualifier against the Cook Islands at the end of the season.

The Broncos lost Hodges, the hard-working prop Mitchell Dodds to Warrington Wolves and the Dally M under-20s Player of the year Ashley Taylor to the Titans (as a halfback he would have had to compete with Milford and Hunt had he stayed in Brisbane). But they still had the personnel to give the 2016 Premiership a real shake.

SYDNEY ROOSTERS (3rd/Minor Premiers)

It takes a great side to win three Minor Premierships (League Leaders Trophies) in a row. That's what the Roosters did in 2015. It was a feat that had not been achieved in a unified competition since Manly did so in 1971-73 (The Storm were stripped of their 2006-08 honours because of salary cap cheating). However the Roosters will still see the 2015 season as a failure as they didn't go on and finish the job with a Grand Final victory.

In reaching the finals series the Roosters strung together a 12-match winning streak. But the turning point had come in the 10th game of that run. In a 12-10 success over the Broncos, the terrifying Kiwi front-rower Jared Waerea-Hargreaves suffered a season-ending knee injury and playmaker Mitchell Pearce a hamstring tear, which left him virtually a passenger when he returned to the fray in the preliminary final. And once again the Sydney club could not make it past the second-last weekend, when they were beaten 31-12 by the Broncos.

Fullback Roger Tuivasa-Sheck, who will play for the New Zealand Warriors in 2016, centre/winger Shaun Kenny-Dowall and forwards Sam Moa, Isaac Liu and Sio Siua Taukeiaho, were members of the Kiwis squad for the end-of-season tour of England. Tuivasa-Sheck, Kenny-Dowall and Moa had earlier played in the Anzac Test, against Roosters' teammate Michael Jennings. Taukeiaho had also represented Tonga in the Test against Samoa in May 2015.

MELBOURNE STORM (4th)

What is it about coach Craig Bellamy? Year after year he defies the critics who write off his Melbourne Storm outfit. And every time he springs a surprise. In 2015 the doomsayers reckoned there were too many old players – notably captain Cameron Smith, scrum-half Cooper Cronk and fullback Billy Slater. And when an injury claimed 'Billy the Kid' for much of the season, the so-called experts reckoned the end was nigh.

But Smith is still one of the finest half-dozen players in the world, Cronk pulls out all stops in the big games and Bellamy found a ready replacement for Slater in Cameron Munster. There is hardly a club on the globe who wouldn't welcome Munster with open arms. He made 19 appearances, ran an average of 180 metres per game and broke 85 vital tackles

Then there was the Storm's defence – the most tackles in the NRL (9314) and the fewest tackles missed (562). These helped in the nine victories in close matches (including one-point wins against the Premiers North Queensland and Minor Premiers Sydney Roosters).

Yes, there was a mid-season slump, in which they lost five out of six games. But they surged back to edge out the Roosters again, in the first round of the finals, before being humbled by North Queensland in the penultimate week of the season.

Kiwi Test prop Jesse Bromwich was the Storm's Player of the Year, ahead of Cronk, with Smith third. Smith was Australia's captain in the Anzac Test, playing with his Melbourne teammates, centre Will Chambers and Cronk. Lined up against them were Bromwich and fellow Storm forwards Tohu Harris and Kevin Proctor who, at the end of the season, toured England with the Kiwis. Hull FC-bound winger Mahe Fonua and prop Felise Kaufusi played internationals for Tonga which has qualified for the 2017 World Cup.

CANTERBURY BULLDOGS (5th)

It was an inconsistent season for the Bulldogs, beaten in the previous year's Grand Final. They were always a chance – but five losses in six games early in the season put them behind the eight-ball. Victory in their final five matches of the regular season saw them just miss out on the vital top four on points-difference. Once in the finals they sorely missed the expertise of playmaker and goal-kicker Trent Hodkinson, injured in the penultimate home-and-away round against Newcastle. They scraped through 11-10 against the Dragons before being outclassed by the Roosters in the second weekend of the finals.

Winger Curtis Rona was one of the best NRL recruits of the season. He blossomed after coming south from the North Queensland Cowboys and finished the year with 23 tries in 25 appearances, second only to Parramatta's Semi Radradra (24). Rona, born in New Zealand but starting his Rugby League career in Western Australia, received his just reward when chosen to tour England with the Kiwis.

The sentimental favourite to win the Bulldogs Player of the Year award was Frank Pritchard. It was arguably his best season since joining Canterbury in 2011. Because of salary cap problems he left to join Hull FC for 2016. But winger Brett Morris, in his first season after joining twin brother Josh at the club, and prop Aiden Tolman were the official winners of the Dr George Peponis award, named after the former Test captain. Sam Kasiano played an international for Samoa in May.

In 2016, the Bulldogs will be without Hodkinson who has left for Newcastle. But the talented Origin representative Josh Reynolds and another of the finds of 2015, Moses Mbye, will be a formidable halfback combination. The pack, led by Englishman James Graham, will be just as strong. Tolman averaged 38 tackles and 155 metres per game. Josh Jackson was Dally M Second-rower of the Year. And look out for young fullback Bradley Abbey, signed from NZ Warriors, who had to make room for Kiwi international Roger Tuivasa-Sheck.

CRONULLA SHARKS (6th)

What a turnaround in 2015! The words of Queen Elizabeth II would have summed up the Sharks' previous season – 'annus horribilis'. The continuing drug investigations, which eventually came to nothing, and the wooden spoon, as Cronulla waited for the return of coach Shane Flanagan who was forced to cool his heels while the probe was conducted.

Then, after a poor opening to the year, with losses in their first four outings, the Sharks came good and surged into the play-offs, with a chance at one stage of earning one of the prized top-four positions. Once in the finals, they hammered the reigning Premiers South Sydney before coming up against a red-hot Cowboys outfit who handed them a 39-0 humiliation. Ironically they had beaten the Cowboys and the Minor Premiers, Sydney Roosters, in each of their games during the regular season.

Sharks stalwart Wade Graham, who has held the fort so many times while captain Paul Gallen was away doing his bit for New South Wales and Australia, again came to the fore and it was no surprise that he was named as Cronulla's Player of the Year. But he was pushed for the honours by recruit Michael Ennis, the ex-Bulldogs captain so shabbily shown the door at Canterbury. Ennis brought a positive, winning mentality to Shark Park and was honoured as Dally M Hooker of the Year.

Ennis was especially important in the Cronulla plans because the Sharks had so many talented young stars needing guidance. There was the future superstar Valentine Holmes, the Junior Kangaroo who is equally at home at fullback or on the wing. And what about stand-off Jack Bird? He was named Dally M Rookie of the Year and looks destined to be a future Test star. In 2016, he will probably move out to the centres where he has played much of his junior career to make way for the arrival of the goal-kicking Roosters Origin No 6 James Maloney.

Centre Gerard Beale was in the Kiwis' squad for the Anglo-New Zealand Test series, veteran utility star Luke Lewis was on Australia's bench for the Anzac Test against the Kiwis while another more than useful utility, Pat Politoni, as well as winger-centre Sosaia Feki and prop David Fifita turned out for Tonga during 2015.

Cronulla's future looks good with the arrival of Maloney. And the Sharks also won the SG Ball (under-18s) and Harold Matthews (under-16s) competitions with a host of future stars including Jack Williams, the grandson of the Immortal Reg Gasnier.

SOUTH SYDNEY RABBITOHS (7th)

Fans keep asking. Why can't NRL clubs put together back-to-back Premierships any more. Remember when St George won 11 straight titles? And what about those consecutive titles won by the Brisbane Broncos in the 1990s? We all thought it could happen in 2015. The euphoria of South Sydney's first Grand Final win in 43 years was still evident when the Rabbitohs thrashed St Helens 39-0 to win the World Club Challenge and followed it up by winning the Auckland Nines a month later. But there was more – wins over Brisbane Broncos, Sydney Roosters and Wests Tigers in the first three rounds of 2015.

Then the wheels fell off. From then on it was backwards, ever backwards.

Why? Critics blamed the loss of England Test man Sam Burgess to the 'Dark Side', where it proved the union media mafia didn't like him and the sweet chariot swung so low that they heaped all the vitriol on Slammin' Sam.

But it was more than that as far as the Rabbitohs were concerned. Souths also lost the much under-rated Ben Te'o to rugby union in the Emerald Isle. And guess who is trying to get Te'o home to Australia? None other than his old Brisbane coach Wayne Bennett.

The Dewsbury-born twins George and Tom Burgess have had their contracts at Redfern extended until the end of 2018 and there was plenty of wheeling and dealing to persuade brother Sam to return. However, the clever ex-Test backrower Glenn Stewart has left to join Catalans Dragons.

Some catalyst is needed after the Rabbitohs lost their final three encounters of the 2015 season proper by big margins (Bulldogs 32-18, Broncos 47-12 and Roosters 30-0) before being bundled out of the play-offs by Cronulla.

The Warriors-bound hooker Issac Luke was named co-captain of the New Zealand touring side after playing a vital role in the Kiwis' 26-12 victory over Australia in the Anzac Test. Fullback Greg Inglis and winger Alex Johnston wore the green and gold in that encounter. Johnston, scrum-half Adam Reynolds and forwards Chris McQueen and Dave Tyrell represented the Prime Minister's XIII in the international against Papua New Guinea.

ST GEORGE ILLAWARRA DRAGONS (8th)

It was a topsy-turvy 2015 for the Dragons. Forgettable performances in the first two rounds had irate fans baying for blood – the blood of coach Paul 'Mary' McGregor. But he had faith in his players. What followed was eight victories in nine outings - largely thanks to some wonderful defence and a great halfback combination between internationals Gareth Widdop and Benji Marshall - and by the start of June the club was sitting equal first in the Premiership race.

Some injuries and a form-slump mid-season, including seven straight losses, brought the Dragons back to the field. But they finished on a high, scraping into the play-offs before a gallant one-point defeat by Canterbury.

Josh Dugan showed his importance to St George Illawarra. When he was in action the Dragons were vastly different, able to threaten the top sides. He made his international debut on the wing for Australia in the Anzac Test. Trent Merrin was on the bench and later captained the Prime Minister's XIII against the Kumuls, with Dragons teammate Euan Aitken on the bench. Merrin will be on the Panthers' roster in 2016. Jason Nightingale played for the Kiwis in the Anzac Test and at the end of the season toured England with the New Zealanders. Dragons teammate Mike Cooper flew home to play for England. Leeson Ah Mau turned out for Samoa in the May Test win over Tonga.

In 2016, coach McGregor is hoping for some wonderful efforts from Super League recruits Mose Masoe (St Helens) and Tyrone McCarthy (Hull KR).

MANLY SEA EAGLES (9th)

Manly missed the finals series for the first time since 2004. However, after sitting in bottom spot on the NRL Ladder and looking as if the wooden spoon was heading their way, a late-season recovery saw the Sea Eagles win seven of their last 10 matches to momentarily challenge for the top-eight.

It was little wonder their season was chaotic with far too many off-field distractions. There was the realisation early in the season that the board planned to move in a different direction and coach Geoff Toovey's days were numbered. It was a real slap in the face for Toovey who had spent three decades with Manly as a player and then on the coaching staff. Everyone knew what was going to happen, especially as his successor, former Test stand-off Trent Barrett was stood down from his role as Penrith's assistant coach and went on indefinite leave.

Then Manly's star half Daly Cherry-Evans announced he would be going to join the Gold Coast, only to do a back-flip at the last moment and decide to stay. His on-pitch partner, Kiwi Test man Keiran Foran accepted a mammoth offer to move to Parramatta. There were rumours he would also renege on his deal but in the end he stood by his commitment. Nevertheless the turmoil took its toil.

But among the good news was the emergence of the two young Trbojevic brothers from the Mona Vale Raiders club in the Manly junior competition. Both made their senior debuts, prop Jake proving to be one of the Sea Eagles' best for 2015. Fullback Tom was equally as impressive, scoring 21 tries in 13 games for the under-20s and eight in nine NRL appearances.

Foran and Peta Hiku made Test appearances for New Zealand. Jake Trbojevic was prop in the Prime Minister's XIII against the Kumuls while Tom Symonds came off the bench. Jorge Taufua turned out for Mate Ma'a Tonga and Dunamis Lui for Samoa as well as Vinny Ngaro for the Cook Islands.

CANBERRA RAIDERS (10th)

The Raiders deserved a better finish than their disappointing spot on the NRL Ladder. Had they reversed the result in just two of the six matches they lost by four points or less they would have made the play-offs. Their appalling record at home didn't help either, winning only three games at Canberra Stadium and losing nine.

Nevertheless, the Raiders played some exciting rugby with coach Ricky Stuart getting yeoman service out of several of his recruits, not the least England Test hooker Josh Hodgson, who played all 24 games and rarely put a foot wrong. His average of 35 tackles per appearance was third only to defensive freak Shaun Fensom (45) and Sia

Soliola (37) who was back in the NRL after five seasons with St Helens. The former Kiwis and Samoan Test representative won the Mal Meninga Medal as Canberra's Player of the Year.

Also back from Super League was ex-Catalans Dragon Sam Williams who formed a devastating halfback partnership with the signing from Wests Tigers, Blake Austin, who became somewhat of a cult figure in Canberra with his distinctive ginger beard. Austin was named Dally M Five-eighth (Stand-off) of the Year. Fullback Jack Wighton and centre Jarrod Croker both played for the Prime Minister's XIII against the Kumuls. Elliott Whitehead will join the Raiders from Catalans Dragons in 2016.

PENRITH PANTHERS (11th)

A horror run of injuries cost Penrith Panthers dearly in a season they had hoped would bring them a top-four finish. They were still a chance after beating South Sydney 20-6 in Round 17 in early July but could only win seven of their final nine outings. Sadly Panthers general manager Phil 'Gus' Gould shattered a long friendship with coach Ivan Cleary and made him the scapegoat, even though Cleary had taken Penrith to the penultimate weekend the previous season. Sacked Broncos coach in 2014 Anthony Griffin will be at the helm in 2016.

The injuries forced the Panthers to use a number of players from their under-20s squad and although they were not up to the task the experience will help them mature in 2016. One of these youngsters was 22-year-old prop Reagan Campbell-Gillard who made his senior debut in the first round victory over the Bulldogs. He went on to appear in every match and win the club members vote as Player of the Year. Bryce Cartwright also established himself a regular in the senior side. What a talent.

Also on the bright side – the Panthers made the finals of the NSW Cup and won the Holden Cup (under-20s) Grand Final convincingly. And they have signed a pair of great kids, two-time Junior Kiwis stand-off Te Maire Martin from Wests Tigers and Fiji's international prop Viliame Kikau. The former left the Tigers because he was stuck behind Mitchell Moses and Luke Brooks, while the latter scored 21 tries for North Queensland Cowboys in 2015, taking his tally to 32 from 42 under-20s games – sensational for a front-rower.

Utility Lewis Brown and centre Dean Whare toured England with the Kiwis squad. Former Kumul James Segeyaro played for the Prime Minister's XIII against his old side alongside Campbell-Gillard and Jeremy Latimore. Hull FC-bound Sika Manu was captain of Tonga.

PARRAMATTA EELS (12th)

The vast majority of newspaper stories about Parramatta during 2015 were about one man – and he wasn't even playing. The Fourth Estate was mesmerised by every move made by the former Eels' star Jarryd Hayne, who had thrown in his Rugby League career to try to break into American Football with the San Francisco 49ers. Day after day the scribes bombarded us with stories about Hayne in the sporting pages in which in previous years NFL would have been lucky to have a got a couple of paragraphs - and only then around the time of Super Bowl.

But the defection of Hayne had a profound effect on Parramatta. He left the announcement of his imminent departure too late for the Eels to shop around for a suitable replacement. And it showed in the inconsistent displays throughout the season. There were some off-pitch dramas concerning management. And it was all topped off by a form slump by playmaker Chris Sandow that saw him dropped to the Eels' feeder club Wentworthville before he headed of to Super League. At the time the Eels were still in with a chance of making the finals series.

Fijian flyer Semi Radradra was named Dally M Winger of the Year after scoring a club record of 24 tries in 18 appearances, bringing his career tally to 48 in 49 matches. Captain Tim Mannah won the Ken Thornett Medal as the Eels Player of the Year. Tepi Moeroa was in the second row for the Prime Minister's XIII in their 40-12 win over Papua New Guinea. Fellow forwards Richie Fa'aoso, Peni Terepo and Manu Ma'u played Tests for Tonga.

NEW ZEALAND WARRIORS (13th)

Every team relies on a small core of key players to put them in a position to make a decisive drive to win the Premiership. But one single man? It seemed that way with the New Zealand Warriors and the current Golden Boot laureate Shaun Johnson. A mid-season roll saw the Auckland club in the top four on the NRL Ladder for the first time in four years.

Johnson was orchestrating his teammates around the pitch with the finesse of a Mozart maestro, silencing the critics who dared to denigrate his selection as the finest player in the world the previous season. Then Johnson broke an ankle and the Warriors had lost their X Factor, losing their final eight games to finish among the cellar-dwellers. The losses included 50-16 thrashings at the hands of both the Cowboys and the Tigers.

Injuries to others didn't help either with England Test man Sam Tomkins, Kiwis Test folk hero Manu 'The Beast' Vatuvei and playmaker Thomas Leuluai among those who missed a significant number of games.

Ben Matulino was the Warriors' Player of the Year. Matulino, Simon Mannering, Vatuvei, Johnson and Leuluai were in New Zealand's winning squad in the Anzac Test, although sadly injuries robbed the Kiwis of the presence of the last three on the tour of Britain. But exciting young utility back Tuimoala Lolohea made the touring side.

Earlier Lolohea played for the Mate Ma'a Tonga side narrowly beaten by Samoa in their May Test on the Gold Coast (together with Konrad Hurrell, Solomone Kata, and Albert Vete), while Sam Lisone and the St Helens-bound Dominique Peyroux were on the bench for the winners.

A homesick Tomkins is back home in Wigan. Kiwis prop Sam Rapira has been signed by Huddersfield Giants and Tongan international Glen Fisiiahi has defected to rugby union. But the 2016 squad will be strengthened by the addition of Kiwis touring co-captain Issac Luke and the brilliant Roosters fullback Roger Tuivasa-Sheck

GOLD COAST TITANS (14th)

It was another disappointing season for the poor cousins of the Queensland game, the Gold Coast Titans. A series of off-pitch problems hardly helped. A number of their players were charged by police with drug offences (although most were eventually exonerated). Then there was a highly-publicised signing of Origin representative half Daly Cherry-Evans only to have him do a back-flip and stay with Manly.

For a long time it looked likely the Titans would end up with the wooden spoon and it was only victories over the Raiders and Dragons as the season neared its conclusion that saved them from that embarrassment.

Prop Luke Douglas won the Paul Broughton Medal as the Titans player of the Year and followed it up with the Ken Stephen Medal, awarded to the NRL player who was best role model for work in the community. It was a far cry from the drugs scandal in which he and other players had been caught up unawares while playing for Cronulla.

Titans forwards Greg Bird and Nate Myles were in Australia's side beaten by the Kiwis in the Anzac Test. But Bird was hit by an eight-match suspension for a dangerous throw in the match. Exciting young stand-off Kane Elgey and utility Daniel Mortimer lined up against the Kumuls for the Prime Minister's XIII. Former 'enfant terrible' James Roberts paid back the Titans for throwing him a lifeline with a sensational season in which the 22-year-old was named Dally M Centre of the Year, scoring 16 tries in 24 appearances.

Captain Nate Myles has left for what he hopes are greener pastures at Brookvale, talented stand-off Aiden Sezer is linking with coach Ricky Stuart in Canberra and the enigmatic Dave Taylor is trying his luck in Perpignan with the Catalans Dragons. But a bright spot on the horizon is the arrival of Australian Schoolboys scrum-half and Dally M under-20s Player of the Year Ash Taylor.

WESTS TIGERS (15th)

As the great coach Jack Gibson was wont to say, a club's success starts not on the pitch but in the front office. In one of his famous quotes he explained: 'The trouble is that the players go through quality control – but there is no quality control with those people (the board and management).' So it was yet again at Wests Tigers in 2015.

As in recent years, the inner turmoil made more headlines than the efforts of the talented young roster containing many of the superstars of the future. And there was the usual public blow-up that ripped the club apart, with captain and coach at loggerheads, players angrily wanting to find a new direction for their career and fans livid.

It all came to a head when late in the season coach Jason Taylor pulled aside the long-serving NSW State of Origin hooker Robbie Farah and told him he was welcome to look for another club to play out his career. It was a real slap in the face for the one-club veteran who had played a record 238 games for the Tigers since making his debut in 2003. Farah had always made it clear he wanted to finish with Wests, which would have given him a chance to beat Darren Lockyer's NRL single-club record of 355 with the Broncos.

Critics reckoned his departure could have catastrophic consequences at a side which was losing its two other experienced veterans to Super League the following season – Pat Richards to Catalans Dragons and Keith Galloway to Leeds Rhinos.

And experience was what was needed to help guide the youngsters, especially the halfback pairing of Luke Brooks and Mitchell Moses, who were targeted by the big opposition forwards during the Tigers' miserable season.

With a rare recent injury-free season fullback James Tedesco was a stand-out Player of Year. Forwards Aaron Woods (Australia) and Martin Taupau (New Zealand) played in the Anzac Test, with the latter in the Kiwis side that toured England at the end of 2015. And in other internationals, winger David Nofoaluma grabbed a brace of tries for the Prime Minister's XIII against the Kumuls, utility back Tim Simona and prop Sauaso Sue played for Samoa, hooker Joel Luani for Tonga and Chance Peni and Esan Marsters for the Cook Islands.

NEWCASTLE KNIGHTS (16th)

What a turnaround! The Knights surprised everyone at the start of the season. They came off a disappointing 2014 season in which they were down among the cellar-dwellers. Coach Wayne Bennett had departed, returning to his alma mater in the Queensland capital after a tumultuous couple of seasons in which the experiment with the private ownership by mining magnate Nathan Tinkler had gone disastrously wrong. With his drift into financial failure, the club had imploded.

But suddenly there was a new sense of hope. The Knights, under new mentor Rick Stone, the man Bennett had originally replaced, won their first four encounters, albeit two of the victories (against the eventual Premiers North Queensland and another club from north of the border, the Gold Coast Titans) were close affairs. However the Novocastrians were up at the top of the ladder.

Then everything went terribly wrong. Newcastle lost 16 of the next 19 matches.

SEASON DOWN UNDER - ROUND-UP

NRL PREMIERSHIP FINALS SERIES

QUALIFYING FINALS

Friday 11th September 2015
Sydney Roosters 18 .... Melbourne Storm 20
Saturday 12th September 2015
Brisbane Broncos 16 .... North Queensland Cowboys 12

ELIMINATION FINALS

Saturday 12th September 2015
Canterbury Bulldogs 11 .... St George Illawarra Dragons 10
(after golden point extra-time)
Sunday 13th September 2015
Cronulla Sharks 28 .... South Sydney Rabbitohs 12
(at Allianz Stadium, Sydney)

SEMI-FINALS

Friday 18th September 2015
Sydney Roosters 38 .... Canterbury Bulldogs 12
Saturday 19th September 2015
North Queensland Cowboys 39 .... Cronulla Sharks 0

PRELIMINARY FINALS

Friday 25th September 2015
Brisbane Broncos 31 .... Sydney Roosters 12
Saturday 26th September 2015
Melbourne Storm 12 .... North Queensland Cowboys 32

GRAND FINAL

Sunday 4th October 2015

BRISBANE BRONCOS 16 NORTH QUEENSLAND COWBOYS 17
(after golden point extra-time)

BRONCOS: 1 Darius Boyd; 2 Corey Oates; 3 Jack Reed; 4 Justin Hodges (C); 5 Jordan Kahu; 6 Anthony Milford; 7 Ben Hunt; 8 Sam Thaiday; 9 Andrew McCullough; 10 Adam Blair; 11 Alex Glenn; 12 Matt Gillett; 13 Corey Parker. Subs (all used): 14 Jarrod Wallace; 15 Mitchell Dodds; 16 Joe Ofahengaue; 17 Kodi Nikorima.
Tries: Oates (6), Reed (34); **Goals:** Parker 2/2, Kahu 2/2.
On report: Hunt (77) - alleged dangerous challenge.
COWBOYS: 1 Lachlan Coote; 2 Kyle Feldt; 3 Justin O'Neill; 4 Kane Linnett; 5 Antonio Winterstein; 6 Michael Morgan; 7 Johnathan Thurston (C); 8 Matt Scott (C); 9 Jake Granville; 10 James Tamou; 11 Gavin Cooper; 12 Ethan Lowe; 13 Jason Taumalolo. Subs (all used): 14 Rory Kostjasyn; 15 John Asiata; 16 Scott Bolton; 17 Ben Hannant.
Tries: O'Neill (10), Tamou (24), Feldt (80); **Goals:** Thurston 2/3;
Field goal: Thurston (82).
Rugby Leaguer & League Express Men of the Match:
Broncos: Corey Parker; *Cowboys:* Johnathan Thurston.
Clive Churchill Medal (Man of the Match):
Johnathan Thurston (North Queensland Cowboys).
Half-time: 14-12; **Referees:** Ben Cummins & Gerard Sutton;
Attendance: 82,758 *(at ANZ Stadium, Sydney).*

FINAL NRL PREMIERSHIP TABLE

	P	W	D	L	B	F	A	D	Pts
Sydney Roosters	24	18	0	6	2	591	300	291	40
Brisbane Broncos	24	17	0	7	2	574	379	195	38
North Queensland Cowboys	24	17	0	7	2	587	454	133	38
Melbourne Storm	24	14	0	10	2	467	348	119	32
Canterbury Bulldogs	24	14	0	10	2	522	480	42	32
Cronulla Sharks	24	14	0	10	2	469	476	- 7	32
South Sydney Rabbitohs	24	13	0	11	2	465	467	- 2	30
St George Illawarra Dragons	24	12	0	12	2	435	408	27	28
Manly Sea Eagles	24	11	0	13	2	458	492	- 34	26
Canberra Raiders	24	10	0	14	2	577	569	8	24
Penrith Panthers	24	10	0	14	2	399	477	- 78	22
Parramatta Eels	24	9	0	15	2	448	573	- 125	22
New Zealand Warriors	24	9	0	15	2	445	588	- 143	22
Gold Coast Titans	24	9	0	15	2	439	636	- 197	22
Wests Tigers	24	8	0	16	2	487	562	- 75	20
Newcastle Knights	24	8	0	16	2	458	612	- 154	20

TOP POINTSCORERS

James Maloney	Sydney Roosters	250
Jarrod Croker	Canberra Raiders	236
Johnathan Thurston	North Queensland Cowboys	208
Pat Richards	Wests Tigers	197
Gareth Widdop	St George Illawarra Dragons	182

TOP TRYSCORERS

Semi Radradra	Parramatta Eels	24
Curtis Rona	Canterbury Bulldogs	23
Alex Johnston	South Sydney Rabbitohs	17
Shaun Kenny-Dowall	Sydney Roosters	17
Pat Richards	Wests Tigers	17
James Tedesco	Wests Tigers	17

HOLDEN CUP GRAND FINAL *(Under-20s)*

Sunday 4th October 2015
Manly Sea Eagles 18 .... Penrith Panthers 34
(at ANZ Stadium, Sydney)

NEW SOUTH WALES CUP GRAND FINAL

Sunday 27th September 2015
Newcastle Knights 20 .... Wyong Roos 10
(at Pirtek Stadium, Parramatta)

QUEENSLAND CUP GRAND FINAL

Sunday 27th September 2015
Ipswich Jets 32 .... Townsville Blackhawks 20
(at Suncorp Stadium, Brisbane)

NRL STATE CHAMPIONSHIP *(NSW Premiers v Queensland Premiers)*

Sunday 4th October 2015
Newcastle Knights 12 .... Ipswich Jets 26
(at ANZ Stadium, Sydney)

DALLY M AWARDS

Dally M Medal (Player of the Year):
Johnathan Thurston (North Queensland Cowboys)
Provan Summons Medal (People's Choice):
Johnathan Thurston (North Queensland Cowboys)
Coach of the Year: Wayne Bennett (Brisbane Broncos)
Captains of the Year:
Johnathan Thurston & Matt Scott (North Queensland Cowboys)
Representative Player of the Year:
Corey Parker (Australia, Queensland & Brisbane Broncos)
Rookie of the Year: Jack Bird (Cronulla Sharks)
Holden Cup (Under-20s) Player of the Year:
Ashley Taylor (Brisbane Broncos)
Female Player of the Year: Jenni-Sue Hoepper (Australian Jillaroos)

Stone was replaced after a 52-6 hammering by the Rabbitohs. His interim successor was one of the club's favourite sons, ex-Leeds Rhinos stalwart Danny Buderus. But the former Test hooker couldn't perform a miracle and Newcastle ended up with the wooden spoon for only the second time in their proud history. Stone, motherless last!

Buderus didn't want the job permanently and former St George Illawarra, Huddersfield and St Helens coach Nathan Brown will in charge in 2016. His task will not be easy with the departure or retirement of players with a total of more than 1,000 matches between them, including Test men, Warrington-bound Kurt Gidley (Australia), Beau Scott (Australia), David Fa'alogo (New Zealand and Samoa), Clint Newton (USA) and Hull FC-signing Carlos Tuimavave (Samoa).

Centre Dane Gagai played for the Prime Minister's XIII against Papua New Guinea. Gidley was the Knights' Player of the Year.

State of Origin

Fans of the NSW Blues were cock-a-hoop when Paul Gallen led them out of nine years in the wilderness in 2014. It had been a long wait and by the time the 2015 series approached the diehards south of the border, especially the parochial media, were predicting a new dynasty to rival that of the Maroons.

But in a different slant to the age-old cliché – don't count your cockroaches before they've hatched. The Queenslanders weren't ready to capitulate a second time without a true blue battle. Cooper Cronk booted a field goal to snatch a late victory in the opening encounter. The Queenslanders came out second-best in the second and then rewrote the record books when giving New South Wales the mother of all thrashings in the decider. Now the Blues would have to start all over again in 2016.

STATE OF ORIGIN - GAME I

Wednesday 27th May 2015

NEW SOUTH WALES 10 QUEENSLAND 11

NEW SOUTH WALES: 1 Josh Dugan (St George Illawarra Dragons); 2 Daniel Tupou (Sydney Roosters); 3 Josh Morris (Canterbury Bulldogs); 4 Michael Jennings (Sydney Roosters); 5 Will Hopoate (Parramatta Eels); 6 Mitchell Pearce (Sydney Roosters); 7 Trent Hodkinson (Canterbury Bulldogs); 8 Aaron Woods (Wests Tigers); 9 Robbie Farah (Wests Tigers) (C); 10 James Tamou (North Queensland Cowboys); 11 Beau Scott (Newcastle Knights); 12 Ryan Hoffman (New Zealand Warriors); 13 Josh Jackson (Canterbury Bulldogs). Subs (all used): 14 Trent Merrin (St George Illawarra Dragons); 15 Boyd Cordner (Sydney Roosters); 16 David Klemmer (Canterbury Bulldogs); 17 Andrew Fifita (Cronulla Sharks).
Tries: J Morris (19), Scott (25); **Goals:** Hodkinson 1/2.
QUEENSLAND: 1 Billy Slater (Melbourne Storm); 2 Darius Boyd (Brisbane Broncos); 3 Greg Inglis (South Sydney Rabbitohs); 4 Justin Hodges (Brisbane Broncos); 5 Will Chambers (Melbourne Storm); 6 Johnathan Thurston (North Queensland Cowboys); 7 Cooper Cronk (Melbourne Storm); 8 Matt Scott (North Queensland Cowboys); 9 Cameron Smith (Melbourne Storm) (C); 10 Nate Myles (Gold Coast Titans); 11 Aidan Guerra (Sydney Roosters); 12 Sam Thaiday (Brisbane Broncos); 13 Corey Parker (Brisbane Broncos). Subs (all used): 14 Michael Morgan (North Queensland Cowboys); 15 Josh McGuire (Brisbane Broncos); 16 Matt Gillett (Brisbane Broncos); 17 Jacob Lillyman (New Zealand Warriors).
Tries: Cronk (12), Chambers (55); **Goals:** Thurston 1/3;
Field goal: Cronk (74).
Rugby Leaguer & League Express Men of the Match:
New South Wales: Aaron Woods; *Queensland:* Cooper Cronk.
Half-time: 10-6; **Referees:** Ben Cummins & Gerard Sutton;
Attendance: 80,122 *(at ANZ Stadium, Sydney).*

Sydney critics had slammed the Maroons' line-up for being too old – with the likes of Cameron Smith, Corey Parker, Billy Slater, Johnathan Thurston and Cronk being on the wrong side of 30. But it was that experience that proved to be the difference in Origin I. The New South Wales halves also blew a chance to snatch a late victory by failing to go for a field goal that would have broken a 10-all deadlock ... and allowing centre Michael Jennings to put in a grubber kick along the ground instead. 'I was thinking they were going to take a shot,' said Queensland skipper Smith. 'And as soon as that ball went dead, Cooper, JT (Thurston) and I realised we had an opportunity to take the one point. Cooper has slotted a few over in recent few years. He struck that one nicely. He struck it when it counted.'

The handwritten acronym on Thurston's wristband said it all. KISS (Keep it simple, stupid). Coach Mal Meninga agreed: 'I was very pleased with the effort. Sensational. Our kicking game was exceptional. All the little things you need at Origin level were performed extremely well.'

The Queenslanders looked to have scored first when Slater managed to get to a kick from Thurston but the video referee ruled he had pushed Trent Hodkinson in the back while the pair was chasing the ball. Eventually the Maroons broke the line. Sam Thaiday made a wonderful burst. Then Smith sent Cronk through a small gap to score the first try of the evening.

The Blues struck back almost immediately. James Tamou made a break and sent fullback Josh Dugan on a long run. When the defence descended on Dugan he put in a clever kick for Test centre Josh Morris to pounce on the ball and score. A few minutes later, NSW half Mitchell Pearce slipped a brilliant pass for Newcastle backrower Beau Scott to dance his way across the stripe. What a reversal of roles from the fellow listed pre-match as the 'hardman' of the Origin opener!

In the second half, the Blues incurred a couple of penalties that gave Queensland a chance to fight back, with Cronk and Thaiday setting up winger Will Chambers for a try to square up the scores 10-all with 15 minutes remaining.

Smith was held up over the line. Then with 10 minutes left on the clock, the Maroons were awarded a penalty for a suspect tackle on Thurston and he took a long-range kick for goal which fell short.

It was finally left to Cronk to swing the result Queensland's way.

Melbourne's 'Three Musketeers' were standouts in the encounter, with Cronk the obvious man of the match and Smith losing little by comparison. Slater, in doubt until the 11th hour with a chronic shoulder injury, was given a solid workout by the New South Welshmen. But the trio weren't alone. As he had always done in the past, centre Justin Hodges lifted in the Origin arena. Thaiday was at his rampaging best and was exhausted as the full-time whistle blew.

For New South Wales, young Aaron Woods showed how he has emerged as one of the best props in the world. Robbie Farah was inspirational in his role as captain, despite carrying a severe injury to his left shoulder for more than half the game.

A rejuvenated NSW Blues side squared the State of Origin series with an eight-point victory over Queensland in an epic encounter at Australia's most famous sporting arena, the Melbourne Cricket Ground. It was a satisfying success for the Blues after their lack-lustre display in Origin I. However the result was not without its controversy. The Queenslanders' feelings were summed up by the front page headline in Brisbane's Courier-Mail newspaper - 'Robbed'.

There was nothing subtle about the single word that dominated the page. It depended upon which side of border you lived as to how you viewed the contentious video referees' decision late in the game, a ruling that virtually determined the result. At the time the New South Welshmen were clinging to a 20-18 lead.

STATE OF ORIGIN - GAME II

Wednesday 17th June 2015

NEW SOUTH WALES 26 QUEENSLAND 18

NEW SOUTH WALES: 1 Josh Dugan (St George Illawarra Dragons); 2 Brett Morris (St George Illawarra Dragons); 3 Michael Jennings (Sydney Roosters); 4 Josh Morris (Canterbury Bulldogs); 5 Will Hopoate (Parramatta Eels); 6 Mitchell Pearce (Sydney Roosters); 7 Trent Hodkinson (Canterbury Bulldogs); 8 Aaron Woods (Wests Tigers); 9 Robbie Farah (Wests Tigers); 10 James Tamou (North Queensland Cowboys); 11 Beau Scott (Newcastle Knights); 12 Ryan Hoffman (New Zealand Warriors); 13 Paul Gallen (Cronulla Sharks) (C). Subs (all used): 14 Trent Merrin (St George Illawarra Dragons); 15 Boyd Cordner (Sydney Roosters); 16 David Klemmer (Canterbury Bulldogs); 17 Josh Jackson (Canterbury Bulldogs).
Tries: Jennings (4), J Morris (26), Woods (61), Dugan (70);
Goals: Hodkinson 5/5.
QUEENSLAND: 1 Billy Slater (Melbourne Storm); 2 Darius Boyd (Brisbane Broncos); 3 Greg Inglis (South Sydney Rabbitohs); 4 Justin Hodges (Brisbane Broncos); 5 Will Chambers (Melbourne Storm); 6 Johnathan Thurston (North Queensland Cowboys); 7 Daly Cherry-Evans (Manly Sea Eagles); 8 Matt Scott (North Queensland Cowboys); 9 Cameron Smith (Melbourne Storm) (C); 10 Nate Myles (Gold Coast Titans); 11 Aidan Guerra (Sydney Roosters); 12 Sam Thaiday (Brisbane Broncos); 13 Corey Parker (Brisbane Broncos). Subs (all used): 14 Michael Morgan (North Queensland Cowboys); 15 Josh McGuire (Brisbane Broncos); 16 Matt Gillett (Brisbane Broncos); 17 Jacob Lillyman (New Zealand Warriors).
Tries: Scott (11), Inglis (32), Gillett (46); **Goals:** Thurston 3/4.
Rugby Leaguer & League Express Men of the Match:
New South Wales: Michael Jennings; *Queensland:* Greg Inglis.
Half-time: 14-10; **Referees:** Ben Cummins & Gerard Sutton;
Attendance: 91,513 *(at Melbourne Cricket Ground).*

Blues' playmaker Mitchell Pearce fumbled during an attack on the Queensland tryline. Greg Inglis scooped up the loose ball and sped more than 90 metres to touch down. However the video referees ruled there had been a Maroons knock-on.

And, to rub salt into the wound, a couple of minutes later NSW fullback Josh Dugan scored a try. Trent Hodkinson converted to stretch the winning lead to 26-18.

Queensland's best player Johnathan Thurston was equally as generous as he was diplomatic: 'Full credit to the Blues. They were just too good for us tonight.'

The match itself was worthy of the Origin record attendance of 91,513. Both the size of the crowd and the display by the elite players justified the decision to take the game away from the two traditional Rugby League states.

The Blues were quickly on the scoreboard after Cameron Smith knocked on trying to take an intercept. From the subsequent set of six tackles, Roosters centre Michael Jennings was across the line to score.

It didn't take Queensland long to strike back. After a clever run from the will-'o'-the wisp Thurston, loose forward Corey Parker surged for the line and slipped a clever pass to prop Matt Scott who touched down next to the left-hand post.

The Blues went back into the lead when the video referees gave Josh Morris the thumbs up after he leaped high over Will Chambers to take a Mitchell Pearce bomb. The decision was controversial – it could have gone either way.

Late in the half Inglis, Slater and Darius Boyd handled in a 55-metre run, before Inglis backed up to score. However, an awful missed conversion attempt by Thurston left the Maroons still trailing by two points. A penalty goal by Hodkinson 90 seconds before the break sent New South Wales to the lead by 14-10.

The Queenslanders snatched back the initiative back early in the second spell when substitute Matt Gillett planted the ball next to the right upright. And a Thurston penalty goal increased the winning margin.

It was a brief lead. Young NSW prop Aaron Woods pushed off three would-be defenders to score. Yet another contentious ruling saw the Blues denied a try after what was deemed a forward pass from Pearce. Then came the Inglis 'no try'.

The game brought an end to Slater's season. He went under the surgeon's scalpel the following week. NSW hooker Robbie Farah played through the encounter suffering excruciating pain and missed the vital Origin III.

The vast majority of State of Origin clashes are won and lost by less than eight points. The 2015 decider was certainly an exception. In posting their 52-6 victory – for their ninth series success in the past 10 seasons – the Maroons set a host of records.

The 46-point margin was the biggest in the 35 years of Origin clashes, eclipsing New South Wales' 56-16 victory in 2000.

The Maroons' 52-point haul was their highest in history.

Johnathan Thurston's nine goals from as many attempts set a new Queensland high and took him to 200 points in his illustrious Origin career (He would have got a 10th goal had he not deferred to teammate Justin Hodges, who booted the final goal to bring down the curtain on his representative career).

Greg Inglis's touchdown just before half-time made him Origin's most prolific tryscorer with 17 in 27 appearances.

An attendance of 52,500 xenophobic fans at Suncorp Stadium helped set a new record as the total crowds for the 2015 series also reached a high of 224,135.

STATE OF ORIGIN - GAME III

Wednesday 8th July 2015

QUEENSLAND 52 NEW SOUTH WALES 6

QUEENSLAND: 1 Greg Inglis (South Sydney Rabbitohs); 2 Darius Boyd (Brisbane Broncos); 3 Will Chambers (Melbourne Storm); 4 Justin Hodges (Brisbane Broncos); 5 Dane Gagai (Newcastle Knights); 6 Johnathan Thurston (North Queensland Cowboys); 7 Cooper Cronk (Melbourne Storm); 8 Matt Scott (North Queensland Cowboys); 9 Cameron Smith (Melbourne Storm) (C); 10 Nate Myles (Gold Coast Titans); 11 Aidan Guerra (Sydney Roosters); 12 Sam Thaiday (Brisbane Broncos); 13 Corey Parker (Brisbane Broncos). Subs (all used): 14 Michael Morgan (North Queensland Cowboys); 18 Josh Papalii (Canberra Raiders); 16 Matt Gillett (Brisbane Broncos); 17 Jacob Lillyman (New Zealand Warriors).
Tries: Gagai (15), Papalii (27), Inglis (34), Gillett (41), Morgan (50), Boyd (56), Chambers (67), Guerra (72);
Goals: Thurston 9/9, Hodges 1/1.
NEW SOUTH WALES: 1 Josh Dugan (St George Illawarra Dragons); 2 Will Hopoate (Parramatta Eels); 3 Michael Jennings (Sydney Roosters); 4 Josh Morris (Canterbury Bulldogs); 5 Brett Morris (St George Illawarra Dragons); 6 Mitchell Pearce (Sydney Roosters); 7 Trent Hodkinson (Canterbury Bulldogs); 8 Aaron Woods (Wests Tigers); 18 Michael Ennis (Cronulla Sharks); 10 James Tamou (North Queensland Cowboys); 11 Ryan Hoffman (New Zealand Warriors); 12 Beau Scott (Newcastle Knights); 13 Paul Gallen (Cronulla Sharks) (C). Subs (all used): 14 Trent Merrin (St George Illawarra Dragons); 15 Boyd Cordner (Sydney Roosters); 16 David Klemmer (Canterbury Bulldogs); 17 Josh Jackson (Canterbury Bulldogs).
Try: Jennings (61); **Goals:** Hodkinson 1/2.
On report: Merrin (33) - alleged dangerous challenge on Parker; Tamou (55) - alleged high tackle on Lillyman.
Rugby Leaguer & League Express Men of the Match:
Queensland: Johnathan Thurston; *New South Wales:* Paul Gallen.
Half-time: 22-2; **Referees:** Ben Cummins & Gerard Sutton;
Attendance: 52,500 *(at Suncorp Stadium, Brisbane).*

Wally Lewis Medal (Man of the Series): Corey Parker (Queensland).

'Geez, I didn't see that coming,' said Laurie Daley, coach of the shell-shocked Blues. 'We were never in it. That wasn't us tonight. I'm shocked it ended up like that.' Captain Paul Gallen agreed: 'That wasn't good enough, simple as that. Absolutely no excuses. I'm a bit shocked. We let ourselves down, we let Laurie down.'

Needless to say it was a different matter in the Queensland dressing room after the match. Thurston, arguably the Maroons' best on the night, summed it all up: 'This is one of the best feelings in your life ... to win an Origin series. They wrote us off before the game. It just goes to show what a champion team this is. It was all about proving a point after losing the series last year. Fifty-two points ... we couldn't ask for a better way to finish the series.'

PERSONALITIES OF 2015

Lizzie & Danny Jones

The singing of 'Abide With Me' at the 2015 Challenge Cup Final at Wembley Stadium was the most moving of any rendition of the hymn.

Lizzie Jones, the wife of former Keighley Cougars and Wales international Danny Jones and a professional singer, wanted to use the occasion to thank the Rugby League family for their support since her husband's tragic death in May.

Danny Jones, at the age of 29, collapsed and died from heart failure triggered by an undetected heart defect whilst playing for Keighley Cougars at London Skolars in a League 1 fixture on 3rd May 2015.

Since that awful day, Rugby League fans, players, administrators and the wider public have donated over 280,000 pounds to a trust fund set up by the RFL Benevolent Fund to secure the futures of Danny and Lizzie's two children.

If Danny had been playing in Super League it is almost certain the heart defect would have been spotted. Cardiac screening has been compulsory for all Super League players since 2012, but not for Championship and League 1 clubs. The policy was extended to all three leagues in July 2015.

Lizzie gave a great performance at Wembley and left the field with her eight-month old twins Phoebe and Bobby held in either arm while acknowledging the cheers of the crowd. It was a wave of emotion never seen before on Rugby League's big stage.

Johnathan Thurston

North Queensland Cowboys, Queensland & Australia

At the end of 2015 it became obvious that there has never been a player quite like Johnathan Thurston.

The fairytale outcome to the NRL's first ever all-Queensland Grand Final was confirmation, at the end of a season in which just about every North Queensland Cowboys game would result in a nail-biting finish.

Needless to say, 32-year-old Thurston inspired a late rally in what was rated as the best Grand Final of all-time. The Cowboys were trailing by four points when JT danced and stepped before his halfback partner Michael Morgan made an amazing flick pass to right winger Kyle Feldt, who touched down as the final siren was sounding. Thurston lined up the conversion attempt from near the right sideline to win the game. It would have been a dramatic ending but the ball bounced off the right upright, sending the game into 'golden-point' extra time.

Of course it was Thurston who kicked the winning field goal to ensure North Queensland snared the first Premiership in their two-decade history.

The previous Monday, an emotional Thurston broke down in tears after winning a record fourth Dally M Player of the Year medal. Thurston had previously won the award in 2005 and 2007 and was equal winner in 2014 with Jarryd Hayne. That surpassed Andrew Johns, who won the award in 1998, 1999 and 2002.

In December, he was named by Rugby League World as the winner of the 2015 Golden Boot for a record third time.

Not bad for a player who was knocked back by clubs who said he too small to make the grade.

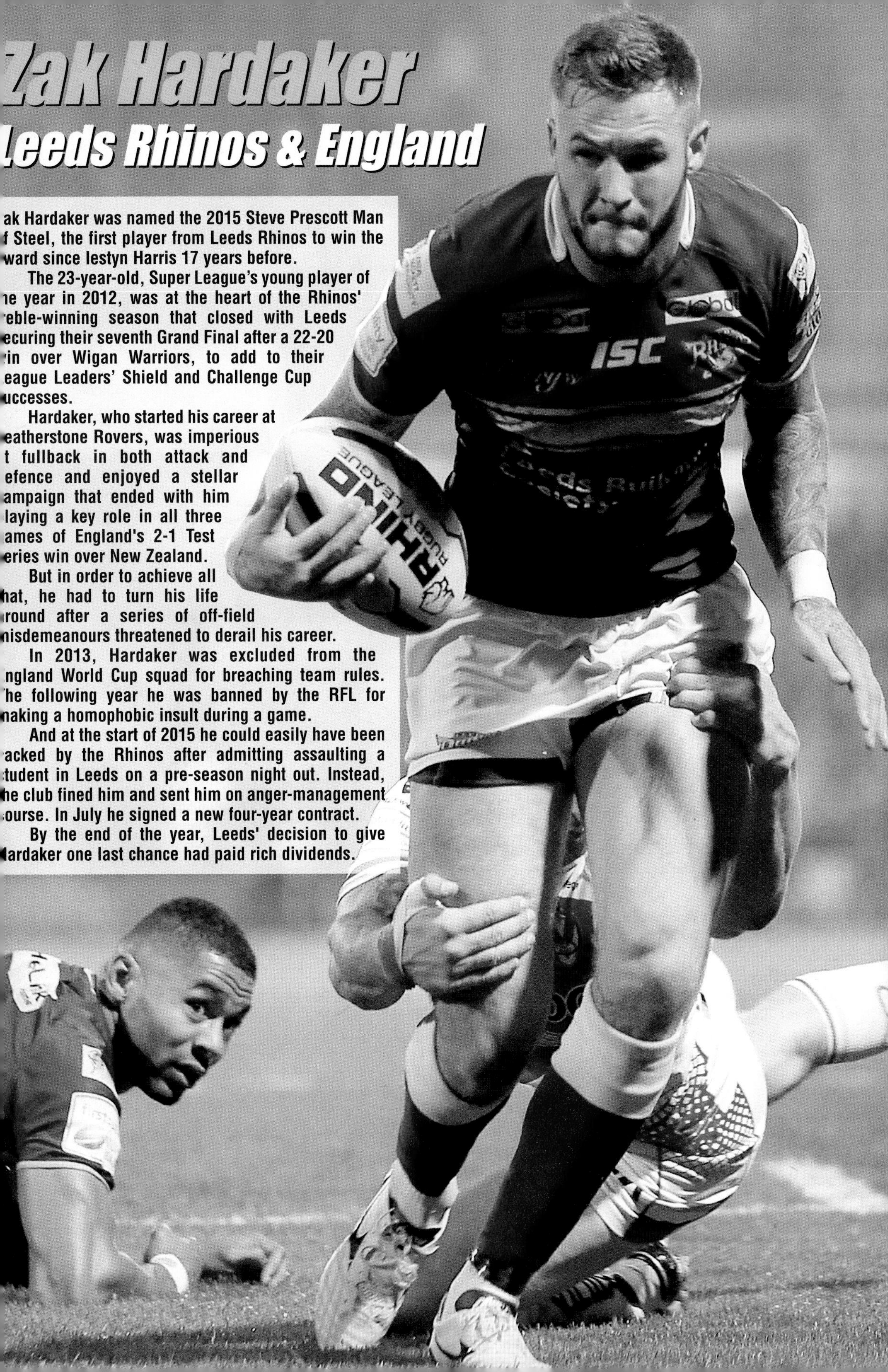

Zak Hardaker

Leeds Rhinos & England

ak Hardaker was named the 2015 Steve Prescott Man f Steel, the first player from Leeds Rhinos to win the ward since Iestyn Harris 17 years before.

The 23-year-old, Super League's young player of ne year in 2012, was at the heart of the Rhinos' eble-winning season that closed with Leeds ecuring their seventh Grand Final after a 22-20 in over Wigan Warriors, to add to their eague Leaders' Shield and Challenge Cup uccesses.

Hardaker, who started his career at eatherstone Rovers, was imperious t fullback in both attack and efence and enjoyed a stellar ampaign that ended with him laying a key role in all three ames of England's 2-1 Test eries win over New Zealand.

But in order to achieve all hat, he had to turn his life round after a series of off-field nisdemeanours threatened to derail his career.

In 2013, Hardaker was excluded from the ngland World Cup squad for breaching team rules. he following year he was banned by the RFL for naking a homophobic insult during a game.

And at the start of 2015 he could easily have been acked by the Rhinos after admitting assaulting a tudent in Leeds on a pre-season night out. Instead, he club fined him and sent him on anger-management ourse. In July he signed a new four-year contract.

By the end of the year, Leeds' decision to give lardaker one last chance had paid rich dividends.

Alex Walmsley

St Helens

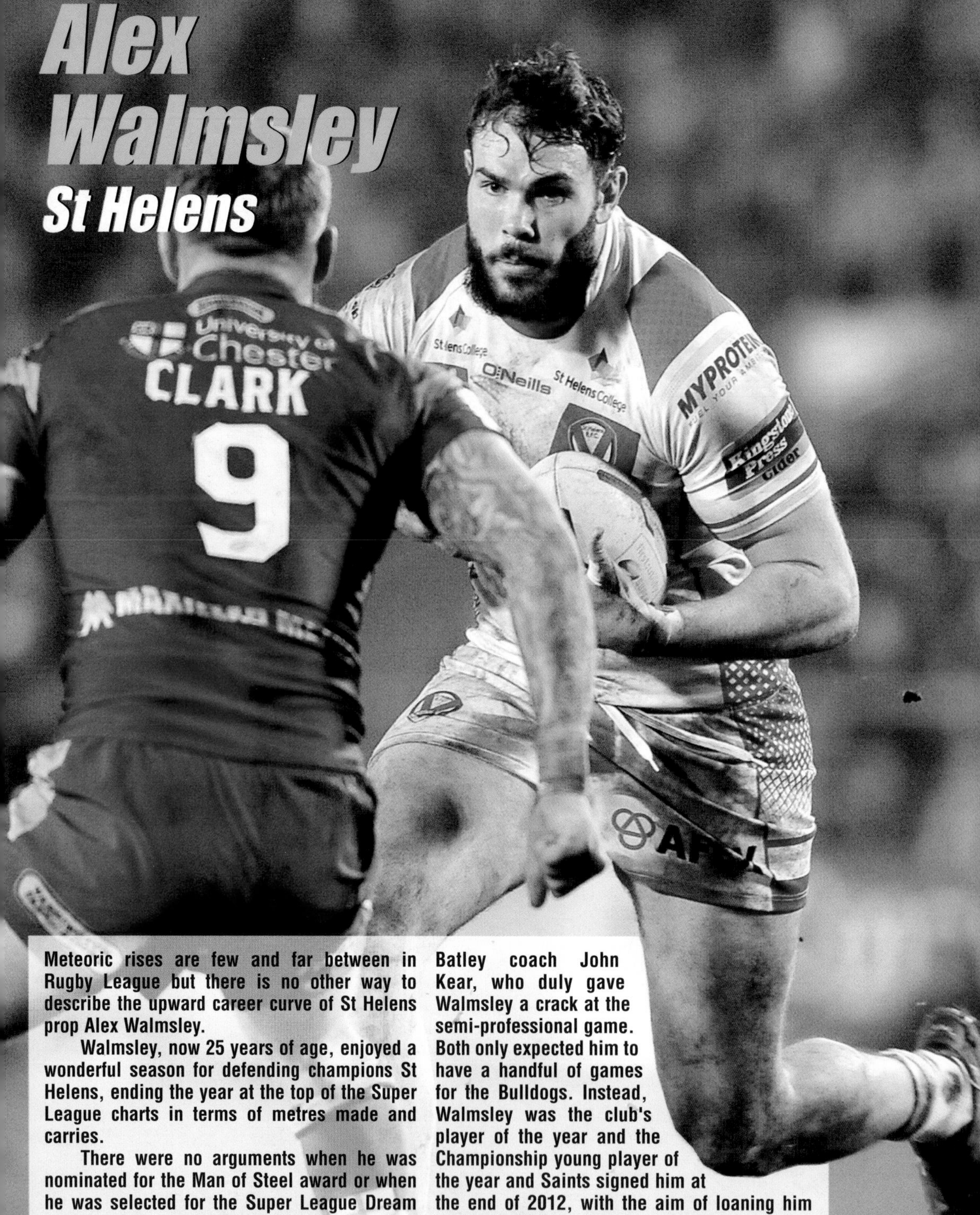

Meteoric rises are few and far between in Rugby League but there is no other way to describe the upward career curve of St Helens prop Alex Walmsley.

Walmsley, now 25 years of age, enjoyed a wonderful season for defending champions St Helens, ending the year at the top of the Super League charts in terms of metres made and carries.

There were no arguments when he was nominated for the Man of Steel award or when he was selected for the Super League Dream Team.

When he was 21, Walmsley was still playing for his boyhood amateur club Dewsbury Celtic. He did win the player of the year award for the Co-operative Summer Conference National League in 2011. He was also studying at then-called Leeds Met University when in his third year he was persuaded to turn out for the all-conquering Met side.

He was named the Student Rugby League player of the year, catching the attention of Batley coach John Kear, who duly gave Walmsley a crack at the semi-professional game. Both only expected him to have a handful of games for the Bulldogs. Instead, Walmsley was the club's player of the year and the Championship young player of the year and Saints signed him at the end of 2012, with the aim of loaning him back to Batley to get more experience.

Alas for Batley supporters he only made three appearances for the Bulldogs that year, making his Saints debut in a round three draw at home against Hull FC and going on to make 26 appearances in 2013.

But for an ankle injury sustained in Saints' semi-final exit at Leeds, Walmsley's would almost certainly have earned a role in England's series against New Zealand in 2015. His first cap can't be too far away.

Jamie Peacock & Kevin Sinfield

Leeds Rhinos

2015 was the year Leeds Rhinos became only the third club to do the treble by winning the Challenge Cup, League Leaders' Shield and the Super League title in the same season, Bradford Bulls in 2003 and St Helens in 2006 also achieving the feat.

On the night the Rhinos secured their third trophy - with the 22-20 victory over Wigan in their seventh Grand Final success - we were also witnessing the end of the long and successful playing careers of two legends of the game.

Rhinos captain Kevin Sinfield and Jamie Peacock had played in over a thousand career games between them when the final whistle blew on that October night.

Sinfield was already the Leeds club's greatest ever captain and that was confirmed when he held the Super League trophy aloft for a record seventh time.

It was the end of an unusual season for Sinfield, who went up from fifth to third in the game's all-time points scorers list, while being relegated to the bench in mid-season and even dropped completely by Brian McDermott, who deservedly ended 2015 as Super League's coach of the year.

With a career total of 4,231 points, only Neil Fox (6,220) and Jim Sullivan (6,022) stand above Sinfield in the all-time list.

Peacock was set to join Hull KR as football manager. The former England captain made 288 appearances for Leeds after joining them from Bradford in 2006, which took his career total to 552. He holds the Grand Final record with 11 appearances. At 37 years of age, he was in the form of his life in Super League XX.

Fellow prop Kylie Leuluai also called it a day, having won six Grand Final rings since he came to Headingley in 2007.

It was truly the end of an era.

2015 SEASON REVIEW

LEFT: Warrington's Ryan Atkins makes a break against St Helens

ABOVE: Super League arrived at Newcastle's St James' Park for the first time in 2015 - the crowd watches on during the Hull FC v Hull KR derby clash

LEFT: Leeds' Kevin Sinfield tackled by Wigan duo Larne Patrick and Matt Bowen

RIGHT: Zak Hardaker - 2015 Man of Steel winner

BELOW: Wigan's Dominic Manfredi dives for the line despite the challenges of Huddersfield's Jake Connor and Aaron Murphy, as the Warriors reach Old Trafford

ABOVE: St Helens' Adam Swift drives forward against Leeds as the Saints fall just short of the Grand Final

BELOW: Leeds' Ryan Hall races away to score the most dramatic of tries against Huddersfield - a score which clinched the League Leaders Shield for the Rhinos (ABOVE)

RIGHT: St George Illawarra's Mitch Rein bursts past Warrington's Ashton Sims

LEFT: Wigan's Josh Charnley halted by Brisbane's Corey Parker and Aaron Whitchurch

ST HELENS 0
SOUTH SYDNEY RABBITOHS 39

ABOVE: Mose Masoe gets the ball away under heavy Souths pressure

ABOVE: John Sutton and Greg Inglis celebrate the Rabbitohs' World Club Challenge victory

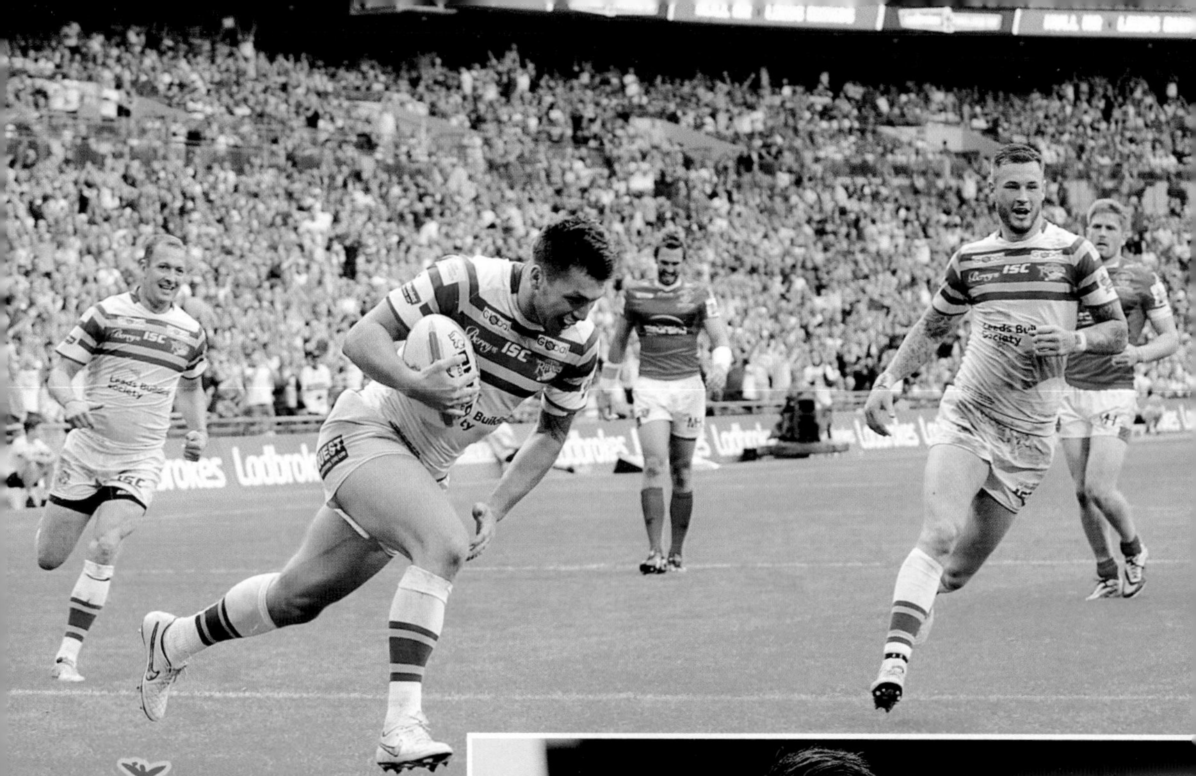

Ladbrokes CHALLENGE CUP FINAL

HULL KINGSTON ROVERS 0
LEEDS RHINOS 50

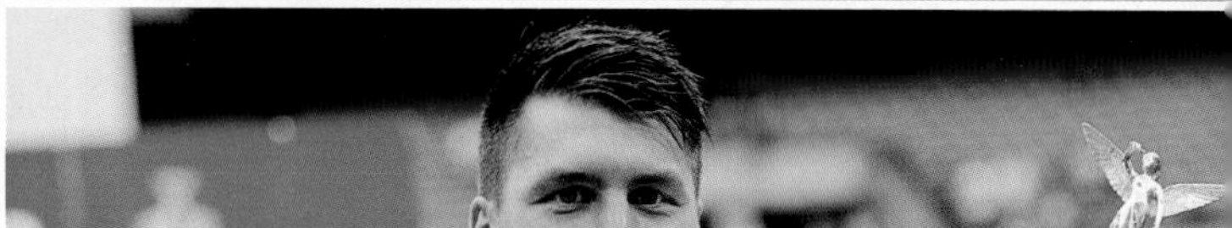

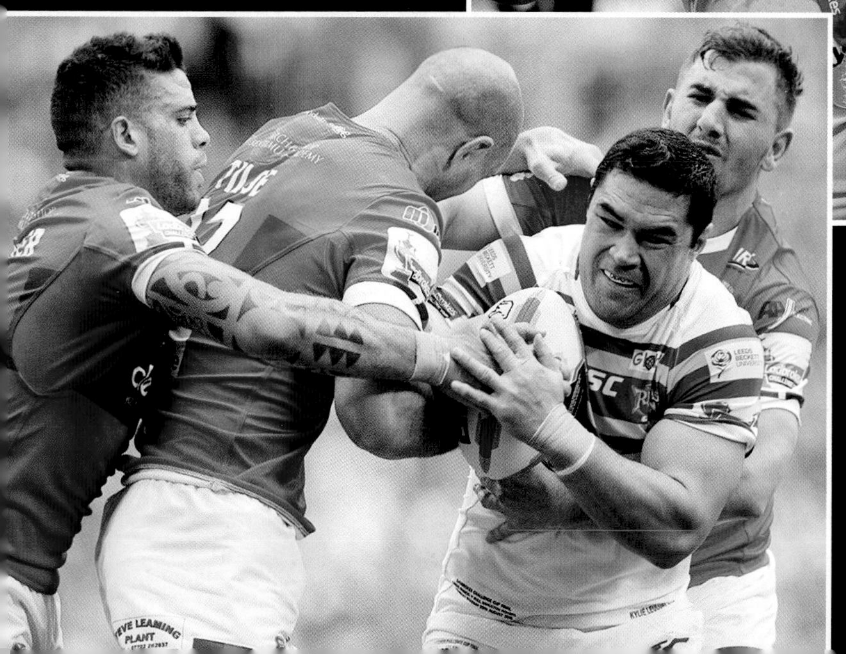

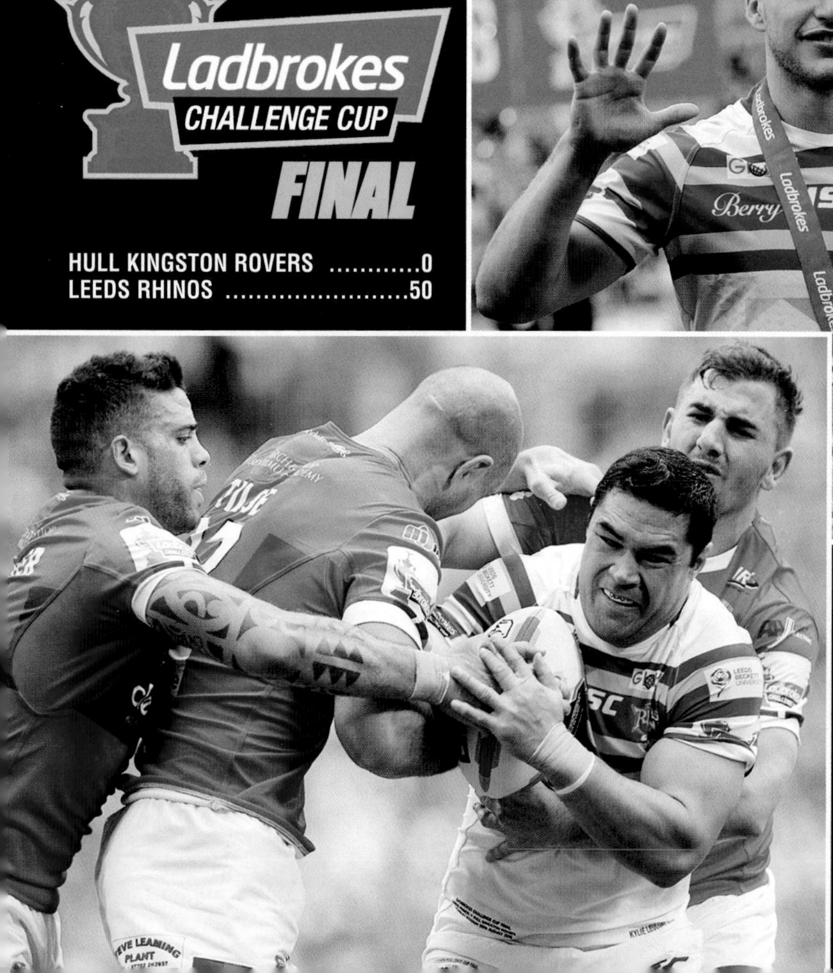

TOP: Leeds' Lance Todd Trophy winner Tom Briscoe shows his delight at crossing for the last of his record-breaking five Challenge Cup Final tries, and (ABOVE) shows off the Challenge Cup

LEFT: Kylie Leuluai meets Hull KR trio Adam Walker, Dane Tilse and Kevin Larroyer head on

BELOW: Oldham celebrate earning promotion to the Championship for 2016

BELOW LEFT: Adam Clay celebrates scoring in the Roughyeds' Promotion Final win against Keighley

RIGHT: Jordan James leads the Swinton celebrations

North Wales Crusaders won the iPRO Sport Cup after victory against Swinton

ABOVE: Swinton's Mike Butt tries to break free from Keighley's Andy Gabriel

Championship League Leaders Leigh Centurions kicked off their campaign in front of a big crowd against rivals Bradford Bulls in February. Ryan Brierley leaves Jake Mullaney grounded in that game

ABOVE LEFT: Featherstone Rovers won the inaugural Championship Shield after defeating London Broncos

ABOVE: Bradford's Dale Ferguson shows the pain of the Bulls' Million Pound Game loss to Wakefield

LEFT: Wildcats loose forward Chris Annakin races away from Bradford's Tom Olbison

RIGHT: Matt Scott shows off the Provan-Summons trophy to the Cowboys' delighted fans

BELOW: Johnathan Thurston beats Brisbane's Darius Boyd to a high ball

GRAND FINAL

BRISBANE BRONCOS..................16
NORTH QUEENSLAND COWBOYS....17

BELOW: The victorious Cowboys rush to Johnathan Thurston after his dramatic winning field goal

first:utility SUPER LEAGUE

GRAND FINAL

XX

LEEDS RHINOS 22
WIGAN WARRIORS 20

ABOVE: Leeds' Josh Walters crashes past Dominic Manfredi and Matt Bowen to score the winning try

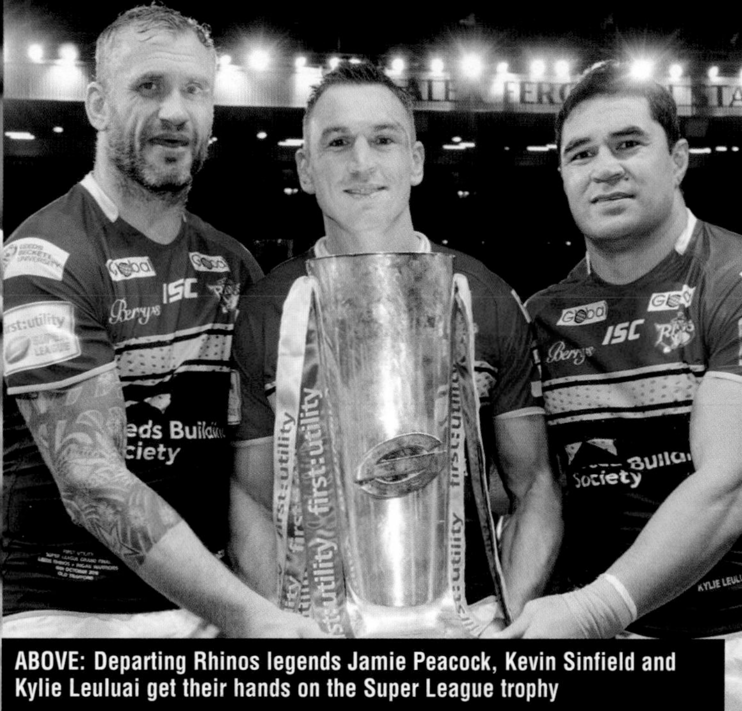

ABOVE: Departing Rhinos legends Jamie Peacock, Kevin Sinfield and Kylie Leuluai get their hands on the Super League trophy

LEFT: Wigan's Liam Farrell makes the break for Joe Burgess' opening try

ABOVE: Queensland celebrate their State of Origin success

BELOW RIGHT: Queensland's Justin Hodges in action during Origin III

ABOVE: Australia's James Tamou closed down by New Zealand's Simon Mannering

BELOW: The Kiwis get their victory party started

BELOW: Wales celebrate winning the 2015 European Championship

FIRST TEST

ENGLAND................................26
NEW ZEALAND 12

ABOVE: Kallum Watkins tackled as George Williams moves in to support

ENGLAND 2
NEW ZEALAND 9

RIGHT: Sean O'Loughlin leads England out at London's Olympic Park

ABOVE: The Kiwis perform the Haka.

SECOND TEST

THIRD TEST

ENGLAND.................................20
NEW ZEALAND 14

ABOVE: Elliott Whitehead crashes over to score his second try of the game

ABOVE: Jordan Kahu slides in for the Kiwis' late try

RIGHT: Mike Cooper meets some heavy New Zealand defensive resistance

ABOVE: England captain Sean O'Loughlin and coach Steve McNamara show off the Baskerville Shield

5
STATISTICAL REVIEW

SUPER LEAGUE PLAYERS
1996-2015

Super League Players 1996-2015

PLAYER	CLUB	YEAR	APP	TRIES	GOALS	FG	PTS
Jordan Abdull	Hull	2014-15	15(10)	4	2	0	20
Carl Ablett	Leeds	2004, 2006-15	194(32)	58	0	0	232
	London	2005	3(2)	0	0	0	0
Darren Abram	Oldham	1996-97	25(2)	11	0	0	44
Mitch Achurch	Leeds	2013-15	16(42)	11	0	0	44
Brad Adams	Bradford	2014	1(1)	0	0	0	0
Darren Adams	Paris	1996	9(1)	1	0	0	4
Guy Adams	Huddersfield	1998	1(2)	0	0	0	0
Luke Adamson	Salford	2006-07, 2009-12	73(39)	11	1	0	46
Matt Adamson	Leeds	2002-04	54(8)	9	0	0	36
Phil Adamson	St Helens	1999	(1)	0	0	0	0
Toby Adamson	Salford	2010	(1)	0	0	0	0
Danny Addy	Bradford	2010-14	49(42)	13	7	0	66
Ade Adebisi	London	2004	(1)	0	0	0	0
Patrick Ah Van	Widnes	2012-15	66	50	54	0	308
	Bradford	2011	26	9	87	0	210
Jamie Ainscough	Wigan	2002-03	30(2)	18	0	0	72
Shaun Ainscough	Bradford	2011-12	27	15	0	0	60
	Wigan	2009-10	12	13	0	0	52
	Castleford	2010	7	4	0	0	16
Glen Air	London	1998-2001	57(13)	27	0	1	109
Paul Aiton	Leeds	2014-15	36(6)	2	0	0	8
	Wakefield	2012-13	43(2)	7	0	0	28
Makali Aizue	Hull KR	2007-09	18(32)	4	0	0	16
Darren Albert	St Helens	2002-05	105	77	0	0	308
Lucas Albert	Catalans	2015	2	0	0	0	0
Paul Alcock	Widnes	2003, 2005	1(7)	1	0	0	4
Neil Alexander	Salford	1998	(1)	0	0	0	0
Malcolm Alker	Salford	1997-2002, 2004-07, 2009-10	271(2)	40	0	1	161
Danny Allan	Leeds	2008-09	2(5)	0	0	0	0
Chris Allen	Castleford	1996	(1)	0	0	0	0
Dave Allen	Widnes	2012-14	50(13)	5	0	0	20
	Wigan	2003, 2005	6(15)	2	0	0	8
Gavin Allen	London	1996	10	0	0	0	0
John Allen	Workington	1996	20(1)	6	0	0	24
Ray Allen	London	1996	5(3)	3	0	0	12
Mitchell Allgood	Hull KR	2015	8	2	0	0	8
Richard Allwood	Gateshead	1999	(4)	0	0	0	0
Sean Allwood	Gateshead	1999	3(17)	1	0	0	4
David Alstead	Warrington	2000-02	23(10)	3	0	0	12
Luke Ambler	Harlequins	2011	5(17)	1	0	0	4
	Leeds	2010	1(8)	1	0	0	4
Asa Amone	Halifax	1996-97	32(7)	10	0	0	40
Kyle Amor	St Helens	2014-15	44(1)	6	0	0	24
	Wakefield	2011-13	51(23)	9	0	0	36
	Leeds	2010	(3)	0	0	0	0
Thibaut Ancely	Catalans	2011	(2)	0	0	0	0
Grant Anderson	Castleford	1996-97	15(6)	3	0	0	12
Louis Anderson	Catalans	2012-15	55(20)	20	0	0	80
	Warrington	2008-11	92	18	0	0	72
Paul Anderson	St Helens	2005-06	48(5)	7	1	0	30
	Bradford	1997-2004	74(104)	30	0	0	120
	Halifax	1996	5(1)	1	0	0	4
Paul Anderson	Sheffield	1999	3(7)	1	0	0	4
	St Helens	1996-98	2(28)	4	1	0	18
Scott Anderson	Wakefield	2014-15	22(7)	2	0	0	8
Vinnie Anderson	Salford	2011-12	33(3)	14	0	0	56
	Warrington	2007-10	57(19)	22	0	0	88
	St Helens	2005-06	28(14)	17	0	0	68
Phil Anderton	St Helens	2004	1	0	0	0	0
Chris Annakin	Wakefield	2013-15	3(24)	1	0	0	4
Eric Anselme	Leeds	2008	2(2)	2	0	0	8
	Halifax	1997	(2)	0	0	0	0
Mark Applegarth	Wakefield	2004-07	20(5)	3	0	0	12
Graham Appo	Warrington	2002-05	60(13)	35	80	0	300
	Huddersfield	2001	7	4	0	0	16
Anthony Armour	London	2005	11(7)	1	0	0	4
Colin Armstrong	Workington	1996	11(2)	1	0	0	4
Tom Armstrong	St Helens	2009-11	10(5)	9	0	0	36
Richard Armswood	Workington	1996	5(1)	1	0	0	4
Danny Arnold	Salford	2001-02	26(13)	13	0	0	52
	Huddersfield	1998-2000	55(7)	26	0	0	104
	Castleford	2000	(4)	0	0	0	0
	St Helens	1996-97	40(1)	33	0	0	132
Joe Arundel	Wakefield	2015	15	2	4	0	16
	Bradford	2014	9(3)	5	0	0	20
	Hull	2013-14	16	7	1	0	30
	Castleford	2008, 2010-12	35(4)	14	2	0	60
Craig Ashall	St Helens	2006	1	1	0	0	4
Nathan Ashe	St Helens	2011-13	6(4)	0	0	0	0
Chris Ashton	Wigan	2005-07	44(2)	25	2	0	104
Matty Ashurst	Wakefield	2015	5	4	0	0	16
	Salford	2012-14	65(7)	11	0	0	44
	St Helens	2009-11	12(39)	8	0	0	32
Jack Ashworth	St Helens	2015	1	0	0	0	0
Roy Asotasi	Warrington	2014-15	16(37)	5	1	0	22
Peter Aspinall	Huddersfield	2013	1(1)	0	0	0	0
Martin Aspinwall	Hull	2012	12(15)	0	0	0	0
	Castleford	2011	12(6)	2	0	0	8
	Huddersfield	2006-10	72(8)	22	0	0	88
	Wigan	2001-05	85(13)	27	0	0	108
Mark Aston	Sheffield	1996-99	67(6)	6	243	6	516
Paul Atcheson	Widnes	2002-04	16(35)	4	0	0	16
	St Helens	1998-2000	58(4)	18	0	0	72
	Oldham	1996-97	40	21	0	0	84
David Atkins	Huddersfield	2001	26(1)	4	0	0	16
Jordan Atkins	London	2014	13(1)	4	0	0	16
Ryan Atkins	Warrington	2010-15	158	99	0	0	396
	Wakefield	2006-09	86(2)	45	0	0	180
Josh Atkinson	Castleford	2012	2	0	0	0	0
Brad Attwood	Halifax	2003	(3)	0	0	0	0
Warren Ayres	Salford	1999	2(9)	1	2	0	8
Jerome Azema	Paris	1997	(1)	0	0	0	0
Marcus Bai	Bradford	2006	24	9	0	0	36
	Leeds	2004-05	57	42	0	0	168
David Baildon	Hull	1998-99	26(2)	4	0	0	16
Jean-Philippe Baile	Catalans	2008-14	62(16)	23	0	0	92
Andy Bailey	Hull	2004-05	2(8)	1	0	0	4
Chris Bailey	Huddersfield	2014-15	17(17)	5	0	0	20
	London	2012-13	41	14	0	0	56
	Harlequins	2011	24	3	0	0	12
Julian Bailey	Huddersfield	2003-04	47	13	0	0	52
Phil Bailey	Wigan	2007-10	84(4)	13	0	0	52
Ricky Bailey	St Helens	2015	1	0	0	0	0
Ryan Bailey	Castleford	2015	3(2)	0	0	0	0
	Hull KR	2015	(1)	1	0	0	4
	Leeds	2002-14	171(102)	17	0	0	68
Jason Baitieri	Catalans	2011-15	91(27)	12	0	0	48
Simon Baldwin	Salford	2004-06	20(29)	3	0	0	12
	Sheffield	1999	7(15)	2	0	0	8
	Halifax	1996-98	41(15)	16	0	1	65
Jordan Baldwinson	Bradford	2014	2(4)	0	0	0	0
	Leeds	2013	(2)	0	0	0	0
Rob Ball	Wigan	1998-2000	3(4)	0	0	0	0
Paul Ballard	Celtic	2009	2	0	0	0	0
	Widnes	2005	3(1)	2	0	0	8
Darren Bamford	Salford	2005	2(1)	0	0	0	0
Michael Banks	Bradford	1998	(1)	0	0	0	0
Steve Bannister	Harlequins	2007	(6)	0	0	0	0
	St Helens	2006-07	(3)	0	0	0	0
Frederic Banquet	Paris	1996	16(2)	7	4	0	36
Lee Bardauskas	Castleford	1996-97	(2)	0	0	0	0
Craig Barker	Workington	1996	(2)	0	0	0	0
Dwayne Barker	Harlequins	2008	5(5)	1	0	0	4
	London	2004	3	1	0	0	4
	Hull	2003	(1)	0	0	0	0
Mark Barlow	Wakefield	2002	(1)	0	0	0	0
Danny Barnes	Halifax	1999	2	0	0	0	0
Richie Barnett	Salford	2007	7	4	0	0	16
	Warrington	2006-07	26(10)	15	0	0	60
	Hull	2004-05	21(5)	21	0	0	84
	Widnes	2005	4	2	0	0	8
Richie Barnett	Hull	2003-04	31(1)	17	0	0	68
	London	2001-02	31(4)	13	0	0	52
David Barnhill	Leeds	2000	20(8)	5	0	0	20
Trent Barrett	Wigan	2007-08	53(1)	22	0	4	92
Paul Barrow	Warrington	1996-97	1(10)	1	0	0	4
Scott Barrow	St Helens	1997-2000	9(13)	1	0	0	4
Steve Barrow	London	2000	2	0	0	0	0
	Hull	1998-99	4(17)	1	0	0	4
	Wigan	1996	(8)	3	0	0	12
William Barthau	Catalans	2010, 2012-14	13(3)	2	15	0	38
Ben Barton	Huddersfield	1998	1(6)	1	0	0	4
Danny Barton	Salford	2001	1	0	0	0	0
Wayne Bartrim	Castleford	2002-03	41(2)	9	157	0	350
Greg Barwick	London	1996-97	30(4)	21	110	2	306
David Bastian	Halifax	1996	(2)	0	0	0	0
Ashley Bateman	Celtic	2009	1	0	0	0	0
John Bateman	Wigan	2014-15	47(8)	13	0	0	52
	Bradford	2011-13	25(5)	7	0	0	28
David Bates	Castleford	2001-02	(4)	0	0	0	0
	Warrington	2001	1(2)	0	0	0	0
Sam Bates	Bradford	2014	(2)	0	0	0	0
Nathan Batty	Wakefield	2001	1(1)	0	0	0	0
Andreas Bauer	Hull KR	2007	10(2)	5	0	0	20
Russell Bawden	London	1996-97, 2002-04	50(49)	15	0	0	60
Neil Baxter	Salford	2001	1	0	0	0	0
Neil Baynes	Salford	1999-2002, 2004	84(19)	10	0	0	40
	Wigan	1996-98	(10)	1	0	0	4
Chris Beasley	Celtic	2009	15(5)	2	0	0	8
Chris Beattie	Catalans	2006	22(5)	3	0	0	12
Richard Beaumont	Hull KR	2011-13	1(16)	1	0	0	4
Robbie Beazley	London	1997-99	48(15)	13	0	0	52
Robbie Beckett	Halifax	2002	27	15	0	0	60
Matty Beharrell	Hull KR	2013	1	0	0	0	0

PLAYER	CLUB	YEAR	APP	TRIES	GOALS	FG	PTS
Dean Bell	Leeds	1996	1	1	0	0	4
Ian Bell	Hull	2003	(1)	0	0	0	0
Mark Bell	Wigan	1998	22	12	0	0	48
Paul Bell	Leeds	2000	1	0	0	0	0
Steven Bell	Catalans	2009-10	43	14	0	0	56
Troy Bellamy	Paris	1997	5(10)	0	0	0	0
Adrian Belle	Huddersfield	1998	10(2)	0	0	0	0
	Oldham	1996	19	8	0	0	32
Jamie Benn	Castleford	1998, 2000	3(8)	1	15	0	34
Andy Bennett	Warrington	1996	6(5)	1	0	0	4
Mike Bennett	St Helens	2000-08	74(70)	15	0	0	60
Andrew Bentley	Catalans	2007-10	9(15)	1	0	0	4
John Bentley	Huddersfield	1999	13(4)	3	0	0	12
	Halifax	1996, 1998	22(3)	24	0	0	96
Kane Bentley	Catalans	2007-10	11(19)	5	0	0	20
Phil Bergman	Paris	1997	20(1)	14	0	0	56
Shaun Berrigan	Hull	2008-10	60(8)	12	0	0	48
Joe Berry	Huddersfield	1998-99	25(14)	3	0	0	12
David Berthezene	Salford	2007	9(1)	0	0	0	0
	Catalans	2006-07	5(14)	0	0	0	0
Colin Best	Hull	2003-04	57	34	0	0	136
Roger Best	London	1997-98	1(5)	1	0	0	4
Bob Beswick	Wigan	2004-05	5(14)	2	0	0	8
Monty Betham	Wakefield	2006	26	2	0	0	8
Mike Bethwaite	Workington	1996	17(3)	1	0	0	4
Denis Betts	Wigan	1998-2001	82(24)	33	0	0	132
Cliff Beverley	Salford	2004-05	47(1)	14	0	0	56
Kyle Bibb	Wakefield	2008-10	1(24)	0	0	0	0
	Harlequins	2010	(2)	0	0	0	0
	Hull KR	2009	(2)	0	0	0	0
Adam Bibey	Widnes	2004	(1)	0	0	0	0
Ricky Bibey	Wakefield	2007-09	32(25)	1	0	0	4
	St Helens	2004	4(14)	0	0	0	0
	Wigan	2001-03	5(29)	0	0	0	0
Chris Birchall	Halifax	2002-03	24(22)	4	0	0	16
	Bradford	2000	(1)	0	0	0	0
Deon Bird	Castleford	2006	17(6)	5	0	0	20
	Widnes	2003-04	39(6)	9	0	0	36
	Wakefield	2002	10(1)	1	0	0	4
	Hull	2000-02	37(22)	20	0	0	80
	Gateshead	1999	19(3)	13	0	0	52
	Paris	1996-97	30	12	2	0	52
Greg Bird	Catalans	2009	20(2)	5	3	0	26
Mike Bishay	London	2013-14	7(11)	2	2	0	12
Nathan Blacklock	Hull	2005-06	44(3)	33	0	0	132
Ben Blackmore	Huddersfield	2013-14	3	4	0	0	16
	Castleford	2012	1	0	0	0	0
Richie Blackmore	Leeds	1997-2000	63	25	0	0	100
Anthony Blackwood	Crusaders	2010	1	0	0	0	0
	Celtic	2009	25	5	0	0	20
Jack Blagbrough	Huddersfield	2013	(1)	0	0	0	0
Maurice Blair	Hull KR	2015	19(2)	2	0	0	8
Luke Blake	Wakefield	2009	(2)	0	0	0	0
Matthew Blake	Wakefield	2003-04	1(5)	0	0	0	0
Steve Blakeley	Salford	1997-2002	103(5)	26	241	2	588
	Warrington	2000	4(3)	1	9	0	22
Richard Blakeway	Castleford	2002-04	1(14)	0	0	0	0
Damien Blanch	Catalans	2011-13	70	42	0	0	168
	Wakefield	2008-10	44(3)	31	0	0	124
	Castleford	2006	3(2)	0	0	0	0
Matt Blaymire	Wakefield	2007-11	96(3)	26	0	1	105
Ian Blease	Salford	1997	(1)	0	0	0	0
Jamie Bloem	Huddersfield	2003	18(4)	3	11	0	34
	Halifax	1998-2002	82(25)	25	100	2	302
Vea Bloomfield	Paris	1996	4(14)	3	0	0	12
Matty Blythe	Bradford	2013-14	24(6)	8	0	0	32
	Warrington	2007-12	28(27)	12	0	0	48
Ben Bolger	London	2012	2(7)	1	0	0	4
	Harlequins	2010-11	4(15)	0	0	0	0
Pascal Bomati	Paris	1996	17(1)	10	0	0	40
Simon Booth	Hull	1998-99	15(9)	2	0	0	8
	St Helens	1996-97	10(4)	1	0	0	4
Steve Booth	Huddersfield	1998-99	16(4)	2	3	0	14
Alan Boothroyd	Halifax	1997	2(3)	0	0	0	0
Thomas Bosc	Catalans	2006-15	186(5)	47	467	11	1133
John Boslem	Paris	1996	(5)	0	0	0	0
Liam Bostock	St Helens	2004	1	0	0	0	0
Liam Botham	Wigan	2005	5	0	0	0	0
	Leeds	2003-05	2(11)	4	0	0	16
	London	2004	6(2)	3	7	0	26
Frano Botica	Castleford	1996	21	5	84	2	190
Matthew Bottom	Leigh	2005	(1)	0	0	0	0
Hadj Boudebza	Paris	1996	(2)	0	0	0	0
John Boudebza	Hull KR	2015	12(6)	2	0	0	8
David Boughton	Huddersfield	1999	26(1)	4	0	0	16
Julian Bousquet	Catalans	2012-15	17(41)	3	0	0	12
David Bouveng	Halifax	1997-99	66(2)	19	0	0	76
Josh Bowden	Hull	2012-15	21(33)	3	0	0	12
Matt Bowen	Wigan	2014-15	43	21	31	0	146
Tony Bowes	Huddersfield	1998	3(2)	0	0	0	0
Radney Bowker	London	2004	3	1	0	0	4
	St Helens	2001	(1)	0	0	0	0
David Boyle	Bradford	1999-2000	36(13)	15	0	1	61
Ryan Boyle	Castleford	2006, 2008-09, 2013-15	10(56)	4	0	0	16
	Salford	2010-13	57(14)	3	0	0	12
Andy Bracek	Crusaders	2011	(2)	0	0	0	0
	Warrington	2005-08	7(49)	7	0	0	28
	St Helens	2004	(1)	0	0	0	0
David Bradbury	Hudds-Sheff	2000	21(2)	1	0	0	4
	Salford	1997-99	23(10)	6	0	0	24
	Oldham	1996-97	19(6)	9	0	0	36
John Braddish	St Helens	2001-02	1(1)	0	3	0	6
Graeme Bradley	Bradford	1996-98	62(1)	29	0	0	116
Nick Bradley-Qalilawa	Harlequins	2006	27	6	0	0	24
	London	2005	28	19	0	0	76
Darren Bradstreet	London	1999-2000	1(3)	0	0	0	0
Dominic Brambani	Castleford	2004	2(2)	0	0	0	0
Liam Bretherton	Wigan	1999	(5)	2	0	0	8
	Warrington	1997	(2)	0	0	0	0
Johnny Brewer	Halifax	1996	4(2)	2	0	0	8
Chris Bridge	Warrington	2005-15	186(17)	89	248	1	853
	Bradford	2003-04	2(14)	4	6	0	28
Danny Bridge	Bradford	2014	4(4)	0	0	0	0
	Warrington	2013	(2)	0	0	0	0
Lee Briers	Warrington	1997-2013	365(12)	130	810	70	2210
	St Helens	1997	3	0	11	0	22
Carl Briggs	Salford	1999	8(5)	3	0	1	13
	Halifax	1996	5(3)	1	0	0	4
Kyle Briggs	Bradford	2011	6	4	0	0	16
	Harlequins	2011	3	0	0	0	0
Mike Briggs	Widnes	2002	1(2)	1	0	0	4
Luke Briscoe	Leeds	2014	(3)	1	0	0	4
	Wakefield	2014	2	0	0	0	0
Shaun Briscoe	Widnes	2012-13	11(2)	4	0	0	16
	Hull KR	2008-11	92	27	0	0	108
	Hull	2004-07	83(9)	50	0	0	200
	Wigan	2002-03	23(5)	11	0	0	44
Tom Briscoe	Leeds	2014-15	41	20	0	0	80
	Hull	2008-13	131(3)	83	0	0	332
Darren Britt	St Helens	2002-03	41	3	0	0	12
Gary Broadbent	Salford	1997-2002	117(2)	22	0	0	88
Paul Broadbent	Wakefield	2002	16(5)	0	0	0	0
	Hull	2000-01	40(9)	3	0	0	12
	Halifax	1999	26(1)	2	0	0	8
	Sheffield	1996-98	63(1)	6	0	0	24
Andrew Brocklehurst	Salford	2004-07	34(23)	5	0	0	20
	London	2004	12(6)	2	0	0	8
	Halifax	2001-03	37(8)	2	0	0	8
Justin Brooker	Wakefield	2001	25	9	0	0	36
	Bradford	2000	17(4)	11	0	0	44
Danny Brough	Huddersfield	2010-15	153(3)	36	542	11	1239
	Wakefield	2008-10	50(1)	14	174	4	408
	Castleford	2006	10	1	31	2	68
	Hull	2005-06	25(12)	3	85	1	183
Jodie Broughton	Huddersfield	2014-15	30	16	0	0	64
	Salford	2010-13	93	53	0	0	212
	Hull	2008-09	9(3)	6	0	0	24
Alex Brown	Hull KR	2013	16	9	0	0	36
	Huddersfield	2009	1	0	0	0	0
Darren Brown	Salford	1999-2001	47(9)	11	6	0	56
Gavin Brown	Leeds	1996-97	5(2)	1	2	0	8
Kevin Brown	Widnes	2013-15	56	36	1	1	147
	Huddersfield	2006-12	156	43	0	1	173
	Wigan	2003-06	46(18)	27	0	0	108
Lee Brown	Hull	1999	(1)	0	0	0	0
Michael Brown	Huddersfield	2008	(1)	0	0	0	0
Michael Brown	London	1996	(2)	0	0	0	0
Todd Brown	Paris	1996	8(1)	2	0	0	8
Adrian Brunker	Wakefield	1999	17	6	0	0	24
Lamont Bryan	Harlequins	2008-11	9(22)	2	0	0	8
Justin Bryant	Paris	1996	4(1)	0	0	0	0
	London	1996	7(8)	1	0	0	4
Mark Bryant	London	2012-13	16(36)	3	1	0	14
	Crusaders	2010-11	42(8)	1	0	0	4
	Celtic	2009	23(3)	0	0	0	0
Austin Buchanan	Wakefield	2005-06	6	2	0	0	8
	London	2003	3(1)	2	0	0	8
Danny Buderus	Leeds	2009-11	57(14)	14	0	0	56
Neil Budworth	Celtic	2009	8(19)	0	0	0	0
	Harlequins	2006	2(19)	0	0	0	0
	London	2002-05	59(11)	4	1	0	18
James Bunyan	Huddersfield	1998-99	8(7)	2	0	0	8
Andy Burgess	Salford	1997	3(12)	0	0	0	0
Joe Burgess	Wigan	2013-15	52	45	0	0	180
Luke Burgess	Leeds	2008-11	10(63)	6	0	0	24
	Harlequins	2007	(3)	0	0	0	0
Sam Burgess	Bradford	2006-09	46(34)	14	5	0	66
Tom Burgess	Bradford	2011-12	1(41)	3	0	0	12
Greg Burke	Hull KR	2015	9(5)	0	0	0	0
	Wigan	2013-14	9(13)	1	0	0	4
	Bradford	2014	(1)	0	0	0	0
Joe Burke	Crusaders	2011	(1)	0	0	0	0

Super League Players 1996-2015

PLAYER	CLUB	YEAR	APP	TRIES	GOALS	FG	PTS
Mike Burnett	Harlequins	2011	16(4)	1	0	0	4
	Hull	2008-10	13(21)	3	0	0	12
Darren Burns	Warrington	2002-04	66(6)	19	0	0	76
Gary Burns	Oldham	1996	6	1	0	0	4
Paul Burns	Workington	1996	5(2)	1	0	0	4
Travis Burns	St Helens	2015	25	4	28	0	72
	Hull KR	2013-14	46	8	81	2	196
Rob Burrow	Leeds	2001-15	284(102)	159	126	5	893
Dean Busby	Warrington	1999-2002	34(34)	7	0	0	28
	Hull	1998	8(6)	0	0	0	0
	St Helens	1996-98	1(7)	0	0	0	0
Tom Bush	Leeds	2010	3(1)	1	0	0	4
Ikram Butt	London	1996	5(1)	0	0	0	0
Shane Byrne	Huddersfield	1998-99	1(5)	0	0	0	0
Todd Byrne	Hull	2008-09	20	4	0	0	16
Didier Cabestany	Paris	1996-97	20(6)	2	0	0	8
Hep Cahill	Widnes	2012-15	65(2)	3	0	0	12
	Crusaders	2011	16	2	0	0	8
Joel Caine	Salford	2004	24	8	13	0	58
	London	2003	6	4	1	0	18
Mark Calderwood	Harlequins	2011	13	2	0	0	8
	Hull	2009-10	23	6	0	0	24
	Wigan	2006-08	64	23	0	0	92
	Leeds	2001-05	117(9)	88	0	0	352
Mike Callan	Warrington	2002	(4)	0	0	0	0
Matt Calland	Huddersfield	2003	2	0	0	0	0
	Hull	1999	1	0	0	0	0
	Bradford	1996-98	44(5)	24	0	0	96
Dean Callaway	London	1999-2000	26(24)	12	0	0	48
Laurent Cambres	Paris	1996	(1)	0	0	0	0
Chris Campbell	Warrington	2000	7(1)	2	0	0	8
Liam Campbell	Wakefield	2005	(1)	0	0	0	0
Logan Campbell	Hull	1998-99, 2001	70(13)	14	0	0	56
	Castleford	2000	14(2)	3	0	0	12
	Workington	1996	7(1)	1	0	0	4
Terry Campese	Hull KR	2015	15	2	0	0	8
Blake Cannova	Widnes	2002	(1)	0	0	0	0
Phil Cantillon	Widnes	2002-03	27(21)	18	0	0	72
	Leeds	1997	(1)	0	0	0	0
Liam Carberry	Widnes	2014-15	2(5)	0	0	0	0
Damien Cardace	Catalans	2012, 2014-15	23	14	0	0	56
Daryl Cardiss	Warrington	2003-04	23(2)	3	4	0	20
	Halifax	1999-2003	91(8)	39	4	0	164
	Wigan	1996-98	12(6)	4	0	0	16
Dale Cardoza	Warrington	2002	5	1	0	0	4
	Halifax	2001	3	1	0	0	4
	Huddersfield	2000-01	20(9)	11	0	0	44
	Sheffield	1998-99	11(7)	3	0	0	12
Paul Carige	Salford	1999	24(1)	7	0	0	28
Dane Carlaw	Catalans	2008-10	58(15)	9	0	0	36
Keal Carlile	Hull KR	2012-15	6(28)	1	0	0	4
	Huddersfield	2009, 2011	2(1)	1	0	0	4
	Bradford	2008	(1)	0	0	0	0
Jim Carlton	Huddersfield	1999	3(11)	2	0	0	8
George Carmont	Wigan	2008-12	136	71	0	0	284
Brian Carney	Warrington	2009	4	2	0	0	8
	Wigan	2001-05	91(10)	42	1	0	170
	Hull	2000	13(3)	7	0	0	28
	Gateshead	1999	3(2)	2	0	0	8
Justin Carney	Castleford	2013-15	58	56	0	0	224
Martin Carney	Warrington	1997	(1)	0	0	0	0
Todd Carney	Catalans	2015	12	5	0	0	20
Omari Caro	Hull KR	2013-14	21	20	0	0	80
	London	2012	11	4	0	0	16
Paul Carr	Sheffield	1996-98	45(5)	15	0	0	60
Bernard Carroll	London	1996	2(1)	1	0	0	4
Mark Carroll	London	1998	15(3)	1	0	0	4
Tonie Carroll	Leeds	2001-02	42(2)	30	0	0	120
Darren Carter	Workington	1996	10(3)	0	1	0	2
Steve Carter	Widnes	2002	14(7)	4	0	0	16
John Cartwright	Salford	1997	9	0	0	0	0
Garreth Carvell	Castleford	2014	1(4)	1	0	0	4
	Hull	2001-08, 2014	75(84)	22	0	0	88
	Warrington	2009-13	77(40)	13	0	0	52
	Leeds	1997-2000	(4)	0	0	0	0
	Gateshead	1999	4(4)	1	0	0	4
Garen Casey	Salford	1999	13(5)	3	23	0	58
Ray Cashmere	Salford	2009-11	63(3)	5	0	0	20
Mick Cassidy	Widnes	2005	24	0	0	0	0
	Wigan	1996-2004	184(36)	30	0	0	120
Remi Casty	Catalans	2006-13, 2015	106(84)	20	0	0	80
Ned Catic	Castleford	2008	7(7)	3	0	0	12
	Wakefield	2006-07	17(29)	4	0	0	16
Mason Caton-Brown	Salford	2014-15	23	5	0	0	20
	London	2013-14	19	15	0	0	60
Chris Causey	Warrington	1997-99	(18)	1	0	0	4
Jason Cayless	St Helens	2006-09	62(9)	7	0	0	28
Arnaud Cervello	Paris	1996	4	4	0	0	16
Marshall Chalk	Celtic	2009	13	4	0	0	16

PLAYER	CLUB	YEAR	APP	TRIES	GOALS	FG	PTS
Gary Chambers	Warrington	1996-2000	65(28)	2	0	0	8
Pierre Chamorin	Paris	1996-97	27(3)	8	3	0	38
Alex Chan	Catalans	2006-08	59(19)	11	0	0	44
Jason Chan	Hull KR	2014	5(1)	3	0	0	12
	Huddersfield	2012-14	46(12)	9	0	0	36
	Crusaders	2010-11	48(1)	10	0	0	40
	Celtic	2009	17(6)	3	0	0	12
Joe Chandler	Leeds	2008	(1)	0	0	0	0
Michael Channing	Castleford	2013-15	27(2)	8	0	0	32
	London	2012-13	15(3)	2	0	0	8
Chris Chapman	Leeds	1999	(1)	0	0	0	0
Damien Chapman	London	1998	6(2)	3	4	1	21
David Chapman	Castleford	1996-98	24(6)	8	0	0	32
Jaymes Chapman	Halifax	2002-03	5(8)	1	0	0	4
Richard Chapman	Sheffield	1996	1	2	0	0	8
Chris Charles	Salford	2004-06	59(16)	6	140	0	304
	Castleford	2001	1(4)	1	0	0	4
Olivier Charles	Catalans	2007	2	2	0	0	8
Josh Charnley	Wigan	2010-15	121(2)	121	72	0	628
	Hull KR	2010	5	5	0	0	20
Lewis Charnock	St Helens	2013, 2015	4(1)	2	6	0	20
Rangi Chase	Salford	2014-15	37	10	13	2	68
	Castleford	2009-13	114(5)	38	0	3	155
Andy Cheetham	Huddersfield	1998-99	30	11	0	0	44
Kris Chesney	London	1998	1(2)	0	0	0	0
Chris Chester	Hull KR	2007-08	28(6)	4	0	0	16
	Hull	2002-06	67(25)	13	0	0	52
	Wigan	1999-2001	21(22)	5	0	0	20
	Halifax	1996-99	47(14)	16	15	1	95
Lee Chilton	Workington	1996	10(3)	6	0	0	24
Dane Chisholm	Hull KR	2015	1	0	0	0	0
Gary Christie	Bradford	1996-97	4(7)	1	0	0	4
James Clare	Castleford	2012-15	33	21	0	0	84
Daryl Clark	Warrington	2015	23(6)	6	0	0	24
	Castleford	2011-14	34(51)	31	0	0	124
Dean Clark	Leeds	1996	11(2)	3	0	0	12
Des Clark	St Helens	1999	4	0	0	0	0
	Halifax	1998-99	35(13)	6	0	0	24
Greg Clarke	Halifax	1997	1(1)	0	0	0	0
John Clarke	Oldham	1996-97	27(4)	5	0	0	20
Jon Clarke	Widnes	2012-14	59(1)	5	0	0	20
	Warrington	2001-11	217(25)	56	2	0	228
	London	2000-01	19(11)	2	0	0	8
	Wigan	1997-99	13(10)	3	0	0	12
Chris Clarkson	Widnes	2015	17(1)	4	0	0	16
	Leeds	2010-14	61(39)	9	0	0	36
Adam Clay	Salford	2011	2	3	0	0	12
Ryan Clayton	Castleford	2004, 2008-10	36(24)	5	0	0	20
	Salford	2006	3(8)	2	0	0	8
	Huddersfield	2005	4(6)	0	0	0	0
	Halifax	2000, 2002-03	28(12)	6	0	0	24
Gavin Clinch	Salford	2004	21(1)	1	0	1	5
	Halifax	1998-99, 2001-02	88(2)	26	45	5	199
	Hudds-Sheff	2000	18(2)	5	0	1	21
	Wigan	1999	10(2)	4	12	0	40
Joel Clinton	Hull KR	2010-12	42(14)	2	0	0	8
John Clough	Salford	2004-06	1(16)	0	0	0	0
Paul Clough	Widnes	2014	4(8)	1	0	0	4
	St Helens	2005-13	53(113)	16	0	0	64
Tony Clubb	Wigan	2014-15	13(33)	9	0	0	36
	London	2012-13	24(8)	7	0	0	28
	Harlequins	2006-11	100(11)	29	0	0	116
Bradley Clyde	Leeds	2001	7(5)	1	0	0	4
Michael Coady	Leeds	2010	1	0	0	0	0
Evan Cochrane	London	1996	5(1)	1	0	0	4
Ben Cockayne	Hull KR	2007-11, 2014-15	109(30)	36	0	0	144
	Wakefield	2012-13	54	28	2	0	116
Liam Colbon	Hull	2014	8	1	0	0	4
	London	2012-13	22	5	0	0	20
	Hull KR	2009-11	51	20	0	0	80
	Wigan	2004-05, 2007-08	37(14)	15	0	0	60
Anthony Colella	Huddersfield	2003	5(1)	2	0	0	8
Liam Coleman	Leigh	2005	1(4)	0	0	0	0
Andy Coley	Wigan	2008-11	100(10)	8	0	0	32
	Salford	2001-02, 2004-07	112(34)	34	0	0	136
Richard Colley	Bradford	2004	1	0	0	0	0
Steve Collins	Hull	2000	28	17	0	0	68
	Gateshead	1999	20(4)	13	0	0	52
Wayne Collins	Leeds	1997	21	3	0	0	12
Dean Collis	Wakefield	2012-15	64	28	0	0	112
Aurelien Cologni	Catalans	2006	4(1)	3	0	0	12
Gary Connolly	Widnes	2005	20	4	1	0	18
	Wigan	1996-2002, 2004	168(10)	70	5	0	290
	Leeds	2003-04	27	6	0	0	24
Jake Connor	Huddersfield	2013-15	26	11	2	0	48

PLAYER	CLUB	YEAR	APP	TRIES	GOALS	FG	PTS
Nathan Conroy	Bradford	2013-14	(4)	0	0	0	0
Matt Cook	Castleford	2008, 2015	6(14)	3	0	0	12
	London	2012-14	50(7)	8	0	0	32
	Hull KR	2010-11	9(16)	7	0	0	28
	Bradford	2005-09	11(52)	4	0	0	16
Mick Cook	Sheffield	1996	9(10)	2	0	0	8
Paul Cook	Huddersfield	1998-99	11(6)	2	13	0	34
	Bradford	1996-97	14(8)	7	38	1	105
Peter Cook	St Helens	2004	(1)	0	0	0	0
Paul Cooke	Wakefield	2010	16(1)	3	36	1	85
	Hull KR	2007-10	54(5)	8	76	2	186
	Hull	1999-2007	177(27)	32	333	4	798
Ben Cooper	Leigh	2005	25(1)	5	0	0	20
	Huddersfield	2000-01, 2003-04	28(12)	3	0	0	12
Michael Cooper	Warrington	2006-13	29(87)	6	0	0	24
	Castleford	2010	1(5)	2	0	0	8
Ged Corcoran	Halifax	2003	1(11)	0	0	0	0
Wayne Corcoran	Halifax	2003	4(2)	0	0	0	0
Jamie Cording	Huddersfield	2011-13	4(21)	5	0	0	20
Josh Cordoba	Hull	2009	8	1	0	0	4
Mark Corvo	Salford	2002	7(5)	0	0	0	0
Neville Costigan	Hull KR	2014	24	3	0	0	12
Brandon Costin	Huddersfield	2001, 2003-04	69	42	93	3	357
	Bradford	2002	20(1)	8	0	0	32
Wes Cotton	London	1997-98	12	3	0	0	12
Phil Coussons	Salford	1997	7(2)	3	0	0	12
Alex Couttet	Paris	1997	1	0	0	0	0
Nick Couttet	Paris	1997	1	0	0	0	0
Jamie Coventry	Castleford	1996	1	0	0	0	0
Jimmy Cowan	Oldham	1996-97	2(8)	0	0	0	0
Will Cowell	Warrington	1998-2000	6(8)	1	0	0	4
Neil Cowie	Wigan	1996-2001	116(27)	10	0	1	41
Danny Cowling	Wakefield	2012-13	2	0	0	0	0
Jordan Cox	Hull KR	2011-15	17(44)	4	0	0	16
	Huddersfield	2015	(2)	0	0	0	0
Mark Cox	London	2003	(3)	0	0	0	0
James Coyle	Wigan	2005	2(3)	1	0	0	4
Thomas Coyle	Wigan	2008	2(1)	0	0	0	0
Eorl Crabtree	Huddersfield	2001, 2003-15	171(160)	50	0	0	200
Andy Craig	Halifax	1999	13(7)	1	3	0	10
	Wigan	1996	5(5)	2	0	0	8
Owen Craigie	Widnes	2005	15	7	0	2	30
Scott Cram	London	1999-2002	65(7)	4	0	0	16
Danny Craven	Widnes	2012-15	27(14)	5	3	2	28
Steve Craven	Hull	1998-2003	53(42)	4	0	0	16
Nicky Crellin	Workington	1996	(2)	0	0	0	0
Jason Critchley	Wakefield	2000	7(1)	4	0	0	16
	Castleford	1997-98	27(3)	11	0	0	44
Jason Croker	Catalans	2007-09	56(2)	11	0	1	45
Martin Crompton	Salford	1998-2000	30(6)	11	6	2	58
	Oldham	1996-97	36(1)	16	0	3	67
Paul Crook	Widnes	2005	2(2)	0	5	1	11
Paul Crook	Oldham	1996	4(9)	0	3	0	6
Jason Crookes	Hull	2013-14	15(1)	5	0	0	20
	Bradford	2009-12	25(1)	7	0	0	28
Ben Crooks	Hull	2012-14	42(3)	30	23	0	166
Lee Crooks	Castleford	1996-97	27(2)	2	14	0	36
Dominic Crosby	Wigan	2012-15	46(30)	6	0	0	24
Alan Cross	St Helens	1997	(2)	0	0	0	0
Ben Cross	Widnes	2012-13	27(1)	2	0	0	8
	Wigan	2011	(4)	0	0	0	0
	Leeds	2011	1(9)	0	0	0	0
Steve Crossley	Castleford	2015	(6)	0	0	0	0
	Bradford	2010-11	(9)	1	0	0	4
Garret Crossman	Hull KR	2008	8(18)	0	0	0	0
Steve Crouch	Castleford	2004	4(1)	2	0	0	8
Kevin Crouthers	Warrington	2001-03	12(1)	4	0	0	16
	London	2000	6(4)	1	0	0	4
	Wakefield	1999	4(4)	1	0	0	4
	Bradford	1997-98	3(9)	2	0	0	8
Jordan Crowther	Wakefield	2014-15	1(7)	1	0	0	4
Matt Crowther	Hull	2001-03	48	20	166	0	412
	Hudds-Sheff	2000	10(4)	5	22	0	64
	Sheffield	1996-99	43(4)	22	10	0	108
Heath Cruckshank	Halifax	2003	19(1)	0	0	0	0
	St Helens	2001	1(12)	0	0	0	0
Leroy Cudjoe	Huddersfield	2008-15	198(1)	86	57	1	459
Paul Cullen	Warrington	1996	19	3	0	0	12
Francis Cummins	Leeds	1996-2005	217(13)	120	26	2	534
James Cunningham	Hull	2012, 2014-15	(9)	0	0	0	0
	London	2014	10(7)	2	0	0	8
Keiron Cunningham	St Helens	1996-2010	357(24)	138	0	0	552
Liam Cunningham	Hull	2010	(1)	0	0	0	0
Ben Currie	Warrington	2012-15	47(29)	31	0	0	124
Andy Currier	Warrington	1996-97	(2)	1	0	0	4
Peter Cusack	Hull	2008-10	34(22)	3	0	0	12

PLAYER	CLUB	YEAR	APP	TRIES	GOALS	FG	PTS
Adam Cuthbertson	Leeds	2015	26(5)	8	0	0	32
Joe Dakuitoga	Sheffield	1996	6(3)	0	0	0	0
Matty Dale	Hull	2006, 2008	(7)	1	0	0	4
	Wakefield	2008	1(1)	0	0	0	0
Brett Dallas	Wigan	2000-06	156	89	0	0	356
Mark Dalle Cort	Celtic	2009	23	4	0	0	16
Paul Darbyshire	Warrington	1997	(6)	0	0	0	0
James Davey	Wakefield	2009-11	3(14)	1	0	0	4
Maea David	Hull	1998	1	0	0	0	0
Alex Davidson	Salford	2011, 2013	(3)	0	0	0	0
Paul Davidson	Halifax	2001-03	22(30)	10	0	0	40
	London	2000	6(10)	4	0	0	16
	St Helens	1998-99	27(16)	7	0	0	28
	Oldham	1996-97	17(18)	14	0	1	57
Ben Davies	Castleford	2011, 2013	3(4)	2	0	0	8
	Widnes	2012-13	10(15)	3	0	0	12
	Wigan	2010	(5)	0	0	0	0
Gareth Davies	Warrington	1996-97	1(6)	0	0	0	0
Geraint Davies	Celtic	2009	(7)	0	0	0	0
John Davies	Castleford	2010-12	1(6)	1	0	0	4
Jordan Davies	Salford	2013	2(3)	0	0	0	0
Wes Davies	Wigan	1998-2001	22(22)	11	0	0	44
Brad Davis	Castleford	1997-2000, 2004, 2006	102(3)	31	43	10	220
	Wakefield	2001-03	51(12)	15	22	5	109
Matty Dawson	St Helens	2014-15	31(1)	8	0	0	32
	Huddersfield	2012-13	4	0	0	0	0
Brad Day	Castleford	2014	(1)	0	0	0	0
Matt Daylight	Hull	2000	17(1)	7	0	0	28
	Gateshead	1999	30	25	0	0	100
Michael De Vere	Huddersfield	2005-06	36	6	74	0	172
Paul Deacon	Wigan	2010-11	32(11)	4	14	0	44
	Bradford	1998-2009	258(43)	72	1029	23	2369
	Oldham	1997	(2)	0	0	0	0
Chris Dean	Widnes	2012-15	75(3)	18	0	0	72
	Wakefield	2011	20	8	0	0	32
	St Helens	2007-10	18(3)	9	0	0	36
Craig Dean	Halifax	1996-97	25(11)	12	1	1	51
Gareth Dean	London	2002	(4)	0	0	0	0
Yacine Dekkiche	Hudds-Sheff	2000	11(3)	3	0	0	12
Brett Delaney	Leeds	2010-15	126(12)	23	0	0	92
Jason Demetriou	Wakefield	2004-10	174(3)	50	2	0	204
	Widnes	2002-03	47(1)	15	1	0	62
Martin Dermott	Warrington	1997	1	0	0	0	0
David Despin	Paris	1996	(1)	0	0	0	0
Fabien Devecchi	Paris	1996-97	17(10)	2	0	0	8
Paul Devlin	Widnes	2002-04	32	16	0	0	64
Stuart Dickens	Salford	2005	4(5)	0	4	0	8
Matt Diskin	Bradford	2011-14	64(16)	11	0	0	44
	Leeds	2001-10	195(37)	40	0	0	160
Andrew Dixon	Salford	2013-14	34(2)	8	0	0	32
	St Helens	2009-12	19(41)	12	0	0	48
Kieran Dixon	Hull KR	2015	15(2)	14	3	0	62
	London	2012-14	49(1)	32	2	0	132
Kirk Dixon	Castleford	2008-14	143(2)	63	267	0	786
	Hull	2004-06	13(4)	7	4	0	36
Paul Dixon	Sheffield	1996-97	5(9)	1	0	0	4
Gareth Dobson	Castleford	1998-2000	(10)	0	0	0	0
Michael Dobson	Salford	2015	13(1)	3	7	1	27
	Hull KR	2008-13	142	51	500	11	1215
	Wigan	2006	14	5	61	0	142
	Catalans	2006	10	4	31	1	79
Michael Docherty	Hull	2000-01	(6)	0	0	0	0
Erjon Dollapi	London	2013-14	(18)	4	0	0	16
Sid Domic	Hull	2006-07	39(4)	15	0	0	60
	Wakefield	2004-05	48	30	0	0	120
	Warrington	2002-03	41(4)	17	0	0	68
Scott Donald	Leeds	2006-10	131	77	0	0	308
James Donaldson	Hull KR	2015	3(13)	0	0	0	0
	Bradford	2009-14	38(35)	4	0	0	16
Glen Donkin	Hull	2002-03	(10)	1	0	0	4
Stuart Donlan	Castleford	2008	20	8	0	0	32
	Huddersfield	2004-06	59(3)	15	0	0	60
	Halifax	2001-03	65(2)	22	0	0	88
Jason Donohue	Bradford	1996	(4)	0	0	0	0
Jeremy Donougher	Bradford	1996-99	40(21)	13	0	0	52
Justin Dooley	London	2000-01	37(18)	2	0	0	8
Dane Dorahy	Halifax	2003	20	7	45	0	118
	Wakefield	2000-01	16(2)	4	19	1	55
Jamie Doran	Wigan	2014	(2)	0	0	0	0
Luke Dorn	Castleford	2008, 2014-15	58(2)	46	0	0	184
	London	2005, 2012-13	58(8)	42	0	0	168
	Harlequins	2006, 2009-11	83(1)	57	0	0	228
	Salford	2007	19(8)	11	0	0	44
Ewan Dowes	Hull	2003-11	169(51)	10	0	0	40
	Leeds	2001-03	1(9)	0	0	0	0
Jack Downs	Hull	2015	2(3)	0	0	0	0
Adam Doyle	Warrington	1998	9(3)	4	0	0	16

Super League Players 1996-2015

PLAYER	CLUB	YEAR	APP	TRIES	GOALS	FG	PTS
Rod Doyle	Sheffield	1997-99	52(10)	10	0	0	40
Brad Drew	Huddersfield	2005-07, 2010	78(13)	18	13	1	99
	Wakefield	2008-09	27(9)	7	14	1	57
Josh Drinkwater	London	2014	23(1)	5	54	0	128
Damien Driscoll	Salford	2001	23(1)	1	0	0	4
James Duckworth	London	2014	3	0	0	0	0
	Leeds	2013	2	1	0	0	4
Gil Dudson	Widnes	2015	16(3)	0	0	0	0
	Wigan	2012-14	26(16)	2	0	0	8
	Crusaders	2011	3(7)	0	0	0	0
	Celtic	2009	(1)	0	0	0	0
Jason Duffy	Leigh	2005	3(1)	0	0	0	0
John Duffy	Leigh	2005	21	6	0	0	24
	Salford	2000	3(11)	0	1	1	3
	Warrington	1997-99	12(12)	0	0	0	0
Tony Duggan	Celtic	2009	4	3	0	0	12
Andrew Duncan	London	1997	2(4)	2	0	0	8
	Warrington	1997	(1)	0	0	0	0
Andrew Dunemann	Salford	2006	25	1	0	2	6
	Leeds	2003-05	76(4)	11	0	2	46
	Halifax	1999-2002	68	19	0	1	77
Matt Dunford	London	1997-98	18(20)	3	0	1	13
Vincent Duport	Catalans	2007-09, 2011-15	106(14)	54	0	0	216
Jamie Durbin	Widnes	2005	1	0	0	0	0
	Warrington	2003	(1)	0	0	0	0
Scott Dureau	Catalans	2011-15	88(1)	29	315	10	756
James Durkin	Paris	1997	(5)	0	0	0	0
Bernard Dwyer	Bradford	1996-2000	65(10)	14	0	0	56
Brad Dwyer	Warrington	2012-15	1(35)	4	0	0	16
	Huddersfield	2013	(6)	0	0	0	0
Luke Dyer	Crusaders	2010	23(1)	5	0	0	20
	Celtic	2009	21	6	0	0	24
	Hull KR	2007	26	13	0	0	52
	Castleford	2006	17(2)	5	0	0	20
Adam Dykes	Hull	2008	12	1	0	2	6
Jim Dymock	London	2001-04	94(1)	15	0	1	61
Leo Dynevor	London	1996	8(11)	5	7	0	34
Jason Eade	Paris	1997	9	4	0	0	16
Michael Eagar	Hull	2004-05	12	4	0	0	16
	Castleford	1999-2003	130(2)	60	0	0	240
	Warrington	1998	21	6	0	0	24
Kyle Eastmond	St Helens	2007-11	46(20)	35	117	3	377
Greg Eastwood	Leeds	2010	5(12)	1	0	0	4
Barry Eaton	Widnes	2002	25	2	49	4	110
	Castleford	2000	1(4)	0	3	0	6
Greg Ebrill	Salford	2002	15(6)	1	0	0	4
Cliff Eccles	Salford	1997-98	30(5)	1	0	0	4
Chris Eckersley	Warrington	1996	1	0	0	0	0
Greg Eden	Hull KR	2013-14	37	23	0	0	92
	Salford	2014	4	1	0	0	4
	Huddersfield	2012	24	8	0	0	32
	Castleford	2011	2	1	0	0	4
Steve Edmed	Sheffield	1997	15(1)	0	0	0	0
Mark Edmondson	Salford	2007	10(2)	0	0	0	0
	St Helens	1999-2005	27(75)	10	0	0	40
Diccon Edwards	Castleford	1996-97	10(5)	1	0	0	4
Grant Edwards	Castleford	2006	(2)	0	0	0	0
Max Edwards	Harlequins	2010	1	0	0	0	0
Peter Edwards	Salford	1997-98	35(2)	4	0	0	16
Shaun Edwards	London	1997-2000	32(8)	16	1	0	66
	Bradford	1998	8(2)	4	0	0	16
	Wigan	1996	17(3)	12	1	0	50
Danny Ekis	Halifax	2001	(1)	0	0	0	0
Abi Ekoku	Bradford	1997-98	21(4)	6	0	0	24
	Halifax	1996	15(1)	5	0	0	20
Shane Elford	Huddersfield	2007-08	26(1)	7	0	0	28
Olivier Elima	Catalans	2008-10, 2013-15	96(29)	33	0	0	132
	Bradford	2011-12	37(3)	12	0	0	48
	Wakefield	2003-07	40(47)	13	0	0	52
	Castleford	2002	(1)	1	0	0	4
Abderazak Elkhalouki	Paris	1997	(1)	0	0	0	0
George Elliott	Leeds	2011	1	0	0	0	0
Andy Ellis	Wakefield	2012	10	0	0	0	0
	Harlequins	2010-11	26(11)	8	0	0	32
Gareth Ellis	Hull	2013-15	50	12	0	0	48
	Leeds	2005-08	109	24	1	0	98
	Wakefield	1999-2004	86(17)	21	2	0	88
Jamie Ellis	Huddersfield	2015	26(2)	11	18	2	82
	Castleford	2012-14	36(8)	10	80	1	201
	Hull	2012	4(5)	1	0	0	4
	St Helens	2009	1(2)	0	1	0	2
Danny Ellison	Castleford	1998-99	7(16)	6	0	0	24
	Wigan	1996-97	15(1)	13	0	0	52
Andrew Emelio	Widnes	2005	22(2)	8	0	0	32
Jake Emmitt	Salford	2013	5(10)	0	0	0	0
	Castleford	2011-13	32(17)	0	0	0	0
	St Helens	2008-10	1(16)	1	0	0	4
Anthony England	Warrington	2014-15	12(21)	3	0	0	12
Patrick Entat	Paris	1996	22	2	0	0	8
Jason Erba	Sheffield	1997	1(4)	0	0	0	0
Morgan Escare	Catalans	2013-15	74	53	1	1	215
Ryan Esders	Harlequins	2009-10	9(11)	3	0	0	12
	Hull KR	2009	(1)	0	0	0	0
Sonny Esslemont	Hull KR	2014-15	(5)	0	0	0	0
Niall Evalds	Salford	2013-15	33(3)	21	0	0	84
Ben Evans	Warrington	2014-15	3(16)	2	0	0	8
	Bradford	2013	3(12)	1	0	0	4
James Evans	Castleford	2009-10	26(1)	13	0	0	52
	Bradford	2007-08	43(5)	20	0	0	80
	Wakefield	2006	6	3	0	0	12
	Huddersfield	2004-06	51	22	0	0	88
Paul Evans	Paris	1997	18	8	0	0	32
Rhys Evans	Warrington	2010-15	48(3)	27	0	0	108
Wayne Evans	London	2002	11(6)	2	0	0	8
Toby Everett	London	2014	(2)	0	0	0	0
Richie Eyres	Warrington	1997	2(5)	0	0	0	0
	Sheffield	1997	2(3)	0	0	0	0
Henry Fa'afili	Warrington	2004-07	90(1)	70	0	0	280
David Fa'alogo	Huddersfield	2010-12	38(16)	13	0	0	52
Sala Fa'alogo	Widnes	2004-05	8(15)	2	0	0	8
Richard Fa'aoso	Castleford	2006	10(15)	5	0	0	20
Maurie Fa'asavalu	St Helens	2004-10	5(137)	29	0	0	116
Bolouagi Fagborun	Huddersfield	2004-06	4(2)	1	0	0	4
Theo Fages	Salford	2013-15	57(5)	18	4	0	80
Esene Faimalo	Salford	1997-99	23(25)	2	0	0	8
	Leeds	1996	3(3)	0	0	0	0
Joe Faimalo	Salford	1998-2000	23(47)	7	0	0	28
	Oldham	1996-97	37(5)	7	0	0	28
Jacob Fairbank	Huddersfield	2011-15	12(3)	0	0	0	0
	Wakefield	2014	1(3)	0	0	0	0
	London	2013	4(1)	1	0	0	4
	Bradford	2013	(2)	0	0	0	0
Karl Fairbank	Bradford	1996	17(2)	4	0	0	16
David Fairleigh	St Helens	2001	26(1)	8	0	0	32
David Faiumu	Huddersfield	2008-14	38(108)	13	0	0	52
Jamal Fakir	Bradford	2014	5(8)	1	0	0	4
	Catalans	2006-14	55(100)	13	0	0	52
Jim Fallon	Leeds	1996	10	5	0	0	20
Ben Farrar	London	2014	22	1	0	0	4
	Catalans	2011	13	3	0	0	12
Danny Farrar	Warrington	1998-2000	76	13	0	0	52
Andy Farrell	Wigan	1996-2004	230	77	1026	16	2376
Anthony Farrell	Widnes	2002-03	24(22)	4	1	0	18
	Leeds	1997-2001	99(23)	18	0	0	72
	Sheffield	1996	14(5)	5	0	0	20
Connor Farrell	Wigan	2014-15	1(8)	1	0	0	4
Craig Farrell	Hull	2000-01	1(3)	0	0	0	0
Liam Farrell	Wigan	2010-15	100(46)	63	0	0	252
Brad Fash	Hull	2015	(7)	0	0	0	0
Abraham Fatnowna	London	1997-98	7(2)	2	0	0	8
	Workington	1996	5	2	0	0	8
Sione Faumuina	Castleford	2009	18	1	0	0	4
	Hull	2005	3	1	0	0	4
Vince Fawcett	Wakefield	1999	13(1)	2	0	0	8
	Warrington	1998	4(7)	1	0	0	4
	Oldham	1997	5	3	0	0	12
Danny Fearon	Huddersfield	2001	(1)	0	0	0	0
	Halifax	1999-2000	5(6)	0	0	0	0
Chris Feather	Castleford	2009	1(23)	0	0	0	0
	Bradford	2007-08	7(20)	1	0	0	4
	Leeds	2003-04, 2006	16(35)	6	0	0	24
	Wakefield	2001-02, 2004-05	29(32)	9	0	0	36
Dom Feaunati	Leigh	2005	4	1	0	0	4
	St Helens	2004	10(7)	7	0	0	28
Adel Fellous	Hull	2008	1(2)	0	0	0	0
	Catalans	2006-07	16(22)	4	0	0	16
Luke Felsch	Hull	2000-01	46(6)	7	0	0	28
	Gateshead	1999	28(1)	2	0	0	8
Leon Felton	Warrington	2002	4(2)	0	0	0	0
	St Helens	2001	1(1)	0	0	0	0
Dale Ferguson	Bradford	2014	3(3)	0	0	0	0
	Huddersfield	2011-13	34(18)	13	0	0	52
	Hull KR	2013	3(1)	1	0	0	4
	Wakefield	2007-11	40(14)	12	0	0	48
Brett Ferres	Huddersfield	2012-15	72	27	0	0	108
	Castleford	2009-12	78(5)	26	0	0	104
	Wakefield	2007-08	36(2)	6	5	0	34
	Bradford	2005-06	18(17)	11	2	0	48
David Ferriol	Catalans	2007-12	72(55)	8	0	0	32
Jason Ferris	Leigh	2005	4	1	0	0	4
Jamie Field	Wakefield	1999-2006	133(59)	19	0	0	76
	Huddersfield	1998	15(5)	0	0	0	0
	Leeds	1996-97	3(11)	0	0	0	0
Mark Field	Wakefield	2003-07	28(7)	3	0	0	12
Jamie Fielden	London	2003	(1)	0	0	0	0
	Huddersfield	1998-2000	4(8)	0	0	0	0

PLAYER	CLUB	YEAR	APP	TRIES	GOALS	FG	PTS
Stuart Fielden	Huddersfield	2013	8(1)	0	0	0	0
	Wigan	2006-12	105(24)	2	0	0	8
	Bradford	1998-2006	142(78)	41	0	0	164
Lafaele Filipo	Workington	1996	15(4)	3	0	0	12
Salesi Finau	Warrington	1996-97	16(15)	8	0	0	32
Brett Finch	Wigan	2011-12	49(3)	16	0	0	64
Vinny Finigan	Bradford	2010	4(1)	4	0	0	16
Liam Finn	Castleford	2014-15	45(2)	8	5	2	44
	Wakefield	2004	1(1)	0	1	0	2
	Halifax	2002-03	16(5)	2	30	1	69
Lee Finnerty	Halifax	2003	18(2)	5	2	0	24
Phil Finney	Warrington	1998	1	0	0	0	0
Simon Finnigan	Widnes	2003-05, 2012	56(24)	21	0	0	84
	Huddersfield	2009-10	22(5)	6	0	0	24
	Bradford	2008	14(13)	8	0	0	32
	Salford	2006-07	50	17	0	0	68
Matt Firth	Halifax	2000-01	12(2)	0	0	0	0
Andy Fisher	Wakefield	1999-2000	31(8)	4	0	0	16
Ben Fisher	London	2013	8(12)	1	0	0	4
	Catalans	2012	9(5)	1	0	0	4
	Hull KR	2007-11	78(46)	18	0	0	72
Craig Fitzgibbon	Hull	2010-11	42(1)	9	8	0	52
Daniel Fitzhenry	Hull KR	2008-09	36(11)	14	0	0	56
Karl Fitzpatrick	Salford	2004-07, 2009-10	89(11)	33	2	0	136
Mark Flanagan	St Helens	2012-15	40(39)	9	0	0	36
	Wigan	2009	3(7)	1	0	0	4
Chris Flannery	St Helens	2007-12	108(11)	32	0	0	128
Darren Fleary	Leigh	2005	24	1	0	0	4
	Huddersfield	2003-04	43(8)	4	0	0	16
	Leeds	1997-2002	98(9)	3	0	0	12
Daniel Fleming	Castleford	2013-14	(15)	1	0	0	4
Greg Fleming	London	1999-2001	64(1)	40	2	0	164
Matty Fleming	St Helens	2015	6	1	0	0	4
Adam Fletcher	Castleford	2006, 2008	16(7)	11	0	0	44
Bryan Fletcher	Wigan	2006-07	47(2)	14	0	0	56
Richard Fletcher	Castleford	2006	13(5)	3	4	0	20
	Hull	1999-2004	11(56)	5	0	0	20
Greg Florimo	Halifax	2000	26	6	4	0	32
	Wigan	1999	18(2)	7	1	0	30
Ben Flower	Wigan	2012-15	56(24)	13	0	0	52
	Crusaders	2010-11	10(23)	2	0	0	8
	Celtic	2009	2(15)	0	0	0	0
Jason Flowers	Salford	2004	6(1)	0	0	0	0
	Halifax	2002	24(4)	4	0	0	16
	Castleford	1996-2001	119(19)	33	0	1	133
Stuart Flowers	Castleford	1996	(3)	0	0	0	0
Adrian Flynn	Castleford	1996-97	19(2)	10	0	0	40
Paddy Flynn	Widnes	2012-15	72	41	0	0	164
Wayne Flynn	Sheffield	1997	3(5)	0	0	0	0
Adam Fogerty	Warrington	1998	4	0	0	0	0
	St Helens	1996	13	1	0	0	4
Liam Foran	Salford	2013	10(3)	1	0	0	4
Carl Forber	Leigh	2005	4	1	0	0	4
	St Helens	2004	1(1)	0	6	0	12
Paul Forber	Salford	1997-98	19(12)	4	0	0	16
Byron Ford	Hull KR	2007	13	6	0	0	24
James Ford	Castleford	2009	3(5)	1	0	0	4
Mike Ford	Castleford	1997-98	25(12)	5	0	3	23
	Warrington	1996	3	0	0	0	0
Jim Forshaw	Salford	1999	(1)	0	0	0	0
Mike Forshaw	Warrington	2004	20(1)	5	0	0	20
	Bradford	1997-2003	162(7)	32	0	0	128
	Leeds	1996	11(3)	5	0	0	20
Carl Forster	Salford	2015	3(6)	1	0	0	4
	St Helens	2011-12, 2014	(4)	0	0	0	0
	London	2014	2(3)	0	0	0	0
Mark Forster	Warrington	1996-2000	102(1)	40	0	0	160
Alex Foster	London	2014	20	3	0	0	12
	Leeds	2013	(8)	1	0	0	4
David Foster	Halifax	2000-01	4(9)	0	0	0	0
Jamie Foster	Bradford	2013-14	32	12	111	0	270
	Hull	2012	9	5	45	0	110
	St Helens	2010-12	44(3)	30	201	0	522
Peter Fox	Wakefield	2007, 2012-14	85	44	0	0	176
	Hull KR	2008-11	95	52	0	0	208
Matty Fozard	St Helens	2014	1	0	0	0	0
Nick Fozzard	Castleford	2011	7(10)	0	0	0	0
	St Helens	2004-08, 2010	100(25)	7	0	0	28
	Hull KR	2009	18(4)	1	0	0	4
	Warrington	2002-03	43(11)	2	0	0	8
	Huddersfield	1998-2000	24(8)	2	0	0	8
	Leeds	1996-97	6(16)	3	0	0	12
David Fraisse	Workington	1996	8	0	0	0	0
Daniel Frame	Widnes	2002-05	100(6)	24	0	0	96
Paul Franze	Castleford	2006	2(1)	0	0	0	0
Laurent Frayssinous	Catalans	2006	14(2)	3	32	0	76
Andrew Frew	Halifax	2003	17	5	0	0	20
	Wakefield	2002	21	8	0	0	32
	Huddersfield	2001	26	15	0	0	60
Dale Fritz	Castleford	1999-2003	120(4)	9	0	0	36
Gareth Frodsham	St Helens	2008-09	1(9)	0	0	0	0
Liam Fulton	Huddersfield	2009	12(3)	4	0	0	16
David Furner	Leeds	2003-04	45	8	23	0	78
	Wigan	2001-02	51(2)	21	13	0	110
David Furness	Castleford	1996	(1)	0	0	0	0
Matt Gafa	Harlequins	2006-09	81	26	16	0	136
Luke Gale	Castleford	2015	28	11	101	1	247
	Bradford	2012-14	56(2)	13	108	4	272
	Harlequins	2009-11	56(12)	18	86	3	247
Ben Galea	Hull	2013	12(2)	3	0	0	12
	Hull KR	2008-12	115(2)	33	0	0	132
Danny Galea	Widnes	2014-15	38(4)	5	0	0	20
Tommy Gallagher	Hull KR	2007	1(7)	0	0	0	0
	Widnes	2004	(6)	0	0	0	0
	London	2003	1(9)	1	0	0	4
Mark Gamson	Sheffield	1996	3	0	0	0	0
Jim Gannon	Hull KR	2007	7(16)	1	0	0	4
	Huddersfield	2003-06	79(14)	11	0	0	44
	Halifax	1999-2002	83(4)	14	0	0	56
Mitch Garbutt	Leeds	2015	7(5)	1	0	0	4
Steve Garces	Salford	2001	(1)	0	0	0	0
Benjamin Garcia	Catalans	2013-15	6(40)	10	0	0	40
Jean-Marc Garcia	Sheffield	1996-97	35(3)	22	0	0	88
Ade Gardner	Hull KR	2014	18	7	0	0	28
	St Helens	2002-13	236(12)	146	0	0	584
Matt Gardner	Harlequins	2009	6(3)	2	0	0	8
	Huddersfield	2006-07	22(3)	7	0	0	28
	Castleford	2004	1	1	0	0	4
Steve Gartland	Oldham	1996	1(1)	0	1	0	2
Daniel Gartner	Bradford	2001-03	74(1)	26	0	0	104
Dean Gaskell	Warrington	2002-05	58(1)	10	0	0	40
Lee Gaskell	Bradford	2014	21	5	0	0	20
	Salford	2013	17	8	2	0	36
	St Helens	2010-13	33(9)	14	12	1	81
George Gatis	Huddersfield	2008	5(5)	1	0	0	4
Richard Gay	Castleford	1996-2002	94(16)	39	0	0	156
Andrew Gee	Warrington	2000-01	33(1)	4	0	0	16
Matty Gee	Salford	2015	(2)	0	0	0	0
Anthony Gelling	Wigan	2012-15	61(1)	34	0	0	136
Stanley Gene	Hull KR	2007-09	37(17)	9	0	0	36
	Bradford	2006	5(16)	8	0	0	32
	Huddersfield	2001, 2003-05	70(6)	27	0	0	108
	Hull	2000-01	5(23)	6	0	0	24
Steve Georgallis	Warrington	2001	5(1)	2	0	0	8
Luke George	Bradford	2014	9(1)	3	0	0	12
	Huddersfield	2012-13	28(2)	18	0	0	72
	Hull KR	2013	4	2	0	0	8
	Wakefield	2007-11	38(3)	24	0	0	96
Shaun Geritas	Warrington	1997	(5)	1	0	0	4
Alex Gerrard	Widnes	2012-15	38(26)	3	0	0	12
Anthony Gibbons	Leeds	1996	9(4)	2	0	1	9
David Gibbons	Leeds	1996	3(4)	2	0	0	8
Scott Gibbs	St Helens	1996	9	3	0	0	12
Ashley Gibson	Castleford	2014-15	27	9	0	0	36
	Salford	2010-13	77(4)	41	0	0	164
	Leeds	2005-09	25(7)	13	9	0	70
Damian Gibson	Castleford	2003-04	40(3)	5	0	0	20
	Salford	2002	28	3	0	0	12
	Halifax	1998-2001	104(1)	39	0	0	156
	Leeds	1997	18	3	0	0	12
Matt Gidley	St Helens	2007-10	105	40	6	0	172
Tony Gigot	Catalans	2010-11, 2015	25(13)	11	3	0	50
	London	2014	2	0	4	0	8
Ian Gildart	Oldham	1996-97	31(7)	0	0	0	0
Oliver Gildart	Wigan	2015	7	4	0	0	16
	Salford	2015	3	1	0	0	4
Chris Giles	Widnes	2003-04	35	12	0	0	48
	St Helens	2002	(1)	0	0	0	0
Peter Gill	London	1996-99	75(6)	20	0	0	80
Carl Gillespie	Halifax	1996-99	47(36)	13	0	0	52
Michael Gillett	London	2001-02	23(21)	12	2	0	52
Simon Gillies	Warrington	1999	28	6	0	0	24
Tom Gilmore	Widnes	2012-15	13(1)	5	3	2	28
Lee Gilmour	Wakefield	2014	10(3)	2	0	0	8
	Castleford	2013	10(2)	0	0	0	0
	Huddersfield	2010-12	71(1)	17	0	0	68
	St Helens	2004-09	149(3)	41	0	0	164
	Bradford	2001-03	44(31)	20	0	0	80
	Wigan	1997-2000	44(39)	22	0	0	88
Marc Glanville	Leeds	1998-99	43(3)	5	0	0	20
Eddie Glaze	Castleford	1996	1	0	0	0	0
Paul Gleadhill	Leeds	1996	4	0	0	0	0
Ben Gledhill	Salford	2012-13	3(10)	1	0	0	4
	Wakefield	2010-11	(16)	0	0	0	0
Mark Gleeson	Warrington	2000-08	38(102)	12	0	0	48
Martin Gleeson	Salford	2013-14	26(1)	4	0	0	16
	Hull	2011	6	4	0	0	16
	Wigan	2009-11	46(1)	19	0	0	76
	Warrington	2005-09	110(1)	44	0	0	176
	St Helens	2002-04	56(1)	25	0	0	100
	Huddersfield	1999-2001	47(9)	18	0	0	72

Super League Players 1996-2015

PLAYER	CLUB	YEAR	APP	TRIES	GOALS	FG	PTS
Sean Gleeson	Hull KR	2013	6	0	0	0	0
	Salford	2011-12	35	14	0	0	56
	Wakefield	2007-10	67(6)	20	0	0	80
	Wigan	2005-06	3(3)	0	0	0	0
Jon Goddard	Hull KR	2007	20	2	0	0	8
	Castleford	2000-01	(2)	0	0	0	0
Richard Goddard	Castleford	1996-97	11(3)	2	10	0	28
Brad Godden	Leeds	1998-99	47	15	0	0	60
Pita Godinet	Wakefield	2014-15	18(19)	10	0	0	40
Wayne Godwin	Salford	2011-13, 2015	43(8)	6	0	0	24
	Bradford	2008-10	16(44)	9	0	0	36
	Hull	2007	3(13)	1	0	0	4
	Wigan	2005-06	9(38)	6	0	0	24
	Castleford	2001-04	30(33)	18	56	0	184
Jason Golden	London	2012	7(2)	1	0	0	4
	Harlequins	2009-11	34(12)	3	0	0	12
	Wakefield	2007-08	26(5)	1	0	0	4
Marvin Golden	Widnes	2003	4	1	0	0	4
	London	2001	17(2)	1	0	0	4
	Halifax	2000	20(2)	5	0	0	20
	Leeds	1996-99	43(11)	19	0	0	76
Ashton Golding	Leeds	2014-15	3(2)	0	0	0	0
Brett Goldspink	Halifax	2000-02	64(5)	2	0	0	8
	Wigan	1999	6(16)	1	0	0	4
	St Helens	1998	19(4)	2	0	0	8
	Oldham	1997	13(2)	0	0	0	0
Lee Gomersall	Hull KR	2008	1	0	0	0	0
Luke Goodwin	London	1998	9(2)	3	1	1	15
	Oldham	1997	16(4)	10	17	2	76
Grant Gore	Widnes	2012-15	6(11)	1	0	0	4
Aaron Gorrell	Catalans	2007-08	23	6	14	0	52
Andy Gorski	Salford	2001-02	(2)	0	0	0	0
Cyrille Gossard	Catalans	2006-12	54(30)	5	0	0	20
Bobbie Goulding	Salford	2001-02	31(1)	2	56	4	124
	Wakefield	2000	12	3	25	3	65
	Huddersfield	1998-99	27(1)	3	65	4	146
	St Helens	1996-98	42(2)	9	210	4	460
Bobbie Goulding (Jnr)	Wakefield	2013	1(2)	0	1	0	2
Darrell Goulding	Hull KR	2015	8	1	0	0	4
	Wigan	2005-14	129(24)	68	0	0	272
	Salford	2009	9	5	0	0	20
Mick Govin	Leigh	2005	5(6)	4	0	0	16
Craig Gower	London	2012-13	40	7	24	0	76
David Gower	Salford	2006-07	(16)	0	0	0	0
Shane Grady	London	2013	5(4)	1	2	0	8
James Graham	St Helens	2003-11	132(63)	47	0	0	188
Nathan Graham	Bradford	1996-98	17(28)	4	0	1	17
Nick Graham	Wigan	2003	13(1)	2	0	0	8
Dalton Grant	Crusaders	2011	(1)	0	0	0	0
Jon Grayshon	Harlequins	2007-09	10(32)	4	0	0	16
	Huddersfield	2003-06	7(43)	5	0	0	20
Blake Green	Wigan	2013-14	42(1)	15	0	0	60
	Hull KR	2011-12	35	14	0	0	56
Brett Green	Gateshead	1999	10(2)	0	0	0	0
Chris Green	Hull	2012-15	12(45)	4	0	0	16
James Green	Hull KR	2012-15	7(46)	1	0	0	4
Toby Green	Huddersfield	2001	3(1)	1	0	0	4
Craig Greenhill	Castleford	2004	21(4)	1	0	0	4
	Hull	2002-03	56	3	2	0	16
Clint Greenshields	Catalans	2007-12	137	81	0	0	324
Brandon Greenwood	Halifax	1996	1	0	0	0	0
Gareth Greenwood	Huddersfield	2003	(1)	0	0	0	0
	Halifax	2002	1	0	0	0	0
James Greenwood	Hull KR	2015	(8)	0	0	0	0
	Salford	2015	1(1)	1	0	0	4
	Wigan	2013, 2015	(2)	0	0	0	0
	London	2014	10(5)	3	0	0	12
Joe Greenwood	St Helens	2012-15	19(26)	15	0	0	60
Lee Greenwood	Huddersfield	2005	7	3	0	0	12
	London	2004-05	30(2)	19	0	0	76
	Halifax	2000-03	38(2)	17	0	0	68
	Sheffield	1999	1(1)	0	0	0	0
James Grehan	Castleford	2012	2(2)	0	0	0	0
Maxime Greseque	Wakefield	2007	2(1)	0	0	0	0
Mathieu Griffi	Catalans	2006-08	1(25)	0	0	0	0
Darrell Griffin	Salford	2013-15	31(27)	1	0	0	4
	Leeds	2012	8(19)	2	0	0	8
	Huddersfield	2007-11	65(60)	13	0	0	52
	Wakefield	2003-06	55(37)	9	3	0	42
George Griffin	Salford	2015	9(4)	1	0	0	4
	Wakefield	2015	5	0	0	0	0
	London	2014	(19)	1	0	0	4
	Hull KR	2012-13	11(7)	0	0	0	0
Josh Griffin	Salford	2014-15	25	14	73	0	202
	Castleford	2012	20	13	1	0	54
	Wakefield	2011	17	5	21	0	62
	Huddersfield	2009	2	0	0	0	0
Jonathan Griffiths	Paris	1996	(4)	1	0	0	4
Andrew Grima	Workington	1996	2(9)	2	0	0	8
Tony Grimaldi	Hull	2000-01	56(1)	14	0	0	56
	Gateshead	1999	27(2)	10	0	0	40
Danny Grimley	Sheffield	1996	4(1)	1	0	0	4
Scott Grix	Huddersfield	2010-15	132(11)	52	32	0	272
	Wakefield	2008-09	39(3)	18	0	0	72
Simon Grix	Warrington	2006-14	133(25)	42	0	0	168
	Halifax	2003	2(4)	0	0	0	0
Brett Grogan	Gateshead	1999	14(7)	3	0	0	12
Brent Grose	Warrington	2003-07	134(1)	55	0	0	220
David Guasch	Catalans	2010	1	0	0	0	0
Joan Guasch	Catalans	2014-15	(6)	0	0	0	0
Renaud Guigue	Catalans	2006	14(4)	3	0	0	12
Jerome Guisset	Catalans	2006-10	102(23)	9	0	0	36
	Wigan	2005	20(2)	3	0	0	12
	Warrington	2000-04	59(65)	21	0	0	84
Awen Guttenbeil	Castleford	2008	19	0	0	0	0
Reece Guy	Oldham	1996	3(4)	0	0	0	0
Josh Guzdek	Hull KR	2013, 2015	2	1	0	0	4
Tom Haberecht	Castleford	2008	2(2)	1	0	0	4
Dean Hadley	Hull	2013-15	22(9)	4	0	0	16
Gareth Haggerty	Harlequins	2008-09	8(28)	6	0	0	24
	Salford	2004-07	1(93)	15	0	0	60
	Widnes	2002	1(2)	1	0	0	4
Kurt Haggerty	Widnes	2012	6(8)	2	0	0	8
Andy Haigh	St Helens	1996-98	20(16)	11	0	0	44
Scott Hale	St Helens	2011	(3)	1	0	0	4
Michael Haley	Leeds	2008	(1)	0	0	0	0
Carl Hall	Leeds	1996	7(2)	3	0	0	12
Craig Hall	Wakefield	2015	15	3	30	0	72
	Hull KR	2011-14	74(3)	38	41	2	236
	Hull	2007-10	59(9)	39	11	0	178
Glenn Hall	Bradford	2010	7(18)	2	0	0	8
Martin Hall	Halifax	1998	2(10)	0	0	0	0
	Hull	1999	7	0	0	0	0
	Castleford	1998	4	0	0	0	0
	Wigan	1996-97	31(5)	7	6	0	40
Ryan Hall	Leeds	2007-15	218(2)	173	0	0	692
Steve Hall	Widnes	2004	1	0	0	0	0
	London	2002-03	35(3)	10	0	0	40
	St Helens	1999-2001	36(22)	19	0	0	76
Graeme Hallas	Huddersfield	2001	1	0	0	0	0
	Hull	1998-99	30(10)	6	39	1	103
	Halifax	1996	11(4)	5	0	0	20
Macauley Hallett	Hull KR	2014	2	3	0	0	12
Dave Halley	Bradford	2007-10	63(12)	20	0	0	80
	Wakefield	2009	5	4	0	0	16
Danny Halliwell	Salford	2007	2(3)	0	0	0	0
	Leigh	2005	5	3	0	0	12
	Halifax	2000-03	17(8)	4	0	0	16
	Warrington	2002	9(1)	8	0	0	32
	Wakefield	2002	3	0	0	0	0
Colum Halpenny	Wakefield	2003-06	103(1)	36	0	0	144
	Halifax	2002	22	12	0	0	48
Jon Hamer	Bradford	1996	(1)	0	0	0	0
Andrew Hamilton	London	1997, 2003	1(20)	3	0	0	12
John Hamilton	St Helens	1998	3	0	0	0	0
Karle Hammond	Halifax	2002	10(2)	2	14	0	36
	Salford	2001	2(3)	1	0	0	4
	London	1999-2000	47	23	2	3	99
	St Helens	1996-98	58(8)	28	0	4	116
Ryan Hampshire	Wigan	2013-15	20(5)	8	24	0	80
Rhys Hanbury	Widnes	2012-15	94	50	34	1	269
	Crusaders	2010-11	26(1)	14	0	0	56
Anthony Hancock	Paris	1997	8(6)	1	0	0	4
Michael Hancock	Salford	2001-02	12(24)	7	0	0	28
Jordan Hand	Wakefield	2015	(2)	0	0	0	0
	St Helens	2013-14	(3)	0	0	0	0
Gareth Handford	Castleford	2001	7(2)	0	0	0	0
	Bradford	2000	1(1)	0	0	0	0
Paul Handforth	Castleford	2006	2(15)	2	1	0	10
	Wakefield	2000-04	17(44)	10	13	0	66
Ash Handley	Leeds	2014-15	19	13	0	0	52
Paddy Handley	Leeds	1996	1(1)	2	0	0	8
Dean Hanger	Warrington	1999	7(11)	3	0	0	12
	Huddersfield	1998	20(1)	5	0	0	20
Josh Hannay	Celtic	2009	17	2	24	0	56
Harrison Hansen	Salford	2014-15	41(2)	7	0	0	28
	Wigan	2004-13	155(62)	39	0	0	156
Lee Hansen	Wigan	1997	10(5)	0	0	0	0
Shontayne Hape	Bradford	2003-08	123(2)	79	0	0	316
Lionel Harbin	Wakefield	2001	(1)	0	0	0	0
Zak Hardaker	Leeds	2011-15	119	56	39	1	303
Ian Hardman	Hull KR	2007	18	4	0	0	16
	St Helens	2003-07	32(11)	9	5	0	46
Jeff Hardy	Hudds-Sheff	2000	20(5)	6	0	1	25
	Sheffield	1999	22(4)	7	0	0	28
Spencer Hargrave	Castleford	1996-99	(6)	0	0	0	0
Bryn Hargreaves	Bradford	2011-12	45(5)	1	0	0	4
	St Helens	2007-10	53(44)	7	0	0	28
	Wigan	2004-06	16(12)	1	0	0	4

PLAYER	CLUB	YEAR	APP	TRIES	GOALS	FG	PTS
Lee Harland	Castleford	1996-2004	148(35)	20	0	0	80
Neil Harmon	Halifax	2003	13(3)	0	0	0	0
	Salford	2001	6(5)	0	0	0	0
	Bradford	1998-2000	15(13)	2	0	0	8
	Huddersfield	1998	12	1	0	0	4
	Leeds	1996	10	1	0	0	4
Ben Harris	Bradford	2005-07	70(4)	24	0	0	96
Iestyn Harris	Bradford	2004-08	109(11)	35	87	2	316
	Leeds	1997-2001	111(7)	57	490	6	1214
	Warrington	1996	16	4	63	2	144
Ben Harrison	Warrington	2007-15	125(59)	14	0	0	56
Karl Harrison	Hull	1999	26	2	0	0	8
	Halifax	1996-98	60(2)	2	0	0	8
Andrew Hart	London	2004	12(1)	2	0	0	8
Tim Hartley	Harlequins	2006	2	1	0	0	4
	Salford	2004-05	6(7)	5	0	0	20
Carlos Hassan	Bradford	1996	6(4)	2	0	0	8
Phil Hassan	Wakefield	2002	9(1)	0	0	0	0
	Halifax	2000-01	25(4)	3	0	0	12
	Salford	1998	15	2	0	0	8
	Leeds	1996-97	38(4)	12	0	0	48
Tom Haughey	Castleford	2006	1(3)	1	0	0	4
	London	2003-04	10(8)	1	0	0	4
	Wakefield	2001-02	5(11)	0	0	0	0
Simon Haughton	Wigan	1996-2002	63(46)	32	0	0	128
Solomon Haumono							
	Harlequins	2006	10(9)	6	0	0	24
	London	2005	24(5)	8	0	0	32
Weller Hauraki	Salford	2015	16	4	0	0	16
	Castleford	2013-14	50(2)	9	0	0	36
	Leeds	2011-12	18(17)	6	0	0	24
	Crusaders	2010	26(1)	11	0	0	44
Richie Hawkyard	Bradford	2007	1(2)	1	0	0	4
Andy Hay	Widnes	2003-04	50(2)	7	0	0	28
	Leeds	1997-2002	112(27)	43	0	0	172
	Sheffield	1996-97	17(3)	5	0	0	20
Adam Hayes	Hudds-Sheff	2000	2(1)	0	0	0	0
Joey Hayes	Salford	1999	9	2	0	0	8
	St Helens	1996-98	11(6)	7	0	0	28
James Haynes	Hull KR	2009	1	0	0	0	0
Mathew Head	Hull	2007	9(1)	1	0	1	5
Mitch Healey	Castleford	2001-03	68(1)	10	16	0	72
Daniel Heckenberg							
	Harlequins	2006-09	31(39)	4	0	0	16
Chris Heil	Hull KR	2012-13	4	2	0	0	8
Ricky Helliwell	Salford	1997-99	(2)	0	0	0	0
Tom Hemingway	Huddersfield	2005-09	7(7)	1	17	0	38
Bryan Henare	St Helens	2000-01	4(12)	1	0	0	4
Richard Henare	Warrington	1996-97	28(2)	24	0	0	96
Andrew Henderson							
	Castleford	2006, 2008	44(11)	4	0	0	16
Ian Henderson	Catalans	2011-15	118(9)	12	0	0	48
	Bradford	2005-07	33(37)	13	0	0	52
Kevin Henderson	Wakefield	2005-11	52(68)	9	0	0	36
	Leigh	2005	(1)	0	0	0	0
Adam Henry	Bradford	2014	23(1)	5	0	0	20
Mark Henry	Salford	2009-11	67	22	0	0	88
Brad Hepi	Castleford	1999, 2001	9(21)	3	0	0	12
	Salford	2000	3(5)	0	0	0	0
	Hull	1998	15(1)	3	0	0	12
Tyla Hepi	Hull KR	2013	(4)	0	0	0	0
Jon Hepworth	Castleford	2003-04	19(23)	7	8	0	44
	Leeds	2003	(1)	0	0	0	0
	London	2002	(2)	0	0	0	0
Marc Herbert	Bradford	2011	20	4	2	0	20
Aaron Heremaia	Widnes	2015	9(14)	3	0	0	12
	Hull	2012-14	27(37)	12	0	0	48
Maxime Herold	London	2014	(2)	0	0	0	0
Ian Herron	Hull	2000	9	1	17	0	38
	Gateshead	1999	25	4	105	0	226
Jason Hetherington							
	London	2001-02	37	9	0	0	36
Gareth Hewitt	Salford	1999	2(1)	0	0	0	0
Andrew Hick	Hull	2000	9(9)	1	0	0	4
	Gateshead	1999	12(5)	2	0	0	8
Jarrad Hickey	Wakefield	2011	(8)	2	0	0	8
Chris Hicks	Warrington	2008-10	72	56	119	0	462
Paul Hicks	Wakefield	1999	(1)	0	0	0	0
Darren Higgins	London	1998	5(6)	2	0	0	8
Iain Higgins	London	1997-98	1(7)	2	0	0	8
Liam Higgins	Wakefield	2011	4(12)	0	0	0	0
	Castleford	2008-10	42(32)	2	0	0	8
	Hull	2003-06	1(34)	0	0	0	0
Mick Higham	Warrington	2009-15	73(78)	34	0	0	136
	Wigan	2006-08	61(28)	13	0	0	52
	St Helens	2001-05	43(56)	32	0	0	128
Chris Highton	Warrington	1997	1(1)	0	0	0	0
David Highton	London	2004-05	21(24)	2	0	0	8
	Salford	2002	4(5)	2	0	0	8
	Warrington	1998-2001	18(14)	2	0	0	8
Paul Highton	Salford	1998-2002,					
		2004-07	114(80)	14	0	0	56
	Halifax	1996-97	12(18)	2	0	0	8
Andy Hill	Huddersfield	1999	(4)	0	0	0	0
	Castleford	1999	4(4)	0	0	0	0

PLAYER	CLUB	YEAR	APP	TRIES	GOALS	FG	PTS
Chris Hill	Warrington	2012-15	106(10)	16	0	0	64
	Leigh	2005	(1)	0	0	0	0
Danny Hill	Wigan	2006-07	1(10)	0	0	0	0
	Hull KR	2007	2	0	0	0	0
	Hull	2004-06	4(6)	0	0	0	0
Howard Hill	Oldham	1996-97	22(12)	4	0	0	16
John Hill	St Helens	2003	(1)	0	0	0	0
	Halifax	2003	1(2)	0	0	0	0
	Warrington	2001-02	(4)	0	0	0	0
Scott Hill	Harlequins	2007-08	41(2)	13	0	0	52
Mark Hilton	Warrington	1996-2000,					
		2002-06	141(40)	7	0	0	28
Ian Hindmarsh	Catalans	2006	25	3	0	0	12
Brendan Hlad	Castleford	2008	(3)	0	0	0	0
Andy Hobson	Widnes	2004	5(13)	0	0	0	0
	Halifax	1998-2003	51(85)	8	0	0	32
Gareth Hock	Salford	2014-15	15(1)	4	0	0	16
	Widnes	2013	15(2)	9	1	0	38
	Wigan	2003-09,					
		2011-12	126(43)	38	0	0	152
Tommy Hodgkinson							
	St Helens	2006	(1)	0	0	0	0
Andy Hodgson	Wakefield	1999	14(2)	2	1	0	10
	Bradford	1997-98	8(2)	4	0	0	16
Brett Hodgson	Warrington	2011-13	66	33	268	1	669
	Huddersfield	2009-10	45	13	166	0	384
David Hodgson	Hull KR	2012-14	51	31	0	0	124
	Huddersfield	2008-11	84	59	0	0	236
	Salford	2005-07	81	30	47	0	214
	Wigan	2000-04	90(19)	43	0	0	172
	Halifax	1999	10(3)	5	0	0	20
Elliot Hodgson	Huddersfield	2009	1	0	0	0	0
Josh Hodgson	Hull KR	2010-14	98(29)	35	0	0	140
	Hull	2009	(2)	0	0	0	0
Ryan Hoffman	Wigan	2011	28(1)	11	0	0	44
Darren Hogg	London	1996	(1)	0	0	0	0
Michael Hogue	Paris	1997	5(7)	0	0	0	0
Lance Hohaia	St Helens	2012-15	67(9)	21	0	1	85
Chris Holden	Warrington	1996-97	2(1)	0	0	0	0
Daniel Holdsworth							
	Hull	2013	19	2	28	2	66
	Salford	2010-12	71	18	183	1	439
Stephen Holgate	Halifax	2000	1(10)	0	0	0	0
	Hull	1999	1	0	0	0	0
	Wigan	1997-98	11(26)	2	0	0	8
	Workington	1996	19	3	0	0	12
Stephen Holker	Hull KR	2015	(1)	0	0	0	0
Martyn Holland	Wakefield	2000-03	52(3)	6	0	0	24
Oliver Holmes	Castleford	2010-15	100(19)	17	0	0	68
Tim Holmes	Widnes	2004-05	15(4)	0	0	0	0
Tom Holmes	Castleford	2015	(1)	0	0	0	0
Graham Holroyd	Huddersfield	2003	3(5)	0	0	0	0
	Salford	2000-02	40(11)	8	75	5	187
	Halifax	1999	24(2)	3	74	5	165
	Leeds	1996-98	40(26)	22	101	8	298
Dallas Hood	Wakefield	2003-04	18(9)	1	0	0	4
Liam Hood	Salford	2015	2(15)	0	0	0	0
	Leeds	2012	1(4)	3	0	0	12
Jason Hooper	St Helens	2003-07	89(6)	35	30	0	200
Will Hope	Salford	2013	1(2)	0	0	0	0
Lee Hopkins	Harlequins	2006-07	44(3)	11	0	0	44
	London	2005	29	6	0	0	24
Sean Hoppe	St Helens	1999-2002	69(16)	32	0	0	128
Graeme Horne	Hull KR	2012-15	67(18)	17	0	0	68
	Huddersfield	2010-11	23(17)	11	0	0	44
	Hull	2003-09	49(74)	24	0	0	96
Richard Horne	Hull	1999-2014	341(16)	115	12	6	490
John Hough	Warrington	1996-97	9	2	0	0	8
Danny Houghton	Hull	2007-15	169(47)	26	0	0	104
Sylvain Houles	Wakefield	2003, 2005	8(1)	1	0	0	4
	London	2001-02	17(10)	11	0	0	44
	Hudds-Sheff	2000	5(2)	1	0	0	4
Harvey Howard	Wigan	2001-02	25(27)	1	0	0	4
	Bradford	1998	4(2)	1	0	0	4
	Leeds	1996	8	0	0	0	0
Kim Howard	London	1997	4(5)	0	0	0	0
Stuart Howarth	Wakefield	2011, 2015	21(2)	1	0	0	4
	Hull	2015	2(3)	0	0	0	0
	Salford	2012-14	25(12)	1	0	0	4
	St Helens	2013	14(1)	0	0	0	0
Stuart Howarth	Workington	1996	(2)	0	0	0	0
David Howell	London	2012-13	24	5	0	0	20
	Harlequins	2008-11	76	26	0	0	104
Phil Howlett	Bradford	1999	5(1)	2	0	0	8
Craig Huby	Huddersfield	2015	29(2)	1	0	0	4
	Castleford	2003-04,					
		2006,					
		2008-14	130(57)	27	41	0	190
Ryan Hudson	Castleford	2002-04,					
		2009-12	138(12)	31	0	0	124
	Huddersfield	1998-99,					
		2007-08	51(22)	10	0	0	40
	Wakefield	2000-01	42(9)	11	0	1	45

Super League Players 1996-2015

PLAYER	CLUB	YEAR	APP	TRIES	GOALS	FG	PTS
Adam Hughes	Widnes	2002-05	89(2)	45	51	0	282
	Halifax	2001	8(8)	8	0	0	32
	Wakefield	1999-2000	43(3)	21	34	0	152
	Leeds	1996-97	4(5)	4	0	0	16
Ian Hughes	Sheffield	1996	9(8)	4	0	0	16
Jack Hughes	Huddersfield	2015	30(1)	5	0	0	20
	Wigan	2011-14	31(33)	9	0	0	36
Mark Hughes	Catalans	2006	23	9	0	0	36
Steffan Hughes	London	1999-2001	1(13)	1	0	0	4
David Hulme	Salford	1997-99	53(1)	5	0	0	20
	Leeds	1996	8(1)	2	0	0	8
Declan Hulme	Widnes	2013-15	5	2	0	0	8
Paul Hulme	Warrington	1996-97	23(1)	2	0	0	8
Gary Hulse	Widnes	2005	12(5)	2	0	0	8
	Warrington	2001-04	20(28)	8	0	1	33
Alan Hunte	Salford	2002	19(2)	9	0	0	36
	Warrington	1999-2001	83	49	0	0	196
	Hull	1998	21	7	0	0	28
	St Helens	1996-97	30(2)	28	0	0	112
Alex Hurst	London	2013	8(2)	2	0	0	8
Kieran Hyde	Wakefield	2010-11	11	4	4	0	24
Nick Hyde	Paris	1997	5(5)	1	0	0	4
Chaz I'Anson	Hull KR	2007-10	17(13)	3	0	0	12
Krisnan Inu	Catalans	2015	12	6	3	0	30
Andy Ireland	Hull	1998-99	22(15)	0	0	0	0
	Bradford	1996	1	0	0	0	0
Kevin Iro	St Helens	1999-2001	76	39	0	0	156
	Leeds	1996	16	9	0	0	36
Willie Isa	Widnes	2012-15	44(33)	3	0	0	12
	Castleford	2011	7(2)	6	0	0	24
Andrew Isherwood	Wigan	1998-99	(5)	0	0	0	0
Olu Iwenofu	London	2000-01	2(1)	0	0	0	0
Chico Jackson	Hull	1999	(4)	0	0	0	0
Lee Jackson	Hull	2001-02	37(9)	12	1	0	50
	Leeds	1999-2000	28(24)	7	0	0	28
Michael Jackson	Sheffield	1998-99	17(17)	2	0	0	8
	Halifax	1996-97	27(6)	11	0	0	44
Paul Jackson	Castleford	2003-04, 2010-12	44(30)	5	0	0	20
	Huddersfield	1998, 2005-09	50(73)	4	0	0	16
	Wakefield	1999-2002	57(42)	2	0	0	8
Rob Jackson	Leigh	2005	20(3)	5	0	0	20
	London	2002-04	26(14)	9	0	0	36
Wayne Jackson	Halifax	1996-97	17(5)	2	0	0	8
Aled James	Crusaders	2011	1	0	0	0	0
	Celtic	2009	3(3)	0	0	0	0
	Widnes	2003	3	0	0	0	0
Andy James	Halifax	1996	(4)	0	0	0	0
Jordan James	Wigan	2006, 2014	3(18)	4	0	0	16
	Salford	2012-13	1(40)	6	0	0	24
	Crusaders	2010-11	5(24)	3	0	0	12
	Celtic	2009	17(4)	1	0	0	4
Matt James	Wakefield	2012	(4)	0	0	0	0
	Harlequins	2010	(2)	0	0	0	0
	Bradford	2006-09	1(23)	0	0	0	0
Pascal Jampy	Catalans	2006	4(7)	0	0	0	0
	Paris	1996-97	3(2)	0	0	0	0
Adam Janowski	Harlequins	2008	(1)	0	0	0	0
Ben Jeffries	Bradford	2008-09, 2011-12	76(3)	20	0	0	80
	Wakefield	2003-07, 2010-11	151(10)	70	20	6	326
Mick Jenkins	Hull	2000	24	2	0	0	8
	Gateshead	1999	16	3	0	0	12
Ed Jennings	London	1998-99	1(2)	0	0	0	0
Rod Jensen	Huddersfield	2007-08	26(3)	13	0	0	52
Anthony Jerram	Warrington	2007	(2)	0	0	0	0
Lee Jewitt	Castleford	2014-15	8(10)	0	0	0	0
	Salford	2007, 2009-13	32(62)	4	0	0	16
	Wigan	2005	(2)	0	0	0	0
Isaac John	Wakefield	2012	13	1	19	0	42
Andrew Johns	Warrington	2005	3	1	12	1	29
Matthew Johns	Wigan	2001	24	3	0	1	13
Andy Johnson	Salford	2004-05	8(26)	7	0	0	28
	Castleford	2002-03	32(16)	11	0	0	44
	London	2000-01	24(21)	12	0	0	48
	Huddersfield	1999	5	1	0	0	4
	Wigan	1996-99	24(20)	19	0	0	76
Bruce Johnson	Widnes	2004-05	(4)	0	0	0	0
Dallas Johnson	Catalans	2010	26	1	0	0	4
Greg Johnson	Salford	2014-15	39	13	1	0	54
	Wakefield	2011	12	2	0	0	8
Jack Johnson	Warrington	2015	4	3	0	0	12
Jason Johnson	St Helens	1997-99	2	0	0	0	0
Josh Johnson	Huddersfield	2013-15	7(10)	0	0	0	0
Mark Johnson	Salford	1999-2000	22(9)	16	0	0	64
	Hull	1998	10(1)	4	0	0	16
	Workington	1996	12	4	0	0	16
Nick Johnson	Hull KR	2012	1	0	0	0	0
Nick Johnson	London	2003	(1)	0	0	0	0
Paul Johnson	Crusaders	2011	6(4)	0	0	0	0
	Wakefield	2010	12(3)	4	0	0	16
	Warrington	2007-09	37(9)	17	0	0	68
	Bradford	2004-06	46(8)	19	0	0	76
	Wigan	1996-2003	74(46)	54	0	0	216
Paul Johnson	Widnes	2014	5(11)	0	0	0	0
	Hull	2013	3(16)	0	0	0	0
	Wakefield	2011-12	25(21)	6	0	0	24
	St Helens	2010	(2)	0	0	0	0
Richard Johnson	Bradford	2008	(2)	0	0	0	0
Ben Johnston	Castleford	2012	2	0	0	0	0
Tom Johnstone	Wakefield	2015	10	9	0	0	36
Ben Jones	Harlequins	2010	(2)	0	0	0	0
Chris Jones	Leigh	2005	1(1)	0	0	0	0
Danny Jones	Halifax	2003	1	0	0	0	0
David Jones	Oldham	1997	14(1)	5	0	0	20
Josh Jones	St Helens	2012-15	88(9)	22	0	0	88
Mark Jones	Warrington	1996	8(11)	2	0	0	8
Phil Jones	Leigh	2005	16	8	31	0	94
	Wigan	1999-2001	14(7)	6	25	0	74
Stacey Jones	Catalans	2006-07	39	11	43	3	133
Stephen Jones	Huddersfield	2005	(1)	0	0	0	0
Stuart Jones	Castleford	2009-12	69(27)	14	0	0	56
	Huddersfield	2004-08	96(22)	17	0	0	68
	St Helens	2003	(18)	2	0	0	8
	Wigan	2002	5(3)	1	0	0	4
Ben Jones-Bishop	Salford	2015	17	12	0	0	48
	Leeds	2008-09, 2011-14	70(2)	46	0	0	184
	Harlequins	2010	17	10	0	0	40
Jamie Jones-Buchanan	Leeds	1999-2015	233(65)	61	0	0	244
Tim Jonkers	Wigan	2006	3(1)	0	0	0	0
	Salford	2004-06	5(11)	0	0	0	0
	St Helens	1999-2004	41(64)	12	0	0	48
Darren Jordan	Wakefield	2003	(1)	0	0	0	0
Phil Joseph	Widnes	2013-15	11(38)	1	0	0	4
	Bradford	2012	(6)	0	0	0	0
	Huddersfield	2004	7(6)	0	0	0	0
Max Jowitt	Wakefield	2014-15	2	0	0	0	0
Warren Jowitt	Hull	2003	(2)	0	0	0	0
	Salford	2001-02	17(4)	2	0	0	8
	Wakefield	2000	19(3)	8	0	0	32
	Bradford	1996-99	13(25)	5	0	0	20
Chris Joynt	St Helens	1996-2004	201(14)	68	0	0	272
Gregory Kacala	Paris	1996	7	1	0	0	4
Andy Kain	Castleford	2004, 2006	9(7)	3	10	0	32
Antonio Kaufusi	Huddersfield	2014	15(2)	1	0	0	4
	Bradford	2014	4	0	0	0	0
	London	2012-13	44(5)	5	0	0	20
Mal Kaufusi	London	2004	1(3)	0	0	0	0
Ben Kavanagh	Wakefield	2015	6(3)	0	0	0	0
	Widnes	2012-15	18(33)	0	0	0	0
Liam Kay	Wakefield	2012-13	4	4	0	0	16
Ben Kaye	Harlequins	2009-10	2(13)	0	0	0	0
	Leeds	2008	2(2)	1	0	0	4
Elliot Kear	Bradford	2012-14	53(2)	17	0	0	68
	Crusaders	2010-11	16(1)	4	0	0	16
	Celtic	2009	3	0	0	0	0
Brett Kearney	Bradford	2010-14	107	55	0	0	220
Stephen Kearney	Hull	2005	22(2)	5	0	0	20
Damon Keating	Wakefield	2002	7(17)	1	0	0	4
Kris Keating	Hull KR	2014	23	5	0	0	20
Shaun Keating	London	1996	1(3)	0	0	0	0
Mark Keenan	Workington	1996	3(4)	1	0	0	4
Jimmy Keinhorst	Leeds	2012-15	21(9)	12	0	0	48
	Wakefield	2014	7	1	0	0	4
Albert Kelly	Hull KR	2015	20	15	2	0	64
Tony Kemp	Wakefield	1999-2000	15(5)	2	0	1	9
	Leeds	1996-98	23(2)	5	0	2	22
Damien Kennedy	London	2003	5(11)	1	0	0	4
Ian Kenny	St Helens	2004	(1)	0	0	0	0
Jason Kent	Leigh	2005	23	1	0	0	4
Liam Kent	Hull	2012-13	1(5)	0	0	0	0
Shane Kenward	Wakefield	1999	28	6	0	0	24
	Salford	1998	1	0	0	0	0
Jason Keough	Paris	1997	2	1	0	0	4
Keiran Kerr	Widnes	2005	6	2	0	0	8
Martin Ketteridge	Halifax	1996	7(5)	0	0	0	0
Ronnie Kettlewell	Warrington	1996	(1)	0	0	0	0
Joe Keyes	London	2014	7	5	0	0	20
Younes Khattabi	Catalans	2006-08	24(4)	10	0	0	40
David Kidwell	Warrington	2001-02	14(12)	9	0	0	36
Andrew King	London	2003	23(1)	15	0	0	60
Dave King	Huddersfield	1998-99	11(17)	2	0	0	8
George King	Warrington	2014-15	4(15)	0	0	0	0
James King	Leigh	2005	5(7)	0	0	0	0
Kevin King	Wakefield	2005	8(1)	2	0	0	8
	Castleford	2004	(1)	0	0	0	0
Matt King	Warrington	2008-11	91	58	0	0	232
Paul King	Wakefield	2010-11	10(19)	0	0	1	1
	Hull	1999-2009	136(93)	20	0	1	81
Toby King	Warrington	2014-15	7(1)	2	0	0	8

PLAYER	CLUB	YEAR	APP	TRIES	GOALS	FG	PTS
Andy Kirk	Wakefield	2005	6(3)	1	0	0	4
	Salford	2004	20	5	0	0	20
	Leeds	2001-02	4(4)	0	0	0	0
Ian Kirke	Wakefield	2015	2(2)	1	0	0	4
	Leeds	2006-14	52(132)	10	0	0	40
John Kirkpatrick	London	2004-05	18(1)	5	0	0	20
	St Helens	2001-03	10(11)	10	0	0	40
	Halifax	2003	4	1	0	0	4
Danny Kirmond	Wakefield	2010, 2012-15	92(4)	32	0	0	128
	Huddersfield	2008-11	18(31)	9	0	0	36
Wayne Kitchin	Workington	1996	11(6)	3	17	1	47
Sione Kite	Widnes	2012	6(8)	1	0	0	4
Ian Knott	Leigh	2005	8(1)	2	0	0	8
	Wakefield	2002-03	34(5)	7	79	0	186
	Warrington	1996-2001	68(41)	24	18	0	132
Matt Knowles	Wigan	1996	(3)	0	0	0	0
Michael Knowles	Castleford	2006	(1)	0	0	0	0
Phil Knowles	Salford	1997	1	0	0	0	0
Simon Knox	Halifax	1999	(6)	0	0	0	0
	Salford	1998	1(1)	0	0	0	0
	Bradford	1996-98	9(19)	7	0	0	28
Toa Kohe-Love	Warrington	1996-2001, 2005-06	166(3)	90	0	0	360
	Bradford	2004	1(1)	0	0	0	0
	Hull	2002-03	42	19	0	0	76
Paul Koloi	Wigan	1997	1(2)	1	0	0	4
Craig Kopczak	Huddersfield	2013-15	48(37)	6	0	0	24
	Bradford	2006-12	32(83)	10	0	0	40
Michael Korkidas	Wakefield	2003-06, 2009-11	133(36)	15	0	0	60
	Huddersfield	2009	4(1)	1	0	0	4
	Castleford	2008	15(6)	1	0	0	4
	Salford	2007	26(1)	1	0	0	4
Nick Kouparitsas	Harlequins	2011	2(13)	1	0	0	4
Olsi Krasniqi	Salford	2015	(3)	0	0	0	0
	London	2012-14	28(34)	3	0	0	12
	Harlequins	2010-11	3(20)	1	0	0	4
David Krause	London	1996-97	22(1)	7	0	0	28
Ben Kusto	Huddersfield	2001	21(4)	9	0	1	37
Anthony Laffranchi	St Helens	2012-14	50(18)	19	0	0	76
James Laithwaite	Warrington	2013-15	23(22)	1	0	0	4
	Hull KR	2012	1(2)	1	0	0	4
Adrian Lam	Wigan	2001-04	105(2)	40	1	9	171
Callum Lancaster	Hull	2014-15	6	9	0	0	36
Mark Lane	Paris	1996	(2)	0	0	0	0
Allan Langer	Warrington	2000-01	47	13	4	0	60
Kevin Langer	London	1996	12(4)	2	0	0	8
Junior Langi	Salford	2005-06	27(7)	7	0	0	28
Chris Langley	Huddersfield	2000-01	18(1)	3	0	0	12
Gareth Langley	St Helens	2006	1	1	3	0	10
Jamie Langley	Hull KR	2014	6(5)	1	0	0	4
	Bradford	2002-13	182(57)	36	0	0	144
Ryan Lannon	Salford	2015	(4)	0	0	0	0
Kevin Larroyer	Hull KR	2014-15	32(10)	8	0	0	32
	Catalans	2012-13	9(10)	6	0	0	24
Andy Last	Hull	1999-2005	16(10)	4	0	0	16
Sam Latus	Hull KR	2010-13	34(3)	13	0	0	52
Epalahame Lauaki	Wigan	2012-13	14(16)	2	0	0	8
	Hull	2009-11	3(50)	4	0	0	16
Dale Laughton	Warrington	2002	15(1)	0	0	0	0
	Huddersfield	2000-01	36(2)	4	0	0	16
	Sheffield	1996-99	48(22)	5	0	0	20
Ali Lauitiiti	Wakefield	2012-15	46(31)	16	0	0	64
	Leeds	2004-11	64(117)	58	0	0	232
Jason Laurence	Salford	1997	1	0	0	0	0
Graham Law	Wakefield	1999-2002	34(30)	6	40	0	104
Neil Law	Wakefield	1999-2002	83	39	0	0	156
	Sheffield	1998	1(1)	1	0	0	4
Dean Lawford	Widnes	2003-04	17(1)	5	2	4	28
	Halifax	2001	1(1)	0	0	0	0
	Leeds	1997-2000	15(8)	2	3	0	14
	Huddersfield	1999	6(1)	0	6	1	13
	Sheffield	1996	9(5)	2	1	1	11
Johnny Lawless	Halifax	2001-03	73(1)	10	0	0	40
	Hudds-Sheff	2000	19(6)	3	0	0	12
	Sheffield	1996-99	76(4)	11	0	0	44
Michael Lawrence	Huddersfield	2007-15	146(33)	40	0	0	160
Adam Lawton	Widnes	2013-14	2(10)	5	0	0	20
Charlie Leaeno	Wakefield	2010	7(3)	2	0	0	8
Mark Leafa	Castleford	2008	5(9)	1	0	0	4
	Leigh	2005	28	2	0	0	8
Leroy Leapai	London	1996	2	0	0	0	0
Jim Leatham	Hull	1998-99	20(18)	4	0	0	16
	Leeds	1997	(1)	0	0	0	0
Andy Leathem	Warrington	1999	2(8)	0	0	0	0
	St Helens	1996-98	20(1)	1	0	0	4
Danny Lee	Gateshead	1999	16(2)	0	0	0	0
Jason Lee	Halifax	2001	10(1)	2	0	0	8
Mark Lee	Salford	1997-2000	25(11)	1	0	4	8
Robert Lee	Hull	1999	4(3)	0	0	0	0

PLAYER	CLUB	YEAR	APP	TRIES	GOALS	FG	PTS
Tommy Lee	Salford	2014-15	29(4)	4	0	0	16
	London	2013	16(4)	2	0	0	8
	Huddersfield	2012	11(7)	3	0	0	12
	Wakefield	2011	25	6	0	0	24
	Crusaders	2010	3(9)	0	0	0	0
	Hull	2005-09	44(27)	6	0	0	24
Kruise Leeming	Huddersfield	2013-15	3(18)	2	0	0	8
Matthew Leigh	Salford	2000	(6)	0	0	0	0
Chris Leikvoll	Warrington	2004-07	72(18)	4	0	0	16
Jim Lenihan	Huddersfield	1999	19(1)	10	0	0	40
Mark Lennon	Celtic	2009	10(3)	1	8	0	20
	Hull KR	2007	11(4)	5	7	0	34
	Castleford	2001-03	30(21)	10	21	0	82
Tevita Leo-Latu	Wakefield	2006-10	28(49)	10	0	0	40
Gary Lester	Hull	1998-99	46	17	0	0	68
Stuart Lester	Wigan	1997	1(3)	0	0	0	0
Heath L'Estrange	Bradford	2010-13	56(35)	7	0	0	28
Afi Leuila	Oldham	1996-97	17(3)	2	0	0	8
Kylie Leuluai	Leeds	2007-15	182(45)	20	0	0	80
Macgraff Leuluai	Widnes	2012-15	38(33)	2	0	0	8
Phil Leuluai	Salford	2007, 2009-10	7(47)	3	0	0	12
Thomas Leuluai	Wigan	2007-12	167(1)	51	0	0	204
	Harlequins	2006	15(2)	6	0	0	24
	London	2005	20	13	0	0	52
Simon Lewis	Castleford	2001	4	3	0	0	12
Paul Leyland	St Helens	2006	1	0	0	0	0
Jon Liddell	Leeds	2001	1	0	0	0	0
Jason Lidden	Castleford	1997	15(1)	7	0	0	28
Jordan Lilley	Leeds	2015	1(3)	0	1	0	2
Danny Lima	Wakefield	2007	(3)	0	0	0	0
	Salford	2006	7(2)	0	0	0	0
	Warrington	2004-06	15(47)	9	0	0	36
Jeff Lima	Catalans	2014-15	37(7)	3	1	0	14
	Wigan	2011-12	24(29)	4	0	0	16
Tom Lineham	Hull	2012-15	61(1)	50	0	0	200
Harry Little	London	2013	2	0	0	0	0
Craig Littler	St Helens	2006	1	1	0	0	4
Stuart Littler	Salford	1998-2002, 2004-07, 2009-10	217(30)	65	0	0	260
Peter Livett	Workington	1996	3(1)	0	0	0	0
Rhodri Lloyd	Wigan	2012-13, 2015	3(4)	0	0	0	0
	Widnes	2014	(4)	0	0	0	0
	London	2013	2	0	0	0	0
Kevin Locke	Wakefield	2015	3	0	0	0	0
	Salford	2014-15	13	6	11	0	46
Jack Logan	Hull	2014-15	15	7	0	0	28
Scott Logan	Wigan	2006	10(11)	0	0	0	0
	Hull	2001-03	27(20)	5	0	0	20
Jamahl Lolesi	Huddersfield	2007-10	75(9)	27	0	0	108
Filimone Lolohea	Harlequins	2006	3(6)	0	0	0	0
	London	2005	8(15)	0	0	0	0
David Lomax	Huddersfield	2000-01	45(9)	4	0	0	16
	Paris	1997	19(2)	1	0	0	4
Jonny Lomax	St Helens	2009-15	109(2)	48	84	2	362
Dave Long	London	1999	(1)	0	0	0	0
Karl Long	London	2003	(1)	0	0	0	0
	Widnes	2002	4	1	0	0	4
Sean Long	Hull	2010-11	22	6	0	0	24
	St Helens	1997-2009	263(8)	126	826	20	2176
	Wigan	1996-97	1(5)	0	0	0	0
Davide Longo	Bradford	1996	1(3)	0	0	0	0
Gary Lord	Oldham	1996-97	28(12)	3	0	0	12
Paul Loughlin	Huddersfield	1998-99	34(2)	4	4	0	24
	Bradford	1996-97	36(4)	15	8	0	76
Rhys Lovegrove	Hull KR	2007-14	75(74)	19	0	0	76
Karl Lovell	Hudds-Sheff	2000	14	5	0	0	20
	Sheffield	1999	22(4)	8	0	0	32
Will Lovell	London	2012-14	16(16)	4	0	0	16
James Lowes	Bradford	1996-2003	205	84	2	2	342
Laurent Lucchese	Paris	1996	13(5)	2	0	0	8
Zebastian Luisi	Harlequins	2006-07	23(2)	4	0	0	16
	London	2004-05	21(1)	7	0	0	28
Keith Lulia	Bradford	2012-13	50	19	0	0	76
Shaun Lunt	Hull KR	2015	9(2)	4	0	0	16
	Huddersfield	2009-15	73(39)	60	0	0	240
	Leeds	2012	10(9)	7	0	0	28
Peter Lupton	Crusaders	2010-11	37(9)	10	0	0	40
	Celtic	2009	16(4)	4	0	0	16
	Castleford	2006, 2008	40	11	0	0	44
	Hull	2003-06	19(26)	10	3	0	46
	London	2000-02	10(15)	2	2	0	12
Andy Lynch	Castleford	1999-2004, 2014-15	131(49)	16	0	0	64
	Hull	2012-13	39(14)	3	0	0	12
	Bradford	2005-11	159(29)	46	0	0	184
Reece Lyne	Wakefield	2013-15	50	17	0	0	68
	Hull	2010-11	11(1)	2	0	0	8
Jamie Lyon	St Helens	2005-06	54(1)	39	172	0	500
Iliess Macani	London	2013-14	12(3)	4	0	0	16
Duncan MacGillivray	Wakefield	2004-08	75(18)	6	0	0	24

Super League Players 1996-2015

PLAYER	CLUB	YEAR	APP	TRIES	GOALS	FG	PTS
Brad Mackay	Bradford	2000	24(2)	8	0	0	32
Graham Mackay	Hull	2002	27	18	24	0	120
	Bradford	2001	16(3)	12	1	0	50
	Leeds	2000	12(8)	10	2	0	44
Keiron Maddocks	Leigh	2005	1(3)	0	0	0	0
Steve Maden	Leigh	2005	23	9	0	0	36
	Warrington	2002	3	0	0	0	0
Mateaki Mafi	Warrington	1996-97	7(8)	7	0	0	28
Shaun Magennis	St Helens	2010-12	7(19)	3	0	0	12
Brendan Magnus	London	2000	3	1	0	0	4
Mark Maguire	London	1996-97	11(4)	7	13	0	54
Adam Maher	Hull	2000-03	88(4)	24	0	0	96
	Gateshead	1999	21(5)	3	0	0	12
Lee Maher	Leeds	1996	4(1)	0	0	0	0
Will Maher	Castleford	2014-15	(9)	0	0	0	0
Shaun Mahony	Paris	1997	5	0	0	0	0
Hutch Maiava	Hull	2007	(19)	1	0	0	4
David Maiden	Hull	2000-01	32(10)	11	0	0	44
	Gateshead	1999	5(16)	8	0	0	32
Craig Makin	Salford	1999-2001	24(20)	2	0	0	8
Tom Makinson	St Helens	2011-15	112(5)	76	94	0	492
Brady Malam	Wigan	2000	5(20)	1	0	0	4
Dominic Maloney	Hull	2009	(7)	0	0	0	0
Francis Maloney	Castleford	1998-99, 2003-04	71(7)	24	33	3	165
	Salford	2001-02	45(1)	26	5	0	114
	Wakefield	2000	11	1	1	0	6
	Oldham	1996-97	39(2)	12	91	2	232
Dominic Manfredi	Wigan	2013-15	31	33	0	0	132
	Salford	2014	1	2	0	0	8
George Mann	Warrington	1997	14(5)	1	0	0	4
	Leeds	1996	11(4)	2	0	0	8
Dane Manning	Leeds	2009	(1)	0	0	0	0
Josh Mantellato	Hull KR	2015	21	14	70	0	196
Misili Manu	Widnes	2005	1	0	0	0	0
Willie Manu	St Helens	2013-14	35(11)	9	0	0	36
	Hull	2007-12	133(18)	33	0	0	132
	Castleford	2006	19(4)	9	0	0	36
Manase Manuokafoa	Widnes	2015	2(20)	3	0	0	12
	Bradford	2012-14	49(21)	3	0	0	12
Darren Mapp	Celtic	2009	9(2)	1	0	0	4
David March	Wakefield	1999-2007	164(23)	34	126	0	388
Paul March	Wakefield	1999-2001, 2007	42(31)	17	23	0	114
	Huddersfield	2003-06	71(19)	17	36	1	141
Nick Mardon	London	1997-98	14	2	0	0	8
Thibaut Margalet	Catalans	2013-15	(5)	0	0	0	0
Remy Marginet	Catalans	2011	2	0	9	0	18
Antoni Maria	Catalans	2012-15	1(24)	0	0	0	0
Frankie Mariano	Castleford	2014-15	12(18)	6	0	0	24
	Wakefield	2011-13	41(12)	20	0	0	80
	Hull KR	2010	(3)	0	0	0	0
Oliver Marns	Halifax	1996-2002	54(19)	23	0	0	92
Paul Marquet	Warrington	2002	23(2)	0	0	0	0
Callum Marriott	Salford	2011	(1)	0	0	0	0
Iain Marsh	Salford	1998-2001	1(4)	0	0	0	0
Lee Marsh	Salford	2001-02	3(4)	0	0	0	0
Matthew Marsh	Hull KR	2015	(1)	0	0	0	0
Stefan Marsh	Widnes	2012-15	71	36	11	0	166
	Wigan	2010-11	12	3	0	0	12
Richard Marshall	Leigh	2005	4(16)	0	0	0	0
	London	2002-03	33(11)	1	0	0	4
	Huddersfield	2000-01	35(14)	1	0	0	4
	Halifax	1996-99	38(34)	2	0	0	8
Charlie Martin	Castleford	2013	(6)	0	0	0	0
Jason Martin	Paris	1997	15(2)	3	0	0	12
Scott Martin	Salford	1997-99	32(18)	8	0	0	32
Tony Martin	Hull	2012	10	1	0	0	4
	Crusaders	2010-11	40(1)	14	1	0	58
	Wakefield	2008-09	33	10	33	0	106
	London	1996-97, 2001-03	97(1)	36	170	1	485
Mick Martindale	Halifax	1996	(4)	0	0	0	0
Sebastien Martins	Catalans	2006, 2009-11	(21)	2	0	0	8
Tommy Martyn	St Helens	1996-2003	125(20)	87	63	12	486
Dean Marwood	Workington	1996	9(6)	0	22	0	44
Martin Masella	Warrington	2001	10(14)	5	0	0	20
	Wakefield	2000	14(8)	4	0	0	16
	Leeds	1997-1999	59(5)	1	0	0	4
Colin Maskill	Castleford	1996	8	1	1	0	6
Mose Masoe	St Helens	2014-15	17(39)	10	0	0	40
Keith Mason	Castleford	2006, 2013	11(6)	0	0	0	0
	Huddersfield	2006-12	118(14)	4	0	0	16
	St Helens	2003-05	33(23)	4	0	0	16
	Wakefield	2000-01	5(17)	0	0	0	0
Nathan Mason	Huddersfield	2013, 2015	(3)	0	0	0	0
Willie Mason	Hull KR	2011	6	1	0	0	4
Sammy Masselot	Wakefield	2011	(1)	0	0	0	0
Nathan Massey	Castleford	2008-15	63(50)	8	0	0	32

PLAYER	CLUB	YEAR	APP	TRIES	GOALS	FG	PTS
Nesiasi Mataitonga	London	2014	11(1)	1	0	0	4
Vila Matautia	St Helens	1996-2001	31(68)	9	0	0	36
Feleti Mateo	London	2005	4(10)	1	0	0	4
Barrie-Jon Mather	Castleford	1998, 2000-02	50(12)	21	0	0	84
Richard Mathers	Wakefield	2012-14	71	24	0	0	96
	Castleford	2011	21(1)	7	0	0	28
	Warrington	2002, 2009-10	42(3)	11	0	0	44
	Wigan	2008-09	23(1)	2	0	0	8
	Leeds	2002-06	85(2)	26	0	0	104
Jamie Mathiou	Leeds	1997-2001	31(82)	3	0	0	12
Masi Matongo	Hull	2015	(1)	0	0	0	0
Terry Matterson	London	1996-98	46	15	90	6	246
Vic Mauro	Salford	2013	1(7)	1	0	0	4
Luke May	Harlequins	2009-10	(3)	0	0	0	0
Casey Mayberry	Halifax	2000	1(1)	0	0	0	0
Chris Maye	Halifax	2003	3(4)	0	0	0	0
Joe Mbu	Harlequins	2006-09	33(20)	3	0	0	12
	London	2003-05	29(19)	4	0	0	16
Danny McAllister	Gateshead	1999	3(3)	1	0	0	4
	Sheffield	1996-97	33(7)	10	0	0	40
John McAtee	St Helens	1996	2(1)	0	0	0	0
Nathan McAvoy	Bradford	1998-2002, 2007	83(31)	46	0	0	184
	Wigan	2006	15(2)	5	0	0	20
	Salford	1997-98, 2004-05	57(4)	18	0	0	72
Tyrone McCarthy	Hull KR	2015	20(1)	4	0	0	16
	Warrington	2009-13	12(24)	2	0	0	8
	Wakefield	2011	2(5)	1	0	0	4
Louie McCarthy-Scarsbrook	St Helens	2011-15	81(58)	25	0	0	100
	Harlequins	2006-10	41(50)	17	0	0	68
Dave McConnell	London	2003	(4)	0	0	0	0
	St Helens	2001-02	3(2)	4	0	0	16
Robbie McCormack	Wigan	1998	24	2	0	0	8
Steve McCurrie	Leigh	2005	7(3)	1	0	0	4
	Widnes	2002-04	55(22)	10	0	0	40
	Warrington	1998-2001	69(26)	31	0	0	124
Barrie McDermott	Leeds	1996-2005	163(69)	28	0	0	112
Brian McDermott	Bradford	1996-2002	138(32)	33	0	0	132
Ryan McDonald	Widnes	2002-03	6(4)	0	0	0	0
Wayne McDonald	Huddersfield	2005-06	11(23)	1	0	0	4
	Wigan	2005	(4)	0	0	0	0
	Leeds	2002-05	34(47)	14	0	0	56
	St Helens	2001	7(11)	4	0	0	16
	Hull	2000	5(8)	4	0	0	16
	Wakefield	1999	9(17)	8	0	0	32
Shannon McDonnell	St Helens	2014-15	10	8	0	0	32
	Hull	2013	19	2	0	0	8
	Hull KR	2012	21	6	0	0	24
Craig McDowell	Huddersfield	2003	(1)	0	0	0	0
	Warrington	2002	(1)	0	0	0	0
	Bradford	2000	(1)	0	0	0	0
Wes McGibbon	Halifax	1999	1	0	0	0	0
Jermaine McGillvary	Huddersfield	2010-15	138	97	0	0	388
Dean McGilvray	Salford	2009-10	14	4	0	0	16
	St Helens	2006-08	5(1)	1	0	0	4
Billy McGinty	Workington	1996	1	0	0	0	0
Ryan McGoldrick	Salford	2013	19(1)	3	0	1	13
	Hull	2012	8	1	0	0	4
	Castleford	2006, 2008-12	129(5)	24	11	0	118
Kevin McGuinness	Salford	2004-07	63(3)	11	0	0	44
Casey McGuire	Catalans	2007-10	87(4)	27	0	0	108
Danny McGuire	Leeds	2001-15	294(38)	230	0	4	924
Gary McGuirk	Workington	1996	(4)	0	0	0	0
Michael McIlorum	Wigan	2007-15	136(52)	19	0	0	76
Richard McKell	Castleford	1997-98	22(7)	2	0	0	8
Chris McKenna	Bradford	2006-07	40(7)	7	0	0	28
	Leeds	2003-05	65(4)	18	0	0	72
Phil McKenzie	Workington	1996	4	0	0	0	0
Chris McKinney	Oldham	1996-97	4(9)	2	0	0	8
Wade McKinnon	Hull	2012	10	4	0	0	16
Mark McLinden	Harlequins	2006-08	46(1)	20	0	1	81
	London	2005	22(3)	8	0	0	32
Mike McMeeken	Castleford	2015	14(5)	1	0	0	4
	London	2012-14	25(9)	5	0	0	20
Shayne McMenemy	Hull	2003-07	80(8)	12	0	0	48
	Halifax	2001-03	63	11	0	0	44
Andy McNally	London	2004	5(3)	0	0	0	0
	Castleford	2001, 2003	2(5)	1	0	0	4
Gregg McNally	Huddersfield	2011	1	0	6	0	12

PLAYER	CLUB	YEAR	APP	TRIES	GOALS	FG	PTS
Steve McNamara	Huddersfield	2001, 2003	41(9)	3	134	1	281
	Wakefield	2000	15(2)	2	32	0	72
	Bradford	1996-99	90(3)	14	348	7	759
Paul McNicholas	Hull	2004-05	28(12)	4	0	0	16
Neil McPherson	Salford	1997	(1)	0	0	0	0
Shannan McPherson	Salford	2012-14	20(11)	0	0	0	0
Duncan McRae	London	1996	11(2)	3	0	1	13
Paul McShane	Castleford	2015	1(5)	0	0	0	0
	Wakefield	2014-15	39(9)	5	0	0	20
	Leeds	2009-13	17(38)	12	0	0	48
	Widnes	2012	6(5)	3	4	0	20
	Hull	2010	(4)	0	0	0	0
Derek McVey	St Helens	1996-97	28(4)	6	1	0	26
Dallas Mead	Warrington	1997	2	0	0	0	0
Robbie Mears	Leigh	2005	8(6)	0	0	0	0
	Leeds	2001	23	6	0	0	24
Paul Medley	Bradford	1996-98	6(35)	9	0	0	36
Francis Meli	Salford	2014	16	11	0	0	44
	St Helens	2006-13	194(1)	122	0	0	488
Vince Mellars	Wakefield	2012-13	21(5)	4	0	0	16
	Crusaders	2010-11	46	17	0	0	68
Chris Melling	London	2012-13	25(12)	5	2	0	24
	Harlequins	2007-11	100(11)	33	6	0	144
	Wigan	2004-05	8(2)	1	3	0	10
Alex Mellor	Bradford	2013-14	(10)	0	0	0	0
Joe Mellor	Widnes	2012-15	74	28	0	0	112
	Wigan	2012	1(1)	1	0	0	4
	Harlequins	2011	(1)	0	0	0	0
Paul Mellor	Castleford	2003-04	36(3)	18	0	0	72
James Mendeika	London	2013	4(2)	2	0	0	8
Craig Menkins	Paris	1997	4(5)	0	0	0	0
Luke Menzies	Hull KR	2008	(1)	0	0	0	0
Steve Menzies	Catalans	2011-13	61(6)	30	0	0	120
	Bradford	2009-10	52(1)	24	1	0	98
Gary Mercer	Castleford	2002	(1)	0	0	0	0
	Leeds	1996-97, 2001	40(2)	9	0	0	36
	Warrington	2001	18	2	0	0	8
	Halifax	1998-2001	73(2)	16	0	0	64
Tony Mestrov	London	1996-97, 2001	59(8)	4	0	0	16
	Wigan	1998-2000	39(39)	3	0	0	12
Keiran Meyer	London	1996	4	1	0	0	4
Brad Meyers	Bradford	2005-06	40(11)	13	0	0	52
Steve Michaels	Hull	2015	23	8	0	0	32
Gary Middlehurst	Widnes	2004	(2)	0	0	0	0
Simon Middleton	Castleford	1996-97	19(3)	8	0	0	32
Constantine Mika	Hull KR	2012-13	45(4)	9	0	0	36
Daryl Millard	Catalans	2011-14	91	38	1	0	154
	Wakefield	2010-11	21(1)	11	0	0	44
Shane Millard	Wigan	2007	19(6)	3	0	0	12
	Leeds	2006	6(21)	3	0	0	12
	Widnes	2003-05	69	23	0	0	92
	London	1998-2001	72(14)	11	1	0	46
Jack Miller	Huddersfield	2013	1	0	1	0	2
Jacob Miller	Wakefield	2015	20	10	17	0	74
	Hull	2013-14	20	6	9	0	42
Grant Millington	Castleford	2012-15	75(23)	14	0	0	56
David Mills	Harlequins	2006-07, 2010	25(32)	2	0	0	8
	Hull KR	2008-09	20(11)	1	0	0	4
	Widnes	2002-05	17(77)	8	0	0	32
Lewis Mills	Celtic	2009	(4)	0	0	0	0
Adam Milner	Castleford	2010-15	77(39)	21	0	0	84
Lee Milner	Halifax	1999	(1)	0	0	0	0
Elliot Minchella	Leeds	2013-14	(6)	1	0	0	4
Mark Minichiello	Hull	2015	27	7	0	0	28
Thomas Minns	London	2014	23	6	0	0	24
	Leeds	2013	2(1)	1	0	0	4
John Minto	London	1996	13	4	0	0	16
Lee Mitchell	Castleford	2012	13(10)	2	0	0	8
	Warrington	2007-11	8(27)	4	0	0	16
	Harlequins	2011	11(1)	1	0	0	4
Sam Moa	Hull	2009-12	29(44)	6	0	0	24
Martin Moana	Salford	2004	6(3)	1	0	0	4
	Halifax	1996-2001, 2003	126(22)	62	0	1	249
	Wakefield	2002	19(2)	10	0	0	40
	Huddersfield	2001	3(3)	2	0	0	8
Adam Mogg	Catalans	2007-10	74	19	0	1	77
Jon Molloy	Wakefield	2013-15	9(13)	2	0	0	8
	Huddersfield	2011-12	2(1)	0	0	0	0
Steve Molloy	Huddersfield	2000-01	26(20)	3	0	0	12
	Sheffield	1998-99	32(17)	3	0	0	12
Chris Molyneux	Huddersfield	2000-01	1(18)	0	0	0	0
	Sheffield	1999	1(2)	0	0	0	0
Joel Monaghan	Warrington	2011-15	127	125	2	0	504
Michael Monaghan	Warrington	2008-14	143(28)	31	0	4	128
Joel Moon	Leeds	2013-15	77	36	0	0	144
	Salford	2012	17	9	0	0	36
Adrian Moore	Huddersfield	1998-99	1(4)	0	0	0	0

PLAYER	CLUB	YEAR	APP	TRIES	GOALS	FG	PTS
Danny Moore	London	2000	7	0	0	0	0
	Wigan	1998-99	49(3)	18	0	0	72
Gareth Moore	Wakefield	2011	5	1	14	1	33
Jason Moore	Workington	1996	(5)	0	0	0	0
Richard Moore	Wakefield	2007-10, 2014	52(57)	10	0	0	40
	Leeds	2012-13	3(27)	1	0	0	4
	Crusaders	2011	11(10)	1	0	0	4
	Leigh	2005	2(5)	0	0	0	0
	Bradford	2002-04	1(26)	0	0	0	0
	London	2002, 2004	5(9)	2	0	0	8
Scott Moore	Wakefield	2015	(1)	0	0	0	0
	Castleford	2008, 2015	24(6)	2	0	0	8
	London	2014	26	3	0	0	12
	Huddersfield	2009, 2012	29(7)	9	0	0	36
	Widnes	2012	3(3)	0	0	0	0
	St Helens	2004-07, 2010-11	29(37)	9	0	0	36
Junior Moors	Castleford	2015	13(11)	4	0	0	16
Dennis Moran	Wigan	2005-06	39	17	1	1	71
	London	2001-04	107(2)	74	2	5	305
Willie Morganson	Sheffield	1997-98	18(12)	5	3	0	26
Paul Moriarty	Halifax	1996	3(2)	0	0	0	0
Adrian Morley	Salford	2014-15	31(14)	2	0	0	8
	Warrington	2007-13	135(21)	8	0	0	32
	Bradford	2005	2(4)	0	0	0	0
	Leeds	1996-2000	95(14)	25	0	0	100
Chris Morley	Salford	1999	3(5)	0	0	0	0
	Warrington	1998	2(8)	0	0	0	0
	St Helens	1996-97	21(16)	4	0	0	16
Glenn Morrison	Wakefield	2010-11	43(1)	9	0	0	36
	Bradford	2007-09	48(2)	19	0	0	76
Iain Morrison	Hull KR	2007	5(6)	1	0	0	4
	Huddersfield	2003-05	11(23)	0	0	0	0
	London	2001	(1)	0	0	0	0
Dale Morton	Wakefield	2009-11	22(3)	8	5	0	42
Gareth Morton	Hull KR	2007	7(4)	3	23	0	58
	Leeds	2001-02	1(1)	0	0	0	0
Lee Mossop	Wigan	2008-13, 2015	70(53)	10	0	0	40
	Huddersfield	2009	1(4)	1	0	0	4
Aaron Moule	Salford	2006-07	45	17	0	0	68
	Widnes	2004-05	29	12	0	0	48
Wilfried Moulinec	Paris	1996	1	0	0	0	0
Gregory Mounis	Catalans	2006-15	145(89)	26	19	0	142
Mark Moxon	Huddersfield	1998-2001	20(5)	1	0	1	5
Rob Mulhern	Leeds	2014-15	(5)	0	0	0	0
Anthony Mullally	Wakefield	2015	(2)	0	0	0	0
	Huddersfield	2013-15	12(24)	5	0	0	20
	Bradford	2014	1(5)	0	0	0	0
	Widnes	2012	(9)	0	0	0	0
Jake Mullaney	Salford	2014	12	2	24	0	56
Brett Mullins	Leeds	2001	5(3)	1	0	0	4
Damian Munro	Widnes	2002	8(2)	1	0	0	4
	Halifax	1996-97	9(6)	8	0	0	32
Matt Munro	Oldham	1996-97	26(5)	8	0	0	32
Craig Murdock	Salford	2000	(2)	0	0	0	0
	Hull	1998-99	21(6)	8	0	2	34
	Wigan	1996-98	18(17)	14	0	0	56
Aaron Murphy	Huddersfield	2012-15	86	50	0	0	200
	Wakefield	2008-11	57(2)	12	0	0	48
Jack Murphy	Wigan	2012, 2014	3	1	0	0	4
	Salford	2013	10	3	1	0	14
Jamie Murphy	Crusaders	2011	(2)	0	0	0	0
Jobe Murphy	Bradford	2013	(4)	0	0	0	0
Justin Murphy	Catalans	2006-08	59	49	0	0	196
	Widnes	2004	5	1	0	0	4
Doc Murray	Warrington	1997	(2)	0	0	0	0
	Wigan	1997	6(2)	0	0	0	0
Scott Murrell	Hull KR	2007-12	114(24)	24	26	1	149
	Leeds	2005	(1)	0	0	0	0
	London	2004	3(3)	2	0	0	8
David Mycoe	Sheffield	1996-97	12(13)	1	0	0	4
Richard Myler	Warrington	2010-15	127(4)	69	1	1	279
	Salford	2009	18	11	0	0	44
Rob Myler	Oldham	1996-97	19(2)	6	0	0	24
Stephen Myler	Salford	2006	4(8)	1	15	0	34
	Widnes	2003-05	35(14)	8	74	0	180
Vinny Myler	Salford	2004	(4)	0	0	0	0
	Bradford	2003	(1)	0	0	0	0
Matt Nable	London	1997	2(2)	1	0	0	4
Brad Nairn	Workington	1996	14	4	0	0	16
Frank Napoli	London	2000	14(6)	2	0	0	8
Carlo Napolitano	Salford	2000	(3)	1	0	0	4
Stephen Nash	Castleford	2012	3(4)	0	0	0	0
	Salford	2007, 2009	2(18)	1	0	0	4
	Widnes	2005	4(1)	0	0	0	0
Curtis Naughton	Hull	2015	11	6	0	0	24
	Bradford	2013	1	0	0	0	0
Jim Naylor	Halifax	2000	7(6)	2	0	0	8
Scott Naylor	Salford	1997-98, 2004	30(1)	9	0	0	36
	Bradford	1999-2003	127(1)	51	0	0	204
Adam Neal	Salford	2010-13	17(28)	0	0	0	0

Super League Players 1996-2015

PLAYER	CLUB	YEAR	APP	TRIES	GOALS	FG	PTS
Mike Neal	Salford	1998	(1)	0	0	0	0
	Oldham	1996-97	6(4)	3	0	0	12
Jonathan Neill	Huddersfield	1998-99	20(11)	0	0	0	0
	St Helens	1996	1	0	0	0	0
Chris Nero	Salford	2011-13	31(16)	7	0	0	28
	Bradford	2008-10	65(5)	24	0	0	96
	Huddersfield	2004-07	97(8)	38	0	0	152
Jason Netherton	Hull KR	2007-14	60(74)	4	0	0	16
	London	2003-04	6	0	0	0	0
	Halifax	2002	2(3)	0	0	0	0
	Leeds	2001	(3)	0	0	0	0
Kirk Netherton	Castleford	2009-10	5(23)	3	0	0	12
	Hull KR	2007-08	9(15)	2	0	0	8
Paul Newlove	Castleford	2004	5	1	0	0	4
	St Helens	1996-2003	162	106	0	0	424
Richard Newlove	Wakefield	2003	17(5)	8	0	0	32
Clint Newton	Hull KR	2008-11	90(3)	37	0	0	148
Terry Newton	Wakefield	2010	(2)	0	0	0	0
	Bradford	2006-09	83(6)	26	0	0	104
	Wigan	2000-05	157(9)	62	0	0	248
	Leeds	1996-1999	55(14)	4	0	0	16
Gene Ngamu	Huddersfield	1999-2000	29(2)	9	67	0	170
Danny Nicklas	Hull	2010, 2012	2(8)	0	0	0	0
Sonny Nickle	St Helens	1999-2002	86(18)	14	0	0	56
	Bradford	1996-98	25(16)	9	0	0	36
Jason Nicol	Salford	2000-02	52(7)	11	0	0	44
Tawera Nikau	Warrington	2000-01	51	7	0	0	28
Rob Nolan	Hull	1998-99	20(11)	6	0	0	24
Paul Noone	Harlequins	2006	5(2)	0	0	0	0
	Warrington	2000-06	60(59)	12	20	0	88
Chris Norman	Halifax	2003	13(3)	2	0	0	8
Paul Norman	Oldham	1996	(1)	0	0	0	0
Andy Northey	St Helens	1996-97	8(17)	2	0	0	8
Danny Nutley	Castleford	2006	28	3	0	0	12
	Warrington	1998-2001	94(1)	3	0	0	12
Tony Nuttall	Oldham	1996-97	1(7)	0	0	0	0
Adam O'Brien	Bradford	2011-14	12(29)	6	0	0	24
Clinton O'Brien	Wakefield	2003	(2)	0	0	0	0
Gareth O'Brien	Warrington	2011-15	48(3)	16	69	3	205
	St Helens	2013	7	0	25	0	50
	Castleford	2013	2	0	0	1	1
	Widnes	2012	4	0	15	0	30
Sam Obst	Hull	2011	17(6)	6	0	0	24
	Wakefield	2005-11	100(28)	40	7	0	174
Jamie O'Callaghan	London	2012-14	44(2)	4	0	0	16
	Harlequins	2008-11	54(3)	12	0	0	48
Eamon O'Carroll	Widnes	2012-15	43(5)	2	0	0	8
	Hull	2012	1(9)	0	0	0	0
	Wigan	2006-11	2(59)	3	0	0	12
Matt O'Connor	Paris	1997	11(4)	1	26	2	58
Terry O'Connor	Widnes	2005	25	2	0	0	8
	Wigan	1996-2004	177(45)	9	0	0	36
Jarrod O'Doherty	Huddersfield	2003	26	3	0	0	12
David O'Donnell	Paris	1997	21	3	0	0	12
Luke O'Donnell	Huddersfield	2011-13	22(2)	2	0	0	8
Martin Offiah	Salford	2000-01	41	20	0	2	82
	London	1996-99	29(3)	21	0	0	84
	Wigan	1996	8	7	0	0	28
Mark O'Halloran	London	2004-05	34(3)	10	0	0	40
Ryan O'Hara	Hull KR	2012	8(7)	1	0	0	4
	Crusaders	2010-11	41(8)	3	0	0	12
	Celtic	2009	27	3	0	0	12
Hefin O'Hare	Huddersfield	2001, 2003-05	72(10)	27	0	0	108
Edwin Okanga-Ajwang	Salford	2013	2	0	0	0	0
Hitro Okesene	Hull	1998	21(1)	0	0	0	0
Anderson Okiwe	Sheffield	1997	1	0	0	0	0
Tom Olbison	Bradford	2009-14	55(26)	11	0	0	44
Michael Oldfield	Catalans	2014-15	41	28	0	0	112
Jamie Olejnik	Paris	1997	11	8	0	0	32
Aaron Ollett	Hull KR	2013-15	5(16)	1	0	0	4
Kevin O'Loughlin	Halifax	1997-98	2(4)	0	0	0	0
	St Helens	1997	(3)	0	0	0	0
Sean O'Loughlin	Wigan	2002-15	300(21)	66	3	2	272
Mark O'Meley	Hull	2010-13	70(13)	13	0	0	52
Jules O'Neill	Widnes	2003-05	57(3)	14	158	7	379
	Wakefield	2005	10(2)	2	4	0	16
	Wigan	2002-03	29(1)	12	72	0	192
Julian O'Neill	Widnes	2002-05	57(39)	3	0	0	12
	Wakefield	2001	24(1)	2	0	0	8
	St Helens	1997-2000	95(8)	5	0	0	20
Mark O'Neill	Hull KR	2007	17	5	0	0	20
	Leeds	2006	1(8)	0	0	0	0
Steve O'Neill	Gateshead	1999	1(1)	0	0	0	0
Tom O'Reilly	Warrington	2001-02	8(6)	1	0	0	4
Matt Orford	Bradford	2010	12	3	31	2	76
Gene Ormsby	Warrington	2014-15	33	23	0	0	92
Chris Orr	Huddersfield	1998	19(3)	2	0	0	8
Danny Orr	Castleford	1997-2003, 2011-12	197(23)	75	308	3	919
	Harlequins	2007-10	90(4)	13	96	0	244
	Wigan	2004-06	66(2)	18	12	0	96

PLAYER	CLUB	YEAR	APP	TRIES	GOALS	FG	PTS
Gareth Owen	Salford	2010, 2012-13	4(32)	6	0	0	24
Nick Owen	Leigh	2005	8(1)	1	11	0	26
Richard Owen	Wakefield	2014-15	29(1)	9	0	0	36
	Castleford	2008-14	109(3)	57	0	0	228
Jack Owens	Widnes	2012-15	53(1)	26	103	0	310
Lopini Paea	Wakefield	2015	1(3)	0	0	0	0
	Catalans	2011-14	41(41)	9	0	0	36
Mickey Paea	Hull	2014-15	44(5)	3	0	0	12
	Hull KR	2012-13	34(17)	5	0	0	20
Mathias Pala	Catalans	2011-15	28(1)	4	0	0	16
Iafeta Palea'aesina	Hull	2014-15	(41)	1	0	0	4
	Salford	2011-12	4(37)	3	0	0	12
	Wigan	2006-10	55(77)	16	0	0	64
Jason Palmada	Workington	1996	12	2	0	0	8
Junior Paramore	Castleford	1996	5(5)	3	0	0	12
Paul Parker	Hull	1999-2002	23(18)	9	0	0	36
Rob Parker	Castleford	2011	4(2)	2	0	0	8
	Salford	2009-11	23(14)	4	0	0	16
	Warrington	2006-08	10(56)	6	0	0	24
	Bradford	2000, 2002-05	19(76)	14	0	0	56
	London	2001	9	1	0	0	4
Wayne Parker	Halifax	1996-97	12(1)	0	0	0	0
Ian Parry	Warrington	2001	(1)	0	0	0	0
Jules Parry	Paris	1996	10(2)	0	0	0	0
Regis Pastre-Courtine	Paris	1996	4(3)	4	0	0	16
Cory Paterson	Salford	2015	14(1)	7	6	0	40
	Hull KR	2013	15	7	0	0	28
Andrew Patmore	Oldham	1996	8(5)	3	0	0	12
Larne Patrick	Wigan	2015	7(20)	4	0	0	16
	Huddersfield	2009-14	25(102)	27	0	0	108
Luke Patten	Salford	2011-12	53	16	0	0	64
Declan Patton	Warrington	2015	8	0	1	1	3
Henry Paul	Harlequins	2006-08	60(1)	8	94	2	222
	Bradford	1999-2001	81(5)	29	350	6	822
	Wigan	1996-98	60	37	23	0	194
Junior Paul	London	1996	3	1	0	0	4
Robbie Paul	Salford	2009	2(24)	2	0	0	8
	Huddersfield	2006-07	44(8)	7	0	0	28
	Bradford	1996-2005	198(31)	121	3	0	490
Jason Payne	Castleford	2006	1(1)	0	0	0	0
Danny Peacock	Bradford	1997-99	32(2)	15	0	0	60
Jamie Peacock	Leeds	2006-15	234(16)	24	0	0	96
	Bradford	1999-2005	163(25)	38	0	0	152
Martin Pearson	Wakefield	2001	21(1)	3	60	3	135
	Halifax	1997-98, 2000	55(6)	24	181	0	458
	Sheffield	1999	17(6)	9	36	2	110
Jacques Pech	Paris	1996	16	0	0	0	0
Mike Pechey	Warrington	1998	6(3)	2	0	0	8
Bill Peden	London	2003	21(3)	7	0	0	28
Adam Peek	Crusaders	2010-11	5(22)	1	0	0	4
	Celtic	2009	5(12)	3	0	0	12
Eloi Pelissier	Catalans	2011-15	18(97)	18	0	1	73
Dimitri Pelo	Catalans	2007-10	79	37	0	0	148
Sean Penkywicz	Huddersfield	2004-05	21(11)	7	0	0	28
	Halifax	2000-03	29(27)	8	0	0	32
Julian Penni	Salford	1998-99	4	0	0	0	0
Kevin Penny	Warrington	2006-09, 2014-15	61(1)	39	0	0	156
	Wakefield	2011	5	1	0	0	4
	Harlequins	2010	5	3	0	0	12
Lee Penny	Warrington	1996-2003	140(5)	54	0	0	216
Paul Penrice	Workington	1996	11(2)	2	0	0	8
Chris Percival	Widnes	2002-03	26	6	0	0	24
Mark Percival	St Helens	2013-15	47(2)	22	81	0	250
Apollo Perelini	St Helens	1996-2000	103(16)	27	0	0	108
Ugo Perez	Catalans	2015	(2)	0	0	0	0
Mark Perrett	Halifax	1996-97	15(4)	4	0	0	16
Josh Perry	St Helens	2011-13	32(9)	2	0	0	8
Shane Perry	Catalans	2009	8(8)	1	0	0	4
Adam Peters	Paris	1997	16(3)	0	0	0	0
Dominic Peters	London	1998-2003	58(11)	12	0	0	48
Mike Peters	Warrington	2000	2(12)	1	0	0	4
	Halifax	2000	1	0	0	0	0
Willie Peters	Widnes	2004	9	3	0	2	14
	Wigan	2000	29	15	5	6	76
	Gateshead	1999	27	11	1	6	52
Dave Petersen	Hull KR	2012	2(2)	1	0	0	4
Matt Petersen	Wakefield	2008-09	14	3	0	0	12
Adrian Petrie	Workington	1996	(1)	0	0	0	0
Eddy Pettybourne	Wigan	2014	1(15)	0	0	0	0
Cameron Phelps	Widnes	2012-15	66(1)	23	2	0	96
	Hull	2011	19	2	0	0	8
	Wigan	2008-10	43(1)	14	4	0	64
Joe Philbin	Warrington	2014-15	6(11)	3	0	0	12
Rowland Phillips	Workington	1996	22	1	0	0	4
Nathan Picchi	Leeds	1996	(1)	0	0	0	0
Ian Pickavance	Hull	1999	4(2)	2	0	0	8
	Huddersfield	1999	3(14)	0	0	0	0
	St Helens	1996-98	12(44)	6	0	0	24

PLAYER	CLUB	YEAR	APP	TRIES	GOALS	FG	PTS
James Pickering	Castleford	1999	1(19)	0	0	0	0
Steve Pickersgill	Widnes	2012-13	27(8)	1	0	0	4
	Warrington	2005-09	1(36)	0	0	0	0
Nick Pinkney	Salford	2000-02	64	29	0	0	116
	Halifax	1999	26(2)	13	0	0	52
	Sheffield	1997-98	33	10	0	0	40
Mikhail Piskunov	Paris	1996	1(1)	1	0	0	4
Darryl Pitt	London	1996	2(16)	4	0	1	17
Jay Pitts	Bradford	2014	15(1)	3	0	0	12
	Hull	2012-14	18(30)	1	0	0	4
	Leeds	2009-12	10(15)	2	0	0	8
	Wakefield	2008-09	9(8)	2	0	0	8
Andy Platt	Salford	1997-98	20(3)	1	0	0	4
Michael Platt	Salford	2001-02, 2014	4(1)	1	0	0	4
	Bradford	2007-13	121(6)	44	0	0	176
	Castleford	2006	26	7	0	0	28
Willie Poching	Leeds	2002-06	58(73)	44	0	0	176
	Wakefield	1999-2001	65(4)	20	0	0	80
Ben Pomeroy	Catalans	2014-15	44	10	0	0	40
Quentin Pongia	Wigan	2003-04	15(10)	0	0	0	0
Justin Poore	Hull KR	2014	7	0	0	0	0
	Wakefield	2013	23	1	0	0	4
Dan Potter	Widnes	2002-03	34(2)	6	0	0	24
	London	2001	1(3)	1	0	0	4
Craig Poucher	Hull	1999-2002	31(5)	5	0	0	20
Andy Powell	Wigan	2013	2(3)	1	0	0	4
Bryn Powell	Salford	2004	1(1)	0	0	0	0
Daio Powell	Sheffield	1999	13(1)	2	0	0	8
	Halifax	1997-98	30(3)	17	0	0	68
Daryl Powell	Leeds	1998-2000	49(30)	12	0	2	50
Sam Powell	Wigan	2012-15	28(30)	8	0	2	34
Karl Pratt	Bradford	2003-05	35(19)	18	0	0	72
	Leeds	1999-2002	62(12)	33	0	0	132
Paul Prescott	Wigan	2004-13	49(75)	4	0	0	16
Steve Prescott	Hull	1998-99, 2001-03	99	46	191	3	569
	Wakefield	2000	22(1)	3	13	0	38
	St Helens	1996-97	32	15	17	0	94
Lee Prest	Workington	1996	(1)	0	0	0	0
Gareth Price	Salford	2002	(2)	0	0	0	0
	London	2002	2(2)	3	0	0	12
	St Helens	1999	(11)	2	0	0	8
Gary Price	Wakefield	1999-2001	55(13)	11	0	0	44
Richard Price	Sheffield	1996	1(2)	0	0	0	0
Tony Priddle	Paris	1997	11(7)	3	0	0	12
Karl Pryce	Bradford	2003-06, 2012	47(19)	46	1	0	186
	Harlequins	2011	11(7)	12	0	0	48
	Wigan	2009-10	11(2)	12	0	0	48
Leon Pryce	Hull	2015	22	6	0	0	24
	Catalans	2012-14	72(2)	15	0	0	60
	St Helens	2006-11	133(3)	64	0	0	256
	Bradford	1998-2005	159(29)	86	0	0	344
Waine Pryce	Wakefield	2007	10(2)	4	0	0	16
	Castleford	2000-06	97(12)	49	0	0	196
Tony Puletua	Hull KR	2015	7	0	0	0	0
	Salford	2014	16(9)	3	0	0	12
	St Helens	2009-13	108(18)	39	0	0	156
Andrew Purcell	Castleford	2000	15(5)	3	0	0	12
	Hull	1999	27	4	0	0	16
Rob Purdham	Harlequins	2006-11	112(3)	18	131	1	335
	London	2002-05	53(15)	16	2	1	69
Adrian Purtell	Bradford	2012-14	45(1)	16	0	0	64
Luke Quigley	Catalans	2007	16(1)	1	0	0	4
Adam Quinlan	St Helens	2015	11	6	0	0	24
Damien Quinn	Celtic	2009	20(1)	4	12	0	40
Scott Quinnell	Wigan	1996	6(3)	1	0	0	4
Florian Quintilla	Catalans	2008-09	1(4)	0	0	0	0
Lee Radford	Hull	1998, 2006-12	138(30)	23	1	0	94
	Bradford	1999-2005	79(65)	18	12	0	96
Kris Radlinski	Wigan	1996-2006	236(1)	134	1	0	538
Sebastien Raguin	Catalans	2007-12	103(22)	28	0	0	112
Adrian Rainey	Castleford	2002	4(7)	1	0	0	4
Andy Raleigh	Wakefield	2012-14	42(21)	9	0	0	36
	Huddersfield	2006-11	74(46)	13	0	0	52
Jean-Luc Ramondou	Paris	1996	1(1)	1	0	0	4
Chad Randall	London	2012-13	29(9)	4	0	0	16
	Harlequins	2006-11	141(2)	37	0	1	149
Craig Randall	Halifax	1999	8(11)	4	0	0	16
	Salford	1997-98	12(18)	4	0	0	16
Jordan Rankin	Hull	2014-15	41(6)	20	43	0	166
Scott Ranson	Oldham	1996-97	19(2)	7	0	0	28
Aaron Raper	Castleford	1999-2001	48(4)	4	2	1	21
Steve Rapira	Salford	2014	5(13)	0	0	0	0
Stefan Ratchford	Warrington	2012-15	103(6)	42	139	2	448
	Salford	2007, 2009-11	65(5)	23	20	0	132
Mike Ratu	Hull KR	2010	5	1	0	0	4
	Leeds	2007, 2009	1(5)	1	0	0	4
Paul Rauhihi	Warrington	2006-09	67(20)	10	0	0	40
Ben Rauter	Wakefield	2001	15(6)	4	0	0	16

PLAYER	CLUB	YEAR	APP	TRIES	GOALS	FG	PTS
Gareth Raynor	Bradford	2011	18	4	0	0	16
	Crusaders	2010	7	4	0	0	16
	Hull	2001-09	186	102	0	0	408
	Leeds	2000	(3)	0	0	0	0
Tony Rea	London	1996	22	4	0	0	16
Stuart Reardon	Crusaders	2011	25	11	0	0	44
	Bradford	2003-05, 2010	78(11)	37	0	0	148
	Warrington	2006-08	48	12	0	0	48
	Salford	2002	7(1)	3	0	0	12
Mark Reber	Wigan	1999-2000	9(9)	5	0	0	20
Alan Reddicliffe	Warrington	2001	1	0	0	0	0
Tahi Reihana	Bradford	1997-98	17(21)	0	0	0	0
Paul Reilly	Wakefield	2008	5(2)	1	0	0	4
	Huddersfield	1999-2001, 2003-07	150(8)	35	1	0	142
Robert Relf	Widnes	2002-04	68(2)	5	0	0	20
Steve Renouf	Wigan	2000-01	55	40	0	0	160
Steele Retchless	London	1998-2004	177(6)	13	0	0	52
Ben Reynolds	Castleford	2013-14	1(3)	0	0	0	0
Scott Rhodes	Hull	2000	2	0	0	0	0
Phillipe Ricard	Paris	1996-97	2	0	0	0	0
Andy Rice	Huddersfield	2000-01	2(13)	1	0	0	4
Basil Richards	Huddersfield	1998-99	28(17)	1	0	0	4
Craig Richards	Oldham	1996	1	0	0	0	0
Greg Richards	St Helens	2013-15	7(34)	0	0	0	0
Pat Richards	Wigan	2006-13	199	147	759	4	2110
Andy Richardson	Hudds-Sheff	2000	(2)	0	0	0	0
Sean Richardson	Widnes	2002	2(18)	1	0	0	4
	Wakefield	1999	5(1)	0	0	0	0
	Castleford	1996-97	3(8)	1	0	0	4
Mark Riddell	Wigan	2009-10	45(11)	5	2	0	24
Neil Rigby	St Helens	2006	(1)	0	0	0	0
Shane Rigon	Bradford	2001	14(11)	12	0	0	48
Craig Rika	Halifax	1996	2	0	0	0	0
Chris Riley	Wakefield	2014-15	44	16	0	0	64
	Warrington	2005-14	146(10)	102	0	0	408
	Harlequins	2011	3	2	0	0	8
Glenn Riley	Warrington	2013-14	(15)	0	0	0	0
Peter Riley	Workington	1996	7(5)	0	0	0	0
Julien Rinaldi	London	2012	4(16)	1	0	0	4
	Wakefield	2002, 2010-11	27(9)	6	0	0	24
	Bradford	2009	(7)	1	0	0	4
	Harlequins	2007-08	4(43)	9	0	0	36
	Catalans	2006	16(6)	3	1	0	14
Dean Ripley	Castleford	2004	3(4)	1	0	0	4
Leroy Rivett	Warrington	2002	9	1	0	0	4
	Hudds-Sheff	2000	5(1)	1	0	0	4
	Leeds	1996-2000	39(15)	21	0	0	84
Jason Roach	Warrington	1998-99	29(7)	15	0	0	60
	Castleford	1997	7	4	0	0	16
Ben Roarty	Castleford	2006	11(6)	2	0	0	8
	Huddersfield	2003-05	52	5	0	0	20
Amos Roberts	Wigan	2009-11	47(2)	27	5	0	118
Ben Roberts	Castleford	2015	17(8)	9	0	2	38
Mark Roberts	Wigan	2003	(3)	0	0	0	0
Oliver Roberts	Bradford	2013-14	(5)	0	0	0	0
Robert Roberts	Huddersfield	2001	(1)	0	0	0	0
	Halifax	2000	(3)	0	0	0	0
	Hull	1999	24(2)	4	13	4	46
Michael Robertson	London	2012-13	35	17	0	0	68
Stanislas Robin	Catalans	2015	5(1)	1	0	0	4
Chad Robinson	Harlequins	2009	13(1)	2	0	0	8
Connor Robinson	Hull KR	2014-15	(2)	0	0	0	0
Craig Robinson	Wakefield	2005	(1)	0	0	0	0
Jason Robinson	Wigan	1996-2000	126(1)	87	0	1	349
Jeremy Robinson	Paris	1997	10(3)	1	21	0	46
John Robinson	Widnes	2003-04	7	1	0	0	4
Luke Robinson	Huddersfield	2008-15	191(18)	45	4	0	188
	Salford	2005-07	79	28	10	2	134
	Wigan	2002-04	17(25)	9	6	1	49
	Castleford	2004	9	4	3	0	22
Will Robinson	Hull	2000	22	4	0	0	16
	Gateshead	1999	28	9	0	0	36
Ash Robson	Castleford	2015	3	1	0	0	4
James Roby	St Helens	2004-15	190(116)	78	1	0	314
Mike Roby	St Helens	2004	(1)	0	0	0	0
Carl Roden	Warrington	1997	1	0	0	0	0
Shane Rodney	London	2012-13	28	3	12	0	36
Matt Rodwell	Warrington	2002	10	3	0	0	12
Darren Rogers	Castleford	1999-2004	162(1)	81	0	0	324
	Salford	1997-98	42	16	0	0	64
Jamie Rooney	Wakefield	2003-09	113(7)	60	321	21	903
	Castleford	2001	2(1)	0	6	0	12
Jonathan Roper	Castleford	2001	13	7	12	0	52
	Salford	2000	1(4)	1	3	0	10
	London	2000	4	0	0	0	0
	Warrington	1996-2000	75(8)	33	71	0	274
Scott Roskell	London	1996-97	30(2)	16	0	0	64
Steve Rosolen	London	1996-98	25(9)	10	0	0	40
Adam Ross	London	1996	(1)	0	0	0	0
Paul Round	Castleford	1996	(3)	0	0	0	0

Super League Players 1996-2015

PLAYER	CLUB	YEAR	APP	TRIES	GOALS	FG	PTS
Steve Rowlands	Widnes	2004-05	18(3)	2	15	0	38
	St Helens	2003	(1)	0	0	0	0
Paul Rowley	Leigh	2005	15(7)	3	0	0	12
	Huddersfield	2001	24	3	0	0	12
	Halifax	1996-2000	107(3)	27	1	3	113
Nigel Roy	London	2001-04	100	39	0	0	156
Nicky Royle	Widnes	2004	13	7	0	0	28
Shad Royston	Bradford	2011	17(1)	10	0	0	40
Chris Rudd	Warrington	1996-98	31(17)	10	16	0	72
Sean Rudder	Catalans	2006	22(1)	6	0	0	24
	Castleford	2004	9(3)	2	0	0	8
James Rushforth	Halifax	1997	(4)	0	0	0	0
Danny Russell	Huddersfield	1998-2000	50(13)	8	0	0	32
Ian Russell	Oldham	1997	1(3)	1	0	0	4
	Paris	1996	3	0	0	0	0
Matthew Russell	Warrington	2014-15	31(4)	7	0	0	28
	Hull	2012	6	0	0	0	0
	Wigan	2012	2	3	0	0	12
Richard Russell	Castleford	1996-98	37(4)	2	0	0	8
Robert Russell	Salford	1998-99	2(1)	0	1	0	2
Sean Rutgerson	Salford	2004-06	60(9)	4	0	0	16
Chris Ryan	London	1998-99	44(3)	17	10	0	88
Matt Ryan	Wakefield	2014-15	28(12)	7	0	0	28
Sean Ryan	Castleford	2004	11(5)	2	0	0	8
	Hull	2002-03	53	8	0	0	32
Justin Ryder	Wakefield	2004	19(3)	11	0	0	44
Jason Ryles	Catalans	2009	19(2)	2	0	0	8
Setaimata Sa	Hull	2014-15	18(6)	6	0	0	24
	Catalans	2010-12	58(5)	21	0	0	84
Teddy Sadaoui	Catalans	2006	7	0	0	0	0
Liam Salter	Hull KR	2012-15	68	16	0	0	64
Matt Salter	London	1997-99	14(34)	0	0	0	0
Ben Sammut	Hull	2000	20	4	67	0	150
	Gateshead	1999	26(2)	6	17	0	58
Jarrod Sammut	Wakefield	2014-15	19(1)	9	52	0	140
	Bradford	2012-13	35(3)	28	47	1	207
	Crusaders	2010-11	17(16)	17	0	0	68
Dean Sampson	Castleford	1996-2003	124(28)	24	0	0	96
Paul Sampson	London	2004	1(2)	1	0	0	4
	Wakefield	2000	17	8	0	0	32
Lee Sanderson	London	2004	1(5)	1	7	0	18
Chris Sandow	Warrington	2015	7	0	16	0	32
Jason Sands	Paris	1996-97	28	0	0	0	0
Mitchell Sargent	Castleford	2008-10	37(21)	6	0	0	24
Dan Sarginson	Wigan	2014-15	43	17	0	0	68
	London	2012-13	35(1)	10	0	0	40
	Harlequins	2011	8	5	0	0	20
Junior Sa'u	Salford	2014-15	42	16	0	0	64
Andre Savelio	St Helens	2014-15	7(21)	2	0	0	8
Lokeni Savelio	Halifax	2000	2(11)	0	0	0	0
	Salford	1997-98	18(20)	0	0	0	0
Tom Saxton	Salford	2007	5	0	0	0	0
	Wakefield	2006	9(6)	2	0	0	8
	Hull	2005	19(8)	3	0	0	12
	Castleford	2002-04	37(12)	11	0	0	44
Jonathan Scales	Halifax	2000	1	0	0	0	0
	Bradford	1996-98	46(4)	24	0	0	96
Andrew Schick	Castleford	1996-98	45(13)	10	0	0	40
Clinton Schifcofske	Crusaders	2010-11	44	5	115	0	250
Garry Schofield	Huddersfield	1998	(2)	0	0	0	0
Gary Schubert	Workington	1996	(1)	0	0	0	0
Matt Schultz	Hull	1998-99	23(9)	2	0	0	8
	Leeds	1996	2(4)	0	0	0	0
John Schuster	Halifax	1996-97	31	9	127	3	293
Nick Scruton	Wakefield	2014-15	40(1)	5	0	0	20
	Bradford	2009-14	70(27)	5	0	0	20
	Leeds	2002, 2004-08	11(53)	3	0	0	12
	Hull	2004	2(16)	3	0	0	12
Danny Sculthorpe	Huddersfield	2009	5(8)	0	0	0	0
	Wakefield	2007-09	14(28)	1	0	0	4
	Castleford	2006	18(1)	4	0	1	17
	Wigan	2002-05	13(49)	7	0	0	28
Paul Sculthorpe	St Helens	1998-2008	223(4)	94	356	7	1095
	Warrington	1996-97	40	6	0	0	24
Mick Seaby	London	1997	3(2)	1	0	0	4
Danny Seal	Halifax	1996-99	8(17)	3	0	0	12
Matt Seers	Wakefield	2003	11(1)	2	0	0	8
Anthony Seibold	London	1999-2000	33(19)	5	0	0	20
Keith Senior	Leeds	1999-2011	319(2)	159	0	0	636
	Sheffield	1996-99	90(2)	40	0	0	160
Fili Seru	Hull	1998-99	37(1)	13	0	0	52
Anthony Seuseu	Halifax	2003	1(11)	1	0	0	4
Jerry Seuseu	Wigan	2005-06	29(9)	1	0	0	4
Brett Seymour	Hull	2012-13	26(1)	7	0	0	28
Will Sharp	Hull	2011-12	27(8)	10	0	0	40
	Harlequins	2008-10	65(1)	19	0	0	76
Jamie Shaul	Hull	2013-15	47	31	0	0	124
Darren Shaw	Salford	2002	5(9)	1	0	0	4
	London	1996, 2002	22(8)	3	0	0	12
	Castleford	2000-01	50(6)	1	0	0	4
	Sheffield	1998-99	51(1)	3	0	1	13
Mick Shaw	Halifax	1999	5	1	0	0	4
	Leeds	1996	12(2)	7	0	0	28
Ryan Shaw	London	2013	2	1	2	0	8
Phil Shead	Paris	1996	3(2)	0	0	0	0
Richard Sheil	St Helens	1997	(1)	0	0	0	0
Kelly Shelford	Warrington	1996-97	25(3)	4	0	2	18
Michael Shenton	Castleford	2004, 2006, 2008-10, 2013-15	177(2)	83	0	0	332
	St Helens	2011-12	51	15	0	0	60
Ryan Sheridan	Castleford	2004	2	0	0	0	0
	Widnes	2003	14(3)	2	0	0	8
	Leeds	1997-2002	123(7)	46	0	1	185
	Sheffield	1996	9(3)	5	0	1	21
Louis Sheriff	Hull KR	2011-12	8	3	0	0	12
Rikki Sheriffe	Bradford	2009-10	51	14	0	0	56
	Harlequins	2006-08	35(1)	16	0	0	64
	Halifax	2003	6(1)	3	0	0	12
Ian Sherratt	Oldham	1996	5(3)	1	0	0	4
Brent Sherwin	Catalans	2010	12	1	0	1	5
	Castleford	2008-10	48(1)	4	0	3	19
Peter Shiels	St Helens	2001-02	44(3)	11	0	0	44
Gary Shillabeer	Huddersfield	1999	(2)	0	0	0	0
Mark Shipway	Salford	2004-05	30(12)	3	0	0	12
Ian Sibbit	Bradford	2011-12	11(7)	0	0	0	0
	Salford	2005-07, 2009-10	64(17)	11	0	0	44
	Warrington	1999-2001, 2003-04	63(18)	24	0	0	96
Mark Sibson	Huddersfield	1999	2	2	0	0	8
Adam Sidlow	Bradford	2013-14	20(22)	8	0	0	32
	Salford	2009-12	34(44)	14	0	0	56
Harry Siejka	Wakefield	2014	6(3)	1	0	0	4
Jordan Sigismeau	Catalans	2015	8	2	0	0	8
Jon Simms	St Helens	2002	(1)	0	0	0	0
Craig Simon	Hull	2000	23(2)	8	0	0	32
	Gateshead	1999	25(4)	6	0	0	24
Mickael Simon	Wakefield	2015	6(10)	0	0	0	0
	Catalans	2010-14	25(40)	2	0	0	8
Darren Simpson	Huddersfield	1998-99	17(1)	5	0	0	20
Jamie Simpson	Huddersfield	2011	8(1)	0	0	0	0
Jared Simpson	Huddersfield	2015	5	2	0	0	8
Robbie Simpson	London	1999	6(7)	0	0	0	0
Ashton Sims	Warrington	2015	24(4)	2	0	0	8
Kevin Sinfield	Leeds	1997-2015	425(29)	70	1566	31	3443
Matt Sing	Hull	2007-08	41	14	0	0	56
Wayne Sing	Paris	1997	18(1)	2	0	0	8
Brad Singleton	Leeds	2011-15	32(38)	10	0	0	40
	Wakefield	2013	(1)	0	0	0	0
Fata Sini	Salford	1997	22	7	0	0	28
Ken Sio	Hull KR	2015	20	14	0	0	56
Michael Sio	Wakefield	2015	2(2)	0	0	0	0
John Skandalis	Huddersfield	2007-08	37(5)	4	0	0	16
Dylan Skee	Harlequins	2008-09	(3)	0	0	0	0
Ben Skerrett	Castleford	2003	(1)	0	0	0	0
Kelvin Skerrett	Halifax	1997-99	31(6)	2	0	0	8
	Wigan	1996	1(8)	0	0	0	0
Troy Slattery	Wakefield	2002-03	33(5)	4	0	0	16
	Huddersfield	1999	3	1	0	0	4
Mick Slicker	Huddersfield	2001, 2003-05	17(48)	2	0	0	8
	Sheffield	1999	(3)	1	0	0	4
	Halifax	1997	2(5)	0	0	0	0
Nick Slyney	London	2014	20(4)	3	0	0	12
Ian Smales	Castleford	1996-97	10(8)	5	0	0	20
Aaron Smith	Castleford	2006	(2)	0	0	0	0
	Bradford	2003-04	12(1)	3	0	0	12
Andy Smith	Harlequins	2007	6(3)	3	0	0	12
	Bradford	2004-06	9(9)	4	0	0	16
	Salford	2005	4	1	0	0	4
Byron Smith	Castleford	2004	(9)	0	0	0	0
	Halifax	2003	6(1)	0	0	0	0
Chris Smith	Hull	2001-02	12	3	0	0	12
	St Helens	1998-2000	62(9)	26	0	0	104
	Castleford	1996-97	36(1)	12	0	0	48
Craig Smith	Wigan	2002-04	77(3)	10	0	0	40
Damien Smith	St Helens	1998	21(1)	8	0	0	32
Daniel Smith	Huddersfield	2015	1(8)	1	0	0	4
	Wakefield	2014-15	21(15)	6	0	0	24
Danny Smith	Paris	1996	10(2)	1	15	0	34
	London	1996	2(1)	1	0	0	4
Darren Smith	St Helens	2003	25(1)	14	0	0	56
Gary Smith	Castleford	2001	(1)	0	0	0	0
Hudson Smith	Bradford	2000	8(22)	2	0	0	8
	Salford	1999	23(2)	5	0	0	20
James Smith	Salford	2000	23(3)	6	0	0	24
Jamie Smith	Hull	1998-99	24(6)	6	12	0	48
	Workington	1996	5(3)	0	1	0	2
Jason Smith	Hull	2001-04	61(3)	17	0	1	69
Jeremy Smith	Wakefield	2011	9(1)	1	0	0	4
	Salford	2009-10	27(17)	2	0	0	8
Kris Smith	London	2001	(1)	0	0	0	0
	Halifax	2001	(1)	0	0	0	0

PLAYER	CLUB	YEAR	APP	TRIES	GOALS	FG	PTS
Lee Smith	Wakefield	2012-13, 2015	30(4)	16	54	2	174
	Leeds	2005-12	125(10)	60	34	1	309
Leigh Smith	Workington	1996	9	4	0	0	16
Mark Smith	Widnes	2005	12(15)	4	0	0	16
	Wigan	1999-2004	35(77)	8	0	0	32
Martyn Smith	Harlequins	2010	(2)	0	0	0	0
Matty Smith	Wigan	2012-15	91(3)	12	190	16	444
	Salford	2010-12	67(4)	13	6	1	65
	St Helens	2006-08, 2010	17(2)	3	10	1	33
	Celtic	2009	15(1)	3	2	1	17
Michael Smith	Hull KR	2007	(3)	1	0	0	4
	Castleford	1998, 2001-04	86(33)	32	0	0	128
	Hull	1999	12(6)	3	0	0	12
Paul Smith	Huddersfield	2004-06	52(17)	13	0	0	52
Paul Smith	Warrington	2001	(1)	0	0	0	0
	Castleford	1997-2000	6(37)	3	0	0	12
Paul Smith	London	1997	7(1)	2	0	0	8
Peter Smith	Oldham	1996	2	0	0	0	0
Richard Smith	Wakefield	2001	8(1)	1	0	0	4
	Salford	1997	(1)	1	0	0	4
Tim Smith	Wakefield	2012-15	79	11	0	0	44
	Salford	2014	12	2	7	0	22
	Wigan	2008-09	13(8)	2	0	0	8
Tony Smith	Hull	2001-03	43(5)	26	0	0	104
	Wigan	1997-2000	66(5)	46	0	0	184
	Castleford	1996-97	18(2)	10	0	0	40
Tony Smith	Workington	1996	9	1	0	0	4
Tyrone Smith	Harlequins	2006-07	49(3)	13	0	0	52
	London	2005	20(4)	11	0	0	44
Rob Smyth	Leigh	2005	15(1)	4	0	0	16
	Warrington	2000-03	65	35	20	0	180
	London	1998-2000	32(2)	9	15	0	66
	Wigan	1996	11(5)	16	0	0	64
Marc Sneyd	Hull	2015	26	3	69	6	156
	Castleford	2014	25(1)	6	100	2	226
	Salford	2010-13	33(12)	4	61	3	141
Steve Snitch	Castleford	2010-12	38(18)	10	0	0	40
	Wakefield	2002-05, 2009	33(55)	9	0	0	36
	Huddersfield	2006-08	24(35)	12	0	0	48
Bright Sodje	Wakefield	2000	15	4	0	0	16
	Sheffield	1996-99	54	34	0	0	136
Iosia Soliola	St Helens	2010-14	83(24)	27	0	0	108
David Solomona	Warrington	2010-12	8(49)	16	1	0	66
	Bradford	2007-09	44(9)	19	0	0	76
	Wakefield	2004-06	73(3)	26	0	0	104
Denny Solomona	Castleford	2015	15	18	0	0	72
	London	2014	19(1)	8	0	0	32
Alfred Songoro	Wakefield	1999	8(5)	4	0	0	16
Romain Sort	Paris	1997	(1)	0	0	0	0
Paul Southern	Salford	1997-2002	79(33)	6	13	0	50
	St Helens	2002	1(1)	0	0	0	0
Steve Southern	Wakefield	2012	7(8)	3	0	0	12
Cain Southernwood	Bradford	2010	2	0	0	0	0
Roy Southernwood	Wakefield	1999	1	0	0	0	0
	Halifax	1996	2	0	0	0	0
Jason Southwell	Huddersfield	2004	(1)	0	0	0	0
Waisale Sovatabua	Wakefield	2001-03	44(3)	19	0	0	76
	Hudds-Sheff	2000	23(1)	8	0	0	32
	Sheffield	1996-99	56(17)	19	0	1	77
Jamie Soward	London	2013	6(1)	4	21	0	58
Yusef Sozi	London	2000-01	(5)	0	0	0	0
Scott Spaven	Hull KR	2010	(2)	0	0	0	0
Andy Speak	Castleford	2001	4(4)	0	0	0	0
	Wakefield	2000	6(5)	2	0	0	8
	Leeds	1999	4	1	0	0	4
Dom Speakman	St Helens	2013	(1)	0	0	0	0
Tim Spears	Castleford	2003	(3)	0	0	0	0
Ady Spencer	London	1996-99	8(36)	5	0	0	20
Jack Spencer	Salford	2009-11	(7)	0	0	0	0
Tom Spencer	Wigan	2012-13	(7)	0	0	0	0
Rob Spicer	Wakefield	2002-05	28(18)	4	0	0	16
Russ Spiers	Wakefield	2011	(2)	0	0	0	0
Gadwin Springer	Castleford	2015	2(8)	0	0	0	0
	Catalans	2014-15	(3)	1	0	0	4
Stuart Spruce	Widnes	2002-03	45(4)	19	0	0	76
	Bradford	1996-2001	107(2)	57	0	0	228
Lee St Hilaire	Castleford	1997	4(2)	0	0	0	0
Marcus St Hilaire	Bradford	2006-07	34(1)	12	0	0	48
	Huddersfield	2003-05	72(2)	30	0	0	120
	Leeds	1996-2002	59(33)	31	0	0	124
Cyril Stacul	Catalans	2007-12	61(1)	18	0	0	72
Dylan Stainton	Workington	1996	2(3)	0	0	0	0
Mark Stamper	Workington	1996	(1)	0	0	0	0
John Stankevitch	Widnes	2005	17(5)	0	0	0	0
	St Helens	2000-04	74(40)	25	0	0	100
Gareth Stanley	Bradford	2000	1	1	0	0	4
Craig Stapleton	Salford	2009	24	2	0	0	8
	Leigh	2005	27(1)	4	0	0	16

PLAYER	CLUB	YEAR	APP	TRIES	GOALS	FG	PTS
Graham Steadman	Castleford	1996-97	11(17)	5	0	0	20
Jon Steel	Hull KR	2007-08	18	6	0	0	24
Jamie Stenhouse	Warrington	2000-01	9(3)	3	0	0	12
Gareth Stephens	Sheffield	1997-99	23(6)	2	0	0	8
David Stephenson	Hull	1998	11(7)	3	0	0	12
	Oldham	1997	10(8)	2	0	0	8
Francis Stephenson	London	2002-05	42(34)	5	0	0	20
	Wigan	2001	2(9)	0	0	0	0
	Wakefield	1999-2000	50(1)	6	0	0	24
Paul Sterling	Leeds	1997-2000	79(12)	50	0	0	200
Paul Stevens	Oldham	1996	2(1)	0	0	0	0
	London	1996	(1)	0	0	0	0
Warren Stevens	Leigh	2005	4(14)	1	0	0	4
	Warrington	1996-99, 2002-05	17(66)	1	0	0	4
	Salford	2001	(8)	0	0	0	0
Anthony Stewart	Harlequins	2006	4	0	0	0	0
	Salford	2004-06	51(2)	15	0	0	60
	St Helens	1997-2003	93(23)	44	0	0	176
Troy Stone	Widnes	2002	18(6)	1	0	0	4
	Huddersfield	2001	12(1)	1	0	0	4
James Stosic	Wakefield	2009	8(10)	1	0	0	4
Lynton Stott	Wakefield	1999	21	4	6	1	29
	Sheffield	1996-98	40(4)	15	0	0	60
Mitchell Stringer	Salford	2005-06	12(4)	0	0	0	0
	London	2004-05	10(19)	0	0	0	0
Graham Strutton	London	1996	9(1)	2	0	0	8
Matt Sturm	Leigh	2005	8(19)	3	0	0	12
	Warrington	2002-04	1(18)	0	0	0	0
	Huddersfield	1998-99	46	8	0	0	32
Anthony Sullivan	St Helens	1996-2001	137(2)	105	0	0	420
Michael Sullivan	Warrington	2006-07	21(16)	8	1	0	34
Phil Sumner	Warrington	1996	(5)	0	0	0	0
Liam Sutcliffe	Leeds	2013-15	33(21)	23	33	0	158
	Bradford	2014	3(1)	1	0	0	4
Ryan Sutton	Wigan	2014-15	6(17)	1	0	0	4
Simon Svabic	Salford	1998-2000	13(5)	3	19	0	50
Luke Swain	Salford	2009-10	54	3	0	0	12
Richard Swain	Hull	2004-07	89	5	0	0	20
Anthony Swann	Warrington	2001	3	1	0	0	4
Logan Swann	Warrington	2005-06	49(1)	17	0	0	68
	Bradford	2004	25	6	0	0	24
Willie Swann	Warrington	1996-97	25(2)	6	0	0	24
Adam Swift	St Helens	2012-15	64	46	0	0	184
Nathan Sykes	Castleford	1996-2004	158(52)	3	0	0	12
Paul Sykes	Wakefield	2012-14	59(1)	12	135	6	324
	Bradford	1999-2002, 2008-12	99(4)	35	64	2	270
	Harlequins	2006-07	31(2)	15	47	1	155
	London	2001-05	95(1)	26	219	3	545
Wayne Sykes	London	1999	(2)	0	0	0	0
Ukuma Ta'ai	Huddersfield	2013-15	40(38)	23	0	0	92
Semi Tadulala	Wakefield	2004-07, 2011	92	37	0	0	148
	Bradford	2008-09	49	30	0	0	120
Whetu Taewa	Sheffield	1997-98	33(7)	8	0	0	32
Zeb Taia	Catalans	2013-15	75	35	0	0	140
Alan Tait	Leeds	1996	3(3)	1	0	0	4
Fetuli Talanoa	Hull	2014-15	50	19	0	0	76
Willie Talau	Salford	2009-10	22	4	0	0	16
	St Helens	2003-08	130(1)	50	0	0	200
Ian Talbot	Wakefield	1999	9(5)	2	31	0	70
	Wigan	1997	3	1	0	0	4
Albert Talipeau	Wakefield	2004	2(3)	0	0	0	0
Gael Tallec	Halifax	2000	5(19)	3	0	0	12
	Castleford	1998-99	19(21)	3	0	0	12
	Wigan	1996-97	8(12)	3	0	0	12
Joe Tamani	Bradford	1996	11(3)	4	0	0	16
Ryan Tandy	Hull KR	2007	8(4)	2	0	0	8
Andrew Tangata-Toa	Huddersfield	1999	15	2	0	0	8
David Tangata-Toa	Celtic	2009	1(18)	4	0	0	16
	Hull KR	2007	(17)	3	0	0	12
Jordan Tansey	Wakefield	2015	4	1	0	0	4
	Castleford	2013-15	44(1)	15	0	0	60
	Crusaders	2011	14(4)	5	0	0	20
	Hull	2009-10	30	9	0	0	36
	Leeds	2006-08	18(32)	19	3	0	82
Lama Tasi	Salford	2014-15	27(11)	2	0	0	8
Kris Tassell	Wakefield	2002	24	10	0	0	40
	Salford	2000-01	35(10)	12	0	0	48
Shem Tatupu	Wigan	1996	(3)	0	0	0	0
Tony Tatupu	Wakefield	2000-01	20	2	0	0	8
	Warrington	1997	21(1)	6	0	0	24
Taulima Tautai	Wigan	2015	5(20)	1	0	0	4
	Wakefield	2013-14	6(19)	2	0	0	8
James Taylor	Leigh	2005	(4)	0	0	0	0
Joe Taylor	Paris	1997	9(5)	2	0	0	8
Lawrence Taylor	Sheffield	1996	(1)	0	0	0	0

Super League Players 1996-2015

PLAYER	CLUB	YEAR	APP	TRIES	GOALS	FG	PTS
Scott Taylor	Salford	2015	23	5	0	0	20
	Wigan	2013-14	18(29)	6	0	0	24
	Hull KR	2009-12	21(29)	8	0	0	32
Frederic Teixido	Sheffield	1999	(4)	0	0	0	0
	Paris	1996-97	2(3)	1	0	0	4
Lionel Teixido	Catalans	2006-07	11(13)	3	0	0	12
Karl Temata	London	2005, 2012	1(8)	1	0	0	4
	Harlequins	2006-11	94(22)	7	0	0	28
Jason Temu	Hull	1998	13(2)	1	0	0	4
	Oldham	1996-97	25(3)	1	0	0	4
Paul Terry	London	1997	(1)	0	0	0	0
Anthony Thackeray	Castleford	2008	3(6)	0	0	0	0
	Hull	2007	2	0	0	0	0
Jamie Thackray	Crusaders	2010	1(16)	2	0	0	8
	Hull	2005-06, 2008-09	37(45)	6	0	0	24
	Leeds	2006-07	5(27)	7	0	0	28
	Castleford	2003-04	7(11)	3	0	0	12
	Halifax	2000-02	10(38)	3	0	0	12
Adam Thaler	Castleford	2002	(1)	0	0	0	0
Gareth Thomas	Crusaders	2010-11	27(1)	6	0	0	24
Giles Thomas	London	1997-99	1(2)	0	0	0	0
Oscar Thomas	London	2014	4(2)	0	1	0	2
Rob Thomas	Harlequins	2011	(2)	0	0	0	0
Steve Thomas	London	2004	4(2)	0	0	0	0
	Warrington	2001	2	0	0	0	0
Alex Thompson	Warrington	2009	(1)	1	0	0	4
Alex Thompson	Sheffield	1997	4(11)	0	0	0	0
Bobby Thompson	Salford	1999	28	5	2	0	24
Jordan Thompson	Hull	2014-15	9(37)	8	0	0	32
	Castleford	2009-13	47(24)	25	0	0	100
Luke Thompson	St Helens	2013-15	19(25)	7	0	0	28
Sam Thompson	Harlequins	2009	(2)	0	0	0	0
	St Helens	2008	(5)	0	0	0	0
Chris Thorman	Hull	2009	19(2)	1	0	0	4
	Huddersfield	2000-01, 2005-08	126(20)	51	320	3	847
	London	2003	26(1)	7	81	1	191
	Sheffield	1999	5(13)	2	8	1	25
Tony Thorniley	Warrington	1997	(5)	0	0	0	0
Andy Thornley	Salford	2009	(1)	1	0	0	4
Iain Thornley	Wigan	2012-14	40	25	0	0	100
Danny Tickle	Widnes	2014-15	33(1)	3	88	0	188
	Hull	2007-13	159(5)	45	528	1	1237
	Wigan	2002-06	94(36)	34	200	2	538
	Halifax	2000-02	25(17)	10	91	2	224
Kris Tickle	Warrington	2001	(1)	0	0	0	0
Lewis Tierney	Wigan	2013-15	5	2	0	0	8
James Tilley	St Helens	2013-14	(3)	0	0	0	0
Dane Tilse	Hull KR	2015	6(1)	1	0	0	4
John Timu	London	1998-2000	57(3)	11	0	0	44
Kerrod Toby	London	1997	2(2)	0	0	0	0
Tulsen Tollett	London	1996-2001	105(5)	38	49	1	251
Joel Tomkins	Wigan	2005-11, 2014-15	132(40)	55	0	0	220
Logan Tomkins	Salford	2014-15	15(10)	3	0	0	12
	Wigan	2012-15	9(32)	1	0	0	4
Sam Tomkins	Wigan	2009-13	124(5)	107	28	1	485
Glen Tomlinson	Wakefield	1999-2000	41(5)	8	0	0	32
	Hull	1998	5	1	0	0	4
	Bradford	1996-97	27(13)	12	0	0	48
Willie Tonga	Catalans	2015	18	6	0	0	24
Ryan Tongia	Wakefield	2011	4	2	0	0	8
Ian Tonks	Castleford	1996-2001	32(50)	11	13	0	70
Tony Tonks	Huddersfield	2012	(1)	0	0	0	0
Motu Tony	Wakefield	2011-12	7(3)	1	0	0	4
	Hull	2005-09	76(20)	25	0	0	100
	Castleford	2004	8(1)	1	0	0	4
Mark Tookey	Harlequins	2006	12(14)	1	0	0	4
	London	2005	13(14)	5	0	0	20
	Castleford	2004	2(8)	1	0	0	4
Clinton Toopi	Leeds	2006-08	40(3)	9	0	0	36
David Tootill	Harlequins	2008	(4)	0	0	0	0
Paul Topping	Oldham	1996-97	23(10)	1	19	0	42
Patrick Torreilles	Paris	1996	9(1)	1	25	0	54
Albert Torrens	Huddersfield	2006	7	5	0	0	20
Mat Toshack	London	1998-2004	120(21)	24	0	0	96
Julien Touxagas	Catalans	2006-11	14(45)	4	0	0	16
Darren Treacy	Salford	2002	24(1)	6	1	0	26
Dean Treister	Hull	2003	16(1)	3	0	0	12
Rocky Trimarchi	Crusaders	2010	16(8)	0	0	0	0
Steve Trindall	London	2003-05	40(20)	3	0	0	12
Shane Tronc	Wakefield	2010	8(3)	2	0	0	8
Kyle Trout	Wakefield	2012-15	6(17)	3	0	0	12
George Truelove	Wakefield	2002	2	1	0	0	4
	London	2000	5	1	0	0	4
Va'aiga Tuigamala	Wigan	1996	21	10	3	0	46
Fereti Tuilagi	St Helens	1999-2000	43(15)	21	0	0	84
	Halifax	1996-98	55(3)	27	0	0	108
Evarn Tuimavave	Hull KR	2013	11(12)	2	0	0	8
Sateki Tuipulotu	Leeds	1996	6(3)	1	2	0	8
Bill Tupou	Wakefield	2015	1	0	0	0	0
Tame Tupou	Bradford	2007-08	10(7)	8	0	0	32

PLAYER	CLUB	YEAR	APP	TRIES	GOALS	FG	PTS
Jansin Turgut	Hull	2015	(4)	0	0	0	0
Neil Turley	Leigh	2005	6(3)	2	20	1	49
Darren Turner	Huddersfield	2000-01, 2003-04	42(13)	13	0	0	52
	Sheffield	1996-99	41(29)	15	0	0	60
Ian Turner	Paris	1996	1(1)	1	0	0	4
Jordan Turner	St Helens	2013-15	81(2)	38	13	2	180
	Hull	2010-12	62(5)	28	0	0	112
	Salford	2006-07, 2009	22(10)	4	1	0	18
Chris Tuson	Hull	2014	10(1)	0	0	0	0
	Wigan	2008, 2010-13	24(49)	13	0	0	52
	Castleford	2010	3(5)	0	0	0	0
Gregory Tutard	Paris	1996	1(1)	0	0	0	0
Brendon Tuuta	Warrington	1998	18(2)	4	0	0	16
	Castleford	1996-97	41(1)	3	0	0	12
Steve Tyrer	Salford	2010	20	6	9	0	42
	Celtic	2009	8	2	5	0	18
	St Helens	2006-08	17(3)	12	42	0	132
Bobby Tyson-Wilson	Hull	2015	(1)	0	0	0	0
Harry Tyson-Wilson	Hull	2014	(1)	0	0	0	0
Wayne Ulugia	Hull KR	2014	3	1	0	0	4
Mike Umaga	Halifax	1996-97	38(1)	16	5	0	74
Kava Utoikamanu	Paris	1996	6(3)	0	0	0	0
Frederic Vaccari	Catalans	2010-11, 2013-14	50	26	0	0	104
David Vaealiki	Wigan	2005-07	67(1)	17	0	0	68
Joe Vagana	Bradford	2001-08	176(44)	17	0	0	68
Nigel Vagana	Warrington	1997	20	17	0	0	68
Tevita Vaikona	Bradford	1998-2004	145(2)	89	0	0	356
Lesley Vainikolo	Bradford	2002-07	132(4)	136	1	0	546
Eric Van Brussell	Paris	1996	2	0	0	0	0
Jace Van Dijk	Celtic	2009	19	1	1	0	6
Richard Varkulis	Warrington	2004	4(1)	3	0	0	12
Marcus Vassilakopoulos	Sheffield	1997-99	15(11)	3	10	2	34
	Leeds	1996-97	1(3)	0	0	0	0
Atelea Vea	St Helens	2015	8(3)	3	0	0	12
	London	2014	19(3)	2	0	0	8
Josh Veivers	Salford	2012	5	2	0	0	8
	Wakefield	2011	10(2)	2	22	0	52
Phil Veivers	Huddersfield	1998	7(6)	1	0	0	4
	St Helens	1996	(1)	1	0	0	4
Michael Vella	Hull KR	2007-11	111(5)	13	0	0	52
Bruno Verges	Catalans	2006	25	6	0	0	24
Eric Vergniol	Paris	1996	14(1)	6	0	0	24
Gray Viane	Salford	2007	9	2	0	0	8
	Castleford	2006	20(7)	14	0	0	56
	Widnes	2005	20	13	0	0	52
	St Helens	2004	4	1	0	0	4
Joe Vickery	Leeds	2013	9	1	0	0	4
Adrian Vowles	Castleford	1997-2001, 2003	125(1)	29	1	1	119
	Wakefield	2002-03	24(3)	6	1	0	26
	Leeds	2002	14(3)	2	0	0	8
Michael Wainwright	Castleford	2008-10	70	22	0	0	88
	Wakefield	2004-05	21(10)	8	0	0	32
Mike Wainwright	Salford	2000-02, 2007	75(3)	9	0	0	36
	Warrington	1996-99, 2003-07	168(14)	23	0	0	92
Adam Walker	Hull KR	2013-15	49(16)	4	0	0	16
	Huddersfield	2010-12	1(5)	0	0	0	0
Alex Walker	London	2014	1	0	0	0	0
Anthony Walker	Wakefield	2015	1(3)	1	0	0	4
	St Helens	2013-14	9(7)	2	0	0	8
Ben Walker	Leeds	2002	23(1)	8	100	0	232
Chev Walker	Bradford	2011-14	44(22)	5	0	0	20
	Hull KR	2008-09	24(7)	5	0	0	20
	Leeds	1999-2006	142(19)	77	0	0	308
Chris Walker	Catalans	2010	11	6	2	0	28
Jonathan Walker	Hull KR	2014	2(6)	0	0	0	0
	Castleford	2010-13	17(31)	4	0	0	16
Jonny Walker	Wigan	2010	(1)	0	0	0	0
Matt Walker	Huddersfield	2001	3(6)	0	0	0	0
Anthony Wall	Paris	1997	9	3	3	0	18
Jon Wallace	London	2014	4(12)	0	0	0	0
Mark Wallace	Workington	1996	14(1)	3	0	0	12
Alex Walmsley	St Helens	2013-15	39(38)	8	0	0	32
Adam Walne	Salford	2012-15	7(23)	1	0	0	4
Jordan Walne	Salford	2013-15	20(21)	3	0	0	12
Joe Walsh	Huddersfield	2009	1(1)	1	0	0	4
	Harlequins	2007-08	1(4)	0	0	0	0
Luke Walsh	St Helens	2014-15	32(2)	12	114	4	280
Lucas Walshaw	Wakefield	2011-14	15(6)	3	0	0	12
Josh Walters	Leeds	2014-15	6(11)	5	0	0	20
Kerrod Walters	Gateshead	1999	10(12)	2	1	0	10
Kevin Walters	Warrington	2001	1	0	0	0	0
Jason Walton	Salford	2009, 2014-15	7(19)	1	0	0	4
Barry Ward	St Helens	2002-03	20(30)	4	0	0	16

PLAYER	CLUB	YEAR	APP	TRIES	GOALS	FG	PTS
Danny Ward	Harlequins	2008-11	89(7)	4	0	0	16
	Hull KR	2007	11(9)	0	0	0	0
	Castleford	2006	18(7)	2	0	0	8
	Leeds	1999-2005	70(48)	9	0	1	37
Robbie Ward	Leeds	2014-15	5(3)	1	0	0	4
Stevie Ward	Leeds	2012-15	50(23)	10	0	0	40
Joe Wardle	Huddersfield	2011-15	112	55	0	0	220
	Bradford	2010	1(1)	0	0	0	0
Phil Waring	Salford	1997-99	6(8)	2	0	0	8
Brett Warton	London	1999-2001	49(7)	14	133	0	322
Kyle Warren	Castleford	2002	13(14)	3	0	0	12
Danny Washbrook	Wakefield	2012-15	93(8)	12	0	0	48
	Hull	2005-11	92(30)	11	0	0	44
Adam Watene	Wakefield	2006-08	45(8)	5	0	0	20
	Bradford	2006	(4)	0	0	0	0
Frank Watene	Wakefield	1999-2001	24(37)	6	0	0	24
Trent Waterhouse	Warrington	2012-14	65(5)	15	0	0	60
Kallum Watkins	Leeds	2008-15	132(7)	80	0	0	320
Dave Watson	Sheffield	1998-99	41(4)	4	0	0	16
Ian Watson	Salford	1997, 2002	24(17)	8	3	5	43
	Workington	1996	4(1)	1	15	0	34
Kris Watson	Warrington	1996	11(2)	2	0	0	8
Anthony Watts	Widnes	2012	(1)	0	0	0	0
Brad Watts	Widnes	2005	6	3	0	0	12
Liam Watts	Hull	2012-15	68(13)	4	0	0	16
	Hull KR	2008, 2010-12	31(26)	6	0	0	24
Michael Watts	Warrington	2002	3	0	0	0	0
Brent Webb	Catalans	2013-14	10	2	0	0	8
	Leeds	2007-12	137(1)	73	0	0	292
Jason Webber	Salford	2000	25(1)	10	0	0	40
Ian Webster	St Helens	2006	1	0	0	0	0
Jake Webster	Castleford	2013-15	36(7)	13	0	0	52
	Hull KR	2008-12	95(1)	34	7	0	150
James Webster	Hull	2008	1	0	0	0	0
	Hull KR	2007-08	36	2	0	2	10
Pat Weisner	Hull KR	2007	(2)	0	0	0	0
	Harlequins	2006	10(6)	3	0	0	12
Taylor Welch	Warrington	2008	1	0	0	0	0
Kris Welham	Hull KR	2007-15	164(2)	90	1	0	362
Paul Wellens	St Helens	1998-2015	399(40)	199	34	1	865
Jon Wells	Harlequins	2006-09	66	10	0	0	40
	London	2004-05	42(2)	19	0	0	76
	Wakefield	2003	22(1)	1	0	0	4
	Castleford	1996-2002	114(14)	49	0	0	196
Dwayne West	St Helens	2000-02	8(16)	6	0	0	24
	Wigan	1999	1(1)	0	0	0	0
Joe Westerman	Hull	2011-15	110(10)	26	52	1	209
	Castleford	2008-10	68(7)	29	151	0	418
Craig Weston	Widnes	2002, 2004	23(9)	2	1	2	12
	Huddersfield	1998-99	46(1)	15	15	0	90
Ben Westwood	Warrington	2002-15	316(8)	107	62	0	552
	Wakefield	1999-2002	31(7)	8	1	0	34
Michael Weyman	Hull KR	2014	22(1)	7	0	0	28
Andrew Whalley	Workington	1996	(2)	0	0	0	0
Paul Whatuira	Huddersfield	2008-10	59	23	0	0	92
Scott Wheeldon	Castleford	2014-15	14(23)	5	0	0	20
	London	2012-13	27(4)	3	0	0	12
	Hull KR	2009-12	30(42)	4	0	0	16
	Hull	2006-08	2(60)	4	0	0	16
Gary Wheeler	Warrington	2015	6(3)	4	0	0	16
	St Helens	2008-14	48(10)	17	13	0	94
Matt Whitaker	Castleford	2006	8(2)	0	0	0	0
	Widnes	2004-05	10(20)	9	0	0	36
	Huddersfield	2003-04	3(14)	0	0	0	0
Ben White	Leeds	2014	1	0	0	0	0
David White	Wakefield	2000	(1)	0	0	0	0
Josh White	Salford	1998	18(3)	5	5	1	31
	London	1997	14(2)	8	0	1	33
Lloyd White	Widnes	2012-15	34(39)	17	7	1	83
	Crusaders	2010-11	13(11)	8	0	0	32
	Celtic	2009	6	1	0	0	4
Paul White	Salford	2009	1	1	0	0	4
	Wakefield	2006-07	24(12)	12	0	0	48
	Huddersfield	2003-05	11(32)	17	16	0	100
Elliott Whitehead	Catalans	2013-15	64(1)	30	0	0	120
	Bradford	2009-13	90(10)	30	0	0	120
Richard Whiting	Hull	2004-15	163(72)	69	19	2	316
Matt Whitley	Widnes	2015	2(8)	2	0	0	8
Emmerson Whittel	Bradford	2014	(1)	0	0	0	0
Danny Whittle	Warrington	1998	(2)	0	0	0	0
David Whittle	St Helens	2002	1(2)	0	0	0	0
	Warrington	2001	1(2)	0	0	0	0
Jon Whittle	Wakefield	2006	8(2)	3	0	0	12
	Widnes	2005	13	2	0	0	8
	Wigan	2003	1	0	0	0	0
Joel Wicks	London	2013-14	3(10)	0	0	0	0
Dean Widders	Castleford	2009-11	25(32)	23	0	0	92
Stephen Wild	Salford	2011-13	71	4	0	0	16
	Huddersfield	2006-10	116(2)	33	0	0	132
	Wigan	2001-05	67(20)	24	0	0	96
Sam Wilde	Warrington	2015	(6)	1	0	0	4
Matty Wildie	Wakefield	2010-14	13(26)	3	0	0	12

PLAYER	CLUB	YEAR	APP	TRIES	GOALS	FG	PTS
Oliver Wilkes	Wakefield	2008-09, 2012-13	55(47)	10	0	0	40
	Harlequins	2010-11	39(13)	4	0	0	16
	Wigan	2006	1(5)	0	0	0	0
	Leigh	2005	13(1)	1	0	0	4
	Huddersfield	2000-01	1(6)	0	0	0	0
	Sheffield	1998	(1)	0	0	0	0
Jon Wilkin	St Helens	2003-15	265(27)	75	0	2	302
Alex Wilkinson	Hull	2003-04	11(4)	1	0	0	4
	Huddersfield	2003	8	4	0	0	16
	London	2002	5(1)	0	0	0	0
	Bradford	2000-01	3(3)	1	0	0	4
Bart Williams	London	1998	5(3)	1	0	0	4
Daley Williams	Salford	2006-07	9(2)	4	0	0	16
Danny Williams	Harlequins	2006	9(13)	4	0	0	16
	London	2005	1(16)	0	0	0	0
Danny Williams	Bradford	2014	7	2	0	0	8
	Salford	2011-14	54	31	0	0	124
	Leeds	2006, 2008	13(2)	7	0	0	28
	Hull	2008	3	0	0	0	0
Dave Williams	Harlequins	2008-11	1(17)	0	0	0	0
Desi Williams	Wigan	2004	2	0	0	0	0
George Williams	Wigan	2013-15	41(12)	14	8	0	72
Jonny Williams	London	2004	(4)	0	0	0	0
Lee Williams	Crusaders	2011	1(7)	0	0	0	0
Rhys Williams	Warrington	2010-13	23(1)	15	0	0	60
	Salford	2013	4	0	0	0	0
	Castleford	2012	8	4	0	0	16
	Crusaders	2011	6	3	0	0	12
Sam Williams	Catalans	2014	11(1)	4	21	0	58
Luke Williamson	Harlequins	2009-10	39	6	0	0	24
John Wilshere	Salford	2006-07, 2009	72(2)	32	142	0	412
	Leigh	2005	26	8	6	0	44
	Warrington	2004	5	2	0	0	8
Craig Wilson	Hull	2000	2(16)	1	0	1	5
	Gateshead	1999	17(11)	5	0	1	21
George Wilson	Paris	1996	7(2)	3	0	0	12
John Wilson	Catalans	2006-08	69	23	0	0	92
Richard Wilson	Hull	1998-99	(13)	0	0	0	0
Scott Wilson	Warrington	1998-99	23(2)	6	0	0	24
Johan Windley	Hull	1999	2(2)	1	0	0	4
Paul Wingfield	Warrington	1997	5(3)	6	1	0	26
Frank Winterstein	Widnes	2012-13	37(9)	16	0	0	64
	Crusaders	2010-11	26(19)	4	0	0	16
	Wakefield	2009	(5)	0	0	0	0
Lincoln Withers	Hull KR	2012-13	18(22)	10	0	0	40
	Crusaders	2010-11	47	4	0	0	16
	Celtic	2009	21	6	0	0	24
Michael Withers	Wigan	2007	6(1)	1	0	0	4
	Bradford	1999-2006	156(6)	94	15	4	410
Michael Witt	London	2012-13	37	10	89	1	219
	Crusaders	2010-11	39	13	47	4	150
Jeff Wittenberg	Huddersfield	1998	18(1)	1	0	0	4
	Bradford	1997	8(9)	4	0	0	16
Josh Wood	Salford	2015	1	0	0	0	0
Kyle Wood	Huddersfield	2011, 2013-15	29(27)	6	0	0	24
	Wakefield	2012-13	5(37)	9	0	0	36
	Castleford	2010	1(4)	0	0	0	0
Martin Wood	Sheffield	1997-98	24(11)	4	18	2	54
Nathan Wood	Warrington	2002-05	90	38	0	3	155
	Wakefield	2002	11	2	0	0	8
Paul Wood	Warrington	2000-14	138(171)	40	0	0	160
Phil Wood	Widnes	2004	2(1)	0	0	0	0
Sam Wood	Bradford	2013-14	7(1)	0	0	0	0
James Woodburn-Hall	London	2013-14	9(4)	2	0	0	8
Darren Woods	Widnes	2005	(1)	0	0	0	0
David Woods	Halifax	2002	18(2)	8	0	0	32
Simon Worrall	Leeds	2008-09	5(16)	1	0	0	4
Michael Worrincy	Bradford	2009-10	12(34)	12	0	0	48
	Harlequins	2006-08	20(12)	10	0	0	40
Rob Worrincy	Castleford	2004	1	0	0	0	0
Troy Wozniak	Widnes	2004	13(7)	1	0	0	4
Matthew Wray	Wakefield	2002-03	13(3)	2	0	0	8
David Wrench	Wakefield	2002-06	28(52)	6	0	0	24
	Leeds	1999-2001	7(17)	0	0	0	0
Callum Wright	Wigan	2014	(2)	0	0	0	0
Craig Wright	Castleford	2000	1(9)	0	0	0	0
Nigel Wright	Huddersfield	1999	4(6)	1	0	0	4
	Wigan	1996-97	5(5)	2	0	1	9
Ricky Wright	Sheffield	1997-99	2(13)	0	0	0	0
Vincent Wulf	Paris	1996	13(4)	4	0	0	16
Andrew Wynyard	London	1999-2000	34(6)	4	0	0	16
Bagdad Yaha	Paris	1996	4(4)	2	4	0	16
Fouad Yaha	Catalans	2015	9	3	0	0	12
Malakai Yasa	Sheffield	1996	1(3)	0	0	0	0
Andy Yates	Leeds	2015	(9)	1	0	0	4
Kirk Yeaman	Hull	2001-15	297(18)	153	0	0	612
Grant Young	London	1998-99	22(2)	2	0	0	8
Nick Youngquest	Castleford	2011-12	37	28	0	0	112
	Crusaders	2010	26(1)	9	0	0	36
Ronel Zenon	Paris	1996	(4)	0	0	0	0
Nick Zisti	Bradford	1999	6(1)	0	0	0	0
Freddie Zitter	Catalans	2006	1	0	0	0	0

NEW FACES - Players making their Super League debuts in 2015

PLAYER	CLUB	DEBUT vs	ROUND	DATE
Lucas Albert	Catalans	Widnes (a)	21	12/7/15
Mitchell Allgood	Hull KR	Leeds (h)	1	8/2/15
Jack Ashworth	St Helens	Hull (h)	9	6/4/15
Ricky Bailey	St Helens	Hull (h)	9	6/4/15
Maurice Blair	Hull KR	Leeds (h)	1	8/2/15
John Boudebza	Hull KR	Wakefield (a)	2	15/2/15
Terry Campese	Hull KR	Leeds (h)	1	8/2/15
Todd Carney	Catalans	Warrington (h)	3	28/2/15
Dane Chisholm	Hull KR	St Helens (a)	23	24/7/15
Adam Cuthbertson	Leeds	Hull KR (a)	1	8/2/15
Jack Downs	Hull	St Helens (a)	S82	14/8/15
Brad Fash	Hull	Castleford (h)	21	12/7/15
Matty Fleming	St Helens	Leeds (h)	11	17/4/15
Mitch Garbutt	Leeds	St Helens (h)	20	3/7/15
Matty Gee	Salford	Leeds (h)	10	12/4/15
Oliver Gildart	Salford	Castleford (h)	12	26/4/15
Stephen Holker	Hull KR	Leeds (a)	15	22/5/15
Tom Holmes	Castleford	Catalans (h)	13	3/5/15
Krisnan Inu	Catalans	Wakefield (h)	19	20/6/15
Jack Johnson	Warrington	Hull (h)	S84	6/9/15
Tom Johnstone	Wakefield	Wigan (a)	7	27/3/15
Albert Kelly	Hull KR	Leeds (h)	1	8/2/15
Ryan Lannon	Salford	Leeds (h)	10	12/4/15
Jordan Lilley	Leeds	Wakefield (a)	17	7/6/15
Josh Mantellato	Hull KR	Leeds (h)	1	8/2/15
Matthew Marsh	Hull KR	Salford (h)	11	30/6/15
Masi Matongo	Hull	Wigan (a)	S85	11/9/15
Steve Michaels	Hull	Warrington (h)	2	13/2/15
Mark Minichiello	Hull	Huddersfield (a)	1	8/2/15
Junior Moors	Castleford	Wakefield (h)	1	8/2/15
Declan Patton	Warrington	Wakefield (h)	10	11/4/15
Ugo Perez	Catalans	Warrington (a)	S86	19/9/15
Adam Quinlan	St Helens	Huddersfield (h)	21	10/7/15
Ben Roberts	Castleford	Catalans (a)	2	14/2/15
Stanislas Robin	Catalans	Wakefield (a)	8	2/4/15
Ash Robson	Castleford	Salford (a)	12	26/4/15
Chris Sandow	Warrington	Leeds (a)	S81	7/8/15
Jordan Sigismeau	Catalans	Widnes (a)	21	12/7/15
Jared Simpson	Huddersfield	Wigan (h)	17	7/6/15
Ashton Sims	Warrington	Salford (h)	1	7/2/15
Ken Sio	Hull KR	Leeds (h)	1	8/2/15
Michael Sio	Wakefield	Hull (h)	11	1/7/15
Dane Tilse	Hull KR	Catalans (a)	12	25/4/15
Willie Tonga	Catalans	St Helens (a)	1	6/2/15
Bill Tupou	Wakefield	Huddersfield (a)	23	26/7/15
Jansin Turgut	Hull	Leeds (h)	4	5/3/15
Bobby Tyson-Wilson	Hull	Salford (h)	13	1/5/15
	(club debut: Sheffield (a), CCR5, 19/4/15)			
Matt Whitley	Widnes	Warrington (h)	8	2/4/15
Sam Wilde	Warrington	Wigan (h)	20	2/7/15
Josh Wood	Salford	Warrington (h)	15	22/5/15
Fouad Yaha	Catalans	Hull KR (h)	12	25/4/15
Andy Yates	Leeds	Widnes (h)	2	13/2/15

Players making their club debuts in other competitions in 2015

PLAYER	CLUB	DEBUT vs	ROUND	DATE
Jake Bibby	Salford	Hull KR (a)	S8-QR7	27/9/15
Jay Chapelhow	Widnes	Leigh (h)	S8-QR7	27/9/15
Olly Davies	St Helens	York (h)	CCR6	15/5/15
Morgan Knowles	St Helens	York (h)	CCR6	15/5/15
George Lawler	Hull KR	Widnes (a)	S8-QR3	23/8/15
Reni Maitua	Salford	Wakefield (h)	S8-QR1	9/8/15
Luke Menzies	Salford	Hull KR (a)	S8-QR7	27/9/15
Charly Runciman	Widnes	Halifax (a)	S8-QR1	9/8/15
Iain Thornley	Salford	Wakefield (h)	S8-QR1	9/8/15
Andy Yates	Wakefield	Halifax (h)	S8-QR6	19/9/15

OLD FACES -
Players making their Super League debuts for new clubs in 2015

PLAYER	CLUB	DEBUT vs	ROUND	DATE
Joe Arundel	Wakefield	Huddersfield (h)	6	22/3/15
Matty Ashurst	Wakefield	Hull KR (h)	2	15/2/15
Ryan Bailey	Castleford	Catalans (h)	13	3/5/15
Ryan Bailey	Hull KR	Wakefield (a)	2	15/2/15
Greg Burke	Hull KR	Leeds (h)	1	8/2/15
Travis Burns	St Helens	Catalans (h)	1	6/2/15
Remi Casty	Catalans	St Helens (a) (D2)	1	6/2/15
Daryl Clark	Warrington	Salford (h)	1	7/2/15
Chris Clarkson	Widnes	Wigan (h)	1	5/2/15
Matt Cook	Castleford	St Helens (a) (D2)	3	27/2/15
Jordan Cox	Huddersfield	St Helens (h)	10	12/4/15
Steve Crossley	Castleford	Wakefield (h)	1	8/2/15
Kieran Dixon	Hull KR	Leeds (h)	1	8/2/15
Michael Dobson	Salford	Warrington (a)	1	7/2/15
James Donaldson	Hull KR	Leeds (h)	1	8/2/15
Gil Dudson	Widnes	Wakefield (h)	3	1/3/15
Jamie Ellis	Huddersfield	Hull (h)	1	8/2/15
Carl Forster	Salford	Widnes (h)	7	26/3/15
Luke Gale	Castleford	Wakefield (h)	1	8/2/15
Tony Gigot	Catalans	Wigan (h)	15	23/5/15
	(club debut: Featherstone (h) (D2), CCR6, 17/5/15)			
Oliver Gildart	Wigan	Warrington (a)	S83	21/8/15
Wayne Godwin	Salford	Castleford (h)	12	26/4/15
	(club debut: Leigh (a) (D2), CCR5, 18/4/15)			
Darrell Goulding	Hull KR	Leeds (h)	1	8/2/15
James Greenwood	Hull KR	Leeds (a)	15	22/5/15
James Greenwood	Salford	Castleford (h)	12	26/4/15
George Griffin	Salford	Castleford (h)	12	26/4/15
	(club debut: Leigh (a), CCR5, 18/4/15)			
George Griffin	Wakefield	Huddersfield (h)	6	22/3/15
Craig Hall	Wakefield	Castleford (a)	1	8/2/15
Jordan Hand	Wakefield	Wigan (a)	7	27/3/15
Weller Hauraki	Salford	Warrington (a)	1	7/2/15
Aaron Heremaia	Widnes	Wigan (h)	1	5/2/15
Liam Hood	Salford	Hull (h)	3	28/2/15
Stuart Howarth	Wakefield	Leeds (h) (D2)	17	7/6/15
Stuart Howarth	Hull	Castleford (a)	7	27/3/15
Craig Huby	Huddersfield	Hull (h)	1	8/2/15
Jack Hughes	Huddersfield	Hull (h)	1	8/2/15
Ben Jones-Bishop	Salford	Warrington (a)	1	7/2/15
Ben Kavanagh	Wakefield	Wigan (h)	12	23/4/15
Ian Kirke	Wakefield	Wigan (h)	12	23/4/15
	(club debut: Halifax (h), CCR5, 17/4/15)			
Olsi Krasniqi	Salford	Catalans (h)	20	5/7/15
Kevin Locke	Wakefield	Hull (h)	11	1/7/15
Shaun Lunt	Hull KR	Catalans (h)	5	15/3/15
Manase Manuokafoa	Widnes	Wigan (h)	1	5/2/15
Tyrone McCarthy	Hull KR	Leeds (h)	1	8/2/15
Mike McMeeken	Castleford	St Helens (a)	3	27/2/15
Paul McShane	Castleford	Hull (h)	S81	7/8/15
Jacob Miller	Wakefield	Castleford (a)	1	8/2/15
Scott Moore	Wakefield	Huddersfield (a)	23	26/7/15
Scott Moore	Castleford	Wakefield (h) (D2)	1	8/2/15
Lee Mossop	Wigan	Hull KR (a) (D2)	3	1/3/15
Anthony Mullally	Wakefield	Castleford (h)	22	19/7/15
Curtis Naughton	Hull	St Helens (a)	9	6/4/15
Lopini Paea	Wakefield	Castleford (a)	1	8/2/15
Cory Paterson	Salford	Warrington (a)	1	7/2/15
Larne Patrick	Wigan	Widnes (a)	1	5/2/15
Leon Pryce	Hull	Huddersfield (a)	1	8/2/15
Tony Puletua	Hull KR	Hull (MW)	16	30/5/15
Mickael Simon	Wakefield	St Helens (h)	4	6/3/15
Daniel Smith	Huddersfield	Catalans (a)	22	18/7/15
Lee Smith	Wakefield	Huddersfield (a) (D2)	23	26/7/15
Marc Sneyd	Hull	Huddersfield (a)	1	8/2/15
Denny Solomona	Castleford	Wakefield (h)	1	8/2/15
Gadwin Springer	Castleford	Widnes (h)	20	5/7/15
Jordan Tansey	Wakefield	Hull (h)	11	1/7/15
Taulima Tautai	Wigan	Widnes (a)	1	5/2/15
Scott Taylor	Salford	Warrington (a)	1	7/2/15
Logan Tomkins	Salford	St Helens (a) (D2)	17	5/6/15
Atelea Vea	St Helens	Catalans (h)	1	6/2/15
Anthony Walker	Wakefield	Hull (a)	20	5/7/15
Gary Wheeler	Warrington	Salford (h)	1	7/2/15

● *All totals in 'Super League Players 1996-2015' include play-off games & Super League Super 8s from 2015. 2015 Super 8s (Qualifiers) not included.*

SUPER LEAGUE XX
Club by Club

6 October 2014 - Daryl Clark named Man of Steel; Daryl Powell coach of the year

30 October 2014 - Ben Reynolds signs for Leigh with Tigers having option for 2016.

6 January 2015 - Kirk Dixon retires on medical advice after off-season neck surgery.

11 January 2015 - 22-14 home win over Bradford as Andy Lynch testimonial goes ahead despite wind damage to Princess Street Stand two nights before.

14 January 2015 - Andy Lynch signs one-year contract extension to end of 2016 season.

8 February 2015 - 24-22 round one defeat at home to Wakefield after leading 22-6 with 15 minutes to go.

14 February 2015 - late field goal means 13-12 loss away at Catalans.

18 February 2015 - Jake Webster escapes ban with EGP for punching in Catalans defeat.

27 February 2015 - Mike McMeeken and Matt Cook make debuts in 21-14 defeat at St Helens. Scott Moore gets one-match ban for dangerous contact.

7 March 2015 - 42-14 home win over Wigan Warriors gets Tigers off the mark.

12 March 2015 - 22-0 Thursday night defeat at Huddersfield.

25 March 2015 - Nathan Massey and Matt Cook suspended for one game each in wake of 30-16 home win over Salford.

27 March 2015 - Luke Gale scores twice in back-to-back 20-14 home win over Hull FC.

1 April 2015 - Luke Dorn signs 12-month contract extension to end of 2016 season.

3 April 2015 - 26-12 Good Friday defeat by Leeds in front of sell-out crowd at the Mend-A-Hose Jungle.

6 April 2015 - 22-14 Easter Monday win at Warrington.

11 April 2015 - Justin Carney dislocates elbow in 25-4 home win over Hull KR.

19 April 2015 - 46-16 defeat at Widnes.

20 April 2015 - Ryan Bailey joins from Hull KR on deal to end of season,

24 April 2015 - Steve Crossley leaves Tigers and joins Bradford.

KEY DATES - CASTLEFORD TIGERS

26 April 2015 - Ash Robson scores matching-winning try in late 22-20 away win over Salford.

30 April 2015 - James Clare to join York on dual-registration.

3 May 2015 - Tigers move up to fifth in table after 36-28 home win over Catalans Dragons.

8 May 2015 – 28-0 defeat at Wigan.

16 May 2015 – 40-14 defeat at Hull means Challenge Cup exit at first hurdle.

31 May 2015 - four tries from Denny Solomona and hat trick from Ashley Gibson in 56-16 win over Wakefield at Magic Weekend in Newcastle.

8 June 2015 - England Academy star Will Maher pens four-year contract extension to end of 2019.

11 June 2015 - 31-24 win at Headingley knocks Leeds off top spot,

12 June 2015 - Gadwin Springer signs two-year deal and joins immediately from Catalans Dragons. Ash Robson signs to end of 2017.

18 June 2015 - last-second Ben Roberts field goal secures 25-24 home win over league leaders St Helens.

26 June 2015 - Jordan Tansey leaves and joins Wakefield.

27 June 2015 - Tigers announce signing of Ben Crooks on three-year deal from 2016.

12 July 2015 - 21-18 loss at Hull ends five-match winning run.

19 July 2015 - Justin Carney gets four tries in 58-20 win at Wakefield.

22 July 2015 - James Clare leaves club and joins Bradford.

23 July 2015 - Paul McShane joins from Wakefield on two-and-a-half year deal with Scott Moore heading the other way on loan.

7 August 2015 - hard-fought 36-30 home win over Hull FC keeps play-off hopes alive.

13 August 2015 - last-gasp Liam Finn field goal seals deserved home 17-16 win over Warrington.

27 August 2015 - Justin Carney is suspended by the club with immediate effect.

3 September 2015 - 40-26 defeat at Huddersfield after Mike McMeeken sin-binned for tripping and Giants score 24 unanswered points in his absence.

10 September 2015 - 42-38 home defeat to St Helens ends top-four play-off hopes.

14 September 2015 - Luke Gale wraps up Albert Goldthorpe Medal.

17 September 2015 - Luke Gale stars in stunning 29-22 win at Leeds.

24 September 2015 - Ashley Gibson, Michael Channing and Brandon Moore all released.

25 September 2015 – 47-12 Friday night defeat at Wigan ends season.

28 September 2015 - club suspension on Justin Carney lifted.

28 September 2015 - new stadium at Five Towns Park gets final planning approval.

29 September 2015 - club announces death of chairman Jack Fulton.

8 October 2015 - Nathan Massey signs four-year contract extension to end of 2019 season.

27 October 2015 - Warrington Wolves winger Joel Monaghan joins on two-year deal.

29 October 2015 - 20-year-old York centre Greg Minikin signs two-year deal

2 November 2015 - centre Jake Webster signs new contract for 2016.

3 November 2015 - winger Justin Carney moves to Salford on year-long loan deal.

CLUB RECORDS

Highest score:
106-0 v Rochdale, 9/9/2007
Highest score against:
12-76 v Leeds, 14/8/2009
Record attendance:
25,449 v Hunslet, 9/3/35

MATCH RECORDS

Tries:
5 Derek Foster v Hunslet, 10/11/72
John Joyner v Millom, 16/9/73
Steve Fenton v Dewsbury, 27/1/78
Ian French v Hunslet, 9/2/86
St John Ellis v Whitehaven, 10/12/89
Goals: 17 Sammy Lloyd v Millom, 16/9/73
Points: 43 Sammy Lloyd v Millom, 16/9/73

SEASON RECORDS

Tries: 40 St John Ellis 1993-94
Goals: 158 Sammy Lloyd 1976-77
Points: 334 Bob Beardmore 1983-84

CAREER RECORDS

Tries: 206 Alan Hardisty 1958-71
Goals: 875 Albert Lunn 1951-63
Points: 1,870 Albert Lunn 1951-63
Appearances: 613 John Joyner 1973-92

CASTLEFORD TIGERS

DATE	FIXTURE	RESULT	SCORERS	LGE	ATT
8/2/15	Wakefield (h)	L22-24	t:Solomona(2),Gale,Carney g:Gale(3)	8th	10,728
14/2/15	Catalans Dragons (a)	L13-12	t:Carney,Tansey g:Gale(2)	9th	9,167
27/2/15	St Helens (a)	L21-14	t:Carney(2),Tansey g:Gale	11th	10,066
6/3/15	Wigan (h)	W42-14	t:Carney(2),Clare,Dorn,Finn,O Holmes,Shenton g:Gale(7)	9th	7,772
12/3/15	Huddersfield (a)	L22-0		11th	5,257
20/3/15	Salford (h)	W30-16	t:Carney(2),Finn,Shenton,Wheeldon,Clare g:Gale(3)	9th	6,901
27/3/15	Hull FC (h)	W20-14	t:Gale(2),Carney,Clare g:Gale(2)	7th	8,744
3/4/15	Leeds (h)	L12-26	t:Shenton(2) g:Gale(2)	10th	11,235
6/4/15	Warrington (a)	W14-22	t:Tansey,Dorn,Milner,Roberts g:Gale(3)	8th	8,518
11/4/15	Hull KR (h)	W25-4	t:Tansey,Gale,Massey,Mariano g:Gale(4) fg:Gale	6th	6,102
19/4/15	Widnes (a)	L46-16	t:Roberts,O Holmes,Shenton g:Finn(2)	7th	5,457
26/4/15	Salford (a)	W20-22	t:Gibson(2),Massey,Robson g:Gale(3)	6th	3,397
3/5/15	Catalans Dragons (h)	W36-28	t:Gibson,Channing,Millington,Shenton,Tansey,Moore g:Gale(6)	5th	5,704
8/5/15	Wigan (a)	L28-0		6th	15,022
16/5/15	Hull FC (a) (CCR6)	L40-14	t:Gibson,Clare,McMeeken g:Gale	N/A	6,715
21/5/15	Huddersfield (h)	L16-24	t:Webster,Roberts,Shenton g:Gale(2)	7th	4,632
31/5/15	Wakefield (MW) ●	W56-16	t:Solomona(4),Tansey,Shenton,Gibson(3),Gale g:Gale(8)	6th	N/A
5/6/15	Hull KR (a)	W22-30	t:Roberts,Solomona,O Holmes,Gale,Finn g:Gale(5)	6th	7,093
11/6/15	Leeds (a)	W24-31	t:Millington,Finn,Shenton,Solomona(2) g:Gale(5) fg:Finn	5th	15,089
18/6/15	St Helens (h)	W25-24	t:Carney,Solomona,Webster,Cook g:Gale(4) fg:Roberts	5th	6,068
5/7/15	Widnes (h)	W34-20	t:Solomona(3),Webster,Cook,Carney g:Gale(5)	5th	7,002
12/7/15	Hull FC (a)	L21-18	t:Solomona(2),Dorn,Roberts g:Finn	5th	10,949
19/7/15	Wakefield (a)	W20-58	t:Millington,Gale,McMeeken,O Holmes,Dorn(2),Carney(4) g:Gale(9)	5th	6,108
26/7/15	Warrington (h)	L6-44	t:Moors g:Finn	5th	7,239
7/8/15	Hull FC (h) (S8)	W36-30	t:Shenton(4),Gale,Gibson g:Gale(6)	5th	6,760
13/8/15	Warrington (h) (S8)	W17-16	t:Carney(2),Shenton g:Gale(2) fg:Finn	5th	5,212
22/8/15	Catalans Dragons (a) (S8)	L44-26	t:Carney,O Holmes,Milner(2),Moors g:Gale(3)	5th	7,473
3/9/15	Huddersfield (a) (S8)	L40-26	t:Gale,Gibson,Dorn,Roberts,Solomona g:Gale(3)	5th	5,350
10/9/15	St Helens (h) (S8)	L38-42	t:Dorn(2),Roberts(2),Solomona,Moors g:Gale(7)	5th	5,253
17/9/15	Leeds (a) (S8)	W22-29	t:Gale(2),Solomona,Dorn,Roberts g:Gale(4) fg:Roberts	5th	15,069
25/9/15	Wigan (a) (S8)	L47-12	t:Dorn,Moors g:Gale(2)	5th	15,017

● Played at St James' Park, Newcastle

	D.O.B.	APP ALL	APP SL	TRIES ALL	TRIES SL	GOALS ALL	GOALS SL	FG ALL	FG SL	PTS ALL	PTS SL
Ryan Bailey	11/11/83	4(2)	3(2)	0	0	0	0	0	0	0	0
Ryan Boyle	17/10/87	1(18)	1(18)	0	0	0	0	0	0	0	0
Justin Carney	16/6/88	18	18	18	18	0	0	0	0	72	72
Michael Channing	30/6/92	10	10	1	1	0	0	0	0	4	4
James Clare	13/4/91	9	8	4	3	0	0	0	0	16	12
Matt Cook	14/11/86	4(13)	4(13)	2	2	0	0	0	0	8	8
Steve Crossley	28/11/89	(6)	(6)	0	0	0	0	0	0	0	0
Luke Dorn	2/7/82	13(1)	13(1)	10	10	0	0	0	0	40	40
Liam Finn	2/11/83	21(3)	21(2)	4	4	4	4	2	2	26	26
Luke Gale	22/6/88	29	28	11	11	102	101	1	1	249	247
Ashley Gibson	25/9/86	22	21	9	8	0	0	0	0	36	32
Oliver Holmes	7/8/92	28	27	5	5	0	0	0	0	20	20
Tom Holmes	2/3/96	(1)	(1)	0	0	0	0	0	0	0	0
Lee Jewitt	14/2/87	1(5)	1(4)	0	0	0	0	0	0	0	0
Andy Lynch	20/10/79	27(1)	26(1)	0	0	0	0	0	0	0	0
Will Maher	4/11/95	(8)	(8)	0	0	0	0	0	0	0	0
Frankie Mariano	10/5/87	5	5	1	1	0	0	0	0	4	4
Nathan Massey	11/7/89	23	22	2	2	0	0	0	0	8	8
Mike McMeeken	10/5/94	14(6)	14(5)	2	1	0	0	0	0	8	4
Paul McShane	19/11/89	1(5)	1(5)	0	0	0	0	0	0	0	0
Grant Millington	1/11/86	25(6)	25(5)	3	3	0	0	0	0	12	12
Adam Milner	19/12/91	17(11)	16(11)	3	3	0	0	0	0	12	12
Scott Moore	23/1/88	13(1)	13(1)	1	1	0	0	0	0	4	4
Junior Moors	30/7/86	14(11)	13(11)	4	4	0	0	0	0	16	16
Ben Roberts	8/7/85	18(8)	17(8)	9	9	0	0	2	2	38	38
Ash Robson	4/11/95	3	3	1	1	0	0	0	0	4	4
Michael Shenton	22/7/86	28	27	14	14	0	0	0	0	56	56
Denny Solomona	27/10/93	15	15	18	18	0	0	0	0	72	72
Gadwin Springer	4/4/93	2(8)	2(8)	0	0	0	0	0	0	0	0
Jordan Tansey	9/9/86	13(1)	12(1)	6	6	0	0	0	0	24	24
Jake Webster	29/10/83	16(3)	15(3)	3	3	0	0	0	0	12	12
Scott Wheeldon	23/2/86	9(6)	9(6)	1	1	0	0	0	0	4	4

'SL' totals include Super 8s; 'All' totals also include Challenge Cup

Luke Gale

LEAGUE RECORD
P30-W16-D0-L14
(5th, SL)
F731, A746, Diff-15
32 points.

CHALLENGE CUP
Round Six

ATTENDANCES
Best - v Leeds (SL - 11,235)
Worst - v Huddersfield
(SL - 4,632)
Total (SL/S8s only) - 99,352
Average (SL/S8s only) - 7,097
(Up by 90 on 2014)

12 December 2014 - Zeb Taia signs new three-year contract to end of 2017.

6 February 2015 - debutant Willie Tonga knocked out just 12 seconds into opening round 18-7 defeat at St Helens. Remi Casty suffers broken hand.

14 February 2015 - Eloi Pelissier banned for two matches for shoulder charge on Scott Wheeldon in 31-12 home win over Castleford. Olivier Elima gets one match for striking.

28 February 2015 - Todd Carney makes debut in 38-18 home win over Warrington.

7 March 2015 - Todd Carney breaks rib in competition-record draw - 40-40 at home to Salford.

15 March 2015 - Ben Pomeroy's 31-match run comes to an end after one-game ban for striking Hull KR forward Mitch Allgood in 50-20 away defeat.

20 March 2015 - Vincent Duport out for season after suffering ruptured tendon in shoulder in 33-22 defeat at Hull FC.

31 March 2015 - Morgan Escaré gets one-match suspension for making dangerous contact with Rob Burrow in 38-22 home defeat by Leeds.

31 March 2015 - coach Laurent Frayssinous fined £500, half suspended, for criticism of the match referee following 40-40 draw with Salford on March 7.

2 April 2015 - Damien Cardace scores hat-trick in Easter Thursday 40-4 win at Wakefield, a first away win of the season.

8 April 2015 - Elliott Whitehead to leave and join Canberra Raiders at end of season.

19 April 2015 - Jeff Lima banned for two matches for dangerous contact on Ukuma Ta'ai in round 11, 28-14 defeat at Huddersfield.

25 April 2015 - Todd Carney returns after six-game absence to inspire first win in three games, a 32-24 home victory over Hull KR. Teenage winger Fouad Yaha makes debut.

12 May 2015 - Avignon's Tony Gigot signs for a second time, on a deal until end of season.

17 May 2015 - Jeff Lima suspended for four matches for shoulder charge on Remi Marginet in 37-34 Challenge Cup home win over Featherstone Rovers.

30 May 2015 - prop Julian Bousquet signs new two-year contract to the end of 2017.

31 May 2015 - Todd Carney tears pectoral muscle in 22-22 draw with Giants at Magic Weekend in Newcastle.

KEY DATES - CATALANS DRAGONS

8 June 2015 - coach Laurent Frayssinous fined £500 for criticising a match official and/or the Match Review Panel and/or an Operational Rules tribunal following the Magic Weekend fixture against the Giants.

9 June 2015 - Mathias Pala joins Leigh Centurions with immediate effect.

10 June 2015 - Benjamin Garcia signs two-year deal with Penrith Panthers from 2016.

11 June 2015 - local products back rower Ugo Perez, three years, and loose forward Thibaut Margalet, one-and-a-half years, sign new contracts.

16 June 2015 - former Kiwi Test centre Krisnan Inu signs from rugby union club Stade Francais on short-term contract to end of season.

3 July 2015 - Jason Baitieri signs new two-year contract.

3 July 2015 - Tony Gigot signs contract extension to end of 2017.

7 July 2015 - Louis Anderson signs new two-year contract to end of 2017 campaign.

8 July 2015 - Pat Richards signs from Wests Tigers on two-year deal from 2016.

9 July 2015 - Scott Dureau to leave for Australia at end of season.

10 July 2015 - Warrington scrum-half Richie Myler signs two-year contract from 2016.

13 July 2015 - winger Fouad Yaha ruled out for six to eight weeks with training ground shoulder injury.

18 July 2015 - Remi Casty ruled out for rest of season after suffering knee injury during 14-12 home defeat by Huddersfield.

27 July 2015 - chairman Bernard Guasch fined £1000 for publicly criticising a match referee following 14-12 defeat by Huddersfield.

3 August 2015 - Australia international Dave Taylor signs for two years from Gold Coast from 2016 season. Hooker Ian Henderson to leave at end of the season to join Sydney Roosters. Zeb Taia to join Gold Coast Titans.

4 August 2015 - academy graduates winger Fouad Yaha, three years, and stand-off Lucas Albert, five-years, sign long-term deals.

4 August 2015 - Leeds Rhinos hooker Paul Aiton signs on three-year contract from 2016.

6 August 2015 - Manly Sea Eagles back-row forward Justin Horo to join from 2016 on two-year contract.

8 August 2015 - centre Ben Pomeroy sent off in 43rd minute for shoulder charge on Josh Jones in 26-16 home win over St Helens in Super Eights opener.

14 August 2015 - 24-12 defeat at Huddersfield ends play-off chances.

18 August 2015 - Huddersfield Giants winger Jodie Broughton signs two-year contract from 2016.

22 August 2015 - Ben Pomeroy sent off and banned for dangerous throw on Ashley Gibson in 29th minute of 44-26 home win over Castleford.

8 September 2015 - Louis Anderson banned for two games for kicking out in 42-16 defeat to Wigan at Millwall the previous Saturday,

9 September 2015 - Souths' former Manly forward Glenn Stewart signs on three-year contract from 2016.

25 September 2015 - Kevin Larroyer, on loan for last two seasons, signs new permanent three-year contract at Hull KR.

25 September 2015 - Krisnan Inu signs 12-month contract for 2016.

27 September 2015 - season ends at Hull FC with second away win of season by 28-24.

30 September 2015 - Todd Carney signs new, improved three-year contract up to end of 2018.

7 October 2015 - Michael Oldfield signs for South Sydney.

CLUB RECORDS

Highest score: 92-8 v York, 12/5/2013
Highest score against:
12-60 v Leeds, 15/9/2006
16-60 v Huddersfield, 28/6/2013
Record attendance: 18,150 v Warrington, 20/6/2009 *(Barcelona)*
11,500 v Warrington, 9/4/2012
(Stade Gilbert Brutus)

MATCH RECORDS

Tries:
4 Justin Murphy v Warrington, 13/9/2008
Damien Cardace v Widnes, 31/3/2012
Kevin Larroyer v York, 12/5/2013
Goals:
11 Thomas Bosc v Featherstone, 31/3/2007
Thomas Bosc v Batley, 29/5/2010
Scott Dureau v Widnes, 31/3/2012
Points:
26 Thomas Bosc v Featherstone, 31/3/2007

SEASON RECORDS

Tries: 29 Morgan Escare 2014
Goals: 134 Scott Dureau 2012
Points: 319 Scott Dureau 2012

CAREER RECORDS

Tries: 86 Clint Greenshields 2007-2012
Goals:
562 *(inc 13fg)* Thomas Bosc 2006-2015
Points: 1,343 Thomas Bosc 2006-2015
Appearances:
251 Gregory Mounis 2006-2015

CATALANS DRAGONS

DATE	FIXTURE	RESULT	SCORERS	LGE	ATT
6/2/15	St Helens (a)	L18-7	t:Pelissier g:Bosc fg:Bosc	10th	12,008
14/2/15	Castleford (h)	W13-12	t:Escare,Whitehead g:Dureau(2) fg:Dureau	7th	9,167
28/2/15	Warrington (h)	W38-18	t:Tonga,Oldfield(2),Duport,Taia(2) g:Dureau(7)	3rd	8,782
7/3/15	Salford (h)	D40-40	t:Taia,Duport,Pomeroy(2),Oldfield,Whitehead,Henderson g:Dureau(6)	4th	8,864
15/3/15	Hull KR (a)	L50-20	t:Tonga,Oldfield,Casty,Pelissier g:Dureau(2)	4th	6,723
20/3/15	Hull FC (a)	L33-22	t:Duport,Bosc,Escare,Taia g:Bosc(3)	6th	11,994
28/3/15	Leeds (h)	L22-38	t:Whitehead(2),Pelissier,Cardace g:Dureau(3)	10th	8,876
2/4/15	Wakefield (a)	W4-40	t:Garcia,Tonga,Pomeroy,Whitehead,Cardace(3) g:Dureau(6)	8th	3,015
6/4/15	Widnes (h)	W32-16	t:Tonga(2),Pelissier(2),Pala,Cardace g:Bosc(3),Dureau	6th	9,683
12/4/15	Wigan (a)	L34-0		8th	12,162
19/4/15	Huddersfield (a)	L38-14	t:Dureau,Bousquet g:Dureau(3)	10th	4,404
25/4/15	Hull KR (h)	W32-24	t:Baitieri,Springer,Oldfield,Pelissier,Garcia,Whitehead g:Bosc(4)	8th	7,938
3/5/15	Castleford (a)	L36-28	t:Yaha,Garcia(3),Taia g:Dureau(4)	8th	5,704
9/5/15	St Helens (h)	W33-26	t:Garcia(2),Taia(2),Escare g:Dureau(6) fg:Dureau	7th	8,884
17/5/15	Featherstone (h) (CCR6)	W37-34	t:Robin,Bousquet,Whitehead,Oldfield,Escare,Bosc g:Bosc(6) fg:Robin	N/A	1,353
23/5/15	Wigan (h)	W58-16	t:Yaha(2),Gigot(3),Taia(3),Oldfield,Escare g:Dureau(9)	6th	10,423
31/5/15	Huddersfield (MW) ●	D22-22	t:Pelissier,Carney(2),Taia g:Dureau(3)	7th	N/A
5/6/15	Warrington (a)	L26-18	t:Gigot,Pelissier,Whitehead g:Dureau(3)	8th	8,611
13/6/15	Hull FC (h)	W20-14	t:Bosc,Gigot,Mounis g:Dureau(4)	7th	7,956
20/6/15	Wakefield (h)	W32-12	t:Pomeroy,Inu,Pelissier,Escare,Anderson g:Dureau(6)	6th	7,834
25/6/15	Hull KR (a) (CCQF)	L32-26	t:Inu(2),Taia,Henderson,Whitehead g:Dureau(3)	N/A	6,073
5/7/15	Salford (a)	L18-14	t:Casty,Anderson g:Dureau(3)	7th	5,078
12/7/15	Widnes (a)	L29-22	t:Anderson,Whitehead(2),Escare g:Dureau(3)	7th	4,822
18/7/15	Huddersfield (h)	L12-14	t:Inu,Escare g:Dureau(2)	8th	8,761
26/7/15	Leeds (a)	L36-22	t:Gigot(2),Escare,Dureau g:Dureau(3)	8th	15,534
8/8/15	St Helens (h) (S8)	W26-16	t:Gigot,Anderson,Escare g:Dureau(6),Inu	7th	7,392
14/8/15	Huddersfield (a) (S8)	L24-12	t:Tonga,Carney g:Inu(2)	8th	4,251
22/8/15	Castleford (h) (S8)	W44-26	t:Gigot(3),Taia,Lima,Carney,Escare(2) g:Bosc(6)	7th	7,473
5/9/15	Wigan (a) (S8) ●●	L42-16	t:Inu,Dureau,Sigismeau g:Dureau(2)	7th	8,101
12/9/15	Leeds (h) (S8)	W46-16	t:Bosc(2),Inu(2),Carney,Sigismeau,Lima,Whitehead g:Bosc,Dureau(5),Lima	7th	8,851
19/9/15	Warrington (a) (S8)	L48-6	t:Robin g:Dureau	7th	7,862
27/9/15	Hull FC (a) (S8)	W24-28	t:Garcia,Henderson,Inu,Whitehead,Bosc g:Dureau(4)	7th	10,832

● Played at St James' Park, Newcastle
●● Played at The Den, Millwall

	D.O.B.	APP ALL	APP SL	TRIES ALL	TRIES SL	GOALS ALL	GOALS SL	FG ALL	FG SL	PTS ALL	PTS SL
Lucas Albert	4/7/98	2	2	0	0	0	0	0	0	0	0
Louis Anderson	27/6/85	15(12)	14(11)	4	4	0	0	0	0	16	16
Jason Baitieri	2/7/89	26(3)	25(3)	1	1	0	0	0	0	4	4
Thomas Bosc	5/8/83	20(1)	19(1)	6	5	24	18	1	1	73	57
Julian Bousquet	18/7/91	3(26)	2(25)	2	1	0	0	0	0	8	4
Damien Cardace	16/10/92	10(1)	10	5	5	0	0	0	0	20	20
Todd Carney	2/6/86	12	12	5	5	0	0	0	0	20	20
Remi Casty	5/2/85	20(1)	18(1)	2	2	0	0	0	0	8	8
Vincent Duport	15/12/87	6	6	3	3	0	0	0	0	12	12
Scott Dureau	29/7/86	27	26	3	3	97	94	2	2	208	202
Olivier Elima	19/5/83	16(8)	16(8)	0	0	0	0	0	0	0	0
Morgan Escare	18/10/91	29	27	12	11	0	0	0	0	48	44
Benjamin Garcia	5/4/93	6(19)	6(18)	8	8	0	0	0	0	32	32
Tony Gigot	27/12/90	18	16	11	11	0	0	0	0	44	44
Joan Guasch	5/7/93	(2)	(2)	0	0	0	0	0	0	0	0
Ian Henderson	23/4/83	28(1)	27(1)	3	2	0	0	0	0	12	8
Krisnan Inu	17/3/87	13	12	8	6	3	3	0	0	38	30
Jeff Lima	4/7/82	19(2)	18(2)	2	2	1	1	0	0	10	10
Thibaut Margalet	3/1/93	(3)	(3)	0	0	0	0	0	0	0	0
Antoni Maria	21/3/87	(8)	(7)	0	0	0	0	0	0	0	0
Gregory Mounis	18/1/85	5(13)	4(12)	1	1	0	0	0	0	4	4
Michael Oldfield	24/11/90	13	12	7	6	0	0	0	0	28	24
Mathias Pala	14/6/89	4	4	1	1	0	0	0	0	4	4
Eloi Pelissier	18/6/91	5(19)	4(18)	9	9	0	0	0	0	36	36
Ugo Perez	30/11/94	(2)	(2)	0	0	0	0	0	0	0	0
Ben Pomeroy	10/1/84	18	17	4	4	0	0	0	0	16	16
Stanislas Robin	21/10/90	7(1)	5(1)	2	1	0	0	1	0	9	4
Jordan Sigismeau	22/12/92	8	8	2	2	0	0	0	0	8	8
Gadwin Springer	4/4/93	(3)	(2)	1	1	0	0	0	0	4	4
Zeb Taia	11/10/84	24	23	13	12	0	0	0	0	52	48
Willie Tonga	8/7/83	19	18	6	6	0	0	0	0	24	24
Elliott Whitehead	4/9/89	32	30	13	11	0	0	0	0	52	44
Fouad Yaha	19/8/96	11	9	3	3	0	0	0	0	12	12

'SL' totals include Super 8s; 'All' totals also include Challenge Cup

Elliott Whitehead

LEAGUE RECORD
P30-W13-D2-L15
(7th, SL)
F739, A770, Diff-31
28 points.

CHALLENGE CUP
Quarter Finalists

ATTENDANCES
Best - v Wigan (SL - 10,423)
Worst - v Featherstone (CC - 1,353)
Total (SL/S8s only) - 120,884
Average (SL/S8s only) - 8,635
(Up by 323 on 2014)

24 November 2014 - Luke Robinson signs contract extension to end of 2017 season.

8 February 2015 - Jack Hughes, Craig Huby and Jamie Ellis make debuts in 19-0 opening-round home defeat to Hull FC.

14 February 2015 - 24-16 defeat at Wigan.

18 February 2015 - Eorl Crabtree escapes ban with EGP for dangerous contact in defeat at Wigan.

6 March 2015 - 24-12 home win over Widnes gets Giants off the mark.

11 March 2015 - Shaun Lunt joins Hull KR on loan for the rest of season.

12 March 2015 - 22-0 home win over Castleford.

3 April 2015 - 18-12 Easter Monday defeat at Salford ends four-match winning run.

8 April 2015 - Jordan Cox joins from Hull KR on one-month loan.

29 April 2015 - Eorl Crabtree signs two-year contract extension to end of 2017.

30 April 2015 - late Liam Sutcliffe penalty secures 24-all draw for Leeds at John Smith's Stadium.

22 May 2015 - prop Anthony Mullally to join Leeds Rhinos on three-year contract at end of season.

23 May 2015 - prop Sam Rapira signs for 2016 from New Zealand Warriors on two-year deal.

28 May 2015 - Brett Ferres rejects advances from NRL to sign contract extension to end of 2019.

31 May 2015 - last-minute Danny Brough touchline conversion earns 22-22 draw with Catalans at Magic Weekend in Newcastle.

3 June 2015 - 19-year-old hooker Kruise Leeming signs two-year contract extension to end of 2017.

5 June 2015 - head coach Paul Anderson signs contract extension to end of 2017.

7 June 2015 - Jared Simpson scores try on debut in 32-18 home defeat to Wigan.

14 June 2015 - Giants overcome 13-6 half-time deficit to mark captain Danny Brough's 400th career appearance with 30-19 home win over Warrington.

21 June 2015 - Brett Ferres returns from injury lay-off and is sent off 11 minutes into 30-22 win at Widnes. He gets two matches for punching Rhys Hanbury.

22 June 2015 - Melbourne Storm forward Ryan Hinchcliffe signs three-year deal from 2016.

KEY DATES - HUDDERSFIELD GIANTS

14 July 2015 - Wakefield prop Daniel Smith signs on four-and-a-half-year contract, with Ireland international Anthony Mullally going the other way on short-term loan.

18 July 2015 - Kyle Wood ruled out for the rest of season after breaking right foot during 14-12 win over Catalans in Perpignan.

23 July 2015 - prop Jacob Fairbank released and joins Halifax for the rest of season.

19 August 2015 - centre Leroy Cudjoe extends contract to end of 2020.

20 August 2015 - Giants overcome sin-binning of Michael Lawrence to leapfrog St Helens into third with a 28-22 win at Langtree Park.

27 August 2015 - hooker Shaun Lunt, on loan at Hull KR in 2015, signs permanent four-year deal at Robins from 2016.

3 September 2015 - Jermaine McGillvary double helps Giants to 40-26 home win over fifth-placed Castleford.

13 September 2015 - Jermaine McGillvary scores four tries in 48-10 home win over Warrington that secures a semi-final spot.

14 September 2015 - forward Ukuma Ta'ai agrees new contract for 2016.

16 September 2015 - Larne Patrick to return from season-loan at Wigan Warriors for 2016.

25 September 2015 - late penalty and last-second Ryan Hall try denies Giants a home play-off tie.

1 October 2015 - 32-8 semi-final exit at Wigan.

6 October 2015 - winger Jermaine McGillvary, top try scorer in 2015, extends contract by further four years to end of 2020 season.

CLUB RECORDS

Highest score:
142-4 v Blackpool G, 26/11/94
Highest score against:
12-94 v Castleford, 18/9/88
Record attendance:
32,912 v Wigan, 4/3/50 *(Fartown)*
15,629 v Leeds, 10/2/2008
(McAlpine/Galpharm/John Smith's Stadium)

MATCH RECORDS

Tries:
10 Lionel Cooper v Keighley, 17/11/51
Goals: 18 Major Holland
v Swinton Park, 28/2/1914
Points: 39 Major Holland
v Swinton Park, 28/2/1914

SEASON RECORDS

Tries: 80 Albert Rosenfeld 1913-14
Goals: 156 *(inc 2fg)* Danny Brough 2013
Points: 346 Danny Brough 2013

CAREER RECORDS

Tries: 420 Lionel Cooper 1947-55
Goals: 958 Frank Dyson 1949-63
Points: 2,072 Frank Dyson 1949-63
Appearances: 485 Douglas Clark 1909-29

HUDDERSFIELD GIANTS

DATE	FIXTURE	RESULT	SCORERS	LGE	ATT
8/2/15	Hull FC (h)	L0-19		12th	7,737
13/2/15	Wigan (a)	L24-16	t:Mullally,Ellis,Murphy g:Brough(2)	10th	12,488
26/2/15	Leeds (a)	L28-24	t:Ellis,Wardle,Wood,Ferres g:Brough(4)	12th	12,878
6/3/15	Widnes (h)	W24-12	t:Grix,McGillvary,Wardle(2),Crabtree g:Brough(2)	11th	5,452
12/3/15	Castleford (h)	W22-0	t:Ellis,Ta'ai,Murphy,McGillvary g:Brough(3)	7th	5,257
22/3/15	Wakefield (a)	W14-44	t:Grix(3),Ferres,Brough,Cudjoe,Ta'ai g:Brough(6),Ellis(2)	4th	4,354
27/3/15	Warrington (a)	W10-29	t:Ellis,Murphy(2),McGillvary,Crabtree g:Brough(4) fg:Brough	3rd	9,019
3/4/15	Salford (h)	L12-18	t:Hughes,Murphy g:Brough(2)	5th	6,003
6/4/15	Hull KR (a)	L20-16	t:Wardle,Ta'ai,Murphy g:Brough(2)	7th	7,827
12/4/15	St Helens (h)	L8-11	t:Cudjoe g:Brough(2)	9th	5,825
19/4/15	Catalans Dragons (h)	W38-14	t:Murphy(2),Ta'ai(2),Cudjoe,McGillvary,Grix g:Brough(5)	5th	4,404
24/4/15	Hull FC (a)	W4-24	t:Brough,Ta'ai,Ellis,Lawrence,McGillvary g:Brough(2)	4th	9,930
30/4/15	Leeds (h)	D24-24	t:Wardle(2),Lawrence,McGillvary g:Brough(4)	6th	6,381
8/5/15	Salford (a)	W0-19	t:Cudjoe,Ellis,Wood g:Brough(3) fg:Brough	4th	1,972
16/5/15	Leeds (a) (CCR6)	L48-16	t:Wood,Ferres,Grix g:Brough(2)	N/A	8,133
21/5/15	Castleford (a)	W16-24	t:Huby,Murphy,Ta'ai,Crabtree g:Brough(4)	4th	4,632
31/5/15	Catalans Dragons (MW) ●	D22-22	t:Broughton(2),McGillvary g:Brough(5)	4th	N/A
7/6/15	Wigan (h)	L18-32	t:Simpson,Wardle,Brough g:Brough(3)	4th	7,307
14/6/15	Warrington (h)	W30-19	t:Connor,Broughton,McGillvary(2),Simpson g:Brough(3),Ellis fg:Ellis(2)	4th	5,797
21/6/15	Widnes (a)	W22-30	t:Ta'ai,Kopczak,Hughes,Robinson,Broughton g:Brough(4),Ellis	4th	5,420
5/7/15	Hull KR (h)	W32-14	t:Lawrence,Murphy,Cudjoe,Brough,McGillvary,Ta'ai g:Brough(3),Ellis	4th	5,596
10/7/15	St Helens (a)	L35-34	t:Hughes,McGillvary(2),Cudjoe,Crabtree,Murphy g:Ellis(5)	4th	11,164
18/7/15	Catalans Dragons (a)	W12-14	t:McGillvary(2) g:Ellis(3)	4th	8,761
26/7/15	Wakefield (h)	W34-24	t:Robinson,Broughton,Lawrence,Smith,Cudjoe,Brough g:Brough(5)	4th	4,839
6/8/15	Wigan (a) (S8)	L30-22	t:McGillvary(2),Hughes,Crabtree g:Brough(3)	4th	11,448
14/8/15	Catalans Dragons (h) (S8)	W24-12	t:Hughes,Murphy,McGillvary(2) g:Brough(4)	4th	4,251
20/8/15	St Helens (a) (S8)	W22-28	t:Ellis,Ta'ai,Wardle,McGillvary,Murphy g:Brough(4)	3rd	10,976
3/9/15	Castleford (h) (S8)	W40-26	t:Ta'ai,McGillvary(2),Connor,Murphy,Wardle,Ellis,Crabtree g:Brough(2),Ellis(2)	3rd	5,350
13/9/15	Warrington (h) (S8)	W48-10	t:Murphy(3),McGillvary(4),Wardle,Ellis g:Brough(3),Ellis(3)	3rd	5,563
18/9/15	Hull FC (a) (S8)	W20-34	t:Murphy,Connor(2),Grix,McGillvary,Ellis g:Brough(5)	3rd	9,332
25/9/15	Leeds (h) (S8)	L16-20	t:McGillvary,Ellis g:Brough(4)	3rd	9,376
1/10/15	Wigan (a) (SF)	L32-8	t:Ferres g:Brough(2)	N/A	10,035

● Played at St James' Park, Newcastle

		APP		TRIES		GOALS		FG		PTS	
	D.O.B.	ALL	SL	ALL	SL	ALL	SL	ALL	SL	ALL	SL
Chris Bailey	5/7/82	4(5)	4(5)	0	0	0	0	0	0	0	0
Danny Brough	15/1/83	32	31	5	5	97	95	2	2	216	212
Jodie Broughton	9/1/88	10	10	5	5	0	0	0	0	20	20
Jake Connor	18/10/94	17	17	4	4	0	0	0	0	16	16
Jordan Cox	27/5/92	(2)	(2)	0	0	0	0	0	0	0	0
Eorl Crabtree	2/10/82	16(14)	15(14)	6	6	0	0	0	0	24	24
Leroy Cudjoe	7/4/88	27	26	7	7	0	0	0	0	28	28
Jamie Ellis	4/10/89	26(3)	26(2)	11	11	18	18	2	2	82	82
Jacob Fairbank	4/3/90	2	2	0	0	0	0	0	0	0	0
Brett Ferres	17/4/86	15	14	4	3	0	0	0	0	16	12
Scott Grix	1/5/84	24	23	7	6	0	0	0	0	28	24
Craig Huby	21/5/86	30(2)	29(2)	1	1	0	0	0	0	4	4
Jack Hughes	4/1/92	31(1)	30(1)	5	5	0	0	0	0	20	20
Josh Johnson	25/7/94	1(4)	1(4)	0	0	0	0	0	0	0	0
Craig Kopczak	20/12/86	9(23)	9(22)	1	1	0	0	0	0	4	4
Michael Lawrence	12/4/90	7(19)	7(18)	4	4	0	0	0	0	16	16
Kruise Leeming	7/9/95	3(12)	3(12)	0	0	0	0	0	0	0	0
Shaun Lunt	15/4/86	3(1)	3(1)	0	0	0	0	0	0	0	0
Nathan Mason	8/9/93	(2)	(2)	0	0	0	0	0	0	0	0
Jermaine McGillvary	16/5/88	32	31	27	27	0	0	0	0	108	108
Anthony Mullally	28/6/91	8(8)	8(7)	1	1	0	0	0	0	4	4
Aaron Murphy	26/11/88	29	28	18	18	0	0	0	0	72	72
Luke Robinson	25/7/84	23(4)	22(4)	2	2	0	0	0	0	8	8
Jared Simpson	4/1/96	5	5	2	2	0	0	0	0	8	8
Daniel Smith	20/3/93	1(8)	1(8)	1	1	0	0	0	0	4	4
Ukuma Ta'ai	17/1/87	22(10)	21(10)	11	11	0	0	0	0	44	44
Joe Wardle	22/9/91	30	29	10	10	0	0	0	0	40	40
Kyle Wood	18/6/89	9(10)	8(10)	3	2	0	0	0	0	12	8

'SL' totals include Super 8s & semi-final; 'All' totals also include Challenge Cup

Jermaine McGillvary

LEAGUE RECORD
P30-W18-D2-L10
(3rd, SL/Semi-Finalists)
F750, A534, Diff+216
38 points.

CHALLENGE CUP
Round Six

ATTENDANCES
Best - v Leeds (S8 - 9,376)
Worst - v Catalans Dragons (S8 - 4,251)
Total (SL/S8s only) - 89,138
Average (SL/S8s only) - 5,942
(Down by 441 on 2014)

5 January 2015 - Stuart Howarth joins on one-year deal.

8 February 2015 - Gareth Ellis makes 250th Super League appearance and Jamie Shaul scores two tries in impressive 19-0 opening-round victory at Huddersfield Giants.

11 February 2015 - Jordan Thompson signs two-year contract extension to end of 2017 season.

13 February 2015 - 7-6 home defeat by Warrington.

11 March 2015 - Mickey Paea handed one-match ban for raising knees in tackle on Jamie Jones-Buchanan during 43-12 home defeat by Leeds, after leading 12-0 at half-time.

26 March 2015 - Fetuli Talanoa signs contract extension to end of 2017 season

2 April 2015 - Easter Thursday 20-6 home defeat to Hull KR leaves FC second from bottom after eight rounds.

24 April 2015 - Mickey Paea banned for two matches for two offences of raising knees in tackle during 24-4 home defeat to Huddersfield.

27 April 2015 - Hull FC reject injury and suspension-hit Salford Red Devils' request to postpone following Friday's match at KC Stadium.

1 May 2015 - late Setaimata Sa try secures 24-20 comeback win over Salford at KC Stadium.

12 May 2015 - Hull FC owner Adam Pearson maintains commitment to club in wake of appointment as executive director at soccer club Leeds United.

19 May 2015 - Mickey Paea to return to Australia with NRL at season end after rejecting offer of new contract.

19 May 2015 - Wigan prop Scott Taylor, currently on loan at Salford, to join on four-year contract at end of season.

30 May 2015 - Fetuli Talanoa scores Newcastle Magic Weekend hat-trick in 46-20 win over Hull KR.

KEY DATES - HULL F.C.

9 June 2015 - leading try-scorer Tom Lineham, with two years left on current contract, to join Warrington from 2016 after the clubs agree £140,000 transfer fee.

10 June 2015 - club take up option to extend contract of Curtis Naughton for 2016, as well as offering him new longer-term deal, which he turns down.

19 June 2015 - former New Zealand Test forward Frank Pritchard signs for 2016 from Canterbury Bulldogs on two-year deal.

21 June 2015 - Marc Sneyd banned for two matches for making dangerous contact with Danny McGuire in 71st minute of 32-20 defeat at Leeds.

2 July 2015 - hooker James Cunningham released and joins London Broncos.

7 July 2015 - Mickey Paea banned for two matches for dangerous throw on Danny Washbrook in shock 26-16 defeat at Wakefield on 1 July.

17 July 2015 - Leon Pryce's 500th career appearance lasts ten minutes due to shoulder injury, and Gareth Ellis snaps Achilles tendon before half-time in 22-12 victory at Hull KR.

25 July 2015 - Newcastle Knights Samoa international Carlos Tuimavave signs three-year deal from 2016.

31 July 2015 - Australian winger or centre Steve Michaels signs new one-year contract for 2016. Jordan Rankin and Setaimata Sa to be released at end of season.

1 August 2015 - Tonga winger Mahe Fonua joins from Melbourne Storm on three-year deal from 2016.

13 August 2015 - Penrith forward Sika Manu signs three-year deal from 2016. Danny Washbrook to return from Wakefield on two-year contract.

14 August 2015 - Curtis Naughton scores hat-trick as 32-22 win at St Helens keeps outside chances of play-offs alive.

21 August 2015 - Jack Downs makes debut in 36-22 home defeat by Leeds that ends semi-final hopes.

3 September 2015 - prop Iafeta Palea'aesina signs new 12-month contract for 2016.

17 September 2015 - Hull FC owner Adam Pearson quits role at Leeds United to devote full attention to Airlie Birds.

18 September 2015 - centres Kirk Yeaman, 12 months, and Jack Logan, to end of 2019, sign new contracts.

CLUB RECORDS

Highest score: 88-0 v Sheffield, 2/3/2003
Highest score against:
18-76 v Huddersfield, 19/9/2013
Record attendance:
28,798 v Leeds, 7/3/36 *(The Boulevard)*
23,004 v Hull KR, 2/9/2007 *(KC Stadium)*

MATCH RECORDS

Tries: 7 Clive Sullivan v Doncaster, 15/4/68
Goals: 14 Jim Kennedy v Rochdale, 7/4/21
Sammy Lloyd v Oldham, 10/9/78
Matt Crowther v Sheffield, 2/3/2003
Points: 36 Jim Kennedy v Keighley, 29/1/21

SEASON RECORDS

Tries: 52 Jack Harrison 1914-15
Goals: 170 Sammy Lloyd 1978-79
Points: 369 Sammy Lloyd 1978-79

CAREER RECORDS

Tries: 250 Clive Sullivan 1961-74; 1981-85
Goals: 687 Joe Oliver 1928-37; 1943-45
Points: 1,842 Joe Oliver 1928-37; 1943-45
Appearances: 500 Edward Rogers 1906-25

HULL F.C.

DATE	FIXTURE	RESULT	SCORERS	LGE	ATT
8/2/15	Huddersfield (a)	W0-19	t:Talanoa,Shaul(2) g:Sneyd(3) fg:Sneyd	1st	7,737
13/2/15	Warrington (h)	L6-7	t:Lineham g:Sneyd	6th	12,002
28/2/15	Salford (a)	L32-28	t:Rankin,Thompson(2),Sa,Lineham g:Sneyd(4)	8th	3,606
5/3/15	Leeds (h)	L12-43	t:Pryce(2) g:Sneyd(2)	10th	10,887
13/3/15	Wigan (a)	L13-12	t:Talanoa,Lancaster g:Sneyd(2)	12th	11,718
20/3/15	Catalans Dragons (h)	W33-22	t:Sneyd,Rankin,Michaels,Talanoa,Lineham(2) g:Sneyd(4) fg:Sneyd	10th	11,994
27/3/15	Castleford (a)	L20-14	t:Lineham(3) g:Sneyd	11th	8,744
2/4/15	Hull KR (h)	L6-20	t:Pryce g:Rankin	11th	20,507
6/4/15	St Helens (a)	W20-28	t:Shaul(2),Naughton,Pryce,Talanoa g:Rankin(4)	11th	11,088
10/4/15	Widnes (h)	W22-8	t:Lineham(3),Shaul g:Rankin(3)	10th	9,295
19/4/15	Sheffield (a) (CCR5) ●	W12-34	t:Minichiello,Paea,Lineham,Shaul,Yeaman,Rankin g:Rankin(5)	N/A	1,620
24/4/15	Huddersfield (h)	L4-24	t:Michaels	11th	9,930
1/5/15	Salford (h)	W24-20	t:Lineham,Talanoa,Minichiello,Sa g:Sneyd(4)	9th	9,385
10/5/15	Warrington (a)	W26-27	t:Thompson,Sa,Sneyd,Minichiello,Lineham g:Sneyd(3) fg:Sneyd	8th	9,697
16/5/15	Castleford (h) (CCR6)	W40-14	t:Naughton(3),Paea,Rankin(2),Yeaman g:Sneyd(6)	N/A	6,715
22/5/15	St Helens (h)	L10-17	t:Pryce,Abdull g:Sneyd	9th	10,320
30/5/15	Hull KR (MW) ●●	W46-20	t:Yeaman(2),Talanoa(3),Ellis,Minichiello,Rankin g:Sneyd(7)	9th	N/A
4/6/15	Widnes (a)	W12-25	t:Lineham(3),Pryce,Sneyd g:Sneyd(2) fg:Sneyd	7th	5,573
13/6/15	Catalans Dragons (a)	L20-14	t:Rankin,Minichiello g:Sneyd(3)	8th	7,956
21/6/15	Leeds (a)	L32-20	t:Thompson,Naughton,Houghton,Talanoa g:Sneyd(2)	8th	16,203
26/6/15	Leeds (h) (CCQF)	L6-24	t:Abdull g:Rankin	N/A	9,261
1/7/15	Wakefield (a)	L26-16	t:Yeaman,Watts,Rankin g:Rankin(2)	9th	3,543
5/7/15	Wakefield (h)	W31-24	t:Westerman,Logan(2),Michaels(2),Rankin g:Sneyd(3) fg:Sneyd	8th	9,558
12/7/15	Castleford (h)	W21-18	t:Whiting,Abdull,Lineham(2) g:Sneyd(2) fg:Sneyd	8th	10,949
17/7/15	Hull KR (a)	W12-22	t:Michaels(2),Lineham(2) g:Sneyd(3)	7th	11,350
23/7/15	Wigan (h)	L12-48	t:Whiting,Westerman g:Sneyd(2)	7th	10,787
7/8/15	Castleford (a) (S8)	L36-30	t:Whiting,Rankin,Michaels,Lineham,Logan g:Sneyd(5)	8th	6,760
14/8/15	St Helens (a) (S8)	W22-32	t:Naughton(3),Lineham,Westerman,Shaul g:Sneyd(4)	7th	10,203
21/8/15	Leeds (h) (S8)	L22-36	t:Minichiello,Michaels,Shaul,Rankin g:Sneyd(3)	8th	10,649
6/9/15	Warrington (a) (S8)	L46-16	t:Hadley,Minichiello(2) g:Sneyd(2)	8th	8,076
11/9/15	Wigan (a) (S8)	L30-24	t:Shaul,Logan(2),Rankin g:Sneyd(4)	8th	12,028
18/9/15	Huddersfield (h) (S8)	L20-34	t:Rankin(2),Bowden,Yeaman g:Sneyd(2)	8th	9,332
27/9/15	Catalans Dragons (h) (S8)	L24-28	t:Lineham(4),Abdull,Naughton	8th	10,832

● Played at Bramall Lane ●● Played at St James' Park, Newcastle

	D.O.B.	APP ALL	APP SL	TRIES ALL	TRIES SL	GOALS ALL	GOALS SL	FG ALL	FG SL	PTS ALL	PTS SL
Jordan Abdull	5/2/96	10(10)	9(9)	4	3	0	0	0	0	16	12
Josh Bowden	14/1/92	7(12)	7(11)	1	1	0	0	0	0	4	4
James Cunningham	3/4/94	(6)	(6)	0	0	0	0	0	0	0	0
Jack Downs	10/11/95	2(3)	2(3)	0	0	0	0	0	0	0	0
Gareth Ellis	3/5/81	15	13	1	1	0	0	0	0	4	4
Brad Fash	24/1/96	(7)	(7)	0	0	0	0	0	0	0	0
Chris Green	3/1/90	(19)	(18)	0	0	0	0	0	0	0	0
Dean Hadley	5/8/92	12(3)	12(3)	1	1	0	0	0	0	4	4
Danny Houghton	25/9/88	32(1)	29(1)	1	1	0	0	0	0	4	4
Stuart Howarth	25/1/90	2(4)	2(3)	0	0	0	0	0	0	0	0
Callum Lancaster	13/10/96	1	1	1	1	0	0	0	0	4	4
Tom Lineham	21/9/91	24	22	26	25	0	0	0	0	104	100
Jack Logan	8/9/95	12	12	5	5	0	0	0	0	20	20
Masi Matongo	15/5/96	(1)	(1)	0	0	0	0	0	0	0	0
Steve Michaels	13/1/87	26	23	8	8	0	0	0	0	32	32
Mark Minichiello	30/1/82	30	27	8	7	0	0	0	0	32	28
Curtis Naughton	25/2/95	13	11	9	6	0	0	0	0	36	24
Mickey Paea	25/3/86	28	25	2	0	0	0	0	0	8	0
Iafeta Palea'aesina	10/2/82	(22)	(20)	0	0	0	0	0	0	0	0
Leon Pryce	9/10/81	25	22	6	6	0	0	0	0	24	24
Jordan Rankin	17/12/91	25(3)	22(3)	14	11	16	10	0	0	88	64
Setaimata Sa	14/9/87	16	14	3	3	0	0	0	0	12	12
Jamie Shaul	1/7/92	15	14	9	8	0	0	0	0	36	32
Marc Sneyd	9/2/91	27	26	3	3	75	69	6	6	168	156
Fetuli Talanoa	23/11/87	26	23	9	9	0	0	0	0	36	36
Jordan Thompson	4/9/91	6(20)	5(18)	4	4	0	0	0	0	16	16
Jansin Turgut	8/3/96	(4)	(4)	0	0	0	0	0	0	0	0
Bobby Tyson-Wilson	6/11/94	(2)	(1)	0	0	0	0	0	0	0	0
Liam Watts	8/7/90	28(2)	25(2)	1	1	0	0	0	0	4	4
Joe Westerman	15/11/89	23	22	3	3	0	0	0	0	12	12
Richard Whiting	20/12/84	6(11)	6(9)	3	3	0	0	0	0	12	12
Kirk Yeaman	15/9/83	18(2)	16(1)	6	4	0	0	0	0	24	16

'SL' totals include Super 8s; 'All' totals also include Challenge Cup

Tom Lineham

LEAGUE RECORD
P30-W12-D0-L18
(8th, SL)
F620, A716, Diff-96
24 points.

CHALLENGE CUP
Quarter Finalists

ATTENDANCES
Best - v Hull KR (SL - 20,507)
Worst - v Castleford (CC - 6,715)
Total (SL/S8s only) - 156,427
Average (SL/S8s only) - 11,173
(Up by 108 on 2014)

KEY DATES - HULL KINGSTON ROVERS

21 November 2014 - Mitchell Allgood signs from Parramatta Eels on three-year deal.

5 December 2014 - Terry Campese signs for 2015 season from Canberra Raiders.

8 February 2015 - opening round 40-30 defeat by Leeds after leading 24-16 at half-time. Record stadium crowd sees debutant Albert Kelly score two tries.

11 March 2015 - Michael Weyman announces retirement with immediate effect at the age of 30 after failing to recover from knee injury.

11 March 2015 - Shaun Lunt joins from Huddersfield Giants on loan for rest of season.

17 March 2015 - hooker Keal Carlile released.

17 March 2015 - Mitch Allgood gets two matches for striking Scott Dureau in 23rd minute of 50-20 home win over Catalans.

27 March 2015 - former Leeds Rhinos prop Ryan Bailey released with immediate effect due to personal reasons.

27 March 2015 - Jamie Peacock MBE to take up new role as Football Manager from 2016.

31 March 2015 - James Green gets one-match suspension for shoulder charge on Travis Burns in 24-22 home win over St Helens.

31 March 2015 - captain Terry Campese, currently on one-year deal, signs new contract to end of 2017 with option for extra year.

2 April 2015 - Kieran Dixon stars in Easter Thursday 20-6 win at Hull FC.

8 April 2015 - Jordan Cox goes to Huddersfield Giants on one-month loan.

1 April 2015 - Canberra Raiders prop forward Dane Tilse signed as replacement for Mick Weyman on two-and-a-half year deal.

25 April 2015 - Dane Tilse, yet to visit Hull, makes debut in 32-24 defeat at Catalans.

20 May 2015 - Wigan Warriors prop James Greenwood signs on loan until end of season.

26 May 2015 - prop Tony Puletua joins on loan from Salford to end of season.

30 May 2015 - 46-20 defeat by Hull FC in second game of Magic Weekend in Newcastle.

1 June 2015 - Darrell Goulding retires at age 27 on medical advice after suffering series of concussion injuries.

2 June 2015 - Albert Kelly and Maurice Blair discard release clauses in contracts to remain at Rovers in 2016.

5 June 2015 - Terry Campese plays last game of season after suffering knee injury in 22-30 home defeat by Castleford.

14 June 2015 - Ken Sio scores hat-trick in 38-16 home win over Widnes.

3 July 2015 - Jordan Cox joins Halifax on dual registration.

3 July 2015 - Leeds Rhinos centre Thomas Minns, on loan at Featherstone, signs three-year contract from 2016.

10 July 2015 - Omari Caro joins Bradford.

15 July 2015 - former France international halfback Dane Chisholm signs from NRL club Canterbury Bulldogs on loan to end of season.

17 July 2015 - 22-12 round 22 home defeat to Hull FC consigns Rovers to Middle Eights.

1 August 2015 - 26-18 Challenge Cup semi-final win over Warrington at Headingley.

5 August 2015 - centre Iain Thornley signs from Wigan on two-year deal.

21 August 2015 - Ben Cockayne signs contract extension for 2016, with further 12-month option.

27 August 2015 - hooker Shaun Lunt, on loan from Huddersfield, signs four-year deal from 2016.

29 August 2015 - record 50-0 Challenge Cup final defeat to Leeds.

6 September 2015 - Super League survival almost ensured with 20-18 home comeback win over Wakefield.

7 September 2015 - captain Tyrone McCarthy to return to Australia at season end on two-year contract with St George Illawarra Dragons.

12 September 2015 - 48-4 home win over Bradford guarantees Super League rugby in 2016.

17 September 2015 - centre Kris Welham to leave at end of season after not being offered new contract.

25 September 2015 - utility Graeme Horne signs new 12-month contract with option for further season

25 September 2015 - Kevin Larroyer, on loan from Catalans for last two seasons, signs new permanent three-year contract.

27 September 2015 - 46-22 home win over Salford means unbeaten record in Middle Eights.

3 October 2015 - Leeds back-row forward Chris Clarkson, on loan at Widnes in 2015, signs three-year deal from 2016.

7 October 2015 - back-rower Sonny Esslemont and fullback Josh Guzdek leave for Keighley and Dewsbury respectively.

14 October 2015 - Wigan prop James Greenwood, on loan in 2015, signs permanent two-year contract.

16 October 2015 - Bradford Bulls outside back Ryan Shaw joins on two-year contract.

CLUB RECORDS

Highest score:
100-6 v Nottingham City, 19/8/90
Highest score against:
6-84 v Wigan, 1/4/2013
Record attendance:
27,670 v Hull FC, 3/4/53 *(Boothferry Park)*
11,811 v Leeds, 8/2/2015 *(Craven Park)*

MATCH RECORDS

Tries: 11 George West
v Brooklands Rovers, 4/3/1905
Goals:
14 Alf Carmichael v Merthyr, 8/10/1910
Mike Fletcher v Whitehaven, 18/3/90
Colin Armstrong v Nottingham City, 19/8/90
Damien Couturier v Halifax, 23/4/2006
Points: 53 George West
v Brooklands Rovers, 4/3/1905

SEASON RECORDS

Tries: 45 Gary Prohm 1984-85
Goals: 199 Mike Fletcher 1989-90
Points: 450 Mike Fletcher 1989-90

CAREER RECORDS

Tries: 207 Roger Millward 1966-80
Goals: 1,268 Mike Fletcher 1987-98
Points: 2,760 Mike Fletcher 1987-98
Appearances: 489 Mike Smith 1975-91

HULL KINGSTON ROVERS

DATE	FIXTURE	RESULT	SCORERS	LGE	ATT
8/2/15	Leeds (h)	L30-40	t:Kelly(2),Allgood,Campese,Welham g:Mantellato(5)	9th	11,811
15/2/15	Wakefield (a)	L44-24	t:Kelly,McCarthy,Sio,Bailey g:Mantellato(4)	11th	5,320
1/3/15	Wigan (h)	W22-20	t:Sio(2),Allgood,Dixon g:Mantellato(3)	9th	7,632
8/3/15	Warrington (a)	L32-24	t:Mantellato(2),Larroyer,Horne g:Mantellato(4)	12th	9,587
15/3/15	Catalans Dragons (h)	W50-20	t:Sio(3),Cockayne(2),Kelly,Lunt(2),Salter g:Mantellato(7)	8th	6,723
22/3/15	Widnes (a)	L20-16	t:Cockayne,Sio,Welham g:Mantellato(2)	11th	5,273
27/3/15	St Helens (h)	W24-22	t:Kelly(2),Sio,Dixon g:Mantellato(4)	8th	7,311
2/4/15	Hull FC (a)	W6-20	t:Campese,Dixon,Lunt g:Mantellato(4)	6th	20,507
6/4/15	Huddersfield (h)	W20-16	t:Goulding,Horne,Kelly,Mantellato g:Mantellato(2)	4th	7,827
11/4/15	Castleford (a)	L25-4	t:Sio	7th	6,102
19/4/15	Bradford (a) (CCR5)	W30-50	t:Mantellato(4),Welham,Kelly,Horne,Larroyer,Boudebza g:Mantellato(7)	N/A	4,538
25/4/15	Catalans Dragons (a)	L32-24	t:Blair,Cockayne,Dixon,Mantellato g:Mantellato(4)	9th	7,938
1/5/15	Wigan (a)	L60-0		10th	11,468
7/5/15	Wakefield (h)	W54-6	t:Welham,Mantellato(2),Kelly,Horne,Dixon(2),Sio,Boudebza,McCarthy g:Mantellato(7)	9th	7,378
15/5/15	Wigan (a) (CCR6) ●	W12-16	t:Blair,Sio g:Mantellato(4)	N/A	4,677
22/5/15	Leeds (a)	L36-16	t:Dixon(2),Cockayne,Mantellato	10th	15,206
30/5/15	Hull FC (MW) ●●	L46-20	t:Mantellato(2),Dixon(2) g:Mantellato(2)	10th	N/A
5/6/15	Castleford (h)	L22-30	t:Kelly(2),Dixon,Ollett g:Dixon(3)	10th	7,093
14/6/15	Widnes (h)	W38-16	t:Welham,Mantellato(2),Kelly,Sio(3) g:Mantellato(3),Kelly(2)	10th	6,982
19/6/15	Warrington (h)	W36-10	t:Sio,Mantellato,Dixon,Salter,McCarthy,Welham g:Mantellato(6)	9th	7,455
25/6/15	Catalans Dragons (h) (CCQF)	W32-26	t:Sio(2),Dixon,Kelly,Horne g:Mantellato(6)	N/A	6,073
30/6/15	Salford (h)	W34-28	t:Cockayne,Dixon,Tilse,Welham,Blair,Kelly g:Mantellato(5)	8th	6,717
5/7/15	Huddersfield (a)	L32-14	t:Welham,Kelly,Mantellato g:Mantellato	9th	5,596
12/7/15	Salford (a)	L31-18	t:McCarthy,Kelly(2) g:Mantellato(3)	9th	4,415
17/7/15	Hull FC (h)	L12-22	t:Lunt,Mantellato g:Mantellato(2)	9th	11,350
24/7/15	St Helens (a)	L52-12	t:Dixon,Boudebza g:Mantellato(2)	10th	10,781
1/8/15	Warrington (CCSF) ●●●	W26-18	t:Mantellato,Sio,Larroyer,Lunt g:Mantellato(5)	N/A	13,049
8/8/15	Leigh (a) (S8-Q)	W26-36	t:Chisholm,Dixon,Blair,Puletua,Lunt,Cockayne g:Mantellato(6)	3rd(S8-Q)	4,459
16/8/15	Halifax (h) (S8-Q)	W34-12	t:Mantellato(3),McCarthy,Sio,Welham g:Mantellato(5)	3rd(S8-Q)	6,837
23/8/15	Widnes (a) (S8-Q)	W8-12	t:Welham,Lawler g:Mantellato(2)	1st(S8-Q)	5,461
29/8/15	Leeds (CCF) ●●●●	L0-50		N/A	80,140
6/9/15	Wakefield (h) (S8-Q)	W20-18	t:Mantellato,Dixon(2),Lunt g:Dixon,Mantellato	1st(S8-Q)	7,495
12/9/15	Bradford (h) (S8-Q)	W48-4	t:Mantellato(2),Dixon(4),Chisholm,Sio,Welham,Horne g:Mantellato(3),Dixon	1st(S8-Q)	6,605
18/9/15	Sheffield (a) (S8-Q) ●●●●●	W28-38	t:Sio(3),Blair,Walker,Welham,Marsh g:Dixon(5)	1st(S8-Q)	2,017
27/9/15	Salford (h) (S8-Q)	W46-22	t:Welham,Lawler,Mantellato,Sio,Chisholm,McCarthy,Cockayne,Blair g:Mantellato(6),Welham	1st(S8-Q)	7,543

● Played at Leigh Sports Village ●● Played at St James' Park, Newcastle
●●● Played at Headingley Carnegie, Leeds ●●●● Played at Wembley Stadium ●●●●● Played at Bramall Lane

		APP		TRIES		GOALS		FG		PTS	
	D.O.B.	ALL	SL	ALL	SL	ALL	SL	ALL	SL	ALL	SL
Mitchell Allgood	27/4/89	11(2)	8	2	2	0	0	0	0	8	8
Ryan Bailey	11/11/83	(1)	(1)	1	1	0	0	0	0	4	4
Maurice Blair	16/10/84	30(2)	19(2)	6	2	0	0	0	0	24	8
John Boudebza	13/6/90	16(11)	12(6)	3	2	0	0	0	0	12	8
Greg Burke	12/2/93	13(8)	9(5)	0	0	0	0	0	0	0	0
Terry Campese	4/8/84	17	15	2	2	0	0	0	0	8	8
Keal Carlile	20/3/90	2	2	0	0	0	0	0	0	0	0
Dane Chisholm	4/7/90	7	1	3	0	0	0	0	0	12	0
Ben Cockayne	20/7/83	22(6)	17(4)	8	6	0	0	0	0	32	24
Jordan Cox	27/5/92	1(8)	1(6)	0	0	0	0	0	0	0	0
Kieran Dixon	22/8/92	26(2)	15(2)	22	14	10	3	0	0	108	62
James Donaldson	14/9/91	4(23)	3(13)	0	0	0	0	0	0	0	0
Sonny Esslemont	29/12/93	(5)	(4)	0	0	0	0	0	0	0	0
Darrell Goulding	3/3/88	8	8	1	1	0	0	0	0	4	4
James Green	29/11/90	6(21)	5(15)	0	0	0	0	0	0	0	0
James Greenwood	17/6/91	(13)	(8)	0	0	0	0	0	0	0	0
Josh Guzdek	22/4/95	1	1	0	0	0	0	0	0	0	0
Stephen Holker	22/11/95	(1)	(1)	0	0	0	0	0	0	0	0
Graeme Horne	22/3/85	25(4)	15(4)	6	3	0	0	0	0	24	12
Albert Kelly	21/3/91	24	20	17	15	2	2	0	0	72	64
Kevin Larroyer	19/6/89	22(5)	13(5)	3	1	0	0	0	0	12	4
George Lawler	1/9/95	1(2)	0	2	0	0	0	0	0	8	0
Shaun Lunt	15/4/86	17(3)	9(2)	7	4	0	0	0	0	28	16
Josh Mantellato	21/4/87	32	21	26	14	115	70	0	0	334	196
Matthew Marsh	21/4/95	4(1)	(1)	1	0	0	0	0	0	4	0
Tyrone McCarthy	21/4/88	30(1)	20(1)	6	4	0	0	0	0	24	16
Aaron Ollett	19/11/92	5(11)	3(8)	1	1	0	0	0	0	4	4
Tony Puletua	25/6/79	14	7	1	0	0	0	0	0	4	0
Connor Robinson	23/10/94	(1)	(1)	0	0	0	0	0	0	0	0
Liam Salter	14/6/93	20	13	2	2	0	0	0	0	8	8
Ken Sio	29/10/90	31	20	24	14	0	0	0	0	96	56
Dane Tilse	24/1/85	10(6)	6(1)	1	1	0	0	0	0	4	4
Adam Walker	20/2/91	25(3)	17(2)	1	0	0	0	0	0	4	0
Kris Welham	12/5/87	31	19	13	7	1	0	0	0	54	28

'SL' totals include regular season only; 'All' totals also include Super 8s (Qualifiers) & Challenge Cup

Josh Mantellato

LEAGUE RECORD
SL: P23-W9-D0-L14 (10th)
F534, A646, Diff-112, 18 points.

S8-Q: P7-W7-D0-L0 (1st)
F234, A118, Diff+116, 14 points.

CHALLENGE CUP
Runners-Up

ATTENDANCES
Best - v Leeds (SL - 11,811)
Worst - v Catalans Dragons (CC - 6,073)
Total (SL/S8s only) - 116,759
Average (SL/S8s only) - 7,784
(Down by 62 on 2014)

KEY DATES - LEEDS RHINOS

29 October 2014 - Kallum Watkins agrees new five-year contract to end of 2019.

14 November 2014 - Brad Singleton signs new four-year contract.

20 November 2014 - Liam Sutcliffe signs new three-year contract.

23 November 2014 - Alex Foster, Thomas Minns, Mason Tonks and Jordan Baldwinson go on loan to Featherstone for 2015 season.

8 December 2014 - Elliot Minchella, 18, and Josh Walters, 20 sign new contracts until end of 2017.

8 February 2015 - opening round 40-30 victory at Hull KR after trailing 24-16 at half-time.

14 February 2015 - Adam Cuthbertson marks home debut with try in 38-6 home win over Widnes.

19 February 2015 - prop Rob Mulhern gets final spot in squad for 2015 and signs new three-year contract.

5 March 2015 - Kevin Sinfield climbs to fourth place in all-time list of RL point-scorers in remarkable 43-12 win, after trailing 12-0 at half-time, at Hull FC.

13 March 2015 - Zak Hardaker missing for disciplinary reasons and Tom Briscoe and Kylie Leuluai suffer long-term shoulder injuries in 18-6 defeat at Warrington. Kevin Sinfield sustains hamstring injury.

20 March 2015 - Ash Handley scores on home debut in hard-fought 26-14 win over Wigan.

27 March 2015 - Jamie Peacock MBE to take up new role as Football Manager of Hull KR from 2016.

31 March 2015 - Kevin Sinfield announces he will join Rhinos' sister club Yorkshire Carnegie at end of season.

1 April 2015 - Elliot Minchella joins London Broncos on loan to the end of season.

3 April 2015 - Liam Sutcliffe stars in 26-12 Good Friday win at Castleford.

8 April 2015 - Zak Hardaker fined one month's salary and takes anger management course after he and Elliot Minchella were arrested, but not charged, by police investigating assault earlier in year. Rob Mulhern, Josh Walters and Ash Handley each receive a fine and verbal warning.

24 April 2015 - Kevin Sinfield comes off bench to make 500th Leeds appearance in 29-10 home defeat to Warrington.

30 April 2015 - Kevin Sinfield dropped from side that draws 24-all at Huddersfield thanks to late Liam Sutcliffe penalty.

21 May 2015 - Rob Burrow signs new two-year contract to end of 2017.

22 May 2015 - Huddersfield prop Anthony Mullally to join Rhinos on three-year contract at end of season.

30 May 2015 - 27-12 defeat by Wigan in front of one-day Magic Weekend record crowd of 40,871 at St James' Park.

24 June 2015 - Brisbane prop Mitch Garbutt released by the Broncos to take up two-and-a-half-year contract with the Rhinos.

21 June 2015 - Liam Sutcliffe out for rest of season with serious knee injury suffered in 32-20 home win over Hull FC.

3 July 2015 - Zak Hardaker signs new four-year contract to end of 2019

3 July 2015 - Thomas Minns, on loan at Featherstone, signs for Hull KR for 2016.

3 July 2015 - Mitch Garbutt makes debut as Ash Handley scores second hat-trick of season in 46-18 home win over St Helens.

24 July 2015 - prop Andy Yates signs for Wakefield with immediate effect.

24 July 2015 - Wests Tigers prop Keith Galloway signs three-year contract from 2016.

26 July 2015 - Tom Briscoe marks return with hat-trick in 36-22 home win over Catalans Dragons.

31 July 2015 - 24-14 Challenge Cup semi-final win over St Helens. Jamie Jones-Buchanan out for season with ruptured quad tendon.

4 August 2015 - hooker Paul Aiton invokes option in contract to leave for Catalans at end of season.

7 August 2015 - prop Brad Singleton signs new four-year deal to end of 2019 season.

7 August 2015 - Paul Aiton suffers broken arm in 49-10 win over Warrington.

15 August 2015 - 25-18 home win over Wigan moves Rhinos four points clear at top.

29 August 2015 - Tom Briscoe scores record five tries in record 50-0 Challenge Cup final win over Hull KR.

11 September 2015 - Danny McGuire signs new two-year contract until end of 2017 season.

25 September 2015 - last-second Ryan Hall clinches 20-16 win at Huddersfield to win League Leaders Shield. Stevie Ward suffers bad knee injury.

2 October 2015 - last-second Kallum Watkins try seals 20-13 home semi-final win over champions St Helens.

6 October 2015 - Zak Hardaker wins Steve Prescott Man of Steel.

10 October 2015 - 22-20 win over Wigan secures record seventh Grand Final win.

16 October 2015 - Championship young player of the year with Featherstone, prop Jordan Baldwinson re-joins on two-year contract.

23 October 2015 - Gold Coast hooker Beau Falloon signs 12-month contract for 2016.

CLUB RECORDS

Highest score:
106-10 v Swinton, 11/2/2001
Highest score against:
6-74 v Wigan, 20/5/92
Record attendance:
40,175 v Bradford, 21/5/47

MATCH RECORDS

Tries:
8 Fred Webster v Coventry, 12/4/1913
Eric Harris v Bradford, 14/9/31
Goals:
17 Iestyn Harris v Swinton, 11/2/2001
Points:
42 Iestyn Harris v Huddersfield, 16/7/99

SEASON RECORDS

Tries: 63 Eric Harris 1935-36
Goals: 173 *(inc 5fg)* Kevin Sinfield 2012
Points: 431 Lewis Jones 1956-57

CAREER RECORDS

Tries: 391 Eric Harris 1930-39
Goals:
1,831 *(inc 39fg)* Kevin Sinfield 1997-2015
Points: 3,967 Kevin Sinfield 1997-2015
Appearances: 625 John Holmes 1968-89

LEEDS RHINOS

DATE	FIXTURE	RESULT	SCORERS	LGE	ATT
8/2/15	Hull KR (a)	W30-40	t:T Briscoe,Sinfield,McGuire(2),Watkins,Hardaker,Singleton g:Sinfield(6)	4th	11,811
13/2/15	Widnes (h)	W38-6	t:Hardaker,Hall,Cuthbertson,T Briscoe,McGuire,Watkins,Sinfield g:Sinfield(5)	2nd	14,132
26/2/15	Huddersfield (h)	W28-24	t:Ablett,Cuthbertson,Hall,T Briscoe,Aiton g:Sinfield(4)	2nd	12,878
5/3/15	Hull FC (a)	W12-43	t:McGuire(2),Singleton,Watkins,Leuluai,Burrow(2) g:Sinfield(7) fg:Sinfield	1st	10,887
13/3/15	Warrington (a)	L18-6	t:T Briscoe g:Sinfield	2nd	10,075
20/3/15	Wigan (h)	W26-14	t:Cuthbertson,Handley,Singleton,Sutcliffe,Burrow g:Sutcliffe(3)	2nd	18,350
28/3/15	Catalans Dragons (a)	W22-38	t:Ablett,S Ward,Singleton,McGuire,Sutcliffe,Watkins,Hardaker g:Sutcliffe(5)	1st	8,876
3/4/15	Castleford (a)	W12-26	t:Moon,Hall(2),S Ward,Cuthbertson g:Sutcliffe(3)	1st	11,235
6/4/15	Wakefield (h)	W48-22	t:Hall,Hardaker,Burrow(2),Watkins(2),Handley,Yates g:Sinfield(8)	1st	17,608
12/4/15	Salford (a)	W18-28	t:Peacock(2),Handley,Burrow,Hardaker g:Sinfield(4)	1st	4,489
17/4/15	St Helens (a)	W16-41	t:Handley(3),Hardaker,McGuire,Sutcliffe,Moon g:Sutcliffe(3),Sinfield(3) fg:Sinfield	1st	12,640
24/4/15	Warrington (h)	L10-29	t:Watkins,Achurch g:Sinfield	1st	17,340
30/4/15	Huddersfield (a)	D24-24	t:Delaney,Ablett,Moon,Watkins g:Sutcliffe(4)	1st	6,381
10/5/15	Widnes (a)	L38-24	t:S Ward,Moon,Watkins(2),Keinhorst g:Sutcliffe(2)	1st	6,113
16/5/15	Huddersfield (h) (CCR6)	W48-16	t:Watkins(2),Hall(2),Aiton,McGuire,Cuthbertson,Ablett g:Sinfield(8)	N/A	8,133
22/5/15	Hull KR (h)	W36-16	t:S Ward,Achurch,Hall(2),Singleton,Sinfield g:Sinfield(6)	1st	15,206
30/5/15	Wigan (MW) ●	L12-27	t:Cuthbertson,Moon g:Sinfield(2)	1st	N/A
7/6/15	Wakefield (a)	W26-58	t:Sutcliffe(3),McGuire,Burrow,Ablett,Handley(2),Keinhorst,Singleton(2) g:Sinfield(5),Sutcliffe(2)	1st	4,597
11/6/15	Castleford (h)	L24-31	t:Ablett,Hall,Cuthbertson,Keinhorst g:Sutcliffe(2),Sinfield(2)	2nd	15,089
21/6/15	Hull FC (h)	W32-20	t:McGuire,Moon(2),Keinhorst,Ablett g:Sutcliffe,Sinfield(5)	1st	16,203
26/6/15	Hull FC (a) (CCQF)	W6-24	t:Moon,Watkins,Hardaker g:Sinfield(6)	N/A	9,261
3/7/15	St Helens (h)	W46-18	t:Watkins,Leuluai,Hall(2),Handley(3),Ablett g:Sinfield(7)	1st	18,514
9/7/15	Wigan (a)	L26-24	t:Aiton,Singleton,Handley,Burrow g:Sinfield(4)	1st	15,009
17/7/15	Salford (h)	W70-6	t:McGuire,Cuthbertson,Watkins,Delaney,Hardaker(2),Hall(2),Moon, Keinhorst,Walters,Ablett(2) g:Hardaker(9)	1st	14,190
26/7/15	Catalans Dragons (h)	W36-22	t:T Briscoe(3),Garbutt,Watkins,Delaney g:Sinfield(6)	1st	15,534
31/7/15	St Helens (CCSF) ●●	W24-14	t:Hardaker,Moon,Peacock,Watkins g:Sinfield(4)	N/A	11,107
7/8/15	Warrington (h) (S8)	W49-10	t:Watkins,T Briscoe,Hardaker(2),McGuire,Moon,Burrow,Ablett g:Sinfield(8) fg:Sinfield	1st	13,118
14/8/15	Wigan (h) (S8)	W25-18	t:McGuire,Moon,Hall,Watkins g:Sinfield(4) fg:Hardaker	1st	15,026
21/8/15	Hull FC (a) (S8)	W22-36	t:Handley,Ablett,Burrow(2),Hall,T Briscoe g:Sinfield(6)	1st	10,649
29/8/15	Hull KR (CCF) ●●●	W0-50	t:Delaney,McGuire,T Briscoe(5),Singleton,Burrow g:Sinfield(7)	N/A	80,140
4/9/15	St Helens (h) (S8)	L18-32	t:Keinhorst,Achurch,Hall g:Sinfield(3)	1st	16,142
12/9/15	Catalans Dragons (a) (S8)	L46-16	t:Hall,McGuire,Moon g:Sinfield(2)	1st	8,851
17/9/15	Castleford (h) (S8)	L22-29	t:Hall(2),Moon,Cuthbertson g:Sinfield(2),Lilley	1st	15,069
25/9/15	Huddersfield (a) (S8)	W16-20	t:S Ward,T Briscoe,Hall g:Sinfield(4)	1st	9,376
2/10/15	St Helens (h) (SF)	W20-13	t:Hardaker,Hall,Watkins g:Sinfield(4)	N/A	17,192
10/10/15	Wigan (GF) ●●●●	W22-20	t:McGuire(2),Moon,Walters g:Sinfield(3)	N/A	73,512

● Played at St James' Park, Newcastle ●● Played at Halliwell Jones Stadium, Warrington
●●● Played at Wembley Stadium ●●●● Played at Old Trafford, Manchester

		APP		TRIES		GOALS		FG		PTS	
	D.O.B.	ALL	SL	ALL	SL	ALL	SL	ALL	SL	ALL	SL
Carl Ablett	19/12/85	36	32	12	11	0	0	0	0	48	44
Mitch Achurch	14/7/88	3(17)	3(15)	3	3	0	0	0	0	12	12
Paul Aiton	29/5/85	26(1)	23(1)	3	2	0	0	0	0	12	8
Tom Briscoe	19/3/90	17	15	15	10	0	0	0	0	60	40
Rob Burrow	26/9/82	12(18)	11(15)	12	11	0	0	0	0	48	44
Adam Cuthbertson	24/2/85	29(5)	26(5)	9	8	0	0	0	0	36	32
Brett Delaney	26/10/85	17(9)	14(8)	4	3	0	0	0	0	16	12
Mitch Garbutt	18/4/89	8(6)	7(5)	1	1	0	0	0	0	4	4
Ashton Golding	4/9/96	3(1)	3(1)	0	0	0	0	0	0	0	0
Ryan Hall	27/11/87	31	27	22	20	0	0	0	0	88	80
Ash Handley	16/2/96	20	18	13	13	0	0	0	0	52	52
Zak Hardaker	17/10/91	31	27	13	11	9	9	1	1	71	63
Jamie Jones-Buchanan	1/8/81	8(3)	7(3)	0	0	0	0	0	0	0	0
Jimmy Keinhorst	14/7/90	13(4)	12(3)	6	6	0	0	0	0	24	24
Kylie Leuluai	29/3/78	8(14)	7(12)	2	2	0	0	0	0	8	8
Jordan Lilley	4/9/96	1(3)	1(3)	0	0	1	1	0	0	2	2
Danny McGuire	6/12/82	32(1)	29(1)	17	15	0	0	0	0	68	60
Joel Moon	20/5/88	32	28	15	13	0	0	0	0	60	52
Rob Mulhern	18/10/94	(2)	(2)	0	0	0	0	0	0	0	0
Jamie Peacock	14/12/77	29(5)	25(5)	3	2	0	0	0	0	12	8
Kevin Sinfield	12/9/80	26(4)	22(4)	3	3	137	112	3	3	289	239
Brad Singleton	29/10/92	14(20)	14(17)	9	8	0	0	0	0	36	32
Liam Sutcliffe	25/11/94	11(4)	11(4)	6	6	25	25	0	0	74	74
Josh Walters	23/12/94	1(9)	1(8)	2	2	0	0	0	0	8	8
Robbie Ward	27/10/95	1(2)	1(1)	0	0	0	0	0	0	0	0
Stevie Ward	17/11/93	27(1)	24(1)	5	5	0	0	0	0	20	20
Kallum Watkins	12/3/91	32	28	20	16	0	0	0	0	80	64
Andy Yates	23/2/90	(10)	(9)	1	1	0	0	0	0	4	4

'SL' totals include Super 8s, semi-final & Grand Final; 'All' totals also include Challenge Cup
Home game v New Zealand (23/10/15) not included - not an official game due to irregular number of substitutes

Jamie Peacock

LEAGUE RECORD
P30-W20-D1-L9 (1st, SL/ Grand Final Winners, Champions)
F944, A650, Diff+294
41 points.

CHALLENGE CUP
Winners

ATTENDANCES
Best - v St Helens (SL - 18,514)
Worst - v Huddersfield (CC - 8,133)
Total (SL/S8s/SF only) - 251,591
Average (SL/S8s/SF only) - 15,724
(Up by 1,252 on 2014)

14 November 2014 - Scott Taylor moves from Wigan on season-long loan for 2015.

25 November 2014 - Cory Paterson, after spell in professional boxing, signs 12-month deal.

9 January 2015 - Andrew Dixon joins Halifax on one-month loan.

22 January 2015 - Andrew Dixon leaves and joins Leigh on permanent deal.

7 February 2015 - Weller Hauraki banned for one match for dangerous contact on Ben Currie in 22-8 round one defeat at Warrington.

12 February 2015 - Gareth Hock suspended for six matches after pleading guilty to two offences of illegal use of the knees in 52-6 home defeat by St Helens.

20 February 2015 - Gareth Hock leaves the club and joins Leigh.

28 February 2015 - short-term coaching advisor, Australia coach Tim Sheens watches on as Rangi Chase inspires 32-28 home win over Hull FC.

24 March 2015 - Theo Fages cops two-match suspension for dangerous contact in 30-16 defeat at Castleford.

26 March 2015 - Red Devils go into fourth spot with resounding 36-8 home win over Widnes.

8 April 2015 - Rangi Chase suspended for seven matches for cannonball tackle on Brett Ferres in Good Friday 18-12 defeat at Huddersfield. Weller Hauraki banned for four games, two for shoulder charge on Scott Grix in same game, two for striking in 24-18 home Easter Monday win over Wigan.

15 April 2015 - hooker Wayne Godwin re-signs on month's loan from Dewsbury.

18 April 2015 - Cory Paterson suspended for shoulder charge on Gregg McNally in first minute of 22-18 Challenge Cup defeat at Leigh Centurions. Darrell Griffin also gets one match for high tackle. Michael Dobson, Junior Sa'u and Ben Jones-Bishop all pick up injuries.

21 April 2015 - James Greenwood and Oliver Gildart join from Wigan on month's loan.

27 April 2015 - Hull FC reject injury and suspension-hit Salford Red Devils' request to postpone following Friday's match at KC Stadium.

1 May 2015 - late Setaimata Sa try secures 24-20 comeback win for Hull at the KC Stadium.

8 May 2015 - Red Devils say they will hand out life bans to fans who caused trouble during 19-0 home defeat by Huddersfield.

KEY DATES - SALFORD RED DEVILS

15 May 2015 - head of youth development Alan Hunte leaves the club.

26 May 2015 - prop Tony Puletua joins Hull KR on loan to end of season.

29 May 2015 - prop Lama Tasi signs for St Helens for 2016.

30 May 2015 - Darrell Griffin sent off for high tackle on Matt Whitley on stroke of half-time of 38-16 defeat by Widnes in first game of Magic Weekend in Newcastle.

4 June 2015 - Wigan hooker Logan Tomkins joins on loan to end of season with an option for 2016. Olsi Krasniqi returns from Australia and signs to end of season.

8 June 2015 - scrum-half Theo Fages, contracted to end of 2016, submits transfer request.

14 June 2015 - eight-match losing run ends with 24-16 win at Wakefield.

18 June 2015 - full-back Kevin Locke quits the club.

23 June 2015 - Australia national coach Tim Sheens to take up role of director of rugby after a month working in an advisory role earlier in year.

24 June 2015 - centre Junior Sa'u signs new contract up to end of 2017 season.

26 June 2015 - forward George Griffin signs two-year contract extension to end of 2017.

30 June 2015 - 34-28 defeat at Hull KR.

5 July 2015 - assistant coach Ian Watson takes over after Iestyn Harris takes sick leave.

12 July 2015 - winning start for new director of rugby Tim Sheens after second-half comeback produces 31-18 home win over Hull KR.

24 July 2015 - Featherstone's former Australian international Reni Maitua and Wigan centre Iain Thornley sign to end of season.

18 August 2015 - Reni Maitua banned for one match for dangerous throw on Jake Emmitt in 46-18 home Qualifiers win over Leigh.

2 September 2015 - head coach Iestyn Harris departs after two-month absence from the club.

3 September 2015 - Rangi Chase suspended pending internal disciplinary investigation.

10 September 2015 - Adrian Morley announces retirement at end of season.

20 September 2015 - 24-10 win at Widnes ensures Super League rugby next season.

25 September 2015 - Cory Paterson, Harrison Hansen and Reni Maitua all move to Leigh Centurions. Salary cap issues prevent Rangi Chase doing the same.

1 October 2015 - Tim Sheens resigns as Australia's national coach to take up three-year contract as full-time director of rugby with Salford.

2 October 2015 - St Helens forward Mark Flanagan, Widnes prop Phil Joseph, Huddersfield prop Craig Kopczak and Warrington halfback Gareth O'Brien sign for next season. North Queensland stand-off Robert Lui and Penrith Panthers prop Ben Murdoch-Masila also sign and Olsi Krasniqi agrees two-year deal after joining in June.

27 October 2015 - prop Matthew Haggarty signs on season-long loan from St Helens.

27 October 2015 - Rangi Chase has contract officially terminated.

3 November 2015 - Castleford Tigers' Australian winger Justin Carney signs on year-long loan deal.

CLUB RECORDS

Highest score:
100-12 v Gateshead, 23/3/2003
Highest score against:
16-96 v Bradford, 25/6/2000
Record attendance:
26,470 v Warrington, 13/2/37 *(The Willows)*
7,102 v Wakefield, 16/2/2014
(AJ Bell Stadium)

MATCH RECORDS

Tries:
6 Frank Miles v Lees, 5/3/1898
Ernest Bone v Goole, 29/3/1902
Jack Hilton v Leigh, 7/10/39
Goals:
14 Steve Blakeley v Gateshead, 23/3/2003
Points:
39 Jim Lomas v Liverpool City, 2/2/1907

SEASON RECORDS

Tries: 46 Keith Fielding 1973-74
Goals: 221 David Watkins 1972-73
Points: 493 David Watkins 1972-73

CAREER RECORDS

Tries: 297 Maurice Richards 1969-83
Goals: 1,241 David Watkins 1967-79
Points: 2,907 David Watkins 1967-79
Appearances:
498 Maurice Richards 1969-83

SALFORD RED DEVILS

DATE	FIXTURE	RESULT	SCORERS	LGE	ATT
7/2/15	Warrington (a)	L22-8	t:Jones-Bishop(2)	11th	11,864
12/2/15	St Helens (h)	L6-52	t:Jones-Bishop g:Dobson	12th	4,975
28/2/15	Hull FC (h)	W32-28	t:Evalds(2),Fages,J Griffin(2),Sa'u g:J Griffin(4)	10th	3,606
7/3/15	Catalans Dragons (a)	D40-40	t:Sa'u,J Griffin,Paterson(2),Lee,Fages,Chase g:J Griffin(6)	8th	8,864
15/3/15	Wakefield (h)	W24-18	t:Johnson,Hauraki,Chase,Sa'u g:J Griffin(4)	6th	2,712
20/3/15	Castleford (a)	L30-16	t:Lee,Hauraki,Jones-Bishop g:J Griffin(2)	8th	6,901
26/3/15	Widnes (h)	W36-8	t:Jones-Bishop,Hauraki,Johnson,Tasi,J Griffin,Paterson,Taylor g:J Griffin(4)	6th	3,476
3/4/15	Huddersfield (a)	W12-18	t:J Griffin,Jones-Bishop,Forster g:J Griffin(3)	4th	6,003
6/4/15	Wigan (h)	W24-18	t:Evalds(2),Dobson,Jones-Bishop g:J Griffin(4)	3rd	6,561
12/4/15	Leeds (h)	L18-28	t:Tasi,Evalds(2) g:Dobson(3)	4th	4,489
18/4/15	Leigh (a) (CCR5)	L22-18	t:Fages,Evalds(2) g:Dobson,Paterson(2)	N/A	6,358
26/4/15	Castleford (h)	L20-22	t:Fages,Locke(2),Taylor g:Locke,Johnson	7th	3,397
1/5/15	Hull FC (a)	L24-20	t:Locke,Greenwood,Gildart g:Fages(4)	7th	9,385
8/5/15	Huddersfield (h)	L0-19		11th	1,972
22/5/15	Warrington (h)	L18-34	t:Paterson,Sa'u,Evalds g:Paterson(3)	11th	6,159
30/5/15	Widnes (MW) ●	L16-38	t:Paterson,Johnson,Jones-Bishop g:J Griffin(2)	11th	N/A
5/6/15	St Helens (a)	L32-12	t:Evalds,Chase g:Paterson(2)	11th	11,664
14/6/15	Wakefield (a)	W16-24	t:Fages,Taylor,Hansen(2) g:J Griffin(4)	11th	3,240
19/6/15	Wigan (a)	L19-12	t:Paterson,G Griffin g:J Griffin(2)	11th	13,710
30/6/15	Hull KR (a)	L34-28	t:Caton-Brown,Jones-Bishop(2),J Walne,Taylor g:J Griffin(4)	11th	6,717
5/7/15	Catalans Dragons (h)	W18-14	t:Evalds,Dobson(2) g:J Griffin(3)	11th	5,078
12/7/15	Hull KR (h)	W31-18	t:Jones-Bishop(2),J Griffin,Hauraki,Fages,Evalds g:Dobson(3) fg:Dobson	11th	4,415
17/7/15	Leeds (a)	L70-6	t:Evalds g:Paterson	11th	14,190
26/7/15	Widnes (a)	L21-20	t:Evalds,Paterson,Taylor g:J Griffin(4)	11th	5,477
9/8/15	Wakefield (h) (S8-Q)	W34-26	t:J Griffin(2),G Griffin,Paterson(2),Chase g:J Griffin(4),Paterson	4th(S8-Q)	3,100
16/8/15	Leigh (h) (S8-Q)	W46-18	t:Jones-Bishop,Taylor,Thornley,Chase(2),Sa'u,Evalds,Johnson g:Dobson(7)	2nd(S8-Q)	4,547
23/8/15	Bradford (a) (S8-Q)	L41-10	t:Chase,Thornley g:Dobson	5th(S8-Q)	6,593
5/9/15	Halifax (a) (S8-Q)	W28-50	t:Evalds(3),Johnson(3),Jones-Bishop(3) g:J Griffin(4),Dobson(3)	3rd(S8-Q)	2,186
13/9/15	Sheffield (h) (S8-Q)	W53-34	t:Hauraki,Hansen,J Griffin(2),Hood,Tasi,Evalds,Thornley,G Griffin g:Dobson(7),J Griffin fg:Dobson	3rd(S8-Q)	3,000
20/9/15	Widnes (a) (S8-Q)	W10-24	t:J Griffin,Taylor,Paterson,Sa'u g:Dobson(4)	2nd(S8-Q)	5,285
27/9/15	Hull KR (a) (S8-Q)	L46-22	t:Johnson,Hansen,Tasi,Lannon g:Jones-Bishop(3)	3rd(S8-Q)	7,543

● Played at St James' Park, Newcastle

		APP		TRIES		GOALS		FG		PTS	
	D.O.B.	ALL	SL	ALL	SL	ALL	SL	ALL	SL	ALL	SL
Jake Bibby	17/6/96	1	0	0	0	0	0	0	0	0	0
Mason Caton-Brown	24/5/93	16	15	1	1	0	0	0	0	4	4
Rangi Chase	11/4/86	17	14	7	3	0	0	0	0	28	12
Michael Dobson	29/5/86	20(1)	13(1)	3	3	30	7	2	1	74	27
Niall Evalds	26/8/93	23(2)	16(1)	19	12	0	0	0	0	76	48
Theo Fages	23/8/94	17(3)	16(3)	6	5	4	4	0	0	32	28
Carl Forster	4/6/92	4(9)	3(6)	1	1	0	0	0	0	4	4
Matty Gee	12/12/94	(2)	(2)	0	0	0	0	0	0	0	0
Oliver Gildart	6/8/96	3	3	1	1	0	0	0	0	4	4
Wayne Godwin	13/3/82	3	2	0	0	0	0	0	0	0	0
James Greenwood	17/6/91	1(1)	1(1)	1	1	0	0	0	0	4	4
Darrell Griffin	19/6/81	2(17)	2(16)	0	0	0	0	0	0	0	0
George Griffin	26/6/92	14(5)	9(4)	3	1	0	0	0	0	12	4
Josh Griffin	9/5/90	21	17	11	6	55	46	0	0	154	116
Harrison Hansen	26/10/85	27(2)	20(2)	4	2	0	0	0	0	16	8
Weller Hauraki	18/2/85	18	16	5	4	0	0	0	0	20	16
Gareth Hock	5/9/83	2	2	0	0	0	0	0	0	0	0
Liam Hood	6/1/92	2(20)	2(15)	1	0	0	0	0	0	4	0
Greg Johnson	20/2/90	26	19	8	3	1	1	0	0	34	14
Ben Jones-Bishop	24/8/88	25	17	16	12	3	0	0	0	70	48
Olsi Krasniqi	26/6/92	2(7)	(3)	0	0	0	0	0	0	0	0
Ryan Lannon	11/1/96	(5)	(4)	1	0	0	0	0	0	4	0
Tommy Lee	1/2/88	13(3)	9	2	2	0	0	0	0	8	8
Kevin Locke	4/4/89	7	7	3	3	1	1	0	0	14	14
Reni Maitua	11/6/82	6	0	0	0	0	0	0	0	0	0
Luke Menzies	29/6/88	(1)	0	0	0	0	0	0	0	0	0
Adrian Morley	10/5/77	14(13)	12(8)	0	0	0	0	0	0	0	0
Cory Paterson	14/7/87	18(3)	14(1)	10	7	9	6	0	0	58	40
Junior Sa'u	18/4/87	23	17	6	4	0	0	0	0	24	16
Lama Tasi	3/5/90	7(13)	4(10)	4	2	0	0	0	0	16	8
Scott Taylor	27/2/91	30	23	7	5	0	0	0	0	28	20
Iain Thornley	11/9/91	6	0	3	0	0	0	0	0	12	0
Logan Tomkins	1/8/91	14(1)	7(1)	0	0	0	0	0	0	0	0
Adam Walne	3/10/90	3(8)	2(6)	0	0	0	0	0	0	0	0
Jordan Walne	28/12/92	13(4)	13(4)	1	1	0	0	0	0	4	4
Jason Walton	13/6/90	3(4)	3(4)	0	0	0	0	0	0	0	0
Josh Wood	15/11/95	2	1	0	0	0	0	0	0	0	0

'SL' totals include regular season only; 'All' totals also include Super 8s (Qualifiers) & Challenge Cup

Niall Evalds

LEAGUE RECORD
SL: P23-W8-D1-L14 (11th)
F447, A617, Diff-170, 17 points.

S8-Q: P7-W5-D0-L2 (3rd)
F239, A203, Diff+36, 10 points.

CHALLENGE CUP
Round Five

ATTENDANCES
Best - v Wigan (SL - 6,561)
Worst - v Huddersfield (SL - 1,972)
Total (SL/S8s only) - 57,487
Average (SL/S8s only) - 4,106
(Down by 409 on 2014)

KEY DATES - ST HELENS

7 November 2014 - Ade Gardner announces retirement and joins club's backroom staff.

17 November 2014 - Sean Long joins backroom staff on two-year contract

21 November 2014 - Paul Wellens extends contract until end of 2015 season.

21 January 2015 - Jon Wilkin replaces Paul Wellens as captain.

6 February 2015 - debutant Atelea Vea scores try in opening round 18-7 victory over Catalans.

9 February 2015 - Dewsbury Rams prop Matthew Haggarty joins on three-year deal.

13 February 2015 - Mark Percival scores two tries and kicks six goals in 10-try, 52-6 away rout of Salford Red Devils.

18 February 2015 - Tommy Makinson signs new four-year contract to end of 2018.

22 February 2015 - Russell Crowe puts World Club Challenge before the Oscars ceremony to watch his club South Sydney hammer Saints 39-0.

27 February 2015 - Saints bounce back with 21-14 home win over Castleford. Kyle Amor gets one-match ban for crusher tackle. Travis Burns gets one-match for high tackle.

6 March 2015 - Jonny Lomax injures knee during 20-16 win at Wakefield and is ruled out for season.

16 March 2015 - Jon Wilkin signs new one-year contract extension until end of season 2016.

31 March 2015 - hundred per cent start to season ends after six wins with 24-22 defeat at Hull KR.

3 April 2015 - capacity 24,054 crowd at DW Stadium witnesses 12-4 defeat to Wigan.

15 April 2015 - Alex Walmsley turns down NRL offers and agrees new contract to end of 2018.

24 April 2015 - Luke Walsh makes first start of season in 34-16 home triumph over Widnes Vikings.

29 April 2015 - Lance Hohaia announces retirement with immediate effect.

30 April 2015 - Shannon McDonnell returns on contract to end of 2016 season.

12 May 2015 - Luke Walsh undergoes minor surgery on ankle injury suffered during 33-26 defeat by Catalans in Perpignan the previous Saturday.

20 May 2015 - coach Keiron Cunningham fined for publicly criticising match referee following 33-26 defeat at Catalans on Saturday May 9.

29 May 2015 - prop Lama Tasi signs for 2016 from Salford on two-year deal.

31 May 2015 - 20-16 win over Warrington at Magic Weekend in Newcastle.

7 June 2015 - winger Tommy Makinson undergoes surgery on ankle damaged in previous Friday's 32-12 win over Salford.

11 June 2015 - scrum-half Luke Walsh takes up third-year option on contract to end of 2016.

17 June 2015 - Josh Jones to join Exeter rugby union club at end of season.

18 June 2015 - fullback Shannon McDonnell to miss the rest of season after snapping Achilles tendon in Saints' last-gasp 25-24 defeat at Castleford.

24 June 2015 - Paul Wellens announces retirement because of ongoing hip problem.

29 June 2015 - Samoan prop Mose Masoe to return to NRL with St George Illawarra at end of season

1 July 2015 - Parramatta Eels reserve Adam Quinlan signs short-term contract to ease full-back crisis.

3 July 2015 - 46-18 defeat at Leeds.

6 July 2015 - Andre Savelio signs two-year contract extension to end of 2017.

10 July 2015 - Adam Quinlan scores hat-trick on debut and Luke Walsh kicks last-gasp field goal in 35-34 win over form team Huddersfield.

16 July 2015 - Jordan Turner try secures last-gasp 20-14 win at Warrington. Jon Wilkin breaks thumb.

23 July 2015 - NZ Warriors' utility Dominque Peyroux signs two-year contract from 2016.

31 July 2015 - 24-14 Challenge Cup semi-final defeat by Leeds.

17 August 2015 - youngsters Matty Fleming and second rower Oliver Davies, both 19, sign new 12-month deals with another year option. Hooker Lewis Charnock extends to end of 2016.

20 August 2015 - 28-22 home defeat by Huddersfield means third straight loss in opening matches of Super 8s.

4 September 2015 - captain Jon Wilkin returns from injury in 32-16 win at Leeds.

24 September 2015 - undisclosed fee paid for transfer of Salford's France international Theo Fages, who signs four-year contract.

2 October 2015 - two late Leeds tries mean 20-13 semi-final exit at Headingley.

4 November 2015 - winger/fullback Jack Owens joins on two-year deal after being released by Widnes.

CLUB RECORDS

Highest score:
112-0 v Carlisle, 14/9/86
Highest score against:
6-78 v Warrington, 12/4/1909
Record attendance:
35,695 v Wigan, 26/12/49 *(Knowsley Road)*
17,980 v Wigan, 6/4/2012
v Wigan, 18/4/2014
v South Sydney, 22/2/2015 *(Langtree Park)*

MATCH RECORDS

Tries: 6 Alf Ellaby v Barrow, 5/3/32
Steve Llewellyn v Castleford, 3/3/56
Steve Llewellyn v Liverpool, 20/8/56
Tom van Vollenhoven v Wakefield, 21/12/57
Tom van Vollenhoven v Blackpool, 23/4/62
Frank Myler v Maryport, 1/9/69
Shane Cooper v Hull, 17/2/88
Goals: 16 Paul Loughlin v Carlisle, 14/9/86
Points:
40 Paul Loughlin v Carlisle, 14/9/86

SEASON RECORDS

Tries 62 Tom van Vollenhoven 1958-59
Goals: 214 Kel Coslett 1971-72
Points: 452 Kel Coslett 1971-72

CAREER RECORDS

Tries: 392 Tom van Vollenhoven 1957-68
Goals: 1,639 Kel Coslett 1962-76
Points: 3,413 Kel Coslett 1962-76
Appearances: 531 Kel Coslett 1962-76

ST HELENS

DATE	FIXTURE	RESULT	SCORERS	LGE	ATT
6/2/15	Catalans Dragons (h)	W18-7	t:Vea,Turner,Savelio,Makinson g:Makinson	3rd	12,008
12/2/15	Salford (a)	W6-52	t:Percival(2),Turner(2),Greenwood(2),Thompson,Makinson, McCarthy-Scarsbrook,Savelio g:Percival(6)	1st	4,975
22/2/15	South Sydney (h) (WCC)	L0-39		N/A	17,980
27/2/15	Castleford (h)	W21-14	t:Swift,Makinson,Jones,Percival g:Percival(2) fg:Wilkin	1st	10,066
6/3/15	Wakefield (a)	W16-20	t:Wellens,Greenwood,Turner g:Percival,Makinson(3)	2nd	4,104
13/3/15	Widnes (a)	W20-30	t:Hohaia(2),Vea,Thompson,Turner g:Burns(5)	1st	7,772
19/3/15	Warrington (h)	W32-24	t:Greenwood,Wilkin,Swift,McCarthy-Scarsbrook,Makinson g:Burns(6)	1st	12,618
27/3/15	Hull KR (a)	L24-22	t:Wilkin,Makinson,McCarthy-Scarsbrook,Turner g:Burns(3)	2nd	7,311
3/4/15	Wigan (a)	L12-4	t:McCarthy-Scarsbrook	2nd	24,054
6/4/15	Hull FC (h)	L20-28	t:Makinson,McCarthy-Scarsbrook,Turner g:Makinson(4)	2nd	11,088
12/4/15	Huddersfield (a)	W8-11	t:Turner g:Burns(3) fg:Walsh	2nd	5,825
17/4/15	Leeds (h)	L16-41	t:Makinson,Turner(2) g:Burns(2)	2nd	12,640
24/4/15	Widnes (h)	W34-16	t:Walsh,Burns,Walmsley,Fleming,Makinson,Percival g:Burns(5)	2nd	11,271
1/5/15	Wakefield (h)	W44-4	t:Walsh(2),Charnock(2),Makinson(2),Turner,Swift,Masoe g:Burns(4)	2nd	10,001
9/5/15	Catalans Dragons (a)	L33-26	t:Swift(4),McDonnell g:Walsh(3)	3rd	8,884
15/5/15	York (h) (CCR6)	W46-6	t:Swift(3),Makinson(4),Percival,Flanagan g:Makinson(3),Charnock(2)	N/A	3,241
22/5/15	Hull FC (a)	W10-17	t:McDonnell,Makinson g:Charnock(3),Makinson fg:Turner	2nd	10,320
31/5/15	Warrington (MW) ●	W20-16	t:McCarthy-Scarsbrook,Swift,Wilkin g:Makinson(4)	2nd	N/A
5/6/15	Salford (h)	W32-12	t:Makinson(2),Swift,Turner,McDonnell g:Makinson(6)	2nd	11,664
12/6/15	Wigan (h)	W30-14	t:Swift,Turner,Burns,McDonnell,Wilkin g:Percival(5)	1st	16,692
18/6/15	Castleford (a)	L25-24	t:Walsh,Walmsley,Greenwood,McDonnell g:Percival(4)	2nd	6,068
28/6/15	Widnes (h) (CCQF)	W36-20	t:Swift,Percival(2),Dawson,Amor,Turner g:Percival(6)	N/A	8,806
3/7/15	Leeds (a)	L46-18	t:Jones,Turner,Amor g:Percival(3)	2nd	18,514
10/7/15	Huddersfield (h)	W35-34	t:Quinlan(3),Percival(2),Greenwood g:Walsh(5) fg:Walsh	2nd	11,164
16/7/15	Warrington (a)	W14-20	t:Roby,Masoe,Turner g:Walsh(4)	2nd	9,618
24/7/15	Hull KR (h)	W52-12	t:Greenwood(2),Burns,Dawson,Vea,Quinlan,Flanagan,Swift(2) g:Walsh(8)	2nd	10,781
31/7/15	Leeds (CCSF) ●●	L24-14	t:Percival(2),Savelio g:Walsh	N/A	11,107
8/8/15	Catalans Dragons (a) (S8)	L26-16	t:Walsh,Dawson,Greenwood g:Walsh(2)	3rd	7,392
14/8/15	Hull FC (h) (S8)	L22-32	t:Thompson,Swift,Roby,Percival g:Walsh(3)	3rd	10,203
20/8/15	Huddersfield (h) (S8)	L22-28	t:Amor,Roby,Makinson,Burns g:Walsh(3)	4th	10,976
4/9/15	Leeds (a) (S8)	W18-32	t:Makinson,Jones,Walsh,Quinlan,Wilkin g:Walsh(6)	4th	16,142
10/9/15	Castleford (a) (S8)	W38-42	t:Swift(3),Percival(2),Quinlan,Makinson g:Walsh(7)	4th	5,253
18/9/15	Wigan (h) (S8)	W18-14	t:Walsh,Swift,Jones g:Walsh(3)	4th	15,808
24/9/15	Warrington (h) (S8)	L16-32	t:Greenwood,Swift,Flanagan g:Walsh(2)	4th	10,966
2/10/15	Leeds (a) (SF)	L20-13	t:Roby,Percival g:Walsh(2) fg:Walsh	N/A	17,192

● Played at St James' Park, Newcastle
●● Played at Halliwell Jones Stadium, Warrington

	D.O.B.	APP ALL	APP SL	TRIES ALL	TRIES SL	GOALS ALL	GOALS SL	FG ALL	FG SL	PTS ALL	PTS SL
Kyle Amor	26/5/87	30(2)	27(1)	3	2	0	0	0	0	12	8
Jack Ashworth	3/7/95	1	1	0	0	0	0	0	0	0	0
Ricky Bailey	25/4/97	1	1	0	0	0	0	0	0	0	0
Travis Burns	6/2/84	29	25	4	4	28	28	0	0	72	72
Lewis Charnock	2/9/94	4	3	2	2	5	3	0	0	18	14
Olly Davies	30/11/95	(1)	0	0	0	0	0	0	0	0	0
Matty Dawson	2/10/90	14(1)	12(1)	3	2	0	0	0	0	12	8
Mark Flanagan	4/12/87	16(13)	13(12)	3	2	0	0	0	0	12	8
Matty Fleming	13/1/96	7	6	1	1	0	0	0	0	4	4
Joe Greenwood	2/4/93	18(5)	15(5)	10	10	0	0	0	0	40	40
Lance Hohaia	1/4/83	6(2)	6(2)	2	2	0	0	0	0	8	8
Josh Jones	12/5/93	25(4)	23(3)	4	4	0	0	0	0	16	16
Morgan Knowles	5/11/96	(1)	0	0	0	0	0	0	0	0	0
Jonny Lomax	4/9/90	5	4	0	0	0	0	0	0	0	0
Tom Makinson	10/10/91	25	23	20	16	22	19	0	0	124	102
Mose Masoe	17/5/89	9(24)	7(22)	2	2	0	0	0	0	8	8
Louie McCarthy-Scarsbrook	14/1/86	24(8)	21(7)	6	6	0	0	0	0	24	24
Shannon McDonnell	5/8/87	8	7	5	5	0	0	0	0	20	20
Mark Percival	29/5/94	25(1)	21(1)	15	10	27	21	0	0	114	82
Adam Quinlan	13/11/92	12	11	6	6	0	0	0	0	24	24
Greg Richards	12/7/95	4(25)	3(24)	0	0	0	0	0	0	0	0
James Roby	22/11/85	30(1)	27(1)	4	4	0	0	0	0	16	16
Andre Savelio	21/3/95	7(22)	7(18)	3	2	0	0	0	0	12	8
Adam Swift	20/2/93	35	31	22	18	0	0	0	0	88	72
Luke Thompson	27/4/95	11(10)	11(9)	3	3	0	0	0	0	12	12
Jordan Turner	9/1/89	30(2)	27(2)	16	15	0	0	1	1	65	61
Atelea Vea	27/11/86	9(4)	8(3)	3	3	0	0	0	0	12	12
Alex Walmsley	10/4/90	22(10)	20(9)	2	2	0	0	0	0	8	8
Luke Walsh	12/5/87	18(2)	16(2)	7	7	49	48	3	3	129	127
Paul Wellens	27/2/80	4	4	1	1	0	0	0	0	4	4
Jon Wilkin	11/1/83	26	23	5	5	0	0	1	1	21	21

'SL' totals include Super 8s & semi-final; 'All' totals also include Challenge Cup & World Club Challenge

Adam Swift

LEAGUE RECORD
P30-W19-D0-L11
(4th, SL/Semi-Finalists)
F766, A624, Diff+142
38 points.

CHALLENGE CUP
Semi-Finalists

ATTENDANCES
Best - v South Sydney (WCC - 17,980)
Worst - v York (CC - 3,241)
Total (SL/S8s only) - 177,946
Average (SL/S8s only) - 11,863
(Up by 320 on 2014)

22 November 2014 - Hull FC halfback Jacob Miller signed on one-year deal.

8 February 2015 - late Danny Washbrook try seals dramatic round one 24-22 win at Castleford after trailing 22-6 with 15 minutes remaining.

15 February 2015 - Chris Riley and Jacob Miller both score hat-tricks in 44-24 home win over Hull KR.

16 February 2015 - Hull FC centre Joe Arundel signs to end of 2015 season.

26 February 2015 - Jarrod Sammut joins London on dual-registration.

1 March 2015 - 58-16 defeat at Widnes.

6 March 2015 - 20-16 home defeat to St Helens

2 April 2015 - Easter Thursday 40-4 defeat to Catalans.

15 April 2015 - Widnes Vikings forward Ben Kavanagh joins on loan for rest of season.

27 April 2015 - Wildcats fined £1,000 for fans throwing smoke flare onto pitch during match at Castleford on February 8.

19 May 2015 - head coach James Webster becomes first coaching casualty of Super League XX, 48 hours after Wildcats suffer 36-30 home defeat to Leigh Centurions in sixth round of Challenge Cup after leading 22-0.

25 May 2015 - prop Lopini Paea leaves club with immediate effect

31 May 2015 - coaching guru Brian Smith announced as new head coach shortly before Wakefield's 56-16 defeat by Castleford on final day of Magic Weekend in Newcastle.

5 June 2015 - Stuart Howarth returns on 18-month contract from Hull FC.

11 June 2015 - centre Dean Collis returns to Australia.

14 June 2015 - 24-16 home defeat by next-to-bottom Salford in Brian Smith's first game in charge.

17 June 2015 - former NZ Warrior and Samoan international Michael Sio joins on 18-month deal.

25 June 2015 - New Zealand full-back Kevin Locke secures release from Salford to join Wildcats to end of season

26 June 2015 - utility back Jordan Tansey moves from Castleford on 18-month contract. Prop Anthony Walker signs from St Helens to end of season.

14 July 2015 - Huddersfield Giants sign prop Daniel Smith on four-and-a-half-year contract, with Leeds bound Anthony Mullally coming the other way on short-term loan.

19 July 2015 - outside back Lee Smith joins on deal to end of season.

KEY DATES - WAKEFIELD T WILDCATS

20 July 2015 - Canberra threequarter Bill Tupou joins until end of season. Australian back-rower Matt Ryan leaves for Bradford.

23 July 2015 - hooker Paul McShane joins Castleford on two-and-a-half-year deal and Scott Moore comes the other way on loan to end of season.

24 July 2015 - Leeds Rhinos prop Andy Yates arrives on 18-month contract.

3 August 2015 - Warrington's Simon Grix, sidelined all season with a leg fracture, signs on loan for the Super 8s campaign, but never plays.

20 August 2015 - Scott Moore expected to be out for season with ruptured bicep suffered in training.

22 August 2015 - Michael Sio sin-binned for crusher tackle on Gregg McNally in 62nd minute of 17-16 win at Leigh. He gets one-match ban.

6 September 2015 - 20-18 defeat at Hull KR after leading 12-0.

12 September 2015 - 46-4 home hammering by Widnes makes 'Million Pound Game' inevitable at best.

17 September 2015 - fullback Kevin Locke, scrum-half Tim Smith and centre Reece Lyne all left out of squad for must-win Qualifier game against Halifax at Belle Vue.

17 September 2015 - Australian halfback Jacob Miller signs new two-year contract to end of 2017.

29 September 2015 - Reece Lyne returns in 24-10 defeat at Sheffield Eagles, warned and fined for his part in off-field transgression.

29 September 2015 - Kevin Locke leaves the club and returns home.

1 October 2015 - scrum-half Tim Smith dismissed for gross misconduct after driving convictions at Beverley Magistrates Court.

3 October 2015 - 24-16 home win over Bradford in 'Million Pound Game' ensures Super League status in 2016.

12 October 2015 - coach Brian Smith agrees new 12-month contract.

14 October 2015 - Warrington Wolves prop Anthony England signs on two-year deal.

20 October 2015 - former academy prop Ben Shulver signs two-year contract on return from Australia. Oxford product Sean Morris signs 12-month deal.

21 October 2015 - scrum-half Liam Finn signs from Castleford on two-year deal.

23 October 2015 - centre Ashley Gibson signs two-year deal after release from Castleford.

27 October 2015 - back-row forward Jon Molloy and Joe Arundel sign new two-year deals.

30 October 2015 - centre Bill Tupou signs one-year contract for 2016.

2 November 2015 - former Australian international forward Anthony Tupou signs from Cronulla on two-year deal.

CLUB RECORDS

Highest score:
90-12 v Highfield, 27/10/92
Highest score against:
0-86 v Castleford, 17/4/95
Record attendance:
30,676 v Huddersfield, 26/2/21

MATCH RECORDS

Tries:
7 Fred Smith v Keighley, 25/4/59
Keith Slater v Hunslet, 6/2/71
Goals:
13 Mark Conway v Highfield, 27/10/92
Points:
36 Jamie Rooney v Chorley, 27/2/2004

SEASON RECORDS

Tries: 38 Fred Smith 1959-60
David Smith 1973-74
Goals: 163 Neil Fox 1961-62
Points: 407 Neil Fox 1961-62

CAREER RECORDS

Tries: 272 Neil Fox 1956-69; 1970-74
Goals: 1,836 Neil Fox 1956-69; 1970-74
Points: 4,488 Neil Fox 1956-69; 1970-74
Appearances:
605 Harry Wilkinson 1930-49

WAKEFIELD T WILDCATS

DATE	FIXTURE	RESULT	SCORERS	LGE	ATT
8/2/15	Castleford (a)	W22-24	t:McShane,Godinet,Lauitiiti,Washbrook g:Hall(4)	5th	10,728
15/2/15	Hull KR (h)	W44-24	t:Ashurst,Miller(3),Kirmond,Riley(3) g:Hall(6)	3rd	5,320
1/3/15	Widnes (a)	L58-16	t:Owen,Ryan,Riley g:Hall(2)	5th	5,810
6/3/15	St Helens (h)	L16-20	t:Ashurst,Lyne,Owen g:Hall(2)	5th	4,104
15/3/15	Salford (a)	L24-18	t:Miller,McShane,Hall g:Hall(3)	9th	2,712
22/3/15	Huddersfield (h)	L14-44	t:Collis,Kirmond,Crowther g:Hall	12th	4,354
27/3/15	Wigan (a)	L52-10	t:Riley,McShane g:Hall	12th	10,787
2/4/15	Catalans Dragons (h)	L4-40	t:Riley	12th	3,015
6/4/15	Leeds (a)	L48-22	t:T Smith,Hall,Sammut,D Smith g:Hall(3)	12th	17,608
11/4/15	Warrington (a)	L80-0		12th	8,036
17/4/15	Halifax (h) (CCR5)	W44-16	t:Owen(2),D Smith,Riley,Hall,Washbrook,Kirke(2) g:Hall(6)	N/A	2,062
23/4/15	Wigan (h)	L22-40	t:Hall,Kirmond,Godinet,Riley g:Hall(3)	12th	3,107
1/5/15	St Helens (a)	L44-4	t:Johnstone	12th	10,001
7/5/15	Hull KR (a)	L54-6	t:Arundel g:Hall	12th	7,378
17/5/15	Leigh (h) (CCR6)	L30-36	t:Riley,Arundel(2),Scruton,Molloy g:Hall(5)	N/A	3,859
24/5/15	Widnes (h)	L18-30	t:Johnstone,Ryan,Collis g:Miller(3)	12th	3,132
31/5/15	Castleford (MW) ●	L56-16	t:Johnstone(2),D Smith g:Miller(2)	12th	N/A
7/6/15	Leeds (h)	L26-58	t:Johnstone(2),Godinet,Kirmond,Scruton g:Hall,Godinet(2)	12th	4,597
14/6/15	Salford (h)	L16-24	t:D Smith,Kirke,Kirmond g:Arundel(2)	12th	3,240
20/6/15	Catalans Dragons (a)	L32-12	t:Riley,Godinet g:Miller(2)	12th	7,834
1/7/15	Hull FC (h)	W26-16	t:Miller,Owen,Arundel,Ryan g:Miller(5)	12th	3,543
5/7/15	Hull FC (a)	L31-24	t:Ashurst,Tansey,Lyne,Johnstone g:Miller(4)	12th	9,558
12/7/15	Warrington (h)	L20-40	t:Miller(4) g:Miller,Hall	12th	3,354
19/7/15	Castleford (h)	L20-58	t:Lyne,Walker,Johnstone(2) g:Arundel(2)	12th	6,108
26/7/15	Huddersfield (a)	L34-24	t:Miller,Anderson,Ashurst,L Smith,Lyne g:Hall(2)	12th	4,839
9/8/15	Salford (a) (S8-Q)	L34-26	t:Miller(2),Washbrook,Lyne g:L Smith(5)	5th(S8-Q)	3,100
15/8/15	Bradford (h) (S8-Q)	W48-18	t:Molloy,Sio,Simon,Scruton,L Smith,Lyne,Ashurst,Miller g:L Smith(7),Arundel	4th(S8-Q)	3,985
22/8/15	Leigh (a) (S8-Q)	W16-17	t:L Smith,Miller(2) g:L Smith(2) fg:L Smith	4th(S8-Q)	4,376
6/9/15	Hull KR (a) (S8-Q)	L20-18	t:Locke(2),L Smith(2) g:L Smith	4th(S8-Q)	7,495
12/9/15	Widnes (h) (S8-Q)	L4-46	t:L Smith	4th(S8-Q)	3,365
19/9/15	Halifax (h) (S8-Q)	W30-12	t:Sio(2),Simon,Mullally,Jowitt g:Arundel(5)	4th(S8-Q)	3,086
27/9/15	Sheffield (a) (S8-Q) ●●	L24-10	t:Kirmond,Kavanagh g:Arundel	4th(S8-Q)	1,712
3/10/15	Bradford (h) (MPG)	W24-16	t:Kirmond,Mullally,Washbrook,Moore g:Arundel,Tansey(3)	N/A	7,236

● Played at St James' Park, Newcastle ●● Played at Bramall Lane

	D.O.B.	APP ALL	APP SL	TRIES ALL	TRIES SL	GOALS ALL	GOALS SL	FG ALL	FG SL	PTS ALL	PTS SL
Scott Anderson	8/1/86	10(6)	3(6)	1	1	0	0	0	0	4	4
Chris Annakin	30/1/91	5(6)	2(5)	0	0	0	0	0	0	0	0
Joe Arundel	22/8/91	23(1)	15	4	2	12	4	0	0	40	16
Matty Ashurst	1/11/89	10(1)	5	5	4	0	0	0	0	20	16
Dean Collis	21/10/85	11	10	2	2	0	0	0	0	8	8
Jordan Crowther	19/2/97	1(7)	1(6)	1	1	0	0	0	0	4	4
Pita Godinet	21/12/87	9(13)	6(9)	4	4	2	2	0	0	20	20
George Griffin	26/6/92	5	5	0	0	0	0	0	0	0	0
Craig Hall	21/2/88	17	15	4	3	41	30	0	0	98	72
Jordan Hand	13/5/93	(2)	(2)	0	0	0	0	0	0	0	0
Stuart Howarth	25/1/90	4	4	0	0	0	0	0	0	0	0
Tom Johnstone	13/8/95	13	10	9	9	0	0	0	0	36	36
Max Jowitt	6/5/97	3	1	1	0	0	0	0	0	4	0
Ben Kavanagh	4/3/88	7(4)	6(3)	1	0	0	0	0	0	4	0
Ian Kirke	26/12/80	2(3)	2(2)	3	1	0	0	0	0	12	4
Danny Kirmond	11/11/85	17(1)	14	7	5	0	0	0	0	28	20
Ali Lauitiiti	13/7/79	6(15)	3(11)	1	1	0	0	0	0	4	4
Kevin Locke	4/4/89	5	3	2	0	0	0	0	0	8	0
Reece Lyne	2/12/92	23	16	6	4	0	0	0	0	24	16
Paul McShane	19/11/89	17(7)	15(7)	3	3	0	0	0	0	12	12
Jacob Miller	22/8/92	30	20	15	10	17	17	0	0	94	74
Jon Molloy	23/3/91	9(4)	6(2)	2	0	0	0	0	0	8	0
Scott Moore	23/1/88	1(2)	(1)	1	0	0	0	0	0	4	0
Anthony Mullally	28/6/91	1(8)	(2)	2	0	0	0	0	0	8	0
Richard Owen	25/4/90	19(1)	15(1)	5	3	0	0	0	0	20	12
Lopini Paea	19/4/84	1(4)	1(3)	0	0	0	0	0	0	0	0
Chris Riley	22/2/88	24	21	10	8	0	0	0	0	40	32
Matt Ryan	13/6/88	14(6)	13(6)	3	3	0	0	0	0	12	12
Jarrod Sammut	15/2/87	3	3	1	1	0	0	0	0	4	4
Nick Scruton	24/12/84	29(2)	21	3	1	0	0	0	0	12	4
Mickael Simon	2/4/87	15(11)	6(10)	2	0	0	0	0	0	8	0
Michael Sio	16/5/93	8(3)	2(2)	3	0	0	0	0	0	12	0
Daniel Smith	20/3/93	11(7)	11(6)	4	3	0	0	0	0	16	12
Lee Smith	8/8/86	6	1	6	1	15	0	1	0	55	4
Tim Smith	13/1/85	25	18	1	1	0	0	0	0	4	4
Jordan Tansey	9/9/86	8	4	1	1	3	0	0	0	10	4
Kyle Trout	1/3/91	(3)	(2)	0	0	0	0	0	0	0	0
Bill Tupou	2/7/90	9	1	0	0	0	0	0	0	0	0
Anthony Walker	28/12/91	3(5)	1(3)	1	1	0	0	0	0	4	4
Danny Washbrook	18/9/85	25(7)	19(3)	4	1	0	0	0	0	16	4
Andy Yates	23/2/90	(3)	0	0	0	0	0	0	0	0	0

'SL' totals include regular season only; 'All' totals also include Super 8s (Qualifiers), Million Pound Game & Challenge Cup

Jacob Miller

LEAGUE RECORD
SL: P23-W3-D0-L20 (12th)
F402, A929, Diff-527, 6 points.

S8-Q: P7-W3-D0-L4 (4th)
F153, A170, Diff-17, 6 points.
(Winners, Million Pound Game)

CHALLENGE CUP
Round Six

ATTENDANCES
Best - v Bradford (MPG - 7,236)
Worst - v Halifax (CC - 2,062)
Total (SL/S8s/MPG only) - 61,546
Average (SL/S8s/MPG only) - 4,103
(Down by 270 on 2014)

7 January 2015 - Paul Wood granted release to join Featherstone Rovers.

15 January 2015 - Matty Russell returns home early from warm-weather training camp in Tenerife with mouth injury.

8 February 2015 - 22-8 opening day home win over Salford.

10 February 2015 - former Lawn Tennis Association boss Roger Draper becomes new CEO.

14 February 2015 - Gareth O'Brien field goal on half-time hooter decides 7-6 win at Hull FC.

20 February 2015 - 18-12 home defeat to St George Illawarra Dragons in the new World Club Series.

13 March 2015 - Ben Westwood stars in 18-6 home win to end Leeds' 100 per cent start to season.

19 March 2015 - Ben Evans ruptures hamstring in 32-24 defeat by St Helens.

3 April 2015 - 30-10 Good Friday loss at Widnes is third successive defeat.

24 April 2015 - 29-10 win at Leeds completes double over league leaders.

30 April 2015 - back rower Sam Wilde signs full-time contract until November 2017.

5 May 2015 - utility player Kurt Gidley to join from NRL side Newcastle Knights for 2016 season on one-year deal.

12 May 2015 - Wolves reject bid from Leigh Centurions for Mickey Higham.

20 May 2015 - Mick Higham joins Leigh for 50,000 pounds transfer fee. Wolves pay fee to London Broncos to bring back on-loan Brad Dwyer on new two-year contract.

31 May 2015 - 20-16 defeat by St Helens at Magic Weekend in Newcastle.

9 June 2015 - Hull FC's leading try-scorer Tom Lineham signs four-year deal from 2016 after the clubs agree £140,000 transfer fee.

15 June 2015 - club issued with formal warning about conduct of supporters following defeat at Widnes on April 2. Wolves fans threw coins, bottles and a smoke canister-type device on to pitch.

16 June 2015 - Anthony England banned for four matches for spitting at an opponent (Danny Brough) in 30-19 defeat at Huddersfield.

17 June 2015 - Ben Currie signs new four-year contract to end of 2019 season.

24 June 2015 - Lee Briers signs new two-year contract as under-19s coach alongside assistant coaching role.

KEY DATES - WARRINGTON WOLVES

30 June 2015 - Ben Currie suspended for two matches for making deliberate physical contact with match official Richard Silverwood during previous Saturday's 34-24 Challenge Cup quarter-final win over Leigh Centurions.

2 July 2015 - back-rower Sam Wilde makes debut in 17-6 home win over Wigan.

14 July 2015 - centre Chris Bridge to join Widnes Vikings at end of season.

23 July 2015 - Parramatta agree to release halfback Chris Sandow immediately to join Wolves on two-year contract.

26 July 2015 - fullback Matty Russell, who missed 13 matches after hurting right ankle at Widnes in early April, ruled out for season with second major ankle injury picked up in 44-6 win at Castleford.

28 July 2015 - Ben Westwood banned for two matches for making Grade B shoulder strike on Luke Gale.

1 August 2015 - 26-18 Challenge Cup semi-final defeat by Hull KR at Headingley.

3 August 2015 - Wakefield sign Simon Grix, sidelined all season with a leg fracture, on loan for Super 8s campaign.

12 August 2015 - Wigan Warriors back-rower Jack Hughes, on season-long loan at Huddersfield in 2015, signs two-year deal from 2016.

13 August 2015 - 17-16 defeat at Castleford ends play-off chances.

3 September 2015 - Jon Clarke to return on two-year contract as head of strength and conditioning.

12 September 2015 - Brisbane Broncos prop Mitchell Dodds signs 12-month deal for 2016.

16 September 2015 - captain Joel Monaghan and halfback Gareth O'Brien, both with a year left on contracts, to leave at season end. Prop Roy Asotasi not offered new deal.

21 September 2015 - released Simon Grix to rejoin home-town club Halifax and will combine playing career with role on Wolves' backroom staff.

23 September 2015 - 20-year-old French centre or second rower Benjamin Jullien signs full-time contract for 2016. Winger Kevin Penny signs new two-year contract to end of 2017 season.

24 September 2015 - season ends on high with 32-16 win at St Helens.

14 October 2015 - prop Anthony England released from final year of contract to join Wakefield Trinity Wildcats.

20 October 2015 - Joe Westerman signs three-year deal from Hull FC.

27 October 2015 - prop Ashton Sims extends contract by 12 months to end of 2017.

CLUB RECORDS

Highest score:
112-0 v Swinton, 20/5/2011
Highest score against:
12-84 v Bradford, 9/9/2001
Record attendance:
34,404 v Wigan, 22/1/49 *(Wilderspool)*
15,000 v St Helens, 30/3/2012
(Halliwell Jones Stadium)

MATCH RECORDS

Tries:
7 Brian Bevan v Leigh, 29/3/48
Brian Bevan v Bramley, 22/4/53
Goals:
16 Lee Briers v Swinton, 20/5/2011
Points:
44 Lee Briers v Swinton, 20/5/2011

SEASON RECORDS

Tries: 66 Brian Bevan 1952-53
Goals: 170 Steve Hesford 1978-79
Points: 363 Harry Bath 1952-53

CAREER RECORDS

Tries: 740 Brian Bevan 1945-62
Goals: 1,159 Steve Hesford 1975-85
Points: 2,586 Lee Briers 1997-2013
Appearances: 620 Brian Bevan 1945-62

WARRINGTON WOLVES

DATE	FIXTURE	RESULT	SCORERS	LGE	ATT
7/2/15	Salford (h)	W22-8	t:Myler,Higham,Atkins,R Evans g:Ratchford(3)	2nd	11,864
13/2/15	Hull FC (a)	W6-7	t:Clark g:O'Brien fg:O'Brien	4th	12,002
20/2/15	St George Illawarra (h) (WCS)	L12-18	t:O'Brien,Atkins g:O'Brien(2)	N/A	13,080
28/2/15	Catalans Dragons (a)	L38-18	t:Monaghan,Wheeler,Philbin g:O'Brien(3)	4th	8,782
8/3/15	Hull KR (h)	W32-24	t:Russell(2),Monaghan,Philbin,Wheeler,Currie g:Ratchford(4)	3rd	9,587
13/3/15	Leeds (h)	W18-6	t:Penny,Ratchford,Atkins g:Ratchford(3)	3rd	10,075
19/3/15	St Helens (a)	L32-24	t:Clark,Higham,Penny,Hill g:Ratchford,O'Brien(3)	3rd	12,618
27/3/15	Huddersfield (h)	L10-29	t:O'Brien,Penny g:O'Brien	4th	9,019
2/4/15	Widnes (a)	L30-10	t:Westwood,Currie g:O'Brien	7th	7,768
6/4/15	Castleford (h)	L14-22	t:Ratchford,Atkins,Penny g:O'Brien	9th	8,518
11/4/15	Wakefield (h)	W80-0	t:Ormsby(2),T King(2),Clark,Myler(3),Sims,Ratchford,Westwood, Monaghan,Currie(2) g:Ratchford(12)	5th	8,036
16/4/15	Wigan (a)	L30-20	t:Monaghan,Bridge(2),Currie g:Ratchford(2)	6th	14,175
24/4/15	Leeds (a)	W10-29	t:Ormsby,Monaghan,Sims,Currie,Asotasi g:Ratchford(4) fg:Patton	5th	17,340
3/5/15	Widnes (h)	W22-20	t:Ormsby,Monaghan(2),Clark,Westwood g:Ratchford	4th	10,856
10/5/15	Hull FC (h)	L26-27	t:Monaghan(2),Currie,Ormsby(2) g:Ratchford(2),Bridge	5th	9,697
15/5/15	Dewsbury (a) (CCR6)	W10-52	t:Dwyer,Atkins,Sims,Currie(2),Patton,Penny(2),Bridge,Myler g:Bridge(6)	N/A	1,771
22/5/15	Salford (a)	W18-34	t:Currie,Ormsby(3),Ratchford,Dwyer g:Ratchford(5)	5th	6,159
31/5/15	St Helens (MW) ●	L20-16	t:Ratchford,Harrison,Atkins g:Bridge(2)	5th	N/A
5/6/15	Catalans Dragons (h)	W26-18	t:Currie(2),Atkins(2),Hill g:O'Brien(3)	5th	8,611
14/6/15	Huddersfield (a)	L30-19	t:Clark,O'Brien,Harrison g:O'Brien(3) fg:O'Brien	6th	5,797
19/6/15	Hull KR (a)	L36-10	t:Hill,Ormsby g:Patton	7th	7,455
27/6/15	Leigh (h) (CCQF)	W34-24	t:Sims,Currie(2),Penny(2),G King g:O'Brien(4),Westwood	N/A	10,119
2/7/15	Wigan (h)	W17-6	t:Myler,Atkins,O'Brien g:O'Brien(2) fg:O'Brien	6th	10,504
12/7/15	Wakefield (a)	W20-40	t:Ratchford,Philbin,Russell(2),Westwood,Clark,Myler g:O'Brien(6)	6th	3,354
16/7/15	St Helens (h)	L14-20	t:Currie,Penny g:O'Brien(3)	6th	9,618
26/7/15	Castleford (a)	W6-44	t:Monaghan(2),Westwood,O'Brien,Ormsby,Currie,Ratchford,Wilde,Myler g:O'Brien(4)	6th	7,239
1/8/15	Hull KR (CCSF) ●●	L26-18	t:Atkins,Myler,Currie g:O'Brien(3)	N/A	13,049
7/8/15	Leeds (a) (S8)	L49-10	t:Penny(2) g:Sandow	6th	13,118
13/8/15	Castleford (a) (S8)	L17-16	t:Myler(2),Penny g:Sandow(2)	6th	5,212
21/8/15	Wigan (h) (S8)	L0-28		6th	10,095
6/9/15	Hull FC (h) (S8)	W46-16	t:Penny(3),Wheeler(2),Currie,Atkins,Monaghan(2) g:Sandow(5)	6th	8,076
13/9/15	Huddersfield (a) (S8)	L48-10	t:Westwood,Asotasi g:Sandow	6th	5,563
19/9/15	Catalans Dragons (h) (S8)	W48-6	t:Monaghan(3),Atkins(2),Johnson(2),Currie,Myler g:Sandow(4),Monaghan,Asotasi	6th	7,862
24/9/15	St Helens (a) (S8)	W16-32	t:Johnson,Monaghan,Hill,Atkins,Asotasi,Penny g:Sandow(3),Monaghan	6th	10,966

● Played at St James' Park, Newcastle ●● Played at Headingley Carnegie, Leeds

	D.O.B.	APP ALL	APP SL	TRIES ALL	TRIES SL	GOALS ALL	GOALS SL	FG ALL	FG SL	PTS ALL	PTS SL
Roy Asotasi	6/1/82	5(25)	5(23)	3	3	1	1	0	0	14	14
Ryan Atkins	7/10/85	29	25	14	11	0	0	0	0	56	44
Chris Bridge	5/7/84	16(2)	15(1)	3	2	9	3	0	0	30	14
Daryl Clark	10/2/93	26(6)	23(6)	6	6	0	0	0	0	24	24
Ben Currie	15/7/94	31	27	19	14	0	0	0	0	76	56
Brad Dwyer	28/4/93	1(18)	(16)	2	1	0	0	0	0	8	4
Anthony England	19/10/86	2(13)	2(10)	0	0	0	0	0	0	0	0
Ben Evans	30/10/92	(4)	(4)	0	0	0	0	0	0	0	0
Rhys Evans	30/10/92	5	4	1	1	0	0	0	0	4	4
Ben Harrison	24/2/88	21(8)	18(7)	2	2	0	0	0	0	8	8
Mick Higham	18/9/80	7(8)	7(7)	2	2	0	0	0	0	8	8
Chris Hill	3/11/87	33(1)	29(1)	4	4	0	0	0	0	16	16
Jack Johnson	25/4/96	4	4	3	3	0	0	0	0	12	12
George King	24/2/95	4(15)	4(13)	1	0	0	0	0	0	4	0
Toby King	9/7/96	6(1)	6(1)	2	2	0	0	0	0	8	8
James Laithwaite	23/9/91	11(11)	9(10)	0	0	0	0	0	0	0	0
Joel Monaghan	22/4/82	27	24	17	17	2	2	0	0	72	72
Richard Myler	21/5/90	25	21	12	10	0	0	0	0	48	40
Gareth O'Brien	31/10/91	18(1)	15	5	4	40	31	3	3	103	81
Gene Ormsby	12/9/92	17	14	11	11	0	0	0	0	44	44
Declan Patton	23/5/95	9	8	1	0	1	1	1	1	7	3
Kevin Penny	3/10/87	23	20	16	12	0	0	0	0	64	48
Joe Philbin	16/11/94	6(10)	6(8)	3	3	0	0	0	0	12	12
Stefan Ratchford	19/7/88	31	29	7	7	37	37	0	0	102	102
Matthew Russell	6/6/93	10	10	4	4	0	0	0	0	16	16
Chris Sandow	9/1/89	7	7	0	0	16	16	0	0	32	32
Ashton Sims	26/2/85	28(4)	24(4)	4	2	0	0	0	0	16	8
Ben Westwood	25/7/81	31	28	6	6	1	0	0	0	26	24
Gary Wheeler	30/9/89	8(3)	6(3)	4	4	0	0	0	0	16	16
Sam Wilde	8/9/95	1(6)	(6)	1	1	0	0	0	0	4	4

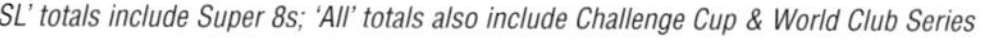

'SL' totals include Super 8s; 'All' totals also include Challenge Cup & World Club Series

Chris Hill

LEAGUE RECORD
P30-W15-D0-L15
(6th, SL)
F714, A636, Diff+78
30 points.

CHALLENGE CUP
Semi-Finalists

ATTENDANCES
Best - v St George Illawarra (WCS - 13,080)
Worst - v Catalans Dragons (S8 - 7,862)
Total (SL/S8s only) - 132,418
Average (SL/S8s only) - 9,458
(Down by 219 on 2014)

25 November 2014 - Vikings fined £20,000 for crowd disturbances at Challenge Cup semi-final in August 2014.

9 January 2015 - head coach Denis Betts signs one-year contract extension to end of 2017 season

12 January 2015 - Gil Dudson signs from Wigan on two-year deal.

5 February 2015 - Patrick Ah Van sent off after 23 minutes for high tackle as Vikings fight back from 16-0 down to draw 22-22 with Wigan in rousing opening match of season in front of 9,286 at the Select Security Stadium.

10 February 2015 - Patrick Ah Van banned for one match after Early Guilty Plea to reckless high tackle on Wigan's Josh Charnley.

12 February 2015 - prop Paul Johnson and hooker Grant Gore join Whitehaven on month's loan.

26 February 2015 - Tom Gilmore joins London Broncos on month loan.

1 March 2015 - Lloyd White scores four tries in 58-16 round 3 home win over Wakefield for first victory of season.

3 April 2015 - Matt Whitley makes debut in 30-10 Good Friday home win over Warrington.

6 April 2015 – Easter Monday 32-16 defeat to Dragons in Perpignan.

10 April 2015 - 22-8 defeat away at Hull FC sinks Vikings to 11th spot.

15 April 2015 - Ben Kavanagh joins Wakefield on loan for rest of season.

16 April 2015 - Danny Craven joins Halifax on loan for rest of season.

19 April 2015 - Patrick Ah Van and Rhys Hanbury score two tries each in 46-16 home win over Castleford.

23 April 2015 - teenage forward Matt Whitley signs full-time three-year contract.

KEY DATES - WIDNES VIKINGS

30 May 2015 - Kevin Brown scores hat-trick in 38-16 victory over Salford in first game of Magic Weekend in Newcastle.

1 June 2015 - winger Patrick Ah Van signs 12-month contract extension to end of 2016.

4 June 2015 - captain Kevin Brown signs two-year contract extension to end of 2018.

23 June 2015 - halfback Grant Gore and threequarter Declan Hulme set to leave club at end of season.

30 June 2015 - Australian centre Cameron Phelps to leave the club at end of season

14 July 2015 - Warrington centre Chris Bridge to join Vikings on two-year deal from start of 2016.

17 July 2015 - two late tries for Wigan end top-eight hopes in 20-10 defeat at the DW Stadium.

21 July 2015 - St George Illawarra Dragons release utility back Charly Runciman to enable him to join Vikings.

26 July 2015 - last-gasp Danny Craven field goal secures round 23, 21-20 home win over Salford and ninth placed Super League finish.

10 August 2015 - Hull centre Setaimata Sa signs for 2016 season.

17 August 2015 - Canterbury Bulldogs winger Corey Thompson signs two-year deal from 2016.

21 August 2015 - Chris Clarkson and Willie Isa to leave at end of season after rejecting new contract offers.

12 September 2015 - 46-4 Qualifiers win at Wakefield ensures Super League place in 2016.

21 September 2015 - Phil Joseph to leave a year before the end of his contract.

27 September 2015 - Patrick Ah Van reaches career milestone of 700 points with brace of tries in 50-6 home win over Leigh on last day of season.

28 October 2015 - Jack Owens released.

CLUB RECORDS

Highest score:
90-4 v Doncaster, 10/6/2007
Highest score against:
6-76 v Catalan Dragons, 31/3/2012
Record attendance:
24,205 v St Helens, 16/2/61

MATCH RECORDS

Tries: 7 Phil Cantillon v York, 18/2/2001
Goals: 14 Mark Hewitt v Oldham, 25/7/99
Tim Hartley v Saddleworth, 7/3/2009
Points:
38 Gavin Dodd v Doncaster, 10/6/2007

SEASON RECORDS

Tries: 58 Martin Offiah 1988-89
Goals: 161 Mick Nanyn 2007
Points: 434 Mick Nanyn 2007

CAREER RECORDS

Tries: 234 Mal Aspey 1964-80
Goals: 1,083 Ray Dutton 1966-78
Points: 2,195 Ray Dutton 1966-78
Appearances: 591 Keith Elwell 1970-86

WIDNES VIKINGS

DATE	FIXTURE	RESULT	SCORERS	LGE	ATT
5/2/15	Wigan (h)	D22-22	t:Mellor,Hanbury,Phelps,Dean g:Tickle(2),Marsh	6th	9,286
13/2/15	Leeds (a)	L38-6	t:Manuokafoa g:Tickle	8th	14,132
1/3/15	Wakefield (h)	W58-16	t:Mellor,Brown(2),White(4),Ah Van(2),Clarkson g:Tickle(5),White(4)	6th	5,810
6/3/15	Huddersfield (a)	L24-12	t:Mellor,Manuokafoa g:Tickle(2)	6th	5,452
13/3/15	St Helens (h)	L20-30	t:O'Carroll,Ah Van,Heremaia g:Tickle,Marsh(3)	10th	7,772
22/3/15	Hull KR (h)	W20-16	t:Flynn(2),Galea g:Owens(4)	5th	5,273
26/3/15	Salford (a)	L36-8	t:Flynn g:Owens(2)	9th	3,476
2/4/15	Warrington (h)	W30-10	t:Phelps,Marsh(2),White,Brown,Owens g:Owens(3)	9th	7,768
6/4/15	Catalans Dragons (a)	L32-16	t:Owens,Marsh,Gerrard g:Owens(2)	10th	9,683
10/4/15	Hull FC (a)	L22-8	t:Brown,Ah Van	11th	9,295
19/4/15	Castleford (h)	W46-16	t:Ah Van(2),Hanbury(2),Owens,Marsh,Brown,Phelps g:Owens(7)	9th	5,457
24/4/15	St Helens (a)	L34-16	t:Brown,Mellor,Whitley g:Owens(2)	10th	11,271
3/5/15	Warrington (a)	L22-20	t:Owens,Flynn,Brown(2) g:Owens(2)	11th	10,856
10/5/15	Leeds (h)	W38-24	t:Clarkson,Marsh,Mellor,Galea,Manuokafoa,Dean,Heremaia g:Owens(5)	10th	6,113
17/5/15	Batley (h) (CCR6)	W26-22	t:White,Ah Van,Brown(2),Phelps g:Owens(3)	N/A	3,866
24/5/15	Wakefield (a)	W18-30	t:Hanbury,Marsh(3),Owens,White g:White(3)	8th	3,132
30/5/15	Salford (MW) ●	W16-38	t:Ah Van(2),Galea,Brown(3),Marsh g:Owens(5)	8th	N/A
4/6/15	Hull FC (h)	L12-25	t:Owens,Whitley g:Owens(2)	9th	5,573
14/6/15	Hull KR (a)	L38-16	t:Marsh,Brown,Dean g:Owens(2)	9th	6,982
21/6/15	Huddersfield (h)	L22-30	t:Ah Van,Owens,Brown(2) g:Owens(3)	10th	5,420
28/6/15	St Helens (a) (CCQF)	L36-20	t:Mellor,Craven,Ah Van,Dean g:Craven,Ah Van	N/A	8,806
5/7/15	Castleford (a)	L34-20	t:Owens,Clarkson,Gilmore,Leuluai g:Owens(2)	10th	7,002
12/7/15	Catalans Dragons (h)	W29-22	t:Ah Van(2),Gilmore,Flynn(2) g:Marsh(3),Gilmore fg:Gilmore	10th	4,822
17/7/15	Wigan (a)	L20-10	t:Gilmore,Dean g:Gilmore	10th	13,194
26/7/15	Salford (h)	W21-20	t:Clarkson,Flynn,Marsh,Heremaia g:Marsh(2) fg:Craven	9th	5,477
9/8/15	Halifax (a) (S8-Q)	W0-14	t:Runciman(2),Gerrard g:White	2nd(S8-Q)	3,022
16/8/15	Sheffield (h) (S8-Q)	W48-12	t:Brown,Marsh(3),Runciman(2),Hanbury,Galea,Mellor,Flynn g:Tickle(2),White(2)	1st(S8-Q)	4,567
23/8/15	Hull KR (h) (S8-Q)	L8-12	t:Runciman,Whitley	2nd(S8-Q)	5,461
6/9/15	Bradford (a) (S8-Q)	W12-56	t:Mellor(3),Ah Van(3),Runciman,Cahill,Hanbury,Brown g:White(2),Tickle(6)	2nd(S8-Q)	6,881
12/9/15	Wakefield (a) (S8-Q)	W4-46	t:White,Hanbury(4),Heremaia,Brown,Flynn g:Tickle(5),Ah Van(2)	2nd(S8-Q)	3,365
20/9/15	Salford (h) (S8-Q)	L10-24	t:Ah Van,White g:Ah Van	3rd(S8-Q)	5,285
27/9/15	Leigh (h) (S8-Q)	W50-6	t:Ah Van(2),Brown,Runciman,Flynn,Gerrard,Hanbury,Mellor,Owens g:Tickle(5),Owens(2)	2nd(S8-Q)	5,550

● Played at St James' Park, Newcastle

		APP		TRIES		GOALS		FG		PTS	
	D.O.B.	ALL	SL	ALL	SL	ALL	SL	ALL	SL	ALL	SL
Patrick Ah Van	17/3/88	23	16	19	11	4	0	0	0	84	44
Kevin Brown	2/10/84	22	13	20	14	0	0	0	0	80	56
Hep Cahill	15/10/86	13(2)	8	1	0	0	0	0	0	4	0
Liam Carberry	24/2/93	2	2	0	0	0	0	0	0	0	0
Jay Chapelhow	21/9/95	(1)	0	0	0	0	0	0	0	0	0
Chris Clarkson	7/4/90	21(4)	17(1)	4	4	0	0	0	0	16	16
Danny Craven	21/11/91	3(5)	3(3)	1	0	1	0	1	1	7	1
Chris Dean	17/1/88	25(2)	17(1)	5	4	0	0	0	0	20	16
Gil Dudson	16/6/90	23(5)	16(3)	0	0	0	0	0	0	0	0
Paddy Flynn	11/12/87	18	10	10	7	0	0	0	0	40	28
Danny Galea	20/9/83	22(3)	17(3)	4	3	0	0	0	0	16	12
Alex Gerrard	5/11/91	22(7)	14(7)	3	1	0	0	0	0	12	4
Tom Gilmore	2/2/94	6	6	3	3	2	2	1	1	17	17
Grant Gore	21/11/91	3(1)	3(1)	0	0	0	0	0	0	0	0
Rhys Hanbury	27/8/85	30	22	11	4	0	0	0	0	44	16
Aaron Heremaia	19/9/82	12(20)	9(14)	4	3	0	0	0	0	16	12
Declan Hulme	14/1/93	2	2	0	0	0	0	0	0	0	0
Willie Isa	1/1/89	10(9)	8(7)	0	0	0	0	0	0	0	0
Phil Joseph	10/1/85	2(8)	1(8)	0	0	0	0	0	0	0	0
Ben Kavanagh	4/3/88	2(4)	2(4)	0	0	0	0	0	0	0	0
Macgraff Leuluai	9/2/90	10(9)	8(8)	1	1	0	0	0	0	4	4
Manase Manuokafoa	24/3/85	4(27)	2(20)	3	3	0	0	0	0	12	12
Stefan Marsh	3/9/90	24	19	14	11	9	9	0	0	74	62
Joe Mellor	28/11/90	30	21	11	5	0	0	0	0	44	20
Eamon O'Carroll	13/6/87	13(1)	13(1)	1	1	0	0	0	0	4	4
Jack Owens	3/6/94	17(1)	16	9	8	46	41	0	0	128	114
Cameron Phelps	11/2/85	13(1)	12(1)	4	3	0	0	0	0	16	12
Charly Runciman	22/7/93	7	0	7	0	0	0	0	0	28	0
Danny Tickle	10/3/83	12(3)	7(1)	0	0	29	11	0	0	58	22
Lloyd White	9/8/88	19(3)	13(1)	9	6	12	7	0	0	60	38
Matt Whitley	20/1/96	6(12)	2(8)	3	2	0	0	0	0	12	8

'SL' totals include regular season only; 'All' totals also include Super 8s (Qualifiers) & Challenge Cup

Aaron Heremaia

LEAGUE RECORD
SL: P23-W9-D1-L13 (9th)
F518, A565, Diff-47, 19 points.

S8-Q: P7-W5-D0-L2 (2nd)
F232, A70, Diff+162, 10 points.

CHALLENGE CUP
Quarter Finalists

ATTENDANCES
Best - v Wigan (SL - 9,286)
Worst - v Batley (CC - 3,866)
Total (SL/S8s only) - 89,634
Average (SL/S8s only) - 5,976
(Up by 340 on 2014)

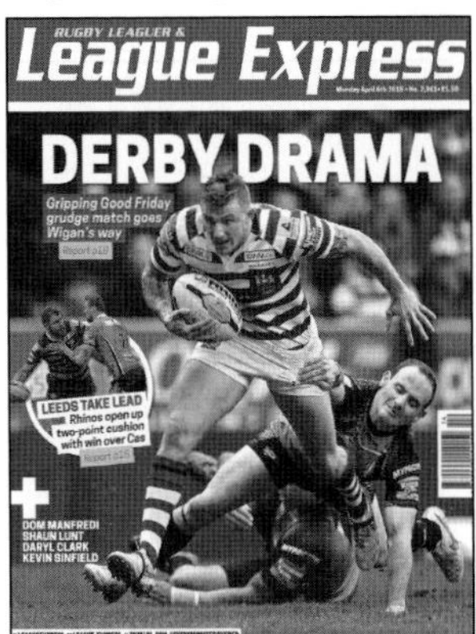

KEY DATES - WIGAN WARRIORS

11 November 2014 - Lee Mossop returns from Parramatta after a year on three-year deal.

14 November 2014 - Scott Taylor moves to Salford Red Devils on season-long loan for 2015.

21 November 2014 - Ben Flower fined 50 per cent of his wages for six months by club, three months suspended.

20 December 2014 - Eddy Pettybourne released for personal reasons halfway through two-year contract.

23 January 2015 - Joe Burgess to leave at end of 2015 season to join Sydney Roosters.

5 February 2015 - Warriors let slip 16-0 lead to draw 22-22 at 12-man Widnes in rousing opening match of SLXX.

10 February 2015 - Matty Smith suspended for one match after Early Guilty Plea to charge of kicking Rhys Hanbury in draw at Widnes.

14 February 2015 - prop Ryan Sutton's first try for the club seven minutes from the end clinches 24-16 home win over Huddersfield.

18 February 2015 - Sam Powell gets one-match ban for dangerous contact in win over Giants.

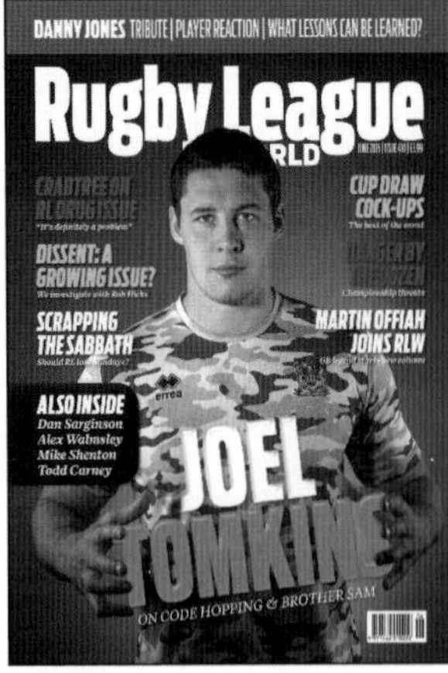

21 February 2015 - last-second Joe Burgess try sets up dramatic 14-12 golden-point extra-time win for Brisbane in second game of three-match World Club Series.

26 February 2015 - Rhodri Lloyd joins Swinton Lions on month's loan.

3 April 2015 - capacity 24,054 crowd at DW Stadium witnesses 12-4 win over St Helens.

4 April 2015 - Dom Manfredi signs new four-year contract.

8 April 2015 - Sam Tomkins to be released from NZ Warriors contract at end of season.

16 April 2015 - Sam Tomkins' return on four-year contract in 2016, having rejected offer from Warrington, announced at half-time of 30-20 home win over Wolves.

21 April 2015 - James Greenwood and Oliver Gildart join Salford on month's loan.

23 April 2015 - Joe Burgess scores his first Super League hat-trick in first away win of season, a 40-22 victory at Wakefield.

19 May 2015 - Scott Taylor, currently on loan at Salford, to join Hull FC at end of season.

20 May 2015 - prop James Greenwood signs for Hull KR on loan until end of season.

27 May 2015 - prop Tony Clubb signs new four-year deal.

30 May 2015 - Michael McIlorum makes 200th appearance for club in 27-12 win over league leaders Leeds Rhinos in front of a one-day Magic Weekend record crowd of 40,871 at St James' Park.

4 June 2015 - hooker Logan Tomkins joins Salford on loan to end of season.

8 June 2015 - coach Shaun Wane warned by RFL as to his future conduct following two incidents in which he criticised match officials.

16 June 2015 - centre Anthony Gelling signs new four-year deal to end of 2019.

9 July 2015 - Matty Smith kicks last-minute penalty to snatch dramatic 26-24 home victory over league leaders Leeds to close to within two points of Rhinos with two games left before Super 8s.

14 July 2015 - Matt Bowen to be released at end of season.

11 August 2015 - hooker Michael McIlorum signs new two-year contract to end of 2019.

5 September 2015 - 42-16 victory over Catalans Dragons at The New Den, Millwall, to confirm place in semi-finals.

8 September 2015 - centre Dan Sarginson out for six months after surgery on hamstring injury.

11 September 2015 - Taulima Tautai banned for three games for dangerous throw on Mickey Paea in 30-24 home win over Hull FC.

26 September 2015 - Dom Manfredi scores four tries in 47-12 home win over Castleford, as Leeds claim League Leaders Trophy with last-gasp win at Huddersfield.

29 September 2015 - Willie Isa signs from Widnes on two-year deal from 2016.

1 October 2015 - third successive Grand Final after 32-8 home semi-final win over Huddersfield.

10 October 2015 - 22-20 Grand Final defeat by Leeds.

20 October 2015 - John Bateman signs three-season contract extension to end of 2019 with conditional final-year option to play in the NRL.

CLUB RECORDS

Highest score:
116-0 v Flimby & Fothergill, 14/2/25
Highest score against:
0-75 v St Helens, 26/6/2005
Record attendance:
47,747 v St Helens, 27/3/59 *(Central Park)*
25,004 v St Helens, 25/3/2005
(JJB/DW Stadium)

MATCH RECORDS

Tries: 10 Martin Offiah v Leeds, 10/5/92
Shaun Edwards v Swinton, 29/9/92
Goals: 22 Jim Sullivan
v Flimby & Fothergill, 14/2/25
Points: 44 Jim Sullivan
v Flimby & Fothergill, 14/2/25

SEASON RECORDS

Tries: 62 Johnny Ring 1925-26
Goals: 186 Frano Botica 1994-95
Points: 462 Pat Richards 2010

CAREER RECORDS

Tries: 478 Billy Boston 1953-68
Goals: 2,317 Jim Sullivan 1921-46
Points: 4,883 Jim Sullivan 1921-46
Appearances: 774 Jim Sullivan 1921-46

WIGAN WARRIORS

DATE	FIXTURE	RESULT	SCORERS	LGE	ATT
5/2/15	Widnes (a)	D22-22	t:J Tomkins,Gelling(2),Burgess g:Smith(3)	6th	9,286
13/2/15	Huddersfield (h)	W24-16	t:J Tomkins(2),Bateman,McIlorum,Sutton g:Hampshire(2)	5th	12,488
21/2/15	Brisbane (h) (WCS)	L12-14 *(aet)*	t:L Farrell,Burgess g:Smith(2)	N/A	20,842
1/3/15	Hull KR (a)	L22-20	t:Burgess,Mossop,Charnley,Williams g:Smith(2)	7th	7,632
6/3/15	Castleford (a)	L42-14	t:Charnley(2),Smith g:Smith	7th	7,772
13/3/15	Hull FC (h)	W13-12	t:J Tomkins,Sarginson g:Smith(2) fg:Smith	5th	11,718
20/3/15	Leeds (a)	L26-14	t:Smith,Burgess g:Smith(3)	7th	18,350
27/3/15	Wakefield (h)	W52-10	t:L Farrell(2),Clubb,Manfredi(2),Gelling(3),Mossop g:Smith(8)	5th	10,787
3/4/15	St Helens (h)	W12-4	t:Manfredi,Burgess g:Smith,Hampshire	3rd	24,054
6/4/15	Salford (a)	L24-18	t:Patrick,Hampshire,Burgess g:Hampshire(3)	5th	6,561
12/4/15	Catalans Dragons (h)	W34-0	t:Burgess(2),Sarginson,Manfredi(3),Gelling,Hampshire g:Hampshire	3rd	12,162
16/4/15	Warrington (h)	W30-20	t:L Farrell,Hampshire,Manfredi(3),Gelling g:Smith(3)	3rd	14,175
23/4/15	Wakefield (a)	W22-40	t:Crosby,Smith,Burgess(3),Manfredi,Mossop g:Smith(6)	3rd	3,107
1/5/15	Hull KR (h)	W60-0	t:Crosby,Burgess(3),L Farrell,J Tomkins,Williams(2),Sarginson, Manfredi,Tautai g:Smith(8)	3rd	11,468
8/5/15	Castleford (h)	W28-0	t:Burgess,McIlorum,Sarginson,Manfredi g:Smith(6)	2nd	15,022
15/5/15	Hull KR (h) (CCR6) ●	L12-16	t:J Tomkins,Burgess g:Smith(2)	N/A	4,677
23/5/15	Catalans Dragons (a)	L58-16	t:Charnley,Sarginson,Burgess g:Smith(2)	3rd	10,423
30/5/15	Leeds (MW) ●●	W12-27	t:Sarginson,Williams,Burgess,Bowen(2) g:Smith(3) fg:Smith	3rd	N/A
7/6/15	Huddersfield (a)	W18-32	t:Burgess,L Farrell(2),Charnley(2),Bateman g:Smith(4)	3rd	7,307
12/6/15	St Helens (a)	L30-14	t:Sarginson,Burgess,J Tomkins g:Smith	3rd	16,692
19/6/15	Salford (h)	W19-12	t:Burgess,L Farrell,Sarginson g:Smith(3) fg:Smith	3rd	13,710
2/7/15	Warrington (a)	L17-6	t:Manfredi g:Bowen	3rd	10,504
9/7/15	Leeds (h)	W26-24	t:L Farrell,O'Loughlin,Bowen,Charnley g:Smith(5)	3rd	15,009
17/7/15	Widnes (h)	W20-10	t:Charnley,Burgess,Hampshire,Gelling g:Smith(2)	3rd	13,194
23/7/15	Hull FC (a)	W12-48	t:Burgess,Bateman,Powell,Williams,Bowen(2),O'Loughlin,Crosby g:Smith(8)	3rd	10,787
6/8/15	Huddersfield (h) (S8)	W30-22	t:L Farrell,Manfredi,Williams,Patrick,Crosby g:Smith(5)	2nd	11,448
14/8/15	Leeds (a) (S8)	L25-18	t:L Farrell(2),Bateman,Manfredi g:Bowen	2nd	15,026
21/8/15	Warrington (a) (S8)	W0-28	t:L Farrell,Flower,Bateman(2),Gildart g:Bowen(4)	2nd	10,095
5/9/15	Catalans Dragons (h) (S8) ●●●	W42-16	t:Flower,Bowen(2),Gildart,Charnley,Patrick,Manfredi g:Bowen(7)	2nd	8,101
11/9/15	Hull FC (h) (S8)	W30-24	t:Gildart,Charnley,Bateman,Flower,Burgess g:Hampshire(5)	2nd	12,028
18/9/15	St Helens (a) (S8)	L18-14	t:J Tomkins,Williams g:Bowen(3)	2nd	15,808
25/9/15	Castleford (h) (S8)	W47-12	t:Manfredi(4),Bowen,Gildart,Williams,Burgess,Patrick g:Bowen(5) fg:Smith	2nd	15,017
1/10/15	Huddersfield (h) (SF)	W32-8	t:Flower,Bateman(2),Manfredi,Clubb g:Bowen(6)	N/A	10,035
10/10/15	Leeds (GF) ●●●●	L22-20	t:Burgess,Manfredi,Bowen g:Bowen(4)	N/A	73,512

● Played at Leigh Sports Village
●● Played at St James' Park, Newcastle
●●● Played at The Den, Millwall
●●●● Played at Old Trafford, Manchester

		APP		TRIES		GOALS		FG		PTS	
	D.O.B.	ALL	SL	ALL	SL	ALL	SL	ALL	SL	ALL	SL
John Bateman	30/9/93	30(1)	28(1)	9	9	0	0	0	0	36	36
Matt Bowen	9/3/82	22	21	9	9	31	31	0	0	98	98
Joe Burgess	14/10/94	29	27	26	24	0	0	0	0	104	96
Josh Charnley	26/6/91	21	19	10	10	0	0	0	0	40	40
Tony Clubb	12/6/87	5(21)	5(20)	2	2	0	0	0	0	8	8
Dominic Crosby	11/12/90	24(1)	22(1)	4	4	0	0	0	0	16	16
Connor Farrell	6/11/93	1(6)	1(6)	0	0	0	0	0	0	0	0
Liam Farrell	2/7/90	28	26	13	12	0	0	0	0	52	48
Ben Flower	19/10/87	15(4)	15(4)	4	4	0	0	0	0	16	16
Anthony Gelling	18/10/90	19(1)	18(1)	8	8	0	0	0	0	32	32
Oliver Gildart	6/8/96	7	7	4	4	0	0	0	0	16	16
James Greenwood	17/6/91	(1)	(1)	0	0	0	0	0	0	0	0
Ryan Hampshire	29/12/94	13(2)	12(2)	4	4	12	12	0	0	40	40
Rhodri Lloyd	22/7/93	1(1)	1(1)	0	0	0	0	0	0	0	0
Dominic Manfredi	1/10/93	18	18	22	22	0	0	0	0	88	88
Michael McIlorum	10/1/88	32	30	2	2	0	0	0	0	8	8
Lee Mossop	17/1/89	16(13)	15(13)	3	3	0	0	0	0	12	12
Sean O'Loughlin	24/11/82	20	19	2	2	0	0	0	0	8	8
Larne Patrick	3/11/88	7(22)	7(20)	4	4	0	0	0	0	16	16
Sam Powell	3/7/92	5(18)	5(17)	1	1	0	0	0	0	4	4
Dan Sarginson	26/5/93	20	18	8	8	0	0	0	0	32	32
Matty Smith	23/7/87	33	31	3	3	80	76	4	4	176	168
Ryan Sutton	2/8/95	6(12)	5(11)	1	1	0	0	0	0	4	4
Taulima Tautai	3/4/88	5(22)	5(20)	1	1	0	0	0	0	4	4
Lewis Tierney	20/10/94	1	1	0	0	0	0	0	0	0	0
Joel Tomkins	21/3/87	33	31	8	7	0	0	0	0	32	28
Logan Tomkins	1/8/91	1(8)	1(7)	0	0	0	0	0	0	0	0
George Williams	31/10/94	30(3)	28(3)	8	8	0	0	0	0	32	32

'SL' totals include Super 8s, semi-final & Grand Final; 'All' totals also include Challenge Cup & World Club Series

Joe Burgess

LEAGUE RECORD
P30-W20-D1-L9
(2nd, SL/Grand Final Runners-Up)
F798, A530, Diff+268
41 points.

CHALLENGE CUP
Round Six

ATTENDANCES
Best - v St Helens (SL - 24,054)
Worst - v Hull KR (CC - 4,677)
Total (SL/S8s/SF only) - 210,416
Average (SL/S8s/SF only) - 13,151
(Down by 651 on 2014)

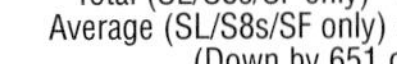

SUPER LEAGUE XX
Round by Round

ROUND 1

Thursday 5th February 2015

WIDNES VIKINGS 22 WIGAN WARRIORS 22

VIKINGS: 1 Rhys Hanbury; 5 Patrick Ah Van; 3 Cameron Phelps; 4 Stefan Marsh; 20 Declan Hulme; 6 Kevin Brown (C); 7 Joe Mellor; 8 Eamon O'Carroll; 22 Liam Carberry; 25 Alex Gerrard; 17 Chris Clarkson (D); 12 Danny Tickle; 13 Hep Cahill. Subs (all used): 10 Manase Manuokafoa (D); 33 Aaron Heremaia (D); 16 Willie Isa; 14 Chris Dean.
Tries: Mellor (35), Hanbury (46), Phelps (66), Dean (77); **Goals:** Tickle 2/2, Marsh 1/2.
Dismissal: Ah Van (23) - high tackle on Charnley.
WARRIORS: 1 Matt Bowen; 2 Josh Charnley; 3 Anthony Gelling; 11 Joel Tomkins; 5 Joe Burgess; 6 George Williams; 7 Matty Smith; 8 Dominic Crosby; 26 Logan Tomkins; 28 Ryan Sutton; 14 John Bateman; 12 Liam Farrell; 13 Sean O'Loughlin (C). Subs (all used): 16 Sam Powell; 24 Taulima Tautai (D); 25 Larne Patrick (D); 17 Tony Clubb.
Tries: J Tomkins (8), Gelling (15, 27), Burgess (55); **Goals:** Smith 3/4.
Sin bin: Smith (78) - kicking Hanbury.
Rugby Leaguer & League Express Men of the Match: *Vikings:* Joe Mellor; *Warriors:* John Bateman.
Penalty count: 7-7; **Half-time:** 6-16; **Referee:** James Child; **Attendance:** 9,286.

Friday 6th February 2015

ST HELENS 18 CATALANS DRAGONS 7

SAINTS: 1 Jonny Lomax; 2 Tom Makinson; 3 Jordan Turner; 17 Mark Percival; 5 Adam Swift; 6 Travis Burns (D); 12 Jon Wilkin (C); 10 Kyle Amor; 9 James Roby; 14 Alex Walmsley; 21 Joe Greenwood; 11 Atelea Vea (D); 4 Josh Jones. Subs (all used): 8 Mose Masoe; 16 Lance Hohaia; 19 Greg Richards; 25 Andre Savelio.
Tries: Vea (7), Turner (44), Savelio (58), Makinson (75); **Goals:** Makinson 1/3, Percival 0/1.
Sin bin: Richards (37) - repeated team offences.
DRAGONS: 1 Morgan Escare; 2 Vincent Duport; 3 Ben Pomeroy; 4 Willie Tonga (D); 5 Michael Oldfield; 14 Thomas Bosc; 9 Ian Henderson; 15 Jeff Lima; 16 Eloi Pelissier; 10 Remi Casty (D2); 11 Zeb Taia; 17 Elliott Whitehead; 12 Louis Anderson. Subs (all used): 8 Olivier Elima; 13 Gregory Mounis (C); 18 Benjamin Garcia; 21 Julian Bousquet.
Try: Pelissier (37); **Goals:** Bosc 1/1; **Field goal:** Bosc (40).
Sin bin: Oldfield (57) - holding down.
Rugby Leaguer & League Express Men of the Match: *Saints:* Alex Walmsley; *Dragons:* Remi Casty.
Penalty count: 8-11; **Half-time:** 6-7; **Referee:** Phil Bentham; **Attendance:** 12,008.

Saturday 7th February 2015

WARRINGTON WOLVES 22 SALFORD RED DEVILS 8

WOLVES: 6 Stefan Ratchford; 2 Rhys Evans; 5 Joel Monaghan (C); 4 Ryan Atkins; 24 Kevin Penny; 20 Gareth O'Brien; 7 Richard Myler; 8 Chris Hill; 9 Daryl Clark (D); 10 Ashton Sims (D); 17 Ben Currie; 18 James Laithwaite; 12 Ben Westwood. Subs (all used): 13 Ben Harrison; 14 Mick Higham; 15 Roy Asotasi; 23 Gary Wheeler (D).
Tries: Myler (26), Higham (30), Atkins (55), R Evans (70); **Goals:** Ratchford 3/4.
Sin bin: Westwood (50) - high tackle on A Walne.
RED DEVILS: 19 Niall Evalds; 2 Ben Jones-Bishop (D); 3 Josh Griffin; 18 Mason Caton-Brown; 5 Greg Johnson; 6 Rangi Chase; 14 Theo Fages; 16 Scott Taylor (D); 9 Tommy Lee; 13 Gareth Hock; 11 Harrison Hansen (C); 12 Weller Hauraki (D); 31 Cory Paterson (D). Subs (all used): 7 Michael Dobson (D); 8 Adrian Morley; 15 Darrell Griffin; 20 Adam Walne.
Tries: Jones-Bishop (58, 78); **Goals:** J Griffin 0/1, Dobson 0/1.
Sin bin: A Walne (37) - repeated team offences.
Rugby Leaguer & League Express Men of the Match: *Wolves:* Stefan Ratchford; *Red Devils:* Gareth Hock.
Penalty count: 11-8; **Half-time:** 12-0; **Referee:** Richard Silverwood; **Attendance:** 11,864.

Sunday 8th February 2015

HUDDERSFIELD GIANTS 0 HULL FC 19

GIANTS: 5 Aaron Murphy; 2 Jermaine McGillvary; 3 Leroy Cudjoe; 4 Joe Wardle; 18 Jodie Broughton; 6 Danny Brough (C); 20 Jamie Ellis (D); 10 Craig Huby (D); 7 Luke Robinson; 15 Craig Kopczak; 11 Brett Ferres; 12 Jack Hughes (D); 13 Chris Bailey. Subs (all used): 8 Eorl Crabtree; 9 Shaun Lunt; 17 Ukuma Ta'ai; 19 Anthony Mullally.
HULL: 1 Jamie Shaul; 2 Tom Lineham; 3 Setaimata Sa; 4 Kirk Yeaman; 5 Fetuli Talanoa; 6 Leon Pryce (D); 7 Marc Sneyd (D); 8 Mickey Paea; 9 Danny Houghton; 10 Liam Watts; 12 Mark Minichiello (D); 11 Gareth Ellis (C); 13 Joe Westerman. Subs (all used): 21 Richard Whiting; 15 Chris Green; 22 Josh Bowden; 16 Jordan Thompson.
Tries: Talanoa (20), Shaul (51, 57); **Goals:** Sneyd 3/4; **Field goal:** Sneyd (63).
Rugby Leaguer & League Express Men of the Match: *Giants:* Aaron Murphy; *Hull:* Marc Sneyd.
Penalty count: 11-6; **Half-time:** 0-6; **Referee:** Tim Roby; **Attendance:** 7,737.

HULL KINGSTON ROVERS 30 LEEDS RHINOS 40

ROVERS: 1 Kieran Dixon (D); 4 Josh Mantellato (D); 19 Kris Welham; 3 Darrell Goulding (D); 5 Ken Sio (D); 23 Terry Campese (C) (D); 7 Albert Kelly (D); 8 Adam Walker; 9 Keal Carlile; 14 Mitchell Allgood (D); 13 Tyrone McCarthy (D); 12 Graeme Horne; 17 Greg Burke (D). Subs (all used): 15 James Donaldson (D); 20 James Green; 6 Maurice Blair (D); 2 Ben Cockayne.
Tries: Kelly (4, 14), Allgood (7), Campese (36), Welham (42); **Goals:** Mantellato 5/5.
RHINOS: 1 Zak Hardaker; 2 Tom Briscoe; 3 Kallum Watkins; 4 Joel Moon; 5 Ryan Hall; 13 Kevin Sinfield (C); 6 Danny McGuire; 11 Jamie Jones-Buchanan; 9 Paul Aiton; 10 Jamie Peacock; 12 Carl Ablett; 14 Stevie Ward; 17 Adam Cuthbertson (D). Subs (all used): 8 Kylie Leuluai; 19 Brad Singleton; 7 Rob Burrow; 16 Mitch Achurch.
Tries: T Briscoe (2), Sinfield (18), McGuire (25, 47), Watkins (54), Hardaker (66), Singleton (76); **Goals:** Sinfield 6/7.
Rugby Leaguer & League Express Men of the Match: *Rovers:* Terry Campese; *Rhinos:* Carl Ablett.
Penalty count: 7-5; **Half-time:** 24-16; **Referee:** Ben Thaler; **Attendance:** 11,811.

CASTLEFORD TIGERS 22 WAKEFIELD TRINITY WILDCATS 24

TIGERS: 22 Jordan Tansey; 20 Denny Solomona (D); 26 Ashley Gibson; 4 Michael Shenton (C); 5 Justin Carney; 7 Luke Gale (D); 21 Liam Finn; 8 Andy Lynch; 17 Scott Moore (D2); 10 Grant Millington; 11 Oliver Holmes; 16 Junior Moors (D); 13 Nathan Massey. Subs (all used): 25 Steve Crossley (D); 9 Adam Milner; 15 Ryan Boyle; 3 Jake Webster.
Tries: Solomona (10, 16), Gale (34), Carney (58); **Goals:** Gale 3/4.
WILDCATS: 1 Craig Hall (D); 2 Chris Riley; 3 Dean Collis; 4 Reece Lyne; 5 Richard Owen; 6 Jacob Miller (D); 7 Tim Smith; 8 Nick Scruton; 9 Paul McShane; 23 Lopini Paea (D); 12 Danny Kirmond (C); 13 Danny Washbrook; 18 Daniel Smith. Subs (all used): 14 Pita Godinet; 10 Scott Anderson; 26 Chris Annakin; 11 Ali Lauitiiti.
Tries: McShane (25), Godinet (69), Lauitiiti (75), Washbrook (77); **Goals:** Hall 4/4.
Rugby Leaguer & League Express Men of the Match: *Tigers:* Luke Gale; *Wildcats:* Danny Washbrook.
Penalty count: 8-6; **Half-time:** 16-6; **Referee:** Robert Hicks; **Attendance:** 10,728.

ROUND 2

Thursday 12th February 2015

SALFORD RED DEVILS 6 ST HELENS 52

RED DEVILS: 1 Kevin Locke; 2 Ben Jones-Bishop; 3 Josh Griffin; 18 Mason Caton-Brown; 5 Greg Johnson; 6 Rangi Chase; 7 Michael Dobson; 16 Scott Taylor; 9 Tommy Lee; 13 Gareth Hock; 11 Harrison Hansen (C); 17 Jordan Walne; 31 Cory Paterson. Subs (all used): 14 Theo Fages; 15 Darrell Griffin; 10 Lama Tasi; 20 Adam Walne.
Try: Jones-Bishop (29); **Goals:** Dobson 1/1.
Sin bin: Hock (61) - use of the knees.
SAINTS: 1 Jonny Lomax; 2 Tom Makinson; 17 Mark Percival; 3 Jordan Turner; 5 Adam Swift; 6 Travis Burns; 12 Jon Wilkin (C); 10 Kyle Amor; 9 James Roby; 8 Mose Masoe; 21 Joe Greenwood; 11 Atelea Vea; 15 Mark Flanagan. Subs (all used): 14 Alex Walmsley; 25 Andre Savelio; 13 Louie McCarthy-Scarsbrook; 18 Luke Thompson.
Tries: Percival (11, 54), Turner (19, 66), Greenwood (22, 62), Thompson (36), Makinson (42), McCarthy-Scarsbrook (59), Savelio (79); **Goals:** Burns 0/1, Percival 6/9.
Rugby Leaguer & League Express Men of the Match: *Red Devils:* Ben Jones-Bishop; *Saints:* Joe Greenwood.
Penalty count: 7-6; **Half-time:** 6-20; **Referee:** Ben Thaler; **Attendance:** 4,975.

Friday 13th February 2015

HULL FC 6 WARRINGTON WOLVES 7

HULL: 1 Jamie Shaul; 2 Tom Lineham; 21 Richard Whiting; 4 Kirk Yeaman; 19 Steve Michaels (D); 6 Leon Pryce; 7 Marc Sneyd; 8 Mickey Paea; 9 Danny Houghton (C); 10 Liam Watts; 17 Dean Hadley; 12 Mark Minichiello; 13 Joe Westerman. Subs (all used): 22 Josh Bowden; 15 Chris Green; 16 Jordan Thompson; 23 James Cunningham.
Try: Lineham (64); **Goals:** Sneyd 1/1.
WOLVES: 6 Stefan Ratchford; 2 Rhys Evans; 4 Ryan Atkins; 5 Joel Monaghan (C); 24 Kevin Penny; 20 Gareth O'Brien; 7 Richard Myler; 8 Chris Hill; 9 Daryl Clark; 10 Ashton Sims; 17 Ben Currie; 18 James Laithwaite; 12 Ben Westwood. Subs (all used): 14 Mick Higham; 13 Ben Harrison; 21 Ben Evans; 23 Gary Wheeler.
Try: Clark (26); **Goals:** O'Brien 1/1; **Field goal:** O'Brien (40).
Rugby Leaguer & League Express Men of the Match: *Hull:* Mark Minichiello; *Wolves:* Ben Westwood.
Penalty count: 4-2; **Half-time:** 0-7; **Referee:** Phil Bentham; **Attendance:** 12,002.

LEEDS RHINOS 38 WIDNES VIKINGS 6

RHINOS: 1 Zak Hardaker; 2 Tom Briscoe; 3 Kallum Watkins; 4 Joel Moon; 5 Ryan Hall; 13 Kevin Sinfield (C); 6 Danny McGuire; 17 Adam Cuthbertson; 9 Paul Aiton; 10 Jamie Peacock; 12 Carl Ablett; 14 Stevie Ward; 11 Jamie Jones-Buchanan. Subs (all used): 19 Brad Singleton; 18 Liam Sutcliffe; 16 Mitch Achurch; 22 Andy Yates (D).
Tries: Hardaker (15), Hall (46), Cuthbertson (54), T Briscoe (67), McGuire (70), Watkins (73), Sinfield (76); **Goals:** Sinfield 5/7.
VIKINGS: 1 Rhys Hanbury; 15 Jack Owens; 3 Cameron Phelps; 14 Chris Dean; 4 Stefan Marsh; 21 Danny Craven; 7 Joe Mellor (C); 8 Eamon O'Carroll; 22 Liam Carberry; 25 Alex Gerrard; 17 Chris Clarkson; 12 Danny Tickle; 13 Hep Cahill. Subs (all used): 10 Manase Manuokafoa; 33 Aaron Heremaia; 11 Danny Galea; 16 Willie Isa.
Try: Manuokafoa (18); **Goals:** Tickle 1/1.
Rugby Leaguer & League Express Men of the Match: *Rhinos:* Adam Cuthbertson; *Vikings:* Aaron Heremaia.
Penalty count: 5-3; **Half-time:** 6-6; **Referee:** Robert Hicks; **Attendance:** 14,132.

WIGAN WARRIORS 24 HUDDERSFIELD GIANTS 16

WARRIORS: 1 Matt Bowen; 2 Josh Charnley; 3 Anthony Gelling; 11 Joel Tomkins; 5 Joe Burgess; 20 Ryan Hampshire; 16 Sam Powell; 8 Dominic Crosby; 9 Michael Mcllorum; 28 Ryan Sutton; 14 John Bateman; 12 Liam Farrell; 13 Sean O'Loughlin (C). Subs (all used): 17 Tony Clubb; 25 Larne Patrick; 26 Logan Tomkins; 31 Connor Farrell.
Tries: J Tomkins (18, 52), Bateman (24), McIlorum (69), Sutton (74); **Goals:** Powell 0/1, Hampshire 2/4.
Sin bin: Powell (28) - dangerous tackle; Sutton (63) - fighting.
GIANTS: 22 Jake Connor; 2 Jermaine McGillvary; 3 Leroy Cudjoe; 4 Joe Wardle; 5 Aaron Murphy; 6 Danny Brough (C); 20 Jamie Ellis; 10 Craig Huby; 9 Shaun Lunt; 19 Anthony Mullally; 11 Brett Ferres; 12 Jack Hughes; 17 Ukuma Ta'ai. Subs (all used): 8 Eorl Crabtree; 7 Luke Robinson; 13 Chris Bailey; 15 Craig Kopczak.
Tries: Mullally (7), Ellis (27), Murphy (36); **Goals:** Brough 2/3.
Sin bin: Huby (63) - fighting.
Rugby Leaguer & League Express Men of the Match: *Warriors:* John Bateman; *Giants:* Danny Brough.
Penalty count: 11-8; **Half-time:** 10-16; **Referee:** Richard Silverwood; **Attendance:** 12,488.

Saturday 14th February 2015

CATALANS DRAGONS 13 CASTLEFORD TIGERS 12

DRAGONS: 1 Morgan Escare; 5 Michael Oldfield; 3 Ben Pomeroy; 4 Willie Tonga; 2 Vincent Duport; 14 Thomas Bosc; 7 Scott Dureau; 15 Jeff Lima; 9 Ian Henderson; 12 Louis Anderson; 11 Zeb Taia; 17 Elliott Whitehead; 13 Gregory Mounis (C). Subs (all used): 8 Olivier Elima; 16 Eloi Pelissier; 18 Benjamin Garcia; 24 Jason Baitieri.
Tries: Escare (48), Whitehead (66); **Goals:** Dureau 2/4; **Field goal:** Dureau (77).
Sin bin: Pelissier (37) - shoulder charge; Elima (37) - fighting.
TIGERS: 22 Jordan Tansey; 20 Denny Solomona; 23 Michael Channing; 4 Michael Shenton (C); 5 Justin Carney; 6 Ben Roberts (D); 7 Luke Gale; 8 Andy Lynch; 17 Scott Moore; 10 Grant Millington; 11 Oliver Holmes; 16 Junior Moors; 13 Nathan Massey. Subs (all used): 3 Jake Webster; 19 Scott Wheeldon; 21 Liam Finn; 25 Steve Crossley.
Tries: Carney (12), Tansey (73); **Goals:** Gale 2/2.
Sin bin: Webster (37) - fighting.
Rugby Leaguer & League Express Men of the Match: *Dragons:* Scott Dureau; *Tigers:* Junior Moors.
Penalty count: 8-8; **Half-time:** 0-6; **Referee:** James Child; **Attendance:** 9,167.

Sunday 15th February 2015

WAKEFIELD TRINITY WILDCATS 44 HULL KINGSTON ROVERS 24

WILDCATS: 1 Craig Hall; 2 Chris Riley; 3 Dean Collis; 4 Reece Lyne; 5 Richard Owen; 6 Jacob Miller; 7 Tim Smith; 18 Daniel Smith; 9 Paul McShane; 8 Nick Scruton; 12 Danny Kirmond (C); 17 Matty Ashurst (D); 13 Danny Washbrook. Subs (all used): 14 Pita Godinet; 11 Ali Lauitiiti; 10 Scott Anderson; 23 Lopini Paea.
Tries: Ashurst (11), Miller (36, 38, 78), Kirmond (47), Riley (60, 69, 72); **Goals:** Hall 6/8.
ROVERS: 2 Ben Cockayne; 4 Josh Mantellato; 18 Liam Salter; 3 Darrell Goulding; 5 Ken Sio; 23 Terry Campese (C); 7 Albert Kelly; 8 Adam Walker; 9 Keal Carlile; 14 Mitchell Allgood; 13 Tyrone McCarthy; 12 Graeme Horne; 17 Greg Burke. Subs (all used): 6 Maurice Blair; 20 James Green; 16 Ryan Bailey (D); 24 John Boudebza (D).
Tries: Kelly (8), McCarthy (31), Sio (52), Bailey (75); **Goals:** Mantellato 4/4.
Rugby Leaguer & League Express Men of the Match: *Wildcats:* Tim Smith; *Rovers:* Tyrone McCarthy.
Penalty count: 5-3; **Half-time:** 16-12; **Referee:** Tim Roby; **Attendance:** 5,320.

ROUND 3

Thursday 26th February 2015

LEEDS RHINOS 28 HUDDERSFIELD GIANTS 24

RHINOS: 1 Zak Hardaker; 2 Tom Briscoe; 3 Kallum Watkins; 4 Joel Moon; 5 Ryan Hall; 13 Kevin Sinfield (C); 6 Danny McGuire; 17 Adam Cuthbertson; 9 Paul Aiton; 10 Jamie Peacock; 12 Carl Ablett; 14 Stevie Ward; 11 Jamie Jones-Buchanan. Subs (all used): 8 Kylie Leuluai; 16 Mitch Achurch; 19 Brad Singleton; 18 Liam Sutcliffe.
Tries: Ablett (6), Cuthbertson (22), Hall (25), T Briscoe (41), Aiton (73); **Goals:** Sinfield 4/5.
GIANTS: 22 Jake Connor; 2 Jermaine McGillvary; 3 Leroy Cudjoe; 4 Joe Wardle; 5 Aaron Murphy; 6 Danny Brough (C); 20 Jamie Ellis; 10 Craig Huby; 9 Shaun Lunt; 19 Anthony Mullally; 11 Brett Ferres; 12 Jack Hughes; 17 Ukuma Ta'ai. Subs (all used): 15 Craig Kopczak; 14 Michael Lawrence; 8 Eorl Crabtree; 16 Kyle Wood.

Tries: Ellis (30), Wardle (36), Wood (63), Ferres (69); **Goals:** Brough 4/4.
Rugby Leaguer & League Express Men of the Match: *Rhinos:* Carl Ablett; *Giants:* Jamie Ellis.
Penalty count: 7-6; **Half-time:** 18-12;
Referee: Phil Bentham; **Attendance:** 12,878.

Friday 27th February 2015

ST HELENS 21 CASTLEFORD TIGERS 14

SAINTS: 1 Jonny Lomax; 2 Tom Makinson; 17 Mark Percival; 4 Josh Jones; 5 Adam Swift; 6 Travis Burns; 12 Jon Wilkin (C); 14 Alex Walmsley; 9 James Roby; 10 Kyle Amor; 21 Joe Greenwood; 11 Atelea Vea; 13 Louie McCarthy-Scarsbrook. Subs (all used): 8 Mose Masoe; 15 Mark Flanagan; 18 Luke Thompson; 19 Greg Richards.
Tries: Swift (11), Makinson (38), Jones (42), Percival (63); **Goals:** Percival 2/4; **Field goal:** Wilkin (73).
Sin bin: Amor (60) - dangerous challenge on Tansey.
TIGERS: 22 Jordan Tansey; 20 Denny Solomona; 23 Michael Channing; 4 Michael Shenton (C); 5 Justin Carney; 21 Liam Finn; 7 Luke Gale; 8 Andy Lynch; 17 Scott Moore; 10 Grant Millington; 11 Oliver Holmes; 16 Junior Moors; 13 Nathan Massey. Subs (all used): 9 Adam Milner; 12 Matt Cook (D2); 15 Ryan Boyle; 24 Mike McMeeken (D).
Tries: Carney (48, 51), Tansey (78); **Goals:** Gale 1/3.
Rugby Leaguer & League Express Men of the Match: *Saints:* Atelea Vea; *Tigers:* Luke Gale.
Penalty count: 6-7; **Half-time:** 10-0;
Referee: Richard Silverwood; **Attendance:** 10,066.

Saturday 28th February 2015

CATALANS DRAGONS 38 WARRINGTON WOLVES 18

DRAGONS: 1 Morgan Escare; 5 Michael Oldfield; 3 Ben Pomeroy; 4 Willie Tonga; 2 Vincent Duport; 6 Todd Carney (D); 7 Scott Dureau; 15 Jeff Lima; 9 Ian Henderson; 12 Louis Anderson; 11 Zeb Taia; 17 Elliott Whitehead; 13 Gregory Mounis (C). Subs (all used): 18 Benjamin Garcia; 21 Julian Bousquet; 23 Antoni Maria; 24 Jason Baitieri.
Tries: Tonga (9), Oldfield (26, 74), Duport (29), Taia (59, 62); **Goals:** Dureau 7/7.
WOLVES: 1 Matthew Russell; 5 Joel Monaghan (C); 3 Chris Bridge; 4 Ryan Atkins; 24 Kevin Penny; 20 Gareth O'Brien; 23 Gary Wheeler; 8 Chris Hill; 9 Daryl Clark; 10 Ashton Sims; 17 Ben Currie; 18 James Laithwaite; 12 Ben Westwood. Subs (all used): 13 Ben Harrison; 14 Mick Higham; 15 Roy Asotasi; 26 Joe Philbin.
Tries: Monaghan (46), Wheeler (50), Philbin (65); **Goals:** O'Brien 3/3.
Rugby Leaguer & League Express Men of the Match: *Dragons:* Scott Dureau; *Wolves:* Roy Asotasi.
Penalty count: 7-4; **Half-time:** 18-0;
Referee: Ben Thaler; **Attendance:** 8,782.

SALFORD RED DEVILS 32 HULL FC 28

RED DEVILS: 19 Niall Evalds; 18 Mason Caton-Brown; 3 Josh Griffin; 4 Junior Sa'u; 5 Greg Johnson; 6 Rangi Chase; 14 Theo Fages; 16 Scott Taylor; 9 Tommy Lee; 10 Lama Tasi; 11 Harrison Hansen (C); 12 Weller Hauraki; 17 Jordan Walne. Subs (all used): 8 Adrian Morley; 15 Darrell Griffin; 24 Liam Hood (D); 20 Adam Walne.
Tries: Evalds (4, 25), Fages (6), J Griffin (61, 64), Sa'u (75); **Goals:** J Griffin 4/6.
Sin bin: Morley (31) - high tackle.
HULL: 32 Jordan Rankin; 2 Tom Lineham; 3 Setaimata Sa; 4 Kirk Yeaman; 5 Fetuli Talanoa; 6 Leon Pryce; 7 Marc Sneyd; 8 Mickey Paea; 9 Danny Houghton (C); 10 Liam Watts; 17 Dean Hadley; 12 Mark Minichiello; 13 Joe Westerman. Subs (all used): 15 Chris Green; 16 Jordan Thompson; 21 Richard Whiting; 23 James Cunningham.
Tries: Rankin (16), Thompson (38, 73), Sa (54), Lineham (78); **Goals:** Sneyd 4/6.
Rugby Leaguer & League Express Men of the Match: *Red Devils:* Rangi Chase; *Hull:* Jordan Thompson.
Penalty count: 7-10; **Half-time:** 16-14;
Referee: Tim Roby; **Attendance:** 3,606.

Sunday 1st March 2015

HULL KINGSTON ROVERS 22 WIGAN WARRIORS 20

ROVERS: 2 Ben Cockayne; 4 Josh Mantellato; 18 Liam Salter; 3 Darrell Goulding; 5 Ken Sio; 23 Terry Campese (C); 7 Albert Kelly; 8 Adam Walker; 24 John Boudebza; 14 Mitchell Allgood; 6 Maurice Blair; 13 Tyrone McCarthy; 17 Greg Burke. Subs (all used): 11 Kevin Larroyer; 20 James Green; 12 Graeme Horne; 1 Kieran Dixon.
Tries: Sio (24, 51), Allgood (58), Dixon (73); **Goals:** Mantellato 3/4.
WARRIORS: 20 Ryan Hampshire; 2 Josh Charnley; 3 Anthony Gelling; 11 Joel Tomkins (C); 5 Joe Burgess; 6 George Williams; 7 Matty Smith; 28 Ryan Sutton; 9 Michael Mcllorum; 24 Taulima Tautai; 31 Connor Farrell; 12 Liam Farrell; 14 John Bateman. Subs (all used): 17 Tony Clubb; 25 Larne Patrick; 23 Lee Mossop (D2); 16 Sam Powell.
Tries: Burgess (29), Mossop (37), Charnley (39), Williams (40); **Goals:** Smith 2/4.
Rugby Leaguer & League Express Men of the Match: *Rovers:* Terry Campese; *Warriors:* George Williams.
Penalty count: 13-8; **Half-time:** 6-14;
Referee: Robert Hicks; **Attendance:** 7,632.

WIDNES VIKINGS 58
WAKEFIELD TRINITY WILDCATS 16

VIKINGS: 1 Rhys Hanbury; 2 Paddy Flynn; 14 Chris Dean; 3 Cameron Phelps; 5 Patrick Ah Van; 6 Kevin Brown (C); 7 Joe Mellor; 35 Gil Dudson (D); 9 Lloyd White; 8 Eamon O'Carroll; 17 Chris Clarkson; 12 Danny Tickle; 13 Hep Cahill. Subs (all used): 19 Ben Kavanagh; 10 Manase Manuokafoa; 33 Aaron Heremaia; 11 Danny Galea.
Tries: Mellor (2), Brown (17, 25), White (22, 55, 61, 78), Ah Van (42, 73), Clarkson (75);
Goals: Tickle 5/7, White 4/4.
WILDCATS: 1 Craig Hall; 2 Chris Riley; 3 Dean Collis; 4 Reece Lyne; 5 Richard Owen; 6 Jacob Miller; 7 Tim Smith; 8 Nick Scruton; 9 Paul McShane; 18 Daniel Smith; 15 Matt Ryan; 12 Danny Kirmond (C); 13 Danny Washbrook. Subs (all used): 10 Scott Anderson; 11 Ali Lauitiiti; 14 Pita Godinet; 23 Lopini Paea.
Tries: Owen (31), Ryan (65), Riley (67); **Goals:** Hall 2/3.
Rugby Leaguer & League Express Men of the Match: *Vikings:* Lloyd White; *Wildcats:* Matt Ryan.
Penalty count: 5-8; **Half-time:** 24-4;
Referee: James Child; **Attendance:** 5,810.

ROUND 4

Thursday 5th March 2015

HULL FC 12 LEEDS RHINOS 43

HULL: 1 Jamie Shaul; 2 Tom Lineham; 19 Steve Michaels; 4 Kirk Yeaman; 5 Fetuli Talanoa; 6 Leon Pryce; 7 Marc Sneyd; 8 Mickey Paea; 9 Danny Houghton; 22 Josh Bowden; 11 Gareth Ellis (C); 12 Mark Minichiello; 13 Joe Westerman. Subs (all used): 14 Iafeta Palea'aesina; 25 Jansin Turgut (D); 27 Jordan Abdull; 32 Jordan Rankin.
Tries: Pryce (7, 23); **Goals:** Sneyd 2/2.
RHINOS: 1 Zak Hardaker; 2 Tom Briscoe; 3 Kallum Watkins; 4 Joel Moon; 5 Ryan Hall; 13 Kevin Sinfield (C); 6 Danny McGuire; 17 Adam Cuthbertson; 9 Paul Aiton; 10 Jamie Peacock; 12 Carl Ablett; 14 Stevie Ward; 11 Jamie Jones-Buchanan. Subs (all used): 19 Brad Singleton; 7 Rob Burrow; 16 Mitch Achurch; 8 Kylie Leuluai.
Tries: McGuire (41, 53), Singleton (44), Watkins (59), Leuluai (62), Burrow (69, 78); **Goals:** Sinfield 7/7;
Field goal: Sinfield (74).
Rugby Leaguer & League Express Men of the Match: *Hull:* Gareth Ellis; *Rhinos:* Brad Singleton.
Penalty count: 6-9; **Half-time:** 12-0;
Referee: Richard Silverwood; **Attendance:** 10,887.

Friday 6th March 2015

CASTLEFORD TIGERS 42 WIGAN WARRIORS 14

TIGERS: 1 Luke Dorn; 2 James Clare; 3 Jake Webster; 4 Michael Shenton (C); 5 Justin Carney; 21 Liam Finn; 7 Luke Gale; 12 Matt Cook; 9 Adam Milner; 10 Grant Millington; 11 Oliver Holmes; 16 Junior Moors; 13 Nathan Massey. Subs (all used): 6 Ben Roberts; 15 Ryan Boyle; 19 Scott Wheeldon; 25 Steve Crossley.
Tries: Carney (2, 13), Clare (4), Dorn (39), Finn (56), O Holmes (62), Shenton (72); **Goals:** Gale 7/8.
WARRIORS: 1 Matt Bowen; 2 Josh Charnley; 3 Anthony Gelling; 4 Dan Sarginson; 22 Dominic Manfredi; 16 Sam Powell; 7 Matty Smith; 17 Tony Clubb; 9 Michael Mcllorum; 23 Lee Mossop; 11 Joel Tomkins (C); 12 Liam Farrell; 14 John Bateman. Subs (all used): 6 George Williams; 24 Taulima Tautai; 25 Larne Patrick; 29 James Greenwood.
Tries: Charnley (17, 50), Smith (79); **Goals:** Smith 1/3.
Rugby Leaguer & League Express Men of the Match: *Tigers:* Luke Gale; *Warriors:* Sam Powell.
Penalty count: 8-8; **Half-time:** 22-4;
Referee: Tim Roby; **Attendance:** 7,772.

HUDDERSFIELD GIANTS 24 WIDNES VIKINGS 12

GIANTS: 1 Scott Grix; 2 Jermaine McGillvary; 3 Leroy Cudjoe; 4 Joe Wardle; 5 Aaron Murphy; 6 Danny Brough (C); 20 Jamie Ellis; 8 Eorl Crabtree; 9 Shaun Lunt; 10 Craig Huby; 11 Brett Ferres; 12 Jack Hughes; 17 Ukuma Ta'ai. Subs (all used): 14 Michael Lawrence; 15 Craig Kopczak; 16 Kyle Wood; 19 Anthony Mullally.
Tries: Grix (27), McGillvary (44), Wardle (60, 68), Crabtree (73); **Goals:** Brough 2/5.
VIKINGS: 1 Rhys Hanbury; 2 Paddy Flynn; 14 Chris Dean; 3 Cameron Phelps; 5 Patrick Ah Van; 6 Kevin Brown (C); 7 Joe Mellor; 8 Eamon O'Carroll; 9 Lloyd White; 35 Gil Dudson; 17 Chris Clarkson; 12 Danny Tickle; 13 Hep Cahill. Subs (all used): 10 Manase Manuokafoa; 19 Ben Kavanagh; 33 Aaron Heremaia; 11 Danny Galea.
Tries: Mellor (10), Manuokafoa (64); **Goals:** Tickle 2/2.
Rugby Leaguer & League Express Men of the Match: *Giants:* Danny Brough; *Vikings:* Joe Mellor.
Penalty count: 6-6; **Half-time:** 6-6;
Referee: Ben Thaler; **Attendance:** 5,452.

WAKEFIELD TRINITY WILDCATS 16 ST HELENS 20

WILDCATS: 1 Craig Hall; 2 Chris Riley; 3 Dean Collis; 4 Reece Lyne; 5 Richard Owen; 6 Jacob Miller; 7 Tim Smith; 18 Daniel Smith; 13 Danny Washbrook; 8 Nick Scruton; 12 Danny Kirmond (C); 17 Matty Ashurst; 15 Matt Ryan. Subs (all used): 11 Ali Lauitiiti; 9 Paul McShane; 16 Mickael Simon (D); 23 Lopini Paea.
Tries: Ashurst (20), Lyne (34), Owen (69);
Goals: Hall 2/3, Collis 0/1.
SAINTS: 1 Jonny Lomax; 2 Tom Makinson; 17 Mark Percival; 3 Jordan Turner; 5 Adam Swift; 20 Paul Wellens; 12 Jon Wilkin (C); 14 Alex Walmsley; 9 James Roby; 19 Greg Richards; 11 Atelea Vea; 21 Joe Greenwood; 15 Mark Flanagan. Subs (all used): 8 Mose Masoe; 13 Louie McCarthy-Scarsbrook; 18 Luke Thompson; 16 Lance Hohaia.
Tries: Wellens (8), Greenwood (46), Turner (54);
Goals: Percival 1/1, Makinson 3/3.

Rugby Leaguer & League Express Men of the Match: *Wildcats:* Craig Hall; *Saints:* Alex Walmsley.
Penalty count: 11-7; **Half-time:** 12-6;
Referee: Robert Hicks; **Attendance:** 4,104.

Saturday 7th March 2015

CATALANS DRAGONS 40 SALFORD RED DEVILS 40

DRAGONS: 1 Morgan Escare; 5 Michael Oldfield; 3 Ben Pomeroy; 4 Willie Tonga; 2 Vincent Duport; 6 Todd Carney; 7 Scott Dureau; 15 Jeff Lima; 9 Ian Henderson; 12 Louis Anderson; 11 Zeb Taia; 17 Elliott Whitehead; 13 Gregory Mounis (C). Subs (all used): 8 Olivier Elima; 18 Benjamin Garcia; 21 Julian Bousquet; 24 Jason Baitieri.
Tries: Taia (23), Duport (30), Pomeroy (34, 50), Oldfield (61), Whitehead (70), Henderson (73);
Goals: Dureau 6/8.
RED DEVILS: 1 Kevin Locke; 5 Greg Johnson; 4 Junior Sa'u; 31 Cory Paterson; 3 Josh Griffin; 6 Rangi Chase; 14 Theo Fages; 16 Scott Taylor; 9 Tommy Lee; 10 Lama Tasi; 11 Harrison Hansen (C); 12 Weller Hauraki; 17 Jordan Walne. Subs (all used): 8 Adrian Morley; 15 Darrell Griffin; 20 Adam Walne; 24 Liam Hood.
Tries: Sa'u (1), J Griffin (10), Paterson (15, 76), Lee (18), Fages (42), Chase (54); **Goals:** J Griffin 6/8.
Rugby Leaguer & League Express Men of the Match: *Dragons:* Zeb Taia; *Red Devils:* Cory Paterson.
Penalty count: 9-4; **Half-time:** 18-22;
Referee: Phil Bentham; **Attendance:** 8,864.

Sunday 8th March 2015

WARRINGTON WOLVES 32
HULL KINGSTON ROVERS 24

WOLVES: 6 Stefan Ratchford; 24 Kevin Penny; 17 Ben Currie; 5 Joel Monaghan (C); 1 Matthew Russell; 20 Gareth O'Brien; 23 Gary Wheeler; 8 Chris Hill; 9 Daryl Clark; 10 Ashton Sims; 26 Joe Philbin; 18 James Laithwaite; 12 Ben Westwood. Subs (all used): 14 Mick Higham; 15 Roy Asotasi; 21 Ben Evans; 27 George King.
Tries: Russell (20, 64), Monaghan (26), Philbin (29), Wheeler (56), Currie (74); **Goals:** Ratchford 4/6.
Sin bin: Sims (18) - retaliation.
ROVERS: 2 Ben Cockayne; 4 Josh Mantellato; 19 Kris Welham; 3 Darrell Goulding; 5 Ken Sio; 23 Terry Campese (C); 7 Albert Kelly; 8 Adam Walker; 24 John Boudebza; 14 Mitchell Allgood; 13 Tyrone McCarthy; 6 Maurice Blair; 17 Greg Burke. Subs (all used): 20 James Green; 12 Graeme Horne; 11 Kevin Larroyer; 1 Kieran Dixon.
Tries: Mantellato (7, 35), Larroyer (52), Horne (68);
Goals: Mantellato 4/5.
Sin bin: McCarthy (18) - high tackle on Sims.
Rugby Leaguer & League Express Men of the Match: *Wolves:* Stefan Ratchford; *Rovers:* Terry Campese.
Penalty count: 8-6; **Half-time:** 14-12;
Referee: James Child; **Attendance:** 9,587.

ROUND 5

Thursday 12th March 2015

HUDDERSFIELD GIANTS 22 CASTLEFORD TIGERS 0

GIANTS: 1 Scott Grix; 2 Jermaine McGillvary; 3 Leroy Cudjoe; 4 Joe Wardle; 5 Aaron Murphy; 6 Danny Brough (C); 20 Jamie Ellis; 10 Craig Huby; 7 Luke Robinson; 15 Craig Kopczak; 11 Brett Ferres; 12 Jack Hughes; 14 Michael Lawrence. Subs (all used): 8 Eorl Crabtree; 16 Kyle Wood; 17 Ukuma Ta'ai; 23 Josh Johnson.
Tries: Ellis (38), Ta'ai (44), Murphy (62), McGillvary (78);
Goals: Brough 3/5.
TIGERS: 1 Luke Dorn (C); 2 James Clare; 23 Michael Channing; 3 Jake Webster; 5 Justin Carney; 21 Liam Finn; 7 Luke Gale; 8 Andy Lynch; 17 Scott Moore; 10 Grant Millington; 11 Oliver Holmes; 16 Junior Moors; 13 Nathan Massey. Subs (all used): 6 Ben Roberts; 12 Matt Cook; 19 Scott Wheeldon; 25 Steve Crossley.
Rugby Leaguer & League Express Men of the Match: *Giants:* Jermaine McGillvary; *Tigers:* Junior Moors.
Penalty count: 7-7; **Half-time:** 6-0;
Referee: James Child; **Attendance:** 5,257.

Friday 13th March 2015

WARRINGTON WOLVES 18 LEEDS RHINOS 6

WOLVES: 6 Stefan Ratchford; 24 Kevin Penny; 17 Ben Currie; 4 Ryan Atkins; 1 Matthew Russell; 3 Chris Bridge; 20 Gareth O'Brien; 8 Chris Hill (C); 9 Daryl Clark; 10 Ashton Sims; 26 Joe Philbin; 18 James Laithwaite; 12 Ben Westwood. Subs (all used): 15 Roy Asotasi; 27 George King; 14 Mick Higham; 21 Ben Evans.
Tries: Penny (16), Ratchford (34), Atkins (56);
Goals: Ratchford 3/4.
RHINOS: 26 Ashton Golding; 2 Tom Briscoe; 3 Kallum Watkins; 4 Joel Moon; 5 Ryan Hall; 13 Kevin Sinfield (C); 6 Danny McGuire; 17 Adam Cuthbertson; 9 Paul Aiton; 10 Jamie Peacock; 14 Stevie Ward; 12 Carl Ablett; 11 Jamie Jones-Buchanan. Subs (all used): 15 Brett Delaney; 19 Brad Singleton; 7 Rob Burrow; 8 Kylie Leuluai.
Try: T Briscoe (60); **Goals:** Sinfield 1/1.
Rugby Leaguer & League Express Men of the Match: *Wolves:* Matthew Russell; *Rhinos:* Tom Briscoe.
Penalty count: 7-5; **Half-time:** 12-0;
Referee: Phil Bentham; **Attendance:** 10,075.

WIDNES VIKINGS 20 ST HELENS 30

VIKINGS: 1 Rhys Hanbury; 2 Paddy Flynn; 14 Chris Dean; 4 Stefan Marsh; 5 Patrick Ah Van; 27 Grant Gore; 7 Joe Mellor (C); 19 Ben Kavanagh; 33 Aaron Heremaia;

8 Eamon O'Carroll; 17 Chris Clarkson; 11 Danny Galea; 12 Danny Tickle. Subs (all used): 24 Macgraff Leuluai; 25 Alex Gerrard; 35 Gil Dudson; 21 Danny Craven.
Tries: O'Carroll (5), Ah Van (31), Heremaia (75);
Goals: Tickle 1/1, Marsh 3/3.
SAINTS: 20 Paul Wellens; 2 Tom Makinson; 3 Jordan Turner; 4 Josh Jones; 5 Adam Swift; 6 Travis Burns; 12 Jon Wilkin (C); 14 Alex Walmsley; 16 Lance Hohaia; 19 Greg Richards; 21 Joe Greenwood; 11 Atelea Vea; 18 Luke Thompson. Subs (all used): 8 Mose Masoe; 13 Louie McCarthy-Scarsbrook; 25 Andre Savelio; 22 Matty Dawson.
Tries: Hohaia (14, 60), Vea (41), Thompson (52), Turner (56); **Goals:** Burns 5/5.
Rugby Leaguer & League Express Men of the Match: *Vikings:* Patrick Ah Van; *Saints:* Atelea Vea.
Penalty count: 8-7; **Half-time:** 14-6;
Referee: Robert Hicks; **Attendance:** 7,772.

WIGAN WARRIORS 13 HULL FC 12

WARRIORS: 1 Matt Bowen; 2 Josh Charnley; 3 Anthony Gelling; 4 Dan Sarginson; 5 Joe Burgess; 16 Sam Powell; 7 Matty Smith; 28 Ryan Sutton; 9 Michael McIlorum (C); 23 Lee Mossop; 11 Joel Tomkins; 12 Liam Farrell; 25 Larne Patrick. Subs (all used): 6 George Williams; 24 Taulima Tautai; 14 John Bateman; 17 Tony Clubb.
Tries: J Tomkins (10), Sarginson (39); **Goals:** Smith 2/3;
Field goal: Smith (66).
HULL: 32 Jordan Rankin; 31 Callum Lancaster; 19 Steve Michaels; 4 Kirk Yeaman; 5 Fetuli Talanoa; 6 Leon Pryce; 7 Marc Sneyd; 22 Josh Bowden; 9 Danny Houghton; 11 Gareth Ellis (C); 17 Dean Hadley; 12 Mark Minichiello; 13 Joe Westerman. Subs (all used): 14 Iafeta Palea'aesina; 15 Chris Green; 10 Liam Watts; 16 Jordan Thompson.
Tries: Talanoa (43), Lancaster (73); **Goals:** Sneyd 2/2.
Rugby Leaguer & League Express Men of the Match: *Warriors:* Ryan Sutton; *Hull:* Leon Pryce.
Penalty count: 7-5; **Half-time:** 12-0;
Referee: Ben Thaler; **Attendance:** 11,718.

Sunday 15th March 2015

HULL KINGSTON ROVERS 50 CATALANS DRAGONS 20

ROVERS: 2 Ben Cockayne; 4 Josh Mantellato; 19 Kris Welham; 18 Liam Salter; 5 Ken Sio; 23 Terry Campese (C); 7 Albert Kelly; 8 Adam Walker; 24 John Boudebza; 14 Mitchell Allgood; 13 Tyrone McCarthy; 6 Maurice Blair; 17 Greg Burke. Subs (all used): 31 Shaun Lunt (D); 11 Kevin Larroyer; 12 Graeme Horne; 20 James Green.
Tries: Sio (17, 49, 57), Cockayne (38, 74), Kelly (44), Lunt (59, 68), Salter (62); **Goals:** Mantellato 7/9.
Sin bin: Allgood (22) - punching.
DRAGONS: 1 Morgan Escare; 5 Michael Oldfield; 3 Ben Pomeroy; 4 Willie Tonga; 2 Vincent Duport; 14 Thomas Bosc; 7 Scott Dureau; 8 Olivier Elima; 9 Ian Henderson; 15 Jeff Lima; 11 Zeb Taia; 17 Elliott Whitehead; 13 Gregory Mounis (C). Subs (all used): 12 Louis Anderson; 10 Remi Casty; 16 Eloi Pelissier; 21 Julian Bousquet.
Tries: Tonga (2), Oldfield (25), Casty (30), Pelissier (34);
Goals: Dureau 2/4.
Rugby Leaguer & League Express Men of the Match: *Rovers:* Albert Kelly; *Dragons:* Ian Henderson.
Penalty count: 7-7; **Half-time:** 10-20;
Referee: Richard Silverwood; **Attendance:** 6,723.

SALFORD RED DEVILS 24
WAKEFIELD TRINITY WILDCATS 18

RED DEVILS: 1 Kevin Locke; 2 Ben Jones-Bishop; 3 Josh Griffin; 4 Junior Sa'u; 5 Greg Johnson; 6 Rangi Chase; 7 Michael Dobson; 16 Scott Taylor; 9 Tommy Lee; 8 Adrian Morley; 11 Harrison Hansen (C); 12 Weller Hauraki; 17 Jordan Walne. Subs (all used): 10 Lama Tasi; 14 Theo Fages; 15 Darrell Griffin; 22 Jason Walton.
Tries: Johnson (19), Hauraki (23), Chase (43), Sa'u (55);
Goals: J Griffin 4/4.
WILDCATS: 1 Craig Hall; 2 Chris Riley; 3 Dean Collis; 4 Reece Lyne; 5 Richard Owen; 6 Jacob Miller; 7 Tim Smith; 8 Nick Scruton; 9 Paul McShane; 18 Daniel Smith; 15 Matt Ryan; 12 Danny Kirmond (C); 13 Danny Washbrook. Subs (all used): 11 Ali Lauitiiti; 14 Pita Godinet; 16 Mickael Simon; 22 Jordan Crowther.
Tries: Miller (15), McShane (49), Hall (76);
Goals: Hall 3/3.
Rugby Leaguer & League Express Men of the Match: *Red Devils:* Rangi Chase; *Wildcats:* Ali Lauitiiti.
Penalty count: 5-9; **Half-time:** 12-6;
Referee: Matthew Thomason; **Attendance:** 2,712.

ROUND 6

Thursday 19th March 2015

ST HELENS 32 WARRINGTON WOLVES 24

SAINTS: 20 Paul Wellens; 2 Tom Makinson; 3 Jordan Turner; 22 Matty Dawson; 5 Adam Swift; 6 Travis Burns; 12 Jon Wilkin (C); 14 Alex Walmsley; 16 Lance Hohaia; 10 Kyle Amor; 21 Joe Greenwood; 11 Atelea Vea; 18 Luke Thompson. Subs (all used): 8 Mose Masoe; 9 James Roby; 13 Louie McCarthy-Scarsbrook; 19 Greg Richards.
Tries: Greenwood (17), Wilkin (29), Swift (33), McCarthy-Scarsbrook (55), Makinson (64);
Goals: Burns 6/7.
WOLVES: 6 Stefan Ratchford; 24 Kevin Penny; 17 Ben Currie; 4 Ryan Atkins; 1 Matthew Russell; 3 Chris Bridge; 20 Gareth O'Brien; 8 Chris Hill; 9 Daryl Clark; 10 Ashton Sims; 26 Joe Philbin; 18 James Laithwaite; 12 Ben Westwood (C). Subs (all used): 14 Mick Higham; 15 Roy Asotasi; 21 Ben Evans; 27 George King.
Tries: Clark (25), Higham (49), Penny (70), Hill (77);
Goals: Ratchford 1/1, O'Brien 3/3.
Rugby Leaguer & League Express Men of the Match: *Saints:* Jon Wilkin; *Wolves:* Chris Hill.
Penalty count: 7-12; **Half-time:** 18-6;
Referee: Ben Thaler; **Attendance:** 12,618.

Friday 20th March 2015

CASTLEFORD TIGERS 30 SALFORD RED DEVILS 16

TIGERS: 1 Luke Dorn; 2 James Clare; 3 Jake Webster; 4 Michael Shenton (C); 5 Justin Carney; 21 Liam Finn; 7 Luke Gale; 12 Matt Cook; 9 Adam Milner; 10 Grant Millington; 11 Oliver Holmes; 16 Junior Moors; 13 Nathan Massey. Subs (all used): 6 Ben Roberts; 15 Ryan Boyle; 19 Scott Wheeldon; 24 Mike McMeeken.
Tries: Carney (5, 65), Finn (13), Shenton (25), Wheeldon (40), Clare (47); **Goals:** Gale 3/7.
Sin bin: Carney (31) - fighting.
RED DEVILS: 19 Niall Evalds; 2 Ben Jones-Bishop; 3 Josh Griffin; 4 Junior Sa'u; 5 Greg Johnson; 6 Rangi Chase; 7 Michael Dobson; 8 Adrian Morley; 9 Tommy Lee; 16 Scott Taylor; 11 Harrison Hansen (C); 12 Weller Hauraki; 17 Jordan Walne. Subs (all used): 10 Lama Tasi; 14 Theo Fages; 15 Darrell Griffin; 22 Jason Walton.
Tries: Lee (19), Hauraki (29), Jones-Bishop (68);
Goals: J Griffin 2/3.
Sin bin: Chase (31) - fighting.
Rugby Leaguer & League Express Men of the Match: *Tigers:* Liam Finn; *Red Devils:* Harrison Hansen.
Penalty count: 8-8; **Half-time:** 22-12;
Referee: Robert Hicks; **Attendance:** 6,901.

HULL FC 33 CATALANS DRAGONS 22

HULL: 32 Jordan Rankin; 2 Tom Lineham; 19 Steve Michaels; 4 Kirk Yeaman; 5 Fetuli Talanoa; 6 Leon Pryce; 7 Marc Sneyd; 8 Mickey Paea; 9 Danny Houghton; 22 Josh Bowden; 11 Gareth Ellis (C); 12 Mark Minichiello; 13 Joe Westerman. Subs (all used): 10 Liam Watts; 14 Iafeta Palea'aesina; 15 Chris Green; 16 Jordan Thompson.
Tries: Sneyd (21), Rankin (32), Michaels (35), Talanoa (38), Lineham (45, 56); **Goals:** Sneyd 4/6;
Field goal: Sneyd (73).
Sin bin: Pryce (79) - dissent.
DRAGONS: 1 Morgan Escare; 5 Michael Oldfield; 20 Damien Cardace; 4 Willie Tonga; 2 Vincent Duport; 6 Todd Carney; 14 Thomas Bosc; 8 Olivier Elima; 9 Ian Henderson; 10 Remi Casty (C); 11 Zeb Taia; 17 Elliott Whitehead; 24 Jason Baitieri. Subs (all used): 12 Louis Anderson; 15 Jeff Lima; 16 Eloi Pelissier; 21 Julian Bousquet.
Tries: Duport (14), Bosc (40), Escare (63), Taia (79);
Goals: Bosc 3/4.
Rugby Leaguer & League Express Men of the Match: *Hull:* Jordan Rankin; *Dragons:* Zeb Taia.
Penalty count: 6-6; **Half-time:** 22-10;
Referee: Phil Bentham; **Attendance:** 11,994.

LEEDS RHINOS 26 WIGAN WARRIORS 14

RHINOS: 1 Zak Hardaker; 27 Ash Handley; 3 Kallum Watkins; 4 Joel Moon; 5 Ryan Hall; 18 Liam Sutcliffe; 6 Danny McGuire (C); 17 Adam Cuthbertson; 9 Paul Aiton; 10 Jamie Peacock; 12 Carl Ablett; 14 Stevie Ward; 11 Jamie Jones-Buchanan. Subs (all used): 7 Rob Burrow; 15 Brett Delaney; 19 Brad Singleton; 22 Andy Yates.
Tries: Cuthbertson (17), Handley (22), Singleton (26), Sutcliffe (61), Burrow (69); **Goals:** Sutcliffe 3/6.
WARRIORS: 1 Matt Bowen; 22 Dominic Manfredi; 3 Anthony Gelling; 4 Dan Sarginson; 5 Joe Burgess; 6 George Williams; 7 Matty Smith; 17 Tony Clubb; 9 Michael McIlorum (C); 23 Lee Mossop; 11 Joel Tomkins; 12 Liam Farrell; 14 John Bateman. Subs (all used): 24 Taulima Tautai; 25 Larne Patrick; 26 Logan Tomkins; 31 Connor Farrell.
Tries: Smith (10), Burgess (37); **Goals:** Smith 3/3.
Sin bin: L Farrell (65) - professional foul.
Rugby Leaguer & League Express Men of the Match: *Rhinos:* Adam Cuthbertson; *Warriors:* Dan Sarginson.
Penalty count: 11-5; **Half-time:** 16-14;
Referee: Richard Silverwood; **Attendance:** 18,350.

Sunday 22nd March 2015

WAKEFIELD TRINITY WILDCATS 14
HUDDERSFIELD GIANTS 44

WILDCATS: 1 Craig Hall; 2 Chris Riley; 3 Dean Collis; 28 Joe Arundel (D); 5 Richard Owen; 6 Jacob Miller; 7 Tim Smith; 8 Nick Scruton; 13 Danny Washbrook; 29 George Griffin (D); 11 Ali Lauitiiti; 12 Danny Kirmond (C); 15 Matt Ryan. Subs (all used): 9 Paul McShane; 16 Mickael Simon; 18 Daniel Smith; 22 Jordan Crowther.
Tries: Collis (16), Kirmond (23), Crowther (48);
Goals: Hall 1/3.
GIANTS: 1 Scott Grix; 2 Jermaine McGillvary; 3 Leroy Cudjoe; 4 Joe Wardle; 5 Aaron Murphy; 6 Danny Brough (C); 20 Jamie Ellis; 10 Craig Huby; 7 Luke Robinson; 15 Craig Kopczak; 11 Brett Ferres; 17 Ukuma Ta'ai; 14 Michael Lawrence. Subs (all used): 8 Eorl Crabtree; 12 Jack Hughes; 16 Kyle Wood; 23 Josh Johnson.
Tries: Grix (2, 6, 9), Ferres (54), Brough (66), Cudjoe (70), Ta'ai (80); **Goals:** Brough 6/6, Ellis 2/2.
Rugby Leaguer & League Express Men of the Match: *Wildcats:* Ali Lauitiiti; *Giants:* Scott Grix.
Penalty count: 8-10; **Half-time:** 8-18;
Referee: Joe Cobb; **Attendance:** 4,354.

WIDNES VIKINGS 20 HULL KINGSTON ROVERS 16

VIKINGS: 1 Rhys Hanbury; 2 Paddy Flynn; 4 Stefan Marsh; 3 Cameron Phelps; 15 Jack Owens; 27 Grant Gore; 7 Joe Mellor (C); 35 Gil Dudson; 33 Aaron Heremaia; 25 Alex Gerrard; 17 Chris Clarkson; 11 Danny Galea; 24 Macgraff Leuluai. Subs (all used): 10 Manase Manuokafoa; 12 Danny Tickle; 19 Ben Kavanagh; 23 Phil Joseph.
Tries: Flynn (4, 53), Galea (29); **Goals:** Owens 4/4.
ROVERS: 2 Ben Cockayne; 4 Josh Mantellato; 19 Kris Welham; 18 Liam Salter; 5 Ken Sio; 23 Terry Campese (C); 7 Albert Kelly; 8 Adam Walker; 31 Shaun Lunt; 17 Greg Burke; 13 Tyrone McCarthy; 6 Maurice Blair; 11 Kevin Larroyer. Subs (all used): 12 Graeme Horne; 15 James Donaldson; 20 James Green; 24 John Boudebza.
Tries: Cockayne (15), Sio (62), Welham (65);
Goals: Mantellato 2/3.
Rugby Leaguer & League Express Men of the Match: *Vikings:* Aaron Heremaia; *Rovers:* Ben Cockayne.
Penalty count: 9-7; **Half-time:** 14-4;
Referee: Matthew Thomason; **Attendance:** 5,273.

ROUND 7

Thursday 26th March 2015

SALFORD RED DEVILS 36 WIDNES VIKINGS 8

RED DEVILS: 1 Kevin Locke; 2 Ben Jones-Bishop; 3 Josh Griffin; 18 Mason Caton-Brown; 5 Greg Johnson; 6 Rangi Chase; 7 Michael Dobson; 16 Scott Taylor; 9 Tommy Lee; 8 Adrian Morley; 12 Weller Hauraki; 31 Cory Paterson; 11 Harrison Hansen (C). Subs (all used): 10 Lama Tasi; 15 Darrell Griffin; 24 Liam Hood; 26 Carl Forster (D).
Tries: Jones-Bishop (4), Hauraki (13), Johnson (30), Tasi (46), J Griffin (52), Paterson (61), Taylor (66);
Goals: J Griffin 4/7.
VIKINGS: 1 Rhys Hanbury; 2 Paddy Flynn; 4 Stefan Marsh; 3 Cameron Phelps; 15 Jack Owens; 33 Aaron Heremaia; 7 Joe Mellor (C); 35 Gil Dudson; 8 Eamon O'Carroll; 25 Alex Gerrard; 14 Chris Dean; 17 Chris Clarkson; 24 Macgraff Leuluai. Subs (all used): 10 Manase Manuokafoa; 19 Ben Kavanagh; 23 Phil Joseph; 27 Grant Gore.
Try: Flynn (34); **Goals:** Owens 2/2.
Sin bin: Marsh (30) - professional foul.
Rugby Leaguer & League Express Men of the Match: *Red Devils:* Cory Paterson; *Vikings:* Paddy Flynn.
Penalty count: 3-5; **Half-time:** 16-8;
Referee: Ben Thaler; **Attendance:** 3,476.

Friday 27th March 2015

CASTLEFORD TIGERS 20 HULL FC 14

TIGERS: 22 Jordan Tansey; 2 James Clare; 26 Ashley Gibson; 4 Michael Shenton (C); 5 Justin Carney; 21 Liam Finn; 7 Luke Gale; 10 Grant Millington; 9 Adam Milner; 16 Junior Moors; 11 Oliver Holmes; 3 Jake Webster; 19 Scott Wheeldon. Subs (all used): 6 Ben Roberts; 8 Andy Lynch; 24 Mike McMeeken; 25 Steve Crossley.
Tries: Gale (24, 41), Carney (60), Clare (70);
Goals: Gale 2/4.
HULL: 32 Jordan Rankin; 2 Tom Lineham; 19 Steve Michaels; 24 Jack Logan; 5 Fetuli Talanoa; 6 Leon Pryce; 7 Marc Sneyd; 8 Mickey Paea; 9 Danny Houghton (C); 10 Liam Watts; 16 Jordan Thompson; 12 Mark Minichiello; 13 Joe Westerman. Subs (all used): 15 Chris Green; 17 Dean Hadley; 22 Josh Bowden; 34 Stuart Howarth (D).
Tries: Lineham (35, 51, 56); **Goals:** Sneyd 1/3.
Rugby Leaguer & League Express Men of the Match: *Tigers:* Luke Gale; *Hull:* Marc Sneyd.
Penalty count: 8-7; **Half-time:** 6-4;
Referee: Matthew Thomason; **Attendance:** 8,744.

HULL KINGSTON ROVERS 24 ST HELENS 22

ROVERS: 1 Kieran Dixon; 4 Josh Mantellato; 19 Kris Welham; 3 Darrell Goulding; 5 Ken Sio; 23 Terry Campese (C); 7 Albert Kelly; 8 Adam Walker; 31 Shaun Lunt; 20 James Green; 12 Graeme Horne; 6 Maurice Blair; 13 Tyrone McCarthy. Subs (all used): 11 Kevin Larroyer; 15 James Donaldson; 21 Aaron Ollett; 24 John Boudebza.
Tries: Kelly (12, 18), Sio (38), Dixon (64);
Goals: Mantellato 4/7.
SAINTS: 16 Lance Hohaia; 2 Tom Makinson; 3 Jordan Turner; 22 Matty Dawson; 5 Adam Swift; 6 Travis Burns; 12 Jon Wilkin (C); 10 Kyle Amor; 9 James Roby; 14 Alex Walmsley; 13 Louie McCarthy-Scarsbrook; 11 Atelea Vea; 15 Mark Flanagan. Subs (all used): 4 Josh Jones; 8 Mose Masoe; 18 Luke Thompson; 19 Greg Richards.
Tries: Wilkin (3), Makinson (26), McCarthy-Scarsbrook (74), Turner (79); **Goals:** Burns 3/4.
Rugby Leaguer & League Express Men of the Match: *Rovers:* Albert Kelly; *Saints:* Jon Wilkin.
Penalty count: 9-7; **Half-time:** 16-12;
Referee: James Child; **Attendance:** 7,311.

WARRINGTON WOLVES 10 HUDDERSFIELD GIANTS 29

WOLVES: 6 Stefan Ratchford; 24 Kevin Penny; 5 Joel Monaghan (C); 4 Ryan Atkins; 1 Matthew Russell; 3 Chris Bridge; 20 Gareth O'Brien; 8 Chris Hill; 9 Daryl Clark; 10 Ashton Sims; 17 Ben Currie; 18 James Laithwaite; 12 Ben Westwood. Subs (all used): 14 Mick Higham; 15 Roy Asotasi; 26 Joe Philbin; 27 George King.
Tries: O'Brien (47), Penny (62); **Goals:** O'Brien 1/2.
GIANTS: 1 Scott Grix; 2 Jermaine McGillvary; 3 Leroy Cudjoe; 4 Joe Wardle; 5 Aaron Murphy; 6 Danny Brough (C); 20 Jamie Ellis; 10 Craig Huby; 7 Luke Robinson; 15 Craig Kopczak; 11 Brett Ferres; 12 Jack Hughes; 17 Ukuma Ta'ai. Subs (all used): 8 Eorl Crabtree; 14 Michael Lawrence; 16 Kyle Wood; 19 Anthony Mullally.
Tries: Ellis (6), Murphy (43, 67), McGillvary (75), Crabtree (80); **Goals:** Brough 4/5;
Field goal: Brough (40).

Rugby Leaguer & League Express Men of the Match: *Wolves:* Stefan Ratchford; *Giants:* Danny Brough.
Penalty count: 6-3; **Half-time:** 0-7;
Referee: Phil Bentham; **Attendance:** 9,019.

WIGAN WARRIORS 52
WAKEFIELD TRINITY WILDCATS 10

WARRIORS: 20 Ryan Hampshire; 22 Dominic Manfredi; 3 Anthony Gelling; 4 Dan Sarginson; 5 Joe Burgess; 6 George Williams; 7 Matty Smith; 17 Tony Clubb; 9 Michael Mcllorum; 23 Lee Mossop; 11 Joel Tomkins (C); 12 Liam Farrell; 14 John Bateman. Subs (all used): 24 Taulima Tautai; 25 Larne Patrick; 26 Logan Tomkins; 31 Connor Farrell.
Tries: L Farrell (3, 60), Clubb (17), Manfredi (21, 48), Gelling (37, 73, 75), Mossop (58); **Goals:** Smith 8/10.
WILDCATS: 5 Richard Owen; 2 Chris Riley; 3 Dean Collis; 28 Joe Arundel; 24 Tom Johnstone (D); 20 Jarrod Sammut; 1 Craig Hall; 8 Nick Scruton; 13 Danny Washbrook (C); 29 George Griffin; 11 Ali Lauitiiti; 15 Matt Ryan; 18 Daniel Smith. Subs (all used): 9 Paul McShane; 16 Mickael Simon; 22 Jordan Crowther; 30 Jordan Hand (D).
Tries: Riley (30), McShane (53); **Goals:** Hall 1/2.
Rugby Leaguer & League Express Men of the Match: *Warriors:* Matty Smith; *Wildcats:* Matt Ryan.
Penalty count: 5-5; **Half-time:** 26-4;
Referee: George Stokes; **Attendance:** 10,787.

Saturday 28th March 2015

CATALANS DRAGONS 22 LEEDS RHINOS 38

DRAGONS: 1 Morgan Escare; 20 Damien Cardace; 3 Ben Pomeroy; 11 Zeb Taia; 4 Willie Tonga; 14 Thomas Bosc; 7 Scott Dureau; 15 Jeff Lima; 9 Ian Henderson; 10 Remi Casty (C); 12 Louis Anderson; 17 Elliott Whitehead; 24 Jason Baitieri. Subs (all used): 8 Olivier Elima; 16 Eloi Pelissier; 18 Benjamin Garcia; 21 Julian Bousquet.
Tries: Whitehead (16, 42), Pelissier (46), Cardace (53); **Goals:** Dureau 3/4.
RHINOS: 1 Zak Hardaker; 27 Ash Handley; 3 Kallum Watkins; 4 Joel Moon; 5 Ryan Hall; 18 Liam Sutcliffe; 6 Danny McGuire (C); 19 Brad Singleton; 9 Paul Aiton; 10 Jamie Peacock; 14 Stevie Ward; 12 Carl Ablett; 17 Adam Cuthbertson. Subs (all used): 7 Rob Burrow; 11 Jamie Jones-Buchanan; 15 Brett Delaney; 16 Mitch Achurch.
Tries: Ablett (6), S Ward (34), Singleton (56), McGuire (58), Sutcliffe (64), Watkins (76), Hardaker (80); **Goals:** Sutcliffe 5/7.
Rugby Leaguer & League Express Men of the Match: *Dragons:* Scott Dureau; *Rhinos:* Rob Burrow.
Penalty count: 7-5; **Half-time:** 6-10;
Referee: Richard Silverwood; **Attendance:** 8,876.

ROUND 8

Thursday 2nd April 2015

HULL FC 6 HULL KINGSTON ROVERS 20

HULL: 1 Jamie Shaul; 2 Tom Lineham; 19 Steve Michaels; 24 Jack Logan; 5 Fetuli Talanoa; 6 Leon Pryce; 32 Jordan Rankin; 8 Mickey Paea; 9 Danny Houghton (C); 10 Liam Watts; 17 Dean Hadley; 12 Mark Minichiello; 13 Joe Westerman. Subs (all used): 14 Iafeta Palea'aesina; 16 Jordan Thompson; 22 Josh Bowden; 23 James Cunningham.
Try: Pryce (30); **Goals:** Rankin 1/1.
ROVERS: 1 Kieran Dixon; 5 Ken Sio; 3 Darrell Goulding; 19 Kris Welham; 4 Josh Mantellato; 23 Terry Campese (C); 7 Albert Kelly; 8 Adam Walker; 31 Shaun Lunt; 14 Mitchell Allgood; 6 Maurice Blair; 12 Graeme Horne; 13 Tyrone McCarthy. Subs (all used): 2 Ben Cockayne; 11 Kevin Larroyer; 15 James Donaldson; 17 Greg Burke.
Tries: Campese (4), Dixon (26), Lunt (37); **Goals:** Mantellato 4/4.
Rugby Leaguer & League Express Men of the Match: *Hull:* Mark Minichiello; *Rovers:* Terry Campese.
Penalty count: 5-9; **Half-time:** 6-18;
Referee: Richard Silverwood; **Attendance:** 20,507.

WAKEFIELD TRINITY WILDCATS 4
CATALANS DRAGONS 40

WILDCATS: 1 Craig Hall; 5 Richard Owen; 3 Dean Collis; 28 Joe Arundel; 2 Chris Riley; 6 Jacob Miller; 7 Tim Smith; 8 Nick Scruton; 9 Paul McShane; 29 George Griffin; 13 Danny Washbrook; 12 Danny Kirmond (C); 16 Mickael Simon. Subs (all used): 11 Ali Lauitiiti; 15 Matt Ryan; 18 Daniel Smith; 27 Kyle Trout.
Try: Riley (80); **Goals:** Hall 0/1.
DRAGONS: 26 Stanislas Robin (D); 20 Damien Cardace; 3 Ben Pomeroy; 4 Willie Tonga; 19 Mathias Pala; 14 Thomas Bosc; 7 Scott Dureau; 18 Benjamin Garcia; 9 Ian Henderson; 10 Remi Casty; 11 Zeb Taia; 17 Elliott Whitehead; 24 Jason Baitieri. Subs (all used): 8 Olivier Elima; 13 Gregory Mounis (C); 16 Eloi Pelissier; 21 Julian Bousquet.
Tries: Garcia (16), Tonga (21), Pomeroy (24), Whitehead (38), Cardace (45, 56, 70); **Goals:** Dureau 6/8.
Rugby Leaguer & League Express Men of the Match: *Wildcats:* Ali Lauitiiti; *Dragons:* Scott Dureau.
Penalty count: 6-7; **Half-time:** 0-26;
Referee: George Stokes; **Attendance:** 3,015.

WIDNES VIKINGS 30 WARRINGTON WOLVES 10

VIKINGS: 1 Rhys Hanbury; 4 Stefan Marsh; 14 Chris Dean; 3 Cameron Phelps; 15 Jack Owens; 6 Kevin Brown (C); 7 Joe Mellor; 35 Gil Dudson; 9 Lloyd White; 8 Eamon O'Carroll; 12 Danny Tickle; 11 Danny Galea; 24 Macgraff Leuluai. Subs (all used): 10 Manase Manuokafoa; 25 Alex Gerrard; 28 Matt Whitley (D); 33 Aaron Heremaia.
Tries: Phelps (10), Marsh (17, 37), White (45), Brown (51), Owens (77); **Goals:** Owens 3/7.
Sin bin: Tickle (64) - high tackle on Clark.
WOLVES: 6 Stefan Ratchford; 24 Kevin Penny; 5 Joel Monaghan (C); 4 Ryan Atkins; 1 Matthew Russell; 3 Chris Bridge; 20 Gareth O'Brien; 8 Chris Hill; 14 Mick Higham; 10 Ashton Sims; 17 Ben Currie; 12 Ben Westwood; 13 Ben Harrison. Subs (all used): 9 Daryl Clark; 15 Roy Asotasi; 18 James Laithwaite; 19 Anthony England.
Tries: Westwood (4), Currie (65); **Goals:** O'Brien 1/2.
Sin bin: Westwood (50) - repeated team offences.
Rugby Leaguer & League Express Men of the Match: *Vikings:* Kevin Brown; *Wolves:* Stefan Ratchford.
Penalty count: 12-8; **Half-time:** 14-6;
Referee: Robert Hicks; **Attendance:** 7,768.

Friday 3rd April 2015

CASTLEFORD TIGERS 12 LEEDS RHINOS 26

TIGERS: 1 Luke Dorn; 2 James Clare; 26 Ashley Gibson; 4 Michael Shenton (C); 5 Justin Carney; 21 Liam Finn; 7 Luke Gale; 8 Andy Lynch; 17 Scott Moore; 10 Grant Millington; 11 Oliver Holmes; 3 Jake Webster; 13 Nathan Massey. Subs (all used): 9 Adam Milner; 12 Matt Cook; 15 Ryan Boyle; 19 Scott Wheeldon.
Tries: Shenton (27, 77); **Goals:** Gale 2/2.
RHINOS: 1 Zak Hardaker; 27 Ash Handley; 3 Kallum Watkins; 4 Joel Moon; 5 Ryan Hall; 18 Liam Sutcliffe; 6 Danny McGuire (C); 19 Brad Singleton; 9 Paul Aiton; 10 Jamie Peacock; 14 Stevie Ward; 12 Carl Ablett; 17 Adam Cuthbertson. Subs (all used): 7 Rob Burrow; 15 Brett Delaney; 16 Mitch Achurch; 22 Andy Yates.
Tries: Moon (15), Hall (21, 63), S Ward (37), Cuthbertson (67); **Goals:** Sutcliffe 3/5.
Sin bin: Hall (4) - holding down.
Rugby Leaguer & League Express Men of the Match: *Tigers:* Andy Lynch; *Rhinos:* Liam Sutcliffe.
Penalty count: 4-4; **Half-time:** 6-16;
Referee: Ben Thaler; **Attendance:** 11,235.

WIGAN WARRIORS 12 ST HELENS 4

WARRIORS: 20 Ryan Hampshire; 22 Dominic Manfredi; 3 Anthony Gelling; 4 Dan Sarginson; 5 Joe Burgess; 6 George Williams; 7 Matty Smith; 17 Tony Clubb; 9 Michael Mcllorum (C); 23 Lee Mossop; 11 Joel Tomkins; 12 Liam Farrell; 14 John Bateman. Subs (all used): 24 Taulima Tautai; 25 Larne Patrick; 26 Logan Tomkins; 28 Ryan Sutton.
Tries: Manfredi (1), Burgess (71); **Goals:** Smith 1/1, Hampshire 1/1.
SAINTS: 20 Paul Wellens (C); 2 Tom Makinson; 22 Matty Dawson; 4 Josh Jones; 5 Adam Swift; 3 Jordan Turner; 16 Lance Hohaia; 10 Kyle Amor; 9 James Roby; 14 Alex Walmsley; 13 Louie McCarthy-Scarsbrook; 21 Joe Greenwood; 18 Luke Thompson. Subs (all used): 8 Mose Masoe; 15 Mark Flanagan; 19 Greg Richards; 25 Andre Savelio.
Try: McCarthy-Scarsbrook (16); **Goals:** Makinson 0/1.
Rugby Leaguer & League Express Men of the Match: *Warriors:* Liam Farrell; *Saints:* Louie McCarthy-Scarsbrook.
Penalty count: 8-2; **Half-time:** 6-4;
Referee: Phil Bentham; **Attendance:** 24,054.

HUDDERSFIELD GIANTS 12 SALFORD RED DEVILS 18

GIANTS: 1 Scott Grix; 2 Jermaine McGillvary; 5 Aaron Murphy; 4 Joe Wardle; 18 Jodie Broughton; 6 Danny Brough (C); 20 Jamie Ellis; 10 Craig Huby; 7 Luke Robinson; 15 Craig Kopczak; 11 Brett Ferres; 12 Jack Hughes; 17 Ukuma Ta'ai. Subs (all used): 8 Eorl Crabtree; 14 Michael Lawrence; 16 Kyle Wood; 23 Josh Johnson.
Tries: Hughes (37), Murphy (72); **Goals:** Brough 2/2.
RED DEVILS: 1 Kevin Locke; 2 Ben Jones-Bishop; 3 Josh Griffin; 4 Junior Sa'u; 5 Greg Johnson; 6 Rangi Chase; 7 Michael Dobson; 8 Adrian Morley; 9 Tommy Lee; 16 Scott Taylor; 31 Cory Paterson; 12 Weller Hauraki; 11 Harrison Hansen (C). Subs (all used): 10 Lama Tasi; 15 Darrell Griffin; 24 Liam Hood; 26 Carl Forster.
Tries: J Griffin (21), Jones-Bishop (31), Forster (55); **Goals:** J Griffin 3/4.
On report: Hauraki (62) - alleged high tackle on Grix.
Rugby Leaguer & League Express Men of the Match: *Giants:* Jamie Ellis; *Red Devils:* Ben Jones-Bishop.
Penalty count: 5-2; **Half-time:** 6-10;
Referee: James Child; **Attendance:** 6,003.

ROUND 9

Monday 6th April 2015

WARRINGTON WOLVES 14 CASTLEFORD TIGERS 22

WOLVES: 6 Stefan Ratchford; 5 Joel Monaghan (C); 3 Chris Bridge; 4 Ryan Atkins; 24 Kevin Penny; 20 Gareth O'Brien; 7 Richard Myler; 8 Chris Hill; 14 Mick Higham; 10 Ashton Sims; 17 Ben Currie; 12 Ben Westwood; 13 Ben Harrison. Subs (all used): 9 Daryl Clark; 15 Roy Asotasi; 19 Anthony England; 18 James Laithwaite.
Tries: Ratchford (16), Atkins (19), Penny (72); **Goals:** O'Brien 1/3.
TIGERS: 1 Luke Dorn; 22 Jordan Tansey; 23 Michael Channing; 4 Michael Shenton (C); 5 Justin Carney; 6 Ben Roberts; 7 Luke Gale; 8 Andy Lynch; 17 Scott Moore; 19 Scott Wheeldon; 18 Frankie Mariano; 12 Matt Cook; 13 Nathan Massey. Subs (all used): 9 Adam Milner; 10 Grant Millington; 15 Ryan Boyle; 28 Will Maher.
Tries: Tansey (6), Dorn (37), Milner (65), Roberts (69); **Goals:** Gale 3/4.
Rugby Leaguer & League Express Men of the Match: *Wolves:* Stefan Ratchford; *Tigers:* Luke Gale.
Penalty count: 6-3; **Half-time:** 10-10;
Referee: James Child; **Attendance:** 8,518.

HULL KINGSTON ROVERS 20
HUDDERSFIELD GIANTS 16

ROVERS: 1 Kieran Dixon; 4 Josh Mantellato; 18 Liam Salter; 3 Darrell Goulding; 2 Ben Cockayne; 23 Terry Campese (C); 7 Albert Kelly; 20 James Green; 31 Shaun Lunt; 14 Mitchell Allgood; 6 Maurice Blair; 12 Graeme Horne; 11 Kevin Larroyer. Subs (all used): 24 John Boudebza; 21 Aaron Ollett; 15 James Donaldson; 8 Adam Walker.
Tries: Goulding (3), Horne (34), Kelly (50), Mantellato (62); **Goals:** Mantellato 2/5.
GIANTS: 1 Scott Grix; 2 Jermaine McGillvary; 3 Leroy Cudjoe; 4 Joe Wardle; 5 Aaron Murphy; 6 Danny Brough (C); 20 Jamie Ellis; 8 Eorl Crabtree; 16 Kyle Wood; 19 Anthony Mullally; 17 Ukuma Ta'ai; 12 Jack Hughes; 13 Chris Bailey. Subs (all used): 7 Luke Robinson; 10 Craig Huby; 14 Michael Lawrence; 15 Craig Kopczak.
Tries: Wardle (31), Ta'ai (45), Murphy (80); **Goals:** Brough 2/3.
Rugby Leaguer & League Express Men of the Match: *Rovers:* Kieran Dixon; *Giants:* Aaron Murphy.
Penalty count: 10-2; **Half-time:** 8-6;
Referee: Phil Bentham; **Attendance:** 7,827.

LEEDS RHINOS 48 WAKEFIELD TRINITY WILDCATS 22

RHINOS: 1 Zak Hardaker; 27 Ash Handley; 3 Kallum Watkins; 4 Joel Moon; 5 Ryan Hall; 18 Liam Sutcliffe; 7 Rob Burrow; 19 Brad Singleton; 9 Paul Aiton; 17 Adam Cuthbertson; 12 Carl Ablett; 15 Brett Delaney; 13 Kevin Sinfield (C). Subs (all used): 6 Danny McGuire; 14 Stevie Ward; 16 Mitch Achurch; 22 Andy Yates.
Tries: Hall (10), Hardaker (19), Burrow (27, 29), Watkins (39, 67), Handley (55), Yates (63); **Goals:** Sinfield 8/8.
WILDCATS: 20 Jarrod Sammut; 2 Chris Riley; 1 Craig Hall; 28 Joe Arundel; 5 Richard Owen; 6 Jacob Miller; 7 Tim Smith; 8 Nick Scruton; 9 Paul McShane; 29 George Griffin; 12 Danny Kirmond (C); 13 Danny Washbrook; 18 Daniel Smith. Subs (all used): 30 Jordan Hand; 11 Ali Lauitiiti; 14 Pita Godinet; 15 Matt Ryan.
Tries: T Smith (15), Hall (24), Sammut (36), D Smith (74); **Goals:** Hall 3/4.
Rugby Leaguer & League Express Men of the Match: *Rhinos:* Paul Aiton; *Wildcats:* Daniel Smith.
Penalty count: 7-3; **Half-time:** 30-16;
Referee: Matthew Thomason; **Attendance:** 17,608.

SALFORD RED DEVILS 24 WIGAN WARRIORS 18

RED DEVILS: 19 Niall Evalds; 2 Ben Jones-Bishop; 3 Josh Griffin; 4 Junior Sa'u; 5 Greg Johnson; 6 Rangi Chase; 7 Michael Dobson; 16 Scott Taylor; 9 Tommy Lee; 8 Adrian Morley; 31 Cory Paterson; 12 Weller Hauraki; 11 Harrison Hansen (C). Subs (all used): 24 Liam Hood; 15 Darrell Griffin; 10 Lama Tasi; 26 Carl Forster.
Tries: Evalds (28, 77), Dobson (37), Jones-Bishop (58); **Goals:** J Griffin 4/4.
Dismissal: Hauraki (79) - fighting.
Sin bin: Hauraki (66) - fighting.
WARRIORS: 20 Ryan Hampshire; 27 Lewis Tierney; 3 Anthony Gelling; 4 Dan Sarginson; 5 Joe Burgess; 6 George Williams; 7 Matty Smith; 24 Taulima Tautai; 9 Michael Mcllorum (C); 23 Lee Mossop; 14 John Bateman; 12 Liam Farrell; 25 Larne Patrick. Subs (all used): 17 Tony Clubb; 26 Logan Tomkins; 28 Ryan Sutton; 31 Connor Farrell.
Tries: Patrick (7), Hampshire (69), Burgess (80); **Goals:** Hampshire 3/4.
Dismissal: Bateman (79) - fighting.
Sin bin: Bateman (66) - fighting.
Rugby Leaguer & League Express Men of the Match: *Red Devils:* Michael Dobson; *Warriors:* Taulima Tautai.
Penalty count: 6-7; **Half-time:** 12-8;
Referee: Richard Silverwood; **Attendance:** 6,561.

ST HELENS 20 HULL FC 28

SAINTS: 2 Tom Makinson; 33 Ricky Bailey (D); 22 Matty Dawson; 28 Jack Ashworth (D); 5 Adam Swift; 3 Jordan Turner; 16 Lance Hohaia; 8 Mose Masoe; 9 James Roby (C); 10 Kyle Amor; 4 Josh Jones; 13 Louie McCarthy-Scarsbrook; 25 Andre Savelio. Subs (all used): 14 Alex Walmsley; 15 Mark Flanagan; 18 Luke Thompson; 19 Greg Richards.
Tries: Makinson (15), McCarthy-Scarsbrook (18), Turner (53); **Goals:** Makinson 4/4.
HULL: 1 Jamie Shaul; 2 Tom Lineham; 19 Steve Michaels; 5 Fetuli Talanoa; 20 Curtis Naughton (D); 6 Leon Pryce; 32 Jordan Rankin; 8 Mickey Paea; 34 Stuart Howarth; 22 Josh Bowden; 17 Dean Hadley; 12 Mark Minichiello; 13 Joe Westerman. Subs (all used): 9 Danny Houghton (C); 14 Iafeta Palea'aesina; 16 Jordan Thompson; 23 James Cunningham.
Tries: Shaul (4, 74), Naughton (24), Pryce (48), Talanoa (67); **Goals:** Rankin 4/6.
Rugby Leaguer & League Express Men of the Match: *Saints:* James Roby; *Hull:* Joe Westerman.
Penalty count: 6-8; **Half-time:** 12-10;
Referee: Robert Hicks; **Attendance:** 11,088.

CATALANS DRAGONS 32 WIDNES VIKINGS 16

DRAGONS: 1 Morgan Escare; 20 Damien Cardace; 3 Ben Pomeroy; 4 Willie Tonga; 19 Mathias Pala; 14 Thomas Bosc; 7 Scott Dureau; 18 Benjamin Garcia; 9 Ian

Henderson; 10 Remi Casty; 11 Zeb Taia; 17 Elliott Whitehead; 24 Jason Baitieri. Subs (all used): 12 Louis Anderson; 13 Gregory Mounis (C); 16 Eloi Pelissier; 21 Julian Bousquet.
Tries: Tonga (6, 12), Pelissier (9, 56), Pala (21), Cardace (64); **Goals:** Bosc 3/4, Dureau 1/2.
VIKINGS: 21 Danny Craven; 5 Patrick Ah Van; 20 Declan Hulme; 4 Stefan Marsh; 15 Jack Owens; 26 Tom Gilmore; 27 Grant Gore; 23 Phil Joseph; 9 Lloyd White (C); 19 Ben Kavanagh; 24 Macgraff Leuluai; 11 Danny Galea; 25 Alex Gerrard. Subs (all used): 3 Cameron Phelps; 10 Manase Manuokafoa; 28 Matt Whitley; 33 Aaron Heremaia.
Tries: Owens (30), Marsh (49), Gerrard (66);
Goals: Owens 2/3.
Sin bin: Whitley (25) - high tackle on Dureau.
Rugby Leaguer & League Express Men of the Match:
Dragons: Ian Henderson; *Vikings:* Lloyd White.
Penalty count: 5-2; **Half-time:** 22-4;
Referee: Ben Thaler; **Attendance:** 9,683.

ROUND 10

Friday 10th April 2015

HULL FC 22 WIDNES VIKINGS 8

HULL: 1 Jamie Shaul; 2 Tom Lineham; 19 Steve Michaels; 5 Fetuli Talanoa; 20 Curtis Naughton; 6 Leon Pryce; 32 Jordan Rankin; 8 Mickey Paea; 9 Danny Houghton (C); 22 Josh Bowden; 3 Setaimata Sa; 12 Mark Minichiello; 13 Joe Westerman. Subs (all used): 14 Iafeta Palea'aesina; 16 Jordan Thompson; 23 James Cunningham; 34 Stuart Howarth.
Tries: Lineham (9, 28, 47), Shaul (67); **Goals:** Rankin 3/5.
VIKINGS: 1 Rhys Hanbury; 15 Jack Owens; 4 Stefan Marsh; 3 Cameron Phelps; 5 Patrick Ah Van; 6 Kevin Brown (C); 7 Joe Mellor; 8 Eamon O'Carroll; 9 Lloyd White; 35 Gil Dudson; 14 Chris Dean; 11 Danny Galea; 25 Alex Gerrard. Subs (all used): 33 Aaron Heremaia; 23 Phil Joseph; 10 Manase Manuokafoa; 28 Matt Whitley.
Tries: Brown (20), Ah Van (69); **Goals:** Owens 0/2.
Rugby Leaguer & League Express Men of the Match:
Hull: Tom Lineham; *Vikings:* Danny Galea.
Penalty count: 8-7; **Half-time:** 10-4;
Referee: Richard Silverwood; **Attendance:** 9,295.

Saturday 11th April 2015

WARRINGTON WOLVES 80 WAKEFIELD TRINITY WILDCATS 0

WOLVES: 6 Stefan Ratchford; 5 Joel Monaghan (C); 3 Chris Bridge; 28 Toby King; 22 Gene Ormsby; 29 Declan Patton (D); 7 Richard Myler; 8 Chris Hill; 14 Mick Higham; 15 Roy Asotasi; 17 Ben Currie; 12 Ben Westwood; 13 Ben Harrison. Subs (all used): 9 Daryl Clark; 10 Ashton Sims; 18 James Laithwaite; 19 Anthony England.
Tries: Ormsby (9, 47), T King (21, 60), Clark (29), Myler (35, 66, 74), Sims (38), Ratchford (49), Westwood (54), Monaghan (57), Currie (67, 77);
Goals: Ratchford 12/15.
WILDCATS: 20 Jarrod Sammut; 2 Chris Riley; 1 Craig Hall; 28 Joe Arundel; 5 Richard Owen; 6 Jacob Miller; 7 Tim Smith; 16 Mickael Simon; 9 Paul McShane; 29 George Griffin; 12 Danny Kirmond (C); 13 Danny Washbrook; 18 Daniel Smith. Subs (all used): 11 Ali Lauitiiti; 14 Pita Godinet; 15 Matt Ryan; 27 Kyle Trout.
Rugby Leaguer & League Express Men of the Match:
Wolves: Richard Myler; *Wildcats:* Chris Riley.
Penalty count: 5-4; **Half-time:** 30-0;
Referee: Robert Hicks; **Attendance:** 8,036.

CASTLEFORD TIGERS 25 HULL KINGSTON ROVERS 4

TIGERS: 22 Jordan Tansey; 26 Ashley Gibson; 23 Michael Channing; 4 Michael Shenton (C); 5 Justin Carney; 6 Ben Roberts; 7 Luke Gale; 8 Andy Lynch; 17 Scott Moore; 19 Scott Wheeldon; 11 Oliver Holmes; 18 Frankie Mariano; 13 Nathan Massey. Subs (all used): 9 Adam Milner; 10 Grant Millington; 14 Lee Jewitt; 15 Ryan Boyle.
Tries: Tansey (9), Gale (25), Massey (31), Mariano (64);
Goals: Gale 4/4; **Field goal:** Gale (60).
ROVERS: 1 Kieran Dixon; 4 Josh Mantellato; 19 Kris Welham; 3 Darrell Goulding; 5 Ken Sio; 23 Terry Campese (C); 7 Albert Kelly; 8 Adam Walker; 31 Shaun Lunt; 14 Mitchell Allgood; 11 Kevin Larroyer; 12 Graeme Horne; 13 Tyrone McCarthy. Subs (all used): 2 Ben Cockayne; 21 Aaron Ollett; 20 James Green; 17 Greg Burke.
Try: Sio (3); **Goals:** Mantellato 0/1.
Rugby Leaguer & League Express Men of the Match:
Tigers: Luke Gale; *Rovers:* Albert Kelly.
Penalty count: 7-4; **Half-time:** 18-4;
Referee: Ben Thaler; **Attendance:** 6,102.

Sunday 12th April 2015

SALFORD RED DEVILS 18 LEEDS RHINOS 28

RED DEVILS: 19 Niall Evalds; 2 Ben Jones-Bishop; 18 Mason Caton-Brown; 4 Junior Sa'u; 5 Greg Johnson; 14 Theo Fages; 7 Michael Dobson; 16 Scott Taylor; 24 Liam Hood; 8 Adrian Morley; 11 Harrison Hansen (C); 22 Jason Walton; 26 Carl Forster. Subs (all used): 32 Ryan Lannon (D); 15 Darrell Griffin; 10 Lama Tasi; 30 Matty Gee (D).
Tries: Tasi (26), Evalds (29, 57); **Goals:** Dobson 3/3.
RHINOS: 26 Ashton Golding; 27 Ash Handley; 12 Carl Ablett; 1 Zak Hardaker; 4 Joel Moon; 6 Danny McGuire; 7 Rob Burrow; 19 Brad Singleton; 9 Paul Aiton; 10 Jamie Peacock; 16 Mitch Achurch; 14 Stevie Ward; 13 Kevin Sinfield (C). Subs (all used): 15 Brett Delaney; 18 Liam Sutcliffe; 17 Adam Cuthbertson; 22 Andy Yates.
Tries: Peacock (22, 32), Handley (39), Burrow (45), Hardaker (60); **Goals:** Sinfield 4/5.
Rugby Leaguer & League Express Men of the Match:
Red Devils: Niall Evalds; *Rhinos:* Zak Hardaker.
Penalty count: 9-8; **Half-time:** 12-16;
Referee: Matthew Thomason; **Attendance:** 4,489.

HUDDERSFIELD GIANTS 8 ST HELENS 11

GIANTS: 1 Scott Grix; 2 Jermaine McGillvary; 3 Leroy Cudjoe; 22 Jake Connor; 5 Aaron Murphy; 6 Danny Brough (C); 20 Jamie Ellis; 8 Eorl Crabtree; 7 Luke Robinson; 15 Craig Kopczak; 17 Ukuma Ta'ai; 12 Jack Hughes; 13 Chris Bailey. Subs (all used): 10 Craig Huby; 16 Kyle Wood; 19 Anthony Mullally; 30 Jordan Cox (D).
Try: Cudjoe (4); **Goals:** Brough 2/3.
SAINTS: 16 Lance Hohaia; 2 Tom Makinson; 22 Matty Dawson; 3 Jordan Turner; 5 Adam Swift; 6 Travis Burns; 12 Jon Wilkin (C); 10 Kyle Amor; 9 James Roby; 14 Alex Walmsley; 13 Louie McCarthy-Scarsbrook; 15 Mark Flanagan; 18 Luke Thompson. Subs (all used): 8 Mose Masoe; 19 Greg Richards; 25 Andre Savelio; 7 Luke Walsh.
Try: Turner (39); **Goals:** Burns 3/4;
Field goal: Walsh (66).
Sin bin: Masoe (58) - late challenge on Ellis.
Rugby Leaguer & League Express Men of the Match:
Giants: Danny Brough; *Saints:* Travis Burns.
Penalty count: 12-8; **Half-time:** 6-6;
Referee: James Child; **Attendance:** 5,825.

WIGAN WARRIORS 34 CATALANS DRAGONS 0

WARRIORS: 20 Ryan Hampshire; 22 Dominic Manfredi; 3 Anthony Gelling; 4 Dan Sarginson; 5 Joe Burgess; 6 George Williams; 7 Matty Smith; 24 Taulima Tautai; 9 Michael McIlorum (C); 23 Lee Mossop; 12 Liam Farrell; 11 Joel Tomkins; 8 Dominic Crosby. Subs (all used): 17 Tony Clubb; 25 Larne Patrick; 26 Logan Tomkins; 28 Ryan Sutton.
Tries: Burgess (15, 71), Sarginson (22), Manfredi (29, 58, 73), Gelling (39), Hampshire (55);
Goals: Hampshire 1/8.
DRAGONS: 1 Morgan Escare; 20 Damien Cardace; 17 Elliott Whitehead; 4 Willie Tonga; 19 Mathias Pala; 14 Thomas Bosc; 7 Scott Dureau; 10 Remi Casty; 9 Ian Henderson; 15 Jeff Lima; 11 Zeb Taia; 12 Louis Anderson; 24 Jason Baitieri. Subs (all used): 8 Olivier Elima; 13 Gregory Mounis (C); 16 Eloi Pelissier; 18 Benjamin Garcia.
Rugby Leaguer & League Express Men of the Match:
Warriors: Ryan Hampshire; *Dragons:* Scott Dureau.
Penalty count: 5-3; **Half-time:** 16-0;
Referee: Phil Bentham; **Attendance:** 12,162.

ROUND 11

Thursday 16th April 2015

WIGAN WARRIORS 30 WARRINGTON WOLVES 20

WARRIORS: 20 Ryan Hampshire; 22 Dominic Manfredi; 3 Anthony Gelling; 4 Dan Sarginson; 5 Joe Burgess; 6 George Williams; 7 Matty Smith; 8 Dominic Crosby; 9 Michael McIlorum (C); 23 Lee Mossop; 12 Liam Farrell; 11 Joel Tomkins; 14 John Bateman. Subs (all used): 10 Ben Flower; 17 Tony Clubb; 24 Taulima Tautai; 26 Logan Tomkins.
Tries: L Farrell (14), Hampshire (17), Manfredi (31, 62, 69), Gelling (52); **Goals:** Smith 3/6.
WOLVES: 6 Stefan Ratchford; 5 Joel Monaghan (C); 3 Chris Bridge; 28 Toby King; 22 Gene Ormsby; 29 Declan Patton; 7 Richard Myler; 8 Chris Hill; 14 Mick Higham; 15 Roy Asotasi; 17 Ben Currie; 12 Ben Westwood; 13 Ben Harrison. Subs (all used): 9 Daryl Clark; 10 Ashton Sims; 18 James Laithwaite; 19 Anthony England.
Tries: Monaghan (7), Bridge (11, 24), Currie (44);
Goals: Ratchford 2/4.
Rugby Leaguer & League Express Men of the Match:
Warriors: Joel Tomkins; *Wolves:* Ben Currie.
Penalty count: 4-8; **Half-time:** 16-14;
Referee: Richard Silverwood; **Attendance:** 14,175.

Friday 17th April 2015

ST HELENS 16 LEEDS RHINOS 41

SAINTS: 2 Tom Makinson; 30 Matty Fleming (D); 3 Jordan Turner; 4 Josh Jones; 5 Adam Swift; 6 Travis Burns; 12 Jon Wilkin (C); 10 Kyle Amor; 9 James Roby; 14 Alex Walmsley; 13 Louie McCarthy-Scarsbrook; 15 Mark Flanagan; 18 Luke Thompson. Subs (all used): 7 Luke Walsh; 8 Mose Masoe; 19 Greg Richards; 25 Andre Savelio.
Tries: Makinson (37), Turner (45, 61); **Goals:** Burns 2/3.
RHINOS: 1 Zak Hardaker; 3 Kallum Watkins; 12 Carl Ablett; 4 Joel Moon; 27 Ash Handley; 18 Liam Sutcliffe; 6 Danny McGuire; 17 Adam Cuthbertson; 9 Paul Aiton; 10 Jamie Peacock; 14 Stevie Ward; 15 Brett Delaney; 19 Brad Singleton. Subs (all used): 7 Rob Burrow; 13 Kevin Sinfield (C); 16 Mitch Achurch; 22 Andy Yates.
Tries: Handley (3, 16, 40), Hardaker (19), McGuire (28), Sutcliffe (67), Moon (80);
Goals: Sutcliffe 3/3, Sinfield 3/4; **Field goal:** Sinfield (71).
Rugby Leaguer & League Express Men of the Match:
Saints: Louie McCarthy-Scarsbrook;
Rhinos: Liam Sutcliffe.
Penalty count: 3-5; **Half-time:** 6-28;
Referee: Ben Thaler; **Attendance:** 12,640.

Sunday 19th April 2015

HUDDERSFIELD GIANTS 38 CATALANS DRAGONS 14

GIANTS: 1 Scott Grix; 2 Jermaine McGillvary; 3 Leroy Cudjoe; 22 Jake Connor; 5 Aaron Murphy; 6 Danny Brough (C); 16 Kyle Wood; 8 Eorl Crabtree; 7 Luke Robinson; 10 Craig Huby; 4 Joe Wardle; 12 Jack Hughes; 13 Chris Bailey. Subs (all used): 15 Craig Kopczak; 17 Ukuma Ta'ai; 20 Jamie Ellis; 30 Jordan Cox.
Tries: Murphy (15, 37), Ta'ai (30, 62), Cudjoe (40), McGillvary (53), Grix (64); **Goals:** Brough 5/7.
DRAGONS: 26 Stanislas Robin; 5 Michael Oldfield; 4 Willie Tonga; 11 Zeb Taia; 20 Damien Cardace; 14 Thomas Bosc; 7 Scott Dureau; 8 Olivier Elima; 9 Ian Henderson; 10 Remi Casty (C); 12 Louis Anderson; 17 Elliott Whitehead; 24 Jason Baitieri. Subs (all used): 15 Jeff Lima; 16 Eloi Pelissier; 18 Benjamin Garcia; 21 Julian Bousquet.
Tries: Dureau (21), Bousquet (45); **Goals:** Dureau 3/3.
Sin bin: Tonga (61) - use of the head on Cudjoe.
Rugby Leaguer & League Express Men of the Match:
Giants: Ukuma Ta'ai; *Dragons:* Ian Henderson.
Penalty count: 5-9; **Half-time:** 22-8;
Referee: Robert Hicks; **Attendance:** 4,404.

WIDNES VIKINGS 46 CASTLEFORD TIGERS 16

VIKINGS: 1 Rhys Hanbury; 15 Jack Owens; 4 Stefan Marsh; 3 Cameron Phelps; 5 Patrick Ah Van; 6 Kevin Brown (C); 26 Tom Gilmore; 35 Gil Dudson; 9 Lloyd White; 8 Eamon O'Carroll; 14 Chris Dean; 11 Danny Galea; 24 Macgraff Leuluai. Subs (all used): 10 Manase Manuokafoa; 25 Alex Gerrard; 33 Aaron Heremaia; 16 Willie Isa.
Tries: Ah Van (4, 39), Hanbury (21, 74), Owens (25), Marsh (30), Brown (44), Phelps (58); **Goals:** Owens 7/8.
TIGERS: 22 Jordan Tansey; 2 James Clare; 4 Michael Shenton (C); 23 Michael Channing; 26 Ashley Gibson; 6 Ben Roberts; 21 Liam Finn; 8 Andy Lynch; 17 Scott Moore; 19 Scott Wheeldon; 11 Oliver Holmes; 10 Grant Millington; 13 Nathan Massey. Subs (all used): 9 Adam Milner; 14 Lee Jewitt; 15 Ryan Boyle; 25 Steve Crossley.
Tries: Roberts (11), O Holmes (49), Shenton (62);
Goals: Finn 2/3.
Rugby Leaguer & League Express Men of the Match:
Vikings: Rhys Hanbury; *Tigers:* Oliver Holmes.
Penalty count: 9-8; **Half-time:** 28-6;
Referee: James Child; **Attendance:** 5,457.

ROUND 12

Thursday 23rd April 2015

WAKEFIELD TRINITY WILDCATS 22 WIGAN WARRIORS 40

WILDCATS: 1 Craig Hall; 5 Richard Owen; 15 Matt Ryan; 4 Reece Lyne; 2 Chris Riley; 14 Pita Godinet; 7 Tim Smith; 8 Nick Scruton; 9 Paul McShane; 31 Ben Kavanagh (D); 13 Danny Washbrook; 12 Danny Kirmond (C); 22 Jordan Crowther. Subs (all used): 11 Ali Lauitiiti; 16 Mickael Simon; 18 Daniel Smith; 25 Ian Kirke.
Tries: Hall (1), Kirmond (25), Godinet (40), Riley (46);
Goals: Hall 3/4.
Sin bin: T Smith (34) - fighting.
WARRIORS: 20 Ryan Hampshire; 22 Dominic Manfredi; 3 Anthony Gelling; 4 Dan Sarginson; 5 Joe Burgess; 6 George Williams; 7 Matty Smith; 23 Lee Mossop; 9 Michael McIlorum (C); 8 Dominic Crosby; 11 Joel Tomkins; 12 Liam Farrell; 14 John Bateman. Subs (all used): 10 Ben Flower; 16 Sam Powell; 17 Tony Clubb; 24 Taulima Tautai.
Tries: Crosby (8), Smith (14), Burgess (21, 44, 64), Manfredi (36), Mossop (57); **Goals:** Smith 6/7.
Sin bin: Powell (34) - fighting.
Rugby Leaguer & League Express Men of the Match:
Wildcats: Danny Washbrook; *Warriors:* Joe Burgess.
Penalty count: 4-4; **Half-time:** 18-24;
Referee: Robert Hicks; **Attendance:** 3,107.

Friday 24th April 2015

HULL FC 4 HUDDERSFIELD GIANTS 24

HULL: 1 Jamie Shaul; 2 Tom Lineham; 5 Fetuli Talanoa; 4 Kirk Yeaman; 19 Steve Michaels; 6 Leon Pryce; 7 Marc Sneyd; 8 Mickey Paea; 9 Danny Houghton (C); 10 Liam Watts; 3 Setaimata Sa; 12 Mark Minichiello; 16 Jordan Thompson. Subs (all used): 14 Iafeta Palea'aesina; 22 Josh Bowden; 23 James Cunningham; 34 Stuart Howarth.
Try: Michaels (65); **Goals:** Sneyd 0/1.
GIANTS: 1 Scott Grix; 2 Jermaine McGillvary; 3 Leroy Cudjoe; 22 Jake Connor; 5 Aaron Murphy; 6 Danny Brough (C); 16 Kyle Wood; 19 Anthony Mullally; 7 Luke Robinson; 10 Craig Huby; 4 Joe Wardle; 12 Jack Hughes; 17 Ukuma Ta'ai. Subs (all used): 8 Eorl Crabtree; 14 Michael Lawrence; 15 Craig Kopczak; 20 Jamie Ellis.
Tries: Brough (9), Ta'ai (25), Ellis (39), Lawrence (58), McGillvary (80); **Goals:** Brough 2/5.
Sin bin: Huby (22) - high tackle on Shaul.
Rugby Leaguer & League Express Men of the Match:
Hull: Mickey Paea; *Giants:* Jermaine McGillvary.
Penalty count: 8-8; **Half-time:** 0-16;
Referee: Ben Thaler; **Attendance:** 9,930.

LEEDS RHINOS 10 WARRINGTON WOLVES 29

RHINOS: 1 Zak Hardaker; 3 Kallum Watkins; 4 Joel Moon; 12 Carl Ablett; 27 Ash Handley; 6 Danny McGuire; 18 Liam Sutcliffe; 17 Adam Cuthbertson; 9 Paul Aiton; 10 Jamie Peacock; 14 Stevie Ward; 15 Brett Delaney; 19 Brad Singleton. Subs (all used): 7 Rob Burrow; 13 Kevin Sinfield (C); 16 Mitch Achurch; 25 Rob Mulhern.
Tries: Watkins (38), Achurch (69);
Goals: Sutcliffe 0/1, Sinfield 1/1.

WOLVES: 6 Stefan Ratchford; 5 Joel Monaghan (C); 3 Chris Bridge; 28 Toby King; 22 Gene Ormsby; 29 Declan Patton; 7 Richard Myler; 8 Chris Hill; 14 Mick Higham; 10 Ashton Sims; 17 Ben Currie; 12 Ben Westwood; 13 Ben Harrison. Subs (all used): 9 Daryl Clark; 15 Roy Asotasi; 18 James Laithwaite; 19 Anthony England.
Tries: Ormsby (9), Monaghan (15), Sims (23), Currie (43), Asotasi (50); **Goals:** Ratchford 4/6;
Field goal: Patton (75).
Rugby Leaguer & League Express Men of the Match: *Rhinos:* Jamie Peacock; *Wolves:* Ben Currie.
Penalty count: 7-4; **Half-time:** 4-14;
Referee: James Child; **Attendance:** 17,340.

ST HELENS 34 WIDNES VIKINGS 16

SAINTS: 2 Tom Makinson; 30 Matty Fleming; 4 Josh Jones; 3 Jordan Turner; 5 Adam Swift; 6 Travis Burns; 7 Luke Walsh; 10 Kyle Amor; 9 James Roby; 8 Mose Masoe; 13 Louie McCarthy-Scarsbrook; 12 Jon Wilkin (C); 18 Luke Thompson. Subs (all used): 14 Alex Walmsley; 17 Mark Percival; 19 Greg Richards; 25 Andre Savelio.
Tries: Walsh (27), Burns (30), Walmsley (52), Fleming (65), Makinson (73), Percival (79);
Goals: Burns 5/6.
VIKINGS: 1 Rhys Hanbury; 15 Jack Owens; 3 Cameron Phelps; 14 Chris Dean; 4 Stefan Marsh; 6 Kevin Brown (C); 7 Joe Mellor; 8 Eamon O'Carroll; 9 Lloyd White; 35 Gil Dudson; 28 Matt Whitley; 11 Danny Galea; 24 Macgraff Leuluai. Subs (all used): 10 Manase Manuokafoa; 16 Willie Isa; 25 Alex Gerrard; 33 Aaron Heremaia.
Tries: Brown (22), Mellor (35), Whitley (62);
Goals: Owens 2/3.
Rugby Leaguer & League Express Men of the Match: *Saints:* Tom Makinson; *Vikings:* Joe Mellor.
Penalty count: 3-5; **Half-time:** 12-12;
Referee: Phil Bentham; **Attendance:** 11,271.

Saturday 25th April 2015

CATALANS DRAGONS 32 HULL KINGSTON ROVERS 24

DRAGONS: 1 Morgan Escare; 5 Michael Oldfield; 20 Damien Cardace; 19 Mathias Pala; 27 Fouad Yaha (D); 6 Todd Carney; 14 Thomas Bosc; 8 Olivier Elima; 9 Ian Henderson; 10 Remi Casty (C); 11 Zeb Taia; 17 Elliott Whitehead; 24 Jason Baitieri. Subs (all used): 16 Eloi Pelissier; 18 Benjamin Garcia; 21 Julian Bousquet; 22 Gadwin Springer.
Tries: Baitieri (7), Springer (30), Oldfield (37), Pelissier (43), Garcia (54), Whitehead (69);
Goals: Bosc 4/6.
ROVERS: 1 Kieran Dixon; 4 Josh Mantellato; 5 Ken Sio; 6 Maurice Blair; 2 Ben Cockayne; 7 Albert Kelly; 23 Terry Campese (C); 32 Dane Tilse (D); 24 John Boudebza; 8 Adam Walker; 12 Graeme Horne; 11 Kevin Larroyer; 13 Tyrone McCarthy. Subs (all used): 17 Greg Burke; 20 James Green; 21 Aaron Ollett; 26 Sonny Esslemont.
Tries: Blair (9), Cockayne (27), Dixon (50), Mantellato (77); **Goals:** Mantellato 4/5.
Rugby Leaguer & League Express Men of the Match: *Dragons:* Jason Baitieri; *Rovers:* Albert Kelly.
Penalty count: 11-7; **Half-time:** 16-12;
Referee: Richard Silverwood; **Attendance:** 7,938.

Sunday 26th April 2015

SALFORD RED DEVILS 20 CASTLEFORD TIGERS 22

RED DEVILS: 19 Niall Evalds; 1 Kevin Locke; 18 Mason Caton-Brown; 34 Oliver Gildart (D); 5 Greg Johnson; 14 Theo Fages; 25 George Griffin; 16 Scott Taylor; 33 Wayne Godwin; 10 Lama Tasi; 11 Harrison Hansen (C); 26 Carl Forster; 35 James Greenwood (D). Subs (all used): 8 Adrian Morley; 24 Liam Hood; 30 Matty Gee; 32 Ryan Lannon.
Tries: Fages (5), Locke (22, 68), Taylor (78);
Goals: Locke 1/3, Johnson 1/1.
TIGERS: 22 Jordan Tansey; 2 James Clare; 26 Ashley Gibson; 4 Michael Shenton (C); 27 Ash Robson (D); 6 Ben Roberts; 7 Luke Gale; 8 Andy Lynch; 17 Scott Moore; 19 Scott Wheeldon; 11 Oliver Holmes; 10 Grant Millington; 13 Nathan Massey. Subs (all used): 9 Adam Milner; 14 Lee Jewitt; 16 Junior Moors; 28 Will Maher.
Tries: Gibson (26, 40), Massey (43), Robson (64);
Goals: Gale 3/4.
Rugby Leaguer & League Express Men of the Match: *Red Devils:* Oliver Gildart; *Tigers:* Ashley Gibson.
Penalty count: 4-6; **Half-time:** 10-10;
Referee: George Stokes *(replaced by Chris Leatherbarrow, 73)*; **Attendance:** 3,397.

ROUND 13

Thursday 30th April 2015

HUDDERSFIELD GIANTS 24 LEEDS RHINOS 24

GIANTS: 1 Scott Grix; 2 Jermaine McGillvary; 3 Leroy Cudjoe; 22 Jake Connor; 5 Aaron Murphy; 6 Danny Brough (C); 20 Jamie Ellis; 19 Anthony Mullally; 16 Kyle Wood; 10 Craig Huby; 12 Jack Hughes; 4 Joe Wardle; 17 Ukuma Ta'ai. Subs (all used): 8 Eorl Crabtree; 14 Michael Lawrence; 15 Craig Kopczak; 24 Kruise Leeming.
Tries: Wardle (4, 66), Lawrence (60), McGillvary (64);
Goals: Brough 4/5.
RHINOS: 1 Zak Hardaker; 3 Kallum Watkins; 20 Jimmy Keinhorst; 4 Joel Moon; 27 Ash Handley; 6 Danny McGuire (C); 18 Liam Sutcliffe; 17 Adam Cuthbertson; 9 Paul Aiton; 10 Jamie Peacock; 15 Brett Delaney; 12 Carl Ablett; 11 Jamie Jones-Buchanan. Subs (all used): 7 Rob Burrow; 16 Mitch Achurch; 19 Brad Singleton; 25 Rob Mulhern.
Tries: Delaney (15), Ablett (22), Moon (30), Watkins (36);
Goals: Sutcliffe 4/5.
Rugby Leaguer & League Express Men of the Match: *Giants:* Danny Brough; *Rhinos:* Zak Hardaker.
Penalty count: 10-8; **Half-time:** 8-22;
Referee: Richard Silverwood; **Attendance:** 6,381.

Friday 1st May 2015

HULL FC 24 SALFORD RED DEVILS 20

HULL: 32 Jordan Rankin; 2 Tom Lineham; 5 Fetuli Talanoa; 4 Kirk Yeaman; 19 Steve Michaels; 6 Leon Pryce; 7 Marc Sneyd; 10 Liam Watts; 9 Danny Houghton (C); 16 Jordan Thompson; 12 Mark Minichiello; 3 Setaimata Sa; 34 Stuart Howarth. Subs (all used): 14 Iafeta Palea'aesina; 21 Richard Whiting; 30 Bobby Tyson-Wilson; 27 Jordan Abdull.
Tries: Lineham (31), Talanoa (50), Minichiello (64), Sa (72); **Goals:** Sneyd 4/4.
Sin bin: Lineham (31) - dissent.
RED DEVILS: 19 Niall Evalds; 34 Oliver Gildart; 22 Jason Walton; 18 Mason Caton-Brown; 5 Greg Johnson; 1 Kevin Locke; 14 Theo Fages; 10 Lama Tasi; 17 Jordan Walne; 16 Scott Taylor; 11 Harrison Hansen (C); 25 George Griffin; 26 Carl Forster. Subs (all used): 24 Liam Hood; 15 Darrell Griffin; 32 Ryan Lannon; 35 James Greenwood.
Tries: Locke (4), Greenwood (44), Gildart (58);
Goals: Fages 4/4.
Rugby Leaguer & League Express Men of the Match: *Hull:* Liam Watts; *Red Devils:* Theo Fages.
Penalty count: 13-7; **Half-time:** 6-8;
Referee: James Child; **Attendance:** 9,385.

ST HELENS 44 WAKEFIELD TRINITY WILDCATS 4

SAINTS: 34 Shannon McDonnell (D2); 2 Tom Makinson; 17 Mark Percival; 3 Jordan Turner; 5 Adam Swift; 6 Travis Burns; 7 Luke Walsh; 10 Kyle Amor; 26 Lewis Charnock; 8 Mose Masoe; 13 Louie McCarthy-Scarsbrook; 12 Jon Wilkin (C); 25 Andre Savelio. Subs (all used): 4 Josh Jones; 14 Alex Walmsley; 15 Mark Flanagan; 19 Greg Richards.
Tries: Walsh (11, 59), Charnock (16, 23), Makinson (29, 77), Turner (43), Swift (45), Masoe (49);
Goals: Burns 4/9.
WILDCATS: 6 Jacob Miller; 24 Tom Johnstone; 4 Reece Lyne; 28 Joe Arundel; 2 Chris Riley; 14 Pita Godinet; 7 Tim Smith; 8 Nick Scruton; 9 Paul McShane; 31 Ben Kavanagh; 19 Jon Molloy; 15 Matt Ryan; 13 Danny Washbrook (C). Subs (all used): 11 Ali Lauitiiti; 16 Mickael Simon; 18 Daniel Smith; 22 Jordan Crowther.
Try: Johnstone (34); **Goals:** Miller 0/1.
Rugby Leaguer & League Express Men of the Match: *Saints:* Luke Walsh; *Wildcats:* Pita Godinet.
Penalty count: 5-6; **Half-time:** 20-4;
Referee: Chris Leatherbarrow; **Attendance:** 10,001.

WIGAN WARRIORS 60 HULL KINGSTON ROVERS 0

WARRIORS: 20 Ryan Hampshire; 22 Dominic Manfredi; 11 Joel Tomkins; 4 Dan Sarginson; 5 Joe Burgess; 6 George Williams; 7 Matty Smith; 8 Dominic Crosby; 9 Michael Mcllorum (C); 10 Ben Flower; 12 Liam Farrell; 14 John Bateman; 25 Larne Patrick. Subs (all used): 17 Tony Clubb; 16 Sam Powell; 24 Taulima Tautai; 28 Ryan Sutton.
Tries: Crosby (4), Burgess (6, 11, 78), L Farrell (9), J Tomkins (15), Williams (21, 63), Sarginson (44), Manfredi (52), Tautai (57); **Goals:** Smith 8/11.
ROVERS: 1 Kieran Dixon; 2 Ben Cockayne; 19 Kris Welham; 5 Ken Sio; 27 Josh Guzdek; 6 Maurice Blair; 7 Albert Kelly; 17 Greg Burke; 24 John Boudebza; 8 Adam Walker; 12 Graeme Horne; 13 Tyrone McCarthy (C); 15 James Donaldson. Subs (all used): 20 James Green; 21 Aaron Ollett; 26 Sonny Esslemont; 28 Connor Robinson.
Rugby Leaguer & League Express Men of the Match: *Warriors:* George Williams; *Rovers:* John Boudebza.
Penalty count: 5-2; **Half-time:** 34-0;
Referee: Phil Bentham; **Attendance:** 11,468.

Sunday 3rd May 2015

WARRINGTON WOLVES 22 WIDNES VIKINGS 20

WOLVES: 6 Stefan Ratchford; 5 Joel Monaghan (C); 3 Chris Bridge; 4 Ryan Atkins; 22 Gene Ormsby; 29 Declan Patton; 7 Richard Myler; 8 Chris Hill; 14 Mick Higham; 19 Anthony England; 17 Ben Currie; 12 Ben Westwood; 13 Ben Harrison. Subs (all used): 9 Daryl Clark; 15 Roy Asotasi; 10 Ashton Sims; 18 James Laithwaite.
Tries: Ormsby (11), Monaghan (31, 80), Clark (34), Westwood (66); **Goals:** Ratchford 1/3, Patton 0/2.
VIKINGS: 1 Rhys Hanbury; 2 Paddy Flynn; 4 Stefan Marsh; 14 Chris Dean; 15 Jack Owens; 6 Kevin Brown (C); 7 Joe Mellor; 8 Eamon O'Carroll; 9 Lloyd White; 25 Alex Gerrard; 12 Danny Tickle; 11 Danny Galea; 16 Willie Isa. Subs (all used): 17 Chris Clarkson; 33 Aaron Heremaia; 23 Phil Joseph; 10 Manase Manuokafoa.
Tries: Owens (22), Flynn (40), Brown (44, 57);
Goals: Owens 2/4.
Rugby Leaguer & League Express Men of the Match: *Wolves:* Stefan Ratchford; *Vikings:* Kevin Brown.
Penalty count: 8-4; **Half-time:** 14-8;
Referee: Ben Thaler; **Attendance:** 10,856.

CASTLEFORD TIGERS 36 CATALANS DRAGONS 28

TIGERS: 22 Jordan Tansey; 23 Michael Channing; 26 Ashley Gibson; 4 Michael Shenton (C); 27 Ash Robson; 21 Liam Finn; 7 Luke Gale; 8 Andy Lynch; 17 Scott Moore; 33 Ryan Bailey (D); 11 Oliver Holmes; 18 Frankie Mariano; 13 Nathan Massey. Subs (all used): 10 Grant Millington; 15 Ryan Boyle; 28 Will Maher; 32 Tom Holmes (D).
Tries: Gibson (24), Channing (29), Millington (35), Shenton (59), Tansey (70), Moore (75); **Goals:** Gale 6/7.
DRAGONS: 1 Morgan Escare; 5 Michael Oldfield; 20 Damien Cardace; 4 Willie Tonga; 27 Fouad Yaha; 14 Thomas Bosc; 7 Scott Dureau; 12 Louis Anderson; 9 Ian Henderson; 10 Remi Casty (C); 11 Zeb Taia; 17 Elliott Whitehead; 24 Jason Baitieri. Subs (all used): 16 Eloi Pelissier; 18 Benjamin Garcia; 21 Julian Bousquet; 22 Gadwin Springer.
Tries: Yaha (39), Garcia (41, 49, 80), Taia (63);
Goals: Dureau 4/4, Bosc 0/1.
Rugby Leaguer & League Express Men of the Match: *Tigers:* Luke Gale; *Dragons:* Zeb Taia.
Penalty count: 7-7; **Half-time:** 20-6;
Referee: Robert Hicks; **Attendance:** 5,704.

ROUND 14

Thursday 7th May 2015

HULL KINGSTON ROVERS 54 WAKEFIELD TRINITY WILDCATS 6

ROVERS: 2 Ben Cockayne; 1 Kieran Dixon; 5 Ken Sio; 19 Kris Welham; 4 Josh Mantellato; 23 Terry Campese (C); 7 Albert Kelly; 8 Adam Walker; 24 John Boudebza; 32 Dane Tilse; 11 Kevin Larroyer; 12 Graeme Horne; 13 Tyrone McCarthy. Subs (all used): 15 James Donaldson; 20 James Green; 21 Aaron Ollett; 22 Jordan Cox.
Tries: Welham (12), Mantellato (17, 35), Kelly (27), Horne (49), Dixon (55, 60), Sio (68), Boudebza (70), McCarthy (77); **Goals:** Mantellato 7/9, Dixon 0/1.
WILDCATS: 6 Jacob Miller; 24 Tom Johnstone; 4 Reece Lyne; 28 Joe Arundel; 2 Chris Riley; 1 Craig Hall; 7 Tim Smith; 8 Nick Scruton; 9 Paul McShane; 31 Ben Kavanagh; 15 Matt Ryan; 13 Danny Washbrook (C); 18 Daniel Smith. Subs (all used): 10 Scott Anderson; 14 Pita Godinet; 16 Mickael Simon; 19 Jon Molloy.
Try: Arundel (25); **Goals:** Hall 1/1.
Rugby Leaguer & League Express Men of the Match: *Rovers:* Terry Campese; *Wildcats:* Scott Anderson.
Penalty count: 4-4; **Half-time:** 20-6;
Referee: Joe Cobb; **Attendance:** 7,378.

Friday 8th May 2015

SALFORD RED DEVILS 0 HUDDERSFIELD GIANTS 19

RED DEVILS: 19 Niall Evalds; 5 Greg Johnson; 18 Mason Caton-Brown; 34 Oliver Gildart; 2 Ben Jones-Bishop; 25 George Griffin; 14 Theo Fages; 16 Scott Taylor; 33 Wayne Godwin; 15 Darrell Griffin; 17 Jordan Walne; 12 Weller Hauraki; 11 Harrison Hansen (C). Subs (all used): 8 Adrian Morley; 10 Lama Tasi; 20 Adam Walne; 24 Liam Hood.
Sin bin: Hauraki (24) - fighting.
On report:
Morley (28) - alleged use of the head on Leeming.
GIANTS: 1 Scott Grix; 2 Jermaine McGillvary; 3 Leroy Cudjoe; 22 Jake Connor; 5 Aaron Murphy; 6 Danny Brough (C); 20 Jamie Ellis; 8 Eorl Crabtree; 16 Kyle Wood; 10 Craig Huby; 12 Jack Hughes; 4 Joe Wardle; 17 Ukuma Ta'ai. Subs (all used): 14 Michael Lawrence; 15 Craig Kopczak; 19 Anthony Mullally; 24 Kruise Leeming.
Tries: Cudjoe (6), Ellis (15), Wood (61);
Goals: Brough 3/4; **Field goal:** Brough (55).
Sin bin: Grix (24) - fighting.
Rugby Leaguer & League Express Men of the Match: *Red Devils:* Theo Fages; *Giants:* Danny Brough.
Penalty count: 9-10; **Half-time:** 0-12;
Referee: Robert Hicks; **Attendance:** 1,972.

WIGAN WARRIORS 28 CASTLEFORD TIGERS 0

WARRIORS: 20 Ryan Hampshire; 22 Dominic Manfredi; 11 Joel Tomkins; 4 Dan Sarginson; 5 Joe Burgess; 6 George Williams; 7 Matty Smith; 8 Dominic Crosby; 9 Michael Mcllorum; 23 Lee Mossop; 30 Rhodri Lloyd; 14 John Bateman; 13 Sean O'Loughlin (C). Subs (all used): 16 Sam Powell; 24 Taulima Tautai; 25 Larne Patrick; 28 Ryan Sutton.
Tries: Burgess (35), Mcllorum (64), Sarginson (71), Manfredi (75); **Goals:** Smith 6/8.
TIGERS: 22 Jordan Tansey; 26 Ashley Gibson; 23 Michael Channing; 4 Michael Shenton (C); 2 James Clare; 21 Liam Finn; 7 Luke Gale; 15 Ryan Boyle; 9 Adam Milner; 33 Ryan Bailey; 18 Frankie Mariano; 16 Junior Moors; 14 Lee Jewitt. Subs (all used): 3 Jake Webster; 6 Ben Roberts; 10 Grant Millington; 19 Scott Wheeldon.
Rugby Leaguer & League Express Men of the Match: *Warriors:* Matty Smith; *Tigers:* Ryan Bailey.
Penalty count: 9-6; **Half-time:** 10-0;
Referee: Ben Thaler; **Attendance:** 15,022.

Saturday 9th May 2015

CATALANS DRAGONS 33 ST HELENS 26

DRAGONS: 1 Morgan Escare; 20 Damien Cardace; 18 Benjamin Garcia; 4 Willie Tonga; 27 Fouad Yaha; 6 Todd Carney; 7 Scott Dureau; 8 Olivier Elima; 9 Ian Henderson; 10 Remi Casty; 11 Zeb Taia; 17 Elliott Whitehead; 24 Jason Baitieri. Subs: 12 Louis Anderson; 13 Gregory Mounis (C); 21 Julian Bousquet; 26 Stanislas Robin (not used).
Tries: Garcia (15, 39), Taia (19, 76), Escare (62);
Goals: Dureau 6/7; **Field goal:** Dureau (80).
SAINTS: 34 Shannon McDonnell; 2 Tom Makinson; 17 Mark Percival; 3 Jordan Turner; 5 Adam Swift; 6 Travis Burns; 7 Luke Walsh; 10 Kyle Amor; 9 James Roby; 14 Alex Walmsley; 12 Jon Wilkin (C); 13 Louie McCarthy-Scarsbrook; 18 Luke Thompson. Subs (all used): 4 Josh Jones; 8 Mose Masoe; 19 Greg Richards; 25 Andre Savelio.

Tries: Swift (3, 26, 32, 71), McDonnell (35);
Goals: Burns 0/2, Walsh 3/3.
Rugby Leaguer & League Express Men of the Match:
Dragons: Zeb Taia; *Saints:* Adam Swift.
Penalty count: 12-7; **Half-time:** 18-20;
Referee: James Child; **Attendance:** 8,884.

Sunday 10th May 2015

WARRINGTON WOLVES 26 HULL FC 27

WOLVES: 6 Stefan Ratchford; 5 Joel Monaghan (C); 28 Toby King; 4 Ryan Atkins; 22 Gene Ormsby; 29 Declan Patton; 7 Richard Myler; 15 Roy Asotasi; 14 Mick Higham; 10 Ashton Sims; 17 Ben Currie; 12 Ben Westwood; 13 Ben Harrison. Subs (all used): 3 Chris Bridge; 8 Chris Hill; 18 James Laithwaite; 19 Anthony England.
Tries: Monaghan (15, 50), Currie (18), Ormsby (53, 62);
Goals: Ratchford 2/4, Bridge 1/1.
HULL: 32 Jordan Rankin; 2 Tom Lineham; 5 Fetuli Talanoa; 4 Kirk Yeaman; 19 Steve Michaels; 6 Leon Pryce; 7 Marc Sneyd; 10 Liam Watts; 9 Danny Houghton; 11 Gareth Ellis (C); 3 Setaimata Sa; 12 Mark Minichiello; 16 Jordan Thompson. Subs (all used): 14 Iafeta Palea'aesina; 15 Chris Green; 21 Richard Whiting; 27 Jordan Abdull.
Tries: Thompson (12), Sa (23), Sneyd (31), Minichiello (69), Lineham (75); **Goals:** Sneyd 3/5;
Field goal: Sneyd (80).
Rugby Leaguer & League Express Men of the Match:
Wolves: Mick Higham; *Hull:* Marc Sneyd.
Penalty count: 6-5; **Half-time:** 12-16;
Referee: Richard Silverwood; **Attendance:** 9,697.

WIDNES VIKINGS 38 LEEDS RHINOS 24

VIKINGS: 1 Rhys Hanbury; 15 Jack Owens; 4 Stefan Marsh; 14 Chris Dean; 5 Patrick Ah Van; 6 Kevin Brown (C); 7 Joe Mellor; 35 Gil Dudson; 9 Lloyd White; 25 Alex Gerrard; 17 Chris Clarkson; 11 Danny Galea; 16 Willie Isa. Subs (all used): 10 Manase Manuokafoa; 33 Aaron Heremaia; 23 Phil Joseph; 28 Matt Whitley.
Tries: Clarkson (4), Marsh (25), Mellor (33), Galea (46), Manuokafoa (53), Dean (72), Heremaia (78);
Goals: Owens 5/7.
RHINOS: 1 Zak Hardaker; 3 Kallum Watkins; 20 Jimmy Keinhorst; 4 Joel Moon; 27 Ash Handley; 18 Liam Sutcliffe; 6 Danny McGuire (C); 17 Adam Cuthbertson; 7 Rob Burrow; 19 Brad Singleton; 14 Stevie Ward; 12 Carl Ablett; 15 Brett Delaney. Subs (all used): 9 Paul Aiton; 10 Jamie Peacock; 16 Mitch Achurch; 21 Josh Walters.
Tries: S Ward (8), Moon (15), Watkins (39, 57), Keinhorst (59); **Goals:** Sutcliffe 2/5.
Rugby Leaguer & League Express Men of the Match:
Vikings: Danny Galea; *Rhinos:* Danny McGuire.
Penalty count: 7-2; **Half-time:** 16-14;
Referee: Phil Bentham; **Attendance:** 6,113.

ROUND 15

Thursday 21st May 2015

CASTLEFORD TIGERS 16 HUDDERSFIELD GIANTS 24

TIGERS: 22 Jordan Tansey; 26 Ashley Gibson; 3 Jake Webster; 4 Michael Shenton (C); 20 Denny Solomona; 6 Ben Roberts; 7 Luke Gale; 8 Andy Lynch; 9 Adam Milner; 33 Ryan Bailey; 11 Oliver Holmes; 18 Frankie Mariano; 13 Nathan Massey. Subs (all used): 10 Grant Millington; 14 Lee Jewitt; 21 Liam Finn; 24 Mike McMeeken.
Tries: Webster (34), Roberts (47), Shenton (66);
Goals: Gale 2/3.
GIANTS: 1 Scott Grix; 2 Jermaine McGillvary; 5 Aaron Murphy; 22 Jake Connor; 18 Jodie Broughton; 6 Danny Brough (C); 16 Kyle Wood; 19 Anthony Mullally; 24 Kruise Leeming; 10 Craig Huby; 4 Joe Wardle; 12 Jack Hughes; 11 Brett Ferres. Subs (all used): 7 Luke Robinson; 8 Eorl Crabtree; 15 Craig Kopczak; 17 Ukuma Ta'ai.
Tries: Huby (21), Murphy (26), Ta'ai (39), Crabtree (74);
Goals: Brough 4/4.
Rugby Leaguer & League Express Men of the Match:
Tigers: Grant Millington; *Giants:* Brett Ferres.
Penalty count: 14-7; **Half-time:** 4-18;
Referee: Richard Silverwood; **Attendance:** 4,632.

Friday 22nd May 2015

HULL FC 10 ST HELENS 17

HULL: 32 Jordan Rankin; 20 Curtis Naughton; 5 Fetuli Talanoa; 4 Kirk Yeaman; 19 Steve Michaels; 6 Leon Pryce; 7 Marc Sneyd; 10 Liam Watts; 9 Danny Houghton; 8 Mickey Paea; 12 Mark Minichiello; 3 Setaimata Sa; 11 Gareth Ellis (C). Subs (all used): 27 Jordan Abdull; 16 Jordan Thompson; 15 Chris Green; 21 Richard Whiting.
Tries: Pryce (36), Abdull (57); **Goals:** Sneyd 1/2.
SAINTS: 34 Shannon McDonnell; 2 Tom Makinson; 30 Matty Fleming; 3 Jordan Turner; 5 Adam Swift; 6 Travis Burns; 26 Lewis Charnock; 14 Alex Walmsley; 9 James Roby (C); 10 Kyle Amor; 15 Mark Flanagan; 13 Louie McCarthy-Scarsbrook; 4 Josh Jones. Subs (all used): 25 Andre Savelio; 8 Mose Masoe; 19 Greg Richards; 18 Luke Thompson.
Tries: McDonnell (20), Makinson (61);
Goals: Charnock 3/4, Makinson 1/1;
Field goal: Turner (80).
Rugby Leaguer & League Express Men of the Match:
Hull: Mark Minichiello; *Saints:* James Roby.
Penalty count: 6-4; **Half-time:** 6-8;
Referee: Matthew Thomason; **Attendance:** 10,320.

Hull FC's Jordan Rankin fends off Warrington's Ben Currie

LEEDS RHINOS 36 HULL KINGSTON ROVERS 16

RHINOS: 1 Zak Hardaker; 27 Ash Handley; 3 Kallum Watkins; 4 Joel Moon; 5 Ryan Hall; 13 Kevin Sinfield (C); 6 Danny McGuire; 17 Adam Cuthbertson; 9 Paul Aiton; 10 Jamie Peacock; 14 Stevie Ward; 16 Mitch Achurch; 12 Carl Ablett. Subs (all used): 7 Rob Burrow; 18 Liam Sutcliffe; 19 Brad Singleton; 21 Josh Walters.
Tries: S Ward (5), Achurch (16), Hall (20, 58), Singleton (48), Sinfield (76); **Goals:** Sinfield 6/7.
ROVERS: 2 Ben Cockayne; 1 Kieran Dixon; 5 Ken Sio; 19 Kris Welham; 4 Josh Mantellato; 23 Terry Campese (C); 6 Maurice Blair; 22 Jordan Cox; 24 John Boudebza; 20 James Green; 11 Kevin Larroyer; 21 Aaron Ollett; 13 Tyrone McCarthy. Subs (all used): 15 James Donaldson; 26 Sonny Esslemont; 30 Stephen Holker (D); 33 James Greenwood (D).
Tries: Dixon (8, 13), Cockayne (32), Mantellato (39);
Goals: Mantellato 0/3, Dixon 0/1.
Rugby Leaguer & League Express Men of the Match:
Rhinos: Danny McGuire; *Rovers:* Tyrone McCarthy.
Penalty count: 7-6; **Half-time:** 18-16;
Referee: Robert Hicks; **Attendance:** 15,206.

SALFORD RED DEVILS 18 WARRINGTON WOLVES 34

RED DEVILS: 19 Niall Evalds; 2 Ben Jones-Bishop; 4 Junior Sa'u; 22 Jason Walton; 5 Greg Johnson; 14 Theo Fages; 36 Josh Wood (D); 16 Scott Taylor; 17 Jordan Walne; 20 Adam Walne; 31 Cory Paterson; 12 Weller Hauraki; 11 Harrison Hansen (C). Subs (all used): 8 Adrian Morley; 24 Liam Hood; 25 George Griffin; 26 Carl Forster.
Tries: Paterson (14), Sa'u (37), Evalds (63);
Goals: Paterson 3/3.
WOLVES: 6 Stefan Ratchford; 24 Kevin Penny; 3 Chris Bridge; 4 Ryan Atkins; 22 Gene Ormsby; 29 Declan Patton; 7 Richard Myler; 8 Chris Hill; 9 Daryl Clark; 10 Ashton Sims; 17 Ben Currie; 12 Ben Westwood (C); 13 Ben Harrison. Subs (all used): 15 Roy Asotasi; 18 James Laithwaite; 25 Brad Dwyer; 27 George King.
Tries: Currie (11), Ormsby (18, 61, 71), Ratchford (25), Dwyer (66); **Goals:** Ratchford 5/6.
Rugby Leaguer & League Express Men of the Match:
Red Devils: Theo Fages; *Wolves:* Ben Currie.
Penalty count: 4-11; **Half-time:** 12-16;
Referee: Ben Thaler; **Attendance:** 6,159.

Saturday 23rd May 2015

CATALANS DRAGONS 58 WIGAN WARRIORS 16

DRAGONS: 1 Morgan Escare; 5 Michael Oldfield; 28 Tony Gigot; 4 Willie Tonga; 27 Fouad Yaha; 6 Todd Carney; 7 Scott Dureau; 8 Olivier Elima; 9 Ian Henderson; 10 Remi Casty; 11 Zeb Taia; 17 Elliott Whitehead; 24 Jason Baitieri. Subs (all used): 12 Louis Anderson; 13 Gregory Mounis (C); 16 Eloi Pelissier; 21 Julian Bousquet.
Tries: Yaha (9, 40), Gigot (15, 37, 70), Taia (26, 33, 60), Oldfield (49), Escare (63); **Goals:** Dureau 9/10.
WARRIORS: 1 Matt Bowen; 2 Josh Charnley; 11 Joel Tomkins; 4 Dan Sarginson; 5 Joe Burgess; 16 Sam Powell; 7 Matty Smith; 8 Dominic Crosby; 9 Michael McIlorum; 23 Lee Mossop; 14 John Bateman; 25 Larne Patrick; 13 Sean O'Loughlin (C). Subs (all used): 6 George Williams; 24 Taulima Tautai; 28 Ryan Sutton; 30 Rhodri Lloyd.
Tries: Charnley (7), Sarginson (29), Burgess (44);
Goals: Smith 2/3.
Rugby Leaguer & League Express Men of the Match:
Dragons: Todd Carney; *Warriors:* Matty Smith.
Penalty count: 9-2; **Half-time:** 34-10;
Referee: James Child; **Attendance:** 10,423.

Sunday 24th May 2015

WAKEFIELD TRINITY WILDCATS 18 WIDNES VIKINGS 30

WILDCATS: 5 Richard Owen; 24 Tom Johnstone; 3 Dean Collis; 4 Reece Lyne; 2 Chris Riley; 6 Jacob Miller; 7 Tim Smith; 8 Nick Scruton; 9 Paul McShane; 19 Jon Molloy; 15 Matt Ryan; 12 Danny Kirmond (C); 13 Danny Washbrook. Subs (all used): 10 Scott Anderson; 14 Pita Godinet; 22 Jordan Crowther; 26 Chris Annakin.
Tries: Johnstone (40), Ryan (65), Collis (72);
Goals: Miller 3/3.
Sin bin: Ryan (54) - professional foul.
VIKINGS: 1 Rhys Hanbury; 15 Jack Owens; 4 Stefan Marsh; 3 Cameron Phelps; 5 Patrick Ah Van; 33 Aaron Heremaia; 7 Joe Mellor (C); 35 Gil Dudson; 9 Lloyd White; 25 Alex Gerrard; 17 Chris Clarkson; 11 Danny Galea; 16 Willie Isa. Subs (all used): 10 Manase Manuokafoa; 23 Phil Joseph; 24 Macgraff Leuluai; 28 Matt Whitley.
Tries: Hanbury (5), Marsh (18, 22, 59), Owens (25), White (49); **Goals:** Owens 0/3, White 3/3.
Sin bin: Phelps (77) - delaying restart.
Rugby Leaguer & League Express Men of the Match:
Wildcats: Matt Ryan; *Vikings:* Aaron Heremaia.
Penalty count: 7-8; **Half-time:** 6-18;
Referee: Richard Silverwood; **Attendance:** 3,132.

ROUND 16 - MAGIC WEEKEND

Saturday 30th May 2015

SALFORD RED DEVILS 16 WIDNES VIKINGS 38

RED DEVILS: 19 Niall Evalds; 2 Ben Jones-Bishop; 4 Junior Sa'u; 3 Josh Griffin; 5 Greg Johnson; 14 Theo Fages; 12 Weller Hauraki; 15 Darrell Griffin; 17 Jordan Walne; 16 Scott Taylor; 11 Harrison Hansen (C); 31 Cory Paterson; 25 George Griffin. Subs (all used): 8 Adrian Morley; 24 Liam Hood; 22 Jason Walton; 26 Carl Forster.
Tries: Paterson (13), Johnson (46), Jones-Bishop (58);
Goals: J Griffin 2/3.
Dismissal: D Griffin (39) - high tackle on Whitley.
Sin bin: J Griffin (77) - fighting.
VIKINGS: 1 Rhys Hanbury; 15 Jack Owens; 4 Stefan Marsh; 3 Cameron Phelps; 5 Patrick Ah Van; 6 Kevin Brown (C); 7 Joe Mellor; 25 Alex Gerrard; 9 Lloyd White; 35 Gil Dudson; 17 Chris Clarkson; 11 Danny Galea; 16 Willie Isa. Subs (all used): 28 Matt Whitley; 10 Manase Manuokafoa; 24 Macgraff Leuluai; 33 Aaron Heremaia.

Tries: Ah Van (16, 27), Galea (20), Brown (36, 42, 62), Marsh (69); **Goals:** Owens 5/7.
Sin bin: Phelps (77) - fighting.
Rugby Leaguer & League Express Men of the Match:
Red Devils: Weller Hauraki; *Vikings:* Kevin Brown.
Penalty count: 2-7; **Half-time:** 4-20;
Referee: James Child.

HULL FC 46 HULL KINGSTON ROVERS 20

HULL: 32 Jordan Rankin; 2 Tom Lineham; 3 Setaimata Sa; 4 Kirk Yeaman; 5 Fetuli Talanoa; 6 Leon Pryce; 7 Marc Sneyd; 8 Mickey Paea; 9 Danny Houghton; 10 Liam Watts; 11 Gareth Ellis (C); 12 Mark Minichiello; 13 Joe Westerman. Subs (all used): 14 Iafeta Palea'aesina; 27 Jordan Abdull; 21 Richard Whiting; 15 Chris Green.
Tries: Yeaman (6, 69), Talanoa (16, 43, 63), Ellis (24), Minichiello (33), Rankin (45); **Goals:** Sneyd 7/8.
ROVERS: 2 Ben Cockayne; 1 Kieran Dixon; 5 Ken Sio; 19 Kris Welham; 4 Josh Mantellato; 23 Terry Campese (C); 6 Maurice Blair; 34 Tony Puletua (D); 24 John Boudebza; 20 James Green; 11 Kevin Larroyer; 21 Aaron Ollett; 13 Tyrone McCarthy. Subs (all used): 33 James Greenwood; 15 James Donaldson; 22 Jordan Cox; 26 Sonny Esslemont.
Tries: Mantellato (9, 56), Dixon (29, 52);
Goals: Mantellato 2/4.
Rugby Leaguer & League Express Men of the Match:
Hull: Fetuli Talanoa; *Rovers:* Terry Campese.
Penalty count: 6-5; **Half-time:** 22-12;
Referee: Robert Hicks.

LEEDS RHINOS 12 WIGAN WARRIORS 27

RHINOS: 1 Zak Hardaker; 27 Ash Handley; 3 Kallum Watkins; 4 Joel Moon; 5 Ryan Hall; 13 Kevin Sinfield (C); 6 Danny McGuire; 17 Adam Cuthbertson; 9 Paul Aiton; 10 Jamie Peacock; 14 Stevie Ward; 15 Brett Delaney; 12 Carl Ablett. Subs (all used): 11 Jamie Jones-Buchanan; 16 Mitch Achurch; 7 Rob Burrow; 19 Brad Singleton.
Tries: Cuthbertson (12), Moon (18); **Goals:** Sinfield 2/2.
WARRIORS: 1 Matt Bowen; 2 Josh Charnley; 11 Joel Tomkins; 4 Dan Sarginson; 5 Joe Burgess; 6 George Williams; 7 Matty Smith; 8 Dominic Crosby; 9 Michael Mcllorum; 23 Lee Mossop; 14 John Bateman; 25 Larne Patrick; 13 Sean O'Loughlin (C). Subs (all used): 10 Ben Flower; 24 Taulima Tautai; 31 Connor Farrell; 28 Ryan Sutton.
Tries: Sarginson (6), Williams (31), Burgess (38), Bowen (58, 76); **Goals:** Smith 3/5; **Field goal:** Smith (78).
Rugby Leaguer & League Express Men of the Match:
Rhinos: Zak Hardaker; *Warriors:* George Williams.
Penalty count: 4-5; **Half-time:** 12-14;
Referee: Phil Bentham.

Attendance: 40,871 *(at St James' Park, Newcastle).*

Sunday 31st May 2015

CATALANS DRAGONS 22 HUDDERSFIELD GIANTS 22

DRAGONS: 1 Morgan Escare; 5 Michael Oldfield; 28 Tony Gigot; 4 Willie Tonga; 27 Fouad Yaha; 6 Todd Carney; 7 Scott Dureau; 8 Olivier Elima; 9 Ian Henderson; 10 Remi Casty; 11 Zeb Taia; 17 Elliott Whitehead; 24 Jason Baitieri. Subs (all used): 12 Louis Anderson; 13 Gregory Mounis (C); 16 Eloi Pelissier; 21 Julian Bousquet.
Tries: Pelissier (47), Carney (63, 72), Taia (70);
Goals: Dureau 3/4.
GIANTS: 1 Scott Grix; 2 Jermaine McGillvary; 5 Aaron Murphy; 22 Jake Connor; 18 Jodie Broughton; 6 Danny Brough (C); 16 Kyle Wood; 15 Craig Kopczak; 7 Luke Robinson; 10 Craig Huby; 4 Joe Wardle; 12 Jack Hughes; 11 Brett Ferres. Subs (all used): 8 Eorl Crabtree; 17 Ukuma Ta'ai; 19 Anthony Mullally; 24 Kruise Leeming.
Tries: Broughton (26, 44), McGillvary (80);
Goals: Brough 5/5.
Rugby Leaguer & League Express Men of the Match:
Dragons: Todd Carney; *Giants:* Danny Brough.
Penalty count: 8-12; **Half-time:** 0-10;
Referee: Ben Thaler.

ST HELENS 20 WARRINGTON WOLVES 16

SAINTS: 34 Shannon McDonnell; 2 Tom Makinson; 30 Matty Fleming; 3 Jordan Turner; 5 Adam Swift; 6 Travis Burns; 12 Jon Wilkin (C); 10 Kyle Amor; 9 James Roby; 14 Alex Walmsley; 13 Louie McCarthy-Scarsbrook; 15 Mark Flanagan; 4 Josh Jones. Subs (all used): 8 Mose Masoe; 25 Andre Savelio; 19 Greg Richards; 18 Luke Thompson.
Tries: McCarthy-Scarsbrook (21), Swift (49), Wilkin (57);
Goals: Makinson 4/5.
WOLVES: 6 Stefan Ratchford; 5 Joel Monaghan (C); 3 Chris Bridge; 4 Ryan Atkins; 22 Gene Ormsby; 29 Declan Patton; 7 Richard Myler; 8 Chris Hill; 9 Daryl Clark; 10 Ashton Sims; 17 Ben Currie; 12 Ben Westwood; 13 Ben Harrison. Subs (all used): 15 Roy Asotasi; 18 James Laithwaite; 25 Brad Dwyer; 27 George King.
Tries: Ratchford (12), Harrison (16), Atkins (28);
Goals: Ratchford 0/2, Bridge 2/2.
Rugby Leaguer & League Express Men of the Match:
Saints: James Roby; *Wolves:* Stefan Ratchford.
Penalty count: 8-7; **Half-time:** 8-16;
Referee: Richard Silverwood.

CASTLEFORD TIGERS 56
WAKEFIELD TRINITY WILDCATS 16

TIGERS: 22 Jordan Tansey; 26 Ashley Gibson; 3 Jake Webster; 4 Michael Shenton (C); 20 Denny Solomona; 21 Liam Finn; 7 Luke Gale; 8 Andy Lynch; 17 Scott Moore; 10 Grant Millington; 11 Oliver Holmes; 24 Mike McMeeken; 13 Nathan Massey. Subs (all used): 9 Adam Milner; 15 Ryan Boyle; 16 Junior Moors; 28 Will Maher.

Catalans Dragons' Scott Dureau gets to grips with Huddersfield's Jake Connor at the Magic Weekend

Tries: Solomona (3, 6, 49, 62), Tansey (10), Shenton (29), Gibson (51, 59, 77), Gale (73);
Goals: Gale 8/10.
WILDCATS: 5 Richard Owen; 24 Tom Johnstone; 3 Dean Collis; 4 Reece Lyne; 2 Chris Riley; 6 Jacob Miller; 7 Tim Smith; 8 Nick Scruton; 9 Paul McShane; 10 Scott Anderson; 13 Danny Washbrook; 12 Danny Kirmond (C); 19 Jon Molloy. Subs (all used): 15 Matt Ryan; 14 Pita Godinet; 16 Mickael Simon; 18 Daniel Smith.
Tries: Johnstone (15, 34), D Smith (17);
Goals: Miller 2/3.
Rugby Leaguer & League Express Men of the Match:
Tigers: Denny Solomona; *Wildcats:* Tom Johnstone.
Penalty count: 5-3; **Half-time:** 22-16; **Referee:** Joe Cobb.

Attendance: 26,917 *(at St James' Park, Newcastle).*

ROUND 17

Thursday 4th June 2015

WIDNES VIKINGS 12 HULL FC 25

VIKINGS: 1 Rhys Hanbury; 15 Jack Owens; 4 Stefan Marsh; 28 Matt Whitley; 5 Patrick Ah Van; 6 Kevin Brown (C); 7 Joe Mellor; 35 Gil Dudson; 9 Lloyd White; 25 Alex Gerrard; 17 Chris Clarkson; 11 Danny Galea; 16 Willie Isa. Subs (all used): 33 Aaron Heremaia; 24 Macgraff Leuluai; 10 Manase Manuokafoa; 23 Phil Joseph.
Tries: Owens (6), Whitley (10); **Goals:** Owens 2/2.
HULL: 1 Jamie Shaul; 2 Tom Lineham; 21 Richard Whiting; 4 Kirk Yeaman; 19 Steve Michaels; 6 Leon Pryce; 7 Marc Sneyd; 8 Mickey Paea; 9 Danny Houghton; 10 Liam Watts; 11 Gareth Ellis (C); 12 Mark Minichiello; 13 Joe Westerman. Subs (all used): 14 Iafeta Palea'aesina; 15 Chris Green; 16 Jordan Thompson; 27 Jordan Abdull.
Tries: Lineham (15, 39, 59), Pryce (30), Sneyd (51);
Goals: Sneyd 2/5; **Field goal:** Sneyd (63).
Rugby Leaguer & League Express Men of the Match:
Vikings: Rhys Hanbury; *Hull:* Gareth Ellis.
Penalty count: 6-5; **Half-time:** 12-14;
Referee: Phil Bentham; **Attendance:** 5,573.

Friday 5th June 2015

HULL KINGSTON ROVERS 22 CASTLEFORD TIGERS 30

ROVERS: 2 Ben Cockayne; 1 Kieran Dixon; 19 Kris Welham; 18 Liam Salter; 5 Ken Sio; 23 Terry Campese (C); 7 Albert Kelly; 20 James Green; 24 John Boudebza; 34 Tony Puletua; 11 Kevin Larroyer; 6 Maurice Blair; 13 Tyrone McCarthy. Subs (all used): 15 James Donaldson; 21 Aaron Ollett; 22 Jordan Cox; 33 James Greenwood.
Tries: Kelly (17, 34), Dixon (30), Ollett (54);
Goals: Dixon 3/4.
TIGERS: 6 Ben Roberts; 26 Ashley Gibson; 3 Jake Webster; 4 Michael Shenton (C); 20 Denny Solomona; 21 Liam Finn; 7 Luke Gale; 8 Andy Lynch; 9 Adam Milner; 10 Grant Millington; 11 Oliver Holmes; 24 Mike McMeeken; 13 Nathan Massey. Subs (all used): 15 Ryan Boyle; 16 Junior Moors; 22 Jordan Tansey; 28 Will Maher.
Tries: Roberts (5), Solomona (10), O Holmes (14), Gale (25), Finn (74); **Goals:** Gale 5/6.
Rugby Leaguer & League Express Men of the Match:
Rovers: Albert Kelly; *Tigers:* Luke Gale.
Penalty count: 3-6; **Half-time:** 16-24;
Referee: Richard Silverwood; **Attendance:** 7,093.

ST HELENS 32 SALFORD RED DEVILS 12

SAINTS: 34 Shannon McDonnell; 2 Tom Makinson; 17 Mark Percival; 3 Jordan Turner; 5 Adam Swift; 6 Travis Burns; 12 Jon Wilkin (C); 10 Kyle Amor; 9 James Roby; 14 Alex Walmsley; 15 Mark Flanagan; 13 Louie McCarthy-Scarsbrook; 4 Josh Jones. Subs (all used): 8 Mose Masoe; 18 Luke Thompson; 19 Greg Richards; 25 Andre Savelio.
Tries: Makinson (10, 39), Swift (22), Turner (25), McDonnell (64); **Goals:** Makinson 6/6.
RED DEVILS: 19 Niall Evalds; 5 Greg Johnson; 4 Junior Sa'u; 18 Mason Caton-Brown; 2 Ben Jones-Bishop; 6 Rangi Chase; 14 Theo Fages; 8 Adrian Morley; 24 Liam Hood; 16 Scott Taylor; 31 Cory Paterson; 12 Weller Hauraki; 25 George Griffin. Subs (all used): 11 Harrison Hansen (C); 15 Darrell Griffin; 17 Jordan Walne; 37 Logan Tomkins (D2).
Tries: Evalds (45), Chase (50); **Goals:** Paterson 2/2.
Rugby Leaguer & League Express Men of the Match:
Saints: Alex Walmsley; *Red Devils:* Theo Fages.
Penalty count: 7-6; **Half-time:** 24-0;
Referee: Ben Thaler; **Attendance:** 11,664.

WARRINGTON WOLVES 26 CATALANS DRAGONS 18

WOLVES: 6 Stefan Ratchford; 5 Joel Monaghan (C); 3 Chris Bridge; 4 Ryan Atkins; 22 Gene Ormsby; 20 Gareth O'Brien; 7 Richard Myler; 8 Chris Hill; 9 Daryl Clark; 10 Ashton Sims; 17 Ben Currie; 12 Ben Westwood; 13 Ben Harrison. Subs (all used): 19 Anthony England; 18 James Laithwaite; 25 Brad Dwyer; 27 George King.
Tries: Currie (24, 67), Atkins (31, 57), Hill (60);
Goals: O'Brien 3/6.
DRAGONS: 1 Morgan Escare; 5 Michael Oldfield; 28 Tony Gigot; 3 Ben Pomeroy; 27 Fouad Yaha; 26 Stanislas Robin; 7 Scott Dureau; 8 Olivier Elima; 9 Ian Henderson; 10 Remi Casty (C); 11 Zeb Taia; 17 Elliott Whitehead; 24 Jason Baitieri. Subs (all used): 12 Louis Anderson; 16 Eloi Pelissier; 21 Julian Bousquet; 23 Antoni Maria.
Tries: Gigot (6), Pelissier (49), Whitehead (52);
Goals: Dureau 3/4.
Rugby Leaguer & League Express Men of the Match:
Wolves: Ben Currie; *Dragons:* Elliott Whitehead.
Penalty count: 7-5; **Half-time:** 12-6;
Referee: Robert Hicks; **Attendance:** 8,611.

Sunday 7th June 2015

HUDDERSFIELD GIANTS 18 WIGAN WARRIORS 32

GIANTS: 31 Jared Simpson (D); 2 Jermaine McGillvary; 12 Jack Hughes; 22 Jake Connor; 18 Jodie Broughton; 6 Danny Brough (C); 16 Kyle Wood; 19 Anthony Mullally; 24 Kruise Leeming; 10 Craig Huby; 4 Joe Wardle; 14 Michael Lawrence; 23 Josh Johnson. Subs (all used): 7 Luke Robinson; 8 Eorl Crabtree; 15 Craig Kopczak; 17 Ukuma Ta'ai.

Tries: Simpson (4), Wardle (28), Brough (50);
Goals: Brough 3/3.
WARRIORS: 1 Matt Bowen; 2 Josh Charnley; 11 Joel Tomkins; 4 Dan Sarginson; 5 Joe Burgess; 6 George Williams; 7 Matty Smith; 23 Lee Mossop; 9 Michael McIlorum; 10 Ben Flower; 14 John Bateman; 12 Liam Farrell; 13 Sean O'Loughlin (C). Subs (all used): 16 Sam Powell; 24 Taulima Tautai; 25 Larne Patrick; 28 Ryan Sutton.
Tries: Burgess (16), L Farrell (37, 54), Charnley (44, 58), Bateman (73); **Goals:** Smith 4/7.
Rugby Leaguer & League Express Men of the Match: *Giants:* Danny Brough; *Warriors:* John Bateman.
Penalty count: 6-10; **Half-time:** 12-12;
Referee: James Child; **Attendance:** 7,307.

WAKEFIELD TRINITY WILDCATS 26 LEEDS RHINOS 58

WILDCATS: 5 Richard Owen; 24 Tom Johnstone; 1 Craig Hall; 28 Joe Arundel; 2 Chris Riley; 14 Pita Godinet; 7 Tim Smith; 8 Nick Scruton; 32 Stuart Howarth (D2); 31 Ben Kavanagh; 13 Danny Washbrook; 12 Danny Kirmond (C); 18 Daniel Smith. Subs (all used): 9 Paul McShane; 16 Mickael Simon; 15 Matt Ryan; 26 Chris Annakin.
Tries: Johnstone (4, 77), Godinet (35), Kirmond (70), Scruton (72); **Goals:** Hall 1/2, Godinet 2/3.
RHINOS: 18 Liam Sutcliffe; 27 Ash Handley; 3 Kallum Watkins; 20 Jimmy Keinhorst; 5 Ryan Hall; 6 Danny McGuire; 7 Rob Burrow; 17 Adam Cuthbertson; 9 Paul Aiton; 10 Jamie Peacock; 14 Stevie Ward; 12 Carl Ablett; 13 Kevin Sinfield (C). Subs (all used): 19 Brad Singleton; 21 Josh Walters; 22 Andy Yates; 29 Jordan Lilley (D).
Tries: Sutcliffe (9, 48, 57), McGuire (25), Burrow (27), Ablett (38), Handley (43, 55), Keinhorst (51), Singleton (60, 63); **Goals:** Sinfield 5/7, Sutcliffe 2/4.
Rugby Leaguer & League Express Men of the Match: *Wildcats:* Tom Johnstone; *Rhinos:* Liam Sutcliffe.
Penalty count: 4-6; **Half-time:** 10-24;
Referee: Joe Cobb; **Attendance:** 4,597.

ROUND 18

Thursday 11th June 2015

LEEDS RHINOS 24 CASTLEFORD TIGERS 31

RHINOS: 18 Liam Sutcliffe; 27 Ash Handley; 3 Kallum Watkins; 20 Jimmy Keinhorst; 5 Ryan Hall; 6 Danny McGuire; 7 Rob Burrow; 19 Brad Singleton; 9 Paul Aiton; 10 Jamie Peacock; 12 Carl Ablett; 14 Stevie Ward; 17 Adam Cuthbertson. Subs: 8 Kylie Leuluai; 13 Kevin Sinfield (C); 22 Andy Yates; 21 Josh Walters (not used).
Tries: Ablett (26), Hall (31), Cuthbertson (38), Keinhorst (56); **Goals:** Sutcliffe 2/3, Sinfield 2/2.
TIGERS: 6 Ben Roberts; 26 Ashley Gibson; 3 Jake Webster; 4 Michael Shenton (C); 20 Denny Solomona; 21 Liam Finn; 7 Luke Gale; 8 Andy Lynch; 17 Scott Moore; 10 Grant Millington; 11 Oliver Holmes; 24 Mike McMeeken; 13 Nathan Massey. Subs (all used): 16 Junior Moors; 9 Adam Milner; 33 Ryan Bailey; 15 Ryan Boyle.
Tries: Millington (8), Finn (11), Shenton (14), Solomona (46, 73); **Goals:** Gale 5/5;
Field goal: Finn (72).
Rugby Leaguer & League Express Men of the Match: *Rhinos:* Danny McGuire; *Tigers:* Grant Millington.
Penalty count: 7-3; **Half-time:** 16-18;
Referee: James Child; **Attendance:** 15,089.

Friday 12th June 2015

ST HELENS 30 WIGAN WARRIORS 14

SAINTS: 34 Shannon McDonnell; 22 Matty Dawson; 17 Mark Percival; 3 Jordan Turner; 5 Adam Swift; 6 Travis Burns; 12 Jon Wilkin (C); 10 Kyle Amor; 9 James Roby; 14 Alex Walmsley; 13 Louie McCarthy-Scarsbrook; 15 Mark Flanagan; 4 Josh Jones. Subs: 8 Mose Masoe; 19 Greg Richards; 25 Andre Savelio; 30 Matty Fleming (not used).
Tries: Swift (29), Turner (32), Burns (43), McDonnell (66), Wilkin (68); **Goals:** Percival 5/7.
WARRIORS: 1 Matt Bowen; 2 Josh Charnley; 11 Joel Tomkins; 4 Dan Sarginson; 5 Joe Burgess; 6 George Williams; 7 Matty Smith; 23 Lee Mossop; 9 Michael McIlorum; 10 Ben Flower; 14 John Bateman; 12 Liam Farrell; 13 Sean O'Loughlin (C). Subs (all used): 8 Dominic Crosby; 16 Sam Powell; 24 Taulima Tautai; 25 Larne Patrick.
Tries: Sarginson (11), Burgess (38), J Tomkins (51);
Goals: Smith 1/3.
Rugby Leaguer & League Express Men of the Match: *Saints:* Jon Wilkin; *Warriors:* Liam Farrell.
Penalty count: 10-7; **Half-time:** 8-10;
Referee: Richard Silverwood; **Attendance:** 16,692.

Saturday 13th June 2015

CATALANS DRAGONS 20 HULL FC 14

DRAGONS: 1 Morgan Escare; 20 Damien Cardace; 28 Tony Gigot; 3 Ben Pomeroy; 27 Fouad Yaha; 14 Thomas Bosc; 7 Scott Dureau; 21 Julian Bousquet; 9 Ian Henderson; 10 Remi Casty; 11 Zeb Taia; 17 Elliott Whitehead; 24 Jason Baitieri. Subs (all used): 12 Louis Anderson; 13 Gregory Mounis (C); 16 Eloi Pelissier; 18 Benjamin Garcia.
Tries: Bosc (16), Gigot (36), Mounis (39);
Goals: Dureau 4/4.
HULL: 32 Jordan Rankin; 5 Fetuli Talanoa; 3 Setaimata Sa; 4 Kirk Yeaman; 19 Steve Michaels; 6 Leon Pryce; 7 Marc Sneyd; 8 Mickey Paea; 9 Danny Houghton; 10 Liam Watts; 11 Gareth Ellis (C); 12 Mark Minichiello; 13 Joe Westerman. Subs (all used): 14 Iafeta Palea'aesina; 15 Chris Green; 16 Jordan Thompson; 21 Richard Whiting.
Tries: Rankin (10), Minichiello (52); **Goals:** Sneyd 3/3.
Rugby Leaguer & League Express Men of the Match: *Dragons:* Remi Casty; *Hull:* Mark Minichiello.
Penalty count: 8-7; **Half-time:** 18-8;
Referee: Ben Thaler; **Attendance:** 7,956.

Sunday 14th June 2015

HUDDERSFIELD GIANTS 30 WARRINGTON WOLVES 19

GIANTS: 31 Jared Simpson; 2 Jermaine McGillvary; 12 Jack Hughes; 22 Jake Connor; 18 Jodie Broughton; 6 Danny Brough (C); 20 Jamie Ellis; 19 Anthony Mullally; 7 Luke Robinson; 10 Craig Huby; 4 Joe Wardle; 14 Michael Lawrence; 21 Jacob Fairbank. Subs (all used): 8 Eorl Crabtree; 15 Craig Kopczak; 17 Ukuma Ta'ai; 24 Kruise Leeming.
Tries: Connor (16), Broughton (43), McGillvary (60, 75), Simpson (64); **Goals:** Brough 3/4, Ellis 1/1;
Field goals: Ellis (70, 73).
Sin bin: Brough (43) - fighting; Connor (78) - fighting.
WOLVES: 6 Stefan Ratchford; 5 Joel Monaghan (C); 3 Chris Bridge; 4 Ryan Atkins; 22 Gene Ormsby; 20 Gareth O'Brien; 7 Richard Myler; 8 Chris Hill; 9 Daryl Clark; 10 Ashton Sims; 17 Ben Currie; 18 James Laithwaite; 13 Ben Harrison. Subs (all used): 19 Anthony England; 15 Roy Asotasi; 25 Brad Dwyer; 27 George King.
Tries: Clark (4), O'Brien (27), Harrison (47);
Goals: O'Brien 3/3; **Field goal:** O'Brien (38).
Sin bin: England (43) - fighting; Clark (78) - fighting.
Rugby Leaguer & League Express Men of the Match: *Giants:* Jamie Ellis; *Wolves:* Stefan Ratchford.
Penalty count: 4-7; **Half-time:** 6-13;
Referee: Phil Bentham; **Attendance:** 5,797.

HULL KINGSTON ROVERS 38 WIDNES VIKINGS 16

ROVERS: 2 Ben Cockayne; 5 Ken Sio; 18 Liam Salter; 19 Kris Welham; 4 Josh Mantellato; 6 Maurice Blair; 7 Albert Kelly; 8 Adam Walker; 24 John Boudebza; 34 Tony Puletua; 11 Kevin Larroyer; 12 Graeme Horne; 13 Tyrone McCarthy (C). Subs (all used): 15 James Donaldson; 22 Jordan Cox; 20 James Green; 33 James Greenwood.
Tries: Welham (7), Mantellato (18, 31), Kelly (33), Sio (38, 46, 68); **Goals:** Mantellato 3/6, Kelly 2/2.
VIKINGS: 1 Rhys Hanbury; 15 Jack Owens; 4 Stefan Marsh; 14 Chris Dean; 5 Patrick Ah Van; 6 Kevin Brown (C); 7 Joe Mellor; 25 Alex Gerrard; 9 Lloyd White; 35 Gil Dudson; 17 Chris Clarkson; 24 Macgraff Leuluai; 16 Willie Isa. Subs (all used): 28 Matt Whitley; 33 Aaron Heremaia; 10 Manase Manuokafoa; 23 Phil Joseph.
Tries: Marsh (15), Brown (23), Dean (50);
Goals: Owens 2/3.
Rugby Leaguer & League Express Men of the Match: *Rovers:* John Boudebza; *Vikings:* Kevin Brown.
Penalty count: 10-4; **Half-time:** 26-10;
Referee: Joe Cobb; **Attendance:** 6,982.

WAKEFIELD TRINITY WILDCATS 16 SALFORD RED DEVILS 24

WILDCATS: 6 Jacob Miller; 24 Tom Johnstone; 28 Joe Arundel; 15 Matt Ryan; 2 Chris Riley; 14 Pita Godinet; 7 Tim Smith; 8 Nick Scruton; 32 Stuart Howarth; 26 Chris Annakin; 13 Danny Washbrook; 12 Danny Kirmond (C); 18 Daniel Smith. Subs (all used): 9 Paul McShane; 16 Mickael Simon; 25 Ian Kirke; 31 Ben Kavanagh.
Tries: D Smith (18), Kirke (42), Kirmond (60);
Goals: Arundel 2/3.
RED DEVILS: 19 Niall Evalds; 18 Mason Caton-Brown; 3 Josh Griffin; 4 Junior Sa'u; 5 Greg Johnson; 6 Rangi Chase; 14 Theo Fages; 8 Adrian Morley; 37 Logan Tomkins; 16 Scott Taylor; 31 Cory Paterson; 17 Jordan Walne; 11 Harrison Hansen (C). Subs (all used): 32 Ryan Lannon; 15 Darrell Griffin; 25 George Griffin; 22 Jason Walton.
Tries: Fages (9), Taylor (15), Hansen (23, 51);
Goals: J Griffin 4/4.
Rugby Leaguer & League Express Men of the Match: *Wildcats:* Pita Godinet; *Red Devils:* Harrison Hansen.
Penalty count: 10-9; **Half-time:** 6-18;
Referee: Robert Hicks; **Attendance:** 3,240.

ROUND 19

Thursday 18th June 2015

CASTLEFORD TIGERS 25 ST HELENS 24

TIGERS: 6 Ben Roberts; 20 Denny Solomona; 3 Jake Webster; 4 Michael Shenton (C); 5 Justin Carney; 21 Liam Finn; 7 Luke Gale; 8 Andy Lynch; 17 Scott Moore; 10 Grant Millington; 11 Oliver Holmes; 24 Mike McMeeken; 13 Nathan Massey. Subs (all used): 9 Adam Milner; 12 Matt Cook; 16 Junior Moors; 33 Ryan Bailey.
Tries: Carney (4), Solomona (27), Webster (46), Cook (59); **Goals:** Gale 4/5; **Field goal:** Roberts (80).
SAINTS: 34 Shannon McDonnell; 22 Matty Dawson; 17 Mark Percival; 3 Jordan Turner; 5 Adam Swift; 6 Travis Burns; 7 Luke Walsh; 10 Kyle Amor; 9 James Roby; 14 Alex Walmsley; 13 Louie McCarthy-Scarsbrook; 12 Jon Wilkin (C); 4 Josh Jones. Subs (all used): 8 Mose Masoe; 15 Mark Flanagan; 19 Greg Richards; 21 Joe Greenwood.
Tries: Walsh (8), Walmsley (15), Greenwood (30), McDonnell (64); **Goals:** Percival 4/4.
Sin bin: Percival (72) - holding down.
Rugby Leaguer & League Express Men of the Match: *Tigers:* Grant Millington; *Saints:* Jon Wilkin.
Penalty count: 10-5; **Half-time:** 10-18;
Referee: Richard Silverwood; **Attendance:** 6,068.

Friday 19th June 2015

HULL KINGSTON ROVERS 36 WARRINGTON WOLVES 10

ROVERS: 1 Kieran Dixon; 5 Ken Sio; 18 Liam Salter; 19 Kris Welham; 4 Josh Mantellato; 6 Maurice Blair; 7 Albert Kelly; 8 Adam Walker; 24 John Boudebza; 34 Tony Puletua; 11 Kevin Larroyer; 12 Graeme Horne; 13 Tyrone McCarthy (C). Subs (all used): 15 James Donaldson; 22 Jordan Cox; 21 Aaron Ollett; 33 James Greenwood.
Tries: Sio (35), Mantellato (38), Dixon (46), Salter (53), McCarthy (64), Welham (72); **Goals:** Mantellato 6/8.
WOLVES: 6 Stefan Ratchford; 5 Joel Monaghan (C); 28 Toby King; 4 Ryan Atkins; 22 Gene Ormsby; 3 Chris Bridge; 29 Declan Patton; 8 Chris Hill; 9 Daryl Clark; 10 Ashton Sims; 12 Ben Westwood; 18 James Laithwaite; 13 Ben Harrison. Subs (all used): 15 Roy Asotasi; 25 Brad Dwyer; 26 Joe Philbin; 27 George King.
Tries: Hill (9), Ormsby (57); **Goals:** Patton 1/2.
Rugby Leaguer & League Express Men of the Match: *Rovers:* Albert Kelly; *Wolves:* Ben Harrison.
Penalty count: 8-4; **Half-time:** 10-6;
Referee: James Child; **Attendance:** 7,455.

WIGAN WARRIORS 19 SALFORD RED DEVILS 12

WARRIORS: 1 Matt Bowen; 22 Dominic Manfredi; 11 Joel Tomkins; 4 Dan Sarginson; 5 Joe Burgess; 6 George Williams; 7 Matty Smith; 8 Dominic Crosby; 9 Michael McIlorum; 10 Ben Flower; 12 Liam Farrell; 14 John Bateman; 13 Sean O'Loughlin (C). Subs (all used): 20 Ryan Hampshire; 23 Lee Mossop; 24 Taulima Tautai; 25 Larne Patrick.
Tries: Burgess (49), L Farrell (64), Sarginson (71);
Goals: Smith 3/4; **Field goal:** Smith (75).
RED DEVILS: 6 Rangi Chase; 18 Mason Caton-Brown; 3 Josh Griffin; 4 Junior Sa'u; 5 Greg Johnson; 14 Theo Fages; 7 Michael Dobson; 8 Adrian Morley; 37 Logan Tomkins; 16 Scott Taylor; 31 Cory Paterson; 12 Weller Hauraki; 11 Harrison Hansen (C). Subs (all used): 10 Lama Tasi; 19 Niall Evalds; 25 George Griffin; 17 Jordan Walne.
Tries: Paterson (9), G Griffin (42); **Goals:** J Griffin 2/2.
Rugby Leaguer & League Express Men of the Match: *Warriors:* Liam Farrell; *Red Devils:* Theo Fages.
Penalty count: 6-4; **Half-time:** 0-6;
Referee: Joe Cobb; **Attendance:** 13,710.

Saturday 20th June 2015

CATALANS DRAGONS 32 WAKEFIELD TRINITY WILDCATS 12

DRAGONS: 1 Morgan Escare; 30 Krisnan Inu (D); 28 Tony Gigot; 3 Ben Pomeroy; 27 Fouad Yaha; 14 Thomas Bosc; 7 Scott Dureau; 15 Jeff Lima; 16 Eloi Pelissier; 10 Remi Casty; 17 Elliott Whitehead; 12 Louis Anderson; 24 Jason Baitieri. Subs (all used): 8 Olivier Elima; 13 Gregory Mounis (C); 18 Benjamin Garcia; 25 Joan Guasch.
Tries: Pomeroy (4), Inu (8), Pelissier (73), Escare (75), Anderson (78); **Goals:** Dureau 6/6.
WILDCATS: 6 Jacob Miller; 24 Tom Johnstone; 28 Joe Arundel; 4 Reece Lyne; 2 Chris Riley; 14 Pita Godinet; 7 Tim Smith; 8 Nick Scruton; 9 Paul McShane; 16 Mickael Simon; 15 Matt Ryan; 25 Ian Kirke; 13 Danny Washbrook (C). Subs (all used): 5 Richard Owen; 19 Jon Molloy; 26 Chris Annakin; 31 Ben Kavanagh.
Tries: Riley (45), Godinet (55); **Goals:** Miller 2/2.
Rugby Leaguer & League Express Men of the Match: *Dragons:* Louis Anderson; *Wildcats:* Tim Smith.
Penalty count: 8-5; **Half-time:** 12-0;
Referee: Phil Bentham; **Attendance:** 7,834.

Sunday 21st June 2015

LEEDS RHINOS 32 HULL FC 20

RHINOS: 1 Zak Hardaker; 27 Ash Handley; 3 Kallum Watkins; 4 Joel Moon; 5 Ryan Hall; 18 Liam Sutcliffe; 6 Danny McGuire; 8 Kylie Leuluai; 9 Paul Aiton; 19 Brad Singleton; 20 Jimmy Keinhorst; 14 Stevie Ward; 12 Carl Ablett. Subs (all used): 13 Kevin Sinfield (C); 21 Josh Walters; 17 Adam Cuthbertson; 10 Jamie Peacock.
Tries: McGuire (6), Moon (22, 52), Keinhorst (37), Ablett (80); **Goals:** Sutcliffe 1/2, Sinfield 5/5.
Sin bin: McGuire (71) - retaliation.
HULL: 1 Jamie Shaul; 20 Curtis Naughton; 3 Setaimata Sa; 5 Fetuli Talanoa; 19 Steve Michaels; 6 Leon Pryce; 7 Marc Sneyd; 8 Mickey Paea; 9 Danny Houghton; 10 Liam Watts; 11 Gareth Ellis (C); 12 Mark Minichiello; 16 Jordan Thompson. Subs (all used): 14 Iafeta Palea'aesina; 27 Jordan Abdull; 21 Richard Whiting; 15 Chris Green.
Tries: Thompson (17), Naughton (45), Houghton (60), Talanoa (74); **Goals:** Sneyd 2/3, Abdull 0/1.
Sin bin: Sneyd (71) - professional foul.
Rugby Leaguer & League Express Men of the Match: *Rhinos:* Jimmy Keinhorst; *Hull:* Jordan Abdull.
Penalty count: 9-9; **Half-time:** 16-6;
Referee: Robert Hicks; **Attendance:** 16,203.

WIDNES VIKINGS 22 HUDDERSFIELD GIANTS 30

VIKINGS: 1 Rhys Hanbury; 15 Jack Owens; 4 Stefan Marsh; 14 Chris Dean; 5 Patrick Ah Van; 6 Kevin Brown (C); 7 Joe Mellor; 10 Manase Manuokafoa; 33 Aaron Heremaia; 25 Alex Gerrard; 17 Chris Clarkson; 11 Danny Galea; 24 Macgraff Leuluai. Subs (all used): 9 Lloyd White; 16 Willie Isa; 28 Matt Whitley; 35 Gil Dudson.
Tries: Ah Van (6), Owens (33), Brown (48, 74);
Goals: Owens 3/4.

GIANTS: 31 Jared Simpson; 2 Jermaine McGillvary; 3 Leroy Cudjoe; 4 Joe Wardle; 18 Jodie Broughton; 6 Danny Brough (C); 20 Jamie Ellis; 8 Eorl Crabtree; 7 Luke Robinson; 10 Craig Huby; 11 Brett Ferres; 12 Jack Hughes; 21 Jacob Fairbank. Subs (all used): 14 Michael Lawrence; 15 Craig Kopczak; 17 Ukuma Ta'ai; 24 Kruise Leeming.
Tries: Ta'ai (29), Kopczak (45), Hughes (54), Robinson (59), Broughton (70);
Goals: Brough 4/4, Ellis 1/1.
Dismissal: Ferres (11) - punching Hanbury.
Rugby Leaguer & League Express Men of the Match: *Vikings:* Manase Manuokafoa; *Giants:* Danny Brough.
Penalty count: 8-7; **Half-time:** 10-6;
Referee: Richard Silverwood; **Attendance:** 5,420.

ROUND 11

Tuesday 30th June 2015

HULL KINGSTON ROVERS 34 SALFORD RED DEVILS 28

ROVERS: 1 Kieran Dixon; 2 Ben Cockayne; 18 Liam Salter; 19 Kris Welham; 4 Josh Mantellato; 6 Maurice Blair; 7 Albert Kelly; 8 Adam Walker; 31 Shaun Lunt; 32 Dane Tilse; 21 Aaron Ollett; 12 Graeme Horne (C); 15 James Donaldson. Subs (all used): 17 Greg Burke; 20 James Green; 29 Matthew Marsh (D); 33 James Greenwood.
Tries: Cockayne (15), Dixon (34), Tilse (51), Welham (53), Blair (58), Kelly (75); **Goals:** Mantellato 5/7.
RED DEVILS: 6 Rangi Chase; 2 Ben Jones-Bishop; 4 Junior Sa'u; 3 Josh Griffin; 18 Mason Caton-Brown; 14 Theo Fages; 7 Michael Dobson; 8 Adrian Morley; 37 Logan Tomkins; 16 Scott Taylor; 31 Cory Paterson; 17 Jordan Walne; 11 Harrison Hansen (C). Subs (all used): 10 Lama Tasi; 20 Adam Walne; 24 Liam Hood; 25 George Griffin.
Tries: Caton-Brown (21), Jones-Bishop (29, 73), J Walne (63), Taylor (67); **Goals:** J Griffin 4/5.
Rugby Leaguer & League Express Men of the Match: *Rovers:* Albert Kelly; *Red Devils:* Theo Fages.
Penalty count: 7-4; **Half-time:** 8-10;
Referee: Richard Silverwood; **Attendance:** 6,717.

Wednesday 1st July 2015

WAKEFIELD TRINITY WILDCATS 26 HULL FC 16

WILDCATS: 33 Kevin Locke (D); 5 Richard Owen; 28 Joe Arundel; 4 Reece Lyne; 35 Jordan Tansey (D); 14 Pita Godinet; 6 Jacob Miller; 8 Nick Scruton (C); 9 Paul McShane; 16 Mickael Simon; 15 Matt Ryan; 25 Ian Kirke; 19 Jon Molloy. Subs (all used): 13 Danny Washbrook; 26 Chris Annakin; 31 Ben Kavanagh; 34 Michael Sio (D).
Tries: Miller (34), Owen (45), Arundel (54), Ryan (70);
Goals: Miller 5/6.
HULL: 1 Jamie Shaul; 20 Curtis Naughton; 5 Fetuli Talanoa; 4 Kirk Yeaman; 19 Steve Michaels; 27 Jordan Abdull; 32 Jordan Rankin; 8 Mickey Paea; 9 Danny Houghton; 10 Liam Watts; 11 Gareth Ellis (C); 3 Setaimata Sa; 13 Joe Westerman. Subs (all used): 17 Dean Hadley; 22 Josh Bowden; 16 Jordan Thompson; 15 Chris Green.
Tries: Yeaman (2), Watts (7), Rankin (18);
Goals: Rankin 2/3.
On report:
Paea (58) - alleged dangerous challenge on Washbrook.
Rugby Leaguer & League Express Men of the Match: *Wildcats:* Nick Scruton; *Hull:* Liam Watts.
Penalty count: 7-7; **Half-time:** 6-16;
Referee: Joe Cobb; **Attendance:** 3,543.

ROUND 20

Thursday 2nd July 2015

WARRINGTON WOLVES 17 WIGAN WARRIORS 6

WOLVES: 1 Matthew Russell; 22 Gene Ormsby; 6 Stefan Ratchford; 4 Ryan Atkins; 24 Kevin Penny; 20 Gareth O'Brien; 7 Richard Myler; 8 Chris Hill (C); 9 Daryl Clark; 10 Ashton Sims; 12 Ben Westwood; 26 Joe Philbin; 13 Ben Harrison. Subs (all used): 25 Brad Dwyer; 15 Roy Asotasi; 27 George King; 31 Sam Wilde (D).
Tries: Myler (12), Atkins (39), O'Brien (51);
Goals: O'Brien 2/3; **Field goal:** O'Brien (37).
WARRIORS: 1 Matt Bowen; 22 Dominic Manfredi; 3 Anthony Gelling; 4 Dan Sarginson; 5 Joe Burgess; 6 George Williams; 7 Matty Smith; 8 Dominic Crosby; 9 Michael McIlorum (C); 10 Ben Flower; 11 Joel Tomkins; 12 Liam Farrell; 28 Ryan Sutton. Subs (all used): 16 Sam Powell; 23 Lee Mossop; 24 Taulima Tautai; 25 Larne Patrick.
Try: Manfredi (56); **Goals:** Bowen 1/1.
Rugby Leaguer & League Express Men of the Match: *Wolves:* Ben Westwood; *Warriors:* Dominic Manfredi.
Penalty count: 6-4; **Half-time:** 13-0;
Referee: Ben Thaler; **Attendance:** 10,504.

Friday 3rd July 2015

LEEDS RHINOS 46 ST HELENS 18

RHINOS: 1 Zak Hardaker; 27 Ash Handley; 3 Kallum Watkins; 4 Joel Moon; 5 Ryan Hall; 13 Kevin Sinfield (C); 6 Danny McGuire; 8 Kylie Leuluai; 9 Paul Aiton; 10 Jamie Peacock; 14 Stevie Ward; 20 Jimmy Keinhorst; 12 Carl Ablett. Subs (all used): 15 Brett Delaney; 17 Adam Cuthbertson; 30 Mitch Garbutt (D); 7 Rob Burrow.
Tries: Watkins (7), Leuluai (11), Hall (14, 74), Handley (38, 56, 69), Ablett (54); **Goals:** Sinfield 7/9.
Sin bin: Hardaker (50) - dangerous challenge on Burns.

SAINTS: 17 Mark Percival; 22 Matty Dawson; 30 Matty Fleming; 3 Jordan Turner; 5 Adam Swift; 6 Travis Burns; 7 Luke Walsh; 8 Mose Masoe; 9 James Roby; 10 Kyle Amor; 21 Joe Greenwood; 12 Jon Wilkin (C); 4 Josh Jones. Subs (all used): 14 Alex Walmsley; 13 Louie McCarthy-Scarsbrook; 25 Andre Savelio; 15 Mark Flanagan.
Tries: Jones (42), Turner (59), Amor (65);
Goals: Percival 3/3.
Rugby Leaguer & League Express Men of the Match: *Rhinos:* Carl Ablett; *Saints:* James Roby.
Penalty count: 7-5; **Half-time:** 22-0;
Referee: Richard Silverwood; **Attendance:** 18,514.

Sunday 5th July 2015

HUDDERSFIELD GIANTS 32
HULL KINGSTON ROVERS 14

GIANTS: 31 Jared Simpson; 2 Jermaine McGillvary; 3 Leroy Cudjoe; 5 Aaron Murphy; 18 Jodie Broughton; 6 Danny Brough (C); 20 Jamie Ellis; 8 Eorl Crabtree; 7 Luke Robinson; 10 Craig Huby; 4 Joe Wardle; 12 Jack Hughes; 14 Michael Lawrence. Subs (all used): 15 Craig Kopczak; 16 Kyle Wood; 17 Ukuma Ta'ai; 19 Anthony Mullally.
Tries: Lawrence (8), Murphy (21), Cudjoe (38), Brough (53), McGillvary (60), Ta'ai (75);
Goals: Brough 3/6, Ellis 1/1.
ROVERS: 2 Ben Cockayne; 4 Josh Mantellato; 19 Kris Welham; 18 Liam Salter; 5 Ken Sio; 6 Maurice Blair; 7 Albert Kelly; 34 Tony Puletua; 24 John Boudebza; 32 Dane Tilse; 11 Kevin Larroyer; 12 Graeme Horne; 13 Tyrone McCarthy (C). Subs (all used): 33 James Greenwood; 20 James Green; 17 Greg Burke; 31 Shaun Lunt.
Tries: Welham (15), Kelly (30), Mantellato (78);
Goals: Mantellato 1/3.
Rugby Leaguer & League Express Men of the Match: *Giants:* Danny Brough; *Rovers:* Maurice Blair.
Penalty count: 5-6; **Half-time:** 16-10;
Referee: Robert Hicks; **Attendance:** 5,596.

HULL FC 31 WAKEFIELD TRINITY WILDCATS 24

HULL: 32 Jordan Rankin; 2 Tom Lineham; 5 Fetuli Talanoa; 24 Jack Logan; 19 Steve Michaels; 6 Leon Pryce; 7 Marc Sneyd; 8 Mickey Paea; 9 Danny Houghton; 10 Liam Watts; 11 Gareth Ellis (C); 3 Setaimata Sa; 13 Joe Westerman. Subs (all used): 15 Chris Green; 14 Iafeta Palea'aesina; 22 Josh Bowden; 16 Jordan Thompson.
Tries: Westerman (5), Logan (24, 48), Michaels (33, 63), Rankin (54); **Goals:** Sneyd 3/7; **Field goal:** Sneyd (67).
WILDCATS: 21 Max Jowitt; 24 Tom Johnstone; 28 Joe Arundel; 4 Reece Lyne; 2 Chris Riley; 35 Jordan Tansey; 6 Jacob Miller; 31 Ben Kavanagh; 32 Stuart Howarth; 36 Anthony Walker (D); 17 Matty Ashurst; 15 Matt Ryan; 34 Michael Sio. Subs (all used): 9 Paul McShane (C); 22 Jordan Crowther; 11 Ali Lauitiiti; 18 Daniel Smith.
Tries: Ashurst (2), Tansey (21), Lyne (49), Johnstone (58); **Goals:** Miller 4/5.
Rugby Leaguer & League Express Men of the Match: *Hull:* Gareth Ellis; *Wildcats:* Tom Johnstone.
Penalty count: 8-4; **Half-time:** 16-14;
Referee: Chris Leatherbarrow; **Attendance:** 9,558.

SALFORD RED DEVILS 18 CATALANS DRAGONS 14

RED DEVILS: 19 Niall Evalds; 2 Ben Jones-Bishop; 4 Junior Sa'u; 3 Josh Griffin; 18 Mason Caton-Brown; 14 Theo Fages; 7 Michael Dobson; 16 Scott Taylor; 37 Logan Tomkins; 20 Adam Walne; 12 Weller Hauraki; 11 Harrison Hansen (C); 25 George Griffin. Subs (all used): 24 Liam Hood; 15 Darrell Griffin; 38 Olsi Krasniqi (D); 17 Jordan Walne.
Tries: Evalds (22), Dobson (33, 74); **Goals:** J Griffin 3/5.
DRAGONS: 28 Tony Gigot; 30 Krisnan Inu; 18 Benjamin Garcia; 3 Ben Pomeroy; 27 Fouad Yaha; 26 Stanislas Robin; 7 Scott Dureau; 15 Jeff Lima; 9 Ian Henderson; 10 Remi Casty; 12 Louis Anderson; 17 Elliott Whitehead; 24 Jason Baitieri. Subs (all used): 8 Olivier Elima; 13 Gregory Mounis (C); 21 Julian Bousquet; 23 Antoni Maria.
Tries: Casty (2), Anderson (16); **Goals:** Dureau 3/3.
Rugby Leaguer & League Express Men of the Match: *Red Devils:* Michael Dobson; *Dragons:* Ian Henderson.
Penalty count: 8-4; **Half-time:** 12-14;
Referee: Ben Thaler; **Attendance:** 5,078.

CASTLEFORD TIGERS 34 WIDNES VIKINGS 20

TIGERS: 1 Luke Dorn; 20 Denny Solomona; 3 Jake Webster; 4 Michael Shenton (C); 5 Justin Carney; 21 Liam Finn; 7 Luke Gale; 8 Andy Lynch; 9 Adam Milner; 10 Grant Millington; 11 Oliver Holmes; 24 Mike McMeeken; 13 Nathan Massey. Subs (all used): 6 Ben Roberts; 12 Matt Cook; 16 Junior Moors; 34 Gadwin Springer (D).
Tries: Solomona (8, 13, 76), Webster (24), Cook (37), Carney (46); **Goals:** Gale 5/6.
Sin bin: Webster (29) - dissent.
VIKINGS: 1 Rhys Hanbury; 2 Paddy Flynn; 14 Chris Dean; 21 Danny Craven; 15 Jack Owens; 26 Tom Gilmore; 7 Joe Mellor (C); 10 Manase Manuokafoa; 33 Aaron Heremaia; 25 Alex Gerrard; 17 Chris Clarkson; 11 Danny Galea; 13 Hep Cahill. Subs (all used): 8 Eamon O'Carroll; 24 Macgraff Leuluai; 35 Gil Dudson; 16 Willie Isa.
Tries: Owens (29), Clarkson (34), Gilmore (51), Leuluai (71); **Goals:** Owens 2/4.
Rugby Leaguer & League Express Men of the Match: *Tigers:* Denny Solomona; *Vikings:* Willie Isa.
Penalty count: 10-7; **Half-time:** 24-10;
Referee: Joe Cobb; **Attendance:** 7,002.

ROUND 21

Thursday 9th July 2015

WIGAN WARRIORS 26 LEEDS RHINOS 24

WARRIORS: 1 Matt Bowen; 2 Josh Charnley; 14 John Bateman; 4 Dan Sarginson; 5 Joe Burgess; 6 George Williams; 7 Matty Smith; 8 Dominic Crosby; 9 Michael McIlorum; 10 Ben Flower; 11 Joel Tomkins; 12 Liam Farrell; 13 Sean O'Loughlin (C). Subs (all used): 17 Tony Clubb; 23 Lee Mossop; 24 Taulima Tautai; 25 Larne Patrick.
Tries: L Farrell (14), O'Loughlin (17), Bowen (33), Charnley (50); **Goals:** Smith 5/5.
RHINOS: 3 Kallum Watkins; 27 Ash Handley; 20 Jimmy Keinhorst; 4 Joel Moon; 5 Ryan Hall; 13 Kevin Sinfield (C); 6 Danny McGuire; 8 Kylie Leuluai; 9 Paul Aiton; 10 Jamie Peacock; 15 Brett Delaney; 12 Carl Ablett; 17 Adam Cuthbertson. Subs (all used): 22 Andy Yates; 21 Josh Walters; 19 Brad Singleton; 7 Rob Burrow.
Tries: Aiton (10), Singleton (26), Handley (53), Burrow (77); **Goals:** Sinfield 4/4.
Rugby Leaguer & League Express Men of the Match: *Warriors:* Matt Bowen; *Rhinos:* Adam Cuthbertson.
Penalty count: 6-5; **Half-time:** 18-12;
Referee: Richard Silverwood; **Attendance:** 15,009.

Friday 10th July 2015

ST HELENS 35 HUDDERSFIELD GIANTS 34

SAINTS: 37 Adam Quinlan (D); 22 Matty Dawson; 17 Mark Percival; 3 Jordan Turner; 5 Adam Swift; 6 Travis Burns; 7 Luke Walsh; 10 Kyle Amor; 9 James Roby (C); 8 Mose Masoe; 13 Louie McCarthy-Scarsbrook; 21 Joe Greenwood; 4 Josh Jones. Subs (all used): 14 Alex Walmsley; 15 Mark Flanagan; 19 Greg Richards; 25 Andre Savelio.
Tries: Quinlan (16, 31, 37), Percival (49, 64), Greenwood (60); **Goals:** Walsh 5/6;
Field goal: Walsh (78).
GIANTS: 1 Scott Grix; 2 Jermaine McGillvary; 3 Leroy Cudjoe; 5 Aaron Murphy; 18 Jodie Broughton; 6 Danny Brough (C); 20 Jamie Ellis; 8 Eorl Crabtree; 7 Luke Robinson; 10 Craig Huby; 4 Joe Wardle; 12 Jack Hughes; 17 Ukuma Ta'ai. Subs (all used): 14 Michael Lawrence; 15 Craig Kopczak; 16 Kyle Wood; 25 Nathan Mason.
Tries: Hughes (22), McGillvary (33, 55), Cudjoe (45), Crabtree (69), Murphy (72); **Goals:** Ellis 5/6, Brough 0/1.
Rugby Leaguer & League Express Men of the Match: *Saints:* James Roby; *Giants:* Joe Wardle.
Penalty count: 2-8; **Half-time:** 18-12;
Referee: Ben Thaler; **Attendance:** 11,164.

Sunday 12th July 2015

HULL FC 21 CASTLEFORD TIGERS 18

HULL: 32 Jordan Rankin; 2 Tom Lineham; 5 Fetuli Talanoa; 24 Jack Logan; 19 Steve Michaels; 6 Leon Pryce; 7 Marc Sneyd; 10 Liam Watts; 9 Danny Houghton (C); 22 Josh Bowden; 17 Dean Hadley; 21 Richard Whiting; 13 Joe Westerman. Subs (all used): 15 Chris Green; 16 Jordan Thompson; 27 Jordan Abdull; 28 Brad Fash (D).
Tries: Whiting (11), Abdull (45), Lineham (59, 69);
Goals: Sneyd 2/4; **Field goal:** Sneyd (71).
Sin bin: Pryce (76) - dissent.
TIGERS: 1 Luke Dorn; 20 Denny Solomona; 3 Jake Webster; 4 Michael Shenton (C); 5 Justin Carney; 21 Liam Finn; 6 Ben Roberts; 8 Andy Lynch; 9 Adam Milner; 10 Grant Millington; 11 Oliver Holmes; 24 Mike McMeeken; 12 Matt Cook. Subs (all used): 15 Ryan Boyle; 16 Junior Moors; 17 Scott Moore; 34 Gadwin Springer.
Tries: Solomona (5, 33), Dorn (17), Roberts (76);
Goals: Finn 1/4.
Rugby Leaguer & League Express Men of the Match: *Hull:* Danny Houghton; *Tigers:* Mike McMeeken.
Penalty count: 5-6; **Half-time:** 6-14;
Referee: Joe Cobb; **Attendance:** 10,949.

SALFORD RED DEVILS 31 HULL KINGSTON ROVERS 18

RED DEVILS: 19 Niall Evalds; 2 Ben Jones-Bishop; 4 Junior Sa'u; 3 Josh Griffin; 18 Mason Caton-Brown; 14 Theo Fages; 7 Michael Dobson; 16 Scott Taylor; 37 Logan Tomkins; 8 Adrian Morley (C); 17 Jordan Walne; 12 Weller Hauraki; 25 George Griffin. Subs (all used): 15 Darrell Griffin; 24 Liam Hood; 31 Cory Paterson; 38 Olsi Krasniqi.
Tries: Jones-Bishop (21, 60), J Griffin (51), Hauraki (58), Fages (76), Evalds (79);
Goals: Dobson 3/4, J Griffin 0/2; **Field goal:** Dobson (78).
ROVERS: 2 Ben Cockayne; 4 Josh Mantellato; 19 Kris Welham; 18 Liam Salter; 5 Ken Sio; 6 Maurice Blair; 7 Albert Kelly; 8 Adam Walker; 31 Shaun Lunt; 32 Dane Tilse; 11 Kevin Larroyer; 13 Tyrone McCarthy (C); 15 James Donaldson. Subs (all used): 20 James Green; 22 Jordan Cox; 24 John Boudebza; 33 James Greenwood.
Tries: McCarthy (3), Kelly (31, 39); **Goals:** Mantellato 3/4.
Sin bin: Larroyer (34) - interference.
Rugby Leaguer & League Express Men of the Match: *Red Devils:* Liam Hood; *Rovers:* Albert Kelly.
Penalty count: 13-9; **Half-time:** 4-18;
Referee: James Child; **Attendance:** 4,415.

WAKEFIELD TRINITY WILDCATS 20
WARRINGTON WOLVES 40

WILDCATS: 33 Kevin Locke; 35 Jordan Tansey; 28 Joe Arundel; 4 Reece Lyne; 2 Chris Riley; 1 Craig Hall; 6 Jacob Miller; 8 Nick Scruton; 9 Paul McShane; 31 Ben Kavanagh; 17 Matty Ashurst; 13 Danny Washbrook (C); 26 Chris Annakin. Subs (all used): 10 Scott Anderson; 15 Matt Ryan; 34 Michael Sio; 36 Anthony Walker.
Tries: Miller (18, 36, 44, 68); **Goals:** Miller 1/3, Hall 1/1.

WOLVES: 1 Matthew Russell; 22 Gene Ormsby; 23 Gary Wheeler; 4 Ryan Atkins; 24 Kevin Penny; 20 Gareth O'Brien; 7 Richard Myler; 8 Chris Hill (C); 9 Daryl Clark; 13 Ben Harrison; 12 Ben Westwood; 26 Joe Philbin; 6 Stefan Ratchford. Subs (all used): 25 Brad Dwyer; 15 Roy Asotasi; 28 Toby King; 31 Sam Wilde.
Tries: Ratchford (7), Philbin (13), Russell (24, 76), Westwood (28), Clark (54), Myler (56);
Goals: O'Brien 6/7.
Rugby Leaguer & League Express Men of the Match: *Wildcats:* Jacob Miller; *Wolves:* Chris Hill.
Penalty count: 4-3; **Half-time:** 10-22;
Referee: Phil Bentham; **Attendance:** 3,354.

WIDNES VIKINGS 29 CATALANS DRAGONS 22

VIKINGS: 1 Rhys Hanbury; 2 Paddy Flynn; 14 Chris Dean; 4 Stefan Marsh; 5 Patrick Ah Van; 26 Tom Gilmore; 7 Joe Mellor (C); 8 Eamon O'Carroll; 33 Aaron Heremaia; 35 Gil Dudson; 17 Chris Clarkson; 11 Danny Galea; 13 Hep Cahill. Subs (all used): 25 Alex Gerrard; 24 Macgraff Leuluai; 10 Manase Manuokafoa; 16 Willie Isa.
Tries: Ah Van (25, 72), Gilmore (27), Flynn (38, 52);
Goals: Marsh 3/3, Gilmore 1/3; **Field goal:** Gilmore (66).
DRAGONS: 1 Morgan Escare; 30 Krisnan Inu; 28 Tony Gigot; 3 Ben Pomeroy; 31 Jordan Sigismeau (D); 32 Lucas Albert (D); 7 Scott Dureau; 15 Jeff Lima; 9 Ian Henderson; 10 Remi Casty; 17 Elliott Whitehead; 12 Louis Anderson; 24 Jason Baitieri. Subs (all used): 13 Gregory Mounis (C); 18 Benjamin Garcia; 21 Julian Bousquet; 29 Thibaut Margalet.
Tries: Anderson (4), Whitehead (12, 77), Escare (78);
Goals: Dureau 3/4.
Rugby Leaguer & League Express Men of the Match: *Vikings:* Tom Gilmore; *Dragons:* Elliott Whitehead.
Penalty count: 8-6; **Half-time:** 18-12;
Referee: Robert Hicks; **Attendance:** 4,822.

ROUND 22

Thursday 16th July 2015

WARRINGTON WOLVES 14 ST HELENS 20

WOLVES: 1 Matthew Russell; 22 Gene Ormsby; 6 Stefan Ratchford; 4 Ryan Atkins; 24 Kevin Penny; 20 Gareth O'Brien; 7 Richard Myler; 8 Chris Hill (C); 9 Daryl Clark; 10 Ashton Sims; 12 Ben Westwood; 17 Ben Currie; 13 Ben Harrison. Subs (all used): 15 Roy Asotasi; 19 Anthony England; 25 Brad Dwyer; 26 Joe Philbin.
Tries: Currie (37), Penny (50); **Goals:** O'Brien 3/3.
SAINTS: 37 Adam Quinlan; 22 Matty Dawson; 17 Mark Percival; 3 Jordan Turner; 5 Adam Swift; 6 Travis Burns; 7 Luke Walsh; 10 Kyle Amor; 9 James Roby; 14 Alex Walmsley; 21 Joe Greenwood; 12 Jon Wilkin (C); 15 Mark Flanagan. Subs (all used): 8 Mose Masoe; 13 Louie McCarthy-Scarsbrook; 19 Greg Richards; 25 Andre Savelio.
Tries: Roby (14), Masoe (55), Turner (78);
Goals: Walsh 4/4.
Rugby Leaguer & League Express Men of the Match: *Wolves:* Matthew Russell; *Saints:* Alex Walmsley.
Penalty count: 9-9; **Half-time:** 6-8;
Referee: James Child; **Attendance:** 9,618.

Friday 17th July 2015

HULL KINGSTON ROVERS 12 HULL FC 22

ROVERS: 1 Kieran Dixon; 4 Josh Mantellato; 19 Kris Welham; 18 Liam Salter; 5 Ken Sio; 6 Maurice Blair; 7 Albert Kelly; 32 Dane Tilse; 31 Shaun Lunt; 34 Tony Puletua; 11 Kevin Larroyer; 12 Graeme Horne; 17 Greg Burke. Subs (all used): 13 Tyrone McCarthy (C); 15 James Donaldson; 2 Ben Cockayne; 8 Adam Walker.
Tries: Lunt (9), Mantellato (26); **Goals:** Mantellato 2/2.
HULL: 32 Jordan Rankin; 2 Tom Lineham; 5 Fetuli Talanoa; 24 Jack Logan; 19 Steve Michaels; 6 Leon Pryce; 7 Marc Sneyd; 22 Josh Bowden; 9 Danny Houghton; 10 Liam Watts; 11 Gareth Ellis (C); 12 Mark Minichiello; 13 Joe Westerman. Subs (all used): 27 Jordan Abdull; 21 Richard Whiting; 16 Jordan Thompson; 15 Chris Green.
Tries: Michaels (16, 54), Lineham (30, 39);
Goals: Sneyd 3/4.
Rugby Leaguer & League Express Men of the Match: *Rovers:* Albert Kelly; *Hull:* Liam Watts.
Penalty count: 5-5; **Half-time:** 12-16;
Referee: Richard Silverwood; **Attendance:** 11,350.

LEEDS RHINOS 70 SALFORD RED DEVILS 6

RHINOS: 1 Zak Hardaker; 27 Ash Handley; 3 Kallum Watkins; 4 Joel Moon; 5 Ryan Hall; 6 Danny McGuire (C); 7 Rob Burrow; 8 Kylie Leuluai; 9 Paul Aiton; 17 Adam Cuthbertson; 20 Jimmy Keinhorst; 12 Carl Ablett; 15 Brett Delaney. Subs (all used): 30 Mitch Garbutt; 19 Brad Singleton; 21 Josh Walters; 24 Robbie Ward.
Tries: McGuire (7), Cuthbertson (10), Watkins (21), Delaney (24), Hardaker (27, 47), Hall (33, 54), Moon (37), Keinhorst (60), Walters (62), Ablett (65, 79);
Goals: Hardaker 9/13.
RED DEVILS: 19 Niall Evalds; 2 Ben Jones-Bishop; 4 Junior Sa'u; 3 Josh Griffin; 18 Mason Caton-Brown; 14 Theo Fages; 7 Michael Dobson; 8 Adrian Morley; 37 Logan Tomkins; 16 Scott Taylor; 31 Cory Paterson; 12 Weller Hauraki; 25 George Griffin. Subs (all used): 24 Liam Hood; 17 Jordan Walne; 15 Darrell Griffin; 11 Harrison Hansen (C).
Try: Evalds (51); **Goals:** Paterson 1/1.
Sin bin: Morley (20) - high tackle on Burrow.
Rugby Leaguer & League Express Men of the Match: *Rhinos:* Danny McGuire; *Red Devils:* Harrison Hansen.
Penalty count: 14-5; **Half-time:** 40-0;
Referee: Ben Thaler; **Attendance:** 14,190.

WIGAN WARRIORS 20 WIDNES VIKINGS 10

WARRIORS: 20 Ryan Hampshire; 2 Josh Charnley; 14 John Bateman; 3 Anthony Gelling; 5 Joe Burgess; 6 George Williams; 7 Matty Smith; 8 Dominic Crosby; 9 Michael Mcllorum; 24 Taulima Tautai; 11 Joel Tomkins; 12 Liam Farrell; 13 Sean O'Loughlin (C). Subs (all used): 10 Ben Flower; 17 Tony Clubb; 23 Lee Mossop; 25 Larne Patrick.
Tries: Charnley (2), Burgess (38), Hampshire (71), Gelling (79); **Goals:** Smith 2/4.
VIKINGS: 1 Rhys Hanbury; 2 Paddy Flynn; 14 Chris Dean; 16 Willie Isa; 5 Patrick Ah Van; 7 Joe Mellor (C); 26 Tom Gilmore; 8 Eamon O'Carroll; 33 Aaron Heremaia; 35 Gil Dudson; 17 Chris Clarkson; 11 Danny Galea; 13 Hep Cahill. Subs (all used): 25 Alex Gerrard; 24 Macgraff Leuluai; 10 Manase Manuokafoa; 21 Danny Craven.
Tries: Gilmore (8), Dean (34); **Goals:** Gilmore 1/2.
Rugby Leaguer & League Express Men of the Match: *Warriors:* John Bateman; *Vikings:* Tom Gilmore.
Penalty count: 5-1; **Half-time:** 10-10;
Referee: Phil Bentham; **Attendance:** 13,194.

Saturday 18th July 2015

CATALANS DRAGONS 12 HUDDERSFIELD GIANTS 14

DRAGONS: 1 Morgan Escare; 30 Krisnan Inu; 28 Tony Gigot; 3 Ben Pomeroy; 31 Jordan Sigismeau; 32 Lucas Albert; 7 Scott Dureau; 15 Jeff Lima; 9 Ian Henderson; 10 Remi Casty; 17 Elliott Whitehead; 12 Louis Anderson; 24 Jason Baitieri. Subs (all used): 13 Gregory Mounis (C); 16 Eloi Pelissier; 18 Benjamin Garcia; 21 Julian Bousquet.
Tries: Inu (39), Escare (45); **Goals:** Dureau 2/3.
GIANTS: 1 Scott Grix; 2 Jermaine McGillvary; 3 Leroy Cudjoe; 4 Joe Wardle; 5 Aaron Murphy; 6 Danny Brough (C); 20 Jamie Ellis; 8 Eorl Crabtree; 7 Luke Robinson; 10 Craig Huby; 11 Brett Ferres; 12 Jack Hughes; 17 Ukuma Ta'ai. Subs (all used): 14 Michael Lawrence; 15 Craig Kopczak; 16 Kyle Wood; 32 Daniel Smith (D).
Tries: McGillvary (28, 49); **Goals:** Ellis 3/3.
Sin bin: Brough (39) - retaliation.
Rugby Leaguer & League Express Men of the Match: *Dragons:* Jason Baitieri; *Giants:* Jack Hughes.
Penalty count: 7-10; **Half-time:** 6-6;
Referee: Joe Cobb; **Attendance:** 8,761.

Sunday 19th July 2015

WAKEFIELD TRINITY WILDCATS 20 CASTLEFORD TIGERS 58

WILDCATS: 33 Kevin Locke; 35 Jordan Tansey; 28 Joe Arundel; 4 Reece Lyne; 24 Tom Johnstone; 6 Jacob Miller; 7 Tim Smith; 8 Nick Scruton (C); 32 Stuart Howarth; 10 Scott Anderson; 11 Ali Lauitiiti; 19 Jon Molloy; 16 Mickael Simon. Subs (all used): 9 Paul McShane; 13 Danny Washbrook; 36 Anthony Walker; 37 Anthony Mullally (D).
Tries: Lyne (4), Walker (35), Johnstone (61, 65);
Goals: Arundel 2/4.
TIGERS: 1 Luke Dorn; 20 Denny Solomona; 26 Ashley Gibson; 4 Michael Shenton (C); 5 Justin Carney; 21 Liam Finn; 7 Luke Gale; 8 Andy Lynch; 9 Adam Milner; 10 Grant Millington; 11 Oliver Holmes; 24 Mike McMeeken; 34 Gadwin Springer. Subs (all used): 6 Ben Roberts; 12 Matt Cook; 15 Ryan Boyle; 16 Junior Moors.
Tries: Millington (13), Gale (16), McMeeken (39), O Holmes (42), Dorn (45, 74), Carney (48, 50, 72, 78);
Goals: Gale 9/10.
Rugby Leaguer & League Express Men of the Match: *Wildcats:* Tom Johnstone; *Tigers:* Luke Gale.
Penalty count: 8-9; **Half-time:** 12-18;
Referee: Robert Hicks; **Attendance:** 6,108.

ROUND 23

Thursday 23rd July 2015

HULL FC 12 WIGAN WARRIORS 48

HULL: 32 Jordan Rankin; 2 Tom Lineham; 5 Fetuli Talanoa; 24 Jack Logan; 19 Steve Michaels; 27 Jordan Abdull; 7 Marc Sneyd; 8 Mickey Paea; 9 Danny Houghton (C); 10 Liam Watts; 12 Mark Minichiello; 21 Richard Whiting; 13 Joe Westerman. Subs (all used): 15 Chris Green; 16 Jordan Thompson; 22 Josh Bowden; 17 Dean Hadley.
Tries: Whiting (20), Westerman (67); **Goals:** Sneyd 2/2.
WARRIORS: 1 Matt Bowen; 2 Josh Charnley; 3 Anthony Gelling; 14 John Bateman; 5 Joe Burgess; 6 George Williams; 7 Matty Smith; 8 Dominic Crosby; 9 Michael Mcllorum; 10 Ben Flower; 11 Joel Tomkins; 12 Liam Farrell; 13 Sean O'Loughlin (C). Subs (all used): 16 Sam Powell; 17 Tony Clubb; 24 Taulima Tautai; 28 Ryan Sutton.
Tries: Burgess (6), Bateman (15), Powell (24), Williams (37), Bowen (45, 71), O'Loughlin (56), Crosby (78); **Goals:** Smith 8/9.
Rugby Leaguer & League Express Men of the Match: *Hull:* Liam Watts; *Warriors:* Sean O'Loughlin.
Penalty count: 6-6; **Half-time:** 6-24;
Referee: Ben Thaler; **Attendance:** 10,787.

Friday 24th July 2015

ST HELENS 52 HULL KINGSTON ROVERS 12

SAINTS: 37 Adam Quinlan; 22 Matty Dawson; 17 Mark Percival; 3 Jordan Turner; 5 Adam Swift; 6 Travis Burns; 7 Luke Walsh (C); 10 Kyle Amor; 26 Lewis Charnock; 25 Andre Savelio; 21 Joe Greenwood; 4 Josh Jones; 18 Luke Thompson. Subs (all used): 8 Mose Masoe; 11 Atelea Vea; 14 Alex Walmsley; 15 Mark Flanagan.
Tries: Greenwood (15, 66), Burns (17), Dawson (21), Vea (25), Quinlan (50), Flanagan (57), Swift (74, 78);
Goals: Walsh 8/10.
ROVERS: 1 Kieran Dixon; 2 Ben Cockayne; 18 Liam Salter; 19 Kris Welham; 4 Josh Mantellato; 6 Maurice Blair; 35 Dane Chisholm (D); 8 Adam Walker; 31 Shaun Lunt; 34 Tony Puletua; 12 Graeme Horne; 13 Tyrone McCarthy (C); 17 Greg Burke. Subs (all used): 15 James Donaldson; 20 James Green; 24 John Boudebza; 32 Dane Tilse.
Tries: Dixon (31), Boudebza (34); **Goals:** Mantellato 2/2.
Rugby Leaguer & League Express Men of the Match: *Saints:* Luke Walsh; *Rovers:* James Green.
Penalty count: 4-3; **Half-time:** 24-12;
Referee: Robert Hicks; **Attendance:** 10,781.

Sunday 26th July 2015

HUDDERSFIELD GIANTS 34 WAKEFIELD TRINITY WILDCATS 24

GIANTS: 31 Jared Simpson; 2 Jermaine McGillvary; 3 Leroy Cudjoe; 5 Aaron Murphy; 18 Jodie Broughton; 6 Danny Brough (C); 20 Jamie Ellis; 8 Eorl Crabtree; 7 Luke Robinson; 10 Craig Huby; 17 Ukuma Ta'ai; 12 Jack Hughes; 14 Michael Lawrence. Subs (all used): 13 Chris Bailey; 15 Craig Kopczak; 24 Kruise Leeming; 32 Daniel Smith.
Tries: Robinson (13), Broughton (19), Lawrence (25), Smith (35), Cudjoe (38), Brough (65); **Goals:** Brough 5/6.
WILDCATS: 38 Lee Smith (D2); 2 Chris Riley; 39 Bill Tupou (D); 28 Joe Arundel; 4 Reece Lyne; 1 Craig Hall (C); 6 Jacob Miller; 8 Nick Scruton; 34 Michael Sio; 10 Scott Anderson; 17 Matty Ashurst; 19 Jon Molloy; 16 Mickael Simon. Subs (all used): 13 Danny Washbrook; 36 Anthony Walker; 37 Anthony Mullally; 40 Scott Moore (D).
Tries: Miller (7), Anderson (30), Ashurst (47), L Smith (50), Lyne (71); **Goals:** Hall 2/4, Miller 0/1.
Rugby Leaguer & League Express Men of the Match: *Giants:* Ukuma Ta'ai; *Wildcats:* Jacob Miller.
Penalty count: 9-8; **Half-time:** 28-12;
Referee: Chris Leatherbarrow; **Attendance:** 4,839.

LEEDS RHINOS 36 CATALANS DRAGONS 22

RHINOS: 1 Zak Hardaker; 2 Tom Briscoe; 3 Kallum Watkins; 20 Jimmy Keinhorst; 5 Ryan Hall; 13 Kevin Sinfield (C); 7 Rob Burrow; 8 Kylie Leuluai; 9 Paul Aiton; 10 Jamie Peacock; 15 Brett Delaney; 12 Carl Ablett; 19 Brad Singleton. Subs: 30 Mitch Garbutt; 11 Jamie Jones-Buchanan; 17 Adam Cuthbertson; 6 Danny McGuire (not used).
Tries: T Briscoe (4, 36, 65), Garbutt (39), Watkins (59), Delaney (63); **Goals:** Sinfield 6/8.
DRAGONS: 1 Morgan Escare; 30 Krisnan Inu; 28 Tony Gigot; 4 Willie Tonga; 31 Jordan Sigismeau; 6 Todd Carney; 7 Scott Dureau; 8 Olivier Elima; 9 Ian Henderson; 15 Jeff Lima; 17 Elliott Whitehead; 3 Ben Pomeroy; 24 Jason Baitieri (C). Subs (all used): 21 Julian Bousquet; 18 Benjamin Garcia; 29 Thibaut Margalet; 16 Eloi Pelissier.
Tries: Gigot (22, 69), Escare (26), Dureau (50);
Goals: Dureau 3/4.
On report:
Lima (53) - alleged dangerous challenge on Leuluai.
Rugby Leaguer & League Express Men of the Match: *Rhinos:* Kallum Watkins; *Dragons:* Tony Gigot.
Penalty count: 10-7; **Half-time:** 16-10;
Referee: James Child; **Attendance:** 15,534.

WIDNES VIKINGS 21 SALFORD RED DEVILS 20

VIKINGS: 1 Rhys Hanbury; 2 Paddy Flynn; 14 Chris Dean; 4 Stefan Marsh; 5 Patrick Ah Van; 26 Tom Gilmore; 7 Joe Mellor (C); 13 Hep Cahill; 33 Aaron Heremaia; 35 Gil Dudson; 17 Chris Clarkson; 11 Danny Galea; 16 Willie Isa. Subs (all used): 25 Alex Gerrard; 24 Macgraff Leuluai; 10 Manase Manuokafoa; 21 Danny Craven.
Tries: Clarkson (22), Flynn (51), Marsh (65), Heremaia (69); **Goals:** Marsh 2/4;
Field goal: Craven (80).
RED DEVILS: 19 Niall Evalds; 2 Ben Jones-Bishop; 4 Junior Sa'u; 3 Josh Griffin; 5 Greg Johnson; 6 Rangi Chase; 7 Michael Dobson; 25 George Griffin; 37 Logan Tomkins; 16 Scott Taylor; 31 Cory Paterson; 11 Harrison Hansen (C); 17 Jordan Walne. Subs (all used): 24 Liam Hood; 8 Adrian Morley; 26 Carl Forster; 38 Olsi Krasniqi.
Tries: Evalds (17), Paterson (27), Taylor (57);
Goals: J Griffin 4/4.
Rugby Leaguer & League Express Men of the Match: *Vikings:* Aaron Heremaia; *Red Devils:* Harrison Hansen.
Penalty count: 9-6; **Half-time:** 6-12;
Referee: Richard Silverwood; **Attendance:** 5,477.

CASTLEFORD TIGERS 6 WARRINGTON WOLVES 44

TIGERS: 1 Luke Dorn; 26 Ashley Gibson; 3 Jake Webster; 4 Michael Shenton (C); 5 Justin Carney; 21 Liam Finn; 7 Luke Gale; 8 Andy Lynch; 9 Adam Milner; 10 Grant Millington; 11 Oliver Holmes; 24 Mike McMeeken; 34 Gadwin Springer. Subs (all used): 15 Ryan Boyle; 12 Matt Cook; 16 Junior Moors; 6 Ben Roberts.
Try: Moors (72); **Goals:** Finn 1/1.
WOLVES: 1 Matthew Russell; 22 Gene Ormsby; 6 Stefan Ratchford; 4 Ryan Atkins; 5 Joel Monaghan (C); 20 Gareth O'Brien; 7 Richard Myler; 8 Chris Hill; 9 Daryl Clark; 10 Ashton Sims; 12 Ben Westwood; 17 Ben Currie; 13 Ben Harrison. Subs (all used): 25 Brad Dwyer; 15 Roy Asotasi; 31 Sam Wilde; 19 Anthony England.
Tries: Monaghan (7, 37), Westwood (12), O'Brien (21), Ormsby (34), Currie (39), Ratchford (52), Wilde (66), Myler (77); **Goals:** O'Brien 4/7, Ratchford 0/2.
Rugby Leaguer & League Express Men of the Match: *Tigers:* Junior Moors; *Wolves:* Richard Myler.
Penalty count: 5-3; **Half-time:** 0-30;
Referee: Phil Bentham; **Attendance:** 7,239.

SUPER 8s

ROUND 1

Thursday 6th August 2015

WIGAN WARRIORS 30 HUDDERSFIELD GIANTS 22

WARRIORS: 1 Matt Bowen; 2 Josh Charnley; 14 John Bateman; 3 Anthony Gelling; 22 Dominic Manfredi; 6 George Williams; 7 Matty Smith; 8 Dominic Crosby; 9 Michael Mcllorum; 23 Lee Mossop; 11 Joel Tomkins; 12 Liam Farrell; 13 Sean O'Loughlin (C). Subs (all used): 16 Sam Powell; 17 Tony Clubb; 24 Taulima Tautai; 25 Larne Patrick.
Tries: L Farrell (33), Manfredi (50), Williams (52), Patrick (67), Crosby (78); **Goals:** Smith 5/5.
GIANTS: 1 Scott Grix; 2 Jermaine McGillvary; 3 Leroy Cudjoe; 4 Joe Wardle; 5 Aaron Murphy; 6 Danny Brough (C); 20 Jamie Ellis; 8 Eorl Crabtree; 7 Luke Robinson; 10 Craig Huby; 17 Ukuma Ta'ai; 12 Jack Hughes; 14 Michael Lawrence. Subs (all used): 13 Chris Bailey; 15 Craig Kopczak; 24 Kruise Leeming; 32 Daniel Smith.
Tries: McGillvary (7, 12), Hughes (62), Crabtree (72); **Goals:** Brough 3/4.
Rugby Leaguer & League Express Men of the Match: *Warriors:* Liam Farrell; *Giants:* Jack Hughes.
Penalty count: 10-6; **Half-time:** 6-10;
Referee: Ben Thaler; **Attendance:** 11,448.

Friday 7th August 2015

CASTLEFORD TIGERS 36 HULL FC 30

TIGERS: 6 Ben Roberts; 26 Ashley Gibson; 3 Jake Webster; 4 Michael Shenton (C); 5 Justin Carney; 21 Liam Finn; 7 Luke Gale; 8 Andy Lynch; 35 Paul McShane (D); 10 Grant Millington; 11 Oliver Holmes; 16 Junior Moors; 13 Nathan Massey. Subs (all used): 9 Adam Milner; 12 Matt Cook; 24 Mike McMeeken; 34 Gadwin Springer.
Tries: Shenton (23, 26, 37, 49), Gale (63), Gibson (76); **Goals:** Gale 6/7.
HULL: 32 Jordan Rankin; 2 Tom Lineham; 3 Setaimata Sa; 24 Jack Logan; 19 Steve Michaels; 7 Marc Sneyd; 27 Jordan Abdull; 8 Mickey Paea; 9 Danny Houghton (C); 10 Liam Watts; 21 Richard Whiting; 12 Mark Minichiello; 13 Joe Westerman. Subs (all used): 16 Jordan Thompson; 14 Iafeta Palea'aesina; 15 Chris Green; 4 Kirk Yeaman.
Tries: Whiting (2), Rankin (5), Michaels (40), Lineham (43), Logan (78); **Goals:** Sneyd 5/5.
Rugby Leaguer & League Express Men of the Match: *Tigers:* Michael Shenton; *Hull:* Jordan Abdull.
Penalty count: 7-9; **Half-time:** 16-18;
Referee: Robert Hicks; **Attendance:** 6,760.

LEEDS RHINOS 49 WARRINGTON WOLVES 10

RHINOS: 1 Zak Hardaker; 2 Tom Briscoe; 3 Kallum Watkins; 4 Joel Moon; 5 Ryan Hall; 13 Kevin Sinfield (C); 6 Danny McGuire; 30 Mitch Garbutt; 9 Paul Aiton; 10 Jamie Peacock; 20 Jimmy Keinhorst; 12 Carl Ablett; 17 Adam Cuthbertson. Subs (all used): 8 Kylie Leuluai; 15 Brett Delaney; 19 Brad Singleton; 7 Rob Burrow.
Tries: Watkins (13), T Briscoe (21), Hardaker (33, 54), McGuire (37), Moon (58), Burrow (73), Ablett (75); **Goals:** Sinfield 8/9; **Field goal:** Sinfield (69).
WOLVES: 6 Stefan Ratchford; 24 Kevin Penny; 2 Rhys Evans; 28 Toby King; 5 Joel Monaghan (C); 33 Chris Sandow (D); 7 Richard Myler; 19 Anthony England; 9 Daryl Clark; 10 Ashton Sims; 26 Joe Philbin; 17 Ben Currie; 8 Chris Hill. Subs (all used): 27 George King; 31 Sam Wilde; 15 Roy Asotasi; 25 Brad Dwyer.
Tries: Penny (11, 46); **Goals:** Sandow 1/2.
Rugby Leaguer & League Express Men of the Match: *Rhinos:* Zak Hardaker; *Wolves:* Stefan Ratchford.
Penalty count: 5-1; **Half-time:** 24-6;
Referee: James Child; **Attendance:** 13,118.

Saturday 8th August 2015

CATALANS DRAGONS 26 ST HELENS 16

DRAGONS: 1 Morgan Escare; 30 Krisnan Inu; 28 Tony Gigot; 3 Ben Pomeroy; 4 Willie Tonga; 14 Thomas Bosc; 7 Scott Dureau; 15 Jeff Lima; 9 Ian Henderson; 8 Olivier Elima; 11 Zeb Taia; 17 Elliott Whitehead; 24 Jason Baitieri (C). Subs (all used): 12 Louis Anderson; 16 Eloi Pelissier; 18 Benjamin Garcia; 21 Julian Bousquet.
Tries: Gigot (12), Anderson (29), Escare (38); **Goals:** Dureau 6/6, Inu 1/1.
Dismissal: Pomeroy (43) - shoulder charge on Jones.
SAINTS: 37 Adam Quinlan; 22 Matty Dawson; 17 Mark Percival; 4 Josh Jones; 5 Adam Swift; 6 Travis Burns; 7 Luke Walsh; 14 Alex Walmsley; 9 James Roby (C); 19 Greg Richards; 21 Joe Greenwood; 15 Mark Flanagan; 18 Luke Thompson. Subs: 8 Mose Masoe; 10 Kyle Amor; 25 Andre Savelio; 29 Olly Davies (not used).
Tries: Walsh (21), Dawson (35), Greenwood (58); **Goals:** Walsh 2/3.
Rugby Leaguer & League Express Men of the Match: *Dragons:* Scott Dureau; *Saints:* Luke Walsh.
Penalty count: 14-8; **Half-time:** 20-10;
Referee: Richard Silverwood; **Attendance:** 7,392.

ROUND 2

Thursday 13th August 2015

CASTLEFORD TIGERS 17 WARRINGTON WOLVES 16

TIGERS: 6 Ben Roberts; 26 Ashley Gibson; 3 Jake Webster; 4 Michael Shenton (C); 5 Justin Carney; 21 Liam Finn; 7 Luke Gale; 8 Andy Lynch; 9 Adam Milner; 10 Grant Millington; 11 Oliver Holmes; 24 Mike McMeeken; 13 Nathan Massey. Subs (all used): 1 Luke Dorn; 12 Matt Cook; 16 Junior Moors; 34 Gadwin Springer.
Tries: Carney (17, 43), Shenton (28); **Goals:** Gale 2/4; **Field goal:** Finn (79).
WOLVES: 6 Stefan Ratchford; 24 Kevin Penny; 2 Rhys Evans; 4 Ryan Atkins; 5 Joel Monaghan (C); 33 Chris Sandow; 7 Richard Myler; 8 Chris Hill; 9 Daryl Clark; 10 Ashton Sims; 12 Ben Westwood; 17 Ben Currie; 13 Ben Harrison. Subs (all used): 15 Roy Asotasi; 23 Gary Wheeler; 25 Brad Dwyer; 27 George King.
Tries: Myler (32, 69), Penny (75); **Goals:** Sandow 2/3.
Rugby Leaguer & League Express Men of the Match: *Tigers:* Justin Carney; *Wolves:* Richard Myler.
Penalty count: 8-7; **Half-time:** 12-6;
Referee: Ben Thaler; **Attendance:** 5,212.

Friday 14th August 2015

HUDDERSFIELD GIANTS 24 CATALANS DRAGONS 12

GIANTS: 1 Scott Grix; 2 Jermaine McGillvary; 3 Leroy Cudjoe; 22 Jake Connor; 5 Aaron Murphy; 6 Danny Brough (C); 20 Jamie Ellis; 8 Eorl Crabtree; 7 Luke Robinson; 10 Craig Huby; 4 Joe Wardle; 12 Jack Hughes; 17 Ukuma Ta'ai. Subs (all used): 14 Michael Lawrence; 15 Craig Kopczak; 24 Kruise Leeming; 32 Daniel Smith.
Tries: Hughes (28), Murphy (33), McGillvary (40, 71); **Goals:** Brough 4/6.
DRAGONS: 1 Morgan Escare; 30 Krisnan Inu; 28 Tony Gigot; 11 Zeb Taia; 4 Willie Tonga; 6 Todd Carney; 7 Scott Dureau; 15 Jeff Lima; 9 Ian Henderson; 8 Olivier Elima; 17 Elliott Whitehead; 12 Louis Anderson; 24 Jason Baitieri (C). Subs (all used): 14 Thomas Bosc; 18 Benjamin Garcia; 21 Julian Bousquet; 23 Antoni Maria.
Tries: Tonga (19), Carney (80); **Goals:** Inu 2/2.
Rugby Leaguer & League Express Men of the Match: *Giants:* Jermaine McGillvary; *Dragons:* Ian Henderson.
Penalty count: 7-9; **Half-time:** 16-6;
Referee: Robert Hicks; **Attendance:** 4,251.

LEEDS RHINOS 25 WIGAN WARRIORS 18

RHINOS: 1 Zak Hardaker; 2 Tom Briscoe; 3 Kallum Watkins; 4 Joel Moon; 5 Ryan Hall; 13 Kevin Sinfield (C); 6 Danny McGuire; 30 Mitch Garbutt; 17 Adam Cuthbertson; 10 Jamie Peacock; 14 Stevie Ward; 12 Carl Ablett; 19 Brad Singleton. Subs (all used): 8 Kylie Leuluai; 16 Mitch Achurch; 7 Rob Burrow; 20 Jimmy Keinhorst.
Tries: McGuire (3), Moon (21), Hall (39), Watkins (65); **Goals:** Sinfield 4/5; **Field goal:** Hardaker (68).
WARRIORS: 1 Matt Bowen; 2 Josh Charnley; 3 Anthony Gelling; 14 John Bateman; 22 Dominic Manfredi; 6 George Williams; 7 Matty Smith; 10 Ben Flower; 9 Michael Mcllorum; 17 Tony Clubb; 11 Joel Tomkins; 12 Liam Farrell; 13 Sean O'Loughlin (C). Subs (all used): 23 Lee Mossop; 28 Ryan Sutton; 16 Sam Powell; 25 Larne Patrick.
Tries: L Farrell (7, 59), Bateman (71), Manfredi (78); **Goals:** Smith 0/2, Bowen 1/2.
Rugby Leaguer & League Express Men of the Match: *Rhinos:* Jamie Peacock; *Warriors:* Matt Bowen.
Penalty count: 8-8; **Half-time:** 20-4;
Referee: Richard Silverwood; **Attendance:** 15,026.

ST HELENS 22 HULL FC 32

SAINTS: 37 Adam Quinlan; 30 Matty Fleming; 17 Mark Percival; 4 Josh Jones; 5 Adam Swift; 6 Travis Burns; 7 Luke Walsh; 14 Alex Walmsley; 9 James Roby (C); 25 Andre Savelio; 15 Mark Flanagan; 13 Louie McCarthy-Scarsbrook; 18 Luke Thompson. Subs (all used): 3 Jordan Turner; 8 Mose Masoe; 19 Greg Richards; 21 Joe Greenwood.
Tries: Thompson (23), Swift (32), Roby (34), Percival (77); **Goals:** Walsh 3/4.
HULL: 1 Jamie Shaul; 20 Curtis Naughton; 5 Fetuli Talanoa; 3 Setaimata Sa; 2 Tom Lineham; 27 Jordan Abdull; 7 Marc Sneyd; 8 Mickey Paea; 9 Danny Houghton (C); 10 Liam Watts; 12 Mark Minichiello; 17 Dean Hadley; 13 Joe Westerman. Subs (all used): 16 Jordan Thompson; 26 Jack Downs (D); 28 Brad Fash; 32 Jordan Rankin.
Tries: Naughton (28, 70, 73), Lineham (43), Westerman (53), Shaul (64); **Goals:** Sneyd 4/6.
Rugby Leaguer & League Express Men of the Match: *Saints:* James Roby; *Hull:* Mark Minichiello.
Penalty count: 4-3; **Half-time:** 18-6;
Referee: James Child; **Attendance:** 10,203.

ROUND 3

Thursday 20th August 2015

ST HELENS 22 HUDDERSFIELD GIANTS 28

SAINTS: 37 Adam Quinlan; 2 Tom Makinson; 17 Mark Percival; 4 Josh Jones; 5 Adam Swift; 6 Travis Burns; 7 Luke Walsh; 14 Alex Walmsley; 9 James Roby (C); 10 Kyle Amor; 21 Joe Greenwood; 13 Louie McCarthy-Scarsbrook; 18 Luke Thompson. Subs (all used): 3 Jordan Turner; 8 Mose Masoe; 19 Greg Richards; 25 Andre Savelio.
Tries: Amor (10), Roby (39), Makinson (47), Burns (50); **Goals:** Walsh 3/5.
GIANTS: 1 Scott Grix; 2 Jermaine McGillvary; 3 Leroy Cudjoe; 22 Jake Connor; 5 Aaron Murphy; 6 Danny Brough (C); 20 Jamie Ellis; 8 Eorl Crabtree; 7 Luke Robinson; 10 Craig Huby; 4 Joe Wardle; 12 Jack Hughes; 17 Ukuma Ta'ai. Subs (all used): 14 Michael Lawrence; 15 Craig Kopczak; 24 Kruise Leeming; 32 Daniel Smith.
Tries: Ellis (14), Ta'ai (19), Wardle (44), McGillvary (61), Murphy (68); **Goals:** Brough 4/6.
Sin bin: Lawrence (38) - persistent team offences.
Rugby Leaguer & League Express Men of the Match: *Saints:* Mark Percival; *Giants:* Jamie Ellis.
Penalty count: 15-11; **Half-time:** 12-14;
Referee: Richard Silverwood; **Attendance:** 10,976.

Friday 21st August 2015

HULL FC 22 LEEDS RHINOS 36

HULL: 1 Jamie Shaul; 20 Curtis Naughton; 5 Fetuli Talanoa; 24 Jack Logan; 19 Steve Michaels; 27 Jordan Abdull; 7 Marc Sneyd; 8 Mickey Paea; 9 Danny Houghton (C); 10 Liam Watts; 12 Mark Minichiello; 17 Dean Hadley; 13 Joe Westerman. Subs (all used): 14 Iafeta Palea'aesina; 32 Jordan Rankin; 28 Brad Fash; 26 Jack Downs.
Tries: Minichiello (8), Michaels (47), Shaul (59), Rankin (64); **Goals:** Sneyd 3/4.
RHINOS: 1 Zak Hardaker; 27 Ash Handley; 2 Tom Briscoe; 12 Carl Ablett; 5 Ryan Hall; 13 Kevin Sinfield (C); 7 Rob Burrow; 30 Mitch Garbutt; 24 Robbie Ward; 19 Brad Singleton; 20 Jimmy Keinhorst; 14 Stevie Ward; 21 Josh Walters. Subs (all used): 10 Jamie Peacock; 8 Kylie Leuluai; 16 Mitch Achurch; 26 Ashton Golding.
Tries: Handley (6), Ablett (51), Burrow (54, 76), Hall (61), T Briscoe (71); **Goals:** Sinfield 6/6.
Rugby Leaguer & League Express Men of the Match: *Hull:* Mark Minichiello; *Rhinos:* Zak Hardaker.
Penalty count: 3-3; **Half-time:** 6-6;
Referee: Joe Cobb; **Attendance:** 10,649.

WARRINGTON WOLVES 0 WIGAN WARRIORS 28

WOLVES: 6 Stefan Ratchford; 24 Kevin Penny; 23 Gary Wheeler; 4 Ryan Atkins; 5 Joel Monaghan (C); 33 Chris Sandow; 7 Richard Myler; 8 Chris Hill; 9 Daryl Clark; 10 Ashton Sims; 12 Ben Westwood; 17 Ben Currie; 13 Ben Harrison. Subs (all used): 25 Brad Dwyer; 15 Roy Asotasi; 26 Joe Philbin; 27 George King.
On report: Sims (27) - alleged stamp on Mossop.
WARRIORS: 1 Matt Bowen; 2 Josh Charnley; 14 John Bateman; 34 Oliver Gildart (D); 22 Dominic Manfredi; 6 George Williams; 7 Matty Smith; 8 Dominic Crosby; 16 Sam Powell; 10 Ben Flower; 11 Joel Tomkins; 12 Liam Farrell; 13 Sean O'Loughlin (C). Subs (all used): 17 Tony Clubb; 20 Ryan Hampshire; 23 Lee Mossop; 28 Ryan Sutton.
Tries: L Farrell (3), Flower (17), Bateman (48, 57), Gildart (61); **Goals:** Bowen 4/6.
On report:
J Tomkins (1) - alleged shoulder charge on Hill.
Rugby Leaguer & League Express Men of the Match: *Wolves:* Chris Hill; *Warriors:* Matt Bowen.
Penalty count: 6-9; **Half-time:** 0-12;
Referee: Robert Hicks; **Attendance:** 10,095.

Saturday 22nd August 2015

CATALANS DRAGONS 44 CASTLEFORD TIGERS 26

DRAGONS: 1 Morgan Escare; 30 Krisnan Inu; 28 Tony Gigot; 3 Ben Pomeroy; 31 Jordan Sigismeau; 6 Todd Carney; 14 Thomas Bosc; 15 Jeff Lima; 16 Eloi Pelissier; 8 Olivier Elima; 11 Zeb Taia; 17 Elliott Whitehead; 24 Jason Baitieri (C). Subs (all used): 9 Ian Henderson; 12 Louis Anderson; 18 Benjamin Garcia; 21 Julian Bousquet.
Tries: Gigot (2, 47, 62), Taia (9), Lima (16), Carney (21), Escare (40, 73); **Goals:** Inu 0/2, Bosc 6/6.
Dismissal: Pomeroy (28) - dangerous throw on Gibson.
TIGERS: 6 Ben Roberts; 26 Ashley Gibson; 23 Michael Channing; 4 Michael Shenton (C); 5 Justin Carney; 21 Liam Finn; 7 Luke Gale; 8 Andy Lynch; 9 Adam Milner; 10 Grant Millington; 11 Oliver Holmes; 24 Mike McMeeken; 13 Nathan Massey. Subs (all used): 12 Matt Cook; 16 Junior Moors; 34 Gadwin Springer; 35 Paul McShane.
Tries: Carney (29), O Holmes (43), Milner (58, 77), Moors (71); **Goals:** Gale 3/5.
On report:
Carney (7) - alleged dangerous challenge on Escare.
Rugby Leaguer & League Express Men of the Match: *Dragons:* Todd Carney; *Tigers:* Luke Gale.
Penalty count: 11-4; **Half-time:** 26-6;
Referee: Ben Thaler; **Attendance:** 7,473.

ROUND 4

Thursday 3rd September 2015

HUDDERSFIELD GIANTS 40 CASTLEFORD TIGERS 26

GIANTS: 1 Scott Grix; 2 Jermaine McGillvary; 3 Leroy Cudjoe; 22 Jake Connor; 5 Aaron Murphy; 6 Danny Brough (C); 20 Jamie Ellis; 8 Eorl Crabtree; 7 Luke Robinson; 10 Craig Huby; 4 Joe Wardle; 12 Jack Hughes; 17 Ukuma Ta'ai. Subs (all used): 14 Michael Lawrence; 15 Craig Kopczak; 24 Kruise Leeming; 32 Daniel Smith.
Tries: Ta'ai (20), McGillvary (23, 26), Connor (28), Murphy (38), Wardle (67), Ellis (71), Crabtree (76); **Goals:** Brough 2/5, Ellis 2/3.
TIGERS: 1 Luke Dorn; 26 Ashley Gibson; 24 Mike McMeeken; 23 Michael Channing; 20 Denny Solomona; 6 Ben Roberts; 7 Luke Gale; 8 Andy Lynch (C); 9 Adam Milner; 19 Scott Wheeldon; 10 Grant Millington; 16 Junior Moors; 13 Nathan Massey. Subs (all used): 12 Matt Cook; 15 Ryan Boyle; 34 Gadwin Springer; 35 Paul McShane.
Tries: Gale (10), Gibson (15), Dorn (43), Roberts (61), Solomona (79); **Goals:** Gale 3/5.
Sin bin: McMeeken (19) - trip on Wardle.
Rugby Leaguer & League Express Men of the Match: *Giants:* Jermaine McGillvary; *Tigers:* Luke Gale.
Penalty count: 5-3; **Half-time:** 24-10;
Referee: Robert Hicks; **Attendance:** 5,350.

Friday 4th September 2015

LEEDS RHINOS 18 ST HELENS 32

RHINOS: 26 Ashton Golding; 2 Tom Briscoe; 20 Jimmy Keinhorst; 4 Joel Moon; 5 Ryan Hall; 13 Kevin Sinfield (C); 6 Danny McGuire; 30 Mitch Garbutt; 17 Adam Cuthbertson; 10 Jamie Peacock; 14 Stevie Ward; 12 Carl Ablett; 15 Brett Delaney. Subs (all used): 19 Brad Singleton; 16 Mitch Achurch; 8 Kylie Leuluai; 29 Jordan Lilley.
Tries: Keinhorst (17), Achurch (39), Hall (70);
Goals: Sinfield 3/3.
SAINTS: 37 Adam Quinlan; 2 Tom Makinson; 17 Mark Percival; 4 Josh Jones; 5 Adam Swift; 6 Travis Burns; 7 Luke Walsh; 10 Kyle Amor; 9 James Roby; 25 Andre Savelio; 13 Louie McCarthy-Scarsbrook; 12 Jon Wilkin (C); 3 Jordan Turner. Subs (all used): 21 Joe Greenwood; 14 Alex Walmsley; 19 Greg Richards; 15 Mark Flanagan.
Tries: Makinson (2), Jones (21), Walsh (44), Quinlan (57), Wilkin (78); **Goals:** Walsh 6/6.
Rugby Leaguer & League Express Men of the Match: *Rhinos:* Mitch Garbutt; *Saints:* Luke Walsh.
Penalty count: 9-7; **Half-time:** 12-14;
Referee: James Child; **Attendance:** 16,142.

Saturday 5th September 2015

WIGAN WARRIORS 42 CATALANS DRAGONS 16

WARRIORS: 1 Matt Bowen; 2 Josh Charnley; 14 John Bateman; 34 Oliver Gildart; 22 Dominic Manfredi; 6 George Williams; 7 Matty Smith; 10 Ben Flower; 9 Michael McIlorum; 8 Dominic Crosby; 11 Joel Tomkins; 25 Larne Patrick; 13 Sean O'Loughlin (C). Subs (all used): 16 Sam Powell; 17 Tony Clubb; 23 Lee Mossop; 24 Taulima Tautai.
Tries: Flower (15), Bowen (24, 50), Gildart (53), Charnley (64), Patrick (67), Manfredi (72);
Goals: Bowen 7/7.
DRAGONS: 1 Morgan Escare; 14 Thomas Bosc; 30 Krisnan Inu; 28 Tony Gigot; 31 Jordan Sigismeau; 6 Todd Carney; 7 Scott Dureau; 15 Jeff Lima; 16 Eloi Pelissier; 8 Olivier Elima; 11 Zeb Taia; 17 Elliott Whitehead; 24 Jason Baitieri (C). Subs (all used): 12 Louis Anderson; 21 Julian Bousquet; 26 Stanislas Robin; 29 Thibaut Margalet.
Tries: Inu (19), Dureau (43), Sigismeau (59);
Goals: Dureau 2/3.
Sin bin: Anderson (29) - kicking out.
Rugby Leaguer & League Express Men of the Match: *Warriors:* Matt Bowen; *Dragons:* Todd Carney.
Penalty count: 7-6; **Half-time:** 12-6; **Referee:** Ben Thaler;
Attendance: 8,101 *(at The Den, Millwall).*

Sunday 6th September 2015

WARRINGTON WOLVES 46 HULL FC 16

WOLVES: 34 Jack Johnson (D); 24 Kevin Penny; 23 Gary Wheeler; 4 Ryan Atkins; 5 Joel Monaghan (C); 6 Stefan Ratchford; 33 Chris Sandow; 8 Chris Hill; 9 Daryl Clark; 15 Roy Asotasi; 12 Ben Westwood; 17 Ben Currie; 27 George King. Subs (all used): 25 Brad Dwyer; 13 Ben Harrison; 26 Joe Philbin; 31 Sam Wilde.
Tries: Penny (6, 25, 49), Wheeler (19, 59), Currie (22), Atkins (56), Monaghan (63, 80); **Goals:** Sandow 5/8 *(last conversion attempt declined).*
On report: Atkins (34) - alleged shoulder charge; Harrison (48) - alleged dangerous challenge.
HULL: 1 Jamie Shaul; 20 Curtis Naughton; 32 Jordan Rankin; 24 Jack Logan; 19 Steve Michaels; 27 Jordan Abdull; 7 Marc Sneyd; 10 Liam Watts; 9 Danny Houghton (C); 8 Mickey Paea; 17 Dean Hadley; 12 Mark Minichiello; 13 Joe Westerman. Subs (all used): 14 Iafeta Palea'aesina; 22 Josh Bowden; 26 Jack Downs; 28 Brad Fash.
Tries: Hadley (13), Minichiello (66, 69); **Goals:** Sneyd 2/3.
Rugby Leaguer & League Express Men of the Match: *Wolves:* Stefan Ratchford; *Hull:* Mark Minichiello.
Penalty count: 8-8; **Half-time:** 22-6;
Referee: Chris Kendall; **Attendance:** 8,076.

ROUND 5

Thursday 10th September 2015

CASTLEFORD TIGERS 38 ST HELENS 42

TIGERS: 1 Luke Dorn; 26 Ashley Gibson; 24 Mike McMeeken; 4 Michael Shenton (C); 20 Denny Solomona; 6 Ben Roberts; 7 Luke Gale; 8 Andy Lynch; 9 Adam Milner; 10 Grant Millington; 11 Oliver Holmes; 16 Junior Moors; 19 Scott Wheeldon. Subs (all used): 15 Ryan Boyle; 28 Will Maher; 34 Gadwin Springer; 35 Paul McShane.
Tries: Dorn (23, 28), Roberts (36, 46), Solomona (66), Moors (79); **Goals:** Gale 7/7.
SAINTS: 37 Adam Quinlan; 2 Tom Makinson; 17 Mark Percival; 4 Josh Jones; 5 Adam Swift; 6 Travis Burns; 7 Luke Walsh; 10 Kyle Amor; 9 James Roby; 14 Alex Walmsley; 13 Louie McCarthy-Scarsbrook; 12 Jon Wilkin (C); 3 Jordan Turner. Subs (all used): 19 Greg Richards; 21 Joe Greenwood; 15 Mark Flanagan; 18 Luke Thompson.
Tries: Swift (7, 13, 69), Percival (16, 52), Quinlan (56), Makinson (60); **Goals:** Walsh 7/7.
Rugby Leaguer & League Express Men of the Match: *Tigers:* Luke Gale; *Saints:* Adam Swift.
Penalty count: 8-6; **Half-time:** 18-18;
Referee: Ben Thaler; **Attendance:** 5,253.

Friday 11th September 2015

WIGAN WARRIORS 30 HULL FC 24

WARRIORS: 20 Ryan Hampshire; 2 Josh Charnley; 3 Anthony Gelling; 34 Oliver Gildart; 5 Joe Burgess; 6 George Williams; 7 Matty Smith; 8 Dominic Crosby; 9 Michael McIlorum (C); 10 Ben Flower; 11 Joel Tomkins; 14 John Bateman; 24 Taulima Tautai. Subs (all used): 16 Sam Powell; 17 Tony Clubb; 23 Lee Mossop; 31 Connor Farrell.
Tries: Gildart (10), Charnley (22), Bateman (32), Flower (61), Burgess (79); **Goals:** Hampshire 5/6.
Sin bin: Tautai (74) - dangerous challenge on Paea.
HULL: 1 Jamie Shaul; 2 Tom Lineham; 32 Jordan Rankin; 24 Jack Logan; 20 Curtis Naughton; 27 Jordan Abdull; 7 Marc Sneyd; 10 Liam Watts; 9 Danny Houghton (C); 8 Mickey Paea; 26 Jack Downs; 12 Mark Minichiello; 17 Dean Hadley. Subs (all used): 14 Iafeta Palea'aesina; 25 Jansin Turgut; 28 Brad Fash; 35 Masi Matongo (D).
Tries: Shaul (36), Logan (38, 72), Rankin (70);
Goals: Sneyd 4/4.
Rugby Leaguer & League Express Men of the Match: *Warriors:* John Bateman; *Hull:* Jack Logan.
Penalty count: 6-4; **Half-time:** 18-12;
Referee: James Child; **Attendance:** 12,028.

Saturday 12th September 2015

CATALANS DRAGONS 46 LEEDS RHINOS 16

DRAGONS: 1 Morgan Escare; 14 Thomas Bosc; 30 Krisnan Inu; 28 Tony Gigot; 31 Jordan Sigismeau; 6 Todd Carney; 7 Scott Dureau; 15 Jeff Lima; 9 Ian Henderson; 8 Olivier Elima; 11 Zeb Taia; 17 Elliott Whitehead; 24 Jason Baitieri (C). Subs (all used): 16 Eloi Pelissier; 18 Benjamin Garcia; 21 Julian Bousquet; 23 Antoni Maria.
Tries: Bosc (15, 45), Inu (20, 55), Carney (30), Sigismeau (57), Lima (67), Whitehead (72);
Goals: Bosc 1/1, Dureau 5/6, Lima 1/1.
RHINOS: 1 Zak Hardaker; 2 Tom Briscoe; 12 Carl Ablett; 4 Joel Moon; 5 Ryan Hall; 13 Kevin Sinfield (C); 6 Danny McGuire; 8 Kylie Leuluai; 17 Adam Cuthbertson; 10 Jamie Peacock; 14 Stevie Ward; 16 Mitch Achurch; 15 Brett Delaney. Subs (all used): 19 Brad Singleton; 21 Josh Walters; 29 Jordan Lilley; 30 Mitch Garbutt.
Tries: Hall (60), McGuire (69), Moon (78);
Goals: Sinfield 2/3.
Rugby Leaguer & League Express Men of the Match: *Dragons:* Todd Carney; *Rhinos:* Stevie Ward.
Penalty count: 5-6; **Half-time:** 18-0;
Referee: Robert Hicks; **Attendance:** 8,851.

Sunday 13th September 2015

HUDDERSFIELD GIANTS 48 WARRINGTON WOLVES 10

GIANTS: 1 Scott Grix; 2 Jermaine McGillvary; 3 Leroy Cudjoe; 22 Jake Connor; 5 Aaron Murphy; 6 Danny Brough (C); 20 Jamie Ellis; 8 Eorl Crabtree; 7 Luke Robinson; 10 Craig Huby; 4 Joe Wardle; 12 Jack Hughes; 17 Ukuma Ta'ai. Subs (all used): 14 Michael Lawrence; 15 Craig Kopczak; 24 Kruise Leeming; 32 Daniel Smith.
Tries: Murphy (10, 63, 66), McGillvary (27, 35, 43, 68), Wardle (46), Ellis (72); **Goals:** Brough 3/5, Ellis 3/4.
Sin bin: Connor (53) - professional foul.
WOLVES: 34 Jack Johnson; 24 Kevin Penny; 23 Gary Wheeler; 4 Ryan Atkins; 5 Joel Monaghan (C); 6 Stefan Ratchford; 33 Chris Sandow; 8 Chris Hill; 9 Daryl Clark; 15 Roy Asotasi; 12 Ben Westwood; 17 Ben Currie; 27 George King. Subs (all used): 10 Ashton Sims; 13 Ben Harrison; 31 Sam Wilde; 25 Brad Dwyer.
Tries: Westwood (53), Asotasi (60); **Goals:** Sandow 1/2.
Rugby Leaguer & League Express Men of the Match: *Giants:* Jermaine McGillvary; *Wolves:* Brad Dwyer.
Penalty count: 6-6; **Half-time:** 18-0;
Referee: James Child; **Attendance:** 5,563.

ROUND 6

Thursday 17th September 2015

LEEDS RHINOS 22 CASTLEFORD TIGERS 29

RHINOS: 1 Zak Hardaker; 2 Tom Briscoe; 3 Kallum Watkins; 4 Joel Moon; 5 Ryan Hall; 13 Kevin Sinfield (C); 6 Danny McGuire; 17 Adam Cuthbertson; 29 Jordan Lilley; 10 Jamie Peacock; 12 Carl Ablett; 14 Stevie Ward; 15 Brett Delaney. Subs: 30 Mitch Garbutt; 19 Brad Singleton; 8 Kylie Leuluai; 21 Josh Walters (not used).
Tries: Hall (11, 29), Moon (14), Cuthbertson (52);
Goals: Sinfield 2/3, Lilley 1/1.
TIGERS: 1 Luke Dorn; 26 Ashley Gibson; 24 Mike McMeeken; 4 Michael Shenton (C); 20 Denny Solomona; 6 Ben Roberts; 7 Luke Gale; 8 Andy Lynch; 9 Adam Milner; 10 Grant Millington; 11 Oliver Holmes; 16 Junior Moors; 19 Scott Wheeldon. Subs (all used): 15 Ryan Boyle; 35 Paul McShane; 12 Matt Cook; 28 Will Maher.
Tries: Gale (4, 45), Solomona (7), Dorn (37), Roberts (47); **Goals:** Gale 4/5; **Field goal:** Roberts (74).
Rugby Leaguer & League Express Men of the Match: *Rhinos:* Jordan Lilley; *Tigers:* Luke Gale.
Penalty count: 7-7; **Half-time:** 16-16;
Referee: James Child; **Attendance:** 15,069.

Friday 18th September 2015

HULL FC 20 HUDDERSFIELD GIANTS 34

HULL: 32 Jordan Rankin; 20 Curtis Naughton; 26 Jack Downs; 4 Kirk Yeaman; 24 Jack Logan; 6 Leon Pryce; 7 Marc Sneyd; 8 Mickey Paea; 9 Danny Houghton (C); 10 Liam Watts; 12 Mark Minichiello; 17 Dean Hadley; 27 Jordan Abdull. Subs (all used): 14 Iafeta Palea'aesina; 25 Jansin Turgut; 28 Brad Fash; 22 Josh Bowden.
Tries: Rankin (4, 35), Bowden (41), Yeaman (48);
Goals: Sneyd 2/4.
GIANTS: 1 Scott Grix; 2 Jermaine McGillvary; 3 Leroy Cudjoe; 22 Jake Connor; 5 Aaron Murphy; 6 Danny Brough (C); 20 Jamie Ellis; 10 Craig Huby; 24 Kruise Leeming; 32 Daniel Smith; 4 Joe Wardle; 12 Jack Hughes; 17 Ukuma Ta'ai. Subs (all used): 13 Chris Bailey; 14 Michael Lawrence; 15 Craig Kopczak; 25 Nathan Mason.
Tries: Murphy (18), Connor (28, 60), Grix (32), McGillvary (78), Ellis (80); **Goals:** Brough 5/7.
Sin bin: Huby (13) - high tackle on Rankin.
Rugby Leaguer & League Express Men of the Match: *Hull:* Jordan Rankin; *Giants:* Aaron Murphy.
Penalty count: 6-10; **Half-time:** 10-18;
Referee: Ben Thaler; **Attendance:** 9,332.

ST HELENS 18 WIGAN WARRIORS 14

SAINTS: 37 Adam Quinlan; 2 Tom Makinson; 17 Mark Percival; 4 Josh Jones; 5 Adam Swift; 3 Jordan Turner; 7 Luke Walsh; 10 Kyle Amor; 9 James Roby; 25 Andre Savelio; 13 Louie McCarthy-Scarsbrook; 21 Joe Greenwood; 12 Jon Wilkin (C). Subs (all used): 8 Mose Masoe; 11 Atelea Vea; 15 Mark Flanagan; 19 Greg Richards.
Tries: Walsh (34), Swift (56), Jones (77);
Goals: Walsh 3/3.
WARRIORS: 1 Matt Bowen; 2 Josh Charnley; 14 John Bateman; 34 Oliver Gildart; 5 Joe Burgess; 6 George Williams; 7 Matty Smith; 8 Dominic Crosby; 9 Michael McIlorum; 10 Ben Flower; 11 Joel Tomkins; 25 Larne Patrick; 13 Sean O'Loughlin (C). Subs (all used): 3 Anthony Gelling; 16 Sam Powell; 17 Tony Clubb; 23 Lee Mossop.
Tries: J Tomkins (12), Williams (51); **Goals:** Bowen 3/3.
Rugby Leaguer & League Express Men of the Match: *Saints:* James Roby; *Warriors:* Sean O'Loughlin.
Penalty count: 6-6; **Half-time:** 6-6;
Referee: Robert Hicks; **Attendance:** 15,808.

Saturday 19th September 2015

WARRINGTON WOLVES 48 CATALANS DRAGONS 6

WOLVES: 34 Jack Johnson; 24 Kevin Penny; 6 Stefan Ratchford; 4 Ryan Atkins; 5 Joel Monaghan (C); 7 Richard Myler; 33 Chris Sandow; 8 Chris Hill; 9 Daryl Clark; 10 Ashton Sims; 17 Ben Currie; 12 Ben Westwood; 27 George King. Subs (all used): 13 Ben Harrison; 15 Roy Asotasi; 25 Brad Dwyer; 26 Joe Philbin.
Tries: Monaghan (5, 22, 64), Atkins (10, 53), Johnson (25, 69), Currie (36), Myler (71);
Goals: Sandow 4/7, Monaghan 1/1, Asotasi 1/1.
DRAGONS: 1 Morgan Escare; 14 Thomas Bosc; 28 Tony Gigot; 30 Krisnan Inu; 31 Jordan Sigismeau; 26 Stanislas Robin; 7 Scott Dureau; 8 Olivier Elima; 9 Ian Henderson; 15 Jeff Lima; 17 Elliott Whitehead; 18 Benjamin Garcia; 24 Jason Baitieri (C). Subs (all used): 21 Julian Bousquet; 23 Antoni Maria; 25 Joan Guasch; 33 Ugo Perez (D).
Try: Robin (76); **Goals:** Dureau 1/1.
Sin bin: Garcia (56) - dangerous challenge on Sims.
Rugby Leaguer & League Express Men of the Match: *Wolves:* Joel Monaghan; *Dragons:* Elliott Whitehead.
Penalty count: 4-7; **Half-time:** 26-0;
Referee: Joe Cobb; **Attendance:** 7,862.

ROUND 7

Thursday 24th September 2015

ST HELENS 16 WARRINGTON WOLVES 32

SAINTS: 37 Adam Quinlan; 2 Tom Makinson; 17 Mark Percival; 4 Josh Jones; 5 Adam Swift; 3 Jordan Turner; 7 Luke Walsh; 10 Kyle Amor; 9 James Roby; 25 Andre Savelio; 13 Louie McCarthy-Scarsbrook; 21 Joe Greenwood; 12 Jon Wilkin (C). Subs (all used): 8 Mose Masoe; 11 Atelea Vea; 15 Mark Flanagan; 19 Greg Richards.
Tries: Greenwood (10), Swift (51), Flanagan (56);
Goals: Walsh 2/3.
WOLVES: 34 Jack Johnson; 24 Kevin Penny; 6 Stefan Ratchford; 4 Ryan Atkins; 5 Joel Monaghan (C); 7 Richard Myler; 33 Chris Sandow; 8 Chris Hill; 9 Daryl Clark; 10 Ashton Sims; 12 Ben Westwood; 17 Ben Currie; 27 George King. Subs (all used): 13 Ben Harrison; 15 Roy Asotasi; 25 Brad Dwyer; 26 Joe Philbin.
Tries: Johnson (13), Monaghan (31), Hill (35), Atkins (48), Asotasi (76), Penny (79);
Goals: Sandow 3/5, Monaghan 1/1.
Rugby Leaguer & League Express Men of the Match: *Saints:* Andre Savelio; *Wolves:* Kevin Penny.
Penalty count: 8-7; **Half-time:** 6-14;
Referee: James Child; **Attendance:** 10,966.

Friday 25th September 2015

HUDDERSFIELD GIANTS 16 LEEDS RHINOS 20

GIANTS: 1 Scott Grix; 2 Jermaine McGillvary; 3 Leroy Cudjoe; 4 Joe Wardle; 5 Aaron Murphy; 6 Danny Brough (C); 20 Jamie Ellis; 15 Craig Kopczak; 7 Luke Robinson; 10 Craig Huby; 11 Brett Ferres; 12 Jack Hughes; 17 Ukuma Ta'ai. Subs (all used): 14 Michael Lawrence; 23 Josh Johnson; 24 Kruise Leeming; 32 Daniel Smith.
Tries: McGillvary (12), Ellis (65); **Goals:** Brough 4/4.
RHINOS: 1 Zak Hardaker; 2 Tom Briscoe; 3 Kallum Watkins; 4 Joel Moon; 5 Ryan Hall; 13 Kevin Sinfield (C); 6 Danny McGuire; 30 Mitch Garbutt; 7 Rob Burrow; 19 Brad Singleton; 12 Carl Ablett; 14 Stevie Ward; 17 Adam Cuthbertson. Subs: 15 Brett Delaney; 8 Kylie Leuluai; 10 Jamie Peacock; 29 Jordan Lilley (not used).

Leeds' Joel Moon tackled by Huddersfield's Leroy Cudjoe and Jamie Ellis during a thrilling Super 8s finale

Tries: S Ward (9), T Briscoe (74), Hall (80);
Goals: Sinfield 4/5.
Rugby Leaguer & League Express Men of the Match: *Giants:* Jermaine McGillvary; *Rhinos:* Danny McGuire.
Penalty count: 4-7; **Half-time:** 6-8;
Referee: Robert Hicks; **Attendance:** 9,376.

WIGAN WARRIORS 47 CASTLEFORD TIGERS 12

WARRIORS: 1 Matt Bowen; 2 Josh Charnley; 34 Oliver Gildart; 5 Joe Burgess; 22 Dominic Manfredi; 6 George Williams; 7 Matty Smith; 8 Dominic Crosby; 9 Michael McIlorum; 10 Ben Flower; 11 Joel Tomkins; 12 Liam Farrell; 13 Sean O'Loughlin (C). Subs (all used): 16 Sam Powell; 17 Tony Clubb; 23 Lee Mossop; 25 Larne Patrick.
Tries: Manfredi (4, 49, 59, 61), Bowen (7), Gildart (69), Williams (73), Burgess (76), Patrick (79);
Goals: Bowen 5/9; **Field goal:** Smith (66).
TIGERS: 1 Luke Dorn; 27 Ash Robson; 24 Mike McMeeken; 26 Ashley Gibson; 20 Denny Solomona; 6 Ben Roberts; 7 Luke Gale; 8 Andy Lynch (C); 9 Adam Milner; 10 Grant Millington; 11 Oliver Holmes; 16 Junior Moors; 19 Scott Wheeldon. Subs (all used): 12 Matt Cook; 28 Will Maher; 34 Gadwin Springer; 35 Paul McShane.
Tries: Dorn (27), Moors (34); **Goals:** Gale 2/2.
Sin bin: Solomona (56) - holding down.
Rugby Leaguer & League Express Men of the Match: *Warriors:* Dominic Manfredi; *Tigers:* Junior Moors.
Penalty count: 10-7; **Half-time:** 10-12;
Referee: Phil Bentham; **Attendance:** 15,017.

Sunday 27th September 2015

HULL FC 24 CATALANS DRAGONS 28

HULL: 32 Jordan Rankin; 2 Tom Lineham; 24 Jack Logan; 4 Kirk Yeaman; 20 Curtis Naughton; 27 Jordan Abdull; 7 Marc Sneyd; 8 Mickey Paea; 9 Danny Houghton (C); 10 Liam Watts; 12 Mark Minichiello; 21 Richard Whiting; 17 Dean Hadley. Subs (all used): 14 Iafeta Palea'aesina; 25 Jansin Turgut; 28 Brad Fash; 22 Josh Bowden.
Tries: Lineham (33, 52, 74, 80), Abdull (37), Naughton (49); **Goals:** Sneyd 0/3, Rankin 0/2 *(last conversion attempt declined).*
DRAGONS: 1 Morgan Escare; 30 Krisnan Inu; 28 Tony Gigot; 18 Benjamin Garcia; 31 Jordan Sigismeau; 14 Thomas Bosc; 7 Scott Dureau; 8 Olivier Elima; 9 Ian Henderson; 21 Julian Bousquet; 17 Elliott Whitehead; 12 Louis Anderson; 24 Jason Baitieri (C). Subs: 23 Antoni Maria; 25 Joan Guasch (not used); 26 Stanislas Robin (not used); 33 Ugo Perez.
Tries: Garcia (4), Henderson (24), Inu (27), Whitehead (30), Bosc (58); **Goals:** Dureau 4/6.
Rugby Leaguer & League Express Men of the Match: *Hull:* Jack Logan; *Dragons:* Ian Henderson.
Penalty count: 11-9; **Half-time:** 8-20;
Referee: Richard Silverwood; **Attendance:** 10,832.

SEMI-FINALS

Thursday 1st October 2015

WIGAN WARRIORS 32 HUDDERSFIELD GIANTS 8

WARRIORS: 1 Matt Bowen; 22 Dominic Manfredi; 14 John Bateman; 34 Oliver Gildart; 5 Joe Burgess; 6 George Williams; 7 Matty Smith; 8 Dominic Crosby; 9 Michael McIlorum; 10 Ben Flower; 11 Joel Tomkins; 12 Liam Farrell; 13 Sean O'Loughlin (C). Subs (all used): 16 Sam Powell; 17 Tony Clubb; 23 Lee Mossop; 25 Larne Patrick.
Tries: Flower (6), Bateman (35, 55 - pen), Manfredi (50), Clubb (80); **Goals:** Bowen 6/7.
GIANTS: 1 Scott Grix; 2 Jermaine McGillvary; 3 Leroy Cudjoe; 22 Jake Connor; 5 Aaron Murphy; 6 Danny Brough (C); 20 Jamie Ellis; 15 Craig Kopczak; 7 Luke Robinson; 10 Craig Huby; 4 Joe Wardle; 12 Jack Hughes; 11 Brett Ferres. Subs (all used): 8 Eorl Crabtree; 13 Chris Bailey; 14 Michael Lawrence; 17 Ukuma Ta'ai.
Try: Ferres (68); **Goals:** Brough 2/2.
Rugby Leaguer & League Express Men of the Match: *Warriors:* John Bateman; *Giants:* Brett Ferres.
Penalty count: 10-7; **Half-time:** 12-2;
Referee: Ben Thaler; **Attendance:** 10,035.

Friday 2nd October 2015

LEEDS RHINOS 20 ST HELENS 13

RHINOS: 1 Zak Hardaker; 2 Tom Briscoe; 3 Kallum Watkins; 4 Joel Moon; 5 Ryan Hall; 6 Danny McGuire; 13 Kevin Sinfield (C); 30 Mitch Garbutt; 7 Rob Burrow; 8 Kylie Leuluai; 12 Carl Ablett; 15 Brett Delaney; 17 Adam Cuthbertson. Subs: 10 Jamie Peacock; 19 Brad Singleton; 20 Jimmy Keinhorst; 29 Jordan Lilley (not used).
Tries: Hardaker (21), Hall (69), Watkins (79);
Goals: Sinfield 4/4.
SAINTS: 37 Adam Quinlan; 2 Tom Makinson; 17 Mark Percival; 4 Josh Jones; 5 Adam Swift; 3 Jordan Turner; 7 Luke Walsh; 8 Mose Masoe; 9 James Roby; 10 Kyle Amor; 11 Atelea Vea; 12 Jon Wilkin (C); 15 Mark Flanagan. Subs (all used): 14 Alex Walmsley; 13 Louie McCarthy-Scarsbrook; 25 Andre Savelio; 21 Joe Greenwood.
Tries: Roby (5), Percival (59); **Goals:** Walsh 2/3;
Field goal: Walsh (39).
Rugby Leaguer & League Express Men of the Match: *Rhinos:* Mitch Garbutt; *Saints:* James Roby.
Penalty count: 5-4; **Half-time:** 8-9;
Referee: Robert Hicks; **Attendance:** 17,192.

GRAND FINAL

Saturday 10th October 2015

LEEDS RHINOS 22 WIGAN WARRIORS 20

RHINOS: 1 Zak Hardaker; 2 Tom Briscoe; 3 Kallum Watkins; 4 Joel Moon; 5 Ryan Hall; 13 Kevin Sinfield (C); 6 Danny McGuire; 30 Mitch Garbutt; 7 Rob Burrow; 10 Jamie Peacock; 12 Carl Ablett; 15 Brett Delaney; 19 Brad Singleton. Subs (all used): 8 Kylie Leuluai; 17 Adam Cuthbertson; 20 Jimmy Keinhorst; 21 Josh Walters.
Tries: McGuire (7, 35), Moon (27), Walters (64);
Goals: Sinfield 3/4.
WARRIORS: 1 Matt Bowen; 22 Dominic Manfredi; 14 John Bateman; 34 Oliver Gildart; 5 Joe Burgess; 6 George Williams; 7 Matty Smith; 8 Dominic Crosby; 9 Michael McIlorum; 10 Ben Flower; 11 Joel Tomkins; 12 Liam Farrell; 13 Sean O'Loughlin (C). Subs (all used): 16 Sam Powell; 17 Tony Clubb; 23 Lee Mossop; 25 Larne Patrick.
Tries: Burgess (4), Manfredi (46), Bowen (49);
Goals: Bowen 4/4.
Rugby Leaguer & League Express Men of the Match: *Rhinos:* Danny McGuire; *Warriors:* Matt Bowen.
Penalty count: 5-4; **Half-time:** 16-6; **Referee:** Ben Thaler;
Attendance: 73,512 *(at Old Trafford, Manchester).*

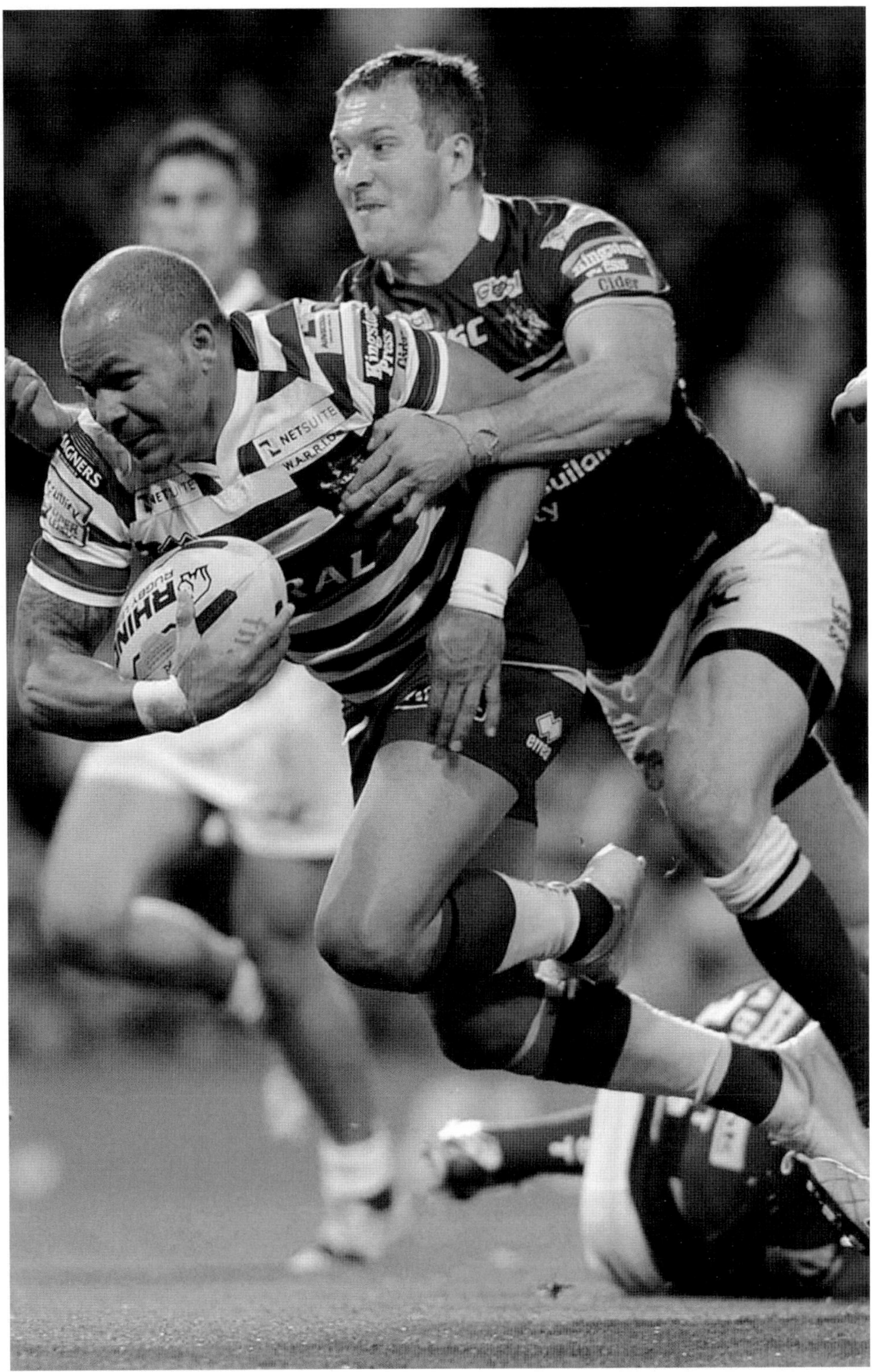

Wigan's Matt Bowen tries to shake off Leeds' Danny McGuire during the Super League Grand Final

SUPER 8s - THE QUALIFIERS
2015 Round by Round

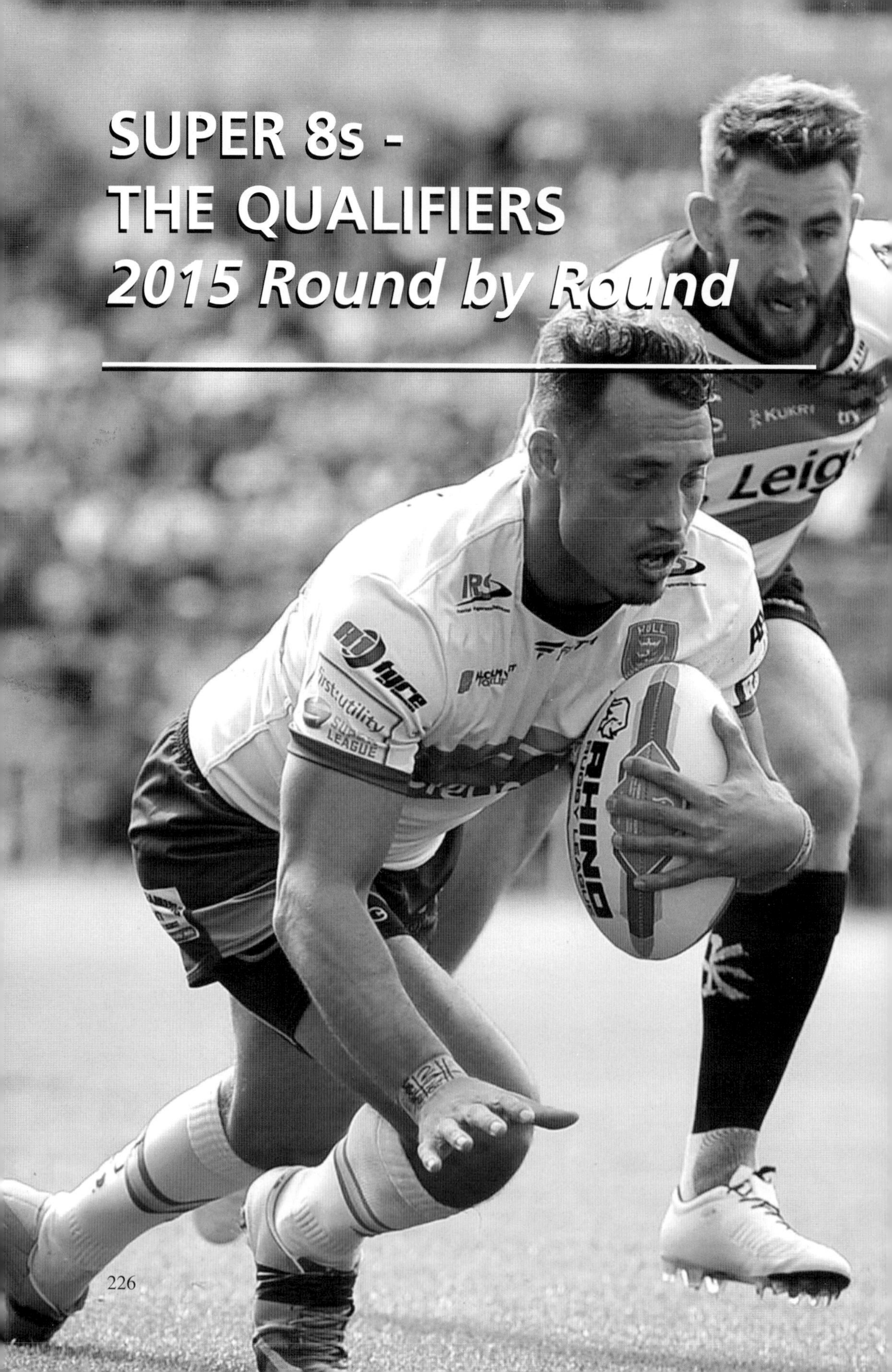

ROUND 1

Saturday 8th August 2015

LEIGH CENTURIONS 26 HULL KINGSTON ROVERS 36

CENTURIONS: 1 Gregg McNally; 2 Adam Higson; 3 Greg Worthington; 4 Tom Armstrong; 5 Liam Kay; 6 Martyn Ridyard; 7 Ryan Brierley; 8 Fuifui Moimoi; 9 Bob Beswick; 29 Jake Emmitt; 22 Andrew Dixon; 12 Tommy Goulden; 26 Gareth Hock. Subs (all used): 30 Mick Higham; 13 Sam Barlow; 10 Oliver Wilkes (C); 20 Sam Hopkins.
Tries: Brierley (19), McNally (23), Dixon (25), Armstrong (40); **Goals:** Ridyard 5/5.
ROVERS: 1 Kieran Dixon; 2 Ben Cockayne; 5 Ken Sio; 19 Kris Welham; 4 Josh Mantellato; 35 Dane Chisholm; 6 Maurice Blair; 8 Adam Walker; 31 Shaun Lunt; 34 Tony Puletua; 11 Kevin Larroyer; 12 Graeme Horne; 13 Tyrone McCarthy (C). Subs (all used): 15 James Donaldson; 21 Aaron Ollett; 32 Dane Tilse; 33 James Greenwood.
Tries: Chisholm (10), Dixon (42), Blair (62), Puletua (68), Lunt (72), Cockayne (77); **Goals:** Mantellato 6/6.
Rugby Leaguer & League Express Men of the Match: *Centurions:* Gregg McNally; *Rovers:* Maurice Blair.
Penalty count: 8-8; **Half-time:** 24-6;
Referee: Ben Thaler; **Attendance:** 4,459.

Sunday 9th August 2015

BRADFORD BULLS 42 SHEFFIELD EAGLES 10

BULLS: 1 Jake Mullaney; 5 Danny Williams; 3 Adrian Purtell (C); 20 Adam Henry; 35 James Clare; 6 Lee Gaskell; 13 Danny Addy; 8 Paul Clough; 9 Adam O'Brien; 10 Adam Sidlow; 11 Tom Olbison; 12 Dale Ferguson; 14 Jay Pitts. Subs (all used): 4 Matty Blythe; 31 Epalahame Lauaki; 32 Steve Crossley; 36 Matt Ryan.
Tries: Williams (4, 8), Gaskell (14, 48, 64), Pitts (26), Henry (39), Clare (72); **Goals:** Addy 5/8.
EAGLES: 1 Quentin Laulu-Togagae; 2 Scott Turner; 3 Menzie Yere; 4 Sam Smeaton; 5 Misi Taulapapa; 6 Kyle Briggs; 7 Dominic Brambani; 17 Steve Thorpe; 24 Keal Carlile; 10 Mitchell Stringer (C); 11 Michael Knowles; 12 Duane Straugheir; 29 Dave Petersen. Subs (all used): 8 Eddie Battye; 9 James Davey; 15 John Davies; 22 Tony Tonks.
Tries: Taulapapa (34), Yere (80); **Goals:** Briggs 1/2.
Rugby Leaguer & League Express Men of the Match: *Bulls:* Lee Gaskell; *Eagles:* Michael Knowles.
Penalty count: 10-8; **Half-time:** 26-6;
Referee: Matthew Thomason; **Attendance:** 6,032.

HALIFAX 0 WIDNES VIKINGS 14

HALIFAX: 7 Ben Johnston; 20 James Saltonstall; 4 Ben Heaton; 3 Steve Tyrer; 2 Tom Saxton; 31 Connor Robinson; 6 Scott Murrell (C); 8 Adam Tangata; 9 Ben Kaye; 17 Mitch Cahalane; 16 Richard Moore; 11 Dane Manning; 22 Jacob Fairbank. Subs (all used): 10 Luke Ambler; 12 Andy Bracek; 21 Ryan Maneely; 29 Ed Barber.
VIKINGS: 1 Rhys Hanbury; 4 Stefan Marsh; 14 Chris Dean; 37 Charly Runciman (D); 5 Patrick Ah Van; 6 Kevin Brown (C); 7 Joe Mellor; 25 Alex Gerrard; 33 Aaron Heremaia; 35 Gil Dudson; 17 Chris Clarkson; 11 Danny Galea; 16 Willie Isa. Subs (all used): 9 Lloyd White; 13 Hep Cahill; 12 Danny Tickle; 10 Manase Manuokafoa.
Tries: Runciman (49, 79), Gerrard (77);
Goals: Marsh 0/1, White 1/2.
Sin bin: Marsh (14) - professional foul.
Rugby Leaguer & League Express Men of the Match: *Halifax:* Dane Manning; *Vikings:* Joe Mellor.
Penalty count: 4-6; **Half-time:** 0-0;
Referee: Robert Hicks; **Attendance:** 3,022.

SALFORD RED DEVILS 34
WAKEFIELD TRINITY WILDCATS 26

RED DEVILS: 2 Ben Jones-Bishop; 3 Josh Griffin; 41 Iain Thornley (D); 4 Junior Sa'u; 5 Greg Johnson; 6 Rangi Chase; 7 Michael Dobson; 16 Scott Taylor; 37 Logan Tomkins; 25 George Griffin; 11 Harrison Hansen (C); 40 Reni Maitua (D); 31 Cory Paterson. Subs (all used): 9 Tommy Lee; 38 Olsi Krasniqi; 19 Niall Evalds; 8 Adrian Morley.
Tries: J Griffin (12, 20), G Griffin (34), Paterson (58, 78), Chase (70); **Goals:** J Griffin 4/5, Paterson 1/1.
WILDCATS: 38 Lee Smith; 5 Richard Owen; 39 Bill Tupou; 28 Joe Arundel; 4 Reece Lyne; 6 Jacob Miller; 7 Tim Smith; 8 Nick Scruton (C); 40 Scott Moore; 10 Scott Anderson; 19 Jon Molloy; 17 Matty Ashurst; 16 Mickael Simon. Subs (all used): 34 Michael Sio; 36 Anthony Walker; 37 Anthony Mullally; 13 Danny Washbrook.
Tries: Miller (39, 45), Washbrook (48), Lyne (51);
Goals: L Smith 5/5.
Rugby Leaguer & League Express Men of the Match: *Red Devils:* Reni Maitua; *Wildcats:* Michael Sio.
Penalty count: 8-5; **Half-time:** 16-6;
Referee: James Child; **Attendance:** 3,100.

ROUND 2

Saturday 15th August 2015

WAKEFIELD TRINITY WILDCATS 48
BRADFORD BULLS 18

WILDCATS: 38 Lee Smith; 5 Richard Owen; 39 Bill Tupou; 28 Joe Arundel; 4 Reece Lyne; 6 Jacob Miller; 7 Tim Smith; 8 Nick Scruton (C); 34 Michael Sio; 10 Scott Anderson; 17 Matty Ashurst; 19 Jon Molloy; 16 Mickael Simon. Subs (all used): 13 Danny Washbrook; 14 Pita Godinet; 36 Anthony Walker; 37 Anthony Mullally.
Tries: Molloy (6), Sio (8), Simon (11), Scruton (18), L Smith (29), Lyne (56), Ashurst (64), Miller (77);
Goals: L Smith 7/8, Arundel 1/1.
BULLS: 35 James Clare; 5 Danny Williams; 3 Adrian Purtell (C); 4 Matty Blythe; 34 Omari Caro; 6 Lee Gaskell; 13 Danny Addy; 8 Paul Clough; 9 Adam O'Brien; 10 Adam Sidlow; 11 Tom Olbison; 12 Dale Ferguson; 14 Jay Pitts. Subs (all used): 36 Matt Ryan; 31 Epalahame Lauaki; 32 Steve Crossley; 7 Harry Siejka.
Tries: Purtell (35), Ferguson (46), Clare (80);
Goals: Addy 3/3.
Rugby Leaguer & League Express Men of the Match: *Wildcats:* Tim Smith; *Bulls:* Dale Ferguson.
Penalty count: 7-7; **Half-time:** 30-6;
Referee: Ben Thaler; **Attendance:** 3,985.

Sunday 16th August 2015

HULL KINGSTON ROVERS 34 HALIFAX 12

ROVERS: 2 Ben Cockayne; 4 Josh Mantellato; 19 Kris Welham; 18 Liam Salter; 5 Ken Sio; 6 Maurice Blair; 35 Dane Chisholm; 8 Adam Walker; 31 Shaun Lunt; 34 Tony Puletua; 11 Kevin Larroyer; 12 Graeme Horne; 13 Tyrone McCarthy (C). Subs (all used): 17 Greg Burke; 14 Mitchell Allgood; 33 James Greenwood; 20 James Green.
Tries: Mantellato (4, 38, 52), McCarthy (11), Sio (76), Welham (80); **Goals:** Mantellato 5/6.
HALIFAX: 7 Ben Johnston; 23 Gareth Potts; 4 Ben Heaton; 3 Steve Tyrer; 20 James Saltonstall; 31 Connor Robinson; 6 Scott Murrell (C); 17 Mitch Cahalane; 9 Ben Kaye; 8 Adam Tangata; 11 Dane Manning; 29 Ed Barber; 22 Jacob Fairbank. Subs (all used): 16 Richard Moore; 12 Andy Bracek; 10 Luke Ambler; 21 Ryan Maneely.
Tries: Manning (21), Tyrer (67); **Goals:** Tyrer 2/2.
Rugby Leaguer & League Express Men of the Match: *Rovers:* Josh Mantellato; *Halifax:* Scott Murrell.
Penalty count: 8-5; **Half-time:** 16-6;
Referee: Joe Cobb; **Attendance:** 6,837.

SALFORD RED DEVILS 46 LEIGH CENTURIONS 18

RED DEVILS: 19 Niall Evalds; 2 Ben Jones-Bishop; 4 Junior Sa'u; 41 Iain Thornley; 5 Greg Johnson; 6 Rangi Chase; 7 Michael Dobson; 25 George Griffin; 37 Logan Tomkins; 16 Scott Taylor; 11 Harrison Hansen (C); 40 Reni Maitua; 31 Cory Paterson. Subs (all used): 9 Tommy Lee; 38 Olsi Krasniqi; 10 Lama Tasi; 8 Adrian Morley.
Tries: Jones-Bishop (4), Taylor (27), Thornley (33), Chase (43, 63), Sa'u (60), Evalds (67), Johnson (71);
Goals: Dobson 7/8.
CENTURIONS: 1 Gregg McNally; 2 Adam Higson; 31 Mathias Pala; 4 Tom Armstrong; 5 Liam Kay; 6 Martyn Ridyard; 7 Ryan Brierley; 29 Jake Emmitt; 30 Mick Higham; 10 Oliver Wilkes (C); 22 Andrew Dixon; 12 Tommy Goulden; 13 Sam Barlow. Subs (all used): 9 Bob Beswick; 19 Kurt Haggerty; 23 Martin Aspinwall; 8 Fuifui Moimoi.
Tries: Higson (51), McNally (53, 77); **Goals:** Ridyard 3/3.
Rugby Leaguer & League Express Men of the Match: *Red Devils:* Rangi Chase; *Centurions:* Mick Higham.
Penalty count: 6-7; **Half-time:** 16-0;
Referee: Richard Silverwood; **Attendance:** 4,547.

WIDNES VIKINGS 48 SHEFFIELD EAGLES 12

VIKINGS: 1 Rhys Hanbury; 2 Paddy Flynn; 14 Chris Dean; 37 Charly Runciman; 4 Stefan Marsh; 6 Kevin Brown (C); 7 Joe Mellor; 25 Alex Gerrard; 9 Lloyd White; 35 Gil Dudson; 12 Danny Tickle; 11 Danny Galea; 24 Macgraff Leuluai. Subs (all used): 33 Aaron Heremaia; 16 Willie Isa; 10 Manase Manuokafoa; 28 Matt Whitley.
Tries: Brown (9), Marsh (20, 22, 76), Runciman (28, 80), Hanbury (32), Galea (35), Mellor (48), Flynn (55);
Goals: Tickle 2/4, White 2/4, Marsh 0/2.
EAGLES: 1 Quentin Laulu-Togagae; 2 Scott Turner; 3 Menzie Yere; 4 Sam Smeaton; 23 Rob Worrincy; 19 Cory Aston; 7 Dominic Brambani; 17 Steve Thorpe; 24 Keal Carlile; 10 Mitchell Stringer (C); 11 Michael Knowles; 12 Duane Straugheir; 5 Misi Taulapapa. Subs (all used): 9 James Davey; 8 Eddie Battye; 13 Pat Walker; 22 Tony Tonks.
Tries: Turner (39), Carlile (64); **Goals:** Walker 2/2.
Rugby Leaguer & League Express Men of the Match: *Vikings:* Kevin Brown; *Eagles:* Steve Thorpe.
Penalty count: 10-4; **Half-time:** 30-6;
Referee: James Child; **Attendance:** 4,567.

ROUND 3

Saturday 22nd August 2015

LEIGH CENTURIONS 16
WAKEFIELD TRINITY WILDCATS 17

CENTURIONS: 1 Gregg McNally; 15 Jonathan Pownall; 3 Greg Worthington; 4 Tom Armstrong; 5 Liam Kay; 6 Martyn Ridyard (C); 7 Ryan Brierley; 8 Fuifui Moimoi; 30 Mick Higham; 29 Jake Emmitt; 19 Kurt Haggerty; 22 Andrew Dixon; 21 Jamie Acton. Subs (all used): 9 Bob Beswick; 13 Sam Barlow; 18 Tom Spencer; 23 Martin Aspinwall.
Tries: Moimoi (12), Pownall (27), Kay (35);
Goals: Ridyard 2/3.
On report: Haggerty (30) - alleged use of the knees.
WILDCATS: 38 Lee Smith; 2 Chris Riley; 39 Bill Tupou; 28 Joe Arundel; 4 Reece Lyne; 6 Jacob Miller; 7 Tim Smith; 8 Nick Scruton (C); 34 Michael Sio; 10 Scott Anderson; 19 Jon Molloy; 17 Matty Ashurst; 16 Mickael Simon. Subs (all used): 11 Ali Lauitiiti; 13 Danny Washbrook; 14 Pita Godinet; 37 Anthony Mullally.
Tries: L Smith (5), Miller (38, 61); **Goals:** L Smith 2/3;
Field goal: L Smith (69).
Sin bin: Sio (65) - dangerous challenge on McNally.
Rugby Leaguer & League Express Men of the Match: *Centurions:* Jake Emmitt; *Wildcats:* Lee Smith.
Penalty count: 6-10; **Half-time:** 16-10;
Referee: James Child; **Attendance:** 4,376.

Sunday 23rd August 2015

BRADFORD BULLS 41 SALFORD RED DEVILS 10

BULLS: 35 James Clare; 34 Omari Caro; 37 Dane Nielsen; 3 Adrian Purtell (C); 5 Danny Williams; 13 Danny Addy; 1 Jake Mullaney; 8 Paul Clough; 9 Adam O'Brien; 10 Adam Sidlow; 12 Dale Ferguson; 11 Tom Olbison; 14 Jay Pitts. Subs (all used): 4 Matty Blythe; 23 Alex Mellor; 31 Epalahame Lauaki; 32 Steve Crossley.
Tries: Ferguson (4), Williams (17), Mullaney (32, 43), Addy (53), Clare (55), Purtell (60); **Goals:** Addy 6/7;
Field goal: Mullaney (39).
RED DEVILS: 19 Niall Evalds; 2 Ben Jones-Bishop; 4 Junior Sa'u; 41 Iain Thornley; 5 Greg Johnson; 6 Rangi Chase; 7 Michael Dobson; 16 Scott Taylor; 37 Logan Tomkins; 10 Lama Tasi; 25 George Griffin; 12 Weller Hauraki; 8 Adrian Morley (C). Subs (all used): 9 Tommy Lee; 26 Carl Forster; 31 Cory Paterson; 38 Olsi Krasniqi.
Tries: Chase (35), Thornley (66); **Goals:** Dobson 1/2.
Rugby Leaguer & League Express Men of the Match: *Bulls:* Danny Addy; *Red Devils:* Niall Evalds.
Penalty count: 7-3; **Half-time:** 17-4;
Referee: Robert Hicks; **Attendance:** 6,593.

WIDNES VIKINGS 8 HULL KINGSTON ROVERS 12

VIKINGS: 1 Rhys Hanbury; 2 Paddy Flynn; 14 Chris Dean; 37 Charly Runciman; 4 Stefan Marsh; 6 Kevin Brown (C); 7 Joe Mellor; 25 Alex Gerrard; 9 Lloyd White; 35 Gil Dudson; 11 Danny Galea; 12 Danny Tickle; 13 Hep Cahill. Subs (all used): 33 Aaron Heremaia; 10 Manase Manuokafoa; 17 Chris Clarkson; 28 Matt Whitley.
Tries: Runciman (45), Whitley (80); **Goals:** White 0/2.
ROVERS: 1 Kieran Dixon; 2 Ben Cockayne; 18 Liam Salter; 19 Kris Welham (C); 4 Josh Mantellato; 29 Matthew Marsh; 35 Dane Chisholm; 14 Mitchell Allgood; 24 John Boudebza; 32 Dane Tilse; 21 Aaron Ollett; 6 Maurice Blair; 17 Greg Burke. Subs (all used): 36 George Lawler (D); 20 James Green; 33 James Greenwood; 15 James Donaldson.
Tries: Welham (36), Lawler (52); **Goals:** Mantellato 2/2.
Rugby Leaguer & League Express Men of the Match: *Vikings:* Alex Gerrard; *Rovers:* James Green.
Penalty count: 10-12; **Half-time:** 0-6;
Referee: Joe Cobb; **Attendance:** 5,461.

SHEFFIELD EAGLES 28 HALIFAX 24

EAGLES: 1 Quentin Laulu-Togagae; 2 Scott Turner; 3 Menzie Yere; 4 Sam Smeaton; 23 Rob Worrincy; 19 Cory Aston; 7 Dominic Brambani; 8 Eddie Battye; 24 Keal Carlile; 10 Mitchell Stringer (C); 11 Michael Knowles; 12 Duane Straugheir; 13 Pat Walker. Subs (all used): 5 Misi Taulapapa; 9 James Davey; 15 John Davies; 22 Tony Tonks.
Tries: Worrincy (12, 54, 77), Walker (37), Laulu-Togagae (67); **Goals:** Walker 4/5.
HALIFAX: 20 James Saltonstall; 23 Gareth Potts; 4 Ben Heaton; 3 Steve Tyrer; 2 Tom Saxton; 7 Ben Johnston; 6 Scott Murrell (C); 8 Adam Tangata; 9 Ben Kaye; 17 Mitch Cahalane; 27 Ross Divorty; 11 Dane Manning; 22 Jacob Fairbank. Subs (all used): 10 Luke Ambler; 12 Andy Bracek; 16 Richard Moore; 21 Ryan Maneely.
Tries: Tangata (9), Tyrer (17), Potts (22), Murrell (58);
Goals: Tyrer 4/4.
Rugby Leaguer & League Express Men of the Match: *Eagles:* Pat Walker; *Halifax:* Adam Tangata.
Penalty count: 8-8; **Half-time:** 12-18;
Referee: Chris Kendall; **Attendance:** 854
(at Keepmoat Stadium, Doncaster).

ROUND 4

Saturday 5th September 2015

HALIFAX 28 SALFORD RED DEVILS 50

HALIFAX: 25 Joe Martin; 4 Ben Heaton; 32 Jake Eccleston; 3 Steve Tyrer; 20 James Saltonstall; 31 Connor Robinson; 6 Scott Murrell (C); 8 Adam Tangata; 9 Ben Kaye; 17 Mitch Cahalane; 16 Richard Moore; 11 Dane Manning; 22 Jacob Fairbank. Subs (all used): 10 Luke Ambler; 12 Andy Bracek; 21 Ryan Maneely; 15 Adam Robinson.
Tries: Manning (18), Murrell (45), Saltonstall (53), Fairbank (57), Tangata (74); **Goals:** Tyrer 4/5.
RED DEVILS: 19 Niall Evalds; 2 Ben Jones-Bishop; 41 Iain Thornley; 3 Josh Griffin; 5 Greg Johnson; 9 Tommy Lee; 7 Michael Dobson; 16 Scott Taylor; 37 Logan Tomkins; 25 George Griffin; 11 Harrison Hansen (C); 40 Reni Maitua; 31 Cory Paterson. Subs (all used): 20 Adam Walne; 24 Liam Hood; 26 Carl Forster; 38 Olsi Krasniqi.
Tries: Evalds (10, 12, 49), Johnson (32, 64, 71), Jones-Bishop (35, 60, 67);
Goals: J Griffin 4/6, Dobson 3/3.
Rugby Leaguer & League Express Men of the Match: *Halifax:* Adam Tangata; *Red Devils:* Liam Hood.
Penalty count: 6-7; **Half-time:** 6-22;
Referee: Joe Cobb; **Attendance:** 2,186.

Sunday 6th September 2015

BRADFORD BULLS 12 WIDNES VIKINGS 56

BULLS: 35 James Clare; 34 Omari Caro; 37 Dane Nielsen; 3 Adrian Purtell (C); 5 Danny Williams; 13

Danny Addy; 1 Jake Mullaney; 8 Paul Clough; 9 Adam O'Brien; 10 Adam Sidlow; 12 Dale Ferguson; 11 Tom Olbison; 14 Jay Pitts. Subs (all used): 4 Matty Blythe; 23 Alex Mellor; 31 Epalahame Lauaki; 32 Steve Crossley.
Tries: Purtell (17), Caro (39); **Goals:** Addy 2/2.
VIKINGS: 1 Rhys Hanbury; 2 Paddy Flynn; 14 Chris Dean; 37 Charly Runciman; 5 Patrick Ah Van; 6 Kevin Brown (C); 7 Joe Mellor; 25 Alex Gerrard; 9 Lloyd White; 35 Gil Dudson; 12 Danny Tickle; 11 Danny Galea; 13 Hep Cahill. Subs (all used): 10 Manase Manuokafoa; 17 Chris Clarkson; 28 Matt Whitley; 33 Aaron Heremaia.
Tries: Mellor (20, 28, 50), Ah Van (25, 66, 77), Runciman (48), Cahill (63), Hanbury (68), Brown (72);
Goals: White 2/4, Tickle 6/7.
Rugby Leaguer & League Express Men of the Match:
Bulls: Dale Ferguson; *Vikings:* Joe Mellor.
Penalty count: 4-7; **Half-time:** 12-14;
Referee: Joe Cobb; **Attendance:** 6,881.

HULL KINGSTON ROVERS 20 WAKEFIELD TRINITY WILDCATS 18

ROVERS: 1 Kieran Dixon; 5 Ken Sio; 12 Graeme Horne; 19 Kris Welham; 4 Josh Mantellato; 29 Matthew Marsh; 35 Dane Chisholm; 8 Adam Walker; 31 Shaun Lunt; 14 Mitchell Allgood; 6 Maurice Blair; 17 Greg Burke; 13 Tyrone McCarthy (C). Subs (all used): 20 James Green; 24 John Boudebza; 15 James Donaldson; 33 James Greenwood.
Tries: Mantellato (29), Dixon (38, 68), Lunt (72);
Goals: Dixon 1/1, Mantellato 1/3.
WILDCATS: 33 Kevin Locke; 38 Lee Smith; 39 Bill Tupou; 4 Reece Lyne; 35 Jordan Tansey; 6 Jacob Miller; 7 Tim Smith; 36 Anthony Walker; 13 Danny Washbrook; 10 Scott Anderson; 11 Ali Lauitiiti; 17 Matty Ashurst; 16 Mickael Simon. Subs (all used): 14 Pita Godinet; 28 Joe Arundel; 8 Nick Scruton (C); 37 Anthony Mullally.
Tries: Locke (5, 21), L Smith (15, 78);
Goals: L Smith 1/3, Tansey 0/1.
Rugby Leaguer & League Express Men of the Match:
Rovers: Kieran Dixon; *Wildcats:* Kevin Locke.
Penalty count: 7-8; **Half-time:** 10-12;
Referee: Robert Hicks; **Attendance:** 7,495.

LEIGH CENTURIONS 52 SHEFFIELD EAGLES 16

CENTURIONS: 1 Gregg McNally; 15 Jonathan Pownall; 3 Greg Worthington; 4 Tom Armstrong; 5 Liam Kay; 6 Martyn Ridyard; 7 Ryan Brierley; 29 Jake Emmitt; 30 Mick Higham; 8 Fuifui Moimoi; 22 Andrew Dixon; 12 Tommy Goulden; 21 Jamie Acton. Subs (all used): 17 Ben Reynolds; 18 Tom Spencer; 10 Oliver Wilkes (C); 23 Martin Aspinwall.
Tries: Higham (11), Dixon (29), Brierley (31, 34, 63), Kay (47), Moimoi (58), Goulden (70), McNally (75);
Goals: Ridyard 8/9.
Sin bin: Ridyard (18) - holding down.
EAGLES: 1 Quentin Laulu-Togagae; 2 Scott Turner; 3 Menzie Yere; 4 Sam Smeaton; 23 Rob Worrincy; 7 Dominic Brambani (C); 19 Cory Aston; 8 Eddie Battye; 24 Keal Carlile; 22 Tony Tonks; 11 Michael Knowles; 12 Duane Straugheir; 13 Pat Walker. Subs (all used): 5 Misi Taulapapa; 15 John Davies; 9 James Davey; 25 Connor Scott.
Tries: Davey (25), Turner (39), Smeaton (60);
Goals: Walker 2/3.
Sin bin: Tonks (67) - high tackle on Pownall.
Rugby Leaguer & League Express Men of the Match:
Centurions: Mick Higham; *Eagles:* Duane Straugheir.
Penalty count: 12-10; **Half-time:** 24-10;
Referee: James Child; **Attendance:** 4,012.

ROUND 5

Saturday 12th September 2015

HULL KINGSTON ROVERS 48 BRADFORD BULLS 4

ROVERS: 5 Ken Sio; 1 Kieran Dixon; 12 Graeme Horne; 19 Kris Welham; 4 Josh Mantellato; 35 Dane Chisholm; 29 Matthew Marsh; 14 Mitchell Allgood; 31 Shaun Lunt; 34 Tony Puletua; 6 Maurice Blair; 13 Tyrone McCarthy (C); 15 James Donaldson. Subs (all used): 32 Dane Tilse; 24 John Boudebza; 17 Greg Burke; 20 James Green.
Tries: Mantellato (12, 33), Dixon (35, 44, 74, 80), Chisholm (46), Sio (57), Welham (60), Horne (70);
Goals: Mantellato 3/9, Dixon 1/1.
BULLS: 33 James Mendeika; 5 Danny Williams; 22 Chev Walker; 37 Dane Nielsen; 34 Omari Caro; 3 Adrian Purtell (C); 13 Danny Addy; 8 Paul Clough; 9 Adam O'Brien; 10 Adam Sidlow; 11 Tom Olbison; 36 Matt Ryan; 14 Jay Pitts. Subs (all used): 7 Harry Siejka; 31 Epalahame Lauaki; 32 Steve Crossley; 12 Dale Ferguson.
Try: Mendeika (25); **Goals:** Addy 0/1.
Sin bin: Williams (7) - professional foul;
Lauaki (39) - dangerous contact on Dixon.
Rugby Leaguer & League Express Men of the Match:
Rovers: Kieran Dixon; *Bulls:* Paul Clough.
Penalty count: 3-4; **Half-time:** 12-4;
Referee: Ben Thaler; **Attendance:** 6,605.

WAKEFIELD TRINITY WILDCATS 4 WIDNES VIKINGS 46

WILDCATS: 33 Kevin Locke; 38 Lee Smith; 39 Bill Tupou; 4 Reece Lyne; 35 Jordan Tansey; 6 Jacob Miller; 7 Tim Smith; 37 Anthony Mullally; 34 Michael Sio; 10 Scott Anderson; 17 Matty Ashurst; 11 Ali Lauitiiti; 16 Mickael Simon. Subs (all used): 13 Danny Washbrook; 14 Pita Godinet; 26 Chris Annakin; 8 Nick Scruton (C).
Try: L Smith (54); **Goals:** L Smith 0/1.
VIKINGS: 1 Rhys Hanbury; 2 Paddy Flynn; 14 Chris Dean; 37 Charly Runciman; 5 Patrick Ah Van; 6 Kevin Brown (C); 7 Joe Mellor; 25 Alex Gerrard; 9 Lloyd White; 35 Gil Dudson; 11 Danny Galea; 12 Danny Tickle; 13 Hep Cahill. Subs (all used): 10 Manase Manuokafoa; 17 Chris Clarkson; 28 Matt Whitley; 33 Aaron Heremaia.
Tries: White (13), Hanbury (25, 31, 43, 60), Heremaia (33), Brown (48), Flynn (65);
Goals: Tickle 5/6, Ah Van 2/2.
Rugby Leaguer & League Express Men of the Match:
Wildcats: Bill Tupou; *Vikings:* Rhys Hanbury.
Penalty count: 5-5; **Half-time:** 0-22;
Referee: Joe Cobb; **Attendance:** 3,365.

Sunday 13th September 2015

HALIFAX 34 LEIGH CENTURIONS 12

HALIFAX: 7 Ben Johnston; 32 Jake Eccleston; 4 Ben Heaton; 3 Steve Tyrer; 20 James Saltonstall; 31 Connor Robinson; 6 Scott Murrell (C); 17 Mitch Cahalane; 21 Ryan Maneely; 10 Luke Ambler; 27 Ross Divorty; 11 Dane Manning; 22 Jacob Fairbank. Subs (all used): 8 Adam Tangata; 9 Ben Kaye; 12 Andy Bracek; 16 Richard Moore.
Tries: Manning (6), Divorty (13), Saltonstall (33), Murrell (56), Tyrer (59); **Goals:** Tyrer 7/7.
On report: Murrell (45) - alleged late challenge.
CENTURIONS: 1 Gregg McNally; 15 Jonathan Pownall; 2 Adam Higson; 4 Tom Armstrong; 5 Liam Kay; 6 Martyn Ridyard; 7 Ryan Brierley; 8 Fuifui Moimoi; 9 Bob Beswick; 21 Jamie Acton; 22 Andrew Dixon; 26 Gareth Hock; 29 Jake Emmitt. Subs (all used): 30 Mick Higham; 10 Oliver Wilkes (C); 18 Tom Spencer; 23 Martin Aspinwall.
Tries: Higson (45), Moimoi (48); **Goals:** Ridyard 2/2.
On report: Acton (68) - alleged late challenge.
Rugby Leaguer & League Express Men of the Match:
Halifax: Steve Tyrer; *Centurions:* Andrew Dixon.
Penalty count: 8-13; **Half-time:** 20-0;
Referee: Chris Kendall; **Attendance:** 3,010.

SALFORD RED DEVILS 53 SHEFFIELD EAGLES 34

RED DEVILS: 19 Niall Evalds; 2 Ben Jones-Bishop; 41 Iain Thornley; 3 Josh Griffin; 5 Greg Johnson; 9 Tommy Lee; 7 Michael Dobson; 25 George Griffin; 37 Logan Tomkins; 16 Scott Taylor; 11 Harrison Hansen (C); 40 Reni Maitua; 12 Weller Hauraki. Subs (all used): 24 Liam Hood; 26 Carl Forster; 10 Lama Tasi; 8 Adrian Morley.
Tries: Hauraki (4), Hansen (24), J Griffin (29, 31), Hood (36), Tasi (38), Evalds (55), Thornley (76), G Griffin (78); **Goals:** Dobson 7/8, J Griffin 1/1;
Field goal: Dobson (74).
EAGLES: 1 Quentin Laulu-Togagae; 2 Scott Turner; 3 Menzie Yere; 4 Sam Smeaton; 23 Rob Worrincy; 7 Dominic Brambani; 19 Cory Aston; 8 Eddie Battye; 24 Keal Carlile; 10 Mitchell Stringer (C); 11 Michael Knowles; 12 Duane Straugheir; 13 Pat Walker. Subs (all used): 5 Misi Taulapapa; 29 Dave Petersen; 9 James Davey; 25 Connor Scott.
Tries: Aston (7), Yere (10), Laulu-Togagae (21), Worrincy (25), Straugheir (55), Turner (68);
Goals: Walker 5/6.
Rugby Leaguer & League Express Men of the Match:
Red Devils: Michael Dobson; *Eagles:* Menzie Yere.
Penalty count: 9-4; **Half-time:** 34-24;
Referee: Gareth Hewer; **Attendance:** 3,000.

ROUND 6

Friday 18th September 2015

SHEFFIELD EAGLES 28 HULL KINGSTON ROVERS 38

EAGLES: 1 Quentin Laulu-Togagae; 30 Ryan Millar; 3 Menzie Yere; 2 Scott Turner; 23 Rob Worrincy; 19 Cory Aston; 7 Dominic Brambani; 8 Eddie Battye; 24 Keal Carlile; 10 Mitchell Stringer (C); 11 Michael Knowles; 12 Duane Straugheir; 13 Pat Walker. Subs (all used): 5 Misi Taulapapa; 29 Dave Petersen; 15 John Davies; 9 James Davey.
Tries: Battye (6), Laulu-Togagae (44), Millar (54, 74, 78);
Goals: Walker 2/3, Brambani 2/2.
Sin bin: Davies (22) - dangerous challenge.
ROVERS: 2 Ben Cockayne; 1 Kieran Dixon; 19 Kris Welham (C); 18 Liam Salter; 5 Ken Sio; 6 Maurice Blair; 29 Matthew Marsh; 32 Dane Tilse; 24 John Boudebza; 34 Tony Puletua; 11 Kevin Larroyer; 21 Aaron Ollett; 17 Greg Burke. Subs (all used): 8 Adam Walker; 15 James Donaldson; 22 Jordan Cox; 36 George Lawler.
Tries: Sio (21, 40, 47), Blair (37), Walker (59), Welham (62), Marsh (70); **Goals:** Dixon 5/7.
Rugby Leaguer & League Express Men of the Match:
Eagles: Eddie Battye; *Rovers:* Ken Sio.
Penalty count: 7-12; **Half-time:** 6-16;
Referee: Chris Kendall; **Attendance:** 2,017
(at Bramall Lane).

Saturday 19th September 2015

LEIGH CENTURIONS 16 BRADFORD BULLS 32

CENTURIONS: 1 Gregg McNally; 2 Adam Higson; 31 Mathias Pala; 4 Tom Armstrong; 5 Liam Kay; 17 Ben Reynolds; 7 Ryan Brierley; 8 Fuifui Moimoi; 30 Mick Higham; 18 Tom Spencer; 19 Kurt Haggerty; 12 Tommy Goulden; 26 Gareth Hock. Subs (all used): 9 Bob Beswick; 10 Oliver Wilkes (C); 15 Jonathan Pownall; 29 Jake Emmitt.
Tries: Higson (37), McNally (40), Beswick (76);
Goals: Brierley 2/3.
BULLS: 1 Jake Mullaney; 5 Danny Williams; 4 Matty Blythe; 37 Dane Nielsen; 35 James Clare; 3 Adrian Purtell (C); 7 Harry Siejka; 8 Paul Clough; 9 Adam O'Brien; 10 Adam Sidlow; 11 Tom Olbison; 14 Jay Pitts; 13 Danny Addy. Subs (all used): 12 Dale Ferguson; 31 Epalahame Lauaki; 32 Steve Crossley; 36 Matt Ryan.
Tries: Mullaney (2), Williams (30, 47), Blythe (63, 79);
Goals: Addy 6/7.
Rugby Leaguer & League Express Men of the Match:
Centurions: Jake Emmitt; *Bulls:* Adam O'Brien.
Penalty count: 7-9; **Half-time:** 10-10;
Referee: Richard Silverwood; **Attendance:** 4,621.

WAKEFIELD TRINITY WILDCATS 30 HALIFAX 12

WILDCATS: 21 Max Jowitt; 24 Tom Johnstone; 39 Bill Tupou; 28 Joe Arundel; 35 Jordan Tansey; 6 Jacob Miller; 14 Pita Godinet; 8 Nick Scruton (C); 34 Michael Sio; 36 Anthony Walker; 13 Danny Washbrook; 16 Mickael Simon; 26 Chris Annakin. Subs (all used): 41 Andy Yates (D); 22 Jordan Crowther; 17 Matty Ashurst; 37 Anthony Mullally.
Tries: Sio (8, 30), Simon (33), Mullally (68), Jowitt (79);
Goals: Arundel 5/6.
HALIFAX: 7 Ben Johnston; 32 Jake Eccleston; 4 Ben Heaton; 3 Steve Tyrer; 20 James Saltonstall; 31 Connor Robinson; 6 Scott Murrell (C); 17 Mitch Cahalane; 21 Ryan Maneely; 10 Luke Ambler; 8 Adam Tangata; 11 Dane Manning; 22 Jacob Fairbank. Subs (all used): 9 Ben Kaye; 12 Andy Bracek; 16 Richard Moore; 27 Ross Divorty.
Tries: Eccleston (11), Murrell (77); **Goals:** Tyrer 2/2.
Rugby Leaguer & League Express Men of the Match:
Wildcats: Jacob Miller; *Halifax:* James Saltonstall.
Penalty count: 4-1; **Half-time:** 18-6;
Referee: Phil Bentham; **Attendance:** 3,086.

Sunday 20th September 2015

WIDNES VIKINGS 10 SALFORD RED DEVILS 24

VIKINGS: 1 Rhys Hanbury; 2 Paddy Flynn; 14 Chris Dean; 37 Charly Runciman; 5 Patrick Ah Van; 6 Kevin Brown (C); 7 Joe Mellor; 25 Alex Gerrard; 9 Lloyd White; 35 Gil Dudson; 17 Chris Clarkson; 28 Matt Whitley; 13 Hep Cahill. Subs (all used): 33 Aaron Heremaia; 10 Manase Manuokafoa; 12 Danny Tickle; 21 Danny Craven.
Tries: Ah Van (12), White (62); **Goals:** Ah Van 1/2.
Dismissal: Brown (71) - fighting.
RED DEVILS: 19 Niall Evalds; 2 Ben Jones-Bishop; 41 Iain Thornley; 4 Junior Sa'u; 3 Josh Griffin; 9 Tommy Lee; 7 Michael Dobson; 16 Scott Taylor; 37 Logan Tomkins; 10 Lama Tasi; 11 Harrison Hansen (C); 40 Reni Maitua; 38 Olsi Krasniqi. Subs (all used): 20 Adam Walne; 8 Adrian Morley; 24 Liam Hood; 31 Cory Paterson.
Tries: J Griffin (2), Taylor (20), Paterson (25), Sa'u (42);
Goals: Dobson 4/5.
Dismissal: J Griffin (71) - fighting.
Sin bin: Hood (36) - high tackle on Brown;
Hansen (58) - dangerous contact on Hanbury.
Rugby Leaguer & League Express Men of the Match:
Vikings: Alex Gerrard; *Red Devils:* Junior Sa'u.
Penalty count: 9-9; **Half-time:** 4-18;
Referee: James Child; **Attendance:** 5,285.

ROUND 7

Saturday 26th September 2015

BRADFORD BULLS 18 HALIFAX 52

BULLS: 27 Ryan Shaw; 34 Omari Caro; 20 Adam Henry; 4 Matty Blythe; 35 James Clare; 33 James Mendeika; 7 Harry Siejka; 8 Paul Clough (C); 26 Vila Halafihi; 31 Epalahame Lauaki; 23 Alex Mellor; 36 Matt Ryan; 14 Jay Pitts. Subs (all used): 6 Lee Gaskell; 15 Daniel Fleming; 17 Jean-Philippe Baile; 32 Steve Crossley.
Tries: Ryan (2), Shaw (25, 29); **Goals:** Shaw 3/3.
HALIFAX: 20 James Saltonstall; 32 Jake Eccleston; 4 Ben Heaton; 3 Steve Tyrer; 2 Tom Saxton; 7 Ben Johnston; 6 Scott Murrell (C); 17 Mitch Cahalane; 9 Ben Kaye; 10 Luke Ambler; 8 Adam Tangata; 11 Dane Manning; 22 Jacob Fairbank. Subs (all used): 13 Jack Spencer; 16 Richard Moore; 21 Ryan Maneely; 36 Mikey Wood.
Tries: Saxton (10, 48), Tyrer (12, 56, 80), Manning (39), Johnston (60, 63), Tangata (68), Heaton (73);
Goals: Tyrer 6/9, Spencer 0/1.
Sin bin: Maneely (42) - dangerous challenge.
Rugby Leaguer & League Express Men of the Match:
Bulls: Matt Ryan; *Halifax:* Ben Johnston.
Penalty count: 4-6; **Half-time:** 18-16;
Referee: Ben Thaler; **Attendance:** 5,163.

Sunday 27th September 2015

HULL KINGSTON ROVERS 46 SALFORD RED DEVILS 22

ROVERS: 5 Ken Sio; 4 Josh Mantellato; 19 Kris Welham; 12 Graeme Horne; 1 Kieran Dixon; 6 Maurice Blair; 35 Dane Chisholm; 8 Adam Walker; 31 Shaun Lunt; 32 Dane Tilse; 11 Kevin Larroyer; 13 Tyrone McCarthy (C); 36 George Lawler. Subs (all used): 2 Ben Cockayne; 15 James Donaldson; 17 Greg Burke; 20 James Green.
Tries: Welham (12), Lawler (16), Mantellato (45), Sio (48), Chisholm (53), McCarthy (58), Cockayne (71), Blair (75); **Goals:** Mantellato 6/7, Welham 1/1.
RED DEVILS: 19 Niall Evalds; 2 Ben Jones-Bishop; 39 Jake Bibby (D); 4 Junior Sa'u; 5 Greg Johnson; 36 Josh Wood; 9 Tommy Lee; 20 Adam Walne; 37 Logan Tomkins; 10 Lama Tasi; 11 Harrison Hansen (C); 40 Reni Maitua; 38 Olsi Krasniqi. Subs (all used): 8 Adrian Morley; 24 Liam Hood; 32 Ryan Lannon; 27 Luke Menzies (D).
Tries: Johnson (5), Hansen (18), Tasi (27), Lannon (31);
Goals: Lee 0/1, Jones-Bishop 3/3.
Rugby Leaguer & League Express Men of the Match:
Rovers: Ken Sio; *Red Devils:* Harrison Hansen.
Penalty count: 8-3; **Half-time:** 10-22;
Referee: Gareth Hewer; **Attendance:** 7,543.

Wakefield's Ali Lauitiiti races away from Bradford's Tom Olbison during the inaugural Million Pound Game

SHEFFIELD EAGLES 24
WAKEFIELD TRINITY WILDCATS 10

EAGLES: 1 Quentin Laulu-Togagae; 2 Scott Turner; 3 Menzie Yere; 4 Sam Smeaton; 23 Rob Worrincy; 7 Dominic Brambani; 19 Cory Aston; 8 Eddie Battye; 24 Keal Carlile; 10 Mitchell Stringer (C); 11 Michael Knowles; 12 Duane Straugheir; 13 Pat Walker. Subs (all used): 5 Misi Taulapapa; 22 Tony Tonks; 15 John Davies; 9 James Davey.
Tries: Turner (18), Aston (25), Yere (35), Laulu-Togagae (72); **Goals:** Walker 3/4, Brambani 1/1.
WILDCATS: 21 Max Jowitt; 4 Reece Lyne; 39 Bill Tupou; 28 Joe Arundel; 24 Tom Johnstone; 6 Jacob Miller; 14 Pita Godinet; 10 Scott Anderson; 34 Michael Sio; 8 Nick Scruton; 16 Mickael Simon; 13 Danny Washbrook; 26 Chris Annakin. Subs (all used): 11 Ali Lauitiiti; 12 Danny Kirmond (C); 31 Ben Kavanagh; 41 Andy Yates.
Tries: Kirmond (28), Kavanagh (39); **Goals:** Arundel 1/2.
Rugby Leaguer & League Express Men of the Match: *Eagles:* Quentin Laulu-Togagae; *Wildcats:* Danny Kirmond.
Penalty count: 10-8; **Half-time:** 16-10;
Referee: Joe Cobb; **Attendance:** 1,712 *(at Bramall Lane).*

WIDNES VIKINGS 50 LEIGH CENTURIONS 6

VIKINGS: 1 Rhys Hanbury; 2 Paddy Flynn; 14 Chris Dean; 37 Charly Runciman; 5 Patrick Ah Van; 6 Kevin Brown (C); 7 Joe Mellor; 25 Alex Gerrard; 33 Aaron Heremaia; 10 Manase Manuokafoa; 28 Matt Whitley; 12 Danny Tickle; 13 Hep Cahill. Subs (all used): 9 Lloyd White; 15 Jack Owens; 34 Jay Chapelhow (D); 35 Gil Dudson.
Tries: Ah Van (15, 74), Brown (23), Runciman (33), Flynn (40), Gerrard (48), Hanbury (57), Mellor (65), Owens (78); **Goals:** Tickle 5/7, Owens 2/2.
CENTURIONS: 1 Gregg McNally; 15 Jonathan Pownall; 3 Greg Worthington; 4 Tom Armstrong; 5 Liam Kay; 17 Ben Reynolds; 7 Ryan Brierley; 18 Tom Spencer; 30 Mick Higham; 10 Oliver Wilkes (C); 26 Gareth Hock; 12 Tommy Goulden; 9 Bob Beswick. Subs (all used): 27 Lewis Foster; 8 Fuifui Moimoi; 22 Andrew Dixon; 29 Jake Emmitt.
Try: Reynolds (5); **Goals:** Brierley 1/1.
Rugby Leaguer & League Express Men of the Match: *Vikings:* Kevin Brown; *Centurions:* Liam Kay.
Penalty count: 13-6; **Half-time:** 20-6;
Referee: Chris Kendall; **Attendance:** 5,550.

MILLION POUND GAME

Saturday 3rd October 2015

WAKEFIELD TRINITY WILDCATS 24
BRADFORD BULLS 16

WILDCATS: 35 Jordan Tansey; 4 Reece Lyne; 39 Bill Tupou; 28 Joe Arundel; 24 Tom Johnstone; 6 Jacob Miller; 14 Pita Godinet; 8 Nick Scruton; 34 Michael Sio; 16 Mickael Simon; 12 Danny Kirmond (C); 13 Danny Washbrook; 26 Chris Annakin. Subs (all used): 41 Andy Yates; 37 Anthony Mullally; 40 Scott Moore; 11 Ali Lauitiiti.
Tries: Kirmond (15), Mullally (44), Washbrook (60), Moore (79); **Goals:** Arundel 1/2, Tansey 3/3.
BULLS: 1 Jake Mullaney; 5 Danny Williams; 3 Adrian Purtell (C); 37 Dane Nielsen; 4 Matty Blythe; 6 Lee Gaskell; 7 Harry Siejka; 8 Paul Clough; 9 Adam O'Brien; 10 Adam Sidlow; 11 Tom Olbison; 12 Dale Ferguson; 13 Danny Addy. Subs (all used): 14 Jay Pitts; 17 Jean-Philippe Baile; 32 Steve Crossley; 31 Epalahame Lauaki.
Tries: Williams (49), Blythe (54), Purtell (65);
Goals: Addy 2/4.
Rugby Leaguer & League Express Men of the Match: *Wildcats:* Scott Moore; *Bulls:* Adrian Purtell.
Penalty count: 6-9; **Half-time:** 6-0;
Referee: Richard Silverwood; **Attendance:** 7,236.

SUPER LEAGUE XX
Opta Analysis

SUPER LEAGUE XX TOP PERFORMERS

TACKLES

Player	Club	Total
Danny Houghton	Hull FC	1359
James Roby	St Helens	1041
Chris Hill	Warrington	976
Alex Gerrard	Widnes	953
Jamie Peacock	Leeds	952
Ian Henderson	Catalans	940
Grant Millington	Castleford	938
Elliott Whitehead	Catalans	937
Stevie Ward	Leeds	926
Jack Hughes	Huddersfield	902

OFFLOADS

Player	Club	Total
Adam Cuthbertson	Leeds	125
Liam Watts	Hull FC	66
Zeb Taia	Catalans	60
Anthony Gelling	Wigan	54
Joel Tomkins	Wigan	54
Alex Walmsley	St Helens	52
Elliott Whitehead	Catalans	52
Junior Moors	Castleford	51
Kallum Watkins	Leeds	47
Grant Millington	Castleford	45

CARRIES

Player	Club	Total
Alex Walmsley	St Helens	531
Jamie Peacock	Leeds	529
Adam Cuthbertson	Leeds	527
Rhys Hanbury	Widnes	503
Andy Lynch	Castleford	499
Chris Hill	Warrington	491
Jermaine McGillvary	Huddersfield	465
Zak Hardaker	Leeds	431
Ben Westwood	Warrington	416
Ashton Sims	Warrington	408

CLEAN BREAKS

Player	Club	Total
Jermaine McGillvary	Huddersfield	33
Kallum Watkins	Leeds	30
Joe Burgess	Wigan	28
Kieran Dixon	Hull KR	26
Josh Mantellato	Hull KR	26
Adam Swift	St Helens	24
Elliott Whitehead	Catalans	24
Rhys Hanbury	Widnes	23
Danny McGuire	Leeds	23
Tom Lineham	Hull FC	22

ERRORS

Player	Club	Total
Scott Dureau	Catalans	51
Albert Kelly	Hull KR	46
Danny McGuire	Leeds	45
Justin Carney	Castleford	44
Rhys Hanbury	Widnes	41
Danny Brough	Huddersfield	39
Jacob Miller	Wakefield	39
Kieran Dixon	Hull KR	38
Marc Sneyd	Hull FC	38
Kevin Brown	Widnes	37

METRES

Player	Club	Total
Alex Walmsley	St Helens	4092
Rhys Hanbury	Widnes	4000
Jermaine McGillvary	Huddersfield	3888
Zak Hardaker	Leeds	3758
Chris Hill	Warrington	3706
Jamie Peacock	Leeds	3701
Andy Lynch	Castleford	3589
Ken Sio	Hull KR	3342
Adam Swift	St Helens	3333
Adam Cuthbertson	Leeds	3238

METRES FROM SCOOTS

Player	Club	Total
James Roby	St Helens	2155
Daryl Clark	Warrington	1775
Danny Houghton	Hull FC	1428
Ian Henderson	Catalans	1425
Luke Robinson	Huddersfield	1234
Michael McIlorum	Wigan	1148
Paul Aiton	Leeds	1134
Aaron Heremaia	Widnes	1424
Adam Milner	Castleford	1053
Lloyd White	Widnes	956

MISSED TACKLES

Player	Club	Total
Ian Henderson	Catalans	93
Mark Minichiello	Hull FC	93
Albert Kelly	Hull KR	88
Scott Dureau	Catalans	86
Michael McIlorum	Wigan	81
Elliott Whitehead	Catalans	78
Aaron Heremaia	Widnes	75
Travis Burns	St Helens	74
Tyrone McCarthy	Hull KR	73
Jon Wilkin	St Helens	72

SUPPORTED BREAKS

Player	Club	Total
Danny McGuire	Leeds	13
Rob Burrow	Leeds	12
Zak Hardaker	Leeds	9
Joe Burgess	Wigan	8
Niall Evalds	Salford	8
Luke Gale	Castleford	8
Richard Myler	Warrington	8
Adam Swift	St Helens	8
Ryan Atkins	Warrington	7
Tom Lineham	Hull FC	7

QUICK PLAY-THE-BALLS

Player	Club	Total
Jermaine McGillvary	Huddersfield	81
Ryan Atkins	Warrington	78
Ryan Hall	Leeds	58
Alex Gerrard	Widnes	57
Stefan Ratchford	Warrington	57
Fetuli Talanoa	Hull FC	54
Mark Minichiello	Hull FC	53
Taulima Tautai	Wigan	51
Ben Westwood	Warrington	49
Liam Farrell	Wigan	48

PENALTIES CONCEDED

Player	Club	Total
Joe Wardle	Huddersfield	27
Louie McCarthy-Scarsbrook	St Helens	25
Ian Henderson	Catalans	24
Travis Burns	St Helens	23
Luke Gale	Castleford	22
Chris Hill	Warrington	22
Mark Minichiello	Hull FC	22
Cory Paterson	Salford	22
Liam Watts	Hull FC	22
Ben Westwood	Warrington	21

TACKLE BUSTS

Player	Club	Total
Mark Minichiello	Hull FC	121
Kieran Dixon	Hull KR	120
Alex Walmsley	St Helens	119
Zak Hardaker	Leeds	109
Kallum Watkins	Leeds	108
Dominic Manfredi	Wigan	107
Jermaine McGillvary	Huddersfield	98
Jordan Rankin	Hull FC	97
Rhys Hanbury	Widnes	95
Fetuli Talanoa	Hull FC	95

All statistics in Opta Analysis include Super League regular season, Super 8s & Super 8s - The Qualifiers. Play-offs not included.

Leeds' Kallum Watkins crosses to score against Salford at Headingley. The Rhinos scored more tries than any other team in Super League XX

SUPER LEAGUE XX AVERAGES PER MATCH

TACKLES

Team	Avg
Widnes Vikings	333.5
Salford Red Devils	329.7
Leeds Rhinos	322.6
Huddersfield Giants	322.4
Warrington Wolves	321.7
Castleford Tigers	321.2
Hull Kingston Rovers	316.1
Wigan Warriors	312.4
Hull FC	311.3
Wakefield T Wildcats	310.2
St Helens	307.0
Catalans Dragons	302.0

MISSED TACKLES

Team	Avg
Hull Kingston Rovers	32.8
Catalans Dragons	31.1
Salford Red Devils	30.7
Hull FC	29.6
Wakefield T Wildcats	29.1
Leeds Rhinos	27.8
Warrington Wolves	26.4
Wigan Warriors	26.0
Widnes Vikings	25.7
Huddersfield Giants	24.7
Castleford Tigers	24.0
St Helens	21.5

OFFLOADS

Team	Avg
Leeds Rhinos	19.1
Catalans Dragons	12.8
Wigan Warriors	11.7
Hull FC	11.6
Warrington Wolves	11.5
St Helens	10.5
Castleford Tigers	9.9
Huddersfield Giants	9.9
Wakefield T Wildcats	9.9
Hull Kingston Rovers	9.6
Widnes Vikings	9.0
Salford Red Devils	8.2

METRES

Team	Avg
Leeds Rhinos	1399.4
Widnes Vikings	1309.5
Wigan Warriors	1299.1
Hull FC	1288.9
Warrington Wolves	1283.7
Hull Kingston Rovers	1234.7
Castleford Tigers	1215.2
St Helens	1212.2
Huddersfield Giants	1208.9
Salford Red Devils	1193.5
Catalans Dragons	1149.1
Wakefield T Wildcats	1146.0

CLEAN BREAKS

Team	Avg
Leeds Rhinos	8.1
Wigan Warriors	6.9
Widnes Vikings	6.4
Hull FC	6.3
Catalans Dragons	6.0
Hull Kingston Rovers	6.0
Castleford Tigers	5.9
Wakefield T Wildcats	5.9
St Helens	5.7
Warrington Wolves	5.4
Huddersfield Giants	5.1
Salford Red Devils	5.1

PASSES

Team	Avg
Leeds Rhinos	224.8
Hull FC	218.9
Wigan Warriors	217.7
Widnes Vikings	214.6
Huddersfield Giants	213.7
St Helens	212.9
Hull Kingston Rovers	208.0
Salford Red Devils	206.1
Catalans Dragons	205.0
Castleford Tigers	202.4
Warrington Wolves	201.3
Wakefield T Wildcats	195.8

ERRORS

Team	Avg
Catalans Dragons	13.8
Warrington Wolves	12.9
Leeds Rhinos	12.7
Hull FC	12.4
Huddersfield Giants	12.1
Wigan Warriors	12.1
St Helens	11.4
Castleford Tigers	11.1
Hull Kingston Rovers	12.6
Wakefield T Wildcats	12.5
Salford Red Devils	10.9
Widnes Vikings	11.2

KICKS IN GENERAL PLAY

Team	Avg
Huddersfield Giants	20.0
St Helens	19.5
Hull FC	19.2
Warrington Wolves	19.2
Wigan Warriors	18.9
Castleford Tigers	18.6
Leeds Rhinos	17.4
Catalans Dragons	17.1
Salford Red Devils	19.4
Widnes Vikings	19.7
Hull Kingston Rovers	18.9
Wakefield T Wildcats	16.7

SUPER LEAGUE XX TRIES SCORED/CONCEDED

(Totals scored/conceded are unequal due to games against Championship teams in Super 8s - The Qualifiers)

TOTAL TRIES SCORED

Team	Tries
Leeds Rhinos	165
Wigan Warriors	144
St Helens	132
Warrington Wolves	132
Huddersfield Giants	131
Castleford Tigers	129
Catalans Dragons	126
Hull FC	114
Hull Kingston Rovers	139
Widnes Vikings	138
Salford Red Devils	121
Wakefield T Wildcats	101

TOTAL TRIES CONCEDED

Team	Tries
Wakefield T Wildcats	194
Salford Red Devils	144
Catalans Dragons	140
Hull Kingston Rovers	138
Castleford Tigers	137
Hull FC	128
Widnes Vikings	117
Warrington Wolves	115
Leeds Rhinos	114
St Helens	113
Huddersfield Giants	96
Wigan Warriors	94

SCORED FROM KICKS

Team	Tries
Wigan Warriors	21
Hull Kingston Rovers	18
Huddersfield Giants	17
Salford Red Devils	17
Leeds Rhinos	16
Castleford Tigers	15
Hull FC	12
Wakefield T Wildcats	12
Warrington Wolves	12
Catalans Dragons	10
St Helens	10
Widnes Vikings	9

CONCEDED FROM KICKS

Team	Tries
Leeds Rhinos	21
Wakefield T Wildcats	19
Castleford Tigers	18
Salford Red Devils	18
Catalans Dragons	15
Widnes Vikings	15
Warrington Wolves	13
Hull Kingston Rovers	12
Hull FC	11
St Helens	11
Wigan Warriors	10
Huddersfield Giants	8

SUPER LEAGUE XX TRIES SCORED/CONCEDED

TRIES SCORED FROM OWN HALF

Wigan Warriors 33
Leeds Rhinos 30
Hull Kingston Rovers 24
Warrington Wolves............23
Widnes Vikings 19
Catalans Dragons..............18
Salford Red Devils 16
St Helens 16
Castleford Tigers 14
Hull FC 13
Huddersfield Giants 11
Wakefield T Wildcats 11

TRIES CONCEDED FROM OVER 50M

Wakefield T Wildcats 39
St Helens 22
Hull FC 21
Leeds Rhinos 21
Catalans Dragons..............19
Salford Red Devils 19
Hull Kingston Rovers 17
Widnes Vikings 17
Castleford Tigers 15
Warrington Wolves............14
Huddersfield Giants 9
Wigan Warriors 8

TRIES SCORED FROM UNDER 10M

Leeds Rhinos 71
Widnes Vikings 67
Salford Red Devils 60
Hull Kingston Rovers 55
Wakefield T Wildcats 53
Castleford Tigers 51
Wigan Warriors 51
Huddersfield Giants 50
St Helens 50
Catalans Dragons..............49
Warrington Wolves............44
Hull FC 43

TRIES CONCEDED FROM UNDER 10M

Castleford Tigers 70
Salford Red Devils 65
Hull Kingston Rovers 64
Wakefield T Wildcats 64
Widnes Vikings 61
Warrington Wolves............57
Hull FC 52
Catalans Dragons..............51
Wigan Warriors 50
Huddersfield Giants 46
St Helens 43
Leeds Rhinos 41

SUPER LEAGUE XX PENALTIES

(Totals awarded/conceded are unequal due to games against Championship teams in Super 8s - The Qualifiers)

TOTAL PENALTIES AWARDED

Catalans Dragons................249
Huddersfield Giants 223
Hull Kingston Rovers..........220
Widnes Vikings 212
Castleford Tigers 208
Leeds Rhinos......................204
Wigan Warriors 202
Hull FC 199
Warrington Wolves 199
St Helens 197
Wakefield T Wildcats 192
Salford Red Devils..............187

TOTAL PENALTIES CONCEDED

Salford Red Devils..............245
St Helens 241
Huddersfield Giants 240
Castleford Tigers 209
Wakefield T Wildcats 209
Catalans Dragons................204
Hull FC 200
Widnes Vikings 196
Wigan Warriors 188
Hull Kingston Rovers..........185
Warrington Wolves 183
Leeds Rhinos......................167

FOUL PLAY - AWARDED

Widnes Vikings 50
Catalans Dragons..................47
Wakefield T Wildcats 43
Leeds Rhinos........................41
Hull Kingston Rovers............39
St Helens 38
Castleford Tigers 37
Warrington Wolves 37
Wigan Warriors 37
Hull FC..................................35
Huddersfield Giants 31
Salford Red Devils................31

FOUL PLAY - CONCEDED

Salford Red Devils................65
Catalans Dragons..................47
Wigan Warriors 43
Huddersfield Giants 41
Widnes Vikings 38
St Helens 37
Castleford Tigers 36
Hull FC..................................34
Hull Kingston Rovers............32
Warrington Wolves 31
Leeds Rhinos........................26
Wakefield T Wildcats 26

OFFSIDE - AWARDED

Warrington Wolves 29
Leeds Rhinos........................28
Huddersfield Giants 25
Salford Red Devils................23
St Helens 23
Catalans Dragons..................21
Hull Kingston Rovers............21
Wigan Warriors 21
Widnes Vikings 20
Wakefield T Wildcats 18
Castleford Tigers 14
Hull FC..................................14

OFFSIDE - CONCEDED

St Helens 43
Huddersfield Giants 39
Salford Red Devils................25
Wakefield T Wildcats 22
Castleford Tigers 21
Hull FC..................................19
Wigan Warriors 18
Hull Kingston Rovers............15
Leeds Rhinos........................15
Warrington Wolves 15
Catalans Dragons..................14
Widnes Vikings 14

INTERFERENCE - AWARDED

Huddersfield Giants 103
Catalans Dragons..................89
Wigan Warriors 89
Wakefield T Wildcats 85
Widnes Vikings 79
Castleford Tigers 76
Hull FC..................................76
Hull Kingston Rovers............73
Leeds Rhinos........................72
Salford Red Devils................72
Warrington Wolves 71
St Helens 70

INTERFERENCE - CONCEDED

St Helens 93
Wakefield T Wildcats 89
Widnes Vikings 89
Salford Red Devils................84
Huddersfield Giants 82
Warrington Wolves 82
Castleford Tigers 80
Hull Kingston Rovers............78
Catalans Dragons..................73
Hull FC..................................71
Wigan Warriors 71
Leeds Rhinos........................60

OBSTRUCTION - AWARDED

Castleford Tigers 17
Leeds Rhinos........................16
Hull FC..................................15
Hull Kingston Rovers............14
Salford Red Devils................14
Catalans Dragons..................12
St Helens 11
Widnes Vikings 11
Wakefield T Wildcats 9
Wigan Warriors 9
Warrington Wolves 8
Huddersfield Giants 6

OBSTRUCTION - CONCEDED

Leeds Rhinos........................19
St Helens 15
Salford Red Devils................14
Hull FC..................................13
Hull Kingston Rovers............11
Huddersfield Giants 10
Wakefield T Wildcats 10
Widnes Vikings 10
Wigan Warriors 10
Castleford Tigers 9
Catalans Dragons....................9
Warrington Wolves 8

BALL STEALING - AWARDED

Catalans Dragons..................39
Hull Kingston Rovers............38
Huddersfield Giants 33
Castleford Tigers 27
Hull FC..................................25
Widnes Vikings 25
St Helens 20
Warrington Wolves 20
Salford Red Devils................19
Wigan Warriors 19
Leeds Rhinos........................14
Wakefield T Wildcats 14

BALL STEALING - CONCEDED

Hull FC..................................36
Huddersfield Giants 31
Catalans Dragons..................30
Castleford Tigers 29
Wakefield T Wildcats 28
Salford Red Devils................26
Hull Kingston Rovers............20
Warrington Wolves 20
Widnes Vikings 20
Leeds Rhinos........................18
St Helens 15
Wigan Warriors 15

OFFSIDE MARKERS - AWARDED

Hull FC..................................12
Hull Kingston Rovers............12
Catalans Dragons..................11
Wigan Warriors 10
Castleford Tigers 7
Leeds Rhinos..........................7
St Helens 7
Warrington Wolves 7
Salford Red Devils..................6
Wakefield T Wildcats 6
Widnes Vikings 4
Huddersfield Giants 3

OFFSIDE MARKERS - CONCEDED

St Helens 17
Widnes Vikings 9
Wigan Warriors 9
Catalans Dragons....................8
Hull Kingston Rovers..............8
Leeds Rhinos..........................7
Castleford Tigers 6
Huddersfield Giants 6
Hull FC....................................6
Wakefield T Wildcats 5
Salford Red Devils..................4
Warrington Wolves 4

OFFSIDE FROM KICK - AWARDED

Castleford Tigers 10
Catalans Dragons....................9
St Helens 8
Salford Red Devils..................7
Hull FC....................................5
Wakefield T Wildcats 5
Widnes Vikings 5
Warrington Wolves 4
Wigan Warriors 4
Hull Kingston Rovers..............3
Leeds Rhinos..........................3
Huddersfield Giants 0

OFFSIDE FROM KICK - CONCEDED

Hull FC....................................9
Salford Red Devils..................8
Castleford Tigers 6
St Helens 6
Wakefield T Wildcats 6
Warrington Wolves 6
Widnes Vikings 6
Huddersfield Giants 5
Hull Kingston Rovers..............5
Catalans Dragons....................3
Leeds Rhinos..........................3
Wigan Warriors 3

DISSENT - AWARDED

St Helens 5
Widnes Vikings 5
Castleford Tigers 4
Leeds Rhinos..........................4
Warrington Wolves 4
Catalans Dragons....................2
Huddersfield Giants 2
Hull FC....................................1
Hull Kingston Rovers..............1
Salford Red Devils..................1
Wakefield T Wildcats 0
Wigan Warriors 0

DISSENT - CONCEDED

Huddersfield Giants 5
Hull Kingston Rovers..............5
Catalans Dragons....................4
Hull FC....................................3
St Helens 3
Warrington Wolves 3
Wakefield T Wildcats 2
Wigan Warriors 2
Castleford Tigers 1
Leeds Rhinos..........................1
Widnes Vikings 1
Salford Red Devils..................0

CASTLEFORD TIGERS

Grant Millington

TACKLES
Grant Millington.............938
Andy Lynch 880
Oliver Holmes 800
Adam Milner 739
Nathan Massey 575

OFFLOADS
Junior Moors....................51
Grant Millington................45
Andy Lynch 36
Mike McMeeken 20
Michael Shenton 18

CLEAN BREAKS
Justin Carney....................21
Michael Shenton 19
Denny Solomona..............19
Luke Dorn 16
Ben Roberts......................14

TRY ASSISTS
Luke Gale..........................27
Ben Roberts......................11
Michael Shenton 11
Liam Finn..........................10
Jake Webster......................7

MARKER TACKLES
Grant Millington.............178
Andy Lynch 140
Oliver Holmes 129
Adam Milner 127
Matt Cook 95

Andy Lynch

METRES
Andy Lynch 3589
Justin Carney................2302
Grant Millington............2284
Michael Shenton 2194
Junior Moors................2158

CARRIES
Andy Lynch 499
Grant Millington.............367
Oliver Holmes 294
Junior Moors..................294
Michael Shenton 291

TACKLE BUSTS
Ben Roberts......................89
Justin Carney....................88
Michael Shenton 65
Luke Gale..........................56
Junior Moors....................56

TOTAL OPTA INDEX
Andy Lynch 16009
Grant Millington..........14335
Oliver Holmes 12929
Luke Gale....................12168
Ben Roberts................10988

CATALANS DRAGONS

Jason Baitieri

TACKLES
Ian Henderson................940
Elliott Whitehead 937
Jason Baitieri..................787
Louis Anderson 570
Benjamin Garcia.............556

OFFLOADS
Zeb Taia 60
Elliott Whitehead 52
Ben Pomeroy....................34
Ian Henderson..................26
Jason Baitieri....................23

CLEAN BREAKS
Elliott Whitehead 24
Morgan Escare 18
Benjamin Garcia...............14
Zeb Taia 14
Tony Gigot........................10

TRY ASSISTS
Scott Dureau 23
Todd Carney......................14
Elliott Whitehead 11
Willie Tonga........................6
Morgan Escare 5

MARKER TACKLES
Elliott Whitehead 165
Jason Baitieri..................146
Ian Henderson................142
Benjamin Garcia.............114
Olivier Elima 111

Elliott Whitehead

METRES
Jason Baitieri................2496
Zeb Taia 2461
Elliott Whitehead 2229
Morgan Escare 2220
Ian Henderson 2128

CARRIES
Jason Baitieri..................392
Zeb Taia 364
Ian Henderson................340
Elliott Whitehead 328
Benjamin Garcia.............267

TACKLE BUSTS
Zeb Taia 79
Elliott Whitehead 79
Tony Gigot 63
Morgan Escare 59
Krisnan Inu 54

TOTAL OPTA INDEX
Elliott Whitehead 15633
Jason Baitieri..............12686
Ian Henderson............11505
Morgan Escare 11029
Benjamin Garcia..........10588

HUDDERSFIELD GIANTS

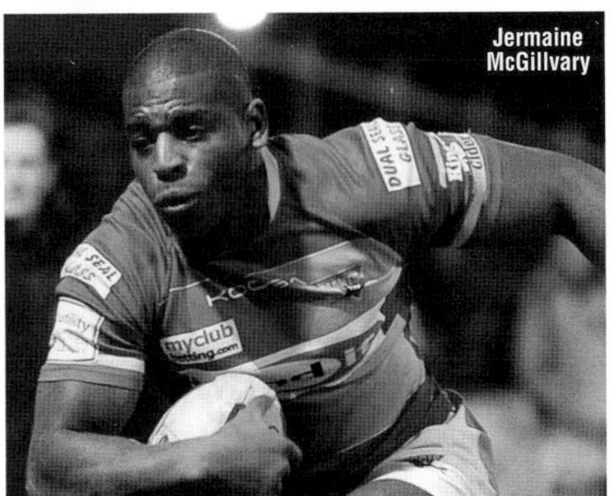
Jermaine McGillvary

MARKER TACKLES
Jack Hughes 148
Michael Lawrence 134
Craig Kopczak 125
Leroy Cudjoe 124
Ukuma Ta'ai 124

METRES
Jermaine McGillvary 3888
Leroy Cudjoe 2554
Aaron Murphy 2504
Craig Huby....................2394
Jack Hughes 2349

CARRIES
Jermaine McGillvary 465
Craig Huby......................378
Jack Hughes 378
Craig Kopczak 334
Aaron Murphy 334

Jack Hughes

TACKLES
Jack Hughes 902
Craig Kopczak 743
Craig Huby.......................738
Ukuma Ta'ai 738
Michael Lawrence 703

OFFLOADS
Craig Huby.........................44
Jack Hughes 35
Leroy Cudjoe 31
Danny Brough 26
Brett Ferres 22

CLEAN BREAKS
Jermaine McGillvary 33
Joe Wardle.........................15
Danny Brough 13
Jamie Ellis 13
Aaron Murphy 13

TRY ASSISTS
Danny Brough 31
Leroy Cudjoe 16
Scott Grix 10
Jamie Ellis 9
Jake Connor 7

TACKLE BUSTS
Jermaine McGillvary 98
Joe Wardle.........................60
Leroy Cudjoe 59
Aaron Murphy 58
Danny Brough 53

TOTAL OPTA INDEX
Jermaine McGillvary ..15031
Jack Hughes 14685
Danny Brough 14057
Leroy Cudjoe 13768
Ukuma Ta'ai...............13346

HULL F.C.

Danny Houghton

MARKER TACKLES
Danny Houghton 234
Liam Watts 229
Joe Westerman 121
Mark Minichiello 118
Mickey Paea 92

METRES
Mickey Paea 2957
Mark Minichiello 2887
Liam Watts 2683
Jordan Rankin 2511
Fetuli Talanoa................2477

CARRIES
Liam Watts 404
Mark Minichiello 397
Mickey Paea 380
Fetuli Talanoa..................321
Jordan Rankin 313

Mark Minichiello

TACKLES
Danny Houghton 1359
Liam Watts 862
Mark Minichiello 745
Joe Westerman 696
Mickey Paea 560

OFFLOADS
Liam Watts 66
Mark Minichiello 36
Leon Pryce 35
Joe Westerman 22
Setaimata Sa 15

CLEAN BREAKS
Tom Lineham 22
Fetuli Talanoa...................21
Mark Minichiello 16
Jordan Rankin 16
Jamie Shaul......................14

TRY ASSISTS
Marc Sneyd 20
Jordan Rankin 12
Danny Houghton 10
Jordan Abdull 8
Jack Logan 5

TACKLE BUSTS
Mark Minichiello 121
Jordan Rankin 97
Fetuli Talanoa...................95
Mickey Paea 66
Tom Lineham....................65

TOTAL OPTA INDEX
Danny Houghton 17057
Mark Minichiello 13976
Liam Watts 12898
Mickey Paea 11595
Jordan Rankin 11467

HULL KINGSTON ROVERS

TACKLES
Tyrone McCarthy 894
Kevin Larroyer 683
John Boudebza 612
Adam Walker 610
Graeme Horne 583

OFFLOADS
Adam Walker 42
Tyrone McCarthy 22
Ben Cockayne 16
James Green 16
James Donaldson 13

CLEAN BREAKS
Kieran Dixon 26
Josh Mantellato 26
Ken Sio 21
Kris Welham 18
Albert Kelly 16

TRY ASSISTS
Ben Cockayne 14
Terry Campese..................12
Maurice Blair 10
Albert Kelly 10
Kris Welham 10

MARKER TACKLES
Tyrone McCarthy 186
Kevin Larroyer 155
John Boudebza 131
Graeme Horne 110
Adam Walker 85

METRES
Ken Sio 3342
Kieran Dixon 2738
Kris Welham 2697
Josh Mantellato 2627
Adam Walker 2233

CARRIES
Ken Sio 364
Adam Walker 353
Kieran Dixon 330
Josh Mantellato 320
Kris Welham 320

TACKLE BUSTS
Kieran Dixon 120
Albert Kelly 75
Ken Sio 69
Ben Cockayne 58
Maurice Blair 55

TOTAL OPTA INDEX
Tyrone McCarthy 12291
Ken Sio 11568
Kieran Dixon 11212
Albert Kelly 10488
Maurice Blair 9935

LEEDS RHINOS

TACKLES
Jamie Peacock................952
Stevie Ward 926
Adam Cuthbertson..........878
Carl Ablett 772
Brad Singleton................726

OFFLOADS
Adam Cuthbertson..........125
Kallum Watkins 47
Jamie Peacock..................45
Kevin Sinfield....................42
Joel Moon 39

CLEAN BREAKS
Kallum Watkins 30
Danny McGuire 23
Zak Hardaker 22
Ryan Hall..........................20
Tom Briscoe......................19

TRY ASSISTS
Danny McGuire 27
Kevin Sinfield....................18
Joel Moon 11
Kallum Watkins 10
Carl Ablett 9

MARKER TACKLES
Brad Singleton................192
Stevie Ward 186
Jamie Peacock................182
Adam Cuthbertson..........148
Paul Aiton 124

METRES
Zak Hardaker 3758
Jamie Peacock..............3701
Adam Cuthbertson........3238
Kallum Watkins 3111
Ryan Hall 2856

CARRIES
Jamie Peacock................529
Adam Cuthbertson..........527
Zak Hardaker 431
Kallum Watkins 386
Ryan Hall 378

TACKLE BUSTS
Zak Hardaker 109
Kallum Watkins 108
Danny McGuire 68
Adam Cuthbertson............67
Stevie Ward 66

TOTAL OPTA INDEX
Adam Cuthbertson......16973
Zak Hardaker 16823
Kallum Watkins 16696
Jamie Peacock............16437
Carl Ablett 13347

SALFORD RED DEVILS

Scott Taylor

TACKLES
Scott Taylor 822
Harrison Hansen 796
Adrian Morley 591
George Griffin 528
Tommy Lee 513

OFFLOADS
Greg Johnson 37
Rangi Chase 22
Cory Paterson 21
Weller Hauraki 20
Junior Sa'u 17

CLEAN BREAKS
Niall Evalds 21
Ben Jones-Bishop 19
Rangi Chase 13
Josh Griffin 12
Greg Johnson 10

TRY ASSISTS
Rangi Chase 16
Michael Dobson................16
Theo Fages 9
Tommy Lee 9
Junior Sa'u 6

MARKER TACKLES
Scott Taylor 138
Harrison Hansen 119
Jordan Walne..................108
George Griffin 97
Adrian Morley 90

METRES
Scott Taylor 2867
Niall Evalds 2417
Ben Jones-Bishop 2262
Josh Griffin 2154
Greg Johnson 2134

CARRIES
Scott Taylor 375
Ben Jones-Bishop 315
Harrison Hansen 309
Niall Evalds 290
Greg Johnson 286

TACKLE BUSTS
Greg Johnson 69
Rangi Chase 67
Niall Evalds 57
Scott Taylor 54
Josh Griffin 51

TOTAL OPTA INDEX
Scott Taylor 14414
Harrison Hansen 11031
Niall Evalds 10469
Rangi Chase 9854
Ben Jones-Bishop 9233

Harrison Hansen

ST HELENS

James Roby

TACKLES
James Roby..................1041
Louie McCarthy-Scarsbrook..708
Kyle Amor 652
Alex Walmsley 603
Jon Wilkin 603

OFFLOADS
Alex Walmsley 52
Louie McCarthy-Scarsbrook....34
James Roby......................26
Travis Burns......................24
Josh Jones 24

CLEAN BREAKS
Adam Swift 24
Jordan Turner 21
Tom Makinson..................13
Mark Percival....................13
James Roby......................13

TRY ASSISTS
Luke Walsh 15
Travis Burns......................13
Jon Wilkin 12
Jordan Turner 10
Mark Percival......................9

MARKER TACKLES
James Roby....................171
Kyle Amor 134
Louie McCarthy-Scarsbrook..134
Alex Walmsley 115
Jon Wilkin 106

METRES
Alex Walmsley 4092
Adam Swift 3333
Kyle Amor 2550
Louie McCarthy-Scarsbrook 2536
James Roby..................2469

CARRIES
Alex Walmsley 531
Louie McCarthy-Scarsbrook..369
Adam Swift 369
Kyle Amor 360
James Roby....................357

TACKLE BUSTS
Alex Walmsley 119
Adam Swift 93
Mark Percival....................53
Mose Masoe 52
Josh Jones 50

TOTAL OPTA INDEX
James Roby................16792
Alex Walmsley 15506
Adam Swift 12516
Louie McCarthy-Scarsbrook..11891
Kyle Amor 10234

Alex Walmsley

WAKEFIELD T WILDCATS

Jacob Miller

TACKLES

Danny Washbrook	863
Nick Scruton	728
Paul McShane	593
Mickael Simon	495
Daniel Smith	463

OFFLOADS

Ali Lauitiiti	30
Mickael Simon	28
Danny Washbrook	24
Nick Scruton	20
Daniel Smith	18

CLEAN BREAKS

Tom Johnstone	20
Jacob Miller	20
Craig Hall	11
Reece Lyne	10
Danny Washbrook	9

TRY ASSISTS

Tim Smith	17
Jacob Miller	7
Pita Godinet	7
Reece Lyne	5
Ali Lauitiiti	5

MARKER TACKLES

Nick Scruton	145
Danny Kirmond	141
Danny Washbrook	138
Paul McShane	124
Mickael Simon	94

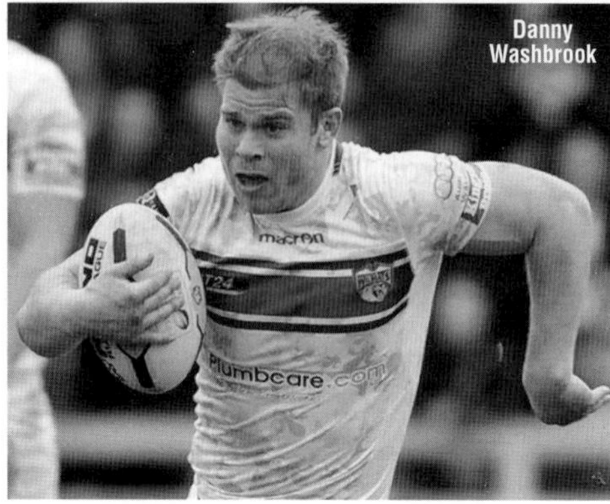
Danny Washbrook

METRES

Nick Scruton	2143
Danny Washbrook	1913
Chris Riley	1908
Mickael Simon	1860
Reece Lyne	1777

CARRIES

Nick Scruton	320
Danny Washbrook	291
Mickael Simon	285
Jacob Miller	277
Chris Riley	257

TACKLE BUSTS

Jacob Miller	75
Chris Riley	47
Danny Washbrook	46
Tom Johnstone	41
Reece Lyne	40

TOTAL OPTA INDEX

Danny Washbrook	13588
Jacob Miller	10733
Nick Scruton	10459
Mickael Simon	8806
Tim Smith	8184

WARRINGTON WOLVES

Stefan Ratchford

TACKLES

Chris Hill	976
Ben Westwood	829
Ashton Sims	783
Daryl Clark	779
Ben Currie	737

OFFLOADS

Ashton Sims	41
Ben Westwood	31
Chris Hill	30
Stefan Ratchford	30
Ben Harrison	29

CLEAN BREAKS

Kevin Penny	16
Stefan Ratchford	15
Richard Myler	13
Gene Ormsby	13
Joel Monaghan	12

TRY ASSISTS

Stefan Ratchford	20
Ben Currie	12
Richard Myler	8
Gareth O'Brien	8
Ben Westwood	5

MARKER TACKLES

Ben Harrison	177
Chris Hill	159
Ben Westwood	148
Ashton Sims	147
Ben Currie	119

Chris Hill

METRES

Chris Hill	3706
Stefan Ratchford	3035
Ben Westwood	2854
Ashton Sims	2617
Daryl Clark	2504

CARRIES

Chris Hill	491
Ben Westwood	416
Ashton Sims	408
Stefan Ratchford	381
Ben Currie	304

TACKLE BUSTS

Stefan Ratchford	87
Daryl Clark	74
Ryan Atkins	58
Ben Westwood	55
Ben Currie	52

TOTAL OPTA INDEX

Chris Hill	17022
Stefan Ratchford	14594
Ben Currie	14270
Ben Westwood	13713
Daryl Clark	12344

WIDNES VIKINGS

TACKLES
Alex Gerrard 953
Aaron Heremaia..............715
Danny Galea 701
Chris Clarkson 680
Lloyd White 612

OFFLOADS
Rhys Hanbury 39
Gil Dudson........................25
Cameron Phelps 20
Hep Cahill 17
Manase Manuokafoa 17

CLEAN BREAKS
Rhys Hanbury 23
Patrick Ah Van..................21
Kevin Brown 18
Jack Owens 18
Joe Mellor 14

TRY ASSISTS
Kevin Brown 29
Rhys Hanbury 23
Aaron Heremaia................14
Joe Mellor 10
Tom Gilmore 7

MARKER TACKLES
Alex Gerrard 195
Chris Clarkson 140
Aaron Heremaia..............129
Chris Dean......................128
Danny Galea 119

METRES
Rhys Hanbury 4000
Manase Manuokafoa 2495
Patrick Ah Van..............2246
Alex Gerrard 2013
Aaron Heremaia............1838

CARRIES
Rhys Hanbury 503
Aaron Heremaia..............315
Manase Manuokafoa 312
Kevin Brown 299
Alex Gerrard 295

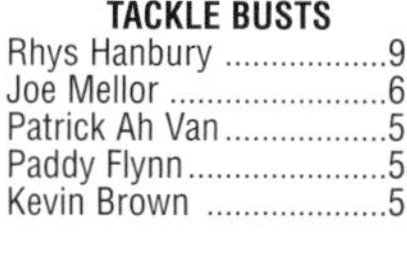

TACKLE BUSTS
Rhys Hanbury 95
Joe Mellor 67
Patrick Ah Van..................57
Paddy Flynn......................53
Kevin Brown 50

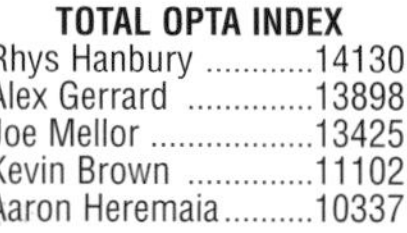

TOTAL OPTA INDEX
Rhys Hanbury 14130
Alex Gerrard 13898
Joe Mellor 13425
Kevin Brown 11102
Aaron Heremaia..........10337

WIGAN WARRIORS

TACKLES
John Bateman 794
Liam Farrell 769
Joel Tomkins 723
Michael McIlorum 688
Lee Mossop....................553

OFFLOADS
Anthony Gelling 54
Joel Tomkins 54
John Bateman 41
George Williams 35
Taulima Tautai 25

CLEAN BREAKS
Joe Burgess......................28
Dominic Manfredi 22
George Williams 19
Matt Bowen 19
Joel Tomkins 15

TRY ASSISTS
George Williams 21
Matty Smith 14
Joe Burgess......................13
Anthony Gelling 11
Joel Tomkins 10

MARKER TACKLES
John Bateman 160
Joel Tomkins 150
Liam Farrell 140
Lee Mossop....................114
Michael McIlorum 88

METRES
Joe Burgess..................2723
John Bateman 2686
Liam Farrell 2611
Joel Tomkins 2384
Anthony Gelling 2333

CARRIES
John Bateman 385
Joel Tomkins 370
Liam Farrell 357
Dan Sarginson................342
Anthony Gelling 318

TACKLE BUSTS
Dominic Manfredi 107
John Bateman 88
Matt Bowen 82
George Williams 78
Joe Burgess......................68

TOTAL OPTA INDEX
John Bateman 17210
Liam Farrell 16468
Joel Tomkins 13886
George Williams 13754
Joe Burgess................12035

CHAMPIONSHIP 2015
Club by Club

BATLEY BULLDOGS

DATE	FIXTURE	RESULT	SCORERS	LGE	ATT
15/2/15	Workington (h)	W30-6	t:Squires(4),Bretherton g:Leatherbarrow(5)	2nd	801
22/2/15	Hunslet (a)	W14-26	t:Craven,Squires,Nicholson,Ainscough,Reittie g:Leatherbarrow(3)	1st	901
1/3/15	Halifax (h)	L2-6	g:Leatherbarrow	4th	1,113
8/3/15	Sheffield (a) ●	L28-16	t:Reittie,Leak,J Brown g:Leatherbarrow(2)	5th	1,358
15/3/15	Bradford (h)	L19-26	t:Squires,Chandler,Hirst g:Southernwood(3) fg:Southernwood	6th	3,019
21/3/15	Normanton (a) (CCR4) ●●	W6-78	t:Thackray,Reittie,Day,Southernwood,Nicholson(2),Lillycrop,Fozard(3),Hey, Campbell(2),Hirst g:Southernwood(11)	N/A	868
29/3/15	Doncaster (a)	W14-16	t:J Brown,Reittie,Southernwood g:Southernwood(2)	6th	1,277
3/4/15	Dewsbury (h)	L6-21	t:Reittie g:Southernwood	8th	1,274
6/4/15	London Broncos (a)	L25-18	t:Hesketh(2),Reittie g:Southernwood(3)	8th	638
12/4/15	Featherstone (h)	L16-23	t:Fozard,Scott,Ainscough g:Southernwood(2)	8th	916
19/4/15	Swinton (h) (CCR5)	W46-14	t:Reittie,Day,Southernwood,Ainscough(2),Morgan,Thackray(2),Leak g:Southernwood(5)	N/A	443
26/4/15	Leigh (a)	L56-8	t:Ainscough,Fozard	9th	3,036
3/5/15	Whitehaven (h)	L22-24	t:Craven(2),Leatherbarrow,Mitchell g:Leatherbarrow(3)	9th	560
10/5/15	Workington (a)	W10-23	t:Reittie,Leak,Craven g:Leatherbarrow(5) fg:Leatherbarrow	8th	596
17/5/15	Widnes (a) (CCR6)	L26-22	t:Rowe,Reittie(2),Fozard g:Leatherbarrow(3)	N/A	3,866
24/5/15	Dewsbury (SB) ●●●	L12-19	t:Day,A Brown g:Leatherbarrow(2)	9th	N/A
31/5/15	Featherstone (a)	L44-16	t:Ainscough,Leak,Mitchell g:Leatherbarrow(2)	9th	2,067
5/6/15	Sheffield (h)	L12-40	t:Mitchell,Ainscough g:Leatherbarrow(2)	10th	525
10/6/15	London Broncos (h)	L22-28	t:Blake,A Brown,Hesketh,Craven g:Leatherbarrow(3)	10th	341
14/6/15	Leigh (h)	L12-26	t:Reittie,Leak g:Leatherbarrow(2)	10th	1,125
21/6/15	Whitehaven (a)	L24-12	t:Ainscough,Chandler g:Leatherbarrow(2)	11th	802
28/6/15	Bradford (a)	L34-16	t:A Brown,Reittie,Rowe g:Leatherbarrow(2)	11th	5,089
5/7/15	Doncaster (h)	W34-6	t:A Brown,Squires(2),Lillycrop,Reittie(2),Southernwood g:Leatherbarrow(3)	9th	537
12/7/15	Halifax (a)	L25-22	t:Day,Reittie(2),Hirst g:Leatherbarrow(3)	10th	1,955
19/7/15	Hunslet (h)	W45-28	t:A Brown(2),Blake,Hesketh,Lillycrop,Day,Squires,Chandler g:Leatherbarrow(6) fg:Leatherbarrow	9th	483
26/7/15	Dewsbury (a)	W12-16	t:A Brown,Ulugia g:Leatherbarrow(4)	9th	1,319
9/8/15	Workington (a) (CS)	L30-12	t:Ulugia,Hesketh g:Leatherbarrow(2)	5th(CS)	864
16/8/15	Dewsbury (h) (CS)	L22-28	t:Ainscough,Blake,A Brown,Scott g:Leatherbarrow(3)	6th(CS)	1,046
23/8/15	Doncaster (a) (CS)	W20-38	t:Cosgrove,Reittie(2),Southernwood,Ainscough(2),Squires g:Leatherbarrow(5)	6th(CS)	735
31/8/15	Featherstone (a) (CS)	L28-26	t:Ainscough(2),Nicholson,Scott g:Leatherbarrow(5)	6th(CS)	1,506
6/9/15	Whitehaven (h) (CS)	W50-0	t:A Brown(3),Day,Squires,Blake,J Brown(2),Hirst,Ainscough g:Leatherbarrow(5)	5th(CS)	499
13/9/15	London Broncos (a) (CS)	L50-16	t:Hesketh,Day,A Brown g:Leatherbarrow(2)	5th(CS)	485
20/9/15	Hunslet (h) (CS)	W60-12	t:Leatherbarrow,Southernwood,Ainscough(2),A Brown(2),Reittie,Squires, Gledhill,Nicholson,Craven g:Leatherbarrow(7),Bretherton	5th(CS)	737

● Played at Keepmoat Stadium, Doncaster ●● Played at Belle Vue, Wakefield ●●● Played at Bloomfield Road, Blackpool

		APP		TRIES		GOALS		FG		PTS	
	D.O.B.	ALL	Ch	ALL	Ch	ALL	Ch	ALL	Ch	ALL	Ch
Shaun Ainscough	27/11/89	29(1)	20(1)	16	6	0	0	0	0	64	24
Luke Blake	10/8/89	24(3)	15(3)	4	2	0	0	0	0	16	8
Alex Bretherton	5/12/82	17(5)	14(1)	1	1	1	0	0	0	6	4
Alex Brown	28/8/87	14(1)	9	14	7	0	0	0	0	56	28
James Brown	6/5/88	15(16)	7(14)	4	2	0	0	0	0	16	8
Johnny Campbell	17/7/87	15	12	2	0	0	0	0	0	8	0
Joe Chandler	2/11/88	21(4)	19(3)	3	3	0	0	0	0	12	12
Elliott Cosgrove	31/3/91	9	4	1	0	0	0	0	0	4	0
James Craven	14/10/88	14(1)	8(1)	6	5	0	0	0	0	24	20
Brad Day	23/9/94	21	13	7	3	0	0	0	0	28	12
Ayden Faal	12/12/86	3	2	0	0	0	0	0	0	0	0
Matty Fozard	3/3/95	2(9)	2(6)	6	2	0	0	0	0	24	8
Adam Gledhill	15/2/93	8(12)	4(8)	1	0	0	0	0	0	4	0
Jordan Grayston	14/9/91	5	5	0	0	0	0	0	0	0	0
Sean Hesketh	17/8/86	6(18)	3(13)	6	4	0	0	0	0	24	16
Brad Hey	4/9/94	5	3	1	0	0	0	0	0	4	0
Keegan Hirst	13/12/88	25(3)	16(3)	4	2	0	0	0	0	16	8
Alistair Leak	5/4/92	15(8)	12(5)	5	4	0	0	0	0	20	16
Scott Leatherbarrow	3/9/90	25	17	2	1	82	50	2	2	174	106
Tom Lillycrop	29/11/91	4(21)	4(13)	3	2	0	0	0	0	12	8
Lee Mitchell	8/9/88	12(3)	12(3)	3	3	0	0	0	0	12	12
Jacob Morgan	3/12/93	2	1	1	0	0	0	0	0	4	0
Anthony Nicholson	28/11/90	7(13)	5(9)	5	1	0	0	0	0	20	4
Wayne Reittie	21/1/88	30	22	19	12	0	0	0	0	76	48
Alex Rowe	11/3/85	23(6)	18(3)	2	1	0	0	0	0	8	4
Sam Scott	5/6/90	25(2)	16(1)	3	1	0	0	0	0	12	4
Cain Southernwood	4/5/92	22(1)	14(1)	6	2	27	11	1	1	79	31
Shaun Squires	20/3/90	26(1)	19(1)	12	9	0	0	0	0	48	36
Tom Thackray	19/2/93	2(4)	1(3)	3	0	0	0	0	0	12	0
Chris Ulugia	15/1/92	3	2	2	1	0	0	0	0	8	4

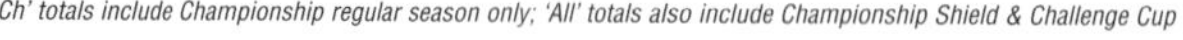

'Ch' totals include Championship regular season only; 'All' totals also include Championship Shield & Challenge Cup

Wayne Reittie

LEAGUE RECORD
Championship, before Super 8 split:
P23-W7-D0-L16 (9th)
F421, A539, Diff-118, 14 points.

After Championship Shield:
P30-W10-D0-L20 (5th)
F645, A707, Diff-62, 20 points.

CHALLENGE CUP
Round Six

ATTENDANCES
Best - v Bradford (Ch - 3,019)
Worst - v London Broncos (Ch - 341)
Total (Championship/ Championship Shield only) - 12,976
Average (Championship/ Championship Shield only) - 927
(Up by 176 on 2014)

CLUB RECORDS **Highest score:** 100-4 v Gateshead, 17/3/2010 **Highest score against:** 9-78 v Wakefield, 26/8/67 **Record attendance:** 23,989 v Leeds, 14/3/25

MATCH RECORDS **Tries:** 5 Joe Oakland v Bramley, 19/12/1908; Tommy Brannan v Swinton, 17/1/20; Jim Wale v Bramley, 4/12/26; Jim Wale v Cottingham, 12/2/27; Tommy Oldroyd v Highfield, 6/3/94; Ben Feehan v Halifax, 10/8/2008; Jermaine McGillvary v Whitehaven, 24/5/2009 **Goals:** 16 Gareth Moore v Gateshead, 17/3/2010 **Points:** 40 Gareth Moore v Gateshead, 17/3/2010

SEASON RECORDS **Tries:** 30 Johnny Campbell 2010 **Goals:** 144 Barry Eaton 2004 **Points:** 308 Richard Price 1997

CAREER RECORDS **Tries:** 142 Craig Lingard 1998-2008 **Goals:** 463 Wharton 'Wattie' Davies 1897-1912 **Points:** 1,297 Wharton 'Wattie' Davies 1897-1912 **Appearances:** 421 Wharton 'Wattie' Davies 1897-1912

BRADFORD BULLS

DATE	FIXTURE	RESULT	SCORERS	LGE	ATT
15/2/15	Leigh (a)	L36-24	t:O'Brien(2),Walker,Mullaney,Uaisele g:Siejka(2)	9th	7,449
22/2/15	Whitehaven (h)	W34-4	t:Purtell,Pitts,Gaskell(3),Sidlow g:Siejka(2),Gaskell(3)	5th	4,891
1/3/15	Featherstone (a)	W4-40	t:Gaskell(2),Purtell,Ulugia(2),O'Brien,Baile g:Shaw(6)	2nd	6,346
8/3/15	Hunslet (h)	W56-6	t:Mullaney(2),Gaskell,O'Brien(2),Shaw(3),Williams,Olbison g:Shaw(8)	2nd	5,119
15/3/15	Batley (a)	W19-26	t:Shaw,Mullaney,Williams,Ulugia g:Shaw(5)	2nd	3,019
22/3/15	Workington (h) (CCR4)	W74-6	t:Purtell(3),Tahraoui(2),Sidlow,Henry,Gaskell,Shaw(2),Williams,Pitts,Siejka g:Shaw(11)	N/A	2,412
29/3/15	Workington (h)	W36-6	t:Pitts,Mullaney,Williams(2),Henry(2),Gaskell g:Shaw(4)	2nd	4,238
3/4/15	Halifax (h)	W32-19	t:Williams,Pitts,Gaskell,Henry,Shaw g:Shaw(6)	2nd	6,134
6/4/15	Dewsbury (a)	W16-30	t:Pitts,Uaisele,Gaskell,Shaw,Addy(2) g:Shaw(3)	2nd	4,068
12/4/15	London Broncos (h)	W28-2	t:Pitts,O'Brien,Gaskell,Ulugia,Uaisele g:Shaw(4)	2nd	4,023
19/4/15	Hull KR (h) (CCR5)	L30-50	t:O'Brien,Ferguson,Addy,Gaskell,Walshaw g:Shaw(5)	N/A	4,538
26/4/15	Doncaster (a)	W38-56	t:Uaisele(2),Gaskell(3),Ferguson(2),Henry,Clough,Shaw g:Shaw(8)	2nd	2,276
3/5/15	Sheffield (h)	W46-12	t:Ferguson(2),Olbison,Uaisele,Williams,Sidlow,Henry,Purtell g:Addy(7)	2nd	4,487
10/5/15	Whitehaven (a)	W16-32	t:Purtell(2),Gaskell,Addy,Williams(2) g:Shaw(4)	2nd	1,338
23/5/15	Halifax (SB) ●	W18-4	t:Shaw,Purtell(2) g:Shaw(2),Addy	2nd	N/A
31/5/15	London Broncos (a)	W18-36	t:Shaw,Williams,Henry,Uaisele,Sidlow,O'Brien g:Shaw(6)	2nd	1,101
7/6/15	Doncaster (h)	W72-6	t:Sidlow,Addy,Shaw,Williams(4),Mendeika(2),Uaisele,Henry,Crossley(2),Gaskell g:Shaw,Addy(7)	2nd	4,982
14/6/15	Dewsbury (h)	W22-18	t:Henry,Purtell(2),Addy g:Shaw(3)	2nd	3,998
21/6/15	Workington (a)	W16-38	t:Henry(2),Sidlow,Mullaney(2),Lauaki,Williams g:Shaw(5)	2nd	1,063
28/6/15	Batley (h)	W34-16	t:Pitts,Mendeika,Henry(2),Williams,Blythe(2) g:Shaw(3)	1st	5,089
1/7/15	Featherstone (h)	L18-37	t:Mendeika(2),Walker g:Shaw(3)	1st	5,044
5/7/15	Hunslet (a)	W6-68	t:O'Brien,Mullaney(4),Blythe,Mendeika,Shaw,Williams(3),Uaisele,Ferguson g:Shaw(8)	1st	1,676
12/7/15	Sheffield (a) ●●	L32-30	t:Mullaney(3),Shaw,Pitts g:Shaw(5)	2nd	2,153
19/7/15	Leigh (h)	D36-36	t:Pitts,Caro(3),Addy,Blythe g:Shaw(6)	2nd	9,181
26/7/15	Halifax (a)	L20-16	t:Pitts,Henry,Caro g:Shaw(2)	2nd	4,589
9/8/15	Sheffield (h) (S8-Q)	W42-10	t:Williams(2),Gaskell(3),Pitts,Henry,Clare g:Addy(5)	1st(S8-Q)	6,032
15/8/15	Wakefield (a) (S8-Q)	L48-18	t:Purtell,Ferguson,Clare g:Addy(3)	5th(S8-Q)	3,985
23/8/15	Salford (h) (S8-Q)	W41-10	t:Ferguson,Williams,Mullaney(2),Addy,Clare,Purtell g:Addy(6) fg:Mullaney	3rd(S8-Q)	6,593
6/9/15	Widnes (h) (S8-Q)	L12-56	t:Purtell,Caro g:Addy(2)	5th(S8-Q)	6,881
12/9/15	Hull KR (a) (S8-Q)	L48-4	t:Mendeika	5th(S8-Q)	6,605
19/9/15	Leigh (a) (S8-Q)	W16-32	t:Mullaney,Williams(2),Blythe(2) g:Addy(6)	5th(S8-Q)	4,621
26/9/15	Halifax (h) (S8-Q)	L18-52	t:Ryan,Shaw(2) g:Shaw(3)	5th(S8-Q)	5,163
3/10/15	Wakefield (a) (MPG)	L24-16	t:Williams,Blythe,Purtell g:Addy(2)	N/A	7,236

● Played at Bloomfield Road, Blackpool ●● Played at Keepmoat Stadium, Doncaster

		APP		TRIES		GOALS		FG		PTS	
	D.O.B.	ALL	Ch	ALL	Ch	ALL	Ch	ALL	Ch	ALL	Ch
Danny Addy	15/1/91	27	19	8	6	39	15	0	0	110	54
Jean-Philippe Baile	7/6/87	4(9)	4(6)	1	1	0	0	0	0	4	4
Matty Blythe	20/11/88	9(6)	5(3)	7	4	0	0	0	0	28	16
Omari Caro	7/3/91	7(1)	2(1)	5	4	0	0	0	0	20	16
James Clare	13/4/91	7	1	3	0	0	0	0	0	12	0
Paul Clough	27/9/87	32	22	1	1	0	0	0	0	4	4
Nathan Conroy	6/3/95	(1)	(1)	0	0	0	0	0	0	0	0
Steve Crossley	28/11/89	1(19)	1(11)	2	2	0	0	0	0	8	8
Dale Ferguson	13/4/88	13(10)	7(7)	8	5	0	0	0	0	32	20
Daniel Fleming	8/7/92	(16)	(14)	0	0	0	0	0	0	0	0
Lee Gaskell	28/10/90	20(1)	15	20	15	3	3	0	0	86	66
Vila Halafihi	24/1/94	2(4)	1(4)	0	0	0	0	0	0	0	0
Adam Henry	2/9/91	23	19	15	13	0	0	0	0	60	52
Epalahame Lauaki	27/1/84	2(22)	1(14)	1	1	0	0	0	0	4	4
Alex Mellor	24/9/94	7(8)	6(5)	0	0	0	0	0	0	0	0
James Mendeika	16/12/91	8(5)	6(5)	7	6	0	0	0	0	28	24
Jake Mullaney	28/5/90	17	11	17	14	0	0	1	0	69	56
Dane Nielsen	10/6/85	5	0	0	0	0	0	0	0	0	0
Adam O'Brien	11/7/93	31(1)	22(1)	9	8	0	0	0	0	36	32
Tom Olbison	20/3/91	28(2)	19(2)	2	2	0	0	0	0	8	8
Jay Pitts	9/12/89	31(2)	22(1)	11	9	0	0	0	0	44	36
Adrian Purtell	31/1/85	26	18	16	9	0	0	0	0	64	36
Matt Ryan	13/6/88	2(3)	0	1	0	0	0	0	0	4	0
Ryan Shaw	27/2/92	22(3)	19(3)	16	12	111	92	0	0	286	232
Adam Sidlow	25/10/87	30	21	6	5	0	0	0	0	24	20
Harry Siejka	3/2/92	13(2)	9	1	0	4	4	0	0	12	8
Samir Tahraoui	28/12/90	1(7)	1(6)	2	0	0	0	0	0	8	0
Etuate Uaisele	8/12/84	15(1)	14	9	9	0	0	0	0	36	36
Chris Ulugia	15/1/92	5(1)	4(1)	4	4	0	0	0	0	16	16
Chev Walker	9/10/82	9(3)	7(3)	2	2	0	0	0	0	8	8
Lucas Walshaw	4/8/92	6(5)	5(4)	1	0	0	0	0	0	4	0
Danny Williams	26/9/86	26	18	25	18	0	0	0	0	100	72

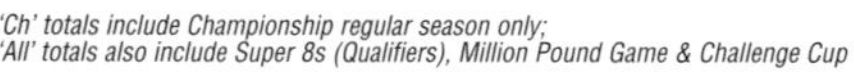
'Ch' totals include Championship regular season only;
'All' totals also include Super 8s (Qualifiers), Million Pound Game & Challenge Cup

Danny Williams

LEAGUE RECORD
Championship, before Super 8 split:
P23-W18-D1-L4 (2nd)
F828, A387, Diff+441, 37 points.

S8-Q: P7-W3-D0-L4 (5th)
F167, A240, Diff-73, 6 points.
(Losers, Million Pound Game)

CHALLENGE CUP
Round Five

ATTENDANCES
Best - v Leigh (Ch - 9,181)
Worst - v Workington (CC - 2,412)
Total (Championship/S8s only) - 81,855
Average (Championship/S8s only) - 5,457
(Down by 1,196 on 2014, SL)

CLUB RECORDS **Highest score:** 98-6 v Toulouse, 19/4/2008 **Highest score against:** 6-84 v Wigan, 21/4/2014 **Record attendance:** 69,429 v Huddersfield, 14/3/53

MATCH RECORDS **Tries:** 6 Eric Batten v Leeds, 15/9/45; Trevor Foster v Wakefield, 10/4/48; Steve McGowan v Barrow, 8/11/92; Lesley Vainikolo v Hull, 2/9/2005 **Goals:** 15 Iestyn Harris v Toulouse, 15/4/2008 **Points:** 36 John Woods v Swinton, 13/10/85

SEASON RECORDS **Tries:** 63 Jack McLean 1951-52 **Goals:** 213 *(inc 5fg)* Henry Paul 2001 **Points:** 457 Henry Paul 2001

CAREER RECORDS **Tries:** 261 Jack McLean 1950-56 **Goals:** 1,165 *(inc 25fg)* Paul Deacon 1998-2009 **Points:** 2,605 Paul Deacon 1998-2009 **Appearances:** 588 Keith Mumby 1973-90; 1992-93

DEWSBURY RAMS

DATE	FIXTURE	RESULT	SCORERS	LGE	ATT
13/2/15	Sheffield (h)	W19-10	t:Grant(2),Thackeray g:Hemingway(3) fg:Thackeray	5th	1,309
1/3/15	Hunslet (a)	L18-6	t:Hepworth g:Hemingway	8th	983
8/3/15	Whitehaven (h)	W23-16	t:Grant,Thackeray,Spicer,L Adamson g:Hemingway(3) fg:Thackeray	7th	911
15/3/15	Halifax (a)	L26-13	t:Pryce,Thackeray g:Hyde(2) fg:Hyde	7th	1,734
18/3/15	Workington (a)	W18-31	t:Morton,L Adamson(2),Wildie,T Adamson g:Hyde(4),Hemingway fg:Hemingway	5th	761
22/3/15	Newcastle (h) (CCR4)	W28-18	t:Hemingway,Grant,Brown,Hale(2) g:Hemingway(4)	N/A	703
27/3/15	Featherstone (h)	L28-38	t:Hale,Thackeray,Grant,Hemingway g:Hyde(5),Hemingway	7th	1,798
3/4/15	Batley (a)	W6-21	t:Grady(2),Farrell,Wildie g:Morton,Hemingway fg:Thackeray	4th	1,274
6/4/15	Bradford (h)	L16-30	t:Morton,Smith,Crookes g:Morton(2)	6th	4,068
12/4/15	Doncaster (a)	W12-24	t:Farrell,Morton,Brown,Hale,Crookes g:Hemingway(2)	5th	1,100
19/4/15	Hunslet (a) (CCR5)	W16-31	t:Haggarty,J Delaney,Crookes,Aizue,Brown g:Hyde(5) fg:Hyde	N/A	536
26/4/15	London Broncos (a)	W16-20	t:Pryce,Beckett,Brown g:Hemingway,Hyde(3)	4th	663
3/5/15	Leigh (h)	L28-32	t:Spicer,Pryce,Grant(2),L Adamson g:Hyde,Seymour(3)	6th	1,551
10/5/15	Hunslet (h)	W40-4	t:L Adamson,Morton(3),Thackeray,T Adamson,Seymour g:Seymour(6)	5th	1,103
15/5/15	Warrington (h) (CCR6)	L10-52	t:Farrell g:B Delaney(3)	N/A	1,771
19/5/15	Sheffield (a) ●	L15-8	t:Thackeray g:Seymour(2)	6th	682
24/5/15	Batley (SB) ●●	W12-19	t:Hale,Brown,Grant g:Seymour(3) fg:Thackeray	4th	N/A
31/5/15	Doncaster (h)	W14-6	t:Hale,Morton,Crookes g:Seymour	4th	763
7/6/15	Workington (h)	D20-20	t:Grant,Brown,Farrell g:Seymour(4)	4th	751
14/6/15	Bradford (a)	L22-18	t:Thackeray,Pryce,Morton g:Seymour(2),Hyde	7th	3,998
21/6/15	Halifax (h)	L16-46	t:T Adamson,Thackeray,Crookes g:Hyde(2)	7th	1,242
5/7/15	Featherstone (a)	W30-32	t:T Adamson,Thackeray(2),Grady,Brown g:Seymour(6)	7th	2,009
12/7/15	London Broncos (h)	W24-12	t:Pryce(2),Conroy g:Seymour(6)	7th	910
19/7/15	Whitehaven (a)	W16-34	t:Morton(2),Conroy,Hale,T Adamson,Farrell g:Seymour(3),Morton(2)	6th	760
22/7/15	Leigh (a)	L40-24	t:Farrell(2),Morton,Fieldhouse g:B Delaney(4)	6th	3,244
26/7/15	Batley (h)	L12-16	t:Grant(2),Morton	6th	1,319
9/8/15	Hunslet (h) (CS)	W32-20	t:Morton,Grady(2),Hale,Fieldhouse,Grant g:B Delaney(4)	2nd(CS)	901
16/8/15	Batley (a) (CS)	W22-28	t:Grady,Uaisele,Grant,Thackeray,Farrell g:Morton(4)	2nd(CS)	1,046
23/8/15	Whitehaven (h) (CS)	L30-42	t:Grady(2),Farrell,Wildie,Pryce,Grant g:Morton(2),Grady	2nd(CS)	709
31/8/15	London Broncos (h) (CS)	W25-16	t:Conroy,Morton,Uaisele,Brown g:Grady(4) fg:Thackeray	2nd(CS)	805
6/9/15	Featherstone (a) (CS)	W16-34	t:Farrell(2),Crookes,Uaisele,Wildie,Thackeray g:Grady,Seymour(4)	2nd(CS)	1,271
13/9/15	Doncaster (a) (CS)	L33-20	t:Grant(3),Aizue g:Seymour(2)	2nd(CS)	725
20/9/15	Workington (h) (CS)	W27-14	t:Brown(2),Fieldhouse,Grant,Uaisele g:Hemingway,Morton(2) fg:Hemingway	2nd(CS)	804
27/9/15	London Broncos (h) (CSSF)	L18-34	t:Thackeray,Morton,Uaisele g:Hemingway,Grady(2)	N/A	940

● Played at Keepmoat Stadium, Doncaster ●● Played at Bloomfield Road, Blackpool

		APP		TRIES		GOALS		FG		PTS	
	D.O.B.	ALL	Ch	ALL	Ch	ALL	Ch	ALL	Ch	ALL	Ch
Luke Adamson	17/11/87	27	19	5	5	0	0	0	0	20	20
Toby Adamson	28/5/90	9(10)	8(10)	5	5	0	0	0	0	20	20
Makali Aizue	30/12/77	8(15)	2(12)	2	0	0	0	0	0	8	0
Callan Beckett	24/3/93	7(2)	4(2)	1	1	0	0	0	0	4	4
Aaron Brown	27/7/92	19(11)	14(8)	10	5	0	0	0	0	40	20
Nathan Conroy	6/3/95	6(10)	1(7)	3	2	0	0	0	0	12	8
Jason Crookes	21/4/90	21(3)	17(1)	6	4	0	0	0	0	24	16
Brad Delaney	25/5/95	3(1)	1(1)	0	0	11	4	0	0	22	8
James Delaney	4/5/92	1(2)	(1)	1	0	0	0	0	0	4	0
Sam Dunn	4/12/94	2	1	0	0	0	0	0	0	0	0
Joel Farrell	15/3/94	9(16)	3(11)	11	6	0	0	0	0	44	24
Ryan Fieldhouse	10/4/88	17	10	3	1	0	0	0	0	12	4
Will Forsyth	6/6/95	2	0	0	0	0	0	0	0	0	0
James Glover	2/12/93	1(3)	(1)	0	0	0	0	0	0	0	0
Wayne Godwin	13/3/82	(4)	(4)	0	0	0	0	0	0	0	0
Shane Grady	13/12/89	14	8	8	3	8	0	0	0	48	12
Dalton Grant	21/4/90	29	18	18	10	0	0	0	0	72	40
Matthew Haggarty	8/1/91	10(4)	7(4)	1	0	0	0	0	0	4	0
Scott Hale	14/12/91	26	20	8	5	0	0	0	0	32	20
Tom Hemingway	6/12/86	13	10	2	1	19	13	2	1	48	31
Ryan Hepworth	16/1/81	29(2)	21(1)	1	1	0	0	0	0	4	4
Kieran Hyde	10/10/89	10(1)	9(1)	0	0	23	18	2	1	48	37
Paul Jackson	29/9/78	14(12)	11(6)	0	0	0	0	0	0	0	0
Joe McLocklan	2/10/86	(2)	0	0	0	0	0	0	0	0	0
Dale Morton	31/10/90	31	22	15	12	13	5	0	0	86	58
Jason Muranka	4/8/89	(4)	(3)	0	0	0	0	0	0	0	0
Stephen Nash	14/1/86	4(9)	4(1)	0	0	0	0	0	0	0	0
Karl Pryce	27/7/86	22	16	7	6	0	0	0	0	28	24
Greg Scott	21/6/91	4	3	0	0	0	0	0	0	0	0
Brett Seymour	27/9/84	11(2)	11	1	1	42	36	0	0	88	76
Byron Smith	5/3/84	3(16)	1(13)	1	1	0	0	0	0	4	4
Rob Spicer	22/9/84	23(1)	16	2	2	0	0	0	0	8	8
Anthony Thackeray	19/2/86	31	22	13	10	0	0	5	4	57	44
Etuate Uaisele	8/12/84	6	0	5	0	0	0	0	0	20	0
Lucas Walshaw	4/8/92	2	2	0	0	0	0	0	0	0	0
Matty Wildie	25/10/90	27(4)	18(4)	4	2	0	0	0	0	16	8
Sam Wood	23/12/93	(1)	(1)	0	0	0	0	0	0	0	0
Ryan Wright	28/10/91	1(1)	0	0	0	0	0	0	0	0	0

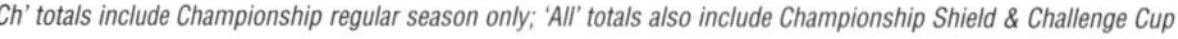

'Ch' totals include Championship regular season only; 'All' totals also include Championship Shield & Challenge Cup

Dalton Grant

LEAGUE RECORD
Championship, before Super 8 split:
P23-W12-D1-L10 (6th)
F490, A461, Diff+29, 25 points.

After Championship Shield:
P30-W17-D1-L12 (2nd/Semi-Finalists)
F686, A624, Diff+62, 35 points.

CHALLENGE CUP
Round Six

ATTENDANCES
Best - v Bradford (Ch - 4,068)
Worst - v Newcastle (CC - 703)
Total (Championship/ Championship Shield only) - 19,884
Average (Championship/ Championship Shield only) - 1,243
(Up by 216 on 2014)

CLUB RECORDS
Highest score: 90-5 v Blackpool, 4/4/93 **Highest score against:** 0-82 v Widnes, 30/11/86
Record attendance: 26,584 v Halifax, 30/10/20 *(Crown Flatt)*; 4,068 v Bradford, 6/4/2015 *(Tetley's Stadium)*

MATCH RECORDS
Tries: 8 Dai Thomas v Liverpool, 13/4/1907
Goals: 13 Greg Pearce v Blackpool Borough, 4/4/93; Francis Maloney v Hunslet, 25/3/2007 **Points:** 32 Les Holliday v Barrow, 11/9/94

SEASON RECORDS
Tries: 40 Dai Thomas 1906-07 **Goals:** 169 Barry Eaton 2000 **Points:** 394 Barry Eaton 2000

CAREER RECORDS
Tries: 144 Joe Lyman 1913-31 **Goals:** 863 Nigel Stephenson 1967-78; 1984-86 **Points:** 2,082 Nigel Stephenson 1967-78; 1984-86
Appearances: 454 Joe Lyman 1913-31

DONCASTER

DATE	FIXTURE	RESULT	SCORERS	LGE	ATT
15/2/15	London Broncos (a)	L26-22	t:Palea'aesina,Doherty(2),Waterman g:Sanderson(3)	7th	976
22/2/15	Featherstone (h)	L6-13	t:Cowling g:Sanderson	9th	950
1/3/15	Workington (a)	L33-6	t:Dunn g:Scott	11th	741
8/3/15	Leigh (h)	L18-54	t:Emmett(2),Doherty g:Sanderson(3)	11th	1,602
15/3/15	Hunslet (a)	L32-12	t:Sanderson,Naughton g:Sanderson(2)	12th	498
22/3/15	North Wales (a) (CCR4)	L40-12	t:Walton(2) g:Scott(2)	N/A	416
29/3/15	Batley (h)	L14-16	t:Turgut,Clark g:Scott(3)	12th	1,277
1/4/15	Sheffield (h)	L4-26	t:Doherty	12th	1,030
6/4/15	Whitehaven (a)	L41-16	t:Nicklas,Fox,Reynolds g:Scott(2)	12th	718
12/4/15	Dewsbury (h)	L12-24	t:Doherty,Emmett g:Sanderson(2)	12th	1,100
26/4/15	Bradford (h)	L38-56	t:Fox(2),Clark,Snitch,Dunn,Groat,Kelly g:Scott(4),Reynolds	12th	2,276
3/5/15	Halifax (a)	L40-6	t:Dunn g:Scott	12th	1,284
8/5/15	Sheffield (a) ●	L30-12	t:Turgut,Hodson g:Scott(2)	12th	863
17/5/15	Workington (h)	L6-37	t:Scott g:Scott	12th	695
24/5/15	Hunslet (SB) ●●	L12-25	t:Wilkinson,Leaf,Hodson	12th	N/A
31/5/15	Dewsbury (a)	L14-6	t:Turgut g:Scott	12th	763
7/6/15	Bradford (a)	L72-6	t:Dunn g:Scott	12th	4,982
14/6/15	London Broncos (h) ●●●	L4-30	t:Welham	12th	530
19/6/15	Featherstone (a)	L54-14	t:Kesik(2),Fox g:Scott	12th	1,624
28/6/15	Whitehaven (h) ●●●	L18-50	t:Mennell,Turgut,Kesik g:Scott(3)	12th	1,000
5/7/15	Batley (a)	L34-6	t:Mennell g:Scott	12th	537
12/7/15	Hunslet (h)	W34-26	t:McLocklan,Fox,Clark,Snitch,Mennell,Groat g:Scott(5)	12th	1,231
19/7/15	Halifax (h)	L0-52		12th	1,506
26/7/15	Leigh (a)	L66-10	t:Fox,Welham g:Naughton	12th	3,311
8/8/15	London Broncos (a) (CS)	L52-12	t:Fox,Emmett g:Scott(2)	8th(CS)	350
16/8/15	Featherstone (h) (CS)	L16-28	t:Fox,Groat,Scott g:Scott(2)	8th(CS)	886
23/8/15	Batley (h) (CS)	L20-38	t:Welham,Waller,Musolino,Hodson g:Scott(2)	8th(CS)	735
31/8/15	Workington (a) (CS)	L62-0		8th(CS)	629
6/9/15	Hunslet (a) (CS)	L25-16	t:Hodson,Verlinden,Wilkinson g:Scott(2)	8th(CS)	599
13/9/15	Dewsbury (h) (CS)	W33-20	t:Welham,Groat,Wright,Fox(3) g:Hodson(4) fg:McLocklan	8th(CS)	725
19/9/15	Whitehaven (a) (CS)	L52-22	t:Doherty,Cowling,Foster,Carr g:McLocklan(3)	8th(CS)	589

● Played at Keepmoat Stadium ●● Played at Bloomfield Road, Blackpool ●●● Played at Castle Park

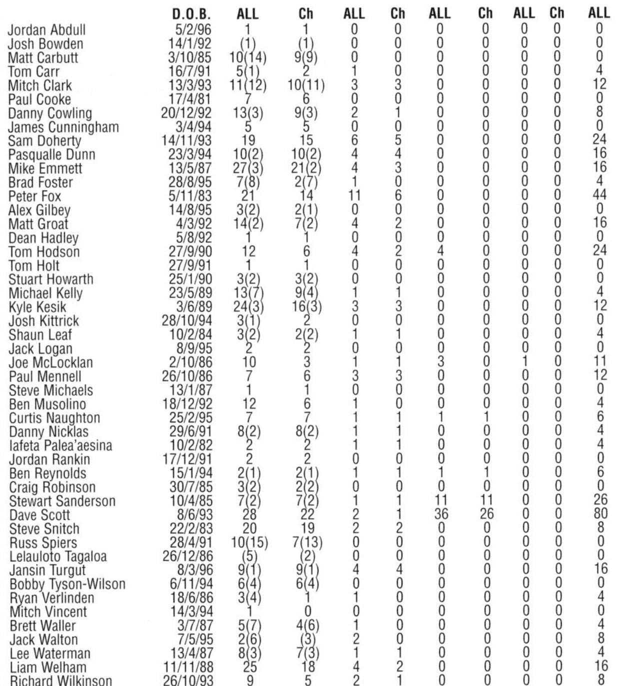

		APP		TRIES		GOALS		FG		PTS	
	D.O.B.	ALL	Ch	ALL	Ch	ALL	Ch	ALL	Ch	ALL	Ch
Jordan Abdull	5/2/96	1	1	0	0	0	0	0	0	0	0
Josh Bowden	14/1/92	(1)	(1)	0	0	0	0	0	0	0	0
Matt Carbutt	3/10/85	10(14)	9(9)	0	0	0	0	0	0	0	0
Tom Carr	16/7/91	5(1)	2	1	0	0	0	0	0	4	0
Mitch Clark	13/3/93	11(12)	10(11)	3	3	0	0	0	0	12	12
Paul Cooke	17/4/81	7	6	0	0	0	0	0	0	0	0
Danny Cowling	20/12/92	13(3)	9(3)	2	1	0	0	0	0	8	4
James Cunningham	3/4/94	5	5	0	0	0	0	0	0	0	0
Sam Doherty	14/11/93	19	15	6	5	0	0	0	0	24	20
Pasqualle Dunn	23/3/94	10(2)	10(2)	4	4	0	0	0	0	16	16
Mike Emmett	13/5/87	27(3)	21(2)	4	3	0	0	0	0	16	12
Brad Foster	28/8/95	7(8)	2(7)	1	0	0	0	0	0	4	0
Peter Fox	5/11/83	21	14	11	6	0	0	0	0	44	24
Alex Gilbey	14/8/95	3(2)	2(1)	0	0	0	0	0	0	0	0
Matt Groat	4/3/92	14(2)	7(2)	4	2	0	0	0	0	16	8
Dean Hadley	5/8/92	1	1	0	0	0	0	0	0	0	0
Tom Hodson	27/9/90	12	6	4	2	4	0	0	0	24	8
Tom Holt	27/9/91	1	1	0	0	0	0	0	0	0	0
Stuart Howarth	25/1/90	3(2)	3(2)	0	0	0	0	0	0	0	0
Michael Kelly	23/5/89	13(7)	9(4)	1	1	0	0	0	0	4	4
Kyle Kesik	3/6/89	24(3)	16(3)	3	3	0	0	0	0	12	12
Josh Kittrick	28/10/94	3(1)	2	0	0	0	0	0	0	0	0
Shaun Leaf	10/2/84	3(2)	2(2)	1	1	0	0	0	0	4	4
Jack Logan	8/9/95	2	2	0	0	0	0	0	0	0	0
Joe McLocklan	2/10/86	10	3	1	1	3	0	1	0	11	4
Paul Mennell	26/10/86	7	6	3	3	0	0	0	0	12	12
Steve Michaels	13/1/87	1	1	0	0	0	0	0	0	0	0
Ben Musolino	18/12/92	12	6	1	0	0	0	0	0	4	0
Curtis Naughton	25/2/95	7	7	1	1	1	1	0	0	6	6
Danny Nicklas	29/6/91	8(2)	8(2)	1	1	0	0	0	0	4	4
Iafeta Palea'aesina	10/2/82	2	2	1	1	0	0	0	0	4	4
Jordan Rankin	17/12/91	2	2	0	0	0	0	0	0	0	0
Ben Reynolds	15/1/94	2(1)	2(1)	1	1	1	1	0	0	6	6
Craig Robinson	30/7/85	3(2)	2(2)	0	0	0	0	0	0	0	0
Stewart Sanderson	10/4/85	7(2)	7(2)	1	1	11	11	0	0	26	26
Dave Scott	8/6/93	28	22	2	1	36	26	0	0	80	56
Steve Snitch	22/2/83	20	19	2	2	0	0	0	0	8	8
Russ Spiers	28/4/91	10(15)	7(13)	0	0	0	0	0	0	0	0
Lelauloto Tagaloa	26/12/86	(5)	(2)	0	0	0	0	0	0	0	0
Jansin Turgut	8/3/96	9(1)	9(1)	4	4	0	0	0	0	16	16
Bobby Tyson-Wilson	6/11/94	6(4)	6(4)	0	0	0	0	0	0	0	0
Ryan Verlinden	18/6/86	3(4)	1	1	0	0	0	0	0	4	0
Mitch Vincent	14/3/94	1	0	0	0	0	0	0	0	0	0
Brett Waller	3/7/87	5(7)	4(6)	1	0	0	0	0	0	4	0
Jack Walton	7/5/95	2(6)	(3)	2	0	0	0	0	0	8	0
Lee Waterman	13/4/87	8(3)	7(3)	1	1	0	0	0	0	4	4
Liam Welham	11/11/88	25	18	4	2	0	0	0	0	16	8
Richard Wilkinson	26/10/93	9	5	2	1	0	0	0	0	8	4
Ryan Wilson	21/12/93	(2)	(1)	0	0	0	0	0	0	0	0
Ryan Wright	28/10/91	1(7)	(3)	1	0	0	0	0	0	4	0

Sam Doherty

LEAGUE RECORD
Championship, before Super 8 split:
P23-W1-D0-L22 (12th)
F282, A851, Diff-569, 2 points.

After Championship Shield:
P30-W2-D0-L28 (8th)
F401, A1128, Diff-727, 4 points.

CHALLENGE CUP
Round Four

ATTENDANCES
Best - v Bradford (Ch - 2,276)
Worst - v London Broncos (Ch - 530)
Total (Championship/ Championship Shield only) - 15,543
Average (Championship/ Championship Shield only) - 1,110
(Up by 304 on 2014)

'Ch' totals include Championship regular season only; 'All' totals also include Championship Shield & Challenge Cup

CLUB RECORDS **Highest score:** 96-0 v Highfield, 20/3/94 **Highest score against:** 4-90 v Widnes, 10/6/2007
Record attendance: 10,000 v Bradford, 16/2/52 *(York Road)*; 6,528 v Castleford, 12/4/2007 *(Keepmoat Stadium)*

MATCH RECORDS **Tries:** 6 Kane Epati v Oldham, 30/7/2006; Lee Waterman v Sharlston, 24/3/2012
Goals: 12 Tony Zelei v Nottingham City, 1/9/91; Robert Turner v Highfield, 20/3/94
Points: 32 Tony Zelei v Nottingham City, 1/9/91; Lee Waterman v Sharlston, 24/3/2012

SEASON RECORDS **Tries:** 36 Lee Waterman 2012 **Goals:** 129 Jonny Woodcock 2002 **Points:** 306 Jonny Woodcock 2002

CAREER RECORDS **Tries:** 112 Mark Roache 1985-97 **Goals:** 850 David Noble 1976-77; 1980-89; 1992 **Points:** 1,751 David Noble 1976-77; 1980-89; 1992
Appearances: 327 Audley Pennant 1980-83; 1985-97

FEATHERSTONE ROVERS

DATE	FIXTURE	RESULT	SCORERS	LGE	ATT
16/2/15	Hunslet (h) ●	W28-14	t:Hardman,Bussey,Blackmore(2),Sykes g:Sykes(3),Marginet	3rd	1,836
22/2/15	Doncaster (a)	W6-13	t:Chappell,Ryan g:Sykes(2) fg:Marginet	3rd	950
1/3/15	Bradford (h)	L4-40	t:Lockwood	6th	6,346
8/3/15	Halifax (a)	W12-24	t:Sykes,Johnstone,Ellis,Arundel g:Sykes(4)	4th	2,187
15/3/15	Leigh (h)	L6-40	t:Chappell g:Sykes	5th	2,695
21/3/15	Whitehaven (a) (CCR4)	W12-36	t:Bostock,Sharp(2),Blackmore,Milner,James,Chappell g:Sykes(3),Marginet	N/A	525
27/3/15	Dewsbury (a)	W28-38	t:Bostock,Sharp,Sykes,Marginet(2),Milner,Cording g:Sykes(2),Marginet(3)	4th	1,798
3/4/15	London Broncos (h)	L8-24	t:Ormondroyd,Chappell	6th	1,654
6/4/15	Sheffield (h)	L4-33	t:Sharp	7th	1,920
12/4/15	Batley (a)	W16-23	t:Blackmore(2),Maitua,Sharp g:Moore(3) fg:Moore	7th	916
19/4/15	North Wales (a) (CCR5)	W12-38	t:Moore,Ellis,Sharp,Blackmore(2),Maitua,Foster g:Moore(5)	N/A	617
26/4/15	Whitehaven (a)	W12-36	t:Minns(2),Sykes(2),Chappell,Moore,Cording g:Moore(3),Sykes	5th	747
3/5/15	Workington (h)	W72-0	t:Hardman,Hitchcox(3),Ellis,Cording(2),Chappell,Moore,Foster(2),Marginet,Bussey g:Moore(8),Marginet(2)	4th	1,547
10/5/15	London Broncos (a)	W32-40	t:Blackmore,Hitchcox,Bostock,Cording,Teasdale,Chappell,Bussey g:Sykes(6)	4th	672
17/5/15	Catalans Dragons (a) (CCR6)	L37-34	t:Foster,Teasdale(2),Ormondroyd,Day,Verlinden g:Marginet(5)	N/A	1,353
24/5/15	Leigh (SB) ●●	L12-31	t:Blackmore,Hardman g:Sykes(2)	5th	N/A
31/5/15	Batley (h)	W44-16	t:Ellis,James,Sykes(4),Ormondroyd,Blackmore g:Sykes(6)	5th	2,067
6/6/15	Halifax (h)	L20-44	t:Sharp,Foster,Moore,Hardman g:Sykes(2)	5th	2,035
14/6/15	Workington (a)	W0-52	t:Hitchcox(2),Sykes,Hardman(2),Moore(2),Minns,Marginet g:Sykes(8)	5th	749
19/6/15	Doncaster (h)	W54-14	t:Hardman(2),Sykes(2),Minns,Marginet(2),Cording,Hitchcox(2),Moore g:Sykes(5)	5th	1,624
28/6/15	Hunslet (a)	W34-42	t:Moore,Cooke(2),Hardman,Sharp(2),Foster g:Sykes(7)	5th	1,056
1/7/15	Bradford (a)	W18-37	t:Hitchcox(3),Maitua,Blackmore,Ellis g:Sykes(6) fg:Marginet	4th	5,044
5/7/15	Dewsbury (h)	L30-32	t:Blackmore,Maitua,Sykes,Milner,Cording,Marginet g:Sykes(3)	5th	2,009
12/7/15	Leigh (a)	L52-18	t:England,Hardman,Blackmore g:Sykes(3)	5th	4,127
19/7/15	Sheffield (a) ●●●	L38-28	t:Minns(4),Sykes,Maitua g:Sykes(2)	5th	2,443
25/7/15	Whitehaven (h)	L0-29		5th	1,305
9/8/15	Whitehaven (h) (CS)	W42-30	t:Foster,Baldwinson,Moore(2),Sharp,Cording,Johnson,James g:Sykes(5)	1st(CS)	1,107
16/8/15	Doncaster (a) (CS)	W16-28	t:Spears,Snitch,Ormondroyd,Foster,Johnson g:Sykes(4)	1st(CS)	886
23/8/15	Workington (a) (CS)	W10-24	t:Foster,Sharp,Snitch,Milner g:Sykes(4)	1st(CS)	906
31/8/15	Batley (h) (CS)	W28-26	t:Ellis,Day,Johnson,Sykes,Sharp g:Sykes(4)	1st(CS)	1,506
6/9/15	Dewsbury (h) (CS)	L16-34	t:Milner,Sharp,Ormondroyd g:Sykes(2)	1st(CS)	1,271
11/9/15	Hunslet (a) (CS)	W10-18	t:Ellis,Sykes,Blackmore g:Sykes(3)	1st(CS)	839
20/9/15	London Broncos (h) (CS)	W20-10	t:Sharp,Blackmore,Milner,Coventry g:Sykes(2)	1st(CS)	1,587
27/9/15	Workington (h) (CSSF)	W52-14	t:Milner,Hardman,Blackmore,Sykes,Knowles-Tagg,Ellis,Moore,Spears,Minns g:Sykes(8)	N/A	1,233
4/10/15	London Broncos (CSF) ●●●●	W36-4	t:James(2),Blackmore,Sykes,Hardman,Moore g:Sykes(6)	N/A	4,179

● Played at Belle Vue, Wakefield ●● Played at Bloomfield Road, Blackpool ●●● Played at Keepmoat Stadium, Doncaster ●●●● Played at Select Security Stadium, Widnes

		APP		TRIES		GOALS		FG		PTS	
	D.O.B.	ALL	Ch	ALL	Ch	ALL	Ch	ALL	Ch	ALL	Ch
Joe Arundel	22/8/91	1	1	1	1	0	0	0	0	4	4
Jordan Baldwinson	10/11/94	31(2)	20(1)	1	0	0	0	0	0	4	0
Ben Blackmore	19/2/93	25	18	17	10	0	0	0	0	68	40
Andrew Bostock	25/2/85	4(14)	3(13)	3	2	0	0	0	0	12	8
Jack Bussey	17/8/92	12(10)	3(9)	3	3	0	0	0	0	12	12
Garreth Carvell	21/4/80	1(4)	1(4)	0	0	0	0	0	0	0	0
Nathan Chappell	4/12/89	11(1)	9(1)	7	6	0	0	0	0	28	24
Paul Cooke	17/4/81	10	4	2	2	0	0	0	0	8	8
Luke Cooper	28/7/94	(9)	(5)	0	0	0	0	0	0	0	0
Jamie Cording	30/12/89	24	21	8	7	0	0	0	0	32	28
Jack Coventry	5/3/94	1(6)	0	1	0	0	0	0	0	4	0
Sam Day	12/6/94	(6)	0	2	0	0	0	0	0	8	0
Andy Ellis	15/12/84	30(1)	20(1)	8	4	0	0	0	0	32	16
Brad England	20/11/94	1(4)	1(3)	1	1	0	0	0	0	4	4
Alex Foster	25/9/93	18(9)	11(8)	9	4	0	0	0	0	36	16
Pita Godinet	21/12/87	1	1	0	0	0	0	0	0	0	0
Ian Hardman	8/12/84	27(1)	18	12	10	0	0	0	0	48	40
Jy Hitchcox	18/8/89	25	23	11	11	0	0	0	0	44	44
Sam Irwin	25/10/92	8(2)	7(2)	0	0	0	0	0	0	0	0
Matt James	26/3/87	13(12)	8(8)	5	1	0	0	0	0	20	4
Kyran Johnson	23/3/94	8(1)	0	3	0	0	0	0	0	12	0
Tom Johnstone	13/8/95	2	2	1	1	0	0	0	0	4	4
Bradley Knowles-Tagg	31/7/93	1(8)	0	1	0	0	0	0	0	4	0
James Lockwood	21/3/86	2(1)	2(1)	1	1	0	0	0	0	4	4
Reni Maitua	11/6/82	13	12	5	4	0	0	0	0	20	16
Remy Marginet	27/5/89	7(8)	5(7)	7	7	12	6	2	2	54	42
James Mendeika	16/12/91	1	1	0	0	0	0	0	0	0	0
Will Milner	28/10/94	12(4)	6(2)	7	2	0	0	0	0	28	8
Thomas Minns	4/9/94	18	11	9	8	0	0	0	0	36	32
Gareth Moore	3/6/89	21	13	12	7	19	14	1	1	87	57
Jack Ormondroyd	7/11/91	3(17)	(10)	5	2	0	0	0	0	20	8
Matt Ryan	13/6/88	1	1	1	1	0	0	0	0	4	4
Will Sharp	12/5/86	31	19	14	6	0	0	0	0	56	24
Steve Snitch	22/2/83	10	1	2	0	0	0	0	0	8	0
Tim Spears	27/7/84	28(2)	17(2)	2	0	0	0	0	0	8	0
Paul Sykes	11/8/81	34	23	18	14	104	63	0	0	280	182
Luke Teasdale	8/6/94	1(8)	(7)	3	1	0	0	0	0	12	4
Mason Tonks	11/10/94	2(4)	1(2)	0	0	0	0	0	0	0	0
Kyle Trout	1/3/91	(1)	(1)	0	0	0	0	0	0	0	0
Ryan Verlinden	18/6/86	4(3)	3(3)	1	0	0	0	0	0	4	0
Paul Wood	10/10/81	13(2)	13(2)	0	0	0	0	0	0	0	0

'Ch' totals include Championship regular season only; 'All' totals also include Championship Shield & Challenge Cup

Paul Sykes

LEAGUE RECORD
Championship, before Super 8 split:
P23-W13-D0-L10 (5th)
F633, A565, Diff+68, 26 points.

After Championship Shield:
P30-W19-D0-L11 (1st/Winners)
F809, A701, Diff+108, 38 points.

CHALLENGE CUP
Round Six

ATTENDANCES
Best - v Bradford (Ch - 6,346)
Worst - v Whitehaven (CS - 1,107)
Total (Championship/Championship Shield only) - 31,742
Average (Championship/Championship Shield only) - 1,984
(Down by 71 on 2014)

CLUB RECORDS **Highest score:** 96-0 v Castleford Lock Lane, 8/2/2004 **Highest score against:** 14-80 v Bradford, 3/4/2005 **Record attendance:** 17,531 v St Helens, 21/3/59

MATCH RECORDS **Tries:** 6 Mike Smith v Doncaster, 13/4/68; Chris Bibb v Keighley, 17/9/89
Goals: 13 Mark Knapper v Keighley, 17/9/89; Liam Finn v Hunslet Old Boys, 25/3/2012; Liam Finn v Swinton, 12/8/2012
Points: 40 Martin Pearson v Whitehaven, 26/11/95

SEASON RECORDS **Tries:** 48 Paul Newlove 1992-93 **Goals:** 183 *(inc 2fg)* Liam Finn 2012 **Points:** 436 Liam Finn 2012

CAREER RECORDS **Tries:** 162 Don Fox 1953-66 **Goals:** 1,210 Steve Quinn 1975-88 **Points:** 2,654 Steve Quinn 1975-88 **Appearances:** 440 Jim Denton 1921-34

HALIFAX

DATE	FIXTURE	RESULT	SCORERS	LGE	ATT
15/2/15	Whitehaven (a)	W16-44	t:Tyrer,Greenwood,Saltonstall(2),Brown(2),A Robinson(2),Ambler g:Tyrer(4)	1st	1,022
22/2/15	Leigh (h)	L6-18	t:Maneely g:Tyrer	6th	2,868
1/3/15	Batley (a)	W2-6	t:Place g:Tyrer	5th	1,113
8/3/15	Featherstone (h)	L12-24	t:Tyrer,Cahalane g:Tyrer(2)	6th	2,187
15/3/15	Dewsbury (h)	W26-13	t:Heaton,Saltonstall,Potts,Tyrer,Ambler g:Tyrer(3)	4th	1,734
22/3/15	Barrow (a) (CCR4)	W16-56	t:Brown,Heaton,Divorty,Tangata,Saltonstall(2),Johnston,Tyrer,Taylor,Potts g:Tyrer(8)	N/A	956
28/3/15	London Broncos (a)	L22-18	t:Saltonstall,Heaton,Cahalane g:Tyrer(3)	5th	724
3/4/15	Bradford (a)	L32-19	t:Cahalane,Divorty,Heaton g:Tyrer(3) fg:Murrell	7th	6,134
6/4/15	Hunslet (h)	W32-24	t:Brown,Heaton,Taylor,Tyrer,Murrell,Saltonstall g:Tyrer(2),Murrell(2)	5th	1,540
12/4/15	Workington (h)	W38-6	t:Ambler,Sheriffe,Heaton,Saltonstall,Manning,Brown,Kaye g:Murrell(4),Saltonstall	4th	1,122
17/4/15	Wakefield (a) (CCR5)	L44-16	t:Saltonstall,Heaton,Potts g:Murrell(2)	N/A	2,062
26/4/15	Sheffield (a) ●	L36-10	t:Moore,Cahalane g:Craven	6th	1,437
3/5/15	Doncaster (h)	W40-6	t:Saltonstall,Maneely,Heaton,Divorty(2),Potts,Murrell,Saxton g:Craven,Murrell(3)	5th	1,284
10/5/15	Leigh (a)	L22-14	t:Murrell,Heaton(2) g:Tyrer	6th	3,647
17/5/15	Whitehaven (h)	W60-18	t:Saxton,Tyrer(2),A Robinson(2),Manning,Saltonstall,Johnston,Murrell,Barber g:Tyrer,Murrell(9)	5th	1,601
23/5/15	Bradford (SB) ●●	L18-4	t:Heaton	6th	N/A
31/5/15	Workington (a)	W6-32	t:Heaton,Potts(2),Manning,Johnston,Cahalane g:Murrell(2),Potts(2)	6th	641
6/6/15	Featherstone (a)	W20-44	t:Saxton(3),Potts(3),Craven(2),Tyrer g:Tyrer(4)	5th	2,035
12/6/15	Hunslet (a)	W8-14	t:Manning,Johnston g:Tyrer(3)	4th	1,061
21/6/15	Dewsbury (a)	W16-46	t:Cahalane(2),Manning(2),Murrell(2),Johnston,Divorty g:Tyrer(7)	4th	1,242
27/6/15	London Broncos (h) ●●●	W46-22	t:Manning,Kaye,Johnston,Tyrer,Saltonstall,Divorty(2),Cahalane g:Tyrer(7)	4th	914
5/7/15	Sheffield (h)	W38-10	t:Saxton,Heaton,Manning(2),Kaye,C Robinson(2) g:Tyrer(5)	4th	1,873
12/7/15	Batley (h)	W25-22	t:Johnston(2),A Robinson,Saltonstall g:Tyrer(4) fg:Murrell	4th	1,955
19/7/15	Doncaster (a)	W0-52	t:Manning(2),Tyrer(2),Saxton,Bracek,Johnston,Maneely(2) g:Tyrer(8)	4th	1,506
26/7/15	Bradford (h)	W20-16	t:Cahalane,Heaton,Tyrer g:Tyrer(4)	4th	4,589
9/8/15	Widnes (h) (S8-Q)	L0-14		7th(S8-Q)	3,022
16/8/15	Hull KR (a) (S8-Q)	L34-12	t:Manning,Tyrer g:Tyrer(2)	6th(S8-Q)	6,837
23/8/15	Sheffield (a) (S8-Q) ●	L28-24	t:Tangata,Tyrer,Potts,Murrell g:Tyrer(4)	8th(S8-Q)	854
5/9/15	Salford (h) (S8-Q)	L28-50	t:Manning,Murrell,Saltonstall,Fairbank,Tangata g:Tyrer(4)	8th(S8-Q)	2,186
13/9/15	Leigh (h) (S8-Q)	W34-12	t:Manning,Divorty,Saltonstall,Murrell,Tyrer g:Tyrer(7)	7th(S8-Q)	3,010
19/9/15	Wakefield (a) (S8-Q)	L30-12	t:Eccleston,Murrell g:Tyrer(2)	7th(S8-Q)	3,086
26/9/15	Bradford (a) (S8-Q)	W18-52	t:Saxton(2),Tyrer(3),Manning,Johnston(2),Tangata,Heaton g:Tyrer(6)	6th(S8-Q)	5,163

● Played at Keepmoat Stadium, Doncaster ●● Played at Bloomfield Road, Blackpool ●●● Played at Cougar Park, Keighley

		APP		TRIES		GOALS		FG		PTS	
	D.O.B.	ALL	Ch	ALL	Ch	ALL	Ch	ALL	Ch	ALL	Ch
Luke Ambler	18/12/89	18(5)	13(1)	3	3	0	0	0	0	12	12
Ed Barber	26/4/90	1(7)	(6)	1	1	0	0	0	0	4	4
Clement Boyer	27/7/94	(2)	(2)	0	0	0	0	0	0	0	0
Andy Bracek	21/3/84	6(20)	6(12)	1	1	0	0	0	0	4	4
Alex Brown	28/8/87	9	7	5	4	0	0	0	0	20	16
Mitch Cahalane	5/5/89	31	23	9	9	0	0	0	0	36	36
Jordan Cox	27/5/92	(1)	(1)	0	0	0	0	0	0	0	0
Danny Craven	21/11/91	6	6	2	2	2	2	0	0	12	12
Tyler Dickinson	18/8/96	(4)	(4)	0	0	0	0	0	0	0	0
Ross Divorty	27/11/88	22(3)	18(2)	8	6	0	0	0	0	32	24
Jake Eccleston	24/4/95	6	2	1	0	0	0	0	0	4	0
Jacob Fairbank	4/3/90	10(5)	3(5)	1	0	0	0	0	0	4	0
Miles Greenwood	30/7/87	4	4	1	1	0	0	0	0	4	4
Ben Heaton	12/3/90	27	18	15	12	0	0	0	0	60	48
Keith Holden	23/6/93	(1)	0	0	0	0	0	0	0	0	0
Ben Johnston	8/3/92	24(2)	17(2)	11	8	0	0	0	0	44	32
Ben Kaye	19/12/88	24(6)	17(4)	3	3	0	0	0	0	12	12
Ryan Maneely	19/10/94	8(16)	6(10)	4	4	0	0	0	0	16	16
Dane Manning	15/4/89	31	23	15	11	0	0	0	0	60	44
Joe Martin	28/3/95	1	0	0	0	0	0	0	0	0	0
Luke Menzies	29/6/88	(2)	(2)	0	0	0	0	0	0	0	0
Richard Moore	2/2/81	17(15)	13(10)	1	1	0	0	0	0	4	4
Scott Murrell	5/9/85	32	23	10	6	22	20	2	2	86	66
Matt Place	11/6/92	3	3	1	1	0	0	0	0	4	4
Gareth Potts	25/7/90	18	14	10	7	2	2	0	0	44	32
Adam Robinson	8/4/87	7(7)	6(6)	5	5	0	0	0	0	20	20
Connor Robinson	23/10/94	7(5)	2(5)	2	2	0	0	0	0	8	8
James Saltonstall	27/9/93	32	23	15	10	1	1	0	0	62	42
Tom Saxton	3/10/83	19	16	9	7	0	0	0	0	36	28
Rikki Sheriffe	5/5/84	2	1	1	1	0	0	0	0	4	4
Jack Spencer	21/12/90	(16)	(13)	0	0	0	0	0	0	0	0
Adam Tangata	17/3/91	16(8)	9(6)	4	0	0	0	0	0	16	0
Chris Taylor	25/10/93	9(1)	8	2	1	0	0	0	0	8	4
Steve Tyrer	16/3/89	26	18	18	11	96	63	0	0	264	170
Mikey Wood	18/4/96	(2)	(1)	0	0	0	0	0	0	0	0

'Ch' totals include Championship regular season only; 'All' totals also include Super 8s (Qualifiers) & Challenge Cup

James Saltonstall

LEAGUE RECORD
Championship, before Super 8 split:
P23-W16-D0-L7 (4th)
F646, A377, Diff+269, 32 points.

S8-Q: P7-W2-D0-L5 (6th)
F162, A186, Diff-24, 4 points.

CHALLENGE CUP
Round Five

ATTENDANCES
Best - v Bradford (Ch - 4,589)
Worst - v London Broncos (Ch - 914)
Total (Championship/S8s only) - 29,885
Average (Championship/S8s only) - 2,135
(Up by 449 on 2014)

CLUB RECORDS **Highest score:** 94-4 v Myton, 25/3/2012 **Highest score against:** 6-88 v Hull KR, 23/4/2006
Record attendance: 29,153 v Wigan, 21/3/59 *(Thrum Hall)*; 9,827 v Bradford, 12/3/2000 *(The Shay)*
MATCH RECORDS **Tries:** 8 Keith Williams v Dewsbury, 9/11/57 **Goals:** 14 Bruce Burton v Hunslet, 27/8/72 **Points:** 32 John Schuster v Doncaster, 9/10/94
SEASON RECORDS **Tries:** 48 Johnny Freeman 1956-57 **Goals:** 156 Graham Holroyd 2008 **Points:** 362 John Schuster 1994-95
CAREER RECORDS **Tries:** 290 Johnny Freeman 1954-67 **Goals:** 1,028 Ronnie James 1961-71 **Points:** 2,191 Ronnie James 1961-71 **Appearances:** 482 Stan Kielty 1946-58

HUNSLET HAWKS

DATE	FIXTURE	RESULT	SCORERS	LGE	ATT
16/2/15	Featherstone (a) ●	L28-14	t:Casey,Mackay g:Brown(3)	10th	1,836
22/2/15	Batley (h)	L14-26	t:Watson,Brennan g:Brown(3)	11th	901
1/3/15	Dewsbury (h)	W18-6	t:Flanagan,Finigan g:Brown(5)	9th	983
8/3/15	Bradford (a)	L56-6	t:Briscoe g:Brown	10th	5,119
15/3/15	Doncaster (h)	W32-12	t:Kain(3),Watson,Brennan g:Ansell(6)	9th	498
22/3/15	Gloucestershire All Golds (a) (CCR4)	W10-28	t:Barnett,Brennan,Cosgrove,Agoro(3) g:Ansell(2)	N/A	137
29/3/15	Sheffield (a) ●●	L28-14	t:Mulhern,Flanagan g:Ansell(3)	9th	1,136
3/4/15	Leigh (h)	L6-42	t:Briscoe g:Brown	10th	1,122
6/4/15	Halifax (a)	L32-24	t:Mulhern,Watson,Briscoe,Finigan g:Brown(4)	10th	1,540
12/4/15	Whitehaven (h)	W26-18	t:Lee,Duckworth,Mvududu,Watson,Flanagan g:Brown(3)	9th	539
19/4/15	Dewsbury (h) (CCR5)	L16-31	t:Mackay,Briscoe,Martin g:Brown(2)	N/A	536
26/4/15	Workington (a)	W16-19	t:Lee,Keinhorst(2),Briscoe g:Brown fg:Brown	8th	689
3/5/15	London Broncos (h)	L12-32	t:Briscoe,Brown g:Brown(2)	8th	514
10/5/15	Dewsbury (a)	L40-4	t:Martin	9th	1,103
24/5/15	Doncaster (SB) ●●●	W12-25	t:Keinhorst,Watson,Maun,Briscoe g:Ansell(4) fg:Ansell	8th	N/A
29/5/15	Sheffield (h)	L10-54	t:Lee,Mackay g:Ansell	8th	521
7/6/15	Whitehaven (a)	L28-12	t:Mackay,Barnett g:Ansell(2)	8th	661
12/6/15	Halifax (h)	L8-14	t:Barnett g:Lilley(2)	8th	1,061
21/6/15	London Broncos (a)	L34-12	t:Gee,Ward g:Lilley(2)	8th	751
28/6/15	Featherstone (h)	L34-42	t:Trout,Kain,Watson,Lee(2),Finigan g:Lilley(5)	9th	1,056
5/7/15	Bradford (h)	L6-68	t:Lee g:Lilley	10th	1,676
8/7/15	Leigh (a)	L72-6	t:Mvududu g:Ansell	10th	2,716
12/7/15	Doncaster (a)	L34-26	t:Maun,Gee(2),Barnett,Casey g:Brown(3)	11th	1,231
19/7/15	Batley (a)	L45-28	t:Casey,Lee(2),Watson,Yates g:Brown(4)	11th	483
26/7/15	Workington (h)	L6-30	t:Mackay g:Brown	11th	706
9/8/15	Dewsbury (a) (CS)	L32-20	t:Lee(2),Maun g:Brown(4)	7th(CS)	901
16/8/15	Workington (h) (CS)	L18-22	t:Grimshaw,Barnett(2) g:Brown(3)	7th(CS)	567
23/8/15	London Broncos (a) (CS)	W24-41	t:Trout,Flanagan,Backhouse,Reed,Duckworth,Lee g:Brown(8) fg:Brown	7th(CS)	225
31/8/15	Whitehaven (a) (CS)	W16-30	t:Gee,Lyons,Castle,Flanagan,Duckworth g:Brown(5)	7th(CS)	804
6/9/15	Doncaster (h) (CS)	W25-16	t:Houston,Ansell,Castle,Lee g:Brown(4) fg:Brown	7th(CS)	599
11/9/15	Featherstone (h) (CS)	L10-18	t:Maun,Flanagan g:Brown	7th(CS)	839
20/9/15	Batley (a) (CS)	L60-12	t:Watson(2) g:Houston,Brown	7th(CS)	737

● Played at Belle Vue, Wakefield ●● Played at Keepmoat Stadium, Doncaster ●●● Played at Bloomfield Road, Blackpool

		APP		TRIES		GOALS		FG		PTS	
	D.O.B.	ALL	Ch	ALL	Ch	ALL	Ch	ALL	Ch	ALL	Ch
Mo Agoro	29/1/93	13	5	3	0	0	0	0	0	12	0
Danny Ansell	9/10/91	16(4)	9(3)	1	0	19	17	1	1	43	35
Ryan Backhouse	8/9/93	14(3)	7(2)	1	0	0	0	0	0	4	0
Richie Barnett	26/4/81	25	16	6	3	0	0	0	0	24	12
Brad Brennan	18/1/93	6(11)	4(7)	3	2	0	0	0	0	12	8
Lee Brickwood	20/7/91	(1)	0	0	0	0	0	0	0	0	0
Luke Briscoe	11/3/94	13(4)	12(4)	7	6	0	0	0	0	28	24
Brooke Broughton	30/10/90	1(1)	(1)	0	0	0	0	0	0	0	0
Simon Brown	23/6/89	25	16	1	1	59	31	3	1	125	67
Callum Casey	6/6/90	19	16	3	3	0	0	0	0	12	12
Mark Castle	19/2/86	(12)	(4)	2	0	0	0	0	0	8	0
Elliott Cosgrove	31/3/91	2(1)	1(1)	1	0	0	0	0	0	4	0
Brett Delaney	26/10/85	1	1	0	0	0	0	0	0	0	0
James Duckworth	9/4/94	15	9	3	1	0	0	0	0	12	4
Marcus Elliott	8/3/94	2	1	0	0	0	0	0	0	0	0
Vinny Finigan	4/8/89	14	14	3	3	0	0	0	0	12	12
George Flanagan	8/10/86	4(18)	3(12)	6	3	0	0	0	0	24	12
Matty Gee	12/12/94	12(2)	5(2)	4	3	0	0	0	0	16	12
Danny Grimshaw	25/2/86	3(4)	1(2)	1	0	0	0	0	0	4	0
Michael Haley	19/9/87	16(4)	14(3)	0	0	0	0	0	0	0	0
James Houston	28/12/82	17(4)	10(4)	1	0	1	0	0	0	6	0
Andy Kain	1/9/85	18	17	4	4	0	0	0	0	16	16
Jimmy Keinhorst	14/7/90	9	9	3	3	0	0	0	0	12	12
Jack Lee	1/11/88	26	18	12	8	0	0	0	0	48	32
Jordan Lilley	4/9/96	4	4	0	0	10	10	0	0	20	20
Aaron Lyons	14/11/90	7(17)	4(12)	1	0	0	0	0	0	4	0
Liam Mackay	26/10/90	22(3)	17(3)	5	4	0	0	0	0	20	16
Charlie Martin	2/12/92	11(2)	9(2)	2	1	0	0	0	0	8	4
Danny Maun	5/1/81	28(1)	20	4	2	0	0	0	0	16	8
Rob Mulhern	18/10/94	13(7)	12(7)	2	2	0	0	0	0	8	8
Mufaro Mvududu	29/8/91	6(9)	5(7)	2	2	0	0	0	0	8	8
Lewis Reed	24/3/91	(4)	(1)	1	0	0	0	0	0	4	0
Matthew Tebb	4/9/90	(2)	(2)	0	0	0	0	0	0	0	0
Kyle Trout	1/3/91	7(9)	1(8)	2	1	0	0	0	0	8	4
Josh Walters	23/12/94	6(1)	6(1)	0	0	0	0	0	0	0	0
Robbie Ward	27/10/95	2(3)	2(3)	1	1	0	0	0	0	4	4
Jimmy Watson	9/9/91	29	21	9	7	0	0	0	0	36	28
Andy Yates	23/2/90	10(1)	10(1)	1	1	0	0	0	0	4	4

'Ch' totals include Championship regular season only; 'All' totals also include Championship Shield & Challenge Cup

Jack Lee

LEAGUE RECORD
Championship, before Super 8 split:
P23-W5-D0-L18 (11th)
F362, A769, Diff-407, 10 points.

After Championship Shield:
P30-W8-D0-L22 (7th)
F518, A957, Diff-439, 16 points.

CHALLENGE CUP
Round Five

ATTENDANCES
Best - v Bradford (Ch - 1,676)
Worst - v Doncaster (Ch - 498)
Total (Championship/ Championship Shield only) - 11,582
Average (Championship/ Championship Shield only) - 827
(Up by 319 on 2014, Championship One)

CLUB RECORDS **Highest score:** 82-0 v Highfield, 21/1/96 **Highest score against:** 0-82 v Bradford, 2/3/2003
Record attendance: 24,700 v Wigan, 15/3/24 *(Parkside)*; 2,454 v Wakefield, 13/4/98 *(South Leeds Stadium)*

MATCH RECORDS **Tries:** 7 George Dennis v Bradford, 20/1/34 **Goals:** 12 Billy Langton v Keighley, 18/8/59 **Points:** 30 Simon Wilson v Highfield, 21/1/96

SEASON RECORDS **Tries:** 34 Alan Snowden 1956-57 **Goals:** 181 Billy Langton 1958-59 **Points:** 380 Billy Langton 1958-59

CAREER RECORDS **Tries:** 154 Fred Williamson 1943-55 **Goals:** 1,044 Billy Langton 1955-66 **Points:** 2,202 Billy Langton 1955-66 **Appearances:** 579 Geoff Gunney 1951-73

LEIGH CENTURIONS

DATE	FIXTURE	RESULT	SCORERS	LGE	ATT
15/2/15	Bradford (h)	W36-24	t:Brierley,Kay,McNally(2),Armstrong,Penkywicz g:Ridyard(6)	4th	7,449
22/2/15	Halifax (a)	W6-18	t:Kay(2),Pownall g:Ridyard(3)	2nd	2,868
1/3/15	London Broncos (h)	W25-12	t:Haggerty,Kay,Armstrong(2),Brierley g:Ridyard(2) fg:Ridyard	1st	4,531
8/3/15	Doncaster (a)	W18-54	t:Brierley(2),Barlow,McNally,Kay(4),Ridyard,Armstrong g:Ridyard(7)	1st	1,602
15/3/15	Featherstone (a)	W6-40	t:Kay(2),Armstrong(2),Goulden,Haggerty,Platt,Brierley g:Ridyard(4)	1st	2,695
20/3/15	London Broncos (h) (CCR4)	W64-12	t:Pownall,Barlow,Brierley(2),Haggerty,Hopkins(2),Armstrong,Kay,McNally,Moimoi g:Ridyard(10)	N/A	2,448
29/3/15	Whitehaven (h)	W60-0	t:Pownall(3),Kay(3),Platt,Ridyard(2),Emmitt,McNally,Brierley g:Ridyard(6)	1st	3,006
3/4/15	Hunslet (a)	W6-42	t:Wilkes,Aspinwall,Kay(2),Barlow,Pownall,Penkywicz,Dixon g:Ridyard(5)	1st	1,122
6/4/15	Workington (h)	W54-6	t:Penkywicz(2),Higson,Brierley,Kay,Hock(2),Platt,McNally g:Ridyard(9)	1st	3,017
12/4/15	Sheffield (a) ●	W22-36	t:Barlow,Goulden,McNally,Brierley(2),Emmitt g:Ridyard(6)	1st	1,454
18/4/15	Salford (h) (CCR5)	W22-18	t:Goulden,McNally,Brierley,Pownall g:Ridyard(3)	N/A	6,358
26/4/15	Batley (h)	W56-8	t:Brierley(3),Kay,Higson(2),Armstrong,Pownall(2),Dixon g:Ridyard(8)	1st	3,036
3/5/15	Dewsbury (a)	W28-32	t:Kay(3),McNally,Ridyard,Worthington g:Ridyard(4)	1st	1,551
10/5/15	Halifax (h)	W22-14	t:Kay,Worthington,Goulden,Beswick g:Ridyard,Brierley(2)	1st	3,647
17/5/15	Wakefield (a) (CCR6)	W30-36	t:Brierley,Pownall,Beswick,Armstrong,Hopkins,Wilkes g:Ridyard(6)	N/A	3,859
24/5/15	Featherstone (SB) ●●	W12-31	t:McNally(3),Worthington,Higham g:Ridyard(5) fg:Brierley	1st	N/A
31/5/15	Whitehaven (a)	W16-46	t:Pownall(2),Sarsfield,Brierley(4),Higson,Worthington g:Brierley(4),Moimoi	1st	841
7/6/15	London Broncos (a)	L29-20	t:Pownall(2),Armstrong,McNally g:Ridyard(2)	1st	1,025
14/6/15	Batley (a)	W12-26	t:Higson(3),Kay,Emmitt g:Ridyard(3)	1st	1,125
21/6/15	Sheffield (h)	W58-18	t:Worthington,McNally(3),Brierley,Higson,Kay(3),Armstrong g:Ridyard(9)	1st	3,572
27/6/15	Warrington (a) (CCQF)	L34-24	t:Worthington,Brierley(2),McNally,Armstrong g:Ridyard(2)	N/A	10,119
5/7/15	Workington (a)	W12-50	t:Brierley(2),Spencer,Ridyard,Pownall,Higson,Haggerty,Higham,Emmitt g:Ridyard(7)	2nd	914
8/7/15	Hunslet (h)	W72-6	t:McNally(5),Ridyard,Higham(2),Haggerty,Sarsfield(2),Aspinwall,Kay(2) g:Ridyard(8)	1st	2,716
12/7/15	Featherstone (h)	W52-18	t:Moimoi(3),Worthington,McNally,Brierley(3),Hock g:Ridyard(7),Emmitt	1st	4,127
19/7/15	Bradford (a)	D36-36	t:Hock,Pownall(3),Worthington,Brierley g:Ridyard(6)	1st	9,181
22/7/15	Dewsbury (h)	W40-24	t:Armstrong,Kay,Brierley(3),Reynolds,Hopkins g:Reynolds(6)	1st	3,244
26/7/15	Doncaster (h)	W66-10	t:Kay(5),Higson,McNally(2),Brierley,Hock,Ridyard,Reynolds g:Ridyard(9)	1st	3,311
8/8/15	Hull KR (h) (S8-Q)	L26-36	t:Brierley,McNally,Dixon,Armstrong g:Ridyard(5)	6th(S8-Q)	4,459
16/8/15	Salford (a) (S8-Q)	L46-18	t:Higson,McNally(2) g:Ridyard(3)	7th(S8-Q)	4,547
22/8/15	Wakefield (h) (S8-Q)	L16-17	t:Moimoi,Pownall,Kay g:Ridyard(2)	7th(S8-Q)	4,376
6/9/15	Sheffield (h) (S8-Q)	W52-16	t:Higham,Dixon,Brierley(3),Kay,Moimoi,Goulden,McNally g:Ridyard(8)	6th(S8-Q)	4,012
13/9/15	Halifax (a) (S8-Q)	L34-12	t:Higson,Moimoi g:Ridyard(2)	6th(S8-Q)	3,010
19/9/15	Bradford (h) (S8-Q)	L16-32	t:Higson,McNally,Beswick g:Brierley(2)	6th(S8-Q)	4,621
27/9/15	Widnes (a) (S8-Q)	L50-6	t:Reynolds g:Brierley	8th(S8-Q)	5,550

● Played at Keepmoat Stadium, Doncaster ●● Played at Bloomfield Road, Blackpool

		APP		TRIES		GOALS		FG		PTS	
	D.O.B.	ALL	Ch	ALL	Ch	ALL	Ch	ALL	Ch	ALL	Ch
Jamie Acton	4/4/92	15(4)	10(4)	0	0	0	0	0	0	0	0
Tom Armstrong	12/9/89	29	18	14	10	0	0	0	0	56	40
Martin Aspinwall	21/10/81	1(11)	1(6)	2	2	0	0	0	0	8	8
Sam Barlow	7/3/88	14(9)	11(6)	4	3	0	0	0	0	16	12
Bob Beswick	8/12/84	20(12)	14(8)	3	1	0	0	0	0	12	4
Ryan Brierley	12/3/92	33	22	37	27	9	6	1	1	167	121
Andrew Dixon	28/2/90	24(2)	16(1)	4	2	0	0	0	0	16	8
Jake Emmitt	4/10/88	18(11)	11(8)	4	4	1	1	0	0	18	18
Lewis Foster	21/12/93	(2)	(1)	0	0	0	0	0	0	0	0
Tommy Goulden	30/6/81	22(1)	13(1)	5	3	0	0	0	0	20	12
Kurt Haggerty	8/1/89	16(3)	13(1)	5	4	0	0	0	0	20	16
Mick Higham	18/9/80	9(9)	4(7)	5	4	0	0	0	0	20	16
Adam Higson	19/5/87	16(1)	12	13	10	0	0	0	0	52	40
Gareth Hock	5/9/83	14(3)	8(2)	5	5	0	0	0	0	20	20
Sam Hopkins	17/2/90	3(20)	3(15)	4	1	0	0	0	0	16	4
Liam Kay	17/12/91	32	21	36	33	0	0	0	0	144	132
Gregg McNally	2/1/91	33	22	30	22	0	0	0	0	120	88
Fuifui Moimoi	26/9/79	20(5)	13(2)	7	3	1	1	0	0	30	14
Mathias Pala	14/6/89	5	3	0	0	0	0	0	0	0	0
Sean Penkywicz	18/5/82	6(3)	5(3)	4	4	0	0	0	0	16	16
Michael Platt	23/3/84	9	6	3	3	0	0	0	0	12	12
Jonathan Pownall	22/8/91	23(1)	15	19	15	0	0	0	0	76	60
Ben Reynolds	15/1/94	5(3)	3(2)	3	2	6	6	0	0	24	20
Martyn Ridyard	25/7/86	30	21	7	7	158	117	1	1	345	263
Matt Sarsfield	10/9/91	4	4	3	3	0	0	0	0	12	12
Tom Spencer	2/1/91	9(11)	6(7)	1	1	0	0	0	0	4	4
Jonathan Walker	20/2/91	1(2)	1(2)	0	0	0	0	0	0	0	0
Oliver Wilkes	2/5/80	8(20)	5(14)	2	1	0	0	0	0	8	4
Greg Worthington	17/7/90	23	18	8	7	0	0	0	0	32	28

'Ch' totals include Championship regular season only; 'All' totals also include Super 8s (Qualifiers) & Challenge Cup

Gregg McNally

LEAGUE RECORD
Championship, before Super 8 split:
P23-W21-D1-L1 (1st)
F972, A343, Diff+629, 43 points.

S8-Q: P7-W1-D0-L6 (8th)
F146, A231, Diff-85, 2 points.

CHALLENGE CUP
Quarter Finalists

ATTENDANCES
Best - v Bradford (Ch - 7,449)
Worst - v London Broncos (CC - 2,448)
Total (Championship/S8s only) - 59,124
Average (Championship/S8s only) - 3,942
(Up by 1,562 on 2014)

CLUB RECORDS **Highest score:** 92-2 v Keighley, 30/4/86 **Highest score against:** 4-94 v Workington, 26/2/95
Record attendance: 31,326 v St Helens, 14/3/53 *(Hilton Park)*; 7,449 v Bradford, 15/2/2015 *(Leigh Sports Village)*

MATCH RECORDS **Tries:** 6 Jack Wood v York, 4/10/47; Neil Turley v Workington, 31/1/2001
Goals: 15 Mick Stacey v Doncaster, 28/3/76 **Points:** 42 Neil Turley v Chorley, 4/4/2004

SEASON RECORDS **Tries:** 55 Neil Turley 2001 **Goals:** 187 Neil Turley 2004 **Points:** 468 Neil Turley 2004

CAREER RECORDS **Tries:** 189 Mick Martyn 1954-67 **Goals:** 1,043 Jimmy Ledgard 1948-58 **Points:** 2,492 John Woods 1976-85; 1990-92
Appearances: 503 Albert Worrall 1920-38

LONDON BRONCOS

DATE	FIXTURE	RESULT	SCORERS	LGE	ATT
15/2/15	Doncaster (h)	W26-22	t:Nasso,Harrison,R Williams(2),Naiqama g:Naiqama(3)	6th	976
22/2/15	Sheffield (a) ●	L40-6	t:R Williams g:Naiqama	8th	850
1/3/15	Leigh (a)	L25-12	t:Dollapi,R Williams g:Naiqama(2)	10th	4,531
8/3/15	Workington (h)	W34-16	t:Dwyer,Garside,Wallace,Gilmore,Lovegrove,Macani g:Naiqama(5)	8th	587
15/3/15	Whitehaven (a)	L18-16	t:Macani,R Williams,Dwyer g:Naiqama(2)	8th	689
20/3/15	Leigh (a) (CCR4)	L64-12	t:Nasso,Harrison g:Naiqama(2)	N/A	2,448
28/3/15	Halifax (h)	W22-18	t:Harrison,Garside,Macani,Dwyer g:Naiqama(3)	8th	724
3/4/15	Featherstone (a)	W8-24	t:Dwyer,Thomas,R Williams(2) g:Naiqama(4)	5th	1,654
6/4/15	Batley (h)	W25-18	t:Garside,Harrison,Hellewell,Minchella g:Naiqama(3),Thomas fg:Thomas	4th	638
12/4/15	Bradford (a)	L28-2	g:Naiqama	6th	4,023
26/4/15	Dewsbury (h)	L16-20	t:Hellewell,Macani(2) g:Naiqama(2)	7th	663
3/5/15	Hunslet (a)	W12-32	t:Minchella,Gilmore,Naiqama,Garside,R Williams(2) g:Naiqama(4)	7th	514
10/5/15	Featherstone (h)	L32-40	t:Thackray,Harrison(2),R Williams,Hellewell,Sammut g:Naiqama(4)	7th	672
23/5/15	Sheffield (SB) ●●	W46-6	t:Kear(2),R Williams(2),Hellewell,Thomas(3) g:Naiqama(7)	7th	N/A
31/5/15	Bradford (h)	L18-36	t:Gilmore,Thackray(2) g:Naiqama(3)	7th	1,101
7/6/15	Leigh (h)	W29-20	t:Thomas,Macani(2),Naiqama,Thackray g:Naiqama(4) fg:Minchella	7th	1,025
10/6/15	Batley (a)	W22-28	t:Dollapi,Garside(2),Gilmore,Macani g:Naiqama(4)	7th	341
14/6/15	Doncaster (a) ●●●	W4-30	t:Hellewell(3),Minchella,R Williams g:Naiqama(5)	6th	530
21/6/15	Hunslet (h)	W34-12	t:Kear,Naiqama(3),Thomas,R Williams g:Naiqama(5)	6th	751
27/6/15	Halifax (a) ●●●●	L46-22	t:R Williams(2),Thomas,Macani g:Naiqama(3)	6th	914
5/7/15	Whitehaven (h)	W40-24	t:Walton(2),Thomas(2),Garside,Macani,Thackray g:Naiqama(5),Barthau	6th	567
12/7/15	Dewsbury (a)	L24-12	t:Naiqama,Thomas g:Naiqama(2)	6th	910
19/7/15	Workington (a)	L29-18	t:Hellewell(2),Keyes g:Naiqama(3)	7th	686
26/7/15	Sheffield (h)	L14-22	t:Naiqama,Garside g:Naiqama(3)	7th	543
8/8/15	Doncaster (h) (CS)	W52-12	t:Hellewell,Kear(3),Walton,Naiqama,R Williams,J Walker,Barthau g:Naiqama(6),Keyes(2)	3rd(CS)	350
15/8/15	Whitehaven (a) (CS)	L40-16	t:Hellewell,Minchella,Barthau g:Naiqama(2)	3rd(CS)	783
23/8/15	Hunslet (h) (CS)	L24-41	t:Garside,Cunningham,Adebiyi,Hellewell(2) g:Barthau(2)	3rd(CS)	225
31/8/15	Dewsbury (a) (CS)	L25-16	t:R Williams,Wallace,Hellewell g:Barthau(2)	3rd(CS)	805
6/9/15	Workington (h) (CS)	W50-10	t:Cunningham(2),R Williams,Davis,Keyes,Morris,Barthau,Hellewell,Dollapi g:Barthau(7)	3rd(CS)	363
13/9/15	Batley (h) (CS)	W50-16	t:Morris(5),Adebiyi,Macani,Hellewell(2) g:Barthau(6),Keyes	3rd(CS)	485
20/9/15	Featherstone (a) (CS)	L20-10	t:Hellewell,Macani g:Kear	3rd(CS)	1,587
27/9/15	Dewsbury (a) (CSSF)	W18-34	t:Hellewell,Keyes,Macani,R Williams,Harrison(2) g:Barthau(5)	N/A	940
4/10/15	Featherstone (CSF) ●●●●●	L36-4	t:R Williams	N/A	4,179

● Played at Keepmoat Stadium, Doncaster ●● Played at Bloomfield Road, Blackpool ●●● Played at Castle Park
●●●● Played at Cougar Park, Keighley ●●●●● Played at Select Security Stadium, Widnes

		APP		TRIES		GOALS		FG		PTS	
	D.O.B.	ALL	Ch	ALL	Ch	ALL	Ch	ALL	Ch	ALL	Ch
Sadiq Adebiyi	8/1/97	(4)	0	2	0	0	0	0	0	8	0
Chris Annakin	30/1/91	(2)	(2)	0	0	0	0	0	0	0	0
William Barthau	30/1/90	12(1)	4(1)	3	0	23	1	0	0	58	2
Harvey Burnett	18/8/95	(1)	0	0	0	0	0	0	0	0	0
Josh Cordoba	29/1/84	2	2	0	0	0	0	0	0	0	0
James Cunningham	3/4/94	7(6)	(4)	3	0	0	0	0	0	12	0
Matt Davis	5/7/96	6(9)	1(5)	1	0	0	0	0	0	4	0
Erjon Dollapi	16/3/93	6(13)	2(11)	3	2	0	0	0	0	12	8
Brad Dwyer	28/4/93	9(3)	9(3)	4	4	0	0	0	0	16	16
Toby Everett	22/12/95	2(18)	1(11)	0	0	0	0	0	0	0	0
Ben Farrar	2/12/86	13	12	0	0	0	0	0	0	0	0
Matt Garside	1/10/90	32	22	9	8	0	0	0	0	36	32
Tom Gilmore	2/2/94	15	15	4	4	0	0	0	0	16	16
Ben Gray	12/11/95	2	0	0	0	0	0	0	0	0	0
Daniel Harrison	15/4/88	23	18	8	5	0	0	0	0	32	20
Ben Hellewell	30/1/92	33	23	19	9	0	0	0	0	76	36
Andrew Henderson	17/6/79	11(6)	8	0	0	0	0	0	0	0	0
Elliot Kear	29/11/88	19(2)	10(2)	6	3	1	0	0	0	26	12
Joe Keyes	17/9/95	17	8	3	1	3	0	0	0	18	4
Rhys Lovegrove	11/3/87	20(1)	20(1)	1	1	0	0	0	0	4	4
Iliess Macani	6/12/93	27(3)	19(2)	13	10	0	0	0	0	52	40
Richard Mathers	24/10/83	4	4	0	0	0	0	0	0	0	0
Elliot Minchella	28/1/96	18	16	4	3	0	0	1	1	17	13
Sean Morris	6/5/89	8	1	6	0	0	0	0	0	24	0
Wes Naiqama	19/10/82	27	23	9	8	88	78	0	0	212	188
Ray Nasso	3/7/87	7(15)	6(15)	2	1	0	0	0	0	8	4
Ben Pointer	25/5/96	1(1)	0	0	0	0	0	0	0	0	0
Glenn Riley	21/9/92	6(6)	(5)	0	0	0	0	0	0	0	0
Jarrod Sammut	15/2/87	5	5	1	1	0	0	0	0	4	4
Nick Slyney	11/2/88	2	2	0	0	0	0	0	0	0	0
Jamie Thackray	30/9/79	12(9)	11(7)	5	5	0	0	0	0	20	20
Oscar Thomas	3/1/94	15(1)	14(1)	10	10	1	1	1	1	43	43
Alex Walker	4/9/95	1	0	0	0	0	0	0	0	0	0
Jonathan Walker	20/2/91	6(10)	2(5)	1	0	0	0	0	0	4	0
Jon Wallace	8/10/94	12(15)	8(12)	2	1	0	0	0	0	8	4
Jason Walton	13/6/90	6	4	3	2	0	0	0	0	12	8
Joel Wicks	27/10/94	6(5)	2(5)	0	0	0	0	0	0	0	0
Dave Williams	29/1/87	4	4	0	0	0	0	0	0	0	0
Rhys Williams	8/12/89	33	23	21	16	0	0	0	0	84	64

'Ch' totals include Championship regular season only; 'All' totals also include Championship Shield & Challenge Cup

Rhys Williams

LEAGUE RECORD

Championship, before Super 8 split:
P23-W12-D0-L11 (7th)
F538, A510, Diff+28, 24 points.

After Championship Shield:
P30-W15-D0-L15 (3rd/Runners-Up)
F756, A674, Diff+82, 30 points.

CHALLENGE CUP

Round Four

ATTENDANCES

Best - v Bradford (Ch - 1,101)
Worst - v Hunslet (CS - 225)
Total (Championship/Championship Shield only) - 9,670
Average (Championship/Championship Shield only) - 645
(Down by 649 on 2014, SL)

CLUB RECORDS **Highest score:** 82-0 v Highfield, 12/11/95; 82-2 v Barrow, 20/5/2006 **Highest score against:** 6-82 v Warrington, 20/3/2011; 10-82 v Warrington, 8/6/2013 **Record attendance:** 15,013 v Wakefield, 15/2/81

MATCH RECORDS **Tries:** 5 Martin Offiah v Whitehaven, 14/3/99; Sean Morris v Batley, 13/9/2015 **Goals:** 13 Rob Purdham v Barrow, 20/5/2006 **Points:** 34 Rob Purdham v Barrow, 20/5/2006

SEASON RECORDS **Tries:** 43 Mark Johnson 1993-94 **Goals:** 159 John Gallagher 1993-94 **Points:** 384 John Gallagher 1993-94

CAREER RECORDS **Tries:** 109 Luke Dorn 2005-2006; 2009-2013 **Goals:** 309 Steve Diamond 1981-84 **Points:** 772 Paul Sykes 2001-2007 **Appearances:** 202 Steele Retchless 1998-2004

SHEFFIELD EAGLES

DATE	FIXTURE	RESULT	SCORERS	LGE	ATT
13/2/15	Dewsbury (a)	L19-10	t:Turner,Davey g:Brambani	8th	1,309
22/2/15	London Broncos (h)	W40-6	t:Knowles,Molloy,Laulu-Togagae,Briggs,Taulapapa,Smeaton,Straugheir,Turner g:Brambani(3),Walker	4th	850
1/3/15	Whitehaven (a)	W6-20	t:Turner(3),Laulu-Togagae,Yere	3rd	701
8/3/15	Batley (h)	W28-16	t:Brambani,Yere(2),Worrincy,Laulu-Togagae g:Walker(4)	3rd	1,358
15/3/15	Workington (a)	W12-14	t:Yere,Smeaton g:Briggs(3)	3rd	682
22/3/15	Oldham (h) (CCR4)	W44-20	t:Yere,Turner,Knowles,Straugheir,Laulu-Togagae,Worrincy,Thorpe(2) g:Walker(6)	N/A	484
29/3/15	Hunslet (h)	W28-14	t:Taulapapa(2),Laulu-Togagae,Knowles,Briggs g:Walker(4)	3rd	1,136
1/4/15	Doncaster (a)	W4-26	t:Langley,Taulapapa,Stringer,Worrincy,Aston g:Briggs,Walker(2)	3rd	1,030
6/4/15	Featherstone (a)	W4-33	t:Yere(2),Turner,Laulu-Togagae,Taulapapa,Walker g:Walker(4) fg:Knowles	3rd	1,920
12/4/15	Leigh (h)	L22-36	t:Aston,Laulu-Togagae(2),Turner g:Walker,Briggs(2)	3rd	1,454
19/4/15	Hull FC (h) (CCR5) ●	L12-34	t:Aston,Yere g:Brambani(2)	N/A	1,620
26/4/15	Halifax (h)	W36-10	t:Laulu-Togagae(2),Worrincy(3),Brambani g:Brambani(6)	3rd	1,437
3/5/15	Bradford (a)	L46-12	t:Turner,Aston g:Knowles(2)	3rd	4,487
8/5/15	Doncaster (h)	W30-12	t:Aston,Stringer,Briggs,Davies,Knowles g:Briggs(5)	3rd	863
19/5/15	Dewsbury (h)	W15-8	t:Turner,Yere,Worrincy g:Briggs fg:Brambani	3rd	682
23/5/15	London Broncos (SB) ●●	L46-6	t:Aston g:Brambani	3rd	N/A
29/5/15	Hunslet (a)	W10-54	t:Yere(4),Smeaton,Tonks,Turner,Worrincy,Knowles,Laulu-Togagae g:Briggs(6),Knowles	3rd	521
5/6/15	Batley (a)	W12-40	t:Yere(3),Smeaton,Davies,Laulu-Togagae,Taulapapa g:Briggs(5),Brambani	3rd	525
13/6/15	Whitehaven (h) ●●●	W26-16	t:Laulu-Togagae,Briggs,Taulapapa(2),Turner g:Briggs(3)	3rd	503
21/6/15	Leigh (a)	L58-18	t:Smeaton,Petersen,Straugheir,Taulapapa g:Briggs	3rd	3,572
28/6/15	Workington (h) ●●●	W26-6	t:Laulu-Togagae(2),Thorpe,Davies,Straugheir g:Briggs(3)	3rd	506
5/7/15	Halifax (a)	L38-10	t:Briggs,Stringer g:Briggs	3rd	1,873
12/7/15	Bradford (h)	W32-30	t:Laulu-Togagae,Briggs,Tonks,Worrincy(2) g:Briggs(6)	3rd	2,153
19/7/15	Featherstone (h)	W38-28	t:Knowles,Straugheir,Worrincy(2),Yere,Turner,Smeaton g:Briggs(5)	3rd	2,443
26/7/15	London Broncos (a)	W14-22	t:Millar(2),Yere,Battye g:Walker(3)	3rd	543
9/8/15	Bradford (a) (S8-Q)	L42-10	t:Taulapapa,Yere g:Briggs	8th(S8-Q)	6,032
16/8/15	Widnes (a) (S8-Q)	L48-12	t:Turner,Carlile g:Walker(2)	8th(S8-Q)	4,567
23/8/15	Halifax (h) (S8-Q)	W28-24	t:Worrincy(3),Walker,Laulu-Togagae g:Walker(4)	6th(S8-Q)	854
6/9/15	Leigh (a) (S8-Q)	L52-16	t:Davey,Turner,Smeaton g:Walker(2)	7th(S8-Q)	4,012
13/9/15	Salford (a) (S8-Q)	L53-34	t:Aston,Yere,Laulu-Togagae,Worrincy,Straugheir,Turner g:Walker(5)	8th(S8-Q)	3,000
18/9/15	Hull KR (h) (S8-Q) ●	L28-38	t:Battye,Laulu-Togagae,Millar(3) g:Walker(2),Brambani(2)	8th(S8-Q)	2,017
27/9/15	Wakefield (h) (S8-Q) ●	W24-10	t:Turner,Aston,Yere,Laulu-Togagae g:Walker(3),Brambani	7th(S8-Q)	1,712

Home games played at Keepmoat Stadium, Doncaster except ● at Bramall Lane and ●●● at Castle Park, Doncaster
●● Played at Bloomfield Road, Blackpool

	D.O.B.	APP ALL	APP Ch	TRIES ALL	TRIES Ch	GOALS ALL	GOALS Ch	FG ALL	FG Ch	PTS ALL	PTS Ch
Cory Aston	1/3/95	19(4)	12(4)	8	5	0	0	0	0	32	20
Eddie Battye	24/7/91	20(12)	13(10)	2	1	0	0	0	0	8	4
Jack Blagbrough	18/1/94	(3)	(2)	0	0	0	0	0	0	0	0
Dominic Brambani	10/5/85	23(1)	15	2	2	17	12	1	1	43	33
Kyle Briggs	7/12/87	21(1)	19(1)	6	6	43	42	0	0	110	108
Greg Burns	25/3/95	(1)	0	0	0	0	0	0	0	0	0
Keal Carlile	20/3/90	22(3)	13(3)	1	0	0	0	0	0	4	0
James Davey	21/8/89	10(19)	10(12)	2	1	0	0	0	0	8	4
John Davies	8/1/91	10(17)	8(12)	3	3	0	0	0	0	12	12
Michael Knowles	2/5/87	28	20	6	5	3	3	1	1	31	27
Jamie Langley	21/12/83	9(3)	8(2)	1	1	0	0	0	0	4	4
Quentin Laulu-Togagae	1/12/84	31	22	20	15	0	0	0	0	80	60
Ryan Millar	12/5/94	2	1	5	2	0	0	0	0	20	8
Jon Molloy	23/3/91	(1)	(1)	1	1	0	0	0	0	4	4
Ben Musolino	18/12/92	(5)	(3)	0	0	0	0	0	0	0	0
Dave Petersen	6/3/92	2(6)	1(4)	1	1	0	0	0	0	4	4
Oliver Roberts	24/12/95	(2)	(2)	0	0	0	0	0	0	0	0
Connor Scott	27/5/93	(3)	(1)	0	0	0	0	0	0	0	0
Sam Smeaton	26/10/88	30	22	7	6	0	0	0	0	28	24
Duane Straugheir	29/9/89	22(3)	14(3)	6	4	0	0	0	0	24	16
Mitchell Stringer	1/11/83	18(6)	12(5)	3	3	0	0	0	0	12	12
Lelauloto Tagaloa	26/12/86	(1)	(1)	0	0	0	0	0	0	0	0
Misi Taulapapa	25/1/82	22(7)	19(2)	10	9	0	0	0	0	40	36
Steve Thorpe	26/9/89	19(7)	16(6)	3	1	0	0	0	0	12	4
Tony Tonks	27/4/85	7(17)	5(13)	2	2	0	0	0	0	8	8
Scott Turner	15/4/88	30	21	17	12	0	0	0	0	68	48
Pat Walker	24/3/86	17(3)	11(2)	2	1	43	19	0	0	94	42
Rob Worrincy	9/7/85	22(3)	14(3)	16	11	0	0	0	0	64	44
Menzie Yere	24/10/83	32	23	21	16	0	0	0	0	84	64

'Ch' totals include Championship regular season only; 'All' totals also include Super 8s (Qualifiers) & Challenge Cup

Eddie Battye

LEAGUE RECORD
Championship, before Super 8 split:
P23-W17-D0-L6 (3rd)
F586, A451, Diff+135, 34 points.

S8-Q: P7-W2-D0-L5 (7th)
F152, A267, Diff-115, 4 points.

CHALLENGE CUP
Round Five

ATTENDANCES
Best - v Featherstone (Ch - 2,443)
Worst - v Oldham (CC - 484)
Total (Championship/S8s only) - 17,968
Average (Championship/S8s only) - 1,283
(Up by 454 on 2014)

CLUB RECORDS **Highest score:** 112-6 v Leigh East, 7/4/2013 **Highest score against:** 0-88 v Hull, 2/3/2003 **Record attendance:** 10,603 v Bradford, 16/8/97
MATCH RECORDS **Tries:** 5 Daryl Powell v Mansfield, 2/1/89; Menzie Yere v Leigh East, 7/4/2013; Quentin Laulu-Togagae v Rochdale, 7/9/2014
Goals: 14 Dominic Brambani v Leigh East, 7/4/2013 **Points:** 32 Roy Rafferty v Fulham, 21/9/86
SEASON RECORDS **Tries:** 46 Menzie Yere 2013 **Goals:** 169 *(inc 1fg)* Dominic Brambani 2013 **Points:** 361 Dominic Brambani 2013
CAREER RECORDS **Tries:** 158 Menzie Yere 2009-2015 **Goals:** 986 Mark Aston 1986-2004 **Points:** 2,142 Mark Aston 1986-2004 **Appearances:** 389 Mark Aston 1986-2004

WHITEHAVEN

DATE	FIXTURE	RESULT	SCORERS	LGE	ATT
15/2/15	Halifax (h)	L16-44	t:Burns,Trout,Gore g:Seymour(2)	12th	1,022
22/2/15	Bradford (a)	L34-4	t:Parker	12th	4,891
1/3/15	Sheffield (h)	L6-20	t:Craven g:Seymour	12th	701
8/3/15	Dewsbury (a)	L23-16	t:McAvoy,Hulme,Parker,Calvert	12th	911
15/3/15	London Broncos (h)	W18-16	t:Burns,Newton,Brocklebank g:Brocklebank(3)	11th	689
21/3/15	Featherstone (h) (CCR4)	L12-36	t:Parker,Aiye g:Brocklebank(2)	N/A	525
29/3/15	Leigh (a)	L60-0		11th	3,006
3/4/15	Workington (a)	L40-0		11th	1,260
6/4/15	Doncaster (h)	W41-16	t:Calvert(2),Chamberlain(2),Hepi,McAvoy,Newton g:Brocklebank(6) fg:Brocklebank	11th	718
12/4/15	Hunslet (a)	L26-18	t:Lepori,Lloyd,Hepi g:Brocklebank(3)	11th	539
26/4/15	Featherstone (h)	L12-36	t:Gore,Brooks g:Brocklebank(2)	11th	747
3/5/15	Batley (a)	W22-24	t:Hulme(2),Newton,Brooks g:Brocklebank(2),Gore(2)	10th	560
10/5/15	Bradford (h)	L16-32	t:McAvoy,Holliday,Newton g:Chamberlain(2)	10th	1,338
17/5/15	Halifax (a)	L60-18	t:Aiye,Calvert,McAvoy g:Johnstone(3)	10th	1,601
23/5/15	Workington (SB) ●	L20-26	t:Gore,Sigismeau,Jouffret,Burns g:Jouffret(2)	11th	N/A
31/5/15	Leigh (h)	L16-46	t:Davies,Johnstone,Lepori g:Jouffret(2)	11th	841
7/6/15	Hunslet (h)	W28-12	t:Allen,Wilde,Aiye,Beaumont,Sigismeau g:Jouffret(4)	11th	661
13/6/15	Sheffield (a) ●●	L26-16	t:Calvert,McAvoy(2) g:Jouffret(2)	11th	503
21/6/15	Batley (h)	W24-12	t:Gore,Calvert(2),Jouffret g:Jouffret(4)	9th	802
28/6/15	Doncaster (a) ●●	W18-50	t:Allen,Gore,Taylor,McAvoy(2),Parker,Sigismeau,Davies,Aiye g:Jouffret(7)	8th	1,000
5/7/15	London Broncos (a)	L40-24	t:Hulme(3),Taylor,Newton g:Gore(2)	8th	567
12/7/15	Workington (h)	L6-28	t:Calvert g:Jouffret	8th	1,722
19/7/15	Dewsbury (h)	L16-34	t:Hulme,Calvert,Davies g:Jouffret(2)	10th	760
25/7/15	Featherstone (a)	W0-29	t:Aiye(2),Taylor,McAvoy,Burns g:Jouffret(4) fg:Gore	10th	1,305
9/8/15	Featherstone (a) (CS)	L42-30	t:T Chapelhow(2),Gore,Taylor,Chamberlain g:Chamberlain(5)	6th(CS)	1,107
15/8/15	London Broncos (h) (CS)	W40-16	t:Newton(2),Davies,Parker,Hepi,Holliday,Fox g:Chamberlain(6)	5th(CS)	783
23/8/15	Dewsbury (a) (CS)	W30-42	t:McAvoy(2),Calvert(2),Aiye,Fox,Gore g:Chamberlain(7)	5th(CS)	709
31/8/15	Hunslet (h) (CS)	L16-30	t:Chamberlain,Griffiths,Taylor g:Chamberlain(2)	5th(CS)	804
6/9/15	Batley (a) (CS)	L50-0		6th(CS)	499
13/9/15	Workington (a) (CS)	L60-20	t:Aiye(3),Coyle g:Chamberlain(2)	6th(CS)	1,559
19/9/15	Doncaster (h) (CS)	W52-22	t:Aiye(2),Newton,Calvert(2),Hepi,Chamberlain,Parker,Brooks g:Chamberlain(6),Robinson(2)	6th(CS)	589

● Played at Bloomfield Road, Blackpool ●● Played at Castle Park, Doncaster

		APP		TRIES		GOALS		FG		PTS	
	D.O.B.	ALL	Ch	ALL	Ch	ALL	Ch	ALL	Ch	ALL	Ch
Dion Aiye	6/11/87	30	22	12	6	0	0	0	0	48	24
Dave Allen	15/9/85	24	22	2	2	0	0	0	0	8	8
Thibaut Ancely	18/5/88	1(4)	(3)	0	0	0	0	0	0	0	0
Steve Bannister	10/10/87	3(2)	3(1)	0	0	0	0	0	0	0	0
Richard Beaumont	2/2/88	15(3)	9(3)	1	1	0	0	0	0	4	4
John-Paul Brocklebank	1/11/89	7	6	1	1	18	16	1	1	41	37
Sam Brooks	29/9/93	15(8)	8(8)	3	2	0	0	0	0	12	8
Jordan Burns	2/9/95	17	12	4	4	0	0	0	0	16	16
Craig Calvert	10/2/84	25	19	13	9	0	0	0	0	52	36
Liam Carberry	24/2/93	1(1)	1(1)	0	0	0	0	0	0	0	0
Ed Chamberlain	8/2/96	12	5	5	2	30	2	0	0	80	12
Jay Chapelhow	21/9/95	(3)	(3)	0	0	0	0	0	0	0	0
Ted Chapelhow	21/9/95	14(7)	11(3)	2	0	0	0	0	0	8	0
Thomas Coyle	10/5/88	24(3)	19(1)	1	0	0	0	0	0	4	0
Danny Craven	21/11/91	2	2	1	1	0	0	0	0	4	4
Ben Davies	2/11/89	14(15)	11(10)	4	3	0	0	0	0	16	12
Steve Fox	13/2/90	7(15)	4(12)	2	0	0	0	0	0	8	0
Grant Gore	21/11/91	22(1)	15(1)	7	5	4	4	1	1	37	29
Owain Griffiths	18/7/91	(3)	0	1	0	0	0	0	0	4	0
Jordan Hand	13/5/93	1	1	0	0	0	0	0	0	0	0
Tyla Hepi	15/6/93	16(10)	9(10)	4	2	0	0	0	0	16	8
Connor Holliday	9/6/95	9(3)	5(1)	2	1	0	0	0	0	8	4
Declan Hulme	14/1/93	10(1)	10(1)	7	7	0	0	0	0	28	28
Paul Johnson	13/3/88	2(1)	2(1)	0	0	0	0	0	0	0	0
Jordan Johnstone	24/5/97	2	2	1	1	3	3	0	0	10	10
Phil Joseph	10/1/85	(3)	(3)	0	0	0	0	0	0	0	0
Louis Jouffret	24/5/95	9	9	2	2	28	28	0	0	64	64
Richard Lepori	22/10/91	11(2)	10(2)	2	2	0	0	0	0	8	8
Macgraff Leuluai	9/2/90	2	2	0	0	0	0	0	0	0	0
Rhodri Lloyd	22/7/93	6	6	1	1	0	0	0	0	4	4
Scott McAvoy	9/4/86	26	21	11	9	0	0	0	0	44	36
Ben Milburn	7/6/95	1	1	0	0	0	0	0	0	0	0
James Newton	20/12/91	8(22)	4(18)	8	5	0	0	0	0	32	20
Jack Owens	3/6/94	1	1	0	0	0	0	0	0	0	0
Jessie Joe Parker	22/8/85	22(1)	16(1)	6	3	0	0	0	0	24	12
Kurtis Quinn	12/1/96	2(3)	(1)	0	0	0	0	0	0	0	0
James Robinson	4/3/79	(7)	(3)	0	0	2	0	0	0	4	0
Brett Seymour	27/9/84	8	7	0	0	3	3	0	0	6	6
Jordan Sigismeau	22/12/92	6	6	3	3	0	0	0	0	12	12
Chris Taylor	25/10/93	13(1)	6(1)	5	3	0	0	0	0	20	12
Kyle Trout	1/3/91	1(1)	1(1)	1	1	0	0	0	0	4	4
Jonathan Walker	20/2/91	5	5	0	0	0	0	0	0	0	0
Greg Wilde	22/12/93	9(3)	6(2)	1	1	0	0	0	0	4	4

'Ch' totals include Championship regular season only; 'All' totals also include Championship Shield & Challenge Cup

Dion Aiye

LEAGUE RECORD
Championship, before Super 8 split:
P23-W7-D0-L16 (10th)
F418, A671, Diff-253, 14 points.

After Championship Shield:
P30-W10-D0-L20 (6th)
F618, A921, Diff-303, 20 points.

CHALLENGE CUP
Round Four

ATTENDANCES
Best - v Workington (Ch - 1,722)
Worst - v Featherstone (CC - 525)
Total (Championship/ Championship Shield only) - 12,177
Average (Championship/ Championship Shield only) - 870
(Up by 72 on 2014)

CLUB RECORDS **Highest score:** 86-6 v Highfield, 25/1/95 **Highest score against:** 8-106 v Wigan, 12/5/2008 **Record attendance:** 18,500 v Wakefield, 19/3/60
MATCH RECORDS **Tries:** 6 Vince Gribbin v Doncaster, 18/11/84 **Goals:** 13 Lee Anderson v Highfield, 25/1/95 **Points:** 32 Mick Nanyn v Batley, 22/8/2004
SEASON RECORDS **Tries:** 34 Mike Pechey 1994-95 **Goals:** 141 John McKeown 1956-57 **Points:** 398 Mick Nanyn 2004
CAREER RECORDS **Tries:** 248 David Seeds 1993-2007 **Goals:** 1,050 John McKeown 1948-61 **Points:** 2,133 John McKeown 1948-61 **Appearances:** 417 John McKeown 1948-61

WORKINGTON TOWN

DATE	FIXTURE	RESULT	SCORERS	LGE	ATT
15/2/15	Batley (a)	L30-6	t:B Phillips g:Forber	11th	801
1/3/15	Doncaster (h)	W33-6	t:Forrester,Manfredi,C Phillips,Whiteley,Olstrum,Forber g:Forber(4) fg:Doran	7th	741
8/3/15	London Broncos (a)	L34-16	t:Whiteley,Stack,Forber g:Forber(2)	9th	587
15/3/15	Sheffield (h)	L12-14	t:Forrester,Whiteley g:Forber(2)	10th	682
18/3/15	Dewsbury (h)	L18-31	t:Forrester,Shackley g:Forber(5)	10th	761
22/3/15	Bradford (a) (CCR4)	L74-6	t:Duerden g:Forber	N/A	2,412
29/3/15	Bradford (a)	L36-6	t:Whiteley g:Forber	10th	4,238
3/4/15	Whitehaven (h)	W40-0	t:McAvoy,Doran,Forber,Stack,Carter,Murphy,Whiteley g:Forber(4),Murphy(2)	9th	1,260
6/4/15	Leigh (a)	L54-6	t:Forber g:Forber	9th	3,017
12/4/15	Halifax (a)	L38-6	t:Whiteley g:Forber	10th	1,122
26/4/15	Hunslet (h)	L16-19	t:Fifita,B Phillips,Doran g:Forber(2)	10th	689
3/5/15	Featherstone (a)	L72-0		11th	1,547
10/5/15	Batley (h)	L10-23	t:C Phillips,Forber g:Forber	11th	596
17/5/15	Doncaster (a)	W6-37	t:Lloyd(2),Tierney(3),B Phillips,Murphy g:Shorrocks(2),Horton(2) fg:Doran	11th	695
23/5/15	Whitehaven (SB) ●	W20-26	t:Stack(2),Shackley,Murphy g:Forber(5)	10th	N/A
31/5/15	Halifax (h)	L6-32	t:Lloyd g:Forber	10th	641
7/6/15	Dewsbury (a)	D20-20	t:Lloyd,Stack,Tierney,Miller g:Forber(2)	9th	751
14/6/15	Featherstone (h)	L0-52		9th	749
21/6/15	Bradford (h)	L16-38	t:Powell(2),Farrell g:Murphy,Forber	10th	1,063
28/6/15	Sheffield (a) ●●	L26-6	t:Carter g:Forber	10th	506
5/7/15	Leigh (h)	L12-50	t:Stack,Tierney g:Sammut,Forber	11th	914
12/7/15	Whitehaven (a)	W6-28	t:Miller(3),Thornley,Sammut g:Sammut(2),Forber(2)	9th	1,722
19/7/15	London Broncos (h)	W29-18	t:Horton,B Phillips,Tierney,Coward g:Sammut(2),Forber(4) fg:Sammut	8th	686
26/7/15	Hunslet (a)	W6-30	t:Sammut,Miller,Carter(2),Murphy g:Sammut(2),Forber(3)	8th	706
9/8/15	Batley (h) (CS)	W30-12	t:Sammut,Stack,Murphy,Horton,C Phillips,Miller g:Sammut(2),Forber	4th(CS)	864
16/8/15	Hunslet (a) (CS)	W18-22	t:Carter,Akehurst,B Phillips,Whiteley g:Sammut,Forber(2)	4th(CS)	567
23/8/15	Featherstone (h) (CS)	L10-24	t:C Phillips,Miller g:Sammut	4th(CS)	906
31/8/15	Doncaster (h) (CS)	W62-0	t:Akehurst,Carter(3),Sammut(3),Doran,Szostak,Miller(2) g:Forber(9)	4th(CS)	629
6/9/15	London Broncos (a) (CS)	L50-10	t:Sammut,Walker g:Forber	4th(CS)	363
13/9/15	Whitehaven (h) (CS)	W60-20	t:Miller(2),Murphy,Carter(3),Stack(2),J Mossop,Forber,Sammut g:Sammut(8)	4th(CS)	1,559
20/9/15	Dewsbury (a) (CS)	L27-14	t:Whiteley,Miller,Sammut g:Forber	4th(CS)	804
27/9/15	Featherstone (a) (CSSF)	L52-14	t:Stack,Sammut(2) g:Sammut	N/A	1,233

● Played at Bloomfield Road, Blackpool ●● Played at Castle Park, Doncaster

		APP		TRIES		GOALS		FG		PTS	
	D.O.B.	ALL	Ch	ALL	Ch	ALL	Ch	ALL	Ch	ALL	Ch
Scott Akehurst	10/8/92	6(1)	1(1)	2	0	0	0	0	0	8	0
Brett Carter	9/7/88	17(1)	10(1)	11	4	0	0	0	0	44	16
Kris Coward	1/10/81	11(9)	4(9)	1	1	0	0	0	0	4	4
Jamie Doran	8/12/94	30	21	3	2	0	0	2	2	14	10
James Duerden	9/10/91	(7)	(6)	1	0	0	0	0	0	4	0
Connor Farrell	6/11/93	3	3	1	1	0	0	0	0	4	4
Latu Fifita	29/10/87	(11)	(10)	1	1	0	0	0	0	4	4
Carl Forber	17/3/85	20(11)	16(6)	6	5	59	44	0	0	142	108
Sam Forrester	28/6/93	13(2)	10(1)	3	3	0	0	0	0	12	12
Oliver Gildart	6/8/96	2	2	0	0	0	0	0	0	0	0
James Greenwood	17/6/91	1(2)	1(2)	0	0	0	0	0	0	0	0
Ryan Hampshire	29/12/94	1	1	0	0	0	0	0	0	0	0
Kurt Horton	13/2/91	15(4)	13(4)	2	1	2	2	0	0	12	8
Rhodri Lloyd	22/7/93	5(1)	5(1)	4	4	0	0	0	0	16	16
Nathan Lucock	2/10/93	3(4)	3(1)	0	0	0	0	0	0	0	0
Dominic Manfredi	1/10/93	2	2	1	1	0	0	0	0	4	4
Graeme Mattinson	24/4/85	16	15	0	0	0	0	0	0	0	0
Liam McAvoy	24/9/93	22(5)	15(3)	1	1	0	0	0	0	4	4
Elliott Miller	14/9/90	18	12	12	5	0	0	0	0	48	20
Jason Mossop	12/9/85	21	14	1	0	0	0	0	0	4	0
Lee Mossop	17/1/89	1	1	0	0	0	0	0	0	0	0
Jack Murphy	18/3/92	31	23	6	4	3	3	0	0	30	22
Karl Olstrum	21/9/91	7(16)	4(11)	1	1	0	0	0	0	4	4
Brett Phillips	25/10/88	27	19	5	4	0	0	0	0	20	16
Callum Phillips	19/2/92	11(8)	6(8)	4	2	0	0	0	0	16	8
Sam Powell	3/7/92	(1)	(1)	2	2	0	0	0	0	8	8
Theerapol Ritson	7/1/96	4	2	0	0	0	0	0	0	0	0
Jarrod Sammut	15/2/87	13	5	11	2	20	7	1	1	85	23
Steve Scholey	7/1/96	3(16)	2(11)	0	0	0	0	0	0	0	0
Marc Shackley	14/1/89	26(3)	21(2)	2	2	0	0	0	0	8	8
Jake Shorrocks	26/10/95	3	3	0	0	2	2	0	0	4	4
Jarrad Stack	13/2/88	25	18	10	6	0	0	0	0	40	24
Ryan Sutton	2/8/95	(2)	(2)	0	0	0	0	0	0	0	0
Alex Szostak	4/3/86	5(3)	(2)	1	0	0	0	0	0	4	0
Iain Thornley	11/9/91	4	4	1	1	0	0	0	0	4	4
Lewis Tierney	20/10/94	13	13	6	6	0	0	0	0	24	24
Logan Tomkins	1/8/91	(2)	(2)	0	0	0	0	0	0	0	0
Tom Walker	25/12/94	23(8)	18(4)	1	0	0	0	0	0	4	0
Perry Whiteley	22/2/93	14(9)	12(4)	8	6	0	0	0	0	32	24

'Ch' totals include Championship regular season only; 'All' totals also include Championship Shield & Challenge Cup

Jack Murphy

LEAGUE RECORD
Championship, before Super 8 split:
P23-W7-D1-L15 (8th)
F379, A631, Diff-252, 15 points.

After Championship Shield:
P30-W11-D1-L18 (4th/Semi-Finalists)
F587, A782, Diff-195, 23 points.

CHALLENGE CUP
Round Four

ATTENDANCES
Best - v Whitehaven (CS - 1,559)
Worst - v Batley (Ch - 596)
Total (Championship/ Championship Shield only) - 12,740
Average (Championship/ Championship Shield only) - 849
(Up by 11 on 2014)

CLUB RECORDS **Highest score:** 94-4 v Leigh, 26/2/95 **Highest score against:** 0-92 v Bradford, 14/2/99 **Record attendance:** 17,741 v Wigan, 3/3/65
MATCH RECORDS **Tries:** 7 Ike Southward v Blackpool, 17/9/55 **Goals:** 14 Darren Holt v Gateshead, 12/6/2011
Points: 42 Dean Marwood v Highfield, 1/11/92; Dean Marwood v Leigh, 26/2/95
SEASON RECORDS **Tries:** 49 Johnny Lawrenson 1951-52 **Goals:** 186 Lyn Hopkins 1981-82 **Points:** 438 Lyn Hopkins 1981-82
CAREER RECORDS **Tries:** 274 Ike Southward 1952-68 **Goals:** 809 Iain MacCorquodale 1972-80 **Points:** 1,800 Iain MacCorquodale 1972-80
Appearances: 419 Paul Charlton 1961-69; 1975-80

CHAMPIONSHIP 2015
Round by Round

ROUND 1

Friday 13th February 2015

DEWSBURY RAMS 19 SHEFFIELD EAGLES 10

RAMS: 3 Karl Pryce; 18 Dalton Grant; 15 Jason Crookes; 4 Shane Grady; 2 Dale Morton; 6 Matty Wildie; 7 Anthony Thackeray; 17 Matthew Haggarty; 23 Tom Hemingway; 10 Ryan Hepworth; 11 Rob Spicer; 12 Scott Hale; 13 Aaron Brown. Subs (all used): 22 Sam Wood; 25 Joel Farrell; 16 Toby Adamson; 32 Makali Aizue.
Tries: Grant (32, 79), Thackeray (37);
Goals: Hemingway 3/3; **Field goal:** Thackeray (74).
EAGLES: 1 Quentin Laulu-Togagae; 2 Scott Turner; 3 Menzie Yere; 4 Sam Smeaton; 5 Misi Taulapapa; 6 Kyle Briggs; 7 Dominic Brambani; 8 Eddie Battye; 9 James Davey; 17 Steve Thorpe; 11 Michael Knowles; 12 Duane Straugheir; 13 Pat Walker. Subs (all used): 19 Cory Aston; 20 Jack Blagbrough; 22 Tony Tonks; 18 Ben Musolino.
Tries: Turner (15), Davey (29); **Goals:** Brambani 1/2.
Rugby Leaguer & League Express Men of the Match: *Rams:* Tom Hemingway; *Eagles:* Eddie Battye.
Penalty count: 11-6; **Half-time:** 12-10;
Referee: Matthew Thomason; **Attendance:** 1,309.

Sunday 15th February 2015

BATLEY BULLDOGS 30 WORKINGTON TOWN 6

BULLDOGS: 1 James Craven; 2 Wayne Reittie; 3 Shaun Ainscough; 20 Shaun Squires; 5 Johnny Campbell; 6 Cain Southernwood; 7 Scott Leatherbarrow; 10 Alex Rowe; 14 Alistair Leak; 18 Tom Lillycrop; 12 Sam Scott; 11 Alex Bretherton; 17 Joe Chandler. Subs (all used): 9 Anthony Nicholson; 13 Luke Blake; 15 Adam Gledhill; 21 James Brown.
Tries: Squires (20, 22, 34, 63), Bretherton (77);
Goals: Leatherbarrow 5/7.
TOWN: 1 Jack Murphy; 32 Dominic Manfredi; 3 Jason Mossop; 4 Perry Whiteley; 5 Brett Carter; 7 Carl Forber; 14 Callum Phillips; 33 Lee Mossop; 9 Graeme Mattinson; 10 Marc Shackley; 11 Brett Phillips; 16 Kurt Horton; 12 Jarrad Stack. Subs (all used): 15 Karl Olstrum; 30 James Greenwood; 25 Steve Scholey; 20 Nathan Lucock.
Try: B Phillips (17); **Goals:** Forber 1/1.
Sin bin: Olstrum (33) - high tackle on Campbell.
Rugby Leaguer & League Express Men of the Match: *Bulldogs:* Shaun Squires; *Town:* Brett Phillips.
Penalty count: 10-9; **Half-time:** 14-6;
Referee: George Stokes; **Attendance:** 801.

LEIGH CENTURIONS 36 BRADFORD BULLS 24

CENTURIONS: 1 Gregg McNally; 2 Adam Higson; 3 Greg Worthington; 4 Tom Armstrong; 5 Liam Kay; 6 Martyn Ridyard; 7 Ryan Brierley; 21 Jamie Acton; 14 Sean Penkywicz; 10 Oliver Wilkes; 19 Kurt Haggerty; 12 Tommy Goulden; 13 Sam Barlow. Subs (all used): 9 Bob Beswick; 20 Sam Hopkins; 8 Fuifui Moimoi; 29 Jake Emmitt.
Tries: Brierley (13), Kay (49), McNally (53, 72), Armstrong (64), Penkywicz (79); **Goals:** Ridyard 6/7.
Sin bin: Acton (21) - punching; McNally (24) - fighting; Haggerty (34) - dangerous challenge on Uaisele.
BULLS: 1 Jake Mullaney; 2 Etuate Uaisele; 3 Adrian Purtell; 22 Chev Walker; 5 Danny Williams; 6 Lee Gaskell; 7 Harry Siejka; 8 Paul Clough; 9 Adam O'Brien; 10 Adam Sidlow; 11 Tom Olbison; 14 Jay Pitts; 13 Danny Addy. Subs (all used): 23 Alex Mellor; 28 Samir Tahraoui; 19 Chris Ulugia; 24 Lucas Walshaw.
Tries: O'Brien (4, 69), Walker (9), Mullaney (29), Uaisele (37); **Goals:** Siejka 2/5.
Sin bin: Williams (24) - fighting;
Siejka (29) - high tackle on Barlow,
(56) - delaying restart.
Rugby Leaguer & League Express Men of the Match: *Centurions:* Gregg McNally; *Bulls:* Adam O'Brien.
Penalty count: 14-12; **Half-time:** 6-20;
Referee: Joe Cobb; **Attendance:** 7,449.

LONDON BRONCOS 26 DONCASTER 22

BRONCOS: 1 Richard Mathers; 2 Rhys Williams; 3 Ben Farrar; 4 Wes Naiqama; 5 Ben Hellewell; 22 Oscar Thomas; 19 Joe Keyes; 8 Nick Slyney; 9 Ray Nasso; 10 Josh Cordoba; 11 Daniel Harrison; 12 Rhys Lovegrove; 15 Matt Garside. Subs (all used): 14 Brad Dwyer; 18 Jon Wallace; 21 Joel Wicks; 23 Toby Everett.
Tries: Nasso (3), Harrison (9), R Williams (15, 22), Naiqama (47); **Goals:** Naiqama 3/5.
DONCASTER: 1 Dave Scott; 26 Sam Doherty; 3 Danny Cowling; 17 Liam Welham; 5 Stewart Sanderson; 6 Paul Cooke; 31 Jordan Rankin; 8 Matt Carbutt; 34 Stuart Howarth; 35 Iafeta Palea'aesina; 12 Steve Snitch; 4 Pasqualle Dunn; 13 Mike Emmett. Subs (all used): 14 Russ Spiers; 15 Mitch Clark; 10 Craig Robinson; 19 Lee Waterman.
Tries: Palea'aesina (53), Doherty (58, 75), Waterman (66);
Goals: Sanderson 3/4.
Rugby Leaguer & League Express Men of the Match: *Broncos:* Nick Slyney; *Doncaster:* Mitch Clark.
Penalty count: 5-8; **Half-time:** 20-0;
Referee: Chris Leatherbarrow; **Attendance:** 976.

WHITEHAVEN 16 HALIFAX 44

WHITEHAVEN: 1 Richard Lepori; 5 Jordan Burns; 3 Jessie Joe Parker; 4 Scott McAvoy; 16 Connor Holliday; 6 Brett Seymour; 14 Thomas Coyle; 8 Ben Davies; 9 James Newton; 10 Jordan Hand; 25 Dion Aiye; 11 Dave Allen; 13 Tyla Hepi. Subs (all used): 15 Grant Gore; 27 Kyle Trout; 28 Paul Johnson; 18 Steve Fox.
Tries: Burns (21), Trout (37), Gore (42);
Goals: Seymour 2/3.
HALIFAX: 1 Miles Greenwood; 20 James Saltonstall; 3 Steve Tyrer; 26 Chris Taylor; 5 Alex Brown; 6 Scott Murrell; 7 Ben Johnston; 17 Mitch Cahalane; 9 Ben Kaye; 16 Richard Moore; 11 Dane Manning; 15 Adam Robinson; 12 Andy Bracek. Subs (all used): 10 Luke Ambler; 13 Jack Spencer; 21 Ryan Maneely; 27 Ross Divorty.
Tries: Tyrer (3), Greenwood (8), Saltonstall (14, 68), Brown (26, 78), A Robinson (34, 39), Ambler (52);
Goals: Tyrer 4/9.
Rugby Leaguer & League Express Men of the Match: *Whitehaven:* Paul Johnson; *Halifax:* Ben Johnston.
Penalty count: 9-5; **Half-time:** 10-28;
Referee: Michael Woodhead; **Attendance:** 1,022.

Monday 16th February 2015

FEATHERSTONE ROVERS 28 HUNSLET HAWKS 14

ROVERS: 21 Jy Hitchcox; 2 Will Sharp; 3 Nathan Chappell; 1 Ian Hardman; 5 Ben Blackmore; 6 Paul Sykes; 14 Sam Irwin; 8 Jordan Baldwinson; 9 Andy Ellis; 10 Paul Wood; 11 James Lockwood; 19 Alex Foster; 13 Tim Spears. Subs (all used): 31 Remy Marginet; 15 Jack Bussey; 16 Andrew Bostock; 17 Matt James.
Tries: Hardman (16), Bussey (43), Blackmore (54, 78), Sykes (69); **Goals:** Sykes 3/4, Marginet 1/1.
Sin bin: Spears (24) - obstruction.
HAWKS: 1 Jimmy Watson; 24 Richie Barnett; 34 Luke Briscoe; 4 Danny Maun; 5 Vinny Finigan; 31 Andy Kain; 6 Simon Brown; 10 James Houston; 9 Jack Lee; 8 Michael Haley; 12 Aaron Lyons; 11 Callum Casey; 15 Liam Mackay. Subs (all used): 19 Brad Brennan; 35 Rob Mulhern; 13 Danny Grimshaw; 23 Elliott Cosgrove.
Tries: Casey (32), Mackay (46); **Goals:** Brown 3/3.
Rugby Leaguer & League Express Men of the Match: *Rovers:* Sam Irwin; *Hawks:* Andy Kain.
Penalty count: 7-9; **Half-time:** 6-8;
Referee: Chris Kendall; **Attendance:** 1,836
(at Belle Vue, Wakefield).

ROUND 2

Sunday 22nd February 2015

DONCASTER 6 FEATHERSTONE ROVERS 13

DONCASTER: 1 Dave Scott; 26 Sam Doherty; 31 Steve Michaels; 3 Danny Cowling; 5 Stewart Sanderson; 6 Paul Cooke; 34 Jordan Rankin; 8 Matt Carbutt; 35 James Cunningham; 33 Iafeta Palea'aesina; 12 Steve Snitch; 4 Pasqualle Dunn; 13 Mike Emmett. Subs (all used): 14 Russ Spiers; 15 Mitch Clark; 19 Lee Waterman; 32 Stuart Howarth.
Try: Cowling (8); **Goals:** Sanderson 1/2.
ROVERS: 21 Jy Hitchcox; 2 Will Sharp; 3 Nathan Chappell; 18 Jamie Cording; 5 Ben Blackmore; 6 Paul Sykes; 14 Sam Irwin; 8 Jordan Baldwinson; 9 Andy Ellis; 10 Paul Wood; 19 Alex Foster; 34 Matt Ryan; 11 James Lockwood. Subs (all used): 13 Tim Spears; 17 Matt James; 16 Andrew Bostock; 31 Remy Marginet.
Tries: Chappell (43), Ryan (71); **Goals:** Sykes 2/3;
Field goal: Marginet (77).
Rugby Leaguer & League Express Men of the Match: *Doncaster:* Paul Cooke; *Rovers:* Nathan Chappell.
Penalty count: 5-6; **Half-time:** 4-0;
Referee: Warren Turley; **Attendance:** 950.

BRADFORD BULLS 34 WHITEHAVEN 4

BULLS: 1 Jake Mullaney; 2 Etuate Uaisele; 3 Adrian Purtell; 17 Jean-Philippe Baile; 5 Danny Williams; 6 Lee Gaskell; 7 Harry Siejka; 8 Paul Clough; 9 Adam O'Brien; 10 Adam Sidlow; 11 Tom Olbison; 14 Jay Pitts; 22 Chev Walker. Subs (all used): 23 Alex Mellor; 28 Samir Tahraoui; 27 Ryan Shaw; 24 Lucas Walshaw.
Tries: Purtell (15), Pitts (18), Gaskell (42, 50, 73), Sidlow (78); **Goals:** Siejka 2/3, Gaskell 3/3.
WHITEHAVEN: 17 Ben Milburn; 1 Richard Lepori; 27 Declan Hulme; 3 Jessie Joe Parker; 26 Greg Wilde; 15 Grant Gore; 6 Brett Seymour; 28 Kyle Trout; 14 Thomas Coyle; 23 Paul Johnson; 4 Scott McAvoy; 25 Dion Aiye; 11 Dave Allen. Subs (all used): 21 Liam Carberry; 18 Steve Fox; 13 Tyla Hepi; 16 Connor Holliday.
Try: Parker (32); **Goals:** Seymour 0/1.
Rugby Leaguer & League Express Men of the Match: *Bulls:* Lee Gaskell; *Whitehaven:* Brett Seymour.
Penalty count: 9-5; **Half-time:** 10-4;
Referee: Chris Kendall; **Attendance:** 4,891.

HALIFAX 6 LEIGH CENTURIONS 18

HALIFAX: 1 Miles Greenwood; 20 James Saltonstall; 3 Steve Tyrer; 26 Chris Taylor; 5 Alex Brown; 6 Scott Murrell; 18 Matt Place; 17 Mitch Cahalane; 9 Ben Kaye; 10 Luke Ambler; 27 Ross Divorty; 11 Dane Manning; 12 Andy Bracek. Subs (all used): 8 Adam Tangata; 13 Jack Spencer; 16 Richard Moore; 21 Ryan Maneely.
Try: Maneely (46); **Goals:** Tyrer 1/1.
Sin bin: Cahalane (27) - punching.
CENTURIONS: 1 Gregg McNally; 15 Jonathan Pownall; 3 Greg Worthington; 4 Tom Armstrong; 5 Liam Kay; 6 Martyn Ridyard; 7 Ryan Brierley; 8 Fuifui Moimoi; 14 Sean Penkywicz; 24 Jonathan Walker; 19 Kurt Haggerty; 12 Tommy Goulden; 29 Jake Emmitt. Subs (all used): 9 Bob Beswick; 10 Oliver Wilkes; 13 Sam Barlow; 20 Sam Hopkins.
Tries: Kay (16, 24), Pownall (78); **Goals:** Ridyard 3/3.
Rugby Leaguer & League Express Men of the Match: *Halifax:* Luke Ambler; *Centurions:* Jake Emmitt.
Penalty count: 3-6; **Half-time:** 0-12;
Referee: Matthew Thomason; **Attendance:** 2,868.

HUNSLET HAWKS 14 BATLEY BULLDOGS 26

HAWKS: 1 Jimmy Watson; 24 Richie Barnett; 34 Luke Briscoe; 4 Danny Maun; 5 Vinny Finigan; 31 Andy Kain; 6 Simon Brown; 10 James Houston; 9 Jack Lee; 8 Michael Haley; 12 Aaron Lyons; 11 Callum Casey; 15 Liam Mackay. Subs (all used): 30 George Flanagan; 18 Brooke Broughton; 19 Brad Brennan; 35 Rob Mulhern.
Tries: Watson (21), Brennan (27); **Goals:** Brown 3/3.
BULLDOGS: 1 James Craven; 2 Wayne Reittie; 3 Shaun Ainscough; 20 Shaun Squires; 5 Johnny Campbell; 6 Cain Southernwood; 7 Scott Leatherbarrow; 10 Alex Rowe; 13 Luke Blake; 18 Tom Lillycrop; 11 Alex Bretherton; 12 Sam Scott; 17 Joe Chandler. Subs (all used): 9 Anthony Nicholson; 15 Adam Gledhill; 21 James Brown; 19 Lee Mitchell.
Tries: Craven (17), Squires (30), Nicholson (43), Ainscough (56), Reittie (79); **Goals:** Leatherbarrow 3/6.
Rugby Leaguer & League Express Men of the Match: *Hawks:* Brad Brennan; *Bulldogs:* Cain Southernwood.
Penalty count: 9-3; **Half-time:** 14-8;
Referee: Tom Crashley; **Attendance:** 901.

SHEFFIELD EAGLES 40 LONDON BRONCOS 6

EAGLES: 1 Quentin Laulu-Togagae; 2 Scott Turner; 3 Menzie Yere; 4 Sam Smeaton; 5 Misi Taulapapa; 6 Kyle Briggs; 7 Dominic Brambani; 8 Eddie Battye; 9 James Davey; 17 Steve Thorpe; 11 Michael Knowles; 12 Duane Straugheir; 13 Pat Walker. Subs (all used): 19 Cory Aston; 22 Tony Tonks; 23 Rob Worrincy; 27 Jon Molloy.
Tries: Knowles (3), Molloy (17), Laulu-Togagae (24), Briggs (35), Taulapapa (43), Smeaton (55), Straugheir (74), Turner (80);
Goals: Brambani 3/6, Walker 1/2.
BRONCOS: 1 Richard Mathers; 2 Rhys Williams; 3 Ben Farrar; 4 Wes Naiqama; 5 Ben Hellewell; 22 Oscar Thomas; 19 Joe Keyes; 8 Nick Slyney; 9 Ray Nasso; 10 Josh Cordoba; 11 Daniel Harrison; 12 Rhys Lovegrove; 15 Matt Garside. Subs (all used): 14 Brad Dwyer; 17 Erjon Dollapi; 18 Jon Wallace; 23 Toby Everett.
Try: R Williams (58); **Goals:** Naiqama 1/1.
Rugby Leaguer & League Express Men of the Match: *Eagles:* Menzie Yere; *Broncos:* Rhys Williams.
Penalty count: 5-7; **Half-time:** 20-0;
Referee: Dave Merrick; **Attendance:** 850
(at Keepmoat Stadium, Doncaster).

ROUND 3

Sunday 1st March 2015

BATLEY BULLDOGS 2 HALIFAX 6

BULLDOGS: 1 James Craven; 2 Wayne Reittie; 4 Ayden Faal; 20 Shaun Squires; 5 Johnny Campbell; 6 Cain Southernwood; 7 Scott Leatherbarrow; 10 Alex Rowe; 14 Alistair Leak; 18 Tom Lillycrop; 11 Alex Bretherton; 19 Lee Mitchell; 17 Joe Chandler. Subs (all used): 9 Anthony Nicholson; 13 Luke Blake; 8 Keegan Hirst; 21 James Brown.
Goals: Leatherbarrow 1/1.
HALIFAX: 1 Miles Greenwood; 2 Tom Saxton; 26 Chris Taylor; 3 Steve Tyrer; 20 James Saltonstall; 18 Matt Place; 6 Scott Murrell; 17 Mitch Cahalane; 9 Ben Kaye; 10 Luke Ambler; 15 Adam Robinson; 11 Dane Manning; 12 Andy Bracek. Subs (all used): 8 Adam Tangata; 16 Richard Moore; 21 Ryan Maneely; 22 Jacob Fairbank.
Try: Place (37); **Goals:** Tyrer 1/2.
Rugby Leaguer & League Express Men of the Match: *Bulldogs:* Johnny Campbell; *Halifax:* Scott Murrell.
Penalty count: 6-13; **Half-time:** 2-6;
Referee: Joe Cobb; **Attendance:** 1,113.

FEATHERSTONE ROVERS 4 BRADFORD BULLS 40

ROVERS: 21 Jy Hitchcox; 2 Will Sharp; 3 Nathan Chappell; 4 Thomas Minns; 5 Ben Blackmore; 6 Paul Sykes; 14 Sam Irwin; 8 Jordan Baldwinson; 9 Andy Ellis; 10 Paul Wood; 24 Mason Tonks; 19 Alex Foster; 15 Jack Bussey. Subs (all used): 31 Remy Marginet; 16 Andrew Bostock; 11 James Lockwood; 17 Matt James.
Try: Lockwood (48); **Goals:** Sykes 0/1.
Sin bin: Bostock (69) - high tackle.
BULLS: 27 Ryan Shaw; 19 Chris Ulugia; 3 Adrian Purtell; 17 Jean-Philippe Baile; 2 Etuate Uaisele; 6 Lee Gaskell; 1 Jake Mullaney; 8 Paul Clough; 9 Adam O'Brien; 10 Adam Sidlow; 24 Lucas Walshaw; 14 Jay Pitts; 23 Alex Mellor. Subs (all used): 31 Epalahame Lauaki; 28 Samir Tahraoui; 12 Dale Ferguson; 11 Tom Olbison.
Tries: Gaskell (18, 71), Purtell (35), Ulugia (40, 76), O'Brien (41), Baile (47); **Goals:** Shaw 6/7.
Rugby Leaguer & League Express Men of the Match: *Rovers:* Paul Wood; *Bulls:* Lee Gaskell.
Penalty count: 5-9; **Half-time:** 0-18;
Referee: Matthew Thomason; **Attendance:** 6,346.

HUNSLET HAWKS 18 DEWSBURY RAMS 6

HAWKS: 1 Jimmy Watson; 33 James Duckworth; 42 Jimmy Keinhorst; 4 Danny Maun; 5 Vinny Finigan; 6 Simon Brown; 7 Danny Ansell; 10 James Houston; 9 Jack Lee; 41 Andy Yates; 40 Josh Walters; 11 Callum Casey; 35 Rob Mulhern. Subs (all used): 30 George Flanagan; 34 Luke Briscoe; 19 Brad Brennan; 15 Liam Mackay.
Tries: Flanagan (40), Finigan (47); **Goals:** Brown 5/6.
RAMS: 3 Karl Pryce; 18 Dalton Grant; 15 Jason Crookes; 4 Shane Grady; 2 Dale Morton; 6 Matty Wildie; 7 Anthony Thackeray; 17 Matthew Haggarty; 23 Tom Hemingway; 10 Ryan Hepworth; 11 Rob Spicer; 12 Scott Hale; 13 Aaron Brown. Subs (all used): 31 Kieran Hyde; 25 Joel Farrell; 16 Toby Adamson; 32 Makali Aizue.
Try: Hepworth (59); **Goals:** Hemingway 1/1.

Rugby Leaguer & League Express Men of the Match: *Hawks:* Jimmy Watson; *Rams:* Toby Adamson.
Penalty count: 9-5; **Half-time:** 12-0;
Referee: Gareth Hewer; **Attendance:** 983.

LEIGH CENTURIONS 25 LONDON BRONCOS 12

CENTURIONS: 1 Gregg McNally; 15 Jonathan Pownall; 3 Greg Worthington; 4 Tom Armstrong; 5 Liam Kay; 6 Martyn Ridyard; 7 Ryan Brierley; 8 Fuifui Moimoi; 9 Bob Beswick; 10 Oliver Wilkes; 22 Andrew Dixon; 19 Kurt Haggerty; 29 Jake Emmitt. Subs (all used): 14 Sean Penkywicz; 24 Jonathan Walker; 20 Sam Hopkins; 13 Sam Barlow.
Tries: Haggerty (7), Kay (12), Armstrong (20, 43), Brierley (29); **Goals:** Ridyard 2/5;
Field goal: Ridyard (80).
BRONCOS: 1 Richard Mathers; 2 Rhys Williams; 3 Ben Farrar; 4 Wes Naiqama; 5 Ben Hellewell; 27 Jarrod Sammut; 28 Tom Gilmore; 17 Erjon Dollapi; 14 Brad Dwyer; 18 Jon Wallace; 11 Daniel Harrison; 15 Matt Garside; 12 Rhys Lovegrove. Subs (all used): 9 Ray Nasso; 21 Joel Wicks; 23 Toby Everett; 20 Iliess Macani.
Tries: Dollapi (15), R Williams (74); **Goals:** Naiqama 2/2.
On report:
Garside (37) - alleged dangerous challenge on Kay.
Rugby Leaguer & League Express Men of the Match: *Centurions:* Tom Armstrong; *Broncos:* Brad Dwyer.
Penalty count: 10-8; **Half-time:** 20-6;
Referee: George Stokes; **Attendance:** 4,531.

WHITEHAVEN 6 SHEFFIELD EAGLES 20

WHITEHAVEN: 7 Danny Craven; 1 Richard Lepori; - Declan Hulme; 3 Jessie Joe Parker; 2 Craig Calvert; 6 Brett Seymour; 15 Grant Gore; 23 Paul Johnson; 14 Thomas Coyle; 28 Macgraff Leuluai; 25 Dion Aiye; 4 Scott McAvoy; 11 Dave Allen. Subs (all used): 18 Steve Fox; 8 Ben Davies; 13 Tyla Hepi; 9 James Newton.
Try: Craven (17); **Goals:** Seymour 1/1.
EAGLES: 1 Quentin Laulu-Togagae; 2 Scott Turner; 3 Menzie Yere; 4 Sam Smeaton; 5 Misi Taulapapa; 6 Kyle Briggs; 7 Dominic Brambani; 8 Eddie Battye; 9 James Davey; 17 Steve Thorpe; 11 Michael Knowles; 12 Duane Straugheir; 13 Pat Walker. Subs (all used): 19 Cory Aston; 22 Tony Tonks; 23 Rob Worrincy; 15 John Davies.
Tries: Turner (11, 26, 53), Laulu-Togagae (28), Yere (70);
Goals: Walker 0/3, Briggs 0/1, Brambani 0/1.
Rugby Leaguer & League Express Men of the Match: *Whitehaven:* Macgraff Leuluai; *Eagles:* Scott Turner.
Penalty count: 10-3; **Half-time:** 6-12;
Referee: Chris Leatherbarrow; **Attendance:** 701.

WORKINGTON TOWN 33 DONCASTER 6

TOWN: 1 Jack Murphy; 2 Sam Forrester; 3 Jason Mossop; 4 Perry Whiteley; 32 Dominic Manfredi; 30 Jamie Doran; 7 Carl Forber; 19 Tom Walker; 9 Graeme Mattinson; 10 Marc Shackley; 11 Brett Phillips; 16 Kurt Horton; 12 Jarrad Stack. Subs (all used): 14 Callum Phillips; 15 Karl Olstrum; 25 Steve Scholey; 17 Latu Fifita.
Tries: Forrester (12), Manfredi (18), C Phillips (42), Whiteley (56), Olstrum (64), Forber (76);
Goals: Forber 4/6; **Field goal:** Doran (80).
DONCASTER: 31 Curtis Naughton; 26 Sam Doherty; 19 Lee Waterman; 17 Liam Welham; 1 Dave Scott; 6 Paul Cooke; 34 Stuart Howarth; 32 Bobby Tyson-Wilson; 13 Mike Emmett; 15 Mitch Clark; 11 Michael Kelly; 4 Pasqualle Dunn; 12 Steve Snitch. Subs (all used): 14 Russ Spiers; 16 Brett Waller; 8 Matt Carbutt; 9 Kyle Kesik.
Try: Dunn (30); **Goals:** Scott 1/1.
Rugby Leaguer & League Express Men of the Match: *Town:* Tom Walker; *Doncaster:* Pasqualle Dunn.
Penalty count: 9-12; **Half-time:** 8-6;
Referee: Andrew Sweet; **Attendance:** 741.

ROUND 4

Sunday 8th March 2015

DONCASTER 18 LEIGH CENTURIONS 54

DONCASTER: 1 Dave Scott; 26 Sam Doherty; 3 Danny Cowling; 19 Lee Waterman; 5 Stewart Sanderson; 29 Tom Holt; 24 Josh Kittrick; 10 Craig Robinson; 9 Kyle Kesik; 16 Brett Waller; 11 Michael Kelly; 12 Steve Snitch; 8 Matt Carbutt. Subs (all used): 14 Russ Spiers; 13 Mike Emmett; 32 Bobby Tyson-Wilson; 4 Pasqualle Dunn.
Tries: Emmett (34, 51), Doherty (67);
Goals: Sanderson 3/3.
CENTURIONS: 1 Gregg McNally; 15 Jonathan Pownall; 3 Greg Worthington; 4 Tom Armstrong; 5 Liam Kay; 6 Martyn Ridyard; 7 Ryan Brierley; 29 Jake Emmitt; 14 Sean Penkywicz; 10 Oliver Wilkes; 19 Kurt Haggerty; 22 Andrew Dixon; 13 Sam Barlow. Subs (all used): 9 Bob Beswick; 21 Jamie Acton; 20 Sam Hopkins; 18 Tom Spencer.
Tries: Brierley (5, 27), Barlow (10), McNally (20), Kay (30, 43, 54, 56), Ridyard (62), Armstrong (73);
Goals: Ridyard 7/10.
Sin bin: Worthington (15) - punching.
Rugby Leaguer & League Express Men of the Match: *Doncaster:* Mike Emmett; *Centurions:* Liam Kay.
Penalty count: 10-7; **Half-time:** 6-26;
Referee: Jamie Bloem; **Attendance:** 1,602.

BRADFORD BULLS 56 HUNSLET HAWKS 6

BULLS: 27 Ryan Shaw; 20 Adam Henry; 3 Adrian Purtell; 17 Jean-Philippe Baile; 5 Danny Williams; 6 Lee Gaskell; 1 Jake Mullaney; 8 Paul Clough; 9 Adam O'Brien; 10 Adam Sidlow; 14 Jay Pitts; 24 Lucas Walshaw; 23 Alex Mellor. Subs (all used): 15 Daniel Fleming; 11 Tom Olbison; 12 Dale Ferguson; 28 Samir Tahraoui.
Tries: Mullaney (5, 78), Gaskell (7), O'Brien (12, 68), Shaw (18, 31, 65), Williams (39), Olbison (57);
Goals: Shaw 8/10.
HAWKS: 1 Jimmy Watson; 33 James Duckworth; 42 Jimmy Keinhorst; 4 Danny Maun; 5 Vinny Finigan; 6 Simon Brown; 7 Danny Ansell; 41 Andy Yates; 9 Jack Lee; 35 Rob Mulhern; 43 Brett Delaney; 11 Callum Casey; 10 James Houston. Subs (all used): 30 George Flanagan; 34 Luke Briscoe; 15 Liam Mackay; 19 Brad Brennan.
Try: Briscoe (62); **Goals:** Brown 1/1.
Rugby Leaguer & League Express Men of the Match: *Bulls:* Ryan Shaw; *Hawks:* Jimmy Watson.
Penalty count: 4-2; **Half-time:** 34-0;
Referee: Chris Leatherbarrow; **Attendance:** 5,119.

DEWSBURY RAMS 23 WHITEHAVEN 16

RAMS: 3 Karl Pryce; 2 Dale Morton; 15 Jason Crookes; 4 Shane Grady; 18 Dalton Grant; 6 Matty Wildie; 7 Anthony Thackeray; 10 Ryan Hepworth; 23 Tom Hemingway; 17 Matthew Haggarty; 11 Rob Spicer; 12 Scott Hale; 34 Luke Adamson. Subs (all used): 32 Makali Aizue; 16 Toby Adamson; 25 Joel Farrell; 13 Aaron Brown.
Tries: Grant (18), Thackeray (29), Spicer (61), L Adamson (64); **Goals:** Hemingway 3/4;
Field goal: Thackeray (36).
WHITEHAVEN: 15 Danny Craven; 5 Jordan Burns; 27 Declan Hulme; 3 Jessie Joe Parker; 2 Craig Calvert; 19 John-Paul Brocklebank; 6 Brett Seymour; 18 Steve Fox; 9 James Newton; 21 Macgraff Leuluai; 25 Dion Aiye; 4 Scott McAvoy; 11 Dave Allen. Subs (all used): 8 Ben Davies; 13 Tyla Hepi; 14 Thomas Coyle; 28 Phil Joseph.
Tries: McAvoy (10), Hulme (37), Parker (48), Calvert (67); **Goals:** Seymour 0/2, Craven 0/2.
Rugby Leaguer & League Express Men of the Match: *Rams:* Rob Spicer; *Whitehaven:* Macgraff Leuluai.
Penalty count: 10-7; **Half-time:** 11-8;
Referee: Joe Cobb; **Attendance:** 911.

HALIFAX 12 FEATHERSTONE ROVERS 24

HALIFAX: 1 Miles Greenwood; 2 Tom Saxton; 4 Ben Heaton; 3 Steve Tyrer; 20 James Saltonstall; 18 Matt Place; 6 Scott Murrell; 17 Mitch Cahalane; 21 Ryan Maneely; 10 Luke Ambler; 15 Adam Robinson; 11 Dane Manning; 12 Andy Bracek. Subs (all used): 8 Adam Tangata; 22 Jacob Fairbank; 16 Richard Moore; 7 Ben Johnston.
Tries: Tyrer (31), Cahalane (75); **Goals:** Tyrer 2/2.
Sin bin: Murrell (58) - late challenge.
ROVERS: 2 Will Sharp; 21 Jy Hitchcox; 34 Joe Arundel; 6 Paul Sykes; 33 Tom Johnstone; 32 Pita Godinet; 7 Gareth Moore; 8 Jordan Baldwinson; 14 Sam Irwin; 10 Paul Wood; 18 Jamie Cording; 19 Alex Foster; 13 Tim Spears. Subs (all used): 9 Andy Ellis; 16 Andrew Bostock; 35 Kyle Trout; 27 Jack Ormondroyd.
Tries: Sykes (4), Johnstone (15), Ellis (60), Arundel (79);
Goals: Sykes 4/5.
Rugby Leaguer & League Express Men of the Match: *Halifax:* Jacob Fairbank; *Rovers:* Jordan Baldwinson.
Penalty count: 10-7; **Half-time:** 6-10;
Referee: George Stokes; **Attendance:** 2,187.

LONDON BRONCOS 34 WORKINGTON TOWN 16

BRONCOS: 1 Richard Mathers; 2 Rhys Williams; 3 Ben Farrar; 4 Wes Naiqama; 5 Ben Hellewell; 27 Jarrod Sammut; 28 Tom Gilmore; 18 Jon Wallace; 14 Brad Dwyer; 17 Erjon Dollapi; 11 Daniel Harrison; 15 Matt Garside; 21 Joel Wicks. Subs (all used): 9 Ray Nasso; 20 Iliess Macani; 23 Toby Everett; 12 Rhys Lovegrove.
Tries: Dwyer (23), Garside (28), Wallace (51), Gilmore (60), Lovegrove (74), Macani (78);
Goals: Naiqama 5/6.
TOWN: 32 Lewis Tierney; 2 Sam Forrester; 12 Jarrad Stack; 4 Perry Whiteley; 1 Jack Murphy; 30 Jamie Doran; 7 Carl Forber; 10 Marc Shackley; 9 Graeme Mattinson; 19 Tom Walker; 11 Brett Phillips; 16 Kurt Horton; 31 Connor Farrell. Subs (all used): 33 Logan Tomkins; 21 James Duerden; 25 Steve Scholey; 17 Latu Fifita.
Tries: Whiteley (43), Stack (48), Forber (65);
Goals: Forber 2/3.
Rugby Leaguer & League Express Men of the Match: *Broncos:* Jarrod Sammut; *Town:* Carl Forber.
Penalty count: 6-4; **Half-time:** 12-0;
Referee: Matthew Thomason; **Attendance:** 587.

SHEFFIELD EAGLES 28 BATLEY BULLDOGS 16

EAGLES: 1 Quentin Laulu-Togagae; 2 Scott Turner; 3 Menzie Yere; 4 Sam Smeaton; 5 Misi Taulapapa; 6 Kyle Briggs; 7 Dominic Brambani; 8 Eddie Battye; 9 James Davey; 17 Steve Thorpe; 15 John Davies; 12 Duane Straugheir; 13 Pat Walker. Subs (all used): 19 Cory Aston; 22 Tony Tonks; 23 Rob Worrincy; 21 Lelauloto Tagaloa.
Tries: Brambani (6), Yere (16, 32), Worrincy (40), Laulu-Togagae (80); **Goals:** Walker 4/6.
BULLDOGS: 22 Jordan Grayston; 2 Wayne Reittie; 3 Shaun Ainscough; 20 Shaun Squires; 5 Johnny Campbell; 6 Cain Southernwood; 7 Scott Leatherbarrow; 18 Tom Lillycrop; 14 Alistair Leak; 10 Alex Rowe; 12 Sam Scott; 19 Lee Mitchell; 17 Joe Chandler. Subs (all used): 8 Keegan Hirst; 9 Anthony Nicholson; 16 Sean Hesketh; 21 James Brown.
Tries: Reittie (12), Leak (21), J Brown (46);
Goals: Leatherbarrow 2/3.
Rugby Leaguer & League Express Men of the Match: *Eagles:* Menzie Yere; *Bulldogs:* Alex Rowe.
Penalty count: 10-8; **Half-time:** 20-10;
Referee: Chris Kendall; **Attendance:** 1,358
(at Keepmoat Stadium, Doncaster).

ROUND 5

Sunday 15th March 2015

BATLEY BULLDOGS 19 BRADFORD BULLS 26

BULLDOGS: 22 Jordan Grayston; 2 Wayne Reittie; 3 Shaun Ainscough; 20 Shaun Squires; 5 Johnny Campbell; 6 Cain Southernwood; 9 Anthony Nicholson; 8 Keegan Hirst; 14 Alistair Leak; 10 Alex Rowe; 11 Alex Bretherton; 12 Sam Scott; 21 James Brown. Subs (all used): 17 Joe Chandler; 15 Adam Gledhill; 16 Sean Hesketh; 19 Lee Mitchell.
Tries: Squires (8), Chandler (49), Hirst (52);
Goals: Southernwood 3/4;
Field goal: Southernwood (70).
BULLS: 1 Jake Mullaney; 5 Danny Williams; 27 Ryan Shaw; 20 Adam Henry; 19 Chris Ulugia; 6 Lee Gaskell; 7 Harry Siejka; 8 Paul Clough; 9 Adam O'Brien; 10 Adam Sidlow; 24 Lucas Walshaw; 11 Tom Olbison; 14 Jay Pitts. Subs (all used): 15 Daniel Fleming; 28 Samir Tahraoui; 31 Epalahame Lauaki; 25 Nathan Conroy.
Tries: Shaw (4), Mullaney (40), Williams (75), Ulugia (80); **Goals:** Shaw 5/5.
Rugby Leaguer & League Express Men of the Match: *Bulldogs:* Johnny Campbell; *Bulls:* Ryan Shaw.
Penalty count: 7-10; **Half-time:** 6-14;
Referee: George Stokes; **Attendance:** 3,019.

FEATHERSTONE ROVERS 6 LEIGH CENTURIONS 40

ROVERS: 2 Will Sharp; 21 Jy Hitchcox; 3 Nathan Chappell; 6 Paul Sykes; 33 Tom Johnstone; 31 Remy Marginet; 14 Sam Irwin; 8 Jordan Baldwinson; 9 Andy Ellis; 10 Paul Wood; 18 Jamie Cording; 19 Alex Foster; 13 Tim Spears. Subs (all used): 23 Luke Teasdale; 16 Andrew Bostock; 17 Matt James; 24 Mason Tonks.
Try: Chappell (25); **Goals:** Sykes 1/1.
CENTURIONS: 1 Gregg McNally; 15 Jonathan Pownall; 16 Michael Platt; 4 Tom Armstrong; 5 Liam Kay; 6 Martyn Ridyard; 7 Ryan Brierley; 8 Fuifui Moimoi; 14 Sean Penkywicz; 21 Jamie Acton; 19 Kurt Haggerty; 12 Tommy Goulden; 13 Sam Barlow. Subs (all used): 9 Bob Beswick; 10 Oliver Wilkes; 20 Sam Hopkins; 29 Jake Emmitt.
Tries: Kay (9, 75), Armstrong (45, 69), Goulden (53), Haggerty (63), Platt (72), Brierley (78);
Goals: Ridyard 4/8.
Rugby Leaguer & League Express Men of the Match: *Rovers:* Sam Irwin; *Centurions:* Fuifui Moimoi.
Penalty count: 7-9; **Half-time:** 6-4;
Referee: Chris Leatherbarrow; **Attendance:** 2,695.

HALIFAX 26 DEWSBURY RAMS 13

HALIFAX: 20 James Saltonstall; 2 Tom Saxton; 4 Ben Heaton; 3 Steve Tyrer; 23 Gareth Potts; 7 Ben Johnston; 6 Scott Murrell; 17 Mitch Cahalane; 21 Ryan Maneely; 10 Luke Ambler; 27 Ross Divorty; 11 Dane Manning; 22 Jacob Fairbank. Subs (all used): 9 Ben Kaye; 12 Andy Bracek; 13 Jack Spencer; 16 Richard Moore.
Tries: Heaton (36), Saltonstall (57), Potts (73), Tyrer (77), Ambler (79); **Goals:** Tyrer 3/5.
RAMS: 3 Karl Pryce; 2 Dale Morton; 4 Shane Grady; 15 Jason Crookes; 18 Dalton Grant; 31 Kieran Hyde; 7 Anthony Thackeray; 24 Byron Smith; 6 Matty Wildie; 10 Ryan Hepworth; 16 Toby Adamson; 12 Scott Hale; 34 Luke Adamson. Subs (all used): 13 Aaron Brown; 9 Wayne Godwin; 33 Paul Jackson; 32 Makali Aizue.
Tries: Pryce (34), Thackeray (39); **Goals:** Hyde 2/2;
Field goal: Hyde (70).
Rugby Leaguer & League Express Men of the Match: *Halifax:* James Saltonstall; *Rams:* Kieran Hyde.
Penalty count: 10-6; **Half-time:** 6-12;
Referee: Chris Kendall; **Attendance:** 1,734.

HUNSLET HAWKS 32 DONCASTER 12

HAWKS: 1 Jimmy Watson; 33 James Duckworth; 42 Jimmy Keinhorst; 4 Danny Maun; 5 Vinny Finigan; 31 Andy Kain; 7 Danny Ansell; 41 Andy Yates; 9 Jack Lee; 35 Rob Mulhern; 11 Callum Casey; 40 Josh Walters; 15 Liam Mackay. Subs (all used): 30 George Flanagan; 19 Brad Brennan; 34 Luke Briscoe; 12 Aaron Lyons.
Tries: Kain (1, 55, 72), Watson (39), Brennan (79);
Goals: Ansell 6/6.
Sin bin: Flanagan (77) - fighting.
DONCASTER: 31 Curtis Naughton; 1 Dave Scott; 3 Danny Cowling; 19 Lee Waterman; 5 Stewart Sanderson; 6 Paul Cooke; 7 Richard Wilkinson; 8 Matt Carbutt; 9 Kyle Kesik; 16 Brett Waller; 30 Jansin Turgut; 12 Steve Snitch; 13 Mike Emmett. Subs (all used): 32 Stuart Howarth; 10 Craig Robinson; 14 Russ Spiers; 34 Bobby Tyson-Wilson.
Tries: Sanderson (13), Naughton (25);
Goals: Sanderson 2/3.
Sin bin: Spiers (77) - fighting.
Rugby Leaguer & League Express Men of the Match: *Hawks:* Andy Kain; *Doncaster:* Curtis Naughton.
Penalty count: 10-8; **Half-time:** 12-10;
Referee: Andrew Sweet; **Attendance:** 498.

WHITEHAVEN 18 LONDON BRONCOS 16

WHITEHAVEN: 15 Jack Owens; 5 Jordan Burns; 27 Declan Hulme; 3 Jessie Joe Parker; 2 Craig Calvert; 19 John-Paul Brocklebank; 6 Brett Seymour; 18 Steve Fox; 14 Thomas Coyle; 13 Tyla Hepi; 11 Dave Allen; 25 Dion Aiye; 21 Liam Carberry. Subs (all used): 8 Ben Davies; 12 Steve Bannister; 9 James Newton; 28 Phil Joseph.
Tries: Burns (5), Newton (48), Brocklebank (51);
Goals: Brocklebank 3/3.
Sin bin: Hepi (67) - dissent.
BRONCOS: 5 Ben Hellewell; 2 Rhys Williams; 3 Ben Farrar; 4 Wes Naiqama; 20 Iliess Macani; 27 Jarrod Sammut; 28 Tom Gilmore; 18 Jon Wallace; 14 Brad

Dwyer; 30 Dave Williams; 11 Daniel Harrison; 15 Matt Garside; 12 Rhys Lovegrove. Subs (all used): 9 Ray Nasso; 21 Joel Wicks; 17 Erjon Dollapi; 29 Jamie Thackray.
Tries: Macani (19), R Williams (56), Dwyer (61);
Goals: Naiqama 2/3.
Rugby Leaguer & League Express Men of the Match: *Whitehaven:* Steve Fox; *Broncos:* Tom Gilmore.
Penalty count: 6-6; **Half-time:** 6-4;
Referee: Jamie Bloem; **Attendance:** 689.

WORKINGTON TOWN 12 SHEFFIELD EAGLES 14

TOWN: 34 Ryan Hampshire; 2 Sam Forrester; 1 Jack Murphy; 4 Perry Whiteley; 32 Lewis Tierney; 30 Jamie Doran; 7 Carl Forber; 19 Tom Walker; 9 Graeme Mattinson; 10 Marc Shackley; 11 Brett Phillips; 16 Kurt Horton; 12 Jarrad Stack. Subs (all used): 13 Liam McAvoy; 33 James Greenwood; 23 Scott Akehurst; 17 Latu Fifita.
Tries: Forrester (60), Whiteley (75); **Goals:** Forber 2/2.
EAGLES: 1 Quentin Laulu-Togagae; 2 Scott Turner; 3 Menzie Yere; 4 Sam Smeaton; 23 Rob Worrincy; 6 Kyle Briggs; 19 Cory Aston; 22 Tony Tonks; 9 James Davey; 17 Steve Thorpe; 11 Michael Knowles; 12 Duane Straugheir; 5 Misi Taulapapa. Subs (all used): 8 Eddie Battye; 15 John Davies; 18 Ben Musolino; 13 Pat Walker.
Tries: Yere (20), Smeaton (48); **Goals:** Briggs 3/3.
Sin bin: Knowles (37) - interference.
Rugby Leaguer & League Express Men of the Match: *Town:* Graeme Mattinson; *Eagles:* Kyle Briggs.
Penalty count: 14-11; **Half-time:** 0-8;
Referee: Joe Cobb; **Attendance:** 682.

ROUND 2

Wednesday 18th March 2015

WORKINGTON TOWN 18 DEWSBURY RAMS 31

TOWN: 2 Sam Forrester; 24 Theerapol Ritson; 1 Jack Murphy; 12 Jarrad Stack; 5 Brett Carter; 30 Jamie Doran; 7 Carl Forber; 25 Steve Scholey; 9 Graeme Mattinson; 19 Tom Walker; 11 Brett Phillips; 4 Perry Whiteley; 15 Karl Olstrum. Subs (all used): 13 Liam McAvoy; 21 James Duerden; 10 Marc Shackley; 17 Latu Fifita.
Tries: Forrester (5), Shackley (50); **Goals:** Forber 5/5.
RAMS: 31 Kieran Hyde; 2 Dale Morton; 4 Shane Grady; 15 Jason Crookes; 18 Dalton Grant; 6 Matty Wildie; 7 Anthony Thackeray; 17 Matthew Haggarty; 23 Tom Hemingway; 10 Ryan Hepworth; 11 Rob Spicer; 34 Luke Adamson; 13 Aaron Brown. Subs (all used): 9 Wayne Godwin; 25 Joel Farrell; 16 Toby Adamson; 33 Paul Jackson.
Tries: Morton (27), L Adamson (36, 53), Wildie (43), T Adamson (76); **Goals:** Hyde 4/4, Hemingway 1/1;
Field goal: Hemingway (73).
Rugby Leaguer & League Express Men of the Match: *Town:* Graeme Mattinson; *Rams:* Anthony Thackeray.
Penalty count: 10-9; **Half-time:** 10-12;
Referee: Chris Leatherbarrow; **Attendance:** 761.

ROUND 6

Friday 27th March 2015

DEWSBURY RAMS 28 FEATHERSTONE ROVERS 38

RAMS: 31 Kieran Hyde; 2 Dale Morton; 15 Jason Crookes; 4 Shane Grady; 18 Dalton Grant; 6 Matty Wildie; 7 Anthony Thackeray; 17 Matthew Haggarty; 23 Tom Hemingway; 10 Ryan Hepworth; 11 Rob Spicer; 12 Scott Hale; 13 Aaron Brown. Subs (all used): 9 Wayne Godwin; 33 Paul Jackson; 16 Toby Adamson; 32 Makali Aizue.
Tries: Hale (6), Thackeray (15), Grant (39), Hemingway (73); **Goals:** Hyde 5/5, Hemingway 1/1.
ROVERS: 21 Jy Hitchcox; 5 Ben Blackmore; 1 Ian Hardman; 3 Nathan Chappell; 2 Will Sharp; 6 Paul Sykes; 31 Remy Marginet; 8 Jordan Baldwinson; 14 Sam Irwin; 16 Andrew Bostock; 18 Jamie Cording; 19 Alex Foster; 13 Tim Spears. Subs (all used): 28 Will Milner; 10 Paul Wood; 17 Matt James; 27 Jack Ormondroyd.
Tries: Bostock (8), Sharp (22), Sykes (31), Marginet (33, 57), Milner (63), Cording (71);
Goals: Sykes 2/4, Marginet 3/4.
Rugby Leaguer & League Express Men of the Match: *Rams:* Anthony Thackeray; *Rovers:* Remy Marginet.
Penalty count: 14-7; **Half-time:** 20-20;
Referee: Warren Turley; **Attendance:** 1,798.

Saturday 28th March 2015

LONDON BRONCOS 22 HALIFAX 18

BRONCOS: 5 Ben Hellewell; 2 Rhys Williams; 3 Ben Farrar; 4 Wes Naiqama; 20 Iliess Macani; 19 Joe Keyes; 28 Tom Gilmore; 23 Toby Everett; 14 Brad Dwyer; 12 Rhys Lovegrove; 15 Matt Garside; 11 Daniel Harrison; 21 Joel Wicks. Subs (all used): 9 Ray Nasso; 29 Jamie Thackray; 17 Erjon Dollapi; 18 Jon Wallace.
Tries: Harrison (1), Garside (21), Macani (61), Dwyer (65); **Goals:** Naiqama 3/4.
HALIFAX: 20 James Saltonstall; 5 Alex Brown; 4 Ben Heaton; 3 Steve Tyrer; 23 Gareth Potts; 7 Ben Johnston; 6 Scott Murrell; 17 Mitch Cahalane; 9 Ben Kaye; 10 Luke Ambler; 27 Ross Divorty; 11 Dane Manning; 22 Jacob Fairbank. Subs (all used): 8 Adam Tangata; 13 Jack Spencer; 16 Richard Moore; 21 Ryan Maneely.
Tries: Saltonstall (10), Heaton (16), Cahalane (53);
Goals: Tyrer 3/3.
Rugby Leaguer & League Express Men of the Match: *Broncos:* Brad Dwyer; *Halifax:* Scott Murrell.
Penalty count: 2-7; **Half-time:** 12-12;
Referee: Gareth Hewer; **Attendance:** 724.

Sunday 29th March 2015

DONCASTER 14 BATLEY BULLDOGS 16

DONCASTER: 1 Dave Scott; 26 Sam Doherty; 17 Liam Welham; 27 Alex Gilbey; 31 Curtis Naughton; 6 Paul Cooke; 24 Josh Kittrick; 8 Matt Carbutt; 9 Kyle Kesik; 10 Craig Robinson; 30 Jansin Turgut; 12 Steve Snitch; 13 Mike Emmett. Subs (all used): 14 Russ Spiers; 15 Mitch Clark; 23 Jack Walton; 32 Bobby Tyson-Wilson.
Tries: Turgut (20), Clark (32); **Goals:** Scott 3/3.
BULLDOGS: 5 Johnny Campbell; 2 Wayne Reittie; 11 Alex Bretherton; 20 Shaun Squires; 3 Shaun Ainscough; 6 Cain Southernwood; 9 Anthony Nicholson; 8 Keegan Hirst; 13 Luke Blake; 10 Alex Rowe; 12 Sam Scott; 19 Lee Mitchell; 17 Joe Chandler. Subs (all used): 15 Adam Gledhill; 18 Tom Lillycrop; 21 James Brown; 26 Matty Fozard.
Tries: J Brown (36), Reittie (69), Southernwood (75);
Goals: Southernwood 2/4.
Rugby Leaguer & League Express Men of the Match: *Doncaster:* Jansin Turgut; *Bulldogs:* Luke Blake.
Penalty count: 6-7; **Half-time:** 14-6;
Referee: Tom Crashley; **Attendance:** 1,277.

BRADFORD BULLS 36 WORKINGTON TOWN 6

BULLS: 1 Jake Mullaney; 5 Danny Williams; 3 Adrian Purtell; 20 Adam Henry; 27 Ryan Shaw; 6 Lee Gaskell; 7 Harry Siejka; 8 Paul Clough; 9 Adam O'Brien; 28 Samir Tahraoui; 11 Tom Olbison; 14 Jay Pitts; 13 Danny Addy. Subs (all used): 12 Dale Ferguson; 17 Jean-Philippe Baile; 31 Epalahame Lauaki; 15 Daniel Fleming.
Tries: Pitts (5), Mullaney (9), Williams (17, 75), Henry (51, 66), Gaskell (54); **Goals:** Shaw 4/7.
TOWN: 32 Lewis Tierney; 2 Sam Forrester; 1 Jack Murphy; 4 Perry Whiteley; 5 Brett Carter; 30 Jamie Doran; 7 Carl Forber; - James Greenwood; 9 Graeme Mattinson; 19 Tom Walker; 11 Brett Phillips; 16 Kurt Horton; 13 Liam McAvoy. Subs (all used): 17 Latu Fifita; 10 Marc Shackley; 15 Karl Olstrum; 14 Callum Phillips.
Try: Whiteley (59); **Goals:** Forber 1/1.
Rugby Leaguer & League Express Men of the Match: *Bulls:* Adam Henry; *Town:* Callum Phillips.
Penalty count: 9-6; **Half-time:** 14-0;
Referee: Chris Kendall; **Attendance:** 4,238.

LEIGH CENTURIONS 60 WHITEHAVEN 0

CENTURIONS: 1 Gregg McNally; 15 Jonathan Pownall; 16 Michael Platt; 4 Tom Armstrong; 5 Liam Kay; 6 Martyn Ridyard; 7 Ryan Brierley; 18 Tom Spencer; 9 Bob Beswick; 21 Jamie Acton; 22 Andrew Dixon; 12 Tommy Goulden; 20 Sam Hopkins. Subs (all used): 14 Sean Penkywicz; 10 Oliver Wilkes; 23 Martin Aspinwall; 29 Jake Emmitt.
Tries: Pownall (2, 22, 37), Kay (9, 30, 51), Platt (12), Ridyard (27, 74), Emmitt (41), McNally (45), Brierley (61);
Goals: Ridyard 6/12.
Sin bin: Acton (58) - fighting.
WHITEHAVEN: 26 Greg Wilde; 5 Jordan Burns; 16 Connor Holliday; 3 Jessie Joe Parker; 2 Craig Calvert; 25 Dion Aiye; 6 Brett Seymour; 8 Ben Davies; 14 Thomas Coyle; 18 Steve Fox; 21 Rhodri Lloyd; 11 Dave Allen; 4 Scott McAvoy. Subs (all used): 13 Tyla Hepi; 20 James Robinson; 9 James Newton; 1 Richard Lepori.
Sin bin: Hepi (58) - fighting.
Rugby Leaguer & League Express Men of the Match: *Centurions:* Gregg McNally; *Whitehaven:* Tyla Hepi.
Penalty count: 6-7; **Half-time:** 32-0;
Referee: Robert Hicks; **Attendance:** 3,006.

SHEFFIELD EAGLES 28 HUNSLET HAWKS 14

EAGLES: 1 Quentin Laulu-Togagae; 2 Scott Turner; 3 Menzie Yere; 4 Sam Smeaton; 5 Misi Taulapapa; 6 Kyle Briggs; 19 Cory Aston; 8 Eddie Battye; 24 Keal Carlile; 22 Tony Tonks; 11 Michael Knowles; 15 John Davies; 13 Pat Walker. Subs (all used): 9 James Davey; 10 Mitchell Stringer; 28 Oliver Roberts; 17 Steve Thorpe.
Tries: Taulapapa (10, 15), Laulu-Togagae (45), Knowles (51), Briggs (75); **Goals:** Walker 4/5.
Dismissal: Taulapapa (40) - headbutt on Flanagan.
HAWKS: 1 Jimmy Watson; 5 Vinny Finigan; 42 Jimmy Keinhorst; 4 Danny Maun; 33 James Duckworth; 6 Simon Brown; 7 Danny Ansell; 41 Andy Yates; 9 Jack Lee; 19 Brad Brennan; 11 Callum Casey; 40 Josh Walters; 15 Liam Mackay. Subs (all used): 30 George Flanagan; 8 Michael Haley; 35 Rob Mulhern; 34 Luke Briscoe.
Tries: Mulhern (49), Flanagan (66); **Goals:** Ansell 3/3.
Rugby Leaguer & League Express Men of the Match: *Eagles:* Michael Knowles; *Hawks:* George Flanagan.
Penalty count: 9-8; **Half-time:** 12-2;
Referee: Chris Leatherbarrow; **Attendance:** 1,136
(at Keepmoat Stadium, Doncaster).

ROUND 7

Wednesday 1st April 2015

DONCASTER 4 SHEFFIELD EAGLES 26

DONCASTER: 1 Dave Scott; 26 Sam Doherty; 17 Liam Welham; 19 Lee Waterman; 5 Stewart Sanderson; 21 Danny Nicklas; 7 Richard Wilkinson; 8 Matt Carbutt; 9 Kyle Kesik; 32 Bobby Tyson-Wilson; 30 Jansin Turgut; 12 Steve Snitch; 13 Mike Emmett. Subs (all used): 11 Michael Kelly; 15 Mitch Clark; 16 Brett Waller; 22 Brad Foster.
Try: Doherty (51); **Goals:** Sanderson 0/1.
Sin bin: Nicklas (60) - dissent.
EAGLES: 1 Quentin Laulu-Togagae; 23 Rob Worrincy; 3 Menzie Yere; 4 Sam Smeaton; 5 Misi Taulapapa; 6 Kyle Briggs; 19 Cory Aston; 8 Eddie Battye; 9 James Davey; 17 Steve Thorpe; 11 Michael Knowles; 16 Jamie Langley; 15 John Davies. Subs (all used): 10 Mitchell Stringer; 13 Pat Walker; 24 Keal Carlile; 28 Oliver Roberts.
Tries: Langley (21), Taulapapa (27), Stringer (39), Worrincy (73), Aston (80); **Goals:** Briggs 1/1, Walker 2/4.
Rugby Leaguer & League Express Men of the Match: *Doncaster:* Lee Waterman; *Eagles:* Kyle Briggs.
Penalty count: 9-7; **Half-time:** 0-16;
Referee: Adam Gill; **Attendance:** 1,030.

Friday 3rd April 2015

HUNSLET HAWKS 6 LEIGH CENTURIONS 42

HAWKS: 1 Jimmy Watson; 33 James Duckworth; 34 Luke Briscoe; 28 Mufaro Mvududu; 24 Richie Barnett; 31 Andy Kain; 6 Simon Brown; 12 Aaron Lyons; 9 Jack Lee; 35 Rob Mulhern; 21 Ryan Backhouse; 23 Elliott Cosgrove; 15 Liam Mackay. Subs (all used): 8 Michael Haley; 7 Danny Ansell; 17 Mark Castle; 19 Brad Brennan.
Try: Briscoe (46); **Goals:** Brown 1/1.
Sin bin: Kain (67) - holding down.
CENTURIONS: 1 Gregg McNally; 15 Jonathan Pownall; 3 Greg Worthington; 4 Tom Armstrong; 5 Liam Kay; 6 Martyn Ridyard; 7 Ryan Brierley; 8 Fuifui Moimoi; 9 Bob Beswick; 18 Tom Spencer; 19 Kurt Haggerty; 22 Andrew Dixon; 13 Sam Barlow. Subs (all used): 10 Oliver Wilkes; 14 Sean Penkywicz; 23 Martin Aspinwall; 24 Jonathan Walker.
Tries: Wilkes (37), Aspinwall (59), Kay (65, 80), Barlow (68), Pownall (73), Penkywicz (77), Dixon (79);
Goals: Ridyard 5/8.
Rugby Leaguer & League Express Men of the Match: *Hawks:* Brad Brennan; *Centurions:* Martin Aspinwall.
Penalty count: 9-14; **Half-time:** 0-6;
Referee: Chris Kendall; **Attendance:** 1,122.

WORKINGTON TOWN 40 WHITEHAVEN 0

TOWN: 1 Jack Murphy; 2 Sam Forrester; 12 Jarrad Stack; 4 Perry Whiteley; 5 Brett Carter; 30 Jamie Doran; 7 Carl Forber; 19 Tom Walker; 9 Graeme Mattinson; 10 Marc Shackley; 11 Brett Phillips; 16 Kurt Horton; 13 Liam McAvoy. Subs (all used): 14 Callum Phillips; 15 Karl Olstrum; 25 Steve Scholey; 17 Latu Fifita.
Tries: McAvoy (8), Doran (16), Forber (29), Stack (46), Carter (49), Murphy (70), Whiteley (75);
Goals: Forber 4/6, Murphy 2/2.
WHITEHAVEN: 1 Richard Lepori; 5 Jordan Burns; 21 Rhodri Lloyd; 16 Connor Holliday; 2 Craig Calvert; 6 Brett Seymour; 14 Thomas Coyle; 18 Steve Fox; 9 James Newton; 8 Ben Davies; 25 Dion Aiye; 11 Dave Allen; 4 Scott McAvoy. Subs (all used): 13 Tyla Hepi; 20 James Robinson; 27 Ted Chapelhow; 3 Jessie Joe Parker.
Sin bin: Lepori (53) - holding down.
Rugby Leaguer & League Express Men of the Match: *Town:* Jamie Doran; *Whitehaven:* Dion Aiye.
Penalty count: 7-9; **Half-time:** 18-0;
Referee: Tom Crashley; **Attendance:** 1,260.

BATLEY BULLDOGS 6 DEWSBURY RAMS 21

BULLDOGS: 22 Jordan Grayston; 2 Wayne Reittie; 23 Brad Day; 20 Shaun Squires; 3 Shaun Ainscough; 6 Cain Southernwood; 9 Anthony Nicholson; 8 Keegan Hirst; 14 Alistair Leak; 10 Alex Rowe; 11 Alex Bretherton; 19 Lee Mitchell; 17 Joe Chandler. Subs (all used): 13 Luke Blake; 18 Tom Lillycrop; 26 Matty Fozard; 21 James Brown.
Try: Reittie (54); **Goals:** Southernwood 1/1.
RAMS: 3 Karl Pryce; 2 Dale Morton; 15 Jason Crookes; 4 Shane Grady; 18 Dalton Grant; 6 Matty Wildie; 7 Anthony Thackeray; 10 Ryan Hepworth; 23 Tom Hemingway; 33 Paul Jackson; 11 Rob Spicer; 12 Scott Hale; 13 Aaron Brown. Subs (all used): 24 Byron Smith; 25 Joel Farrell; 16 Toby Adamson; 32 Makali Aizue.
Tries: Grady (2, 49), Farrell (22), Wildie (71);
Goals: Morton 1/3, Hemingway 1/3;
Field goal: Thackeray (40).
Rugby Leaguer & League Express Men of the Match: *Bulldogs:* Tom Lillycrop; *Rams:* Anthony Thackeray.
Penalty count: 8-6; **Half-time:** 0-11;
Referee: Chris Leatherbarrow; **Attendance:** 1,274.

FEATHERSTONE ROVERS 8 LONDON BRONCOS 24

ROVERS: 21 Jy Hitchcox; 2 Will Sharp; 3 Nathan Chappell; 1 Ian Hardman; 5 Ben Blackmore; 6 Paul Sykes; 31 Remy Marginet; 8 Jordan Baldwinson; 14 Sam Irwin; 16 Andrew Bostock; 18 Jamie Cording; 19 Alex Foster; 13 Tim Spears. Subs (all used): 28 Will Milner; 17 Matt James; 10 Paul Wood; 27 Jack Ormondroyd.
Tries: Ormondroyd (33), Chappell (78);
Goals: Sykes 0/2, Marginet 0/1.
On report:
Ormondroyd (43) - alleged late challenge on Dwyer.
BRONCOS: 5 Ben Hellewell; 2 Rhys Williams; 3 Ben Farrar; 4 Wes Naiqama; 20 Iliess Macani; 22 Oscar Thomas; 19 Joe Keyes; 12 Rhys Lovegrove; 14 Brad Dwyer; 30 Dave Williams; 11 Daniel Harrison; 15 Matt Garside; 31 Elliot Minchella. Subs (all used): 9 Ray Nasso; 29 Jamie Thackray; 17 Erjon Dollapi; 23 Toby Everett.
Tries: Dwyer (23), Thomas (44), R Williams (58, 73);
Goals: Naiqama 4/4.
Rugby Leaguer & League Express Men of the Match: *Rovers:* Jamie Cording; *Broncos:* Rhys Lovegrove.
Penalty count: 8-6; **Half-time:** 4-6;
Referee: Michael Woodhead; **Attendance:** 1,654.

BRADFORD BULLS 32 HALIFAX 19

BULLS: 27 Ryan Shaw; 5 Danny Williams; 20 Adam Henry; 3 Adrian Purtell; 19 Chris Ulugia; 6 Lee Gaskell; 7 Harry Siejka; 8 Paul Clough; 9 Adam O'Brien; 10 Adam Sidlow; 11 Tom Olbison; 14 Jay Pitts; 13 Danny Addy. Subs (all used): 12 Dale Ferguson; 31 Epalahame Lauaki; 15 Daniel Fleming; 17 Jean-Philippe Baile.
Tries: Williams (42), Pitts (45), Gaskell (49), Henry (62), Shaw (77); **Goals:** Shaw 6/6.
Sin bin: Shaw (28) - holding down.
HALIFAX: 20 James Saltonstall; 5 Alex Brown; 4 Ben Heaton; 3 Steve Tyrer; 23 Gareth Potts; 7 Ben Johnston; 6 Scott Murrell; 17 Mitch Cahalane; 9 Ben Kaye; 10 Luke Ambler; 27 Ross Divorty; 11 Dane Manning; 16 Richard Moore. Subs (all used): 12 Andy Bracek; 13 Jack Spencer; 15 Adam Robinson; 21 Ryan Maneely.
Tries: Cahalane (12), Divorty (31), Heaton (69);
Goals: Tyrer 3/3; **Field goal:** Murrell (39).
Rugby Leaguer & League Express Men of the Match:
Bulls: Adam O'Brien; *Halifax:* Luke Ambler.
Penalty count: 6-4; **Half-time:** 2-13;
Referee: Matthew Thomason; **Attendance:** 6,134.

ROUND 8

Monday 6th April 2015

LEIGH CENTURIONS 54 WORKINGTON TOWN 6

CENTURIONS: 1 Gregg McNally; 2 Adam Higson; 16 Michael Platt; 3 Greg Worthington; 5 Liam Kay; 6 Martyn Ridyard; 7 Ryan Brierley; 8 Fuifui Moimoi; 14 Sean Penkywicz; 21 Jamie Acton; 22 Andrew Dixon; 12 Tommy Goulden; 20 Sam Hopkins. Subs (all used): 9 Bob Beswick; 13 Sam Barlow; 26 Gareth Hock; 29 Jake Emmitt.
Tries: Penkywicz (4, 16), Higson (36), Brierley (42), Kay (45), Hock (57, 79), Platt (63), McNally (73);
Goals: Ridyard 9/9.
TOWN: 1 Jack Murphy; 2 Sam Forrester; 12 Jarrad Stack; 4 Perry Whiteley; 5 Brett Carter; 33 Jamie Doran; 7 Carl Forber; 19 Tom Walker; 9 Graeme Mattinson; 10 Marc Shackley; 11 Brett Phillips; 16 Kurt Horton; 13 Liam McAvoy. Subs (all used): 14 Callum Phillips; 17 Latu Fifita; 21 James Duerden; 25 Steve Scholey.
Try: Forber (11); **Goals:** Forber 1/1.
Rugby Leaguer & League Express Men of the Match:
Centurions: Sean Penkywicz; *Town:* Jack Murphy.
Penalty count: 5-7; **Half-time:** 18-6;
Referee: Chris Leatherbarrow; **Attendance:** 3,017.

DEWSBURY RAMS 16 BRADFORD BULLS 30

RAMS: 3 Karl Pryce; 2 Dale Morton; 15 Jason Crookes; 12 Scott Hale; 18 Dalton Grant; 13 Aaron Brown; 7 Anthony Thackeray; 10 Ryan Hepworth; 23 Tom Hemingway; 33 Paul Jackson; 11 Rob Spicer; 16 Toby Adamson; 34 Luke Adamson. Subs (all used): 24 Byron Smith; 17 Matthew Haggarty; 6 Matty Wildie; 32 Makali Aizue.
Tries: Morton (39), Smith (55), Crookes (79);
Goals: Morton 2/2, Hemingway 0/1.
BULLS: 27 Ryan Shaw; 5 Danny Williams; 3 Adrian Purtell; 20 Adam Henry; 2 Etuate Uaisele; 6 Lee Gaskell; 7 Harry Siejka; 8 Paul Clough; 9 Adam O'Brien; 10 Adam Sidlow; 24 Lucas Walshaw; 14 Jay Pitts; 13 Danny Addy. Subs (all used): 28 Samir Tahraoui; 15 Daniel Fleming; 22 Chev Walker; 26 Vila Halafihi.
Tries: Pitts (12), Uaisele (37), Gaskell (44), Shaw (48), Addy (71, 77); **Goals:** Shaw 3/6.
Rugby Leaguer & League Express Men of the Match:
Rams: Aaron Brown; *Bulls:* Danny Addy.
Penalty count: 6-10; **Half-time:** 6-10;
Referee: George Stokes; **Attendance:** 4,068.

HALIFAX 32 HUNSLET HAWKS 24

HALIFAX: 20 James Saltonstall; 5 Alex Brown; 4 Ben Heaton; 3 Steve Tyrer; 23 Gareth Potts; 26 Chris Taylor; 6 Scott Murrell; 17 Mitch Cahalane; 9 Ben Kaye; 10 Luke Ambler; 27 Ross Divorty; 11 Dane Manning; 22 Jacob Fairbank. Subs (all used): 15 Adam Robinson; 21 Ryan Maneely; 13 Jack Spencer; 16 Richard Moore.
Tries: Brown (8), Heaton (22), Taylor (24), Tyrer (28), Murrell (73), Saltonstall (80);
Goals: Tyrer 2/4, Murrell 2/2.
HAWKS: 1 Jimmy Watson; 24 Richie Barnett; 34 Luke Briscoe; 4 Danny Maun; 5 Vinny Finigan; 6 Simon Brown; 31 Andy Kain; 35 Rob Mulhern; 30 George Flanagan; 12 Aaron Lyons; 42 Jimmy Keinhorst; 21 Ryan Backhouse; 15 Liam Mackay. Subs (all used): 7 Danny Ansell; 44 Charlie Martin; 19 Brad Brennan; 28 Mufaro Mvududu.
Tries: Mulhern (11), Watson (18), Briscoe (36), Finigan (58); **Goals:** Brown 4/4.
Rugby Leaguer & League Express Men of the Match:
Halifax: James Saltonstall; *Hawks:* Jimmy Watson.
Penalty count: 3-3; **Half-time:** 20-18;
Referee: Dave Merrick; **Attendance:** 1,540.

LONDON BRONCOS 25 BATLEY BULLDOGS 18

BRONCOS: 5 Ben Hellewell; 2 Rhys Williams; 3 Ben Farrar; 4 Wes Naiqama; 20 Iliess Macani; 19 Joe Keyes; 22 Oscar Thomas; 12 Rhys Lovegrove; 14 Brad Dwyer; 30 Dave Williams; 11 Daniel Harrison; 15 Matt Garside; 31 Elliot Minchella. Subs (all used): 9 Ray Nasso; 29 Jamie Thackray; 17 Erjon Dollapi; 23 Toby Everett.
Tries: Garside (9), Harrison (12), Hellewell (39), Minchella (52); **Goals:** Naiqama 3/3, Thomas 1/1;
Field goal: Thomas (79).
BULLDOGS: 22 Jordan Grayston; 2 Wayne Reittie; 24 Brad Hey; 11 Alex Bretherton; 3 Shaun Ainscough; 6 Cain Southernwood; 14 Alistair Leak; 8 Keegan Hirst; 13 Luke Blake; 10 Alex Rowe; 12 Sam Scott; 25 Tom Thackray; 21 James Brown. Subs (all used): 9 Anthony Nicholson; 15 Adam Gledhill; 16 Sean Hesketh; 19 Lee Mitchell.
Tries: Hesketh (47, 75), Reittie (72);
Goals: Southernwood 3/3.
Rugby Leaguer & League Express Men of the Match:
Broncos: Oscar Thomas; *Bulldogs:* Sean Hesketh.
Penalty count: 3-8; **Half-time:** 18-0;
Referee: Andrew Sweet; **Attendance:** 638.

WHITEHAVEN 41 DONCASTER 16

WHITEHAVEN: 1 Richard Lepori; 28 Ed Chamberlain; 3 Jessie Joe Parker; 12 Steve Bannister; 2 Craig Calvert; 25 Dion Aiye; 19 John-Paul Brocklebank; 8 Ben Davies; 14 Thomas Coyle; 27 Ted Chapelhow; 21 Rhodri Lloyd; 4 Scott McAvoy; 11 Dave Allen. Subs (all used): 13 Tyla Hepi; 23 Sam Brooks; 9 James Newton; 18 Steve Fox.
Tries: Calvert (2, 79), Chamberlain (11, 65), Hepi (32), McAvoy (40), Newton (45); **Goals:** Brocklebank 6/7;
Field goal: Brocklebank (72).
DONCASTER: 1 Dave Scott; 26 Sam Doherty; 17 Liam Welham; 19 Lee Waterman; 31 Peter Fox; 6 Paul Cooke; 21 Danny Nicklas; 8 Matt Carbutt; 9 Kyle Kesik; 32 Bobby Tyson-Wilson; 30 Jansin Turgut; 12 Steve Snitch; 13 Mike Emmett. Subs (all used): 28 Ben Reynolds; 4 Pasqualle Dunn; 15 Mitch Clark; 16 Brett Waller.
Tries: Nicklas (15), Fox (54), Reynolds (57);
Goals: Scott 2/3.
Rugby Leaguer & League Express Men of the Match:
Whitehaven: Richard Lepori; *Doncaster:* Ben Reynolds.
Penalty count: 5-4; **Half-time:** 24-6;
Referee: Warren Turley; **Attendance:** 718.

FEATHERSTONE ROVERS 4 SHEFFIELD EAGLES 33

ROVERS: 21 Jy Hitchcox; 2 Will Sharp; 3 Nathan Chappell; 1 Ian Hardman; 5 Ben Blackmore; 6 Paul Sykes; 7 Gareth Moore; 17 Matt James; 9 Andy Ellis; 10 Paul Wood; 18 Jamie Cording; 19 Alex Foster; 15 Jack Bussey. Subs (all used): 14 Sam Irwin; 8 Jordan Baldwinson; 16 Andrew Bostock; 27 Jack Ormondroyd.
Try: Sharp (60); **Goals:** Moore 0/1.
Sin bin: Bussey (39) - holding down;
Hardman (70) - fighting; Sharp (70) - fighting;
Ellis (72) - interference.
EAGLES: 1 Quentin Laulu-Togagae; 2 Scott Turner; 3 Menzie Yere; 4 Sam Smeaton; 5 Misi Taulapapa; 6 Kyle Briggs; 7 Dominic Brambani; 8 Eddie Battye; 24 Keal Carlile; 22 Tony Tonks; 11 Michael Knowles; 16 Jamie Langley; 13 Pat Walker. Subs (all used): 9 James Davey; 17 Steve Thorpe; 10 Mitchell Stringer; 15 John Davies.
Tries: Yere (3, 51), Turner (27), Laulu-Togagae (37), Taulapapa (46), Walker (80); **Goals:** Walker 4/7;
Field goal: Knowles (74).
Sin bin: Davies (39) - interference, (60) - interference;
Tonks (70) - fighting.
Rugby Leaguer & League Express Men of the Match:
Rovers: Will Sharp; *Eagles:* Menzie Yere.
Penalty count: 14-14; **Half-time:** 0-20;
Referee: Joe Cobb; **Attendance:** 1,920.

ROUND 9

Sunday 12th April 2015

DONCASTER 12 DEWSBURY RAMS 24

DONCASTER: 1 Dave Scott; 26 Sam Doherty; 17 Liam Welham; 18 Shaun Leaf; 5 Stewart Sanderson; 21 Danny Nicklas; 28 Ben Reynolds; 32 Bobby Tyson-Wilson; 9 Kyle Kesik; 16 Brett Waller; 11 Michael Kelly; 12 Steve Snitch; 13 Mike Emmett. Subs (all used): 8 Matt Carbutt; 14 Russ Spiers; 15 Mitch Clark; 22 Brad Foster.
Tries: Doherty (14), Emmett (20); **Goals:** Sanderson 2/2.
RAMS: 31 Kieran Hyde; 2 Dale Morton; 15 Jason Crookes; 12 Scott Hale; 18 Dalton Grant; 13 Aaron Brown; 7 Anthony Thackeray; 10 Ryan Hepworth; 23 Tom Hemingway; 33 Paul Jackson; 25 Joel Farrell; 16 Toby Adamson; 34 Luke Adamson. Subs (all used): 6 Matty Wildie; 17 Matthew Haggarty; 24 Byron Smith; 19 Callan Beckett.
Tries: Farrell (4), Morton (8), Brown (32), Hale (53), Crookes (66); **Goals:** Hemingway 2/3, Hyde 0/2.
Rugby Leaguer & League Express Men of the Match:
Doncaster: Kyle Kesik; *Rams:* Aaron Brown.
Penalty count: 6-6; **Half-time:** 12-14;
Referee: Tom Crashley; **Attendance:** 1,100.

BATLEY BULLDOGS 16 FEATHERSTONE ROVERS 23

BULLDOGS: 22 Jordan Grayston; 2 Wayne Reittie; 11 Alex Bretherton; 20 Shaun Squires; 3 Shaun Ainscough; 6 Cain Southernwood; 14 Alistair Leak; 8 Keegan Hirst; 26 Matty Fozard; 10 Alex Rowe; 12 Sam Scott; 19 Lee Mitchell; 17 Joe Chandler. Subs (all used): 9 Anthony Nicholson; 18 Tom Lillycrop; 16 Sean Hesketh; 21 James Brown.
Tries: Fozard (3), Scott (12), Ainscough (30);
Goals: Southernwood 2/4.
ROVERS: 21 Jy Hitchcox; 5 Ben Blackmore; 1 Ian Hardman; 4 Thomas Minns; 2 Will Sharp; 6 Paul Sykes; 7 Gareth Moore; 8 Jordan Baldwinson; 9 Andy Ellis; 16 Andrew Bostock; 18 Jamie Cording; 12 Reni Maitua; 13 Tim Spears. Subs (all used): 14 Sam Irwin; 19 Alex Foster; 24 Mason Tonks; 15 Jack Bussey.
Tries: Blackmore (55, 57), Maitua (67), Sharp (78);
Goals: Moore 3/4; **Field goal:** Moore (79).
Rugby Leaguer & League Express Men of the Match:
Bulldogs: Alex Rowe; *Rovers:* Reni Maitua.
Penalty count: 6-6; **Half-time:** 14-0;
Referee: George Stokes; **Attendance:** 916.

BRADFORD BULLS 28 LONDON BRONCOS 2

BULLS: 27 Ryan Shaw; 2 Etuate Uaisele; 3 Adrian Purtell; 20 Adam Henry; 19 Chris Ulugia; 6 Lee Gaskell; 7 Harry Siejka; 8 Paul Clough; 9 Adam O'Brien; 10 Adam Sidlow; 11 Tom Olbison; 14 Jay Pitts; 13 Danny Addy. Subs (all used): 12 Dale Ferguson; 23 Alex Mellor; 31 Epalahame Lauaki; 15 Daniel Fleming.
Tries: Pitts (15), O'Brien (19), Gaskell (48), Ulugia (69), Uaisele (72); **Goals:** Shaw 4/5.
BRONCOS: 5 Ben Hellewell; 2 Rhys Williams; 3 Ben Farrar; 4 Wes Naiqama; 20 Iliess Macani; 22 Oscar Thomas; 28 Tom Gilmore; 12 Rhys Lovegrove; 14 Brad Dwyer; 30 Dave Williams; 11 Daniel Harrison; 15 Matt Garside; 31 Elliot Minchella. Subs (all used): 9 Ray Nasso; 29 Jamie Thackray; 17 Erjon Dollapi; 23 Toby Everett.
Goals: Naiqama 1/1.
Rugby Leaguer & League Express Men of the Match:
Bulls: Adam O'Brien; *Broncos:* Wes Naiqama.
Penalty count: 9-13; **Half-time:** 12-2;
Referee: Joe Cobb; **Attendance:** 4,023.

HALIFAX 38 WORKINGTON TOWN 6

HALIFAX: 20 James Saltonstall; 5 Alex Brown; 4 Ben Heaton; 24 Rikki Sheriffe; 23 Gareth Potts; 26 Chris Taylor; 6 Scott Murrell; 17 Mitch Cahalane; 9 Ben Kaye; 10 Luke Ambler; 27 Ross Divorty; 11 Dane Manning; 16 Richard Moore. Subs (all used): 8 Adam Tangata; 12 Andy Bracek; 13 Jack Spencer; 21 Ryan Maneely.
Tries: Ambler (12), Sheriffe (14), Heaton (21), Saltonstall (24), Manning (37), Brown (79), Kaye (80);
Goals: Murrell 4/5, Taylor 0/1, Saltonstall 1/1.
TOWN: 1 Jack Murphy; 2 Sam Forrester; 31 Oliver Gildart; 4 Perry Whiteley; 5 Brett Carter; 14 Callum Phillips; 7 Carl Forber; 19 Tom Walker; 9 Graeme Mattinson; 10 Marc Shackley; 11 Brett Phillips; 16 Kurt Horton; 15 Karl Olstrum. Subs (all used): 8 Kris Coward; 13 Liam McAvoy; 17 Latu Fifita; 21 James Duerden.
Try: Whiteley (72); **Goals:** Forber 1/1.
Rugby Leaguer & League Express Men of the Match:
Halifax: James Saltonstall; *Town:* Carl Forber.
Penalty count: 5-5; **Half-time:** 28-0;
Referee: Warren Turley; **Attendance:** 1,122.

HUNSLET HAWKS 26 WHITEHAVEN 18

HAWKS: 1 Jimmy Watson; 33 James Duckworth; 34 Luke Briscoe; 4 Danny Maun; 24 Richie Barnett; 31 Andy Kain; 6 Simon Brown; 35 Rob Mulhern; 9 Jack Lee; 19 Brad Brennan; 42 Jimmy Keinhorst; 44 Charlie Martin; 15 Liam Mackay. Subs (all used): 30 George Flanagan; 28 Mufaro Mvududu; 8 Michael Haley; 12 Aaron Lyons.
Tries: Lee (11), Duckworth (22), Mvududu (45), Watson (50), Flanagan (55); **Goals:** Brown 3/5.
WHITEHAVEN: 1 Richard Lepori; 5 Jordan Burns; 12 Steve Bannister; 3 Jessie Joe Parker; 2 Craig Calvert; 25 Dion Aiye; 19 John-Paul Brocklebank; 8 Ben Davies; 14 Thomas Coyle; 27 Ted Chapelhow; 21 Rhodri Lloyd; 4 Scott McAvoy; 11 Dave Allen. Subs (all used): 13 Tyla Hepi; 23 Sam Brooks; 9 James Newton; 18 Steve Fox.
Tries: Lepori (5), Lloyd (24), Hepi (41);
Goals: Brocklebank 3/3.
Rugby Leaguer & League Express Men of the Match:
Hawks: Jimmy Watson; *Whitehaven:* Dion Aiye.
Penalty count: 3-2; **Half-time:** 10-12;
Referee: Chris Leatherbarrow; **Attendance:** 539.

SHEFFIELD EAGLES 22 LEIGH CENTURIONS 36

EAGLES: 1 Quentin Laulu-Togagae; 2 Scott Turner; 3 Menzie Yere; 4 Sam Smeaton; 5 Misi Taulapapa; 6 Kyle Briggs; 19 Cory Aston; 8 Eddie Battye; 24 Keal Carlile; 22 Tony Tonks; 11 Michael Knowles; 16 Jamie Langley; 13 Pat Walker. Subs (all used): 9 James Davey; 10 Mitchell Stringer; 15 John Davies; 17 Steve Thorpe.
Tries: Aston (10), Laulu-Togagae (25, 64), Turner (57);
Goals: Walker 1/2, Briggs 2/2.
CENTURIONS: 1 Gregg McNally; 15 Jonathan Pownall; 16 Michael Platt; 4 Tom Armstrong; 5 Liam Kay; 6 Martyn Ridyard; 7 Ryan Brierley; 26 Gareth Hock; 9 Bob Beswick; 29 Jake Emmitt; 22 Andrew Dixon; 12 Tommy Goulden; 13 Sam Barlow. Subs: 27 Lewis Foster (not used); 20 Sam Hopkins; 23 Martin Aspinwall; 21 Jamie Acton.
Tries: Barlow (14), Goulden (27), McNally (32), Brierley (69, 80), Emmitt (78); **Goals:** Ridyard 6/7.
Sin bin: McNally (54) - dissent.
Rugby Leaguer & League Express Men of the Match:
Eagles: Eddie Battye; *Centurions:* Sam Barlow.
Penalty count: 11-6; **Half-time:** 10-16;
Referee: Michael Woodhead; **Attendance:** 1,454
(at Keepmoat Stadium, Doncaster).

ROUND 10

Sunday 26th April 2015

DONCASTER 38 BRADFORD BULLS 56

DONCASTER: 1 Dave Scott; 26 Sam Doherty; 17 Liam Welham; 4 Pasqualle Dunn; 31 Peter Fox; 34 Jordan Abdull; 28 Ben Reynolds; 32 Bobby Tyson-Wilson; 9 Kyle Kesik; 14 Russ Spiers; 12 Steve Snitch; 30 Jansin Turgut; 13 Mike Emmett. Subs (all used): 11 Michael Kelly; 15 Mitch Clark; 21 Danny Nicklas; 38 Matt Groat.
Tries: Fox (6, 68), Clark (22), Snitch (40), Dunn (43), Groat (46), Kelly (76); **Goals:** Scott 4/6, Reynolds 1/1.
BULLS: 27 Ryan Shaw; 2 Etuate Uaisele; 22 Chev Walker; 17 Jean-Philippe Baile; 20 Adam Henry; 6 Lee Gaskell; 13 Danny Addy; 8 Paul Clough; 9 Adam O'Brien; 10 Adam Sidlow; 11 Tom Olbison; 12 Dale Ferguson; 14 Jay Pitts. Subs (all used): 15 Daniel Fleming; 23 Alex Mellor; 26 Vila Halafihi; 32 Steve Crossley.

Tries: Uaisele (3, 52), Gaskell (11, 14, 60), Ferguson (29, 34), Henry (38), Clough (57), Shaw (79); **Goals:** Shaw 8/11.
Rugby Leaguer & League Express Men of the Match: *Doncaster:* Matt Groat; *Bulls:* Lee Gaskell.
Penalty count: 4-6; **Half-time:** 16-34;
Referee: Chris Kendall; **Attendance:** 2,276.

LEIGH CENTURIONS 56 BATLEY BULLDOGS 8

CENTURIONS: 15 Jonathan Pownall; 2 Adam Higson; 3 Greg Worthington; 4 Tom Armstrong; 5 Liam Kay; 6 Martyn Ridyard; 7 Ryan Brierley; 18 Tom Spencer; 9 Bob Beswick; 20 Sam Hopkins; 22 Andrew Dixon; 19 Kurt Haggerty; 13 Sam Barlow. Subs (all used): 10 Oliver Wilkes; 21 Jamie Acton; 27 Lewis Foster; 29 Jake Emmitt.
Tries: Brierley (3, 5, 33), Kay (7), Higson (19, 49), Armstrong (22), Pownall (31, 71), Dixon (66);
Goals: Ridyard 8/10.
Sin bin: Barlow (36) - punching; Emmitt (79) - dissent.
BULLDOGS: 27 Jacob Morgan; 2 Wayne Reittie; 11 Alex Bretherton; 20 Shaun Squires; 3 Shaun Ainscough; 6 Cain Southernwood; 14 Alistair Leak; 8 Keegan Hirst; 13 Luke Blake; 16 Sean Hesketh; 19 Lee Mitchell; 23 Brad Day; 17 Joe Chandler. Subs (all used): 15 Adam Gledhill; 18 Tom Lillycrop; 25 Tom Thackray; 26 Matty Fozard.
Tries: Ainscough (17), Fozard (77);
Goals: Southernwood 0/1, Fozard 0/1.
Rugby Leaguer & League Express Men of the Match: *Centurions:* Jonathan Pownall; *Bulldogs:* Joe Chandler.
Penalty count: 10-13; **Half-time:** 38-4;
Referee: Joe Cobb; **Attendance:** 3,036.

LONDON BRONCOS 16 DEWSBURY RAMS 20

BRONCOS: 5 Ben Hellewell; 2 Rhys Williams; 3 Ben Farrar; 4 Wes Naiqama; 20 Iliess Macani; 19 Joe Keyes; 28 Tom Gilmore; 12 Rhys Lovegrove; 14 Brad Dwyer; 18 Jon Wallace; 11 Daniel Harrison; 15 Matt Garside; 31 Elliot Minchella. Subs (all used): 9 Ray Nasso; 29 Jamie Thackray; 17 Erjon Dollapi; 23 Toby Everett.
Tries: Hellewell (6), Macani (51, 79); **Goals:** Naiqama 2/3.
RAMS: 31 Kieran Hyde; 2 Dale Morton; 19 Callan Beckett; 3 Karl Pryce; 15 Jason Crookes; 44 Brett Seymour; 7 Anthony Thackeray; 10 Ryan Hepworth; 23 Tom Hemingway; 33 Paul Jackson; 11 Rob Spicer; 16 Toby Adamson; 34 Luke Adamson. Subs (all used): 32 Makali Aizue; 24 Byron Smith; 13 Aaron Brown; 6 Matty Wildie.
Tries: Pryce (20), Beckett (42), Brown (65);
Goals: Hemingway 1/1, Hyde 3/3.
Rugby Leaguer & League Express Men of the Match: *Broncos:* Brad Dwyer; *Rams:* Tom Hemingway.
Penalty count: 6-8; **Half-time:** 6-6;
Referee: Michael Woodhead; **Attendance:** 663.

WHITEHAVEN 12 FEATHERSTONE ROVERS 36

WHITEHAVEN: 1 Richard Lepori; 28 Ed Chamberlain; 12 Steve Bannister; 21 Rhodri Lloyd; 2 Craig Calvert; 19 John-Paul Brocklebank; 25 Dion Aiye; 8 Ben Davies; 15 Grant Gore; 30 Jonathan Walker; 4 Scott McAvoy; 13 Tyla Hepi; 11 Dave Allen. Subs (all used): 27 Ted Chapelhow; 18 Steve Fox; 9 James Newton; 23 Sam Brooks.
Tries: Gore (34), Brooks (37); **Goals:** Brocklebank 2/2.
ROVERS: 22 James Mendeika; 5 Ben Blackmore; 1 Ian Hardman; 4 Thomas Minns; 21 Jy Hitchcox; 6 Paul Sykes; 7 Gareth Moore; 8 Jordan Baldwinson; 9 Andy Ellis; 17 Matt James; 12 Reni Maitua; 18 Jamie Cording; 13 Tim Spears. Subs (all used): 19 Alex Foster; 16 Andrew Bostock; 3 Nathan Chappell; 30 Garreth Carvell.
Tries: Minns (10, 71), Sykes (25, 62), Chappell (50), Moore (68), Cording (76); **Goals:** Moore 3/6, Sykes 1/1.
Rugby Leaguer & League Express Men of the Match: *Whitehaven:* Tyla Hepi; *Rovers:* Gareth Moore.
Penalty count: 10-8; **Half-time:** 12-10;
Referee: Andrew Sweet; **Attendance:** 747.

WORKINGTON TOWN 16 HUNSLET HAWKS 19

TOWN: 32 Lewis Tierney; 2 Sam Forrester; 1 Jack Murphy; 4 Perry Whiteley; 24 Theerapol Ritson; 30 Jamie Doran; 7 Carl Forber; 19 Tom Walker; 9 Graeme Mattinson; 10 Marc Shackley; 11 Brett Phillips; 16 Kurt Horton; 15 Karl Olstrum. Subs (all used): 14 Callum Phillips; 8 Kris Coward; 33 Ryan Sutton; 17 Latu Fifita.
Tries: Fifita (24), B Phillips (59), Doran (67);
Goals: Forber 2/3.
HAWKS: 1 Jimmy Watson; 33 James Duckworth; 34 Luke Briscoe; 4 Danny Maun; 24 Richie Barnett; 31 Andy Kain; 6 Simon Brown; 8 Michael Haley; 9 Jack Lee; 41 Andy Yates; 44 Charlie Martin; 42 Jimmy Keinhorst; 15 Liam Mackay. Subs (all used): 40 Josh Walters; 10 James Houston; 28 Mufaro Mvududu; 12 Aaron Lyons.
Tries: Lee (13), Keinhorst (27, 46), Briscoe (33);
Goals: Brown 1/4; **Field goal:** Brown (40).
Sin bin: Watson (65) - professional foul.
Rugby Leaguer & League Express Men of the Match: *Town:* Brett Phillips; *Hawks:* Simon Brown.
Penalty count: 7-9; **Half-time:** 6-15;
Referee: Tom Crashley; **Attendance:** 689.

SHEFFIELD EAGLES 36 HALIFAX 10

EAGLES: 1 Quentin Laulu-Togagae; 2 Scott Turner; 3 Menzie Yere; 4 Sam Smeaton; 23 Rob Worrincy; 19 Cory Aston; 7 Dominic Brambani; 8 Eddie Battye; 24 Keal Carlile; 17 Steve Thorpe; 11 Michael Knowles; 15 John Davies; 5 Misi Taulapapa. Subs (all used): 9 James Davey; 18 Ben Musolino; 6 Kyle Briggs; 10 Mitchell Stringer.
Tries: Laulu-Togagae (9, 74), Worrincy (17, 20, 39), Brambani (80); **Goals:** Brambani 6/7.
HALIFAX: 20 James Saltonstall; 23 Gareth Potts; 4 Ben Heaton; 26 Chris Taylor; 5 Alex Brown; 28 Danny Craven; 7 Ben Johnston; 17 Mitch Cahalane; 9 Ben Kaye; 10 Luke Ambler; 27 Ross Divorty; 11 Dane Manning; 6 Scott Murrell. Subs (all used): 8 Adam Tangata; 13 Jack Spencer; 16 Richard Moore; 21 Ryan Maneely.
Tries: Moore (40), Cahalane (65); **Goals:** Craven 1/2.
Rugby Leaguer & League Express Men of the Match: *Eagles:* Rob Worrincy; *Halifax:* Mitch Cahalane.
Penalty count: 7-5; **Half-time:** 22-4;
Referee: Matthew Thomason; **Attendance:** 1,437
(at Keepmoat Stadium, Doncaster).

ROUND 11

Sunday 3rd May 2015

BATLEY BULLDOGS 22 WHITEHAVEN 24

BULLDOGS: 1 James Craven; 2 Wayne Reittie; 20 Shaun Squires; 24 Brad Hey; 3 Shaun Ainscough; 7 Scott Leatherbarrow; 14 Alistair Leak; 8 Keegan Hirst; 13 Luke Blake; 10 Alex Rowe; 12 Sam Scott; 19 Lee Mitchell; 17 Joe Chandler. Subs (all used): 16 Sean Hesketh; 26 Matty Fozard; 18 Tom Lillycrop; 21 James Brown.
Tries: Craven (11, 27), Leatherbarrow (40), Mitchell (44);
Goals: Leatherbarrow 3/4.
WHITEHAVEN: 1 Richard Lepori; 16 Connor Holliday; 21 Rhodri Lloyd; 27 Declan Hulme; 2 Craig Calvert; 25 Dion Aiye; 19 John-Paul Brocklebank; 8 Ben Davies; 15 Grant Gore; 30 Jonathan Walker; 4 Scott McAvoy; 13 Tyla Hepi; 11 Dave Allen. Subs (all used): 9 James Newton; 18 Steve Fox; 23 Sam Brooks; 29 Richard Beaumont.
Tries: Hulme (22, 33), Newton (67), Brooks (80);
Goals: Brocklebank 2/2, Gore 2/2.
Rugby Leaguer & League Express Men of the Match: *Bulldogs:* Scott Leatherbarrow; *Whitehaven:* Declan Hulme.
Penalty count: 10-3; **Half-time:** 16-12;
Referee: Jamie Bloem; **Attendance:** 560.

BRADFORD BULLS 46 SHEFFIELD EAGLES 12

BULLS: 1 Jake Mullaney; 5 Danny Williams; 3 Adrian Purtell; 20 Adam Henry; 2 Etuate Uaisele; 6 Lee Gaskell; 13 Danny Addy; 8 Paul Clough; 9 Adam O'Brien; 10 Adam Sidlow; 11 Tom Olbison; 12 Dale Ferguson; 14 Jay Pitts. Subs (all used): 27 Ryan Shaw; 23 Alex Mellor; 31 Epalahame Lauaki; 15 Daniel Fleming.
Tries: Ferguson (6, 48), Olbison (20), Uaisele (30), Williams (33), Sidlow (59), Henry (61), Purtell (79);
Goals: Addy 7/8.
EAGLES: 1 Quentin Laulu-Togagae; 2 Scott Turner; 3 Menzie Yere; 4 Sam Smeaton; 23 Rob Worrincy; 19 Cory Aston; 7 Dominic Brambani; 17 Steve Thorpe; 9 James Davey; 10 Mitchell Stringer; 11 Michael Knowles; 16 Jamie Langley; 13 Pat Walker. Subs (all used): 24 Keal Carlile; 15 John Davies; 8 Eddie Battye; 22 Tony Tonks.
Tries: Turner (68), Aston (76); **Goals:** Knowles 2/2.
Rugby Leaguer & League Express Men of the Match: *Bulls:* Adam Henry; *Eagles:* Cory Aston.
Penalty count: 10-5; **Half-time:** 22-0;
Referee: Matthew Thomason; **Attendance:** 4,487.

DEWSBURY RAMS 28 LEIGH CENTURIONS 32

RAMS: 31 Kieran Hyde; 2 Dale Morton; 19 Callan Beckett; 3 Karl Pryce; 18 Dalton Grant; 44 Brett Seymour; 7 Anthony Thackeray; 10 Ryan Hepworth; 23 Tom Hemingway; 33 Paul Jackson; 11 Rob Spicer; 16 Toby Adamson; 34 Luke Adamson. Subs (all used): 32 Makali Aizue; 24 Byron Smith; 13 Aaron Brown; 6 Matty Wildie.
Tries: Spicer (8), Pryce (38), Grant (49, 72), L Adamson (58); **Goals:** Hyde 1/3, Seymour 3/3.
CENTURIONS: 1 Gregg McNally; 2 Adam Higson; 3 Greg Worthington; 16 Michael Platt; 5 Liam Kay; 6 Martyn Ridyard; 7 Ryan Brierley; 18 Tom Spencer; 9 Bob Beswick; 23 Martin Aspinwall; 19 Kurt Haggerty; 12 Tommy Goulden; 13 Sam Barlow. Subs (all used): 10 Oliver Wilkes; 21 Jamie Acton; 22 Andrew Dixon; 29 Jake Emmitt.
Tries: Kay (22, 32, 62), McNally (27), Ridyard (36), Worthington (52); **Goals:** Ridyard 4/6.
Sin bin: Barlow (17) - dissent.
Rugby Leaguer & League Express Men of the Match: *Rams:* Dalton Grant; *Centurions:* Liam Kay.
Penalty count: 10-4; **Half-time:** 10-22;
Referee: Dave Merrick; **Attendance:** 1,551.

FEATHERSTONE ROVERS 72 WORKINGTON TOWN 0

ROVERS: 21 Jy Hitchcox; 5 Ben Blackmore; 1 Ian Hardman; 3 Nathan Chappell; 4 Thomas Minns; 6 Paul Sykes; 7 Gareth Moore; 10 Paul Wood; 9 Andy Ellis; 17 Matt James; 18 Jamie Cording; 19 Alex Foster; 13 Tim Spears. Subs (all used): 31 Remy Marginet; 15 Jack Bussey; 16 Andrew Bostock; 30 Garreth Carvell.
Tries: Hardman (2), Hitchcox (5, 75, 80), Ellis (10), Cording (24, 39), Chappell (31), Moore (35), Foster (38, 73), Marginet (44), Bussey (46);
Goals: Moore 8/10, Marginet 2/3.
TOWN: 1 Jack Murphy; 2 Sam Forrester; 3 Jason Mossop; 4 Perry Whiteley; 22 Elliott Miller; 33 Jamie Doran; 7 Carl Forber; 19 Tom Walker; 9 Graeme Mattinson; 10 Marc Shackley; 11 Brett Phillips; 16 Kurt Horton; 25 Steve Scholey. Subs (all used): 17 Latu Fifita; 8 Kris Coward; 14 Callum Phillips; 5 Brett Carter.
Rugby Leaguer & League Express Men of the Match: *Rovers:* Alex Foster; *Town:* Carl Forber.
Penalty count: 7-4; **Half-time:** 44-0;
Referee: Joe Cobb; **Attendance:** 1,547.

HALIFAX 40 DONCASTER 6

HALIFAX: 7 Ben Johnston; 23 Gareth Potts; 4 Ben Heaton; 20 James Saltonstall; 2 Tom Saxton; 6 Scott Murrell; 28 Danny Craven; 10 Luke Ambler; 21 Ryan Maneely; 17 Mitch Cahalane; 27 Ross Divorty; 11 Dane Manning; 16 Richard Moore. Subs (all used): 9 Ben Kaye; 12 Andy Bracek; 13 Jack Spencer; 15 Adam Robinson.
Tries: Saltonstall (6), Maneely (8), Heaton (15), Divorty (19, 80), Potts (23), Murrell (38), Saxton (68);
Goals: Craven 1/4, Murrell 3/4.
DONCASTER: 34 Curtis Naughton; 39 Tom Hodson; 17 Liam Welham; 4 Pasqualle Dunn; 31 Peter Fox; 1 Dave Scott; 21 Danny Nicklas; 8 Matt Carbutt; 33 James Cunningham; 14 Russ Spiers; 12 Steve Snitch; 11 Michael Kelly; 13 Mike Emmett. Subs (all used): 15 Mitch Clark; 22 Brad Foster; 9 Kyle Kesik; 23 Jack Walton.
Try: Dunn (60); **Goals:** Scott 1/1.
Rugby Leaguer & League Express Men of the Match: *Halifax:* Scott Murrell; *Doncaster:* Mitch Clark.
Penalty count: 8-6; **Half-time:** 28-0;
Referee: Gareth Hewer; **Attendance:** 1,284.

HUNSLET HAWKS 12 LONDON BRONCOS 32

HAWKS: 1 Jimmy Watson; 33 James Duckworth; 34 Luke Briscoe; 4 Danny Maun; 24 Richie Barnett; 31 Andy Kain; 6 Simon Brown; 8 Michael Haley; 30 George Flanagan; 41 Andy Yates; 44 Charlie Martin; 40 Josh Walters; 15 Liam Mackay. Subs (all used): 36 Robbie Ward; 28 Mufaro Mvududu; 10 James Houston; 12 Aaron Lyons.
Tries: Briscoe (13), Brown (55); **Goals:** Brown 2/2.
Sin bin: Ward (43) - interference.
BRONCOS: 5 Ben Hellewell; 2 Rhys Williams; 3 Ben Farrar; 4 Wes Naiqama; 20 Iliess Macani; 27 Jarrod Sammut; 28 Tom Gilmore; 12 Rhys Lovegrove; 9 Ray Nasso; 29 Jamie Thackray; 11 Daniel Harrison; 15 Matt Garside; 31 Elliot Minchella. Subs (all used): 14 Brad Dwyer; 32 Elliot Kear; 18 Jon Wallace; 33 Chris Annakin.
Tries: Minchella (1), Gilmore (20), Naiqama (22), Garside (35), R Williams (46, 77); **Goals:** Naiqama 4/6.
Sin bin: Garside (61) - delaying restart.
Rugby Leaguer & League Express Men of the Match: *Hawks:* Simon Brown; *Broncos:* Tom Gilmore.
Penalty count: 8-8; **Half-time:** 6-22;
Referee: Warren Turley; **Attendance:** 514.

ROUND 12

Friday 8th May 2015

SHEFFIELD EAGLES 30 DONCASTER 12

EAGLES: 5 Misi Taulapapa; 2 Scott Turner; 3 Menzie Yere; 4 Sam Smeaton; 23 Rob Worrincy; 6 Kyle Briggs; 19 Cory Aston; 8 Eddie Battye; 24 Keal Carlile; 10 Mitchell Stringer; 11 Michael Knowles; 16 Jamie Langley; 15 John Davies. Subs (all used): 9 James Davey; 22 Tony Tonks; 12 Duane Straugheir; 20 Jack Blagbrough.
Tries: Aston (38), Stringer (58), Briggs (63), Davies (70), Knowles (79); **Goals:** Briggs 5/5.
DONCASTER: 1 Dave Scott; 39 Tom Hodson; 30 Jack Logan; 4 Pasqualle Dunn; 31 Peter Fox; 21 Danny Nicklas; 34 Curtis Naughton; 14 Russ Spiers; 13 Mike Emmett; 32 Bobby Tyson-Wilson; 28 Jansin Turgut; 11 Michael Kelly; 12 Steve Snitch. Subs (all used): 15 Mitch Clark; 38 Matt Groat; 3 Danny Cowling; 22 Brad Foster.
Tries: Turgut (11), Hodson (49); **Goals:** Scott 2/3.
Rugby Leaguer & League Express Men of the Match: *Eagles:* Michael Knowles; *Doncaster:* Mike Emmett.
Penalty count: 6-4; **Half-time:** 6-6;
Referee: Chris Leatherbarrow; **Attendance:** 863
(at Keepmoat Stadium).

Sunday 10th May 2015

DEWSBURY RAMS 40 HUNSLET HAWKS 4

RAMS: 1 Ryan Fieldhouse; 2 Dale Morton; 3 Karl Pryce; 19 Callan Beckett; 18 Dalton Grant; 44 Brett Seymour; 7 Anthony Thackeray; 10 Ryan Hepworth; 6 Matty Wildie; 33 Paul Jackson; 11 Rob Spicer; 12 Scott Hale; 34 Luke Adamson. Subs (all used): 32 Makali Aizue; 13 Aaron Brown; 16 Toby Adamson; 15 Jason Crookes.
Tries: L Adamson (13), Morton (26, 59, 76), Thackeray (53), T Adamson (62), Seymour (68);
Goals: Seymour 6/6, Morton 0/1.
Sin bin: Seymour (24) - repeated team offences.
On report: Hepworth (73) - alleged late challenge.
HAWKS: 1 Jimmy Watson; 33 James Duckworth; 34 Luke Briscoe; 4 Danny Maun; 24 Richie Barnett; 31 Andy Kain; 6 Simon Brown; 41 Andy Yates; 30 George Flanagan; 8 Michael Haley; 44 Charlie Martin; 11 Callum Casey; 15 Liam Mackay. Subs (all used): 28 Mufaro Mvududu; 7 Danny Ansell; 35 Rob Mulhern; 12 Aaron Lyons.
Try: Martin (2); **Goals:** Brown 0/1.
Sin bin: Ansell (26) - repeated team offences.
Rugby Leaguer & League Express Men of the Match: *Rams:* Dale Morton; *Hawks:* Andy Yates.
Penalty count: 12-10; **Half-time:** 10-4;
Referee: Andrew Sweet; **Attendance:** 1,103.

LEIGH CENTURIONS 22 HALIFAX 14

CENTURIONS: 1 Gregg McNally; 15 Jonathan Pownall; 3 Greg Worthington; 4 Tom Armstrong; 5 Liam Kay; 6 Martyn Ridyard; 7 Ryan Brierley; 8 Fuifui Moimoi; 9 Bob Beswick; 21 Jamie Acton; 19 Kurt Haggerty; 22 Andrew Dixon; 13 Sam Barlow. Subs (all used): 12 Tommy Goulden; 17 Ben Reynolds; 10 Oliver Wilkes; 20 Sam Hopkins.
Tries: Kay (9), Worthington (52), Goulden (64), Beswick (80); **Goals:** Ridyard 1/1, Brierley 2/3.
Dismissals:
Armstrong (70) - use of the head on Saltonstall;
Acton (74) - fighting.
Sin bin: Haggerty (74) - fighting.

HALIFAX: 7 Ben Johnston; 20 James Saltonstall; 4 Ben Heaton; 3 Steve Tyrer; 2 Tom Saxton; 6 Scott Murrell; 28 Danny Craven; 10 Luke Ambler; 21 Ryan Maneely; 17 Mitch Cahalane; 27 Ross Divorty; 11 Dane Manning; 12 Andy Bracek. Subs (all used): 9 Ben Kaye; 16 Richard Moore; 15 Adam Robinson; 13 Jack Spencer.
Tries: Murrell (6), Heaton (27, 45); **Goals:** Tyrer 1/3.
Dismissals: Bracek (74) - fighting; Tyrer (74) - fighting.
Sin bin: Cahalane (74) - fighting.
Rugby Leaguer & League Express Men of the Match: *Centurions:* Andrew Dixon; *Halifax:* Mitch Cahalane.
Penalty count: 7-9; **Half-time:** 6-10;
Referee: Matthew Thomason; **Attendance:** 3,647.

LONDON BRONCOS 32 FEATHERSTONE ROVERS 40

BRONCOS: 5 Ben Hellewell; 2 Rhys Williams; 3 Ben Farrar; 4 Wes Naiqama; 20 Iliess Macani; 27 Jarrod Sammut; 28 Tom Gilmore; 12 Rhys Lovegrove; 14 Brad Dwyer; 29 Jamie Thackray; 11 Daniel Harrison; 15 Matt Garside; 31 Elliot Minchella. Subs (all used): 9 Ray Nasso; 32 Elliot Kear; 18 Jon Wallace; 33 Chris Annakin.
Tries: Thackray (3), Harrison (21, 80), R Williams (64), Hellewell (68), Sammut (71); **Goals:** Naiqama 4/6.
ROVERS: 21 Jy Hitchcox; 5 Ben Blackmore; 1 Ian Hardman; 3 Nathan Chappell; 2 Will Sharp; 6 Paul Sykes; 7 Gareth Moore; 10 Paul Wood; 9 Andy Ellis; 17 Matt James; 12 Reni Maitua; 18 Jamie Cording; 13 Tim Spears. Subs (all used): 23 Luke Teasdale; 15 Jack Bussey; 16 Andrew Bostock; 30 Garreth Carvell.
Tries: Blackmore (28), Hitchcox (32), Bostock (35), Cording (47), Teasdale (57), Chappell (61), Bussey (75);
Goals: Sykes 6/7.
Rugby Leaguer & League Express Men of the Match: *Broncos:* Tom Gilmore; *Rovers:* Andrew Bostock.
Penalty count: 6-8; **Half-time:** 12-16;
Referee: Gareth Hewer; **Attendance:** 672.

WHITEHAVEN 16 BRADFORD BULLS 32

WHITEHAVEN: 1 Richard Lepori; 28 Ed Chamberlain; 16 Connor Holliday; 27 Declan Hulme; 2 Craig Calvert; 25 Dion Aiye; 15 Grant Gore; 8 Ben Davies; 14 Thomas Coyle; 30 Jonathan Walker; 4 Scott McAvoy; 13 Tyla Hepi; 11 Dave Allen. Subs (all used): 29 Richard Beaumont; 18 Steve Fox; 9 James Newton; 23 Sam Brooks.
Tries: McAvoy (34), Holliday (39), Newton (50);
Goals: Chamberlain 2/3.
Sin bin: Hepi (53) - fighting.
BULLS: 27 Ryan Shaw; 5 Danny Williams; 3 Adrian Purtell; 20 Adam Henry; 2 Etuate Uaisele; 6 Lee Gaskell; 13 Danny Addy; 8 Paul Clough; 9 Adam O'Brien; 10 Adam Sidlow; 11 Tom Olbison; 14 Jay Pitts; 23 Alex Mellor. Subs (all used): 12 Dale Ferguson; 17 Jean-Philippe Baile; 31 Epalahame Lauaki; 15 Daniel Fleming.
Tries: Purtell (20, 30), Gaskell (33), Addy (66), Williams (71, 76); **Goals:** Shaw 4/6.
Sin bin: Pitts (53) - fighting.
Rugby Leaguer & League Express Men of the Match: *Whitehaven:* Scott McAvoy; *Bulls:* Adam Sidlow.
Penalty count: 5-9; **Half-time:** 10-16;
Referee: Warren Turley; **Attendance:** 1,338.

WORKINGTON TOWN 10 BATLEY BULLDOGS 23

TOWN: 1 Jack Murphy; 22 Elliott Miller; 3 Jason Mossop; 12 Jarrad Stack; 32 Lewis Tierney; 30 Jamie Doran; 7 Carl Forber; 19 Tom Walker; 9 Graeme Mattinson; 10 Marc Shackley; 11 Brett Phillips; 4 Perry Whiteley; 13 Liam McAvoy. Subs (all used): 14 Callum Phillips; 15 Karl Olstrum; 25 Steve Scholey; 8 Kris Coward.
Tries: C Phillips (41), Forber (53); **Goals:** Forber 1/2.
BULLDOGS: 1 James Craven; 2 Wayne Reittie; 4 Ayden Faal; 20 Shaun Squires; 3 Shaun Ainscough; 14 Alistair Leak; 7 Scott Leatherbarrow; 8 Keegan Hirst; 13 Luke Blake; 21 James Brown; 12 Sam Scott; 23 Brad Day; 17 Joe Chandler. Subs (all used): 10 Alex Rowe; 16 Sean Hesketh; 18 Tom Lillycrop; 25 Tom Thackray.
Tries: Reittie (33), Leak (69), Craven (75);
Goals: Leatherbarrow 5/5;
Field goal: Leatherbarrow (78).
Rugby Leaguer & League Express Men of the Match: *Town:* Carl Forber; *Bulldogs:* Luke Blake.
Penalty count: 8-7; **Half-time:** 0-8;
Referee: Michael Woodhead; **Attendance:** 596.

ROUND 13

Sunday 17th May 2015

DONCASTER 6 WORKINGTON TOWN 37

DONCASTER: 1 Dave Scott; 39 Tom Hodson; 30 Jack Logan; 4 Pasqualle Dunn; 31 Peter Fox; 32 James Cunningham; 21 Danny Nicklas; 14 Russ Spiers; 34 Stuart Howarth; 38 Matt Groat; 28 Jansin Turgut; 12 Steve Snitch; 13 Mike Emmett. Subs (all used): 33 Bobby Tyson-Wilson; 15 Mitch Clark; 11 Michael Kelly; 3 Danny Cowling.
Try: Scott (13); **Goals:** Scott 1/1.
Dismissal: Clark (72) - punching.
TOWN: 1 Jack Murphy; 30 Lewis Tierney; - Rhodri Lloyd; 3 Jason Mossop; 22 Elliott Miller; 31 Jake Shorrocks; 38 Jamie Doran; 19 Tom Walker; 9 Graeme Mattinson; 10 Marc Shackley; 11 Brett Phillips; 12 Jarrad Stack; 13 Liam McAvoy. Subs (all used): 16 Kurt Horton; 32 Logan Tomkins; 15 Karl Olstrum; 8 Kris Coward.
Tries: Lloyd (29, 56), Tierney (32, 58, 64), B Phillips (73), Murphy (78); **Goals:** Murphy 0/1, Shorrocks 2/4, Horton 2/4; **Field goal:** Doran (80).
Rugby Leaguer & League Express Men of the Match: *Doncaster:* Mike Emmett; *Town:* Lewis Tierney.
Penalty count: 6-6; **Half-time:** 6-10;
Referee: Gareth Hewer; **Attendance:** 695.

HALIFAX 60 WHITEHAVEN 18

HALIFAX: 7 Ben Johnston; 20 James Saltonstall; 4 Ben Heaton; 3 Steve Tyrer; 2 Tom Saxton; 6 Scott Murrell; 28 Danny Craven; 10 Luke Ambler; 21 Ryan Maneely; 17 Mitch Cahalane; 27 Ross Divorty; 11 Dane Manning; 15 Adam Robinson. Subs (all used): 29 Ed Barber; 16 Richard Moore; 12 Andy Bracek; 9 Ben Kaye.
Tries: Saxton (3), Tyrer (6, 58), A Robinson (13, 67), Manning (43), Saltonstall (49), Johnston (55), Murrell (66), Barber (80); **Goals:** Tyrer 1/2, Murrell 9/9.
WHITEHAVEN: 1 Richard Lepori; 15 Ed Chamberlain; 3 Jessie Joe Parker; 27 Declan Hulme; 2 Craig Calvert; 25 Dion Aiye; 28 Jordan Johnstone; 8 Ben Davies; 14 Thomas Coyle; 30 Jonathan Walker; 4 Scott McAvoy; 13 Tyla Hepi; 11 Dave Allen. Subs (all used): 23 Sam Brooks; 29 Richard Beaumont; 9 James Newton; 18 Steve Fox.
Tries: Aiye (27), Calvert (31), McAvoy (60);
Goals: Johnstone 3/3.
Rugby Leaguer & League Express Men of the Match: *Halifax:* Danny Craven; *Whitehaven:* Scott McAvoy.
Penalty count: 9-2; **Half-time:** 18-12;
Referee: Chris Kendall; **Attendance:** 1,601.

Tuesday 19th May 2015

SHEFFIELD EAGLES 15 DEWSBURY RAMS 8

EAGLES: 1 Quentin Laulu-Togagae; 2 Scott Turner; 3 Menzie Yere; 4 Sam Smeaton; 23 Rob Worrincy; 6 Kyle Briggs; 7 Dominic Brambani; 17 Steve Thorpe; 24 Keal Carlile; 10 Mitchell Stringer; 11 Michael Knowles; 12 Duane Straugheir; 5 Misi Taulapapa. Subs (all used): 8 Eddie Battye; 9 James Davey; 22 Tony Tonks; 15 John Davies.
Tries: Turner (34), Yere (44), Worrincy (73);
Goals: Briggs 1/4; **Field goal:** Brambani (80).
RAMS: 1 Ryan Fieldhouse; 2 Dale Morton; 3 Karl Pryce; 15 Jason Crookes; 18 Dalton Grant; 44 Brett Seymour; 7 Anthony Thackeray; 17 Matthew Haggarty; 6 Matty Wildie; 33 Paul Jackson; 11 Rob Spicer; 12 Scott Hale; 34 Luke Adamson. Subs (all used): 13 Aaron Brown; 16 Toby Adamson; 9 Wayne Godwin; 10 Ryan Hepworth.
Try: Thackeray (66); **Goals:** Seymour 2/2.
Rugby Leaguer & League Express Men of the Match: *Eagles:* Scott Turner; *Rams:* Matty Wildie.
Penalty count: 7-8; **Half-time:** 4-2;
Referee: Tom Crashley; **Attendance:** 682 *(at Keepmoat Stadium, Doncaster).*

ROUND 14 - SUMMER BASH

Saturday 23rd May 2015

WHITEHAVEN 20 WORKINGTON TOWN 26

WHITEHAVEN: 32 Louis Jouffret; - Jordan Sigismeau; 26 Greg Wilde; 3 Jessie Joe Parker; 5 Jordan Burns; 25 Dion Aiye; 15 Grant Gore; 30 Jonathan Walker; 14 Thomas Coyle; 29 Richard Beaumont; 4 Scott McAvoy; 13 Tyla Hepi; 11 Dave Allen. Subs (all used): 27 Ted Chapelhow; 18 Steve Fox; 9 James Newton; 23 Sam Brooks.
Tries: Gore (7), Sigismeau (10), Jouffret (22), Burns (27);
Goals: Jouffret 2/5.
Sin bin: Hepi (23) - punching.
TOWN: 1 Jack Murphy; 22 Elliott Miller; 3 Jason Mossop; 30 Oliver Gildart; 32 Lewis Tierney; 34 Jake Shorrocks; 33 Jamie Doran; 10 Marc Shackley; 9 Graeme Mattinson; 19 Tom Walker; 11 Brett Phillips; 12 Jarrad Stack; 13 Liam McAvoy. Subs (all used): 7 Carl Forber; 15 Karl Olstrum; 8 Kris Coward; 16 Kurt Horton.
Tries: Stack (37, 53), Shackley (62), Murphy (75);
Goals: Forber 5/5.
Rugby Leaguer & League Express Men of the Match: *Whitehaven:* Louis Jouffret; *Town:* Jarrad Stack.
Penalty count: 8-9; **Half-time:** 18-6;
Referee: Tom Crashley.

LONDON BRONCOS 46 SHEFFIELD EAGLES 6

BRONCOS: 32 Elliot Kear; 2 Rhys Williams; 5 Ben Hellewell; 4 Wes Naiqama; 20 Iliess Macani; 22 Oscar Thomas; 28 Tom Gilmore; 12 Rhys Lovegrove; 35 Andrew Henderson; 29 Jamie Thackray; 11 Daniel Harrison; 15 Matt Garside; 31 Elliot Minchella. Subs (all used): 9 Ray Nasso; 34 Matt Davis; 18 Jon Wallace; 23 Toby Everett.
Tries: Kear (4, 17), R Williams (11, 69), Hellewell (14), Thomas (27, 48, 60); **Goals:** Naiqama 7/8.
EAGLES: 1 Quentin Laulu-Togagae; 2 Scott Turner; 3 Menzie Yere; 4 Sam Smeaton; 23 Rob Worrincy; 19 Cory Aston; 7 Dominic Brambani; 8 Eddie Battye; 24 Keal Carlile; 10 Mitchell Stringer; 16 Jamie Langley; 12 Duane Straugheir; 5 Misi Taulapapa. Subs (all used): 9 James Davey; 15 John Davies; 22 Tony Tonks; 17 Steve Thorpe.
Try: Aston (33); **Goals:** Brambani 1/1.
Rugby Leaguer & League Express Men of the Match: *Broncos:* Oscar Thomas; *Eagles:* Tony Tonks.
Penalty count: 4-5; **Half-time:** 28-6;
Referee: Chris Kendall.

BRADFORD BULLS 18 HALIFAX 4

BULLS: 27 Ryan Shaw; 5 Danny Williams; 3 Adrian Purtell; 20 Adam Henry; 2 Etuate Uaisele; 6 Lee Gaskell; 13 Danny Addy; 8 Paul Clough; 9 Adam O'Brien; 10 Adam Sidlow; 11 Tom Olbison; 14 Jay Pitts; 23 Alex Mellor. Subs (all used): 31 Epalahame Lauaki; 32 Steve Crossley; 17 Jean-Philippe Baile; 33 James Mendeika.
Tries: Shaw (35), Purtell (39, 55);
Goals: Shaw 2/2, Addy 1/1.
HALIFAX: 7 Ben Johnston; 20 James Saltonstall; 4 Ben Heaton; 26 Chris Taylor; 2 Tom Saxton; 6 Scott Murrell; 28 Danny Craven; 10 Luke Ambler; 9 Ben Kaye; 17 Mitch Cahalane; 27 Ross Divorty; 11 Dane Manning; 15 Adam Robinson. Subs (all used): 16 Richard Moore; 21 Ryan Maneely; 29 Ed Barber; 30 Tyler Dickinson.
Try: Heaton (44); **Goals:** Murrell 0/1.
Rugby Leaguer & League Express Men of the Match: *Bulls:* Lee Gaskell; *Halifax:* Ben Johnston.
Penalty count: 5-4; **Half-time:** 12-0; **Referee:** Joe Cobb.

Attendance: 8,360 *(at Bloomfield Road, Blackpool).*

Sunday 24th May 2015

BATLEY BULLDOGS 12 DEWSBURY RAMS 19

BULLDOGS: 1 James Craven; 2 Wayne Reittie; 3 Shaun Ainscough; 11 Alex Bretherton; 28 Alex Brown; 14 Alistair Leak; 7 Scott Leatherbarrow; 15 Adam Gledhill; 13 Luke Blake; 10 Alex Rowe; 19 Lee Mitchell; 23 Brad Day; 21 James Brown. Subs (all used): 8 Keegan Hirst; 26 Matty Fozard; 18 Tom Lillycrop; 17 Joe Chandler.
Tries: Day (21), A Brown (43); **Goals:** Leatherbarrow 2/3.
RAMS: 1 Ryan Fieldhouse; 15 Jason Crookes; 3 Karl Pryce; 19 Callan Beckett; 18 Dalton Grant; 44 Brett Seymour; 7 Anthony Thackeray; 10 Ryan Hepworth; 6 Matty Wildie; 33 Paul Jackson; 11 Rob Spicer; 12 Scott Hale; 34 Luke Adamson. Subs (all used): 17 Matthew Haggarty; 25 Joel Farrell; 32 Makali Aizue; 13 Aaron Brown.
Tries: Hale (14), Brown (35), Grant (68);
Goals: Seymour 3/4; **Field goal:** Thackeray (78).
Rugby Leaguer & League Express Men of the Match: *Bulldogs:* Shaun Ainscough; *Rams:* Luke Adamson.
Penalty count: 7-11; **Half-time:** 6-12;
Referee: Gareth Hewer.

DONCASTER 12 HUNSLET HAWKS 25

DONCASTER: 1 Dave Scott; 26 Sam Doherty; 17 Liam Welham; 3 Danny Cowling; 39 Tom Hodson; 21 Danny Nicklas; 7 Richard Wilkinson; 38 Matt Groat; 13 Mike Emmett; 15 Mitch Clark; 12 Steve Snitch; 11 Michael Kelly; 4 Pasqualle Dunn. Subs (all used): 14 Russ Spiers; 8 Matt Carbutt; 9 Kyle Kesik; 18 Shaun Leaf.
Tries: Wilkinson (13), Leaf (34), Hodson (55);
Goals: Scott 0/2, Hodson 0/1.
HAWKS: 1 Jimmy Watson; 34 Luke Briscoe; 42 Jimmy Keinhorst; 4 Danny Maun; 5 Vinny Finigan; 31 Andy Kain; 7 Danny Ansell; 41 Andy Yates; 36 Robbie Ward; 8 Michael Haley; 44 Charlie Martin; 11 Callum Casey; 15 Liam Mackay. Subs (all used): 30 George Flanagan; 35 Rob Mulhern; 12 Aaron Lyons; 28 Mufaro Mvududu.
Tries: Keinhorst (8), Watson (19), Maun (25), Briscoe (64); **Goals:** Ansell 4/5; **Field goal:** Ansell (76).
Rugby Leaguer & League Express Men of the Match: *Doncaster:* Kyle Kesik; *Hawks:* Andy Kain.
Penalty count: 8-5; **Half-time:** 8-16;
Referee: Jamie Bloem.

FEATHERSTONE ROVERS 12 LEIGH CENTURIONS 31

ROVERS: 21 Jy Hitchcox; 5 Ben Blackmore; 1 Ian Hardman; 4 Thomas Minns; 2 Will Sharp; 6 Paul Sykes; 7 Gareth Moore; 8 Jordan Baldwinson; 9 Andy Ellis; 10 Paul Wood; 12 Reni Maitua; 18 Jamie Cording; 17 Matt James. Subs (all used): 23 Luke Teasdale; 16 Andrew Bostock; 30 Garreth Carvell; 20 Ryan Verlinden.
Tries: Blackmore (2), Hardman (73); **Goals:** Sykes 2/2.
Dismissal: Wood (27) - gouging Beswick.
Sin bin: Moore (68) - punching.
CENTURIONS: 1 Gregg McNally; 15 Jonathan Pownall; 16 Michael Platt; 3 Greg Worthington; 5 Liam Kay; 6 Martyn Ridyard; 7 Ryan Brierley; 8 Fuifui Moimoi; 9 Bob Beswick; 29 Jake Emmitt; 22 Andrew Dixon; 12 Tommy Goulden; 13 Sam Barlow. Subs (all used): 30 Mick Higham; 10 Oliver Wilkes; 20 Sam Hopkins; 26 Gareth Hock.
Tries: McNally (10, 33, 51), Worthington (43), Higham (45); **Goals:** Ridyard 5/6;
Field goal: Brierley (40).
Sin bin: Barlow (27) - punching; Hock (65) - running in to altercation; Kay (72) - holding down.
Rugby Leaguer & League Express Men of the Match: *Rovers:* Jy Hitchcox; *Centurions:* Martyn Ridyard.
Penalty count: 6-7; **Half-time:** 6-15;
Referee: Chris Leatherbarrow.

Attendance: 7,021 *(at Bloomfield Road, Blackpool).*

ROUND 15

Friday 29th May 2015

HUNSLET HAWKS 10 SHEFFIELD EAGLES 54

HAWKS: 1 Jimmy Watson; 34 Luke Briscoe; 42 Jimmy Keinhorst; 4 Danny Maun; 5 Vinny Finigan; 31 Andy Kain; 7 Danny Ansell; 8 Michael Haley; 9 Jack Lee; 19 Brad Brennan; 21 Ryan Backhouse; 11 Callum Casey; 41 Andy Yates. Subs (all used): 14 Matthew Tebb; 12 Aaron Lyons; 10 James Houston; 15 Liam Mackay.
Tries: Lee (26), Mackay (57); **Goals:** Ansell 1/2.
EAGLES: 1 Quentin Laulu-Togagae; 2 Scott Turner; 3 Menzie Yere; 4 Sam Smeaton; 23 Rob Worrincy; 6 Kyle Briggs; 19 Cory Aston; 17 Steve Thorpe; 9 James Davey; 10 Mitchell Stringer; 11 Michael Knowles; 12 Duane Straugheir; 15 John Davies. Subs (all used): 24 Keal Carlile; 8 Eddie Battye; 5 Misi Taulapapa; 22 Tony Tonks.
Tries: Yere (33, 44, 46, 63), Smeaton (40), Tonks (41), Turner (50), Worrincy (67), Knowles (71), Laulu-Togagae (80); **Goals:** Briggs 6/9, Knowles 1/1.
Rugby Leaguer & League Express Men of the Match: *Hawks:* Andy Kain; *Eagles:* Menzie Yere.
Penalty count: 4-5; **Half-time:** 6-10;
Referee: Adam Gill; **Attendance:** 521.

Sunday 31st May 2015

DEWSBURY RAMS 14 DONCASTER 6

RAMS: 1 Ryan Fieldhouse; 2 Dale Morton; 15 Jason Crookes; 3 Karl Pryce; 18 Dalton Grant; 44 Brett Seymour; 7 Anthony Thackeray; 17 Matthew Haggarty; 6 Matty Wildie; 10 Ryan Hepworth; 11 Rob Spicer; 12 Scott Hale; 34 Luke Adamson. Subs (all used): 47 Nathan Conroy; 25 Joel Farrell; 24 Byron Smith; 32 Makali Aizue.
Tries: Hale (19), Morton (63), Crookes (79);
Goals: Seymour 1/3.
DONCASTER: 1 Dave Scott; 26 Sam Doherty; 17 Liam Welham; 27 Alex Gilbey; 31 Peter Fox; 9 Kyle Kesik; 34 James Cunningham; 38 Matt Groat; 13 Mike Emmett; 15 Mitch Clark; 11 Michael Kelly; 28 Jansin Turgut; 4 Pasqualle Dunn. Subs (all used): 14 Russ Spiers; 8 Matt Carbutt; 22 Brad Foster; 5 Stewart Sanderson.
Try: Turgut (31); **Goals:** Scott 1/1.
Sin bin: Emmett (18) - dissent.
On report: Clark (72) - alleged high tackle.
Rugby Leaguer & League Express Men of the Match:
Rams: Ryan Hepworth; *Doncaster:* Dave Scott.
Penalty count: 10-7; **Half-time:** 6-6;
Referee: Chris Leatherbarrow; **Attendance:** 763.

FEATHERSTONE ROVERS 44 BATLEY BULLDOGS 16

ROVERS: 21 Jy Hitchcox; 5 Ben Blackmore; 1 Ian Hardman; 6 Paul Sykes; 2 Will Sharp; 28 Will Milner; 7 Gareth Moore; 8 Jordan Baldwinson; 9 Andy Ellis; 10 Paul Wood; 12 Reni Maitua; 18 Jamie Cording; 17 Matt James. Subs (all used): 23 Luke Teasdale; 16 Andrew Bostock; 20 Ryan Verlinden; 27 Jack Ormondroyd.
Tries: Ellis (12), James (16), Sykes (22, 26, 30, 79), Ormondroyd (34), Blackmore (65); **Goals:** Sykes 6/8.
BULLDOGS: 3 Shaun Ainscough; 2 Wayne Reittie; 20 Shaun Squires; 11 Alex Bretherton; 28 Alex Brown; 14 Alistair Leak; 7 Scott Leatherbarrow; 8 Keegan Hirst; 13 Luke Blake; 10 Alex Rowe; 19 Lee Mitchell; 23 Brad Day; 21 James Brown. Subs (all used): 15 Adam Gledhill; 16 Sean Hesketh; 12 Sam Scott; 17 Joe Chandler.
Tries: Ainscough (46), Leak (57), Mitchell (60);
Goals: Leatherbarrow 2/3.
Rugby Leaguer & League Express Men of the Match:
Rovers: Paul Sykes; *Bulldogs:* Alex Rowe.
Penalty count: 6-14; **Half-time:** 34-0;
Referee: Michael Woodhead; **Attendance:** 2,067.

LONDON BRONCOS 18 BRADFORD BULLS 36

BRONCOS: 32 Elliot Kear; 2 Rhys Williams; 5 Ben Hellewell; 4 Wes Naiqama; 20 Iliess Macani; 22 Oscar Thomas; 28 Tom Gilmore; 12 Rhys Lovegrove; 35 Andrew Henderson; 29 Jamie Thackray; 11 Daniel Harrison; 15 Matt Garside; 31 Elliot Minchella. Subs (all used): 21 Joel Wicks; 34 Matt Davis; 18 Jon Wallace; 36 Jonathan Walker.
Tries: Gilmore (5), Thackray (9, 67); **Goals:** Naiqama 3/3.
BULLS: 27 Ryan Shaw; 5 Danny Williams; 3 Adrian Purtell; 20 Adam Henry; 2 Etuate Uaisele; 6 Lee Gaskell; 13 Danny Addy; 8 Paul Clough; 9 Adam O'Brien; 10 Adam Sidlow; 11 Tom Olbison; 14 Jay Pitts; 23 Alex Mellor. Subs (all used): 31 Epalahame Lauaki; 32 Steve Crossley; 17 Jean-Philippe Baile; 33 James Mendeika.
Tries: Shaw (18), Williams (21), Henry (48), Uaisele (58), Sidlow (61), O'Brien (78); **Goals:** Shaw 6/6.
Rugby Leaguer & League Express Men of the Match:
Broncos: Jamie Thackray; *Bulls:* Adam O'Brien.
Penalty count: 5-11; **Half-time:** 12-12;
Referee: Gareth Hewer; **Attendance:** 1,101.

WHITEHAVEN 16 LEIGH CENTURIONS 46

WHITEHAVEN: 32 Louis Jouffret; 28 Jordan Sigismeau; 26 Greg Wilde; 3 Jessie Joe Parker; 5 Jordan Burns; 15 Grant Gore; 24 Jordan Johnstone; 22 Ted Chapelhow; 14 Thomas Coyle; 23 Sam Brooks; 8 Ben Davies; 13 Tyla Hepi; 11 Dave Allen. Subs: 4 Scott McAvoy (not used); 18 Steve Fox; 9 James Newton; 1 Richard Lepori.
Tries: Davies (11), Johnstone (67), Lepori (70);
Goals: Jouffret 2/2, Parker 0/1.
Sin bin: T Chapelhow (20) - interference.
CENTURIONS: 1 Gregg McNally; 15 Jonathan Pownall; 2 Adam Higson; 3 Greg Worthington; 5 Liam Kay; 17 Ben Reynolds; 7 Ryan Brierley; 26 Gareth Hock; 9 Bob Beswick; 21 Jamie Acton; 22 Andrew Dixon; 11 Matt Sarsfield; 18 Tom Spencer. Subs (all used): 30 Mick Higham; 10 Oliver Wilkes; 29 Jake Emmitt; 8 Fuifui Moimoi.
Tries: Pownall (5, 30), Sarsfield (19), Brierley (21, 36, 43, 79), Higson (25), Worthington (54);
Goals: Brierley 4/8, Moimoi 1/1.
Rugby Leaguer & League Express Men of the Match:
Whitehaven: Ben Davies; *Centurions:* Ryan Brierley.
Penalty count: 11-8; **Half-time:** 6-30;
Referee: Jamie Bloem; **Attendance:** 841.

WORKINGTON TOWN 6 HALIFAX 32

TOWN: 1 Jack Murphy; 22 Elliott Miller; 3 Jason Mossop; 30 Rhodri Lloyd; 32 Lewis Tierney; 7 Carl Forber; 34 Jake Shorrocks; 19 Tom Walker; 33 Jamie Doran; 10 Marc Shackley; 11 Brett Phillips; 12 Jarrad Stack; 13 Liam McAvoy. Subs (all used): 4 Perry Whiteley; 8 Kris Coward; 16 Kurt Horton; 25 Steve Scholey.
Try: Lloyd (49); **Goals:** Forber 1/1.
HALIFAX: 20 James Saltonstall; 23 Gareth Potts; 4 Ben Heaton; 26 Chris Taylor; 2 Tom Saxton; 6 Scott Murrell; 7 Ben Johnston; 8 Adam Tangata; 9 Ben Kaye; 17 Mitch Cahalane; 27 Ross Divorty; 11 Dane Manning; 16 Richard Moore. Subs (all used): 12 Andy Bracek; 22 Jacob Fairbank; 29 Ed Barber; 30 Tyler Dickinson.
Tries: Heaton (3), Potts (19, 43), Manning (32), Johnston (37), Cahalane (69);
Goals: Murrell 2/3, Potts 2/3.
Rugby Leaguer & League Express Men of the Match:
Town: Jarrad Stack; *Halifax:* Scott Murrell.
Penalty count: 8-5; **Half-time:** 0-22;
Referee: Andrew Sweet; **Attendance:** 641.

ROUND 16

Friday 5th June 2015

BATLEY BULLDOGS 12 SHEFFIELD EAGLES 40

BULLDOGS: 3 Shaun Ainscough; 2 Wayne Reittie; 29 Elliott Cosgrove; 24 Brad Hey; 28 Alex Brown; 19 Lee Mitchell; 7 Scott Leatherbarrow; 8 Keegan Hirst; 26 Matty Fozard; 10 Alex Rowe; 12 Sam Scott; 23 Brad Day; 17 Joe Chandler. Subs (all used): 16 Sean Hesketh; 14 Alistair Leak; 18 Tom Lillycrop; 21 James Brown.
Tries: Mitchell (11), Ainscough (21);
Goals: Leatherbarrow 2/3.
EAGLES: 1 Quentin Laulu-Togagae; 2 Scott Turner; 3 Menzie Yere; 4 Sam Smeaton; 23 Rob Worrincy; 6 Kyle Briggs; 7 Dominic Brambani; 17 Steve Thorpe; 24 Keal Carlile; 10 Mitchell Stringer; 11 Michael Knowles; 12 Duane Straugheir; 5 Misi Taulapapa. Subs (all used): 8 Eddie Battye; 9 James Davey; 15 John Davies; 29 Dave Petersen.
Tries: Yere (35, 39, 52), Smeaton (43), Davies (47), Laulu-Togagae (66), Taulapapa (77);
Goals: Briggs 5/6, Brambani 1/1.
Rugby Leaguer & League Express Men of the Match:
Bulldogs: Shaun Ainscough; *Eagles:* Kyle Briggs.
Penalty count: 11-13; **Half-time:** 12-10;
Referee: Michael Woodhead; **Attendance:** 525.

Saturday 6th June 2015

FEATHERSTONE ROVERS 20 HALIFAX 44

ROVERS: 21 Jy Hitchcox; 5 Ben Blackmore; 1 Ian Hardman; 4 Thomas Minns; 2 Will Sharp; 6 Paul Sykes; 7 Gareth Moore; 8 Jordan Baldwinson; 9 Andy Ellis; 30 Garreth Carvell; 18 Jamie Cording; 19 Alex Foster; 13 Tim Spears. Subs (all used): 23 Luke Teasdale; 34 Brad England; 20 Ryan Verlinden; 35 Luke Cooper.
Tries: Sharp (16), Foster (52), Moore (57), Hardman (76);
Goals: Sykes 2/4.
Sin bin: Cooper (30) - persistent team offences.
HALIFAX: 20 James Saltonstall; 23 Gareth Potts; 4 Ben Heaton; 3 Steve Tyrer; 2 Tom Saxton; 28 Danny Craven; 6 Scott Murrell; 8 Adam Tangata; 9 Ben Kaye; 17 Mitch Cahalane; 27 Ross Divorty; 11 Dane Manning; 16 Richard Moore. Subs (all used): 7 Ben Johnston; 12 Andy Bracek; 22 Jacob Fairbank; 29 Ed Barber.
Tries: Saxton (4, 25, 36), Potts (31, 36, 76), Craven (60, 78), Tyrer (64); **Goals:** Tyrer 4/9.
Rugby Leaguer & League Express Men of the Match:
Rovers: Ian Hardman; *Halifax:* Danny Craven.
Penalty count: 7-11; **Half-time:** 4-26;
Referee: Chris Kendall; **Attendance:** 2,035.

Sunday 7th June 2015

BRADFORD BULLS 72 DONCASTER 6

BULLS: 27 Ryan Shaw; 5 Danny Williams; 3 Adrian Purtell; 20 Adam Henry; 2 Etuate Uaisele; 6 Lee Gaskell; 13 Danny Addy; 8 Paul Clough; 9 Adam O'Brien; 10 Adam Sidlow; 11 Tom Olbison; 14 Jay Pitts; 23 Alex Mellor. Subs (all used): 31 Epalahame Lauaki; 32 Steve Crossley; 17 Jean-Philippe Baile; 33 James Mendeika.
Tries: Sidlow (6), Addy (10), Shaw (13), Williams (22, 47, 76, 79), Mendeika (44, 73), Uaisele (50), Henry (53), Crossley (56, 62), Gaskell (58);
Goals: Shaw 1/4, Addy 7/10.
DONCASTER: 1 Dave Scott; 26 Sam Doherty; 3 Danny Cowling; 17 Liam Welham; 31 Peter Fox; 9 Kyle Kesik; 34 James Cunningham; 38 Matt Groat; 13 Mike Emmett; 15 Mitch Clark; 22 Brad Foster; 28 Jansin Turgut; 4 Pasqualle Dunn. Subs (all used): 14 Russ Spiers; 8 Matt Carbutt; 23 Jack Walton; 5 Stewart Sanderson.
Try: Dunn (18); **Goals:** Scott 1/1.
Sin bin: Groat (61) - dangerous challenge.
Rugby Leaguer & League Express Men of the Match:
Bulls: Tom Olbison; *Doncaster:* Kyle Kesik.
Penalty count: 11-3; **Half-time:** 18-6;
Referee: Tom Crashley; **Attendance:** 4,982.

DEWSBURY RAMS 20 WORKINGTON TOWN 20

RAMS: 1 Ryan Fieldhouse; 2 Dale Morton; 12 Scott Hale; 15 Jason Crookes; 18 Dalton Grant; 44 Brett Seymour; 7 Anthony Thackeray; 10 Ryan Hepworth; 6 Matty Wildie; 32 Makali Aizue; 11 Rob Spicer; 25 Joel Farrell; 34 Luke Adamson. Subs (all used): 13 Aaron Brown; 47 Nathan Conroy; 17 Matthew Haggarty; 33 Paul Jackson.
Tries: Grant (10), Brown (22), Farrell (39);
Goals: Seymour 4/4.
TOWN: 1 Jack Murphy; 22 Elliott Miller; 3 Jason Mossop; - Rhodri Lloyd; 32 Lewis Tierney; 7 Carl Forber; 33 Jamie Doran; 10 Marc Shackley; 20 Nathan Lucock; 19 Tom Walker; 11 Brett Phillips; 12 Jarrad Stack; 13 Liam McAvoy. Subs (all used): 15 Karl Olstrum; 4 Perry Whiteley; 25 Steve Scholey; 21 James Duerden.
Tries: Lloyd (4), Stack (25), Tierney (27), Miller (79);
Goals: Forber 2/4.
Rugby Leaguer & League Express Men of the Match:
Rams: Aaron Brown; *Town:* Jack Murphy.
Penalty count: 7-5; **Half-time:** 18-14;
Referee: Dave Merrick; **Attendance:** 751.

LONDON BRONCOS 29 LEIGH CENTURIONS 20

BRONCOS: 32 Elliot Kear; 2 Rhys Williams; 5 Ben Hellewell; 4 Wes Naiqama; 20 Iliess Macani; 22 Oscar Thomas; 28 Tom Gilmore; 12 Rhys Lovegrove; 35 Andrew Henderson; 29 Jamie Thackray; 11 Daniel Harrison; 15 Matt Garside; 31 Elliot Minchella. Subs (all used): 9 Ray Nasso; 18 Jon Wallace; 23 Toby Everett; 17 Erjon Dollapi.
Tries: Thomas (8), Macani (14, 21), Naiqama (30), Thackray (55); **Goals:** Naiqama 4/5;
Field goal: Minchella (70).
CENTURIONS: 1 Gregg McNally; 15 Jonathan Pownall; 3 Greg Worthington; 4 Tom Armstrong; 5 Liam Kay; 6 Martyn Ridyard; 7 Ryan Brierley; 29 Jake Emmitt; 30 Mick Higham; 10 Oliver Wilkes; 22 Andrew Dixon; 12 Tommy Goulden; 13 Sam Barlow. Subs (all used): 9 Bob Beswick; 19 Kurt Haggerty; 18 Tom Spencer; 20 Sam Hopkins.
Tries: Pownall (26, 35), Armstrong (37), McNally (65);
Goals: Ridyard 2/4.
Rugby Leaguer & League Express Men of the Match:
Broncos: Tom Gilmore; *Centurions:* Gregg McNally.
Penalty count: 8-11; **Half-time:** 22-16;
Referee: Chris Leatherbarrow; **Attendance:** 1,025.

WHITEHAVEN 28 HUNSLET HAWKS 12

WHITEHAVEN: 32 Louis Jouffret; 28 Jordan Sigismeau; 26 Greg Wilde; 3 Jessie Joe Parker; 2 Craig Calvert; 25 Dion Aiye; 15 Grant Gore; 29 Ted Chapelhow; 14 Thomas Coyle; 30 Richard Beaumont; 4 Scott McAvoy; 11 Dave Allen; 23 Sam Brooks. Subs (all used): 18 Steve Fox; 9 James Newton; 27 Jay Chapelhow; 8 Ben Davies.
Tries: Allen (41), Wilde (53), Aiye (58), Beaumont (60), Sigismeau (74); **Goals:** Jouffret 4/5.
HAWKS: 1 Jimmy Watson; 24 Richie Barnett; 4 Danny Maun; 34 Luke Briscoe; 5 Vinny Finigan; 31 Andy Kain; 7 Danny Ansell; 19 Brad Brennan; 9 Jack Lee; 10 James Houston; 11 Callum Casey; 21 Ryan Backhouse; 15 Liam Mackay. Subs (all used): 12 Aaron Lyons; 28 Mufaro Mvududu; 44 Charlie Martin; 45 Kyle Trout.
Tries: Mackay (21), Barnett (36); **Goals:** Ansell 2/2.
Rugby Leaguer & League Express Men of the Match:
Whitehaven: Dave Allen; *Hawks:* Jimmy Watson.
Penalty count: 8-10; **Half-time:** 0-12;
Referee: Andrew Sweet; **Attendance:** 661.

ROUND 13

Wednesday 10th June 2015

BATLEY BULLDOGS 22 LONDON BRONCOS 28

BULLDOGS: 1 James Craven; 2 Wayne Reittie; 29 Elliott Cosgrove; 20 Shaun Squires; 28 Alex Brown; 19 Lee Mitchell; 7 Scott Leatherbarrow; 8 Keegan Hirst; 13 Luke Blake; 10 Alex Rowe; 12 Sam Scott; 17 Joe Chandler; 21 James Brown. Subs (all used): 15 Adam Gledhill; 26 Matty Fozard; 16 Sean Hesketh; 3 Shaun Ainscough.
Tries: Blake (10), A Brown (24), Hesketh (39), Craven (69); **Goals:** Leatherbarrow 3/4.
BRONCOS: 32 Elliot Kear; 2 Rhys Williams; 5 Ben Hellewell; 4 Wes Naiqama; 20 Iliess Macani; 22 Oscar Thomas; 28 Tom Gilmore; 12 Rhys Lovegrove; 35 Andrew Henderson; 29 Jamie Thackray; 11 Daniel Harrison; 15 Matt Garside; 31 Elliot Minchella. Subs (all used): 9 Ray Nasso; 17 Erjon Dollapi; 36 Jonathan Walker; 18 Jon Wallace.
Tries: Dollapi (33), Garside (41, 44), Gilmore (50), Macani (61); **Goals:** Naiqama 4/5.
Rugby Leaguer & League Express Men of the Match:
Bulldogs: Scott Leatherbarrow; *Broncos:* Tom Gilmore.
Penalty count: 8-6; **Half-time:** 18-6;
Referee: Jamie Bloem; **Attendance:** 341.

ROUND 17

Friday 12th June 2015

HUNSLET HAWKS 8 HALIFAX 14

HAWKS: 1 Jimmy Watson; 24 Richie Barnett; 34 Luke Briscoe; 4 Danny Maun; 5 Vinny Finigan; 46 Jordan Lilley; 31 Andy Kain; 8 Michael Haley; 9 Jack Lee; 10 James Houston; 11 Callum Casey; 21 Ryan Backhouse; 15 Liam Mackay. Subs (all used): 36 Robbie Ward; 35 Rob Mulhern; 12 Aaron Lyons; 45 Kyle Trout.
Try: Barnett (17); **Goals:** Lilley 2/2.
HALIFAX: 20 James Saltonstall; 23 Gareth Potts; 32 Jake Eccleston; 3 Steve Tyrer; 2 Tom Saxton; 6 Scott Murrell; 7 Ben Johnston; 8 Adam Tangata; 9 Ben Kaye; 17 Mitch Cahalane; 27 Ross Divorty; 11 Dane Manning; 16 Richard Moore. Subs (all used): 12 Andy Bracek; 29 Ed Barber; 30 Tyler Dickinson; 31 Connor Robinson.
Tries: Manning (42), Johnston (74); **Goals:** Tyrer 3/3.
Sin bin: Potts (70) - holding down.
Rugby Leaguer & League Express Men of the Match:
Hawks: Jordan Lilley; *Halifax:* Steve Tyrer.
Penalty count: 4-3; **Half-time:** 6-0;
Referee: Tom Crashley; **Attendance:** 1,061.

Saturday 13th June 2015

SHEFFIELD EAGLES 26 WHITEHAVEN 16

EAGLES: 1 Quentin Laulu-Togagae; 2 Scott Turner; 3 Menzie Yere; 4 Sam Smeaton; 23 Rob Worrincy; 6 Kyle Briggs; 7 Dominic Brambani; 17 Steve Thorpe; 24 Keal Carlile; 10 Mitchell Stringer; 11 Michael Knowles; 12 Duane Straugheir; 29 Dave Petersen. Subs (all used): 8 Eddie Battye; 16 Jamie Langley; 5 Misi Taulapapa; 9 James Davey.

Tries: Laulu-Togagae (11), Briggs (30), Taulapapa (40, 72), Turner (60); **Goals:** Briggs 3/5.
WHITEHAVEN: 32 Louis Jouffret; 28 Jordan Sigismeau; 26 Greg Wilde; 3 Jessie Joe Parker; 2 Craig Calvert; 25 Dion Aiye; 15 Grant Gore; 29 Ted Chapelhow; 14 Thomas Coyle; 30 Richard Beaumont; 4 Scott McAvoy; 11 Dave Allen; 23 Sam Brooks. Subs (all used): 21 Chris Taylor; 9 James Newton; 27 Jay Chapelhow; 8 Ben Davies.
Tries: Calvert (26), McAvoy (45, 58); **Goals:** Jouffret 2/3.
Rugby Leaguer & League Express Men of the Match: *Eagles:* Misi Taulapapa; *Whitehaven:* Jessie Joe Parker.
Penalty count: 12-10; **Half-time:** 16-4;
Referee: Jon Roberts; **Attendance:** 503
(at Castle Park, Doncaster).

Sunday 14th June 2015

BATLEY BULLDOGS 12 LEIGH CENTURIONS 26

BULLDOGS: 1 James Craven; 2 Wayne Reittie; 3 Shaun Ainscough; 20 Shaun Squires; 28 Alex Brown; 19 Lee Mitchell; 7 Scott Leatherbarrow; 15 Adam Gledhill; 13 Luke Blake; 10 Alex Rowe; 11 Alex Bretherton; 23 Brad Day; 17 Joe Chandler. Subs (all used): 14 Alistair Leak; 16 Sean Hesketh; 18 Tom Lillycrop; 25 Tom Thackray.
Tries: Reittie (36), Leak (49); **Goals:** Leatherbarrow 2/2.
Dismissal: Lillycrop (79) - fighting.
CENTURIONS: 1 Gregg McNally; 2 Adam Higson; 3 Greg Worthington; 4 Tom Armstrong; 5 Liam Kay; 6 Martyn Ridyard; 17 Ben Reynolds; 8 Fuifui Moimoi; 9 Bob Beswick; 26 Gareth Hock; 22 Andrew Dixon; 12 Tommy Goulden; 21 Jamie Acton. Subs (all used): 18 Tom Spencer; 20 Sam Hopkins; 29 Jake Emmitt; 30 Mick Higham.
Tries: Higson (2, 65, 72), Kay (10), Emmitt (69);
Goals: Ridyard 3/5.
Dismissal: Acton (79) - fighting.
Sin bin: Hock (62) - holding down; (79) - fighting.
Rugby Leaguer & League Express Men of the Match: *Bulldogs:* Brad Day; *Centurions:* Bob Beswick.
Penalty count: 14-8; **Half-time:** 6-10;
Referee: Chris Kendall; **Attendance:** 1,125.

BRADFORD BULLS 22 DEWSBURY RAMS 18

BULLS: 33 James Mendeika; 5 Danny Williams; 3 Adrian Purtell; 20 Adam Henry; 2 Etuate Uaisele; 1 Jake Mullaney; 13 Danny Addy; 8 Paul Clough; 9 Adam O'Brien; 10 Adam Sidlow; 11 Tom Olbison; 12 Dale Ferguson; 14 Jay Pitts. Subs (all used): 31 Epalahame Lauaki; 32 Steve Crossley; 4 Matty Blythe; 27 Ryan Shaw.
Tries: Henry (52), Purtell (55, 73), Addy (66);
Goals: Shaw 3/4.
RAMS: 31 Kieran Hyde; 2 Dale Morton; 3 Karl Pryce; 12 Scott Hale; 18 Dalton Grant; 44 Brett Seymour; 7 Anthony Thackeray; 10 Ryan Hepworth; 6 Matty Wildie; 33 Paul Jackson; 11 Rob Spicer; 34 Luke Adamson; 13 Aaron Brown. Subs (all used): 19 Callan Beckett; 24 Byron Smith; 35 James Delaney; 27 Jason Muranka.
Tries: Thackeray (34), Pryce (45), Morton (76);
Goals: Seymour 2/2, Hyde 1/1.
Rugby Leaguer & League Express Men of the Match: *Bulls:* Jake Mullaney; *Rams:* Anthony Thackeray.
Penalty count: 2-2; **Half-time:** 0-6;
Referee: Chris Leatherbarrow; **Attendance:** 3,998.

DONCASTER 4 LONDON BRONCOS 30

DONCASTER: 28 Curtis Naughton; 31 Peter Fox; 17 Liam Welham; 3 Danny Cowling; 39 Tom Hodson; 37 Paul Mennell; 7 Richard Wilkinson; 38 Matt Groat; 9 Kyle Kesik; 15 Mitch Clark; 22 Brad Foster; 12 Steve Snitch; 13 Mike Emmett. Subs (all used): 14 Russ Spiers; 18 Shaun Leaf; 20 Ryan Wilson; 35 Josh Bowden.
Try: Welham (17); **Goals:** Naughton 0/1.
BRONCOS: 26 Sean Morris; 2 Rhys Williams; 5 Ben Hellewell; 4 Wes Naiqama; 20 Iliess Macani; 22 Oscar Thomas; 28 Tom Gilmore; 12 Rhys Lovegrove; 35 Andrew Henderson; 29 Jamie Thackray; 11 Daniel Harrison; 15 Matt Garside; 31 Elliot Minchella. Subs (all used): 9 Ray Nasso; 17 Erjon Dollapi; 18 Jon Wallace; 36 Jonathan Walker.
Tries: Hellewell (10, 62, 68), Minchella (38), R Williams (65); **Goals:** Naiqama 5/6.
Rugby Leaguer & League Express Men of the Match: *Doncaster:* Matt Groat; *Broncos:* Ben Hellewell.
Penalty count: 7-8; **Half-time:** 4-10;
Referee: Dave Merrick; **Attendance:** 530 *(at Castle Park).*

WORKINGTON TOWN 0 FEATHERSTONE ROVERS 52

TOWN: 1 Jack Murphy; 22 Elliott Miller; 3 Jason Mossop; 30 Rhodri Lloyd; 32 Lewis Tierney; 33 Jamie Doran; 7 Carl Forber; 19 Tom Walker; 20 Nathan Lucock; 10 Marc Shackley; 11 Brett Phillips; 12 Jarrad Stack; 13 Liam McAvoy. Subs (all used): 2 Sam Forrester; 4 Perry Whiteley; 21 James Duerden; 25 Steve Scholey.
ROVERS: 1 Ian Hardman; 2 Will Sharp; 6 Paul Sykes; 4 Thomas Minns; 21 Jy Hitchcox; 28 Will Milner; 7 Gareth Moore; 8 Jordan Baldwinson; 9 Andy Ellis; 17 Matt James; 18 Jamie Cording; 12 Reni Maitua; 13 Tim Spears. Subs (all used): 31 Remy Marginet; 16 Andrew Bostock; 15 Jack Bussey; 19 Alex Foster.
Tries: Hitchcox (12, 60), Sykes (16), Hardman (22, 33), Moore (24, 28), Minns (48), Marginet (69);
Goals: Sykes 8/9.
Rugby Leaguer & League Express Men of the Match: *Town:* Elliott Miller; *Rovers:* Paul Sykes.
Penalty count: 9-8; **Half-time:** 0-36;
Referee: Michael Woodhead; **Attendance:** 749.

ROUND 18

Friday 19th June 2015

FEATHERSTONE ROVERS 54 DONCASTER 14

ROVERS: 1 Ian Hardman; 2 Will Sharp; 6 Paul Sykes; 4 Thomas Minns; 21 Jy Hitchcox; 28 Will Milner; 7 Gareth Moore; 8 Jordan Baldwinson; 9 Andy Ellis; 17 Matt James; 18 Jamie Cording; 12 Reni Maitua; 13 Tim Spears. Subs (all used): 31 Remy Marginet; 16 Andrew Bostock; 15 Jack Bussey; 19 Alex Foster.
Tries: Hardman (14, 17), Sykes (32, 67), Minns (34), Marginet (38, 58), Cording (48), Hitchcox (55, 70), Moore (78); **Goals:** Sykes 5/11.
DONCASTER: 1 Dave Scott; 39 Tom Hodson; 3 Danny Cowling; 17 Liam Welham; 31 Peter Fox; 7 Richard Wilkinson; 37 Paul Mennell; 14 Russ Spiers; 9 Kyle Kesik; 15 Mitch Clark; 33 Dean Hadley; 34 Ben Musolino; 13 Mike Emmett. Subs (all used): 21 Danny Nicklas; 8 Matt Carbutt; 16 Brett Waller; 27 Alex Gilbey.
Tries: Kesik (10, 79), Fox (43); **Goals:** Scott 1/3.
Rugby Leaguer & League Express Men of the Match: *Rovers:* Ian Hardman; *Doncaster:* Kyle Kesik.
Penalty count: 3-2; **Half-time:** 24-6;
Referee: Chris Leatherbarrow; **Attendance:** 1,624.

Sunday 21st June 2015

DEWSBURY RAMS 16 HALIFAX 46

RAMS: 31 Kieran Hyde; 2 Dale Morton; 15 Jason Crookes; 51 Lucas Walshaw; 18 Dalton Grant; 13 Aaron Brown; 7 Anthony Thackeray; 10 Ryan Hepworth; 6 Matty Wildie; 33 Paul Jackson; 11 Rob Spicer; 12 Scott Hale; 34 Luke Adamson. Subs (all used): 16 Toby Adamson; 47 Nathan Conroy; 24 Byron Smith; 46 James Glover.
Tries: T Adamson (27), Thackeray (33), Crookes (63);
Goals: Hyde 2/2, Morton 0/1.
HALIFAX: 20 James Saltonstall; 23 Gareth Potts; 4 Ben Heaton; 3 Steve Tyrer; 2 Tom Saxton; 6 Scott Murrell; 7 Ben Johnston; 8 Adam Tangata; 9 Ben Kaye; 17 Mitch Cahalane; 27 Ross Divorty; 11 Dane Manning; 16 Richard Moore. Subs (all used): 12 Andy Bracek; 30 Tyler Dickinson; 31 Connor Robinson; 33 Luke Menzies.
Tries: Cahalane (11, 73), Manning (15, 36), Murrell (23, 69), Johnston (53), Divorty (59);
Goals: Tyrer 7/8.
Rugby Leaguer & League Express Men of the Match: *Rams:* Scott Hale; *Halifax:* Scott Murrell.
Penalty count: 6-6; **Half-time:** 12-24;
Referee: Chris Kendall; **Attendance:** 1,242.

LEIGH CENTURIONS 58 SHEFFIELD EAGLES 18

CENTURIONS: 1 Gregg McNally; 2 Adam Higson; 3 Greg Worthington; 4 Tom Armstrong; 5 Liam Kay; 6 Martyn Ridyard; 7 Ryan Brierley; 8 Fuifui Moimoi; 9 Bob Beswick; 29 Jake Emmitt; 22 Andrew Dixon; 12 Tommy Goulden; 26 Gareth Hock. Subs (all used): 30 Mick Higham; 20 Sam Hopkins; 18 Tom Spencer; 10 Oliver Wilkes.
Tries: Worthington (7), McNally (10, 49, 51), Brierley (17), Higson (32), Kay (39, 56, 70), Armstrong (73); **Goals:** Ridyard 9/10.
Sin bin: Hock (66) - fighting.
EAGLES: 1 Quentin Laulu-Togagae; 2 Scott Turner; 3 Menzie Yere; 4 Sam Smeaton; 23 Rob Worrincy; 6 Kyle Briggs; 19 Cory Aston; 17 Steve Thorpe; 24 Keal Carlile; 10 Mitchell Stringer; 11 Michael Knowles; 15 John Davies; 5 Misi Taulapapa. Subs (all used): 29 Dave Petersen; 12 Duane Straugheir; 8 Eddie Battye; 22 Tony Tonks.
Tries: Smeaton (37), Petersen (43), Straugheir (59), Taulapapa (78); **Goals:** Briggs 1/4.
Dismissal: Aston (4) - high tackle on McNally.
Sin bin: Taulapapa (66) - fighting.
On report: Smeaton (70) - alleged high tackle.
Rugby Leaguer & League Express Men of the Match: *Centurions:* Gregg McNally; *Eagles:* John Davies.
Penalty count: 10-12; **Half-time:** 28-4;
Referee: Michael Woodhead; **Attendance:** 3,572.

LONDON BRONCOS 34 HUNSLET HAWKS 12

BRONCOS: 32 Elliot Kear; 2 Rhys Williams; 5 Ben Hellewell; 4 Wes Naiqama; 20 Iliess Macani; 22 Oscar Thomas; 28 Tom Gilmore; 12 Rhys Lovegrove; 35 Andrew Henderson; 29 Jamie Thackray; 11 Daniel Harrison; 15 Matt Garside; 31 Elliot Minchella. Subs (all used): 9 Ray Nasso; 18 Jon Wallace; 7 William Barthau; 17 Erjon Dollapi.
Tries: Kear (9), Naiqama (14, 64, 69), Thomas (51), R Williams (71); **Goals:** Naiqama 5/7.
HAWKS: 1 Jimmy Watson; 24 Richie Barnett; 11 Callum Casey; 28 Mufaro Mvududu; 5 Vinny Finigan; 46 Jordan Lilley; 31 Andy Kain; 8 Michael Haley; 9 Jack Lee; 10 James Houston; 21 Ryan Backhouse; 44 Charlie Martin; 15 Liam Mackay. Subs (all used): 47 Matty Gee; 45 Kyle Trout; 35 Rob Mulhern; 36 Robbie Ward.
Tries: Gee (21), Ward (35); **Goals:** Lilley 2/2.
Rugby Leaguer & League Express Men of the Match: *Broncos:* Wes Naiqama; *Hawks:* Andy Kain.
Penalty count: 7-6; **Half-time:** 12-12;
Referee: Jamie Bloem; **Attendance:** 751.

WHITEHAVEN 24 BATLEY BULLDOGS 12

WHITEHAVEN: 32 Louis Jouffret; 28 Jordan Sigismeau; 21 Chris Taylor; 3 Jessie Joe Parker; 2 Craig Calvert; 25 Dion Aiye; 15 Grant Gore; 30 Richard Beaumont; 14 Thomas Coyle; 29 Ted Chapelhow; 11 Dave Allen; 4 Scott McAvoy; 23 Sam Brooks. Subs (all used): 27 Declan Hulme; 8 Ben Davies; 9 James Newton; 20 James Robinson.
Tries: Gore (4), Calvert (14, 37), Jouffret (61);
Goals: Jouffret 4/4.
Sin bin: Sigismeau (20) - dissent; Calvert (22) - use of the head.
BULLDOGS: 3 Shaun Ainscough; 2 Wayne Reittie; 29 Elliott Cosgrove; 20 Shaun Squires; 5 Johnny Campbell; 17 Joe Chandler; 7 Scott Leatherbarrow; 8 Keegan Hirst; 13 Luke Blake; 15 Adam Gledhill; 12 Sam Scott; 23 Brad Day; 21 James Brown. Subs (all used): 6 Cain Southernwood; 14 Alistair Leak; 16 Sean Hesketh; 11 Alex Bretherton.
Tries: Ainscough (46), Chandler (71);
Goals: Leatherbarrow 2/2.
Rugby Leaguer & League Express Men of the Match: *Whitehaven:* Sam Brooks; *Bulldogs:* Shaun Ainscough.
Penalty count: 7-7; **Half-time:** 18-0;
Referee: Tom Crashley; **Attendance:** 802.

WORKINGTON TOWN 16 BRADFORD BULLS 38

TOWN: 1 Jack Murphy; 22 Elliott Miller; 3 Jason Mossop; 23 Scott Akehurst; 5 Brett Carter; 33 Jamie Doran; 7 Carl Forber; 8 Kris Coward; 9 Graeme Mattinson; 10 Marc Shackley; 31 Connor Farrell; 13 Liam McAvoy; 15 Karl Olstrum. Subs (all used): 14 Callum Phillips; 19 Tom Walker; 25 Steve Scholey; 34 Sam Powell.
Tries: Powell (28, 33), Farrell (73);
Goals: Murphy 1/2, Forber 1/1.
BULLS: 1 Jake Mullaney; 5 Danny Williams; 3 Adrian Purtell; 20 Adam Henry; 27 Ryan Shaw; 7 Harry Siejka; 13 Danny Addy; 8 Paul Clough; 9 Adam O'Brien; 10 Adam Sidlow; 11 Tom Olbison; 12 Dale Ferguson; 14 Jay Pitts. Subs (all used): 31 Epalahame Lauaki; 32 Steve Crossley; 4 Matty Blythe; 33 James Mendeika.
Tries: Henry (4, 23), Sidlow (12), Mullaney (61, 69), Lauaki (64), Williams (66); **Goals:** Shaw 5/7.
Rugby Leaguer & League Express Men of the Match: *Town:* Karl Olstrum; *Bulls:* Adam O'Brien.
Penalty count: 11-8; **Half-time:** 10-16;
Referee: Gareth Hewer; **Attendance:** 1,063.

ROUND 19

Saturday 27th June 2015

HALIFAX 46 LONDON BRONCOS 22

HALIFAX: 20 James Saltonstall; 23 Gareth Potts; 4 Ben Heaton; 3 Steve Tyrer; 2 Tom Saxton; 7 Ben Johnston; 6 Scott Murrell; 8 Adam Tangata; 9 Ben Kaye; 17 Mitch Cahalane; 16 Richard Moore; 11 Dane Manning; 15 Adam Robinson. Subs (all used): 12 Andy Bracek; 13 Jack Spencer; 27 Ross Divorty; 31 Connor Robinson.
Tries: Manning (5), Kaye (13), Johnston (18), Tyrer (29), Saltonstall (37), Divorty (49, 73), Cahalane (77);
Goals: Tyrer 7/8.
BRONCOS: 32 Elliot Kear; 2 Rhys Williams; 5 Ben Hellewell; 4 Wes Naiqama; 20 Iliess Macani; 7 William Barthau; 28 Tom Gilmore; 36 Jonathan Walker; 35 Andrew Henderson; 29 Jamie Thackray; 31 Elliot Minchella; 15 Matt Garside; 12 Rhys Lovegrove. Subs (all used): 9 Ray Nasso; 22 Oscar Thomas; 18 Jon Wallace; 16 Glenn Riley.
Tries: R Williams (2, 47), Thomas (61), Macani (68);
Goals: Naiqama 3/4.
Rugby Leaguer & League Express Men of the Match: *Halifax:* Dane Manning; *Broncos:* Iliess Macani.
Penalty count: 2-3; **Half-time:** 30-6;
Referee: Chris Leatherbarrow; **Attendance:** 914
(at Cougar Park, Keighley).

Sunday 28th June 2015

BRADFORD BULLS 34 BATLEY BULLDOGS 16

BULLS: 33 James Mendeika; 5 Danny Williams; 3 Adrian Purtell; 20 Adam Henry; 27 Ryan Shaw; 4 Matty Blythe; 13 Danny Addy; 8 Paul Clough; 9 Adam O'Brien; 10 Adam Sidlow; 11 Tom Olbison; 12 Dale Ferguson; 14 Jay Pitts. Subs (all used): 26 Vila Halafihi; 15 Daniel Fleming; 22 Chev Walker; 32 Steve Crossley.
Tries: Pitts (8), Mendeika (25), Henry (28, 32), Williams (66), Blythe (74, 79); **Goals:** Shaw 3/7.
BULLDOGS: 5 Johnny Campbell; 2 Wayne Reittie; 3 Shaun Ainscough; 23 Brad Day; 28 Alex Brown; 6 Cain Southernwood; 7 Scott Leatherbarrow; 8 Keegan Hirst; 13 Luke Blake; 16 Sean Hesketh; 11 Alex Bretherton; 12 Sam Scott; 17 Joe Chandler. Subs (all used): 9 Anthony Nicholson; 10 Alex Rowe; 21 James Brown; 20 Shaun Squires.
Tries: A Brown (4), Reittie (36), Rowe (70);
Goals: Leatherbarrow 2/3.
Dismissal: Ainscough (65) - dissent.
Sin bin: Ainscough (65) - holding down.
Rugby Leaguer & League Express Men of the Match: *Bulls:* Adam Henry; *Bulldogs:* Johnny Campbell.
Penalty count: 9-5; **Half-time:** 20-10;
Referee: Jamie Bloem; **Attendance:** 5,089.

DONCASTER 18 WHITEHAVEN 50

DONCASTER: 19 Lee Waterman; 1 Dave Scott; 18 Shaun Leaf; 17 Liam Welham; 31 Peter Fox; 37 Paul Mennell; 21 Danny Nicklas; 15 Mitch Clark; 9 Kyle Kesik; 16 Brett Waller; 12 Steve Snitch; 32 Ben Musolino; 13 Mike Emmett. Subs (all used): 3 Danny Cowling; 8 Matt Carbutt; 14 Russ Spiers; 28 Jansin Turgut.
Tries: Mennell (54), Turgut (60), Kesik (76);
Goals: Scott 3/3.
WHITEHAVEN: 32 Louis Jouffret; 28 Jordan Sigismeau; 21 Chris Taylor; 3 Jessie Joe Parker; 2 Craig Calvert; 25 Dion Aiye; 15 Grant Gore; 30 Richard Beaumont; 14 Thomas Coyle; 29 Ted Chapelhow; 11 Dave Allen; 4

Scott McAvoy; 23 Sam Brooks. Subs (all used): 8 Ben Davies; 9 James Newton; 24 Phil Joseph; 26 Greg Wilde.
Tries: Allen (5), Gore (15), Taylor (19), McAvoy (24, 29), Parker (33), Sigismeau (38), Davies (42), Aiye (45);
Goals: Jouffret 7/9.
Sin bin: Parker (3) - dangerous challenge on Leaf.
Rugby Leaguer & League Express Men of the Match: *Doncaster:* Ben Musolino; *Whitehaven:* Dion Aiye.
Penalty count: 8-7; **Half-time:** 0-38;
Referee: Tom Crashley; **Attendance:** 1,000
(at Castle Park).

HUNSLET HAWKS 34 FEATHERSTONE ROVERS 42

HAWKS: 1 Jimmy Watson; 24 Richie Barnett; 4 Danny Maun; 28 Mufaro Mvududu; 5 Vinny Finigan; 31 Andy Kain; 46 Jordan Lilley; 8 Michael Haley; 9 Jack Lee; 10 James Houston; 44 Charlie Martin; 21 Ryan Backhouse; 35 Rob Mulhern. Subs (all used): 30 George Flanagan; 47 Matty Gee; 45 Kyle Trout; 12 Aaron Lyons.
Tries: Trout (18), Kain (39), Watson (48), Lee (69, 77), Finigan (72); **Goals:** Lilley 5/6.
ROVERS: 1 Ian Hardman; 2 Will Sharp; 6 Paul Sykes; 4 Thomas Minns; 21 Jy Hitchcox; 36 Paul Cooke; 7 Gareth Moore; 8 Jordan Baldwinson; 9 Andy Ellis; 20 Ryan Verlinden; 18 Jamie Cording; 12 Reni Maitua; 13 Tim Spears. Subs (all used): 31 Remy Marginet; 35 Luke Cooper; 27 Jack Ormondroyd; 19 Alex Foster.
Tries: Moore (5), Cooke (11, 32), Hardman (29), Sharp (52, 64), Foster (75); **Goals:** Sykes 7/7.
Rugby Leaguer & League Express Men of the Match: *Hawks:* Jimmy Watson; *Rovers:* Paul Cooke.
Penalty count: 6-3; **Half-time:** 12-24;
Referee: Gareth Hewer; **Attendance:** 1,056.

SHEFFIELD EAGLES 26 WORKINGTON TOWN 6

EAGLES: 1 Quentin Laulu-Togagae; 2 Scott Turner; 3 Menzie Yere; 4 Sam Smeaton; 5 Misi Taulapapa; 19 Cory Aston; 6 Kyle Briggs; 8 Eddie Battye; 9 James Davey; 22 Tony Tonks; 11 Michael Knowles; 15 John Davies; 13 Pat Walker. Subs (all used): 17 Steve Thorpe; 29 Dave Petersen; 16 Jamie Langley; 12 Duane Straugheir.
Tries: Laulu-Togagae (30, 58), Thorpe (44), Davies (71), Straugheir (78); **Goals:** Briggs 3/5.
TOWN: 1 Jack Murphy; 22 Elliott Miller; 3 Jason Mossop; 32 Iain Thornley; 5 Brett Carter; 28 Jarrod Sammut; 33 Jamie Doran; 10 Marc Shackley; 20 Nathan Lucock; 19 Tom Walker; 30 Rhodri Lloyd; 12 Jarrad Stack; 13 Liam McAvoy. Subs (all used): 16 Kurt Horton; 25 Steve Scholey; 8 Kris Coward; 7 Carl Forber.
Try: Carter (20); **Goals:** Sammut 0/1, Forber 1/1.
Rugby Leaguer & League Express Men of the Match: *Eagles:* Quentin Laulu-Togagae; *Town:* Jarrod Sammut.
Penalty count: 10-7; **Half-time:** 6-6;
Referee: Andrew Sweet; **Attendance:** 506
(at Castle Park, Doncaster).

ROUND 13

Wednesday 1st July 2015

BRADFORD BULLS 18 FEATHERSTONE ROVERS 37

BULLS: 33 James Mendeika; 5 Danny Williams; 3 Adrian Purtell; 20 Adam Henry; 27 Ryan Shaw; 7 Harry Siejka; 13 Danny Addy; 8 Paul Clough; 9 Adam O'Brien; 10 Adam Sidlow; 11 Tom Olbison; 12 Dale Ferguson; 14 Jay Pitts. Subs (all used): 4 Matty Blythe; 15 Daniel Fleming; 22 Chev Walker; 32 Steve Crossley.
Tries: Mendeika (16, 78), Walker (55); **Goals:** Shaw 3/4.
ROVERS: 1 Ian Hardman; 5 Ben Blackmore; 6 Paul Sykes; 4 Thomas Minns; 21 Jy Hitchcox; 28 Will Milner; 31 Remy Marginet; 8 Jordan Baldwinson; 9 Andy Ellis; 20 Ryan Verlinden; 18 Jamie Cording; 12 Reni Maitua; 13 Tim Spears. Subs (all used): 34 Brad England; 35 Luke Cooper; 27 Jack Ormondroyd; 19 Alex Foster.
Tries: Hitchcox (3, 8, 27), Maitua (29), Blackmore (45), Ellis (74); **Goals:** Sykes 6/7; **Field goal:** Marginet (68).
Rugby Leaguer & League Express Men of the Match: *Bulls:* James Mendeika; *Rovers:* Jy Hitchcox.
Penalty count: 11-7; **Half-time:** 6-22;
Referee: Chris Kendall; **Attendance:** 5,044.

ROUND 20

Sunday 5th July 2015

BATLEY BULLDOGS 34 DONCASTER 6

BULLDOGS: 5 Johnny Campbell; 3 Shaun Ainscough; 2 Wayne Reittie; 20 Shaun Squires; 28 Alex Brown; 6 Cain Southernwood; 7 Scott Leatherbarrow; 8 Keegan Hirst; 13 Luke Blake; 16 Sean Hesketh; 23 Brad Day; 12 Sam Scott; 17 Joe Chandler. Subs (all used): 9 Anthony Nicholson; 10 Alex Rowe; 18 Tom Lillycrop; 21 James Brown.
Tries: A Brown (12), Squires (20, 63), Lillycrop (29), Reittie (38, 40), Southernwood (43);
Goals: Leatherbarrow 3/7.
DONCASTER: 1 Dave Scott; 26 Sam Doherty; 17 Liam Welham; 19 Lee Waterman; 31 Peter Fox; 5 Stewart Sanderson; 37 Paul Mennell; 8 Matt Carbutt; 9 Kyle Kesik; 14 Russ Spiers; 11 Michael Kelly; 32 Ben Musolino; 12 Steve Snitch. Subs (all used): 13 Mike Emmett; 16 Brett Waller; 15 Mitch Clark; 22 Brad Foster.
Try: Mennell (74); **Goals:** Scott 1/1.
Sin bin: Mennell (40) - holding down.
Rugby Leaguer & League Express Men of the Match: *Bulldogs:* Wayne Reittie; *Doncaster:* Mike Emmett.
Penalty count: 9-6; **Half-time:** 24-0;
Referee: Adam Gill; **Attendance:** 537.

FEATHERSTONE ROVERS 30 DEWSBURY RAMS 32

ROVERS: 1 Ian Hardman; 5 Ben Blackmore; 6 Paul Sykes; 21 Jy Hitchcox; 2 Will Sharp; 28 Will Milner; 31 Remy Marginet; 8 Jordan Baldwinson; 9 Andy Ellis; 20 Ryan Verlinden; 18 Jamie Cording; 12 Reni Maitua; 13 Tim Spears. Subs (all used): 34 Brad England; 35 Luke Cooper; 15 Jack Bussey; 19 Alex Foster.
Tries: Blackmore (1), Maitua (7), Sykes (28), Milner (36), Cording (58), Marginet (73); **Goals:** Sykes 3/6.
Sin bin: Verlinden (72) - high tackle on L Adamson.
RAMS: 1 Ryan Fieldhouse; 2 Dale Morton; 4 Shane Grady; 51 Lucas Walshaw; 3 Karl Pryce; 44 Brett Seymour; 7 Anthony Thackeray; 10 Ryan Hepworth; 6 Matty Wildie; 8 Stephen Nash; 12 Scott Hale; 34 Luke Adamson; 13 Aaron Brown. Subs (all used): 47 Nathan Conroy; 24 Byron Smith; 25 Joel Farrell; 16 Toby Adamson.
Tries: T Adamson (33), Thackeray (42, 70), Grady (51), Brown (55); **Goals:** Seymour 6/6.
Rugby Leaguer & League Express Men of the Match: *Rovers:* Remy Marginet; *Rams:* Anthony Thackeray.
Penalty count: 5-5; **Half-time:** 20-8;
Referee: Phil Bentham; **Attendance:** 2,009.

HALIFAX 38 SHEFFIELD EAGLES 10

HALIFAX: 20 James Saltonstall; 23 Gareth Potts; 4 Ben Heaton; 3 Steve Tyrer; 2 Tom Saxton; 7 Ben Johnston; 6 Scott Murrell; 8 Adam Tangata; 9 Ben Kaye; 17 Mitch Cahalane; 27 Ross Divorty; 11 Dane Manning; 16 Richard Moore. Subs (all used): 12 Andy Bracek; 15 Adam Robinson; 31 Connor Robinson; 34 Jordan Cox.
Tries: Saxton (13), Heaton (33), Manning (39, 41), Kaye (59), C Robinson (64, 73); **Goals:** Tyrer 5/7.
EAGLES: 1 Quentin Laulu-Togagae; 2 Scott Turner; 3 Menzie Yere; 12 Duane Straugheir; 5 Misi Taulapapa; 6 Kyle Briggs; 7 Dominic Brambani; 17 Steve Thorpe; 24 Keal Carlile; 10 Mitchell Stringer; 11 Michael Knowles; 16 Jamie Langley; 13 Pat Walker. Subs (all used): 9 James Davey; 8 Eddie Battye; 15 John Davies; 22 Tony Tonks.
Tries: Briggs (6), Stringer (55); **Goals:** Briggs 1/2.
Rugby Leaguer & League Express Men of the Match: *Halifax:* Scott Murrell; *Eagles:* John Davies.
Penalty count: 11-9; **Half-time:** 14-6;
Referee: Chris Kendall; **Attendance:** 1,873.

HUNSLET HAWKS 6 BRADFORD BULLS 68

HAWKS: 46 Jordan Lilley; 24 Richie Barnett; 4 Danny Maun; 28 Mufaro Mvududu; 2 Mo Agoro; 13 Danny Grimshaw; 6 Simon Brown; 8 Michael Haley; 9 Jack Lee; 10 James Houston; 40 Josh Walters; 47 Matty Gee; 35 Rob Mulhern. Subs (all used): 30 George Flanagan; 12 Aaron Lyons; 45 Kyle Trout; 21 Ryan Backhouse.
Try: Lee (34); **Goals:** Lilley 1/1.
BULLS: 27 Ryan Shaw; 5 Danny Williams; 4 Matty Blythe; 33 James Mendeika; 2 Etuate Uaisele; 1 Jake Mullaney; 13 Danny Addy; 8 Paul Clough; 9 Adam O'Brien; 10 Adam Sidlow; 11 Tom Olbison; 22 Chev Walker; 14 Jay Pitts. Subs (all used): 26 Vila Halafihi; 15 Daniel Fleming; 12 Dale Ferguson; 32 Steve Crossley.
Tries: O'Brien (6), Mullaney (7, 25, 30, 76), Blythe (13), Mendeika (23), Shaw (39), Williams (53, 67, 71), Uaisele (58), Ferguson (64); **Goals:** Shaw 8/13.
Rugby Leaguer & League Express Men of the Match: *Hawks:* Josh Walters; *Bulls:* Jake Mullaney.
Penalty count: 3-5; **Half-time:** 6-38;
Referee: Tom Crashley; **Attendance:** 1,676.

LONDON BRONCOS 40 WHITEHAVEN 24

BRONCOS: 32 Elliot Kear; 2 Rhys Williams; 5 Ben Hellewell; 4 Wes Naiqama; 20 Iliess Macani; 22 Oscar Thomas; 7 William Barthau; 18 Jon Wallace; 9 Ray Nasso; 29 Jamie Thackray; 37 Jason Walton; 15 Matt Garside; 12 Rhys Lovegrove. Subs (all used): 38 James Cunningham; 34 Matt Davis; 16 Glenn Riley; 36 Jonathan Walker.
Tries: Walton (6, 69), Thomas (16, 75), Garside (35), Macani (38), Thackray (64);
Goals: Naiqama 5/6, Barthau 1/1.
WHITEHAVEN: 21 Chris Taylor; 5 Jordan Burns; 27 Declan Hulme; 3 Jessie Joe Parker; 2 Craig Calvert; 25 Dion Aiye; 15 Grant Gore; 30 Richard Beaumont; 14 Thomas Coyle; 24 Ted Chapelhow; 11 Dave Allen; 4 Scott McAvoy; 23 Sam Brooks. Subs (all used): 9 James Newton; 8 Ben Davies; 13 Tyla Hepi; 29 Thibault Ancely.
Tries: Hulme (21, 50, 60), Taylor (24), Newton (56);
Goals: Gore 2/5.
On report: Taylor (58) - alleged dangerous challenge.
Rugby Leaguer & League Express Men of the Match: *Broncos:* Wes Naiqama; *Whitehaven:* Declan Hulme.
Penalty count: 4-5; **Half-time:** 24-10;
Referee: Michael Woodhead; **Attendance:** 567.

WORKINGTON TOWN 12 LEIGH CENTURIONS 50

TOWN: 1 Jack Murphy; 32 Lewis Tierney; 3 Jason Mossop; 34 Iain Thornley; 5 Brett Carter; 33 Jamie Doran; 28 Jarrod Sammut; 19 Tom Walker; 14 Callum Phillips; 10 Marc Shackley; 31 Connor Farrell; 12 Jarrad Stack; 13 Liam McAvoy. Subs (all used): 7 Carl Forber; 15 Karl Olstrum; 8 Kris Coward; 30 Rhodri Lloyd.
Tries: Stack (43), Tierney (63);
Goals: Sammut 1/1, Forber 1/1.
CENTURIONS: 1 Gregg McNally; 2 Adam Higson; 3 Greg Worthington; 4 Tom Armstrong; 15 Jonathan Pownall; 6 Martyn Ridyard; 7 Ryan Brierley; 29 Jake Emmitt; 9 Bob Beswick; 26 Gareth Hock; 11 Matt Sarsfield; 19 Kurt Haggerty; 18 Tom Spencer. Subs: 30 Mick Higham; 20 Sam Hopkins; 12 Tommy Goulden (not used); 10 Oliver Wilkes.
Tries: Brierley (17, 40), Spencer (19), Ridyard (25), Pownall (32), Higson (37), Haggerty (53), Higham (67), Emmitt (70); **Goals:** Ridyard 7/9.
Rugby Leaguer & League Express Men of the Match: *Town:* Jarrod Sammut; *Centurions:* Bob Beswick.
Penalty count: 6-13; **Half-time:** 0-32;
Referee: Jamie Bloem; **Attendance:** 914.

ROUND 13

Wednesday 8th July 2015

LEIGH CENTURIONS 72 HUNSLET HAWKS 6

CENTURIONS: 1 Gregg McNally; 2 Adam Higson; 31 Mathias Pala; 4 Tom Armstrong; 5 Liam Kay; 6 Martyn Ridyard; 7 Ryan Brierley; 8 Fuifui Moimoi; 30 Mick Higham; 21 Jamie Acton; 11 Matt Sarsfield; 19 Kurt Haggerty; 13 Sam Barlow. Subs (all used): 9 Bob Beswick; 10 Oliver Wilkes; 18 Tom Spencer; 23 Martin Aspinwall.
Tries: McNally (5, 24, 47, 61, 70), Ridyard (9), Higham (12, 66), Haggerty (18), Sarsfield (30, 40), Aspinwall (34), Kay (49, 80); **Goals:** Ridyard 8/14.
HAWKS: 26 Marcus Elliott; 2 Mo Agoro; 11 Callum Casey; 28 Mufaro Mvududu; 5 Vinny Finigan; 6 Simon Brown; 7 Danny Ansell; 35 Rob Mulhern; 36 Robbie Ward; 10 James Houston; 47 Matty Gee; 44 Charlie Martin; 45 Kyle Trout. Subs (all used): 14 Matthew Tebb; 16 Lewis Reed; 17 Mark Castle; 21 Ryan Backhouse.
Try: Mvududu (72); **Goals:** Ansell 1/1.
Rugby Leaguer & League Express Men of the Match: *Centurions:* Gregg McNally; *Hawks:* Matty Gee.
Penalty count: 6-4; **Half-time:** 46-0;
Referee: Chris Leatherbarrow; **Attendance:** 2,716.

ROUND 21

Sunday 12th July 2015

DONCASTER 34 HUNSLET HAWKS 26

DONCASTER: 2 Tom Carr; 1 Dave Scott; 26 Sam Doherty; 17 Liam Welham; 31 Peter Fox; 28 Joe McLocklan; 37 Paul Mennell; 38 Matt Groat; 9 Kyle Kesik; 15 Mitch Clark; 12 Steve Snitch; 32 Ben Musolino; 13 Mike Emmett. Subs (all used): 14 Russ Spiers; 16 Brett Waller; 19 Lee Waterman; 30 Ryan Wright.
Tries: McLocklan (26), Fox (54), Clark (58), Snitch (60), Mennell (65), Groat (73); **Goals:** Scott 5/7.
HAWKS: 1 Jimmy Watson; 2 Mo Agoro; 4 Danny Maun; 47 Matty Gee; 24 Richie Barnett; 6 Simon Brown; 31 Andy Kain; 35 Rob Mulhern; 9 Jack Lee; 8 Michael Haley; 11 Callum Casey; 40 Josh Walters; 15 Liam Mackay. Subs (all used): 12 Aaron Lyons; 30 George Flanagan; 41 Andy Yates; 45 Kyle Trout.
Tries: Maun (30), Gee (36, 47), Barnett (44), Casey (49);
Goals: Brown 3/5.
Rugby Leaguer & League Express Men of the Match: *Doncaster:* Mitch Clark; *Hawks:* Matty Gee.
Penalty count: 5-6; **Half-time:** 6-8;
Referee: Jamie Bloem; **Attendance:** 1,231.

DEWSBURY RAMS 24 LONDON BRONCOS 12

RAMS: 1 Ryan Fieldhouse; 2 Dale Morton; 3 Karl Pryce; 12 Scott Hale; 5 Greg Scott; 44 Brett Seymour; 7 Anthony Thackeray; 8 Stephen Nash; 6 Matty Wildie; 10 Ryan Hepworth; 34 Luke Adamson; 16 Toby Adamson; 13 Aaron Brown. Subs (all used): 47 Nathan Conroy; 25 Joel Farrell; 24 Byron Smith; 33 Paul Jackson.
Tries: Pryce (6, 15), Conroy (35); **Goals:** Seymour 6/7.
Dismissal: Fieldhouse (21) - high tackle on Barthau.
Sin bin: Nash (32) - fighting.
BRONCOS: 32 Elliot Kear; 2 Rhys Williams; 5 Ben Hellewell; 4 Wes Naiqama; 20 Iliess Macani; 22 Oscar Thomas; 7 William Barthau; 18 Jon Wallace; 9 Ray Nasso; 29 Jamie Thackray; 37 Jason Walton; 15 Matt Garside; 31 Elliot Minchella. Subs (all used): 38 James Cunningham; 34 Matt Davis; 16 Glenn Riley; 36 Jonathan Walker.
Tries: Naiqama (19), Thomas (59); **Goals:** Naiqama 2/2.
Sin bin: Kear (32) - fighting;
Minchella (47) - use of the elbow.
Rugby Leaguer & League Express Men of the Match: *Rams:* Paul Jackson; *Broncos:* Iliess Macani.
Penalty count: 15-5; **Half-time:** 18-6;
Referee: Tom Crashley; **Attendance:** 910.

HALIFAX 25 BATLEY BULLDOGS 22

HALIFAX: 20 James Saltonstall; 32 Jake Eccleston; 4 Ben Heaton; 3 Steve Tyrer; 2 Tom Saxton; 7 Ben Johnston; 6 Scott Murrell; 8 Adam Tangata; 9 Ben Kaye; 17 Mitch Cahalane; 27 Ross Divorty; 11 Dane Manning; 16 Richard Moore. Subs (all used): 13 Jack Spencer; 15 Adam Robinson; 31 Connor Robinson; 33 Luke Menzies.
Tries: Johnston (31, 62), A Robinson (36), Saltonstall (55); **Goals:** Tyrer 4/4;
Field goal: Murrell (76).
BULLDOGS: 5 Johnny Campbell; 2 Wayne Reittie; 29 Elliott Cosgrove; 20 Shaun Squires; - Chris Ulugia; 6 Cain Southernwood; 7 Scott Leatherbarrow; 8 Keegan Hirst; 9 Anthony Nicholson; 10 Alex Rowe; 23 Brad Day; 12 Sam Scott; 17 Joe Chandler. Subs (all used): 1 James Craven; 14 Alistair Leak; 18 Tom Lillycrop; 21 James Brown.
Tries: Day (46), Reittie (69, 78), Hirst (74);
Goals: Leatherbarrow 3/4.
Rugby Leaguer & League Express Men of the Match: *Halifax:* Ben Johnston; *Bulldogs:* Alex Rowe.
Penalty count: 11-7; **Half-time:** 12-0;
Referee: Gareth Hewer; **Attendance:** 1,955.

LEIGH CENTURIONS 52 FEATHERSTONE ROVERS 18

CENTURIONS: 1 Gregg McNally; 15 Jonathan Pownall; 3 Greg Worthington; 4 Tom Armstrong; 5 Liam Kay; 6 Martyn Ridyard; 7 Ryan Brierley; 8 Fuifui Moimoi; 9 Bob Beswick; 29 Jake Emmitt; 19 Kurt Haggerty; 22 Andrew Dixon; 26 Gareth Hock. Subs (all used): 13 Sam Barlow; 20 Sam Hopkins; 10 Oliver Wilkes; 30 Mick Higham.
Tries: Moimoi (7, 44, 49), Worthington (27), McNally (31), Brierley (33, 38, 58), Hock (80);
Goals: Ridyard 7/8, Emmitt 1/1.
ROVERS: 1 Ian Hardman; 5 Ben Blackmore; 6 Paul Sykes; 34 Brad England; 21 Jy Hitchcox; 36 Paul Cooke; 7 Gareth Moore; 8 Jordan Baldwinson; 9 Andy Ellis; 10 Paul Wood; 12 Reni Maitua; 18 Jamie Cording; 13 Tim Spears. Subs (all used): 15 Jack Bussey; 19 Alex Foster; 27 Jack Ormondroyd; 35 Luke Cooper.
Tries: England (10), Hardman (23), Blackmore (70);
Goals: Sykes 3/3.
Rugby Leaguer & League Express Men of the Match:
Centurions: Fuifui Moimoi; *Rovers:* Reni Maitua.
Penalty count: 9-11; **Half-time:** 28-12;
Referee: Chris Kendall; **Attendance:** 4,127.

WHITEHAVEN 6 WORKINGTON TOWN 28

WHITEHAVEN: 32 Louis Jouffret; 5 Jordan Burns; 21 Chris Taylor; - Declan Hulme; 2 Craig Calvert; 25 Dion Aiye; 15 Grant Gore; 30 Richard Beaumont; 14 Thomas Coyle; 29 Ted Chapelhow; 11 Dave Allen; 4 Scott McAvoy; 23 Sam Brooks. Subs (all used): 27 Thibault Ancely; 8 Ben Davies; 9 James Newton; 13 Tyla Hepi.
Try: Calvert (78); **Goals:** Jouffret 1/1.
TOWN: 1 Jack Murphy; 22 Elliott Miller; 3 Jason Mossop; 34 Iain Thornley; 32 Lewis Tierney; 33 Jamie Doran; 28 Jarrod Sammut; 8 Kris Coward; 14 Callum Phillips; 10 Marc Shackley; 16 Kurt Horton; 12 Jarrad Stack; 13 Liam McAvoy. Subs (all used): 7 Carl Forber; 15 Karl Olstrum; 19 Tom Walker; - Ryan Sutton.
Tries: Miller (16, 29, 71), Thornley (51), Sammut (68);
Goals: Sammut 2/2, Forber 2/3.
Rugby Leaguer & League Express Men of the Match:
Whitehaven: Scott McAvoy; *Town:* Jarrod Sammut.
Penalty count: 7-6; **Half-time:** 0-12;
Referee: Dave Merrick; **Attendance:** 1,722.

SHEFFIELD EAGLES 32 BRADFORD BULLS 30

EAGLES: 1 Quentin Laulu-Togagae; 2 Scott Turner; 3 Menzie Yere; 4 Sam Smeaton; 23 Rob Worrincy; 6 Kyle Briggs; 7 Dominic Brambani; 17 Steve Thorpe; 24 Keal Carlile; 10 Mitchell Stringer; 11 Michael Knowles; 12 Duane Straugheir; 5 Misi Taulapapa. Subs (all used): 9 James Davey; 22 Tony Tonks; 15 John Davies; 8 Eddie Battye.
Tries: Laulu-Togagae (15), Briggs (29), Tonks (33), Worrincy (36, 43); **Goals:** Briggs 6/7.
BULLS: 33 James Mendeika; 27 Ryan Shaw; 4 Matty Blythe; 20 Adam Henry; 2 Etuate Uaisele; 1 Jake Mullaney; 13 Danny Addy; 31 Epalahame Lauaki; 9 Adam O'Brien; 10 Adam Sidlow; 12 Dale Ferguson; 22 Chev Walker; 14 Jay Pitts. Subs (all used): 34 Omari Caro; 24 Lucas Walshaw; 32 Steve Crossley; 15 Daniel Fleming.
Tries: Mullaney (12, 63, 70), Shaw (68), Pitts (75);
Goals: Shaw 5/5.
Rugby Leaguer & League Express Men of the Match:
Eagles: Tony Tonks; *Bulls:* Jake Mullaney.
Penalty count: 6-8; **Half-time:** 22-6;
Referee: Chris Leatherbarrow; **Attendance:** 2,153
(at Keepmoat Stadium, Doncaster).

ROUND 22

Sunday 19th July 2015

DONCASTER 0 HALIFAX 52

DONCASTER: 2 Tom Carr; 1 Dave Scott; 26 Sam Doherty; 17 Liam Welham; 31 Peter Fox; 28 Joe McLocklan; 13 Mike Emmett; 38 Matt Groat; 9 Kyle Kesik; 14 Russ Spiers; 12 Steve Snitch; 32 Ben Musolino; 15 Mitch Clark. Subs (all used): 8 Matt Carbutt; 11 Michael Kelly; 30 Ryan Wright; 35 Lelauloto Tagaloa.
HALIFAX: 7 Ben Johnston; 23 Gareth Potts; 20 James Saltonstall; 3 Steve Tyrer; 2 Tom Saxton; 31 Connor Robinson; 6 Scott Murrell; 8 Adam Tangata; 9 Ben Kaye; 17 Mitch Cahalane; 27 Ross Divorty; 11 Dane Manning; 16 Richard Moore. Subs (all used): 12 Andy Bracek; 13 Jack Spencer; 21 Ryan Maneely; 35 Clement Boyer.
Tries: Manning (4, 15), Tyrer (39, 47), Saxton (42), Bracek (50), Johnston (54), Maneely (68, 71);
Goals: Tyrer 8/10.
Rugby Leaguer & League Express Men of the Match:
Doncaster: Liam Welham; *Halifax:* Steve Tyrer.
Penalty count: 7-12; **Half-time:** 0-18;
Referee: Tom Crashley; **Attendance:** 1,506.

BATLEY BULLDOGS 45 HUNSLET HAWKS 28

BULLDOGS: 5 Johnny Campbell; 2 Wayne Reittie; 3 Shaun Ainscough; 20 Shaun Squires; 28 Alex Brown; 6 Cain Southernwood; 7 Scott Leatherbarrow; 8 Keegan Hirst; 13 Luke Blake; 10 Alex Rowe; 12 Sam Scott; 23 Brad Day; 17 Joe Chandler. Subs (all used): 16 Sean Hesketh; 9 Anthony Nicholson; 18 Tom Lillycrop; 21 James Brown.
Tries: A Brown (18, 48), Blake (21), Hesketh (33), Lillycrop (37), Day (55), Squires (58), Chandler (68);
Goals: Leatherbarrow 6/8;
Field goal: Leatherbarrow (78).
HAWKS: 1 Jimmy Watson; 2 Mo Agoro; 4 Danny Maun; 47 Matty Gee; 24 Richie Barnett; 6 Simon Brown; 31 Andy Kain; 41 Andy Yates; 9 Jack Lee; 8 Michael Haley; 11 Callum Casey; 15 Liam Mackay; 35 Rob Mulhern. Subs (all used): 30 George Flanagan; 17 Mark Castle; 13 Danny Grimshaw; 45 Kyle Trout.
Tries: Casey (14), Lee (25, 73), Watson (30), Yates (61);
Goals: Brown 4/5.
Sin bin: Mackay (39) - persistent team offences.
Rugby Leaguer & League Express Men of the Match:
Bulldogs: Alex Rowe; *Hawks:* Danny Grimshaw.
Penalty count: 10-9; **Half-time:** 22-18;
Referee: Chris Kendall; **Attendance:** 483.

BRADFORD BULLS 36 LEIGH CENTURIONS 36

BULLS: 27 Ryan Shaw; 5 Danny Williams; 4 Matty Blythe; 20 Adam Henry; 34 Omari Caro; 3 Adrian Purtell; 13 Danny Addy; 8 Paul Clough; 9 Adam O'Brien; 10 Adam Sidlow; 11 Tom Olbison; 14 Jay Pitts; 22 Chev Walker. Subs (all used): 24 Lucas Walshaw; 31 Epalahame Lauaki; 32 Steve Crossley; 33 James Mendeika.
Tries: Pitts (1), Caro (21, 27, 76), Addy (57), Blythe (66);
Goals: Shaw 6/7.
CENTURIONS: 1 Gregg McNally; 15 Jonathan Pownall; 3 Greg Worthington; 4 Tom Armstrong; 2 Adam Higson; 6 Martyn Ridyard; 7 Ryan Brierley; 8 Fuifui Moimoi; 9 Bob Beswick; 26 Gareth Hock; 22 Andrew Dixon; 12 Tommy Goulden; 29 Jake Emmitt. Subs (all used): 13 Sam Barlow; 18 Tom Spencer; 20 Sam Hopkins; 30 Mick Higham.
Tries: Hock (11), Pownall (19, 63, 70), Worthington (44), Brierley (48); **Goals:** Ridyard 6/6.
Rugby Leaguer & League Express Men of the Match:
Bulls: Danny Addy; *Centurions:* Mick Higham.
Penalty count: 10-5; **Half-time:** 20-12;
Referee: James Child; **Attendance:** 9,181.

WHITEHAVEN 16 DEWSBURY RAMS 34

WHITEHAVEN: 32 Louis Jouffret; 5 Jordan Burns; 21 Chris Taylor; - Declan Hulme; 2 Craig Calvert; 25 Dion Aiye; 15 Grant Gore; 30 Richard Beaumont; 14 Thomas Coyle; 29 Ted Chapelhow; 11 Dave Allen; 4 Scott McAvoy; 8 Ben Davies. Subs (all used): 27 Thibault Ancely; 23 Sam Brooks; 9 James Newton; 13 Tyla Hepi.
Tries: Hulme (31), Calvert (43), Davies (69);
Goals: Jouffret 2/3.
RAMS: 1 Ryan Fieldhouse; 2 Dale Morton; 15 Jason Crookes; 12 Scott Hale; 5 Greg Scott; 44 Brett Seymour; 7 Anthony Thackeray; 8 Stephen Nash; 6 Matty Wildie; 10 Ryan Hepworth; 34 Luke Adamson; 16 Toby Adamson; 13 Aaron Brown. Subs (all used): 47 Nathan Conroy; 25 Joel Farrell; 24 Byron Smith; 33 Paul Jackson.
Tries: Morton (22, 63), Conroy (35), Hale (54), T Adamson (60), Farrell (76);
Goals: Seymour 3/3, Morton 2/3.
Rugby Leaguer & League Express Men of the Match:
Whitehaven: Ben Davies; *Rams:* Toby Adamson.
Penalty count: 4-7; **Half-time:** 6-12;
Referee: Jamie Bloem; **Attendance:** 760.

WORKINGTON TOWN 29 LONDON BRONCOS 18

TOWN: 1 Jack Murphy; 22 Elliott Miller; 12 Jarrad Stack; 34 Iain Thornley; 32 Lewis Tierney; 33 Jamie Doran; 28 Jarrod Sammut; 8 Kris Coward; 14 Callum Phillips; 10 Marc Shackley; 16 Kurt Horton; 11 Brett Phillips; 13 Liam McAvoy. Subs (all used): 7 Carl Forber; 4 Perry Whiteley; 19 Tom Walker; 27 Alex Szostak.
Tries: Horton (9), B Phillips (12), Tierney (42), Coward (58); **Goals:** Sammut 2/3, Forber 4/4;
Field goal: Sammut (68).
BRONCOS: 32 Elliot Kear; 2 Rhys Williams; 5 Ben Hellewell; 4 Wes Naiqama; 20 Iliess Macani; 19 Joe Keyes; 7 William Barthau; 36 Jonathan Walker; 9 Ray Nasso; 18 Jon Wallace; 31 Elliot Minchella; 37 Jason Walton; 34 Matt Davis. Subs (all used): 38 James Cunningham; 21 Joel Wicks; 29 Jamie Thackray; 16 Glenn Riley.
Tries: Hellewell (38, 72), Keyes (48); **Goals:** Naiqama 3/3.
Rugby Leaguer & League Express Men of the Match:
Town: Jarrod Sammut; *Broncos:* Jonathan Walker.
Penalty count: 12-5; **Half-time:** 12-6;
Referee: Andrew Sweet; **Attendance:** 686.

SHEFFIELD EAGLES 38 FEATHERSTONE ROVERS 28

EAGLES: 1 Quentin Laulu-Togagae; 2 Scott Turner; 3 Menzie Yere; 4 Sam Smeaton; 23 Rob Worrincy; 6 Kyle Briggs; 7 Dominic Brambani; 17 Steve Thorpe; 24 Keal Carlile; 10 Mitchell Stringer; 11 Michael Knowles; 12 Duane Straugheir; 5 Misi Taulapapa. Subs (all used): 9 James Davey; 22 Tony Tonks; 15 John Davies; 8 Eddie Battye.
Tries: Knowles (32), Straugheir (35), Worrincy (40, 58), Yere (41), Turner (68), Smeaton (76); **Goals:** Briggs 5/7.
ROVERS: 2 Will Sharp; 5 Ben Blackmore; 1 Ian Hardman; 4 Thomas Minns; 21 Jy Hitchcox; 36 Paul Cooke; 6 Paul Sykes; 8 Jordan Baldwinson; 9 Andy Ellis; 10 Paul Wood; 18 Jamie Cording; 12 Reni Maitua; 15 Jack Bussey. Subs (all used): 13 Tim Spears; 17 Matt James; 27 Jack Ormondroyd; 23 Luke Teasdale.
Tries: Minns (8, 54, 61, 72), Sykes (15), Maitua (44);
Goals: Sykes 2/6.
Rugby Leaguer & League Express Men of the Match:
Eagles: Eddie Battye; *Rovers:* Thomas Minns.
Penalty count: 4-5; **Half-time:** 18-10;
Referee: Michael Woodhead; **Attendance:** 2,443
(at Keepmoat Stadium, Doncaster).

ROUND 19

Wednesday 22nd July 2015

LEIGH CENTURIONS 40 DEWSBURY RAMS 24

CENTURIONS: 1 Gregg McNally; 2 Adam Higson; 31 Mathias Pala; 4 Tom Armstrong; 5 Liam Kay; 17 Ben Reynolds; 7 Ryan Brierley; 8 Fuifui Moimoi; 30 Mick Higham; 21 Jamie Acton; 11 Matt Sarsfield; 19 Kurt Haggerty; 10 Oliver Wilkes. Subs (all used): 9 Bob Beswick; 18 Tom Spencer; 20 Sam Hopkins; 23 Martin Aspinwall.
Tries: Armstrong (2), Kay (13), Brierley (54, 61, 67), Reynolds (59), Hopkins (76); **Goals:** Reynolds 6/7.
RAMS: 1 Ryan Fieldhouse; 2 Dale Morton; 40 Sam Dunn; 12 Scott Hale; 5 Greg Scott; 36 Brad Delaney; 7 Anthony Thackeray; 8 Stephen Nash; 47 Nathan Conroy; 10 Ryan Hepworth; 34 Luke Adamson; 16 Toby Adamson; 13 Aaron Brown. Subs (all used): 24 Byron Smith; 25 Joel Farrell; 27 Jason Muranka; 35 James Delaney.
Tries: Farrell (37, 78), Morton (50), Fieldhouse (72);
Goals: B Delaney 4/5.
Rugby Leaguer & League Express Men of the Match:
Centurions: Ryan Brierley; *Rams:* Joel Farrell.
Penalty count: 8-9; **Half-time:** 12-6;
Referee: Chris Leatherbarrow; **Attendance:** 3,244.

ROUND 23

Saturday 25th July 2015

FEATHERSTONE ROVERS 0 WHITEHAVEN 29

ROVERS: 2 Will Sharp; 5 Ben Blackmore; 18 Jamie Cording; 28 Will Milner; 21 Jy Hitchcox; 6 Paul Sykes; 36 Paul Cooke; 8 Jordan Baldwinson; 9 Andy Ellis; 10 Paul Wood; 19 Alex Foster; 39 Steve Snitch; 13 Tim Spears. Subs (all used): 15 Jack Bussey; 27 Jack Ormondroyd; 23 Luke Teasdale; 17 Matt James.
Sin bin: Wood (78) - dangerous contact.
WHITEHAVEN: 32 Louis Jouffret; 5 Jordan Burns; 21 Chris Taylor; 28 Ed Chamberlain; 2 Craig Calvert; 25 Dion Aiye; 15 Grant Gore; 30 Richard Beaumont; 9 James Newton; 24 Ted Chapelhow; 4 Scott McAvoy; 13 Tyla Hepi; 23 Sam Brooks. Subs (all used): 22 Kurtis Quinn; 8 Ben Davies; 27 Jay Chapelhow; 26 Greg Wilde.
Tries: Aiye (26, 40), Taylor (48), McAvoy (50), Burns (72);
Goals: Jouffret 4/5; **Field goal:** Gore (79).
Rugby Leaguer & League Express Men of the Match:
Rovers: Steve Snitch; *Whitehaven:* Grant Gore.
Penalty count: 7-7; **Half-time:** 0-12;
Referee: Tom Crashley; **Attendance:** 1,305.

Sunday 26th July 2015

DEWSBURY RAMS 12 BATLEY BULLDOGS 16

RAMS: 1 Ryan Fieldhouse; 2 Dale Morton; 3 Karl Pryce; 15 Jason Crookes; 18 Dalton Grant; 31 Kieran Hyde; 13 Aaron Brown; 33 Paul Jackson; 6 Matty Wildie; 32 Makali Aizue; 12 Scott Hale; 25 Joel Farrell; 34 Luke Adamson. Subs (all used): 24 Byron Smith; 47 Nathan Conroy; 27 Jason Muranka; 8 Stephen Nash.
Tries: Grant (27, 49), Morton (62); **Goals:** Hyde 0/3.
Sin bin: Nash (20) - punching Rowe.
BULLDOGS: 5 Johnny Campbell; 3 Shaun Ainscough; 20 Shaun Squires; - Chris Ulugia; 28 Alex Brown; 9 Anthony Nicholson; 7 Scott Leatherbarrow; 15 Adam Gledhill; 13 Luke Blake; 10 Alex Rowe; 11 Alex Bretherton; 23 Brad Day; 17 Joe Chandler. Subs (all used): 14 Alistair Leak; 16 Sean Hesketh; 18 Tom Lillycrop; 21 James Brown.
Tries: A Brown (30), Ulugia (69);
Goals: Leatherbarrow 4/5.
Sin bin: Campbell (27) - high tackle on Grant.
Rugby Leaguer & League Express Men of the Match:
Rams: Dalton Grant; *Bulldogs:* Scott Leatherbarrow.
Penalty count: 8-12; **Half-time:** 4-8;
Referee: Dave Merrick; **Attendance:** 1,319.

HALIFAX 20 BRADFORD BULLS 16

HALIFAX: 7 Ben Johnston; 20 James Saltonstall; 4 Ben Heaton; 3 Steve Tyrer; 2 Tom Saxton; 31 Connor Robinson; 6 Scott Murrell; 8 Adam Tangata; 21 Ryan Maneely; 17 Mitch Cahalane; 16 Richard Moore; 11 Dane Manning; 12 Andy Bracek. Subs (all used): 22 Jacob Fairbank; 29 Ed Barber; 35 Clement Boyer; 36 Mikey Wood.
Tries: Cahalane (11), Heaton (30), Tyrer (76);
Goals: Tyrer 4/5.
BULLS: 27 Ryan Shaw; 35 James Clare; 4 Matty Blythe; 20 Adam Henry; 34 Omari Caro; 33 James Mendeika; 13 Danny Addy; 8 Paul Clough; 26 Vila Halafihi; 32 Steve Crossley; 11 Tom Olbison; 24 Lucas Walshaw; 22 Chev Walker. Subs (all used): 15 Daniel Fleming; 31 Epalahame Lauaki; 14 Jay Pitts; 9 Adam O'Brien.
Tries: Pitts (44), Henry (53), Caro (61); **Goals:** Shaw 2/3.
Sin bin: Walker (75) - interference.
Rugby Leaguer & League Express Men of the Match:
Halifax: Richard Moore; *Bulls:* Danny Addy.
Penalty count: 8-6; **Half-time:** 14-0;
Referee: Joe Cobb; **Attendance:** 4,589.

Leigh celebrate as captain Oliver Wilkes lifts the Championship League Leaders Shield

HUNSLET HAWKS 6 WORKINGTON TOWN 30

HAWKS: 1 Jimmy Watson; 2 Mo Agoro; 11 Callum Casey; 4 Danny Maun; 24 Richie Barnett; 6 Simon Brown; 7 Danny Ansell; 8 Michael Haley; 9 Jack Lee; 35 Rob Mulhern; 44 Charlie Martin; 47 Matty Gee; 15 Liam Mackay. Subs (all used): 30 George Flanagan; 17 Mark Castle; 45 Kyle Trout; 10 James Houston.
Try: Mackay (5); **Goals:** Brown 1/1.
TOWN: 1 Jack Murphy; 22 Elliott Miller; 3 Jason Mossop; 12 Jarrad Stack; 5 Brett Carter; 28 Jarrod Sammut; 33 Jamie Doran; 8 Kris Coward; 14 Callum Phillips; 10 Marc Shackley; 11 Brett Phillips; 16 Kurt Horton; 13 Liam McAvoy. Subs (all used): 7 Carl Forber; 15 Karl Olstrum; 19 Tom Walker; 27 Alex Szostak.
Tries: Sammut (20), Miller (24), Carter (43, 70), Murphy (72); **Goals:** Sammut 2/3, Forber 3/3.
Rugby Leaguer & League Express Men of the Match: *Hawks:* Jack Lee; *Town:* Jarrod Sammut.
Penalty count: 6-6; **Half-time:** 6-12;
Referee: Michael Woodhead; **Attendance:** 706.

LEIGH CENTURIONS 66 DONCASTER 10

CENTURIONS: 1 Gregg McNally; 2 Adam Higson; 3 Greg Worthington; 31 Mathias Pala; 5 Liam Kay; 6 Martyn Ridyard; 7 Ryan Brierley; 21 Jamie Acton; 30 Mick Higham; 29 Jake Emmitt; 22 Andrew Dixon; 12 Tommy Goulden; 26 Gareth Hock. Subs (all used): 10 Oliver Wilkes; 13 Sam Barlow; 17 Ben Reynolds; 23 Martin Aspinwall.
Tries: Kay (6, 36, 52, 67, 79), Higson (10), McNally (38, 50), Brierley (47), Hock (57), Ridyard (61), Reynolds (75); **Goals:** Ridyard 9/11, Emmitt 0/1.
DONCASTER: 34 Curtis Naughton; 1 Dave Scott; 3 Danny Cowling; 17 Liam Welham; 31 Peter Fox; 28 Joe McLocklan; 37 Paul Mennell; 33 Ryan Verlinden; 9 Kyle Kesik; 15 Mitch Clark; 11 Michael Kelly; 35 Ben Musolino; 13 Mike Emmett. Subs (all used): 30 Ryan Wright; 8 Matt Carbutt; 32 Lelauloto Tagaloa; 22 Brad Foster.
Tries: Fox (30), Welham (73); **Goals:** Naughton 1/2.
Rugby Leaguer & League Express Men of the Match: *Centurions:* Liam Kay; *Doncaster:* Ryan Wright.
Penalty count: 8-8; **Half-time:** 22-4;
Referee: Andrew Sweet; **Attendance:** 3,311.

LONDON BRONCOS 14 SHEFFIELD EAGLES 22

BRONCOS: 32 Elliot Kear; 2 Rhys Williams; 4 Wes Naiqama; 5 Ben Hellewell; 20 Iliess Macani; 22 Oscar Thomas; 19 Joe Keyes; 12 Rhys Lovegrove; 35 Andrew Henderson; 18 Jon Wallace; 15 Matt Garside; 37 Jason Walton; 31 Elliot Minchella. Subs (all used): 38 James Cunningham; 34 Matt Davis; 23 Toby Everett; 16 Glenn Riley.
Tries: Naiqama (5), Garside (61); **Goals:** Naiqama 3/4.
EAGLES: 1 Quentin Laulu-Togagae; 30 Ryan Millar; 3 Menzie Yere; 4 Sam Smeaton; 23 Rob Worrincy; 19 Cory Aston; 7 Dominic Brambani; 8 Eddie Battye; 9 James Davey; 10 Mitchell Stringer; 16 Jamie Langley; 12 Duane Straugheir; 13 Pat Walker. Subs (all used): 29 Dave Petersen; 25 Connor Scott; 15 John Davies; 17 Steve Thorpe.
Tries: Millar (42, 50), Yere (74), Battye (77);
Goals: Walker 3/4.
Rugby Leaguer & League Express Men of the Match: *Broncos:* Matt Davis; *Eagles:* Ryan Millar.
Penalty count: 3-5; **Half-time:** 6-0;
Referee: Jamie Bloem; **Attendance:** 543.

CHAMPIONSHIP SHIELD
2015 *Round by Round*

ROUND 1

Saturday 8th August 2015

LONDON BRONCOS 52 DONCASTER 12

BRONCOS: 32 Elliot Kear; 2 Rhys Williams; 5 Ben Hellewell; 4 Wes Naiqama; 20 Iliess Macani; 7 William Barthau; 19 Joe Keyes; 36 Jonathan Walker; 35 Andrew Henderson; 18 Jon Wallace; 15 Matt Garside; 37 Jason Walton; 31 Elliot Minchella. Subs (all used): 38 James Cunningham; 34 Matt Davis; 16 Glenn Riley; 23 Toby Everett.
Tries: Hellewell (4), Kear (25, 53, 80), Walton (37), Naiqama (40), R Williams (49), J Walker (58), Barthau (77); **Goals:** Naiqama 6/7, Keyes 2/2.
DONCASTER: 1 Dave Scott; 39 Tom Hodson; 26 Sam Doherty; 17 Liam Welham; 31 Peter Fox; 28 Joe McLocklan; 24 Josh Kittrick; 15 Mitch Clark; 9 Kyle Kesik; 38 Matt Groat; 22 Brad Foster; 35 Ben Musolino; 13 Mike Emmett. Subs (all used): 14 Russ Spiers; 32 Lelauloto Tagaloa; 11 Michael Kelly; 33 Ryan Verlinden.
Tries: Fox (9), Emmett (70); **Goals:** Scott 2/2.
Rugby Leaguer & League Express Men of the Match: *Broncos:* Wes Naiqama; *Doncaster:* Dave Scott.
Penalty count: 6-8; **Half-time:** 24-6;
Referee: Chris Leatherbarrow; **Attendance:** 350.

Sunday 9th August 2015

DEWSBURY RAMS 32 HUNSLET HAWKS 20

RAMS: 1 Ryan Fieldhouse; 2 Dale Morton; 48 Etuate Uaisele; 4 Shane Grady; 18 Dalton Grant; 36 Brad Delaney; 7 Anthony Thackeray; 33 Paul Jackson; 6 Matty Wildie; 10 Ryan Hepworth; 34 Luke Adamson; 12 Scott Hale; 13 Aaron Brown. Subs (all used): 47 Nathan Conroy; 25 Joel Farrell; 8 Stephen Nash; 24 Byron Smith.
Tries: Morton (15), Grady (32, 54), Hale (62), Fieldhouse (66), Grant (75); **Goals:** B Delaney 4/6.
HAWKS: 1 Jimmy Watson; 2 Mo Agoro; 11 Callum Casey; 4 Danny Maun; 24 Richie Barnett; 6 Simon Brown; 7 Danny Ansell; 8 Michael Haley; 9 Jack Lee; 10 James Houston; 47 Matty Gee; 44 Charlie Martin; 15 Liam Mackay. Subs (all used): 45 Kyle Trout; 13 Danny Grimshaw; 17 Mark Castle; 21 Ryan Backhouse.
Tries: Lee (22, 47), Maun (77); **Goals:** Brown 4/4.
Rugby Leaguer & League Express Men of the Match: *Rams:* Shane Grady; *Hawks:* Mark Castle.
Penalty count: 8-8; **Half-time:** 10-6;
Referee: Gareth Hewer; **Attendance:** 901.

FEATHERSTONE ROVERS 42 WHITEHAVEN 30

ROVERS: 1 Ian Hardman; 26 Kyran Johnson; 6 Paul Sykes; 19 Alex Foster; 2 Will Sharp; 36 Paul Cooke; 7 Gareth Moore; 8 Jordan Baldwinson; 9 Andy Ellis; 15 Jack Bussey; 18 Jamie Cording; 39 Steve Snitch; 13 Tim Spears. Subs (all used): 27 Jack Ormondroyd; 23 Luke Teasdale; 17 Matt James; 40 Bradley Knowles-Tagg.
Tries: Foster (13), Baldwinson (26), Moore (28, 39), Sharp (34), Cording (37), Johnson (43), James (52);
Goals: Sykes 5/8.
WHITEHAVEN: 21 Chris Taylor; 5 Jordan Burns; 26 Greg Wilde; 28 Ed Chamberlain; 2 Craig Calvert; 25 Dion Aiye; 15 Grant Gore; 24 Ted Chapelhow; 9 James Newton; 8 Ben Davies; 4 Scott McAvoy; 13 Tyla Hepi; 23 Sam Brooks. Subs (all used): 18 Steve Fox; 22 Kurtis Quinn; 14 Thomas Coyle; 29 Thibault Ancely.
Tries: T Chapelhow (5, 69), Gore (54), Taylor (74), Chamberlain (80); **Goals:** Chamberlain 5/5.
Rugby Leaguer & League Express Men of the Match: *Rovers:* Gareth Moore; *Whitehaven:* Grant Gore.
Penalty count: 7-7; **Half-time:** 32-6;
Referee: Chris Kendall; **Attendance:** 1,107.

WORKINGTON TOWN 30 BATLEY BULLDOGS 12

TOWN: 1 Jack Murphy; 22 Elliott Miller; 3 Jason Mossop; 12 Jarrad Stack; 5 Brett Carter; 33 Jamie Doran; 28 Jarrod Sammut; 8 Kris Coward; 14 Callum Phillips; 10 Marc Shackley; 11 Brett Phillips; 16 Kurt Horton; 13 Liam McAvoy. Subs (all used): 7 Carl Forber; 15 Karl Olstrum; 19 Tom Walker; 27 Alex Szostak.
Tries: Sammut (20), Stack (27), Murphy (34), Horton (41), C Phillips (74), Miller (79);
Goals: Sammut 2/3, Forber 1/3.
BULLDOGS: 5 Johnny Campbell; 2 Wayne Reittie; 20 Shaun Squires; 30 Chris Ulugia; 28 Alex Brown; 6 Cain Southernwood; 7 Scott Leatherbarrow; 8 Keegan Hirst; 13 Luke Blake; 10 Alex Rowe; 11 Alex Bretherton; 12 Sam Scott; 15 Adam Gledhill. Subs (all used): 9 Anthony Nicholson; 16 Sean Hesketh; 18 Tom Lillycrop; 21 James Brown.
Tries: Ulugia (39), Hesketh (49);
Goals: Leatherbarrow 2/2.
Rugby Leaguer & League Express Men of the Match: *Town:* Jarrod Sammut; *Bulldogs:* Anthony Nicholson.
Penalty count: 7-8; **Half-time:** 16-6;
Referee: Jamie Bloem; **Attendance:** 864.

ROUND 2

Saturday 15th August 2015

WHITEHAVEN 40 LONDON BRONCOS 16

WHITEHAVEN: 24 Ed Chamberlain; 5 Jordan Burns; 21 Chris Taylor; 3 Jessie Joe Parker; 2 Craig Calvert; 25 Dion Aiye; 15 Grant Gore; 30 Richard Beaumont; 9 James Newton; 29 Thibault Ancely; 23 Sam Brooks; 13 Tyla Hepi; 8 Ben Davies. Subs (all used): 28 Ted Chapelhow; 18 Steve Fox; 16 Connor Holliday; 38 Owain Griffiths.
Tries: Newton (34, 63), Davies (39), Parker (56), Hepi (66), Holliday (69), Fox (77);
Goals: Chamberlain 6/7.
BRONCOS: 32 Elliot Kear; 2 Rhys Williams; 5 Ben Hellewell; 4 Wes Naiqama; 20 Iliess Macani; 7 William Barthau; 19 Joe Keyes; 36 Jonathan Walker; 35 Andrew Henderson; 16 Glenn Riley; 15 Matt Garside; 31 Elliot Minchella; 21 Joel Wicks. Subs (all used): 38 James Cunningham; 34 Matt Davis; 18 Jon Wallace; 23 Toby Everett.
Tries: Hellewell (15), Minchella (24), Barthau (28);
Goals: Naiqama 2/4.
Sin bin: Walker (68) - punching.
Rugby Leaguer & League Express Men of the Match: *Whitehaven:* Dion Aiye; *Broncos:* Joe Keyes.
Penalty count: 14-8; **Half-time:** 12-16;
Referee: Gareth Hewer; **Attendance:** 783.

Sunday 16th August 2015

DONCASTER 16 FEATHERSTONE ROVERS 28

DONCASTER: 1 Dave Scott; 39 Tom Hodson; 26 Sam Doherty; 17 Liam Welham; 31 Peter Fox; 28 Joe McLocklan; 37 Paul Mennell; 38 Matt Groat; 9 Kyle Kesik; 33 Ryan Verlinden; 11 Michael Kelly; 35 Ben Musolino; 13 Mike Emmett. Subs (all used): 14 Russ Spiers; 22 Brad Foster; 30 Ryan Wright; 32 Lelauloto Tagaloa.
Tries: Fox (3), Groat (12), Scott (73); **Goals:** Scott 2/3.
ROVERS: 1 Ian Hardman; 26 Kyran Johnson; 6 Paul Sykes; 19 Alex Foster; 2 Will Sharp; 36 Paul Cooke; 7 Gareth Moore; 8 Jordan Baldwinson; 9 Andy Ellis; 15 Jack Bussey; 18 Jamie Cording; 39 Steve Snitch; 13 Tim Spears. Subs (all used): 32 Sam Day; 17 Matt James; 40 Bradley Knowles-Tagg; 27 Jack Ormondroyd.
Tries: Spears (5), Snitch (37), Ormondroyd (54), Foster (68), Johnson (79); **Goals:** Sykes 4/5.
Rugby Leaguer & League Express Men of the Match: *Doncaster:* Dave Scott; *Rovers:* Alex Foster.
Penalty count: 8-9; **Half-time:** 10-12;
Referee: Dave Merrick; **Attendance:** 886.

BATLEY BULLDOGS 22 DEWSBURY RAMS 28

BULLDOGS: 5 Johnny Campbell; 2 Wayne Reittie; 3 Shaun Ainscough; 29 Elliott Cosgrove; 28 Alex Brown; 9 Anthony Nicholson; 7 Scott Leatherbarrow; 8 Keegan Hirst; 13 Luke Blake; 16 Sean Hesketh; 15 Adam Gledhill; 12 Sam Scott; 21 James Brown. Subs (all used): 14 Alistair Leak; 10 Alex Rowe; 18 Tom Lillycrop; 11 Alex Bretherton.
Tries: Ainscough (6), Blake (30), A Brown (50), Scott (70); **Goals:** Leatherbarrow 3/4.
RAMS: 1 Ryan Fieldhouse; 2 Dale Morton; 48 Etuate Uaisele; 4 Shane Grady; 18 Dalton Grant; 6 Matty Wildie; 7 Anthony Thackeray; 33 Paul Jackson; 47 Nathan Conroy; 10 Ryan Hepworth; 11 Rob Spicer; 12 Scott Hale; 34 Luke Adamson. Subs (all used): 13 Aaron Brown; 25 Joel Farrell; 8 Stephen Nash; 24 Byron Smith.
Tries: Grady (38), Uaisele (42), Grant (58), Thackeray (63), Farrell (72); **Goals:** Morton 4/5.
Sin bin: Farrell (26) - dangerous challenge.
Rugby Leaguer & League Express Men of the Match: *Bulldogs:* James Brown; *Rams:* Anthony Thackeray.
Penalty count: 10-6; **Half-time:** 12-6;
Referee: Chris Kendall; **Attendance:** 1,046.

HUNSLET HAWKS 18 WORKINGTON TOWN 22

HAWKS: 1 Jimmy Watson; 2 Mo Agoro; 4 Danny Maun; 11 Callum Casey; 24 Richie Barnett; 6 Simon Brown; 13 Danny Grimshaw; 10 James Houston; 9 Jack Lee; 45 Kyle Trout; 47 Matty Gee; 21 Ryan Backhouse; 15 Liam Mackay. Subs (all used): 7 Danny Ansell; 12 Aaron Lyons; 17 Mark Castle; 28 Mufaro Mvududu.
Tries: Grimshaw (23), Barnett (54, 65); **Goals:** Brown 3/3.
TOWN: 2 Sam Forrester; 22 Elliott Miller; 3 Jason Mossop; 23 Scott Akehurst; 5 Brett Carter; 33 Jamie Doran; 28 Jarrod Sammut; 8 Kris Coward; 14 Callum Phillips; 10 Marc Shackley; 11 Brett Phillips; 12 Jarrad Stack; 13 Liam McAvoy. Subs (all used): 4 Perry Whiteley; 15 Karl Olstrum; 19 Tom Walker; 7 Carl Forber.
Tries: Carter (2), Akehurst (28), B Phillips (32), Whiteley (34); **Goals:** Sammut 1/2, Forber 2/2.
Rugby Leaguer & League Express Men of the Match: *Hawks:* Simon Brown; *Town:* Jarrod Sammut.
Penalty count: 4-5; **Half-time:** 6-22;
Referee: Chris Leatherbarrow; **Attendance:** 567.

ROUND 3

Sunday 23rd August 2015

DONCASTER 20 BATLEY BULLDOGS 38

DONCASTER: 1 Dave Scott; 39 Tom Hodson; 3 Danny Cowling; 17 Liam Welham; 31 Peter Fox; 28 Joe McLocklan; 30 Ryan Wright; 38 Matt Groat; 9 Kyle Kesik; 33 Ryan Verlinden; 11 Michael Kelly; 35 Ben Musolino; 13 Mike Emmett. Subs (all used): 8 Matt Carbutt; 16 Brett Waller; 23 Jack Walton; 32 Lelauloto Tagaloa.
Tries: Welham (14), Waller (33), Musolino (37), Hodson (69); **Goals:** Scott 2/4.
BULLDOGS: 1 James Craven; 2 Wayne Reittie; 3 Shaun Ainscough; 29 Elliott Cosgrove; 20 Shaun Squires; 6 Cain Southernwood; 7 Scott Leatherbarrow; 8 Keegan Hirst; 13 Luke Blake; 15 Adam Gledhill; 12 Sam Scott; 23 Brad Day; 21 James Brown. Subs (all used): 10 Alex Rowe; 11 Alex Bretherton; 14 Alistair Leak; 18 Tom Lillycrop.
Tries: Cosgrove (30), Reittie (43, 60), Southernwood (53), Ainscough (56, 76), Squires (65);
Goals: Leatherbarrow 5/7.
Rugby Leaguer & League Express Men of the Match: *Doncaster:* Liam Welham; *Bulldogs:* Scott Leatherbarrow.
Penalty count: 7-8; **Half-time:** 14-6;
Referee: Michael Woodhead; **Attendance:** 735.

DEWSBURY RAMS 30 WHITEHAVEN 42

RAMS: 1 Ryan Fieldhouse; 2 Dale Morton; 3 Karl Pryce; 4 Shane Grady; 18 Dalton Grant; 6 Matty Wildie; 7 Anthony Thackeray; 10 Ryan Hepworth; 47 Nathan Conroy; 32 Makali Aizue; 11 Rob Spicer; 34 Luke Adamson; 13 Aaron Brown. Subs (all used): 33 Paul Jackson; 8 Stephen Nash; 25 Joel Farrell; 15 Jason Crookes.
Tries: Grady (6, 9), Farrell (45), Wildie (47), Pryce (56), Grant (79); **Goals:** Morton 2/5, Grady 1/1.
WHITEHAVEN: 24 Ed Chamberlain; 5 Jordan Burns; 21 Chris Taylor; 3 Jessie Joe Parker; 2 Craig Calvert; 25 Dion Aiye; 15 Grant Gore; 18 Steve Fox; 14 Thomas Coyle; 30 Richard Beaumont; 4 Scott McAvoy; 13 Tyla Hepi; 23 Sam Brooks. Subs (all used): 9 James Newton; 8 Ben Davies; 28 Ted Chapelhow; 16 Connor Holliday.
Tries: McAvoy (21, 50), Calvert (27, 59), Aiye (35), Fox (68), Gore (77); **Goals:** Chamberlain 7/7.
Rugby Leaguer & League Express Men of the Match: *Rams:* Shane Grady; *Whitehaven:* Thomas Coyle.
Penalty count: 9-4; **Half-time:** 10-18;
Referee: Tom Crashley; **Attendance:** 709.

LONDON BRONCOS 24 HUNSLET HAWKS 41

BRONCOS: 32 Elliot Kear; 2 Rhys Williams; 5 Ben Hellewell; 4 Wes Naiqama; 26 Sean Morris; 7 William Barthau; 38 James Cunningham; 36 Jonathan Walker; 35 Andrew Henderson; 39 Ben Gray; 15 Matt Garside; 37 Jason Walton; 21 Joel Wicks. Subs (all used): 41 Ben Pointer; 34 Matt Davis; 40 Sadiq Adebiyi; 17 Erjon Dollapi.
Tries: Garside (11), Cunningham (27), Adebiyi (35), Hellewell (67, 73); **Goals:** Naiqama 0/2, Barthau 2/3.
Sin bin: Walton (57) - professional foul.
HAWKS: 1 Jimmy Watson; 2 Mo Agoro; 33 James Duckworth; 4 Danny Maun; 24 Richie Barnett; 6 Simon Brown; 7 Danny Ansell; 10 James Houston; 9 Jack Lee; 45 Kyle Trout; 47 Matty Gee; 21 Ryan Backhouse; 15 Liam Mackay. Subs (all used): 30 George Flanagan; 17 Mark Castle; 12 Aaron Lyons; 16 Lewis Reed.
Tries: Trout (22), Flanagan (31), Backhouse (44), Reed (52), Duckworth (56), Lee (78); **Goals:** Brown 8/8;
Field goal: Brown (65).
Rugby Leaguer & League Express Men of the Match: *Broncos:* Sadiq Adebiyi; *Hawks:* Simon Brown.
Penalty count: 7-15; **Half-time:** 14-12;
Referee: Dave Merrick; **Attendance:** 225.

WORKINGTON TOWN 10 FEATHERSTONE ROVERS 24

TOWN: 1 Jack Murphy; 22 Elliott Miller; 3 Jason Mossop; 23 Scott Akehurst; 5 Brett Carter; 33 Jamie Doran; 28 Jarrod Sammut; 8 Kris Coward; 14 Callum Phillips; 10 Marc Shackley; 11 Brett Phillips; 27 Alex Szostak; 15 Karl Olstrum. Subs (all used): 4 Perry Whiteley; 13 Liam McAvoy; 19 Tom Walker; 7 Carl Forber.
Tries: C Phillips (3), Miller (28);
Goals: Sammut 1/1, Forber 0/1.
Sin bin: Olstrum (65) - dissent.
ROVERS: 1 Ian Hardman; 26 Kyran Johnson; 6 Paul Sykes; 19 Alex Foster; 2 Will Sharp; 36 Paul Cooke; 28 Will Milner; 8 Jordan Baldwinson; 9 Andy Ellis; 15 Jack Bussey; 13 Tim Spears; 39 Steve Snitch; 27 Jack Ormondroyd. Subs (all used): 32 Sam Day; 40 Bradley Knowles-Tagg; 35 Luke Cooper; 38 Jack Coventry.
Tries: Foster (10), Sharp (45), Snitch (51), Milner (73);
Goals: Sykes 4/5.
Rugby Leaguer & League Express Men of the Match: *Town:* Brett Phillips; *Rovers:* Alex Foster.
Penalty count: 10-9; **Half-time:** 10-4;
Referee: Andrew Sweet; **Attendance:** 906.

ROUND 4

Monday 31st August 2015

DEWSBURY RAMS 25 LONDON BRONCOS 16

RAMS: 1 Ryan Fieldhouse; 2 Dale Morton; 3 Karl Pryce; 48 Etuate Uaisele; 18 Dalton Grant; 6 Matty Wildie; 7 Anthony Thackeray; 32 Makali Aizue; 47 Nathan Conroy; 10 Ryan Hepworth; 11 Rob Spicer; 4 Shane Grady; 25 Joel Farrell. Subs (all used): 8 Stephen Nash; 33 Paul Jackson; 46 James Glover; 13 Aaron Brown.
Tries: Conroy (6), Morton (13), Uaisele (30), Brown (52);
Goals: Grady 4/5; **Field goal:** Thackeray (74).
BRONCOS: 26 Sean Morris; 2 Rhys Williams; 5 Ben Hellewell; 32 Elliot Kear; 20 Iliess Macani; 7 William Barthau; 19 Joe Keyes; 17 Erjon Dollapi; 38 James Cunningham; 39 Ben Gray; 15 Matt Garside; 21 Joel Wicks; 34 Matt Davis. Subs (all used): 35 Andrew Henderson; 18 Jon Wallace; 36 Jonathan Walker; 40 Sadiq Adebiyi.
Tries: R Williams (37), Wallace (60), Hellewell (68);
Goals: Barthau 2/3.
Rugby Leaguer & League Express Men of the Match: *Rams:* Rob Spicer; *Broncos:* James Cunningham.
Penalty count: 5-9; **Half-time:** 16-4;
Referee: Jamie Bloem; **Attendance:** 805.

FEATHERSTONE ROVERS 28 BATLEY BULLDOGS 26

ROVERS: 1 Ian Hardman; 26 Kyran Johnson; 6 Paul Sykes; 19 Alex Foster; 2 Will Sharp; 36 Paul Cooke; 28 Will Milner; 8 Jordan Baldwinson; 9 Andy Ellis; 15 Jack Bussey; 13 Tim Spears; 39 Steve Snitch; 27 Jack Ormondroyd. Subs (all used): 32 Sam Day; 40 Bradley Knowles-Tagg; 35 Luke Cooper; 38 Jack Coventry.

Tries: Ellis (34), Day (74), Johnson (76), Sykes (79), Sharp (80); **Goals:** Sykes 4/5.
BULLDOGS: 1 James Craven; 2 Wayne Reittie; 20 Shaun Squires; 29 Elliott Cosgrove; 3 Shaun Ainscough; 6 Cain Southernwood; 7 Scott Leatherbarrow; 8 Keegan Hirst; 13 Luke Blake; 16 Sean Hesketh; 12 Sam Scott; 23 Brad Day; 21 James Brown. Subs (all used): 9 Anthony Nicholson; 10 Alex Rowe; 18 Tom Lillycrop; 28 Alex Brown.
Tries: Ainscough (39, 70), Nicholson (45), Scott (48); **Goals:** Leatherbarrow 5/5.
Rugby Leaguer & League Express Men of the Match: *Rovers:* Jordan Baldwinson; *Bulldogs:* Shaun Ainscough.
Penalty count: 8-6; **Half-time:** 6-6;
Referee: Gareth Hewer; **Attendance:** 1,506.

WHITEHAVEN 16 HUNSLET HAWKS 30

WHITEHAVEN: 24 Ed Chamberlain; 5 Jordan Burns; 21 Chris Taylor; 3 Jessie Joe Parker; 16 Connor Holliday; 14 Thomas Coyle; 15 Grant Gore; 30 Richard Beaumont; 9 James Newton; 22 Kurtis Quinn; 25 Dion Aiye; 23 Sam Brooks; 8 Ben Davies. Subs (all used): 38 Owain Griffiths; 28 Ted Chapelhow; 20 James Robinson; 26 Greg Wilde.
Tries: Chamberlain (15), Griffiths (42), Taylor (66); **Goals:** Chamberlain 2/3.
Sin bin: Gore (75) - dissent.
HAWKS: 1 Jimmy Watson; 2 Mo Agoro; 33 James Duckworth; 4 Danny Maun; 24 Richie Barnett; 6 Simon Brown; 7 Danny Ansell; 10 James Houston; 9 Jack Lee; 12 Aaron Lyons; 47 Matty Gee; 21 Ryan Backhouse; 45 Kyle Trout. Subs (all used): 30 George Flanagan; 19 Brad Brennan; 17 Mark Castle; 16 Lewis Reed.
Tries: Gee (2), Lyons (8), Castle (29), Flanagan (45), Duckworth (58); **Goals:** Brown 5/6.
Rugby Leaguer & League Express Men of the Match: *Whitehaven:* Dion Aiye; *Hawks:* Danny Maun.
Penalty count: 11-3; **Half-time:** 6-16;
Referee: Dave Merrick; **Attendance:** 804.

WORKINGTON TOWN 62 DONCASTER 0

TOWN: 1 Jack Murphy; 22 Elliott Miller; 3 Jason Mossop; 23 Scott Akehurst; 5 Brett Carter; 28 Jarrod Sammut; 7 Carl Forber; 19 Tom Walker; 33 Jamie Doran; 10 Marc Shackley; 11 Brett Phillips; 27 Alex Szostak; 13 Liam McAvoy. Subs (all used): 2 Sam Forrester; 4 Perry Whiteley; 20 Nathan Lucock; 25 Steve Scholey.
Tries: Akehurst (4), Carter (8, 46, 80), Sammut (13, 22, 50), Doran (27), Szostak (58), Miller (61, 73); **Goals:** Forber 9/10, McAvoy 0/1.
DONCASTER: 1 Dave Scott; 39 Tom Hodson; 27 Alex Gilbey; 3 Danny Cowling; 31 Peter Fox; 2 Tom Carr; 28 Joe McLocklan; 8 Matt Carbutt; 9 Kyle Kesik; 38 Matt Groat; 22 Brad Foster; 35 Ben Musolino; 11 Michael Kelly. Subs (all used): 30 Ryan Wright; 24 Josh Kittrick; 33 Ryan Verlinden; 13 Mike Emmett.
Sin bin: Groat (21) - dangerous challenge.
Rugby Leaguer & League Express Men of the Match: *Town:* Jarrod Sammut; *Doncaster:* Joe McLocklan.
Penalty count: 10-8; **Half-time:** 28-0;
Referee: Jon Roberts; **Attendance:** 629.

ROUND 5

Sunday 6th September 2015

BATLEY BULLDOGS 50 WHITEHAVEN 0

BULLDOGS: 1 James Craven; 3 Shaun Ainscough; 20 Shaun Squires; 29 Elliott Cosgrove; 28 Alex Brown; 6 Cain Southernwood; 7 Scott Leatherbarrow; 8 Keegan Hirst; 13 Luke Blake; 10 Alex Rowe; 12 Sam Scott; 23 Brad Day; 21 James Brown. Subs (all used): 9 Anthony Nicholson; 18 Tom Lillycrop; 16 Sean Hesketh; 11 Alex Bretherton.
Tries: A Brown (9, 14, 54), Day (23), Squires (36), Blake (48), J Brown (61, 78), Hirst (70), Ainscough (73); **Goals:** Leatherbarrow 5/11.
WHITEHAVEN: 24 Ed Chamberlain; 26 Greg Wilde; 21 Chris Taylor; 4 Scott McAvoy; 3 Jessie Joe Parker; 25 Dion Aiye; 15 Grant Gore; 14 Thomas Coyle; 30 Richard Beaumont; 18 Steve Fox; 11 Dave Allen; 13 Tyla Hepi; 23 Sam Brooks. Subs (all used): 9 James Newton; 28 Ted Chapelhow; 38 Owain Griffiths; 8 Ben Davies.
Rugby Leaguer & League Express Men of the Match: *Bulldogs:* Alex Brown; *Whitehaven:* Tyla Hepi.
Penalty count: 8-3; **Half-time:** 20-0;
Referee: Jon Roberts; **Attendance:** 499.

FEATHERSTONE ROVERS 16 DEWSBURY RAMS 34

ROVERS: 1 Ian Hardman; 26 Kyran Johnson; 6 Paul Sykes; 4 Thomas Minns; 2 Will Sharp; 28 Will Milner; 7 Gareth Moore; 8 Jordan Baldwinson; 9 Andy Ellis; 27 Jack Ormondroyd; 13 Tim Spears; 39 Steve Snitch; 40 Bradley Knowles-Tagg. Subs (all used): 32 Sam Day; 17 Matt James; 38 Jack Coventry; 34 Brad England.
Tries: Milner (34), Sharp (37), Ormondroyd (65); **Goals:** Sykes 2/3.
RAMS: 1 Ryan Fieldhouse; 15 Jason Crookes; 48 Etuate Uaisele; 3 Karl Pryce; 18 Dalton Grant; 6 Matty Wildie; 7 Anthony Thackeray; 32 Makali Aizue; 47 Nathan Conroy; 10 Ryan Hepworth; 4 Shane Grady; 34 Luke Adamson; 25 Joel Farrell. Subs (all used): 33 Paul Jackson; 8 Stephen Nash; 44 Brett Seymour; 46 James Glover.
Tries: Farrell (20, 50), Crookes (25), Uaisele (31), Wildie (56), Thackeray (78); **Goals:** Grady 1/2, Seymour 4/4.
Rugby Leaguer & League Express Men of the Match: *Rovers:* Will Sharp; *Rams:* Matty Wildie.
Penalty count: 10-6; **Half-time:** 10-16;
Referee: Michael Woodhead; **Attendance:** 1,271.

HUNSLET HAWKS 25 DONCASTER 16

HAWKS: 1 Jimmy Watson; 2 Mo Agoro; 33 James Duckworth; 4 Danny Maun; 24 Richie Barnett; 6 Simon Brown; 7 Danny Ansell; 10 James Houston; 9 Jack Lee; 12 Aaron Lyons; 21 Ryan Backhouse; 47 Matty Gee; 45 Kyle Trout. Subs (all used): 30 George Flanagan; 16 Lewis Reed; 17 Mark Castle; 19 Brad Brennan.
Tries: Houston (17), Ansell (24), Castle (46), Lee (61); **Goals:** Brown 4/5; **Field goal:** Brown (72).
DONCASTER: 1 Dave Scott; 39 Tom Hodson; 26 Sam Doherty; 17 Liam Welham; 31 Peter Fox; 28 Joe McLocklan; 7 Richard Wilkinson; 38 Matt Groat; 9 Kyle Kesik; 14 Russ Spiers; 32 Ben Musolino; 22 Brad Foster; 11 Michael Kelly. Subs (all used): 2 Tom Carr; 33 Ryan Verlinden; 8 Matt Carbutt; 23 Jack Walton.
Tries: Hodson (40), Verlinden (57), Wilkinson (66); **Goals:** Scott 2/3.
Dismissal: Kesik (80) - dissent.
Rugby Leaguer & League Express Men of the Match: *Hawks:* George Flanagan; *Doncaster:* Richard Wilkinson.
Penalty count: 7-9; **Half-time:** 12-4;
Referee: Jamie Bloem; **Attendance:** 599.

LONDON BRONCOS 50 WORKINGTON TOWN 10

BRONCOS: 26 Sean Morris; 2 Rhys Williams; 5 Ben Hellewell; 32 Elliot Kear; 20 Iliess Macani; 7 William Barthau; 19 Joe Keyes; 16 Glenn Riley; 38 James Cunningham; 17 Erjon Dollapi; 15 Matt Garside; 34 Matt Davis; 18 Jon Wallace. Subs: 35 Andrew Henderson; 40 Sadiq Adebiyi (not used); 23 Toby Everett; 36 Jonathan Walker.
Tries: Cunningham (13, 80), R Williams (20), Davis (27), Keyes (32), Morris (44), Barthau (53), Hellewell (71), Dollapi (75); **Goals:** Barthau 7/9.
TOWN: 1 Jack Murphy; 2 Sam Forrester; 3 Jason Mossop; 23 Scott Akehurst; 5 Brett Carter; 28 Jarrod Sammut; 7 Carl Forber; 8 Kris Coward; 33 Jamie Doran; 19 Tom Walker; 11 Brett Phillips; 12 Jarrad Stack; 13 Liam McAvoy. Subs (all used): 15 Karl Olstrum; 4 Perry Whiteley; 25 Steve Scholey; 10 Marc Shackley.
Tries: Sammut (17), Walker (67); **Goals:** Forber 1/2.
Rugby Leaguer & League Express Men of the Match: *Broncos:* James Cunningham; *Town:* Liam McAvoy.
Penalty count: 7-6; **Half-time:** 22-6;
Referee: Sam Ansell; **Attendance:** 363.

ROUND 6

Friday 11th September 2015

HUNSLET HAWKS 10 FEATHERSTONE ROVERS 18

HAWKS: 1 Jimmy Watson; 2 Mo Agoro; 33 James Duckworth; 4 Danny Maun; 24 Richie Barnett; 6 Simon Brown; 7 Danny Ansell; 10 James Houston; 9 Jack Lee; 12 Aaron Lyons; 47 Matty Gee; 21 Ryan Backhouse; 45 Kyle Trout. Subs (all used): 30 George Flanagan; 13 Danny Grimshaw; 17 Mark Castle; 19 Brad Brennan.
Tries: Maun (65), Flanagan (80); **Goals:** Brown 1/2.
ROVERS: 2 Will Sharp; 26 Kyran Johnson; 6 Paul Sykes; 4 Thomas Minns; 5 Ben Blackmore; 36 Paul Cooke; 7 Gareth Moore; 8 Jordan Baldwinson; 9 Andy Ellis; 17 Matt James; 13 Tim Spears; 39 Steve Snitch; 15 Jack Bussey. Subs (all used): 1 Ian Hardman; 40 Bradley Knowles-Tagg; 27 Jack Ormondroyd; 38 Jack Coventry.
Tries: Ellis (38), Sykes (44), Blackmore (70); **Goals:** Sykes 3/3.
Rugby Leaguer & League Express Men of the Match: *Hawks:* Simon Brown; *Rovers:* Will Sharp.
Penalty count: 7-4; **Half-time:** 0-6;
Referee: Chris Leatherbarrow; **Attendance:** 839.

Sunday 13th September 2015

DONCASTER 33 DEWSBURY RAMS 20

DONCASTER: 2 Tom Carr; 39 Tom Hodson; 3 Danny Cowling; 17 Liam Welham; 31 Peter Fox; 28 Joe McLocklan; 7 Richard Wilkinson; 38 Matt Groat; 9 Kyle Kesik; 14 Russ Spiers; 23 Jack Walton; 22 Brad Foster; 13 Mike Emmett. Subs (all used): 8 Matt Carbutt; 11 Michael Kelly; 30 Ryan Wright; 33 Ryan Verlinden.
Tries: Welham (11), Groat (13), Wright (29), Fox (37, 43, 80); **Goals:** Hodson 4/5, Emmett 0/1;
Field goal: McLocklan (75).
RAMS: 3 Karl Pryce; 2 Dale Morton; 12 Scott Hale; 15 Jason Crookes; 18 Dalton Grant; 6 Matty Wildie; 7 Anthony Thackeray; 32 Makali Aizue; 47 Nathan Conroy; 10 Ryan Hepworth; 11 Rob Spicer; 25 Joel Farrell; 34 Luke Adamson. Subs (all used): 8 Stephen Nash; 13 Aaron Brown; 33 Paul Jackson; 44 Brett Seymour.
Tries: Grant (32, 51, 55), Aizue (61); **Goals:** Seymour 2/4.
Rugby Leaguer & League Express Men of the Match: *Doncaster:* Matt Groat; *Rams:* Dalton Grant.
Penalty count: 11-6; **Half-time:** 22-4;
Referee: Chris Campbell; **Attendance:** 725.

LONDON BRONCOS 50 BATLEY BULLDOGS 16

BRONCOS: 26 Sean Morris; 2 Rhys Williams; 5 Ben Hellewell; 32 Elliot Kear; 20 Iliess Macani; 7 William Barthau; 19 Joe Keyes; 16 Glenn Riley; 38 James Cunningham; 36 Jonathan Walker; 15 Matt Garside; 11 Daniel Harrison; 18 Jon Wallace. Subs (all used): 35 Andrew Henderson; 34 Matt Davis; 23 Toby Everett; 40 Sadiq Adebiyi.
Tries: Morris (7, 39, 42, 67, 79), Adebiyi (23), Macani (29), Hellewell (44, 54);
Goals: Barthau 6/6, Kear 0/1, Keyes 1/2.
BULLDOGS: 1 James Craven; 3 Shaun Ainscough; 20 Shaun Squires; 29 Elliott Cosgrove; 28 Alex Brown; 6 Cain Southernwood; 7 Scott Leatherbarrow; 8 Keegan Hirst; 13 Luke Blake; 10 Alex Rowe; 12 Sam Scott; 23 Brad Day; 21 James Brown. Subs (all used): 14 Alastair Leak; 16 Sean Hesketh; 15 Adam Gledhill; 18 Tom Lillycrop.
Tries: Hesketh (33), Day (35), A Brown (62); **Goals:** Leatherbarrow 2/3.
Rugby Leaguer & League Express Men of the Match: *Broncos:* Sean Morris; *Bulldogs:* Scott Leatherbarrow.
Penalty count: 2-10; **Half-time:** 24-12;
Referee: Jamie Bloem; **Attendance:** 485.

WORKINGTON TOWN 60 WHITEHAVEN 20

TOWN: 1 Jack Murphy; 22 Elliott Miller; 3 Jason Mossop; 12 Jarrad Stack; 5 Brett Carter; 33 Jamie Doran; 28 Jarrod Sammut; 8 Kris Coward; 14 Callum Phillips; 10 Marc Shackley; 11 Brett Phillips; 27 Alex Szostak; 13 Liam McAvoy. Subs (all used): 7 Carl Forber; 15 Karl Olstrum; 19 Tom Walker; 25 Steve Scholey.
Tries: Miller (1, 34), Murphy (13), Carter (20, 42, 54), Stack (24, 71), J Mossop (27), Forber (30), Sammut (48); **Goals:** Sammut 8/11.
WHITEHAVEN: 24 Ed Chamberlain; 16 Connor Holliday; 21 Chris Taylor; 25 Dion Aiye; 2 Craig Calvert; 9 James Newton; 15 Grant Gore; 30 Richard Beaumont; 22 Kurtis Quinn; 28 Ted Chapelhow; 4 Scott McAvoy; 13 Tyla Hepi; 23 Sam Brooks. Subs (all used): 20 James Robinson; 18 Steve Fox; 8 Ben Davies; 14 Thomas Coyle.
Tries: Aiye (10, 17, 59), Coyle (64); **Goals:** Chamberlain 2/4.
Rugby Leaguer & League Express Men of the Match: *Town:* Brett Carter; *Whitehaven:* Dion Aiye.
Penalty count: 4-7; **Half-time:** 40-10;
Referee: Michael Woodhead; **Attendance:** 1,559.

ROUND 7

Saturday 19th September 2015

WHITEHAVEN 52 DONCASTER 22

WHITEHAVEN: 24 Ed Chamberlain; 26 Greg Wilde; 21 Chris Taylor; 16 Connor Holliday; 2 Craig Calvert; 25 Dion Aiye; 15 Grant Gore; 30 Richard Beaumont; 14 Thomas Coyle; 28 Ted Chapelhow; 3 Jessie Joe Parker; 13 Tyla Hepi; 23 Sam Brooks. Subs (all used): 9 James Newton; 20 James Robinson; 8 Ben Davies; 22 Kurtis Quinn.
Tries: Aiye (15, 42), Newton (21), Calvert (23, 39), Hepi (32), Chamberlain (55), Parker (67), Brooks (77); **Goals:** Chamberlain 6/7, Robinson 2/2.
DONCASTER: 2 Tom Carr; 26 Sam Doherty; 3 Danny Cowling; 17 Liam Welham; 31 Peter Fox; 28 Joe McLocklan; 7 Richard Wilkinson; 38 Matt Groat; 9 Kyle Kesik; 14 Russ Spiers; 32 Ben Musolino; 22 Brad Foster; 13 Mike Emmett. Subs (all used): 8 Matt Carbutt; 23 Jack Walton; 30 Ryan Wright; 27 Alex Gilbey.
Tries: Doherty (36), Cowling (62), Foster (71), Carr (79); **Goals:** McLocklan 3/4.
Rugby Leaguer & League Express Men of the Match: *Whitehaven:* Dion Aiye; *Doncaster:* Mike Emmett.
Penalty count: 6-11; **Half-time:** 28-4;
Referee: Sam Ansell; **Attendance:** 589.

Sunday 20th September 2015

BATLEY BULLDOGS 60 HUNSLET HAWKS 12

BULLDOGS: 1 James Craven; 2 Wayne Reittie; 3 Shaun Ainscough; 20 Shaun Squires; 28 Alex Brown; 6 Cain Southernwood; 7 Scott Leatherbarrow; 8 Keegan Hirst; 13 Luke Blake; 10 Alex Rowe; 12 Sam Scott; 23 Brad Day; 21 James Brown. Subs (all used): 9 Anthony Nicholson; 15 Adam Gledhill; 16 Sean Hesketh; 11 Alex Bretherton.
Tries: Leatherbarrow (11), Southernwood (13), Ainscough (21, 67), A Brown (36, 77), Reittie (43), Squires (49), Gledhill (55), Nicholson (63), Craven (78); **Goals:** Leatherbarrow 7/10, Bretherton 1/1.
HAWKS: 1 Jimmy Watson; 2 Mo Agoro; 4 Danny Maun; 33 James Duckworth; 24 Richie Barnett; 6 Simon Brown; 7 Danny Ansell; 10 James Houston; 9 Jack Lee; 45 Kyle Trout; 21 Ryan Backhouse; 47 Matty Gee; 13 Danny Grimshaw. Subs (all used): 30 George Flanagan; 12 Aaron Lyons; 19 Brad Brennan; 17 Mark Castle.
Tries: Watson (61, 72); **Goals:** Houston 1/1, Brown 1/1.
Rugby Leaguer & League Express Men of the Match: *Bulldogs:* Shaun Ainscough; *Hawks:* Jimmy Watson.
Penalty count: 5-7; **Half-time:** 20-0;
Referee: Chris Leatherbarrow; **Attendance:** 737.

DEWSBURY RAMS 27 WORKINGTON TOWN 14

RAMS: 1 Ryan Fieldhouse; 2 Dale Morton; 48 Etuate Uaisele; 3 Karl Pryce; 18 Dalton Grant; 6 Matty Wildie; 7 Anthony Thackeray; 10 Ryan Hepworth; 23 Tom Hemingway; 32 Makali Aizue; 11 Rob Spicer; 34 Luke Adamson; 13 Aaron Brown. Subs (all used): 25 Joel Farrell; 47 Nathan Conroy; 33 Paul Jackson; 8 Stephen Nash.
Tries: Brown (8, 47), Fieldhouse (15), Grant (24), Uaisele (34); **Goals:** Hemingway 1/3, Morton 2/4;
Field goal: Hemingway (77).
TOWN: 1 Jack Murphy; 2 Sam Forrester; 3 Jason Mossop; 12 Jarrad Stack; 22 Elliott Miller; 28 Jarrod Sammut; 33 Jamie Doran; 8 Kris Coward; 14 Callum Phillips; 19 Tom Walker; 11 Brett Phillips; 27 Alex Szostak; 13 Liam McAvoy. Subs (all used): 7 Carl Forber; 15 Karl Olstrum; 4 Perry Whiteley; 25 Steve Scholey.
Tries: Whiteley (44), Miller (62), Sammut (67); **Goals:** Forber 1/3.
Rugby Leaguer & League Express Men of the Match: *Rams:* Aaron Brown; *Town:* Jarrod Sammut.
Penalty count: 9-6; **Half-time:** 20-0;
Referee: Jon Roberts; **Attendance:** 804.

Featherstone's Jordan Baldwinson tackled by London Broncos' Glenn Riley during the Championship Shield Final

FEATHERSTONE ROVERS 20 LONDON BRONCOS 10

ROVERS: 1 Ian Hardman; 5 Ben Blackmore; 6 Paul Sykes; 4 Thomas Minns; 2 Will Sharp; 36 Paul Cooke; 7 Gareth Moore; 8 Jordan Baldwinson; 9 Andy Ellis; 38 Jack Coventry; 13 Tim Spears; 39 Steve Snitch; 15 Jack Bussey. Subs (all used): 32 Sam Day; 28 Will Milner; 35 Luke Cooper; 40 Bradley Knowles-Tagg.
Tries: Sharp (50), Blackmore (62), Milner (63), Coventry (69); **Goals:** Sykes 2/4.
BRONCOS: 26 Sean Morris; 2 Rhys Williams; 5 Ben Hellewell; 32 Elliot Kear; 20 Iliess Macani; 41 Ben Pointer; 19 Joe Keyes; 16 Glenn Riley; 38 James Cunningham; 17 Erjon Dollapi; 11 Daniel Harrison; 15 Matt Garside; 34 Matt Davis. Subs (all used): 35 Andrew Henderson; 40 Sadiq Adebiyi; 36 Jonathan Walker; 23 Toby Everett.
Tries: Hellewell (7), Macani (77); **Goals:** Kear 1/2.
Rugby Leaguer & League Express Men of the Match: *Rovers:* Jack Bussey; *Broncos:* Ben Hellewell.
Penalty count: 6-7; **Half-time:** 0-4;
Referee: Chris Campbell; **Attendance:** 1,587.

SEMI-FINALS

Sunday 27th September 2015

DEWSBURY RAMS 18 LONDON BRONCOS 34

RAMS: 1 Ryan Fieldhouse; 2 Dale Morton; 3 Karl Pryce; 48 Etuate Uaisele; 18 Dalton Grant; 6 Matty Wildie; 7 Anthony Thackeray; 10 Ryan Hepworth; 23 Tom Hemingway; 32 Makali Aizue; 4 Shane Grady; 34 Luke Adamson; 25 Joel Farrell. Subs (all used): 47 Nathan Conroy; 33 Paul Jackson; 15 Jason Crookes; 8 Stephen Nash.
Tries: Thackeray (13), Morton (28), Uaisele (31);
Goals: Hemingway 1/1, Grady 2/3.
BRONCOS: 24 Alex Walker; 2 Rhys Williams; 5 Ben Hellewell; 32 Elliot Kear; 20 Iliess Macani; 7 William Barthau; 19 Joe Keyes; 16 Glenn Riley; 38 James Cunningham; 17 Erjon Dollapi; 11 Daniel Harrison; 15 Matt Garside; 34 Matt Davis. Subs (all used): 35 Andrew Henderson; 29 Jamie Thackray; 23 Toby Everett; 36 Jonathan Walker.
Tries: Hellewell (15), Keyes (35), Macani (39), R Williams (55), Harrison (70, 78); **Goals:** Barthau 5/6.
Rugby Leaguer & League Express Men of the Match: *Rams:* Dale Morton; *Broncos:* Alex Walker.
Penalty count: 8-10; **Half-time:** 16-16;
Referee: Jon Roberts; **Attendance:** 940.

FEATHERSTONE ROVERS 52 WORKINGTON TOWN 14

ROVERS: 1 Ian Hardman; 5 Ben Blackmore; 6 Paul Sykes; 4 Thomas Minns; 2 Will Sharp; 28 Will Milner; 7 Gareth Moore; 8 Jordan Baldwinson; 9 Andy Ellis; 17 Matt James; 13 Tim Spears; 39 Steve Snitch; 15 Jack Bussey. Subs (all used): 26 Kyran Johnson; 40 Bradley Knowles-Tagg; 38 Jack Coventry; 27 Jack Ormondroyd.
Tries: Milner (5), Hardman (19), Blackmore (24), Sykes (30), Knowles-Tagg (40), Ellis (69), Moore (74), Spears (77), Minns (80); **Goals:** Sykes 8/9.
TOWN: 1 Jack Murphy; 24 Theerapol Ritson; 23 Scott Akehurst; 4 Perry Whiteley; 15 Karl Olstrum; 28 Jarrod Sammut; 7 Carl Forber; 8 Kris Coward; 33 Jamie Doran; 19 Tom Walker; 12 Jarrad Stack; 27 Alex Szostak; 13 Liam McAvoy. Subs (only three named): 20 Nathan Lucock; 25 Steve Scholey; 18 Daniel Rooney (not used).
Tries: Stack (37), Sammut (42, 65);
Goals: Forber 0/2, Sammut 1/1.
Rugby Leaguer & League Express Men of the Match: *Rovers:* Will Milner; *Town:* Jarrod Sammut.
Penalty count: 6-7; **Half-time:** 28-4;
Referee: Michael Woodhead; **Attendance:** 1,233.

FINAL

Sunday 4th October 2015

FEATHERSTONE ROVERS 36 LONDON BRONCOS 4

ROVERS: 1 Ian Hardman; 5 Ben Blackmore; 6 Paul Sykes; 4 Thomas Minns; 2 Will Sharp; 28 Will Milner; 7 Gareth Moore; 8 Jordan Baldwinson; 9 Andy Ellis; 17 Matt James; 13 Tim Spears; 39 Steve Snitch; 15 Jack Bussey. Subs (all used): 19 Alex Foster; 40 Bradley Knowles-Tagg; 38 Jack Coventry; 27 Jack Ormondroyd.
Tries: James (10, 59), Blackmore (16), Sykes (36), Hardman (66), Moore (68); **Goals:** Sykes 6/7.
BRONCOS: 26 Sean Morris; 2 Rhys Williams; 5 Ben Hellewell; 32 Elliot Kear; 20 Iliess Macani; 7 William Barthau; 19 Joe Keyes; 16 Glenn Riley; 38 James Cunningham; 29 Jamie Thackray; 11 Daniel Harrison; 15 Matt Garside; 34 Matt Davis. Subs (all used): 35 Andrew Henderson; 18 Jon Wallace; 23 Toby Everett; 36 Jonathan Walker.
Try: R Williams (48); **Goals:** Barthau 0/1.
Rugby Leaguer & League Express Men of the Match: *Rovers:* Gareth Moore; *Broncos:* William Barthau.
Penalty count: 7-7; **Half-time:** 16-0;
Referee: Chris Campbell; **Attendance:** 4,179
(at Select Security Stadium, Widnes).

LEAGUE 1 2015
Club by Club

BARROW RAIDERS

DATE	FIXTURE	RESULT	SCORERS	LGE	ATT
1/3/15	Gloucestershire All Golds (h) (L1CR1)	W16-14	t:Hankinson,Campbell,Bate g:Ward,Fleming	N/A	836
8/3/15	Keighley (h) (CCR3)	W38-22	t:Haney,Ward,Wiper,Heaton,Mossop(2),Campbell(2) g:Hankinson(3)	N/A	929
15/3/15	Oldham (h) (L1CR2)	L10-32	t:Ward,Nicholson g:Ward	N/A	844
22/3/15	Halifax (h) (CCR4)	L16-56	t:Marwood,Pitman,Wiper g:Ward(2)	N/A	956
3/4/15	Newcastle (a)	L34-22	t:Fleming,Haney(2),Bate,Lupton g:Hankinson	10th	1,522
11/4/15	Swinton (h)	W50-12	t:Dolan,Hankinson,Mossop(2),Heaton,D Toal(2),Bullock,Marwood g:Ward(7)	4th	1,064
18/4/15	Rochdale (a)	L48-12	t:Briscoe(2) g:Hankinson(2)	8th	580
25/4/15	South Wales (h)	W86-0	t:D Toal,Campbell(2),Mossop(4),Ward(2),Lupton,Litherland(2),Tyson,S Toal(2) g:Ward(13)	4th	836
3/5/15	North Wales (a)	L24-16	t:Campbell,Tyson,Haney g:Ward(2)	6th	612
9/5/15	Oldham (h)	W30-18	t:Pitman(2),Dolan,Campbell,Litherland,Harrison g:Ward(3)	5th	935
17/5/15	London Skolars (a)	W6-42	t:Pitman,Dawson,Harrison,Ward,Bate,S Toal g:Ward(9)	5th	331
31/5/15	Coventry (a)	W4-22	t:Hankinson,Pitman,Hambley,Litherland g:Ward(3)	5th	552
7/6/15	Keighley (h)	L22-24	t:Tyson,Mossop,Bullock,Lupton g:Ward(3)	8th	1,141
14/6/15	Hemel (a)	W10-38	t:Hankinson(2),Mossop(2),Campbell,Wiper g:Ward(7)	7th	192
20/6/15	Gloucestershire All Golds (h)	W26-18	t:S Toal(2),Hankinson,Lupton,Hambley g:Ward(3)	5th	841
27/6/15	Newcastle (h)	W16-4	t:D Toal,Fleming,Campbell g:Ward(2)	4th	927
5/7/15	Swinton (a)	L30-20	t:Ward,Briscoe,Fleming g:Ward(4)	6th	485
11/7/15	London Skolars (h)	W38-12	t:Harrison,Campbell,Briscoe,Marwood,S Toal,D Toal(2) g:Ward(4),Hankinson	5th	793
18/7/15	North Wales (h)	L6-23	t:Briscoe g:Ward	7th	1,010
25/7/15	Oxford (a) ●	W22-34	t:Tracey,Campbell,Wiper,Ward,Dolan(2) g:Ward(5)	6th	233
1/8/15	Hemel (h)	W44-22	t:Lupton,Briscoe,Duerden,Dolan,Litherland,Marwood,Bullock,Hankinson g:Ward(6)	7th	828
8/8/15	Coventry (h)	W44-22	t:S Toal,Ward,Pitman,Nicholson,Lupton,Hankinson(2),Briscoe g:Ward(6)	6th	848
16/8/15	Keighley (a)	L18-17	t:Crellin,Lupton,Duerden g:Marwood(2) fg:Marwood	6th	903
23/8/15	Oldham (a)	L28-12	t:Wiper,Dolan g:Hankinson(2)	7th	740
5/9/15	Rochdale (h)	W46-28	t:Fleming(2),Mossop,Campbell,Marwood,Ward(2),Hankinson g:Ward(7)	7th	865
13/9/15	York (a) ●●	W16-18	t:Mossop,Pitman(2) g:Ward(2),Hankinson	7th	468

● Played at Prince of Wales Stadium, Cheltenham
●● Played at Elmpark Way, Heworth

		APP		TRIES		GOALS		FG		PTS	
	D.O.B.	ALL	L1	ALL	L1	ALL	L1	ALL	L1	ALL	L1
Anthony Bate	28/4/93	15(5)	12(4)	3	2	0	0	0	0	12	8
Craig Briscoe	8/12/92	23(1)	20(1)	7	7	0	0	0	0	28	28
Joe Bullock	27/11/92	25	21	3	3	0	0	0	0	12	12
Liam Campbell	5/6/86	19(1)	16(1)	12	9	0	0	0	0	48	36
Bradd Crellin	2/7/89	7(12)	6(12)	1	1	0	0	0	0	4	4
Andrew Dawson	12/3/89	(20)	(17)	1	1	0	0	0	0	4	4
Kyle Dolan	22/10/94	13(1)	10(1)	6	6	0	0	0	0	24	24
James Duerden	9/10/91	2(4)	2(4)	2	2	0	0	0	0	8	8
Chris Fleming	11/1/91	16	13	5	5	1	0	0	0	22	20
Joe Hambley	2/12/95	5(3)	5(3)	2	2	0	0	0	0	8	8
Lee Haney	11/6/88	7	6	4	3	0	0	0	0	16	12
Chris Hankinson	30/11/93	25	21	10	9	10	7	0	0	60	50
Liam Harrison	3/12/82	24	21	3	3	0	0	0	0	12	12
Matt Heaton	19/11/94	1(7)	1(4)	2	1	0	0	0	0	8	4
Danny Jones	12/11/92	6(4)	4(2)	0	0	0	0	0	0	0	0
Andy Litherland	15/5/90	14(2)	12(2)	5	5	0	0	0	0	20	20
Peter Lupton	7/3/82	16(8)	13(7)	7	7	0	0	0	0	28	28
Brad Marwood	4/11/93	2(11)	2(10)	5	4	2	2	1	1	25	21
Ruairi McGoff	5/1/85	1	1	0	0	0	0	0	0	0	0
Nathan Mossop	21/2/88	21(5)	19(3)	13	11	0	0	0	0	52	44
Adam Nicholson	22/9/89	8(6)	5(5)	2	1	0	0	0	0	8	4
Cameron Pitman	9/7/89	19	18	8	7	0	0	0	0	32	28
Dan Toal	22/9/89	7(12)	7(10)	6	6	0	0	0	0	24	24
Shane Toal	11/11/95	11	11	7	7	0	0	0	0	28	28
Jamie Tracey	22/4/94	3(1)	3(1)	1	1	0	0	0	0	4	4
Kris Tyson	3/12/94	10	7	3	3	0	0	0	0	12	12
Josh Ward	16/6/95	24	20	10	8	91	87	0	0	222	206
Max Wiper	18/9/90	14	10	5	3	0	0	0	0	20	12

'L1' totals League 1 regular season only; 'All' totals also include League 1 Cup & Challenge Cup

Josh Ward

LEAGUE RECORD
P22-W14-D0-L8 (7th)
F661, A423, Diff+238, 28 points.

LEAGUE 1 CUP
Round Two

CHALLENGE CUP
Round Four

ATTENDANCES
Best - v Keighley (L1 - 1,141)
Worst - v London Skolars (L1 - 793)
Total (League 1/ League 1 Cup only) - 11,768
Average (League 1/ League 1 Cup only) - 905
(Down by 125 on 2014, Championship)

CLUB RECORDS **Highest score:** 138-0 v Nottingham City, 27/11/94 **Highest score against:** 0-90 v Leeds, 11/2/90 **Record attendance:** 21,651 v Salford, 15/4/38

MATCH RECORDS **Tries:** 6 Val Cumberbatch v Batley, 21/11/36; Jim Thornburrow v Maryport, 19/2/38; Steve Rowan v Nottingham City, 15/11/92 **Goals:** 17 Darren Carter v Nottingham City, 27/11/94 **Points:** 42 Darren Carter v Nottingham City, 27/11/94

SEASON RECORDS **Tries:** 50 Jim Lewthwaite 1956-57 **Goals:** 135 Joe Ball 1956-57 **Points:** 323 Jamie Rooney 2010

CAREER RECORDS **Tries:** 352 Jim Lewthwaite 1943-57 **Goals:** 1,099 *(inc 63fg)* Darren Holt 1998-2002; 2004-2009; 2012 **Points:** 2,403 Darren Holt 1998-2002; 2004-2009; 2012 **Appearances:** 500 Jim Lewthwaite 1943-57

COVENTRY BEARS

DATE	FIXTURE	RESULT	SCORERS	LGE	ATT
1/3/15	Oldham (a) (L1CR1)	L42-6	t:Tyers g:Coleman	N/A	291
8/3/15	Oldham (a) (CCR3)	L46-6	t:Cooper g:Coleman	N/A	256
3/4/15	Oxford (h)	W32-10	t:Sheen,Cooper,Medforth(2),Guzdek,Brophy g:Coleman(4)	2nd	721
12/4/15	Oldham (a)	L38-10	t:Reid,Guzdek g:Coleman	9th	322
19/4/15	Hemel (h)	W52-16	t:Sheen(3),Hunte(2),Cooper,Marsh(3) g:Robinson(8)	5th	425
26/4/15	York (a) ●	L42-10	t:Hughes,Hunte g:Coleman	7th	498
3/5/15	Rochdale (h)	L10-35	t:Parker,Boulter g:Coleman	9th	496
10/5/15	Keighley (a)	L52-10	t:Medforth(2) g:Coleman	11th	4,066
16/5/15	Gloucestershire All Golds (a)	L66-6	t:Hunte g:Parker	11th	308
31/5/15	Barrow (h)	L4-22	t:Hunte	11th	552
7/6/15	London Skolars (a)	W20-46	t:Hughes,Parry,Hunte,Cooper,Parker(2),Winfield,Chapman-Carry g:Parker(7)	11th	259
14/6/15	Swinton (h)	L8-78	t:Hunte,Sheen	11th	454
21/6/15	South Wales (a)	W14-42	t:Sheen(2),Hughes,Hunte,Hall,Kelliher,Francis,Evans g:Coleman(3),Parker(2)	9th	307
27/6/15	Oxford (a)	L24-20	t:Coleman,Thompson,Parry g:Parker(4)	10th	502
5/7/15	North Wales (h)	L4-50	t:Cooper	11th	467
12/7/15	Keighley (h)	L10-42	t:Morrison,Bass g:Parker	11th	441
19/7/15	Rochdale (a)	L50-22	t:Phillips,Hughes,Cooper(2) g:Parker(3)	11th	315
26/7/15	Hemel (a)	L16-12	t:Barratt,Parker g:Parker(2)	12th	117
2/8/15	York (h)	L10-38	t:James,Parker g:Parker	13th	442
8/8/15	Barrow (a)	L44-22	t:Hughes,Thompson,Hunte,Francis g:Parker(3)	13th	848
16/8/15	South Wales (h)	W44-18	t:Parker,Harper,Price,Hunte(2),Taylor,Hughes,Thompson g:Parker(6)	10th	200
23/8/15	Newcastle (a)	L24-16	t:Hughes,Unsworth,Boulter g:Price,Parker	11th	503
6/9/15	London Skolars (h)	L18-28	t:Barratt,Morrison,Hunte,Phillips g:Price	12th	400
13/9/15	Gloucestershire All Golds (h)	L22-48	t:Hunte,Parry,Hughes,Parker g:Parker(3)	12th	441

● Played at Clifton Park

		APP		TRIES		GOALS		FG		PTS	
	D.O.B.	ALL	L1	ALL	L1	ALL	L1	ALL	L1	ALL	L1
John Aldred	3/10/89	3	1	0	0	0	0	0	0	0	0
Dylan Bale	23/5/96	(6)	(6)	0	0	0	0	0	0	0	0
Chris Barratt	7/2/93	24	22	2	2	0	0	0	0	8	8
Jason Bass	10/5/96	11	11	1	1	0	0	0	0	4	4
Alex Beddows	1/8/94	2(4)	2(4)	0	0	0	0	0	0	0	0
Cameron Boulter	5/7/96	17	16	2	2	0	0	0	0	8	8
Troy Brophy	21/7/91	5	3	1	1	0	0	0	0	4	4
Alex Brown	2/6/81	6(2)	4(2)	0	0	0	0	0	0	0	0
Alex Calvert	24/3/94	1(3)	(2)	0	0	0	0	0	0	0	0
Reece Chapman-Carry	16/12/95	7	7	1	1	0	0	0	0	4	4
Stephen Coleman	23/2/87	10(6)	8(6)	1	1	13	11	0	0	30	26
Matt Cooper	28/4/88	16(8)	16(6)	7	6	0	0	0	0	28	24
Chris Dixon	26/5/88	4	4	0	0	0	0	0	0	0	0
Morgan Evans	23/3/92	(8)	(8)	1	1	0	0	0	0	4	4
Jack Francis	17/12/92	6(5)	6(5)	2	2	0	0	0	0	8	8
James Geurtjens	28/4/86	16(3)	14(3)	0	0	0	0	0	0	0	0
Josh Guzdek	22/4/95	4	4	2	2	0	0	0	0	8	8
Tom Hall	1/11/93	5(13)	5(13)	1	1	0	0	0	0	4	4
Jordan Harper	11/2/95	2	2	1	1	0	0	0	0	4	4
Elliot Holton	22/7/96	2	2	0	0	0	0	0	0	0	0
Richard Hughes	28/3/93	17(2)	17(2)	8	8	0	0	0	0	32	32
Jamahl Hunte	27/4/94	19	17	13	13	0	0	0	0	52	52
Joel James	17/2/95	5	5	1	1	0	0	0	0	4	4
Kenneth Kelliher	9/10/89	4(5)	4(5)	1	1	0	0	0	0	4	4
Matthew Marsh	21/4/95	3	3	3	3	0	0	0	0	12	12
Andy McGrory	15/11/85	(1)	(1)	0	0	0	0	0	0	0	0
Rob Meadows	18/1/96	(1)	0	0	0	0	0	0	0	0	0
Eddie Medforth	30/3/95	8	6	4	4	0	0	0	0	16	16
Jack Morrison	16/9/92	9(1)	9(1)	2	2	0	0	0	0	8	8
David O'Conner	13/4/91	(1)	(1)	0	0	0	0	0	0	0	0
Dan Parker	11/3/93	20(1)	20(1)	7	7	34	34	0	0	96	96
Ben Parry	6/11/94	9	9	3	3	0	0	0	0	12	12
Simon Phillips	28/4/83	15	13	2	2	0	0	0	0	8	8
Dan Poulton	17/11/81	4	2	0	0	0	0	0	0	0	0
Dan Price	5/10/92	6	6	1	1	2	2	0	0	8	8
Matt Reid	16/9/92	3(3)	3(3)	1	1	0	0	0	0	4	4
Connor Robinson	23/10/94	1(2)	1(2)	0	0	8	8	0	0	16	16
Dan Rundle	30/7/92	3	3	0	0	0	0	0	0	0	0
Billy Sheen	8/12/89	8(2)	7(1)	7	7	0	0	0	0	28	28
Nick Taylor	5/12/93	3(9)	3(8)	1	1	0	0	0	0	4	4
Liam Thompson	7/2/91	19(4)	17(4)	3	3	0	0	0	0	12	12
Ben Tyers	22/3/91	(2)	0	1	0	0	0	0	0	4	0
Andy Unsworth	14/9/92	3(4)	3(4)	1	1	0	0	0	0	4	4
Andy Winfield	8/7/91	12	11	1	1	0	0	0	0	4	4

'L1' totals League 1 regular season only; 'All' totals also include League 1 Cup & Challenge Cup

Andy Winfield

LEAGUE RECORD
P22-W5-D0-L17 (12th)
F430, A775, Diff-345, 10 points.

LEAGUE 1 CUP
Round One

CHALLENGE CUP
Round Three

ATTENDANCES
Best - v Oxford (L1 - 721)
Worst - v South Wales (L1 - 200)
Total (League 1 only) - 5,039
Average (League 1 only) - 458

GLOUCESTERSHIRE ALL GOLDS

DATE	FIXTURE	RESULT	SCORERS	LGE	ATT
1/3/15	Barrow (a) (L1CR1)	L16-14	t:Martin,Mulkeen,Cowburn g:Bradley	N/A	836
8/3/15	Skirlaugh (h) (CCR3)	W66-4	t:Cowburn,Claridge(2),Parry(3),Davies(3),Topham,Pywell,Purslow g:Bradley(7),Cowburn(2)	N/A	87
22/3/15	Hunslet (h) (CCR4)	L10-28	t:Parry,McClean g:Bradley	N/A	137
3/4/15	South Wales (h)	W36-6	t:Bradley,Martin,Mulkeen(2),Vitalini,Topham,Whittel g:Bradley(4)	1st	404
11/4/15	Rochdale (h)	L18-38	t:Pywell,McClean,Mulkeen g:Bradley(3)	6th	218
19/4/15	London Skolars (a)	W10-36	t:Mulkeen(2),Cowburn,Bradley,Murphy,Crowther,Davies g:Bradley(4)	4th	243
26/4/15	Swinton (h)	L18-60	t:Topham,Martin,Murphy g:Bradley(3)	8th	314
3/5/15	Oldham (a)	L33-30	t:Reece,Martin,McClean(2),Mulkeen g:Bradley(5)	8th	413
9/5/15	York (h)	L6-46	t:Vitalini g:Bradley	10th	212
16/5/15	Coventry (h)	W66-6	t:Bowen(3),Pywell(2),Bradley(2),Cowburn,Murphy(2),Mulkeen,Topham g:Bradley(8),Reece	9th	308
31/5/15	Oxford (a)	L20-12	t:Davidson,Murphy g:Bradley(2)	9th	252
6/6/15	Hemel (h)	L30-34	t:Parker,Parry,Cowburn,Vitalini,Bowen g:Bradley(5)	10th	153
13/6/15	Newcastle (a)	L38-6	t:Bradley g:Bradley	10th	452
20/6/15	Barrow (a)	L26-18	t:Mapals,Whittel,Purslow g:Bradley(3)	11th	841
27/6/15	Oldham (h)	L30-42	t:Vitalini,Mapals(3),Purslow g:Bradley(5)	11th	146
5/7/15	South Wales (a)	W16-36	t:Reece,Parry(2),Cowburn,Mulkeen,Davidson,Pywell g:Bradley(4)	10th	211
11/7/15	York (a) ●	L50-10	t:Mulkeen,Cowburn g:Bradley	10th	350
18/7/15	Oxford (h)	W38-24	t:Reece,Parry,Pywell,Whittel,Davidson,Mapals,Vitalini g:Bradley(5)	9th	235
25/7/15	London Skolars (h)	L10-34	t:Okanga-Ajwang,Mapals g:Bradley	9th	233
2/8/15	North Wales (a)	L38-20	t:Parry(2),Mapals g:Leroyer(4)	9th	420
8/8/15	Newcastle (h)	W26-10	t:Pywell,Mapals,Parry(2),Mulkeen g:Davies,Leroyer(2)	9th	265
16/8/15	Hemel (a)	W34-38	t:Davidson(2),Parry(2),O'Keeffe,Whittel,Murphy g:Davies(2),Bradley(3)	9th	277
23/8/15	Swinton (a)	L42-6	t:Leroyer g:Bradley	9th	368
6/9/15	Keighley (h) ●●	L24-48	t:Pywell,Mapals,Davies,Whittel,Davidson g:Bradley(2)	9th	170
13/9/15	Coventry (a)	W22-48	t:Mapals(2),Okanga-Ajwang,Murphy(2),Mulkeen,Davies,Davidson,Pywell g:Bradley(6)	9th	441

● Played at Elmpark Way, Heworth
●● Played at Beavis Memorial Ground, Cinderford

		APP		TRIES		GOALS		FG		PTS	
	D.O.B.	ALL	L1	ALL	L1	ALL	L1	ALL	L1	ALL	L1
Kevin Aparicio	20/9/93	1(2)	1(2)	0	0	0	0	0	0	0	0
Yann Bertrand	12/9/86	4	4	0	0	0	0	0	0	0	0
Mark Bowen	1/5/90	4(2)	4(2)	4	4	0	0	0	0	16	16
Matt Bradley	2/8/91	20(3)	17(3)	5	5	76	67	0	0	172	154
Casey Canterbury	1/1/94	(1)	0	0	0	0	0	0	0	0	0
Scott Claridge	22/1/91	1	0	2	0	0	0	0	0	8	0
Phil Cowburn	15/10/90	24(1)	21(1)	7	5	2	0	0	0	32	20
Jamie Crowther	28/10/92	3(8)	2(6)	1	1	0	0	0	0	4	4
Alex Davidson	1/11/92	8(8)	8(8)	7	7	0	0	0	0	28	28
Courtney Davies	1/7/94	13(1)	10(1)	6	3	3	3	0	0	30	18
Izaak Duffy	16/2/89	5(8)	3(7)	0	0	0	0	0	0	0	0
Brad England	20/11/94	5(2)	5(2)	0	0	0	0	0	0	0	0
Danny Fallon	26/7/95	2(3)	2(3)	0	0	0	0	0	0	0	0
Owain Griffiths	18/7/91	(3)	(3)	0	0	0	0	0	0	0	0
Ash Haynes	11/3/94	4(2)	2(2)	0	0	0	0	0	0	0	0
Yvan Leroyer	29/6/91	4	4	1	1	6	6	0	0	16	16
Lee Mapals	17/7/85	12	12	11	11	0	0	0	0	44	44
Joe Martin	28/3/95	9	8	4	3	0	0	0	0	16	12
Joe McClean	10/8/89	11(9)	11(6)	4	3	0	0	0	0	16	12
Callum Mulkeen	10/12/90	24(1)	21(1)	12	11	0	0	0	0	48	44
Jamie Murphy	29/12/89	13(3)	13(3)	8	8	0	0	0	0	32	32
Graham O'Keeffe	13/5/91	7(5)	7(5)	1	1	0	0	0	0	4	4
Edwin Okanga-Ajwang	29/11/94	8(2)	8(2)	2	2	0	0	0	0	8	8
Yannic Parker	29/12/90	1	1	1	1	0	0	0	0	4	4
Steve Parry	19/10/88	25	22	14	10	0	0	0	0	56	40
Dan Poulton	17/11/81	2(1)	2(1)	0	0	0	0	0	0	0	0
Oliver Purslow	17/9/87	24	21	3	2	0	0	0	0	12	8
Ryan Pywell	26/6/91	23	20	9	8	0	0	0	0	36	32
Nathan Rainer	16/10/89	(5)	(2)	0	0	0	0	0	0	0	0
Lewis Reece	17/6/91	23(1)	20(1)	3	3	1	1	0	0	14	14
Brett Scriven	5/12/78	3(2)	3(2)	0	0	0	0	0	0	0	0
Joel Thomas	11/11/94	3(5)	2(5)	0	0	0	0	0	0	0	0
Toby Topham	28/1/90	8(8)	7(6)	4	3	0	0	0	0	16	12
Chris Vitalini	5/5/87	10(7)	7(7)	5	5	0	0	0	0	20	20
James Walter	11/9/91	(6)	(6)	0	0	0	0	0	0	0	0
Emmerson Whittel	13/9/94	22	19	5	5	0	0	0	0	20	20

'L1' totals League 1 regular season only; 'All' totals also include League 1 Cup & Challenge Cup

Steve Parry

LEAGUE RECORD
P22-W8-D0-L14 (9th)
F562, A677, Diff-115, 16 points.

LEAGUE 1 CUP
Round One

CHALLENGE CUP
Round Four

ATTENDANCES
Best - v South Wales (L1 - 404)
Worst - v Skirlaugh (CC - 87)
Total (League 1 only) - 2,658
Average (League 1 only) - 242
(Up by 31 on 2014)

CLUB RECORDS **Highest score:** 66-4 v Skirlaugh, 8/3/2015; 66-6 v Coventry, 16/5/2015 **Highest score against:** 6-82 v Salford, 21/4/2013 **Record attendance:** 867 v Salford, 21/4/2013

MATCH RECORDS **Tries:** 3 *(4 players)* **Goals:** 8 Matt Bradley v Coventry, 16/5/2015 **Points:** 24 Matt Bradley v Coventry, 16/5/2015

SEASON RECORDS **Tries:** 14 Steve Parry 2015 **Goals:** 76 Matt Bradley 2015 **Points:** 172 Matt Bradley 2015

CAREER RECORDS **Tries:** 23 Phil Cowburn 2013-2015 **Goals:** 153 Matt Bradley 2013-2015 **Points:** 338 Matt Bradley 2013-2015 **Appearances:** 63 Phil Cowburn 2013-2015

HEMEL STAGS

DATE	FIXTURE	RESULT	SCORERS	LGE	ATT
1/3/15	Swinton (a) (L1CR1)	L34-0		N/A	349
8/3/15	Oxford (h) (CCR3)	L10-22	t:Mbaraga,Helliwell g:Gale	N/A	125
3/4/15	London Skolars (a)	W12-34	t:Agoro(2),J O'Callaghan,Helliwell,Olpherts,Anthony g:Swindells(5)	3rd	376
12/4/15	Keighley (h)	L20-54	t:Mbaraga,Anthony,Darby,L O'Callaghan g:Swindells,Jy-mel Coleman	10th	272
19/4/15	Coventry (a)	L52-16	t:Jy-mel Coleman,Brown(2) g:Swindells(2)	10th	425
26/4/15	Oxford (a)	L31-28	t:Brown,Anthony(2),Finigan(2),J O'Callaghan g:Swindells(2)	11th	278
3/5/15	South Wales (h)	W18-6	t:McNamara,Mbaraga,Finigan,Swindells g:Swindells	10th	137
10/5/15	Newcastle (h)	L12-58	t:Brown,Olpherts g:Swindells,Jy-mel Coleman	12th	179
16/5/15	North Wales (a)	L74-14	t:Anthony,Cosgrove(2) g:Jy-mel Coleman	12th	503
31/5/15	Swinton (h)	L8-32	t:Agoro,Chester	12th	154
6/6/15	Gloucestershire All Golds (a)	W30-34	t:Hrbek(3),Woodburn-Hall,Flanagan,Stewart g:Young(5)	12th	153
14/6/15	Barrow (h)	L10-38	t:Anthony,Stewart g:Young	12th	192
21/6/15	York (h)	L10-70	t:Ingarfield,Boyd-Barnes g:Swindells	12th	145
27/6/15	Rochdale (a)	L32-14	t:Mbaraga(2),Brown g:Young	12th	310
5/7/15	London Skolars (h)	L12-26	t:Ingarfield,Hrbek g:Young(2)	12th	481
12/7/15	Newcastle (a)	L40-26	t:Jy-mel Coleman(2),Olpherts,Brown,Anthony g:Young(3)	12th	1,027
19/7/15	South Wales (a)	W28-46	t:Olpherts(3),Crowther,Hrbek,Wilson(2),Woodburn-Hall,Anthony(2) g:Jy-mel Coleman,Lawrence,Woodburn-Hall	12th	175
26/7/15	Coventry (h)	W16-12	t:Lawrence,Ross g:Lawrence(4)	10th	117
1/8/15	Barrow (a)	L44-22	t:Anthony(2),Brown,Cousine g:Lawrence(3)	10th	828
9/8/15	Oldham (h)	L6-70	t:Lloyd-Jones g:Woodburn-Hall	11th	145
16/8/15	Gloucestershire All Golds (h)	L34-38	t:Ross,Anthony(2),Olpherts,Woodburn-Hall,Brown g:Swindells(4),Woodburn-Hall	11th	277
23/8/15	York (a) ●	L50-10	t:Anthony,Lawrence g:Lawrence	12th	384
6/9/15	Oxford (h)	L16-38	t:L O'Callaghan,Fyson,Cousine g:Lawrence,Jy-mel Coleman	13th	144
13/9/15	Keighley (a)	L68-16	t:Woodburn-Hall,Darby,Hrbek g:Lawrence(2)	13th	692

● Played at Elmpark Way, Heworth

		APP		TRIES		GOALS		FG		PTS	
	D.O.B.	ALL	L1	ALL	L1	ALL	L1	ALL	L1	ALL	L1
Mo Agoro	29/1/93	5	5	3	3	0	0	0	0	12	12
Jamaine Akaidere	19/5/91	1	1	0	0	0	0	0	0	0	0
Alex Anthony	24/12/91	19	17	14	14	0	0	0	0	56	56
Adam Booth	13/12/91	(1)	(1)	0	0	0	0	0	0	0	0
Connor Boyd-Barnes	7/4/92	1(2)	1(2)	1	1	0	0	0	0	4	4
Brooke Broughton	30/10/90	1(2)	1(2)	0	0	0	0	0	0	0	0
Michael Brown	9/9/86	24	22	8	8	0	0	0	0	32	32
Mark Castle	19/2/86	4(2)	4(2)	0	0	0	0	0	0	0	0
Ryan Chester	19/3/92	2(15)	2(13)	1	1	0	0	0	0	4	4
Jermaine Coleman	17/6/82	2	0	0	0	0	0	0	0	0	0
Jy-mel Coleman	13/10/88	21	21	3	3	5	5	0	0	22	22
Liam Coleman	17/6/86	(1)	(1)	0	0	0	0	0	0	0	0
Brandon Conway	4/5/95	2	2	0	0	0	0	0	0	0	0
Elliott Cosgrove	31/3/91	1	1	2	2	0	0	0	0	8	8
Thibault Cousine	16/4/93	2(6)	2(6)	2	2	0	0	0	0	8	8
Victor Croker	28/6/91	(2)	(2)	0	0	0	0	0	0	0	0
Jamie Crowther	28/10/92	5(2)	5(2)	1	1	0	0	0	0	4	4
Nathan Darby	12/4/95	1(8)	1(8)	2	2	0	0	0	0	8	8
Vinny Finigan	4/8/89	3	3	3	3	0	0	0	0	12	12
George Flanagan	8/10/86	(2)	(2)	1	1	0	0	0	0	4	4
Ashley Fyson	13/3/85	1	1	1	1	0	0	0	0	4	4
Jordan Gale	30/9/95	2	0	0	0	1	0	0	0	2	0
James Helliwell	27/2/91	21	19	2	1	0	0	0	0	8	4
James Howitt	2/3/83	5(4)	5(3)	0	0	0	0	0	0	0	0
Simon Hrbek	15/10/94	10	10	6	6	0	0	0	0	24	24
Alex Ingarfield	18/10/91	13	11	2	2	0	0	0	0	8	8
Charlie Lawrence	6/10/94	9(9)	9(9)	2	2	12	12	0	0	32	32
Dan Ljazouli	14/8/89	16(1)	16(1)	0	0	0	0	0	0	0	0
Malikhi Lloyd-Jones	29/8/94	3(9)	3(8)	1	1	0	0	0	0	4	4
Jason Long	11/8/94	(1)	(1)	0	0	0	0	0	0	0	0
Frank Mayfield	11/8/82	2	0	0	0	0	0	0	0	0	0
Eddie Mbaraga	9/9/87	20(1)	19(1)	5	4	0	0	0	0	20	16
Miles McLeod	9/11/92	1	1	0	0	0	0	0	0	0	0
Chris McNamara	13/7/88	20	20	1	1	0	0	0	0	4	4
Kaizer Muroi	6/9/96	(2)	(2)	0	0	0	0	0	0	0	0
Jamie O'Callaghan	21/9/90	9	7	2	2	0	0	0	0	8	8
Liam O'Callaghan	24/9/94	6(6)	5(6)	2	2	0	0	0	0	8	8
Derrell Olpherts	7/1/92	22	20	7	7	0	0	0	0	28	28
Aidan Pritchard	1/6/88	2	0	0	0	0	0	0	0	0	0
Lewis Reed	24/3/91	(1)	0	0	0	0	0	0	0	0	0
Jesse Richardson	7/8/93	1	1	0	0	0	0	0	0	0	0
Matt Ross	2/9/92	7(2)	7(2)	2	2	0	0	0	0	8	8
Tom Sadler	30/10/87	1(5)	1(3)	0	0	0	0	0	0	0	0
Mike Stewart	14/2/89	16(4)	15(3)	2	2	0	0	0	0	8	8
Barry-John Swindells	6/4/82	13(2)	11(2)	1	1	17	17	0	0	38	38
Rob Thomas	9/10/90	2(2)	1(2)	0	0	0	0	0	0	0	0
Aston Wilson	23/10/90	1	1	2	2	0	0	0	0	8	8
James Woodburn-Hall	2/2/95	13	13	4	4	3	3	0	0	22	22
Ben Young	16/9/93	6	6	0	0	12	12	0	0	24	24

'L1' totals League 1 regular season only; 'All' totals also include League 1 Cup & Challenge Cup

Derrell Olpherts

LEAGUE RECORD
P22-W5-D0-L17 (13th)
F422, A903, Diff-481, 10 points.

LEAGUE 1 CUP
Round One

CHALLENGE CUP
Round Three

ATTENDANCES
Best - v London Skolars (L1 - 481)
Worst - v Coventry (L1 - 117)
Total (League 1 only) - 2,243
Average (League 1 only) - 204
(Down by 15 on 2014)

CLUB RECORDS **Highest score:** 52-24 v South Wales, 26/5/2013 **Highest score against:** 14-74 v North Wales, 16/5/2015 **Record attendance:** 679 v Oldham, 12/5/2013

MATCH RECORDS **Tries:** 3 *(3 players)* **Goals:** 8 Mike Bishay v South Wales, 26/5/2013; Jy-mel Coleman v Oldham, 8/6/2014 **Points:** 16 Mike Bishay v South Wales, 26/5/2013; Jy-mel Coleman v Oldham, 8/6/2014

SEASON RECORDS **Tries:** 14 Alex Anthony 2015 **Goals:** 62 Barry-John Swindells 2014 **Points:** 160 Barry-John Swindells 2014

CAREER RECORDS **Tries:** 17 Eddie Mbaraga 2013-2015; Barry-John Swindells 2013-2015 **Goals:** 126 Barry-John Swindells 2013-2015 **Points:** 320 Barry-John Swindells 2013-2015 **Appearances:** 56 Barry-John Swindells 2013-2015

KEIGHLEY COUGARS

DATE	FIXTURE	RESULT	SCORERS	LGE	ATT
1/3/15	East Leeds (h) (L1CR1)	W64-0	t:Graham(3),R Sheriffe,Lawton,Lindsay(3),Handforth(2),White g:Jones(10)	N/A	423
8/3/15	Barrow (a) (CCR3)	L38-22	t:Handforth,Lynam,D March,Jode Sheriffe g:Jones(3)	N/A	929
15/3/15	Swinton (h) (L1CR2)	L22-24	t:R Sheriffe,Law,Rawlins,Jesse Sheriffe g:Jones(3)	N/A	472
3/4/15	York (h)	W28-12	t:White(2),Lynam,R Sheriffe,Law g:Jones(4)	4th	903
12/4/15	Hemel (a)	W20-54	t:Lynam(2),Jones,Handforth(2),Barnes(2),Duffy(2),White g:Jones(7)	1st	272
19/4/15	Newcastle (a)	W16-36	t:Barnes,White(3),Jesse Sheriffe,Feather,P March g:Jones(4)	2nd	750
26/4/15	North Wales (h)	W23-22	t:Handforth(3),Gabriel g:Jones(3) fg:Jones	2nd	1,011
10/5/15	Coventry (h)	W52-10	t:Rawlins,Feather(3),P March,Barnes,Jesse Sheriffe,White,Pursglove g:Handforth(8)	1st	4,066
17/5/15	Swinton (a)	L29-16	t:Feather,Pursglove,Handforth g:Handforth(2)	3rd	561
31/5/15	Oldham (h)	W32-24	t:P March,Handforth(2),Lynam,White(2) g:Handforth(4)	3rd	931
7/6/15	Barrow (a)	W22-24	t:Brook,Lynam,White,Handforth g:Handforth(4)	1st	1,141
14/6/15	South Wales (h)	W66-6	t:Lynam,Brook(2),R Sheriffe,Lawton(2),Gabriel(3),Lindsay,Cherryholme,Handforth g:Handforth,Lawton(8)	1st	671
21/6/15	Rochdale (h)	W54-20	t:Handforth,Gabriel(2),White(2),P March,Lynam,Brook,Jesse Sheriffe g:Lawton(9)	1st	907
28/6/15	North Wales (a)	L34-10	t:White,R Sheriffe g:Lawton	2nd	747
5/7/15	Oxford (h)	W44-14	t:Gabriel,White(2),P March,Lynam,R Sheriffe,Lindsay,Barnes g:Handforth(6)	2nd	701
12/7/15	Coventry (a)	W10-42	t:White(2),R Sheriffe,Lynam(2),Brook,Tahraoui,Feather g:Handforth(3),Brook(2)	1st	441
19/7/15	Swinton (h)	L14-22	t:Lee,D March,White g:Brook	2nd	831
26/7/15	Newcastle (h)	W28-10	t:Gabriel,Darville,Brook,Cherryholme,Guzdek g:Lawton(4)	2nd	753
2/8/15	Oldham (a)	L38-8	t:Guzdek,Gabriel	3rd	888
9/8/15	South Wales (a)	W10-48	t:Guzdek(3),White(3),Gabriel(3),Pursglove g:Lawton(4)	3rd	224
16/8/15	Barrow (h)	W18-17	t:White,P March,R Sheriffe,Gabriel g:Lawton	3rd	903
23/8/15	Rochdale (a)	W8-10	t:Tahraoui,Gabriel g:Handforth	3rd	671
31/8/15	London Skolars (a) ●	W16-36	t:Gabriel(2),Barnes,R Sheriffe,Darville,Rawlins,White g:Lawton(4)	2nd	115
6/9/15	Gloucestershire All Golds (a) ●●	W24-48	t:White(2),Rawlins,Darville,Gabriel,Handforth,Feather,Dickinson g:Lawton(8)	2nd	170
13/9/15	Hemel (h)	W68-16	t:Feather(4),Rawlins(2),Gabriel(2),Lynam,Law(2),Handforth,Guzdek g:Lawton(8)	2nd	692
20/9/15	Oldham (a) (PF)	L31-20	t:Bailey,White,Handforth,Gabriel g:Lawton(2)	N/A	1,405
27/9/15	North Wales (h) (SF)	W32-6	t:White(3),Bailey,P March,Gabriel g:Lawton(4)	N/A	1,103
4/10/15	Swinton (POF) ●●●	L28-29	t:Law(2),Lynam,Pursglove,P March g:Lawton(4)	N/A	N/A

● Played at Pennine Way, Hemel
●● Played at Beavis Memorial Ground, Cinderford
●●● Played at Select Security Stadium, Widnes

		APP		TRIES		GOALS		FG		PTS	
	D.O.B.	ALL	L1	ALL	L1	ALL	L1	ALL	L1	ALL	L1
Matthew Bailey	1/12/91	5(18)	5(17)	2	2	0	0	0	0	8	8
Hamish Barnes	22/5/92	13	13	6	6	0	0	0	0	24	24
Adam Brook	29/9/94	9	9	6	6	3	3	0	0	30	30
Neil Cherryholme	20/12/86	8(18)	6(17)	2	2	0	0	0	0	8	8
Liam Darville	7/7/94	9	9	3	3	0	0	0	0	12	12
Tyler Dickinson	18/8/96	9(2)	9(2)	1	1	0	0	0	0	4	4
Gavin Duffy	9/4/87	6	5	2	2	0	0	0	0	8	8
James Feather	15/4/84	21(2)	18(2)	11	11	0	0	0	0	44	44
Andy Gabriel	21/12/93	20	20	21	21	0	0	0	0	84	84
Lewis Graham	3/10/93	2	0	3	0	0	0	0	0	12	0
Josh Guzdek	22/4/95	10	10	6	6	0	0	0	0	24	24
Paul Handforth	6/10/81	22	19	17	14	29	29	0	0	126	114
Danny Jones	6/3/86	7	4	1	1	34	18	1	1	73	41
Sean Kelly	2/4/91	(5)	(3)	0	0	0	0	0	0	0	0
Scott Law	19/2/85	26(2)	25	6	5	0	0	0	0	24	20
Danny Lawton	10/3/90	23	20	3	2	57	57	0	0	126	122
Scott Lee	20/10/94	3(4)	3(4)	1	1	0	0	0	0	4	4
Ashley Lindsay	31/7/83	18(1)	15(1)	5	2	0	0	0	0	20	8
Josh Lynam	16/2/93	20(5)	19(3)	13	12	0	0	0	0	52	48
David March	25/7/79	10(7)	8(7)	2	1	0	0	0	0	8	4
Paul March	25/7/79	9(12)	9(11)	8	8	0	0	0	0	32	32
Adam Mitchell	7/8/81	3	3	0	0	0	0	0	0	0	0
Ryan Patchett	7/10/92	1(1)	1(1)	0	0	0	0	0	0	0	0
Ross Peltier	24/4/92	(4)	(4)	0	0	0	0	0	0	0	0
Oliver Pursglove	18/1/86	20(3)	17(3)	4	4	0	0	0	0	16	16
Brendan Rawlins	28/1/86	24(2)	21(2)	6	5	0	0	0	0	24	20
Jesse Sheriffe	12/1/90	18(1)	15(1)	4	3	0	0	0	0	16	12
Jode Sheriffe	4/7/86	1(10)	1(7)	1	0	0	0	0	0	4	0
Rikki Sheriffe	5/5/84	20	18	9	7	0	0	0	0	36	28
Samir Tahraoui	28/12/90	5(11)	5(11)	2	2	0	0	0	0	8	8
Paul White	7/12/82	25	22	30	29	0	0	0	0	120	116
Daley Williams	15/5/86	1	0	0	0	0	0	0	0	0	0

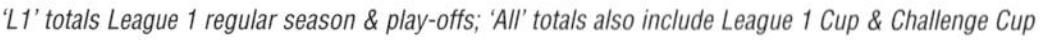
'L1' totals League 1 regular season & play-offs; 'All' totals also include League 1 Cup & Challenge Cup

Danny Jones
1986-2015

LEAGUE RECORD
P22-W18-D0-L4
(2nd/Losers, Play-off Final)
F759, A400, Diff+359, 36 points.

LEAGUE 1 CUP
Round Two

CHALLENGE CUP
Round Three

ATTENDANCES
Best - v Coventry (L1 - 4,066)
Worst - v East Leeds (L1C - 423)
Total (League 1, inc SF, & League 1 Cup only) - 14,367
Average (League 1, inc SF, & League 1 Cup only) - 1,026
(Up by 35 on 2014, Championship)

CLUB RECORDS **Highest score:** 104-4 v Highfield, 23/4/95 **Highest score against:** 2-92 v Leigh, 30/4/86 **Record attendance:** 14,500 v Halifax, 3/3/51

MATCH RECORDS **Tries:** 6 Jason Critchley v Widnes, 18/8/96 **Goals:** 15 John Wasyliw v Nottingham City, 1/11/92; Martyn Wood v Lancashire Lynx, 1/5/2000 **Points:** 36 John Wasyliw v Nottingham City, 1/11/92

SEASON RECORDS **Tries:** 45 Nick Pinkney 1994-95 **Goals:** 187 John Wasyliw 1992-93 **Points:** 490 John Wasyliw 1992-93

CAREER RECORDS **Tries:** 155 Sam Stacey 1904-20 **Goals:** 967 Brian Jefferson 1965-77 **Points:** 2,116 Brian Jefferson 1965-77 **Appearances:** 372 Hartley Tempest 1902-15; David McGoun 1925-38

LONDON SKOLARS

DATE	FIXTURE	RESULT	SCORERS	LGE	ATT
1/3/15	York (h) (L1CR1)	L10-78	t:Fatouri(2) g:Druce	N/A	156
7/3/15	Swinton (h) (CCR3)	L4-86	t:Lovell	N/A	165
3/4/15	Hemel (h)	L12-34	t:Fairhurst(2) g:Druce(2)	12th	376
12/4/15	South Wales (a)	W12-30	t:Anthony(2),Connick,Boot,Burnett g:Connick,Fairhurst(4)	8th	328
19/4/15	Gloucestershire All Golds (h)	L10-36	t:Morgan,Wallace g:Druce	9th	243
26/4/15	Oldham (a)	L48-6	t:Spurr g:Druce	12th	423
10/5/15	Oxford (a)	L38-24	t:Kittrick,Sykes,Cook,Wicks g:M Bishay(4)	13th	255
17/5/15	Barrow (h)	L6-42	t:Benson g:Thomas	13th	331
31/5/15	North Wales (a) ●	L18-10	t:Small,Burnett g:Druce	13th	432
7/6/15	Coventry (h)	L20-46	t:Cook(2),Driver,Morgan g:Druce,Elliott	13th	259
14/6/15	York (a) ●●	L40-10	t:Anthony,Price g:Elliott	13th	401
21/6/15	Newcastle (h)	L12-19	t:Lovell,Wicks g:Elliott(2)	13th	327
28/6/15	South Wales (h)	L20-26	t:Small,Anthony,C Bishay,Coleman g:M Bishay(2)	13th	304
5/7/15	Hemel (a)	W12-26	t:Anthony(2),Price,Bryan g:M Bishay(5)	13th	481
11/7/15	Barrow (a)	L38-12	t:Chisholm,C Bishay g:Druce,M Bishay	13th	793
19/7/15	Oldham (h)	L6-32	t:Cox g:M Bishay	13th	314
25/7/15	Gloucestershire All Golds (a)	W10-34	t:M Bishay,Bryan(2),Driver,Nash,C Bishay g:M Bishay(5)	13th	233
2/8/15	Oxford (h)	W42-12	t:Fatouri,Williams(2),Cook,Driver,Lovell,M Bishay,Paxton g:M Bishay(4),Cook	12th	340
9/8/15	Swinton (a)	L74-4	t:Nash	12th	401
16/8/15	York (h)	L22-30	t:Nash,Bryan,Williams,Martin g:Connick(3)	13th	323
28/8/15	North Wales (h)	L16-24	t:Small(2),Martin g:Connick(2)	13th	1,018
31/8/15	Keighley (h) ●●●	L16-36	t:M Bishay,Williams,Paxton g:M Bishay,Druce	13th	115
6/9/15	Coventry (a)	W18-28	t:Paxton,Williams,Driver(2),Anthony g:Connick(4)	11th	400
12/9/15	Rochdale (a)	L26-22	t:Anthony(3),Morgan g:Connick(3)	11th	305

● Played at The Rock, Wrexham ●● Played at Elmpark Way, Heworth ●●● Played at Pennine Way, Hemel

		APP		TRIES		GOALS		FG		PTS	
	D.O.B.	ALL	L1	ALL	L1	ALL	L1	ALL	L1	ALL	L1
James Anthony	18/2/86	22(1)	21	10	10	0	0	0	0	40	40
Mike Benson	27/11/80	6(6)	5(5)	1	1	0	0	0	0	4	4
Chris Bishay	24/2/87	11	11	3	3	0	0	0	0	12	12
Mike Bishay	8/2/93	16	16	3	3	23	23	0	0	58	58
Oliver Bloom	16/4/86	(4)	(3)	0	0	0	0	0	0	0	0
Craig Boot	10/10/85	2	2	1	1	0	0	0	0	4	4
Chris Brown	7/4/90	1	0	0	0	0	0	0	0	0	0
Lamont Bryan	12/4/88	10(2)	10(2)	4	4	0	0	0	0	16	16
Danny Burke	26/7/86	(3)	(2)	0	0	0	0	0	0	0	0
Harvey Burnett	18/8/95	8	7	2	2	0	0	0	0	8	8
James Carty	13/9/91	2	0	0	0	0	0	0	0	0	0
Dion Chapman	16/2/92	3(1)	3(1)	0	0	0	0	0	0	0	0
Jamel Chisholm	7/11/92	4	4	1	1	0	0	0	0	4	4
Cariern Clement-Pascall	28/9/90	2(2)	2(2)	0	0	0	0	0	0	0	0
Jermaine Coleman	17/6/82	15	15	1	1	0	0	0	0	4	4
Tommy Connick	19/1/90	7	5	1	1	13	13	0	0	30	30
Mathew Cook	28/6/94	18	18	4	4	1	1	0	0	18	18
Anthony Cox	19/1/94	2(12)	(12)	1	1	0	0	0	0	4	4
Billy Driver	18/9/90	(16)	(16)	5	5	0	0	0	0	20	20
Sam Druce	23/9/93	9(1)	7(1)	0	0	9	8	0	0	18	16
Max Edwards	29/11/90	(2)	(2)	0	0	0	0	0	0	0	0
Marcus Elliott	8/3/94	9	9	0	0	4	4	0	0	8	8
Dave Ellison	2/4/82	2(5)	2(3)	0	0	0	0	0	0	0	0
Will Fairhurst	22/2/94	10	8	2	2	4	4	0	0	16	16
Kazeem Fatouri	22/10/93	12(4)	10(4)	3	1	0	0	0	0	12	4
Liam Foran	25/4/88	1	0	0	0	0	0	0	0	0	0
Judd Greenhalgh	16/1/93	3	3	0	0	0	0	0	0	0	0
Josh Kittrick	28/10/94	1	1	1	1	0	0	0	0	4	4
Sebastian Kolasa	27/3/95	2	1	0	0	0	0	0	0	0	0
Will Lovell	10/5/93	20(1)	19(1)	3	2	0	0	0	0	12	8
Will Martin	28/12/93	8(1)	8(1)	2	2	0	0	0	0	8	8
Jimmy Morgan	1/6/93	13	13	3	3	0	0	0	0	12	12
Sam Nash	1/5/89	6	6	3	3	0	0	0	0	12	12
John Paxton	20/4/85	10	10	3	3	0	0	0	0	12	12
Joe Price	7/10/85	13	13	2	2	0	0	0	0	8	8
Lewis Reed	24/3/91	5(5)	5(5)	0	0	0	0	0	0	0	0
Glenn Riley	21/9/92	(1)	(1)	0	0	0	0	0	0	0	0
Louis Robinson	9/1/91	3(11)	1(11)	0	0	0	0	0	0	0	0
Aaron Small	28/10/91	14(7)	12(7)	4	4	0	0	0	0	16	16
Vince Spurr	23/9/90	3	2	1	1	0	0	0	0	4	4
Louie Sutherland	8/2/94	(1)	0	0	0	0	0	0	0	0	0
Michael Sykes	10/12/86	11(8)	11(7)	1	1	0	0	0	0	4	4
Oscar Thomas	3/1/94	1	1	0	0	1	1	0	0	2	2
Jon Wallace	8/10/94	(1)	(1)	1	1	0	0	0	0	4	4
Joel Wicks	27/10/94	7(1)	7(1)	2	2	0	0	0	0	8	8
Dave Williams	29/1/87	20	18	5	5	0	0	0	0	20	20

'L1' totals League 1 regular season only; 'All' totals also include League 1 Cup & Challenge Cup

Lamont Bryan

LEAGUE RECORD
P22-W5-D0-L17 (11th)
F388, A671, Diff-283, 10 points.

LEAGUE 1 CUP
Round One

CHALLENGE CUP
Round Three

ATTENDANCES
Best - v North Wales (L1 - 1,018)
Worst - v Keighley (L1 - 115)
Total (League 1/ League 1 Cup only) - 4,106
Average (League 1/ League 1 Cup only) - 342
(Down by 122 on 2014)

CLUB RECORDS **Highest score:** 70-28 v St Albans, 19/3/2006 **Highest score against:** 4-98 v Sheffield, 3/8/2003 **Record attendance:** 1,427 v Keighley, 29/8/2008

MATCH RECORDS **Tries:** 5 Mark Cantoni v Gateshead, 27/6/2004 **Goals:** 10 Jake Johnstone v Gateshead, 24/8/2003; Dylan Skee v South Wales, 29/7/2012; Dylan Skee v Rochdale, 5/8/2012 **Points:** 28 Dylan Skee v South Wales, 29/7/2012

SEASON RECORDS **Tries:** 20 Mark Cantoni 2004; James Anthony 2013 **Goals:** 100 Dylan Skee 2013 **Points:** 248 Dylan Skee 2013

CAREER RECORDS **Tries:** 57 Austen Aggrey 2004-2012 **Goals:** 230 *(inc 1fg)* Dylan Skee 2011-2013 **Points:** 579 Dylan Skee 2011-2013 **Appearances:** 198 Gareth Honor 2003-2011

NEWCASTLE THUNDER

NEWCASTLE THUNDER

DATE	FIXTURE	RESULT	SCORERS	LGE	ATT
28/2/15	Oxford (a) (L1CR1)	W20-56	t:Kain,Brown,Mapals(3),Wabo,Tali,Beharrell,Hardcastle,Stoker g:Beharrell(8)	N/A	252
7/3/15	Wath Brow (a) (CCR3)	W4-26	t:Meads,Hardcastle,Tali(2),Beharrell g:Hardcastle(3)	N/A	400
15/3/15	York (a) (L1CR2) ●	W24-38	t:Hardcastle,Mapals,Tali,Mexico,Payne,Wabo g:Hardcastle(7)	N/A	358
22/3/15	Dewsbury (a) (CCR4)	L28-18	t:Stamp,Capper,Hardcastle g:Hardcastle(3)	N/A	703
3/4/15	Barrow (h)	W34-22	t:Tali(3),Hardcastle,Sheriff,Fewlass g:Hardcastle(5)	5th	1,522
7/4/15	Swinton (a) (L1CSF)	L36-28	t:Meads(3),Sheriff,Wabo g:Beharrell(4)	N/A	351
12/4/15	North Wales (a)	W18-24	t:Craig,Mapals,Sheriff,Simons g:Hardcastle(4)	3rd	789
19/4/15	Keighley (h)	L16-36	t:Tali,Meads(2) g:Hardcastle(2)	6th	750
26/4/15	Rochdale (a)	W15-16	t:Mapals,Meads,Brown,Craig	3rd	411
3/5/15	Oxford (h)	W36-20	t:Tali(2),Kain,Craig(2),Meads,Capper g:Craig(4)	3rd	552
10/5/15	Hemel (a)	W12-58	t:Craig(2),Blair(2),Beharrell,Simons,Marsh(3),Holker g:Beharrell(9)	3rd	179
17/5/15	Oldham (a)	L45-20	t:Craig(2),Brown,Payne g:Beharrell(2)	4th	491
29/5/15	York (h)	W32-14	t:Hallett,Sheriff(2),Beharrell,Marsh g:Beharrell(5),Craig	4th	2,576
7/6/15	Swinton (a)	L44-32	t:Hallett(2),Sheriff,Marsh,Stamp(2) g:Beharrell(4)	4th	455
13/6/15	Gloucestershire All Golds (h)	W38-6	t:Hallett(3),Payne,Bowring(2),Craig,Clarke g:Beharrell(3)	4th	452
21/6/15	London Skolars (a)	W12-19	t:Marsh,Clarke,Simons g:Beharrell(3) fg:Beharrell	3rd	327
27/6/15	Barrow (a)	L16-4	t:Blair	6th	927
5/7/15	Rochdale (h)	L28-32	t:Capper,Brown,Blair,Beharrell,Marsh g:Beharrell(4)	7th	678
12/7/15	Hemel (h)	W40-26	t:Hardcastle,Wabo,Blades,Craig(2),Kain,Blair g:Beharrell(6)	7th	1,027
19/7/15	York (a) ●●	L40-8	t:Craig,Hallett	8th	430
26/7/15	Keighley (a)	L28-10	t:Hallett,Simons g:Beharrell	8th	753
2/8/15	Swinton (h)	L18-30	t:Welsh,Blair,Hallett,Sheriff g:Craig	8th	514
8/8/15	Gloucestershire All Golds (a)	L26-10	t:Tali,Hallett g:Hardcastle	8th	265
16/8/15	Oldham (h)	L16-28	t:Hardcastle,Hallett,Tali g:Hardcastle(2)	8th	1,003
23/8/15	Coventry (h)	W24-16	t:Tali,Wabo,Simons,Sheriff g:Hardcastle(4)	8th	503
6/9/15	South Wales (a)	W16-50	t:Tali(2),Barron,Capper,Craig(3),Beharrell,Wabo g:Hardcastle(7)	8th	160
13/9/15	North Wales (h)	L22-50	t:Tali,Craig,Esslemont,Beharrell g:Hardcastle(3)	8th	810

● Played at Clifton Park
●● Played at Elmpark Way, Heworth

		APP		TRIES		GOALS		FG		PTS	
	D.O.B.	ALL	L1	ALL	L1	ALL	L1	ALL	L1	ALL	L1
Matt Barron	17/11/86	20(2)	18(1)	1	1	0	0	0	0	4	4
Matty Beharrell	29/3/94	24(2)	19(2)	7	5	49	37	1	1	127	95
Jacob Blades	9/8/93	8	8	1	1	0	0	0	0	4	4
Ali Blair	21/2/90	19	19	6	6	0	0	0	0	24	24
Craig Boot	10/10/85	1(2)	(2)	0	0	0	0	0	0	0	0
Sam Bowring	1/7/91	4(3)	4(3)	2	2	0	0	0	0	8	8
Joe Brown	24/4/87	24	19	4	3	0	0	0	0	16	12
Tom Capper	10/10/92	13	9	4	3	0	0	0	0	16	12
Rhys Clarke	12/3/91	16(3)	11(3)	2	2	0	0	0	0	8	8
Dayne Craig	2/4/90	25	20	16	16	6	6	0	0	76	76
Sonny Esslemont	29/12/93	11(4)	10(2)	1	1	0	0	0	0	4	4
Lee Fewlass	29/4/89	8(13)	4(13)	1	1	0	0	0	0	4	4
Josh Guzdek	22/4/95	2	2	0	0	0	0	0	0	0	0
Macauley Hallett	27/11/95	12	12	11	11	0	0	0	0	44	44
Benn Hardcastle	4/1/90	16	12	7	3	41	28	0	0	110	68
Stephen Holker	22/11/95	1(3)	1(3)	1	1	0	0	0	0	4	4
Ricky Hough	22/8/95	(1)	(1)	0	0	0	0	0	0	0	0
Stuart Kain	18/9/85	8(1)	7(1)	3	2	0	0	0	0	12	8
Ryan MacDonald	24/2/78	(4)	(4)	0	0	0	0	0	0	0	0
Lee Mapals	17/7/85	9	4	6	2	0	0	0	0	24	8
Matthew Marsh	21/4/95	9	9	7	7	0	0	0	0	28	28
Sebastien Martins	18/11/84	9(3)	9(3)	0	0	0	0	0	0	0	0
Jordan Meads	16/2/92	12	7	8	4	0	0	0	0	32	16
Mark Mexico	21/5/89	13(5)	10(4)	1	0	0	0	0	0	4	0
Iain Murray	9/5/90	(1)	(1)	0	0	0	0	0	0	0	0
Jason Payne	20/1/88	14(2)	10(2)	3	2	0	0	0	0	12	8
Stewart Sanderson	10/4/85	2	2	0	0	0	0	0	0	0	0
Louis Sheriff	6/9/92	14(6)	13(2)	8	7	0	0	0	0	32	28
Evan Simons	11/10/91	15(9)	15(7)	5	5	0	0	0	0	20	20
Paul Stamp	25/1/89	4(8)	3(6)	3	2	0	0	0	0	12	8
Josh Stoker	26/7/92	3(15)	3(11)	1	0	0	0	0	0	4	0
Jason Tali	7/7/89	15	10	16	12	0	0	0	0	64	48
Dan Turland	11/1/94	1(1)	1(1)	0	0	0	0	0	0	0	0
Charlie Wabo	19/9/83	13(5)	9(5)	6	3	0	0	0	0	24	12
Francis Welsh	9/11/92	6(15)	6(11)	1	1	0	0	0	0	4	4

'L1' totals League 1 regular season only; 'All' totals also include League 1 Cup & Challenge Cup

Charlie Wabo

LEAGUE RECORD
P22-W11-D0-L11 (8th)
F555, A552, Diff+3, 22 points.

LEAGUE 1 CUP
Semi-Finalists

CHALLENGE CUP
Round Four

ATTENDANCES
Best - v York (L1 - 2,576)
Worst - v Gloucestershire All Golds (L1 - 452)
Total (League 1 only) - 10,387
Average (League 1 only) - 944
(Up by 661 on 2014)

CLUB RECORDS **Highest score:** 66-6 v Wakefield, 5/9/99; 66-6 v London Skolars, 29/6/2014 **Highest score against:** 0-132 v Blackpool Panthers, 16/5/2010 **Record attendance:** 6,631 v Bradford, 16/5/99

MATCH RECORDS **Tries:** 5 Andy Walker v London Skolars, 22/6/2003 **Goals:** 11 Ian Herron v Wakefield, 5/9/99 **Points:** 26 Ian Herron v Wakefield, 5/9/99

SEASON RECORDS **Tries:** 25 Matt Daylight 1999 **Goals:** 129 *(inc 1fg)* Dan Russell 2008 **Points:** 293 Dan Russell 2008

CAREER RECORDS **Tries:** 74 Kevin Neighbour 2001-2006; 2008-2010 **Goals:** 151 Paul Thorman 2001-2004 **Points:** 387 Paul Thorman 2001-2004 **Appearances:** 218 Robin Peers 2002-2012

NORTH WALES CRUSADERS

DATE	FIXTURE	RESULT	SCORERS	LGE	ATT
28/2/15	West Hull (a) (L1CR1)	W10-36	t:Turner(2),Massam,Smith(2),Johnson,Wright g:Johnson(4)	N/A	150
8/3/15	West Bank Bears (h) (CCR3)	W60-12	t:Thompson,Smith,Dallimore,Turner,Johnson(2),Davies,Ashall,Mort,Burke g:Johnson(8),Turner(2)	N/A	523
15/3/15	Rochdale (h) (L1CR2)	W28-4	t:Dallimore,Middlehurst,Turner(2),Ashall g:Johnson(4)	N/A	465
22/3/15	Doncaster (h) (CCR4)	W40-12	t:Thompson,Reardon,Johnson,Massam(4) g:Johnson(6)	N/A	416
3/4/15	Swinton (a)	D14-14	t:Smith,Turner g:Johnson(3)	7th	561
8/4/15	Oldham (a) (L1CSF)	W16-18	t:Massam,Duffy,Dallimore g:Johnson(3)	N/A	444
12/4/15	Newcastle (h)	L18-24	t:King,Reardon,Smith g:Johnson(3)	11th	789
19/4/15	Featherstone (h) (CCR5)	L12-38	t:Dallimore,Johnson g:Johnson(2)	N/A	617
26/4/15	Keighley (a)	L23-22	t:Penny,Massam,Smith g:Johnson(5)	13th	1,011
3/5/15	Barrow (h)	W24-16	t:Dallimore(2),Thompson,King g:Johnson(4)	11th	612
10/5/15	South Wales (a) ●	W18-50	t:Thompson,Dallimore,O'Brien,Davies,Johnson,Smith(2),Reardon,Massam g:Johnson(7)	7th	1,025
16/5/15	Hemel (h)	W74-14	t:Mort,Smith(5),Massam(3),Thompson,Wild,Ashall,Wright g:Mort(11)	6th	503
23/5/15	Swinton (L1CF) ●●	W14-8	t:Turner,Dallimore g:Johnson(3)	N/A	1,200
31/5/15	London Skolars (h) ●●●	W18-10	t:Massam(2),Peet g:Johnson(3)	6th	432
7/6/15	Oldham (a)	W28-38	t:Thompson,Dallimore,Penny(2),Smith,Wild,Johnson g:Johnson(5)	5th	671
14/6/15	Rochdale (h) ●●●	L12-14	t:Massam,Wild g:Johnson(2)	8th	661
21/6/15	Oxford (a)	W12-36	t:Dallimore(2),White,Jullien,Massam,Johnson g:Johnson(2),Turner(4)	7th	357
28/6/15	Keighley (h)	W34-10	t:Turner(2),Hudson,Massam,Smith,Burke g:Johnson(5)	7th	747
5/7/15	Coventry (a)	W4-50	t:Smith(2),Massam(3),Ashall(2),Peet,Johnson g:Johnson(7)	4th	467
12/7/15	South Wales (h)	W56-10	t:Peet,Wild(2),Dallimore(2),Turner(2),Moulsdale,Smith,Johnson g:Johnson(8)	3rd	703
18/7/15	Barrow (a)	W6-23	t:Dallimore,Turner,Smith,Burke g:Johnson(3) fg:Middlehurst	3rd	1,010
26/7/15	Oldham (h)	L6-23	t:Evans g:Johnson	4th	905
2/8/15	Gloucestershire All Golds (h)	W38-20	t:Turner,Burke,Reid(2),Massam(4) g:Johnson(3)	4th	420
9/8/15	Rochdale (a)	L19-18	t:Jullien(2),Oakden,Massam g:Johnson	7th	530
16/8/15	Swinton (h)	L14-30	t:Massam(2),Roets g:Johnson	7th	737
20/8/15	York (a) ●●●●	W28-30	t:Oakden(2),Massam,Jullien(2) g:Johnson(5)	6th	607
28/8/15	London Skolars (a)	W16-24	t:Jullien(2),Joy,Duffy,Dallimore g:Johnson(2)	5th	1,018
6/9/15	York (h)	L28-30	t:Oakden,Burke,Roets,Johnson,Reid g:Johnson(4)	5th	720
13/9/15	Newcastle (a)	W22-50	t:Walker,Massam(2),Johnson,Oakden(3),Roets,Hudson g:Johnson(4),Dallimore(3)	5th	810
27/9/15	Keighley (a) (SF)	L32-6	t:Thompson g:Johnson	N/A	1,103

● Played at Cardiff Arms Park ●● Played at Bloomfield Road, Blackpool ●●● Played at The Rock, Wrexham ●●●● Played at Elmpark Way, Heworth

		APP		TRIES		GOALS		FG		PTS	
	D.O.B.	ALL	L1	ALL	L1	ALL	L1	ALL	L1	ALL	L1
Karl Ashall	3/11/89	21(6)	16(4)	5	3	0	0	0	0	20	12
Joe Burke	18/5/90	28(2)	21(2)	5	4	0	0	0	0	20	16
Jamie Dallimore	20/8/88	29	22	15	10	3	3	0	0	66	46
Elliott Davies	15/9/91	1(18)	1(13)	2	1	0	0	0	0	8	4
Ryan Duffy	13/5/93	7(23)	7(16)	2	1	0	0	0	0	8	4
Rhys Evans	30/10/92	1	1	1	1	0	0	0	0	4	4
Mark Hobson	14/1/87	3(14)	2(10)	0	0	0	0	0	0	0	0
Lee Hudson	28/9/90	10(9)	10(8)	2	2	0	0	0	0	8	8
Tommy Johnson	19/4/91	29	22	12	7	109	79	0	0	266	186
Andrew Joy	7/2/94	(8)	(7)	1	1	0	0	0	0	4	4
Benjamin Jullien	1/3/95	14	14	7	7	0	0	0	0	28	28
George King	24/2/95	(5)	(4)	2	2	0	0	0	0	8	8
Rob Massam	29/11/87	26	20	29	23	0	0	0	0	116	92
Gary Middlehurst	24/10/83	18	12	1	0	0	0	1	1	5	1
Paddy Mooney	28/3/94	(1)	0	0	0	0	0	0	0	0	0
Ian Mort	21/6/88	4(1)	3	2	1	11	11	0	0	30	26
Andy Moulsdale	22/1/87	7(4)	7(4)	1	1	0	0	0	0	4	4
Gareth O'Brien	31/10/91	2	2	1	1	0	0	0	0	4	4
Andrew Oakden	8/8/93	8(1)	8(1)	7	7	0	0	0	0	28	28
Gene Ormsby	12/9/92	1(1)	(1)	0	0	0	0	0	0	0	0
Declan Patton	23/5/95	1(1)	1	0	0	0	0	0	0	0	0
Sam Peet	21/2/94	7(5)	7(5)	3	3	0	0	0	0	12	12
Kevin Penny	3/10/87	4	4	3	3	0	0	0	0	12	12
Joe Philbin	16/11/94	1(2)	1(2)	0	0	0	0	0	0	0	0
Stuart Reardon	13/10/81	15	9	3	2	0	0	0	0	12	8
Matt Reid	16/9/92	8(5)	7(4)	3	3	0	0	0	0	12	12
Christiaan Roets	5/9/80	20(1)	15(1)	3	3	0	0	0	0	12	12
Jono Smith	12/11/88	20	14	19	16	0	0	0	0	76	64
Alex Thompson	11/2/90	18(2)	13(1)	7	5	0	0	0	0	28	20
Scott Turner	7/5/94	15	10	13	7	6	4	0	0	64	36
Jonny Walker	26/9/86	28(1)	21(1)	1	1	0	0	0	0	4	4
Gary Wheeler	30/9/89	1	1	0	0	0	0	0	0	0	0
Craig White	13/1/88	5(1)	2	1	1	0	0	0	0	4	4
Stephen Wild	26/4/81	24	18	5	5	0	0	0	0	20	20
Callum Wright	18/10/94	14(7)	8(6)	2	1	0	0	0	0	8	4

'L1' totals League 1 regular season & semi-final; 'All' totals also include League 1 Cup & Challenge Cup

Rob Massam

LEAGUE RECORD
P22-W14-D1-L7 (5th/Semi-Finalists)
F677, A391, Diff+286, 29 points.

LEAGUE 1 CUP
Winners

CHALLENGE CUP
Round Five

ATTENDANCES
Best - v Oldham (L1 - 905)
Worst - v Doncaster (CC - 416)
Total (League 1/ League 1 Cup only) - 7,694
Average (League 1/ League 1 Cup only) - 641
(Down by 205 on 2014, Championship)

CLUB RECORDS **Highest score:** 82-6 v West Hull, 6/4/2013 **Highest score against:** 4-98 v Wigan, 15/4/2012 **Record attendance:** 1,562 v South Wales, 1/9/2013

MATCH RECORDS **Tries:** 5 Rob Massam v Rochdale, 30/6/2013; Jono Smith v Hemel, 16/5/2015 **Goals:** 11 Tommy Johnson v West Hull, 6/4/2013; Ian Mort v Hemel, 16/5/2015 **Points:** 30 Tommy Johnson v West Hull, 6/4/2013

SEASON RECORDS **Tries:** 29 Rob Massam 2015 **Goals:** 109 Tommy Johnson 2015 **Points:** 266 Tommy Johnson 2015

CAREER RECORDS **Tries:** 75 Rob Massam 2012-2015 **Goals:** 320 Tommy Johnson 2012-2015 **Points:** 780 Tommy Johnson 2012-2015 **Appearances:** 98 Tommy Johnson 2012-2015

OLDHAM

DATE	FIXTURE	RESULT	SCORERS	LGE	ATT
1/3/15	Coventry (h) (L1CR1)	W42-6	t:Neal,Holmes,Clay(2),Mason,J Ward(2) g:Palfrey(7)	N/A	291
8/3/15	Coventry (h) (CCR3)	W46-6	t:Gee,J Ward,Tyson,Thompson,M Ward,Clay(2),Learmonth,Holmes g:Palfrey(5)	N/A	256
15/3/15	Barrow (a) (L1CR2)	W10-32	t:M Ward,Clay(2),Broughton(2),Gee g:Palfrey(4)	N/A	844
22/3/15	Sheffield (a) (CCR4) ●	L44-20	t:Learmonth,Clay,Crowley(2) g:Palfrey,Roper	N/A	484
3/4/15	Rochdale (a)	W16-23	t:Crowley(2),Palfrey g:Palfrey(5) fg:Roper	6th	1,201
8/4/15	North Wales (h) (L1CSF)	L16-18	t:Tyson,Langtree g:Palfrey(4)	N/A	444
12/4/15	Coventry (h)	W38-10	t:Holmes(2),M Ward,Ford,Ashton,R Joy,Johnson g:Roper(5)	2nd	322
19/4/15	South Wales (a)	W12-50	t:Mason,Tyson(2),Ford(2),Holmes(2),J Ward,Langtree(2) g:Palfrey(5)	1st	224
26/4/15	London Skolars (h)	W48-6	t:Tyson(2),Thompson,Ford(4),R Joy,Dempsey g:Palfrey(6)	1st	423
3/5/15	Gloucestershire All Golds (h)	W33-30	t:Nield(3),Johnson,Gee,Thompson g:Palfrey(2),Dempsey(2) fg:Dempsey	1st	413
9/5/15	Barrow (a)	L30-18	t:Clay(2),Holmes,Owen g:Palfrey	2nd	935
17/5/15	Newcastle (h)	W45-20	t:Roper,Owen,Clay(3),Langtree,Nield,Palfrey g:Palfrey(6) fg:Palfrey	1st	491
31/5/15	Keighley (a)	L32-24	t:Roper,Roberts,Palfrey,Crowley g:Palfrey(4)	2nd	931
7/6/15	North Wales (h)	L28-38	t:Crowley(2),Palfrey,Roberts,Holmes g:Palfrey(4)	3rd	671
14/6/15	Oxford (h)	W64-0	t:Clay(2),P Joy,Holmes(3),Files,Owen,Tyson(2),Thompson,Hughes g:Palfrey(8)	3rd	433
21/6/15	Swinton (a)	W26-32	t:Langtree,Tyson(2),Crowley,Clay g:Palfrey(6)	2nd	625
27/6/15	Gloucestershire All Golds (a)	W30-42	t:Clay(2),P Joy,Hewitt(2),Langtree,Holmes g:Palfrey(7)	1st	146
5/7/15	York (h)	W34-12	t:Langtree,M Ward,Holmes,P Joy,Crowley(2) g:Palfrey(5)	1st	581
12/7/15	Rochdale (h)	W38-18	t:Clay,Connor,Palfrey,Fairbank,Gee,Owen,Crowley g:Palfrey(5)	2nd	725
19/7/15	London Skolars (a)	W6-32	t:Palfrey(2),M Ward(2),Roper,Thompson g:Palfrey(4)	1st	314
26/7/15	North Wales (a)	W6-23	t:Neal,Gee,Tyson g:Palfrey(5) fg:Roper	1st	905
2/8/15	Keighley (h)	W38-8	t:Gee,Lepori,Holmes,Palfrey,Langtree,Thompson g:Palfrey(7)	1st	888
9/8/15	Hemel (a)	W6-70	t:Owen,Langtree(2),M Ward(2),Hewitt,Tyson,Thompson,Palfrey(3),Gee g:Palfrey(11)	1st	145
16/8/15	Newcastle (a)	W16-28	t:Ford(2),Hewitt,Liku,Ashton g:Palfrey(4)	1st	1,003
23/8/15	Barrow (h)	W28-12	t:Ashton,M Ward(2),Hewitt,Thompson g:Palfrey(4)	1st	740
6/9/15	Swinton (h)	W28-16	t:Lepori,Roper,Langtree(2),Clay g:Palfrey(4)	1st	1,004
12/9/15	Oxford (a)	W12-76	t:Crowley(2),Ford,Hope(2),P Joy(2),Hughes,Liku,Holmes,Files(2),Dempsey g:Roper(12)	1st	246
20/9/15	Keighley (h) (PF)	W31-20	t:Ford,Neal,Langtree,Tyson,Clay g:Palfrey(5) fg:Palfrey	N/A	1,405

● Played at Keepmoat Stadium, Doncaster

		APP		TRIES		GOALS		FG		PTS	
	D.O.B.	ALL	L1	ALL	L1	ALL	L1	ALL	L1	ALL	L1
Tom Ashton	26/6/92	6	6	3	3	0	0	0	0	12	12
Jodie Broughton	9/1/88	1	0	2	0	0	0	0	0	8	0
Adam Clay	7/10/90	23	18	20	13	0	0	0	0	80	52
Jake Connor	18/10/94	2	2	1	1	0	0	0	0	4	4
Josh Crowley	24/9/91	27(1)	23	13	11	0	0	0	0	52	44
Tom Dempsey	9/11/96	7(1)	7(1)	2	2	2	2	1	1	13	13
Jacob Fairbank	4/3/90	1	1	1	1	0	0	0	0	4	4
Adam Files	7/1/93	(24)	(19)	3	3	0	0	0	0	12	12
Jonathan Ford	1/11/93	16	15	11	11	0	0	0	0	44	44
Sam Gee	28/2/87	19(3)	14(3)	7	5	0	0	0	0	28	20
Dave Hewitt	4/11/95	6	6	5	5	0	0	0	0	20	20
Jack Holmes	5/1/94	22	17	15	13	0	0	0	0	60	52
Will Hope	2/6/93	3	3	2	2	0	0	0	0	8	8
Kenny Hughes	30/3/90	3(21)	3(17)	2	2	0	0	0	0	8	8
Josh Johnson	25/7/94	5	4	2	2	0	0	0	0	8	8
Phil Joy	4/9/91	26(1)	21(1)	5	5	0	0	0	0	20	20
Richard Joy	7/2/94	1(5)	1(5)	2	2	0	0	0	0	8	8
Danny Langtree	18/2/91	24	22	13	12	0	0	0	0	52	48
Mick Learmonth	8/2/95	(2)	0	2	0	0	0	0	0	8	0
Richard Lepori	22/10/91	7	7	2	2	0	0	0	0	8	8
Elliot Liku	21/4/96	(4)	(4)	2	2	0	0	0	0	8	8
Nathan Mason	8/9/93	4(12)	4(9)	2	1	0	0	0	0	8	4
Adam Neal	21/5/90	24	19	3	2	0	0	0	0	12	8
Steven Nield	20/11/90	8	7	4	4	0	0	0	0	16	16
Gareth Owen	3/7/92	25	20	5	5	0	0	0	0	20	20
Lewis Palfrey	25/2/90	26	21	11	11	129	108	2	2	304	262
Oliver Roberts	24/12/95	5(3)	4(3)	2	2	0	0	0	0	8	8
Steve Roper	10/11/86	21	16	4	4	18	17	2	2	54	52
Liam Thompson	3/1/92	17(10)	13(9)	8	7	0	0	0	0	32	28
George Tyson	1/10/93	23	18	13	11	0	0	0	0	52	44
Jarrod Ward	21/10/93	12	7	4	1	0	0	0	0	16	4
Michael Ward	10/2/91	(25)	(21)	10	8	0	0	0	0	40	32

'L1' totals League 1 regular season & Promotion Final; 'All' totals also include League 1 Cup & Challenge Cup

Sam Gee

LEAGUE RECORD
P22-W19-D0-L3
(1st/Winners, Promotion Final)
F840, A362, Diff+478, 38 points.

LEAGUE 1 CUP
Semi-Finalists

CHALLENGE CUP
Round Four

ATTENDANCES
Best - v Keighley (L1PF - 1,405)
Worst - v Coventry (CC - 256)
Total (League 1, inc PF, & League 1 Cup only) - 8,831
Average (League 1, inc PF, & League 1 Cup only) - 631
(Up by 132 on 2014)

CLUB RECORDS **Highest score:** 80-6 v Blackwood, 7/3/2010 **Highest score against:** 0-84 v Widnes, 25/7/99
Record attendance: 28,000 v Huddersfield, 24/2/1912 *(Watersheddings)*; 1,405 v Keighley, 20/9/2015 *(Whitebank Stadium)*

MATCH RECORDS **Tries:** 7 James Miller v Barry, 31/10/1908 **Goals:** 14 Bernard Ganley v Liverpool City, 4/4/59
Points: 34 Andy Ballard v London Skolars, 2/5/2009; Chris Baines v Hunslet, 20/9/2009; Lewis Palfrey v Hemel, 9/8/2015

SEASON RECORDS **Tries:** 49 Reg Farrar 1921-22 **Goals:** 200 Bernard Ganley 1957-58 **Points:** 412 Bernard Ganley 1957-58

CAREER RECORDS **Tries:** 174 Alan Davies 1950-61 **Goals:** 1,358 Bernard Ganley 1951-61 **Points:** 2,761 Bernard Ganley 1951-61 **Appearances:** 627 Joe Ferguson 1899-1923

OXFORD

DATE	FIXTURE	RESULT	SCORERS	LGE	ATT
28/2/15	Newcastle (h) (L1CR1)	L20-56	t:S Morris,Jones-Bishop,Watkins,Brooker g:Allan(2)	N/A	252
8/3/15	Hemel (a) (CCR3)	W10-22	t:Hoggins(2),Brooker,Allan,Jones-Bishop g:Allan	N/A	125
21/3/15	Leigh Miners Rangers (a) (CCR4) ●	L32-6	t:Payne g:Allan	N/A	787
3/4/15	Coventry (a)	L32-10	t:J Scott,Brooker g:Allan	13th	721
12/4/15	York (h)	L20-44	t:Conroy,Hoggins(2),Payne g:Allan(2)	13th	200
26/4/15	Hemel (h)	W31-28	t:Brook,S Morris,Brooker,Conroy(2),Richards g:Barlow(3) fg:Barlow	10th	278
3/5/15	Newcastle (a)	L36-20	t:Petersen,Thomas,S Morris(2) g:Kitson(2)	12th	552
10/5/15	London Skolars (h)	W38-24	t:Hoggins,Blythe,K Davies,Thomas,Gardiner(2),Jones-Bishop g:Brook(5)	9th	255
16/5/15	Rochdale (a)	L76-16	t:Hoggins,Nasso,Gardiner g:Kitson(2)	10th	652
31/5/15	Gloucestershire All Golds (h)	W20-12	t:Hoggins,J Scott,Jones-Bishop,Matthews g:Kitson(2)	10th	252
7/6/15	South Wales (h)	W38-30	t:J Scott,Matthews(3),Evans,Blythe,Thomas g:Richards(5)	9th	286
14/6/15	Oldham (a)	L64-0		9th	433
21/6/15	North Wales (h)	L12-36	t:Halafihi,Thomas g:Kitson(2)	10th	357
27/6/15	Coventry (h)	W24-20	t:Mignacca,Kitson(3),Matthews g:Kitson,Richards	9th	502
5/7/15	Keighley (a)	L44-14	t:S Morris,Jones-Bishop,Brooker g:Kitson	9th	701
12/7/15	Swinton (h) ●●	L4-96	t:Withington	9th	497
18/7/15	Gloucestershire All Golds (a)	L38-24	t:Kitson(2),Nathaniel,Hoggins,Tyson-Wilson g:Kitson(2)	10th	235
25/7/15	Barrow (h) ●●●	L22-34	t:Cook,Hoggins,Withington,Kitson g:Kitson(3)	11th	233
2/8/15	London Skolars (a)	L42-12	t:Nathaniel,Thomas g:Richards(2)	11th	340
9/8/15	York (a) ●●●●	L36-26	t:Nathaniel(2),Cook,Danns,Hoggins g:Kitson(3)	10th	519
15/8/15	Rochdale (h) ●●	L16-54	t:Land,Thomas,Gardiner g:Kitson(2)	12th	51
23/8/15	South Wales (a)	W26-40	t:Matthews,S Scott,Kitson,J Scott,Cook(2),Jones-Bishop g:Kitson(6)	10th	148
31/8/15	Swinton (a)	L84-16	t:S Scott,T Davies,Kitson g:Kitson(2)	10th	487
6/9/15	Hemel (a)	W16-38	t:Danns,Withington,Nathaniel,Evans,Speake,Richards,Cook g:Kitson(5)	10th	144
12/9/15	Oldham (h)	L12-76	t:Gardiner,Richards g:Kitson(2)	10th	246

● Played at Leigh Sports Village ●● Played at Pennine Way, Hemel
●●● Played at Prince of Wales Stadium, Cheltenham ●●●● Played at Elmpark Way, Heworth

		APP		TRIES		GOALS		FG		PTS	
	D.O.B.	ALL	L1	ALL	L1	ALL	L1	ALL	L1	ALL	L1
Danny Allan	9/4/89	6	3	1	0	7	3	0	0	18	6
Jordan Andrade	24/1/92	9(7)	7(7)	0	0	0	0	0	0	0	0
Mark Barlow	16/2/84	9(2)	9(2)	0	0	3	3	1	1	7	7
Stuart Biscomb	16/12/91	5(1)	5(1)	0	0	0	0	0	0	0	0
Sam Blaney	4/12/89	(2)	(1)	0	0	0	0	0	0	0	0
Matty Blythe	20/11/88	5	5	2	2	0	0	0	0	8	8
Adam Brook	29/9/94	4	4	1	1	5	5	0	0	14	14
Marcus Brooker	2/9/89	25	22	5	3	0	0	0	0	20	12
Ian Clark	1/9/92	1	1	0	0	0	0	0	0	0	0
Nathan Conroy	6/3/95	2	2	3	3	0	0	0	0	12	12
Craig Cook	26/5/83	5	5	5	5	0	0	0	0	20	20
Kyle Danns	19/12/87	9(11)	6(11)	2	2	0	0	0	0	8	8
Karl Davies	3/5/92	3	3	1	1	0	0	0	0	4	4
Tom Davies	14/4/89	(5)	(3)	1	1	0	0	0	0	4	4
Erjon Dollapi	16/3/93	1	1	0	0	0	0	0	0	0	0
Luke Evans	9/5/90	6(11)	5(10)	2	2	0	0	0	0	8	8
Daniel Fleming	8/7/92	1	1	0	0	0	0	0	0	0	0
Luke Gardiner	5/8/91	12(2)	12(2)	5	5	0	0	0	0	20	20
Charlie Greene	23/10/95	2(1)	2(1)	0	0	0	0	0	0	0	0
Vila Halafihi	24/1/94	2	2	1	1	0	0	0	0	4	4
Ed Hayles	10/6/83	4(1)	1(1)	0	0	0	0	0	0	0	0
Andrew Hoggins	7/8/88	22	19	10	8	0	0	0	0	40	32
Ricky Hopwood	19/4/89	2(2)	1(1)	0	0	0	0	0	0	0	0
Aaron Jones-Bishop	18/1/90	17(5)	14(5)	6	4	0	0	0	0	24	16
Harry Kaufman	20/12/91	3(1)	2(1)	0	0	0	0	0	0	0	0
Nathan Kitson	11/12/88	19(4)	16(4)	8	8	35	35	0	0	102	102
Josh Kittrick	28/10/94	4(1)	4(1)	0	0	0	0	0	0	0	0
Lee Land	10/6/88	5(1)	5(1)	1	1	0	0	0	0	4	4
James Mason	27/1/95	(1)	(1)	0	0	0	0	0	0	0	0
Andy Matthews	2/10/88	16	16	6	6	0	0	0	0	24	24
Dean Mignacca	4/4/88	5(7)	5(7)	1	1	0	0	0	0	4	4
James Milburn	11/6/91	8(2)	8(2)	0	0	0	0	0	0	0	0
Jonny Morris	7/5/92	3	2	0	0	0	0	0	0	0	0
Sean Morris	6/5/89	8	7	5	4	0	0	0	0	20	16
Ray Nasso	3/7/87	1	1	1	1	0	0	0	0	4	4
Josh Nathaniel	24/5/91	10	10	5	5	0	0	0	0	20	20
Wes Newton	26/2/90	(1)	0	0	0	0	0	0	0	0	0
Graham O'Keeffe	13/5/91	(4)	(2)	0	0	0	0	0	0	0	0
Chris Palser-Thorne	27/12/93	(2)	(2)	0	0	0	0	0	0	0	0
Jonny Payne	13/11/91	11(1)	8(1)	2	1	0	0	0	0	8	4
Dave Petersen	6/3/92	3	3	1	1	0	0	0	0	4	4
Simon Price	30/1/85	(1)	(1)	0	0	0	0	0	0	0	0
Louis Richards	29/12/87	9(4)	7(4)	3	3	8	8	0	0	28	28
Josh Scott	22/12/89	10(4)	9(2)	4	4	0	0	0	0	16	16
Steve Scott	14/11/86	5(5)	5(5)	2	2	0	0	0	0	8	8
Andy Speake	28/9/86	10	7	1	1	0	0	0	0	4	4
Danny Thomas	21/12/83	19(1)	19(1)	6	6	0	0	0	0	24	24
Bobby Tyson-Wilson	6/11/94	4	4	1	1	0	0	0	0	4	4
Chris Ulugia	15/1/92	2	2	0	0	0	0	0	0	0	0
Edd Vickers	7/3/89	(1)	0	0	0	0	0	0	0	0	0
Jack Walton	7/5/95	4	4	0	0	0	0	0	0	0	0
Kash Watkins	20/6/88	3	1	1	0	0	0	0	0	4	0
Adam Withington	29/8/86	15(5)	15(4)	3	3	0	0	0	0	12	12

'L1' totals League 1 regular season only; 'All' totals also include League 1 Cup & Challenge Cup

Sean Morris

LEAGUE RECORD
P22-W7-D0-L15 (10th)
F453, A948, Diff-495, 14 points.

LEAGUE 1 CUP
Round One

CHALLENGE CUP
Round Four

ATTENDANCES
Best - v Coventry (L1 - 502)
Worst - v Rochdale (L1 - 51)
Total (League 1/League 1 Cup only) - 3,409
Average (League 1/League 1 Cup only) - 284
(Up by 13 on 2014)

CLUB RECORDS **Highest score:** 40-30 v Gloucestershire All Golds, 29/3/2013; 40-24 v South Wales, 18/5/2014; 40-26 v South Wales, 23/8/2015
Highest score against: 4-96 v Swinton, 12/7/2015 **Record attendance:** 502 v Coventry, 27/6/2015

MATCH RECORDS **Tries:** 3 *(4 players)* **Goals:** 6 Jonny Leather v Gloucestershire All Golds, 29/3/2013; Nathan Kitson v South Wales, 23/8/2015
Points: 16 Jonny Leather v Gloucestershire All Golds, 29/3/2013; Nathan Kitson v South Wales, 23/8/2015

SEASON RECORDS **Tries:** 17 Sean Morris 2014 **Goals:** 46 *(inc 2fg)* Jimmy Rowland 2014 **Points:** 118 Jimmy Rowland 2014

CAREER RECORDS **Tries:** 29 Sean Morris 2013-2015 **Goals:** 49 *(inc 2fg)* Jimmy Rowland 2013-2014 **Points:** 124 Jimmy Rowland 2013-2014
Appearances: 56 Andrew Hoggins 2013-2015

ROCHDALE HORNETS

DATE	FIXTURE	RESULT	SCORERS	LGE	ATT
1/3/15	South Wales (h) (L1CR1)	W40-0	t:Bridge,Hargreaves,McClurg,Yates,Bloomfield,Case,Suffolk g:Crook(6)	N/A	260
7/3/15	Kells (a) (CCR3) ●	W12-29	t:Suffolk,Dandy,Bloomfield,Langley,Case g:Crook(4) fg:Yates	N/A	587
15/3/15	North Wales (a) (L1CR2)	L28-4	t:Hull	N/A	465
22/3/15	Swinton (a) (CCR4)	L30-12	t:Case,Tilley g:Crook(2)	N/A	502
3/4/15	Oldham (h)	L16-23	t:Bloomfield,Crook g:Crook(3),Charnock	9th	1,201
11/4/15	Gloucestershire All Golds (a)	W18-38	t:Bridge,Crook(2),Bloomfield,Tilley,Yates,Hargreaves g:Crook(3),Charnock(2)	5th	218
18/4/15	Barrow (h)	W48-12	t:Ratu(2),Crook(2),Bridge(2),Tilley,Bloomfield,Smith g:Crook(5),Langley	3rd	580
26/4/15	Newcastle (h)	L15-16	t:Yates,Bridge,Langley g:Crook fg:Crook	5th	411
3/5/15	Coventry (a)	W10-35	t:Bloomfield,English,Walker(2),W Thompson,Bridge g:Langley(5) fg:Yates	4th	496
9/5/15	Swinton (h)	W28-16	t:Hull,Yates(2),Walker,Ashworth g:Charnock(2),Crook(2)	4th	662
16/5/15	Oxford (h)	W76-16	t:Bloomfield(3),Yates,W Thompson,Ashworth,Hadden(2),Walker,Bridge, Hargreaves,Suffolk,Crook g:Crook(9),Yates(3)	2nd	652
31/5/15	South Wales (a)	W10-64	t:Crook(3),Yates(3),Bridge(2),English(2),Hargreaves,Paterson g:Crook(5),Case(2),Yates	1st	172
7/6/15	York (a) ●●	L34-20	t:Trumper,Yates,Ashworth,Dawson g:Crook,Yates	2nd	386
14/6/15	North Wales (a) ●●●	W12-14	t:English,Bloomfield g:Crook(2),Yates	2nd	661
21/6/15	Keighley (a)	L54-20	t:Bloomfield,Hargreaves,Walker,Crook g:Crook(2)	6th	907
27/6/15	Hemel (h)	W32-14	t:Bridge(2),Smith,Cookson,Yates,Case g:Yates(4)	5th	310
5/7/15	Newcastle (a)	W28-32	t:English,Bridge,Fozard,Smith,Paterson g:Crook(4),Yates(2)	3rd	678
12/7/15	Oldham (a)	L38-18	t:Crook,Paterson,Bridge g:Crook(2),Yates	6th	725
19/7/15	Coventry (h)	W50-22	t:Crook(3),Bridge,Haggarty,Jones,Case,Hull,Bloomfield g:Crook(7)	5th	315
26/7/15	Swinton (a)	L20-16	t:English,Bloomfield,Paterson g:Crook(2)	7th	494
2/8/15	South Wales (h)	W74-4	t:Bloomfield(4),Yates(2),Ratu(2),Hadden,Crook,Smith,Paterson,Bridge g:Crook(11)	6th	300
9/8/15	North Wales (h)	W19-18	t:Hargreaves,Case(2) g:Crook(3) fg:Yates	5th	530
15/8/15	Oxford (a) ●●●●	W16-54	t:Hargreaves,Case,Ratu,Hull,Yates,Bloomfield(2),McClurg,Dandy,Fozard g:Crook(7)	5th	51
23/8/15	Keighley (h)	L8-10	t:Ratu g:Crook(2)	5th	671
5/9/15	Barrow (a)	L46-28	t:Yates,Bloomfield,Ratu,Crook(2) g:Crook(4)	6th	865
12/9/15	London Skolars (h)	W26-22	t:Fozard,English,Trumper,Bloomfield,Bridge g:Crook(2),Langley	6th	305

● Played at Recreation Ground, Whitehaven ●● Played at BigFella's Stadium, Featherstone
●●● Played at The Rock, Wrexham ●●●● Played at Pennine Way, Hemel

		APP		TRIES		GOALS		FG		PTS	
	D.O.B.	ALL	L1	ALL	L1	ALL	L1	ALL	L1	ALL	L1
Jack Ashworth	3/7/95	9(2)	9(1)	3	3	0	0	0	0	12	12
Richard Beaumont	2/2/88	2(1)	2	0	0	0	0	0	0	0	0
Dale Bloomfield	24/10/87	23	20	21	19	0	0	0	0	84	76
Danny Bridge	4/1/93	24	21	16	15	0	0	0	0	64	60
Sam Brooks	29/9/93	2(2)	(1)	0	0	0	0	0	0	0	0
Jordan Case	10/4/93	19(1)	15(1)	8	5	2	2	0	0	36	24
Lewis Charnock	2/9/94	6(2)	6(2)	0	0	5	5	0	0	10	10
John Cookson	12/12/84	(5)	(3)	1	1	0	0	0	0	4	4
Paul Crook	28/8/86	23(1)	19(1)	17	17	89	77	1	1	247	223
James Dandy	23/5/90	11(3)	9(2)	2	1	0	0	0	0	8	4
Matty Dawson	2/10/90	1	1	1	1	0	0	0	0	4	4
Wayne English	8/3/80	22	19	7	7	0	0	0	0	28	28
Matty Fozard	3/3/95	7(2)	7(2)	3	3	0	0	0	0	12	12
Liam Gilchrist	28/3/89	(1)	(1)	0	0	0	0	0	0	0	0
Matty Hadden	7/6/90	6(17)	5(15)	3	3	0	0	0	0	12	12
Matthew Haggarty	8/1/91	3(3)	3(3)	1	1	0	0	0	0	4	4
Jordan Hand	13/5/93	(1)	(1)	0	0	0	0	0	0	0	0
Bradley Hargreaves	13/12/93	16(2)	14(2)	7	6	0	0	0	0	28	24
Dave Hull	3/11/85	14(1)	10(1)	4	3	0	0	0	0	16	12
Danny Jones	12/11/92	3(7)	3(7)	1	1	0	0	0	0	4	4
Gareth Langley	24/10/84	13	10	2	1	7	7	0	0	22	18
Dave Llewellyn	3/12/82	1(2)	1	0	0	0	0	0	0	0	0
Alex McClurg	28/8/89	3(19)	(19)	2	1	0	0	0	0	8	4
Dean Mignacca	4/4/88	1(2)	(1)	0	0	0	0	0	0	0	0
Lee Paterson	20/7/82	22	18	5	5	0	0	0	0	20	20
Mike Ratu	16/10/87	7(1)	7	7	7	0	0	0	0	28	28
Ryan Smith	25/9/89	17(5)	16(3)	4	4	0	0	0	0	16	16
Tony Suffolk	7/11/86	12(1)	9(1)	3	1	0	0	0	0	12	4
Luke Thompson	27/4/95	1	1	0	0	0	0	0	0	0	0
Warren Thompson	24/2/90	24(2)	20(2)	2	2	0	0	0	0	8	8
James Tilley	11/11/93	9(15)	8(13)	3	2	0	0	0	0	12	8
Alex Trumper	5/4/91	5(4)	5(4)	2	2	0	0	0	0	8	8
Anthony Walker	28/12/91	6(2)	6(2)	5	5	0	0	0	0	20	20
Danny Yates	28/5/94	26	22	15	14	13	13	3	2	89	84

'L1' totals League 1 regular season only; 'All' totals also include League 1 Cup & Challenge Cup

Dale Bloomfield

LEAGUE RECORD
P22-W14-D0-L8 (6th)
F731, A459, Diff+272, 28 points.

LEAGUE 1 CUP
Round Two

CHALLENGE CUP
Round Four

ATTENDANCES
Best - v Oldham (L1 - 1,201)
Worst - v South Wales (L1C - 260)
Total (League 1/ League 1 Cup only) - 6,197
Average (League 1/ League 1 Cup only) - 516
(Down by 248 on 2014, Championship)

CLUB RECORDS **Highest score:** 120-4 v Illingworth, 13/3/2005 **Highest score against:** 0-106 v Castleford, 9/9/2007 **Record attendance:** 26,664 v Oldham, 25/3/22 *(Athletic Grounds)*; 8,061 v Oldham, 26/12/89 *(Spotland)*

MATCH RECORDS **Tries:** 5 Jack Corsi v Barrow, 31/12/21; Jack Corsi v Broughton Moor, 25/2/22; Jack Williams v St Helens, 4/4/33; Norman Brelsford v Whitehaven, 3/9/73; Marlon Billy v York, 8/4/2001 **Goals:** 18 Lee Birdseye v Illingworth, 13/3/2005 **Points:** 44 Lee Birdseye v Illingworth, 13/3/2005

SEASON RECORDS **Tries:** 31 Marlon Billy 2001 **Goals:** 150 Martin Strett 1994-95 **Points:** 350 Mick Nanyn 2003

CAREER RECORDS **Tries:** 103 Jack Williams 1931-37 **Goals:** 741 Walter Gowers 1922-36 **Points:** 1,497 Walter Gowers 1922-36 **Appearances:** 456 Walter Gowers 1922-36

SOUTH WALES SCORPIONS

DATE	FIXTURE	RESULT	SCORERS	LGE	ATT
1/3/15	Rochdale (a) (L1CR1)	L40-0		N/A	260
8/3/15	York (h) (CCR3)	L4-20	t:Songhurst	N/A	247
3/4/15	Gloucestershire All Golds (a)	L36-6	t:R Davies g:Emanuelli	14th	404
12/4/15	London Skolars (h)	L12-30	t:Newbury,Sheridan g:Emanuelli(2)	14th	328
19/4/15	Oldham (h)	L12-50	t:Farrer,Petelo g:Emanuelli(2)	14th	224
25/4/15	Barrow (a)	L86-0		14th	836
3/5/15	Hemel (a)	L18-6	t:Curtis Davies g:Emanuelli	14th	137
10/5/15	North Wales (h) ●	L18-50	t:Leather,Symons,Curtis Davies g:Emanuelli(3)	14th	1,025
22/5/15	York (a) ●●	L70-0		14th	246
31/5/15	Rochdale (h)	L10-64	t:Parker,Scrivens g:Emanuelli	14th	172
7/6/15	Oxford (a)	L38-30	t:Newbury(2),Joy,Sheridan,Connor Davies g:Emanuelli(5)	14th	286
14/6/15	Keighley (a)	L66-6	t:Petelo g:Emanuelli	14th	671
21/6/15	Coventry (h)	L14-42	t:Parker(2),Joy g:Emanuelli	14th	307
28/6/15	London Skolars (a)	W20-26	t:Parker(2),Hellard,Petelo,Newbury g:Emanuelli(3)	14th	304
5/7/15	Gloucestershire All Golds (h)	L16-36	t:Hill,Leather,Farrer g:Emanuelli(2)	14th	211
12/7/15	North Wales (a)	L56-10	t:Newbury,Hill g:Emanuelli	14th	703
19/7/15	Hemel (h)	L28-46	t:Parker(2),Farrer(2),Williams g:Emanuelli(4)	14th	175
25/7/15	York (h)	L0-64		14th	202
2/8/15	Rochdale (a)	L74-4	t:Farrer	14th	300
9/8/15	Keighley (h)	L10-48	t:Newbury,Farrer g:Emanuelli	14th	224
16/8/15	Coventry (a)	L44-18	t:Farrer,Parker,Newbury g:Emanuelli(3)	14th	200
23/8/15	Oxford (h)	L26-40	t:Edwards,Farrer,Newbury,Petelo,Williams g:Emanuelli(3)	14th	148
6/9/15	Newcastle (h)	L16-50	t:B Phillips,Leather(2) g:Emanuelli(2)	14th	160
13/9/15	Swinton (a)	L94-6	t:Hellard g:Jones	14th	417

● Played at Cardiff Arms Park
●● Played at BigFella's Stadium, Featherstone

	D.O.B.	APP ALL	APP L1	TRIES ALL	TRIES L1	GOALS ALL	GOALS L1	FG ALL	FG L1	PTS ALL	PTS L1
Mike Connor	27/3/94	11(3)	9(3)	0	0	0	0	0	0	0	0
Neil Dallimore	24/2/81	10(1)	8(1)	0	0	0	0	0	0	0	0
Connor Davies	17/1/97	12(1)	12(1)	1	1	0	0	0	0	4	4
Curtis Davies	17/1/97	15(4)	13(4)	2	2	0	0	0	0	8	8
Rhys Davies	9/6/96	4(5)	4(5)	1	1	0	0	0	0	4	4
Paul Edwards	18/5/96	16(1)	14(1)	1	1	0	0	0	0	4	4
Paul Emanuelli	3/1/84	23	21	0	0	36	36	0	0	72	72
Morgan Evans	23/3/92	4	2	0	0	0	0	0	0	0	0
Connor Farrer	6/6/95	16(4)	14(4)	8	8	0	0	0	0	32	32
Scott Giles	5/7/86	3(3)	3(1)	0	0	0	0	0	0	0	0
Dafydd Hellard	21/2/85	2(13)	2(13)	2	2	0	0	0	0	8	8
Bradley Hill	14/11/92	18	17	2	2	0	0	0	0	8	8
Ben Jones	7/9/96	4(1)	4(1)	0	0	1	1	0	0	2	2
Andrew Joy	7/2/94	6(1)	6(1)	2	2	0	0	0	0	8	8
Gethin King	23/11/85	(4)	(4)	0	0	0	0	0	0	0	0
Jonny Leather	29/7/89	16	16	4	4	0	0	0	0	16	16
Craig Lewis	15/10/86	5	3	0	0	0	0	0	0	0	0
Dafydd Lloyd	7/5/92	(2)	(1)	0	0	0	0	0	0	0	0
Bradley Mais	6/4/96	2(2)	2(2)	0	0	0	0	0	0	0	0
Micah Manuokafoa	10/7/97	(1)	(1)	0	0	0	0	0	0	0	0
Ryan Millington	14/1/87	14(2)	14(2)	0	0	0	0	0	0	0	0
Tom Morgan	18/10/89	4	4	0	0	0	0	0	0	0	0
Ian Newbury	17/9/86	18	16	8	8	0	0	0	0	32	32
Andrew Oakden	8/8/93	1	1	0	0	0	0	0	0	0	0
Yannic Parker	29/12/90	15	15	8	8	0	0	0	0	32	32
Tala Petelo	25/4/82	4(13)	4(12)	4	4	0	0	0	0	16	16
Barrie Phillips	27/5/86	11(2)	11(2)	1	1	0	0	0	0	4	4
Osian Phillips	2/5/94	13(1)	11(1)	0	0	0	0	0	0	0	0
Nathan Rainer	16/10/89	(4)	(4)	0	0	0	0	0	0	0	0
Kyle Scrivens	7/8/88	20	18	1	1	0	0	0	0	4	4
Jordan Sheridan	19/7/94	16	16	2	2	0	0	0	0	8	8
Paul Songhurst	26/1/91	2	0	1	0	0	0	0	0	4	0
Christopher Speck	21/2/90	1(8)	1(8)	0	0	0	0	0	0	0	0
Anthony Symons	1/6/90	6(7)	5(6)	1	1	0	0	0	0	4	4
Lewis Tutt	15/10/85	(1)	0	0	0	0	0	0	0	0	0
Marcus Webb	11/1/97	4(1)	4	0	0	0	0	0	0	0	0
Zak Williams	17/9/96	16(5)	16(5)	2	2	0	0	0	0	8	8

'L1' totals League 1 regular season only; 'All' totals also include League 1 Cup & Challenge Cup

Paul Emanuelli

LEAGUE RECORD
P22-W1-D0-L21 (14th)
F274, A1122, Diff-848, 2 points.

LEAGUE 1 CUP
Round One

CHALLENGE CUP
Round Three

ATTENDANCES
Best - v North Wales (L1 - 1,025)
Worst - v Oxford (L1 - 148)
Total (League 1 only) - 3,176
Average (League 1 only) - 289
(Up by 10 on 2014)

CLUB RECORDS **Highest score:** 70-22 v London Skolars, 23/5/2010; 70-16 v Gateshead, 11/7/2010 **Highest score against:** 6-94 v Swinton, 13/9/2015 **Record attendance:** 1,025 v North Wales, 10/5/2015

MATCH RECORDS **Tries:** 4 Dalton Grant v Gateshead, 22/5/2011 **Goals:** 11 Lewis Reece v Gateshead, 11/7/2010 **Points:** 30 Lewis Reece v Gateshead, 11/7/2010

SEASON RECORDS **Tries:** 19 Steve Parry 2010 **Goals:** 55 Lewis Reece 2011 **Points:** 130 Lewis Reece 2011

CAREER RECORDS **Tries:** 43 Steve Parry 2010-2013 **Goals:** 79 *(inc 2fg)* Paul Emanuelli 2014-2015 **Points:** 188 Lewis Reece 2010-2013 **Appearances:** 101 Ashley Bateman 2010-2014

SWINTON LIONS

DATE	FIXTURE	RESULT	SCORERS	LGE	ATT
1/3/15	Hemel (h) (L1CR1)	W34-0	t:R Hawkyard(3),Ackers(2),Robinson,Dwyer g:Atkin(3)	N/A	349
7/3/15	London Skolars (a) (CCR3)	W4-86	t:Rowland(2),R Hawkyard,White(3),Atkin(2),Littler,R Lloyd(3),Rothwell,Lever, Dwyer g:Atkin(13)	N/A	165
15/3/15	Keighley (a) (L1CR2)	W22-24	t:Beecham,White,Atkin,Littler g:Atkin(4)	N/A	472
22/3/15	Rochdale (h) (CCR4)	W30-12	t:Rothwell,Beecham(2),Atkin(2),R Hawkyard g:Rowland(3)	N/A	502
3/4/15	North Wales (h)	D14-14	t:Robinson,Littler,R Hawkyard g:Atkin	7th	561
7/4/15	Newcastle (h) (L1CSF)	W36-28	t:James,Atkin(2),D Hawkyard,Gardner,Ackers g:Atkin(6)	N/A	351
11/4/15	Barrow (a)	L50-12	t:Gallagher,Gardner g:Atkin(2)	12th	1,064
19/4/15	Batley (a) (CCR5)	L46-14	t:Rothwell,Littler,Robinson g:Atkin	N/A	443
26/4/15	Gloucestershire All Golds (a)	W18-60	t:Robinson(2),White,R Hawkyard(2),Gardner,Beecham,Littler,A Lloyd,Ackers,Atkin g:Atkin(8)	9th	314
3/5/15	York (h)	W34-24	t:Littler(3),Atkin,White,Ackers g:Atkin(5)	5th	444
9/5/15	Rochdale (a)	L28-16	t:R Hawkyard(2),Rothwell g:Atkin(2)	8th	662
17/5/15	Keighley (h)	W29-16	t:Dwyer(2),Rothwell,Butt,Robinson,White g:R Hawkyard(2) fg:White	7th	561
23/5/15	North Wales (L1CF) ●	L14-8	t:Robinson g:Atkin(2)	N/A	1,200
31/5/15	Hemel (a)	W8-32	t:Rothwell,Ball,Robinson(2),Ackers,Govin g:R Hawkyard(4)	7th	154
7/6/15	Newcastle (h)	W44-32	t:Rothwell(2),White(2),Beecham,D Hawkyard,Butt,Ackers g:White(6)	6th	455
14/6/15	Coventry (a)	W8-78	t:Aaronson(2),Lever,Atkin,Ackers(2),Littler(2),White(2),Robinson(3),Austin,A Lloyd g:White(5),Atkin(4)	5th	454
21/6/15	Oldham (h)	L26-32	t:Robinson,Govin,A Lloyd,Butt,Thornley g:Atkin(3)	8th	625
28/6/15	York (a) ●●	L26-16	t:Atkin,Ackers,D Hawkyard g:White(2)	8th	511
5/7/15	Barrow (h)	W30-20	t:Robinson,White,Rothwell,Gallagher(2),James g:Mort(3)	8th	485
12/7/15	Oxford (a) ●●●	W4-96	t:White,R Hawkyard(2),Mort(5),Lever,Atkin(2),D Hawkyard,Dwyer,Rothwell, Ackers,M Morrison,Robinson g:Mort(14)	8th	497
19/7/15	Keighley (a)	W14-22	t:Ackers,Littler,Robinson,Butt g:Atkin(3)	6th	831
26/7/15	Rochdale (h)	W20-16	t:Robinson,Thornley,Rothwell,Beecham g:Mort(2)	5th	494
2/8/15	Newcastle (a)	W18-30	t:Robinson,Atkin(2),Littler,Ackers g:Mort(5)	5th	514
9/8/15	London Skolars (h)	W74-4	t:R Hawkyard(3),Butt(3),R Lloyd,White(2),Ackers,Littler,Barlow,Aaronson(2) g:Atkin(9)	4th	401
16/8/15	North Wales (a)	W14-30	t:White,Atkin,R Lloyd(2),Thornley g:Atkin(5)	4th	737
23/8/15	Gloucestershire All Golds (h)	W42-6	t:Littler,James,White,R Lloyd,Beecham,Butt,Aaronson,Ackers g:Atkin(5)	4th	368
31/8/15	Oxford (h)	W84-16	t:Littler(5),Atkin(2),White,Mort,Austin,Beecham(2),Rothwell,Barlow,Robinson g:Atkin(12)	3rd	487
6/9/15	Oldham (a)	L28-16	t:Ackers,Lever,Gallagher g:Atkin(2)	4th	1,004
13/9/15	South Wales (h)	W94-6	t:Robinson(2),Aaronson,A Lloyd(2),R Lloyd,Gallagher(4),Rowland,Atkin,Govin(2), Butt(2),Littler,Ackers g:Atkin(10),Gallagher	3rd	417
27/9/15	York (h) (SF)	W18-17 *(aet)*	t:Atkin,Dwyer,Butt g:Atkin(2) fg:White,Atkin	N/A	684
4/10/15	Keighley (POF) ●●●●	W28-29	t:Atkin,Butt,White,R Lloyd,Robinson g:Atkin(4) fg:Atkin	N/A	N/A

● Played at Bloomfield Road, Blackpool ●● Played at Elmpark Way, Heworth ●●● Played at Pennine Way, Hemel ●●●● Played at Select Security Stadium, Widnes

	D.O.B.	APP ALL	APP L1	TRIES ALL	TRIES L1	GOALS ALL	GOALS L1	FG ALL	FG L1	PTS ALL	PTS L1
Harry Aaronson	28/3/98	4	4	6	6	0	0	0	0	24	24
Andy Ackers	25/12/93	28(3)	21(3)	17	14	0	0	0	0	68	56
Chris Atkin	7/2/93	26(1)	19(1)	21	14	106	77	2	2	298	212
Ben Austin	3/5/95	6(20)	5(15)	2	2	0	0	0	0	8	8
Andy Ball	24/7/91	4(2)	3(2)	1	1	0	0	0	0	4	4
Josh Barlow	15/5/91	8(10)	7(9)	2	2	0	0	0	0	8	8
Grant Beecham	25/10/94	16(6)	10(6)	9	6	0	0	0	0	36	24
Mike Butt	6/5/95	13	13	12	12	0	0	0	0	48	48
Connor Dwyer	29/12/93	14(7)	9(7)	6	4	0	0	0	0	24	16
Tommy Gallagher	10/9/83	(22)	(17)	8	8	1	1	0	0	34	34
Matt Gardner	24/8/84	5(2)	4	3	2	0	0	0	0	12	8
Mick Govin	5/11/84	4(11)	4(10)	4	4	0	0	0	0	16	16
Darren Hawkyard	14/10/84	4(12)	4(9)	4	3	0	0	0	0	16	12
Ritchie Hawkyard	21/1/86	24	17	15	10	6	6	0	0	72	52
Keith Holden	23/6/93	1(1)	1(1)	0	0	0	0	0	0	0	0
Alex Hurst	17/3/90	1	0	0	0	0	0	0	0	0	0
Jordan James	24/5/80	26(2)	20(2)	3	2	0	0	0	0	12	8
Rob Lever	13/7/95	24(6)	21(2)	4	3	0	0	0	0	16	12
Stuart Littler	19/2/79	30	23	20	17	0	0	0	0	80	68
Aaron Lloyd	28/6/92	10(10)	9(4)	5	5	0	0	0	0	20	20
Rhodri Lloyd	22/7/93	12	8	9	6	0	0	0	0	36	24
Jack Morrison	16/9/92	1	0	0	0	0	0	0	0	0	0
Mike Morrison	9/9/87	24(4)	18(3)	1	1	0	0	0	0	4	4
Ian Mort	21/6/88	6	6	6	6	24	24	0	0	72	72
Mick Nanyn	3/6/82	1	1	0	0	0	0	0	0	0	0
Shaun Robinson	13/7/89	30	23	22	19	0	0	0	0	88	76
Chris Rothwell	7/10/88	27	20	12	9	0	0	0	0	48	36
Jimmy Rowland	8/4/94	9	3	3	1	3	0	0	0	18	4
Tom Thackray	19/2/93	1(3)	1(3)	0	0	0	0	0	0	0	0
Andy Thornley	1/3/89	15(2)	15(2)	3	3	0	0	0	0	12	12
Ben White	27/10/94	29	23	19	15	13	13	2	2	104	88

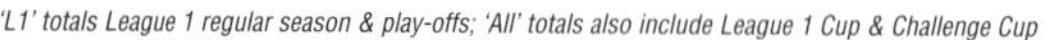

'L1' totals League 1 regular season & play-offs; 'All' totals also include League 1 Cup & Challenge Cup

Stuart Littler

LEAGUE RECORD
P22-W16-D1-L5
(3rd/Winners, Play-off Final)
F899, A402, Diff+497, 33 points.

LEAGUE 1 CUP
Runners-Up

CHALLENGE CUP
Round Five

ATTENDANCES
Best - v York (L1SF - 684)
Worst - v Hemel (L1C - 349)
Total (League 1, inc SF, & League 1 Cup only) - 6,682
Average (League 1, inc SF, & League 1 Cup only) - 477
(Down by 53 on 2014, Championship)

CLUB RECORDS **Highest score:** 96-4 v Oxford, 12/7/2015 **Highest score against:** 0-112 v Warrington, 20/5/2011 **Record attendance:** 26,891 v Wigan, 12/2/64
MATCH RECORDS **Tries:** 6 Mark Riley v Prescot, 11/8/96 **Goals:** 14 Ian Mort v Oxford, 12/7/2015 **Points:** 48 Ian Mort v Oxford, 12/7/2015
SEASON RECORDS **Tries:** 42 John Stopford 1963-64 **Goals:** 128 Albert Blan 1960-61 **Points:** 338 Ian Mort 2011
CAREER RECORDS **Tries:** 197 Frank Evans 1921-31 **Goals:** 970 Ken Gowers 1954-73 **Points:** 2,105 Ken Gowers 1954-73 **Appearances:** 601 Ken Gowers 1954-73

YORK CITY KNIGHTS

DATE	FIXTURE	RESULT	SCORERS	LGE	ATT
1/3/15	London Skolars (a) (L1CR1)	W10-78	t:E Smith,Morrison(3),Aspinall(2),Cunningham,Brining,P Smith(2),Minikin,Carter,Joynt, Haynes g:Haynes(11)	N/A	156
8/3/15	South Wales (a) (CCR3)	W4-20	t:Presley,Riley,Brining,Aspinall g:Haynes,P Smith	N/A	247
15/3/15	Newcastle (h) (L1CR2) ●	L24-38	t:Brining,Cunningham,Morrison,Presley g:Haynes(4)	N/A	358
20/3/15	Featherstone Lions (a) (CCR4) ●●	W8-58	t:Brining(2),Aspinall,Cunningham(3),Carter,E Smith,Haynes,Roche g:Haynes(9)	N/A	1,200
3/4/15	Keighley (a)	L28-12	t:P Smith,Presley g:Haynes(2)	11th	903
12/4/15	Oxford (a)	W20-44	t:Tonks,Craig(2),Haynes,Cunningham,Iley,Minikin,Morrison,Presley g:Haynes(3),P Smith	7th	200
19/4/15	Leigh Miners Rangers (a) (CCR5) ●●●	W14-44	t:B Dent,Morrison,Brining(3),Presley,A Dent,E Smith g:B Dent(6)	N/A	1,191
26/4/15	Coventry (h) ●	W42-10	t:P Smith(2),Brining,Minikin,Carter,Craig,A Dent(2) g:B Dent(5)	6th	498
3/5/15	Swinton (a)	L34-24	t:E Smith,Minikin,Clare,Cunningham,Tonks g:Waterman,B Dent	7th	444
9/5/15	Gloucestershire All Golds (a)	W6-46	t:P Smith(2),Craig,Tonks(2),B Dent,Morrison,Minikin g:B Dent(7)	6th	212
15/5/15	St Helens (a) (CCR6)	L46-6	t:Craig g:B Dent	N/A	3,241
22/5/15	South Wales (h) ●●	W70-0	t:Minikin(3),P Smith,Pickles,B Dent,Waterman,Tonks,Craig,Nicholson(2),E Smith, Canterbury g:B Dent(9)	5th	246
29/5/15	Newcastle (a)	L32-14	t:Tonks,Waterman,Cunningham g:B Dent	8th	2,576
7/6/15	Rochdale (h) ●●	W34-20	t:Cunningham,P Smith,Clare(2),B Dent(2),Channing g:B Dent(3)	7th	386
14/6/15	London Skolars (h) ●●●●	W40-10	t:Morrison,Howden(2),Mallinder,Aldous,Minikin,Tonks,Cunningham g:B Dent(4)	6th	401
21/6/15	Hemel (a)	W10-70	t:Howden(2),Brining(3),B Dent(2),Minikin,Carter,Morrison(2),Clare,E Smith g:B Dent(3),Howden(6)	4th	145
28/6/15	Swinton (h) ●●●●	W26-16	t:E Smith,B Dent,Howden,Clare,Minikin g:Howden(2),B Dent	3rd	511
5/7/15	Oldham (a)	L34-12	t:Nicholson,Applegarth g:B Dent(2)	5th	581
11/7/15	Gloucestershire All Golds (h) ●●●●	W50-10	t:Howden,Aldous,Clare(4),Carter(2),E Smith,B Dent g:Haynes(3),B Dent(2)	4th	350
19/7/15	Newcastle (h) ●●●●	W40-8	t:E Smith(2),Presley,Brining(3),Nicholson g:Haynes(6)	4th	430
25/7/15	South Wales (a)	W0-64	t:Morrison,Minikin(2),Nicholson(2),Brining(3),Presley,Craig,Mallinder g:Haynes(9),B Dent	3rd	202
2/8/15	Coventry (a)	W10-38	t:Tonks,Cunningham,Nicholson,P Smith,E Smith,Carter,Mallinder g:Howden(3),A Dent(2)	2nd	442
9/8/15	Oxford (h) ●●●●	W36-26	t:B Dent,Blagbrough(2),Haynes,Minikin(2),Tonks g:Haynes(3),B Dent	2nd	519
16/8/15	London Skolars (a)	W22-30	t:Minikin(2),Mallinder,Chisholm,Hey g:B Dent(5)	2nd	323
20/8/15	North Wales (h) ●●●●	L28-30	t:Tonks,Mallinder,A Dent,E Smith,Brining g:B Dent(4)	2nd	607
23/8/15	Hemel (h) ●●●●	W50-10	t:P Smith,Howden,B Dent(2),Brining(2),Morrison,Nicholson(2) g:B Dent(7)	2nd	384
6/9/15	North Wales (a)	W28-30	t:Morland(2),Aldous,P Smith,Brining g:B Dent(4),Howden	3rd	720
13/9/15	Barrow (h) ●●●●	L16-18	t:A Dent,E Smith,Howden g:B Dent(2)	4th	468
27/9/15	Swinton (a) (SF)	L18-17 *(aet)*	t:E Smith,Brining,Minikin,Presley fg:Howden	N/A	684

● Played at Clifton Park ●● Played at BigFellas Stadium, Featherstone
●●● Played at Leigh Sports Village ●●●● Played at Elmpark Way, Heworth

	D.O.B.	APP ALL	APP L1	TRIES ALL	TRIES L1	GOALS ALL	GOALS L1	FG ALL	FG L1	PTS ALL	PTS L1
Jack Aldous	3/4/91	28	22	3	3	0	0	0	0	12	12
Mark Applegarth	10/12/84	29	23	1	1	0	0	0	0	4	4
Peter Aspinall	4/4/94	3(3)	(1)	4	0	0	0	0	0	16	0
Jack Blagbrough	18/1/94	2(10)	2(10)	2	2	0	0	0	0	8	8
Kris Brining	16/11/93	10(9)	6(8)	23	15	0	0	0	0	92	60
Casey Canterbury	1/1/94	1(4)	1(4)	1	1	0	0	0	0	4	4
Harry Carter	10/2/94	8(10)	6(7)	7	5	0	0	0	0	28	20
Michael Channing	30/6/92	7	7	1	1	0	0	0	0	4	4
Jamel Chisholm	7/11/92	3	1	1	1	0	0	0	0	4	4
James Clare	13/4/91	7	7	9	9	0	0	0	0	36	36
Tyler Craig	4/7/93	12(1)	10(1)	7	6	0	0	0	0	28	24
Liam Cunningham	28/10/89	16(5)	11(4)	11	6	0	0	0	0	44	24
Adam Dent	2/11/93	7	5	5	4	2	2	0	0	24	20
Ben Dent	27/9/91	23	21	12	11	69	62	0	0	186	168
Scott Glassell	14/8/88	(2)	(2)	0	0	0	0	0	0	0	0
James Haynes	22/3/89	10	6	4	2	51	26	0	0	118	60
Brad Hey	4/9/94	(4)	(4)	1	1	0	0	0	0	4	4
Jordan Howden	6/5/96	17	17	8	8	12	12	1	1	57	57
Jack Iley	26/5/90	(3)	(2)	1	1	0	0	0	0	4	4
Jake Joynt	24/10/92	(2)	0	1	0	0	0	0	0	4	0
Mick Learmonth	8/2/95	4(6)	4(6)	0	0	0	0	0	0	0	0
Jay Leary	8/9/92	(2)	(2)	0	0	0	0	0	0	0	0
Ryan Mallinder	17/7/88	12(9)	10(8)	5	5	0	0	0	0	20	20
Luke Menzies	29/6/88	(1)	0	0	0	0	0	0	0	0	0
Greg Minikin	29/3/95	27	21	18	17	0	0	0	0	72	68
James Morland	29/6/95	4	4	2	2	0	0	0	0	8	8
Nev Morrison	27/5/90	23	18	12	7	0	0	0	0	48	28
Brad Nicholson	20/8/95	7(16)	6(15)	9	9	0	0	0	0	36	36
Jack Pickles	3/6/92	3(8)	1(5)	1	1	0	0	0	0	4	4
Jon Presley	8/7/84	27	21	8	5	0	0	0	0	32	20
Liam Richmond	17/10/96	(4)	(3)	0	0	0	0	0	0	0	0
Kane Riley	11/3/95	1(2)	(1)	1	0	0	0	0	0	4	0
Colton Roche	23/6/93	3(11)	2(7)	1	0	0	0	0	0	4	0
Ed Smith	12/11/92	28	22	14	11	0	0	0	0	56	44
Pat Smith	4/3/90	28	22	12	10	2	1	0	0	52	42
Josh Tonks	14/8/91	25(2)	21	10	10	0	0	0	0	40	40
Lee Waterman	13/4/87	2(2)	2(2)	2	2	1	1	0	0	10	10

'L1' totals League 1 regular season & semi-final; 'All' totals also include League 1 Cup & Challenge Cup

Ben Dent

LEAGUE RECORD
P22-W16-D0-6 (4th/Semi-Finalists)
F816, A382, Diff+434, 32 points.

LEAGUE 1 CUP
Round Two

CHALLENGE CUP
Round Six

ATTENDANCES
Best - v North Wales (L1 - 607)
Worst - v South Wales (L1 - 246)
Total (League 1/League 1 Cup only) - 5,158
Average (League 1/League 1 Cup only) - 430
(Down by 215 on 2014)

CLUB RECORDS
Highest score: 132-0 v Northumbria University, 6/3/2011 **Highest score against:** 0-98 v Rochdale, 8/4/2001
Record attendance: 14,689 v Swinton, 10/2/34 *(Clarence Street)*; 4,977 v Halifax, 5/1/90 *(Ryedale/Huntington Stadium)*

MATCH RECORDS
Tries: 7 Brad Davis v Highfield, 17/9/95 **Goals:** 20 Chris Thorman v Northumbria University, 6/3/2011
Points: 56 Chris Thorman v Northumbria University, 6/3/2011

SEASON RECORDS
Tries: 35 John Crossley 1980-81 **Goals:** 178 *(inc 4fg)* Danny Brough 2004 **Points:** 412 Danny Brough 2004

CAREER RECORDS
Tries: 167 Peter Foster 1955-67 **Goals:** 1,060 Vic Yorke 1954-67 **Points:** 2,159 Vic Yorke 1954-67 **Appearances:** 449 Willie Hargreaves 1952-65

LEAGUE 1 2015
Round by Round

ROUND 1

Friday 3rd April 2015

COVENTRY BEARS 32 OXFORD 10

BEARS: 1 Troy Brophy; 37 Josh Guzdek; 4 Eddie Medforth; 21 Stephen Coleman; 20 Jamahl Hunte; 6 Billy Sheen; 39 Matthew Marsh; 27 James Geurtjens; 9 Alex Brown; 26 Matt Cooper; 29 Liam Thompson; 12 Chris Barratt; 13 Simon Phillips. Subs (all used): 40 Connor Robinson; 38 Tom Hall; 17 Alex Calvert; - Nick Taylor.
Tries: Sheen (3), Cooper (12), Medforth (17, 80), Guzdek (20), Brophy (70); **Goals:** Coleman 4/6.
OXFORD: 28 Jonny Morris; 21 Luke Gardiner; 14 Marcus Brooker; 5 Aaron Jones-Bishop; 20 Ricky Hopwood; 6 Danny Allan; 9 Nathan Kitson; 8 Jordan Andrade; 7 Andy Speake; 12 Ed Hayles; 4 Kash Watkins; 3 Andrew Hoggins; 10 Jonny Payne. Subs (all used): 11 Josh Scott; 25 Luke Evans; 16 Graham O'Keeffe; 19 Kyle Danns.
Tries: J Scott (34), Brooker (42); **Goals:** Allan 1/2.
Rugby Leaguer & League Express Men of the Match: *Bears:* Billy Sheen; *Oxford:* Danny Allan.
Penalty count: 7-7; **Half-time:** 20-6;
Referee: Scott Mikalauskas; **Attendance:** 721.

GLOUCESTERSHIRE ALL GOLDS 36 SOUTH WALES SCORPIONS 6

ALL GOLDS: 1 Phil Cowburn; 23 Joe Martin; 3 Lewis Reece; 4 Callum Mulkeen; 28 Ryan Pywell; 20 Courtney Davies; 7 Matt Bradley; 10 Izaak Duffy; 9 Steve Parry; 14 Joe McClean; 30 Emmerson Whittel; 16 Ash Haynes; 33 Mark Bowen. Subs (all used): 6 Toby Topham; 13 Chris Vitalini; 8 Oliver Purslow; 32 Brad England.
Tries: Bradley (8), Martin (10), Mulkeen (25, 79), Vitalini (53), Topham (56), Whittel (67);
Goals: Bradley 4/7.
Sin bin: McClean (74) - late challenge on Farrer.
SCORPIONS: 1 Jordan Sheridan; 2 Ian Newbury; 3 Paul Edwards; 4 Kyle Scrivens; 24 Craig Lewis; 26 Marcus Webb; 7 Paul Emanuelli; 8 Osian Phillips; 9 Connor Farrer; 10 Morgan Evans; 11 Mike Connor; 18 Bradley Hill; 13 Neil Dallimore. Subs (all used): 6 Curtis Davies; 15 Rhys Davies; 17 Zak Williams; 23 Anthony Symons.
Try: R Davies (30); **Goals:** Emanuelli 1/1.
Rugby Leaguer & League Express Men of the Match: *All Golds:* Matt Bradley; *Scorpions:* Neil Dallimore.
Penalty count: 11-10; **Half-time:** 16-6;
Referee: Tom Grant; **Attendance:** 404.

KEIGHLEY COUGARS 28 YORK CITY KNIGHTS 12

COUGARS: 1 Jesse Sheriffe; 2 Gavin Duffy; 4 Danny Lawton; - Rikki Sheriffe; 5 Paul White; 6 Danny Jones; 7 Paul Handforth; 8 Scott Law; 9 James Feather; 12 Brendan Rawlins; 28 Josh Lynam; 17 Oliver Pursglove; 11 Ashley Lindsay. Subs (all used): 15 Neil Cherryholme; 16 Jode Sheriffe; 19 Matthew Bailey; 26 Paul March.
Tries: White (9, 24), Lynam (47), R Sheriffe (55), Law (60); **Goals:** Jones 4/6.
CITY KNIGHTS: 1 James Haynes; 5 Nev Morrison; 3 Greg Minikin; 4 Liam Cunningham; 2 Ben Dent; 6 Jon Presley; 7 Pat Smith; 8 Mark Applegarth; 14 Kris Brining; 10 Jack Aldous; 15 Josh Tonks; 12 Ed Smith; 21 Jack Pickles. Subs (all used): 13 Colton Roche; 20 Jay Leary; 22 Jack Iley; 29 Brad Nicholson.
Tries: P Smith (5), Presley (28); **Goals:** Haynes 2/2.
Rugby Leaguer & League Express Men of the Match: *Cougars:* Josh Lynam; *City Knights:* Jon Presley.
Penalty count: 8-4; **Half-time:** 10-12;
Referee: Gareth Hewer; **Attendance:** 903.

LONDON SKOLARS 12 HEMEL STAGS 34

SKOLARS: 1 Mathew Cook; 2 Sebastian Kolasa; 3 Kazeem Fatouri; 4 Mike Benson; 5 Judd Greenhalgh; 6 James Anthony; 7 Vince Spurr; 21 Dave Ellison; 9 Sam Druce; 10 Dion Chapman; 11 Will Lovell; 12 Harvey Burnett; 13 Will Fairhurst. Subs (all used): 16 Oliver Bloom; 24 Michael Sykes; 17 Anthony Cox; - Max Edwards.
Tries: Fairhurst (20, 76); **Goals:** Druce 2/2.
STAGS: 1 Derrell Olpherts; 31 Mo Agoro; 4 Michael Brown; 3 Jamie O'Callaghan; 5 Alex Anthony; 7 Charlie Lawrence; 24 James Woodburn-Hall; 26 James Howitt; 9 James Helliwell; 16 Mike Stewart; 15 Liam O'Callaghan; 11 Barry-John Swindells; 13 Eddie Mbaraga. Subs (all used): 8 Rob Thomas; 30 Nathan Darby; 14 Ryan Chester; 23 Tom Sadler.
Tries: Agoro (9, 62), J O'Callaghan (26), Helliwell (44), Olpherts (67), Anthony (71); **Goals:** Swindells 5/8.
Rugby Leaguer & League Express Men of the Match: *Skolars:* Will Fairhurst; *Stags:* Eddie Mbaraga.
Penalty count: 9-5; **Half-time:** 6-12;
Referee: Chris Campbell; **Attendance:** 376.

NEWCASTLE THUNDER 34 BARROW RAIDERS 22

THUNDER: 7 Jordan Meads; 1 Louis Sheriff; 3 Jason Tali; 4 Joe Brown; 21 Lee Mapals; 23 Benn Hardcastle; 6 Matty Beharrell; 15 Lee Fewlass; 13 Charlie Wabo; 36 Sonny Esslemont; 12 Rhys Clarke; 11 Jason Payne; 9 Dayne Craig. Subs (all used): 25 Evan Simons; 10 Mark Mexico; 18 Josh Stoker; 16 Francis Welsh.
Tries: Tali (1, 8, 35), Hardcastle (50), Sheriff (70), Fewlass (76); **Goals:** Hardcastle 5/6.
RAIDERS: 23 Chris Fleming; 2 Lee Haney; 3 Chris Hankinson; 27 Cameron Pitman; 4 Max Wiper; 29 Peter Lupton; 7 Liam Campbell; - Ruairi McGoff; 9 Nathan Mossop; 21 Anthony Bate; 24 Andy Litherland; 16 Adam Nicholson; 11 Liam Harrison. Subs (all used): 6 Brad Marwood; 13 Dan Toal; 19 Matt Heaton; 18 Danny Jones.
Tries: Fleming (25), Haney (27, 65), Bate (34), Lupton (79); **Goals:** Hankinson 1/5.
Rugby Leaguer & League Express Men of the Match: *Thunder:* Jason Tali; *Raiders:* Lee Haney.
Penalty count: 3-6; **Half-time:** 16-14;
Referee: Jamie Bloem; **Attendance:** 1,522.

ROCHDALE HORNETS 16 OLDHAM 23

HORNETS: 2 Gareth Langley; 20 Bradley Hargreaves; 24 Dave Hull; 4 Lee Paterson; 5 Dale Bloomfield; 21 Ryan Smith; 7 Danny Yates; 25 Richard Beaumont; 6 Paul Crook; 10 Warren Thompson; 11 Jordan Case; 19 Danny Bridge; 13 Tony Suffolk. Subs (all used): 15 Lewis Charnock; 9 Alex McClurg; 28 Matty Hadden; 17 Sam Brooks.
Tries: Bloomfield (15), Crook (18);
Goals: Crook 3/3, Charnock 1/1.
Sin bin: Charnock (60) - late challenge.
OLDHAM: 4 Jack Holmes; 2 Adam Clay; 17 George Tyson; 3 Jonathan Ford; 5 Jarrod Ward; 6 Lewis Palfrey; 7 Steve Roper; 8 Phil Joy; 15 Gareth Owen; 10 Adam Neal; 11 Josh Crowley; 12 Danny Langtree; 13 Liam Thompson. Subs (all used): 9 Sam Gee; 19 Michael Ward; 16 Kenny Hughes; 22 Nathan Mason.
Tries: Crowley (27, 74), Palfrey (39); **Goals:** Palfrey 5/5;
Field goal: Roper (77).
Rugby Leaguer & League Express Men of the Match: *Hornets:* Danny Bridge; *Oldham:* Josh Crowley.
Penalty count: 6-6; **Half-time:** 14-12;
Referee: Sam Ansell; **Attendance:** 1,201.

SWINTON LIONS 14 NORTH WALES CRUSADERS 14

LIONS: 7 Chris Atkin; 2 Shaun Robinson; 3 Stuart Littler; 22 Chris Rothwell; 1 Ritchie Hawkyard; 6 Ben White; 16 Jimmy Rowland; 8 Mike Morrison; 9 Andy Ackers; 24 Jordan James; 11 Grant Beecham; 21 Andy Ball; 31 Rob Lever. Subs (all used): 18 Aaron Lloyd; 13 Tommy Gallagher; 10 Ben Austin; 12 Darren Hawkyard.
Tries: Robinson (29), Littler (44), R Hawkyard (47);
Goals: Atkin 1/2, Rowland 0/2.
Sin bin: Rowland (21) - fighting.
CRUSADERS: 1 Tommy Johnson; 5 Rob Massam; 3 Christiaan Roets; 17 Stuart Reardon; 2 Scott Turner; 29 Declan Patton; 7 Jamie Dallimore; 8 Jonny Walker; 14 Karl Ashall; 16 Joe Burke; 11 Jono Smith; 12 Stephen Wild; 13 Gary Middlehurst. Subs (all used): 9 Callum Wright; 30 Gene Ormsby; 22 Alex Thompson; 10 Ryan Duffy.
Tries: Smith (2), Turner (33); **Goals:** Johnson 3/4.
Sin bin: Wild (14) - high tackle on Robinson; Smith (21) - fighting; Ashall (66) - kicking Atkin.
Rugby Leaguer & League Express Men of the Match: *Lions:* Mike Morrison; *Crusaders:* Jonny Walker.
Penalty count: 12-5; **Half-time:** 4-12;
Referee: Jon Roberts; **Attendance:** 561.

ROUND 2

Saturday 11th April 2015

GLOUCESTERSHIRE ALL GOLDS 18 ROCHDALE HORNETS 38

ALL GOLDS: 1 Phil Cowburn; 4 Callum Mulkeen; 2 Jamie Murphy; 3 Lewis Reece; 28 Ryan Pywell; 23 Joe Martin; 7 Matt Bradley; 8 Oliver Purslow; 9 Steve Parry; 14 Joe McClean; 30 Emmerson Whittel; 32 Brad England; 18 Jamie Crowther. Subs (all used): 6 Toby Topham; 16 Ash Haynes; 13 Chris Vitalini; 10 Izaak Duffy.
Tries: Pywell (2), McClean (16), Mulkeen (42);
Goals: Bradley 3/4.
Sin bin: Purslow (12) - high tackle on Yates.
HORNETS: 20 Bradley Hargreaves; 2 Gareth Langley; 24 Dave Hull; 22 Mike Ratu; 5 Dale Bloomfield; 21 Ryan Smith; 7 Danny Yates; 25 Richard Beaumont; 6 Paul Crook; 10 Warren Thompson; 11 Jordan Case; 19 Danny Bridge; 13 Tony Suffolk. Subs (all used): 14 James Tilley; 9 Alex McClurg; 28 Matty Hadden; 15 Lewis Charnock.
Tries: Bridge (13), Crook (29, 71), Bloomfield (36), Tilley (46), Yates (60), Hargreaves (65);
Goals: Crook 3/5, Charnock 2/2.
Rugby Leaguer & League Express Men of the Match: *All Golds:* Joe McClean; *Hornets:* Paul Crook.
Penalty count: 7-5; **Half-time:** 12-18;
Referee: Chris Campbell; **Attendance:** 218.

BARROW RAIDERS 50 SWINTON LIONS 12

RAIDERS: 23 Chris Fleming; 5 Kyle Dolan; 3 Chris Hankinson; 27 Cameron Pitman; 2 Lee Haney; 14 Josh Ward; 29 Peter Lupton; 8 Joe Bullock; 9 Nathan Mossop; 18 Danny Jones; 11 Liam Harrison; 12 Craig Briscoe; 21 Anthony Bate. Subs (all used): 6 Brad Marwood; 13 Dan Toal; 19 Matt Heaton; 10 Andrew Dawson.
Tries: Dolan (6), Hankinson (20), Mossop (33, 70), Heaton (45), D Toal (55, 69), Bullock (64), Marwood (67);
Goals: Ward 7/10.
LIONS: 7 Chris Atkin; 2 Shaun Robinson; 3 Stuart Littler; 22 Chris Rothwell; 1 Ritchie Hawkyard; 6 Ben White; 16 Jimmy Rowland; 8 Mike Morrison; 9 Andy Ackers; 31 Rob Lever; 11 Grant Beecham; 30 Matt Gardner; 12 Darren Hawkyard. Subs (all used): 29 Mick Govin; 13 Tommy Gallagher; 10 Ben Austin; 21 Andy Ball.
Tries: Gallagher (25), Gardner (27); **Goals:** Atkin 2/2.
Sin bin: D Hawkyard (63) - high tackle.
Rugby Leaguer & League Express Men of the Match: *Raiders:* Joe Bullock; *Lions:* Stuart Littler.
Penalty count: 9-4; **Half-time:** 16-12;
Referee: Andrew Sweet; **Attendance:** 1,064.

Sunday 12th April 2015

HEMEL STAGS 20 KEIGHLEY COUGARS 54

STAGS: 1 Derrell Olpherts; 5 Alex Anthony; 18 Chris McNamara; 3 Jamie O'Callaghan; 19 Miles McLeod; 4 Michael Brown; 7 Charlie Lawrence; 15 Liam O'Callaghan; 9 James Helliwell; 29 Nathan Darby; 13 Eddie Mbaraga; 11 Barry-John Swindells; 6 Jy-mel Coleman. Subs (all used): 21 Malikhi Lloyd-Jones; 22 Victor Croker; 23 Tom Sadler; 14 Ryan Chester.
Tries: Mbaraga (16), Anthony (25), Darby (64), L O'Callaghan (66);
Goals: Swindells 1/2, Jy-mel Coleman 1/2.
COUGARS: 1 Jesse Sheriffe; 2 Gavin Duffy; 4 Danny Lawton; - Hamish Barnes; 5 Paul White; 6 Danny Jones; 7 Paul Handforth; 12 Brendan Rawlins; 9 James Feather; 8 Scott Law; 28 Josh Lynam; 17 Oliver Pursglove; 19 Matthew Bailey. Subs (all used): 10 Ross Peltier; 15 Neil Cherryholme; 16 Jode Sheriffe; 26 Paul March.
Tries: Lynam (4, 77), Jones (20), Handforth (29, 32), Barnes (48, 80), Duffy (51, 72), White (54);
Goals: Jones 7/10.
Rugby Leaguer & League Express Men of the Match: *Stags:* Jy-mel Coleman; *Cougars:* Paul Handforth.
Penalty count: 1-6; **Half-time:** 10-24;
Referee: Adam Gill; **Attendance:** 272.

NORTH WALES CRUSADERS 18 NEWCASTLE THUNDER 24

CRUSADERS: 1 Tommy Johnson; 21 Ian Mort; 17 Stuart Reardon; 3 Christiaan Roets; 5 Rob Massam; 26 Craig White; 7 Jamie Dallimore; 8 Jonny Walker; 14 Karl Ashall; 16 Joe Burke; 29 Joe Philbin; 12 Stephen Wild; 11 Jono Smith. Subs (all used): 9 Callum Wright; 23 Mark Hobson; 10 Ryan Duffy; 30 George King.
Tries: King (49), Reardon (55), Smith (69);
Goals: Johnson 3/3.
THUNDER: 1 Louis Sheriff; 21 Lee Mapals; 31 Ali Blair; 3 Jason Tali; 22 Sam Bowring; 23 Benn Hardcastle; 7 Jordan Meads; 10 Mark Mexico; 13 Charlie Wabo; 8 Matt Barron; 36 Sonny Esslemont; 9 Dayne Craig; 16 Francis Welsh. Subs (all used): 25 Evan Simons; 15 Lee Fewlass; 18 Josh Stoker; 24 Ryan MacDonald.
Tries: Craig (36), Mapals (60), Sheriff (64), Simons (71);
Goals: Hardcastle 4/4.
Rugby Leaguer & League Express Men of the Match: *Crusaders:* Stuart Reardon; *Thunder:* Benn Hardcastle.
Penalty count: 6-8; **Half-time:** 0-6;
Referee: Gareth Hewer; **Attendance:** 789.

OLDHAM 38 COVENTRY BEARS 10

OLDHAM: 1 Steven Nield; 2 Adam Clay; 3 Jonathan Ford; 25 Tom Ashton; 5 Jarrod Ward; 7 Steve Roper; 4 Jack Holmes; 10 Adam Neal; 16 Kenny Hughes; 22 Nathan Mason; 11 Josh Crowley; 12 Danny Langtree; 23 Josh Johnson. Subs (all used): 14 Adam Files; 19 Michael Ward; 18 Richard Joy; 20 Tom Dempsey.
Tries: Holmes (9, 16), M Ward (26), Ford (37), Ashton (40), R Joy (47), Johnson (61); **Goals:** Roper 5/7.
BEARS: 1 Troy Brophy; 37 Josh Guzdek; 4 Eddie Medforth; 30 Dan Parker; 20 Jamahl Hunte; 6 Billy Sheen; 39 Matthew Marsh; 27 James Geurtjens; 9 Alex Brown; 38 Tom Hall; 29 Liam Thompson; 12 Chris Barratt; 13 Simon Phillips. Subs (all used): 21 Stephen Coleman; 26 Matt Cooper; 50 Matt Reid; 40 Connor Robinson.
Tries: Reid (53), Guzdek (57); **Goals:** Coleman 1/2.
Rugby Leaguer & League Express Men of the Match: *Oldham:* Michael Ward; *Bears:* Billy Sheen.
Penalty count: 5-5; **Half-time:** 26-0;
Referee: Jamie Bloem; **Attendance:** 322.

OXFORD 20 YORK CITY KNIGHTS 44

OXFORD: 9 Nathan Kitson; 1 Ian Clark; 14 Marcus Brooker; 3 Andrew Hoggins; 5 Aaron Jones-Bishop; 6 Danny Allan; 21 Adam Brook; 10 Jonny Payne; 32 Nathan Conroy; 19 Kyle Danns; 11 Josh Scott; 37 Adam Withington; 31 Dave Petersen. Subs (all used): 20 Ricky Hopwood; 24 Sam Blaney; 16 Graham O'Keeffe; 12 Ed Hayles.
Tries: Conroy (21), Hoggins (33, 38), Payne (64);
Goals: Allan 2/4.
Sin bin: Brook (68) - fighting.
CITY KNIGHTS: 1 James Haynes; 24 Tyler Craig; 3 Greg Minikin; 4 Liam Cunningham; 5 Nev Morrison; 6 Jon Presley; 7 Pat Smith; 8 Mark Applegarth; 9 Harry Carter; 10 Jack Aldous; 15 Josh Tonks; 12 Ed Smith; 13 Colton Roche. Subs (all used): 22 Jack Iley; 11 Ryan Mallinder; 16 Peter Aspinall; 20 Jay Leary.
Tries: Tonks (2), Craig (9, 80), Haynes (24), Cunningham (35), Iley (50), Minikin (57), Morrison (70), Presley (73); **Goals:** Haynes 3/6, P Smith 1/3.
Dismissal: Aspinall (68) - fighting.
Sin bin: Haynes (68) - fighting.
Rugby Leaguer & League Express Men of the Match: *Oxford:* Nathan Conroy; *City Knights:* Josh Tonks.
Penalty count: 4-9; **Half-time:** 16-18;
Referee: Scott Mikalauskas; **Attendance:** 200.

SOUTH WALES SCORPIONS 12 LONDON SKOLARS 30

SCORPIONS: 1 Jordan Sheridan; 2 Ian Newbury; 3 Paul Edwards; 4 Kyle Scrivens; 28 Yannic Parker; 6 Curtis Davies; 7 Paul Emanuelli; 8 Osian Phillips; 9 Connor Farrer; 10 Morgan Evans; 11 Mike Connor; 18 Bradley Hill; 13 Neil Dallimore. Subs (all used): 14 Dafydd Hellard; 15 Rhys Davies; 17 Zak Williams; 23 Anthony Symons.
Tries: Newbury (8), Sheridan (33); **Goals:** Emanuelli 2/2.
SKOLARS: 1 Aaron Small; 2 Jimmy Morgan; 3 Mike Benson; 4 Kazeem Fatouri; 24 Judd Greenhalgh; 6 Tommy Connick; 7 James Anthony; 16 Dave Ellison; 9 Joel Wicks;

10 Dion Chapman; 19 Craig Boot; 12 Harvey Burnett; 13 Will Fairhurst. Subs (all used): 14 Oliver Bloom; 15 Danny Burke; 8 Michael Sykes; 17 Anthony Cox.
Tries: Anthony (20, 36), Connick (27), Boot (53), Burnett (73); **Goals:** Connick 1/1, Fairhurst 4/4.
Rugby Leaguer & League Express Men of the Match: *Scorpions:* Connor Farrer; *Skolars:* Joel Wicks.
Penalty count: 7-5; **Half-time:** 12-18;
Referee: Sam Ansell; **Attendance:** 328.

ROUND 3

Saturday 18th April 2015

ROCHDALE HORNETS 48 BARROW RAIDERS 12

HORNETS: 1 Wayne English; 5 Dale Bloomfield; 4 Lee Paterson; 22 Mike Ratu; 2 Gareth Langley; 21 Ryan Smith; 7 Danny Yates; 13 Tony Suffolk; 6 Paul Crook; 10 Warren Thompson; 23 James Dandy; 19 Danny Bridge; 15 Lewis Charnock. Subs (all used): 11 Jordan Case; 9 Alex McClurg; 28 Matty Hadden; 14 James Tilley.
Tries: Ratu (2, 65), Crook (5, 18), Bridge (14, 77), Tilley (39), Bloomfield (51), Smith (58);
Goals: Crook 5/7, Langley 1/2.
RAIDERS: 23 Chris Fleming; 5 Kyle Dolan; 3 Chris Hankinson; 27 Cameron Pitman; 2 Lee Haney; 29 Peter Lupton; 14 Josh Ward; 8 Joe Bullock; 9 Nathan Mossop; 18 Danny Jones; 11 Liam Harrison; 12 Craig Briscoe; 21 Anthony Bate. Subs (all used): 7 Liam Campbell; 10 Andrew Dawson; 13 Dan Toal; 19 Matt Heaton.
Tries: Briscoe (32, 62); **Goals:** Hankinson 2/2.
Rugby Leaguer & League Express Men of the Match: *Hornets:* Mike Ratu; *Raiders:* Peter Lupton.
Penalty count: 15-8; **Half-time:** 28-6;
Referee: Jon Roberts; **Attendance:** 580.

Sunday 19th April 2015

COVENTRY BEARS 52 HEMEL STAGS 16

BEARS: 37 Josh Guzdek; 20 Jamahl Hunte; 30 Dan Parker; 4 Eddie Medforth; 1 Troy Brophy; 6 Billy Sheen; 39 Matthew Marsh; 27 James Geurtjens; 40 Connor Robinson; 38 Tom Hall; 12 Chris Barratt; 29 Liam Thompson; 13 Simon Phillips. Subs (all used): 16 Alex Beddows; 26 Matt Cooper; 21 Stephen Coleman; 50 Matt Reid.
Tries: Sheen (17, 48, 75), Hunte (29, 45), Cooper (42), Marsh (59, 70, 78); **Goals:** Robinson 8/9.
STAGS: 33 Brandon Conway; 5 Alex Anthony; 3 Jamie O'Callaghan; 4 Michael Brown; 32 Jamaine Akaidere; 6 Jy-mel Coleman; 7 Charlie Lawrence; 26 James Howitt; 9 James Helliwell; 16 Mike Stewart; 11 Barry-John Swindells; 18 Chris McNamara; 13 Eddie Mbaraga. Subs (all used): 15 Liam O'Callaghan; 14 Ryan Chester; 29 Nathan Darby; 31 Brooke Broughton.
Tries: Jy-mel Coleman (5), Brown (55, 65);
Goals: Swindells 2/3.
Rugby Leaguer & League Express Men of the Match: *Bears:* Matthew Marsh; *Stags:* Jy-mel Coleman.
Penalty count: 8-7; **Half-time:** 12-6;
Referee: Sam Ansell; **Attendance:** 425.

LONDON SKOLARS 10 GLOUCESTERSHIRE ALL GOLDS 36

SKOLARS: 1 Mathew Cook; 2 Jimmy Morgan; 3 Aaron Small; 4 Mike Benson; 24 Judd Greenhalgh; 6 James Anthony; 7 Sam Druce; 10 Dave Williams; 9 Joel Wicks; 8 Michael Sykes; 11 Harvey Burnett; 19 Craig Boot; 13 Will Fairhurst. Subs (all used): 16 Will Lovell; 20 Dave Ellison; 17 Jon Wallace; 15 Danny Burke.
Tries: Morgan (42), Wallace (50); **Goals:** Druce 1/2.
ALL GOLDS: 23 Joe Martin; 28 Ryan Pywell; 3 Lewis Reece; 1 Phil Cowburn; 4 Callum Mulkeen; 20 Courtney Davies; 7 Matt Bradley; 8 Oliver Purslow; 9 Steve Parry; 13 Chris Vitalini; 30 Emmerson Whittel; 32 Brad England; 18 Jamie Crowther. Subs (all used): 33 Jamie Murphy; 14 Joe McClean; 19 Brett Scriven; 10 Izaak Duffy.
Tries: Mulkeen (2, 19), Cowburn (29), Bradley (39), Murphy (56), Crowther (73), Davies (75);
Goals: Bradley 4/7.
Rugby Leaguer & League Express Men of the Match: *Skolars:* Jon Wallace; *All Golds:* Matt Bradley.
Penalty count: 9-6; **Half-time:** 0-20;
Referee: Jamie Bloem; **Attendance:** 243.

NEWCASTLE THUNDER 16 KEIGHLEY COUGARS 36

THUNDER: 1 Louis Sheriff; 21 Lee Mapals; 3 Jason Tali; 31 Ali Blair; 22 Sam Bowring; 23 Benn Hardcastle; 7 Jordan Meads; 8 Matt Barron; 13 Charlie Wabo; 15 Lee Fewlass; 9 Dayne Craig; 4 Joe Brown; 16 Francis Welsh. Subs (all used): 10 Mark Mexico; 25 Evan Simons; 18 Josh Stoker; 6 Matty Beharrell.
Tries: Tali (33), Meads (38, 79);
Goals: Hardcastle 2/2, Beharrell 0/1.
COUGARS: 1 Jesse Sheriffe; 25 Andy Gabriel; 4 Danny Lawton; - Hamish Barnes; 5 Paul White; 6 Danny Jones; 7 Paul Handforth; 12 Brendan Rawlins; 9 James Feather; 8 Scott Law; 28 Josh Lynam; 17 Oliver Pursglove; 11 Ashley Lindsay. Subs (all used): 26 Paul March; 15 Neil Cherryholme; 16 Jode Sheriffe; 19 Matthew Bailey.
Tries: Barnes (5), White (13, 17, 76), Jesse Sheriffe (26), Feather (72), P March (80); **Goals:** Jones 4/8.
Rugby Leaguer & League Express Men of the Match: *Thunder:* Jordan Meads; *Cougars:* Paul White.
Penalty count: 5-11; **Half-time:** 12-18;
Referee: Andrew Sweet; **Attendance:** 750.

SOUTH WALES SCORPIONS 12 OLDHAM 50

SCORPIONS: 1 Jordan Sheridan; 20 Tala Petelo; 3 Paul Edwards; 4 Kyle Scrivens; 28 Yannic Parker; 6 Curtis Davies; 7 Paul Emanuelli; 16 Scott Giles; 9 Connor Farrer; 18 Bradley Hill; 11 Mike Connor; 30 Bradley Mais; 13 Neil Dallimore. Subs (all used): 14 Dafydd Hellard; 15 Rhys Davies; 17 Zak Williams; 29 Dafydd Lloyd.
Tries: Farrer (26), Petelo (53); **Goals:** Emanuelli 2/2.
OLDHAM: 1 Steven Nield; 3 Jonathan Ford; 17 George Tyson; 25 Tom Ashton; 5 Jarrod Ward; 4 Jack Holmes; 6 Lewis Palfrey; 8 Phil Joy; 15 Gareth Owen; 22 Nathan Mason; 11 Josh Crowley; 12 Danny Langtree; 13 Liam Thompson. Subs (all used): 16 Kenny Hughes; 9 Sam Gee; 18 Richard Joy; 19 Michael Ward.
Tries: Mason (8), Tyson (11, 62), Ford (16, 76), Holmes (24, 40), J Ward (46), Langtree (56, 73);
Goals: Palfrey 5/10.
Rugby Leaguer & League Express Men of the Match: *Scorpions:* Connor Farrer; *Oldham:* Jonathan Ford.
Penalty count: 4-6; **Half-time:** 6-26;
Referee: Tom Grant; **Attendance:** 224.

ROUND 4

Saturday 25th April 2015

BARROW RAIDERS 86 SOUTH WALES SCORPIONS 0

RAIDERS: 1 Kris Tyson; 20 Shane Toal; 3 Chris Hankinson; 27 Cameron Pitman; 2 Lee Haney; 14 Josh Ward; 7 Liam Campbell; 8 Joe Bullock; 9 Nathan Mossop; 21 Anthony Bate; 24 Andy Litherland; 12 Craig Briscoe; 13 Dan Toal. Subs (all used): 19 Matt Heaton; 29 Peter Lupton; 18 Danny Jones; 30 Bradd Crellin.
Tries: D Toal (10), Campbell (14, 43), Mossop (21, 61, 74, 76), Ward (24, 36), Lupton (32), Litherland (48, 52), Tyson (64), S Toal (67, 79);
Goals: Ward 13/15.
SCORPIONS: 1 Jordan Sheridan; 2 Ian Newbury; 10 Jonny Leather; 4 Kyle Scrivens; 28 Yannic Parker; 17 Zak Williams; 7 Paul Emanuelli; 23 Anthony Symons; 9 Connor Farrer; 16 Scott Giles; - Bradley Mais; 18 Bradley Hill; 27 Ryan Millington. Subs (all used): 11 Mike Connor; 20 Tala Petelo; 30 Micah Manuokafoa; 12 Andrew Joy.
Rugby Leaguer & League Express Men of the Match: *Raiders:* Josh Ward; *Scorpions:* Paul Emanuelli.
Penalty count: 6-6; **Half-time:** 36-0;
Referee: Sam Ansell; **Attendance:** 836.

Sunday 26th April 2015

GLOUCESTERSHIRE ALL GOLDS 18 SWINTON LIONS 60

ALL GOLDS: 23 Joe Martin; 31 Jamie Murphy; 3 Lewis Reece; 1 Phil Cowburn; 4 Callum Mulkeen; 20 Courtney Davies; 7 Matt Bradley; 13 Chris Vitalini; 9 Steve Parry; 10 Izaak Duffy; 16 Ash Haynes; 32 Brad England; 6 Toby Topham. Subs (all used): 33 Mark Bowen; 34 Nathan Rainer; 18 Jamie Crowther; 14 Joe McClean.
Tries: Topham (7), Martin (34), Murphy (79);
Goals: Bradley 3/3.
LIONS: 7 Chris Atkin; 2 Shaun Robinson; 3 Stuart Littler; 22 Chris Rothwell; 1 Ritchie Hawkyard; 6 Ben White; 18 Aaron Lloyd; 8 Mike Morrison; 9 Andy Ackers; 24 Jordan James; 11 Grant Beecham; 17 Matt Gardner; 31 Rob Lever. Subs (all used): 10 Ben Austin; 30 Josh Barlow; 12 Darren Hawkyard; 29 Mick Govin.
Tries: Robinson (12, 66), White (18), R Hawkyard (21, 70), Gardner (24), Beecham (45), Littler (52), A Lloyd (57), Ackers (74), Atkin (77);
Goals: Atkin 8/11.
Rugby Leaguer & League Express Men of the Match: *All Golds:* Lewis Reece; *Lions:* Ritchie Hawkyard.
Penalty count: 8-4; **Half-time:** 12-24;
Referee: Scott Mikalauskas; **Attendance:** 314.

KEIGHLEY COUGARS 23 NORTH WALES CRUSADERS 22

COUGARS: 1 Jesse Sheriffe; 25 Andy Gabriel; 4 Danny Lawton; - Hamish Barnes; 5 Paul White; 6 Danny Jones; 7 Paul Handforth; 8 Scott Law; 9 James Feather; 12 Brendan Rawlins; 28 Josh Lynam; 17 Oliver Pursglove; 11 Ashley Lindsay. Subs (all used): 13 David March; 15 Neil Cherryholme; 16 Jode Sheriffe; 26 Paul March.
Tries: Handforth (8, 47, 75), Gabriel (66);
Goals: Jones 3/4; **Field goal:** Jones (80).
CRUSADERS: 1 Tommy Johnson; 5 Rob Massam; 3 Christiaan Roets; 17 Stuart Reardon; 29 Kevin Penny; 30 Gary Wheeler; 7 Jamie Dallimore; 8 Jonny Walker; 9 Callum Wright; 16 Joe Burke; 11 Jono Smith; 22 Alex Thompson; 13 Gary Middlehurst. Subs (all used): 10 Ryan Duffy; 14 Karl Ashall; 31 Joe Philbin; 32 George King.
Tries: Penny (11), Massam (14), Smith (23);
Goals: Johnson 5/5.
Rugby Leaguer & League Express Men of the Match: *Cougars:* Paul Handforth; *Crusaders:* Tommy Johnson.
Penalty count: 12-3; **Half-time:** 6-18;
Referee: Jamie Bloem; **Attendance:** 1,011.

OLDHAM 48 LONDON SKOLARS 6

OLDHAM: 20 Tom Dempsey; 3 Jonathan Ford; 17 George Tyson; 9 Sam Gee; 1 Steven Nield; 6 Lewis Palfrey; 7 Steve Roper; 10 Adam Neal; 15 Gareth Owen; 8 Phil Joy; 11 Josh Crowley; 12 Danny Langtree; 13 Liam Thompson. Subs (all used): 14 Adam Files; 18 Richard Joy; 16 Kenny Hughes; 22 Nathan Mason.
Tries: Tyson (4, 52), Thompson (27), Ford (35, 64, 72, 76), R Joy (44), Dempsey (79);
Goals: Palfrey 6/9.
SKOLARS: 1 Mathew Cook; 2 Jimmy Morgan; 4 Aaron Small; 3 Mike Benson; 5 Marcus Elliott; 6 Vince Spurr; 7 Sam Druce; 10 Dave Williams; 9 Joel Wicks; 16 Dion Chapman; 11 Harvey Burnett; 12 Will Lovell; 19 Will Fairhurst. Subs (all used): 8 Michael Sykes; 22 Oliver Bloom; 14 Anthony Cox; 17 Cariern Clement-Pascall.
Try: Spurr (80); **Goals:** Druce 1/1.
Sin bin: Small (73) - dissent.
Rugby Leaguer & League Express Men of the Match: *Oldham:* Danny Langtree; *Skolars:* Marcus Elliott.
Penalty count: 6-3; **Half-time:** 18-0;
Referee: Adam Gill; **Attendance:** 423.

OXFORD 31 HEMEL STAGS 28

OXFORD: 28 Sean Morris; 1 Louis Richards; 14 Marcus Brooker; 3 Andrew Hoggins; 5 Aaron Jones-Bishop; 6 Danny Allan; 21 Adam Brook; 11 Josh Scott; 32 Nathan Conroy; 10 Jonny Payne; 33 Dave Petersen; 27 Matty Blythe; 31 Mark Barlow. Subs (all used): 23 Tom Davies; 37 Adam Withington; 36 Danny Thomas; 19 Kyle Danns.
Tries: Brook (6), S Morris (25), Brooker (32), Conroy (40, 69), Richards (63);
Goals: Allan 0/1, Barlow 3/5; **Field goal:** Barlow (75).
STAGS: 1 Derrell Olpherts; 5 Alex Anthony; 3 Jamie O'Callaghan; 4 Michael Brown; 30 Vinny Finigan; 6 Jy-mel Coleman; 7 Charlie Lawrence; 16 Mike Stewart; 9 James Helliwell; 8 Rob Thomas; 11 Barry-John Swindells; 18 Chris McNamara; 13 Eddie Mbaraga. Subs (all used): 14 Ryan Chester; 26 James Howitt; 15 Liam O'Callaghan; 29 Nathan Darby.
Tries: Brown (11), Anthony (14, 29), Finigan (37, 77), J O'Callaghan (71);
Goals: Swindells 2/4, Jy-mel Coleman 0/2.
Rugby Leaguer & League Express Men of the Match: *Oxford:* Nathan Conroy; *Stags:* Vinny Finigan.
Penalty count: 8-2; **Half-time:** 22-20;
Referee: Tom Grant; **Attendance:** 278.

ROCHDALE HORNETS 15 NEWCASTLE THUNDER 16

HORNETS: 1 Wayne English; 5 Dale Bloomfield; 4 Lee Paterson; 22 Mike Ratu; 2 Gareth Langley; 21 Ryan Smith; 7 Danny Yates; 13 Tony Suffolk; 6 Paul Crook; 10 Warren Thompson; 23 James Dandy; 19 Danny Bridge; 15 Lewis Charnock. Subs (all used): 29 Jack Ashworth; 18 Dean Mignacca; 30 Anthony Walker; 14 James Tilley.
Tries: Yates (6), Bridge (26), Langley (45);
Goals: Crook 1/2, Langley 0/2; **Field goal:** Crook (68).
THUNDER: 7 Jordan Meads; 21 Lee Mapals; 4 Joe Brown; 31 Ali Blair; 5 Tom Capper; 27 Matthew Marsh; 6 Matty Beharrell; 8 Matt Barron; 13 Charlie Wabo; 10 Mark Mexico; 9 Dayne Craig; 11 Jason Payne; 12 Rhys Clarke. Subs (all used): 1 Louis Sheriff; 25 Evan Simons; 15 Lee Fewlass; 16 Francis Welsh.
Tries: Mapals (32), Meads (52), Brown (70), Craig (77);
Goals: Beharrell 0/4.
Rugby Leaguer & League Express Men of the Match: *Hornets:* Mike Ratu; *Thunder:* Lee Mapals.
Penalty count: 8-7; **Half-time:** 10-4;
Referee: Warren Turley; **Attendance:** 411.

YORK CITY KNIGHTS 42 COVENTRY BEARS 10

CITY KNIGHTS: 2 Ben Dent; 5 Nev Morrison; 3 Greg Minikin; 24 Tyler Craig; 25 Adam Dent; 7 Pat Smith; 6 Jon Presley; 8 Mark Applegarth; 14 Kris Brining; 10 Jack Aldous; 12 Ed Smith; 15 Josh Tonks; 11 Ryan Mallinder. Subs (all used): 9 Harry Carter; 21 Jack Pickles; 29 Brad Nicholson; 28 Mick Learmonth.
Tries: P Smith (3, 73), Brining (7), Minikin (18), Carter (20), Craig (28), A Dent (41, 70);
Goals: B Dent 5/8.
BEARS: 37 Josh Guzdek; 20 Jamahl Hunte; 30 Dan Parker; 4 Eddie Medforth; 41 Reece Chapman-Carry; 6 Billy Sheen; 7 Cameron Boulter; 27 James Geurtjens; 9 Alex Brown; 38 Tom Hall; 29 Liam Thompson; 12 Chris Barratt; 13 Simon Phillips. Subs (all used): 24 Richard Hughes; 50 Matt Reid; 26 Matt Cooper; 21 Stephen Coleman.
Tries: Hughes (49), Hunte (77); **Goals:** Coleman 1/2.
Rugby Leaguer & League Express Men of the Match: *City Knights:* Pat Smith; *Bears:* Eddie Medforth.
Penalty count: 6-4; **Half-time:** 24-0;
Referee: Jon Roberts; **Attendance:** 498 *(at Clifton Park).*

ROUND 5

Sunday 3rd May 2015

HEMEL STAGS 18 SOUTH WALES SCORPIONS 6

STAGS: 5 Alex Anthony; 33 Mo Agoro; 4 Michael Brown; 18 Chris McNamara; 30 Vinny Finigan; 6 Jy-mel Coleman; 24 James Woodburn-Hall; 16 Mike Stewart; 9 James Helliwell; 26 James Howitt; 11 Barry-John Swindells; 3 Jamie O'Callaghan; 13 Eddie Mbaraga. Subs (all used): 14 Ryan Chester; 7 Charlie Lawrence; 22 Victor Croker; 17 Dan Ljazouli.
Tries: McNamara (4), Mbaraga (14), Finigan (48), Swindells (69); **Goals:** Swindells 1/4.
Sin bin: Woodburn-Hall (67) - fighting.
SCORPIONS: 1 Jordan Sheridan; 2 Ian Newbury; 26 Marcus Webb; 4 Kyle Scrivens; 28 Yannic Parker; 6 Curtis Davies; 7 Paul Emanuelli; 11 Mike Connor; 9 Connor Farrer; 16 Scott Giles; 29 Tom Morgan; 12 Andy Joy; 13 Neil Dallimore. Subs (all used): 14 Dafydd Hellard; 15 Rhys Davies; 30 Bradley Mais; 17 Zak Williams.
Try: Curtis Davies (63); **Goals:** Emanuelli 1/1.
Sin bin: Hellard (67) - fighting.
Rugby Leaguer & League Express Men of the Match: *Stags:* Jy-mel Coleman; *Scorpions:* Paul Emanuelli.
Penalty count: 8-8; **Half-time:** 10-0;
Referee: Jon Roberts; **Attendance:** 137.

NORTH WALES CRUSADERS 24 BARROW RAIDERS 16

CRUSADERS: 1 Tommy Johnson; 29 Kevin Penny; 17 Stuart Reardon; 3 Christiaan Roets; 5 Rob Massam; 30 Gareth O'Brien; 7 Jamie Dallimore; 8 Jonny Walker; 9 Callum Wright; 16 Joe Burke; 11 Jono Smith; 22 Alex Thompson; 13 Gary Middlehurst. Subs (all used): 14 Karl Ashall; 31 Joe Philbin; 32 George King; 10 Ryan Duffy.
Tries: Dallimore (11, 68), Thompson (39), King (66);
Goals: Johnson 4/4.
Sin bin: Smith (58) - dissent.
RAIDERS: 1 Kris Tyson; 2 Lee Haney; 3 Chris Hankinson; 31 Cameron Pitman; 20 Shane Toal; 14 Josh Ward; 7 Liam Campbell; 8 Joe Bullock; 9 Nathan Mossop; 21 Anthony Bate; 11 Liam Harrison; 12 Craig Briscoe; 13 Dan Toal. Subs: 29 Peter Lupton; 30 Bradd Crellin; 10 Andrew Dawson; 18 Danny Jones (not used).
Tries: Campbell (22), Tyson (25), Haney (33);
Goals: Ward 2/3.
Sin bin: Bate (19) - punching;
Pitman (65) - professional foul.
Rugby Leaguer & League Express Men of the Match:
Crusaders: Jamie Dallimore; *Raiders:* Joe Bullock.
Penalty count: 9-14; **Half-time:** 12-16;
Referee: Tom Crashley; **Attendance:** 612.

COVENTRY BEARS 10 ROCHDALE HORNETS 35

BEARS: 7 Cameron Boulter; 42 Dan Rundle; 4 Eddie Medforth; 13 Simon Phillips; 41 Reece Chapman-Carry; 30 Dan Parker; 18 Dan Poulton; 27 James Geurtjens; 9 Alex Brown; 38 Tom Hall; 50 Matt Reid; 12 Chris Barratt; 21 Stephen Coleman. Subs (all used): 24 Richard Hughes; 26 Matt Cooper; 17 Alex Calvert; 32 Kenneth Kelliher.
Tries: Parker (8), Boulter (74); **Goals:** Coleman 1/2.
HORNETS: 1 Wayne English; 2 Gareth Langley; 4 Lee Paterson; 24 Dave Hull; 5 Dale Bloomfield; 21 Ryan Smith; 7 Danny Yates; 28 Matty Hadden; 23 James Dandy; 10 Warren Thompson; 19 Danny Bridge; 29 Jack Ashworth; 14 James Tilley. Subs (all used): 30 Anthony Walker; 20 Bradley Hargreaves; 8 John Cookson; 9 Alex McClurg.
Tries: Bloomfield (27), English (38), Walker (43, 48), W Thompson (54), Bridge (59); **Goals:** Langley 5/6;
Field goal: Yates (80).
Rugby Leaguer & League Express Men of the Match:
Bears: Dan Rundle; *Hornets:* Anthony Walker.
Penalty count: 7-7; **Half-time:** 4-10;
Referee: Tom Grant; **Attendance:** 496.

NEWCASTLE THUNDER 36 OXFORD 20

THUNDER: 7 Jordan Meads; 17 Stuart Kain; 3 Jason Tali; 4 Joe Brown; 5 Tom Capper; 6 Matty Beharrell; 27 Matthew Marsh; 8 Matt Barron; 25 Evan Simons; 10 Mark Mexico; 11 Jason Payne; 9 Dayne Craig; 12 Rhys Clarke. Subs (all used): 1 Louis Sheriff; 15 Lee Fewlass; 18 Josh Stoker; 16 Francis Welsh.
Tries: Tali (5, 13), Kain (44), Craig (52, 72), Meads (55), Capper (75); **Goals:** Craig 4/7.
Sin bin: Meads (63) - fighting.
OXFORD: 28 Sean Morris; 1 Louis Richards; 14 Marcus Brooker; 3 Andrew Hoggins; 5 Aaron Jones-Bishop; 21 Adam Brook; 36 Danny Thomas; 10 Jonny Payne; 31 Mark Barlow; 34 Karl Davies; 11 Josh Scott; 27 Matty Blythe; 33 Dave Petersen. Subs (all used): 9 Nathan Kitson; 8 Jordan Andrade; 19 Kyle Danns; 37 Adam Withington.
Tries: Petersen (30), Thomas (36), S Morris (59, 80);
Goals: Kitson 2/3, Barlow 0/1.
Sin bin: Brook (8) - dangerous challenge;
Blythe (63) - fighting.
Rugby Leaguer & League Express Men of the Match:
Thunder: Dayne Craig; *Oxford:* Sean Morris.
Penalty count: 9-5; **Half-time:** 12-10;
Referee: Andrew Sweet; **Attendance:** 552.

OLDHAM 33 GLOUCESTERSHIRE ALL GOLDS 30

OLDHAM: 20 Tom Dempsey; 1 Steven Nield; 17 George Tyson; 9 Sam Gee; 5 Jarrod Ward; 6 Lewis Palfrey; 4 Jack Holmes; 10 Adam Neal; 15 Gareth Owen; 8 Phil Joy; 11 Josh Crowley; 12 Danny Langtree; 23 Josh Johnson. Subs (all used): 14 Adam Files; 13 Liam Thompson; 19 Michael Ward; 22 Nathan Mason.
Tries: Nield (20, 50, 64), Johnson (36), Gee (39), Thompson (71); **Goals:** Palfrey 2/3, Dempsey 2/3;
Field goal: Dempsey (77).
ALL GOLDS: 23 Joe Martin; 31 Jamie Murphy; 1 Phil Cowburn; 32 Brad England; 28 Ryan Pywell; 20 Courtney Davies; 7 Matt Bradley; 8 Oliver Purslow; 9 Steve Parry; 19 Brett Scriven; 3 Lewis Reece; 4 Callum Mulkeen; 30 Emmerson Whittel. Subs (all used): 33 Mark Bowen; 16 Ash Haynes; 18 Jamie Crowther; 14 Joe McClean.
Tries: Reece (4), Martin (14), McClean (43, 67), Mulkeen (78); **Goals:** Bradley 5/5.
Sin bin: Mulkeen (30) - holding down;
Parry (80) - dissent.
Rugby Leaguer & League Express Men of the Match:
Oldham: Tom Dempsey; *All Golds:* Matt Bradley.
Penalty count: 16-5; **Half-time:** 16-12;
Referee: Adam Gill; **Attendance:** 413.

SWINTON LIONS 34 YORK CITY KNIGHTS 24

LIONS: 7 Chris Atkin; 2 Shaun Robinson; 3 Stuart Littler; 4 Mick Nanyn; 1 Ritchie Hawkyard; 6 Ben White; 18 Aaron Lloyd; 8 Mike Morrison; 9 Andy Ackers; 24 Jordan James; 30 Josh Barlow; 17 Matt Gardner; 31 Rob Lever. Subs (all used): 29 Mick Govin; 10 Ben Austin; 13 Tommy Gallagher; 23 Connor Dwyer.
Tries: Littler (11, 53, 57), Atkin (24), White (60), Ackers (69); **Goals:** Atkin 5/6.
CITY KNIGHTS: 2 Ben Dent; 19 James Clare; 3 Greg Minikin; 4 Liam Cunningham; 5 Nev Morrison; 6 Jon Presley; 7 Pat Smith; 8 Mark Applegarth; 9 Harry Carter; 10 Jack Aldous; 12 Ed Smith; 15 Josh Tonks; 28 Mick Learmonth. Subs (all used): 27 Casey Canterbury; 29 Brad Nicholson; 13 Colton Roche; 30 Lee Waterman.
Tries: E Smith (30), Minikin (44), Clare (65), Cunningham (78), Tonks (80);
Goals: Waterman 1/2, B Dent 1/3.
Rugby Leaguer & League Express Men of the Match:
Lions: Stuart Littler; *City Knights:* Greg Minikin.
Penalty count: 3-7; **Half-time:** 12-6;
Referee: Michael Woodhead; **Attendance:** 444.

ROUND 6

Saturday 9th May 2015

GLOUCESTERSHIRE ALL GOLDS 6
YORK CITY KNIGHTS 46

ALL GOLDS: 23 Joe Martin; 28 Ryan Pywell; 3 Lewis Reece; 32 Brad England; 1 Phil Cowburn; 20 Courtney Davies; 7 Matt Bradley; 8 Oliver Purslow; 9 Steve Parry; 19 Brett Scriven; 30 Emmerson Whittel; 4 Callum Mulkeen; 14 Joe McClean. Subs (all used): 35 Owain Griffiths; 34 Alex Davidson; 13 Chris Vitalini; 10 Izaak Duffy.
Try: Vitalini (18); **Goals:** Bradley 1/1.
Dismissal: Scriven (77) - punching.
CITY KNIGHTS: 2 Ben Dent; 24 Tyler Craig; 3 Greg Minikin; 4 Liam Cunningham; 5 Nev Morrison; 6 Jon Presley; 7 Pat Smith; 8 Mark Applegarth; 9 Harry Carter; 10 Jack Aldous; 12 Ed Smith; 15 Josh Tonks; 13 Colton Roche. Subs (all used): 30 Liam Richmond; 32 Kane Riley; 11 Ryan Mallinder; 29 Brad Nicholson.
Tries: P Smith (2, 45), Craig (11), Tonks (34, 55), B Dent (36), Morrison (60), Minikin (73);
Goals: B Dent 7/8.
Rugby Leaguer & League Express Men of the Match:
All Golds: Brad England; *City Knights:* Pat Smith.
Penalty count: 11-5; **Half-time:** 6-22;
Referee: Jon Roberts; **Attendance:** 212.

ROCHDALE HORNETS 28 SWINTON LIONS 16

HORNETS: 1 Wayne English; 5 Dale Bloomfield; 4 Lee Paterson; 24 Dave Hull; 2 Gareth Langley; 21 Ryan Smith; 7 Danny Yates; 30 Anthony Walker; 15 Lewis Charnock; 10 Warren Thompson; 29 Jack Ashworth; 19 Danny Bridge; 14 James Tilley. Subs (all used): 6 Paul Crook; 20 Bradley Hargreaves; 28 Matty Hadden; 13 Tony Suffolk.
Tries: Hull (4), Yates (18, 72), Walker (36), Ashworth (48); **Goals:** Charnock 2/2, Crook 2/3.
LIONS: 7 Chris Atkin; 2 Shaun Robinson; 3 Stuart Littler; 22 Chris Rothwell; 1 Ritchie Hawkyard; 6 Ben White; 18 Aaron Lloyd; 8 Mike Morrison; 9 Andy Ackers; 24 Jordan James; 30 Josh Barlow; 12 Darren Hawkyard; 31 Rob Lever. Subs (all used): 13 Tommy Gallagher; 23 Connor Dwyer; 10 Ben Austin; 29 Mick Govin.
Tries: R Hawkyard (10, 57), Rothwell (32);
Goals: Atkin 2/3.
Rugby Leaguer & League Express Men of the Match:
Hornets: Jack Ashworth; *Lions:* Chris Atkin.
Penalty count: 3-5; **Half-time:** 18-10;
Referee: Jamie Bloem; **Attendance:** 662.

BARROW RAIDERS 30 OLDHAM 18

RAIDERS: 1 Kris Tyson; 5 Kyle Dolan; 24 Andy Litherland; 31 Cameron Pitman; 20 Shane Toal; 14 Josh Ward; 7 Liam Campbell; 8 Joe Bullock; 9 Nathan Mossop; 21 Anthony Bate; 11 Liam Harrison; 12 Craig Briscoe; 13 Dan Toal. Subs (all used): 30 Bradd Crellin; 29 Peter Lupton; 10 Andrew Dawson; 16 Adam Nicholson.
Tries: Pitman (6, 19), Dolan (38), Campbell (50), Litherland (70), Harrison (79); **Goals:** Ward 3/7.
Dismissal: Campbell (79) - fighting.
OLDHAM: 1 Steven Nield; 2 Adam Clay; 17 George Tyson; 4 Jack Holmes; 5 Jarrod Ward; 6 Lewis Palfrey; 7 Steve Roper; 10 Adam Neal; 15 Gareth Owen; 22 Nathan Mason; 11 Josh Crowley; 12 Danny Langtree; 23 Josh Johnson. Subs (all used): 19 Michael Ward; 8 Phil Joy; 13 Liam Thompson; 16 Kenny Hughes.
Tries: Clay (14, 23), Holmes (46), Owen (76);
Goals: Palfrey 1/4.
Dismissal: Owen (79) - fighting.
Rugby Leaguer & League Express Men of the Match:
Raiders: Anthony Bate; *Oldham:* Lewis Palfrey.
Penalty count: 9-4; **Half-time:** 12-8;
Referee: Chris Campbell; **Attendance:** 935.

Sunday 10th May 2015

HEMEL STAGS 12 NEWCASTLE THUNDER 58

STAGS: 1 Derrell Olpherts; 30 Vinny Finigan; 13 Eddie Mbaraga; 18 Chris McNamara; 5 Alex Anthony; 4 Michael Brown; 6 Jy-mel Coleman; 16 Mike Stewart; 9 James Helliwell; 26 James Howitt; 3 Jamie O'Callaghan; 11 Barry-John Swindells; 17 Dan Ljazouli. Subs (all used): 8 Rob Thomas; 7 Charlie Lawrence; 14 Ryan Chester; 31 Nathan Darby.
Tries: Brown (23), Olpherts (80);
Goals: Swindells 1/1, Jy-mel Coleman 1/1.
THUNDER: 1 Louis Sheriff; 17 Stuart Kain; 31 Ali Blair; 4 Joe Brown; 5 Tom Capper; 6 Matty Beharrell; 27 Matthew Marsh; 8 Matt Barron; 25 Evan Simons; 18 Josh Stoker; 11 Jason Payne; 9 Dayne Craig; 12 Rhys Clarke. Subs (all used): 19 Craig Boot; 36 Sonny Esslemont; 28 Stephen Holker; 16 Francis Welsh.
Tries: Craig (9, 40), Blair (17, 20), Beharrell (26), Simons (34), Marsh (37, 55, 68), Holker (61);
Goals: Beharrell 9/10.
Rugby Leaguer & League Express Men of the Match:
Stags: Derrell Olpherts; *Thunder:* Matty Beharrell.
Penalty count: 8-10; **Half-time:** 6-40;
Referee: Jack Smith; **Attendance:** 179.

KEIGHLEY COUGARS 52 COVENTRY BEARS 10

COUGARS: 1 Jesse Sheriffe; 25 Andy Gabriel; 32 Hamish Barnes; 30 Rikki Sheriffe; 5 Paul White; 26 Paul March; 7 Paul Handforth; 8 Scott Law; 9 James Feather; 12 Brendan Rawlins; 28 Josh Lynam; 17 Oliver Pursglove; 11 Ashley Lindsay. Subs (all used): 15 Neil Cherryholme; 16 Jode Sheriffe; 20 Ryan Patchett; 21 Sean Kelly.
Tries: Rawlins (4), Feather (10, 77, 80), P March (21), Barnes (31), Jesse Sheriffe (43), White (61), Pursglove (73); **Goals:** Handforth 8/9.
BEARS: 7 Cameron Boulter; 42 Dan Rundle; 21 Stephen Coleman; 4 Eddie Medforth; 41 Reece Chapman-Carry; 18 Dan Poulton; 30 Dan Parker; 27 James Geurtjens; 24 Richard Hughes; 38 Tom Hall; 12 Chris Barratt; 29 Liam Thompson; 50 Matt Reid. Subs (all used): 9 Alex Brown; 16 Alex Beddows; 26 Matt Cooper; 32 Kenneth Kelliher.
Tries: Medforth (27, 39); **Goals:** Coleman 1/2.
Sin bin: Parker (72) - professional foul.
Rugby Leaguer & League Express Men of the Match:
Cougars: Brendan Rawlins; *Bears:* Reece Chapman-Carry.
Penalty count: 6-6; **Half-time:** 24-10;
Referee: Dave Merrick; **Attendance:** 4,066.

OXFORD 38 LONDON SKOLARS 24

OXFORD: - Sean Morris; 21 Luke Gardiner; 14 Marcus Brooker; 3 Andrew Hoggins; 28 Jonny Morris; 32 Adam Brook; 36 Danny Thomas; 34 Karl Davies; 31 Mark Barlow; 10 Jonny Payne; 11 Josh Scott; 37 Adam Withington; 27 Matty Blythe. Subs (all used): 9 Nathan Kitson; 8 Jordan Andrade; 19 Kyle Danns; 5 Aaron Jones-Bishop.
Tries: Hoggins (5), Blythe (21), K Davies (24), Thomas (35), Gardiner (39, 75), Jones-Bishop (54);
Goals: Brook 5/7.
SKOLARS: 1 James Anthony; 2 Marcus Elliott; 3 Mathew Cook; 4 Aaron Small; 5 Jimmy Morgan; 6 Josh Kittrick; 7 Mike Bishay; 8 Michael Sykes; 9 Joel Wicks; 10 Dave Williams; 11 Cariern Clement-Pascall; 12 Will Lovell; 14 Will Fairhurst. Subs (all used): 25 Anthony Cox; 20 Max Edwards; 24 Lewis Reed; 16 Mike Benson.
Tries: Kittrick (50), Sykes (61), Cook (63), Wicks (66);
Goals: M Bishay 4/4.
Rugby Leaguer & League Express Men of the Match:
Oxford: Adam Brook; *Skolars:* Josh Kittrick.
Penalty count: 4-8; **Half-time:** 28-0;
Referee: Scott Mikalauskas; **Attendance:** 255.

SOUTH WALES SCORPIONS 18
NORTH WALES CRUSADERS 50

SCORPIONS: 1 Jordan Sheridan; 2 Ian Newbury; 3 Paul Edwards; 10 Jonny Leather; 28 Yannic Parker; 6 Curtis Davies; 7 Paul Emanuelli; 8 Osian Phillips; 9 Connor Farrer; 4 Kyle Scrivens; 11 Mike Connor; 29 Tom Morgan; 13 Neil Dallimore. Subs (all used): 14 Dafydd Hellard; 16 Scott Giles; 17 Zak Williams; 23 Anthony Symons.
Tries: Leather (13), Symons (29), Curtis Davies (73);
Goals: Emanuelli 3/4.
CRUSADERS: 1 Tommy Johnson; 17 Stuart Reardon; 3 Christiaan Roets; 22 Alex Thompson; 5 Rob Massam; 30 Gareth O'Brien; 7 Jamie Dallimore; 16 Joe Burke; 14 Karl Ashall; 10 Ryan Duffy; 11 Jono Smith; 12 Stephen Wild; 13 Gary Middlehurst. Subs (all used): 32 George King; 15 Lee Hudson; 20 Elliott Davies; 23 Mark Hobson.
Tries: Thompson (5), Dallimore (10), O'Brien (38), Davies (40), Johnson (49), Smith (59, 65), Reardon (63), Massam (78); **Goals:** Johnson 7/9.
Rugby Leaguer & League Express Men of the Match:
Scorpions: Curtis Davies; *Crusaders:* Tommy Johnson.
Penalty count: 6-6; **Half-time:** 14-24;
Referee: Callum Straw; **Attendance:** 1,025
(at Cardiff Arms Park).

ROUND 7

Saturday 16th May 2015

GLOUCESTERSHIRE ALL GOLDS 66
COVENTRY BEARS 6

ALL GOLDS: 23 Joe Martin; 31 Jamie Murphy; 6 Toby Topham; 1 Phil Cowburn; 28 Ryan Pywell; 33 Mark Bowen; 7 Matt Bradley; 8 Oliver Purslow; 9 Steve Parry; 34 Alex Davidson; 3 Lewis Reece; 4 Callum Mulkeen; 30 Emmerson Whittel. Subs (all used): 35 Owain Griffiths; 32 Brad England; 19 Brett Scriven; 14 Joe McClean.
Tries: Bowen (2, 13, 67), Pywell (4, 74), Bradley (10, 54), Cowburn (22), Murphy (25, 79), Mulkeen (64), Topham (77); **Goals:** Bradley 8/10, Reece 1/2.
Sin bin: England (73) - fighting.
BEARS: 7 Cameron Boulter; 20 Jamahl Hunte; 5 Ben Parry; 13 Simon Phillips; 42 Dan Rundle; 6 Billy Sheen; 30 Dan Parker; 27 James Geurtjens; 24 Richard Hughes; 10 John Aldred; 12 Chris Barratt; 29 Liam Thompson; 50 Matt Reid. Subs (all used): 14 Dylan Bale; 26 Matt Cooper; 38 Tom Hall; 21 Stephen Coleman.
Try: Hunte (30); **Goals:** Parker 1/1.
Dismissal: Sheen (73) - fighting.
Rugby Leaguer & League Express Men of the Match:
All Golds: Mark Bowen; *Bears:* Jamahl Hunte.
Penalty count: 4-9; **Half-time:** 34-6;
Referee: Scott Mikalauskas; **Attendance:** 308.

NORTH WALES CRUSADERS 74 HEMEL STAGS 14

CRUSADERS: 21 Ian Mort; 5 Rob Massam; 29 Sam Peet; 22 Alex Thompson; 17 Stuart Reardon; 14 Karl Ashall; 7 Jamie Dallimore; 8 Jonny Walker; 9 Callum Wright; 16 Joe Burke; 11 Jono Smith; 12 Stephen Wild; 13 Gary Middlehurst. Subs (all used): 10 Ryan Duffy; 20 Elliott Davies; 15 Lee Hudson; 23 Mark Hobson.
Tries: Mort (6), Smith (8, 26, 48, 56, 74), Massam (12, 44, 62), Thompson (40), Wild (51), Ashall (65), Wright (79); **Goals:** Mort 11/13.
STAGS: 1 Derrell Olpherts; 33 Mo Agoro; 4 Michael Brown; 18 Chris McNamara; 5 Alex Anthony; 6 Jy-mel Coleman; 24 James Woodburn-Hall; 17 Dan Ljazouli; 9 James Helliwell; 26 James Howitt; 11 Barry-John Swindells; 30 Elliott Cosgrove; 13 Eddie Mbaraga. Subs (all used): 14 Ryan Chester; 7 Charlie Lawrence; 31 Nathan Darby; 32 Mark Castle.
Tries: Anthony (20), Cosgrove (54, 68);
Goals: Swindells 0/1, Jy-mel Coleman 1/2.
Rugby Leaguer & League Express Men of the Match: *Crusaders:* Jono Smith; *Stags:* Elliott Cosgrove.
Penalty count: 2-5; **Half-time:** 30-4;
Referee: Sam Ansell; **Attendance:** 503.

ROCHDALE HORNETS 76 OXFORD 16

HORNETS: 1 Wayne English; 5 Dale Bloomfield; 25 Jack Ashworth; 24 Dave Hull; 20 Bradley Hargreaves; 21 Ryan Smith; 7 Danny Yates; 30 Anthony Walker; 6 Paul Crook; 13 Tony Suffolk; 12 Alex Trumper; 19 Danny Bridge; - Luke Thompson. Subs (all used): 9 Alex McClurg; 14 James Tilley; 28 Matty Hadden; 10 Warren Thompson.
Tries: Bloomfield (5, 19, 38), Yates (12), W Thompson (28), Ashworth (34), Hadden (42, 47), Walker (53), Bridge (58), Hargreaves (63), Suffolk (67), Crook (80); **Goals:** Crook 9/9, Yates 3/4.
OXFORD: 36 Danny Thomas; 21 Luke Gardiner; 14 Marcus Brooker; 3 Andrew Hoggins; 5 Aaron Jones-Bishop; 9 Nathan Kitson; 31 Mark Barlow; 34 Karl Davies; 32 Ray Nasso; 33 Erjon Dollapi; 11 Josh Scott; 37 Adam Withington; 10 Jonny Payne. Subs (all used): 19 Kyle Danns; 8 Jordan Andrade; 25 Luke Evans; 23 Tom Davies.
Tries: Hoggins (36), Nasso (74), Gardiner (77);
Goals: Kitson 2/3.
Rugby Leaguer & League Express Men of the Match: *Hornets:* Jack Ashworth; *Oxford:* Aaron Jones-Bishop.
Penalty count: 7-5; **Half-time:** 34-6;
Referee: Andrew Sweet; **Attendance:** 652.

Sunday 17th May 2015

LONDON SKOLARS 6 BARROW RAIDERS 42

SKOLARS: 1 James Anthony; 2 Jimmy Morgan; 3 Mathew Cook; 4 Aaron Small; 5 Marcus Elliott; 6 Mike Bishay; 7 Oscar Thomas; 24 Lewis Reed; 9 Joel Wicks; 10 Dave Williams; 11 Mike Benson; 12 Will Lovell; 19 Will Fairhurst. Subs (all used): 8 Michael Sykes; 15 Billy Driver; 21 Dave Ellison; 16 Cariern Clement-Pascall.
Try: Benson (53); **Goals:** Thomas 1/1.
RAIDERS: 1 Kris Tyson; 20 Shane Toal; 3 Chris Hankinson; 31 Cameron Pitman; 5 Kyle Dolan; 14 Josh Ward; 7 Liam Campbell; 8 Joe Bullock; 9 Nathan Mossop; 21 Anthony Bate; 11 Liam Harrison; 12 Craig Briscoe; 13 Dan Toal. Subs (all used): 29 Peter Lupton; 24 Andy Litherland; 30 Bradd Crellin; 10 Andrew Dawson.
Tries: Pitman (5), Dawson (21), Harrison (63), Ward (66), Bate (73), S Toal (78); **Goals:** Ward 9/9.
Rugby Leaguer & League Express Men of the Match: *Skolars:* Dave Ellison; *Raiders:* Andrew Dawson.
Penalty count: 5-11; **Half-time:** 0-16;
Referee: Tom Grant; **Attendance:** 331.

OLDHAM 45 NEWCASTLE THUNDER 20

OLDHAM: 1 Steven Nield; 2 Adam Clay; 17 George Tyson; 9 Sam Gee; 5 Jarrod Ward; 6 Lewis Palfrey; 7 Steve Roper; 10 Adam Neal; 15 Gareth Owen; 8 Phil Joy; 11 Josh Crowley; 12 Danny Langtree; 23 Josh Johnson. Subs (all used): 22 Nathan Mason; 13 Liam Thompson; 19 Michael Ward; 16 Kenny Hughes.
Tries: Roper (10), Owen (16), Clay (18, 71, 79), Langtree (25), Nield (37), Palfrey (65); **Goals:** Palfrey 6/8;
Field goal: Palfrey (76).
THUNDER: 7 Jordan Meads; 17 Stuart Kain; 31 Ali Blair; 4 Joe Brown; 5 Tom Capper; 6 Matty Beharrell; 27 Matthew Marsh; 8 Matt Barron; 25 Evan Simons; 18 Josh Stoker; 11 Jason Payne; 9 Dayne Craig; 12 Rhys Clarke. Subs (all used): 14 Paul Stamp; 26 Sebastien Martins; 28 Stephen Holker; 16 Francis Welsh.
Tries: Craig (3, 58), Brown (28), Payne (46);
Goals: Beharrell 2/4.
Rugby Leaguer & League Express Men of the Match: *Oldham:* Gareth Owen; *Thunder:* Francis Welsh.
Penalty count: 6-7; **Half-time:** 28-8;
Referee: Dave Merrick; **Attendance:** 491.

SWINTON LIONS 29 KEIGHLEY COUGARS 16

LIONS: 1 Ritchie Hawkyard; 2 Shaun Robinson; 3 Stuart Littler; 22 Chris Rothwell; 28 Mike Butt; 6 Ben White; 18 Aaron Lloyd; 24 Jordan James; 9 Andy Ackers; 10 Ben Austin; 30 Josh Barlow; 23 Connor Dwyer; 31 Rob Lever. Subs (all used): 29 Mick Govin; 12 Darren Hawkyard; 8 Mike Morrison; 21 Andy Ball.
Tries: Dwyer (17, 67), Rothwell (27), Butt (36), Robinson (49), White (75); **Goals:** White 0/2, Govin 0/1, R Hawkyard 2/3; **Field goal:** White (47).
COUGARS: 1 Jesse Sheriffe; 25 Andy Gabriel; 4 Danny Lawton; 32 Hamish Barnes; 5 Paul White; 26 Paul March; 7 Paul Handforth; 12 Brendan Rawlins; 9 James Feather; 8 Scott Law; 28 Josh Lynam; 17 Oliver Pursglove; 11 Ashley Lindsay. Subs (all used): 21 Sean Kelly; 15 Neil Cherryholme; 10 Ross Peltier; 19 Matthew Bailey.
Tries: Feather (7), Pursglove (56), Handforth (71);
Goals: Handforth 2/3.
Rugby Leaguer & League Express Men of the Match: *Lions:* Ritchie Hawkyard; *Cougars:* Paul March.
Penalty count: 8-8; **Half-time:** 12-6;
Referee: Jon Roberts; **Attendance:** 561.

Friday 22nd May 2015

YORK CITY KNIGHTS 70 SOUTH WALES SCORPIONS 0

CITY KNIGHTS: 2 Ben Dent; 17 Lee Waterman; 3 Greg Minikin; 4 Liam Cunningham; 24 Tyler Craig; 7 Pat Smith; 32 Jordan Howden; 8 Mark Applegarth; 27 Casey Canterbury; 10 Jack Aldous; 12 Ed Smith; 15 Josh Tonks; 11 Ryan Mallinder. Subs (all used): 34 Scott Glassell; 21 Jack Pickles; 29 Brad Nicholson; 28 Liam Richmond.
Tries: Minikin (14, 25, 74), P Smith (21), Pickles (29), B Dent (33), Waterman (38), Tonks (42), Craig (45), Nicholson (55, 71), E Smith (61), Canterbury (65);
Goals: B Dent 9/13.
SCORPIONS: 1 Jordan Sheridan; 24 Craig Lewis; 3 Paul Edwards; 10 Jonny Leather; 28 Yannic Parker; 6 Curtis Davies; 7 Paul Emanuelli; 8 Osian Phillips; 17 Zak Williams; 23 Anthony Symons; 29 Tom Morgan; 20 Tala Petelo; 18 Bradley Hill. Subs (all used): 9 Connor Farrer; 19 Ryan Millington; 14 Dafydd Hellard; 30 Bradley Mais.
Rugby Leaguer & League Express Men of the Match: *City Knights:* Greg Minikin; *Scorpions:* Tom Morgan.
Penalty count: 12-5; **Half-time:** 32-0;
Referee: Andrew Sweet; **Attendance:** 246
(at BigFella's Stadium, Featherstone).

ROUND 8

Friday 29th May 2015

NEWCASTLE THUNDER 32 YORK CITY KNIGHTS 14

THUNDER: 1 Stuart Kain; 2 Louis Sheriff; 3 Ali Blair; 4 Joe Brown; 5 Macauley Hallett; 6 Matty Beharrell; 7 Matthew Marsh; 8 Matt Barron; 9 Evan Simons; 10 Sebastien Martins; 11 Francis Welsh; 12 Dayne Craig; 13 Rhys Clarke. Subs (all used): 14 Paul Stamp; 15 Lee Fewlass; 16 Sam Bowring; 24 Ryan MacDonald.
(All players except MacDonald wore special edition shirts, numbered 1-17).
Tries: Hallett (7), Sheriff (15, 25), Beharrell (38), Marsh (45); **Goals:** Beharrell 5/5, Craig 1/1.
CITY KNIGHTS: 2 Ben Dent; 17 Lee Waterman; 3 Greg Minikin; 4 Liam Cunningham; 24 Tyler Craig; 32 Jordan Howden; 7 Pat Smith; 8 Mark Applegarth; 9 Harry Carter; 10 Jack Aldous; 12 Ed Smith; 15 Josh Tonks; 11 Ryan Mallinder. Subs (all used): 34 Scott Glassell; 29 Brad Nicholson; 21 Jack Pickles; 27 Casey Canterbury.
Tries: Tonks (5), Waterman (61), Cunningham (71);
Goals: B Dent 1/3.
Rugby Leaguer & League Express Men of the Match: *Thunder:* Matty Beharrell; *City Knights:* Greg Minikin.
Penalty count: 5-10; **Half-time:** 24-4;
Referee: Andrew Sweet; **Attendance:** 2,576.

Sunday 31st May 2015

HEMEL STAGS 8 SWINTON LIONS 32

STAGS: 1 Derrell Olpherts; 31 Mo Agoro; 4 Michael Brown; 18 Chris McNamara; 32 Brandon Conway; 6 Jy-mel Coleman; 33 Ben Young; 17 Dan Ljazouli; 9 James Helliwell; 16 Mike Stewart; 12 Alex Ingarfield; 13 Eddie Mbaraga; 3 Jamie O'Callaghan. Subs (all used): 30 George Flanagan; 26 James Howitt; 14 Ryan Chester; 7 Charlie Lawrence.
Tries: Agoro (56), Chester (72);
Goals: Jy-mel Coleman 0/2.
LIONS: 1 Ritchie Hawkyard; 2 Shaun Robinson; 21 Andy Ball; 22 Chris Rothwell; 28 Mike Butt; 6 Ben White; 29 Mick Govin; 8 Mike Morrison; 14 Keith Holden; 12 Darren Hawkyard; 11 Grant Beecham; 30 Matt Gardner; 23 Connor Dwyer. Subs (all used): 9 Andy Ackers; 13 Tommy Gallagher; 24 Jordan James; 31 Rob Lever.
Tries: Rothwell (17), Ball (28), Robinson (39, 80), Ackers (52), Govin (77); **Goals:** R Hawkyard 4/6.
Rugby Leaguer & League Express Men of the Match: *Stags:* Jy-mel Coleman; *Lions:* Ritchie Hawkyard.
Penalty count: 7-7; **Half-time:** 0-14;
Referee: Tom Grant; **Attendance:** 154.

NORTH WALES CRUSADERS 18 LONDON SKOLARS 10

CRUSADERS: 1 Tommy Johnson; 21 Ian Mort; 22 Alex Thompson; 4 Matt Reid; 5 Rob Massam; 14 Karl Ashall; 7 Jamie Dallimore; 8 Jonny Walker; 15 Lee Hudson; 10 Ryan Duffy; 11 Jono Smith; 12 Stephen Wild; 13 Gary Middlehurst. Subs (all used): 16 Joe Burke; 20 Elliott Davies; 30 Sam Peet; 9 Callum Wright.
Tries: Massam (5, 67), Peet (56); **Goals:** Johnson 3/4.
SKOLARS: 1 James Anthony; 2 Jimmy Morgan; 3 Mathew Cook; 4 Aaron Small; 5 John Paxton; 6 Jermaine Coleman; 7 Marcus Elliott; 23 Lewis Reed; 9 Sam Druce; 10 Dave Williams; 11 Harvey Burnett; 12 Will Lovell; 19 Will Fairhurst. Subs (all used): 15 Billy Driver; 20 Dave Ellison; 8 Michael Sykes; 13 Lamont Bryan.
Tries: Small (16), Burnett (21); **Goals:** Druce 1/2.
Rugby Leaguer & League Express Men of the Match: *Crusaders:* Stephen Wild; *Skolars:* Lamont Bryan.
Penalty count: 10-7; **Half-time:** 8-10;
Referee: Chris Campbell; **Attendance:** 432
(at The Rock, Wrexham).

COVENTRY BEARS 4 BARROW RAIDERS 22

BEARS: 7 Cameron Boulter; 41 Reece Chapman-Carry; 5 Ben Parry; 13 Simon Phillips; 20 Jamahl Hunte; 30 Dan Parker; 6 Billy Sheen; 27 James Geurtjens; 24 Richard Hughes; 46 Jack Francis; 29 Liam Thompson; 12 Chris Barratt; 26 Matt Cooper. Subs (all used): 14 Dylan Bale; 50 Morgan Evans; 38 Tom Hall; 3 Nick Taylor.
Try: Hunte (7); **Goals:** Parker 0/1.
RAIDERS: 1 Kris Tyson; 5 Kyle Dolan; 3 Chris Hankinson; 31 Cameron Pitman; 22 Joe Hambley; 29 Peter Lupton; 14 Josh Ward; 8 Joe Bullock; 9 Nathan Mossop; 19 Matt Heaton; 11 Liam Harrison; 12 Craig Briscoe; 21 Anthony Bate. Subs (all used): 6 Brad Marwood; 10 Andrew Dawson; 24 Andy Litherland; 30 Bradd Crellin.
Tries: Hankinson (25), Pitman (32), Hambley (52), Litherland (69); **Goals:** Ward 3/4.
Sin bin: Heaton (60) - dissent.
Rugby Leaguer & League Express Men of the Match: *Bears:* Jamahl Hunte; *Raiders:* Anthony Bate.
Penalty count: 4-6; **Half-time:** 4-12;
Referee: Scott Mikalauskas; **Attendance:** 552.

KEIGHLEY COUGARS 32 OLDHAM 24

COUGARS: 1 Jesse Sheriffe; 2 Gavin Duffy; 32 Hamish Barnes; 30 Rikki Sheriffe; 5 Paul White; 24 Liam Darville; 7 Paul Handforth; 8 Scott Law; 26 Paul March; 19 Matthew Bailey; 28 Josh Lynam; 12 Brendan Rawlins; 11 Ashley Lindsay. Subs (all used): 10 Ross Peltier; 15 Neil Cherryholme; 16 Jode Sheriffe; 21 Sean Kelly.
Tries: P March (3), Handforth (6, 62), Lynam (20), White (32, 39); **Goals:** Handforth 4/5, Duffy 0/1.
OLDHAM: 1 Steven Nield; 2 Adam Clay; 9 Sam Gee; 3 Jonathan Ford; 5 Jarrod Ward; 6 Lewis Palfrey; 7 Steve Roper; 10 Adam Neal; 16 Kenny Hughes; 8 Phil Joy; 11 Josh Crowley; 12 Danny Langtree; 13 Liam Thompson. Subs (all used): 14 Adam Files; 19 Michael Ward; 22 Nathan Mason; 26 Oliver Roberts.
Tries: Roper (43), Roberts (45), Palfrey (68), Crowley (74); **Goals:** Palfrey 4/4.
Rugby Leaguer & League Express Men of the Match: *Cougars:* Scott Law; *Oldham:* Oliver Roberts.
Penalty count: 3-5; **Half-time:** 26-0;
Referee: Sam Ansell; **Attendance:** 931.

OXFORD 20 GLOUCESTERSHIRE ALL GOLDS 12

OXFORD: 28 Sean Morris; 32 Andy Matthews; 14 Marcus Brooker; 3 Andrew Hoggins; 5 Aaron Jones-Bishop; 36 Danny Thomas; 31 Mark Barlow; 10 Jonny Payne; 9 Nathan Kitson; 34 Steve Scott; 27 Matty Blythe; 37 Adam Withington; 13 James Milburn. Subs (all used): 21 Dean Mignacca; 11 Josh Scott; 8 Jordan Andrade; 25 Luke Evans.
Tries: Hoggins (39), J Scott (56), Jones-Bishop (64), Matthews (73); **Goals:** Kitson 2/4.
Sin bin: Withington (49) - high tackle.
ALL GOLDS: 23 Joe Martin; 31 Jamie Murphy; 6 Toby Topham; 1 Phil Cowburn; 28 Ryan Pywell; 33 Mark Bowen; 7 Matt Bradley; 8 Oliver Purslow; 9 Steve Parry; 34 Alex Davidson; 3 Lewis Reece; 4 Callum Mulkeen; 30 Emmerson Whittel. Subs (all used): 35 Owain Griffiths; 18 Jamie Crowther; 14 Joe McClean; 10 Izaak Duffy.
Tries: Davidson (9), Murphy (27); **Goals:** Bradley 2/3.
Rugby Leaguer & League Express Men of the Match: *Oxford:* Andrew Hoggins; *All Golds:* Mark Bowen.
Penalty count: 8-5; **Half-time:** 6-12;
Referee: Andrew Bentham; **Attendance:** 252.

SOUTH WALES SCORPIONS 10 ROCHDALE HORNETS 64

SCORPIONS: 2 Ian Newbury; 3 Paul Edwards; 17 Zak Williams; 10 Jonny Leather; 28 Yannic Parker; 6 Curtis Davies; 7 Paul Emanuelli; 13 Neil Dallimore; 9 Connor Farrer; 29 Tom Morgan; 18 Bradley Hill; 4 Kyle Scrivens; 19 Connor Davies. Subs: 8 Osian Phillips; 14 Dafydd Hellard (not used); 20 Tala Petelo; 23 Anthony Symons.
Tries: Parker (34), Scrivens (61); **Goals:** Emanuelli 1/2.
HORNETS: 1 Wayne English; 20 Bradley Hargreaves; 12 Alex Trumper; 4 Lee Paterson; 5 Dale Bloomfield; 21 Ryan Smith; 7 Danny Yates; 30 Anthony Walker; 6 Paul Crook; 10 Warren Thompson; 25 Jordan Case; 19 Danny Bridge; 13 Tony Suffolk. Subs (all used): 14 James Tilley; 9 Alex McClurg; 28 Matty Hadden; 29 Jordan Hand.
Tries: Crook (2, 64, 69), Yates (27, 30, 71), Bridge (37, 43), English (45, 74), Hargreaves (55), Paterson (57); **Goals:** Crook 5/5, Case 2/6, Yates 1/1.
Rugby Leaguer & League Express Men of the Match: *Scorpions:* Kyle Scrivens; *Hornets:* Danny Bridge.
Penalty count: 4-4; **Half-time:** 4-20;
Referee: Jack Smith; **Attendance:** 172.

ROUND 9

Saturday 6th June 2015

GLOUCESTERSHIRE ALL GOLDS 30 HEMEL STAGS 34

ALL GOLDS: 1 Phil Cowburn; 5 Yannic Parker; 4 Callum Mulkeen; 31 Edwin Okanga-Ajwang; 28 Ryan Pywell; 7 Matt Bradley; 32 Mark Bowen; 19 Brett Scriven; 9 Steve Parry; 33 Alex Davidson; 14 Joe McClean; 30 Emmerson Whittel; 8 Oliver Purslow. Subs (all used): 6 Toby Topham; 29 Joel Thomas; 13 Chris Vitalini; 10 Izaak Duffy.
Tries: Parker (10), Parry (23), Cowburn (30), Vitalini (50), Bowen (55); **Goals:** Bradley 5/5.
STAGS: 1 Derrell Olpherts; 33 Simon Hrbek; 4 Michael Brown; 23 Ben Young; 18 Chris McNamara; 6 Jy-mel Coleman; 24 James Woodburn-Hall; 17 Dan Ljazouli; 9 James Helliwell; 16 Mike Stewart; 15 Liam O'Callaghan;

12 Alex Ingarfield; 13 Eddie Mbaraga. Subs (all used): 30 George Flanagan; 32 Mark Castle; 11 Barry-John Swindells; 14 Ryan Chester.
Tries: Hrbek (3, 36, 42), Woodburn-Hall (15), Flanagan (46), Stewart (73); **Goals:** Young 5/6.
Rugby Leaguer & League Express Men of the Match: *All Golds:* Phil Cowburn; *Stags:* Simon Hrbek.
Penalty count: 6-7; **Half-time:** 18-18;
Referee: Tom Grant; **Attendance:** 153.

Sunday 7th June 2015

BARROW RAIDERS 22 KEIGHLEY COUGARS 24

RAIDERS: 1 Kris Tyson; 2 Lee Haney; 3 Chris Hankinson; 4 Max Wiper; 23 Chris Fleming; 29 Peter Lupton; 14 Josh Ward; 8 Joe Bullock; 9 Nathan Mossop; 21 Anthony Bate; 11 Liam Harrison; 12 Craig Briscoe; 13 Dan Toal. Subs (all used): 6 Brad Marwood; 30 Bradd Crellin; 10 Andrew Dawson; 16 Adam Nicholson.
Tries: Tyson (39), Mossop (45), Bullock (57), Lupton (68); **Goals:** Ward 3/4.
Dismissal: Haney (53) - punching.
Sin bin: Haney (29) - fighting.
COUGARS: 1 Jesse Sheriffe; 5 Paul White; 30 Rikki Sheriffe; 4 Danny Lawton; 2 Gavin Duffy; - Adam Brook; 7 Paul Handforth; 8 Scott Law; 31 Scott Lee; 19 Matthew Bailey; 28 Josh Lynam; 12 Brendan Rawlins; 11 Ashley Lindsay. Subs (all used): 26 Paul March; 15 Neil Cherryholme; 17 Oliver Pursglove; 16 Jode Sheriffe.
Tries: Brook (11), Lynam (23), White (30), Handforth (47); **Goals:** Handforth 4/4.
Sin bin: Rawlins (29) - fighting.
Rugby Leaguer & League Express Men of the Match: *Raiders:* Joe Bullock; *Cougars:* Paul Handforth.
Penalty count: 10-6; **Half-time:** 4-18;
Referee: Adam Gill; **Attendance:** 1,141.

LONDON SKOLARS 20 COVENTRY BEARS 46

SKOLARS: 1 James Anthony; 2 Jimmy Morgan; 3 Mathew Cook; 4 Aaron Small; 5 John Paxton; 7 Marcus Elliott; 6 Mike Bishay; 8 Michael Sykes; 9 Sam Druce; 10 Dave Williams; 11 Will Lovell; 12 Cariern Clement-Pascall; 13 Lamont Bryan. Subs (all used): 15 Billy Driver; 24 Lewis Reed; 22 Louis Robinson; 14 Kazeem Fatouri.
Tries: Cook (4, 61), Driver (46), Morgan (58);
Goals: Druce 1/2, Elliott 1/2.
BEARS: 28 Andy Winfield; 20 Jamahl Hunte; 5 Ben Parry; 13 Simon Phillips; 41 Reece Chapman-Carry; 7 Cameron Boulter; 30 Dan Parker; 27 James Geurtjens; 24 Richard Hughes; 46 Jack Francis; 12 Chris Barratt; 29 Liam Thompson; 26 Matt Cooper. Subs (all used): 21 Stephen Coleman; 50 Morgan Evans; 38 Tom Hall; 32 Kenneth Kelliher.
Tries: Hughes (16), Parry (19), Hunte (28), Cooper (30), Parker (35, 40), Winfield (53), Chapman-Carry (73);
Goals: Parker 7/8.
Rugby Leaguer & League Express Men of the Match: *Skolars:* Billy Driver; *Bears:* Dan Parker.
Penalty count: 7-9; **Half-time:** 6-34;
Referee: Scott Mikalauskas; **Attendance:** 259.

OLDHAM 28 NORTH WALES CRUSADERS 38

OLDHAM: 20 Tom Dempsey; 2 Adam Clay; 4 Jack Holmes; 9 Sam Gee; 3 Jonathan Ford; 6 Lewis Palfrey; 7 Steve Roper; 10 Adam Neal; 16 Kenny Hughes; 8 Phil Joy; 11 Josh Crowley; 12 Danny Langtree; 13 Liam Thompson. Subs (all used): 14 Adam Files; 22 Nathan Mason; 19 Michael Ward; 26 Oliver Roberts.
Tries: Crowley (3, 11), Palfrey (54), Roberts (72), Holmes (80); **Goals:** Palfrey 4/5.
CRUSADERS: 1 Tommy Johnson; 29 Kevin Penny; 4 Matt Reid; 22 Alex Thompson; 5 Rob Massam; 14 Karl Ashall; 7 Jamie Dallimore; 8 Jonny Walker; 9 Callum Wright; 16 Joe Burke; 11 Jono Smith; 12 Stephen Wild; 13 Gary Middlehurst. Subs (all used): 10 Ryan Duffy; 20 Elliott Davies; 23 Mark Hobson; 15 Lee Hudson.
Tries: Thompson (5), Dallimore (21), Penny (24, 47), Smith (30), Wild (34), Johnson (63); **Goals:** Johnson 5/7.
Sin bin: Johnson (69) - high tackle.
Rugby Leaguer & League Express Men of the Match: *Oldham:* Josh Crowley; *Crusaders:* Karl Ashall.
Penalty count: 10-3; **Half-time:** 10-28;
Referee: Sam Ansell; **Attendance:** 671.

OXFORD 38 SOUTH WALES SCORPIONS 30

OXFORD: 36 Danny Thomas; 32 Andy Matthews; 14 Marcus Brooker; 33 Chris Ulugia; 5 Aaron Jones-Bishop; 31 Mark Barlow; 1 Louis Richards; 8 Jordan Andrade; 20 Dean Mignacca; 37 Adam Withington; 11 Josh Scott; 27 Matty Blythe; 13 James Milburn. Subs (all used): 9 Nathan Kitson; 10 Jonny Payne; 21 Luke Gardiner; 25 Luke Evans.
Tries: J Scott (13), Matthews (26, 29, 46), Evans (60), Blythe (69), Thomas (72); **Goals:** Richards 5/7.
SCORPIONS: 1 Jordan Sheridan; 2 Ian Newbury; 3 Paul Edwards; 10 Jonny Leather; 17 Zak Williams; 27 Ryan Millington; 7 Paul Emanuelli; 8 Osian Phillips; 9 Connor Farrer; 13 Neil Dallimore; 18 Bradley Hill; 12 Andrew Joy; 19 Connor Davies. Subs: 14 Dafydd Hellard; - Barrie Phillips; 6 Curtis Davies (not used); 20 Tala Petelo.
Tries: Newbury (3, 54), Joy (20), Sheridan (40), Connor Davies (42); **Goals:** Emanuelli 5/5.
Rugby Leaguer & League Express Men of the Match: *Oxford:* Matty Blythe; *Scorpions:* Paul Emanuelli.
Penalty count: 6-4; **Half-time:** 18-18;
Referee: Chris Campbell; **Attendance:** 286.

SWINTON LIONS 44 NEWCASTLE THUNDER 32

LIONS: 28 Mike Butt; 2 Shaun Robinson; 3 Stuart Littler; 22 Chris Rothwell; 17 Andy Thornley; 6 Ben White; 18 Aaron Lloyd; 24 Jordan James; 9 Andy Ackers; 31 Rob Lever; 11 Grant Beecham; 30 Josh Barlow; 10 Ben Austin. Subs (all used): 29 Mick Govin; 12 Darren Hawkyard; 8 Mike Morrison; 13 Tommy Gallagher.
Tries: Rothwell (1, 61), White (15, 70), Beecham (29), D Hawkyard (37), Butt (43), Ackers (65);
Goals: White 6/8.
THUNDER: 17 Stuart Kain; 1 Louis Sheriff; 31 Ali Blair; 4 Joe Brown; 38 Macauley Hallett; 6 Matty Beharrell; 27 Matthew Marsh; 8 Matt Barron; 25 Evan Simons; 26 Sebastien Martins; 36 Sonny Esslemont; 9 Dayne Craig; 28 Stephen Holker. Subs (all used): 14 Paul Stamp; 15 Lee Fewlass; 16 Francis Welch; 22 Sam Bowring.
Tries: Hallett (13, 57), Sheriff (23), Marsh (48), Stamp (61, 73); **Goals:** Beharrell 4/6.
Rugby Leaguer & League Express Men of the Match: *Lions:* Aaron Lloyd; *Thunder:* Macauley Hallett.
Penalty count: 4-4; **Half-time:** 22-8;
Referee: Jamie Bloem; **Attendance:** 455.

YORK CITY KNIGHTS 34 ROCHDALE HORNETS 20

CITY KNIGHTS: 2 Ben Dent; 26 James Clare; 3 Greg Minikin; 24 Michael Channing; 5 Nev Morrison; 6 Jon Presley; 32 Jordan Howden; 8 Mark Applegarth; 7 Pat Smith; 10 Jack Aldous; 12 Ed Smith; 4 Liam Cunningham; 29 Brad Nicholson. Subs (all used): 27 Casey Canterbury; 21 Jack Pickles; 11 Ryan Mallinder; 17 Lee Waterman.
Tries: Cunningham (5), P Smith (8), Clare (23, 34), B Dent (27, 72), Channing (31); **Goals:** B Dent 3/7.
HORNETS: 20 Bradley Hargreaves; 12 Alex Trumper; 3 Dave Llewellyn; 29 Jack Ashworth; - Matty Dawson; 21 Ryan Smith; 7 Danny Yates; 30 Anthony Walker; 6 Paul Crook; 10 Warren Thompson; 19 Danny Bridge; 25 Jordan Case; 13 Tony Suffolk. Subs (all used): 14 James Tilley; 9 Alex McClurg; 28 Matty Hadden; 16 Liam Gilchrist.
Tries: Trumper (19), Yates (40), Ashworth (51), Dawson (62); **Goals:** Crook 1/1, Yates 1/3.
Rugby Leaguer & League Express Men of the Match: *City Knights:* Jack Aldous; *Hornets:* Danny Yates.
Penalty count: 8-8; **Half-time:** 30-12;
Referee: Jon Roberts; **Attendance:** 386
(at BigFella's Stadium, Featherstone).

ROUND 10

Saturday 13th June 2015

NEWCASTLE THUNDER 38 GLOUCESTERSHIRE ALL GOLDS 6

THUNDER: 2 Jacob Blades; 1 Louis Sheriff; 31 Ali Blair; 4 Joe Brown; 38 Macauley Hallett; 6 Matty Beharrell; 27 Matthew Marsh; 37 Sebastien Martins; 14 Paul Stamp; 8 Matt Barron; 9 Dayne Craig; 11 Jason Payne; 12 Rhys Clarke. Subs (all used): 25 Evan Simons; 28 Stephen Holker; 22 Sam Bowring; 24 Ryan MacDonald.
Tries: Hallett (12, 15, 33), Payne (22), Bowring (37, 42), Craig (58), Clarke (62); **Goals:** Beharrell 3/8.
Dismissal: Sheriff (12) - fighting.
Sin bin: Barron (12) - fighting.
ALL GOLDS: 1 Phil Cowburn; 31 Lee Mapals; 3 Lewis Reece; 32 Edwin Okanga-Ajwang; 28 Ryan Pywell; 6 Toby Topham; 7 Matt Bradley; 8 Oliver Purslow; 9 Steve Parry; 34 Alex Davidson; 14 Joe McClean; 4 Callum Mulkeen; 30 Emmerson Whittel. Subs (all used): 27 Danny Fallon; 18 Jamie Crowther; 29 Joel Thomas; 13 Chris Vitalini.
Try: Bradley (73); **Goals:** Bradley 1/1.
Sin bin: Davidson (12) - fighting;
Mapals (21) - high tackle.
Rugby Leaguer & League Express Men of the Match: *Thunder:* Jacob Blades; *All Golds:* Matt Bradley.
Penalty count: 3-8; **Half-time:** 24-0;
Referee: Andrew Sweet; **Attendance:** 452.

Sunday 14th June 2015

HEMEL STAGS 10 BARROW RAIDERS 38

STAGS: 1 Derrell Olpherts; 33 Simon Hrbek; 18 Chris McNamara; 4 Michael Brown; 5 Alex Anthony; 6 Jy-mel Coleman; 23 Ben Young; 16 Mike Stewart; 9 James Helliwell; 17 Dan Ljazouli; 13 Eddie Mbaraga; 12 Alex Ingarfield; 11 Barry-John Swindells. Subs (all used): 15 Liam O'Callaghan; 30 Brooke Broughton; 32 Mark Castle; 7 Charlie Lawrence.
Tries: Anthony (15), Stewart (71); **Goals:** Young 1/2.
RAIDERS: 1 Kris Tyson; 20 Shane Toal; 3 Chris Hankinson; 4 Max Wiper; 23 Chris Fleming; 7 Liam Campbell; 14 Josh Ward; 8 Joe Bullock; 9 Nathan Mossop; 18 Danny Jones; 11 Liam Harrison; 12 Craig Briscoe; 30 Bradd Crellin. Subs (all used): 29 Peter Lupton; 13 Dan Toal; 16 Adam Nicholson; 10 Andrew Dawson.
Tries: Hankinson (2, 64), Mossop (7, 58), Campbell (24), Wiper (34); **Goals:** Ward 7/7.
Sin bin: Fleming (77) - holding down.
Rugby Leaguer & League Express Men of the Match: *Stags:* Jy-mel Coleman; *Raiders:* Liam Campbell.
Penalty count: 5-8; **Half-time:** 4-24;
Referee: Adam Gill; **Attendance:** 192.

NORTH WALES CRUSADERS 12 ROCHDALE HORNETS 14

CRUSADERS: 1 Tommy Johnson; 2 Scott Turner; 31 Benjamin Jullien; 4 Matt Reid; 5 Rob Massam; 14 Karl Ashall; 7 Jamie Dallimore; 8 Jonny Walker; 9 Callum Wright; 16 Joe Burke; 11 Jono Smith; 12 Stephen Wild; 22 Alex Thompson. Subs (all used): 10 Ryan Duffy; 15 Lee Hudson; 23 Mark Hobson; 20 Elliott Davies.
Tries: Massam (15), Wild (42); **Goals:** Johnson 2/3.
Sin bin: Davies (50) - fighting.
HORNETS: 1 Wayne English; 20 Bradley Hargreaves; 4 Lee Paterson; 29 Jack Ashworth; 5 Dale Bloomfield; 21 Ryan Smith; 7 Danny Yates; 30 Anthony Walker; 6 Paul Crook; 10 Warren Thompson; 25 Jordan Case; 19 Danny Bridge; 13 Tony Suffolk. Subs (all used): 14 James Tilley; 28 Matty Hadden; 9 Alex McClurg; 12 Alex Trumper.
Tries: English (9), Bloomfield (77);
Goals: Crook 2/3, Yates 1/1.
Sin bin: Suffolk (50) - fighting.
Rugby Leaguer & League Express Men of the Match: *Crusaders:* Jamie Dallimore; *Hornets:* Tony Suffolk.
Penalty count: 10-8; **Half-time:** 6-10;
Referee: Gareth Hewer; **Attendance:** 661
(at The Rock, Wrexham).

COVENTRY BEARS 8 SWINTON LIONS 78

BEARS: 28 Andy Winfield; 41 Reece Chapman-Carry; 5 Ben Parry; 21 Stephen Coleman; 20 Jamahl Hunte; 7 Cameron Boulter; 30 Dan Parker; 27 James Geurtjens; 24 Richard Hughes; 26 Matt Cooper; 29 Liam Thompson; 12 Chris Barratt; 32 Kenneth Kelliher. Subs (all used): 6 Billy Sheen; 46 Jack Francis; 38 Tom Hall; 3 Nick Taylor.
Tries: Hunte (58), Sheen (66);
Goals: Coleman 0/1, Parker 0/1.
LIONS: 7 Chris Atkin; 2 Shaun Robinson; 3 Stuart Littler; 21 Andy Ball; 25 Harry Aaronson; 6 Ben White; 18 Aaron Lloyd; 24 Jordan James; 9 Andy Ackers; 10 Ben Austin; 11 Grant Beecham; 30 Josh Barlow; 31 Rob Lever. Subs (all used): 13 Tommy Gallagher; 17 Andy Thornley; 12 Darren Hawkyard; 14 Keith Holden.
Tries: Aaronson (5, 13), Lever (10), Atkin (20), Ackers (23, 74), Littler (26, 51), White (30, 47), Robinson (36, 44, 78), Austin (55), A Lloyd (76);
Goals: White 5/9, Atkin 4/6.
Rugby Leaguer & League Express Men of the Match: *Bears:* Billy Sheen; *Lions:* Tommy Gallagher.
Penalty count: 5-6; **Half-time:** 0-42;
Referee: Tom Grant; **Attendance:** 454.

KEIGHLEY COUGARS 66 SOUTH WALES SCORPIONS 6

COUGARS: 24 Liam Darville; 2 Gavin Duffy; 4 Danny Lawton; 30 Rikki Sheriffe; 25 Andy Gabriel; - Adam Brook; 7 Paul Handforth; 8 Scott Law; 31 Scott Lee; 16 Jode Sheriffe; 28 Josh Lynam; 12 Brendan Rawlins; 11 Ashley Lindsay. Subs (all used): 9 James Feather; 13 David March; 15 Neil Cherryholme; - Samir Tahraoui.
Tries: Lynam (6), Brook (10, 51), R Sheriffe (15), Lawton (26, 39), Gabriel (33, 37, 62), Lindsay (56), Cherryholme (68), Handforth (78);
Goals: Handforth 1/4, Lawton 8/8.
SCORPIONS: 1 Jordan Sheridan; 2 Ian Newbury; 3 Paul Edwards; 10 Jonny Leather; 21 Andrew Oakden; 7 Paul Emanuelli; 27 Ryan Millington; 20 Tala Petelo; 17 Zak Williams; 29 Andrew Joy; 4 Kyle Scrivens; 16 Christopher Speck; 18 Bradley Hill. Subs: 5 Ben Jones; 14 Dafydd Hellard (not used); 23 Anthony Symons; 30 Gethin King.
Try: Petelo (48); **Goals:** Emanuelli 1/1.
Rugby Leaguer & League Express Men of the Match: *Cougars:* Ashley Lindsay; *Scorpions:* Anthony Symons.
Penalty count: 7-5; **Half-time:** 36-0;
Referee: Chris Campbell; **Attendance:** 671.

OLDHAM 64 OXFORD 0

OLDHAM: 20 Tom Dempsey; 2 Adam Clay; 17 George Tyson; 9 Sam Gee; 4 Jack Holmes; 6 Lewis Palfrey; 7 Steve Roper; 10 Adam Neal; 15 Gareth Owen; 8 Phil Joy; 11 Josh Crowley; 12 Danny Langtree; 13 Liam Thompson. Subs (all used): 14 Adam Files; 22 Nathan Mason; 16 Kenny Hughes; 18 Richard Joy.
Tries: Clay (6, 67), P Joy (16), Holmes (26, 34, 73), Files (30), Owen (47), Tyson (54, 59), Thompson (62), Hughes (77); **Goals:** Palfrey 8/12.
OXFORD: 36 Danny Thomas; 32 Andy Matthews; 14 Marcus Brooker; 28 Josh Nathaniel; 5 Aaron Jones-Bishop; 30 Josh Kittrick; 9 Nathan Kitson; 31 Daniel Fleming; 27 Vila Halafihi; 10 Jonny Payne; 11 Josh Scott; 33 Chris Ulugia; 13 James Milburn. Subs (all used): 20 Dean Mignacca; 19 Kyle Danns; 8 Jordan Andrade; 1 Louis Richards.
Sin bin: Kitson (72) - dissent.
Rugby Leaguer & League Express Men of the Match: *Oldham:* George Tyson; *Oxford:* Vila Halafihi.
Penalty count: 10-4; **Half-time:** 26-0;
Referee: Jamie Bloem; **Attendance:** 433.

YORK CITY KNIGHTS 40 LONDON SKOLARS 10

CITY KNIGHTS: 2 Ben Dent; 26 James Clare; 3 Greg Minikin; 24 Michael Channing; 5 Nev Morrison; 6 Jon Presley; 32 Jordan Howden; 8 Mark Applegarth; 7 Pat Smith; 10 Jack Aldous; 12 Ed Smith; 15 Josh Tonks; 11 Ryan Mallinder. Subs (all used): 9 Harry Carter; 21 Jack Pickles; 4 Liam Cunningham; 34 Jack Blagbrough.
Tries: Morrison (8), Howden (11, 26), Mallinder (20), Aldous (39), Minikin (47), Tonks (50), Cunningham (59);
Goals: B Dent 4/8.
SKOLARS: 1 James Anthony; 5 Jimmy Morgan; 3 Mathew Cook; 4 Joe Price; 2 Chris Bishay; 6 Jermaine Coleman; 7 Marcus Elliott; 8 Michael Sykes; 9 Mike Bishay; 10 Lewis Reed; 11 Harvey Burnett; 12 Kazeem Fatouri; 13 Lamont Bryan. Subs (all used): 14 Anthony Cox; 15 Billy Driver; 16 Louis Robinson; 17 Aaron Small.
Tries: Anthony (32), Price (64); **Goals:** Elliott 1/2.
Rugby Leaguer & League Express Men of the Match: *City Knights:* Josh Tonks; *Skolars:* Jermaine Coleman.
Penalty count: 10-4; **Half-time:** 26-6;
Referee: Sam Ansell; **Attendance:** 401
(at Elmpark Way, Heworth).

ROUND 11

Saturday 20th June 2015

BARROW RAIDERS 26 GLOUCESTERSHIRE ALL GOLDS 18

RAIDERS: 23 Chris Fleming; 20 Shane Toal; 3 Chris Hankinson; 4 Max Wiper; 22 Joe Hambley; 14 Josh Ward; 7 Liam Campbell; 8 Joe Bullock; 9 Nathan Mossop; 18 Danny Jones; 11 Liam Harrison; 12 Craig Briscoe; 30 Bradd Crellin. Subs (all used): 29 Peter Lupton; 13 Dan Toal; 10 Andrew Dawson; 16 Adam Nicholson.
Tries: S Toal (16, 19), Hankinson (46), Lupton (55), Hambley (79); **Goals:** Ward 3/6.
ALL GOLDS: 7 Matt Bradley; 31 Lee Mapals; 3 Lewis Reece; 32 Edwin Okanga-Ajwang; 4 Callum Mulkeen; - Jamie Murphy; 1 Phil Cowburn; 8 Oliver Purslow; 9 Steve Parry; 29 Joel Thomas; 14 Joe McClean; 30 Emmerson Whittel; 13 Chris Vitalini. Subs (all used): 27 Danny Fallon; 33 Graham O'Keeffe; 18 Jamie Crowther; 34 Alex Davidson.
Tries: Mapals (4), Whittel (43), Purslow (63); **Goals:** Bradley 3/5.
Rugby Leaguer & League Express Men of the Match: *Raiders:* Liam Harrison; *All Golds:* Matt Bradley.
Penalty count: 11-7; **Half-time:** 8-8;
Referee: Chris Campbell; **Attendance:** 841.

Sunday 21st June 2015

HEMEL STAGS 10 YORK CITY KNIGHTS 70

STAGS: 1 Derrell Olpherts; 18 Chris McNamara; 11 Barry-John Swindells; 4 Michael Brown; 5 Alex Anthony; 24 James Woodburn-Hall; 6 Jy-mel Coleman; 16 Mike Stewart; 9 James Helliwell; 32 Mark Castle; 12 Alex Ingarfield; 13 Eddie Mbaraga; 23 Tom Sadler. Subs (all used): 31 Nathan Darby; 33 Thibault Cousine; 14 Ryan Chester; 28 Connor Boyd-Barnes.
Tries: Ingarfield (25), Boyd-Barnes (78); **Goals:** Swindells 1/1, Jy-mel Coleman 0/1.
CITY KNIGHTS: 2 Ben Dent; 5 Nev Morrison; 3 Greg Minikin; 24 Michael Channing; 19 James Clare; 32 Jordan Howden; 6 Jon Presley; 8 Mark Applegarth; 14 Kris Brining; 10 Jack Aldous; 12 Ed Smith; 15 Josh Tonks; 29 Brad Nicholson. Subs (all used): 9 Harry Carter; 4 Liam Cunningham; 34 Jack Blagbrough; 28 Mick Learmonth.
Tries: Howden (4, 6), Brining (15, 18, 80), B Dent (35, 49), Minikin (41), Carter (46), Morrison (55, 68), Clare (58), E Smith (61); **Goals:** B Dent 3/5, Howden 6/8.
Rugby Leaguer & League Express Men of the Match: *Stags:* Eddie Mbaraga; *City Knights:* Jordan Howden.
Penalty count: 10-5; **Half-time:** 6-26;
Referee: Tom Grant; **Attendance:** 145.

KEIGHLEY COUGARS 54 ROCHDALE HORNETS 20

COUGARS: 1 Jesse Sheriffe; 25 Andy Gabriel; 4 Danny Lawton; 30 Rikki Sheriffe; 5 Paul White; - Adam Brook; 7 Paul Handforth; 8 Scott Law; 31 Scott Lee; 15 Neil Cherryholme; 28 Josh Lynam; 12 Brendan Rawlins; 11 Ashley Lindsay. Subs (all used): 13 David March; 19 Matthew Bailey; 26 Paul March; - Samir Tahraoui.
Tries: Handforth (8), Gabriel (10, 29), White (20, 67), P March (23), Lynam (53), Brook (60), Jesse Sheriffe (70); **Goals:** Lawton 9/9.
HORNETS: 1 Wayne English; 20 Bradley Hargreaves; 4 Lee Paterson; 29 Jack Ashworth; 5 Dale Bloomfield; 21 Ryan Smith; 7 Danny Yates; 30 Anthony Walker; 6 Paul Crook; 10 Warren Thompson; 19 Danny Bridge; 25 Jordan Case; 15 Lewis Charnock. Subs (all used): 9 Alex McClurg; 12 Alex Trumper; 14 James Tilley; 28 Matty Hadden.
Tries: Bloomfield (16), Hargreaves (26), Walker (57), Crook (73); **Goals:** Crook 2/3, Charnock 0/1.
Rugby Leaguer & League Express Men of the Match: *Cougars:* Paul Handforth; *Hornets:* Anthony Walker.
Penalty count: 8-8; **Half-time:** 30-8;
Referee: Dave Merrick; **Attendance:** 907.

LONDON SKOLARS 12 NEWCASTLE THUNDER 19

SKOLARS: 1 Marcus Elliott; 2 Jimmy Morgan; 3 Mathew Cook; 4 Joe Price; 5 Chris Bishay; 6 Jermaine Coleman; 7 James Anthony; 8 Michael Sykes; 9 Joel Wicks; 10 Lewis Reed; 11 Harvey Burnett; 12 Will Lovell; 13 Lamont Bryan. Subs (all used): 15 Billy Driver; 16 Aaron Small; 17 Kazeem Fatouri; 21 Glenn Riley.
Tries: Lovell (4), Wicks (12); **Goals:** Elliott 2/2.
THUNDER: 34 Josh Guzdek; 2 Jacob Blades; 22 Sam Bowring; 4 Joe Brown; 38 Macauley Hallett; 6 Matty Beharrell; 27 Matthew Marsh; 8 Matt Barron; 14 Paul Stamp; 37 Sebastien Martins; 11 Jason Payne; 16 Francis Welsh; 12 Rhys Clarke. Subs (all used): 25 Evan Simons; 10 Mark Mexico; 18 Josh Stoker; 24 Ryan MacDonald.
Tries: Marsh (35), Clarke (57), Simons (64); **Goals:** Beharrell 3/3; **Field goal:** Beharrell (75).
Rugby Leaguer & League Express Men of the Match: *Skolars:* Will Lovell; *Thunder:* Matty Beharrell.
Penalty count: 11-6; **Half-time:** 12-6;
Referee: Jon Roberts; **Attendance:** 327.

OXFORD 12 NORTH WALES CRUSADERS 36

OXFORD: 36 Danny Thomas; 32 Andy Matthews; 14 Marcus Brooker; 28 Josh Nathaniel; 21 Luke Gardiner; 27 Mark Barlow; 9 Nathan Kitson; 34 Steve Scott; 31 Vila Halafihi; 8 Jordan Andrade; 37 Adam Withington; 11 Josh Scott; 13 James Milburn. Subs (all used): 20 Dean Mignacca; 25 Luke Evans; 19 Kyle Danns; 5 Aaron Jones-Bishop.
Tries: Halafihi (61), Thomas (64); **Goals:** Kitson 2/2.
CRUSADERS: 29 Kevin Penny; 5 Rob Massam; 31 Benjamin Jullien; 1 Tommy Johnson; 2 Scott Turner; 7 Jamie Dallimore; 26 Craig White; 8 Jonny Walker; 14 Karl Ashall; 16 Joe Burke; 32 Sam Peet; 12 Stephen Wild; 11 Jono Smith. Subs (all used): 15 Lee Hudson; 10 Ryan Duffy; 23 Mark Hobson; 4 Matt Reid.
Tries: Dallimore (8, 35), White (28), Jullien (40), Massam (41), Johnson (74); **Goals:** Johnson 2/2, Turner 4/4.
Rugby Leaguer & League Express Men of the Match: *Oxford:* Vila Halafihi; *Crusaders:* Jamie Dallimore.
Penalty count: 4-4; **Half-time:** 0-24;
Referee: Adam Gill; **Attendance:** 357.

SOUTH WALES SCORPIONS 14 COVENTRY BEARS 42

SCORPIONS: 1 Jordan Sheridan; 28 Yannic Parker; 3 Paul Edwards; 10 Jonny Leather; 5 Ben Jones; 27 Ryan Millington; 7 Paul Emanuelli; 23 Anthony Symons; 17 Zak Williams; 13 Neil Dallimore; 4 Kyle Scrivens; 29 Andrew Joy; 18 Bradley Hill. Subs (all used): 9 Connor Farrer; 20 Tala Petelo; 16 Christopher Speck; 12 Barrie Phillips.
Tries: Parker (3, 8), Joy (61); **Goals:** Emanuelli 1/3.
Dismissal: Hill (72) - dissent.
Sin bin: Dallimore (55) - obstruction; Hill (72) - high tackle.
BEARS: 28 Andy Winfield; 20 Jamahl Hunte; 30 Dan Parker; 21 Stephen Coleman; 41 Reece Chapman-Carry; 6 Billy Sheen; 7 Cameron Boulter; 27 James Geurtjens; 24 Richard Hughes; 46 Jack Francis; 32 Kenneth Kelliher; 12 Chris Barratt; 26 Matt Cooper. Subs (all used): 29 Liam Thompson; 38 Tom Hall; - Andy Unsworth; 50 Morgan Evans.
Tries: Sheen (12, 34), Hughes (16), Hunte (28), Hall (39), Kelliher (56), Francis (71), Evans (80); **Goals:** Coleman 3/6, Parker 2/2.
Rugby Leaguer & League Express Men of the Match: *Scorpions:* Yannic Parker; *Bears:* Billy Sheen.
Penalty count: 7-11; **Half-time:** 10-26;
Referee: Callum Straw; **Attendance:** 307.

SWINTON LIONS 26 OLDHAM 32

LIONS: 7 Chris Atkin; 2 Shaun Robinson; 3 Stuart Littler; 22 Chris Rothwell; 28 Mike Butt; 6 Ben White; 18 Aaron Lloyd; 24 Jordan James; 9 Andy Ackers; 10 Ben Austin; 11 Grant Beecham; 30 Andy Thornley; 31 Rob Lever. Subs (all used): 8 Mike Morrison; 12 Darren Hawkyard; 13 Tommy Gallagher; 29 Mick Govin.
Tries: Robinson (36), Govin (42), A Lloyd (45), Butt (49), Thornley (80); **Goals:** Atkin 3/5.
OLDHAM: 9 Sam Gee; 2 Adam Clay; 3 Jonathan Ford; 17 George Tyson; 4 Jack Holmes; 6 Lewis Palfrey; 7 Steve Roper; 10 Adam Neal; 15 Gareth Owen; 8 Phil Joy; 11 Josh Crowley; 12 Danny Langtree; 13 Liam Thompson. Subs (all used): 22 Nathan Mason; 19 Michael Ward; 14 Adam Files; 26 Oliver Roberts.
Tries: Langtree (2), Tyson (4, 60), Crowley (12), Clay (31); **Goals:** Palfrey 6/8.
Rugby Leaguer & League Express Men of the Match: *Lions:* Mick Govin; *Oldham:* Lewis Palfrey.
Penalty count: 6-12; **Half-time:** 4-22;
Referee: Andrew Sweet; **Attendance:** 625.

ROUND 12

Saturday 27th June 2015

GLOUCESTERSHIRE ALL GOLDS 30 OLDHAM 42

ALL GOLDS: 1 Phil Cowburn; 31 Lee Mapals; 3 Lewis Reece; 32 Edwin Okanga-Ajwang; 28 Ryan Pywell; 27 Danny Fallon; 7 Matt Bradley; 8 Oliver Purslow; 9 Steve Parry; 13 Chris Vitalini; 33 Graham O'Keeffe; 4 Callum Mulkeen; 30 Emmerson Whittel. Subs (all used): 6 Toby Topham; 35 Nathan Rainer; 18 Jamie Crowther; 29 Joel Thomas.
Tries: Vitalini (12), Mapals (28, 56, 62), Purslow (49); **Goals:** Bradley 5/6.
OLDHAM: 20 Tom Dempsey; 2 Adam Clay; 17 George Tyson; 9 Sam Gee; 4 Jack Holmes; 6 Lewis Palfrey; 27 Dave Hewitt; 8 Phil Joy; 15 Gareth Owen; 22 Nathan Mason; 11 Josh Crowley; 12 Danny Langtree; 26 Oliver Roberts. Subs (all used): 19 Michael Ward; 16 Kenny Hughes; 14 Adam Files; 13 Liam Thompson.
Tries: Clay (4, 39), P Joy (21), Hewitt (25, 35), Langtree (44), Holmes (67); **Goals:** Palfrey 7/8.
Rugby Leaguer & League Express Men of the Match: *All Golds:* Lee Mapals; *Oldham:* Lewis Palfrey.
Penalty count: 10-8; **Half-time:** 12-30;
Referee: Scott Mikalauskas; **Attendance:** 146.

OXFORD 24 COVENTRY BEARS 20

OXFORD: 36 Danny Thomas; 32 Andy Matthews; 3 Andrew Hoggins; 14 Marcus Brooker; 5 Aaron Jones-Bishop; 27 Mark Barlow; 9 Nathan Kitson; 25 Luke Evans; 20 Dean Mignacca; 19 Kyle Danns; 28 Josh Nathaniel; 37 Adam Withington; 13 James Milburn. Subs (all used): 31 Josh Kittrick; 22 Harry Kaufman; 1 Louis Richards; 34 Steve Scott.
Tries: Mignacca (21), Kitson (54, 62, 65), Matthews (79); **Goals:** Kitson 1/2, Richards 1/3.
BEARS: 28 Andy Winfield; 20 Jamahl Hunte; 21 Stephen Coleman; 5 Ben Parry; 45 Jason Bass; 30 Dan Parker; 7 Cameron Boulter; 27 James Geurtjens; 24 Richard Hughes; 46 Jack Francis; 32 Kenneth Kelliher; 12 Chris Barratt; 26 Matt Cooper. Subs (all used): 15 Andy Unsworth; 31 Morgan Evans; 29 Liam Thompson; 14 Dylan Bale.
Tries: Coleman (3), Thompson (30), Parry (44); **Goals:** Parker 4/4.
Sin bin: Winfield (40) - holding down.
Rugby Leaguer & League Express Men of the Match: *Oxford:* Nathan Kitson; *Bears:* Matt Cooper.
Penalty count: 5-9; **Half-time:** 6-12;
Referee: Callum Straw; **Attendance:** 502.

ROCHDALE HORNETS 32 HEMEL STAGS 14

HORNETS: 1 Wayne English; 20 Bradley Hargreaves; 4 Lee Paterson; 24 Dave Hull; 12 Alex Trumper; 21 Ryan Smith; 7 Danny Yates; 28 Matty Hadden; 27 Matty Fozard; 10 Warren Thompson; 29 Jack Ashworth; 19 Danny Bridge; 25 Jordan Case. Subs (all used): 14 James Tilley; 8 John Cookson; 9 Alex McClurg; 23 James Dandy.
Tries: Bridge (13, 78), Smith (28), Cookson (33), Yates (36), Case (55); **Goals:** Yates 4/6.
STAGS: 1 Derrell Olpherts; 18 Chris McNamara; 5 Alex Anthony; 4 Michael Brown; 33 Mo Agoro; 6 Jy-mel Coleman; 2 Ben Young; 32 Mark Castle; 23 Thibault Cousine; 17 Dan Ljazouli; 13 Eddie Mbaraga; 12 Alex Ingarfield; 24 James Woodburn-Hall. Subs (all used): 31 Nathan Darby; 10 Adam Booth; 7 Charlie Lawrence; 21 Malikhi Lloyd-Jones.
Tries: Mbaraga (40, 74), Brown (65); **Goals:** Young 1/3.
Sin bin: Lloyd-Jones (25) - dangerous challenge on Cookson.
Rugby Leaguer & League Express Men of the Match: *Hornets:* Matty Hadden; *Stags:* Eddie Mbaraga.
Penalty count: 7-5; **Half-time:** 20-4;
Referee: Sam Ansell; **Attendance:** 310.

BARROW RAIDERS 16 NEWCASTLE THUNDER 4

RAIDERS: 23 Chris Fleming; 20 Shane Toal; 3 Chris Hankinson; 4 Max Wiper; 31 Cameron Pitman; 14 Josh Ward; 7 Liam Campbell; 8 Joe Bullock; 9 Nathan Mossop; 21 Anthony Bate; 24 Andy Litherland; 12 Craig Briscoe; 11 Liam Harrison. Subs (all used): 29 Peter Lupton; 13 Dan Toal; 30 Bradd Crellin; 22 Joe Hambley.
Tries: D Toal (29), Fleming (32), Campbell (65); **Goals:** Ward 2/4.
THUNDER: 34 Josh Guzdek; 22 Sam Bowring; 31 Ali Blair; 4 Joe Brown; 38 Macauley Hallett; 6 Matty Beharrell; 7 Jordan Meads; 39 Sebastien Martins; 25 Evan Simons; 10 Mark Mexico; 9 Dayne Craig; 36 Sonny Esslemont; 12 Rhys Clarke. Subs (all used): 13 Charlie Wabo; 17 Stuart Kain; 18 Josh Stoker; 16 Francis Welsh.
Try: Blair (79); **Goals:** Beharrell 0/1.
Rugby Leaguer & League Express Men of the Match: *Raiders:* Craig Briscoe; *Thunder:* Mark Mexico.
Penalty count: 13-7; **Half-time:** 10-0;
Referee: Tom Grant; **Attendance:** 927.

Sunday 28th June 2015

NORTH WALES CRUSADERS 34 KEIGHLEY COUGARS 10

CRUSADERS: 1 Tommy Johnson; 2 Scott Turner; 31 Benjamin Jullien; 32 Sam Peet; 5 Rob Massam; 14 Karl Ashall; 7 Jamie Dallimore; 8 Jonny Walker; 15 Lee Hudson; 16 Joe Burke; 11 Jono Smith; 12 Stephen Wild; 13 Gary Middlehurst. Subs (all used): 3 Christiaan Roets; 9 Callum Wright; 10 Ryan Duffy; 20 Elliott Davies.
Tries: Turner (10, 68), Hudson (14), Massam (32), Smith (62), Burke (80); **Goals:** Johnson 5/6.
Sin bin: Johnson (50) - dissent.
COUGARS: 1 Jesse Sheriffe; 25 Andy Gabriel; 4 Danny Lawton; 30 Rikki Sheriffe; 5 Paul White; - Adam Brook; 7 Paul Handforth; 8 Scott Law; 9 James Feather; 15 Neil Cherryholme; 28 Josh Lynam; 12 Brendan Rawlins; 11 Ashley Lindsay. Subs (all used): 13 David March; 19 Matthew Bailey; 26 Paul March; - Samir Tahraoui.
Tries: White (45), R Sheriffe (59); **Goals:** Lawton 1/2.
Rugby Leaguer & League Express Men of the Match: *Crusaders:* Karl Ashall; *Cougars:* Andy Gabriel.
Penalty count: 1-5; **Half-time:** 16-0;
Referee: Dave Merrick; **Attendance:** 747.

LONDON SKOLARS 20 SOUTH WALES SCORPIONS 26

SKOLARS: 1 Marcus Elliott; 2 Jimmy Morgan; 3 Mathew Cook; 4 Joe Price; 5 Chris Bishay; 6 Jermaine Coleman; 7 James Anthony; 8 Michael Sykes; 9 Mike Bishay; 10 Dave Williams; 11 Aaron Small; 12 Will Lovell; 13 Lamont Bryan. Subs (all used): 14 Louis Robinson; 21 Lewis Reed; 19 Sam Druce; 17 Joel Wicks.
Tries: Small (4), Anthony (22), C Bishay (38), Coleman (64); **Goals:** Elliott 0/1, M Bishay 2/2, Druce 0/1.
SCORPIONS: 10 Jonny Leather; 28 Yannic Parker; 3 Paul Edwards; 4 Kyle Scrivens; 2 Ian Newbury; 21 Ryan Millington; 7 Paul Emanuelli; 23 Anthony Symons; 17 Zak Williams; 12 Barrie Phillips; 29 Andrew Joy; 18 Bradley Hill; 19 Connor Davies. Subs (all used): 14 Dafydd Hellard; 6 Curtis Davies; 30 Christopher Speck; 20 Tala Petelo.
Tries: Parker (10, 62), Hellard (36), Petelo (73), Newbury (76); **Goals:** Emanuelli 3/5.
Rugby Leaguer & League Express Men of the Match: *Skolars:* Aaron Small; *Scorpions:* Paul Emanuelli.
Penalty count: 9-10; **Half-time:** 14-10;
Referee: Chris Campbell; **Attendance:** 304.

YORK CITY KNIGHTS 26 SWINTON LIONS 16

CITY KNIGHTS: 2 Ben Dent; 19 James Clare; 24 Michael Channing; 3 Greg Minikin; 5 Nev Morrison; 32 Jordan Howden; 6 Jon Presley; 8 Mark Applegarth; 7 Pat Smith; 10 Jack Aldous; 12 Ed Smith; 15 Josh Tonks; 29 Brad Nicholson. Subs (all used): 14 Kris Brining; 4 Liam Cunningham; 34 Jack Blagbrough; 28 Mick Learmonth.
Tries: E Smith (1), B Dent (7), Howden (26), Clare (55), Minikin (61); **Goals:** Howden 2/3, B Dent 1/3.

LIONS: 1 Ritchie Hawkyard; 2 Shaun Robinson; 3 Stuart Littler; 22 Chris Rothwell; 7 Chris Atkin; 6 Ben White; 18 Aaron Lloyd; 8 Mike Morrison; 29 Mick Govin; 12 Darren Hawkyard; 27 Tom Thackray; 23 Connor Dwyer; 30 Andy Thornley. Subs (all used): 24 Jordan James; 13 Tommy Gallagher; 31 Rob Lever; 9 Andy Ackers.
Tries: Atkin (12), Ackers (42), D Hawkyard (74);
Goals: White 2/3.
Dismissal: Govin (72) - high tackle.
Rugby Leaguer & League Express Men of the Match:
City Knights: Mark Applegarth; *Lions:* Andy Ackers.
Penalty count: 8-6; **Half-time:** 16-4;
Referee: Jon Roberts; **Attendance:** 511
(at Elmpark Way, Heworth).

ROUND 13

Sunday 5th July 2015

HEMEL STAGS 12 LONDON SKOLARS 26

STAGS: 1 Derrell Olpherts; 2 Simon Hrbek; 4 Michael Brown; 18 Chris McNamara; 5 Alex Anthony; 6 Jy-mel Coleman; 33 Ben Young; 8 Dan Ljazouli; 9 James Helliwell; 32 Mark Castle; 12 Alex Ingarfield; 13 Eddie Mbaraga; 24 James Woodburn-Hall. Subs (all used): 16 Mike Stewart; 7 Charlie Lawrence; 11 Barry-John Swindells; 21 Malikhi Lloyd-Jones.
Tries: Ingarfield (45), Hrbek (69); **Goals:** Young 2/3.
Sin bin: Mbaraga (75) - fighting.
SKOLARS: 1 James Anthony; 2 Marcus Elliott; 3 Mathew Cook; 4 Joe Price; 5 Jamel Chisholm; 6 Jermaine Coleman; 7 Mike Bishay; 24 Lewis Reed; 9 Joel Wicks; 10 Dave Williams; 11 Aaron Small; 12 Will Lovell; 13 Lamont Bryan. Subs (all used): 8 Michael Sykes; 16 Louis Robinson; 15 Billy Driver; 17 Kazeem Fatouri.
Tries: Anthony (19, 80), Price (52), Bryan (58);
Goals: M Bishay 5/6.
Sin bin: Wicks (75) - fighting.
Rugby Leaguer & League Express Men of the Match:
Stags: Mike Stewart; *Skolars:* Jermaine Coleman.
Penalty count: 7-6; **Half-time:** 0-6;
Referee: Sam Ansell; **Attendance:** 481.

COVENTRY BEARS 4 NORTH WALES CRUSADERS 50

BEARS: 28 Andy Winfield; 2 Chris Dixon; 5 Ben Parry; 21 Stephen Coleman; 45 Jason Bass; 30 Dan Parker; 7 Cameron Boulter; 27 James Geurtjens; 24 Richard Hughes; 16 Alex Beddows; 32 Kenneth Kelliher; 12 Chris Barratt; 26 Matt Cooper. Subs (all used): 29 Liam Thompson; 15 Andy Unsworth; 50 Morgan Evans; 17 Jack Morrison.
Try: Cooper (42); **Goals:** Parker 0/1.
CRUSADERS: 1 Tommy Johnson; 2 Scott Turner; 31 Benjamin Jullien; 3 Christiaan Roets; 5 Rob Massam; 14 Karl Ashall; 7 Jamie Dallimore; 8 Jonny Walker; 15 Lee Hudson; 16 Joe Burke; 11 Jono Smith; 12 Stephen Wild; 13 Gary Middlehurst. Subs (all used): 6 Andy Moulsdale; 32 Sam Peet; 23 Mark Hobson; 10 Ryan Duffy.
Tries: Smith (6, 20), Massam (17, 38, 65), Ashall (22, 69), Peet (52), Johnson (72);
Goals: Johnson 7/9.
Rugby Leaguer & League Express Men of the Match:
Bears: Matt Cooper; *Crusaders:* Lee Hudson.
Penalty count: 5-4; **Half-time:** 0-26;
Referee: Chris Campbell; **Attendance:** 467.

KEIGHLEY COUGARS 44 OXFORD 14

COUGARS: 1 Jesse Sheriffe; 25 Andy Gabriel; 32 Hamish Barnes; 30 Rikki Sheriffe; 5 Paul White; - Adam Brook; 7 Paul Handforth; 8 Scott Law; 9 James Feather; 12 Brendan Rawlins; 28 Josh Lynam; 17 Oliver Pursglove; 11 Ashley Lindsay. Subs (all used): 13 David March; 19 Matthew Bailey; 26 Paul March; - Samir Tahraoui.
Tries: Gabriel (9), White (27, 80), P March (33), Lynam (42), R Sheriffe (47), Lindsay (69), Barnes (73);
Goals: Handforth 6/8.
OXFORD: 28 Sean Morris; 32 Andy Matthews; 14 Marcus Brooker; 3 Andrew Hoggins; 5 Aaron Jones-Bishop; 36 Danny Thomas; 31 Josh Kittrick; 25 Luke Evans; 9 Nathan Kitson; 19 Kyle Danns; 33 Jack Walton; 22 Harry Kaufman; 37 Adam Withington. Subs (all used): 21 Luke Gardiner; 27 Mark Barlow; 30 Chris Palser-Thorne; 34 Steve Scott.
Tries: S Morris (1), Jones-Bishop (37), Brooker (63);
Goals: Kitson 1/1, Kittrick 0/2.
Rugby Leaguer & League Express Men of the Match:
Cougars: Ashley Lindsay; *Oxford:* Jack Walton.
Penalty count: 9-5; **Half-time:** 16-10;
Referee: Tom Grant; **Attendance:** 701.

NEWCASTLE THUNDER 28 ROCHDALE HORNETS 32

THUNDER: 17 Stuart Kain; 5 Tom Capper; 31 Ali Blair; 4 Joe Brown; 38 Macauley Hallett; 6 Matty Beharrell; 27 Matthew Marsh; 8 Matt Barron; 25 Evan Simons; 10 Mark Mexico; 9 Dayne Craig; 11 Jason Payne; 13 Charlie Wabo. Subs (all used): 14 Paul Stamp; 15 Lee Fewlass; 39 Sebastien Martins; 16 Francis Welsh.
Tries: Capper (18), Brown (28), Blair (51), Beharrell (60), Marsh (77); **Goals:** Beharrell 4/5.
HORNETS: 1 Wayne English; 20 Bradley Hargreaves; 4 Lee Paterson; 23 Jack Ashworth; 5 Dale Bloomfield; 21 Ryan Smith; 7 Danny Yates; 10 Warren Thompson; 6 Paul Crook; 28 Matty Hadden; 19 Danny Bridge; 29 Jordan Case; 14 James Tilley. Subs (all used): 8 John Cookson; 25 Danny Jones; 9 Alex McClurg; 27 Matty Fozard.
Tries: English (6), Bridge (9), Fozard (36), Smith (45), Paterson (69); **Goals:** Crook 4/5, Yates 2/2.
Rugby Leaguer & League Express Men of the Match:
Thunder: Matty Beharrell; *Hornets:* Danny Bridge.
Penalty count: 8-11; **Half-time:** 12-18;
Referee: Gareth Hewer; **Attendance:** 678.

OLDHAM 34 YORK CITY KNIGHTS 12

OLDHAM: 9 Sam Gee; 2 Adam Clay; 26 Oliver Roberts; 21 Jake Connor; 4 Jack Holmes; 6 Lewis Palfrey; 27 Dave Hewitt; 10 Adam Neal; 15 Gareth Owen; 8 Phil Joy; 11 Josh Crowley; 12 Danny Langtree; 13 Liam Thompson. Subs (all used): 14 Adam Files; 22 Nathan Mason; 16 Kenny Hughes; 19 Michael Ward.
Tries: Langtree (4), M Ward (54), Holmes (63), P Joy (71), Crowley (74, 77); **Goals:** Palfrey 5/6.
CITY KNIGHTS: 2 Ben Dent; 19 James Clare; 24 Michael Channing; 3 Greg Minikin; 5 Nev Morrison; 32 Jordan Howden; 6 Jon Presley; 8 Mark Applegarth; 7 Pat Smith; 10 Jack Aldous; 12 Ed Smith; 15 Josh Tonks; 29 Brad Nicholson. Subs (all used): 14 Kris Brining; 4 Liam Cunningham; 34 Jack Blagbrough; 11 Ryan Mallinder.
Tries: Nicholson (12), Applegarth (15); **Goals:** B Dent 2/2.
Rugby Leaguer & League Express Men of the Match:
Oldham: Michael Ward; *City Knights:* Brad Nicholson.
Penalty count: 5-6; **Half-time:** 6-12;
Referee: Dave Merrick; **Attendance:** 581.

SOUTH WALES SCORPIONS 16 GLOUCESTERSHIRE ALL GOLDS 36

SCORPIONS: 10 Jonny Leather; 2 Ian Newbury; 1 Jordan Sheridan; 4 Kyle Scrivens; 28 Yannic Parker; 21 Ryan Millington; 7 Paul Emanuelli; 14 Dafydd Hellard; 17 Zak Williams; 18 Bradley Hill; 29 Andrew Joy; 12 Barrie Phillips; 19 Connor Davies. Subs (all used): 13 Neil Dallimore; 9 Connor Farrer; 34 Christopher Speck; 20 Tala Petelo.
Tries: Hill (28), Leather (43), Farrer (78);
Goals: Emanuelli 2/4.
Sin bin: Farrer (28) - fighting; Hill (28) - fighting.
ALL GOLDS: 1 Phil Cowburn; 31 Lee Mapals; 3 Lewis Reece; 6 Toby Topham; 28 Ryan Pywell; 35 Dan Poulton; 7 Matt Bradley; 8 Oliver Purslow; 9 Steve Parry; 13 Chris Vitalini; 14 Joe McClean; 4 Callum Mulkeen; 30 Emmerson Whittel. Subs (all used): 33 Graham O'Keeffe; 32 Edwin Okanga-Ajwang; 34 Alex Davidson; 29 Joel Thomas.
Tries: Reece (3), Parry (8, 67), Cowburn (11), Mulkeen (61), Davidson (70), Pywell (79);
Goals: Bradley 4/7.
Sin bin: Mapals (28) - fighting.
Rugby Leaguer & League Express Men of the Match:
Scorpions: Ryan Millington; *All Golds:* Steve Parry.
Penalty count: 12-12; **Half-time:** 6-12;
Referee: Scott Mikalauskas; **Attendance:** 211.

SWINTON LIONS 30 BARROW RAIDERS 20

LIONS: 1 Ritchie Hawkyard; 2 Shaun Robinson; 3 Stuart Littler; 22 Chris Rothwell; 28 Ian Mort; 29 Mick Govin; 6 Ben White; 24 Jordan James; 9 Andy Ackers; 8 Mike Morrison; 30 Andy Thornley; 23 Connor Dwyer; 31 Rob Lever. Subs (all used): 32 Tom Thackray; 12 Darren Hawkyard; 13 Tommy Gallagher; 10 Ben Austin.
Tries: Robinson (19), White (30), Rothwell (60), Gallagher (69, 76), James (80); **Goals:** Mort 3/6.
RAIDERS: 23 Chris Fleming; 31 Cameron Pitman; 3 Chris Hankinson; 4 Max Wiper; 20 Shane Toal; 7 Liam Campbell; 14 Josh Ward; 8 Joe Bullock; 29 Peter Lupton; 11 Liam Harrison; 24 Andy Litherland; 12 Craig Briscoe; 30 Bradd Crellin. Subs (all used): 9 Nathan Mossop; 10 Andrew Dawson; 13 Dan Toal; 21 Anthony Bate.
Tries: Ward (16), Briscoe (44), Fleming (53);
Goals: Ward 4/4.
Sin bin:
Lupton (34) - dangerous challenge on R Hawkyard.
Rugby Leaguer & League Express Men of the Match:
Lions: Rob Lever; *Raiders:* Craig Briscoe.
Penalty count: 8-9; **Half-time:** 10-6;
Referee: Andrew Sweet; **Attendance:** 485.

ROUND 14

Saturday 11th July 2015

YORK CITY KNIGHTS 50 GLOUCESTERSHIRE ALL GOLDS 10

CITY KNIGHTS: 1 James Haynes; 26 James Clare; - Michael Channing; 24 Tyler Craig; 2 Ben Dent; 6 Jon Presley; 32 Jordan Howden; 8 Mark Applegarth; 7 Pat Smith; 10 Jack Aldous; 12 Ed Smith; 15 Josh Tonks; 28 Mick Learmonth. Subs (all used): 9 Harry Carter; 34 Jack Blagbrough; 11 Ryan Mallinder; 29 Brad Nicholson.
Tries: Howden (10), Aldous (22), Clare (25, 39, 50, 77), Carter (35, 56), E Smith (62), B Dent (66);
Goals: Haynes 3/7, B Dent 2/3.
ALL GOLDS: 32 Jamie Murphy; 31 Lee Mapals; 3 Lewis Reece; 6 Toby Topham; 28 Ryan Pywell; 27 Danny Fallon; 1 Phil Cowburn; 8 Oliver Purslow; 9 Steve Parry; 29 Joel Thomas; 33 Graham O'Keeffe; 14 Joe McClean; 30 Emmerson Whittel. Subs (all used): 7 Matt Bradley; 4 Callum Mulkeen; 34 Alex Davidson; 10 Izaak Duffy.
Tries: Mulkeen (29), Cowburn (53);
Goals: Reece 0/1, Bradley 1/1.
Rugby Leaguer & League Express Men of the Match:
City Knights: Pat Smith; *All Golds:* Graham O'Keeffe.
Penalty count: 9-9; **Half-time:** 26-4;
Referee: Jon Roberts; **Attendance:** 350
(at Elmpark Way, Heworth).

BARROW RAIDERS 38 LONDON SKOLARS 12

RAIDERS: 23 Chris Fleming; 20 Shane Toal; 3 Chris Hankinson; 4 Max Wiper; 5 Kyle Dolan; 14 Josh Ward; 7 Liam Campbell; 8 Joe Bullock; 9 Nathan Mossop; 21 Anthony Bate; 11 Liam Harrison; 12 Craig Briscoe; 29 Peter Lupton. Subs (all used): 6 Brad Marwood; 13 Dan Toal; 22 Joe Hambley; 30 Bradd Crellin.
Tries: Harrison (2), Campbell (8), Briscoe (25), Marwood (42), S Toal (51), D Toal (57, 64);
Goals: Ward 4/6, Hankinson 1/1.
SKOLARS: 1 James Anthony; 2 Chris Bishay; 3 Mathew Cook; 4 Joe Price; 5 Jamel Chisholm; 6 Mike Bishay; 7 Jermaine Coleman; 8 Michael Sykes; 9 Sam Druce; 10 Dave Williams; 11 Aaron Small; 12 Will Lovell; 13 Lamont Bryan. Subs (all used): 14 Will Martin; 15 Billy Driver; 16 Louis Robinson; 17 Kazeem Fatouri.
Tries: Chisholm (20), C Bishay (61);
Goals: Druce 1/1, M Bishay 1/1.
Sin bin: Lovell (31) - high tackle on Dolan.
Rugby Leaguer & League Express Men of the Match:
Raiders: Joe Hambley; *Skolars:* Jermaine Coleman.
Penalty count: 6-6; **Half-time:** 16-6;
Referee: Adam Gill; **Attendance:** 793.

Sunday 12th July 2015

NORTH WALES CRUSADERS 56 SOUTH WALES SCORPIONS 10

CRUSADERS: 1 Tommy Johnson; 29 Andrew Oakden; 3 Christiaan Roets; 32 Sam Peet; 2 Scott Turner; 6 Andy Moulsdale; 7 Jamie Dallimore; 8 Jonny Walker; 14 Karl Ashall; 16 Joe Burke; 11 Jono Smith; 12 Stephen Wild; 23 Mark Hobson. Subs (all used): 9 Callum Wright; 34 Andrew Joy; 10 Ryan Duffy; 20 Elliott Davies.
Tries: Peet (4), Wild (26, 71), Dallimore (35, 65), Turner (37, 49), Moulsdale (45), Smith (56), Johnson (78); **Goals:** Johnson 8/10.
Sin bin: Smith (69) - dissent.
SCORPIONS: 5 Ben Jones; 2 Ian Newbury; 1 Jordan Sheridan; 4 Kyle Scrivens; 28 Yannic Parker; 21 Ryan Millington; 6 Curtis Davies; 12 Barrie Phillips; 7 Paul Emanuelli; 8 Osian Phillips; 18 Bradley Hill; 11 Mike Connor; 19 Connor Davies. Subs (all used): 9 Connor Farrer; 16 Nathan Rainer; 34 Christopher Speck; 20 Tala Petelo.
Tries: Newbury (18), Hill (61); **Goals:** Emanuelli 1/2.
Rugby Leaguer & League Express Men of the Match:
Crusaders: Stephen Wild; *Scorpions:* Paul Emanuelli.
Penalty count: 4-5; **Half-time:** 22-6;
Referee: Michael Woodhead; **Attendance:** 703.

COVENTRY BEARS 10 KEIGHLEY COUGARS 42

BEARS: 28 Andy Winfield; 2 Chris Dixon; 30 Dan Parker; 5 Ben Parry; 45 Jason Bass; 39 Joel James; 7 Cameron Boulter; 46 Jack Francis; 24 Richard Hughes; 17 Jack Morrison; 29 Liam Thompson; 12 Chris Barratt; 26 Matt Cooper. Subs (all used): 3 Nick Taylor; 14 Dylan Bale; 16 Alex Beddows; 38 Tom Hall.
Tries: Morrison (12), Bass (54); **Goals:** Parker 1/2.
COUGARS: 1 Jesse Sheriffe; 32 Hamish Barnes; 17 Oliver Pursglove; 30 Rikki Sheriffe; 5 Paul White; - Adam Brook; 7 Paul Handforth; 8 Scott Law; 9 James Feather; 15 Neil Cherryholme; 28 Josh Lynam; 13 David March; 11 Ashley Lindsay. Subs (all used): 12 Brendan Rawlins; 19 Matthew Bailey; 26 Paul March; - Samir Tahraoui.
Tries: White (7, 35), R Sheriffe (14), Lynam (28, 49), Brook (39), Tahraoui (60), Feather (70);
Goals: Handforth 3/6, Brook 2/2.
Sin bin: Lynam (11) - professional foul.
Rugby Leaguer & League Express Men of the Match:
Bears: Alex Beddows; *Cougars:* Samir Tahraoui.
Penalty count: 6-2; **Half-time:** 6-26;
Referee: Scott Mikalauskas; **Attendance:** 441.

NEWCASTLE THUNDER 40 HEMEL STAGS 26

THUNDER: 17 Stuart Kain; 2 Jacob Blades; 31 Ali Blair; 4 Joe Brown; 5 Tom Capper; 6 Matty Beharrell; 23 Benn Hardcastle; 8 Matt Barron; 13 Charlie Wabo; 39 Sebastien Martins; 11 Jason Payne; 9 Dayne Craig; 12 Rhys Clarke. Subs (all used): 25 Evan Simons; 19 Craig Boot; 15 Lee Fewlass; 16 Francis Welsh.
Tries: Hardcastle (11), Wabo (21), Blades (31), Craig (39, 64), Kain (55), Blair (68); **Goals:** Beharrell 6/7.
STAGS: 1 Derrell Olpherts; 5 Alex Anthony; 4 Michael Brown; 18 Chris McNamara; 23 Simon Hrbek; 6 Jy-mel Coleman; 33 Ben Young; 16 Mike Stewart; 9 James Helliwell; 17 Dan Ljazouli; 13 Eddie Mbaraga; 12 Alex Ingarfield; 11 Barry-John Swindells. Subs (all used): 7 Charlie Lawrence; 31 Matt Ross; 21 Malikhi Lloyd-Jones; 32 Jamie Crowther.
Tries: Jy-mel Coleman (5, 45), Olpherts (17), Brown (52), Anthony (73); **Goals:** Young 3/5.
Rugby Leaguer & League Express Men of the Match:
Thunder: Dayne Craig; *Stags:* Jy-mel Coleman.
Penalty count: 2-2; **Half-time:** 22-12;
Referee: Chris Campbell; **Attendance:** 1,027.

OLDHAM 38 ROCHDALE HORNETS 18

OLDHAM: 27 Jake Connor; 2 Adam Clay; 17 George Tyson; 26 Oliver Roberts; 4 Jack Holmes; 6 Lewis Palfrey; 7 Steve Roper; 10 Adam Neal; 15 Gareth Owen; 8 Phil Joy; 11 Josh Crowley; 12 Danny Langtree; 21 Jacob Fairbank. Subs (all used): 14 Adam Files; 13 Liam Thompson; 9 Sam Gee; 19 Michael Ward.
Tries: Clay (17), Connor (21), Palfrey (33), Fairbank (49), Gee (53), Owen (75), Crowley (79); **Goals:** Palfrey 5/8.
HORNETS: 1 Wayne English; 2 Gareth Langley; 4 Lee Paterson; 23 Jack Ashworth; 5 Dale Bloomfield; 21 Ryan Smith; 7 Danny Yates; 10 Warren Thompson; 6 Paul Crook; 28 Matty Hadden; 19 Danny Bridge; 29 Jordan Case; 15 Lewis Charnock. Subs (all used): - Matthew Haggarty; 27 Danny Jones; 9 Alex McClurg; 14 James Tilley.
Tries: Crook (6), Paterson (37), Bridge (44);
Goals: Crook 2/2, Yates 1/2.
Rugby Leaguer & League Express Men of the Match:
Oldham: Josh Crowley; *Hornets:* Danny Bridge.
Penalty count: 12-10; **Half-time:** 14-14;
Referee: Andrew Sweet; **Attendance:** 725.

OXFORD 4 SWINTON LIONS 96

OXFORD: 28 Sean Morris; 32 Andy Matthews; 14 Marcus Brooker; 3 Andrew Hoggins; 21 Luke Gardiner; 36 Danny Thomas; 31 Josh Kittrick; 19 Kyle Danns; 9 Nathan Kitson; 25 Luke Evans; 33 Jack Walton; 22 Harry Kaufman; 37 Adam Withington. Subs (all used): 27 Mark Barlow; 34 Steve Scott; 30 Chris Palser-Thorne; 18 Simon Price.
Try: Withington (62); **Goals:** S Morris 0/1.
LIONS: 1 Ritchie Hawkyard; 2 Shaun Robinson; 3 Stuart Littler; 22 Chris Rothwell; 28 Ian Mort; 6 Ben White; 7 Chris Atkin; 8 Mike Morrison; 9 Andy Ackers; 24 Jordan James; 30 Andy Thornley; 23 Connor Dwyer; 31 Rob Lever. Subs (all used): 32 Tom Thackray; 12 Darren Hawkyard; 11 Grant Beecham; 10 Ben Austin.
Tries: White (8), R Hawkyard (11, 26), Mort (13, 31, 34, 48, 62), Lever (20), Atkin (36, 65), D Hawkyard (40), Dwyer (44), Rothwell (55), Ackers (57), M Morrison (75), Robinson (79); **Goals:** Mort 14/17.
Rugby Leaguer & League Express Men of the Match: *Oxford:* Jack Walton; *Lions:* Ian Mort.
Penalty count: 4-8; **Half-time:** 0-52;
Referee: Sam Ansell; **Attendance:** 497
(at Pennine Way, Hemel).

ROUND 15

Saturday 18th July 2015

GLOUCESTERSHIRE ALL GOLDS 38 OXFORD 24

ALL GOLDS: 7 Matt Bradley; 31 Lee Mapals; 4 Callum Mulkeen; 32 Edwin Okanga-Ajwang; 28 Ryan Pywell; 33 Jamie Murphy; 1 Phil Cowburn; 8 Oliver Purslow; 9 Steve Parry; 10 Izaak Duffy; 3 Lewis Reece; 30 Emmerson Whittel; 13 Chris Vitalini. Subs (all used): 6 Toby Topham; 34 Graham O'Keeffe; 29 Joel Thomas; 35 Alex Davidson.
Tries: Reece (1), Parry (4), Pywell (22), Whittel (26), Davidson (47), Mapals (59), Vitalini (78);
Goals: Bradley 5/7.
OXFORD: 28 Sean Morris; 32 Andy Matthews; 37 Adam Withington; 3 Andrew Hoggins; 1 Louis Richards; 36 Danny Thomas; 20 Dean Mignacca; 27 Bobby Tyson-Wilson; 31 Josh Kittrick; 8 Jordan Andrade; 14 Marcus Brooker; 33 Jack Walton; 29 Josh Nathaniel. Subs (all used): 9 Nathan Kitson; 19 Kyle Danns; 34 Steve Scott; 5 Aaron Jones-Bishop.
Tries: Kitson (43, 73), Nathaniel (53), Hoggins (67), Tyson-Wilson (71); **Goals:** Kitson 2/5.
Sin bin: Nathaniel (39) - dissent.
Rugby Leaguer & League Express Men of the Match: *All Golds:* Steve Parry; *Oxford:* Jordan Andrade.
Penalty count: 8-10; **Half-time:** 22-0;
Referee: Chris Campbell; **Attendance:** 235.

BARROW RAIDERS 6 NORTH WALES CRUSADERS 23

RAIDERS: 23 Chris Fleming; 22 Joe Hambley; 3 Chris Hankinson; 4 Max Wiper; 31 Cameron Pitman; 7 Liam Campbell; 14 Josh Ward; 8 Joe Bullock; 29 Peter Lupton; 11 Liam Harrison; 24 Andy Litherland; 12 Craig Briscoe; 27 Jamie Tracey. Subs (all used): 10 Andrew Dawson; 9 Nathan Mossop; 21 Anthony Bate; 30 Bradd Crellin.
Try: Briscoe (62); **Goals:** Ward 1/1.
Sin bin: Pitman (60) - fighting.
CRUSADERS: 1 Tommy Johnson; 29 Andrew Oakden; 3 Christiaan Roets; 31 Benjamin Jullien; 2 Scott Turner; 14 Karl Ashall; 7 Jamie Dallimore; 8 Jonny Walker; 9 Callum Wright; 16 Joe Burke; 11 Jono Smith; 12 Stephen Wild; 13 Gary Middlehurst. Subs (all used): 15 Lee Hudson; 6 Andy Moulsdale; 23 Mark Hobson; 10 Ryan Duffy.
Tries: Dallimore (12), Turner (18), Smith (43), Burke (68);
Goals: Johnson 3/5; **Field goal:** Middlehurst (75).
Sin bin: Ashall (14) - high tackle on Harrison; Middlehurst (60) - fighting.
Rugby Leaguer & League Express Men of the Match: *Raiders:* Joe Bullock; *Crusaders:* Jamie Dallimore.
Penalty count: 9-8; **Half-time:** 0-10;
Referee: Gareth Hewer; **Attendance:** 1,010.

Sunday 19th July 2015

KEIGHLEY COUGARS 14 SWINTON LIONS 22

COUGARS: 1 Jesse Sheriffe; 25 Andy Gabriel; 32 Hamish Barnes; 30 Rikki Sheriffe; 5 Paul White; 33 Adam Brook; 26 Paul March; 8 Scott Law; 9 James Feather; 15 Neil Cherryholme; 17 Oliver Pursglove; 13 David March; 12 Brendan Rawlins. Subs (all used): 19 Matthew Bailey; 31 Scott Lee; 34 Samir Tahraoui; - Tyler Dickinson.
Tries: Lee (19), D March (46), White (60);
Goals: Brook 1/3.
LIONS: 1 Ritchie Hawkyard; 2 Shaun Robinson; 3 Stuart Littler; 22 Chris Rothwell; 28 Mike Butt; 6 Ben White; 7 Chris Atkin; 8 Mike Morrison; 9 Andy Ackers; 24 Jordan James; 30 Andy Thornley; 23 Connor Dwyer; 31 Rob Lever. Subs (all used): 10 Ben Austin; 11 Grant Beecham; 12 Darren Hawkyard; 29 Mick Govin.
Tries: Ackers (14), Littler (50), Robinson (68), Butt (74);
Goals: Atkin 3/4.
Rugby Leaguer & League Express Men of the Match: *Cougars:* Oliver Pursglove; *Lions:* Chris Atkin.
Penalty count: 9-9; **Half-time:** 6-6;
Referee: Jon Roberts; **Attendance:** 831.

LONDON SKOLARS 6 OLDHAM 32

SKOLARS: 1 Chris Bishay; 2 Sam Nash; 3 John Paxton; 4 Joe Price; 5 Jamel Chisholm; 6 James Anthony; 7 Jermaine Coleman; 21 Will Martin; 9 Mike Bishay; 10 Dave Williams; 11 Kazeem Fatouri; 12 Will Lovell; 13 Lamont Bryan. Subs (all used): 14 Billy Driver; 24 Lewis Reed; 17 Anthony Cox; 16 Aaron Small.
Try: Cox (72); **Goals:** M Bishay 1/1.
OLDHAM: 20 Tom Dempsey; 2 Adam Clay; 26 Oliver Roberts; 17 George Tyson; 4 Jack Holmes; 6 Lewis Palfrey; 7 Steve Roper; 10 Adam Neal; 15 Gareth Owen; 8 Phil Joy; 11 Josh Crowley; 12 Danny Langtree; 13 Liam Thompson. Subs (all used): 14 Adam Files; 16 Kenny Hughes; 19 Michael Ward; 18 Richard Joy.
Tries: Palfrey (12, 65), M Ward (37, 47), Roper (40), Thompson (80); **Goals:** Palfrey 4/6.
Rugby Leaguer & League Express Men of the Match: *Skolars:* Lamont Bryan; *Oldham:* Lewis Palfrey.
Penalty count: 5-8; **Half-time:** 0-18;
Referee: Sam Ansell; **Attendance:** 314.

ROCHDALE HORNETS 50 COVENTRY BEARS 22

HORNETS: 1 Wayne English; 2 Gareth Langley; 4 Lee Paterson; 24 Dave Hull; 5 Dale Bloomfield; 21 Ryan Smith; 7 Danny Yates; 25 Danny Jones; 6 Paul Crook; 10 Warren Thompson; 11 Jordan Case; 19 Danny Bridge; 15 Lewis Charnock. Subs (all used): 29 Matthew Haggarty; - Matty Fozard; 9 Alex McClurg; 14 James Tilley.
Tries: Crook (12, 46, 66), Bridge (17), Haggarty (40), Jones (55), Case (58), Hull (63), Bloomfield (77);
Goals: Crook 7/9.
On report: Charnock (69) - alleged late challenge.
BEARS: 28 Andy Winfield; 20 Jamahl Hunte; 3 Nick Taylor; 13 Simon Phillips; 45 Jason Bass; 42 Joel James; 30 Dan Parker; 35 Jack Morrison; 24 Richard Hughes; 46 Jack Francis; 29 Liam Thompson; 12 Chris Barratt; 26 Matt Cooper. Subs (all used): 27 James Geurtjens; 21 Stephen Coleman; 38 Tom Hall; 14 Dylan Bale.
Tries: Phillips (5), Hughes (24), Cooper (28, 72);
Goals: Parker 3/5.
Rugby Leaguer & League Express Men of the Match: *Hornets:* Paul Crook; *Bears:* Matt Cooper.
Penalty count: 7-5; **Half-time:** 18-14;
Referee: Chris Leatherbarrow; **Attendance:** 315.

SOUTH WALES SCORPIONS 28 HEMEL STAGS 46

SCORPIONS: 10 Jonny Leather; 17 Zak Williams; 1 Jordan Sheridan; 4 Kyle Scrivens; 28 Yannic Parker; 21 Ryan Millington; 7 Paul Emanuelli; 8 Osian Phillips; 9 Connor Farrer; 14 Dafydd Hellard; 11 Mike Connor; 12 Barrie Phillips; 19 Connor Davies. Subs (all used): 6 Curtis Davies; 33 Nathan Rainer; 34 Christopher Speck; 20 Tala Petelo.
Tries: Parker (10, 36), Farrer (18, 23), Williams (70);
Goals: Emanuelli 4/5.
STAGS: 1 Derrell Olpherts; 2 Alex Anthony; - Aston Wilson; 4 Michael Brown; 33 Simon Hrbek; 6 Jy-mel Coleman; 23 James Woodburn-Hall; 17 Dan Ljazouli; 9 James Helliwell; 16 Mike Stewart; 13 Eddie Mbaraga; 12 Alex Ingarfield; 32 Jamie Crowther. Subs (all used): 31 Matt Ross; 28 Brooke Broughton; 7 Charlie Lawrence; 21 Malikhi Lloyd-Jones.
Tries: Olpherts (2, 13, 67), Crowther (26), Hrbek (28), Wilson (44, 47), Woodburn-Hall (52), Anthony (58, 62);
Goals: Jy-mel Coleman 1/5, Lawrence 1/4, Woodburn-Hall 1/1.
Rugby Leaguer & League Express Men of the Match: *Scorpions:* Connor Farrer; *Stags:* Derrell Olpherts.
Penalty count: 7-10; **Half-time:** 22-18;
Referee: Scott Mikalauskas; **Attendance:** 175.

YORK CITY KNIGHTS 40 NEWCASTLE THUNDER 8

CITY KNIGHTS: 1 James Haynes; 5 Nev Morrison; 26 Michael Channing; 3 Greg Minikin; 2 Ben Dent; 6 Jon Presley; 32 Jordan Howden; 8 Mark Applegarth; 7 Pat Smith; 10 Jack Aldous; 12 Ed Smith; 15 Josh Tonks; 29 Brad Nicholson. Subs (all used): 14 Kris Brining; 13 Colton Roche; 11 Ryan Mallinder; 28 Mick Learmonth.
Tries: E Smith (13, 78), Presley (20), Brining (31, 49, 52), Nicholson (63); **Goals:** Haynes 6/8.
THUNDER: 1 Louis Sheriff; 38 Macauley Hallett; 31 Ali Blair; 4 Joe Brown; 5 Tom Capper; 6 Matty Beharrell; 23 Benn Hardcastle; 8 Matt Barron; 25 Evan Simons; 39 Sebastien Martins; 16 Francis Welsh; 9 Dayne Craig; 12 Rhys Clarke. Subs (all used): 13 Charlie Wabo; 10 Mark Mexico; 15 Lee Fewlass; 36 Sonny Esslemont.
Tries: Craig (27), Hallett (75); **Goals:** Beharrell 0/2.
Sin bin: Brown (66) - dissent.
Rugby Leaguer & League Express Men of the Match: *City Knights:* Ed Smith; *Thunder:* Matt Barron.
Penalty count: 7-6; **Half-time:** 18-4;
Referee: Dave Merrick; **Attendance:** 430
(at Elmpark Way, Heworth).

ROUND 16

Saturday 25th July 2015

GLOUCESTERSHIRE ALL GOLDS 10 LONDON SKOLARS 34

ALL GOLDS: 7 Matt Bradley; 31 Lee Mapals; 6 Toby Topham; 32 Edwin Okanga-Ajwang; 28 Ryan Pywell; 1 Phil Cowburn; - Jamie Murphy; 8 Oliver Purslow; 9 Steve Parry; 34 Alex Davidson; 3 Lewis Reece; 4 Callum Mulkeen; 33 Graham O'Keeffe. Subs (all used): 27 Danny Fallon; 35 Dan Poulton; 13 Chris Vitalini; 10 Izaak Duffy.
Tries: Okanga-Ajwang (64), Mapals (76);
Goals: Bradley 1/1, Murphy 0/1.
SKOLARS: 1 Chris Bishay; 2 Sam Nash; 3 Mathew Cook; 4 Joe Price; 5 Jamel Chisholm; 6 James Anthony; 7 Jermaine Coleman; 21 Will Martin; 9 Mike Bishay; 10 Dave Williams; 12 Will Lovell; 11 Kazeem Fatouri; 13 Lamont Bryan. Subs (all used): 15 Billy Driver; 24 Lewis Reed; 16 Anthony Cox; 17 Aaron Small.
Tries: M Bishay (14), Bryan (24, 72), Driver (44), Nash (58), C Bishay (78);
Goals: M Bishay 5/7, C Bishay 0/1, Coleman 0/1.
Rugby Leaguer & League Express Men of the Match: *All Golds:* Lee Mapals; *Skolars:* Lamont Bryan.
Penalty count: 9-6; **Half-time:** 0-12;
Referee: Adam Gill; **Attendance:** 233.

OXFORD 22 BARROW RAIDERS 34

OXFORD: 36 Danny Thomas; 32 Andy Matthews; 14 Marcus Brooker; 5 Aaron Jones-Bishop; 21 Luke Gardiner; 1 Louis Richards; 9 Nathan Kitson; 8 Jordan Andrade; 31 Craig Cook; 27 Bobby Tyson-Wilson; 33 Jack Walton; 3 Andrew Hoggins; 13 James Milburn. Subs (all used): 20 Dean Mignacca; 18 Lee Land; 25 Luke Evans; 37 Adam Withington.
Tries: Cook (9), Hoggins (34), Withington (72), Kitson (73); **Goals:** Kitson 3/4.
RAIDERS: 7 Liam Campbell; 5 Kyle Dolan; 3 Chris Hankinson; 31 Cameron Pitman; 4 Max Wiper; 29 Peter Lupton; 14 Josh Ward; 8 Joe Bullock; 9 Nathan Mossop; 11 Liam Harrison; 24 Andy Litherland; 27 Jamie Tracey; 30 Bradd Crellin. Subs (all used): 6 Brad Marwood; 28 James Duerden; 12 Craig Briscoe; 10 Andrew Dawson.
Tries: Tracey (17), Campbell (21), Wiper (28), Ward (40), Dolan (51, 60); **Goals:** Ward 5/6.
Rugby Leaguer & League Express Men of the Match: *Oxford:* Jordan Andrade; *Raiders:* Kyle Dolan.
Penalty count: 7-6; **Half-time:** 10-24;
Referee: Jon Roberts; **Attendance:** 233
(at Prince of Wales Stadium, Cheltenham).

SOUTH WALES SCORPIONS 0 YORK CITY KNIGHTS 64

SCORPIONS: 10 Jonny Leather; 17 Zak Williams; 3 Paul Edwards; 4 Kyle Scrivens; 28 Yannic Parker; 6 Curtis Davies; 7 Paul Emanuelli; 8 Osian Phillips; 9 Connor Farrer; 20 Tala Petelo; 23 Anthony Symons; 12 Barrie Phillips; 19 Connor Davies. Subs (all used): 11 Mike Connor; 15 Rhys Davies; 33 Nathan Rainer; 21 Ryan Millington.
Sin bin: Leather (71) - persistent offside; O Phillips (76) - fighting.
CITY KNIGHTS: 1 James Haynes; 2 Ben Dent; 3 Greg Minikin; 24 Tyler Craig; 5 Nev Morrison; 6 Jon Presley; 7 Pat Smith; 8 Mark Applegarth; 9 Harry Carter; 34 Jack Blagbrough; 4 Liam Cunningham; 12 Ed Smith; 11 Ryan Mallinder. Subs (all used): 14 Kris Brining; 26 Brad Hey; 29 Brad Nicholson; 13 Colton Roche.
Tries: Morrison (6), Minikin (13, 53), Nicholson (28, 80), Brining (33, 50, 76), Presley (35), Craig (45), Mallinder (59); **Goals:** Haynes 9/10, B Dent 1/1.
Sin bin: E Smith (76) - fighting.
Rugby Leaguer & League Express Men of the Match: *Scorpions:* Barrie Phillips; *City Knights:* Kris Brining.
Penalty count: 7-15; **Half-time:** 0-28;
Referee: Tom Grant; **Attendance:** 202.

Sunday 26th July 2015

HEMEL STAGS 16 COVENTRY BEARS 12

STAGS: 1 Derrell Olpherts; 30 Jamie Crowther; 18 Chris McNamara; 4 Michael Brown; 23 Simon Hrbek; 24 James Woodburn-Hall; 6 Jy-mel Coleman; 31 Matt Ross; 9 James Helliwell; 16 Mike Stewart; 13 Eddie Mbaraga; 12 Alex Ingarfield; 17 Dan Ljazouli. Subs (all used): 7 Charlie Lawrence; 21 Malikhi Lloyd-Jones; 15 Liam Coleman; 14 Ryan Chester.
Tries: Lawrence (33), Ross (39); **Goals:** Lawrence 4/5.
BEARS: 7 Cameron Boulter; 2 Chris Dixon; 45 Jason Bass; 3 Nick Taylor; 20 Jamahl Hunte; 30 Dan Parker; 42 Joel James; 17 Jack Morrison; 24 Richard Hughes; 27 James Geurtjens; 29 Liam Thompson; 12 Chris Barratt; 26 Matt Cooper. Subs (all used): 9 Alex Brown; 38 Tom Hall; 46 Jack Francis; 32 Kenneth Kelliher.
Tries: Barratt (36), Parker (60); **Goals:** Parker 2/2.
Dismissal: Francis (77) - high tackle on Olpherts.
Rugby Leaguer & League Express Men of the Match: *Stags:* Charlie Lawrence; *Bears:* Dan Parker.
Penalty count: 8-10; **Half-time:** 12-6;
Referee: Chris Campbell; **Attendance:** 117.

NORTH WALES CRUSADERS 6 OLDHAM 23

CRUSADERS: 1 Tommy Johnson; 5 Rob Massam; 3 Christiaan Roets; 32 Rhys Evans; 2 Scott Turner; 14 Karl Ashall; 7 Jamie Dallimore; 8 Jonny Walker; 9 Callum Wright; 16 Joe Burke; 31 Benjamin Jullien; 22 Alex Thompson; 13 Gary Middlehurst. Subs (all used): 6 Andy Moulsdale; 15 Lee Hudson; 10 Ryan Duffy; 23 Mark Hobson.
Try: Evans (13); **Goals:** Johnson 1/2.
OLDHAM: 21 Richard Lepori; 2 Adam Clay; 17 George Tyson; 3 Jonathan Ford; 4 Jack Holmes; 6 Lewis Palfrey; 7 Steve Roper; 10 Adam Neal; 15 Gareth Owen; 8 Phil Joy; 11 Josh Crowley; 12 Danny Langtree; 9 Sam Gee. Subs (all used): 19 Michael Ward; 13 Liam Thompson; 14 Adam Files; 16 Kenny Hughes.
Tries: Neal (2), Gee (6), Tyson (52); **Goals:** Palfrey 5/5;
Field goal: Roper (59).
Rugby Leaguer & League Express Men of the Match: *Crusaders:* Rhys Evans; *Oldham:* Lewis Palfrey.
Penalty count: 13-9; **Half-time:** 6-12;
Referee: Gareth Hewer; **Attendance:** 905.

KEIGHLEY COUGARS 28 NEWCASTLE THUNDER 10

COUGARS: 24 Liam Darville; 25 Andy Gabriel; 4 Danny Lawton; 30 Rikki Sheriffe; - Josh Guzdek; 33 Adam Brook; 26 Paul March; 8 Scott Law; 9 James Feather; 15 Neil Cherryholme; 17 Oliver Pursglove; 13 David March; 12 Brendan Rawlins. Subs (all used): 19 Matthew Bailey; 28 Josh Lynam; 34 Samir Tahraoui; - Tyler Dickinson.
Tries: Gabriel (15), Darville (35), Brook (50), Cherryholme (65), Guzdek (77); **Goals:** Lawton 4/5.
Sin bin: R Sheriffe (70) - fighting.

THUNDER: 1 Louis Sheriff; 38 Macauley Hallett; 31 Ali Blair; 4 Joe Brown; 37 Stewart Sanderson; 6 Matty Beharrell; 23 Benn Hardcastle; 39 Sebastien Martins; 25 Evan Simons; 10 Mark Mexico; 9 Dayne Craig; 36 Sonny Esslemont; 13 Charlie Wabo. Subs (all used): 8 Matt Barron; 12 Rhys Clarke; 15 Lee Fewlass; 16 Francis Welsh.
Tries: Hallett (19), Simons (58); **Goals:** Beharrell 1/2.
Sin bin: Hardcastle (70) - fighting.
Rugby Leaguer & League Express Men of the Match: *Cougars:* Liam Darville; *Thunder:* Sonny Esslemont.
Penalty count: 6-4; **Half-time:** 12-4;
Referee: Sam Ansell; **Attendance:** 753.

SWINTON LIONS 20 ROCHDALE HORNETS 16

LIONS: 1 Ritchie Hawkyard; 2 Shaun Robinson; 3 Stuart Littler; 22 Chris Rothwell; 28 Ian Mort; 6 Ben White; 29 Mick Govin; 24 Jordan James; 9 Andy Ackers; 8 Mike Morrison; 17 Andy Thornley; 11 Grant Beecham; 31 Rob Lever. Subs (all used): 10 Ben Austin; 23 Connor Dwyer; 30 Josh Barlow; 7 Chris Atkin.
Tries: Robinson (1), Thornley (20), Rothwell (24), Beecham (67); **Goals:** Mort 2/4.
On report: Morrison (56) - alleged high tackle on Tilley.
HORNETS: 1 Wayne English; 2 Gareth Langley; 4 Lee Paterson; 24 Dave Hull; 5 Dale Bloomfield; 21 Ryan Smith; 7 Danny Yates; 25 Danny Jones; 6 Paul Crook; 10 Warren Thompson; 19 Danny Bridge; 23 James Dandy; 17 Jordan Case. Subs (all used): 14 James Tilley; 27 Matthew Haggarty; 9 Alex McClurg; 28 Matty Hadden.
Tries: English (13), Bloomfield (60), Paterson (72);
Goals: Crook 2/3.
Dismissal: Langley (9) - dissent.
Rugby Leaguer & League Express Men of the Match: *Lions:* Grant Beecham; *Hornets:* Paul Crook.
Penalty count: 7-11; **Half-time:** 16-4;
Referee: Matthew Thomason; **Attendance:** 494.

ROUND 17

Saturday 1st August 2015

BARROW RAIDERS 44 HEMEL STAGS 22

RAIDERS: 7 Liam Campbell; 5 Kyle Dolan; 3 Chris Hankinson; 24 Andy Litherland; 31 Cameron Pitman; 29 Peter Lupton; 14 Josh Ward; 8 Joe Bullock; 9 Nathan Mossop; 11 Liam Harrison; 27 Jamie Tracey; 12 Craig Briscoe; 30 Bradd Crellin. Subs (all used): 6 Brad Marwood; 28 James Duerden; 16 Adam Nicholson; 10 Andrew Dawson.
Tries: Lupton (10), Briscoe (23), Duerden (40), Dolan (42), Litherland (52), Marwood (57), Bullock (72), Hankinson (74); **Goals:** Ward 6/8.
STAGS: 1 Derrell Olpherts; 5 Alex Anthony; 4 Michael Brown; 18 Chris McNamara; 33 Simon Hrbek; 6 Jy-mel Coleman; 7 Charlie Lawrence; 31 Matt Ross; 9 James Helliwell; 16 Mike Stewart; 12 Alex Ingarfield; 30 Jamie Crowther; 17 Dan Ljazouli. Subs (all used): 23 Thibault Cousine; 21 Malikhi Lloyd-Jones; 15 Liam O'Callaghan; 13 Eddie Mbaraga.
Tries: Anthony (7, 67), Brown (19), Cousine (48);
Goals: Lawrence 3/4.
Rugby Leaguer & League Express Men of the Match: *Raiders:* Adam Nicholson; *Stags:* Derrell Olpherts.
Penalty count: 7-3; **Half-time:** 18-12;
Referee: Sam Ansell; **Attendance:** 828.

Sunday 2nd August 2015

NORTH WALES CRUSADERS 38 GLOUCESTERSHIRE ALL GOLDS 20

CRUSADERS: 1 Tommy Johnson; 2 Scott Turner; 17 Stuart Reardon; 32 Benjamin Jullien; 5 Rob Massam; 6 Andy Moulsdale; 7 Jamie Dallimore; 8 Jonny Walker; 15 Lee Hudson; 16 Joe Burke; 4 Matt Reid; 23 Mark Hobson; 13 Gary Middlehurst. Subs (all used): 34 Andrew Joy; 20 Elliott Davies; 10 Ryan Duffy; 31 Sam Peet.
Tries: Turner (8), Burke (16), Reid (45, 61), Massam (51, 56, 67, 80); **Goals:** Johnson 3/8, Turner 0/1.
Sin bin: Middlehurst (28) - punching.
ALL GOLDS: 1 Phil Cowburn; 31 Lee Mapals; 4 Callum Mulkeen; 12 Yann Bertrand; 28 Ryan Pywell; 20 Courtney Davies; - Yvan Leroyer; 8 Oliver Purslow; 9 Steve Parry; 35 Graham O'Keeffe; 32 Edwin Okanga-Ajwang; 24 Kevin Aparicio; 14 Joe McClean. Subs (all used): 33 Jamie Murphy; 3 Lewis Reece; 17 James Walter; 34 Alex Davidson.
Tries: Parry (38, 42), Mapals (59); **Goals:** Leroyer 4/4.
Dismissal:
McClean (70) - dangerous challenge on Walker.
Rugby Leaguer & League Express Men of the Match: *Crusaders:* Rob Massam; *All Golds:* Steve Parry.
Penalty count: 12-8; **Half-time:** 10-8;
Referee: Chris Campbell; **Attendance:** 420.

COVENTRY BEARS 10 YORK CITY KNIGHTS 38

BEARS: 45 Jason Bass; 49 Elliot Holton; 13 Simon Phillips; 3 Nick Taylor; 2 Chris Dixon; 39 Dan Price; 42 Joel James; 17 Jack Morrison; 24 Richard Hughes; 34 Andy Unsworth; 26 Matt Cooper; 12 Chris Barratt; 30 Dan Parker. Subs (all used): 38 Tom Hall; 29 Liam Thompson; 14 Dylan Bale; 50 Morgan Evans.
Tries: James (70), Parker (75); **Goals:** Parker 1/2.
CITY KNIGHTS: 32 Jordan Howden; 5 Nev Morrison; 4 Liam Cunningham; 24 Tyler Craig; 25 Adam Dent; 6 Jon Presley; 7 Pat Smith; 8 Mark Applegarth; 9 Harry Carter; 10 Jack Aldous; 15 Josh Tonks; 12 Ed Smith; 11 Ryan Mallinder. Subs (all used): 27 Casey Canterbury; - Brad Hey; 29 Brad Nicholson; 28 Mick Learmonth.
Tries: Tonks (21), Cunningham (25), Nicholson (33), P Smith (47), E Smith (56), Carter (66), Mallinder (80);
Goals: Howden 3/3, A Dent 2/4.
Rugby Leaguer & League Express Men of the Match: *Bears:* Dan Parker; *City Knights:* Nev Morrison.
Penalty count: 8-6; **Half-time:** 0-18;
Referee: Jon Roberts; **Attendance:** 442.

LONDON SKOLARS 42 OXFORD 12

SKOLARS: 1 Chris Bishay; 2 Sam Nash; 3 Mathew Cook; 4 Joe Price; 5 John Paxton; 6 James Anthony; 7 Jermaine Coleman; 21 Will Martin; 9 Mike Bishay; 10 Dave Williams; 11 Kazeem Fatouri; 12 Will Lovell; 13 Lamont Bryan. Subs (all used): 14 Louis Robinson; 15 Billy Driver; 16 Anthony Cox; 17 Mike Benson.
Tries: Fatouri (8), Williams (16, 20), Cook (26), Driver (29), Lovell (55), M Bishay (73), Paxton (80);
Goals: M Bishay 4/6, Cook 1/2.
OXFORD: 36 Danny Thomas; 32 Andy Matthews; 14 Marcus Brooker; 28 Josh Nathaniel; 21 Luke Gardiner; 1 Louis Richards; 7 Andy Speake; 27 Bobby Tyson-Wilson; 20 Dean Mignacca; 8 Jordan Andrade; 18 Lee Land; 3 Andrew Hoggins; 37 Adam Withington. Subs (all used): 19 Kyle Danns; 5 Aaron Jones-Bishop; 25 Luke Evans; 31 Charlie Greene.
Tries: Nathaniel (59), Thomas (65); **Goals:** Richards 2/2.
Rugby Leaguer & League Express Men of the Match: *Skolars:* Dave Williams; *Oxford:* Dean Mignacca.
Penalty count: 11-6; **Half-time:** 28-0;
Referee: Scott Mikalauskas; **Attendance:** 340.

NEWCASTLE THUNDER 18 SWINTON LIONS 30

THUNDER: 1 Louis Sheriff; 2 Jacob Blades; 3 Jason Tali; 31 Ali Blair; 38 Macauley Hallett; 23 Benn Hardcastle; 6 Matty Beharrell; 10 Mark Mexico; 25 Evan Simons; 37 Sebastien Martins; 9 Dayne Craig; 11 Jason Payne; 36 Sonny Esslemont. Subs (all used): 13 Charlie Wabo; 15 Lee Fewlass; 18 Josh Stoker; 16 Francis Welsh.
Tries: Welsh (34), Blair (47), Hallett (70), Sheriff (79);
Goals: Craig 1/4.
LIONS: 1 Ritchie Hawkyard; 2 Shaun Robinson; 3 Stuart Littler; 22 Chris Rothwell; 28 Ian Mort; 6 Ben White; 7 Chris Atkin; 8 Mike Morrison; 9 Andy Ackers; 24 Jordan James; 17 Andy Thornley; 29 Rhodri Lloyd; 31 Rob Lever. Subs (all used): 10 Ben Austin; 23 Connor Dwyer; 30 Josh Barlow; 11 Grant Beecham.
Tries: Robinson (5), Atkin (13, 64), Littler (29), Ackers (74); **Goals:** Mort 5/7.
Rugby Leaguer & League Express Men of the Match: *Thunder:* Benn Hardcastle; *Lions:* Chris Atkin.
Penalty count: 7-10; **Half-time:** 6-16;
Referee: Gareth Hewer; **Attendance:** 514.

OLDHAM 38 KEIGHLEY COUGARS 8

OLDHAM: 21 Richard Lepori; 2 Adam Clay; 17 George Tyson; 3 Jonathan Ford; 4 Jack Holmes; 6 Lewis Palfrey; 7 Steve Roper; 10 Adam Neal; 15 Gareth Owen; 8 Phil Joy; 11 Josh Crowley; 12 Danny Langtree; 9 Sam Gee. Subs (all used): 14 Adam Files; 13 Liam Thompson; 16 Kenny Hughes; 19 Michael Ward.
Tries: Gee (3), Lepori (10), Holmes (21), Palfrey (45), Langtree (55), Thompson (80); **Goals:** Palfrey 7/8.
COUGARS: 1 Jesse Sheriffe; 25 Andy Gabriel; 4 Danny Lawton; 30 Rikki Sheriffe; - Josh Guzdek; 33 Adam Brook; 24 Liam Darville; 8 Scott Law; 9 James Feather; - Tyler Dickinson; 28 Josh Lynam; 13 David March; 12 Brendan Rawlins. Subs (all used): 19 Matthew Bailey; 17 Oliver Pursglove; 34 Samir Tahraoui; 15 Neil Cherryholme.
Tries: Guzdek (18), Gabriel (65); **Goals:** Lawton 0/2.
Rugby Leaguer & League Express Men of the Match: *Oldham:* Steve Roper; *Cougars:* Josh Guzdek.
Penalty count: 7-5; **Half-time:** 18-4;
Referee: Matthew Thomason; **Attendance:** 888.

ROCHDALE HORNETS 74 SOUTH WALES SCORPIONS 4

HORNETS: 1 Wayne English; 5 Dale Bloomfield; 4 Lee Paterson; 22 Mike Ratu; 20 Bradley Hargreaves; 6 Paul Crook; 7 Danny Yates; 27 Matthew Haggarty; 29 Matty Fozard; 10 Warren Thompson; 23 James Dandy; 19 Danny Bridge; 14 James Tilley. Subs (all used): 21 Ryan Smith; 28 Matty Hadden; 12 Alex Trumper; 17 Danny Jones.
Tries: Bloomfield (3, 38, 46, 77), Yates (13, 23), Ratu (19, 64), Hadden (28), Crook (30), Smith (48), Paterson (50), Bridge (70); **Goals:** Crook 11/13.
SCORPIONS: 10 Jonny Leather; 17 Zak Williams; 3 Paul Edwards; 6 Curtis Davies; 2 Ian Newbury; 21 Ryan Millington; 7 Paul Emanuelli; 12 Barrie Phillips; 9 Connor Farrer; 8 Osian Phillips; 4 Kyle Scrivens; 18 Bradley Hill; 19 Connor Davies. Subs (all used): 14 Dafydd Hellard; 11 Mike Connor; 23 Anthony Symons; 30 Gethin King.
Try: Farrer (67); **Goals:** Emanuelli 0/1.
Dismissal: Emanuelli (73) - high tackle.
Sin bin: Leather (76) - dissent.
Rugby Leaguer & League Express Men of the Match: *Hornets:* Danny Bridge; *Scorpions:* Connor Farrer.
Penalty count: 9-8; **Half-time:** 40-0;
Referee: Tom Grant; **Attendance:** 300.

ROUND 18

Saturday 8th August 2015

GLOUCESTERSHIRE ALL GOLDS 26 NEWCASTLE THUNDER 10

ALL GOLDS: 33 Jamie Murphy; 31 Lee Mapals; 4 Callum Mulkeen; 12 Yann Bertrand; 28 Ryan Pywell; 20 Courtney Davies; 15 Yvan Leroyer; 8 Oliver Purslow; 9 Steve Parry; 35 Graham O'Keeffe; 3 Lewis Reece; 30 Emmerson Whittel; 14 Joe McClean. Subs (all used): 1 Phil Cowburn; 32 Kevin Aparicio; 34 Alex Davidson; 17 James Walter.
Tries: Pywell (9), Mapals (15), Parry (25, 44), Mulkeen (70); **Goals:** Davies 1/4, Leroyer 2/3.
THUNDER: 1 Louis Sheriff; 38 Macauley Hallett; 31 Ali Blair; 3 Jason Tali; 2 Jacob Blades; 14 Paul Stamp; 23 Benn Hardcastle; 8 Matt Barron; 25 Evan Simons; 10 Mark Mexico; 16 Francis Welsh; 32 Dan Turland; 18 Josh Stoker. Subs (all used): 6 Matty Beharrell; 39 Sebastien Martins; 15 Lee Fewlass; 26 Ricky Hough.
Tries: Tali (4), Hallett (52); **Goals:** Hardcastle 1/2.
Rugby Leaguer & League Express Men of the Match: *All Golds:* Lee Mapals; *Thunder:* Benn Hardcastle.
Penalty count: 7-8; **Half-time:** 14-4;
Referee: Chris Campbell; **Attendance:** 265.

BARROW RAIDERS 44 COVENTRY BEARS 22

RAIDERS: 5 Kyle Dolan; 20 Shane Toal; 3 Chris Hankinson; 24 Andy Litherland; 31 Cameron Pitman; 29 Peter Lupton; 14 Josh Ward; 8 Joe Bullock; 6 Brad Marwood; 16 Adam Nicholson; 11 Liam Harrison; 12 Craig Briscoe; 13 Dan Toal. Subs (all used): 9 Nathan Mossop; 28 James Duerden; 30 Bradd Crellin; 27 Jamie Tracey.
Tries: S Toal (8), Ward (18), Pitman (27), Nicholson (34), Lupton (42), Hankinson (58, 70), Briscoe (73);
Goals: Ward 6/8.
BEARS: 45 Jason Bass; 20 Jamahl Hunte; 30 Dan Parker; 13 Simon Phillips; 49 Elliot Holton; 40 Dan Price; 42 Joel James; 35 Jack Morrison; 24 Richard Hughes; 34 Andy Unsworth; 29 Liam Thompson; 12 Chris Barratt; 26 Matt Cooper. Subs (all used): 38 Tom Hall; 3 Nick Taylor; 16 Alex Beddows; 46 Jack Francis.
Tries: Hughes (14), Thompson (20), Hunte (25), Francis (38); **Goals:** Parker 3/4.
Rugby Leaguer & League Express Men of the Match: *Raiders:* Peter Lupton; *Bears:* Joel James.
Penalty count: 12-10; **Half-time:** 20-22;
Referee: Tom Grant; **Attendance:** 848.

Sunday 9th August 2015

HEMEL STAGS 6 OLDHAM 70

STAGS: 1 Derrell Olpherts; 5 Alex Anthony; 4 Michael Brown; 25 Jesse Richardson; 18 Chris McNamara; 6 Jy-mel Coleman; 24 James Woodburn-Hall; 31 Matt Ross; 9 James Helliwell; 13 Eddie Mbaraga; 30 Jamie Crowther; 17 Dan Ljazouli; 16 Mike Stewart. Subs (all used): 33 Thibault Cousine; 21 Malikhi Lloyd-Jones; 14 Ryan Chester; 15 Liam O'Callaghan.
Try: Lloyd-Jones (4); **Goals:** Woodburn-Hall 1/1.
Sin bin: Olpherts (38) - high tackle on Gee.
OLDHAM: 9 Sam Gee; 21 Richard Lepori; 17 George Tyson; 24 Tom Ashton; 3 Jonathan Ford; 6 Lewis Palfrey; 27 Dave Hewitt; 10 Adam Neal; 15 Gareth Owen; 8 Phil Joy; 11 Josh Crowley; 12 Danny Langtree; 13 Liam Thompson. Subs (all used): 19 Michael Ward; 25 Elliot Liku; 16 Kenny Hughes; 14 Adam Files.
Tries: Owen (10), Langtree (28, 80), M Ward (36, 63), Hewitt (38), Tyson (42), Thompson (54), Palfrey (58, 66, 77), Gee (69); **Goals:** Palfrey 11/12.
Rugby Leaguer & League Express Men of the Match: *Stags:* Jesse Richardson; *Oldham:* Lewis Palfrey.
Penalty count: 3-8; **Half-time:** 6-22;
Referee: Sam Ansell; **Attendance:** 145.

ROCHDALE HORNETS 19 NORTH WALES CRUSADERS 18

HORNETS: 1 Wayne English; 20 Bradley Hargreaves; 24 Dave Hull; 4 Lee Paterson; 5 Dale Bloomfield; 6 Paul Crook; 7 Danny Yates; 27 Matthew Haggarty; 29 Matty Fozard; 10 Warren Thompson; 19 Danny Bridge; 11 Jordan Case; 14 James Tilley. Subs (all used): 28 Matty Hadden; 23 James Dandy; 17 Danny Jones; 9 Alex McClurg.
Tries: Hargreaves (34), Case (43, 63); **Goals:** Crook 3/4;
Field goal: Yates (75).
Dismissal: Bloomfield (30) - fighting.
CRUSADERS: 1 Tommy Johnson; 2 Scott Turner; 17 Stuart Reardon; 31 Benjamin Jullien; 5 Rob Massam; 6 Andy Moulsdale; 7 Jamie Dallimore; 16 Joe Burke; 15 Lee Hudson; 8 Jonny Walker; 32 Sam Peet; 4 Matt Reid; 10 Ryan Duffy. Subs (all used): 9 Callum Wright; 34 Andrew Joy; 20 Elliott Davies; 29 Andrew Oakden.
Tries: Jullien (7, 51), Oakden (68), Massam (78);
Goals: Johnson 1/4.
Dismissal: Turner (30) - fighting.
Rugby Leaguer & League Express Men of the Match: *Hornets:* Jordan Case; *Crusaders:* Benjamin Jullien.
Penalty count: 7-9; **Half-time:** 4-4;
Referee: Dave Merrick; **Attendance:** 530.

SOUTH WALES SCORPIONS 10 KEIGHLEY COUGARS 48

SCORPIONS: 10 Jonny Leather; 17 Zak Williams; 2 Ian Newbury; 1 Jordan Sheridan; 28 Yannic Parker; 21 Ryan Millington; 7 Paul Emanuelli; 12 Barrie Phillips; 9 Connor Farrer; 11 Mike Connor; 4 Kyle Scrivens; 18 Bradley Hill; 19 Connor Davies. Subs (all used): 14 Dafydd Hellard; 6 Curtis Davies; 34 Christopher Speck; 20 Tala Petelo.
Tries: Newbury (29), Farrer (48); **Goals:** Emanuelli 1/2.
COUGARS: 36 Josh Guzdek; 25 Andy Gabriel; 32 Hamish Barnes; 4 Danny Lawton; 5 Paul White; 24 Liam Darville; 26 Paul March; 8 Scott Law; 9 James Feather; 15 Neil Cherryholme; 17 Oliver Pursglove; 28 Josh Lynam; 35 Tyler Dickinson. Subs (all used): 1 Jesse Sheriffe; 34 Samir Tahraoui; 19 Matthew Bailey; 20 Ryan Patchett.
Tries: Guzdek (3, 13, 44), White (16, 64, 74), Gabriel (56, 59, 78), Pursglove (71); **Goals:** Lawton 4/10.
Dismissal: Tahraoui (36) - punching.

Rugby Leaguer & League Express Men of the Match: *Scorpions:* Kyle Scrivens; *Cougars:* Josh Guzdek.
Penalty count: 5-5; **Half-time:** 6-16;
Referee: Adam Gill; **Attendance:** 224.

SWINTON LIONS 74 LONDON SKOLARS 4

LIONS: 1 Ritchie Hawkyard; 25 Harry Aaronson; 3 Stuart Littler; 29 Rhodri Lloyd; 28 Mike Butt; 6 Ben White; 7 Chris Atkin; 8 Mike Morrison; 9 Andy Ackers; 24 Jordan James; 17 Andy Thornley; 23 Connor Dwyer; 31 Rob Lever. Subs (all used): 10 Ben Austin; 13 Tommy Gallagher; 30 Josh Barlow; 11 Grant Beecham.
Tries: R Hawkyard (3, 58, 69), Butt (6, 10, 18), R Lloyd (15), White (20, 46), Ackers (32), Littler (44), Barlow (50), Aaronson (57, 73); **Goals:** Atkin 9/14.
SKOLARS: 1 Chris Bishay; 2 Sam Nash; 3 Mathew Cook; 4 Joe Price; 5 John Paxton; 6 James Anthony; 7 Jermaine Coleman; 8 Michael Sykes; 9 Mike Bishay; 10 Dave Williams; 11 Kazeem Fatouri; 12 Will Lovell; 13 Lamont Bryan. Subs (all used): 17 Anthony Cox; 16 Louis Robinson; 14 Aaron Small; 15 Billy Driver.
Try: Nash (32); **Goals:** M Bishay 0/1.
Rugby Leaguer & League Express Men of the Match: *Lions:* Stuart Littler; *Skolars:* Lamont Bryan.
Penalty count: 6-4; **Half-time:** 38-4;
Referee: Jon Roberts; **Attendance:** 401.

YORK CITY KNIGHTS 36 OXFORD 26

CITY KNIGHTS: 1 James Haynes; 5 Nev Morrison; 26 James Morland; 3 Greg Minikin; 2 Ben Dent; 6 Jon Presley; 32 Jordan Howden; 8 Mark Applegarth; 7 Pat Smith; 10 Jack Aldous; 4 Liam Cunningham; 15 Josh Tonks; 34 Jack Blagbrough. Subs (all used): 14 Kris Brining; 29 Brad Nicholson; 13 Colton Roche; 24 Tyler Craig.
Tries: B Dent (13), Blagbrough (20, 76), Haynes (31), Minikin (40, 52), Tonks (49);
Goals: Haynes 3/6, B Dent 1/1.
Dismissal: Aldous (6) - punching Land.
OXFORD: 36 Danny Thomas; 32 Andy Matthews; 28 Josh Nathaniel; 14 Marcus Brooker; 21 Luke Gardiner; 9 Nathan Kitson; 7 Andy Speake; 27 Bobby Tyson-Wilson; 31 Craig Cook; 25 Luke Evans; 37 Adam Withington; 3 Andrew Hoggins; 33 Lee Land. Subs (all used): 20 Dean Mignacca; 19 Kyle Danns; 8 Jordan Andrade; 18 Stuart Biscomb.
Tries: Nathaniel (25, 43), Cook (35), Danns (62), Hoggins (70); **Goals:** Kitson 3/5.
Rugby Leaguer & League Express Men of the Match: *City Knights:* Greg Minikin; *Oxford:* Josh Nathaniel.
Penalty count: 11-4; **Half-time:** 22-12;
Referee: Scott Mikalauskas; **Attendance:** 519
(at Elmpark Way, Heworth).

ROUND 19

Saturday 15th August 2015

OXFORD 16 ROCHDALE HORNETS 54

OXFORD: 36 Danny Thomas; 32 Andy Matthews; 14 Marcus Brooker; 28 Josh Nathaniel; 21 Luke Gardiner; 9 Nathan Kitson; 7 Andy Speake; 34 Steve Scott; 27 Mark Barlow; 18 Stuart Biscomb; 3 Andrew Hoggins; 5 Aaron Jones-Bishop; 33 Lee Land. Subs (all used): 37 Adam Withington; 19 Kyle Danns; 8 Jordan Andrade; 1 Louis Richards.
Tries: Land (15), Thomas (54), Gardiner (76);
Goals: Kitson 2/3.
Sin bin: Land (58) - high tackle.
HORNETS: 1 Wayne English; 20 Bradley Hargreaves; 24 Dave Hull; 22 Mike Ratu; 5 Dale Bloomfield; 6 Paul Crook; 7 Danny Yates; 29 Matthew Haggarty; 25 Matty Fozard; 28 Matty Hadden; 17 Jordan Case; 23 James Dandy; 14 James Tilley. Subs (all used): 9 Alex McClurg; 12 Alex Trumper; 10 Warren Thompson; 27 Danny Jones.
Tries: Hargreaves (12), Case (22), Ratu (26), Hull (33), Yates (35), Bloomfield (42, 73), McClurg (51), Dandy (64), Fozard (70); **Goals:** Crook 7/10.
Rugby Leaguer & League Express Men of the Match: *Oxford:* Stuart Biscomb; *Hornets:* Danny Yates.
Penalty count: 8-14; **Half-time:** 6-26;
Referee: Andrew Bentham; **Attendance:** 51
(at Pennine Way, Hemel).

Sunday 16th August 2015

HEMEL STAGS 34 GLOUCESTERSHIRE ALL GOLDS 38

STAGS: 1 Derrell Olpherts; 2 Simon Hrbek; 4 Michael Brown; 18 Chris McNamara; 5 Alex Anthony; 6 Jy-mel Coleman; 24 James Woodburn-Hall; 21 Malikhi Lloyd-Jones; 9 James Helliwell; 31 Matt Ross; 11 Barry-John Swindells; 13 Eddie Mbaraga; 17 Dan Ljazouli. Subs (all used): 30 Jamie Crowther; 33 Thibault Cousine; 14 Ryan Chester; 16 Mike Stewart.
Tries: Ross (22), Anthony (24, 30), Olpherts (27), Woodburn-Hall (55), Brown (65);
Goals: Swindells 4/6, Woodburn-Hall 1/1.
ALL GOLDS: 33 Jamie Murphy; 1 Phil Cowburn; 4 Callum Mulkeen; 12 Yann Bertrand; 28 Ryan Pywell; 20 Courtney Davies; 15 Yvan Leroyer; 8 Oliver Purslow; 9 Steve Parry; 35 Graham O'Keeffe; 3 Lewis Reece; 30 Emmerson Whittel; 13 Chris Vitalini. Subs (all used): 32 Kevin Aparicio; 34 Alex Davidson; 7 Matt Bradley; 17 James Walter.
Tries: Davidson (19, 78), Parry (33, 50), O'Keeffe (59), Whittel (67), Murphy (73); **Goals:** Davies 2/2, Bradley 3/5.
Rugby Leaguer & League Express Men of the Match: *Stags:* Alex Anthony; *All Golds:* Steve Parry.
Penalty count: 7-12; **Half-time:** 22-12;
Referee: Scott Mikalauskas; **Attendance:** 277.

NORTH WALES CRUSADERS 14 SWINTON LIONS 30

CRUSADERS: 1 Tommy Johnson; 29 Andrew Oakden; 31 Benjamin Jullien; 3 Christiaan Roets; 5 Rob Massam; 6 Andy Moulsdale; 14 Karl Ashall; 8 Jonny Walker; 9 Callum Wright; 16 Joe Burke; 22 Alex Thompson; 12 Stephen Wild; 10 Ryan Duffy. Subs (all used): 15 Lee Hudson; 20 Elliott Davies; 4 Matt Reid; 32 Sam Peet.
Tries: Massam (39, 80), Roets (60); **Goals:** Johnson 1/3.
LIONS: 1 Ritchie Hawkyard; 2 Shaun Robinson; 3 Stuart Littler; 22 Chris Rothwell; 28 Mike Butt; 6 Ben White; 7 Chris Atkin; 8 Mike Morrison; 9 Andy Ackers; 24 Jordan James; 17 Andy Thornley; 29 Rhodri Lloyd; 31 Rob Lever. Subs (all used): 13 Tommy Gallagher; 30 Josh Barlow; 10 Ben Austin; 11 Grant Beecham.
Tries: White (2), Atkin (6), R Lloyd (20, 53), Thornley (27); **Goals:** Atkin 5/5.
Rugby Leaguer & League Express Men of the Match: *Crusaders:* Stephen Wild; *Lions:* Andy Ackers.
Penalty count: 12-4; **Half-time:** 4-24;
Referee: Sam Ansell; **Attendance:** 737.

COVENTRY BEARS 44 SOUTH WALES SCORPIONS 18

BEARS: 28 Andy Winfield; 45 Jason Bass; 40 Jordan Harper; 30 Dan Parker; 20 Jamahl Hunte; 39 Dan Price; 7 Cameron Boulter; 17 Jack Morrison; 24 Richard Hughes; 16 Alex Beddows; 29 Liam Thompson; 12 Chris Barratt; 26 Matt Cooper. Subs (all used): 3 Nick Taylor; 38 Tom Hall; 34 Andy McGrory; 46 Jack Francis.
Tries: Parker (9), Harper (13), Price (19), Hunte (22, 29), Taylor (54), Hughes (57), Thompson (80);
Goals: Parker 6/8.
SCORPIONS: 10 Jonny Leather; 17 Zak Williams; 2 Ian Newbury; 1 Jordan Sheridan; 28 Yannic Parker; 6 Curtis Davies; 7 Paul Emanuelli; 12 Barrie Phillips; 9 Connor Farrer; 15 Rhys Davies; 4 Kyle Scrivens; 19 Connor Davies; 21 Ryan Millington. Subs (all used): 14 Dafydd Hellard; 3 Paul Edwards; 20 Tala Petelo; 34 Christopher Speck.
Tries: Farrer (38), Parker (40), Newbury (68);
Goals: Emanuelli 3/3.
Rugby Leaguer & League Express Men of the Match: *Bears:* Jamahl Hunte; *Scorpions:* Ian Newbury.
Penalty count: 9-6; **Half-time:** 28-12;
Referee: Jon Roberts; **Attendance:** 200.

KEIGHLEY COUGARS 18 BARROW RAIDERS 17

COUGARS: 36 Josh Guzdek; 25 Andy Gabriel; 4 Danny Lawton; 30 Rikki Sheriffe; 5 Paul White; 26 Paul March; 24 Liam Darville; 8 Scott Law; 9 James Feather; 34 Samir Tahraoui; 28 Josh Lynam; 17 Oliver Pursglove; 35 Tyler Dickinson. Subs (all used): 1 Jesse Sheriffe; 10 Ross Peltier; 15 Neil Cherryholme; 19 Matthew Bailey.
Tries: White (22), P March (59), R Sheriffe (76), Gabriel (80); **Goals:** Lawton 1/4.
RAIDERS: 7 Liam Campbell; 31 Cameron Pitman; 3 Chris Hankinson; 24 Andy Litherland; 20 Shane Toal; 29 Peter Lupton; 14 Josh Ward; 8 Joe Bullock; 9 Nathan Mossop; 11 Liam Harrison; 16 Adam Nicholson; 12 Craig Briscoe; 13 Dan Toal. Subs (all used): 6 Brad Marwood; 10 Andrew Dawson; 28 James Duerden; 30 Bradd Crellin.
Tries: Crellin (39), Lupton (46), Duerden (65);
Goals: Marwood 2/3; **Field goal:** Marwood (63).
Rugby Leaguer & League Express Men of the Match: *Cougars:* Rikki Sheriffe; *Raiders:* Peter Lupton.
Penalty count: 7-5; **Half-time:** 4-6;
Referee: Andrew Sweet; **Attendance:** 903.

LONDON SKOLARS 22 YORK CITY KNIGHTS 30

SKOLARS: 1 James Anthony; 2 Sam Nash; 3 Mathew Cook; 4 Joe Price; 5 John Paxton; 6 Tommy Connick; 7 Jermaine Coleman; 21 Will Martin; 9 Mike Bishay; 10 Dave Williams; 11 Will Lovell; 12 Kazeem Fatouri; 13 Aaron Small. Subs (all used): 14 Louis Robinson; 15 Billy Driver; 18 Anthony Cox; 17 Lamont Bryan.
Tries: Nash (4), Bryan (48), Williams (61), Martin (75);
Goals: M Bishay 0/1, Connick 3/3.
CITY KNIGHTS: 2 Ben Dent; 5 Nev Morrison; 3 Greg Minikin; 24 Tyler Craig; 19 Jamel Chisholm; 32 Jordan Howden; 6 Jon Presley; 8 Mark Applegarth; 7 Pat Smith; 10 Jack Aldous; 12 Ed Smith; 15 Josh Tonks; 11 Ryan Mallinder. Subs (all used): 14 Kris Brining; 27 Brad Hey; 34 Jack Blagbrough; 17 Brad Nicholson.
Tries: Minikin (6, 80), Mallinder (13), Chisholm (17), Hey (71); **Goals:** Howden 0/1, B Dent 5/5.
Rugby Leaguer & League Express Men of the Match: *Skolars:* Lamont Bryan; *City Knights:* Greg Minikin.
Penalty count: 3-8; **Half-time:** 4-16;
Referee: Tom Crashley; **Attendance:** 323.

NEWCASTLE THUNDER 16 OLDHAM 28

THUNDER: 37 Stewart Sanderson; 38 Macauley Hallett; 31 Ali Blair; 4 Joe Brown; 1 Louis Sheriff; 6 Matty Beharrell; 23 Benn Hardcastle; 8 Matt Barron; 25 Evan Simons; 10 Mark Mexico; 9 Dayne Craig; 3 Jason Tali; 36 Sonny Esslemont. Subs (all used): 13 Charlie Wabo; 14 Paul Stamp; 18 Josh Stoker; 15 Lee Fewlass.
Tries: Hardcastle (23), Hallett (33), Tali (69);
Goals: Hardcastle 2/3.
Dismissal: Hallett (62) - fighting.
OLDHAM: 9 Sam Gee; 21 Richard Lepori; 17 George Tyson; 24 Tom Ashton; 3 Jonathan Ford; 6 Lewis Palfrey; 27 Dave Hewitt; 10 Adam Neal; 15 Gareth Owen; 8 Phil Joy; 11 Josh Crowley; 12 Danny Langtree; 13 Liam Thompson. Subs (all used): 19 Michael Ward; 25 Elliot Liku; 16 Kenny Hughes; 14 Adam Files.
Tries: Ford (25, 78), Hewitt (46), Liku (57), Ashton (80);
Goals: Palfrey 4/6.
Dismissal: Gee (62) - fighting.
Rugby Leaguer & League Express Men of the Match: *Thunder:* Jason Tali; *Oldham:* Lewis Palfrey.
Penalty count: 7-7; **Half-time:** 10-4;
Referee: Jamie Bloem; **Attendance:** 1,003.

ROUND 3

Thursday 20th August 2015

YORK CITY KNIGHTS 28 NORTH WALES CRUSADERS 30

CITY KNIGHTS: 2 Ben Dent; 25 Adam Dent; 4 Liam Cunningham; 3 Greg Minikin; 5 Nev Morrison; 6 Jon Presley; 18 Jordan Howden; 8 Mark Applegarth; 7 Pat Smith; 10 Jack Aldous; 12 Ed Smith; 15 Josh Tonks; 11 Ryan Mallinder. Subs (all used): 14 Kris Brining; 29 Brad Nicholson; 13 Colton Roche; 28 Mick Learmonth.
Tries: Tonks (50), Mallinder (55), A Dent (59), E Smith (67), Brining (72); **Goals:** B Dent 4/5.
CRUSADERS: 1 Tommy Johnson; 5 Rob Massam; 31 Benjamin Jullien; 3 Christiaan Roets; 29 Andrew Oakden; 7 Jamie Dallimore; 6 Andy Moulsdale; 10 Ryan Duffy; 15 Lee Hudson; 20 Elliott Davies; 12 Stephen Wild; 4 Matt Reid; 22 Alex Thompson. Subs (all used, only three named): 16 Joe Burke; 34 Andrew Joy; 8 Jonny Walker.
Tries: Oakden (5, 9), Massam (26), Jullien (29, 38);
Goals: Johnson 5/6.
Rugby Leaguer & League Express Men of the Match: *City Knights:* Josh Tonks; *Crusaders:* Stephen Wild.
Penalty count: 1-2; **Half-time:** 0-28;
Referee: Chris Leatherbarrow; **Attendance:** 607
(at Elmpark Way, Heworth).

ROUND 20

Sunday 23rd August 2015

NEWCASTLE THUNDER 24 COVENTRY BEARS 16

THUNDER: 1 Louis Sheriff; 38 Macauley Hallett; 2 Jacob Blades; 4 Joe Brown; 31 Ali Blair; 6 Matty Beharrell; 23 Benn Hardcastle; 8 Matt Barron; 25 Evan Simons; 10 Mark Mexico; 9 Dayne Craig; 3 Jason Tali; 36 Sonny Esslemont. Subs (all used): 13 Charlie Wabo; 14 Paul Stamp; 18 Josh Stoker; 15 Lee Fewlass.
Tries: Tali (8), Wabo (55), Simons (73), Sheriff (75);
Goals: Hardcastle 4/4.
BEARS: 28 Andy Winfield; 45 Jason Bass; 13 Simon Phillips; 40 Jordan Harper; 20 Jamahl Hunte; 39 Dan Price; 7 Cameron Boulter; 35 Jack Morrison; 24 Richard Hughes; 26 Matt Cooper; 29 Liam Thompson; 12 Chris Barratt; 30 Dan Parker. Subs (all used): 38 Tom Hall; 34 Andy Unsworth; 3 Nick Taylor; 46 Jack Francis.
Tries: Hughes (28), Unsworth (33), Boulter (49);
Goals: Price 1/1, Parker 1/2.
Rugby Leaguer & League Express Men of the Match: *Thunder:* Benn Hardcastle; *Bears:* Dan Parker.
Penalty count: 1-5; **Half-time:** 6-10;
Referee: Jack Smith; **Attendance:** 503.

OLDHAM 28 BARROW RAIDERS 12

OLDHAM: 21 Richard Lepori; 2 Adam Clay; 17 George Tyson; 24 Tom Ashton; 3 Jonathan Ford; 6 Lewis Palfrey; 27 Dave Hewitt; 10 Adam Neal; 15 Gareth Owen; 8 Phil Joy; 11 Josh Crowley; 12 Danny Langtree; 9 Sam Gee. Subs (all used): 14 Adam Files; 16 Kenny Hughes; 19 Michael Ward; 13 Liam Thompson.
Tries: Ashton (39), M Ward (48, 77), Hewitt (69), Thompson (72); **Goals:** Palfrey 4/5.
Sin bin: Neal (35) - high tackle.
RAIDERS: 23 Chris Fleming; 5 Kyle Dolan; 31 Cameron Pitman; 3 Chris Hankinson; 4 Max Wiper; 29 Peter Lupton; 7 Liam Campbell; 8 Joe Bullock; 9 Nathan Mossop; 21 Anthony Bate; 11 Liam Harrison; 12 Craig Briscoe; 28 James Duerden. Subs (all used): 6 Brad Marwood; 10 Andrew Dawson; 22 Joe Hambley; 30 Bradd Crellin.
Tries: Wiper (12), Dolan (16); **Goals:** Hankinson 2/4.
Rugby Leaguer & League Express Men of the Match: *Oldham:* Dave Hewitt; *Raiders:* Joe Bullock.
Penalty count: 11-5; **Half-time:** 4-12;
Referee: Jon Roberts; **Attendance:** 740.

ROCHDALE HORNETS 8 KEIGHLEY COUGARS 10

HORNETS: 1 Wayne English; 20 Bradley Hargreaves; 22 Mike Ratu; 4 Lee Paterson; 5 Dale Bloomfield; 6 Paul Crook; 7 Danny Yates; 14 James Tilley; 29 Matty Fozard; 10 Warren Thompson; 19 Danny Bridge; 23 James Dandy; 11 Jordan Case. Subs (all used): 28 Matty Hadden; 24 Dave Hull; 17 Danny Jones; 9 Alex McClurg.
Try: Ratu (19); **Goals:** Crook 2/5.
COUGARS: 36 Josh Guzdek; 25 Andy Gabriel; 4 Danny Lawton; 32 Hamish Barnes; 5 Paul White; 24 Liam Darville; 7 Paul Handforth; 8 Scott Law; 9 James Feather; 34 Samir Tahraoui; 17 Oliver Pursglove; 28 Josh Lynam; 35 Tyler Dickinson. Subs (all used): 13 David March; 12 Brendan Rawlins; 19 Matthew Bailey; 15 Neil Cherryholme.
Tries: Tahraoui (4), Gabriel (56);
Goals: Lawton 0/1, Handforth 1/2.
Rugby Leaguer & League Express Men of the Match: *Hornets:* Jordan Case; *Cougars:* Paul Handforth.
Penalty count: 11-6; **Half-time:** 4-4;
Referee: Tom Grant; **Attendance:** 671.

SOUTH WALES SCORPIONS 26 OXFORD 40

SCORPIONS: 10 Jonny Leather; 17 Zak Williams; 2 Ian

Newbury; 1 Jordan Sheridan; 3 Paul Edwards; 6 Curtis Davies; 7 Paul Emanuelli; 15 Rhys Davies; 9 Connor Farrer; 12 Barrie Phillips; 4 Kyle Scrivens; 18 Bradley Hill; 21 Ryan Millington. Subs (all used): 14 Dafydd Hellard; 34 Christopher Speck; 19 Connor Davies; 20 Tala Petelo.
Tries: Edwards (20), Farrer (23), Newbury (45), Petelo (62), Williams (76); **Goals:** Emanuelli 3/5.
OXFORD: 36 Danny Thomas; 32 Andy Matthews; 3 Andrew Hoggins; 21 Luke Gardiner; 5 Aaron Jones-Bishop; 14 Marcus Brooker; 9 Nathan Kitson; 34 Steve Scott; 31 Craig Cook; 18 Stuart Biscomb; 11 Josh Scott; 37 Adam Withington; 33 Lee Land. Subs (all used): 13 James Milburn; 8 Jordan Andrade; 20 Dean Mignacca; 25 Luke Evans.
Tries: Matthews (6), S Scott (9), Kitson (17), J Scott (52), Cook (67, 79), Jones-Bishop (80); **Goals:** Kitson 6/7.
Rugby Leaguer & League Express Men of the Match: *Scorpions:* Dafydd Hellard; *Oxford:* Craig Cook.
Penalty count: 8-9; **Half-time:** 10-16;
Referee: Callum Straw; **Attendance:** 148.

SWINTON LIONS 42 GLOUCESTERSHIRE ALL GOLDS 6

LIONS: 28 Mike Butt; 2 Shaun Robinson; 3 Stuart Littler; 29 Rhodri Lloyd; 25 Harry Aaronson; 6 Ben White; 7 Chris Atkin; 8 Mike Morrison; 9 Andy Ackers; 24 Jordan James; 17 Andy Thornley; 11 Grant Beecham; 23 Connor Dwyer. Subs (all used): 18 Aaron Lloyd; 13 Tommy Gallagher; 30 Josh Barlow; 27 Tom Thackray.
Tries: Littler (3), James (8), White (18), R Lloyd (31), Beecham (38), Butt (46), Aaronson (57), Ackers (68);
Goals: Atkin 5/8.
ALL GOLDS: 1 Phil Cowburn; 31 Lee Mapals; 4 Callum Mulkeen; 12 Yann Bertrand; 28 Ryan Pywell; 20 Courtney Davies; 15 Yvan Leroyer; 8 Oliver Purslow; 9 Steve Parry; 34 Alex Davidson; 3 Lewis Reece; 30 Emmerson Whittel; 35 Graham O'Keeffe. Subs (all used): 7 Matt Bradley; 33 Jamie Murphy; 13 Chris Vitalini; 17 James Walter.
Try: Leroyer (66); **Goals:** Bradley 1/1.
Sin bin: Reece (30) - high tackle on R Lloyd.
Rugby Leaguer & League Express Men of the Match: *Lions:* Grant Beecham; *All Golds:* Ryan Pywell.
Penalty count: 10-7; **Half-time:** 26-0;
Referee: Andrew Bentham; **Attendance:** 368.

YORK CITY KNIGHTS 50 HEMEL STAGS 10

CITY KNIGHTS: 32 Jordan Howden; 2 Ben Dent; 3 Greg Minikin; 12 Ed Smith; 5 Nev Morrison; 6 Jon Presley; 7 Pat Smith; 8 Mark Applegarth; 14 Kris Brining; 10 Jack Aldous; 11 Ryan Mallinder; 15 Josh Tonks; 29 Brad Nicholson. Subs (all used): 34 Jack Blagbrough; 9 Harry Carter; 28 Liam Richmond; 19 Brad Hey.
Tries: P Smith (2), Howden (7), B Dent (15, 40), Brining (27, 66), Morrison (54), Nicholson (59, 80);
Goals: B Dent 7/9.
STAGS: 1 Derrell Olpherts; 18 Chris McNamara; 4 Michael Brown; 16 Jamie Crowther; 5 Alex Anthony; 7 Charlie Lawrence; 6 Jy-mel Coleman; 21 Malikhi Lloyd-Jones; 9 James Helliwell; 31 Matt Ross; 13 Eddie Mbaraga; 14 Ryan Chester; 17 Dan Ljazouli. Subs (all used): 2 Thibault Cousine; 23 Tom Sadler; 15 Liam O'Callaghan; 33 Kaizer Muroi.
Tries: Anthony (21), Lawrence (44); **Goals:** Lawrence 1/2.
Rugby Leaguer & League Express Men of the Match: *City Knights:* Kris Brining; *Stags:* Jy-mel Coleman.
Penalty count: 9-4; **Half-time:** 28-6;
Referee: Tom Hudson; **Attendance:** 384
(at Elmpark Way, Heworth).

Friday 28th August 2015

LONDON SKOLARS 16 NORTH WALES CRUSADERS 24

SKOLARS: 1 James Anthony; 2 Sam Nash; 3 Aaron Small; 4 Joe Price; 5 John Paxton; 6 Tommy Connick; 7 Jermaine Coleman; 21 Will Martin; 9 Mike Bishay; 10 Dave Williams; 11 Kazeem Fatouri; 12 Will Lovell; 19 Will Fairhurst. Subs (all used): 14 Louis Robinson; 15 Billy Driver; 16 Anthony Cox; 8 Michael Sykes.
Tries: Small (2, 69), Martin (75); **Goals:** Connick 2/5.
CRUSADERS: 1 Tommy Johnson; 5 Rob Massam; 31 Benjamin Jullien; 3 Christiaan Roets; 29 Andrew Oakden; 6 Andy Moulsdale; 7 Jamie Dallimore; 8 Jonny Walker; 15 Lee Hudson; 16 Joe Burke; 22 Alex Thompson; 12 Stephen Wild; 10 Ryan Duffy. Subs (all used, only three named): 14 Karl Ashall; 20 Elliott Davies; 34 Andrew Joy.
Tries: Jullien (10, 48), Joy (40), Duffy (57), Dallimore (70); **Goals:** Johnson 2/5.
Rugby Leaguer & League Express Men of the Match: *Skolars:* Aaron Small; *Crusaders:* Jamie Dallimore.
Penalty count: 8-6; **Half-time:** 6-8;
Referee: Chris Kendall; **Attendance:** 1,018.

ROUND 3

Monday 31st August 2015

SWINTON LIONS 84 OXFORD 16

LIONS: 14 Mike Butt; 2 Shaun Robinson; 3 Stuart Littler; 22 Chris Rothwell; 28 Ian Mort; 6 Ben White; 7 Chris Atkin; 24 Jordan James; 9 Andy Ackers; 31 Rob Lever; 30 Josh Barlow; 11 Grant Beecham; 23 Connor Dwyer. Subs (all used): 17 Andy Thornley; 10 Ben Austin; 18 Aaron Lloyd; 29 Mick Govin.
Tries: Littler (3, 21, 25, 31, 53), Atkin (10, 28), White (13), Mort (35), Austin (45), Beecham (63, 77), Rothwell (65), Barlow (73), Robinson (75);
Goals: Atkin 12/15.
OXFORD: 36 Danny Thomas; 32 Andy Matthews; 14 Marcus Brooker; 3 Andrew Hoggins; 5 Aaron Jones-Bishop; 7 Andy Speake; 9 Nathan Kitson; 18 Stuart Biscomb; 31 Craig Cook; 25 Luke Evans; 13 James Milburn; 27 Josh Nathaniel; 33 Lee Land. Subs (all used): 20 Dean Mignacca; - James Mason; 23 Tom Davies; 34 Steve Scott.
Tries: S Scott (18), T Davies (60), Kitson (80);
Goals: Kitson 2/3.
Rugby Leaguer & League Express Men of the Match: *Lions:* Stuart Littler; *Oxford:* Nathan Kitson.
Penalty count: 8-4; **Half-time:** 42-4;
Referee: Tom Grant; **Attendance:** 487.

ROUND 5

Monday 31st August 2015

LONDON SKOLARS 16 KEIGHLEY COUGARS 36

SKOLARS: 1 James Anthony; 2 Jimmy Morgan; 3 Chris Bishay; 4 Joe Price; 5 John Paxton; 6 Mike Bishay; 7 Jermaine Coleman; 20 Michael Sykes; 9 Sam Druce; 10 Will Martin; 11 Dave Williams; 12 Will Lovell; 13 Louis Robinson. Subs (all used): 14 Anthony Cox; 15 Billy Driver; 16 Mike Benson; 17 Dion Chapman.
Tries: M Bishay (32), Williams (49), Paxton (67);
Goals: M Bishay 1/2, Druce 1/1.
COUGARS: 5 Paul White; 25 Andy Gabriel; 4 Danny Lawton; 30 Rikki Sheriffe; 32 Hamish Barnes; 24 Liam Darville; 26 Paul March; 8 Scott Law; 9 James Feather; 34 Samir Tahraoui; 17 Oliver Pursglove; 12 Brendan Rawlins; 35 Tyler Dickinson. Subs (all used): 13 David March; 15 Neil Cherryholme; 19 Matthew Bailey; 31 Scott Lee.
Tries: Gabriel (7, 78), Barnes (21), R Sheriffe (53), Darville (61), Rawlins (75), White (80);
Goals: Lawton 4/7.
Rugby Leaguer & League Express Men of the Match: *Skolars:* Dave Williams; *Cougars:* James Feather.
Penalty count: 5-8; **Half-time:** 4-10;
Referee: Chris Campbell; **Attendance:** 115
(at Pennine Way, Hemel).

ROUND 21

Saturday 5th September 2015

BARROW RAIDERS 46 ROCHDALE HORNETS 28

RAIDERS: 23 Chris Fleming; 31 Cameron Pitman; 3 Chris Hankinson; 24 Andy Litherland; 22 Joe Hambley; 7 Liam Campbell; 14 Josh Ward; 8 Joe Bullock; 9 Nathan Mossop; 11 Liam Harrison; 16 Adam Nicholson; 12 Craig Briscoe; 30 Bradd Crellin. Subs (all used): 13 Dan Toal; 10 Andrew Dawson; 6 Brad Marwood; 21 Anthony Bate.
Tries: Fleming (11, 46), Mossop (25), Campbell (37), Marwood (39), Ward (50, 60), Hankinson (70);
Goals: Ward 7/8.
HORNETS: 1 Wayne English; 20 Bradley Hargreaves; 22 Mike Ratu; 4 Lee Paterson; 5 Dale Bloomfield; 6 Paul Crook; 7 Danny Yates; 17 Danny Jones; 29 Matty Fozard; 10 Warren Thompson; 19 Danny Bridge; 23 James Dandy; 13 Jordan Case. Subs (all used): 21 Ryan Smith; 28 Matty Hadden; 9 Alex McClurg; 14 James Tilley.
Tries: Yates (3), Bloomfield (12), Ratu (23), Crook (73, 79); **Goals:** Crook 4/5.
Rugby Leaguer & League Express Men of the Match: *Raiders:* Joe Bullock; *Hornets:* Paul Crook.
Penalty count: 6-5; **Half-time:** 24-16;
Referee: Gareth Hewer; **Attendance:** 865.

Sunday 6th September 2015

SOUTH WALES SCORPIONS 16 NEWCASTLE THUNDER 50

SCORPIONS: 10 Jonny Leather; 17 Zak Williams; 2 Ian Newbury; 26 Marcus Webb; 5 Ben Jones; 6 Curtis Davies; 21 Ryan Millington; 8 Osian Phillips; 7 Paul Emanuelli; 15 Rhys Davies; 18 Bradley Hill; 12 Barrie Phillips; 19 Connor Davies. Subs (all used): 14 Dafydd Hellard; 20 Tala Petelo; 33 Nathan Rainer; 30 Gethin King.
Tries: B Phillips (30), Leather (34, 38);
Goals: Emanuelli 2/3.
THUNDER: 2 Jacob Blades; 31 Ali Blair; 3 Jason Tali; 4 Joe Brown; 5 Tom Capper; 6 Matty Beharrell; 23 Benn Hardcastle; 8 Matt Barron; 25 Evan Simons; 15 Lee Fewlass; 36 Sonny Esslemont; 9 Dayne Craig; 13 Charlie Wabo. Subs (all used): 11 Jason Payne; 12 Rhys Clarke; 32 Dan Turland; 18 Josh Stoker.
Tries: Tali (5, 75), Barron (9), Capper (12), Craig (16, 55, 78), Beharrell (22), Wabo (42);
Goals: Hardcastle 7/9.
Rugby Leaguer & League Express Men of the Match: *Scorpions:* Jonny Leather; *Thunder:* Dayne Craig.
Penalty count: 7-6; **Half-time:** 16-26;
Referee: Andrew Bentham; **Attendance:** 160.

HEMEL STAGS 16 OXFORD 38

STAGS: 1 Derrell Olpherts; 5 Ashley Fyson; 18 Chris McNamara; 4 Michael Brown; 2 Simon Hrbek; 24 James Woodburn-Hall; 6 Jy-mel Coleman; 21 Malikhi Lloyd-Jones; 7 Charlie Lawrence; 31 Matt Ross; 14 Ryan Chester; 12 Alex Ingarfield; 17 Dan Ljazouli. Subs (all used): 15 Liam O'Callaghan; 33 Thibault Cousine; 28 Connor Boyd-Barnes; 16 Mike Stewart.
Tries: L O'Callaghan (30), Fyson (41), Cousine (44);
Goals: Lawrence 1/1, Woodburn-Hall 0/1, Jy-mel Coleman 1/1.
OXFORD: 9 Nathan Kitson; 32 Andy Matthews; 14 Marcus Brooker; 3 Andrew Hoggins; 21 Luke Gardiner; 36 Danny Thomas; 7 Andy Speake; 19 Kyle Danns; 31 Craig Cook; 18 Stuart Biscomb; 27 Charlie Greene; 37 Adam Withington; 28 Josh Nathaniel. Subs (all used): 20 Dean Mignacca; 25 Luke Evans; 1 Louis Richards; 13 James Milburn.
Tries: Danns (10), Withington (14), Nathaniel (22), Evans (34), Speake (47), Richards (58), Cook (60);
Goals: Kitson 5/7.
Rugby Leaguer & League Express Men of the Match: *Stags:* James Woodburn-Hall; *Oxford:* Nathan Kitson.
Penalty count: 9-12; **Half-time:** 6-22;
Referee: Scott Mikalauskas; **Attendance:** 144.

NORTH WALES CRUSADERS 28
YORK CITY KNIGHTS 30

CRUSADERS: 1 Tommy Johnson; 29 Andrew Oakden; 31 Benjamin Jullien; 3 Christiaan Roets; 5 Rob Massam; 6 Andy Moulsdale; 7 Jamie Dallimore; 8 Jonny Walker; 15 Lee Hudson; 16 Joe Burke; 4 Matt Reid; 12 Stephen Wild; 10 Ryan Duffy. Subs (all used): 14 Karl Ashall; 20 Elliott Davies; 34 Andrew Joy; 32 Sam Peet.
Tries: Oakden (11), Burke (30), Roets (37), Johnson (60), Reid (73); **Goals:** Johnson 4/5.
CITY KNIGHTS: 32 Jordan Howden; 2 Ben Dent; 24 James Morland; 3 Greg Minikin; 5 Nev Morrison; 6 Jon Presley; 7 Pat Smith; 8 Mark Applegarth; 14 Kris Brining; 28 Mick Learmonth; 12 Ed Smith; 15 Josh Tonks; 10 Jack Aldous. Subs (all used): 9 Harry Carter; 11 Ryan Mallinder; 29 Brad Nicholson; 34 Jack Blagbrough.
Tries: Morland (20, 22), Aldous (34), P Smith (44), Brining (66); **Goals:** B Dent 4/6, Howden 1/1.
Rugby Leaguer & League Express Men of the Match: *Crusaders:* Karl Ashall; *City Knights:* Jack Aldous.
Penalty count: 8-9; **Half-time:** 16-16;
Referee: Tom Grant; **Attendance:** 720.

COVENTRY BEARS 18 LONDON SKOLARS 28

BEARS: 28 Andy Winfield; 45 Jason Bass; 5 Ben Parry; 13 Simon Phillips; 20 Jamahl Hunte; 40 Dan Price; 7 Cameron Boulter; 17 Jack Morrison; 24 Richard Hughes; 34 Andy Unsworth; 29 Liam Thompson; 12 Chris Barratt; 26 Matt Cooper. Subs (all used): 27 James Geurtjens; 50 Morgan Evans; 30 Dan Parker; 3 Nick Taylor.
Tries: Barratt (29), Morrison (37), Hunte (44), Phillips (50); **Goals:** Price 1/1, Parker 0/3.
Sin bin: Geurtjens (70) - late challenge.
SKOLARS: 1 James Anthony; 2 Jimmy Morgan; 3 Mathew Cook; 4 Chris Bishay; 5 John Paxton; 6 Tommy Connick; 7 Jermaine Coleman; 8 Michael Sykes; 9 Mike Bishay; 10 Will Martin; 11 Kazeem Fatouri; 12 Will Lovell; 13 Dave Williams. Subs (all used): 14 Louis Robinson; 15 Billy Driver; 16 Mike Benson; 17 Aaron Small.
Tries: Paxton (3), Williams (23), Driver (33, 54), Anthony (75); **Goals:** Connick 4/6.
Dismissal: Robinson (36) - headbutt on Hughes.
Sin bin: Small (29) - dissent.
Rugby Leaguer & League Express Men of the Match: *Bears:* Dan Price; *Skolars:* Billy Driver.
Penalty count: 5-5; **Half-time:** 10-14;
Referee: Dave Merrick; **Attendance:** 400.

GLOUCESTERSHIRE ALL GOLDS 24
KEIGHLEY COUGARS 48

ALL GOLDS: 33 Jamie Murphy; 31 Lee Mapals; 4 Callum Mulkeen; 1 Phil Cowburn; 28 Ryan Pywell; 35 Dan Poulton; 7 Matt Bradley; 8 Oliver Purslow; 9 Steve Parry; 34 Alex Davidson; 3 Lewis Reece; 30 Emmerson Whittel; 14 Joe McClean. Subs (all used): - Graham O'Keeffe; 17 James Walter; 20 Courtney Davies; 32 Edwin Okanga-Ajwang.
Tries: Pywell (14), Mapals (21), Davies (36), Whittel (39), Davidson (55); **Goals:** Bradley 2/5.
Sin bin: Mapals (60) - punching R Sheriffe.
COUGARS: 36 Josh Guzdek; 25 Andy Gabriel; 4 Danny Lawton; 30 Rikki Sheriffe; 5 Paul White; 24 Liam Darville; 7 Paul Handforth; 8 Scott Law; 9 James Feather; 34 Samir Tahraoui; 13 David March; 12 Brendan Rawlins; 35 Tyler Dickinson. Subs (all used): 15 Neil Cherryholme; 17 Oliver Pursglove; 19 Matthew Bailey; 31 Scott Lee.
Tries: White (12, 28), Rawlins (26), Darville (31), Gabriel (49), Handforth (58), Feather (62), Dickinson (77);
Goals: Lawton 8/8.
Sin bin: Handforth (36) - dissent.
Rugby Leaguer & League Express Men of the Match: *All Golds:* Lee Mapals; *Cougars:* Samir Tahraoui.
Penalty count: 7-8; **Half-time:** 18-24;
Referee: Andrew Sweet; **Attendance:** 170
(at Beavis Memorial Ground, Cinderford).

OLDHAM 28 SWINTON LIONS 16

OLDHAM: 21 Richard Lepori; 2 Adam Clay; 17 George Tyson; 3 Jonathan Ford; 4 Jack Holmes; 6 Lewis Palfrey; 7 Steve Roper; 13 Liam Thompson; 15 Gareth Owen; 8 Phil Joy; 11 Josh Crowley; 12 Danny Langtree; 26 Will Hope. Subs (all used): 19 Michael Ward; 14 Adam Files; 16 Kenny Hughes; 24 Elliott Liku.
Tries: Lepori (10), Roper (15), Langtree (57, 77), Clay (75); **Goals:** Palfrey 4/6.
LIONS: 28 Ian Mort; 2 Shaun Robinson; 3 Stuart Littler; 22 Chris Rothwell; 14 Mike Butt; 6 Ben White; 7 Chris Atkin; 8 Mike Morrison; 9 Andy Ackers; 24 Jordan James; 17 Andy Thornley; 29 Rhodri Lloyd; 31 Rob Lever. Subs (all used): 10 Ben Austin; 13 Tommy Gallagher; 30 Josh Barlow; 11 Grant Beecham.
Tries: Ackers (46), Lever (52), Gallagher (80);
Goals: Atkin 2/3.
Rugby Leaguer & League Express Men of the Match: *Oldham:* Gareth Owen; *Lions:* Andy Ackers.
Penalty count: 9-11; **Half-time:** 10-0;
Referee: Chris Campbell; **Attendance:** 1,004.

Oldham's Danny Langtree on the charge during the Roughyeds' Promotion Final victory against Keighley

ROUND 22

Saturday 12th September 2015

OXFORD 12 OLDHAM 76

OXFORD: 9 Nathan Kitson; 32 Andy Matthews; 14 Marcus Brooker; 3 Andrew Hoggins; 21 Luke Gardiner; 36 Danny Thomas; 7 Andy Speake; 18 Stuart Biscomb; 13 James Milburn; 34 Steve Scott; 27 Charlie Greene; 37 Adam Withington; 28 Josh Nathaniel. Subs (all used): 25 Luke Evans; 5 Aaron Jones-Bishop; 1 Louis Richards; 19 Kyle Danns.
Tries: Gardiner (30), Richards (63); **Goals:** Kitson 2/2.
OLDHAM: 20 Tom Dempsey; 2 Adam Clay; 24 Tom Ashton; 3 Jonathan Ford; 4 Jack Holmes; 7 Steve Roper; 27 Dave Hewitt; 8 Phil Joy; 15 Gareth Owen; 18 Richard Joy; 11 Josh Crowley; 13 Liam Thompson; 26 Will Hope. Subs (all used): 16 Kenny Hughes; 14 Adam Files; 19 Michael Ward; 25 Elliot Liku.
Tries: Crowley (2, 36), Ford (5), Hope (12, 77), P Joy (15, 68), Hughes (25), Liku (41), Holmes (44), Files (50, 56), Dempsey (69); **Goals:** Roper 12/13.
Rugby Leaguer & League Express Men of the Match: *Oxford:* Charlie Greene; *Oldham:* Steve Roper.
Penalty count: 3-10; **Half-time:** 6-34;
Referee: Callum Straw; **Attendance:** 246.

ROCHDALE HORNETS 26 LONDON SKOLARS 22

HORNETS: 1 Wayne English; 2 Gareth Langley; 12 Alex Trumper; 4 Lee Paterson; 5 Dale Bloomfield; 6 Paul Crook; 7 Danny Yates; 14 James Tilley; 29 Matty Fozard; 10 Warren Thompson; 19 Danny Bridge; 23 James Dandy; 13 Tony Suffolk. Subs (all used): 28 Matty Hadden; 21 Ryan Smith; 17 Danny Jones; 9 Alex McClurg.
Tries: Fozard (14), English (26), Trumper (39), Bloomfield (62), Bridge (65);
Goals: Crook 2/4, Langley 1/1.
SKOLARS: 1 James Anthony; 2 Jimmy Morgan; 3 Mathew Cook; 4 Chris Bishay; 5 John Paxton; 6 Tommy Connick; 7 Jermaine Coleman; 20 Michael Sykes; 9 Mike Bishay; 10 Will Martin; 11 Joe Price; 12 Will Lovell; 13 Dave Williams. Subs (all used): 14 Mike Benson; 15 Billy Driver; 16 Louis Robinson; 17 Aaron Small.
Tries: Anthony (30, 34, 45), Morgan (72);
Goals: Connick 3/4.
Rugby Leaguer & League Express Men of the Match: *Hornets:* Warren Thompson; *Skolars:* James Anthony.
Penalty count: 7-3; **Half-time:** 16-12;
Referee: Scott Mikalauskas; **Attendance:** 305.

Sunday 13th September 2015

SWINTON LIONS 94 SOUTH WALES SCORPIONS 6

LIONS: 28 Mike Butt; 2 Shaun Robinson; 3 Stuart Littler; 22 Chris Rothwell; 25 Harry Aaronson; 16 Jimmy Rowland; 7 Chris Atkin; 8 Mike Morrison; 18 Aaron Lloyd; 31 Rob Lever; 17 Andy Thornley; 29 Rhodri Lloyd; 30 Josh Barlow. Subs (all used): 13 Tommy Gallagher; 9 Andy Ackers; 23 Connor Dwyer; 27 Mick Govin.
Tries: Robinson (7, 38), Aaronson (9), A Lloyd (15, 17), R Lloyd (21), Gallagher (26, 68, 73, 79), Rowland (36), Atkin (44), Govin (49, 54), Butt (60, 75), Littler (66), Ackers (80); **Goals:** Atkin 10/17, Gallagher 1/1.
SCORPIONS: 3 Paul Edwards; 24 Craig Lewis; 18 Bradley Hill; 26 Marcus Webb; 5 Ben Jones; 6 Curtis Davies; 21 Ryan Millington; 8 Osian Phillips; 17 Zak Williams; 15 Rhys Davies; 12 Barrie Phillips; 11 Mike Connor; 19 Connor Davies. Subs (both used, only two named): 14 Dafydd Hellard; 30 Gethin King.
Try: Hellard (29); **Goals:** Jones 1/1.
Sin bin: Lewis (77) - high tackle on Barlow.
Rugby Leaguer & League Express Men of the Match: *Lions:* Tommy Gallagher; *Scorpions:* Ryan Millington.
Penalty count: 10-6; **Half-time:** 38-6;
Referee: Andrew Sweet; **Attendance:** 417.

COVENTRY BEARS 22 GLOUCESTERSHIRE ALL GOLDS 48

BEARS: 28 Andy Winfield; 45 Jason Bass; 30 Dan Parker; 5 Ben Parry; 20 Jamahl Hunte; 39 Dan Price; 7 Cameron Boulter; 17 Jack Morrison; 24 Richard Hughes; 26 Matt Cooper; 29 Liam Thompson; 12 Chris Barratt; 21 Stephen Coleman. Subs (all used): 11 David O'Conner; 27 James Geurtjens; 32 Kenneth Kelliher; 50 Morgan Evans.
Tries: Hunte (9), Parry (14), Hughes (27), Parker (32);
Goals: Parker 3/4.
ALL GOLDS: 33 Jamie Murphy; 31 Lee Mapals; 4 Callum Mulkeen; 1 Phil Cowburn; 28 Ryan Pywell; 20 Courtney Davies; 7 Matt Bradley; 8 Oliver Purslow; 9 Steve Parry; 34 Alex Davidson; 32 Edwin Okanga-Ajwang; 3 Lewis Reece; 30 Emmerson Whittel. Subs (all used): 6 Toby Topham; 14 Joe McClean; 35 Graham O'Keeffe; 17 James Walter.
Tries: Mapals (2, 49), Okanga-Ajwang (7), Murphy (20, 57), Mulkeen (23), Davies (60), Davidson (65), Pywell (73); **Goals:** Bradley 6/9.
Rugby Leaguer & League Express Men of the Match: *Bears:* Cameron Boulter; *All Golds:* Joe McClean.
Penalty count: 10-8; **Half-time:** 22-22;
Referee: Andrew Bentham; **Attendance:** 441.

KEIGHLEY COUGARS 68 HEMEL STAGS 16

COUGARS: 36 Josh Guzdek; 25 Andy Gabriel; 4 Danny Lawton; 32 Hamish Barnes; 5 Paul White; - Adam Mitchell; 7 Paul Handforth; 8 Scott Law; 9 James Feather; 19 Matthew Bailey; 17 Oliver Pursglove; 12 Brendan Rawlins; 35 Tyler Dickinson. Subs (all used): 11 Ashley Lindsay; 15 Neil Cherryholme; 28 Josh Lynam; 31 Scott Lee.
Tries: Feather (9, 19, 61, 69), Rawlins (32, 74), Gabriel (37, 44), Lynam (55), Law (63, 65), Handforth (77), Guzdek (80); **Goals:** Lawton 8/13.
STAGS: 1 Derrell Olpherts; 18 Chris McNamara; 4 Michael Brown; 33 Thibault Cousine; 27 Simon Hrbek; 24 James Woodburn-Hall; 6 Jy-mel Coleman; 16 Mike Stewart; 7 Charlie Lawrence; 31 Matt Ross; 15 Liam O'Callaghan; 28 Connor Boyd-Barnes; 17 Dan Ljazouli. Subs (all used): 9 Kaizer Muroi; 26 James Howitt; 30 Nathan Darby; 32 Jason Long.
Tries: Woodburn-Hall (5), Darby (40), Hrbek (52);
Goals: Lawrence 2/3.
Rugby Leaguer & League Express Men of the Match: *Cougars:* James Feather; *Stags:* James Woodburn-Hall.
Penalty count: 7-5; **Half-time:** 20-12;
Referee: Tom Grant; **Attendance:** 692.

NEWCASTLE THUNDER 22 NORTH WALES CRUSADERS 50

THUNDER: 2 Jacob Blades; 31 Ali Blair; 4 Joe Brown; 3 Jason Tali; 5 Tom Capper; 6 Matty Beharrell; 23 Benn Hardcastle; 8 Matt Barron; 25 Evan Simons; 15 Lee Fewlass; 9 Dayne Craig; 36 Sonny Esslemont; 13 Charlie Wabo. Subs (all used): 18 Josh Stoker; 26 Iain Murray; 11 Jason Payne; 12 Rhys Clarke.
Tries: Tali (3), Craig (21), Esslemont (69), Beharrell (74);
Goals: Hardcastle 3/4.
CRUSADERS: 1 Tommy Johnson; 5 Rob Massam; 3 Christiaan Roets; 31 Benjamin Jullien; 29 Andrew Oakden; 14 Karl Ashall; 7 Jamie Dallimore; 8 Jonny Walker; 15 Lee Hudson; 16 Joe Burke; 22 Alex Thompson; 32 Sam Peet;

Swinton's Stuart Littler takes on the Keighley defence during the League 1 Play-off Final

12 Stephen Wild. Subs (all used): 34 Andrew Joy; 20 Elliott Davies; 10 Ryan Duffy; 4 Matt Reid.
Tries: Walker (6), Massam (13, 33), Johnson (36), Oakden (58, 72, 76), Roets (62), Hudson (67);
Goals: Johnson 4/6, Dallimore 3/3.
Rugby Leaguer & League Express Men of the Match: *Thunder:* Benn Hardcastle; *Crusaders:* Andrew Oakden.
Penalty count: 5-4; **Half-time:** 10-24;
Referee: Sam Ansell; **Attendance:** 810.

YORK CITY KNIGHTS 16 BARROW RAIDERS 18

CITY KNIGHTS: 32 Jordan Howden; 25 Adam Dent; 3 Greg Minikin; 24 James Morland; 2 Ben Dent; 6 Jon Presley; 7 Pat Smith; 8 Mark Applegarth; 14 Kris Brining; 28 Mick Learmonth; 12 Ed Smith; 15 Josh Tonks; 10 Jack Aldous. Subs (all used): 9 Harry Carter; 11 Ryan Mallinder; 29 Brad Nicholson; 34 Jack Blagbrough.
Tries: A Dent (12), E Smith (21), Howden (43);
Goals: B Dent 2/4.
RAIDERS: 23 Chris Fleming; 31 Cameron Pitman; 3 Chris Hankinson; 24 Andy Litherland; 22 Joe Hambley; 6 Brad Marwood; 14 Josh Ward; 8 Joe Bullock; 9 Nathan Mossop; 11 Liam Harrison; 16 Adam Nicholson; 12 Craig Briscoe; 28 James Duerden. Subs (all used): 5 Kyle Dolan; 10 Andrew Dawson; 13 Dan Toal; 21 Anthony Bate.
Tries: Mossop (15), Pitman (68, 78);
Goals: Ward 2/3, Hankinson 1/1.
Dismissal: Bate (38) - dangerous contact on A Dent.
Sin bin: Briscoe (26) - dissent;
Litherland (28) - punching.
Rugby Leaguer & League Express Men of the Match: *City Knights:* Greg Minikin; *Raiders:* Cameron Pitman.
Penalty count: 16-8; **Half-time:** 12-8;
Referee: Dave Merrick; **Attendance:** 468
(at Elmpark Way, Heworth).

PROMOTION FINAL

Sunday 20th September 2015

OLDHAM 31 KEIGHLEY COUGARS 20

OLDHAM: 21 Richard Lepori; 2 Adam Clay; 17 George Tyson; 3 Jonathan Ford; 4 Jack Holmes; 6 Lewis Palfrey; 7 Steve Roper; 10 Adam Neal; 15 Gareth Owen; 8 Phil Joy; 12 Danny Langtree; 11 Josh Crowley; 26 Will Hope. Subs (all used): 13 Liam Thompson; 19 Michael Ward; 14 Adam Files; 16 Kenny Hughes.
Tries: Ford (12), Neal (32), Langtree (38), Tyson (66), Clay (78); **Goals:** Palfrey 5/6; **Field goal:** Palfrey (71).
COUGARS: 36 Josh Guzdek; 25 Andy Gabriel; 4 Danny Lawton; 30 Rikki Sheriffe; 5 Paul White; - Adam Mitchell; 7 Paul Handforth; 8 Scott Law; 13 David March; 35 Tyler Dickinson; 17 Oliver Pursglove; 12 Brendan Rawlins; 11 Ashley Lindsay. Subs (all used): 26 Paul March; 19 Matthew Bailey; 28 Josh Lynam; 34 Samir Tahraoui.
Tries: Bailey (25), White (59), Handforth (69), Gabriel (80); **Goals:** Lawton 2/4.
Rugby Leaguer & League Express Men of the Match: *Oldham:* Steve Roper; *Cougars:* Paul Handforth.
Penalty count: 6-4; **Half-time:** 18-6;
Referee: Michael Woodhead; **Attendance:** 1,405.

SEMI-FINALS

Sunday 27th September 2015

KEIGHLEY COUGARS 32 NORTH WALES CRUSADERS 6

COUGARS: 36 Josh Guzdek; 25 Andy Gabriel; 4 Danny Lawton; 30 Rikki Sheriffe; 5 Paul White; 37 Adam Mitchell; 7 Paul Handforth; 8 Scott Law; 13 David March; 35 Tyler Dickinson; 28 Josh Lynam; 12 Brendan Rawlins; 11 Ashley Lindsay. Subs (all used): 15 Neil Cherryholme; 19 Matthew Bailey; 26 Paul March; 34 Samir Tahraoui.
Tries: White (4, 44, 47), Bailey (50), P March (53), Gabriel (80); **Goals:** Lawton 4/6.
CRUSADERS: 1 Tommy Johnson; 17 Stuart Reardon; 3 Christiaan Roets; 31 Benjamin Jullien; 29 Andrew Oakden; 14 Karl Ashall; 7 Jamie Dallimore; 8 Jonny Walker; 15 Lee Hudson; 16 Joe Burke; 22 Alex Thompson; 32 Sam Peet; 12 Stephen Wild. Subs (all used): 4 Matt Reid; 6 Andy Moulsdale; 10 Ryan Duffy; 23 Mark Hobson.
Try: Thompson (24); **Goals:** Johnson 1/1.
Rugby Leaguer & League Express Men of the Match: *Cougars:* Ashley Lindsay; *Crusaders:* Alex Thompson.
Penalty count: 7-8; **Half-time:** 6-6;
Referee: Sam Ansell; **Attendance:** 1,103.

SWINTON LIONS 18 YORK CITY KNIGHTS 17
(after golden point extra-time)

LIONS: 1 Ritchie Hawkyard; 2 Shaun Robinson; 3 Stuart Littler; 22 Chris Rothwell; 28 Mike Butt; 6 Ben White; 7 Chris Atkin; 8 Mike Morrison; 9 Andy Ackers; 24 Jordan James; 17 Andy Thornley; 29 Rhodri Lloyd; 31 Rob Lever. Subs (all used): 13 Tommy Gallagher; 30 Josh Barlow; 10 Ben Austin; 23 Connor Dwyer.
Tries: Atkin (10), Dwyer (48), Butt (60); **Goals:** Atkin 2/4;
Field goals: White (80), Atkin (83).
CITY KNIGHTS: 2 Ben Dent; 25 Adam Dent; 3 Greg Minikin; 26 James Morland; 24 Tyler Craig; 6 Jon Presley; 22 Jordan Howden; 8 Mark Applegarth; 7 Pat Smith; 11 Ryan Mallinder; 15 Josh Tonks; 12 Ed Smith; 10 Jack Aldous. Subs (all used): 14 Kris Brining; 13 Colton Roche; 34 Jack Blagbrough; 23 Brad Nicholson.
Tries: E Smith (17), Brining (28), Minikin (38), Presley (43); **Goals:** B Dent 0/2, Howden 0/2;
Field goal: Howden (74).
Rugby Leaguer & League Express Men of the Match: *Lions:* Josh Barlow; *City Knights:* Jon Presley.
Penalty count: 4-5; **Half-time:** 6-12;
Referee: Chris Campbell; **Attendance:** 684.

PLAY-OFF FINAL

Sunday 4th October 2015

KEIGHLEY COUGARS 28 SWINTON LIONS 29

COUGARS: 36 Josh Guzdek; 25 Andy Gabriel; 4 Danny Lawton; 30 Rikki Sheriffe; 5 Paul White; 26 Paul March; 7 Paul Handforth; 8 Scott Law; 13 David March; 12 Brendan Rawlins; 28 Josh Lynam; 17 Oliver Pursglove; 11 Ashley Lindsay. Subs (all used): 9 James Feather; 19 Matthew Bailey; 15 Neil Cherryholme; 34 Samir Tahraoui.
Tries: Law (12, 15), Lynam (28), Pursglove (50), P March (70); **Goals:** Lawton 4/5.
LIONS: 1 Ritchie Hawkyard; 2 Shaun Robinson; 3 Stuart Littler; 22 Chris Rothwell; 28 Mike Butt; 6 Ben White; 7 Chris Atkin; 24 Jordan James; 9 Andy Ackers; 10 Ben Austin; 17 Andy Thornley; 29 Rhodri Lloyd; 31 Rob Lever. Subs (all used): 13 Tommy Gallagher; 30 Josh Barlow; 23 Connor Dwyer; 18 Aaron Lloyd.
Tries: Atkin (7), Butt (20), White (22), R Lloyd (36), Robinson (40); **Goals:** Atkin 4/6; **Field goal:** Atkin (63).
Rugby Leaguer & League Express Men of the Match: *Cougars:* Paul Handforth; *Lions:* Rhodri Lloyd.
Penalty count: 8-4; **Half-time:** 16-26;
Referee: Chris Kendall.
(at Select Security Stadium, Widnes).

iPRO Sport Cup 2015 *Round by Round*

ROUND 1

Saturday 28th February 2015

WEST HULL 10 NORTH WALES CRUSADERS 36

WEST HULL: 1 Brett Turner; 2 Chris Whinn; 3 Tom Radley; 4 Dan Parker; 5 Josh Hart; 6 Ryan Steen; 7 Ian Kerman; 8 Ash Shaw; 9 Callum Windley; 10 Paul Shaw; 11 Dean Thompson; 12 Sam Cator; 13 Ricky Hough. Subs (all used): 19 Callum King; 16 Louis Crowther; 14 Matt Plummer; 18 Ben Parker.
Tries: D Parker (66, 78); **Goals:** Kerman 1/2.
CRUSADERS: 1 Tommy Johnson; 2 Scott Turner; 17 Stuart Reardon; 3 Christiaan Roets; 5 Rob Massam; 14 Karl Ashall; 7 Jamie Dallimore; 16 Joe Burke; 9 Callum Wright; 8 Jonny Walker; 11 Jono Smith; 22 Alex Thompson; 13 Gary Middlehurst. Subs (all used): 26 Craig White; 10 Ryan Duffy; 29 George King; 23 Mark Hobson.
Tries: Turner (15, 70), Massam (25), Smith (37, 53), Johnson (49), Wright (61); **Goals:** Johnson 4/7.
Rugby Leaguer & League Express Men of the Match: *West Hull:* Dan Parker; *Crusaders:* Jono Smith.
Penalty count: 8-8; **Half-time:** 0-14;
Referee: Chris Campbell; **Attendance:** 150
(at YPI Sports Ground).

OXFORD 20 NEWCASTLE THUNDER 56

OXFORD: 31 Sean Morris; 22 Harry Kaufman; 14 Marcus Brooker; 4 Kash Watkins; 5 Aaron Jones-Bishop; 6 Danny Allan; 7 Andy Speake; 25 Luke Evans; 9 Nathan Kitson; 19 Kyle Danns; 12 Ed Hayles; 3 Andrew Hoggins; 10 Jonny Payne. Subs (all used): 20 Ricky Hopwood; 11 Josh Scott; 18 Edd Vickers; 23 Tom Davies.
Tries: S Morris (6), Jones-Bishop (9), Watkins (46), Brooker (63); **Goals:** Allan 2/4.
THUNDER: 7 Jordan Meads; 21 Lee Mapals; 3 Jason Tali; 4 Joe Brown; 17 Stuart Kain; 6 Matty Beharrell; 23 Benn Hardcastle; 8 Matt Barron; 9 Dayne Craig; 10 Mark Mexico; 11 Jason Payne; 12 Rhys Clarke; 13 Charlie Wabo. Subs (all used): 1 Louis Sheriff; 18 Josh Stoker; 16 Francis Welsh; 36 Sonny Esslemont.
Tries: Kain (2), Brown (17), Mapals (23, 44, 79), Wabo (29), Tali (32), Beharrell (38), Hardcastle (39), Stoker (57); **Goals:** Beharrell 8/10.
Rugby Leaguer & League Express Men of the Match: *Oxford:* Sean Morris; *Thunder:* Lee Mapals.
Penalty count: 9-5; **Half-time:** 10-40;
Referee: Jon Roberts; **Attendance:** 252.

Sunday 1st March 2015

BARROW RAIDERS 16
GLOUCESTERSHIRE ALL GOLDS 14

RAIDERS: 1 Kris Tyson; 5 Kyle Dolan; 3 Chris Hankinson; 4 Max Wiper; 23 Chris Fleming; 7 Liam Campbell; 14 Josh Ward; 8 Joe Bullock; 9 Nathan Mossop; 18 Danny Jones; 16 Adam Nicholson; 12 Craig Briscoe; 21 Anthony Bate. Subs (all used): 29 Peter Lupton; 13 Dan Toal; 10 Andrew Dawson; 19 Matt Heaton.
Tries: Hankinson (13), Campbell (48), Bate (64);
Goals: Ward 1/2, Fleming 1/1.
ALL GOLDS: 23 Joe Martin; 4 Callum Mulkeen; 3 Lewis Reece; 1 Phil Cowburn; 28 Ryan Pywell; 20 Courtney Davies; 7 Matt Bradley; 10 Izaak Duffy; 9 Steve Parry; 8 Oliver Purslow; 30 Emmerson Whittel; 16 Ash Haynes; 13 Chris Vitalini. Subs (all used): 6 Toby Topham; 18 Jamie Crowther; 14 Joe McClean; 34 Nathan Rainer.
Tries: Martin (6), Mulkeen (16), Cowburn (25);
Goals: Bradley 1/3.
Rugby Leaguer & League Express Men of the Match: *Raiders:* Adam Nicholson; *All Golds:* Matt Bradley.
Penalty count: 8-6; **Half-time:** 4-14;
Referee: Jamie Bloem; **Attendance:** 836.

KEIGHLEY COUGARS 64 EAST LEEDS 0

COUGARS: 1 Jesse Sheriffe; 18 Lewis Graham; - Rikki Sheriffe; 4 Danny Lawton; 5 Paul White; 6 Danny Jones; 7 Paul Handforth; 15 Neil Cherryholme; 9 James Feather; 12 Brendan Rawlins; 13 David March; 17 Oliver Pursglove; 11 Ashley Lindsay. Subs (all used): 8 Scott Law; 16 Jode Sheriffe; 21 Sean Kelly; 28 Josh Lynam.
Tries: Graham (5, 31, 65), R Sheriffe (8), Lawton (20), Lindsay (34, 49, 62), Handforth (39, 52), White (79);
Goals: Jones 10/11.
EAST LEEDS: 1 Nathan West; 2 Jordan Normington; 3 Declan Tomlinson; 4 Kyle Quinlan; 5 Jason Priestley; 6 Tom Sheldrake; 7 Ryan Gaunt; 8 Ashley James; 20 David Nurse; 10 Luke Pettman; 11 Ben Walkin; 12 Dale Pattison; 13 Jake Normington. Subs (all used): 9 Jonny Carter; 14 Lee Priestley; 18 Lee Fisher; 21 Joey Walkin.
Rugby Leaguer & League Express Men of the Match: *Cougars:* Ashley Lindsay; *East Leeds:* Ashley James.
Penalty count: 10-6; **Half-time:** 36-0;
Referee: Tom Grant; **Attendance:** 423.

LONDON SKOLARS 10 YORK CITY KNIGHTS 78

SKOLARS: 1 Aaron Small; 2 Sebastian Kolasa; 3 Mike Benson; 4 Kazeem Fatouri; 5 James Carty; 6 Tommy Connick; 7 Liam Foran; 13 Louis Robinson; 9 Sam Druce; 10 Dave Williams; 11 Harvey Burnett; 12 Anthony Cox; 22 Will Fairhurst. Subs (all used): 8 Michael Sykes; 21 Dave Ellison; 15 James Anthony; 16 Louie Sutherland.
Tries: Fatouri (8, 64); **Goals:** Connick 0/1, Druce 1/1.
Sin bin: Small (32) - trip on Morrison.
CITY KNIGHTS: 1 James Haynes; 5 Nev Morrison; 3 Greg Minikin; 16 Peter Aspinall; 24 Tyler Craig; 6 Jon Presley; 7 Pat Smith; 28 Brad Nicholson; 9 Harry Carter; 10 Jack Aldous; 12 Ed Smith; 15 Josh Tonks; 8 Mark Applegarth. Subs (all used): 14 Kris Brining; 13 Colton Roche; 4 Liam Cunningham; 18 Jake Joynt.

Tries: E Smith (25), Morrison (32, 59, 75), Aspinall (37, 63), Cunningham (40), Brining (43), P Smith (45, 77), Minikin (50), Carter (68), Joynt (73), Haynes (80); **Goals:** Haynes 11/15.
Rugby Leaguer & League Express Men of the Match: *Skolars:* Kazeem Fatouri; *City Knights:* Nev Morrison.
Penalty count: 3-10; **Half-time:** 4-14;
Referee: Warren Turley; **Attendance:** 156.

OLDHAM 42 COVENTRY BEARS 6

OLDHAM: 4 Jack Holmes; 2 Adam Clay; 17 George Tyson; 9 Sam Gee; 5 Jarrod Ward; 6 Lewis Palfrey; 7 Steve Roper; 10 Adam Neal; 15 Gareth Owen; 8 Phil Joy; 11 Josh Crowley; 26 Oliver Roberts; 23 Josh Johnson. Subs (all used): 13 Liam Thompson; 14 Adam Files; 19 Michael Ward; 22 Nathan Mason.
Tries: Neal (10), Holmes (24), Clay (30, 38), Mason (43), J Ward (47, 57); **Goals:** Palfrey 7/7.
BEARS: 1 Troy Brophy; 20 Jamahl Hunte; 21 Stephen Coleman; 4 Eddie Medforth; 28 Andy Winfield; 18 Dan Poulton; 7 Cameron Boulter; 27 James Geurtjens; 9 Alex Brown; 10 John Aldred; 29 Liam Thompson; 12 Chris Barratt; 13 Simon Phillips. Subs (all used): 6 Billy Sheen; 8 Ben Tyers; 17 Alex Calvert; 26 Matt Cooper.
Try: Tyers (26); **Goals:** Coleman 1/1.
Rugby Leaguer & League Express Men of the Match: *Oldham:* Lewis Palfrey; *Bears:* Dan Poulton.
Penalty count: 4-6; **Half-time:** 24-6;
Referee: Dave Merrick; **Attendance:** 291.

ROCHDALE HORNETS 40 SOUTH WALES SCORPIONS 0

HORNETS: 1 Wayne English; 20 Bradley Hargreaves; 24 Dave Hull; 4 Lee Paterson; 5 Dale Bloomfield; 6 Paul Crook; 7 Danny Yates; 13 Tony Suffolk; 9 Alex McClurg; 10 Warren Thompson; 19 Danny Bridge; 23 James Dandy; 11 Jordan Case. Subs (all used): 8 John Cookson; 3 Dave Llewellyn; 18 Dean Mignacca; 28 Matty Hadden.
Tries: Bridge (5), Hargreaves (9), McClurg (19), Yates (38), Bloomfield (43), Case (65), Suffolk (73); **Goals:** Crook 6/7.
SCORPIONS: 2 Ian Newbury; 24 Craig Lewis; 3 Paul Edwards; 4 Kyle Scrivens; 21 Paul Songhurst; 6 Curtis Davies; 7 Paul Emanuelli; 8 Osian Phillips; 9 Connor Farrer; 10 Morgan Evans; 11 Mike Connor; 23 Anthony Symons; 13 Neil Dallimore. Subs: 14 Dafydd Lloyd; 16 Scott Giles; - Marcus Webb (not used); 20 Tala Petelo.
Rugby Leaguer & League Express Men of the Match: *Hornets:* Tony Suffolk; *Scorpions:* Osian Phillips.
Penalty count: 5-6; **Half-time:** 22-0;
Referee: Chris Kendall; **Attendance:** 260.

SWINTON LIONS 34 HEMEL STAGS 0

LIONS: 7 Chris Atkin; 2 Shaun Robinson; 3 Stuart Littler; 22 Chris Rothwell; 1 Ritchie Hawkyard; 6 Ben White; 16 Jimmy Rowland; 8 Mike Morrison; 9 Andy Ackers; 24 Jordan James; 29 Rhodri Lloyd; 11 Grant Beecham; 23 Connor Dwyer. Subs (all used): 18 Aaron Lloyd; 13 Tommy Gallagher; 10 Ben Austin; 31 Rob Lever.
Tries: R Hawkyard (4, 33, 56), Ackers (16, 76), Robinson (43), Dwyer (55); **Goals:** Atkin 3/7.
STAGS: 21 Derrell Olpherts; 26 Frank Mayfield; 3 Jamie O'Callaghan; 4 Michael Brown; 15 Alex Anthony; 18 Jordan Gale; 7 Jermaine Coleman; 8 Mike Stewart; 6 James Helliwell; 13 Aidan Pritchard; 19 Barry-John Swindells; 11 Alex Ingarfield; 10 Liam O'Callaghan. Subs (all used): 17 Tom Sadler; 12 Lewis Reed; 20 Ryan Chester; 22 Malikhi Lloyd-Jones.
Rugby Leaguer & League Express Men of the Match: *Lions:* Ritchie Hawkyard; *Stags:* Jermaine Coleman.
Penalty count: 7-5; **Half-time:** 14-0;
Referee: Michael Woodhead; **Attendance:** 349.

ROUND 2

Sunday 15th March 2015

BARROW RAIDERS 10 OLDHAM 32

RAIDERS: 23 Chris Fleming; 5 Kyle Dolan; 3 Chris Hankinson; 24 Andy Litherland; 4 Max Wiper; 14 Josh Ward; 7 Liam Campbell; 8 Joe Bullock; 29 Peter Lupton; 11 Liam Harrison; 16 Adam Nicholson; 12 Craig Briscoe; 21 Anthony Bate. Subs (all used): 9 Nathan Mossop; 10 Andrew Dawson; 13 Dan Toal; 18 Danny Jones.
Tries: Ward (3), Nicholson (17); **Goals:** Ward 1/2.
On report: Toal (53) - alleged high tackle on M Ward.
OLDHAM: 5 Jarrod Ward; 2 Adam Clay; 9 Sam Gee; 4 Jack Holmes; 27 Jodie Broughton; 6 Lewis Palfrey; 7 Steve Roper; 10 Adam Neal; 15 Gareth Owen; 8 Phil Joy; 11 Josh Crowley; 17 George Tyson; 13 Liam Thompson. Subs (all used): 14 Adam Files; 16 Kenny Hughes; 22 Nathan Mason; 19 Michael Ward.
Tries: M Ward (32), Clay (37, 56), Broughton (39, 47), Gee (68); **Goals:** Palfrey 4/7.
Rugby Leaguer & League Express Men of the Match: *Raiders:* Adam Nicholson; *Oldham:* George Tyson.
Penalty count: 5-6; **Half-time:** 10-18;
Referee: Michael Woodhead; **Attendance:** 844.

NORTH WALES CRUSADERS 28 ROCHDALE HORNETS 4

CRUSADERS: 1 Tommy Johnson; 5 Rob Massam; 31 Gene Ormsby; 17 Stuart Reardon; 2 Scott Turner; 14 Karl Ashall; 7 Jamie Dallimore; 8 Jonny Walker; 9 Callum Wright; 16 Joe Burke; 11 Jono Smith; 12 Stephen Wild; 13 Gary Middlehurst. Subs (all used): 30 Declan Patton; 22 Alex Thompson; 10 Ryan Duffy; 33 Paddy Mooney.
Tries: Dallimore (2), Middlehurst (15), Turner (42, 78), Ashall (75); **Goals:** Johnson 4/6.

North Wales Crusaders' Ryan Duffy finds his path blocked by Swinton's Josh Barlow during the iPRO Sport Cup Final

HORNETS: 1 Wayne English; 2 Gareth Langley; 24 Dave Hull; 4 Lee Paterson; 20 Bradley Hargreaves; 6 Paul Crook; 7 Danny Yates; 17 Sam Brooks; 9 Alex McClurg; 10 Warren Thompson; 19 Danny Bridge; 11 Jordan Case; 13 Tony Suffolk. Subs (all used): 8 John Cookson; 21 Ryan Smith; - Jack Ashworth; 14 James Tilley.
Try: Hull (26); **Goals:** Crook 0/1.
Rugby Leaguer & League Express Men of the Match: *Crusaders:* Gary Middlehurst; *Hornets:* Sam Brooks.
Penalty count: 9-7; **Half-time:** 12-4;
Referee: Gareth Hewer; **Attendance:** 465.

KEIGHLEY COUGARS 22 SWINTON LIONS 24

COUGARS: 1 Jesse Sheriffe; 2 Gavin Duffy; 4 Danny Lawton; - Rikki Sheriffe; 5 Paul White; 6 Danny Jones; 7 Paul Handforth; 8 Scott Law; 9 James Feather; 12 Brendan Rawlins; 28 Josh Lynam; 17 Oliver Pursglove; 11 Ashley Lindsay. Subs (all used): 15 Neil Cherryholme; 16 Jode Sheriffe; 19 Matthew Bailey; 26 Paul March.
Tries: R Sheriffe (10), Law (56), Rawlins (69), Jesse Sheriffe (73); **Goals:** Jones 3/4.
LIONS: 7 Chris Atkin; 2 Shaun Robinson; 3 Stuart Littler; 22 Chris Rothwell; 1 Ritchie Hawkyard; 6 Ben White; 16 Jimmy Rowland; 8 Mike Morrison; 9 Andy Ackers; 24 Jordan James; 11 Grant Beecham; 29 Rhodri Lloyd; 23 Connor Dwyer. Subs (all used): 10 Ben Austin; 13 Tommy Gallagher; 18 Aaron Lloyd; 31 Rob Lever.
Tries: Beecham (24), White (36), Atkin (44), Littler (63); **Goals:** Atkin 4/5.
Rugby Leaguer & League Express Men of the Match: *Cougars:* Ashley Lindsay; *Lions:* Chris Atkin.
Penalty count: 6-7; **Half-time:** 6-12;
Referee: Dave Merrick; **Attendance:** 472.

YORK CITY KNIGHTS 24 NEWCASTLE THUNDER 38

CITY KNIGHTS: 1 James Haynes; 19 Jamel Chisholm; 4 Liam Cunningham; 3 Greg Minikin; 5 Nev Morrison; 6 Jon Presley; 7 Pat Smith; 8 Mark Applegarth; 14 Kris Brining; 21 Jack Pickles; 12 Ed Smith; 15 Josh Tonks; 10 Jack Aldous. Subs (all used): 9 Harry Carter; 13 Colton Roche; 16 Peter Aspinall; 29 Luke Menzies.
Tries: Brining (6), Cunningham (9), Morrison (19), Presley (61); **Goals:** Haynes 4/4.
THUNDER: 7 Jordan Meads; 21 Lee Mapals; 3 Jason Tali; 4 Joe Brown; 5 Tom Capper; 23 Benn Hardcastle; 6 Matty Beharrell; 15 Lee Fewlass; 13 Charlie Wabo; 10 Mark Mexico; 11 Jason Payne; 12 Rhys Clarke; 9 Dayne Craig. Subs (all used): 36 Sonny Esslemont; 1 Louis Sheriff; 18 Josh Stoker; 14 Paul Stamp.
Tries: Hardcastle (34), Mapals (40), Tali (44), Mexico (65), Payne (73), Wabo (78); **Goals:** Hardcastle 7/8.
Rugby Leaguer & League Express Men of the Match: *City Knights:* Ed Smith; *Thunder:* Benn Hardcastle.
Penalty count: 10-14; **Half-time:** 18-10;
Referee: Tom Crashley; **Attendance:** 358 *(at Clifton Park).*

SEMI-FINALS

Tuesday 7th April 2015

SWINTON LIONS 36 NEWCASTLE THUNDER 28

LIONS: 7 Chris Atkin; 2 Shaun Robinson; 3 Stuart Littler; 22 Chris Rothwell; 1 Ritchie Hawkyard; 6 Ben White; 16 Jimmy Rowland; 8 Mike Morrison; 9 Andy Ackers; 24 Jordan James; 11 Grant Beecham; 21 Andy Ball; 31 Rob Lever. Subs (all used): 18 Aaron Lloyd; 30 Matt Gardner; 10 Ben Austin; 12 Darren Hawkyard.
Tries: James (13), Atkin (17, 52), D Hawkyard (26), Gardner (49), Ackers (80); **Goals:** Atkin 6/7.
THUNDER: 1 Louis Sheriff; 21 Lee Mapals; 4 Joe Brown; 3 Jason Tali; 5 Tom Capper; 6 Matty Beharrell; 7 Jordan Meads; 15 Lee Fewlass; 13 Charlie Wabo; 36 Sonny Esslemont; 12 Rhys Clarke; 11 Jason Payne; 9 Dayne Craig. Subs (all used): 10 Mark Mexico; 8 Matt Barron; 16 Francis Welsh; 25 Evan Simons.
Tries: Meads (6, 33, 76), Sheriff (23), Wabo (71); **Goals:** Beharrell 4/5.
Rugby Leaguer & League Express Men of the Match: *Lions:* Chris Atkin; *Thunder:* Charlie Wabo.
Penalty count: 7-6; **Half-time:** 18-16;
Referee: Michael Woodhead; **Attendance:** 351.

Wednesday 8th April 2015

OLDHAM 16 NORTH WALES CRUSADERS 18

OLDHAM: 4 Jack Holmes; 2 Adam Clay; 17 George Tyson; 9 Sam Gee; 5 Jarrod Ward; 6 Lewis Palfrey; 7 Steve Roper; 10 Adam Neal; 15 Gareth Owen; 8 Phil Joy; 11 Josh Crowley; 12 Danny Langtree; 13 Liam Thompson. Subs (all used): 14 Adam Files; 16 Kenny Hughes; 19 Michael Ward; 22 Nathan Mason.
Tries: Tyson (17), Langtree (77); **Goals:** Palfrey 4/4.
Sin bin: Tyson (41) - late challenge on Dallimore.
CRUSADERS: 1 Tommy Johnson; 2 Scott Turner; 17 Stuart Reardon; 3 Christiaan Roets; 5 Rob Massam; 26 Craig White; 7 Jamie Dallimore; 8 Jonny Walker; 9 Callum Wright; 16 Joe Burke; 11 Jono Smith; 12 Stephen Wild; 22 Alex Thompson. Subs (all used): 10 Ryan Duffy; 14 Karl Ashall; 20 Elliott Davies; 23 Mark Hobson.
Tries: Massam (20), Duffy (48), Dallimore (63); **Goals:** Johnson 3/3.
Rugby Leaguer & League Express Men of the Match: *Oldham:* Adam Neal; *Crusaders:* Jamie Dallimore.
Penalty count: 10-5; **Half-time:** 10-6;
Referee: Dave Merrick; **Attendance:** 444.

FINAL

Saturday 23rd May 2015

NORTH WALES CRUSADERS 14 SWINTON LIONS 8

CRUSADERS: 1 Tommy Johnson; 2 Scott Turner; 4 Matt Reid; 22 Alex Thompson; 5 Rob Massam; 14 Karl Ashall; 7 Jamie Dallimore; 16 Joe Burke; 9 Callum Wright; 8 Jonny Walker; 11 Jono Smith; 12 Stephen Wild; 13 Gary Middlehurst. Subs (all used): 15 Lee Hudson; 23 Mark Hobson; 10 Ryan Duffy; 20 Elliott Davies.
Tries: Turner (30), Dallimore (65); **Goals:** Johnson 3/5.
LIONS: 7 Chris Atkin; 2 Shaun Robinson; 3 Stuart Littler; 22 Chris Rothwell; 1 Ritchie Hawkyard; 6 Ben White; 18 Aaron Lloyd; 24 Jordan James; 9 Andy Ackers; 10 Ben Austin; 30 Josh Barlow; 23 Connor Dwyer; 31 Rob Lever. Subs (all used): 8 Mike Morrison; 12 Darren Hawkyard; 17 Matt Gardner; 29 Mick Govin.
Try: Robinson (10); **Goals:** Atkin 2/2.
Rugby Leaguer & League Express Men of the Match: *Crusaders:* Jamie Dallimore; *Lions:* Chris Atkin.
Penalty count: 12-5; **Half-time:** 6-8;
Referee: Michael Woodhead; **Attendance:** 1,200 *(at Bloomfield Road, Blackpool).*

CHALLENGE CUP 2015
Round by Round

ROUND 3

Saturday 7th March 2015

ELLAND 14 FEATHERSTONE LIONS 26

ELLAND: 1 James Marshall; 2 Oliver Fairbank; 3 Richard Crawshaw; 4 Thomas Harnett; 5 Christopher Dyson; 6 Bradley Radcliffe; 7 Philip Taylor; 8 Cayci Pearson; 9 Chris Cullimore; 10 Ben Bottomley; 11 Ben Hinsley; 12 Jack Fairbank; 13 Andy Shickell. Subs (all used): 14 Dehran Gibson; 15 Ben Fairbank; 16 Joe Fradgley; 17 Luke Reed.
Tries: Cullimore (17), Hinsley (48); **Goals:** Taylor 3/4.
LIONS: 1 Ian Jackson; 5 Kieran Redfearn; 4 Ricky Williams; 3 Josh Hardcastle; 2 David Garahan; 7 Lewis Young; 6 Sam Candlin; 10 Liam Jackson; 9 Dean Gamble; 8 Scott Wilson; 14 Matty Johnson; 17 Joe Fox; 13 Brendan Gibbins. Subs (all used): 20 Richard Frankland; 15 George Nuttall; 16 Adam Curtis; 11 Adam Hepworth.
Tries: Young (10), Hardcastle (22), Candlin (68), L Jackson (75); **Goals:** Young 4/4, Frankland 1/1.
Rugby Leaguer & League Express Men of the Match: *Elland:* Andy Shickell; *Lions:* Matty Johnson.
Half-time: 8-12; **Referee:** Scott Mikalauskas; **Attendance:** 350.

OULTON RAIDERS 8 NORMANTON KNIGHTS 34

RAIDERS: 1 Matty Bullough; 2 Adrian Holdsworth; 3 Nathan Batty; 4 Andy Tillett; 5 Scott Macdonald; 6 Danny Macintosh; 7 Tommy Griffiths; 21 Rob Stanley; 9 Craig Savage; 22 Danny Stanley; 18 Clayton Stott; 12 Chris Hope; 20 Andy Williamson. Subs (all used): 14 Josh Murray; 15 Carlos Sanchez; 8 Lawrence Dibb; 17 Brendan Shepherd.
Tries: Holdsworth (33), Tillett (60);
Goals: Griffiths 0/1, D Stanley 0/1.
Sin bin: Tillet (2), D Stanley (68), R Stanley (71).
KNIGHTS: 1 Jonathan Hodgson; 2 Aaron Butterfield; 3 Steven Lewis; 4 Connor Taylor; 5 Lee Hammond; 6 Thomas Alexander; 7 Adrian Mulcahy; 8 Patrick Waterton; 9 Chris Woolford; 10 David Evans; 11 Stuart Biscomb; 12 Ryan Kelsey; 13 Michael Butterfield. Subs (all used): 14 Tom Carroll; 15 Jordan Ratcliffe; 16 Ian Hoult; 17 Lee Starbuck.
Tries: Biscomb (4), Woolford (15), Mulcahy (39, 43), Hodgson (57, 72); **Goals:** Mulcahy 5/8.
Rugby Leaguer & League Express Men of the Match: *Raiders:* Carlos Sanchez; *Knights:* Adrian Mulcahy.
Half-time: 4-16; **Referee:** John McMullen; **Attendance:** 1,200.

WATH BROW HORNETS 4 NEWCASTLE THUNDER 26

HORNETS: 1 Jamie Devine; 2 Gregg Dawson; 3 Luke Davidson; 4 Peter Caddy; 5 Scott Pink; 6 Karl Dixon; 7 Cole Walker-Taylor; 8 Richard Huby; 9 Lewis McCarron; 15 James Dixon; 11 Callum Farrer; 12 James McClennan; 13 Charlie Thomlinson. Subs (all used): 14 Ryan Doran; 20 Jamie Sharpe; 16 Liam Martin; 22 Ben Agnew.
Try: K Dixon (1); **Goals:** Caddy 0/1.
THUNDER: 7 Jordan Meads; 21 Lee Mapals; 3 Jason Tali; 4 Joe Brown; 5 Tom Capper; 6 Matty Beharrell; 23 Benn Hardcastle; 8 Matt Barron; 14 Paul Stamp; 15 Lee Fewlass; 19 Craig Boot; 12 Rhys Clarke; 9 Dayne Craig. Subs (all used): 1 Louis Sheriff; 18 Josh Stoker; 16 Francis Welsh; 25 Evan Simons.
Tries: Meads (3), Hardcastle (21), Tali (27, 60), Beharrell (38); **Goals:** Hardcastle 3/5.
Rugby Leaguer & League Express Men of the Match: *Hornets:* Karl Dixon; *Thunder:* Jason Tali.
Penalty count: 5-11; **Half-time:** 4-20; **Referee:** Warren Turley; **Attendance:** 400.

LEIGH MINERS RANGERS 32 WEST HULL 28

MINERS RANGERS: 1 Johnny Youds; 2 Harry Gagen; 3 Adam Thomason; 4 Bradley Hargreaves; 5 Haydn Skinkis; 6 Tony Doyle; 7 Scott O'Brien; 8 Matt Astley; 9 Danny Jones; 10 Darryl Kay; 11 Tommy Parkinson; 12 Ellis Grimes; 13 Connor Ratcliffe. Subs (all used): 14 Shaun Dowie; 15 Mick O'Boyle; 16 Martin Gray; 17 Tom Farrimond.
Tries: Youds (1), Skinkis (13, 79), Kay (20), Hargreaves (26), Doyle (39); **Goals:** Youds 4/6.
WEST HULL: 1 Brett Turner; 2 Chris Whinn; 3 Matt Plummer; 4 Callum King; 5 Dillon Price; 6 Ben Arbon; 7 Scott Partis; 8 Ash Shaw; 9 Callum Windley; 19 Aiden Morton; 11 Jamie Edwards; 12 Tom Radley; 13 Ryan Steen. Subs (all used): 14 Josh Hart; 10 Lee Roberts; 18 Ben Parker; 17 Calvin Parker.
Tries: King (30), Whinn (33, 75), Price (47), Turner (62), Arbon (66); **Goals:** Hart 2/6.
Rugby Leaguer & League Express Men of the Match: *Miners Rangers:* Scott O'Brien; *West Hull:* Ryan Steen.
Half-time: 28-10; **Referee:** Jack Smith; **Attendance:** 350.

LONDON SKOLARS 4 SWINTON LIONS 86

SKOLARS: 1 James Anthony; 2 Chris Brown; 3 Kazeem Fatouri; 4 Aaron Small; 5 James Carty; 6 Tommy Connick; 7 Vince Spurr; 13 Louis Robinson; 9 Sam Druce; 10 Dave Williams; 11 Will Lovell; 12 Anthony Cox; 22 Will Fairhurst. Subs (all used): 21 Dave Ellison; 17 Oliver Bloom; 15 Danny Burke; 16 Mike Benson.
Try: Lovell (35); **Goals:** Spurr 0/1.
LIONS: 7 Chris Atkin; 2 Shaun Robinson; 3 Stuart Littler; 22 Chris Rothwell; 1 Ritchie Hawkyard; 6 Ben White; 16 Jimmy Rowland; 8 Mike Morrison; 9 Andy Ackers; 24 Jordan James; 11 Grant Beecham; 29 Rhodri Lloyd; 23 Connor Dwyer. Subs (all used): 18 Aaron Lloyd; 13 Tommy Gallagher; 10 Ben Austin; 31 Rob Lever.
Tries: Rowland (10, 47), R Hawkyard (12), White (15, 59, 80), Atkin (19, 62), Littler (21), R Lloyd (30, 32, 73), Rothwell (40), Lever (43), Dwyer (71); **Goals:** Atkin 13/15.
Rugby Leaguer & League Express Men of the Match: *Skolars:* James Anthony; *Lions:* Jimmy Rowland.
Penalty count: 5-5; **Half-time:** 4-46; **Referee:** Adam Gill; **Attendance:** 165.

KELLS 12 ROCHDALE HORNETS 29

KELLS: 1 Dominic Wear; 2 Reece O'Neil; 3 Craig Benson; 4 Scott Lofthouse; 5 Daniel Joyce; 6 Tyrone Dalton; 7 Ross Gainford; 8 David Lowery; 9 Troy Armstrong; 10 Ross Ainley; 11 Lewis Wilson; 12 Ryan Watson; 13 Tony Burns. Subs (all used): 14 Conner Hetherington; 15 Martin O'Neil; 16 Lewis White; 17 David Ford.
Tries: Dalton (2), Joyce (48); **Goals:** Gainford 2/2.
Dismissal: Wilson (78) - fighting.
Sin bin: Lowery (77) - dissent; Ford (78) - fighting.
HORNETS: 1 Wayne English; 2 Gareth Langley; 24 Dave Hull; 4 Lee Paterson; 5 Dale Bloomfield; 6 Paul Crook; 7 Danny Yates; 10 Warren Thompson; 9 Alex McClurg; 28 Matty Hadden; 11 Jordan Case; 23 James Dandy; 13 Tony Suffolk. Subs (all used): 14 James Tilley; 17 Sam Brooks; 21 Ryan Smith; 22 Mike Ratu.
Tries: Suffolk (17), Dandy (32), Bloomfield (52), Langley (72), Case (79); **Goals:** Crook 4/5;
Field goal: Yates (77).
Sin bin: Suffolk (78) - fighting.
Rugby Leaguer & League Express Men of the Match: *Kells:* Tyrone Dalton; *Hornets:* Tony Suffolk.
Penalty count: 4-15; **Half-time:** 6-12; **Referee:** Tom Grant; **Attendance:** 587
(at Recreation Ground, Whitehaven).

Sunday 8th March 2015

BARROW RAIDERS 38 KEIGHLEY COUGARS 22

RAIDERS: 1 Kris Tyson; 2 Lee Haney; 3 Chris Hankinson; 4 Max Wiper; 23 Chris Fleming; 14 Josh Ward; 7 Liam Campbell; 8 Joe Bullock; 29 Peter Lupton; 11 Liam Harrison; 16 Adam Nicholson; 12 Craig Briscoe; 21 Anthony Bate. Subs (all used): 9 Nathan Mossop; 10 Andrew Dawson; 18 Danny Jones; 19 Matt Heaton.
Tries: Haney (5), Ward (14), Wiper (16), Heaton (33), Mossop (36, 78), Campbell (62, 67);
Goals: Ward 0/4, Fleming 0/1, Hankinson 3/3.
COUGARS: 1 Jesse Sheriffe; 18 Lewis Graham; 4 Danny Lawton; 3 Daley Williams; 5 Paul White; 6 Danny Jones; 7 Paul Handforth; 12 Brendan Rawlins; 9 James Feather; 15 Neil Cherryholme; 13 David March; 17 Oliver Pursglove; 11 Ashley Lindsay. Subs (all used): 21 Sean Kelly; 8 Scott Law; 16 Jode Sheriffe; 28 Josh Lynam.
Tries: Handforth (11), Lynam (30), D March (40), Jode Sheriffe (80); **Goals:** Jones 3/4.
Rugby Leaguer & League Express Men of the Match: *Raiders:* Craig Briscoe; *Cougars:* Danny Jones.
Penalty count: 9-9; **Half-time:** 20-16; **Referee:** Gareth Hewer; **Attendance:** 929.

SOUTH WALES SCORPIONS 4 YORK CITY KNIGHTS 20

SCORPIONS: 2 Ian Newbury; 24 Craig Lewis; 3 Paul Edwards; 4 Kyle Scrivens; 21 Paul Songhurst; 6 Curtis Davies; 7 Paul Emanuelli; 8 Osian Phillips; 9 Connor Farrer; 10 Morgan Evans; 11 Mike Connor; 18 Bradley Hill; 13 Neil Dallimore. Subs (all used): 16 Scott Giles; 22 Lewis Tutt; 23 Anthony Symons; - Marcus Webb.
Try: Songhurst (37); **Goals:** Emanuelli 0/1.
CITY KNIGHTS: 1 James Haynes; 28 Kane Riley; 3 Greg Minikin; 16 Peter Aspinall; 5 Nev Morrison; 6 Jon Presley; 7 Pat Smith; 8 Mark Applegarth; 14 Kris Brining; 10 Jack Aldous; 4 Liam Cunningham; 12 Ed Smith; 21 Jack Pickles. Subs (all used): 9 Harry Carter; 15 Josh Tonks; 18 Jake Joynt; 30 Liam Richmond.
Tries: Presley (17), Riley (51), Brining (68), Aspinall (70);
Goals: Haynes 1/1, P Smith 1/3.
Rugby Leaguer & League Express Men of the Match: *Scorpions:* Neil Dallimore; *City Knights:* Mark Applegarth.
Penalty count: 8-4; **Half-time:** 4-6;
Referee: Chris Campbell; **Attendance:** 247.

HEMEL STAGS 10 OXFORD 22

STAGS: 20 Derrell Olpherts; 21 Frank Mayfield; 4 Michael Brown; 3 Jamie O'Callaghan; 16 Alex Anthony; 18 Jordan Gale; 7 Jermaine Coleman; 24 Rob Thomas; 6 James Helliwell; 10 Aidan Pritchard; 11 Barry-John Swindells; 12 Alex Ingarfield; 13 Eddie Mbaraga. Subs (all used): 8 Ryan Chester; 26 Mike Stewart; 17 Tom Sadler; 25 James Howitt.
Tries: Mbaraga (6), Helliwell (55);
Goals: Swindells 0/1, Gale 1/1.
Sin bin: Swindells (50) - use of the elbow on O'Keeffe.
OXFORD: 1 Louis Richards; 20 Ricky Hopwood; 14 Marcus Brooker; 3 Andrew Hoggins; 5 Aaron Jones-Bishop; 6 Danny Allan; 7 Andy Speake; 19 Kyle Danns; 9 Nathan Kitson; 8 Jordan Andrade; 4 Kash Watkins; 12 Ed Hayles; 10 Jonny Payne. Subs (all used): 24 Sam Blaney; 11 Josh Scott; 16 Graham O'Keeffe; 37 Adam Withington.
Tries: Hoggins (51, 75), Brooker (58), Allan (61), Jones-Bishop (80); **Goals:** Allan 1/5.
Sin bin: O'Keeffe (50) - retaliation.
Rugby Leaguer & League Express Men of the Match: *Stags:* Derrell Olpherts; *Oxford:* Danny Allan.
Penalty count: 9-11; **Half-time:** 4-0;
Referee: Andrew Sweet; **Attendance:** 125.

NORTH WALES CRUSADERS 60 WEST BANK BEARS 12

CRUSADERS: 1 Tommy Johnson; 17 Stuart Reardon; 22 Alex Thompson; 3 Christiaan Roets; 2 Scott Turner; 14 Karl Ashall; 7 Jamie Dallimore; 8 Jonny Walker; 9 Callum Wright; 16 Joe Burke; 11 Jono Smith; 12 Stephen Wild; 13 Gary Middlehurst. Subs (all used): 21 Ian Mort; 4 Matt Reid; 10 Ryan Duffy; 20 Elliott Davies.
Tries: Thompson (8), Smith (13), Dallimore (23), Turner (26), Johnson (29, 33), Davies (39), Ashall (41), Mort (51), Burke (77); **Goals:** Johnson 8/8, Turner 2/2.
Sin bin: Thompson (46) - fighting.
BEARS: 1 Greg Pickilingi; 2 Keiron Butterworth; 3 Brendan Kavanagh; 4 David Jones; 5 Danny Stapleton; 6 Tommy Arrowsmith; 7 Jamie Durbin; 8 Shaun McDermott; 9 Steve McDermott; 10 Ryan Bates; 11 Danny Yates; 12 Lloyd Hankin; 13 Ryan Millington. Subs (all used): 14 Eddie McAdam; 15 Gregg Forbes; 16 Josh Simms; 17 Jack Murphy.
Tries: Simms (43), Durbin (47); **Goals:** Arrowsmith 2/2.
Sin bin: McAdam (46) - fighting.
Rugby Leaguer & League Express Men of the Match: *Crusaders:* Callum Wright; *Bears:* Jamie Durbin.
Penalty count: 7-8; **Half-time:** 42-0;
Referee: Dave Merrick; **Attendance:** 523.

GLOUCESTERSHIRE ALL GOLDS 66 SKIRLAUGH 4

ALL GOLDS: 1 Phil Cowburn; 4 Callum Mulkeen; 3 Lewis Reece; 2 Scott Claridge; 28 Ryan Pywell; 20 Courtney Davies; 7 Matt Bradley; 10 Izaak Duffy; 9 Steve Parry; 8 Oliver Purslow; 30 Emmerson Whittel; 16 Ash Haynes; 13 Chris Vitalini. Subs (all used): 6 Toby Topham; 18 Jamie Crowther; 14 Joe McClean; 34 Nathan Rainer.
Tries: Cowburn (7), Claridge (10, 48), Parry (13, 63, 71), Davies (18, 25, 43), Topham (35), Pywell (53), Purslow (79); **Goals:** Bradley 7/9, Cowburn 2/3.
SKIRLAUGH: 1 Kieren Jones; 2 Tom Saltmar; 3 Matty Bower; 4 Stuart Smith; 5 Mike Johnson; 6 James Higginbotham; 7 Carl Puckering; 8 Kane Larvin; 9 Tommy Harrison; 10 Luke Thompson; 11 Connor Myers; 12 Scott Mountain; 13 Chris Brown. Subs (all used): 14 John Gay; 15 Marc Smith; 16 Shaun Painter; 17 Jed Carter.
Try: Saltmar (40); **Goals:** Puckering 0/1.
Rugby Leaguer & League Express Men of the Match: *All Golds:* Courtney Davies; *Skirlaugh:* Tom Saltmar.
Penalty count: 3-6; **Half-time:** 34-4;
Referee: Jon Roberts; **Attendance:** 87.

OLDHAM 46 COVENTRY BEARS 6

OLDHAM: 1 Steven Nield; 2 Adam Clay; 4 Jack Holmes; 9 Sam Gee; 5 Jarrod Ward; 6 Lewis Palfrey; 7 Steve Roper; 10 Adam Neal; 15 Gareth Owen; 8 Phil Joy; 11 Josh Crowley; 17 George Tyson; 13 Liam Thompson. Subs (all used): 16 Kenny Hughes; 14 Adam Files; 19 Michael Ward; 27 Mick Learmonth.
Tries: Gee (18), J Ward (24), Tyson (28), Thompson (31), M Ward (37), Clay (50, 67), Learmonth (53), Holmes (64); **Goals:** Palfrey 5/9.
BEARS: 6 Billy Sheen; 20 Jamahl Hunte; 21 Stephen Coleman; 4 Eddie Medforth; 1 Troy Brophy; 13 Simon Phillips; 18 Dan Poulton; 27 James Geurtjens; 9 Alex Brown; 10 John Aldred; 29 Liam Thompson; 12 Chris Barratt; 17 Alex Calvert. Subs (all used): 8 Ben Tyers; 26 Matt Cooper; 39 Rob Meadows; 3 Nick Taylor.
Try: Cooper (44); **Goals:** Coleman 1/1.
Rugby Leaguer & League Express Men of the Match: *Oldham:* Michael Ward; *Bears:* Billy Sheen.
Penalty count: 9-4; **Half-time:** 26-0;
Referee: Tom Crashley; **Attendance:** 256.

ROUND 4

Friday 20th March 2015

FEATHERSTONE LIONS 8 YORK CITY KNIGHTS 58

LIONS: 1 Ian Jackson; 5 Kieran Redfearn; 4 Ricky Williams; 3 Reece Dyas; 2 Jake Perkins; 6 Sam Candlin; 7 Lewis Young; 8 Scott Wilson; 9 Dean Gamble; 16 Adam Curtis; 21 Danny Glassell; 14 Matty Johnson; 13 Brendan Gibbins. Subs (all used): 20 Richard Frankland; 15 Adam Hepworth; 10 Craig Barker; 17 Sam Millard.
Tries: Redfearn (56), Candlin (75); **Goals:** Jackson 0/2.
Sin bin: Gamble (26) - late challenge.
CITY KNIGHTS: 1 James Haynes; 19 Jamel Chisholm; 3 Greg Minikin; 4 Liam Cunningham; 5 Nev Morrison; 6 Jon Presley; 7 Pat Smith; 8 Mark Applegarth; 14 Kris Brining; 10 Jack Aldous; 16 Peter Aspinall; 12 Ed Smith; 11 Ryan Mallinder. Subs (all used): 9 Harry Carter; 13 Colton Roche; 15 Josh Tonks; 21 Jack Pickles.
Tries: Brining (15, 22), Aspinall (28), Cunningham (32, 71, 80), Carter (39), E Smith (51), Haynes (69), Roche (77); **Goals:** Haynes 9/10.
Rugby Leaguer & League Express Men of the Match: *Lions:* Ian Jackson; *City Knights:* Kris Brining.
Penalty count: 5-12; **Half-time:** 0-30;
Referee: Scott Mikalauskas; **Attendance:** 1,200
(at BigFellas Stadium).

LEIGH CENTURIONS 64 LONDON BRONCOS 12

CENTURIONS: 1 Gregg McNally; 15 Jonathan Pownall; 16 Michael Platt; 4 Tom Armstrong; 5 Liam Kay; 6 Martyn Ridyard; 7 Ryan Brierley; 8 Fuifui Moimoi; 14 Sean Penkywicz; 21 Jamie Acton; 19 Kurt Haggerty; 12 Tommy Goulden; 13 Sam Barlow. Subs (all used): 9 Bob Beswick; 10 Oliver Wilkes; 20 Sam Hopkins; 29 Jake Emmitt.
Tries: Pownall (8), Barlow (16), Brierley (19, 28), Haggerty (21), Hopkins (34, 54), Armstrong (50), Kay (54), McNally (60), Moimoi (78);
Goals: Ridyard 10/11.
On report: Acton (71) - alleged dangerous challenge.
BRONCOS: 22 Oscar Thomas; 2 Rhys Williams; 3 Ben Farrar; 5 Ben Hellewell; 26 Sean Morris; 4 Wes Naiqama; 19 Joe Keyes; 18 Jon Wallace; 9 Ray Nasso; 23 Toby Everett; 11 Daniel Harrison; 15 Matt Garside; 21 Joel Wickes. Subs (all used): 20 Iliess Macani; 29 Jamie Thackray; 25 Harvey Burnett; 17 Erjon Dollapi.
Tries: Nasso (43), Harrison (70); **Goals:** Naiqama 2/2.

Rugby Leaguer & League Express Men of the Match: *Centurions:* Ryan Brierley; *Broncos:* Jamie Thackray.
Penalty count: 5-6; **Half-time:** 36-0;
Referee: Michael Woodhead; **Attendance:** 2,448.

Saturday 21st March 2015

NORMANTON KNIGHTS 6 BATLEY BULLDOGS 78

KNIGHTS: 1 Jonathan Hodgson; 2 Aaron Butterfield; 3 Steven Lewis; 4 Connor Taylor; 5 Lee Hammond; 6 Thomas Alexander; 7 Adrian Mulcahy; 8 Patrick Waterton; 9 Chris Woolford; 10 David Evans; 11 Ryan Kelsey; 12 Stuart Biscomb; 13 Michael Butterfield. Subs (all used): 14 Tom Carroll; 15 Luke Molloy; 16 Ian Hoult; 17 Jordan Ratcliffe.
Try: Hodgson (25); **Goals:** Mulcahy 1/1.
BULLDOGS: 3 Shaun Ainscough; 2 Wayne Reittie; 23 Brad Day; 24 Brad Hey; 5 Johnny Campbell; 6 Cain Southernwood; 9 Anthony Nicholson; 8 Keegan Hirst; 14 Alistair Leak; 21 James Brown; 11 Alex Bretherton; 25 Tom Thackray; 17 Joe Chandler. Subs (all used): 12 Sam Scott; 15 Adam Gledhill; 18 Tom Lillycrop; 26 Matty Fozard.
Tries: Thackray (8), Reittie (17), Day (21), Southernwood (28), Nicholson (33, 66), Lillycrop (46), Fozard (53, 59, 63), Hey (70), Campbell (72, 78), Hirst (74); **Goals:** Southernwood 11/14.
Rugby Leaguer & League Express Men of the Match: *Knights:* Thomas Alexander; *Bulldogs:* Matty Fozard.
Penalty count: 7-9; **Half-time:** 6-28; **Referee:** Adam Gill; **Attendance:** 868 *(at Belle Vue, Wakefield).*

LEIGH MINERS RANGERS 32 OXFORD 6

MINERS RANGERS: 1 Johnny Youds; 2 Haydn Skinkis; 3 Mick O'Boyle; 4 Adam Thomason; 5 Harry Gagen; 6 Shaun Dowie; 7 Scott O'Brien; 8 Matt Astley; 9 Danny Jones; 10 Darryl Kay; 11 Tommy Parkinson; 12 Ellis Grimes; 13 Connor Ratcliffe. Subs (all used): 14 Tony Doyle; 15 Martin Gray; 16 Tom Farrimond; 18 Chris Bowers.
Tries: Grimes (21), O'Brien (26), O'Boyle (37), Gagen (53), Ratcliffe (61), Thomason (73);
Goals: Youds 4/6.
OXFORD: 1 Louis Richards; 28 Jonny Morris; 14 Marcus Brooker; 3 Andrew Hoggins; 5 Aaron Jones-Bishop; 6 Danny Allan; 7 Andy Speake; 8 Jordan Andrade; 9 Nathan Kitson; 19 Kyle Danns; 11 Josh Scott; 12 Ed Hayles; 10 Jonny Payne. Subs (all used): 15 Wes Newton; 16 Graham O'Keeffe; 23 Tom Davies; 25 Luke Evans.
Try: Payne (9); **Goals:** Allan 1/1.
Rugby Leaguer & League Express Men of the Match: *Miners Rangers:* Tommy Parkinson; *Oxford:* Andrew Hoggins.
Penalty count: 5-4; **Half-time:** 16-6;
Referee: Chris Campbell; **Attendance:** 787 *(at Leigh Sports Village).*

WHITEHAVEN 12 FEATHERSTONE ROVERS 36

WHITEHAVEN: 1 Richard Lepori; 5 Jordan Burns; 16 Connor Holliday; 3 Jessie Joe Parker; 2 Craig Calvert; 19 John-Paul Brocklebank; 6 Brett Seymour; 18 Steve Fox; 14 Thomas Coyle; 13 Tyla Hepi; 11 Dave Allen; 4 Scott McAvoy; 25 Dion Aiye. Subs (all used): 8 Ben Davies; 12 Steve Bannister; 9 James Newton; 20 James Robinson.
Tries: Parker (13), Aiye (29); **Goals:** Brocklebank 2/3.
ROVERS: 2 Will Sharp; 26 Kyran Johnson; 3 Nathan Chappell; 21 Jy Hitchcox; 5 Ben Blackmore; 6 Paul Sykes; 31 Remy Marginet; 8 Jordan Baldwinson; 14 Sam Irwin; 16 Andrew Bostock; 18 Jamie Cording; 19 Alex Foster; 13 Tim Spears. Subs (all used): 28 Will Milner; 17 Matt James; 27 Jack Ormondroyd; 24 Mason Tonks.
Tries: Bostock (9), Sharp (23, 39), Blackmore (45), Milner (66), James (70), Chappell (78);
Goals: Sykes 3/5, Marginet 1/2.
Rugby Leaguer & League Express Men of the Match: *Whitehaven:* Dion Aiye; *Rovers:* Paul Sykes.
Penalty count: 12-13; **Half-time:** 12-16;
Referee: Chris Kendall; **Attendance:** 525.

Sunday 22nd March 2015

BARROW RAIDERS 16 HALIFAX 56

RAIDERS: 1 Kris Tyson; 5 Kyle Dolan; 3 Chris Hankinson; 4 Max Wiper; 27 Cameron Pitman; 29 Peter Lupton; 14 Josh Ward; 8 Joe Bullock; 9 Nathan Mossop; 18 Danny Jones; 30 Bradd Crellin; 24 Andy Litherland; 11 Liam Harrison. Subs (all used): 6 Brad Marwood; 21 Anthony Bate; 16 Adam Nicholson; 19 Matt Heaton.
Tries: Marwood (43), Pitman (57), Wiper (62);
Goals: Ward 2/3.
HALIFAX: 20 James Saltonstall; 5 Alex Brown; 4 Ben Heaton; 3 Steve Tyrer; 23 Gareth Potts; 7 Ben Johnston; 6 Scott Murrell; 16 Richard Moore; 9 Ben Kaye; 10 Luke Ambler; 27 Ross Divorty; 15 Adam Robinson; 8 Adam Tangata. Subs (all used): 12 Andy Bracek; 13 Jack Spencer; 19 Keith Holden; 26 Chris Taylor.
Tries: Brown (10), Heaton (12), Divorty (23), Tangata (26), Saltonstall (28, 77), Johnston (34), Tyrer (40), Taylor (47), Potts (74); **Goals:** Tyrer 8/10.
Rugby Leaguer & League Express Men of the Match: *Raiders:* Brad Marwood; *Halifax:* Ben Johnston.
Penalty count: 4-9; **Half-time:** 0-40;
Referee: Tom Crashley; **Attendance:** 956.

NORTH WALES CRUSADERS 40 DONCASTER 12

CRUSADERS: 1 Tommy Johnson; 5 Rob Massam; 3 Christiaan Roets; 22 Alex Thompson; 17 Stuart Reardon; 26 Craig White; 7 Jamie Dallimore; 8 Jonny Walker; 14 Karl Ashall; 16 Joe Burke; 11 Jono Smith; 12 Stephen Wild; 13 Gary Middlehurst. Subs (all used): 9 Callum Wright; 23 Mark Hobson; 10 Ryan Duffy; 20 Elliott Davies.
Tries: Thompson (15), Reardon (28), Johnson (36), Massam (49, 58, 62, 65); **Goals:** Johnson 6/8.
DONCASTER: 19 Lee Waterman; 1 Dave Scott; 17 Liam Welham; 18 Shaun Leaf; 25 Mitch Vincent; 6 Paul Cooke; 7 Richard Wilkinson; 10 Craig Robinson; 9 Kyle Kesik; 16 Brett Waller; 23 Jack Walton; 12 Steve Snitch; 13 Mike Emmett. Subs (all used): 20 Ryan Wilson; 11 Michael Kelly; 15 Mitch Clark; 8 Matt Carbutt.
Tries: Walton (10, 43); **Goals:** Scott 2/2.
Rugby Leaguer & League Express Men of the Match: *Crusaders:* Rob Massam; *Doncaster:* Jack Walton.
Penalty count: 11-5; **Half-time:** 18-6;
Referee: Warren Turley; **Attendance:** 416.

BRADFORD BULLS 74 WORKINGTON TOWN 6

BULLS: 1 Jake Mullaney; 5 Danny Williams; 3 Adrian Purtell; 20 Adam Henry; 27 Ryan Shaw; 6 Lee Gaskell; 7 Harry Siejka; 8 Paul Clough; 9 Adam O'Brien; 10 Adam Sidlow; 24 Lucas Walshaw; 11 Tom Olbison; 14 Jay Pitts. Subs (all used): 12 Dale Ferguson; 28 Samir Tahraoui; 31 Epalahame Lauaki; 2 Etuate Uaisele.
Tries: Purtell (13, 46, 61), Tahraoui (32, 36), Sidlow (38), Henry (40), Gaskell (50), Shaw (57, 77), Williams (69), Pitts (72), Siejka (75);
Goals: Shaw 11/13.
TOWN: 1 Jack Murphy; 24 Theerapol Ritson; 4 Perry Whiteley; 12 Jarrad Stack; 5 Brett Carter; 30 Jamie Doran; 7 Carl Forber; 19 Tom Walker; 9 Graeme Mattinson; 25 Steve Scholey; 11 Brett Phillips; 16 Kurt Horton; 15 Karl Olstrum. Subs (all used): 17 Latu Fifita; 13 Liam McAvoy; 20 Nathan Lucock; 21 James Duerden.
Try: Duerden (25); **Goals:** Forber 1/1.
Rugby Leaguer & League Express Men of the Match: *Bulls:* Lee Gaskell; *Town:* Carl Forber.
Penalty count: 6-3; **Half-time:** 28-6;
Referee: Chris Leatherbarrow; **Attendance:** 2,412.

DEWSBURY RAMS 28 NEWCASTLE THUNDER 18

RAMS: 39 Will Forsyth; 2 Dale Morton; 15 Jason Crookes; 19 Callan Beckett; 18 Dalton Grant; 13 Aaron Brown; 23 Tom Hemingway; 24 Byron Smith; 35 James Delaney; 17 Matthew Haggarty; 11 Rob Spicer; 12 Scott Hale; 25 Joel Farrell. Subs (all used): 14 Ryan Wright; 29 Joe McLocklan; 27 Jason Muranka; 32 Makali Aizue.
Tries: Hemingway (10), Grant (20), Brown (49), Hale (61, 74); **Goals:** Hemingway 4/7.
THUNDER: 7 Jordan Meads; 21 Lee Mapals; 3 Jason Tali; 4 Joe Brown; 5 Tom Capper; 6 Matty Beharrell; 23 Benn Hardcastle; 15 Lee Fewlass; 13 Charlie Wabo; 10 Mark Mexico; 11 Jason Payne; 12 Rhys Clarke; 9 Dayne Craig. Subs (all used): 14 Paul Stamp; 18 Josh Stoker; 1 Louis Sheriff; 16 Francis Welsh.
Tries: Stamp (28), Capper (32), Hardcastle (70);
Goals: Hardcastle 3/4.
Rugby Leaguer & League Express Men of the Match: *Rams:* Joel Farrell; *Thunder:* Mark Mexico.
Penalty count: 8-5; **Half-time:** 10-10;
Referee: Dave Merrick; **Attendance:** 703.

GLOUCESTERSHIRE ALL GOLDS 10 HUNSLET HAWKS 28

ALL GOLDS: 20 Courtney Davies; 4 Callum Mulkeen; 3 Lewis Reece; 1 Phil Cowburn; 28 Ryan Pywell; 6 Toby Topham; 7 Matt Bradley; 8 Oliver Purslow; 9 Steve Parry; 29 Joel Thomas; 30 Emmerson Whittel; 18 Jamie Crowther; 13 Chris Vitalini. Subs (all used): 15 Casey Canterbury; 14 Joe McClean; 10 Izaak Duffy; 34 Nathan Rainer.
Tries: Parry (23), McClean (42); **Goals:** Bradley 1/2.
HAWKS: 26 Marcus Elliott; 2 Mo Agoro; 28 Mufaro Mvududu; 23 Elliott Cosgrove; 24 Richie Barnett; 6 Simon Brown; 7 Danny Ansell; 19 Brad Brennan; 30 George Flanagan; 8 Michael Haley; 18 Brooke Broughton; 21 Ryan Backhouse; 15 Liam Mackay. Subs (all used): 12 Aaron Lyons; 17 Mark Castle; 3 Lee Brickwood; 4 Danny Maun.
Tries: Barnett (14), Brennan (17), Cosgrove (46), Agoro (50, 58, 68); **Goals:** Ansell 2/6, Brown 0/1.
Rugby Leaguer & League Express Men of the Match: *All Golds:* Lewis Reece; *Hawks:* Mo Agoro.
Penalty count: 7-6; **Half-time:** 4-12;
Referee: Jon Roberts; **Attendance:** 137.

SHEFFIELD EAGLES 44 OLDHAM 20

EAGLES: 1 Quentin Laulu-Togagae; 2 Scott Turner; 3 Menzie Yere; 4 Sam Smeaton; 23 Rob Worrincy; 13 Pat Walker; 7 Dominic Brambani; 8 Eddie Battye; 24 Keal Carlile; 22 Tony Tonks; 11 Michael Knowles; 12 Duane Straugheir; 15 John Davies. Subs (all used): 17 Steve Thorpe; 26 Greg Burns; 18 Ben Musolino; 16 Jamie Langley.
Tries: Yere (2), Turner (9), Knowles (28), Straugheir (38), Laulu-Togagae (40), Worrincy (48), Thorpe (54, 74);
Goals: Walker 6/8.
OLDHAM: 4 Jack Holmes; 2 Adam Clay; 9 Sam Gee; 3 Jonathan Ford; 5 Jarrod Ward; 6 Lewis Palfrey; 7 Steve Roper; 10 Adam Neal; 15 Gareth Owen; 8 Phil Joy; 17 George Tyson; 12 Danny Langtree; 13 Liam Thompson. Subs (all used): 14 Adam Files; 16 Kenny Hughes; 27 Mick Learmonth; 11 Josh Crowley.
Tries: Learmonth (32), Clay (61), Crowley (67, 77);
Goals: Palfrey 1/2, Roper 1/2.
Rugby Leaguer & League Express Men of the Match: *Eagles:* Menzie Yere; *Oldham:* Josh Crowley.
Penalty count: 5-6; **Half-time:** 30-6;
Referee: Andrew Sweet; **Attendance:** 484 *(at Keepmoat Stadium, Doncaster).*

SWINTON LIONS 30 ROCHDALE HORNETS 12

LIONS: 7 Chris Atkin; 2 Shaun Robinson; 3 Stuart Littler; 22 Chris Rothwell; 1 Ritchie Hawkyard; 6 Ben White; 16 Jimmy Rowland; 8 Mike Morrison; 9 Andy Ackers; 24 Jordan James; 11 Grant Beecham; 29 Rhodri Lloyd; 23 Connor Dwyer. Subs (all used): 18 Aaron Lloyd; 13 Tommy Gallagher; 10 Ben Austin; 31 Rob Lever.
Tries: Rothwell (20), Beecham (25, 40), Atkin (48, 77), R Hawkyard (75); **Goals:** Atkin 0/3, Rowland 3/4.
HORNETS: 21 Ryan Smith; 2 Gareth Langley; 24 Dave Hull; 4 Lee Paterson; 5 Dale Bloomfield; 6 Paul Crook; 7 Danny Yates; 17 Sam Brooks; 18 Dean Mignacca; 10 Warren Thompson; 19 Danny Bridge; 11 Jordan Case; 14 James Tilley. Subs (all used): 25 Richard Beaumont; 28 Matty Hadden; 3 Dave Llewellyn; 23 James Dandy.
Tries: Case (11), Tilley (58); **Goals:** Crook 2/3.
Rugby Leaguer & League Express Men of the Match: *Lions:* Andy Ackers; *Hornets:* Ryan Smith.
Penalty count: 12-7; **Half-time:** 12-6;
Referee: Jamie Bloem; **Attendance:** 502.

ROUND 5

Friday 17th April 2015

WAKEFIELD TRINITY WILDCATS 44 HALIFAX 16

WILDCATS: 1 Craig Hall; 5 Richard Owen; 15 Matt Ryan; 28 Joe Arundel; 2 Chris Riley; 6 Jacob Miller; 7 Tim Smith; 8 Nick Scruton; 9 Paul McShane; 16 Mickael Simon; 11 Ali Lauitiiti; 12 Danny Kirmond (C); 13 Danny Washbrook. Subs (all used): 18 Daniel Smith; 19 Jon Molloy; 25 Ian Kirke (D); 27 Kyle Trout.
Tries: Owen (11, 20), D Smith (37), Riley (49), Hall (63), Washbrook (69), Kirke (72, 75);
Goals: Hall 6/8, T Smith 0/1.
HALIFAX: 20 James Saltonstall; 5 Alex Brown; 4 Ben Heaton; 24 Rikki Sheriffe; 23 Gareth Potts; 26 Chris Taylor; 6 Scott Murrell; 17 Mitch Cahalane; 9 Ben Kaye; 10 Luke Ambler; 27 Ross Divorty; 11 Dane Manning; 16 Richard Moore. Subs (all used): 8 Adam Tangata; 12 Andy Bracek; 13 Jack Spencer; 21 Ryan Maneely.
Tries: Saltonstall (17), Heaton (30), Potts (46);
Goals: Murrell 2/3.
Rugby Leaguer & League Express Men of the Match: *Wildcats:* Craig Hall; *Halifax:* Mitch Cahalane.
Penalty count: 3-3; **Half-time:** 18-10;
Referee: Joe Cobb; **Attendance:** 2,062.

Saturday 18th April 2015

LEIGH CENTURIONS 22 SALFORD RED DEVILS 18

CENTURIONS: 1 Gregg McNally; 15 Jonathan Pownall; 16 Michael Platt; 4 Tom Armstrong; 5 Liam Kay; 6 Martyn Ridyard; 7 Ryan Brierley; 18 Tom Spencer; 9 Bob Beswick; 29 Jake Emmitt; 22 Andrew Dixon; 12 Tommy Goulden; 13 Sam Barlow. Subs: 20 Sam Hopkins; 23 Martin Aspinwall; 26 Gareth Hock; 3 Greg Worthington (not used).
Tries: Goulden (25), McNally (27), Brierley (65), Pownall (68); **Goals:** Ridyard 3/4.
RED DEVILS: 19 Niall Evalds; 2 Ben Jones-Bishop; 18 Mason Caton-Brown; 4 Junior Sa'u; 5 Greg Johnson; 14 Theo Fages; 7 Michael Dobson; 8 Adrian Morley; 33 Wayne Godwin (D2); 16 Scott Taylor; 11 Harrison Hansen (C); 31 Cory Paterson; 26 Carl Forster. Subs (all used): 15 Darrell Griffin; 25 George Griffin (D); 10 Lama Tasi; 24 Liam Hood.
Tries: Fages (9), Evalds (34, 45);
Goals: Dobson 1/1, Paterson 2/2.
On report:
Paterson (1) - alleged late challenge on McNally.
Rugby Leaguer & League Express Men of the Match: *Centurions:* Jake Emmitt; *Red Devils:* Theo Fages.
Penalty count: 5-7; **Half-time:** 12-12;
Referee: Phil Bentham; **Attendance:** 6,358.

Sunday 19th April 2015

LEIGH MINERS RANGERS 14 YORK CITY KNIGHTS 44

MINERS RANGERS: 1 Johnny Youds; 2 Harry Gagen; 3 Bradley Hargreaves; 4 Adam Thomason; 5 Jack Probert; 6 Shaun Dowie; 7 Scott O'Brien; 8 Matt Astley; 9 Danny Jones; 10 Darryl Kay; 11 Danny Jackson; 12 Tommy Parkinson; 13 Connor Ratcliffe. Subs (all used): 14 Tony Doyle; 15 Mick O'Boyle; 16 Ellis Grimes; 17 Martin Gray.
Tries: Gagen (28), O'Brien (32), Thomason (70);
Goals: Youds 1/3.
CITY KNIGHTS: 2 Ben Dent; 25 Adam Dent; 3 Greg Minikin; 4 Liam Cunningham; 5 Nev Morrison; 6 Jon Presley; 7 Pat Smith; 8 Mark Applegarth; 14 Kris Brining; 10 Jack Aldous; 15 Josh Tonks; 12 Ed Smith; 11 Ryan Mallinder. Subs (all used): 13 Colton Roche; 16 Peter Aspinall; 21 Jack Pickles; 22 Jack Iley.
Tries: B Dent (12), Morrison (15), Brining (20, 37, 50), Presley (39), A Dent (63), E Smith (74);
Goals: B Dent 6/8.
Rugby Leaguer & League Express Men of the Match: *Miners Rangers:* Shaun Dowie; *City Knights:* Kris Brining.
Penalty count: 8-8; **Half-time:** 10-30;
Referee: Gareth Hewer; **Attendance:** 1,191 *(at Leigh Sports Village).*

NORTH WALES CRUSADERS 12 FEATHERSTONE ROVERS 38

CRUSADERS: 1 Tommy Johnson; 5 Rob Massam; 3 Christiaan Roets; 17 Stuart Reardon; 21 Ian Mort; 26 Craig White; 7 Jamie Dallimore; 8 Jonny Walker; 9 Callum Wright; 16 Joe Burke; 23 Mark Hobson; 12 Stephen Wild; 13 Gary Middlehurst. Subs (all used): 10 Ryan Duffy; 14 Karl Ashall; 20 Elliott Davies; 27 Andrew Joy.
Tries: Dallimore (15), Johnson (43); **Goals:** Johnson 2/2.

ROVERS: 21 Jy Hitchcox; 5 Ben Blackmore; 1 Ian Hardman; 4 Thomas Minns; 2 Will Sharp; 6 Paul Sykes; 7 Gareth Moore; 8 Jordan Baldwinson; 9 Andy Ellis; 17 Matt James; 12 Reni Maitua; 19 Alex Foster; 13 Tim Spears. Subs (all used): 15 Jack Bussey; 16 Andrew Bostock; 24 Mason Tonks; 31 Remy Marginet.
Tries: Moore (6), Ellis (8), Sharp (23), Blackmore (54, 65), Maitua (61), Foster (78);
Goals: Moore 5/7.
Rugby Leaguer & League Express Men of the Match: *Crusaders:* Gary Middlehurst; *Rovers:* Ian Hardman.
Penalty count: 6-5; **Half-time:** 6-16;
Referee: Dave Merrick; **Attendance:** 617.

BATLEY BULLDOGS 46 SWINTON LIONS 14

BULLDOGS: 27 Jacob Morgan; 2 Wayne Reittie; 20 Shaun Squires; 24 Brad Hey; 3 Shaun Ainscough; 6 Cain Southernwood; 14 Alistair Leak; 8 Keegan Hirst; 13 Luke Blake; 16 Sean Hesketh; 12 Sam Scott; 23 Brad Day; 17 Joe Chandler. Subs (all used): 26 Matty Fozard; 15 Adam Gledhill; 21 James Brown; 25 Tom Thackray.
Tries: Reittie (8), Day (13), Southernwood (18), Ainscough (26, 57), Morgan (42), Thackray (62, 72), Leak (74); **Goals:** Southernwood 5/9.
LIONS: 1 Ritchie Hawkyard; 2 Shaun Robinson; 3 Stuart Littler; 22 Chris Rothwell; 5 Alex Hurst; 7 Chris Atkin; 16 Jimmy Rowland; 8 Mike Morrison; 9 Andy Ackers; 19 Jack Morrison; 11 Grant Beecham; 29 Matt Gardner; 31 Rob Lever. Subs (all used): 12 Darren Hawkyard; 13 Tommy Gallagher; 30 Josh Barlow; 18 Aaron Lloyd.
Tries: Rothwell (3), Littler (30), Robinson (68);
Goals: Atkin 1/3.
Sin bin: D Hawkyard (52) - high tackle.
Rugby Leaguer & League Express Men of the Match: *Bulldogs:* Cain Southernwood; *Lions:* Ritchie Hawkyard.
Penalty count: 10-7; **Half-time:** 20-8;
Referee: Chris Kendall; **Attendance:** 443.

BRADFORD BULLS 30 HULL KINGSTON ROVERS 50

BULLS: 27 Ryan Shaw; 2 Etuate Uaisele; 22 Chev Walker; 20 Adam Henry; 19 Chris Ulugia; 6 Lee Gaskell; 13 Danny Addy; 8 Paul Clough; 9 Adam O'Brien; 10 Adam Sidlow; 11 Tom Olbison; 12 Dale Ferguson; 14 Jay Pitts. Subs (all used): 15 Daniel Fleming; 17 Jean-Philippe Baile; 23 Alex Mellor; 24 Lucas Walshaw.
Tries: O'Brien (6), Ferguson (12), Addy (42), Gaskell (58), Walshaw (62); **Goals:** Shaw 5/5.
Sin bin: Sidlow (39) - fighting.
ROVERS: 1 Kieran Dixon; 4 Josh Mantellato; 19 Kris Welham; 18 Liam Salter; 5 Ken Sio; 23 Terry Campese (C); 7 Albert Kelly; 8 Adam Walker; 31 Shaun Lunt; 17 Greg Burke; 11 Kevin Larroyer; 12 Graeme Horne; 13 Tyrone McCarthy. Subs (all used): 2 Ben Cockayne; 15 James Donaldson; 21 Aaron Ollett; 24 John Boudebza.
Tries: Mantellato (18, 65, 67, 72), Welham (29), Kelly (34), Horne (45), Larroyer (55), Boudebza (80);
Goals: Mantellato 7/9.
Sin bin: Walker (39) - fighting.
Rugby Leaguer & League Express Men of the Match: *Bulls:* Adam O'Brien; *Rovers:* Josh Mantellato.
Penalty count: 8-5; **Half-time:** 12-18;
Referee: Matthew Thomason; **Attendance:** 4,538.

HUNSLET HAWKS 16 DEWSBURY RAMS 31

HAWKS: 1 Jimmy Watson; 33 James Duckworth; 34 Luke Briscoe; 4 Danny Maun; 24 Richie Barnett; 6 Simon Brown; 31 Andy Kain; 35 Rob Mulhern; 9 Jack Lee; 19 Brad Brennan; 11 Callum Casey; 44 Charlie Martin; 15 Liam Mackay. Subs (all used): 30 George Flanagan; 28 Mufaro Mvududu; 8 Michael Haley; 12 Aaron Lyons.
Tries: Mackay (20), Briscoe (64), Martin (70);
Goals: Brown 2/4.
RAMS: 31 Kieran Hyde; 2 Dale Morton; 15 Jason Crookes; 19 Callan Beckett; 18 Dalton Grant; 13 Aaron Brown; 7 Anthony Thackeray; 33 Paul Jackson; 6 Matty Wildie; 17 Matthew Haggarty; 11 Rob Spicer; 12 Scott Hale; 34 Luke Adamson. Subs (all used): 32 Makali Aizue; 24 Byron Smith; 25 Joel Farrell; 35 James Delaney.
Tries: Haggarty (5), J Delaney (34), Crookes (50), Aizue (53), Brown (80); **Goals:** Hyde 5/6;
Field goal: Hyde (71).
Rugby Leaguer & League Express Men of the Match: *Hawks:* Jimmy Watson; *Rams:* Kieran Hyde.
Penalty count: 6-6; **Half-time:** 6-14;
Referee: Chris Leatherbarrow; **Attendance:** 536.

SHEFFIELD EAGLES 12 HULL FC 34

EAGLES: 1 Quentin Laulu-Togagae; 2 Scott Turner; 3 Menzie Yere; 4 Sam Smeaton; 23 Rob Worrincy; 6 Kyle Briggs; 19 Cory Aston; 8 Eddie Battye; 24 Keal Carlile; 17 Steve Thorpe; 15 John Davies; 16 Jamie Langley; 5 Misi Taulapapa. Subs (all used): 7 Dominic Brambani; 20 Jack Blagbrough; 18 Ben Musolino; 10 Mitchell Stringer.
Tries: Aston (55), Yere (59); **Goals:** Brambani 2/2.
HULL: 1 Jamie Shaul; 2 Tom Lineham; 19 Steve Michaels; 5 Fetuli Talanoa; 20 Curtis Naughton; 6 Leon Pryce; 32 Jordan Rankin; 8 Mickey Paea; 9 Danny Houghton (C); 10 Liam Watts; 3 Setaimata Sa; 12 Mark Minichiello; 16 Jordan Thompson. Subs (all used): 14 Iafeta Palea'aesina; 30 Bobby Tyson-Wilson (D); 4 Kirk Yeaman; 34 Stuart Howarth.
Tries: Minichiello (19), Paea (22), Lineham (26), Shaul (34), Yeaman (70), Rankin (73); **Goals:** Rankin 5/6.
Rugby Leaguer & League Express Men of the Match: *Eagles:* Eddie Battye; *Hull:* Jordan Thompson.
Penalty count: 5-6; **Half-time:** 0-22;
Referee: George Stokes; **Attendance:** 1,620
(at Bramall Lane).

ROUND 6

Friday 15th May 2015

DEWSBURY RAMS 10 WARRINGTON WOLVES 52

RAMS: 39 Will Forsyth; 18 Dalton Grant; 19 Callan Beckett; 40 Sam Dunn; 5 Greg Scott; 46 James Glover; 36 Brad Delaney; 17 Matthew Haggarty; 14 Ryan Wright; 24 Byron Smith; 12 Scott Hale; 16 Toby Adamson; 25 Joel Farrell. Subs (all used): 29 Joe McLocklan; 11 Rob Spicer; 10 Ryan Hepworth; 32 Makali Aizue.
Try: Farrell (31); **Goals:** B Delaney 3/3.
WOLVES: 24 Kevin Penny; 5 Joel Monaghan (C); 3 Chris Bridge; 4 Ryan Atkins; 22 Gene Ormsby; 29 Declan Patton; 7 Richard Myler; 8 Chris Hill; 25 Brad Dwyer; 10 Ashton Sims; 17 Ben Currie; 12 Ben Westwood; 13 Ben Harrison. Subs (all used): 18 James Laithwaite; 20 Gareth O'Brien; 19 Anthony England; 27 George King.
Tries: Dwyer (6), Atkins (13), Sims (16), Currie (19, 68), Patton (22), Penny (42, 45), Bridge (50), Myler (61);
Goals: Bridge 6/10.
Rugby Leaguer & League Express Men of the Match: *Rams:* Joel Farrell; *Wolves:* Brad Dwyer.
Penalty count: 11-6; **Half-time:** 8-26;
Referee: Matthew Thomason; **Attendance:** 1,771.

ST HELENS 46 YORK CITY KNIGHTS 6

SAINTS: 34 Shannon McDonnell; 2 Tom Makinson; 17 Mark Percival; 30 Matty Fleming; 5 Adam Swift; 6 Travis Burns; 12 Jon Wilkin (C); 8 Mose Masoe; 26 Lewis Charnock; 19 Greg Richards; 13 Louie McCarthy-Scarsbrook; 15 Mark Flanagan; 4 Josh Jones. Subs (all used): 10 Kyle Amor; 25 Andre Savelio; 29 Olly Davies (D); 36 Morgan Knowles (D).
Tries: Swift (3, 34, 73), Makinson (11, 29, 51, 56), Percival (39), Flanagan (67);
Goals: Burns 0/3, Makinson 3/4, Charnock 2/2.
CITY KNIGHTS: 2 Ben Dent; 25 Adam Dent; 4 Liam Cunningham; 3 Greg Minikin; 24 Tyler Craig; 6 Jon Presley; 7 Pat Smith; 8 Mark Applegarth; 9 Harry Carter; 10 Jack Aldous; 12 Ed Smith; 15 Josh Tonks; 13 Colton Roche. Subs (all used): 11 Ryan Mallinder; 21 Jack Pickles; 29 Brad Nicholson; 32 Kane Riley.
Try: Craig (77); **Goals:** B Dent 1/1.
Rugby Leaguer & League Express Men of the Match: *Saints:* Tom Makinson; *City Knights:* Greg Minikin.
Penalty count: 2-3; **Half-time:** 22-0;
Referee: Chris Leatherbarrow; **Attendance:** 3,241.

WIGAN WARRIORS 12 HULL KINGSTON ROVERS 16

WARRIORS: 20 Ryan Hampshire; 2 Josh Charnley; 11 Joel Tomkins; 4 Dan Sarginson; 5 Joe Burgess; 6 George Williams; 7 Matty Smith; 8 Dominic Crosby; 9 Michael McIlorum; 23 Lee Mossop; 12 Liam Farrell; 14 John Bateman; 13 Sean O'Loughlin (C). Subs (all used): 16 Sam Powell; 24 Taulima Tautai; 25 Larne Patrick; 28 Ryan Sutton.
Tries: J Tomkins (37), Burgess (64); **Goals:** Smith 2/2.
ROVERS: 2 Ben Cockayne; 1 Kieran Dixon; 5 Ken Sio; 19 Kris Welham; 4 Josh Mantellato; 6 Maurice Blair; 23 Terry Campese (C); 20 James Green; 24 John Boudebza; 32 Dane Tilse; 11 Kevin Larroyer; 12 Graeme Horne; 13 Tyrone McCarthy. Subs (all used): 15 James Donaldson; 26 Sonny Esslemont; 21 Aaron Ollett; 22 Jordan Cox.
Tries: Blair (18), Sio (73); **Goals:** Mantellato 4/4.
Rugby Leaguer & League Express Men of the Match: *Warriors:* Taulima Tautai; *Rovers:* Terry Campese.
Penalty count: 13-11; **Half-time:** 6-6;
Referee: Richard Silverwood; **Attendance:** 4,677
(at Leigh Sports Village).

Saturday 16th May 2015

LEEDS RHINOS 48 HUDDERSFIELD GIANTS 16

RHINOS: 1 Zak Hardaker; 27 Ash Handley; 3 Kallum Watkins; 4 Joel Moon; 5 Ryan Hall; 13 Kevin Sinfield (C); 6 Danny McGuire; 17 Adam Cuthbertson; 9 Paul Aiton; 10 Jamie Peacock; 14 Stevie Ward; 12 Carl Ablett; 15 Brett Delaney. Subs (all used): 16 Mitch Achurch; 19 Brad Singleton; 7 Rob Burrow; 21 Josh Walters.
Tries: Watkins (7, 13), Hall (16, 65), Aiton (21), McGuire (50), Cuthbertson (63), Ablett (76);
Goals: Sinfield 8/9.
GIANTS: 1 Scott Grix; 2 Jermaine McGillvary; 3 Leroy Cudjoe; 4 Joe Wardle; 5 Aaron Murphy; 6 Danny Brough (C); 16 Kyle Wood; 8 Eorl Crabtree; 7 Luke Robinson; 10 Craig Huby; 11 Brett Ferres; 12 Jack Hughes; 17 Ukuma Ta'ai. Subs (all used): 15 Craig Kopczak; 14 Michael Lawrence; 20 Jamie Ellis; 19 Anthony Mullally.
Tries: Wood (35), Ferres (70), Grix (74);
Goals: Brough 2/3.
Rugby Leaguer & League Express Men of the Match: *Rhinos:* Zak Hardaker; *Giants:* Joe Wardle.
Penalty count: 8-9; **Half-time:** 22-4;
Referee: Phil Bentham *(replaced by Jon Roberts, half-time)*; **Attendance:** 8,133.

HULL FC 40 CASTLEFORD TIGERS 14

HULL: 32 Jordan Rankin; 20 Curtis Naughton; 5 Fetuli Talanoa; 4 Kirk Yeaman; 19 Steve Michaels; 6 Leon Pryce; 7 Marc Sneyd; 10 Liam Watts; 9 Danny Houghton; 8 Mickey Paea; 12 Mark Minichiello; 3 Setaimata Sa; 11 Gareth Ellis (C). Subs (all used): 27 Jordan Abdull; 16 Jordan Thompson; 15 Chris Green; 21 Richard Whiting.
Tries: Naughton (4, 13, 70), Paea (17), Rankin (61, 73), Yeaman (80); **Goals:** Sneyd 6/8.
TIGERS: 22 Jordan Tansey; 26 Ashley Gibson; 3 Jake Webster; 4 Michael Shenton (C); 2 James Clare; 6 Ben Roberts; 7 Luke Gale; 8 Andy Lynch; 9 Adam Milner; 33 Ryan Bailey; 11 Oliver Holmes; 16 Junior Moors; 13 Nathan Massey. Subs (all used): 10 Grant Millington; 14 Lee Jewitt; 24 Mike McMeeken; 21 Liam Finn.
Tries: Gibson (32), Clare (43), McMeeken (47);
Goals: Gale 1/3.
Rugby Leaguer & League Express Men of the Match: *Hull:* Curtis Naughton; *Tigers:* Oliver Holmes.
Penalty count: 5-5; **Half-time:** 16-4;
Referee: James Child; **Attendance:** 6,715.

Sunday 17th May 2015

WAKEFIELD TRINITY WILDCATS 30
LEIGH CENTURIONS 36

WILDCATS: 1 Craig Hall; 5 Richard Owen; 3 Dean Collis; 28 Joe Arundel; 2 Chris Riley; 6 Jacob Miller; 7 Tim Smith; 8 Nick Scruton; 9 Paul McShane; 10 Scott Anderson; 13 Danny Washbrook; 12 Danny Kirmond (C); 31 Ben Kavanagh. Subs (all used): 11 Ali Lauitiiti; 23 Lopini Paea; 19 Jon Molloy; 16 Mickael Simon.
Tries: Riley (8), Arundel (18, 31), Scruton (25), Molloy (62); **Goals:** Hall 5/6.
Sin bin: Kirmond (46) - fighting.
CENTURIONS: 1 Gregg McNally; 15 Jonathan Pownall; 16 Michael Platt; 4 Tom Armstrong; 5 Liam Kay; 6 Martyn Ridyard; 7 Ryan Brierley; 8 Fuifui Moimoi; 9 Bob Beswick; 26 Gareth Hock; 12 Tommy Goulden; 22 Andrew Dixon; 21 Jamie Acton. Subs (all used): 19 Kurt Haggerty; 20 Sam Hopkins; 10 Oliver Wilkes; 13 Sam Barlow.
Tries: Brierley (33), Pownall (47), Beswick (55), Armstrong (58), Hopkins (69), Wilkes (73);
Goals: Ridyard 6/7.
Sin bin: Kay (46) - fighting.
Rugby Leaguer & League Express Men of the Match: *Wildcats:* Joe Arundel; *Centurions:* Bob Beswick.
Penalty count: 10-7; **Half-time:** 24-6;
Referee: Ben Thaler; **Attendance:** 3,859.

WIDNES VIKINGS 26 BATLEY BULLDOGS 22

VIKINGS: 15 Jack Owens; 5 Patrick Ah Van; 4 Stefan Marsh; 3 Cameron Phelps; 2 Paddy Flynn; 6 Kevin Brown (C); 7 Joe Mellor; 35 Gil Dudson; 9 Lloyd White; 23 Phil Joseph; 17 Chris Clarkson; 28 Matt Whitley; 16 Willie Isa. Subs (all used): 33 Aaron Heremaia; 10 Manase Manuokafoa; 24 Macgraff Leuluai; 14 Chris Dean.
Tries: White (18), Ah Van (30), Brown (34, 36), Phelps (44); **Goals:** Owens 3/5.
BULLDOGS: 1 James Craven; 2 Wayne Reittie; 4 Ayden Faal; 11 Alex Bretherton; 3 Shaun Ainscough; 14 Alistair Leak; 7 Scott Leatherbarrow; 15 Adam Gledhill; 13 Luke Blake; 10 Alex Rowe; 12 Sam Scott; 23 Brad Day; 21 James Brown. Subs (all used): 17 Joe Chandler; 26 Matty Fozard; 18 Tom Lillycrop; 16 Sean Hesketh.
Tries: Rowe (21), Reittie (52, 68), Fozard (59);
Goals: Leatherbarrow 3/4.
Rugby Leaguer & League Express Men of the Match: *Vikings:* Patrick Ah Van; *Bulldogs:* Alex Rowe.
Penalty count: 4-11; **Half-time:** 20-6;
Referee: Joe Cobb; **Attendance:** 3,866.

CATALANS DRAGONS 37 FEATHERSTONE ROVERS 34

DRAGONS: 1 Morgan Escare; 5 Michael Oldfield; 28 Tony Gigot (D2); 4 Willie Tonga; 27 Fouad Yaha; 14 Thomas Bosc; 26 Stanislas Robin; 15 Jeff Lima; 16 Eloi Pelissier; 10 Remi Casty; 17 Elliott Whitehead; 12 Louis Anderson; 13 Gregory Mounis (C). Subs (all used): 20 Damien Cardace; 21 Julian Bousquet; 22 Gadwin Springer; 23 Antoni Maria.
Tries: Robin (19), Bousquet (21), Whitehead (35), Oldfield (57), Escare (72), Bosc (74); **Goals:** Bosc 6/6;
Field goal: Robin (79).
Dismissal: Lima (48) - shoulder charge on Marginet.
ROVERS: 26 Kyran Johnson; 5 Ben Blackmore; 4 Thomas Minns; 3 Nathan Chappell; 2 Will Sharp; 28 Will Milner; 31 Remy Marginet; 20 Ryan Verlinden; 23 Luke Teasdale; 17 Matt James; 19 Alex Foster; 24 Mason Tonks; 15 Jack Bussey. Subs (all used): 8 Jordan Baldwinson; 27 Jack Ormondroyd; 32 Sam Day; 35 Luke Cooper.
Tries: Foster (10), Teasdale (27, 52), Ormondroyd (49), Day (61), Verlinden (80); **Goals:** Marginet 5/6.
Rugby Leaguer & League Express Men of the Match: *Dragons:* Thomas Bosc; *Rovers:* Ben Blackmore.
Penalty count: 7-7; **Half-time:** 18-12;
Referee: Robert Hicks; **Attendance:** 1,353.

QUARTER FINALS

Thursday 25th June 2015

HULL KINGSTON ROVERS 32 CATALANS DRAGONS 26

ROVERS: 1 Kieran Dixon; 5 Ken Sio; 18 Liam Salter; 19 Kris Welham; 4 Josh Mantellato; 6 Maurice Blair; 7 Albert Kelly; 8 Adam Walker; 24 John Boudebza; 34 Tony Puletua; 11 Kevin Larroyer; 12 Graeme Horne; 13 Tyrone McCarthy (C). Subs (all used): 31 Shaun Lunt; 15 James Donaldson; 33 James Greenwood; 32 Dane Tilse.
Tries: Sio (8, 65), Dixon (16), Kelly (19), Horne (29);
Goals: Mantellato 6/7.
DRAGONS: 1 Morgan Escare; 30 Krisnan Inu; 28 Tony Gigot; 3 Ben Pomeroy; 27 Fouad Yaha; 26 Stanislas Robin; 7 Scott Dureau; 21 Julian Bousquet; 9 Ian Henderson; 10 Remi Casty; 11 Zeb Taia; 17 Elliott Whitehead; 24 Jason Baitieri. Subs (all used): 12 Louis Anderson; 13 Gregory Mounis (C); 16 Eloi Pelissier; 18 Benjamin Garcia.

Hull KR's Albert Kelly closed down by Warrington duo Ryan Atkins and Stefan Ratchford

Tries: Inu (35, 56), Taia (50), Henderson (67), Whitehead (78); **Goals:** Dureau 3/5.
On report:
Baitieri (70) - alleged dangerous challenge on Dixon.
Rugby Leaguer & League Express Men of the Match:
Rovers: Albert Kelly; *Dragons:* Louis Anderson.
Penalty count: 7-10; **Half-time:** 26-4;
Referee: Phil Bentham; **Attendance:** 6,073.

Friday 26th June 2015

HULL FC 6 LEEDS RHINOS 24

HULL: 32 Jordan Rankin; 2 Tom Lineham; 5 Fetuli Talanoa; 4 Kirk Yeaman; 19 Steve Michaels; 6 Leon Pryce; 27 Jordan Abdull; 8 Mickey Paea; 9 Danny Houghton; 10 Liam Watts; 11 Gareth Ellis (C); 12 Mark Minichiello; 13 Joe Westerman. Subs (all used): 14 Iafeta Palea'aesina; 22 Josh Bowden; 16 Jordan Thompson; 21 Richard Whiting.
Try: Abdull (76); **Goals:** Rankin 1/1.
RHINOS: 1 Zak Hardaker; 27 Ash Handley; 3 Kallum Watkins; 4 Joel Moon; 5 Ryan Hall; 13 Kevin Sinfield (C); 7 Rob Burrow; 8 Kylie Leuluai; 9 Paul Aiton; 10 Jamie Peacock; 14 Stevie Ward; 20 Jimmy Keinhorst; 12 Carl Ablett. Subs (all used): 15 Brett Delaney; 19 Brad Singleton; 22 Andy Yates; 24 Robbie Ward.
Tries: Moon (6), Watkins (43), Hardaker (71);
Goals: Sinfield 6/8.
Rugby Leaguer & League Express Men of the Match:
Hull: Gareth Ellis; *Rhinos:* Kevin Sinfield.
Penalty count: 6-6; **Half-time:** 0-10;
Referee: James Child; **Attendance:** 9,261.

Saturday 27th June 2015

WARRINGTON WOLVES 34 LEIGH CENTURIONS 24

WOLVES: 6 Stefan Ratchford; 22 Gene Ormsby; 18 James Laithwaite; 4 Ryan Atkins; 24 Kevin Penny; 20 Gareth O'Brien; 7 Richard Myler; 8 Chris Hill (C); 9 Daryl Clark; 10 Ashton Sims; 12 Ben Westwood; 17 Ben Currie; 13 Ben Harrison. Subs (all used): 25 Brad Dwyer; 15 Roy Asotasi; 26 Joe Philbin; 27 George King.
Tries: Sims (8), Currie (19, 70), Penny (41, 44), G King (56); **Goals:** O'Brien 4/5, Westwood 1/1.
Sin bin: O'Brien (47) - professional foul.
CENTURIONS: 1 Gregg McNally; 15 Jonathan Pownall; 3 Greg Worthington; 4 Tom Armstrong; 5 Liam Kay; 6 Martyn Ridyard; 7 Ryan Brierley; 10 Oliver Wilkes; 9 Bob Beswick; 26 Gareth Hock; 22 Andrew Dixon; 12 Tommy Goulden; 29 Jake Emmitt. Subs (all used): 2 Adam Higson; 20 Sam Hopkins; 8 Fuifui Moimoi; 18 Tom Spencer.
Tries: Worthington (12), Brierley (23, 65), McNally (37), Armstrong (72); **Goals:** Ridyard 2/5.
Rugby Leaguer & League Express Men of the Match:
Wolves: Chris Hill; *Centurions:* Jake Emmitt.
Penalty count: 7-7; **Half-time:** 12-14;
Referee: Richard Silverwood; **Attendance:** 10,119.

Sunday 28th June 2015

ST HELENS 36 WIDNES VIKINGS 20

SAINTS: 17 Mark Percival; 22 Matty Dawson; 4 Josh Jones; 3 Jordan Turner; 5 Adam Swift; 6 Travis Burns; 7 Luke Walsh; 10 Kyle Amor; 9 James Roby; 14 Alex Walmsley; 12 Jon Wilkin (C); 21 Joe Greenwood; 13 Louie McCarthy-Scarsbrook. Subs (all used): 8 Mose Masoe; 15 Mark Flanagan; 19 Greg Richards; 25 Andre Savelio.
Tries: Swift (6), Percival (30, 80), Dawson (33), Amor (64), Turner (72); **Goals:** Percival 6/8.
VIKINGS: 1 Rhys Hanbury; 2 Paddy Flynn; 4 Stefan Marsh; 14 Chris Dean; 5 Patrick Ah Van; 6 Kevin Brown (C); 7 Joe Mellor; 10 Manase Manuokafoa; 33 Aaron Heremaia; 25 Alex Gerrard; 17 Chris Clarkson; 28 Matt Whitley; 24 Macgraff Leuluai. Subs (all used): 13 Hep Cahill; 16 Willie Isa; 21 Danny Craven; 35 Gil Dudson.
Tries: Mellor (16), Craven (37), Ah Van (44), Dean (53);
Goals: Craven 1/2, Ah Van 1/2.
Rugby Leaguer & League Express Men of the Match:
Saints: Jon Wilkin; *Vikings:* Willie Isa.
Penalty count: 8-4; **Half-time:** 18-12;
Referee: Robert Hicks; **Attendance:** 8,806.

SEMI-FINALS

Friday 31st July 2015

LEEDS RHINOS 24 ST HELENS 14

RHINOS: 1 Zak Hardaker; 2 Tom Briscoe; 3 Kallum Watkins; 4 Joel Moon; 5 Ryan Hall; 13 Kevin Sinfield (C); 6 Danny McGuire; 17 Adam Cuthbertson; 9 Paul Aiton; 10 Jamie Peacock; 15 Brett Delaney; 12 Carl Ablett; 11 Jamie Jones-Buchanan. Subs (all used): 8 Kylie Leuluai; 7 Rob Burrow; 30 Mitch Garbutt; 20 Jimmy Keinhorst.
Tries: Hardaker (3), Moon (24), Peacock (46), Watkins (66); **Goals:** Sinfield 4/5.
SAINTS: 37 Adam Quinlan; 22 Matty Dawson; 17 Mark Percival; 3 Jordan Turner; 5 Adam Swift; 6 Travis Burns; 7 Luke Walsh; 10 Kyle Amor; 9 James Roby (C); 14 Alex Walmsley; 13 Louie McCarthy-Scarsbrook; 21 Joe Greenwood; 15 Mark Flanagan. Subs (all used): 8 Mose Masoe; 11 Atelea Vea; 25 Andre Savelio; 4 Josh Jones.
Tries: Percival (38, 54), Savelio (51); **Goals:** Walsh 1/3.
Rugby Leaguer & League Express Men of the Match:
Rhinos: Zak Hardaker; *Saints:* Alex Walmsley.
Penalty count: 3-4; **Half-time:** 12-4;
Referee: Ben Thaler; **Attendance:** 11,107
(at Halliwell Jones Stadium, Warrington).

Saturday 1st August 2015

HULL KINGSTON ROVERS 26 WARRINGTON WOLVES 18

ROVERS: 1 Kieran Dixon; 4 Josh Mantellato; 19 Kris Welham; 18 Liam Salter; 5 Ken Sio; 6 Maurice Blair; 7 Albert Kelly; 8 Adam Walker; 31 Shaun Lunt; 34 Tony Puletua; 11 Kevin Larroyer; 12 Graeme Horne; 13 Tyrone McCarthy (C). Subs (all used): 24 John Boudebza; 15 James Donaldson; 20 James Green; 32 Dane Tilse.
Tries: Mantellato (24), Sio (27), Larroyer (47), Lunt (76);
Goals: Mantellato 5/6.
WOLVES: 6 Stefan Ratchford; 22 Gene Ormsby; 23 Gary Wheeler; 4 Ryan Atkins; 5 Joel Monaghan (C); 20 Gareth O'Brien; 7 Richard Myler; 8 Chris Hill; 9 Daryl Clark; 10 Ashton Sims; 31 Sam Wilde; 17 Ben Currie; 13 Ben Harrison. Subs (all used): 25 Brad Dwyer; 15 Roy Asotasi; 26 Joe Philbin; 19 Anthony England.
Tries: Atkins (2), Myler (58), Currie (67);
Goals: O'Brien 3/3.
Rugby Leaguer & League Express Men of the Match:
Rovers: Albert Kelly; *Wolves:* Chris Hill.
Penalty count: 7-7; **Half-time:** 12-6;
Referee: Richard Silverwood; **Attendance:** 13,049
(at Headingley Carnegie, Leeds).

FINAL

Saturday 29th August 2015

HULL KINGSTON ROVERS 0 LEEDS RHINOS 50

ROVERS: 1 Kieran Dixon; 4 Josh Mantellato; 19 Kris Welham; 18 Liam Salter; 5 Ken Sio; 6 Maurice Blair; 7 Albert Kelly; 8 Adam Walker; 31 Shaun Lunt; 34 Tony Puletua; 11 Kevin Larroyer; 12 Graeme Horne; 13 Tyrone McCarthy (C). Subs (all used): 24 John Boudebza; 15 James Donaldson; 32 Dane Tilse; 14 Mitchell Allgood.
RHINOS: 1 Zak Hardaker; 2 Tom Briscoe; 3 Kallum Watkins; 4 Joel Moon; 5 Ryan Hall; 13 Kevin Sinfield (C); 6 Danny McGuire; 30 Mitch Garbutt; 17 Adam Cuthbertson; 10 Jamie Peacock; 14 Stevie Ward; 12 Carl Ablett; 15 Brett Delaney. Subs (all used): 7 Rob Burrow; 8 Kylie Leuluai; 16 Mitch Achurch; 19 Brad Singleton.
Tries: Delaney (7), McGuire (17), T Briscoe (20, 47, 66, 75, 79), Singleton (58), Burrow (73); **Goals:** Sinfield 7/9.
Rugby Leaguer & League Express Men of the Match:
Rovers: Albert Kelly; *Rhinos:* Tom Briscoe.
Penalty count: 2-3; **Half-time:** 0-16; **Referee:** Ben Thaler;
Attendance: 80,140 *(at Wembley Stadium).*

Leeds' Tom Briscoe beats Hull KR's Graeme Horne and Kris Welham to score the first of a record five Challenge Cup Final tries

SUPER LEAGUE 2016 FIXTURES

ROUND 1

Thursday February 4
Leeds Rhinos v Warrington Wolves 8:00pm
Friday February 5
Hull FC v Salford Red Devils 8:00pm
St Helens v Huddersfield Giants 8:00pm
Wigan Warriors v Catalans Dragons 8:00pm
Sunday February 7
Hull Kingston Rovers v Castleford Tigers 3:00pm
Wakefield T Wildcats v Widnes Vikings 3:00pm

ROUND 2

Thursday February 11
Salford Red Devils v St Helens 8:00pm
Friday February 12
Huddersfield Giants v Wigan Warriors 8:00pm
Saturday February 13
Catalans Dragons v Hull FC..........................6:00pm
Sunday February 14
Castleford Tigers v Wakefield T Wildcats 3:30pm
Warrington Wolves v Hull Kingston Rovers..3:00pm
Widnes Vikings v Leeds Rhinos 3:00pm

WORLD CLUB SERIES

Friday February 19
St Helens v Sydney Roosters 8:00pm
Saturday February 20
Wigan Warriors v Brisbane Broncos 8:00pm
Sunday February 21
Leeds Rhinos v North Queensland Cowboys..7:00pm

ROUND 11

Sunday February 21
Hull Kingston Rovers v Wakefield T Wildcats..3:00pm
Salford Red Devils v Widnes Vikings 3:00pm

ROUND 3

Thursday February 25
Hull FC v Castleford Tigers 8:00pm
Friday February 26
Hull Kingston Rovers v St Helens 8:00pm
Warrington Wolves v Wakefield T Wildcats..8:00pm
Wigan Warriors v Salford Red Devils 8:00pm
Saturday February 27
Catalans Dragons v Leeds Rhinos................6:00pm
Sunday February 28
Huddersfield Giants v Widnes Vikings 3:00pm

ROUND 4

Thursday March 3
Salford Red Devils v Warrington Wolves 8:00pm
Friday March 4
Hull FC v Wigan Warriors 8:00pm
Leeds Rhinos v Huddersfield Giants 8:00pm
St Helens v Castleford Tigers 8:00pm
Widnes Vikings v Hull Kingston Rovers 8:00pm
Sunday March 6
Wakefield T Wildcats v Catalans Dragons....3:00pm

ROUND 5

Thursday March 10
Widnes Vikings v Hull FC 8:00pm
Friday March 11
St Helens v Wakefield T Wildcats 8:00pm
Wigan Warriors v Leeds Rhinos 8:00pm
Saturday March 12
Catalans Dragons v Warrington Wolves 6:00pm
Sunday March 13
Castleford Tigers v Salford Red Devils 3:30pm
Huddersfield Giants v Hull Kingston Rovers..3:00pm

ROUND 6

Thursday March 17
Wigan Warriors v Widnes Vikings................8:00pm
Friday March 18
Hull FC v Wakefield T Wildcats 8:00pm
Leeds Rhinos v St Helens 8:00pm
Warrington Wolves v Castleford Tigers........8:00pm
Sunday March 20
Huddersfield Giants v Catalans Dragons......3:00pm
Hull Kingston Rovers v Salford Red Devils..3:00pm

ROUND 7

Thursday March 24
Castleford Tigers v Leeds Rhinos 8:00pm
Friday March 25
Hull Kingston Rovers v Hull FC..........................TBC
Salford Red Devils v Catalans Dragons ....TBC
St Helens v Wigan Warriors ....TBC
Wakefield T Wildcats v Huddersfield Giants..3:00pm
Warrington Wolves v Widnes Vikings..........3:00pm

ROUND 8

Monday March 28
Catalans Dragons v Castleford Tigers................TBC
Huddersfield Giants v Salford Red Devils 3:00pm
Hull FC v Warrington Wolves 3:00pm
Leeds Rhinos v Wakefield T Wildcats 3:00pm
Widnes Vikings v St Helens 3:00pm
Wigan Warriors v Hull Kingston Rovers ....TBC

ROUND 9

Friday April 1
Leeds Rhinos v Hull Kingston Rovers..........8:00pm
St Helens v Hull FC 8:00pm
Wigan Warriors v Warrington Wolves..........8:00pm
Saturday April 2
Catalans Dragons v Widnes Vikings 6:00pm
Wakefield T Wildcats v Salford Red Devils ....TBC
Sunday April 3
Castleford Tigers v Huddersfield Giants 3:30pm

ROUND 10

Thursday April 7
Hull Kingston Rovers v Catalans Dragons....8:00pm
Friday April 8
Hull FC v Huddersfield Giants 8:00pm
Salford Red Devils v Leeds Rhinos 8:00pm
Warrington Wolves v St Helens....................8:00pm
Sunday April 10
Wakefield T Wildcats v Wigan Warriors 3:00pm
Widnes Vikings v Castleford Tigers.............3:00pm

ROUND 11

Thursday April 14
St Helens v Catalans Dragons......................8:00pm
Friday April 15
Huddersfield Giants v Warrington Wolves....8:00pm
Leeds Rhinos v Hull FC................................8:00pm
Wigan Warriors v Castleford Tigers 8:00pm

ROUND 12

Thursday April 21
Wigan Warriors v Huddersfield Giants 8:00pm
Friday April 22
St Helens v Leeds Rhinos 8:00pm
Widnes Vikings v Warrington Wolves..........8:00pm
Saturday April 23
Catalans Dragons v Salford Red Devils........6:00pm
Sunday April 24
Castleford Tigers v Hull Kingston Rovers 3:30pm
Wakefield T Wildcats v Hull FC 3:00pm

ROUND 13

Thursday April 28
Warrington Wolves v Wigan Warriors..........8:00pm
Friday April 29
Castleford Tigers v St Helens 8:00pm
Huddersfield Giants v Leeds Rhinos 8:00pm
Hull FC v Catalans Dragons..........................8:00pm
Salford Red Devils v Hull Kingston Rovers ..8:00pm
Widnes Vikings v Wakefield T Wildcats 8:00pm

ROUND 14

Thursday May 12
Leeds Rhinos v Castleford Tigers 8:00pm
Friday May 13
St Helens v Salford Red Devils 8:00pm
Wigan Warriors v Hull FC 8:00pm
Saturday May 14
Catalans Dragons v Huddersfield Giants......6:00pm
Sunday May 15
Hull Kingston Rovers v Widnes Vikings 3:00pm
Wakefield T Wildcats v Warrington Wolves..3:00pm

ROUND 15 - MAGIC WEEKEND

Saturday May 21
Salford Red Devils v Widnes Vikings 2:30pm
Warrington Wolves v Castleford Tigers........4:45pm
Leeds Rhinos v Wigan Warriors 7:00pm
Sunday May 22
Wakefield T Wildcats v Catalans Dragons....1:00pm
St Helens v Huddersfield Giants 3:15pm
Hull FC v Hull Kingston Rovers....................5:30pm

ROUND 16

Thursday May 26
Castleford Tigers v Wigan Warriors 8:00pm
Friday May 27
Salford Red Devils v Wakefield T Wildcats ..8:00pm
Warrington Wolves v Leeds Rhinos 8:00pm
Saturday May 28
Catalans Dragons v Hull Kingston Rovers....6:00pm
Hull FC v St Helens 3:00pm
Sunday May 29
Widnes Vikings v Huddersfield Giants 3:00pm

ROUND 17

Thursday June 2
Wakefield T Wildcats v Hull Kingston Rovers..8:00pm
Friday June 3
Huddersfield Giants v Castleford Tigers 8:00pm
Hull FC v Widnes Vikings 8:00pm
Leeds Rhinos v Catalans Dragons................8:00pm
Salford Red Devils v Wigan Warriors 8:00pm
St Helens v Warrington Wolves....................8:00pm

ROUND 18

Thursday June 9
Castleford Tigers v Widnes Vikings.............8:00pm
Friday June 10
Hull Kingston Rovers v Wigan Warriors 8:00pm
Leeds Rhinos v Salford Red Devils.............8:00pm
Saturday June 11
Catalans Dragons v St Helens......................6:00pm
Sunday June 12
Huddersfield Giants v Wakefield T Wildcats..3:00pm
Warrington Wolves v Hull FC 3:00pm

ROUND 19

Thursday June 16
Widnes Vikings v Wigan Warriors................8:00pm
Friday June 17
Salford Red Devils v Huddersfield Giants 8:00pm
St Helens v Hull Kingston Rovers 8:00pm
Sunday June 19
Castleford Tigers v Hull FC 3:30pm
Wakefield T Wildcats v Leeds Rhinos 3:00pm
Warrington Wolves v Catalans Dragons 3:00pm

ROUND 20

Thursday June 30
Huddersfield Giants v Hull FC 8:00pm
Friday July 1
Hull Kingston Rovers v Warrington Wolves..8:00pm
Salford Red Devils v Castleford Tigers 8:00pm
Saturday July 2
Catalans Dragons v Wigan Warriors 6:00pm
Sunday July 3
Leeds Rhinos v Widnes Vikings 3:00pm
Wakefield T Wildcats v St Helens 3:00pm

ROUND 21

Thursday July 7
Warrington Wolves v Salford Red Devils 8:00pm
Friday July 8
Hull FC v Leeds Rhinos................................8:00pm
Hull Kingston Rovers v Huddersfield Giants..8:00pm
St Helens v Widnes Vikings 8:00pm
Wigan Warriors v Wakefield T Wildcats 8:00pm
Sunday July 10
Castleford Tigers v Catalans Dragons 3:30pm

ROUND 22

Thursday July 14
Hull FC v Hull Kingston Rovers....................8:00pm
Friday July 15
Leeds Rhinos v Wigan Warriors 8:00pm
Widnes Vikings v Salford Red Devils 8:00pm
Saturday July 16
Catalans Dragons v Wakefield T Wildcats....6:00pm
Sunday July 17
Castleford Tigers v Warrington Wolves........3:30pm
Huddersfield Giants v St Helens 3:00pm

ROUND 23

Thursday July 21
Hull Kingston Rovers v Leeds Rhinos..........8:00pm
Friday July 22
Salford Red Devils v Hull FC 8:00pm
Wigan Warriors v St Helens 8:00pm
Sunday July 24
Wakefield T Wildcats v Castleford Tigers 3:00pm
Warrington Wolves v Huddersfield Giants....3:00pm
Widnes Vikings v Catalans Dragons 3:00pm

SUPER LEAGUE KEY DATES

FEBRUARY
Weekend of 4th-7th - Super League Round 1
Weekend of 19th-21st - World Club Series

MARCH
Weekend of 24th-28th - Easter Weekend

APRIL
Weekend of 14th-17th - Challenge Cup Round 5
(teams who finished 9th-12th in 2015 enter)

MAY
Weekend of 5th-8th - Challenge Cup Round 6
(teams who finished 1st-8th in 2015 enter)
Weekend of 21st-22nd - Magic Weekend

JUNE
Weekend of 23rd-26th -
Challenge Cup Quarter Finals

JULY
Weekend of 29th-31st -
Challenge Cup Semi-Finals

AUGUST
Weekend of 4th-7th - Super 8s, Round 1
27th - Challenge Cup Final

OCTOBER
Weekend of 1st-2nd - Super League Semi-Finals
and Million Pound Game
8th - Super League Grand Final

All kick-offs given as local time, and all fixtures are subject to change.

The RFL and Super League (Europe) Ltd will endeavour to keep them as accurate as possible.

CHAMPIONSHIP 2016 FIXTURES

ROUND 1
Sunday February 7
Batley Bulldogs v Leigh Centurions..............3:00pm
Bradford Bulls v Featherstone Rovers..........3:00pm
Halifax v Whitehaven....................................3:00pm
Oldham v London Broncos 3:00pm
Swinton Lions v Dewsbury Rams.................3:00pm
Workington Town v Sheffield Eagles............3:00pm

ROUND 2
Saturday February 13
Whitehaven v Bradford Bulls........................6:30pm
Sunday February 14
Dewsbury Rams v Workington Town 3:00pm
Featherstone Rovers v Batley Bulldogs........3:00pm
Leigh Centurions v Oldham...........................3:00pm
London Broncos v Swinton Lions.................3:00pm
Sheffield Eagles v Halifax ....TBC

ROUND 3
Saturday February 20
Whitehaven v Featherstone Rovers..............6:30pm
Sunday February 21
Batley Bulldogs v Sheffield Eagles 3:00pm
Leigh Centurions v London Broncos.............3:00pm
Oldham v Dewsbury Rams 3:00pm
Swinton Lions v Bradford Bulls....................3:00pm
Workington Town v Halifax 3:00pm

ROUND 4
Sunday February 28
Bradford Bulls v Leigh Centurions 3:00pm
Dewsbury Rams v Whitehaven 3:00pm
Featherstone Rovers v Oldham 3:00pm
Halifax v Batley Bulldogs..............................3:00pm
Sheffield Eagles v Swinton Lions ....TBC
Workington Town v London Broncos 3:00pm

ROUND 5
Saturday March 5
Whitehaven v Swinton Lions........................6:30pm
Sunday March 6
Batley Bulldogs v Workington Town 3:00pm
Featherstone Rovers v Dewsbury Rams 3:00pm
Leigh Centurions v Sheffield Eagles 3:00pm
London Broncos v Halifax............................3:00pm
Oldham v Bradford Bulls..............................3:00pm

ROUND 6
Saturday March 12
London Broncos v Dewsbury Rams 3:00pm
Sunday March 13
Batley Bulldogs v Bradford Bulls..................3:00pm
Halifax v Leigh Centurions 3:00pm
Sheffield Eagles v Whitehaven ....TBC
Swinton Lions v Featherstone Rovers..........3:00pm
Workington Town v Oldham 3:00pm

ROUND 7
Thursday March 24
Leigh Centurions v Swinton Lions 8:00pm
Friday March 25
Bradford Bulls v London Broncos................3:00pm
Dewsbury Rams v Batley Bulldogs 7:30pm
Featherstone Rovers v Sheffield Eagles 7:30pm
Oldham v Halifax..3:00pm
Whitehaven v Workington Town 1:30pm

ROUND 8
Monday March 28
Batley Bulldogs v Whitehaven......................3:00pm
Halifax v Bradford Bulls................................3:00pm
London Broncos v Featherstone Rovers.......3:00pm
Sheffield Eagles v Dewsbury Rams ....TBC
Swinton Lions v Oldham..............................3:00pm
Workington Town v Leigh Centurions..........3:00pm

ROUND 9
Saturday April 2
Whitehaven v London Broncos 6:30pm
Sunday April 3
Bradford Bulls v Sheffield Eagles 3:00pm
Dewsbury Rams v Leigh Centurions............3:00pm
Featherstone Rovers v Halifax......................3:00pm
Oldham v Batley Bulldogs 3:00pm
Swinton Lions v Workington Town 3:00pm

ROUND 10
Sunday April 10
Dewsbury Rams v Bradford Bulls 3:00pm
Halifax v Swinton Lions................................3:00pm
Leigh Centurions v Whitehaven....................3:00pm
London Broncos v Batley Bulldogs 3:00pm
Oldham v Sheffield Eagles............................3:00pm
Workington Town v Featherstone Rovers 3:00pm

ROUND 11
Saturday April 23
Whitehaven v Oldham 6:30pm
Sunday April 24
Batley Bulldogs v Swinton Lions..................3:00pm
Bradford Bulls v Workington Town 3:00pm
Featherstone Rovers v Leigh Centurions......3:00pm
Halifax v Dewsbury Rams 3:00pm
Sheffield Eagles v London Broncos ....TBC

ROUND 12
Sunday May 1
Dewsbury Rams v Sheffield Eagles.............3:00pm
Halifax v Workington Town 3:00pm
Leigh Centurions v Batley Bulldogs.............3:00pm
London Broncos v Bradford Bulls................3:00pm
Oldham v Featherstone Rovers 3:00pm
Swinton Lions v Whitehaven........................3:00pm

ROUND 13
Saturday May 14
Whitehaven v Dewsbury Rams 6:30pm
Sunday May 15
Batley Bulldogs v Halifax..............................3:00pm
Bradford Bulls v Swinton Lions....................3:00pm
Featherstone Rovers v London Broncos.......3:00pm
Oldham v Leigh Centurions..........................3:00pm
Sheffield Eagles v Workington Town..................TBC

ROUND 14
Sunday May 22
Dewsbury Rams v Featherstone Rovers 3:00pm
Halifax v Oldham..3:00pm
London Broncos v Whitehaven 3:00pm
Sheffield Eagles v Bradford Bulls ....TBC
Swinton Lions v Leigh Centurions 3:00pm
Workington Town v Batley Bulldogs 3:00pm

ROUND 15 - SUMMER BASH
Saturday May 28
Sheffield Eagles v London Broncos..............2:30pm
Workington Town v Whitehaven 4:45pm
Bradford Bulls v Leigh Centurions 7:00pm
Sunday May 29
Dewsbury Rams v Batley Bulldogs 12:45pm
Oldham v Swinton Lions 3:00pm
Halifax v Featherstone Rovers......................5:15pm

ROUND 16
Saturday June 4
Whitehaven v Leigh Centurions....................6:30pm
Sunday June 5
Batley Bulldogs v Oldham 3:00pm
Bradford Bulls v Dewsbury Rams 3:00pm
Featherstone Rovers v Swinton Lions..........3:00pm
Halifax v Sheffield Eagles 3:00pm
London Broncos v Workington Town 3:00pm

ROUND 17
Saturday June 11
Whitehaven v Halifax....................................6:30pm
Sunday June 12
Dewsbury Rams v Oldham 3:00pm
Leigh Centurions v Featherstone Rovers......3:00pm
Sheffield Eagles v Batley Bulldogs ....TBC
Swinton Lions v London Broncos................3:00pm
Workington Town v Bradford Bulls 3:00pm

ROUND 18
Sunday June 19
Bradford Bulls v Batley Bulldogs..................3:00pm
Dewsbury Rams v Halifax............................3:00pm
Featherstone Rovers v Whitehaven..............3:00pm
Leigh Centurions v Workington Town 3:00pm
London Broncos v Oldham 3:00pm
Swinton Lions v Sheffield Eagles 3:00pm

ROUND 19
Sunday June 26
Batley Bulldogs v Dewsbury Rams 3:00pm
Bradford Bulls v Halifax...............................3:00pm
London Broncos v Leigh Centurions............3:00pm
Oldham v Whitehaven 3:00pm
Sheffield Eagles v Featherstone Rovers ....TBC
Workington Town v Swinton Lions 3:00pm

ROUND 20
Saturday July 2
Whitehaven v Batley Bulldogs......................6:30pm
Sunday July 3
Dewsbury Rams v London Broncos 3:00pm
Featherstone Rovers v Workington Town 3:00pm
Leigh Centurions v Bradford Bulls 3:00pm
Sheffield Eagles v Oldham ....TBC
Swinton Lions v Halifax................................3:00pm

ROUND 21
Sunday July 10
Batley Bulldogs v Featherstone Rovers........3:00pm
Bradford Bulls v Whitehaven........................3:00pm
Leigh Centurions v Halifax 3:00pm
London Broncos v Sheffield Eagles..............3:00pm
Oldham v Swinton Lions..............................3:00pm
Workington Town v Dewsbury Rams 3:00pm

ROUND 22
Sunday July 17
Batley Bulldogs v London Broncos..............3:00pm
Bradford Bulls v Oldham..............................3:00pm
Dewsbury Rams v Swinton Lions 3:00pm
Halifax v Featherstone Rovers......................3:00pm
Sheffield Eagles v Leigh Centurions ....TBC
Workington Town v Whitehaven 3:00pm

ROUND 23
Saturday July 23
Whitehaven v Sheffield Eagles 6:30pm
Sunday July 24
Featherstone Rovers v Bradford Bulls..........3:00pm
Halifax v London Broncos............................3:00pm
Leigh Centurions v Dewsbury Rams............3:00pm
Oldham v Workington Town 3:00pm
Swinton Lions v Batley Bulldogs..................3:00pm

All kick-offs given as local time, and all fixtures are subject to change.

The RFL will endeavour to keep them as accurate as possible.

LEAGUE 1 2016 FIXTURES

ROUND 1
Saturday March 5
Toulouse Olympique v Coventry Bears 3:30pm
Sunday March 6
Doncaster v Gloucestershire AG 3:00pm
North Wales Crusaders v Barrow Raiders....2:30pm
Oxford v Newcastle Thunder 2:30pm
Rochdale Hornets v Hunslet Hawks 3:00pm
South Wales Scorpions v Keighley Cougars ..3:00pm
York City Knights v London Skolars 3:00pm
Bye: Hemel Stags

ROUND 2
Saturday March 12
London Skolars v Oxford 6:00pm
Toulouse Olympique v Hemel Stags 6:30pm
Sunday March 13
Barrow Raiders v Hunslet Hawks 3:30pm
Coventry Bears v Rochdale Hornets 3:00pm
Keighley Cougars v Doncaster 3:00pm
Newcastle Thunder v North Wales Crusaders..3:00pm
Wednesday March 16
Gloucestershire AG v South Wales Scorpions..7:00pm
Bye: York City Knights

ROUND 3
Friday March 25
Barrow Raiders v Newcastle Thunder 3:00pm
Doncaster v York City Knights.....................3:00pm
Gloucestershire AG v Coventry Bears 7:30pm
Hemel Stags v London Skolars 2:30pm
Hunslet Hawks v Keighley Cougars...............2:00pm
North Wales Crusaders v Rochdale Hornets..2:30pm
Oxford v South Wales Scorpions 2:30pm
Bye: Toulouse Olympique

ROUND 4
Sunday April 10
Coventry Bears v Barrow Raiders 3:00pm
Doncaster v North Wales Crusaders 3:00pm
Hemel Stags v York City Knights..................2:30pm
Keighley Cougars v Oxford 3:00pm
Newcastle Thunder v Hunslet Hawks 3:00pm
Rochdale Hornets v Gloucestershire AG 3:00pm
South Wales Scorpions v Toulouse Olympique..3:00pm
Bye: London Skolars

ROUND 5
Saturday April 16
Toulouse Olympique v Oxford......................6:30pm
Sunday April 17
Barrow Raiders v Rochdale Hornets 3:30pm
Hunslet Hawks v Doncaster 3:00pm
Keighley Cougars v Gloucestershire AG 3:00pm
North Wales Crusaders v London Skolars ..2:30pm
South Wales Scorpions v Hemel Stags........3:00pm
York City Knights v Coventry Bears..............3:00pm
Bye: Newcastle Thunder

ROUND 6
Saturday April 23
London Skolars v Coventry Bears................6:00pm
Sunday April 24
Doncaster v Barrow Raiders 3:00pm
Gloucestershire AG v Newcastle Thunder 3:00pm
Hemel Stags v North Wales Crusaders 2:30pm
Oxford v Hunslet Hawks 2:30pm
Rochdale Hornets v Toulouse Olympique 3:00pm
York City Knights v South Wales Scorpions ..3:00pm
Bye: Keighley Cougars

ROUND 7
Saturday May 7
Toulouse Olympique v Gloucestershire AG ..3:30pm
Sunday May 8
Barrow Raiders v York City Knights 3:30pm
Coventry Bears v Keighley Cougars 3:00pm
Hunslet Hawks v Hemel Stags 3:00pm
Newcastle Thunder v Doncaster 3:00pm
North Wales Crusaders v Oxford..................2:30pm
Rochdale Hornets v London Skolars............3:00pm
Bye: South Wales Scorpions

ROUND 8
Saturday May 14
London Skolars v Newcastle Thunder..........6:00pm
Sunday May 15
Coventry Bears v Doncaster 3:00pm
Hunslet Hawks v Toulouse Olympique 3:00pm
Keighley Cougars v Hemel Stags 3:00pm
Oxford v Rochdale Hornets..........................2:30pm
South Wales Scorpions v Barrow Raiders ..3:00pm
York City Knights v North Wales Crusaders..3:00pm
Bye: Gloucestershire All Golds

ROUND 9
Friday May 20
Newcastle Thunder v York City Knights 8:00pm
Saturday May 21
London Skolars v Keighley Cougars 6:00pm
Sunday May 22
Barrow Raiders v Toulouse Olympique 3:30pm
Doncaster v Oxford 3:00pm
Gloucestershire AG v Hunslet Hawks 3:00pm
Hemel Stags v Coventry Bears 2:30pm
Rochdale Hornets v South Wales Scorpions ..3:00pm
Bye: North Wales Crusaders

ROUND 10
Saturday June 4
S Wales Scorpions v N Wales Crusaders 5:00pm
Toulouse Olympique v Doncaster 6:30pm
Sunday June 5
Gloucestershire AG v Barrow Raiders..........3:00pm
Hunslet Hawks v London Skolars 3:00pm
Keighley Cougars v Newcastle Thunder 3:00pm
Oxford v Hemel Stags 2:30pm
York City Knights v Rochdale Hornets 3:00pm
Bye: Coventry Bears

ROUND 11
Saturday June 11
London Skolars v Barrow Raiders................2:00pm
Sunday June 12
Coventry Bears v Oxford 3:00pm
Doncaster v South Wales Scorpions............3:00pm
Hemel Stags v Gloucestershire AG 2:30pm
Newcastle Thunder v Toulouse Olympique ..3:00pm
North Wales Crusaders v Keighley Cougars..2:30pm
York City Knights v Hunslet Hawks..............3:00pm
Bye: Rochdale Hornets

ROUND 12
Saturday June 18
Toulouse Olympique v Keighley Cougars 6:30pm
Sunday June 19
Barrow Raiders v Hemel Stags 3:30pm
Gloucestershire AG v North Wales Crusaders ..3:00pm
Hunslet Hawks v Coventry Bears 3:00pm
Newcastle Thunder v Rochdale Hornets 3:00pm
Oxford v York City Knights 2:30pm
South Wales Scorpions v London Skolars ..3:00pm
Bye: Doncaster

ROUND 13
Saturday June 25
Coventry Bears v Newcastle Thunder 3:00pm
London Skolars v Doncaster........................3:00pm
Sunday June 26
Hemel Stags v Rochdale Hornets 2:30pm
Keighley Cougars v Barrow Raiders 3:00pm
North Wales Crusaders v Toulouse Olympique ..2:30pm
South Wales Scorpions v Hunslet Hawks 3:00pm
York City Knights v Gloucestershire AG 3:00pm
Bye: Oxford

ROUND 14
Saturday July 2
Toulouse Olympique v York City Knights 6:30pm
Sunday July 3
Barrow Raiders v Oxford.............................3:30pm
Doncaster v Hemel Stags 3:00pm
Gloucestershire AG v London Skolars..........3:00pm
Newcastle Thunder v South Wales Scorpions..3:00pm
North Wales Crusaders v Coventry Bears 2:30pm
Rochdale Hornets v Keighley Cougars 3:00pm
Bye: Hunslet Hawks

CHAMPIONSHIP KEY DATES

FEBRUARY
Weekend of 5th-7th - Championship Round 1

MARCH
Weekend of 18th-20th - Challenge Cup Round 4
(Championship clubs enter)

APRIL
Weekend of 14th-17th - Challenge Cup Round 5

MAY
Weekend of 5th-8th - Challenge Cup Round 6
Weekend of 28th-29th - Summer Bash

JUNE
Weekend of 23rd-26th -
Challenge Cup Quarter Finals

JULY
Weekend of 29th-31st -
Challenge Cup Semi-Finals

AUGUST
Weekend of 4th-7th - Super 8s, Round 1
27th - Challenge Cup Final

OCTOBER
Weekend of 1st-2nd - Million Pound Game
and Championship Shield Final

LEAGUE 1 KEY DATES

FEBRUARY
Weekend of 20th-21st - League 1 Cup Round 1
Weekend of 27th-28th - Challenge Cup Round 3
(League 1 clubs enter)

MARCH
Weekend of 5th-6th - League 1 Round 1
Weekend of 18th-20th - Challenge Cup Round 4

APRIL
Weekend of 14th-17th - Challenge Cup Round 5

MAY
Weekend of 5th-8th - Challenge Cup Round 6
28th - League 1 Cup Final *(at Summer Bash)*

JUNE
Weekend of 23rd-26th -
Challenge Cup Quarter Finals

JULY
Weekend of 23rd-24th -
League 1 Super 8s Round 1

SEPTEMBER
Weekend of 17th-18th - League 1 Play-off Final
(winner promoted) and League 1 Shield Final
Weekend of 24th-25th - League 1 Semi-Finals

OCTOBER
Weekend of 1st-2nd - League 1 Super 8s Final
(winner promoted)

ROUND 15
Saturday July 9
Coventry Bears v South Wales Scorpions....3:00pm
London Skolars v Toulouse Olympique........3:00pm
Sunday July 10
Hemel Stags v Newcastle Thunder 2:30pm
Hunslet Hawks v North Wales Crusaders 3:00pm
Keighley Cougars v York City Knights..........3:00pm
Oxford v Gloucestershire AG........................2:30pm
Rochdale Hornets v Doncaster 3:00pm
Bye: Barrow Raiders

Following Round 15, division splits into League 1 Super 8s and a seven-team League 1 Shield

GRAND FINALS

1998-2014

1998

DIVISION ONE GRAND FINAL

Saturday 26th September 1998

FEATHERSTONE ROVERS 22 WAKEFIELD TRINITY 24

ROVERS: 1 Steve Collins; 2 Carl Hall; 3 Shaun Irwin; 4 Danny Baker; 5 Karl Pratt; 6 Jamie Coventry; 7 Ty Fallins; 8 Chico Jackson; 9 Richard Chapman; 10 Stuart Dickens; 11 Gary Price; 12 Neil Lowe; 13 Richard Slater. Subs: 14 Paddy Handley for Coventry (70); 15 Asa Amone for Lowe (50); 16 Micky Clarkson for Jackson (50); 17 Steve Dooler (not used).
Tries: Baker (15), Jackson (45), Collins (49), Hall (69); **Goals:** Chapman 3.
TRINITY: 1 Martyn Holland; 2 Josh Bostock; 3 Adam Hughes; 4 Martin Law; 5 Kevin Gray; 6 Garen Casey; 7 Roger Kenworthy; 8 Francis Stephenson; 9 Roy Southernwood; 10 Gary Lord; 11 Ian Hughes; 12 Sonny Whakarau; 13 Matt Fuller. Subs: 14 Sean Richardson for I Hughes (32); 15 Andy Fisher for Lord (26); 16 David Mycoe (not used); 17 Wayne McDonald for Whakarau (70); Lord for Stephenson (40); Stephenson for Lord (70).
Tries: Southernwood (2), Bostock (7, 25), Casey (58), Stephenson (76); **Goals:** Casey 2.
League Express Men of the Match:
Rovers: Richard Chapman; *Trinity:* Garen Casey.
Penalty count: 8-3; **Half time:** 6-12;
Referee: Nick Oddy (Halifax); **Attendance:** 8,224
(at McAlpine Stadium, Huddersfield).

SUPER LEAGUE GRAND FINAL

Saturday 24th October 1998

LEEDS RHINOS 4 WIGAN WARRIORS 10

RHINOS: 1 Iestyn Harris (C); 22 Leroy Rivett; 3 Richie Blackmore; 4 Brad Godden; 5 Francis Cummins; 13 Daryl Powell; 7 Ryan Sheridan; 8 Martin Masella; 21 Terry Newton; 25 Darren Fleary; 11 Adrian Morley; 17 Anthony Farrell; 12 Marc Glanville. Subs: 20 Jamie Mathiou for Masella (25); 24 Marcus St Hilaire for Powell (40); 14 Graham Holroyd for Newton (49); 27 Andy Hay for Fleary (54); Powell for Godden (58); Masella for Mathiou (71).
Try: Blackmore (20).
WARRIORS: 1 Kris Radlinski; 2 Jason Robinson; 3 Danny Moore; 4 Gary Connolly; 5 Mark Bell; 6 Henry Paul; 7 Tony Smith; 16 Terry O'Connor; 9 Robbie McCormack; 10 Tony Mestrov; 20 Lee Gilmour; 17 Stephen Holgate; 13 Andy Farrell (C). Subs: 8 Neil Cowie for O'Connor (18BB, rev 48); 14 Mick Cassidy for McCormack (19BB, rev 27); 25 Paul Johnson for Moore (37); 12 Simon Haughton for Gilmour (27BB, rev 33); Haughton for Holgate (33); Cowie for Mestrov (54); Cassidy for Haughton (64); Holgate for Cowie (68); Haughton for Gilmour (71BB, rev 75); Mestrov for O'Connor (75BB).
Try: Robinson (37); **Goals:** Farrell 3.
League Express Men of the Match:
Rhinos: Iestyn Harris; *Warriors:* Jason Robinson.
Penalty count: 7-13; **Half-time:** 4-6;
Referee: Russell Smith (Castleford); **Attendance:** 43,553
(at Old Trafford, Manchester).

1999

NORTHERN FORD PREMIERSHIP GRAND FINAL

Saturday 25th September 1999

DEWSBURY RAMS 11 HUNSLET HAWKS 12

RAMS: 1 Nathan Graham; 2 Alex Godfrey; 3 Paul Evans; 4 Brendan O'Meara; 5 Adrian Flynn; 6 Richard Agar; 7 Barry Eaton; 8 Alan Boothroyd; 9 Paul Delaney; 10 Matthew Long; 11 Andy Spink; 12 Mark Haigh; 13 Damian Ball. Subs: 14 Brendan Williams for Eaton (5BB, rev 15); 15 Sean Richardson for Haigh (50); 16 Simon Hicks for Long (25); 17 Paul Medley for Spink (50); Williams for Evans (61); Long for Boothroyd (71); Spink for Long (78).
Tries: Flynn (27), Ball (54); **Goal:** Eaton; **Field goal:** Agar.
HAWKS: 1 Abraham Fatnowna; 2 Chris Ross; 3 Shaun Irwin; 4 Paul Cook; 5 Iain Higgins; 6 Marcus Vassilakopoulos; 7 Latham Tawhai; 8 Richard Hayes; 9 Richard Pachniuk; 10 Steve Pryce; 11 Rob Wilson; 12 Jamie Leighton; 13 Lee St Hilaire. Subs: 14 Mick Coyle for Wilson (57); 15 Phil Kennedy for Pryce (35); 16 Jamie Thackray for St Hilaire (25); 17 Richard Baker for Higgins (55); Higgins for Fatnowna (62); Pryce for Kennedy (65).
Tries: Cook (31), Higgins (46); **Goal:** Ross;
Field goals: Tawhai, Leighton.
League Express Men of the Match:
Rams: Barry Eaton; *Hawks:* Latham Tawhai.
Penalty count: 8-5; **Half-time:** 7-7;
Referee: Steve Ganson (St Helens); **Attendance:** 5,783
(at Headingley Stadium, Leeds).

SUPER LEAGUE GRAND FINAL

Saturday 9th October 1999

BRADFORD BULLS 6 ST HELENS 8

BULLS: 28 Stuart Spruce; 2 Tevita Vaikona; 20 Scott Naylor; 5 Michael Withers; 17 Leon Pryce; 6 Henry Paul; 1 Robbie Paul (C); 10 Paul Anderson; 9 James Lowes; 29 Stuart Fielden; 15 David Boyle; 23 Bernard Dwyer; 13 Steve McNamara. Subs: 14 Paul Deacon for R Paul (53); 4 Nathan McAvoy (not used); 12 Mike Forshaw for McNamara (18); 22 Brian McDermott for Anderson (18); Anderson for Fielden (61); Fielden for Dwyer (65); R Paul for Deacon (72).
Try: H Paul (18); **Goal:** H Paul.
SAINTS: 1 Paul Atcheson; 14 Chris Smith; 3 Kevin Iro; 4 Paul Newlove; 5 Anthony Sullivan; 13 Paul Sculthorpe; 20 Tommy Martyn; 8 Apollo Perelini; 9 Keiron Cunningham; 10 Julian O'Neill; 2 Fereti Tuilagi; 21 Sonny Nickle; 11 Chris Joynt (C). Subs: 26 Paul Wellens for Martyn (52); 6 Sean Hoppe for Newlove (43); 16 Vila Matautia for O'Neill (20); 7 Sean Long for Perelini (24); Perelini for Matautia (46); O'Neill for Perelini (69).
Tries: Iro (65); **Goals:** Long 2.
League Express Men of the Match:
Bulls: Henry Paul; *Saints:* Kevin Iro.
Penalty count: 4-7; **Half-time:** 6-2;
Referee: Stuart Cummings (Widnes);
Attendance: 50,717 *(at Old Trafford, Manchester).*

2000

NORTHERN FORD PREMIERSHIP GRAND FINAL

Saturday 29th July 2000

DEWSBURY RAMS 13 LEIGH CENTURIONS 12

RAMS: 1 Nathan Graham; 2 Richard Baker; 4 Dan Potter; 3 Brendan O'Meara; 5 Adrian Flynn; 6 Richard Agar; 7 Barry Eaton; 8 Shayne Williams; 9 David Mycoe; 10 Mark Haigh; 11 Sean Richardson; 12 Daniel Frame; 13 Damian Ball. Subs: 14 Gavin Wood (not used); 15 Paul Delaney for Mycoe (53); 16 Ryan McDonald for Haigh (30); 17 Matthew Long for Williams (23); Haigh for McDonald (64).
Tries: Eaton (2), Long (23); **Goals:** Eaton 2;
Field goal: Agar.
Sin bin: Williams (66) - use of the elbow.
On report: Richardson (20) - high tackle on Donlan.
CENTURIONS: 1 Stuart Donlan; 5 David Ingram; 3 Paul Anderson; 4 Andy Fairclough; 2 Alan Cross; 6 Liam Bretherton; 7 Kieron Purtill; 8 Tim Street; 9 Mick Higham; 10 Andy Leathem; 11 Simon Baldwin; 12 Heath Cruckshank; 13 Adam Bristow. Subs: 14 James Arkwright for Cross (68); 15 Paul Norman for Street (36); 16 Radney Bowker (not used); 17 David Whittle for Leathem (24); Street for Norman (62).
Tries: Higham (29, 69); **Goals:** Bretherton 2.
Sin bin: Whittle (66) - retaliation.
League Express Men of the Match:
Rams: Richard Agar; *Centurions:* Mick Higham.
Penalty count: 4-4; **Half-time:** 10-6;
Referee: Robert Connolly (Wigan); **Attendance:** 8,487
(at Gigg Lane, Bury).

SUPER LEAGUE GRAND FINAL

Saturday 14th October 2000

ST HELENS 29 WIGAN WARRIORS 16

SAINTS: 17 Paul Wellens; 24 Steve Hall; 3 Kevin Iro; 15 Sean Hoppe; 5 Anthony Sullivan; 20 Tommy Martyn; 7 Sean Long; 8 Apollo Perelini; 9 Keiron Cunningham; 10 Julian O'Neill; 11 Chris Joynt (C); 22 Tim Jonkers; 13 Paul Sculthorpe. Subs: 14 Fereti Tuilagi for O'Neill (20); 12 Sonny Nickle for Perelini (28); 26 John Stankevitch for Jonkers (50); 23 Scott Barrow (not used); Perelini for Nickle (52); Jonkers for Stankevitch (66); Stankevitch for Perelini (67BB); O'Neill for Hall (74).
Tries: Hoppe (7), Joynt (28, 50), Tuilagi (69), Jonkers (80); **Goals:** Long 4; **Field goal:** Sculthorpe.
WARRIORS: 5 Jason Robinson; 2 Brett Dallas; 1 Kris Radlinski; 3 Steve Renouf; 26 David Hodgson; 6 Tony Smith; 7 Willie Peters; 8 Terry O'Connor; 9 Terry Newton; 10 Neil Cowie; 11 Mick Cassidy; 12 Denis Betts; 13 Andy Farrell (C). Subs: 23 Brady Malam for Cowie (30); 17 Tony Mestrov for O'Connor (43); 19 Chris Chester for Cassidy (47BB, rev 69); 14 Lee Gilmour for Betts (51); O'Connor for Mestrov (61); Cowie for Malam (67); Chester for Newton (75).
Tries: Farrell (13), Hodgson (58), Smith (61);
Goals: Farrell 2.
League Express Men of the Match:
Saints: Chris Joynt; *Warriors:* Andy Farrell.
Penalty count: 10-6; **Half-time:** 11-4;
Referee: Russell Smith (Castleford); **Attendance:** 58,132
(at Old Trafford, Manchester).

2001

NORTHERN FORD PREMIERSHIP GRAND FINAL

Saturday 28th July 2001

OLDHAM 14 WIDNES VIKINGS 24

OLDHAM: 1 Mark Sibson; 2 Joey Hayes; 3 Anthony Gibbons; 4 Pat Rich; 5 Joe McNicholas; 6 David Gibbons; 7 Neil Roden; 8 Leo Casey; 9 Keith Brennan; 10 Paul Norton; 11 Phil Farrell; 12 Bryan Henare; 13 Kevin Mannion. Subs: 14 Mike Ford for Mannion (27); 15 Jason Clegg for Casey (18); 16 John Hough for Brennan (44); 17 Danny Guest for Norton (40BB, rev 54); Mannion for Henare (66); Guest for Clegg (73).
Tries: Brennan (9), Ford (74), Mannion (80); **Goal:** Rich.
VIKINGS: 1 Paul Atcheson; 2 Damian Munro; 3 Craig Weston; 4 Jason Demetriou; 5 Chris Percival; 6 Richard Agar; 7 Martin Crompton; 8 Simon Knox; 9 Phil Cantillon; 10 Stephen Holgate; 11 Steve Gee; 12 Sean Richardson; 13 Tommy Hodgkinson. Subs: 14 Andy Craig for Percival (65); 15 Chris McKinney for Gee (41); 16 Joe Faimalo for Knox (32); 17 Matthew Long for Holgate (23); Knox for Long (49BB, rev 61); Holgate for Long (74).
Tries: Gee (17), Demetriou (38, 60), Cantillon (50), Munro (69); **Goals:** Weston 2.
League Express Men of the Match:
Oldham: Jason Clegg; *Vikings:* Phil Cantillon.
Penalty count: 8-5; **Half-time:** 4-10;
Referee: Steve Ganson (St Helens); **Attendance:** 8,974
(at Spotland, Rochdale).

SUPER LEAGUE GRAND FINAL

Saturday 13th October 2001

BRADFORD BULLS 37 WIGAN WARRIORS 6

BULLS: 5 Michael Withers; 2 Tevita Vaikona; 20 Scott Naylor; 23 Graham Mackay; 3 Leon Pryce; 6 Henry Paul; 1 Robbie Paul (C); 8 Joe Vagana; 9 James Lowes; 22 Brian McDermott; 11 Daniel Gartner; 19 Jamie Peacock; 12 Mike Forshaw. Subs: 29 Stuart Fielden for McDermott (21BB, rev 65); 10 Paul Anderson for Vagana (22); 15 Shane Rigon for Pryce (40); 7 Paul Deacon for R Paul (69); Vagana for Anderson (53); Fielden for Gartner (72); Anderson for Vagana (74).
Tries: Lowes (9), Withers (11, 27, 31), Fielden (65), Mackay (72); **Goals:** H Paul 5, Mackay;
Field goal: H Paul.

WARRIORS: 1 Kris Radlinski; 2 Brett Dallas; 4 Gary Connolly; 3 Steve Renouf; 5 Brian Carney; 6 Matthew Johns; 7 Adrian Lam; 8 Terry O'Connor; 9 Terry Newton; 20 Harvey Howard; 11 Mick Cassidy; 14 David Furner; 13 Andy Farrell (C). Subs: 15 Paul Johnson for Carney (12BB); 10 Neil Cowie for Howard (17); 12 Denis Betts for O'Connor (32); 19 Chris Chester for Farrell (59); O'Connor for Cowie (55); Howard for Newton (64); Cowie for Cassidy (72).
Try: Lam (63); **Goal:** Furner.
League Express Men of the Match:
Bulls: Michael Withers; *Warriors:* Adrian Lam.
Penalty count: 6-7; **Half-time:** 26-0;
Referee: Stuart Cummings (Widnes);
Attendance: 60,164 *(at Old Trafford, Manchester).*

2002

NORTHERN FORD PREMIERSHIP GRAND FINAL

Saturday 12th October 2002

HUDDERSFIELD GIANTS 38 LEIGH CENTURIONS 16

GIANTS: 1 Ben Cooper; 2 Hefin O'Hare; 3 Eorl Crabtree; 4 Graeme Hallas; 5 Marcus St Hilaire; 6 Stanley Gene; 7 Chris Thorman; 8 Michael Slicker; 9 Paul March; 10 Jeff Wittenberg; 11 David Atkins; 12 Robert Roberts; 13 Steve McNamara. Subs: 14 Heath Cruckshank for Roberts (24BB); 15 Chris Molyneux for Slicker (53); 16 Darren Turner for March (21); 17 Andy Rice for Cruckshank (57); Roberts for Wittenberg (34); Wittenberg for Roberts (74).
Tries: O'Hare (12, 78), St Hilaire (34, 53), Thorman (46), Gene (57); **Goals:** McNamara 7.
Sin bin: Roberts (47) - fighting.
CENTURIONS: 1 Neil Turley; 2 Leon Felton; 4 Jon Roper; 3 Dale Cardoza; 5 Oliver Marns; 6 Willie Swann; 7 Bobbie Goulding; 8 Vila Matautia; 9 Paul Rowley; 10 David Bradbury; 11 Simon Baldwin; 12 Andrew Isherwood; 13 Adam Bristow. Subs: 14 Gareth Price for Bradbury (24BB, rev 35); 15 John Duffy for Swann (32); 16 John Hamilton for Bristow (46BB, rev 57); 17 David Whittle for Matautia (22); Matautia for Bradbury (53BB); Swann for Goulding (58); Hamilton for Whittle (67); Bradbury for Turley (72); Goulding for Swann (75).
Tries: Cardoza (9), Marns (18), Hamilton (70);
Goals: Turley 2.
Sin bin: Whittle (47) - fighting;
Bristow (74) - interference.
On report: Isherwood (66) - high tackle on Roberts.
Rugby Leaguer & League Express Men of the Match:
Giants: Chris Thorman; *Centurions:* Adam Bristow.
Penalty count: 11-11; **Half-time:** 14-10;
Referee: Karl Kirkpatrick (Warrington);
Attendance: 9,051 *(at Halton Stadium, Widnes).*

SUPER LEAGUE GRAND FINAL

Saturday 19th October 2002

BRADFORD BULLS 18 ST HELENS 19

BULLS: 6 Michael Withers; 2 Tevita Vaikona; 20 Scott Naylor; 15 Brandon Costin; 5 Lesley Vainikolo; 1 Robbie Paul (C); 7 Paul Deacon; 8 Joe Vagana; 9 James Lowes; 29 Stuart Fielden; 11 Daniel Gartner; 12 Jamie Peacock; 13 Mike Forshaw. Subs: 14 Lee Gilmour for Gartner (21); 10 Paul Anderson for Vagana (25); 22 Brian McDermott for Fielden (34); 3 Leon Pryce for Vainikolo (53); Fielden for Anderson (55); Vainikolo for Paul (77).
Tries: Naylor (3), Paul (44), Withers (47);
Goals: Deacon 3.
SAINTS: 1 Paul Wellens; 5 Darren Albert; 3 Martin Gleeson; 4 Paul Newlove; 19 Anthony Stewart; 13 Paul Sculthorpe; 7 Sean Long; 8 Darren Britt; 9 Keiron Cunningham; 10 Barry Ward; 23 Mike Bennett; 15 Tim Jonkers; 11 Chris Joynt (C). Subs: 2 Sean Hoppe for Wellens (3); 12 Peter Shiels for Ward (27); 14 John Stankevitch for Britt (31BB, rev 58); 17 Mick Higham for Joynt (54); Stankevitch for Shiels (58); Joynt for Britt (75); Shiels for Jonkers (77).
Tries: Bennett (24), Long (32), Gleeson (56);
Goals: Long 3; **Field goal:** Long.
Rugby Leaguer & League Express Men of the Match:
Bulls: Paul Deacon; *Saints:* Mike Bennett.
Penalty count: 5-4; **Half-time:** 12-8;
Referee: Russell Smith (Castleford); **Attendance:** 61,138 *(at Old Trafford, Manchester).*

2003

NATIONAL LEAGUE TWO GRAND FINAL

Sunday 5th October 2003

KEIGHLEY COUGARS 13 SHEFFIELD EAGLES 11

COUGARS: 1 Matt Foster; 2 Max Tomlinson; 3 David Foster; 4 James Rushforth; 5 Andy Robinson; 6 Paul Ashton; 7 Matt Firth; 8 Phil Stephenson; 9 Simeon Hoyle; 10 Danny Ekis; 11 Oliver Wilkes; 12 Ian Sinfield; 13 Lee Patterson. Subs (all used): 14 Chris Wainwright; 15 Richard Mervill; 16 Mick Durham; 17 Jason Ramshaw.
Tries: M Foster (7), Robinson (74); **Goals:** Ashton 2;
Field goal: Firth.
EAGLES: 1 Andy Poynter; 2 Tony Weller; 3 Richard Goddard; 4 Tom O'Reilly; 5 Greg Hurst; 6 Gavin Brown; 7 Mark Aston; 8 Jack Howieson; 9 Gareth Stanley; 10 Dale Laughton; 11 Andy Raleigh; 12 Craig Brown; 13 Wayne Flynn. Subs (all used): 14 Peter Reilly; 15 Simon Tillyer; 16 Nick Turnbull; 17 Mitchell Stringer.
Try: O'Reilly (51); **Goals:** G Brown 3; **Field goal:** Reilly.

Rugby Leaguer & League Express Men of the Match:
Cougars: Simeon Hoyle; *Eagles:* Andy Raleigh.
Penalty count: 6-8; **Half-time:** 9-4;
Referee: Peter Taberner (Wigan).
(at Halton Stadium, Widnes).

NATIONAL LEAGUE ONE GRAND FINAL

Sunday 5th October 2003

LEIGH CENTURIONS 14 SALFORD CITY REDS 31

CENTURIONS: 1 Neil Turley; 2 Damian Munro; 3 Alan Hadcroft; 4 Danny Halliwell; 5 Leroy Rivett; 6 John Duffy; 7 Tommy Martyn; 8 Sonny Nickle; 9 Patrick Weisner; 10 Paul Norman; 11 Sean Richardson; 12 Willie Swann; 13 Adam Bristow. Subs (all used): 14 David Bradbury; 15 Lee Sanderson; 16 Bryan Henare; 17 Ricky Bibey.
Tries: Richardson (33), Halliwell (38), Swann (65);
Goal: Turley.
On report: Nickle (60) - late tackle on Clinch.
CITY REDS: 1 Jason Flowers; 2 Danny Arnold; 3 Stuart Littler; 4 Alan Hunte; 5 Andy Kirk; 6 Cliff Beverley; 7 Gavin Clinch; 8 Neil Baynes; 9 Malcolm Alker; 10 Andy Coley; 11 Simon Baldwin; 12 Paul Highton; 13 Chris Charles. Subs (all used): 14 Steve Blakeley; 15 David Highton; 16 Martin Moana; 17 Gareth Haggerty.
Tries: Hunte (3, 52), Beverley (23), Littler (73);
Goals: Charles 6, Blakeley; **Field goal:** Blakeley.
Rugby Leaguer & League Express Men of the Match:
Centurions: Willie Swann; *City Reds:* Gavin Clinch.
Penalty count: 10-10; **Half-time:** 10-16;
Referee: Richard Silverwood (Dewsbury);
Attendance: 9,186 *(at Halton Stadium, Widnes).*

SUPER LEAGUE GRAND FINAL

Saturday 18th October 2003

BRADFORD BULLS 25 WIGAN WARRIORS 12

BULLS: 17 Stuart Reardon; 2 Tevita Vaikona; 6 Michael Withers; 4 Shontayne Hape; 5 Lesley Vainikolo; 15 Karl Pratt; 7 Paul Deacon; 8 Joe Vagana; 9 James Lowes; 29 Stuart Fielden; 11 Daniel Gartner; 12 Jamie Peacock; 13 Mike Forshaw. Subs (all used): 10 Paul Anderson; 18 Lee Radford; 3 Leon Pryce; 1 Robbie Paul (C).
Tries: Reardon (51), Hape (59), Lowes (75);
Goals: Deacon 6/6; **Field goal:** Deacon.
WARRIORS: 1 Kris Radlinski; 5 Brian Carney; 18 Martin Aspinwall; 14 David Hodgson; 2 Brett Dallas; 15 Sean O'Loughlin; 20 Luke Robinson; 30 Quentin Pongia; 9 Terry Newton; 10 Craig Smith; 11 Mick Cassidy; 12 Danny Tickle; 13 Andy Farrell (C). Subs (all used): 4 Paul Johnson; 8 Terry O'Connor; 23 Gareth Hock; 17 Mark Smith.
Tries: Tickle (17), Radlinski (72); **Goals:** Farrell 2/3.
Rugby Leaguer & League Express Men of the Match:
Bulls: Stuart Reardon; *Warriors:* Kris Radlinski.
Penalty count: 7-6; **Half-time:** 4-6;
Referee: Karl Kirkpatrick (Warrington);
Attendance: 65,537 *(at Old Trafford, Manchester).*

2004

NATIONAL LEAGUE ONE GRAND FINAL

Sunday 10th October 2004

LEIGH CENTURIONS 32 WHITEHAVEN 16
(after extra time)

CENTURIONS: 1 Neil Turley; 2 Rob Smyth; 3 Danny Halliwell; 4 Ben Cooper; 5 David Alstead; 6 John Duffy; 7 Tommy Martyn; 8 Simon Knox; 9 Paul Rowley; 10 Matt Sturm; 11 David Larder; 12 Oliver Wilkes; 13 Ian Knott. Subs (all used): 14 Dave McConnell; 15 Heath Cruckshank; 16 Richard Marshall; 17 Willie Swann.
Tries: Cooper (27, 83), Martyn (61), Turley (87);
Goals: Turley 6/8; **Field goals:** Turley 2, Rowley, Martyn.
WHITEHAVEN: 1 Gary Broadbent; 2 Craig Calvert; 3 David Seeds; 4 Mick Nanyn; 5 Wesley Wilson; 6 Leroy Joe; 7 Sam Obst; 8 Marc Jackson; 9 Aaron Lester; 10 David Fatialofa; 11 Paul Davidson; 12 Howard Hill; 13 Craig Walsh. Subs (all used): 14 Spencer Miller; 15 Carl Sice; 16 Chris McKinney; 17 Ryan Tandy.
Tries: Wilson (2, 71), Calvert (45); **Goals:** Nanyn 2/6.
Rugby Leaguer & League Express Men of the Match:
Centurions: Neil Turley; *Whitehaven:* Aaron Lester.
Penalty count: 5-9; **Half-time:** 7-6; **Full-time:** 16-16;
Referee: Ronnie Laughton (Barnsley);
Attendance: 11,005 *(at Halton Stadium, Widnes).*

SUPER LEAGUE GRAND FINAL

Saturday 16th October 2004

BRADFORD BULLS 8 LEEDS RHINOS 16

BULLS: 6 Michael Withers; 17 Stuart Reardon; 16 Paul Johnson; 4 Shontayne Hape; 5 Lesley Vainikolo; 18 Iestyn Harris; 7 Paul Deacon; 8 Joe Vagana; 1 Robbie Paul (C); 29 Stuart Fielden; 12 Jamie Peacock; 13 Logan Swann; 11 Lee Radford. Subs: 10 Paul Anderson for Vagana (14); 15 Karl Pratt for Paul (23); 27 Rob Parker for Anderson (24); 19 Jamie Langley for Peacock (32); Paul for Withers (ht); Peacock for Radford (48); Radford for Swann (54); Vagana for Parker (56); Parker for Fielden (63); Fielden for Vagana (67); Swann for Langley (68).
Tries: Vainikolo (7), Hape (43); **Goals:** Deacon 0/2.

RHINOS: 21 Richard Mathers; 18 Mark Calderwood; 5 Chev Walker; 4 Keith Senior; 22 Marcus Bai; 13 Kevin Sinfield (C); 6 Danny McGuire; 19 Danny Ward; 9 Matt Diskin; 8 Ryan Bailey; 3 Chris McKenna; 29 Ali Lauitiiti; 11 David Furner. Subs: 16 Willie Poching for Furner (19); 10 Barrie McDermott for Ward (22); Ward for Bailey (29); 7 Rob Burrow for Lauitiiti (30); Bailey for McDermott (41); 20 Jamie Jones-Buchanan for McKenna (48); Lauitiiti for Ward (50); Furner for Sinfield (60); McKenna for Poching (63); Sinfield for Diskin (67); Poching for McKenna (72); Ward for Bailey (73).
Tries: Diskin (15), McGuire (75); **Goals:** Sinfield 4/4.
Rugby Leaguer & League Express Men of the Match:
Bulls: Lesley Vainikolo; *Rhinos:* Richard Mathers.
Penalty count: 5-5; **Half-time:** 4-10;
Referee: Steve Ganson (St Helens);
Attendance: 65,547 *(at Old Trafford, Manchester).*

2005

NATIONAL LEAGUE ONE GRAND FINAL

Sunday 9th October 2005

CASTLEFORD TIGERS 36 WHITEHAVEN 8

TIGERS: 1 Michael Platt; 2 Waine Pryce; 3 Michael Shenton; 4 Jon Hepworth; 5 Damien Blanch; 6 Brad Davis; 7 Andrew Henderson; 8 Adam Watene; 9 Aaron Smith; 10 Richard Fletcher; 11 Tom Haughey; 12 Steve Crouch; 13 Deon Bird. Subs (all used): 14 Paul Handforth; 15 Craig Huby; 16 Adrian Vowles; 17 Frank Watene.
Tries: Huby (22), Crouch (24), Blanch (26), Davis (33, 45), Haughey (52);
Goals: Fletcher 2/3, Huby 3/4, Hepworth 1/1.
WHITEHAVEN: 1 Gary Broadbent; 2 Craig Calvert; 3 David Seeds; 4 Mick Nanyn; 5 Wesley Wilson; 6 Leroy Joe; 7 Joel Penny; 8 Ryan Tandy; 9 Carl Sice; 10 David Fatialofa; 11 Spencer Miller; 12 Howard Hill; 13 Aaron Lester. Subs (all used): 14 Carl Rudd; 15 Aaron Summers; 16 Craig Chambers; 17 Marc Jackson.
Tries: Seeds (56), Calvert (78); **Goals:** Nanyn 0/2.
Sin bin: Joe (16) - late tackle on Davis.
On report: Joe (16) - late tackle on Davis;
Sice (40) - alleged biting.
Rugby Leaguer & League Express Men of the Match:
Tigers: Brad Davis; *Whitehaven:* Wesley Wilson.
Penalty count: 4-9; **Half-time:** 26-0;
Referee: Steve Ganson (St Helens);
Attendance: 13,300 *(at Halton Stadium, Widnes).*

SUPER LEAGUE GRAND FINAL

Saturday 15th October 2005

BRADFORD BULLS 15 LEEDS RHINOS 6

BULLS: 6 Michael Withers; 3 Leon Pryce; 13 Ben Harris; 4 Shontayne Hape; 5 Lesley Vainikolo; 18 Iestyn Harris; 7 Paul Deacon; 12 Jamie Peacock (C); 9 Ian Henderson; 29 Stuart Fielden; 16 Paul Johnson; 10 Brad Meyers; 11 Lee Radford. Subs (all used): 24 Adrian Morley for Johnson (5); 19 Jamie Langley for Peacock (24); 8 Joe Vagana for Fielden (24); Johnson for Radford (24); 1 Robbie Paul for Henderson (31); Peacock for Vagana (45); Fielden for Morley (49); Henderson for Paul (54); Radford for Meyers (60); Morley for Peacock (62); Meyers for Langley (73); Peacock for Johnson (74).
Tries: L Pryce (29), Vainikolo (53); **Goals:** Deacon 3/5;
Field goal: I Harris.
RHINOS: 1 Richard Mathers; 2 Mark Calderwood; 3 Chev Walker; 12 Chris McKenna; 5 Marcus Bai; 6 Danny McGuire; 7 Rob Burrow; 8 Ryan Bailey; 14 Andrew Dunemann; 15 Danny Ward; 20 Gareth Ellis; 16 Willie Poching; 13 Kevin Sinfield (C). Subs (all used): 10 Barrie McDermott for Ward (17); 11 Ali Lauitiiti for Poching (21); 18 Jamie Jones-Buchanan for Bailey (31); Ward for McDermott (34); 9 Matt Diskin for Ellis (48); Poching for Lauitiiti (48); McDermott for Ward (54); Ellis for Poching (54); Lauitiiti for McDermott (61); Poching for Dunemann (65); Ward for Jones-Buchanan (68); Dunemann for Ellis (71).
Try: McGuire (22); **Goals:** Sinfield 1/2.
Rugby Leaguer & League Express Men of the Match:
Bulls: Leon Pryce; *Rhinos:* Danny McGuire.
Penalty count: 6-8; **Half-time:** 8-6;
Referee: Ashley Klein (Keighley); **Attendance:** 65,537 *(at Old Trafford, Manchester).*

2006

NATIONAL LEAGUE TWO GRAND FINAL

Sunday 8th October 2006

SHEFFIELD EAGLES 35 SWINTON LIONS 10

EAGLES: 1 Johnny Woodcock; 5 Greg Hurst; 4 Jimmy Walker; 3 James Ford; 2 Rob Worrincy; 6 Brendon Lindsay; 7 Gavin Brown; 8 Jack Howieson; 9 Paul Pickering; 10 Mitchell Stringer; 11 Andy Hay; 12 Dale Holdstock; 13 Andy Smith. Subs (all used): 14 Craig Poucher; 15 Martin Ostler; 16 Sean Dickinson; 17 Waisale Sovatabua.
Tries: Worrincy (21, 43), Lindsay (38), Woodcock (39), Walker (51), Hay (60); **Goals:** Woodcock 5/6;
Field goal: G Brown.
LIONS: 1 Wayne English; 2 Andy Saywell; 3 Darren Woods; 4 David Alstead; 5 Marlon Billy; 6 Martin Moana; 7 Chris Hough; 8 Bruce Johnson; 9 Phil Wood; 10 Dave Newton; 11 Kris Smith; 12 Ian Sinfield; 13 Lee Marsh. Subs (all used): 14 Liam McGovern; 15 Chris Morley; 16 Danny Aboushakra; 17 Ian Parry.
Tries: Saywell (35), Alstead (74); **Goals:** McGovern 1/2.

Rugby Leaguer & League Express Men of the Match: *Eagles:* Johnny Woodcock; *Lions:* Wayne English.
Penalty count: 3-4; **Half-time:** 16-4;
Referee: Peter Taberner (Wigan).
(at Halliwell Jones Stadium, Warrington).

Dewsbury Rams were National League Two Champions in 2006. This game was to determine who took the second promotion place.

NATIONAL LEAGUE ONE GRAND FINAL

Sunday 8th October 2006

HULL KINGSTON ROVERS 29 WIDNES VIKINGS 16

ROVERS: 1 Ben Cockayne; 2 Leroy Rivett; 3 Gareth Morton; 4 Jon Goddard; 5 Byron Ford; 6 Scott Murrell; 7 James Webster; 8 Makali Aizue; 9 Ben Fisher; 10 David Tangata-Toa; 11 Iain Morrison; 12 Michael Smith; 13 Tommy Gallagher. Subs (all used): 14 Pat Weisner; 15 Dwayne Barker; 16 Jason Netherton; 17 Dave Wilson.
Tries: Ford (6), Goddard (18, 36), Murrell (24), Weisner (43); **Goals:** Morton 4/6; **Field goal:** Murrell.
VIKINGS: 1 Gavin Dodd; 2 Damien Blanch; 3 Sean Gleeson; 4 Daryl Cardiss; 5 John Kirkpatrick; 6 Dennis Moran; 7 Ian Watson; 8 Terry O'Connor; 9 Mark Smith; 10 Barrie McDermott; 11 Mick Cassidy; 12 David Allen; 13 Bob Beswick. Subs (all used): 14 Aaron Summers; 15 Oliver Wilkes; 16 Jordan James; 17 Ryan Tandy.
Tries: Dodd (32), Tandy (57), Blanch (70);
Goals: Dodd 2/3.
Rugby Leaguer & League Express Men of the Match: *Rovers:* James Webster; *Vikings:* Mark Smith.
Penalty count: 8-5; **Half-time:** 22-4;
Referee: Phil Bentham (Warrington); **Attendance:** 13,024
(at Halliwell Jones Stadium, Warrington).

SUPER LEAGUE GRAND FINAL

Saturday 14th October 2006

HULL FC 4 ST HELENS 26

HULL: 1 Shaun Briscoe; 14 Motu Tony; 4 Sid Domic; 3 Kirk Yeaman; 5 Gareth Raynor; 13 Paul Cooke; 7 Richard Horne; 8 Ewan Dowes; 9 Richard Swain (C); 10 Garreth Carvell; 11 Lee Radford; 12 Shayne McMenemy; 24 Danny Washbrook. Subs: 15 Paul King for Carvell (17); 19 Graeme Horne for Radford (23); 26 Scott Wheeldon for Dowes (27); 6 Richard Whiting for McMenemy (29); Dowes for Wheeldon (49); Carvell for King (49); Radford for G Horne (51); McMenemy for Whiting (54); King for Carvell (68); Wheeldon for Dowes (73); Whiting for Tony (76); G Horne for Radford (77).
Try: Domic (24); **Goals:** Cooke 0/1.
SAINTS: 1 Paul Wellens; 2 Ade Gardner; 3 Jamie Lyon; 4 Willie Talau; 5 Francis Meli; 6 Leon Pryce; 7 Sean Long (C); 17 Paul Anderson; 9 Keiron Cunningham; 10 Jason Cayless; 11 Lee Gilmour; 12 Jon Wilkin; 16 Jason Hooper. Subs: 23 Maurie Fa'asavalu for P Anderson (12); 19 James Graham for Cayless (25); 15 Mike Bennett for Fa'asavalu (28); 14 James Roby for Cunningham (31); P Anderson for Wilkin (33); Cunningham for Gilmour (49); Cayless for P Anderson (52); Wilkin for Hooper (56); Fa'asavalu for Cayless (58); Gilmour for Graham (66); Cayless for Fa'asavalu (72); P Anderson for Wilkin (75).
Tries: Meli (17), Pryce (29), Talau (49), Gardner (52), Cunningham (62); **Goals:** Lyon 3/5.
Rugby Leaguer & League Express Men of the Match: *Hull:* Shaun Briscoe; *Saints:* Paul Wellens.
Penalty count: 4-2; **Half-time:** 4-10;
Referee: Karl Kirkpatrick (Warrington);
Attendance: 72,582 *(at Old Trafford, Manchester).*

2007

NATIONAL LEAGUE TWO GRAND FINAL

Sunday 7th October 2007

FEATHERSTONE ROVERS 24 OLDHAM 6

ROVERS: 1 Loz Wildbore; 2 Danny Kirmond; 3 Jon Whittle; 4 Wayne McHugh; 5 Ade Adebisi; 6 Andy Kain; 7 Paul Handforth; 8 Gareth Handford; 9 Joe McLocklan; 10 Stuart Dickens; 11 Jamie Field; 12 Richard Blakeway; 13 Tom Haughey. Subs (all used): 14 Jamie Benn; 15 Ian Tonks; 16 James Houston; 17 Gavin Swinson.
Tries: McHugh (39, 49), Handforth (46);
Goals: Dickens 5/6; **Field goals:** Wildbore (66, 70).
Dismissal: Blakeway (64) – head butt on Roberts.
OLDHAM: 1 Gareth Langley; 2 Byron Ford; 3 Craig Littler; 4 Adam Hughes; 5 Lucas Onyango; 6 Neil Roden; 7 James Coyle; 8 Anthony Tonks; 9 Simeon Hoyle; 10 Richard Mervill; 11 Ian Sinfield; 12 Robert Roberts; 13 Geno Costin. Subs (all used): 14 Ian Hodson; 15 Alex Wilkinson; 16 Said Tamghart; 17 Matty Brooks.
Try: Hughes (31); **Goals:** Langley 1/2.
Rugby Leaguer & League Express Men of the Match: *Rovers:* Paul Handforth; *Oldham:* Robert Roberts.
Penalty count: 9-5; **Half-time:** 10-6;
Referee: Gareth Hewer. *(at Headingley Carnegie, Leeds).*

Celtic Crusaders were National League Two Champions in 2007. This game was to determine who took the second promotion place.

NATIONAL LEAGUE ONE GRAND FINAL

Sunday 7th October 2007

CASTLEFORD TIGERS 42 WIDNES VIKINGS 10

TIGERS: 1 Stuart Donlan; 2 Danny Williams; 3 Michael Shenton; 4 Ryan McGoldrick; 5 Kirk Dixon; 6 Anthony Thackeray; 7 Danny Brough; 8 Liam Higgins; 9 Andrew Henderson; 10 Awen Guttenbeil; 11 Joe Westerman; 12 Ryan Clayton; 13 Peter Lupton. Subs (all used): 14 Mark Leafa; 15 Chris Charles; 16 Michael Wainwright; 17 Ryan Boyle.
Tries: Wainwright (20), McGoldrick (29), Guttenbeil (44, 76), M Shenton (52), Westerman (62), Clayton (66);
Goals: Brough 6/9; **Field goals:** Brough (25, 55).
VIKINGS: 1 Scott Grix; 2 Damien Blanch; 3 Toa Kohe-Love; 4 Mick Nanyn; 5 Gavin Dodd; 6 Dennis Moran; 7 Joel Penny; 8 Mick Cassidy; 9 Mark Smith; 10 Oliver Wilkes; 11 Joel Tomkins; 12 Paul Noone; 13 Bob Beswick. Subs (all used): 14 Aaron Summers; 15 Jordan James; 16 Ian Webster; 17 Lee Doran.
Tries: Nanyn (35), Wilkes (69); **Goals:** Nanyn 1/2.
Rugby Leaguer & League Express Men of the Match: *Tigers:* Danny Brough; *Vikings:* Scott Grix.
Penalty count: 7-2; **Half-time:** 13-4;
Referee: Phil Bentham; **Attendance:** 20,814
(at Headingley Carnegie, Leeds).

SUPER LEAGUE GRAND FINAL

Saturday 13th October 2007

LEEDS RHINOS 33 ST HELENS 6

RHINOS: 1 Brent Webb; 5 Lee Smith; 3 Clinton Toopi; 4 Keith Senior; 2 Scott Donald; 6 Danny McGuire; 7 Rob Burrow; 8 Kylie Leuluai; 9 Matt Diskin; 10 Jamie Peacock; 11 Jamie Jones-Buchanan; 12 Gareth Ellis; 13 Kevin Sinfield (C). Subs (all used): 14 Ali Lauitiiti for Diskin (23); 16 Ryan Bailey for Leuluai (18); 18 Ian Kirke for Jones-Buchanan (33); 22 Carl Ablett for Kirke (57); Leuluai for Bailey (55); Jones-Buchanan for Lauitiiti (60); Diskin for Ablett (63); Kirke for Leuluai (65); Bailey for Kirke (76).
Tries: Webb (19), Lauitiiti (50), Donald (52), Smith (69), Jones-Buchanan (80); **Goals:** Sinfield 6/7;
Field goal: Burrow (55).
SAINTS: 1 Paul Wellens; 2 Ade Gardner; 3 Matt Gidley; 4 Willie Talau; 5 Francis Meli; 6 Leon Pryce; 7 Sean Long; 8 Nick Fozzard; 9 Keiron Cunningham (C); 10 Jason Cayless; 11 Lee Gilmour; 30 Chris Flannery; 12 Jon Wilkin. Subs (all used): 17 James Graham for Cayless (15); 14 James Roby for Cunningham (23); 23 Maurie Fa'asavalu for Fozzard (23); 15 Mike Bennett for Wilkin (31); Cayless for Fa'asavalu (34); Cunningham for Flannery (51); Wilkin for Bennett (55); Fa'asavalu for Cayless (55); Fozzard for Graham (57); Cayless for Fozzard (68); Graham for Fa'asavalu (68); Bennett for Gilmour (72).
Try: Roby (27); **Goals:** Long 1/2.
Rugby Leaguer & League Express Men of the Match: *Rhinos:* Rob Burrow; *Saints:* Sean Long.
Penalty count: 4-5; **Half-time:** 8-6; **Referee:** Ashley Klein;
Attendance: 71,352 *(at Old Trafford, Manchester).*

2008

NATIONAL LEAGUE TWO GRAND FINAL

Sunday 28th September 2008

DONCASTER 18 OLDHAM 10

DONCASTER: 1 Zebastian Luisi; 2 Dean Colton; 3 Andreas Bauer; 4 Shaun Leaf; 5 Wayne Reittie; 6 Kyle Wood; 7 Luke Gale; 8 Nathan Freer; 9 Corey Lawrie; 10 Alex Benson; 11 Peter Green; 12 Craig Lawton; 13 Josh Weeden. Subs (all used): 14 Kyle Briggs; 15 Chris Buttery; 16 Michael Haley; 17 Mark Castle.
Tries: Buttery (44), Gale (49), Briggs (73);
Goals: Gale 3/4.
OLDHAM: 1 Paul O'Connor; 2 Gareth Langley; 3 Marcus St Hilaire; 4 Mick Nanyn; 5 Daryl Cardiss; 6 Phil Joseph; 7 James Coyle; 8 Adam Robinson; 9 Matty Brooks; 10 Richard Mervill; 11 Tommy Goulden; 12 Danny Halliwell; 13 Robert Roberts. Subs (all used): 14 Ian Hodson; 15 Luke Menzies; 16 Chris Baines; 17 Said Tamghart.
Tries: Hodson (34), Nanyn (62); **Goals:** Nanyn 1/4.
Rugby Leaguer & League Express Men of the Match: *Doncaster:* Luke Gale; *Oldham:* Adam Robinson.
Penalty count: 7-8; **Half-time:** 2-6;
Referee: Ronnie Laughton.
(at Halliwell Jones Stadium, Warrington).

Gateshead Thunder were National League Two Champions in 2008. This game was to determine who took the second promotion place.

NATIONAL LEAGUE ONE GRAND FINAL

Sunday 28th September 2008

CELTIC CRUSADERS 18 SALFORD CITY REDS 36
(after extra time)

CRUSADERS: 1 Tony Duggan; 2 Luke Dyer; 3 Josh Hannay; 4 Mark Dalle Cort; 5 Anthony Blackwood; 6 Damien Quinn; 7 Jace Van Dijk; 8 Jordan James; 9 Neil Budworth; 10 David Tangata-Toa; 11 Chris Beasley; 12 Darren Mapp; 13 Terry Martin. Subs (all used): 14 Aaron Summers; 15 Ian Webster; 16 Mark Lennon; 17 Neale Wyatt.
Tries: Blackwood (38), Dyer (50), J James (54), Tangata-Toa (66); **Goals:** Hannay 0/1, Lennon 1/3.
CITY REDS: 1 Karl Fitzpatrick; 2 Matt Gardner; 3 Stuart Littler; 4 John Wilshere; 5 Paul White; 6 Robbie Paul; 7 Richard Myler; 8 Paul Highton; 9 Malcolm Alker; 10 Craig Stapleton; 11 Ian Sibbit; 12 Luke Adamson; 13 Jordan Turner. Subs (all used): 14 Stefan Ratchford; 15 Steve Bannister; 16 Lee Jewitt; 17 Phil Leuluai.
Tries: White (5, 86), Gardner (26), Fitzpatrick (63), Sibbit (83), Myler (99); **Goals:** Wilshere 6/7.
Rugby Leaguer & League Express Men of the Match: *Crusaders:* Tony Duggan; *City Reds:* John Wilshere.
Penalty count: 5-5; **Half-time:** 4-10; **Full-time:** 18-18;
Referee: Ben Thaler; **Attendance:** 7,104
(at Halliwell Jones Stadium, Warrington).

SUPER LEAGUE GRAND FINAL

Saturday 4th October 2008

LEEDS RHINOS 24 ST HELENS 16

RHINOS: 5 Lee Smith; 22 Ryan Hall; 19 Carl Ablett; 4 Keith Senior; 2 Scott Donald; 6 Danny McGuire; 7 Rob Burrow; 8 Kylie Leuluai; 9 Matt Diskin; 10 Jamie Peacock; 11 Jamie Jones-Buchanan; 12 Gareth Ellis; 13 Kevin Sinfield (C). Subs (all used): 17 Nick Scruton; 14 Ali Lauitiiti; 18 Ian Kirke; 16 Ryan Bailey.
Tries: Smith (23), Hall (37), McGuire (49, 63);
Goals: Sinfield 4/4.
SAINTS: 1 Paul Wellens; 2 Ade Gardner; 3 Matt Gidley; 4 Willie Talau; 5 Francis Meli; 6 Leon Pryce; 7 Sean Long; 18 Bryn Hargreaves; 9 Keiron Cunningham (C); 17 James Graham; 11 Lee Gilmour; 12 Jon Wilkin; 16 Chris Flannery. Subs (all used): 8 Nick Fozzard; 21 Paul Clough; 14 James Roby; 23 Maurie Fa'asavalu.
Tries: Graham (6), Gidley (43), Gardner (59);
Goals: Long 2/3.
Rugby Leaguer & League Express Men of the Match: *Rhinos:* Jamie Peacock; *Saints:* Sean Long.
Penalty count: 6-8; **Half-time:** 12-6;
Referee: Ashley Klein; **Attendance:** 68,810
(at Old Trafford, Manchester).

2009

CHAMPIONSHIP ONE GRAND FINAL

Sunday 4th October 2009

KEIGHLEY COUGARS 28 OLDHAM 26

COUGARS: 1 George Rayner; 2 Sam Gardner; 3 Dan Potter; 4 Oliver Pursglove; 5 Gavin Duffy; 6 Jon Presley; 7 Danny Jones; 17 Scott Law; 14 Jamaine Wray; 8 Andy Shickell; 11 Will Cartledge; 18 Greg Nicholson; 13 Carl Hughes. Subs (all used): 21 Ryan Smith; 28 Ryan Benjafield; 9 James Feather; 16 Brendan Rawlins.
Tries: Gardner (24), Jones (42, 50), Presley (63), Pursglove (67); **Goals:** Jones 4/5.
OLDHAM: 4 Paul Reilly; 21 Lucas Onyango; 24 Marcus St Hilaire; 22 Phil Joseph; 1 Paul O'Connor; 18 Neil Roden; 7 Thomas Coyle; 15 Jason Boults; 30 Martin Roden; 16 Wayne Kerr; 23 Chris Baines; 12 Tommy Goulden; 28 Craig Lawton. Subs (all used): 10 Jamie I'Anson; 25 Luke Menzies; 27 Matt Ashe; 29 Ben Heaton.
Tries: Menzies (35, 76), N Roden (54), St Hilaire (70), Kerr (78); **Goals:** Baines 3/4, Ashe 0/1.
Rugby Leaguer & League Express Men of the Match: *Cougars:* Danny Jones; *Oldham:* Luke Menzies.
Penalty count: 9-2; **Half-time:** 4-6;
Referee: Ronnie Laughton.
(at Halliwell Jones Stadium, Warrington).

Dewsbury Rams were Championship One Champions in 2009. This game was to determine who took the second promotion place.

CHAMPIONSHIP GRAND FINAL

Sunday 4th October 2009

BARROW RAIDERS 26 HALIFAX 18

RAIDERS: 1 Gary Broadbent; 36 Andy Ballard; 32 Andreas Bauer; 4 Liam Harrison; 5 James Nixon; 24 Jamie Rooney; 31 James Coyle; 34 Rob Roberts; 9 Andy Ellis; 8 Brett McDermott; 33 Dave Allen; 22 Ned Catic; 26 Zebastian Luisi. Subs (all used): 15 Chris Young; 13 Andy Bracek; 35 Danny Halliwell; 14 Paul Noone.
Tries: Harrison (33), Ballard (37), Allen (61), Bauer (66, 78); **Goals:** Rooney 3/5.
HALIFAX: 4 Shad Royston; 5 James Haley; 15 Mark Roberts; 2 Lee Paterson; 23 Rob Worrincy; 19 Mick Govin; 7 Ben Black; 21 Neil Cherryholme; 9 Sean Penkywicz; 22 David Wrench; 11 David Larder; 27 Steve Bannister; 12 Paul Smith. Subs (all used): 13 Bob Beswick; 14 Mark Gleeson; 16 Said Tamghart; 26 Dominic Maloney.
Tries: Haley (12), Royston (31), Black (45), Govin (70);
Goals: Paterson 1/5.
Rugby Leaguer & League Express Men of the Match: *Raiders:* Gary Broadbent; *Halifax:* Mick Govin.
Penalty count: 8-5; **Half-time:** 10-10;
Referee: Phil Bentham; **Attendance:** 11,398
(at Halliwell Jones Stadium, Warrington).

SUPER LEAGUE GRAND FINAL

Saturday 10th October 2009

LEEDS RHINOS 18 ST HELENS 10

RHINOS: 1 Brent Webb; 2 Scott Donald; 3 Lee Smith; 4 Keith Senior; 5 Ryan Hall; 6 Danny McGuire; 7 Rob Burrow; 8 Kylie Leuluai; 14 Matt Diskin; 10 Jamie Peacock; 11 Jamie Jones-Buchanan; 18 Carl Ablett; 13 Kevin Sinfield (C). Subs (all used): 16 Ryan Bailey for Leuluai (19); 19 Luke Burgess for Peacock (29); 17 Ian Kirke for Jones-Buchanan (29); 12 Ali Lauitiiti for Ablett (29); Jones-Buchanan for Lauitiiti (36); Peacock for Burgess (46); Leuluai for Bailey (53); Ablett for Kirke (57); Burgess for Diskin (62); Bailey for Leuluai (67); Diskin for Burgess (69); Kirke for Jones-Buchanan (76).
Tries: Diskin (30), Smith (37, 72); **Goals:** Sinfield 2/4;
Field goals: Sinfield (42), Burrow (78).
SAINTS: 1 Paul Wellens; 2 Ade Gardner; 3 Matt Gidley; 18 Kyle Eastmond; 5 Francis Meli; 6 Leon Pryce; 7 Sean Long; 10 James Graham; 9 Keiron Cunningham (C); 16 Tony Puletua; 12 Jon Wilkin; 11 Lee Gilmour; 13 Chris Flannery. Subs (all used): 14 James Roby for Cunningham (25); 15 Bryn Hargreaves for Puletua (24); 17 Paul Clough for Gilmour (31); 23 Maurie Fa'asavalu for Graham (31); Graham for Fa'asavalu (48); Puletua for Hargreaves (50); Gilmour for Wilkin (55); Cunningham for Clough (61); Wilkin for Roby (65); Roby for Flannery (73).
Try: Eastmond (13); **Goals:** Eastmond 3/3.
Rugby Leaguer & League Express Men of the Match:
Rhinos: Kevin Sinfield; *Saints:* James Graham.
Penalty count: 8-7; **Half-time:** 8-8;
Referee: Steve Ganson; **Attendance:** 63,259
(at Old Trafford, Manchester).

2010

CHAMPIONSHIP ONE GRAND FINAL

Sunday 26th September 2010

OLDHAM 4 YORK CITY KNIGHTS 25

OLDHAM: 1 Paul O'Connor; 2 Lucas Onyango; 24 Marcus St Hilaire; 4 Mick Fogerty; 5 John Gillam; 6 Neil Roden; 28 Gregg McNally; 8 Jason Boults; 9 Martin Roden; 16 Wayne Kerr; 18 Chris Clarke; 13 Joe Chandler; 21 Valu Bentley. Subs (all used): 10 Dave Ellison; 19 Ben Heaton; 17 Danny Whitmore; 7 Matt Ashe.
Try: Fogerty (20); **Goals:** McNally 0/1.
CITY KNIGHTS: 31 James Haynes; 2 Wayne Reittie; 3 Mike Mitchell; 4 Lee Waterman; 28 Danny Wilson; 6 Chris Thorman; 1 Danny Ratcliffe; 17 Nathan Freer; 33 Jack Lee; 10 Alex Benson; 11 Jordan Ross; 29 Ryan Esders; 15 Luke Hardbottle. Subs (all used): 32 Paul Stamp; 36 Callum Dinsdale; 26 Steve Lewis; 30 Jack Stearman.
Tries: Reittie (7), Haynes (26), Thorman (64), Lewis (74);
Goals: Waterman 2/3, Thorman 2/2;
Field goal: Thorman (69).
Rugby Leaguer & League Express Men of the Match:
Oldham: Neil Roden; *City Knights:* Chris Thorman.
Penalty count: 2-7; **Half-time:** 4-10;
Referee: Gareth Hewer.
(at Halliwell Jones Stadium, Warrington).

Hunslet Hawks were Championship One Champions in 2010. This game was to determine who took the second promotion place.

CHAMPIONSHIP GRAND FINAL

Sunday 26th September 2010

FEATHERSTONE ROVERS 22 HALIFAX 23
(after golden point extra time)

ROVERS: 1 Ian Hardman; 26 Zak Hardaker; 3 Sam Smeaton; 4 Liam Welham; 2 Tom Saxton; 6 Kyle Briggs; 9 Liam Finn; 17 Tony Tonks; 31 Ben Kaye; 10 Stuart Dickens; 18 Tim Spears; 13 Jamie Field; 11 Matty Dale. Subs (all used): 19 Ross Divorty; 16 Dane Manning; 12 Jon Grayshon; 7 Andy Kain.
Tries: Briggs (28), Hardaker (30, 52), Dale (45);
Goals: Briggs 3/4.
HALIFAX: 4 Shad Royston; 2 Lee Paterson; 6 Luke Branighan; 18 Dylan Nash; 23 Rob Worrincy; 26 Graham Holroyd; 7 Ben Black; 10 Neil Cherryholme; 13 Bob Beswick; 8 Makali Aizue; 11 David Larder; 22 David Wrench; 27 Sam Barlow. Subs (all used): 9 Sean Penkywicz; 17 Frank Watene; 19 Dominic Maloney; 24 Steve Bannister.
Tries: Worrincy (20), Black (58), Branighan (60), Bannister (75); **Goals:** Paterson 3/4;
Field goal: Black (82).
On report: Barlow (35) - alleged high tackle on Divorty.
Rugby Leaguer & League Express Men of the Match:
Rovers: Tom Saxton; *Halifax:* Ben Black.
Penalty count: 6-3; **Half-time:** 12-4; **Full-time:** 22-22;
Referee: Robert Hicks; **Attendance:** 9,443
(at Halliwell Jones Stadium, Warrington).

SUPER LEAGUE GRAND FINAL

Saturday 2nd October 2010

ST HELENS 10 WIGAN WARRIORS 22

SAINTS: 1 Paul Wellens; 30 Jamie Foster; 3 Matt Gidley; 5 Francis Meli; 24 Jonny Lomax; 12 Jon Wilkin; 34 Matty Smith; 10 James Graham; 9 Keiron Cunningham (C); 15 Bryn Hargreaves; 4 Iosia Soliola; 13 Chris Flannery; 11 Tony Puletua. Subs (all used): 17 Paul Clough; 14 James Roby; 22 Andrew Dixon; 25 Jacob Emmitt.
Tries: Dixon (28), Meli (74); **Goals:** Foster 1/2.
WARRIORS: 6 Sam Tomkins; 24 Darrell Goulding; 3 Martin Gleeson; 4 George Carmont; 5 Pat Richards; 19 Paul Deacon; 7 Thomas Leuluai; 8 Stuart Fielden; 15 Michael McIlorum; 10 Andy Coley; 11 Harrison Hansen; 12 Joel Tomkins; 13 Sean O'Loughlin (C). Subs (all used): 9 Mark Riddell; 17 Iafeta Palea'aesina; 25 Liam Farrell; 14 Paul Prescott.
Tries: Gleeson (4, 16), Goulding (20), S Tomkins (53);
Goals: Richards 2/3, Riddell 1/3, S Tomkins 0/1.
Rugby Leaguer & League Express Men of the Match:
Saints: Tony Puletua; *Warriors:* Thomas Leuluai.
Penalty count: 6-11; **Half time:** 6-16;
Referee: Richard Silverwood; **Attendance:** 71,526
(at Old Trafford, Manchester).

2011

CHAMPIONSHIP ONE GRAND FINAL

Sunday 2nd October 2011

KEIGHLEY COUGARS 32 WORKINGTON TOWN 12

COUGARS: 18 James Haythornthwaite; 4 Danny Lawton; 22 Ben Sagar; 33 Jake Normington; 5 Gavin Duffy; 6 Jason Demetriou; 36 Jy-Mel Coleman; 17 Ryan Benjafield; 9 James Feather; 10 Scott Law; 11 Will Cartledge; 12 Oliver Pursglove; 21 Richard Jones. Subs (all used): 14 Jamaine Wray; 8 Andy Shickell; 16 Brendan Rawlins; 7 Ryan Smith.
Tries: Lawton (5), Feather (20), Rawlins (25), Pursglove (32), Normington (69, 77); **Goals:** Lawton 4/6.
TOWN: 1 Brett Carter; 2 Elliott Miller; 3 Jason Mossop; 4 Aaron Low; 5 Neil Frazer; 24 Darren Holt; 7 Scott Kaighan; 10 Kris Coward; 13 Karl Olstrum; 29 Dave Armitstead; 11 Mike Whitehead; 18 Joe McKenna; 12 Jarrad Stack. Subs (all used): 23 Marc Bainbridge; 15 Ruairi McGoff; 32 Chris Clough; 17 James Robinson.
Tries: Kaighan (65), Frazer (74); **Goals:** Holt 2/2.
Rugby Leaguer & League Express Men of the Match:
Cougars: Jason Demetriou; *Town:* Jarrad Stack.
Penalty count: 7-5; **Half-time:** 22-0; **Referee:** Tim Roby.
(at Halliwell Jones Stadium, Warrington).

Swinton Lions were Championship One Champions in 2011. This game was to determine who took the second promotion place.

CHAMPIONSHIP GRAND FINAL

Sunday 2nd October 2011

FEATHERSTONE ROVERS 40 SHEFFIELD EAGLES 4

ROVERS: 1 Ian Hardman; 33 Ben Cockayne; 3 Sam Smeaton; 17 Greg Worthington; 5 Tom Saxton; 6 Andy Kain; 7 Liam Finn; 8 Tony Tonks; 9 Ben Kaye; 10 Stuart Dickens; 11 Jon Grayshon; 12 Tim Spears; 28 Jon Hepworth. Subs (all used): 18 Ross Divorty; 13 Matty Dale; 4 Andrew Bostock; 30 Kirk Netherton.
Tries: Spears (4), Finn (7, 39), Hardman (42), Cockayne (56), Hepworth (59), Saxton (79);
Goals: Finn 6/7.
Sin bin: Netherton (54) - fighting.
EAGLES: 6 Quentin Laulu-Togagae; 5 Tim Bergin; 26 Corey Hanson; 1 Misi Taulapapa; 16 Vinny Finigan; 13 Dane McDonald; 7 Simon Brown; 8 Jack Howieson; 9 Andrew Henderson; 10 Mitchell Stringer; 11 Alex Szostak; 12 Peter Green; 19 Joe Hirst. Subs (all used): 22 Ryan Hepworth; 30 Sam Scott; 20 Pat Smith; 14 Jonny Woodcock.
Try: McDonald (12); **Goals:** Brown 0/1.
Sin bin: Hirst (54) - fighting.
Rugby Leaguer & League Express Men of the Match:
Rovers: Liam Finn; *Eagles:* Joe Hirst.
Penalty count: 7-11; **Half-time:** 18-4;
Referee: Matthew Thomason; **Attendance:** 7,263
(at Halliwell Jones Stadium, Warrington).

SUPER LEAGUE GRAND FINAL

Saturday 8th October 2011

LEEDS RHINOS 32 ST HELENS 16

RHINOS: 1 Brent Webb; 23 Ben Jones-Bishop; 27 Zak Hardaker; 12 Carl Ablett; 5 Ryan Hall; 13 Kevin Sinfield (C); 6 Danny McGuire; 8 Kylie Leuluai; 9 Danny Buderus; 10 Jamie Peacock; 11 Jamie Jones-Buchanan; 3 Brett Delaney; 21 Chris Clarkson. Subs (all used): 7 Rob Burrow; 16 Ryan Bailey; 17 Ian Kirke; 14 Ali Lauitiiti.
Tries: Burrow (34), Webb (65), Hall (70), Ablett (74), Hardaker (80); **Goals:** Sinfield 6/7.
SAINTS: 1 Paul Wellens (C); 28 Tom Makinson; 3 Michael Shenton; 5 Francis Meli; 22 Jamie Foster; 25 Lee Gaskell; 20 Jonny Lomax; 10 James Graham (C); 9 James Roby; 11 Tony Puletua; 12 Jon Wilkin; 4 Iosia Soliola; 16 Paul Clough. Subs (all used): 19 Andrew Dixon; 14 Scott Moore; 15 Louie McCarthy-Scarsbrook; 17 Gary Wheeler.
Tries: Makinson (50), Shenton (55); **Goals:** Foster 4/5.
Rugby Leaguer & League Express Men of the Match:
Rhinos: Rob Burrow; *Saints:* Lee Gaskell.
Penalty count: 5-7; **Half-time:** 8-2;
Referee: Phil Bentham; **Attendance:** 69,107
(at Old Trafford, Manchester).

2012

CHAMPIONSHIP ONE GRAND FINAL

Sunday 30th September 2012

BARROW RAIDERS 13 DONCASTER 16

RAIDERS: 1 Andy Ballard; 2 Lee Haney; 3 Chris Larkin; 4 Aaron Low; 5 James Nixon; 6 Scott Kaighan; 7 Liam Campbell; 8 Jamie Butler; 9 James Dandy; 10 Ryan Duffy; 11 Liam Harrison; 12 James Gordon; 13 Daniel Toal. Subs (all used): 14 Liam Finch; 15 Martin Ostler; 16 Ruairi McGoff; 17 Andrew Dawson.
Tries: Larkin (4), Low (77); **Goals:** Ballard 2/3;
Field goal: Kaighan (39).
DONCASTER: 1 Lee Waterman; 2 Tom Hodson; 3 Chris Spurr; 4 Danny Cowling; 5 Stewart Sanderson; 6 Kyle Kesik; 7 Craig Fawcett; 8 Mark Castle; 9 Mike Emmett; 10 Russ Spiers; 11 Lucas Walshaw; 12 Michael Kelly; 13 Carl Hughes. Subs (all used): 14 Nathan Powley; 15 Craig Robinson; 16 Grant Edwards; 17 Liam Cunningham.
Tries: Sanderson (11), Waterman (46), Fawcett (57);
Goals: Hodson 2/3.
Rugby Leaguer & League Express Men of the Match:
Raiders: Liam Harrison; *Doncaster:* Craig Fawcett.
Penalty count: 4-5; **Half-time:** 7-4; **Referee:** Jamie Leahy.
(at Halliwell Jones Stadium, Warrington).

CHAMPIONSHIP GRAND FINAL

Sunday 30th September 2012

FEATHERSTONE ROVERS 16 SHEFFIELD EAGLES 20

ROVERS: 1 Ian Hardman; 2 Tangi Ropati; 3 Nathan Chappell; 4 Greg Worthington; 5 Tom Saxton; 6 Andy Kain; 7 Liam Finn; 8 Anthony England; 9 Ben Kaye; 10 James Lockwood; 11 Matty Dale; 12 Tim Spears; 13 Kyle Briggs. Subs (all used): 14 Dominic Maloney; 15 Stuart Dickens; 16 Andrew Bostock; 17 Jon Hepworth.
Tries: Hardman (17), Hepworth (51); **Goals:** Finn 4/4.
On report:
Maloney (57) - alleged use of the elbow on Turner.
EAGLES: 1 Quentin Laulu-Togagae; 2 Misi Taulapapa; 3 Duane Straugheir; 4 Menzie Yere; 5 Scott Turner; 6 Simon Brown; 7 Dominic Brambani; 8 Jack Howieson; 9 Andrew Henderson; 10 Mitchell Stringer; 11 Michael Knowles; 12 Sam Scott; 13 Alex Szostak. Subs (all used): 14 James Davey; 15 Peter Green; 16 Dane McDonald; 17 Liam Higgins.
Tries: Turner (9), Laulu-Togagae (32), McDonald (46), Taulapapa (57); **Goals:** Brown 2/5.
Rugby Leaguer & League Express Men of the Match:
Rovers: Ian Hardman; *Eagles:* Michael Knowles.
Penalty count: 4-6; **Half-time:** 8-10; **Referee:** Tim Roby;
Attendance: 6,409
(at Halliwell Jones Stadium, Warrington).

SUPER LEAGUE GRAND FINAL

Saturday 6th October 2012

LEEDS RHINOS 26 WARRINGTON WOLVES 18

RHINOS: 4 Zak Hardaker; 2 Ben Jones-Bishop; 3 Kallum Watkins; 12 Carl Ablett; 5 Ryan Hall; 13 Kevin Sinfield (C); 6 Danny McGuire; 8 Kylie Leuluai; 7 Rob Burrow; 10 Jamie Peacock; 11 Jamie Jones-Buchanan; 15 Brett Delaney; 16 Ryan Bailey. Subs (all used): 17 Ian Kirke; 20 Darrell Griffin; 25 Stevie Ward; 31 Shaun Lunt.
Tries: Sinfield (19), Jones-Bishop (28), Ablett (59), Hall (72); **Goals:** Sinfield 5/5.
WOLVES: 1 Brett Hodgson; 5 Joel Monaghan; 19 Stefan Ratchford; 4 Ryan Atkins; 2 Chris Riley; 6 Lee Briers; 7 Richard Myler; 20 Chris Hill; 14 Mick Higham; 13 Ben Harrison; 12 Ben Westwood; 11 Trent Waterhouse; 15 Simon Grix. Subs (all used): 8 Adrian Morley (C); 9 Michael Monaghan; 16 Paul Wood; 17 Michael Cooper.
Tries: Myler (4), J Monaghan (38), Atkins (45);
Goals: Hodgson 3/4.
Rugby Leaguer & League Express Men of the Match:
Rhinos: Kevin Sinfield; *Wolves:* Richard Myler.
Penalty count: 6-5; **Half-time:** 14-14;
Referee: Richard Silverwood; **Attendance:** 70,676
(at Old Trafford, Manchester).

2013

CHAMPIONSHIP ONE GRAND FINAL

Sunday 29th September 2013

OLDHAM 18 ROCHDALE HORNETS 32

OLDHAM: 1 Richard Lepori; 2 Mo Agoro; 21 David Cookson; 25 Jonathan Ford; 5 Dale Bloomfield; 23 Lewis Palfrey; 16 Kenny Hughes; 18 Phil Joy; 9 Sam Gee; 10 Jason Boults; 11 Josh Crowley; 12 Danny Langtree; 13 Mark Hobson. Subs (all used): 14 Adam Files; 19 Michael Ward; 22 Liam Thompson; 28 Matthew Haggarty.
Tries: Ford (12), Hughes (38), Cookson (44);
Goals: Palfrey 3/3.
HORNETS: 1 Wayne English; 2 Gareth Langley; 20 Daniel Davies; 23 Dave Hull; 17 Martin Waring; 6 Paul Crook; 7 Steve Roper; 29 Carl Forster; 31 Chris Hough; 10 Warren Thompson; 26 Dave Llewellyn; 14 Alex Trumper; 18 Joe Greenwood. Subs (all used): 8 John Cookson; 9 Alex McClurg; 11 Chris Baines; 13 Jordan Case.
Tries: Llewellyn (5), Davies (20), Hull (58), Cookson (71), English (78); **Goals:** Crook 6/6.

St Helens' Mose Masoe takes on Wigan's Blake Green and Liam Farrell during the 2014 Super League Grand Final

Rugby Leaguer & League Express Men of the Match: *Oldham:* Lewis Palfrey; *Hornets:* Paul Crook.
Penalty count: 1-2; **Half-time:** 12-12;
Referee: Chris Leatherbarrow. *(at Leigh Sports Village).*

North Wales Crusaders were Championship One Champions in 2013. This game was to determine who took the second promotion place.

CHAMPIONSHIP GRAND FINAL

Sunday 29th September 2013

BATLEY BULLDOGS 12 SHEFFIELD EAGLES 19

BULLDOGS: 1 Miles Greenwood; 5 Johnny Campbell; 3 Jason Walton; 4 Danny Maun; 21 Greg Johnson; 6 Ben Black; 7 Gareth Moore; 8 Byron Smith; 9 Paul Mennell; 28 Anthony Mullally; 11 Alex Bretherton; 16 John Davies; 13 Ashley Lindsay. Subs (all used): 14 George Flanagan; 15 Keegan Hirst; 19 Alex Rowe; 17 Liam Walmsley.
Try: Campbell (13); **Goals:** Moore 4/5.
EAGLES: 1 Quentin Laulu-Togagae; 5 Misi Taulapapa; 4 Tom Armstrong; 3 Menzie Yere; 2 Scott Turner; 6 Pat Walker; 7 Dominic Brambani; 25 Eddie Battye; 9 Andrew Henderson; 10 Mitchell Stringer; 11 Michael Knowles; 15 Alex Szostak; 13 Joe Hirst. Subs (all used): 14 James Davey; 12 Peter Green; 16 Duane Straugheir; 21 Matt Garside.
Tries: Turner (56, 67), Yere (61), Laulu-Togagae (70);
Goals: Brambani 1/5; **Field goal:** Walker (74).
Rugby Leaguer & League Express Men of the Match: *Bulldogs:* Keegan Hirst; *Eagles:* Dominic Brambani.
Penalty count: 6-7; **Half-time:** 12-0;
Referee: Matthew Thomason; **Attendance:** 6,374 *(at Leigh Sports Village).*

SUPER LEAGUE GRAND FINAL

Saturday 5th October 2013

WARRINGTON WOLVES 16 WIGAN WARRIORS 30

WOLVES: 19 Stefan Ratchford; 5 Joel Monaghan; 3 Chris Bridge; 4 Ryan Atkins; 2 Chris Riley; 6 Lee Briers; 7 Richard Myler; 16 Paul Wood; 14 Mick Higham; 18 Chris Hill; 13 Ben Harrison; 12 Ben Westwood; 15 Simon Grix. Subs (all used): 9 Michael Monaghan; 8 Adrian Morley (C); 17 Michael Cooper; 10 Garreth Carvell.
Tries: J Monaghan (20), Grix (24), Westwood (27);
Goals: Ratchford 2/3.
On report: Westwood (2) - alleged punch on Green.
WARRIORS: 1 Sam Tomkins; 2 Josh Charnley; 3 Darrell Goulding; 17 Iain Thornley; 5 Pat Richards; 6 Blake Green; 7 Matty Smith; 10 Lee Mossop; 9 Michael McIlorum; 20 Gil Dudson; 11 Harrison Hansen; 12 Liam Farrell; 13 Sean O'Loughlin (C). Subs (all used): 15 Ben Flower; 4 Jack Hughes; 26 Dominic Crosby; 21 Scott Taylor.
Tries: Goulding (37), McIlorum (47), Charnley (53), Green (65), Richards (74); **Goals:** Richards 5/6.
Rugby Leaguer & League Express Men of the Match: *Wolves:* Chris Hill; *Warriors:* Michael McIlorum.
Penalty count: 7-10; **Half-time:** 16-6;
Referee: Richard Silverwood; **Attendance:** 66,281 *(at Old Trafford, Manchester).*

2014

CHAMPIONSHIP ONE GRAND FINAL

Sunday 5th October 2014

HUNSLET HAWKS 17 OLDHAM 16
(after golden point extra-time)

HAWKS: 2 Jimmy Watson; 36 Gavin Duffy; 4 Danny Maun; 3 Lee Brickwood; 37 James Duckworth; 6 Thomas Coyle; 20 Danny Ansell; 38 Richard Moore; 9 David March; 10 James Houston; 11 John Oakes; 12 Aaron Lyons; 31 Luke Briscoe. Subs (all used): 27 Liam Hood; 8 Michael Haley; 1 Stuart Kain; 40 Luke Hardbottle.
Tries: Watson (22), Duckworth (45), T Coyle (53);
Goals: March 2/3; **Field goal:** T Coyle (85).
OLDHAM: 4 Steven Nield; 29 Adam Clay; 21 David Cookson; 25 Jonathan Ford; 5 Dale Bloomfield; 6 Lewis Palfrey; 26 Steve Roper; 8 Phil Joy; 30 Gareth Owen; 10 Jason Boults; 11 Josh Crowley; 12 Danny Langtree; 22 Liam Thompson. Subs (all used): 19 Michael Ward; 28 Nathan Mason; 16 Kenny Hughes; 20 George Tyson.
Tries: Roper (5), Bloomfield (31), Langtree (74);
Goals: Roper 2/3.
Rugby Leaguer & League Express Men of the Match: *Hawks:* Liam Hood; *Oldham:* Jonathan Ford.
Penalty count: 4-3; **Half-time:** 6-10; **Referee:** Joe Cobb. *(at Headingley Carnegie, Leeds).*

CHAMPIONSHIP GRAND FINAL

Sunday 5th October 2014

FEATHERSTONE ROVERS 12 LEIGH CENTURIONS 36

ROVERS: 2 Will Sharp; 35 Jason Crookes; 1 Ian Hardman; 18 Jamie Cording; 36 Ben Blackmore; 23 Andy Kain; 7 Gareth Moore; 8 Steve Crossley; 9 Andy Ellis; 13 Matt James; 31 Shaun Pick; 11 James Lockwood; 12 Tim Spears. Subs (all used): 30 Luke Teasdale; 6 Jack Bussey; 42 Chris Annakin; 10 Keegan Hirst.
Tries: Sharp (27, 51); **Goals:** Moore 2/2.
Sin bin: Crookes (68) - high tackle on Armstrong.
CENTURIONS: 1 Gregg McNally; 22 Adam Higson; 34 Michael Platt; 4 Tom Armstrong; 15 Liam Kay; 6 Martyn Ridyard; 7 Ryan Brierley; 29 Jake Emmitt; 14 Sean Penkywicz; 10 Oliver Wilkes; 11 Matt Sarsfield; 30 Kurt Haggerty; 13 Sam Barlow. Subs (all used): 9 Bob Beswick; 18 Jamie Acton; 16 Martin Aspinwall; 33 Jonathan Walker.
Tries: Sarsfield (5), McNally (17), Armstrong (22), Higson (65), Barlow (70), Brierley (80);
Goals: Ridyard 6/8.
Sin bin: Penkywicz (68) - retaliation.
Rugby Leaguer & League Express Men of the Match: *Rovers:* Jack Bussey; *Centurions:* Tom Armstrong.
Penalty count: 6-8; **Half-time:** 6-20;
Referee: Matthew Thomason; **Attendance:** 9,164 *(at Headingley Carnegie, Leeds).*

SUPER LEAGUE GRAND FINAL

Saturday 11th October 2014

ST HELENS 14 WIGAN WARRIORS 6

SAINTS: 17 Paul Wellens (C); 2 Tom Makinson; 22 Mark Percival; 4 Josh Jones; 5 Adam Swift; 15 Mark Flanagan; 6 Lance Hohaia; 16 Kyle Amor; 9 James Roby; 8 Mose Masoe; 10 Louie McCarthy-Scarsbrook; 11 Iosia Soliola; 3 Jordan Turner. Subs (all used): 28 Luke Thompson; 13 Willie Manu; 18 Alex Walmsley; 27 Greg Richards.
Tries: Soliola (54), Makinson (69); **Goals:** Percival 3/3.
WARRIORS: 1 Matt Bowen; 2 Josh Charnley; 5 Anthony Gelling; 23 Dan Sarginson; 32 Joe Burgess; 6 Blake Green; 7 Matty Smith; 10 Ben Flower; 19 Sam Powell; 17 Dominic Crosby; 11 Joel Tomkins; 12 Liam Farrell; 13 Sean O'Loughlin (C). Subs (all used): 22 Eddy Pettybourne; 24 Tony Clubb; 25 John Bateman; 27 George Williams.
Try: Burgess (40); **Goals:** Smith 1/3.
Dismissal: Flower (2) - punching Hohaia.
Rugby Leaguer & League Express Men of the Match: *Saints:* James Roby; *Warriors:* Liam Farrell.
Penalty count: 9-7; **Half-time:** 2-6;
Referee: Phil Bentham; **Attendance:** 70,102 *(at Old Trafford, Manchester).*

2015 SEASON
Stats round-up

ATTENDANCES

SUPER LEAGUE CLUBS - AVERAGES

	2015 Avg	*2014 Avg*	*Diff*
Leeds Rhinos	15,724	14,472	+1,252
Wigan Warriors	13,151	13,802	-651
St Helens	11,863	11,543	+320
Hull FC	11,173	11,065	+108
Warrington Wolves	9,458	9,677	-219
Catalans Dragons	8,635	8,312	+323
Hull Kingston Rovers	7,784	7,846	-62
Castleford Tigers	7,097	7,007	+90
Widnes Vikings	5,976	5,636	+340
Huddersfield Giants	5,942	6,383	-441
Salford Red Devils	4,106	4,515	-409
Wakefield Trinity Wildcats	4,103	4,373	-270

2015 Average 8,751
2014 Average 8,041
Difference +710

CHAMPIONSHIP CLUBS - AVERAGES

	2015 Avg	*2014 Avg*	*Diff*
Bradford Bulls	5,457	6,653 *(Super League)*	-1,196
Leigh Centurions	3,942	2,380	+1,562
Halifax	2,135	1,686	+449
Featherstone Rovers	1,984	2,055	-71
Sheffield Eagles	1,283	829	+454
Dewsbury Rams	1,243	1,027	+216
Doncaster	1,110	806	+304
Batley Bulldogs	927	751	+176
Whitehaven	870	798	+72
Workington Town	849	838	+11
Hunslet Hawks	827	508 *(Championship One)*	+319
London Broncos	645	1,294 *(Super League)*	-649

2015 Average 1,773
2014 Average 1,095
Difference +678

LEAGUE 1 CLUBS - AVERAGES

	2015 Avg	*2014 Avg*	*Diff*
Keighley Cougars	1,026	991 *(Championship)*	+35
Newcastle Thunder	944	283	+661
Barrow Raiders	905	1,030 *(Championship)*	-125
North Wales Crusaders	641	846 *(Championship)*	-205
Oldham	631	499	+132
Rochdale Hornets	516	764 *(Championship)*	-248
Swinton Lions	477	530 *(Championship)*	-53
Coventry Bears	458	N/A	N/A
York City Knights	430	645	-215
London Skolars	342	464	-122
South Wales Scorpions	289	279	+10
Oxford	284	271	+13
Gloucestershire All Golds	242	211	+31
Hemel Stags	204	219	-15

2015 Average 528
2014 Average 375
Difference +153

BEST ATTENDANCES

		Round	*Date*
80,140	Hull KR v Leeds *(at Wembley Stadium)*	CCF	29/8/15
73,512	Leeds v Wigan *(at Old Trafford, Manchester)*	SLGF	10/10/15
24,054	Wigan v St Helens	SLR8	3/4/15
20,842	Wigan v Brisbane	WCS	21/2/15
20,507	Hull FC v Hull KR	SLR8	2/4/15
18,514	Leeds v St Helens	SLR20	3/7/15
18,350	Leeds v Wigan	SLR6	20/3/15
17,980	St Helens v South Sydney	WCC	22/2/15
17,608	Leeds v Wakefield	SLR9	6/4/15
17,340	Leeds v Warrington	SLR12	24/4/15
17,192	Leeds v St Helens	SLSF	2/10/15
16,692	St Helens v Wigan	SLR18	12/6/15
16,203	Leeds v Hull FC	SLR19	21/6/15
16,142	Leeds v St Helens	SLS8R4	4/9/15
15,808	St Helens v Wigan	SLS8R6	18/9/15
15,534	Leeds v Catalans Dragons	SLR23	26/7/15
15,206	Leeds v Hull KR	SLR15	22/5/15
15,089	Leeds v Castleford	SLR18	11/6/15
15,069	Leeds v Castleford	SLS8R6	17/9/15
15,026	Leeds v Wigan	SLS8R2	14/8/15

LEADING SCORERS

SUPER LEAGUE

(Regular season, Super 8s, Semi-finals & Grand Final. Super 8s (Qualifiers) not included)

TRIES

	Player	Club	
1	Jermaine McGillvary	Huddersfield Giants	27
2	Tom Lineham	Hull FC	25
3	Joe Burgess	Wigan Warriors	24
4	Dominic Manfredi	Wigan Warriors	22
5	Ryan Hall	Leeds Rhinos	20
6	Justin Carney	Castleford Tigers	18
	Denny Solomona	Castleford Tigers	18
	Aaron Murphy	Huddersfield Giants	18
	Adam Swift	St Helens	18
10	Joel Monaghan	Warrington Wolves	17

GOALS

	Player	Club	
1	Kevin Sinfield	Leeds Rhinos	112
2	Luke Gale	Castleford Tigers	101
3	Danny Brough	Huddersfield Giants	95
4	Scott Dureau	Catalans Dragons	94
5	Matty Smith	Wigan Warriors	76
6	Josh Mantellato	Hull Kingston Rovers	70
7	Marc Sneyd	Hull FC	69
8	Luke Walsh	St Helens	48
9	Josh Griffin	Salford Red Devils	46
10	Jack Owens	Widnes Vikings	41

GOALS PERCENTAGE

	Player	Club	*G*	*Att*	*%*
1	Scott Dureau	Catalans Dragons	94	109	86.23
2	Jamie Ellis	Huddersfield Giants	18	21	85.71
3	Kevin Sinfield	Leeds Rhinos	112	131	85.49
4	Danny Tickle	Widnes Vikings	11	13	84.61
5	Luke Walsh	St Helens	48	57	84.21
6	Tom Makinson	St Helens	19	23	82.60
7	Matt Bowen	Wigan Warriors	31	39	79.48
8	Luke Gale	Castleford Tigers	101	129	78.29
9	Thomas Bosc	Catalans Dragons	18	23	78.26
10	Stefan Marsh	Widnes Vikings	9	12	75.00

(10 minimum attempts to qualify)

POINTS

	Player	Club	*T*	*G*	*FG*	*Pts*
1	Luke Gale	Castleford Tigers	11	101	1	247
2	Kevin Sinfield	Leeds Rhinos	3	112	3	239
3	Danny Brough	Huddersfield Giants	5	95	2	212
4	Scott Dureau	Catalans Dragons	3	94	2	202
5	Josh Mantellato	Hull Kingston Rovers	14	70	0	196
6	Matty Smith	Wigan Warriors	3	76	4	168
7	Marc Sneyd	Hull FC	3	69	6	156
8	Luke Walsh	St Helens	7	48	3	127
9	Josh Griffin	Salford Red Devils	6	46	0	116
10	Jack Owens	Widnes Vikings	8	41	0	114

CONSECUTIVE APPEARANCES

(all club games included)

	Player	Club	
1	Elliott Whitehead	Catalans Dragons	50
2	Jermaine McGillvary	Huddersfield Giants	47
	Chris Hill	Warrington Wolves	47
4	Craig Kopczak	Huddersfield Giants	45
5	Danny Houghton	Hull FC	43
6	Carl Ablett	Leeds Rhinos	41
7	Ukuma Ta'ai	Huddersfield Giants	38
	Adam Swift	St Helens	38
9	Craig Huby	Huddersfield Giants/Castleford Tigers	35
	Aaron Heremaia	Widnes Vikings/Hull FC	35

CHAMPIONSHIP

(Regular season only)

TRIES

	Player	Club	
1	Liam Kay	Leigh Centurions	33
2	Ryan Brierley	Leigh Centurions	27
3	Gregg McNally	Leigh Centurions	22
4	Danny Williams	Bradford Bulls	18
5	Rhys Williams	London Broncos	16
	Menzie Yere	Sheffield Eagles	16
7	Lee Gaskell	Bradford Bulls	15
	Jonathan Pownall	Leigh Centurions	15
	Quentin Laulu-Togagae	Sheffield Eagles	15
10	Jake Mullaney	Bradford Bulls	14
	Paul Sykes	Featherstone Rovers	14

GOALS

	Player	Club	
1	Martyn Ridyard	Leigh Centurions	117
2	Ryan Shaw	Bradford Bulls	92
3	Wes Naiqama	London Broncos	78
4	Paul Sykes	Featherstone Rovers	63
	Steve Tyrer	Halifax	63
6	Scott Leatherbarrow	Batley Bulldogs	50
7	Carl Forber	Workington Town	44
8	Kyle Briggs	Sheffield Eagles	42
9	Brett Seymour *	Dewsbury Rams	39
10	Simon Brown	Hunslet Hawks	31

** includes 3 for Whitehaven*

POINTS

	Player	Club	*T*	*G*	*FG*	*Pts*
1	Martyn Ridyard	Leigh Centurions	7	117	1	263
2	Ryan Shaw	Bradford Bulls	12	92	0	232
3	Wes Naiqama	London Broncos	8	78	0	188
4	Paul Sykes	Featherstone Rovers	14	63	0	182
5	Steve Tyrer	Halifax	11	63	0	170
6	Liam Kay	Leigh Centurions	33	0	0	132
7	Ryan Brierley	Leigh Centurions	27	6	1	121
8	Kyle Briggs	Sheffield Eagles	6	42	0	108
	Carl Forber	Workington Town	5	44	0	108
10	Scott Leatherbarrow	Batley Bulldogs	1	50	2	106

LEAGUE 1

(Regular season & play-offs)

TRIES

	Player	Club	
1	Paul White	Keighley Cougars	29
2	Rob Massam	North Wales Crusaders	23
3	Andy Gabriel	Keighley Cougars	21
4	Dale Bloomfield	Rochdale Hornets	19
	Shaun Robinson	Swinton Lions	19
6	Paul Crook	Rochdale Hornets	17
	Stuart Littler	Swinton Lions	17
	Greg Minikin	York City Knights	17
9	Dayne Craig	Newcastle Thunder	16
	Jono Smith	North Wales Crusaders	16

GOALS

	Player	Club	
1	Lewis Palfrey	Oldham	108
2	Josh Ward	Barrow Raiders	87
3	Tommy Johnson	North Wales Crusaders	79
4	Chris Atkin	Swinton Lions	77
	Paul Crook	Rochdale Hornets	77
6	Matt Bradley	Gloucestershire All Golds	67
7	Ben Dent	York City Knights	62
8	Danny Lawton	Keighley Cougars	57
9	Matty Beharrell	Newcastle Thunder	37
10	Paul Emanuelli	South Wales Scorpions	36

LEADING SCORERS

POINTS

			T	G	FG	Pts
1	Lewis Palfrey	Oldham	11	108	2	262
2	Paul Crook	Rochdale Hornets	17	77	1	223
3	Chris Atkin	Swinton Lions	14	77	2	212
4	Josh Ward	Barrow Raiders	8	87	0	206
5	Tommy Johnson	North Wales Crusaders	7	79	0	186
6	Ben Dent	York City Knights	11	62	0	168
7	Matt Bradley	Gloucestershire All Golds	5	67	0	154
8	Danny Lawton	Keighley Cougars	2	57	0	122
9	Paul White	Keighley Cougars	29	0	0	116
10	Paul Handforth	Keighley Cougars	14	29	0	114

SUPER 8s - THE QUALIFIERS

TRIES

1	Kieran Dixon	Hull Kingston Rovers	7
	Josh Mantellato	Hull Kingston Rovers	7
	Rhys Hanbury	Widnes Vikings	7
	Charly Runciman	Widnes Vikings	7
5	Danny Williams	Bradford Bulls	6
	Steve Tyrer	Halifax	6
	Ken Sio	Hull Kingston Rovers	6
	Patrick Ah Van	Widnes Vikings	6

GOALS

1	Steve Tyrer	Halifax	25
2	Danny Addy	Bradford Bulls	24
3	Josh Mantellato	Hull Kingston Rovers	23
4	Michael Dobson	Salford Red Devils	22
5	Martyn Ridyard	Leigh Centurions	20

POINTS

			T	G	FG	Pts
1	Josh Mantellato	Hull Kingston Rovers	7	23	0	74
	Steve Tyrer	Halifax	6	25	0	74
3	Danny Addy	Bradford Bulls	1	24	0	52
4	Lee Smith	Wakefield Trinity Wildcats	5	15	1	51
5	Michael Dobson	Salford Red Devils	0	22	1	45

CHAMPIONSHIP SHIELD

TRIES

1	Ben Hellewell	London Broncos	10
2	Jarrod Sammut	Workington Town	9
3	Shaun Ainscough	Batley Bulldogs	8
4	Alex Brown	Batley Bulldogs	7
	Dalton Grant	Dewsbury Rams	7
	Brett Carter	Workington Town	7
	Elliott Miller	Workington Town	7

GOALS

1	Paul Sykes	Featherstone Rovers	38
2	Scott Leatherbarrow	Batley Bulldogs	29
3	Ed Chamberlain	Whitehaven	28
4	Simon Brown	Hunslet Hawks	26
5	William Barthau	London Broncos	22

POINTS

			T	G	FG	Pts
1	Paul Sykes	Featherstone Rovers	4	38	0	92
2	Ed Chamberlain	Whitehaven	3	28	0	68
3	Scott Leatherbarrow	Batley Bulldogs	1	29	0	62
	Jarrod Sammut	Workington Town	9	13	0	62
5	William Barthau	London Broncos	3	22	0	56

CHALLENGE CUP

TRIES

1	Ryan Brierley	Leigh Centurions	6
	Kris Brining	York City Knights	6
3	Josh Mantellato	Hull Kingston Rovers	5
	Tom Briscoe	Leeds Rhinos	5
	Mark Percival	St Helens	5
	Ben Currie	Warrington Wolves	5

GOALS

1	Kevin Sinfield	Leeds Rhinos	25
2	Josh Mantellato	Hull Kingston Rovers	22
3	Martyn Ridyard	Leigh Centurions	21
4	Tommy Johnson	North Wales Crusaders	16
	Ryan Shaw	Bradford Bulls	16
	Cain Southernwood	Batley Bulldogs	16

POINTS

			T	G	FG	Pts
1	Josh Mantellato	Hull Kingston Rovers	5	22	0	64
2	Kevin Sinfield	Leeds Rhinos	0	25	0	50
3	Tommy Johnson	North Wales Crusaders	4	16	0	48
4	Chris Atkin	Swinton Lions	4	14	0	44
5	Martyn Ridyard	Leigh Centurions	0	21	0	42

LEAGUE 1 CUP

TRIES

1	Scott Turner	North Wales Crusaders	5
2	Lee Mapals	Newcastle Thunder	4
	Adam Clay	Oldham	4
	Nev Morrison	York City Knights	4

(8 players tied on 3)

GOALS

1	Chris Atkin	Swinton Lions	15
	James Haynes	York City Knights	15
	Lewis Palfrey	Oldham	15
4	Tommy Johnson	North Wales Crusaders	14
5	Danny Jones	Keighley Cougars	13

POINTS

			T	G	FG	Pts
1	Chris Atkin	Swinton Lions	3	15	0	42
2	James Haynes	York City Knights	1	15	0	34
3	Tommy Johnson	North Wales Crusaders	1	14	0	32
4	Lewis Palfrey	Oldham	0	15	0	30
5	Matty Beharrell	Newcastle Thunder	1	12	0	28

ALL COMPETITIONS

TRIES

1	Ryan Brierley	Leigh Centurions	37
2	Liam Kay	Leigh Centurions	36
3	Gregg McNally	Leigh Centurions	30
	Paul White	Keighley Cougars	30
5	Rob Massam	North Wales Crusaders	29
6	Jermaine McGillvary	Huddersfield Giants	27
7	Tom Lineham	Hull FC	26
	Josh Mantellato	Hull Kingston Rovers	26
	Joe Burgess	Wigan Warriors	26
10	Danny Williams	Bradford Bulls	25

GOALS

1	Martyn Ridyard	Leigh Centurions	158
2	Kevin Sinfield	Leeds Rhinos	137
3	Lewis Palfrey	Oldham	129
4	Josh Mantellato	Hull Kingston Rovers	115
5	Ryan Shaw	Bradford Bulls	111
6	Tommy Johnson	North Wales Crusaders	109
7	Chris Atkin	Swinton Lions	106
8	Paul Sykes	Featherstone Rovers	104
9	Luke Gale	Castleford Tigers	102
10	Danny Brough	Huddersfield Giants	97
	Scott Dureau	Catalans Dragons	97

POINTS

			T	G	FG	Pts
1	Martyn Ridyard	Leigh Centurions	7	158	1	345
2	Josh Mantellato	Hull Kingston Rovers	26	115	0	334
3	Lewis Palfrey	Oldham	11	129	2	304
4	Chris Atkin	Swinton Lions	21	106	2	298
5	Kevin Sinfield	Leeds Rhinos	3	137	3	289
6	Ryan Shaw	Bradford Bulls	16	111	0	286
7	Paul Sykes	Featherstone Rovers	18	104	0	280
8	Tommy Johnson	North Wales Crusaders	12	109	0	266
9	Steve Tyrer	Halifax	18	96	0	264
10	Luke Gale	Castleford Tigers	11	102	1	249

FINAL TABLES

SUPER LEAGUE - SUPER 8s

	P	W	D	L	F	A	D	Pts
Leeds Rhinos	30	20	1	9	944	650	294	41
Wigan Warriors	30	20	1	9	798	530	268	41
Huddersfield Giants	30	18	2	10	750	534	216	38
St Helens	30	19	0	11	766	624	142	38
Castleford Tigers	30	16	0	14	731	746	-15	32
Warrington Wolves	30	15	0	15	714	636	78	30
Catalans Dragons	30	13	2	15	739	770	-31	28
Hull FC	30	12	0	18	620	716	-96	24

SUPER 8s - THE QUALIFIERS

	P	W	D	L	F	A	D	Pts
Hull Kingston Rovers	7	7	0	0	234	118	116	14
Widnes Vikings	7	5	0	2	232	70	162	10
Salford Red Devils	7	5	0	2	239	203	36	10
Wakefield Trinity Wildcats	7	3	0	4	153	170	-17	6
Bradford Bulls	7	3	0	4	167	240	-73	6
Halifax	7	2	0	5	162	186	-24	4
Sheffield Eagles	7	2	0	5	152	267	-115	4
Leigh Centurions	7	1	0	6	146	231	-85	2

CHAMPIONSHIP SHIELD

	P	W	D	L	F	A	D	Pts
Featherstone Rovers	30	19	0	11	809	701	108	38
Dewsbury Rams	30	17	1	12	686	624	62	35
London Broncos	30	15	0	15	756	674	82	30
Workington Town	30	11	1	18	587	782	-195	23
Batley Bulldogs	30	10	0	20	645	707	-62	20
Whitehaven	30	10	0	20	618	921	-303	20
Hunslet Hawks	30	8	0	22	518	957	-439	16
Doncaster	30	2	0	28	401	1128	-727	4

LEAGUE 1

	P	W	D	L	F	A	D	Pts
Oldham	22	19	0	3	840	362	478	38
Keighley Cougars	22	18	0	4	759	400	359	36
Swinton Lions	22	16	1	5	899	402	497	33
York City Knights	22	16	0	6	816	382	434	32
North Wales Crusaders	22	14	1	7	677	391	286	29
Rochdale Hornets	22	14	0	8	731	459	272	28
Barrow Raiders	22	14	0	8	661	423	238	28
Newcastle Thunder	22	11	0	11	555	552	3	22
Gloucestershire All Golds	22	8	0	14	562	677	-115	16
Oxford	22	7	0	15	453	948	-495	14
London Skolars	22	5	0	17	388	671	-283	10
Coventry Bears	22	5	0	17	430	775	-345	10
Hemel Stags	22	5	0	17	422	903	-481	10
South Wales Scorpions	22	1	0	21	274	1122	-848	2

SUPER LEAGUE - REGULAR SEASON

	P	W	D	L	F	A	D	Pts
Leeds Rhinos	23	16	1	6	758	477	281	33
St Helens	23	16	0	7	598	436	162	32
Wigan Warriors	23	15	1	7	589	413	176	31
Huddersfield Giants	23	13	2	8	538	394	144	28
Castleford Tigers	23	13	0	10	547	505	42	26
Warrington Wolves	23	12	0	11	552	456	96	24
Hull FC	23	11	0	12	452	484	-32	22
Catalans Dragons	23	9	2	12	561	574	-13	20
Widnes Vikings	23	9	1	13	518	565	-47	19
Hull Kingston Rovers	23	9	0	14	534	646	-112	18
Salford Red Devils	23	8	1	14	447	617	-170	17
Wakefield Trinity Wildcats	23	3	0	20	402	929	-527	6

CHAMPIONSHIP - REGULAR SEASON

	P	W	D	L	F	A	D	Pts
Leigh Centurions	23	21	1	1	972	343	629	43
Bradford Bulls	23	18	1	4	828	387	441	37
Sheffield Eagles	23	17	0	6	586	451	135	34
Halifax	23	16	0	7	646	377	269	32
Featherstone Rovers	23	13	0	10	633	565	68	26
Dewsbury Rams	23	12	1	10	490	461	29	25
London Broncos	23	12	0	11	538	510	28	24
Workington Town	23	7	1	15	379	631	-252	15
Batley Bulldogs	23	7	0	16	421	539	-118	14
Whitehaven	23	7	0	16	418	671	-253	14
Hunslet Hawks	23	5	0	18	362	769	-407	10
Doncaster	23	1	0	22	282	851	-569	2